FIELDING'S
THE WORLD'S
MOST DANGEROUS
PLACES™

Fielding Titles

Fielding's Alaska Cruises/Inside Passage

Fielding's Amazon

Fielding's Australia

Fielding's Bahamas

Fielding's Belgium

Fielding's Bermuda

Fielding's Borneo

Fielding's Brazil

Fielding's Britain

Fielding's Budget Europe

Fielding's Caribbean

Fielding's Caribbean Cruises

Fielding's Caribbean East

Fielding's Caribbean West

Fielding's Europe

Fielding's European Cruises

Fielding's Far East

Fielding's France

Fielding's Freewheelin' USA

Fielding's Guide to the World's Most Dangerous Places

Fielding's Guide to Kenya's Best Hotels, Lodges & Homestays

Fielding's Guide to the World's Great Voyages

Fielding's Hawaii

Fielding's Holland

Fielding's Italy

Fielding's Las Vegas Agenda

Fielding's London Agenda

Fielding's Los Angeles Agenda

Fielding's Malaysia and Singapore

Fielding's Mexico

Fielding's New York Agenda

Fielding's New Zealand

Fielding's Paris Agenda

Fielding's Portugal

Fielding's Rome Agenda

Fielding's San Diego Agenda

Fielding's Scandinavia

Fielding's Southeast Asia

Fielding's Southern Vietnam on Two Wheels

Fielding's Spain

Fielding's Thailand Including Cambodia, Laos, Myanmar

Fielding's Vacation Places Rated

Fielding's Vietnam

Fielding's Worldwide Cruises

The Indiana Jones Survival Guide

FIELDING'S THE WORLD'S MOST DANGEROUS PLACES™

Robert Young Pelton

Coskun Aral

Fielding Worldwide, Inc.

308 South Catalina Avenue

Redondo Beach, California 90277 U.S.A.

Fielding's Guide to The World's Most Dangerous Places

Published by Fielding Worldwide, Inc.

Text Copyright ©1995 Robert Young Pelton

Icons & Illustrations Copyright ©1995 FWI

Photo Copyrights ©1995 to Individual Photographers

FIELDING WORLDWIDE INC.

PUBLISHER AND CEO **Robert Young Pelton**
PUBLISHING DIRECTOR **Paul T. Snapp**
ELEC. PUBLISHING DIRECTOR **Larry E. Hart**
PUBLIC RELATIONS DIRECTOR **Beverly Riess**
ACCOUNT SERVICES MANAGER **Christy Harp**

EDITORS

Linda Charlton   **Kathy Knoles**

PRODUCTION

Gini Sardo-Martin   **Chris Snyder**
Craig South   **Janice Whitby**
COVER DESIGNED BY **Digital Artists, Inc.**
COVER PHOTOGRAPHERS **Coskun Aral**
INSIDE PHOTOS **Werner Funk, Franck Jolot**
Blackstar: Sebastian Bolesch, Francois Charton, Charles Crowell, Caren Firouz, Cindy Karp, Erica Lanser, Vera Lentz, Malcolm Linton, Paul Miller, Debbi Morello, Christopher Morris, Rob Nelson, Rogerio Reis, Klaus Reisinger, Joseph Rodriguez, Robert Semeniuk, Joao Silva, Jay Ullal, Munesuke Yamamoto
National Geographic: Rebecca Abrams, James P. Blair, Bruce Dale, James Staufield
Sipa Press: Coskun Aral, Philippe Fabry, Albert Facelly, Patrick Frilet, Andy Hernandez, Armineh Johannes, Barbier A Kachgar, Francois Lehr, Richard Manin, John Mantel, Marc Simon, Bob Strong, Sergio Zalis
Westlight: Robert Young Pelton

Inquiries should be addressed to: Fielding Worldwide, Inc., 308 South Catalina Ave., Redondo Beach, California 90277 U.S.A., Telephone *(310) 372-4474*, Facsimile *(310) 376-8064*, 8:30 a.m.–5:30 p.m. Pacific Standard Time.

ISBN 1-56952-031-3

Library of Congress Catalog Card Number

94-068334

Printed in the United States of America

Letter from the Publisher

In 1946, Temple Fielding began the first of what would be a remarkable new series of well-written, highly personalized guidebooks for independent travelers. Temple's opinionated, witty and oft-imitated books have now guided travelers for almost a half-century. More important to some was Fielding's humorous and direct method of steering travelers away from the dull and the insipid. Today, the Fielding Travel Guides are still written by experienced travelers for experienced travelers. Our authors carry on Fielding's reputation for creating travel experiences that deliver insight with a sense of discovery and style.

This guide was written to help people understand just what the less traveled parts of the world can offer.

Today the concept of independent travel has never been bigger. Our policy of *brutal honesty* and a highly personal point of view has never changed; it just seems the travel world has caught up with us.

RYP

Robert Young Pelton
Publisher and CEO
Fielding Worldwide, Inc.

M₨. D🅿'S DA🅝G🄴🅆 🅆A🅁

FACE FEAR WITH STYLE!

LOOK SHARP WHILE YOU LAUGH AT DANGER IN YOUR 100% HEAVYWEIGHT COTTON T SHIRT (MAKES GREAT BANDAGES!). AVAILABLE ONLY IN XL AND APOCALYPTIC BLACK. ORDER WHILE THERE IS STILL TIME!

ONLY $18 PLUS $4 SHIPPING AND HANDLING. CA RESIDENTS ADD $1.50 SALES TAX. ALLOW 2 TO 4 WEEKS FOR DELIVERY.

NAME:

ADDRESS:

CITY:

STATE   ZIP

SHIRT NAME:
QUANTITY

SEND CHECK OR MONEY ORDER WITH YOUR ORDER FORM TO:
FIELDING WORLDWIDE, INC.
308 SOUTH CATALINA AVE.
REDONDO BEACH, CA 90277
OR
ORDER YOUR SHIRTS BY PHONE.:

1-800-FW-2-GUIDE

VISA, MC, AMEX ACCEPTED

FRONT

BACK

TOUR OF DUTY

Hit the hard road with a fashion statement for our times. Visit all 35 of Mr. DP's favorite nasty places (If they still exist) and cross 'em off one by one. Make sure you send us postcards and pictures. Warning: DP's Dangerwear T-shirts are not bullet-proof or politically correct.

FRONT

BACK

DANGER SPOT

If the smiling countenance of Mr. DP wasn't enough to attract attention we've added a red bull's eye. Guaranteed readable at over a mile through a sniper's scope. This bright shirt also makes rescue and retrieval easier (Make sure you lie face down).

FRONT

BACK

NO LIMITS

No borders will hold you in this stunning fashion accessory. Mr. DP is captured in an elegant post-Soviet design that will ensure that even complacent customs inspectors will strip search you, your dog and the guy in line behind you.

Introduction

Welcome to the *World's Most Dangerous Places.* This book has been a long time in coming—combining research, personal experiences, a lot of opinions and four lifetimes of adventure, travel and experiences.

No one person could travel to every one of these countries every year and stay alive. We do, however, visit places we feel are important. In the past two years that it has taken to put this book together, the authors have been on the ground in Bosnia, Chechnya, Chile, Cambodia, Guyana, Rwanda, Burundi, Turkey, India, Indonesia, Iraq, Kenya, Lebanon, Tanzania, Malaysia, Paraguay, Vietnam. We also have been doing our homework at home spending time in Los Angeles, Miami, New York and Washington.

Along the way we chatted with some interesting characters, from the leaders of *Hezbollah* to head of the PKK. We also have hit the books and tried to keep track of and make sense out of the rapidly changing world.

We have been to a lot of countries besides the ones mentioned here and managed to have a good time in most of them. We are a whole lot smarter and a whole lot wiser.

Please view this book as embryonic. There is much more work to do in future years. Also understand that your opinions or numbers may not agree with ours. We hold no political affiliations. We have no axe to grind. We happily make fun of the pedantic and the fanatic. We are fascinated equally by the relevant and irrelevant facts we stumble across.

If you like what you read, send us a letter. If you don't, give this book to your worst enemy, maybe he or she will use it as a travel guide.

A Message to Fellow Adventurers

If you have been in dangerous places and think you can help our readers with practical info (no diatribes on political theory, please), jot down your experience with a liberal application of facts, dates, specifics and backup sources and if we use your material we will send you a **Dangerous Places** (DP) T-shirt. Also, we are looking for outrageous photos to appear in our next book. All photos will be returned if sent with a SASE. If we use your photo you will get a DP T-shirt (guaranteed to make your friends question your sanity).

The Authors

Robert Young Pelton

Pelton has led an adventurous life. It started with being the youngest student ever (10) to attend a Canadian survival school in Selkirk, Manitoba. Whether it was canoeing 1000 miles in the early spring or snowshoeing marathons in 50 degrees below zero temperatures, Pelton had an early exposure to adversity and adventure. He has worked as a lumberjack, boundary cutter, tunneler, driller and blaster's assistant. His quest for knowledge and understanding has taken him through the remote and exotic areas of more than 50 countries. Stories about his adventures have been featured in publications ranging from *Soldier of Fortune* to *Road & Track*.

Some of Pelton's adventures include: living with the Dogon people in the Sahel, breaking American citizens out of jail in Colombia, running forbidden rivers in Indonesia in leaky native canoes, traveling across East Africa with the U.S. team in the Camel Trophy series, hitchhiking through war-torn Central America, climbing the smoking volcano of Anak Krakatau and leading one of the first expeditions to explore The Lost World (Maliau Basin) in Borneo.

Along the way, he survived car accidents, muggings, illness, attacks by killer bees, even a plane crash in the central highlands of Kalimantan. He still looks forward to each encounter with danger with a sense of humor and an irreverent wit.

Pelton's approach to adventure can be quite humorous. Whether it's challenging Iban headhunters to a chug-a-lug contest, filling expedition members' packs with rocks, indulging in a little target practice with Kurdish warlords in Turkey or filling up the hotel pool with stewardesses, waiters and furniture in Burundi during an all-night party, he brings a certain element of fun and excitement to dangerous places.

Pelton is a Fellow of the Royal Geographical Society in London and is also author/coauthor of *Borneo*, *Southeast Asia*, *L.A. Agenda* and *Far East* for Fielding Worldwide.

Coskun Aral

Coskun Aral coauthor of *The World's Most Dangerous Places,* was thrust into the spotlight as a photographer when he was caught aboard a Turkish 727 hijacked by terrorists in 1980. He turned the event into world theater. His photojournalist career was launched.

Since then, photojournalist Aral has made a living covering dangerous and forbidden places. One of the few people on earth who has photographed Mecca and to be on first-name terms with the major warlords in Beirut during the '80s, he has seen more than most people see in a lifetime. His special relationships with some of the world's most dangerous people make him uniquely suited to contribute to this book.

He has covered wars on the front lines in Afghanistan, Azerbaijan, Bosnia, Cambodia, Chad, Iran, Iraq, Kuwait, Libya, the Philippines, Nicaragua, Northern Ireland, Panama, Romania, Sri Lanka, Yugoslavia and other areas. He is also the only nine-time participant of the Camel Trophy.

Aral was the only reporter in the world to interview the hijacker of the TWA plane in Beirut airport in 1985 and spent over 10 years in Lebanon. He covered the Gulf War from downtown Baghdad and has two *TIME* covers to his credit, as well as numerous photo stories.

Aral and Pelton have traveled to many places, and together they bring an intimate knowledge of the workings of the world at war, along with Pelton's intimate knowledge of the world's wild places.

Jack Kramer

Kramer has been sent to the world's most dangerous places on assignment for *TIME, Business Week* and *PBS.* He began his career by covering the civil rights movement in the Deep South during the mid-60s. In the late '60s, he went from covering the battles at home to experiencing and reporting on some of the bloodiest fighting of the Vietnam War, from Cam Lo to Khe Sanh. Later, his beat was the turbulent Middle East, including the Six-Day War, Sudan and Eritrea. He worked as a television producer for PBS on "Behind the Lines" and was *Business Week's* Cairo bureau chief, covering Saudi Arabia, the Gulf States and Iran. He covered Iran before, during and after the revolution and then restarted the defunct *Beirut Daily Star* in 1984. Kramer has covered Kenya, Rhodesia (Zimbabwe), Tanzania, Laos, Thailand, Tunisia, Turkey, Syria, South Africa and the Somalia crisis. He has traveled with the Innuit in northern Canada and traveled with the Polisario guerrillas in Morocco. He is author of *Our French Connection in Africa,* a major investigative report published in *Foreign Policy* and *Travels with the Celestial Dog,* an historical analysis of the 1960s. He lives in Washington, D.C. with his wife and their two children.

Wink Dulles

Dulles is the author of *Fielding's Vietnam, Southern Vietnam on Two Wheels* and is coauthor of *Fielding's Southeast Asia* and the *Far East.* He has spent considerable time in Cambodia, Thailand and Vietnam, traveling by motorcycle. Dulles covered the 1993 elections in Cambodia and the subsequent breakdown of order in that perpetually-besieged country, being in-country at a time when few foreigners dared. Articles on Wink's adventures have been published in *Newsday* and *Escape* magazine. He lives in Los Angeles and Bangkok.

TABLE OF CONTENTS

DANGEROUS THINGS

Security/Health

LIST OF MAPS

Criminal Places

Forbidden Places

Coming Attractions

Fielding's
The World's
Most Dangerous
Places

Foreword

While working on this book, I was asked who would read a book about places they would never want to go to. Many people make the assumption that they know the difference between dangerous and safe. Unfortunately, as travelers are kidnapped and executed in Cambodia, a recognized dangerous place, they also are hunted down and murdered in Florida. Danger is all around us. It's found in the black hearts of junkies looking for a quick hit, terrorists looking for publicity, in the poorly-maintained tin buckets that pass as airplanes you fly in across the Himalayas, the water you drink in Kenya or even in the air conditioning ducts on a cruise ship.

Danger is all around and for the traveler faced with a new environment and strange cultures, it is important to at least have a level playing field. This book will not tell all or even attempt to provide a comprehensive list. It will provide fairly candid appraisals of the dangers that await the unsuspecting. Along the way, you will learn and understand things and places that are rarely talked about in polite circles: how drugs are smuggled, how much money mercenaries make, the cost to bribe your way out of jail and more. If you have never set foot in the world's most dangerous places, you now will have plenty of reasons never to leave your armchair.

Who This Book is For

Intelligence junkies

Those who have an unabashed curiosity about the world may be looking for a central source on dangerous places. This book can never compete with the files of the world's intelligence agencies, but it makes for good disposable reading. If you want real up-to-the-minute INTEL, join the CIA. If you want to have a general grounding on the political complexities of the world, go to school.

Journalists and expats

The hard-boiled who travel on business probably require a basic grounding in the regions' danger zones and a rudimentary background on the dangers that await them. Journalists usually know more about the country they are traveling to than the people who live there. Others could care less. For those in need of the latest info, call the local embassy and tap into the State Department's on-line incident reports. Keep in mind, the State Department information is gathered by American government employees from outside news services; their reports are very Western and subject to reporting embassies' intelligence abilities and political slants. Government warnings also seem to reflect a siege mentality. Most journalists pride themselves on their up-to-the-minute knowledge of their beat. The problem is that most of that information is filtered through the Western press, government sources and other writers. Many journalists are content to cover civil wars from plush hotels and to rely on official tours of the war zones for their coverage. Others remain on the side, completely unaware of the dangers posed by opposing armies. We have tried to present information from both sides with a minor slant toward covering terrorist and criminal operations, as well as opposition forces.

Adventure travelers

The legions of healthy professionals looking for a two-week recharge may or may not be aware of the dangers that await them. The rapid increase in travel to exotic regions will continue to attract travelers as they venture to more and more far-flung countries. Many of the new countries currently in favor are "destinations" such as Cambodia, Kenya, India, Pakistan and Turkey. They all possess both dangerous and safe regions.

Few know the difference. Most will return robust and suntanned. Others will die, the result of bus crashes, robberies, kidnappings, land mines and diseases. Most adventure travelers rely on politically correct but militarily-naive guidebooks such as Lonely Planet, Moon and Rough Guides. They provide minimal coverage of war zones and simply tell you to stay away. Very few backpacker guide writers will risk their lives for the paltry sums earned writing these books. Their hesitation in covering the untouristy subjects of land mines, street executions, kidnapping of foreigners and drug smuggling is also understandable, in light of the fact that book sales are based on the number of travelers who go there.

Adrenaline junkies and war freaks

People with a need for danger look for nerve-tingling destinations. The world has many areas that attract ghouls, mercenaries, thrill seekers and the intellectually curious. In many cases, the invasion of a country is followed within hours by the invasion of the press. Hungry for bang-bang, eager to make headlines and reputations, they swarm small countries in their Banana Republic safari jackets with Sony camcorders and Nikons blazing. Some are real journalists; some are spies. Soon the hotels fill up with arms dealers, doctors, pilots, advisors, embassy attaches and spooks. Yes, Virginia, there is a Satan; he can usually be found at the bar in the Holiday Inn.

The curious and easily amused

The intellectual and bored will find this book contains information not available in any other guidebook: everything from defusing land mines to where to find pirates. If nothing else, some of the stories make for ripping yarns and an entertaining read.

This book covers a very narrow period of about two years and describes situations as they were as of June 1995. Naturally, we fully expect major developments in each and every region the day after we go to press. It is important that you read between the lines to understand ongoing feuds (Northern Ireland vs England or Hutu vs Tutsi) and flash-in-the-pan uprisings like in Yemen (destabilized by Iran), Haiti (same country, different dictator), Kuwait (Hussein's punitive expedition fueled by delusions of grandeur based on a premise of stealing oil) or more importantly, long-term vows by terrorists of covert warfare that occur on anniversaries of some event (bombings, demonstrations, stonings and assassinations).

A Polite Discourse on Liability (ours) and Gullibility (yours)

This book is more likely to kill you than save your life. We can advise you not to try this at home, but more people are injured in their homes than outside them, so you may be safer traveling to some of the places in this book. At least you will be paying attention to the dangers that await you. Much of the information is gathered from secondhand sources where we feel it is more accurate than our firsthand reports. War zones, third-world countries and danger zones are very mercurial places with no one really knowing what's going on at any one time. Situations change by the hour. So use this book and other sources as pieces of the puzzle. If you choose to travel to dangerous places, get your situation reports updated by everyone all the time. Ask the embassy, the police, locals, bus drivers and farmers what's going on. But remember, even if you have all the pieces, you're still left with a puzzle.

A disclaimer: Please understand that due to the nature of this book and the unusual sources of information, we ask that you do not make any decisions based on the material presented in this book. In fact, this book is about places you should not go (they *are* dangerous). This book is written by a group of people with help from correspondents, friends and contacts around the world. To protect many of our sources, we have not credited all of them. We cannot guarantee this information is accurate or reliable. And, it shouldn't be used for the planning of any activity. We encourage you always to investigate other sources of information regarding areas where you wish to travel. Fielding and the authors cannot take responsibility for any misfortune, liability or inconvenience due to your interpretation, application or even understanding of the information in this book.

THE AUTHORS AND PUBLISHERS ASSUME NO LIABILITY NOR DO THEY ENCOURAGE YOU TO DO, SEE, VISIT OR TRY ANY OF THE ACTIVITIES OR ACTIONS DISCUSSED IN THIS BOOK. THIS BOOK IS INTENDED FOR ENTERTAINMENT ONLY AND SHOULD BE VIEWED AS BEING INFORMATION BUT NOT NECESSARILY RELIABLE.

The modest goal of the authors: Unemployment

This book is not all doom and gloom. There is a chapter on "Making a Difference." Here we show you how actually to connect with other people and organizations to effect change. It might be washing bandages in Burundi, sleeping in a hammock high up in a first-growth forest to fight off loggers, protecting oil workers in Angola as a paid mercenary or even discussing politics with other folks in an effort to build a better understanding between people who don't see eye-to-eye.

So you have our primitive formula for success: Tell people what is going on and then show them how to fix it. Knowledge fights fear, builds hope, exposes cowards, supports the just and makes the world a better place. We do not aspire to greatness, but we do hope that we intrigue enough people to want to know how to gather information and then do something with it.

It is our goal not to find enough dangerous places in the world to justify writing a book about the subject.

The World's Most Dangerous People

"Davis, come in here and take a bullet."

Terrorists

Terrorism draws the attention of a lot of security analysts. The difference is the PR-spin terrorist groups are able to put on common crimes. A kidnapping becomes a political crime; robbery, extortion and murder all calculated to achieve a political aim. All are followed with the requisite press communique to attach political significance to the act of thuggery.

Pinkerton's does an excellent job of keeping track of every murder, kidnapping, maiming and bombing by various terrorist groups. In its most recent report on terrorism, the security firm comes up with some interesting if not numerically sterile, conclusions.

As of May 1993, Pinkerton determined that the total casualties of terrorism as of 1992 involved 21,103 people. All, by definition, innocent people. Attacks against buildings were up 361 over 1992 to 2043 in 1993 and 6.9 people were killed per facility attack.

Between 50% and 70% of facility attacks involved police, military and governmental targets as opposed to businesses. This means little to the innocent bystanders who are wounded or maimed and statistics mean little when trying to predict the danger or timing of an attack.

When I or our other contributors travel, we are not only aware of but we are prepared for danger. The fact that the authors have survived their travels is reason enough to write a book. Most of the people we see hurt, killed or terrorized tend to be innocent victims, not travelers. Soldiers have no problem killing other soldiers in battle, but it takes a unique person to murder innocent people. If these individuals have a political agenda they are called terrorists. Terrorists, due to their effective publicity efforts and well-groomed public images, are the number one fear of most Americans. Terrorists, however, rarely target travelers but are responsible for much of the fear among them.

The world's dispossessed now know how to play to American sensitivities. And, of course, the press plays a willing role in delivering their messages: images of starvation, the rape of innocents, murders of nuns, genocide, ethnic cleansing, executions of civilians, bloody mortar attacks, kidnapping and murders of attachés. Many of these incidents are carefully staged to elicit opinions and emotions, as well as financial and military support.

Terrorism is a method of waging war against the innocent. It conveys the perpetrators' feelings of injustice, outrage and powerlessness. The more innocent you are, the more effective their message.

Worse yet is the systematic targeting of tourists and foreigners to strangle the flow of foreign currency. War of this type is being waged in Algeria by Iranian-backed fundamentalists, in Sri Lanka by the Tamil LTTE and in Turkey by the Kurdish PKK. This new and frightening development means that the happy-go-lucky traveler is apt to be targeted specifically to send a message to his home country.

The last and most ominous danger is terror in our own backyard. The bombing of the World Trade Center in New York at 12:18 p.m. on February 26, 1993 was not the opening shot in an East vs West Holy War, but a well-planned press release sent from Iran to show hatred of Western indifference and lack of support for Muslims in Bosnia.

There have been other incidents that lead many to believe that *jihad* (Holy War), once confined to the Middle East, is filtering into the United States. The March 1989 pipe bomb attack in San Diego on the wife of the captain of the U.S.S. Vincennes (the ship that shot down the Air Iran Airbus in July 1988) is an indication of this infiltration. The fatal shooting of two CIA employees on January 25, 1993 by Pakistani Mir Amail Kansi with an AK-47 assault rifle was a signal that the war is here.

But there is one last "ultimate fear." What if the van that was driven and parked on the B2 Level at the World Trade Center wasn't carrying a $400 bomb made of simple industrial chemicals (nitric acid, sulfuric acid and urea)? The 1000 lbs. of gooey explosives were packed into cheap cardboard boxes and then detonated by simple blasting caps timed by a cheap metal alarm clock. The only melodrama was that the bottles of compressed hydrogen gas were designed to create a Hollywood-style fireball. What if it had been a small nuclear bomb instead—donated by North Korea or some other disgruntled group? That thought should send terror into the heart of every American.

The Politically Incorrect Bad Boys

The most comprehensive report on global terrorism is released every April by the United States Department of State (Patterns of Global Terrorism, publication #10136). The report gives a comprehensive overview of terrorism activities on a country by country basis. The numbers tell us that of the 427 terrorist attacks in 1993 there have been only 88 attacks against Americans (down from 142 in 1992). It would have been a much better year if it weren't for the PKK racking up terrorist attacks like Michael Jordan racking up points in a playoff game. The PKK managed to claim 150 of those incidents, most of them in a two-day orgy of bombings in Western Europe on November 4 and June 24.

The government report mentions that if it weren't for the PKK the number of terrorist incidents would be down, something that irritates those chart-loving bureaucrats. Luckily they come clean and mention that 1993 was actually the highest casualty total in five years with 109 people killed and 1393 wounded. You don't win wars by counting battles but by the body count, something the State Department report tries to ignore.

The good news is that terrorism costs money and the former bad boys of the World (Cuba, Libya, Soviet Union, Syria and Iran) need their folding money for boring things like food and armored limousines. The bad news is that the current crop of terrorist boys are getting very politically savvy and are working away on the hearts and minds of their core groups while maiming and killing their enemies (Hamas, *Hezbollah*, Sikhs, the LTTE, the PKK). These groups are learning to be self-sufficient although Iran is still the major supporter of terrorism at this point.

When it comes to where terrorist acts occur, the report says that Western Europe was the site for 180 attacks, the Middle East was runner up with 101, and Latin America came in a close third with 97. What they don't mention is that your life is far safer shopping at Harrods than strolling through downtown Kabul during a rocket attack.

Criminals

Career criminals come in a close second in image to terrorists, but are number one with a bullet for real damage. Criminals are usually a product of society. The more desperate the needs of some, the more likely they are to turn to crime. As of 1994, America became the first nation to have more than a million people in jail. In fact, we have more people in jail than any other country. The British point to Australia, the former Soviets nod toward Siberia and China points to the ground as the best place to put criminals. The reality is that there are more criminals on the street than there are in jail.

Travelers are ideal targets for crooks; they carry lots of cash and expensive equipment and keep it in handy luggage, cars or hotel rooms. They can't or won't hang around to pursue the case and they are, in the majority of cases, unarmed and unsuspecting. The most likely bad experience you will face, war zone or not, is finding someone's fingers wandering through your pockets, or your luggage running down the street attached to a teenage kid.

Criminals are not all shifty-eyed opportunists. Criminals can also run countries, protecting drug smugglers, poachers, terrorists and even leaders of terrorist groups.

Countries alleged to support and/or protect criminals include Syria, Libya, Sudan and Myanmar.

Other countries have little or no control over major criminal organizations that operate with impunity. These include Russia, Thailand, Pakistan, Afghanistan, Zaire, Colombia, Italy and the United States. There are some areas, like Chechnya in southern Russia, The Golden Triangle in Laos and Myanmar, that are essentially criminal countries within countries that have their own government, armies and laws.

Criminal Places

Americans like to think that they enjoy a certain level of safety because of their standard of living. They do. But if you don't have a certain standard of living, you live in one of the world's most violent and dangerous places. The chances are the person who is going to do you in is sitting across the table during breakfast. Crime is big business in some countries and you are part of their expansion plan. Travel to these countries is laughably easy and getting whacked is even easier. Staying alive or solvent in these countries requires a lot of common sense (don't go out at night, travel in groups, don't stray of the beaten path, etc.)

Violent countries where your wallet or life stand a good chance of enhancing their GDP include:

Brazil	**Colombia**
Kenya	**Mexico**
Nigeria	**Panama**
Russia	**Tanzania**
United States of America	**Zaire**

Bugs

Bugs are the number three bad guy: the zillions of microbes that enter every orifice of your body when you travel. Whether the nasty things are from aedes aegypti mosquitos deciding whether or not to give you yellow fever, Iranian flies vomiting on your kebab or Nigerian snails delivering unseen parasites into your intestines, bugs like big, fleshy European stock. Once smitten, you will wish you were a hostage in a Khmer Rouge camp instead of voiding fluids out of both ends of your body. This book won't try to tell you all the nasty things that are out there. (But we do dabble enough in the sensational to send you screaming with stool, blood and urine sample in hand, to the nearest tropical disease specialist.)

The Most Dangerous Trends: War of the Innocents

It used to be that young men marched off to war. Nowadays, war marches directly into your home. Whether the war is delivered by CNN, the pointed end of a SCUD missile, a letter bomb or in a beat-up Ford van parked under the World Trade Center, it no longer involves two clearly defined groups battling for superiority. Wars are being fought on the ground, in the newsrooms, boardrooms and in peoples' homes.

It is hard to define war today. There are few uniforms, few battlefields that become tourist attractions and even fewer marching songs and flying colors. In the past, 90 percent of casualties used to be soldiers; today, 90 percent of the casualties are civilians. This is the new face of war. Or is it war? In Rwanda, Somalia, Bosnia, Haiti, Turkey and Azerbaijan we see the mass graves, the frightened refugees, the crying babies, the atrocities, the horror—but where are the soldiers? The flags? The marching columns? The War? In Algeria, Egypt, Turkey, Sri Lanka, Cambodia and Pakistan, foreigners are the favored target of the fundamentalists. Is this a war or a turkey shoot?

As in the words of General George S. Patton: "The idea is not to die for your country but to make the other poor bastard die for his." George never lived to see the sad irony of terrorism: where we die for our enemies' countries. Worse yet, we're dying so the poor bastards can have a country to die for.

Terrorism as a form of war has actually died down in direct proportion to the dwindling amount of money dedicated to this black art by the former Soviet Union, Libya, Syria, Cuba, the former East Germany and Iraq. They've all had their financial fingers slapped and have resorted to minor sulking support of outlawed groups.

It does not mean that terrorism is on the decline. In 1993, there were 109 people killed by terrorists in 427 incidents. As of August 1994, there had been 130 people killed. Terrorism seems to be here to stay. According to the U.N., of the 82 armed conflicts that were fought in the past three years, only three were between nations. The rest were civil wars or insurgencies.

These wonderful facts and figures are brought to you by the world's working press, who once could sit on a hill overlooking a battlefield and report on both sides with relative immunity. Today, you can get more publicity by shooting journalists than just mere soldiers. The numbers do not mean much and even can lead to speculation as to their purpose. According to Reporters Without Borders, in 1993, 63 journalists were killed on the job. An additional 30 were slain, but it could not be determined if they were working at the time. All, however, agree that they were dead and unable to work after being killed. A total of 124 journalists were detained by local governments who objected to their reports.

Dangerous Places

Where are the world's most dangerous places? I guess wherever you are the most terrified for your life. For some people it's in a state-of-the-art Boeing 767 lifting off on their way to visit Grannie, for others it's looking for a gas station after midnight after taking the wrong off-ramp. Many people assume that other places are more dangerous than where they are right now. Californians watch with some relief when terrorists blow up the World Trade Center in New York, while New Yorkers feel thankful not to be among the victims of L.A.'s earthquakes, fires and mudslides.

Where are the hot spots? In 1994, Algeria, Afghanistan, Angola, Burma (Myanmar), Burundi, Egypt, Georgia, Haiti, Iraq, Liberia, Mexico, Mozambique, Nigeria, Sudan, Tajikistan, Rwanda and Zaire were described by the U.N. as nations in crisis and in danger of social disintegration. It is an interesting assumption that some of these countries had something to disintegrate from.

The U.N. knows who its landlord is, so there was no mention of the L.A. riots, refugees in Guantanamo Bay, gang wars in U.S. inner cities, executions by Colombian drug dealers or political murders by Peruvian Maoists. The U.N.'s list of dangerous places is made more modest by its budget restrictions in keeping the world safe. The reality is that most countries from Germany to Indonesia have dangerous places. And, there seems to be more and more of these places popping up without warning. Four years ago, UNICEF spent 4 percent of its budget on emergencies; now it spends almost 30 percent. During the creation of this book, Rwanda was fanned from a thin smoking wisp of danger into a bona fide hell. It then turned into a major human exodus. The tiny city of Goma turned into a new city/country on the verge of civil unrest. Historically, the elimination of half the Tutsi population did not come as a surprise. What was surprising was how the world watched passively from the comfort of Barclay loungers as hell on earth played out competing with the O.J Simpson trial and the baseball strike. Rwanda faded to the back page and then disappeared entirely. There were some mentions of a similar bloodbath in Burundi, but like most sequels, the ratings suffered, so the holocaust was canceled. At least by the press.

Politically Incorrect Places

It probably doesn't matter whether the guy shooting you wants your wallet or is desirous of making a political statement. Dead is dead. But it does help to know that there are some countries where they are picky about who they kill, kidnap and terrorize. In fact, being an American or just a tourist is politically incorrect in the following countries:

Algeria	**India**
Israel and the Occupied Territories	**Sri Lanka**
Turkey	

The Apocalyptic Paradises

There are many areas where they just can't afford terrorists simply because there is no government to overthrow. Countries like Afghanistan, Angola, Somalia, Zaire and Rwanda have more important things to do like survive, rather than balance road building or military budgets. Every once in awhile someone will run the country for a week or so, but then his opponents will violently disagree with the political interpretation of his stranglehold. Travel to these places is truly the zenith of thrill seeking because you will see the absolute lowest level of human existence, atrocities and civilizations. Your friends will not really care about your trip since it won't be covered on any news programs and you will probably wonder why you risked your life to see such a depressing world.

These countries are the most frustrating and dangerous to travel to since there is little to no infrastructure (electricity, phone, money, etc.) and rampant lawlessness. Consider your chances of survival when traveling to these countries on par with premeditated human sacrifice or skinny dipping with piranhas.

Afghanistan	**Angola**
Liberia	**Somalia**
Zaire	

The Evil Druglords

There is another group of bombers, shooters and evil people who need to be terrorists to continue to manufacture, sell and transport drugs. Sometimes they are listed as terrorist groups but usually as druglords or gangs. These groups stay local but are more vicious than the politically motivated groups. The triads in China, the Wa and Shan army in Northern Thailand, the Shining Path in Peru, the Russian mafia, the mujahadeen of Afghanistan, even the Crips and Bloods in L.A. and New York kill and maim people in their ongoing business activities. Some claim a mild political agenda but in reality view that as a way to extend their dramatically shortened life span should they decide to retire. All and any are equally deadly if you appear in the wrong place at the wrong time regardless of their political persuasion. Travel to these areas is very dangerous due to summary executions, opportunistic kidnappings and absolute hatred of publicity or visitors.

These groups operate in the countryside and police can inform you of their turf. Contrary to what Hollywood would have you believe, the leaders of these groups are not slobbering maniacs with greasy hair and bad teeth. They are in fact multimillionaires who live better (and in many cases longer) than the rulers of the countries in which they operate. You can arrange visits or trips if the drug lord is working his political angle. (Imagine the influence of a politician who never talked to the press!) Since these people are regularly tracked down and killed by the governments they operate in, expect your film and your visit to be of extreme interest to the police when you leave (or try to leave) the country.

Lebanon	**Peru**
Colombia	**Laos**
Myanmar	**Pakistan**
Thailand	

The Death of Bang-Bang

The media love wars. Conflict, pathos and bright colors: green tracers, red blood, bright flashes and big ratings. The chance to dust off the old safari jackets and get in a little talking-head time. Out to the front with the military: close-ups of the heads and wide shots of the pieces. Burning buildings, talking generals and back to the bar.

There are dangers that make little news because they contain no pitiful children, no raging inferno; no bang-bang, as the journos like to call it.

AIDS continues to spread and devastate in the Third World. Then there's the wholesale trade in nuclear materials from the former Soviet Union. To date, German police have uncovered over 700 attempts to sell nuclear materials since the breakup of the former Soviet Union. In August 1994, police stopped a man carrying a pound of plutonium from Moscow. Dumped into a city's water supply, that much plutonium could kill hundreds of thousands of people. Iraq, Iran, Libya and North Korea all are itching to join the nuclear club and actively are seeking the bits and pieces they need to make phantom bombs. They like the world trade scenario and are taking full advantage of America's, "peace-at-any-price" campaign where they literally buy peace from Israel, the PLO and other cash-poor but idealistic countries. Right now, Cuba, Haiti, Sudan, Libya and North Korea are squealing for U.S. attention (and the resultant aid they hope reconciliation brings) now that Mother Russia's teats have dried up. But the U.S. can't write blank checks to countries like Iran, China, Albania or other more fundamental centers. Saddam even tried a fourth-down quarterback sneak in an attempt to negotiate a lucrative settlement with the United States and divert his countrymen's attention from their plight. It didn't work.

The collapse of the totalitarian regime in Russia has allowed strongmen to carve out their own turf, sending most of the Russian and many former Marxist countries into small, tribal and feudal kingdoms. Nationalist groups that were once vigorously suppressed are rising up. Cultural, tribal and religious groups who were forced to live together in uneasy harmony now vent their pent-up hatred in Africa and Eastern Europe. Elections are ignored in Myanmar and Haiti. Rescue missions turn into ugly gang wars, as in Somalia and Bosnia-Herzegovina, with the white knight becoming the military oppressor.

The World's Least Covered Dangerous Places	
Afghanistan	Algeria
Burundi	Cambodia
China	India
Iran	Liberia
The Philippines	Tajikistan

War-In-Our-Time Places

There are of course the classic war zones available to the adventurous traveler, places like Nagorno Karabakh, Bosnia-Herzegovina, Azerbaijan and a rotating weekly series of guest wars (Rwanda, Iraq, Afghanistan, Liberia, Angola) that flare up, boil over and then go back down to a simmer until they can find enough money to kill each other properly. These places are tough to get into unless you are a professional journalist or don't mind being put in jail while war wages around you. These are great places if you want to be the next Robert Capa, but expect a lot of shooters (with cameras, not guns). In fact, in Somalia and Haiti there have been more journalists than combatants at skirmishes. Some journalists have been so desperate to get gripping images that they actually run ahead of the soldiers in firefights to get those great shots. Travel in war zones is expensive, boring and fraught with paperwork and checkpoints required to move around. So bring plenty of cash and patience.

There are some places like Turkey, India or Russia where there are all-out wars but the government in charge prefers to call them "ongoing campaigns against terrorism." All one has to do is read the weekly body counts coming out of these minor clashes to realize that there is more to it.

Azerbaijan	BosniaHerzegovina
Cambodia	Chechnya
Nagorno Karabakh	Haiti

Clear geographic and political lines have resulted in new horrors. Ethnic cleansing is now a regular feature of these dirty little wars, as in Rwanda and Bosnia-Herzegovina. Terrorism takes the war into the shopping malls of the oppressor. Television takes the agony of the entire world into our homes. Even the April 1992 riots in Los Angeles show that no one is immune from hate and fractionalism. Could we be as equally third world? The question is does TV journalism cause hatred and war?

Domestic Terrorism

In the Third World, there is a blurred line between terrorism and warfare. Here in America, we pretend that a terrorist act is an anomaly, a fluke—something that will go away if we flip the channel. The heyday of domestic terrorism was 1982 and the death knell for global terrorism was the collapse of the Soviet Union. In the U.S., we forget we have our own problems. Jewish and Muslim extremists, abortion rights activists, white supremacist groups and Cubans are just some of the players involved.

There were 51 incidents of domestic terrorism in 1982, four in 1992. There were 165 incidents in the past 11 years. Of that number, 77 took place in Puerto Rico, 23 were committed by left wing groups, 16 by Jewish extremists, 12 by anti-Castro Cubans, six by right wing groups and 31 by other groups.

Their targets were businesses (60), military (33), state and federal government property (31), private property (18) and diplomatic establishments (17).

What this means is that there are terrorist attacks in the United States. And that you live in a dangerous place. Who would have thought that downtown Oklahoma City would have the most dangerous place in America in 1995?

More proof of how you get more for your TV dollar.

Using a single day's programming on similar services between 1992 and 1994, a recent study determined that violence was up 41%. Broadcast network violence was up 72% and violence on cable was up 37%.

Center for Media and Public Affairs, Washington, D.C.

What Is Dangerous?

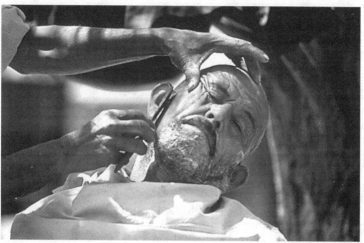

All right, let's get to it. What is dangerous and what isn't? Since most of us start to think about danger only when we travel, let's look at the odds. There's a one in 10 million chance of dying in a plane crash. Not bad. The odds of getting killed on a train is 10 times higher, about one in a million.

If you think that pilot error or cannibis-smoking railroad engineers are the cause of most accidents, try driving across the country. The chances of getting killed are one in 14,000—worse odds yet. And a full third of American drivers don't even bother to buckle up.

What Should You Worry About?

There are three danger zones in life. First is making it through the first year of life. The second major hurdle is surviving until the ripe old age of 37 where accidental death is the grim reaper's best friend. Unintentional injuries are the fifth leading cause of death. The third stage is making it past the list of debilitating diseases that claim most people and surviving into old age. It's important to understand the relative dangers of normal living to appreciate the numbers that you will read about in later chapters.

Time

The number one killer is Father Time. Although there is a slow lengthening of our lives, we are all subject to deterioration of tissues. Most of us can expect to live to our mid-70s before getting nervous about getting our money's worth on a five-year carpet.

In 1890, life expectancy was 31.1 years. In 1995, it is up to 75.4 years.

How to live longer? First, don't let accidental causes get in the way. Second, exercise and eat right and maintain a positive mental attitude. How is that done? Travel, of course. People who live the longest have an insatiable curiosity as well as a love for travel. Those wiry little octogenarians that seem perfectly healthy, have inquiring minds, travel a lot and are always looking for a good time. They stay out of the house as much as possible, fully understanding that the home is the world's most dangerous place (see "Accidents") for people over the age of 75.

Accidental Death

Young and Tender

In 1991, there were 36,766 children who did not make it past the first year of life in the U.S. If you make it out of the womb (16,591 didn't) without a major congenital abnormality (7685 did), there's Sudden Infant Death Syndrome to deal with (5349). The next most dangerous incidents are choking (961), car crashes (174), ingesting a foreign object (130), burns or fires (114) and drowning (105).

Young and Reckless

Young male teenagers in cars seem to have a death wish. Eighteen may be a magic age for most people, but it is a very profitable target demographic for undertakers. Of every 100,000 18-year-olds, 42.5 will die in car crashes.

Middle-aged and Reckless

What is the #2 accidental killer of people between the ages of 18 and 49 (after car accidents of course)? Dying to know the answer? It's accidental poisoning; a curious manner of death, with a rate highest for men aged 37. Most of this poisoning is the result of the deadly side effects of ingesting normal medicines.

Old and Clumsy

The next time you send Gramps downstairs to find his glasses, don't be surprised if he doesn't come back. Falls collect a number of victims in the age group above 75. Although the number pales in comparison to heart disease, it is worth remembering: 8169 people died from falls last year vs. 437,973 from heart disease.

Disease

The last time these numbers were totalled up (in 1991), the leading cause of death in America was heart disease (720,862 deaths). Cancer claimed 514,657 lives, strokes accounted for 143,481 fatalities and chronic obstructive pulmonary disease claimed 90,650 victims. It's a long way down to the next killer. Are there any trends to give us hope? The rates of incidence of stomach, uterus and liver cancer has dropped since 1930. Lung cancer and leukemia cases have climbed dramatically. Men are the most likely victims of all these maladies, except stroke. And there are no cures for any of these afflictions except early diagnosis and treatment. Don't smoke, don't work in coal mines and stay away from nuclear waste sites.

Criminal Places	
Afghanistan	Banditry
Aruba	Street Crime
Belize	Petty Crime
Benin	Street Crime
Bolivia	Kidnapping
Brazil	Violent Crime
Burundi	Violent Crime
Cambodia	Kidnapping, Murder
Cameroon	Street Crime
Cent. African Rep.	Street Crime
Chad	Banditry
Chile	Petty Crime
China	Petty Theft, Robbery
Colombia	You name it
Congo	Street Crime
Cote d'Ivoire	Street Crime
Cuba	Street Crime
Dominican Rep.	Petty Theft
Equatorial Guinea	Violent Crime
Ethiopia	Banditry
Ghana	Petty Theft
India	Petty Theft, Kidnapping
Liberia	Lawlessness
Mali	Banditry
Morocco	Banditry
Nigeria	Con Artists
Pakistan	Kidnapping, Banditry
Peru	Murder, Kidnapping
Philippines	Kidnapping

Criminal Places	
Russia	The Works
Rwanda	Nobody left to steal anything
Somalia	Banditry
Spain	Tourist Crime
Uganda	Violent Crime
Western Sahara	Banditry
Zaire	Violent Crime

Automobile Accidents

We weren't joking in saying that if you want to live longer, stay out of the house. People between the age of 70 and 90 are attracted to stairs like lemmings to cliffs. But even at younger ages, if you really want to live dangerously, stay at home. Most accidents happen at home. Any student of statistics will tell you that home is where people spend the majority of their time. Each year slippery floors, kitchen knives and glass coffee tables will do more damage than all the world's terrorists.

The most dangerous month for accidents is August, with 9000 unintentional injuries versus a monthly incidence average of 7500. The safest month is February with only 5700. Curious to know the other most dangerous months?

Cause of Death	Most Dangerous Month	#	Least Dangerous Month	#	Avg
Car Accidents	August	4243	January	2869	3628
Falls	December	1145	February	959	1055
Drownings	July	886	November	147	385
Firearms	November	164	September	83	120
Fire	January	539	June	194	343
Poisoning	August	572	January	412	475

Source: National Center for Health Statistics and National Safety Council

Danger On the Road

From the moment you grasp your airline seat with sweaty palms to the minute your cab rolls to a stop at your front door, most travelers have a nervous feeling that their life has become more dangerous. The reality is quite the opposite. Fewer accidents happen to people when they travel than when they are at home.

Why? Think about your takeoff. You're in a multimillion dollar aircraft, the culmination of more than 100 years of aviation safety engineering. Up front, you have two pilots who must not only take training in emergency procedures, but are the best of their kind. Many American pilots are Vietnam-era pilots who have flown in combat. All have racked up tens of thousands of hours in the air. You are given flight safety procedures by individuals trained in emergency situations. You're under the control of a global traffic network that tracks all major aircraft and weather patterns. Buses, trains and cars are subject to stringent safety laws in both construction and operation. Hotels have sophisticated sprinkler systems. Restaurants are inspected by health inspectors and so on.

Naturally, you can throw this entire scenario out the window when you leave Europe, America or Australia. The point is, danger is not something you can control but at least Uncle Sam is looking out for you.

What Danger Awaits the Weary Traveler?

What do people worry about when they are on vacation? Well, a recent survey in Europe came up with the following:

What me Worry?	%
Burglary of home while away	90%
Illness and accidents on holiday	40%
Family's safety	33%
Bad Accommodation	26%
Bad Weather	19%
Bad Food	18%
Work	6%

By the very definition of travel, you will be forced to choose some form of transportation. Planes are the safest means; cars are the most dangerous. In America, the death rate per miles traveled is comforting for those who fly but unsettling for the majority of people who like to drive:

Type of Passenger Transport	Death Rate (per billion passenger miles)	Passenger Miles (in billions)
Passenger Cars	.89	2393.2
Intercity Buses	.03	23.7
Transit Buses	.01	20.6
Trains	.02	13.5
Airplanes	.01	354.3

Europeans' most dangerous places	%
Florida	42%
North Africa	9%
Turkey	7%
California	7%
Kenya	7%

Expect danger every time you decide to get into a taxi; but expect death in a small minivan. You may prefer to travel by bus, cab, rickshaw, trishaw, *becek* or even roller-blades.

The most dangerous form of travel in the world is the fabled minibus. These Third World creations are small Japanese-made transports with a drive train that has a hard time pushing around a family of four built with a "cargo" hold for up to 16 passengers. Most minivans are designed to seat seven, but ingenuity and greed prevail.

The minivans are used primarily for rush hour transportation of poor people to work. Unlike the large, regulated buses, minivans are run by entrepreneurs who make their money by carrying as many people, as many times as they can. For example, in South Africa 60,000 accidents involving minibuses killed more than 900 people in 1993. In Peru, where they are called "killer combis," the death toll also includes non- passengers trying to get out of the way of the weaving, speeding vans. The deadly driving style is a function of drivers who must make their money within the two hours of rush hour in order to make a profit on their rental owner's charge. Last year, 375 pedestrians were killed by the 30,000 or so minivans in Lima, Peru. The numbers are not available for most third world countries. A rough estimate puts the chances of a fatality in a minibus, *matatu* or combi at about 30 times the normal U.S. accident rate. So the next time you plunk down between a quarter to fifty cents for one of these rides, consider how much you just sold your life for.

Minibuses

Imagine what happens when your body decelerates from 60-0 m.p.h. in two milliseconds. Not pretty. Having been at the site of many small bus crashes in my travels, I can best compare the scenes to putting a dozen mice in a coffee can along with glass and nails, slamming it against a wall and then shaking it for a few minutes more. Then spray the bloody contents across the path of oncoming traffic. That pretty much sums up the bloody and confused scene of a *matatu* accident.

Americans tend to be a little diffident about the goings-on in other countries. Very few Americans list any of their own tourist destinations as potentially dangerous places. You may be surprised to learn what Europeans think of as dangerous:

Tips on surviving minibuses

There is a reason for the multitude of religious symbols, slogans and prayers painted on Third World buses. Once they cram their doors shut and the wobbly wheels start forward, your life is in the hands of a supreme being. If you travel via small buses, remember the following:

- Avoid mountainous areas and/or winter conditions.
- Bring water and food with you.
- Ask whether the route goes through areas frequented by bandits or terrorist groups.
- Sit near an exit or on top. At least make sure you are near an open window.
- Remember your luggage is prey for slashers, rummagers and thieves. Put your luggage in a standard trash bag.
- Watch for shirt slashers if you doze off.
- Do not accept food or drink from fellow passengers.

Taxis

Our esteemed founder was reputed to have once lost a libel case wherein he described a particular cab company as the biggest crooks in Italy. The cab company easily won the case because they proved not that they were innocent but that there were bigger criminal operations in Italy at the time.

When you get into a taxi driven by a stranger in a strange land, watch out. The odds for damage to your body, your sense of well being and your wallet just jumped. Cabs in most countries have no seatbelts, no brakes, no licence and no top end on what can be charged. In many countries such as Colombia, you could get robbed in the bargain. Taxis can be controlled by telling the driver to drive slowly in his native language. I do remember a friend of mine during one particularly terrifying cab ride, rummaging through his Greek phrase book yelling what he thought meant "slower" at the top of his lungs. As the driver divided his time between staring at us incredulously and trying to maintain control of his over-revved cab, we thought we were in the hands of a lunatic. At the end of our ride, the wide-eyed cabdriver was visibly relieved to see the last of us. Upon closer examination, we realized in our haste to translate, we had been requesting him to drive "faster, faster." To be fair, I also had a cab driver in Malaysia carry around stacks of expensive luggage well beyond any chance of recovery all day long for less than $20. Based on courtesy, cleanliness, knowledge and respect for human life, the world's best cab drivers are in London and the world's worst cabbies are in New York City.

Tips on surviving cab rides

- Never get into a taxi with another passenger already inside.

- Do not take gypsy cabs; ask the airline people how much it should cost to go to your city and then agree upon a fare before you get in.

- Keep your luggage in the back seat.

- Memorize the local phrase for "slower," "stop" and "That costs too much."

- Have the hotel doorman or guide negotiate cab fares in advance.

- Check your change before you get into the cab or get change. It is a global law that cabbies never carry change.

- Many cabbies will rent themselves out for flat fees. Do not be afraid to engage the services of a trusted cabby as guide and protector of baggage.

Cars

If you rent or drive a car, you can expect a few thrills and spills along the way. First, you should know the most dangerous places to drive in the United States:

State	Deaths per 100,000 population
South Carolina	25.2
Mississippi	31.3
New Mexico	27.9
Tennessee	23.4
Arkansas	27.0
Alabama	30.0
West Virginia	24.0
Wyoming	24.2
Idaho	24.3
Kentucky	22.1

The accident rate for international travel is clouded by lack of reporting and the skew in numbers caused by the large numbers of people who don't own cars. Countries like Mexico, Pakistan, Australia, Egypt and China have horrendous accident rates but do not figure prominently in studies. Obviously, in the U.S., travel "down South" behind the wheel of a car can be nasty business. Here's what it's like outside the country:

Country	Deaths per 100,000 population
South Korea	30.4
Portugal	28.1
Brazil	22.7
Hungary	22.7
Greece	22.0
Venezuela	20.7
Spain	20.5
Ecuador	20.0
New Zealand	19.5
Luxembourg	19.4
Poland	19.2
Belgium	18.4
United States	18.4

Great Britain has the safest roads in Europe, according to figures collated by the travel insurance company Home & Overseas Insurance, a subsidiary of Eagle Star. The death rate is 1.5 per 10,000 vehicles. The next safest country is West Germany with 1.9, followed by Switzerland at 2.1, Turkey at 2.1, Italy at 2.4, Belgium at 3.5, France at 3.6, Austria at 3.6, Spain at 4.7 and Portugal at 8.6. Motorway driving is most dangerous in Spain, with almost four times as many deaths as in France.

Poland has one of the highest road-accident mortality rates in Europe; 11.4 people killed for every 100 injured. This is three to four times higher than Western figures. Police officers from the National Police Headquarters Traffic Office advise foreigners to be aware of this upon crossing the Polish border. Foreigners were involved in 2020 road accidents in Poland last year; 209 of the foreigners ended up dead and 1030 were injured. In 308 cases, foreigners were to blame and 132 of these incidents involved drivers under the influence of alcohol. The most dangerous road in Poland is the E30, a road used by more than 7000 vehicles per day. In 1991 there were 314 accidents on the E-30, in which 109 people were killed and 355 were injured.

Cause of Accident	
Alcohol/Drugs influenced	90%
Speeding	83%
Running red traffic lights	78%
Not concentrating on driving	76%
Aggressive driving	68%
Tailgating	63%

Source: National Sheriff's Association

How to get killed driving

If you have a death wish, you could find a 16-year-old to drive you around: sixteen-year-olds are the most dangerous drivers in America, being involved in 1200 deadly accidents during 1994. But more driving-related fatalities involve the use of alcohol. Many more. A nationwide organization of 25,000 sheriffs, deputy sheriffs and municipal, state and federal law enforcement officers were polled to find out what causes accidents.

Tips on staying alive while driving

There is little to be said that hasn't been said in every driver's education class you have ever taken.

- Be familiar with road warning signs. For example, in Borneo there are signs telling you to stick to the left or right of the road to choreograph the intentions of oncoming logging trucks.

- Avoid driving if possible. Nobody gets up in the morning and plans on having an accident. The fact that you are rubbernecking or checking maps while on the wrong side of the road increases the chances of an accident.

- Avoid driving in inclement weather conditions, night time or on weekends. Fog kills, rain kills, drunks kill, other tourists kill. It is estimated that after midnight on Friday and Saturday nights in rural America, three out of five drivers on the road have been drinking.

- Stay off the road in high-risk countries. You may think the Italians, Portuguese and Spaniards display amazing bravery as they skid around winding mountain roads. The accident rate says they are just lousy drivers.

- Reduce your speed. To see the difference in impact at various speeds, try running as fast as you can into the nearest wall. Now walk slowly and do it again.

- Wear a seat belt.

- Select a large car instead of a small compact.

- Don't drive tired or while suffering from jet lag.

Flying

North America is the safest place to fly. If you fly any First World airline, your chances of being killed in a crash are one in 4.4 million, according to Massachusetts Institute of Technology. If you are on a U.S. carrier, flying coast to coast , the odds are even better, one in 11 million. Other studies say that your odds of getting on a plane that is going to crash are one in every 20,000. About two-thirds of major airline crashes have been blamed on flight crew error. When you change from a big bird to a puddle-jumper you have just increased your chances of crashing by a factor of four. Commuter flights (flights with 30 or fewer seats) carry about 12 percent of all passengers. These small planes not only fly lower, take off and land more often, but are piloted by less experienced, more overworked pilots and are not subject to the same safety standards as large airliners.

	Dangerous Airports	Crimes per 10,000 passengers
1	Kennedy Airport, New York	2.5
2	Newark International, New Jersey	1.2
3	Philadelphia International, Pennsylvania	1.1
4	Miami International, Florida	.9
5	LAX, Los Angeles, California	.8
6	La Guardia, New York	.7
7	Lambert, St Louis, Missouri	.5
8	San Francisco International, California	.4
9	Sea-Tac, Seattle, Washington	.4
10	Washington, Baltimore, Maryland	.4

Source: Business Traveler, 1993 statistics, based on various reporting methods from each airport.

U.S. puddle-jumpers are as safe as houses compared to Third World airlines. If you are flying anywhere in Africa, the chances of crashing are multiplied by 20—about the same odds as getting killed in an automobile accident in the States. Get on a smaller plane or a charter and the odds multiply again.

Some experts calculate the odds of being killed in a plane crash are less than one in a million for North America, Canada and Western Europe versus one in 50,000 for the dark continent. Flying in Latin America, the Middle East, Asia and Eastern Europe are the next most dangerous areas of the world. Colombia's Avianca has one of the worst flight safety records in the world. Not surprising considering that poorer countries fly old aircraft usually purchased from major carriers who have already wrung every useful mile from their airframes. The safety of these aircraft is aggravated by substandard maintenance programs and less-developed facilities.

There are about 25 airlines banned from landing in the U.S. due to their poor safety and maintenance standards. Which are the airlines? The list is kept under wraps to avoid diplomatic repercussions.

The most dangerous places to fly are on local carriers in **China**, **North Korea**, **Colombia**, all countries in **Central Africa** and all countries in the **CIS**. It is wise to avoid all flights inside **India** and through the **Andes**. But faced with taking a clapped-out bus over rugged mountains, most people choose clapped-out airplanes. China has the world's worst air piracy record and Russian flight crews are known to accept bribes to overload planes with extra passengers, baggage and cargo.

Russian Roulette

Aeroflot and the many other new airlines created by the breakup of the Soviet Union are the most dangerous airlines in the world. The U.S. State Department has instructed government employees to avoid using all Russian airlines unless absolutely necessary. Britain, Canada and other nations have issued similar warnings. The International Airline Passengers Association issued an unprecedented warning that flying anywhere in the former Soviet Union is unsafe. DP flew to Lake Baikal in Siberia where the passenger exit of a Tupelov had to be sealed with gaffers tape before takeoff. It's said that if the flight doesn't nail you, the food will. Worldwide, the fatality rate for commercial passengers is less than one in a million. In Russia, the figure is 5.5 per million. In one 18-month period, there were more than a dozen air crashes in the former Soviet Union, involving both commercial and military aircraft, killing more than 500 people.

Before the Soviet break up in 1991, Aeroflot was the largest airline in the world with more than 4000 planes, carrying more than 100 million passengers annually and it maintained a safety record in line with the international average. Now the CIS has more than 300 separate carriers. The Russian version of our national system of maintenance and safety inspections has been discontinued. The ITAR-Tass news agency reported: "The American flying public is entitled to know that we have concerns with the safety of the Russian air transportation system."

Russian pilots make as little as 20 dollars a day or 40,000 rubles. In May 1994, Alfred Malinovsky, president of the Russian Pilots' Association, commented during a one-day strike to protest lack of aircraft safety standards, "We are as scared as anyone to fly, perhaps even more, because we know more."

To give you a taste of just how bad it is, in March 1994, an Airbus A-310 crashed, killing all 75 people on board—apparently while the pilot was giving an impromptu flight lesson to his teenage son.

Colombian Roulette

In Colombia in May 1994 alone, there were seven accidents that resulted in 16 deaths. At Bogota's international airport, air traffic controllers sometimes work 12-hour shifts; many of the nation's aircraft navigation radio beacons have not been serviced since 1986.

Colombia has the worst air-safety record in the Americas, according to the International Airline Passengers Association, a consumer group based in Dallas. Citing aircraft accident rates, India and Colombia were declared the two most dangerous countries to fly in.

After deregulation in Colombia in 1990, the number of passenger and cargo airlines serving El Dorado Airport in Bogota surged from 24, three years ago, to 68 today. In the same four years, the volume of international passengers arriving in Colombia jumped by 55 percent. Last year El Dorado handled 170,000 takeoffs and landings. By comparison, Gatwick Airport in London registered 180,000 takeoffs and landings in 1992.

Chinese Roulette

In June 1994, a Chinese Northwest airliner crashed after takeoff from the city of Xian, killing all 160 onboard. On the same day, a lone hijacker commandeered a China Southern Airlines plane to Taiwan, the 12th hijacking in the past year. There are about 40 different airlines flying in China. China is a leading contender for the title of the most dangerous place in the world to fly.

China's biggest problem is a shortage of pilots. Passenger air travel is expected to grow 20 percent annually until the year 2000. To keep up with demand, the country needs 600 new pilots a year. But China can only turn out less than half that number. Once a pilot is on the job, the workday is excruciating. Although Chinese regulations set the limit at 100 hours of flight time a month to avoid pilot fatigue, pilots average an astounding 280 hours. China's airspace is controlled by the military and civilian airlines must request use of it; then they are allotted narrow air corridors. There is a severe shortage of radar and ground equipment. Some parts of the country have no IFR controls, meaning that flying can be done only in good weather.

Evidently, there are a lot more dangerous things to be doing other than flying. There are seven million commercial flights a year in the States, giving you a year and a half after a major crash to fly with impunity. Assuming that God starts the clock on your first flight.

Tips on staying alive while flying

- Stick to U.S.-based national carriers.
- Fly between major airports on nonstop flights.
- Avoid bad weather or flying at night.
- You can sit in the back if you want but above the wing (structurally stronger) or near an exit might be just as advisable.

Remember that travel by airliner is the safest method of travel and that your odds of surviving a plane crash are about 50 percent.

Trains

Trains are supposed to be safe. After all they run on rails, are usually pointed in one direction and are immune to the inclement weather that dogs airplanes, buses and cars. There's a joke that asks "what is the last thing a bug sees when it hits the windshield of a train?" The answer: its asshole. When trains do hit, they hit hard.

Heavy sleepers on the night train

Beware of the 10-hour night train from Budapest to Vienna. The first two hours during the stretch between Gyoer on the Austro-Hungarian border and Budapest are the most dangerous. The train leaves from the West Vienna station. The railway line to Vienna via Hungary is one of the last links with Yugoslavia after United Nations sanctions were imposed. Several Serbians working in Germany, Switzerland and Austria take the route back home. The train is targeted because Serbs working in Germany and loaded with cash and gifts, take the train. The bandits will inject sleeping gas into each compartment and then methodically rob each compartment. The criminals comprise a United Nations of crooks: Serbs, Croats, Russians, Hungarians, Slovaks and Albanians from Kosovo in Rump, Yugoslavia. Some suspect that the Hungarian conductors and engineers collaborate with the criminals. At some time after a robbery the train will stop so that the robbers can escape.

Trains tend to run into substantial objects like trucks stalled on crossings or trains coming the other way. The fact that trains have limited mobility make them ideal targets for terrorists. Criminals enjoy the opportunities trains afford, as passengers leave their belongings in their seats when they leave for the dining car.

Using the death rate per billion miles as a guide, American trains are about twice as dangerous as flying, four times safer than driving and a lot safer than local buses.

Tips on avoiding danger on trains

- Ask whether the train is a target for bandits (this is appropriate in Cambodia and Egypt where terrorists, bandits and insurgents regularly target tourist routes).
- Beware of train routes where thieves are known to ride as passengers. When in doubt sleep with the window cracked open to avoid being gassed.
- Stash your valuables in secret spots making it more difficult for robbers to locate your belongings.
- The back of the train is traditionally the safest area in the event of a collision.

- Keep your luggage with you at all times if possible.
- Trains are preferable to buses when traveling through mountainous areas, deserts and jungles.

War & Terrorism

War is organized armed conflict between groups of people. Man is the only animal that engages in organized warfare. Wars are fought over control, land, money, religious beliefs, national security, border security, freedom and, of course, ironically enough, for peace. You can safely assume that there will be warfare in a large number of countries for as long as you are alive.

Few U.S. travelers head for war zones. (See the overview for "Who's Doing What to Whom" this year.) Even fewer Americans are victims of war. There is, however, an immediate run on no-discount, full-fare business class tickets by journalists whenever a war breaks out. Others find themselves in the middle of a revolution or firefight with little knowledge of who the players are. The chances are better that war will find you. This is called terrorism. Various countries around the world are looking for a few good victims. Of the 427 terrorist attacks in 1994, Western Europe was the most popular venue with 180 attacks since 1993, the Middle East placed second, then Latin America with only 97,109 people were killed and 1393 were wounded. Eighty-eight, or 21%, of all terrorist attacks were directed at American interests.

Countries with Terrorist Activity	Group
Afghanistan	Hezbollah, mujahadeen
Algeria	Islamic Salvation Front (FIS)
Angola	Renovada (FLEC)
Bangladesh	Mujahadeen

Countries with Terrorist Activity	Group
Bolivia	National Liberation Army (ELN),Tupac Katari Guerilla Army (EGTK)
Myanmar (Burma)	Karens
Cambodia	Khmer Rouge
Chile	The Dissident Faction of the Manual Rodriguez Patriot-ric Front (FPMR/D), Lautaro Youth Movement (MJL)
Colombia	Revolutionary Armed Forces of Colombia (FARC), Army of National Liberation (ELN)
Ecuador	Puka Inti (Red Sun)
Egypt	The Islamic Group (IG)
El Salvador	Farabundo Marti National Liberation Front (FMLN)
Gaza	Fatah Hawks, Hamas, Popular Front for the Liberation of Palestine General Command (PFLP-GC)
Germany	Red Army Faction (RAF), PKK
Greece	Greek Revolutionary Organization, 17 November
India	Sikhs
Indonesia	Timorese
Israel	Hamas, PFLP-GC
Italy	Red Brigades
Japan	Chukaka-ha (Middle Core Faction), subway gassings
Mali	Turag Groups
Morocco	Polisario
Nigeria	Nigerian Movement for the Advance of Democracy
Pakistan	Mujahadeen Groups
Peru	Sendero Luminoso (SL or Shining Path), Tupac Amaru Revolutionary Movement (MRTA)
Philippines	Abu Sayeef
Russia	Chechens
South Africa	White Supremacists
Spain	Basque Fatherland and Liberty (ETA)
Sri Lanka	Tamils of Tiger Eelam (LTTE)
Turkey	Kurdistan Workers Party (PKK), Dev Sol, Hezbollah
United States	Puerto Rican Seccesionist Groups, Antiabortion activ-ists, Islamic Fundamentalists, militia hotheads
West Bank	Hamas

There are many more terrorist groups that operate in other countries. The list does not include narco/trafficking groups or criminal groups allied under a political banner.

Over the past few years, war has killed so few travelers that the statistic doesn't even record as a blip. Even so, the most likely victim in a war these days is probably going to be a noncombatant. The most likely forms of warfare to impact (literally) civilians are terrorist acts or land mines.

The best advice on staying healthy is to downplay your image as an American. Stay away from blatantly American businesses or installations and avoid countries that have inadequate security. (Unfortunately, this includes the U.S.) *D.P's* list of countries at war includes areas where armies occupy major regions and there is significant fighting between opposing factions on a regular basis.

Countries at war	Cause
Afghanistan	Power
Albania	Power
Algeria	Religion
Angola	Tribal
Armenia	Land
Azerbaijan	Land, Oil
Bolivia	Drugs, Ideology
Bosnia-Herzegovina	Religion
Burundi	Ethnic
Cambodia	Ideology
Chad	Land, Oil
Colombia	Drugs, Ideology
Croatia	Ethnic
Cyprus	Ethnic
Djibouti	Self-Rule
Gaza	Self-Rule
India	Ethnic, Religious, Self-Rule
Indonesia	Self-Rule
Iran	Land, Oil
Iraq	Land, Oil
Israel	Land, Religion
Lebanon	Land, Religion
Liberia	Tribal
Mali	Self-Rule, Ethnic
Morocco	Ethnic
Myanmar (Burma)	Drugs, Ethnic
Pakistan	Religion, Land
Papua New Guinea	Tribal
Peru	Ideology, Drugs
Russia	Self-Rule, Oil

Countries at war	Cause
Rwanda	Tribal
Serbia	Ethnic, Land
Somalia	Tribal
Sri Lanka	Ethnic
Sudan	Religion
Tajikistan	Religion, Ethnic
Turkey	Ideology, Self-Rule
West Bank	Self-Rule

Who's looking for a fight?

Are you curious to know who may be the most bellicose nations are? Here is a list of who has pumped up their forces recently:

Country	% Growth in military '82-'92	Current Forces
Cambodia	575%	135,000
Uganda	833%	70,000
Angola	286%	128,000
Iran	171%	528,000
Bahrain	146%	6000
Fiji	144%	5000
Colombia	99%	139,000
Venezuela	84%	75,000
Syria	83%	408,000
Saudi Arabia	97%	102,000

Source: AsiaWeek

Reasons for War

This book is designed to help you understand why certain areas are more dangerous than others. There are many reasons for war and, evidently, it appears there are more reasons for people to hate one another than to leave each other alone.

Food, shelter, land, greed and plain capriciousness are causing warfare right now. Another reason for increased warfare has been the artificial controls implemented by outside forces on a third party involved in civil conflict.

It is questionable whether the United Nations relieves or aggravates or prolongs regional tensions. Do Russia and the United States have the right to militarily interfere in foreign countries? Do aid programs actually create starvation and suffering by artificially shifting populations to refugee camps and thereby increasing the birth rate?

Much of the anger toward Americans is a direct result of others' perception of our need to control foreign governments. If the government feels it lacks sufficient political clout in certain regions of the world, it brings out the checkbook. The U.S. bought peace in the Middle East by writing checks to both sides. We also support a wide variety of dictators, despots and other non-democratically elected rulers because they are less antagonistic toward the U.S. than the opposition. The U.S. also wages moralistic, covert (and not so covert) operations against enemies of the state, such as the Islamic fundamentalists, drug dealers, unfriendly dictators and gangsters. We do this by supporting (or sometimes creating) opposition forces with money, weapons and military training.

You may find it surprising to see how obvious the U.S. "covert" presence is in Third World countries. Terrorist groups keep very good tabs on CIA and other government agents in their countries.

The problem for the traveler is that in some areas, such as the Middle East, Southeast Asia, Central Africa and areas where Americans are rarely seen, you will be assumed to be working for or allied with American intelligence agencies. Although I'm Canadian,

I have been accused on numerous occasions of being "CIA" in war zones simply because I had no plausible explanation as to why I was there.

If you look and act like a an American you will be assumed to be gathering information. You'll run the risk of confrontation, kidnapping, detainment or harassment. Execution is rare, since Americans are worth more alive (financially and politically) than dead.

What the World Needs Now Is Love, Sweet Love

The biggest lessons learned from travel in war zones is that there are at least two sides to every story and that it's love of a cause rather than hatred of an enemy that causes war. I have yet to meet a warlord or soldier who said that he was on the side of evil and not fighting the good fight. It is helpful to all travelers to approach even the most obscene situation (by Western standards) with an open mind.

Also, do not challenge the beliefs of your host. Talking politics with soldiers is like reading *Playboy* with the Pope.

Finally, there is much to be said for tolerance and understanding. The first place to practice it is with the people you consider to be your enemy.

For the Love of God

What can be said about religious strife that hasn't been said before? Despite what most Americans assume, the most popular religious deity in the world is Mohammed. Over one billion of the world's inhabitants are Muslims. Only 18 percent are found in the Arab world. Most live east of Karachi; 30 percent of Muslims are found on the Indian subcontinent, 20 percent in sub-Saharan Africa, 17 percent in Southeast Asia and 10 percent in the CIS and China. There are an estimated 5 million Muslims in the United States.

This is not to say that there is a basic antagonism between Christianity and Islam. There tends to be much confusion and distrust generated by the media. Unable to understand the basic similarities between Islam and Christianity, the media focuses on the disparities and usually the most extreme examples. The presentation of Islamic fundamentalism as a religion rather than a political agenda is one example. Christian fundamentalism is just as dangerous and skewed as is any hard-core belief. Currently, there are dozens of wars between Hindus and Muslims (Kashmir), Muslims and Christians (Bosnia) and Christians and Marxists (Central America).

For the Love of Money

Wealth has always been a source of both war and peace. The most successful formula seems to be to create of a strong middle class where the majority are property owners, workers and community leaders. The most volatile seems to be having a wealthy ruling class and a poor working class. Maoists, the military and fundamentalists, add a wild card to the standard class struggle now and then, but chances are poor countries with disparate social classes are going to be the most volatile.

Brotherly Love

Most of us are well versed in the effects on native peoples that colonialism has traditionally had. Today, these tensions continue not only in Africa, but also in Asia and the Middle East. Many of these tribal schisms are aggravated in Rwanda, Burundi, Northern Ireland, Bosnia and India, where governments step in with remedial action and actually force minorities into equal or superior positions.

Needless to say, all hell breaks loose once the colonial-dominating power is gone resulting in the Balkanization of the world—a world where brutality forced unity and disparate peoples have been scattered by force, leaving a ragged patchwork quilt of hate and tension. Russia shattered into its basic units. Then those basic units broke into tiny fiefdoms. Now religious, criminal, ethnic and tribal groups are trying to glue together new alliances. The process is also taking place in Africa where tribal hatred and forced cohabitation explode into mass bloodletting and hatred. Armenians have removed virtually 100 percent of all Azeri Muslims from Nagorno Karabakh, and Chechens were trying to figure out how to get rid of the 100,000 or so ethnic Russians left in their breakaway republic. This process will continue until the natural counterforce emerges. These small warring states will fall victim to a powerful outside military consolidator. Our fractured world awaits the next Alexander the Great, Charlemagne, Garibaldi, Mao Zedong or Tito.

One good indicator of what is going on and where the hot spots might be is to look at just who the players are militarily. Keep in mind that these figures do not reflect the ability of a country to raise a militia or call upon its neighbors should there be a conflict. However, it is interesting to note the disparity between the size of the population of countries like North Korea and Vietnam and the size of their armies. Although Vietnam—reentering the world community after decades of isolation—is under no imminent threat from its neighbors or faraway powers, fully 50 percent of its annual budget goes into defense spending.

Who's Getting Ready for WWIII		
Country	**Armed Forces**	**Growth '82-'92**
China	3,030,000	-36%
Russia	2,720,000	-26%
United States of America	1,914,000	-7%
India	1,265,000	+15%
North Korea	1,132,000	+45%
Vietnam	857,000	-17%
South Korea	633,000	+5%
Pakistan	580,000	+29%
Turkey	560,000	-2%
Iran	528,000	+171

Love It or Leave It

Many of the world's wars are caused by the massive displacement of ethnic groups. Elective or forced migration is an important means of transmitting instability, mainly because ethnic minorities are easy targets for hostility from the native population. Their arrival in a new country—even a new area of their own nation—creates conflict with the indigenous community.

Most migration takes place between developing countries. Pakistan receives workers from Myanmar and Bangladesh; Colombians go to Venezuela; Sudanese and Thais migrate to the Persian Gulf states. Migration has been influenced by government programs such as the Indonesian government's policy of moving city dwellers into undeveloped jungle regions.

There have also been massive movements of people as a result of war and famine. Many of these movements are actually encouraged by aid organizations and NGOs, who create camps away from water, fertile land and cities to deal with the initial flow. Once word gets out that there is food, medicine and shelter at these oases, the numbers crawling in can swell as we witnessed in Rwanda, where the camps were the only hope of staying alive for hundreds of thousands.

In other countries such as Somalia, Sudan and Angola there simply is no other source of food for the millions of people who create new tent cities in arid wastelands. There is little chance they will ever return home. Ethnic cleansing has displaced entire populations in Turkey, Nagorno-Karabakh, Israel, Bosnia, Iraq and many parts of Africa. The displaced people tend to support freedom movements from their new homes even after the situation is hopeless.

United Nations peacekeeping troops are doing their best to keep a lid on many of the world's hot spots. The fact that they have proven completely ineffective in Somalia and Bosnia has raised the serious question of just how influential the world body is.To an emerging generation of both freedom fighters and their foes, it is impotent.

Countries With U.N. Peace Keeping Forces	Number of Troops	Annual Cost in $million	Mission Began	Mission Ended
Cyprus	1218	47	Mar-64	ongoing
Israel	1251	62	Jun-48	Jun-74
El Salvador	250	24	Jul-91	ongoing
Western Sahara	310	40	Sep-91	ongoing
Liberia	370	70	Sep-93	ongoing
Angola	77	25	Jun-91	ongoing
Mozambique	5929	329	Dec-92	ongoing
Rwanda	706	98	Jun-93	ongoing
Somalia	18,952	1000	Apr-92	Dec 94
India/Pakistan	40	8	Jan-49	ongoing
Iraq & Kuwait	1147	73	Apr-91	ongoing
Georgia	21	7	Aug-93	ongoing
Lebanon	5231	145	Mar-78	ongoing
Ex-Yugoslavia	34,940	1002	Mar-92	ongoing

Source: U.N.

If you have ever wondered who is doing the dirty work, you will not be surprised to see countries like Pakistan, India and Bangladesh providing a major chunk of the manpower in U.N. peacekeeping missions. Some accuse these countries of collecting Western-level fees for providing soldiers, paying them less and pocketing the difference. On the other hand, employing highly trained combat troops in noncombat positions is demoralizing, frustrating and, in the end, counterproductive to the morale of combat-trained soldiers.

# of U.N. Peacekeepers by Country of Origin	
Pakistan	7256
France	7094
India	5914
Britain	3880
Jordan	3550
Bangladesh	3287
Malaysia	2707
Canada	2406
Holland	2259
Egypt	2245
Nepal	1995
Sri Lanka	11
Indonesia	10
Greece	8
South Korea	8
Germany	7
Singapore	7
Turkey	7
Guyana	6
Thailand	6
Malawi	5
Morocco	2
Guinea	1

Source: U.N.

Just Plain Love

The trend in emerging dangerous places—normally underdeveloped nations—is that exploding population rates are creating tensions.

In 1950, 33 percent of the world's population lived in the developed, industrialized nations. Today, that share is approximately 23 percent. By the year 2025, it will fall to 16 percent; Africa then will have 19 percent of the world's inhabitants. Today, Western and Southeast Asia are home to more people than any other part of the world. The population of India will overtake that of China early in the next century. This area is also home to the most diverse mix of languages, religions and peoples in the world, many of whom have been at war for centuries and will continue to fight over land, religion and tribal feuds.

As populations grow and standards of living drop, people will live at ever-greater densities, creating more tension. *The World Bank's World Development Report* 1992 noted that only Bangladesh, South Korea, the Netherlands and the island of Java now have population densities of more than 400 people per square kilometer. By the middle of the next century, one-third of the world's people will probably live at these density levels. Given the current trends, the population density of Bangladesh will rise to a hardly conceivable 1700 people per square kilometer. Population growth on such a large scale is intrinsically destabilizing. The wars in India show that even minor terrorist incidents can kill hundreds of people. The world's most dangerous places will also be the most crowded and impoverished places.

Poorest People	% of Population in Poverty	Foreign Aid % per Poor Person 1992
Bangladesh	80	19
Ethiopia	60	41
Vietnam	55	16
Philippines	55	49
Brazil	50	3
India	40	7
Nigeria	40	7
Indonesia	25	44
China	10	28

On the African continent, 45 percent of the population is under the age of 15; in South America, it's 35 percent; in Asia, 32 percent. Only 21 percent of the population of the United States and 19 percent of Europe's is under 15.

The World Resources Institute reports that only 3 percent of the world's inhabitants lived in urban areas in the mid-eighteenth century. By the 1950s, that proportion had risen to 29 percent. Today, it is more than 40 percent; by 2025, 60 percent of the world's people are expected to be living in or around cities. Almost all of that increase will be in what is now the Third World. The young people tend to migrate to major urban centers seeking Western-style jobs instead of backbreaking menial labor. Once in the city, they find that the competition for jobs is fierce and that petty crime against the more wealthy is the only source of income. But despite this, the cities continue to grow. Mexico City, which had 17 million inhabitants in 1985, will have 24 million by the end of the century; Sao Paulo will jump from 15 million to 24 million.

For the Love of Money

When Von Clauswitz said that war was a continuation of politics on a higher level, he was wrong. What he should have said was that war is simply business negotiations carried on at a higher level. Whether it is over land, minerals, resources or waterways, war is a zero sum game. What are the benefits versus the costs? In some cases, we go to war to protect worthless islands inhabited by penguins, but there are spoils for the victor and riches for the industrial society that supports the winning government. Here are what the wars of the future will be fought over:

Oil

Oil and war do mix. There is usually enough financial incentive to send in the troops at the first sign of instability in oil-rich countries. One has to wonder why America has been so quick to help Kuwait and so slow to help the Kurds. Kurdistan (Northern Iraq), where the Kurds were banished, has now been discovered to contain substantial oil reserves, but the people there do not have the funds to exploit the region. So it is interesting that Kurdistan is under American protection.

Oil will also cause future wars in Southeast Asia, the Middle East, Southern Africa and Russia. Breakaway governments will see the financial benefits of keeping their oil resources while the central government balances the military costs to retake the region against the income lost. Many people are not aware that under all the Jihad rhetoric, Chechnya straddles an important oil pipeline that extends from Azerbaijan to Russia.

Look at a map of the world's major oil reserves and you will see not only the wars of the last fifty years but the next fifty.

Food

The World Bank estimates suggest that it would be technically possible to feed a world population of 11.4 billion people with a daily diet that would provide 6000 calories of "plant energy" (grain, seed and animal feed) a day. That is roughly twice the calories found in the typical diet in South Asia today. In a number of ways, there is enough food: not only for today's population, but for one twice as large.

Such calculations, however, rely on a sizable increase in yields in developing countries. Such increases are theoretically possible. Cereal yield in the United States at the start of the 1980s was 4.2 tons per hectare of harvested area, compared with 1.5 tons for fertile Kenya or 2 tons for hungry Bangladesh. For a growing number of countries, increasing yields will be the only way to raise food output, as the growing population competes for crop land. The alternative to increasing yields is to increase the amount of land taken into cultivation. That usually means destroying forests and cultivating ever-steeper hillsides. Starvation is also used as a weapon of war in Biafra, Somalia, Bosnia and Iraq.

Water

It may seem odd that water is a major source of conflict and warfare. There are the usual territorial problems such as in the Spratleys, where a host of nations including China, Vietnam and Malaysia claim sovereignty over the tiny but oil-rich islands. More important is the fight for control of fishing grounds and territorial waters.

Since 1989, the world marine catch has been on a steady decline. Throughout the 1980s, catches of the most valuable species, such as cod and halibut, were lower than they had been the previous decade, even though the capacity of world fishing fleets was greater. Catches were maintained by a rising take of less-valuable fish, such as pollock and anchovies. Fish are the most important source of animal protein in many developing and poor countries.

Fresh water is also a major source of friction, since it is used for irrigation and transportation and sustains the economy of many poor countries. Where watersheds are shared by several countries, the availability of water will become a source of political tension. Three parts of the world are particularly short of water: Africa, the Middle East and South Asia. In each of those areas, rainfall is low. India is already using half the rain that runs from land into rivers and lakes and half as much again from underground wells and springs. By the year 2025, India is likely to be using 92 percent of its freshwater resources. Irrigation in India utilizes 360 times as much water as industry. Worldwide, 70 percent of the world's fresh water is used for irrigation and the proportion is higher in poorer countries. Irrigation has been essential to the increase in food output over the past 20 years. Although only a fifth of the world's croplands are irrigated, a third of the world's food now comes from irrigated land.

Nearly 50 countries on four continents have more than three-quarters of their land in international river basins; 214 river basins are multinational, while 13 are shared by five or more countries. And nearly 40 percent of the world's population lives in an international river basin. The Jordan, the Ganges, the Nile and the Rio Grande Rivers have been at the center of international disputes. Since rivers in many areas serve as borderlines, water will continue to be a source of conflict. Europe needs more than 175 international treaties to regulate its four river basins shared by more than four countries. The Iraqis are busy draining their southern marches to displace people, while the Turks are busy building dams in east Turkey to flood out others.

Land

There is little to say about warfare for *Lebensraum,* or living room. It is the natural tendency of man to extend his domain to meet the needs of larger populations. Contrary to popular images, nomadic hunter-gatherers are less warlike than farmers since they need less land to survive on. They tend to be less concerned about borders and ownership. Farmers, on the other hand, count their wealth in acres or hectares; the more the better. The colonial powers of Britain, Russia, France, the Netherlands and Portugal are good examples of this. The United States could never really be called a colonial power, although they have been known to be somewhat heavy-handed in gaining financial and political clout in the potentially rich countries of Central America, the Middle East and South America.

Minerals

Need we even discuss why the West was won? "Gold rushes" have displaced more native populations than any other reason. Prospectors are soon followed by armies, police, government, railroads and cities. The turbulent countries of South Africa and Angola have been propped up by diamonds and gold.

Drugs

War and drugs go hand-in-hand. In fact, many of the world's terrorist organizations finance their operations through drug sales or levies on drug smuggling. The profits from illicit drugs keep countries like Afghanistan, Pakistan, Thailand, Myanmar, Colombia, Peru and Mexico on or teetering-on the brink of total anarchy, as drug lords command armies and control domains that easily intimidate local officials and leaders into submission in one form or another.

Some countries have found that being a conduit for drug smuggling (Pakistan, Laos, Myanmar, Cambodia, Panama, Cuba and Iran are alleged to be major drug transport routes) usually ends up with profits in the *el jefe's* Swiss bank account. The "bad guys" should actually be the consumers or end packagers (i.e., the United States, France, the Netherlands), but in the Western tradition of "I am a victim," it seems easier to denounce the sellers rather than the buyers. One wonders how quickly recreational drug usage would stop if all the special forces, executions and paramilitary operations were turned on users instead of growers.

Terrorism

Although terrorism is specifically designed to capture the world's attention, it poses a lesser threat than disease, car accidents, plane crashes and other afflictions that haunt the traveler. Having taken the lightly–booked anniversary flight of Pan Am flight 103, I can attest to the effectiveness of terrorism in deterring tourists.

The number of terrorist attacks in 1993 increased to 427, up from 361 in 1992; not an impressive figure in terms of the number of dangerous incidents compared to muggings. When you localize some of these activities though, it gets a little scarier.

The increase in terrorism was primarily due to activities of the Kurdistan Workers Party, or PKK, against Turkish targets during two black days throughout Western Europe in 1993. The attacks occurred on two separate days in June and November, with about 75 attacks each day.

Although some experts point to this sudden rash of attacks or incidents, combined with the large numbers injured in the World Trade Center bombing, as an anomaly, the fact is that terrorism is still with us. Americans have been given a little relief mostly by the descent in frequency of South American terrorist attacks. The number of anti-American attacks decreased in 1993 to 88, down from 142 the previous year. This was attributed to fewer bombings by the National Liberation Army in Colombia and by the Lautaro Youth Movement in Chile, as well as fewer armed attacks against Americans by Dev Sol in Turkey. But before you brush these statistics aside as being insignificant, remember that the highest casualty total in a single terrorist attack ever recorded was the bombing of the World Trade Center in the good old U.S. of A. That bombing killed six Americans and wounded more than 1000. The highest death toll was the 167 people killed in the 1995 blast in Oklahoma City.

Seven nations are currently designated as states that sponsor international terrorism: **Iran**, **Iraq**, **Libya**, **Syria**, **Sudan**, **Cuba** and **North Korea**. Most European adventure travelers consider these countries quasi-safe for travel except for southern Sudan and the rougher parts of Cuba. Most are off-limits for Americans and there is an understandably high level of antagonism in Iraq, Iran and North Korea toward Americans, especially toward those who make it in—usually nuts or spooks. The fact that two Americans were slapped with eight year jail sentences for illegally entering Iraq should keep most travelers out.

Iran remains the most dangerous sponsor of sanctioned terrorism and the greatest source of concern. Iran's surrogate political and military arm, Hezbollah, was responsible for the bombing of the Israeli Embassy in Buenos Aires in early 1992. Iran opposes the Middle East peace process and arms and funds rejectionist groups who espouse violence.

Libya's ties with terrorists are ongoing despite the continual pleading by Qaddafi to be allowed back into the political and financial playpen of the world market. He continues to harbor those responsible for placing the bomb on Pan Am flight 103 in 1988 and the French want to chat with him regarding the bombing of UTA flight 772. United Nations Security Council Resolution 883 froze selected Libyan assets and banned the sale of many categories of oil-industry equipment. Qaddafi has made a series of silly demands in exchange for the suspected terrorists but has yet to show any good faith.

In late March, Qaddafi held a little barbecue in Tripoli for all Palestinian groups and the infamous international contract terrorist Abu Nidal continues to live there comfortably.

Syria continues to support groups that carry out terrorist attacks against its two neighbors, Israel and Turkey. Syria harbors the leader of the PKK and provides a safe headquarters for other terrorist groups.

Sudan has provided safe haven to a number of international terrorist groups, not least the Abu Nidal organization. Sudan-based fundamentalist organizations have carried out acts of terrorism in Egypt, Tunisia and Algeria.

Cuba and **North Korea** have not been tied directly to acts of international terrorism for some years now. In Cuba's case, it appears to be more a result of its disastrous economic situation and loss of Soviet support. However, the island continues to serve as a sanctuary for members of some regional and international terrorist organizations.

Turkey is still home to the most active terrorist organization in the world. The ruthless PKK continues to execute relentless attacks against tourists in resort towns, as well as to execute villagers. None are spared their wrath, apparently, including school teachers. As well, businesses have been targeted more frequently than diplomatic, government or military facilities.

Algeria poses the most dangerous threat to Western tourists, though not through government sanctioned terrorism but rather through Islamic fundamentalists opposed to the Western-backed military government of President Liamine Zeroual. The Salvation Islamic Front, which is seeking to transform Algeria into a fundamentalist Islamic state, is using terrorism to frighten Western nations supporting Zeroual's authoritarian government, particularly in the wake of canceled elections in 1991 and 1992. On December 24, 1994, four Algerian terrorists seized an Air France *Airbus A300* jetliner in Algiers with 239 passengers and crew members aboard. The gunmen killed three passengers, including a Vietnamese diplomat, before the plane was stormed by French commandos in Marseille. The raid killed all four hostages and wounded 13 passengers. Since the canceled 1992 Algerian elections, radical fundamentalists have assassinated more than 11,000 people, including 70 foreigners and 22 French nationals, in an effort to topple the government. Among the victims are playwrights, journalists, politicians and even school girls who refuse to don the *hejab* Muslim head scarf. At press time, the Algerian threat to the U.S. is minimal—however, if Uncle Sam gets more involved in its support for Zeroual, this situation will change quickly.

In 1993, 70 percent of all international terrorist actions were targeted at businesses—nearly 300 attacks in all, the highest number of terrorist strikes in that category since statistics on organized terrorism began to be compiled 25 years ago. Sixty of those 1993 attacks were against American businesses.

Terrorists tend to strike countries where there is the potential for the greatest amount of economic damage. Tourists and tourism facilities are prime targets because crippled tourism cuts off vital foreign hard currency. Following the 1985 hijacking of TWA flight 847 enroute to Athens, the Greek government estimated that the subsequent tourism damage topped out at more than US$100 million.

In **Egypt**, Islamic fundamentalists have been waging a bloody terrorist campaign for the past two years against foreign tourists. Cruise ships, tour buses and public gathering areas have especially been targeted. It's estimated that earnings from Egypt's tourism industry may be down by as much as 50 percent since the start of that campaign.

The Kurdistan Workers Party in Turkey in 1993 began targeting the tourism industry by bombing restaurants, hotels and tourist sites, as well as planting grenades on Mediterranean beaches.

The "Shining Path" in Peru has a long, bloody history of singling out tourists for attack.

There were 38 percent fewer anti-U.S. attacks in 1993 than the previous year. Terrorist activity against American diplomatic facilities fell sharply. Attacks on international business targets, however, rose overall in 1993. What does this mean for travelers in dangerous places? American tourists and business travelers are the preferred targets of many of the world's nastiest terrorist organizations.

Iraq is under the heavy hand of Hussein for now but only because he has survived numerous assassination attempts. Once he is gone hell will break loose as the various factions set upon each other like dogs in a dumpster.

Business Travel: Professional Victims

We know that money makes the world go 'round. We also know that money makes businesspeople go 'round the world.

Many companies pay a premium for foreign expertise and will convince normally rational people to set out for the front lines in the new war against America. American workers in oil, mining, construction, technology and computer companies are in big demand abroad and are exposed to major risks on an increasing basis.

Business travel is perhaps the most dangerous form of travel. Why? Namely, one becomes a target by most of the world's terrorists simply by representing an American company. You also lose the ability to be discerning about when and where to travel. Most tourists wouldn't consider flying into a Colombian war zone for a week. Yet folks from oil, computer, agricultural and food companies do it regularly. Most victims of terrorism tend to be working on a daily basis in a foreign country in areas where no sane traveler would go.

Finally, by doing business, you tend to frequent establishments and locations where thieves, terrorists and opportunists seek victims—luxury hotels, expensive restaurants, expat compounds, airports, embassies, etc. As a business person, you cannot adopt the cloak of anonymity, since you will more than likely be wearing an expensive suit, staying in expensive hotels and have scads of luggage, cash and gifts.

Business travel exposes you to frequent car and, air travel and other means of transportation. Many trips are also undertaken in bad weather conditions and at congested travel periods (i.e., Monday out, Friday back). You are fed very carefully through a chain of businesses that cater to business travelers and become high profile targets for criminals who prey on business travelers. I often shudder when I see oil field technicians, complete with cowboy hats, pointed boots and silver Halliburton briefcases, tossing beer-soaked profanities around the world's transit lounges. Can you think of a more inviting target?

Dangerous Places for Business Travel

Business travelers are by far the juiciest targets for terrorists and thugs alike. They make great kidnap victims as well as willing dispensers of cash. Any Third World country with oil should be considered dangerous. **Nigeria** is probably the most overt place for scams, con artists and extortion-based crime. **Colombia** gets five stars for brutality, pervasiveness and ingenuity.

Algeria is by far one of the countries most dependent on foreign expertise and yet it is the most dangerous place in the world in which to provide this aid. In Algeria, about 12,000 people have died in political violence, and in a ten-month period 53 foreigners were killed, 14 of them during a four-day period in the beginning of July 1994.

The southern **Philippines** is where Abu Sayeef and a host of motley terrorists-turned-brigands compete for hostages. They prefer Chinese victims and priests but dabble with Westerners when they get lucky.

In **Angola,** oil and diamonds shore up this shattered country. However, impotent cease-fires are signed as frequently as bad checks and there is no foreseeable lull in the fighting there. Some tribes in **Pakistan** are insulted when you tell them that kidnapping for ransom is a crime. The climate for business is unhealthy to say the least.

Cambodia is essentially lawless, thanks to the Khmer Rouge and banditry in rural areas. There is little business left to conduct in this post-election, war-torn country. Rising crime and armed carjackings in Phnom Penh are turning the capital into an anarchist's heaven. **Russia**, specifically Moscow and St. Petersburg, is a quagmire for American business people who are faced with extortion, lawlessness and politically instability. There is growing disenchantment with the new Russian revolution. Many had a much better go at it with the communists. It's estimated that there will be more than 120 foreigners killed in Russia in 1995.

Business travelers in all Third World countries can expect to be hit up for tips, bribes, gifts and dinner checks.

Gangsters: The Businessman's Friend

Wherever there is money, there are gangsters. They have an amazing ability to ignore governments and streamline collection procedures. Do not be surprised if your business partner in Eastern Europe or Russia turns out to be a person of ill repute. Italian and Russian gangs are busy establishing links and are now working together in Germany to control a number of businesses: 17 percent of the 776 investigations into organized crime in Germany last year involved attempts to influence politics, big business or government administration. The main activities of organized crime were drug trafficking, weapons smuggling, money laundering and gambling. In 1992, police uncovered profits from organized crime in those areas alone totalling US$438 million or 700 million Deutschemarks.

Tips on Surviving Business Travel

- Spend very little time in dangerous places: airports, remote regions and inner cities. Stay inside after dark. Avoid American chain hotels and stay on the lower, but not ground, floors.
- Avoid traveling in cars with foreign or rental identification plates and tags.
- Avoid restaurants frequented by expats and tourists.
- Be especially alert during dangerous times such as public holidays, anniversary dates of terrorist or political parties or during visits by foreign delegations.
- Retain copies of important papers.
- Divide your money in half and keep it in separate places.
- Choose nonstop flights.
- Show no name, country or hotel ID on luggage or clothing.
- Do not discuss plans, accommodations, finances or politics with strangers.
- Wear a cheap watch and no jewelry.
- Get used to sitting near emergency exits, fire escapes, locking your doors and being aware at all times.
- Avoid American symbols or logos. Wear drab colors with conservative accessories.
- Stay away from the front of the plane (terrorists use it to control the aircraft).
- Do not carry unmarked prescription drugs.
- Leave questionable reading material at home (i.e., *Playboy*, political materials, financial magazines).
- Do not pack alcohol.
- Do not take foreign women (or men) up on questionable offers.

- Watch your drink being poured.
- Do not hang the "Make Up Room" sign on your hotel room door. Rather, use the "Do Not Disturb" sign. Keep the TV or radio on even when you leave.

After all this, what if you come home in a box? First of all, you'd better have an insurance policy or plan that facilitates the sometimes complicated and lengthy paperwork required for repatriation. See the list of providers under "Insurance" in the back of the book. According to International SOS Assistance in Geneva, Switzerland—a company that specializes in health, security and insurance for travelers—a deadly traffic accident is the most likely reason you'll be flown home dead. Cardiac arrest is the second most likely reason. Tropical diseases are the third. Have fun.

Tourists: Fodder for Fiends

"The scenery is terrible but the people are interesting!"

Usually, when you are on vacation, you do a few things that make local police shudder. You carry a lot of money, you dress funny, you drive an easy-to-spot rental car, you stay in concentrated high risk areas and you probably drink too much or stay out too late.

Criminals, given a choice between rolling a next-door neighbor or a Rotarian from Cleveland, don't have to think too hard. They know where, when and how to find tourists. And they know exactly what to say to them. They're nice. They'll ask you where you're from—and then jack you up for your wallet, camera and jewelry. You'll then have to leave town or spend all day in the police station filing a report. You'll have to rebook airline tickets and then hit the VISA or AMEX office to get new credit cards. You'll never be back to file a charge or testify.

Think this is bad? In Kenya bandits routinely rob tourist buses, perform violent carjackings and prey on tourists in the Masai Mara, the world's most popular safari park. In August 1993, a band of robbers shot a bus driver dead and robbed all 50 passengers between Malindi and Lamu. Tourists are robbed and beaten in most countries, but many never bother to report the incidents knowing full well the futility.

Tourists congregate in the same places. They drive in a state of rubbernecking ecstasy. And they are terrified of local law enforcement. They're even more terrified of damaging that nice new rental car they were too cheap to take out insurance on. In Florida, thugs looked for European tourists driving rental cars with "Y" and "Z" plates until someone finally figured out that discretion is better than advertising. Route A46 south of Lyon, France is the site of more than five robberies a month during the summer. Crooks race up behind cars with foreign licence plates, rear-end them and then, when the unsuspecting tourist gets out, rob them at gunpoint.

The chance of being injured or slain by a terrorist is much less than an attack by a common criminal. But as you will learn in this book, crooks in **Algeria**, **Egypt**, **Turkey**, **Cambodia**, **Myanmar**, **Colombia**, **the Philippines** and **Peru** are deliberately targeting tourists and foreigners as victims of kidnap and/or murder. Their need for negative publicity is designed to curtail tourism and the prosperity it brings in to convolute what they view as elemental societal disfavor with the present political structure. They also demand ransoms for the release of their hostages. In Cambodia, if you're abducted by the Khmer Rouge, you may as well kiss your life "adios" if their demands aren't met—and in some instances, even if they are.

Dangerous Places for Tourists

Despite the charming pictures of happy travelers having a good time in Third World countries, there is much to be said for the evils of tourism. As soon as you don that Hawaiian shirt or throw on that Eagle Creek backpack, you may as well paint a bulls-eye on your back. Nobody likes to be considered a tourist; we are travelers, cultural ambassadors yearning to soak up new experiences and sights. The first place to look for danger is in the eyes of the people who wait your table, drive your minibus or clean your toilet. Many countries simply refuse to let tourism interfere with their cultures. Brunei, Saudi Arabia, the Gulf States and North Korea all view tourism as an evil and do their best to restrict outside influences.

Other countries are averse to tourism, but need the bucks. Tourism has destroyed areas like Nepal, the Caribbean, Mexico and the Riviera. Invading armies of cash-spewing oglers have enslaved thousands of young girls as prostitutes in Thailand, Amsterdam, Hamburg, New York and Berlin. Entire villages like Bagan in Myanmar, have been bulldozed because they cluttered the scenery. Hundreds of tiny rustic seaports have turned into T-shirt-spewing tourist traps as cruise ships send waves of tourists armed with VISA cards off in landing crafts.

Tourism from the other side ain't pretty.

To some locals in some countries, you are simply a capitalistic, imperialistic, overfed, money-lined symbol of the inequalities of the world. Feeling like caged animals, the locals watch as Westerners corrupt their women, raise the cost of living, force them to work in menial jobs and live in shantytowns. I've spent many ganja-filled nights talking revolution with Caribbean busboys who would be more than happy to see every white face dumped into the ocean. So the next time you feel you're doing the locals a favor by taking their picture or flipping them spare change, be warned: You're part of the problem, not its solution.

Inner Cities

In America, few local people stray downtown after dark. Unfortunately, many tourists stay in business hotels built downtown and go for early morning jogs or late night strolls. Are they Crazy? No they're just tourists.

Trains

In Russia, China, Central and Southeast Asia, Georgia and Eastern Europe, trains are a target of organized thefts and abductions. Bandits, terrorists and marauding militias use drugs injected into sleeping cars. Others place logs or vehicles across the tracks and then leisurely rob passengers one at a time. Others, such as the Khmer Rouge in Cambodia, simply rocket trains before they rob and kill the passengers.

Buses

Buses are prime targets of criminals and terrorists because they hold a lot of people in a confined area, have few exits and generally travel rural routes—the unarmed passengers are usually carrying most of their earthly belongings with them. Buses also follow regular routes along remote thoroughfares which allows the civilized bandit to pull off an 11:30 ambush and make it home for lunch.

Resorts

If you are looking for tourists, what better place than where they sleep and store all their stuff? No need to kick in the door since the criminal will already have a key; the manager splits the booty with them. Hotels are also convenient places to put bombs. The Kurdish separatist movement in Turkey (PKK) deliberately targets tourist resorts along the Aegean Sea, even though they're fighting a war in Eastern Turkey. The Basque separatists (ETA) cause havoc along the Spanish Mediterranean coast and Corsican terrorists (FLNC and MNA) have tried to scare away French tourists with random bombings in French resorts.

Dangerous Regions for Tourists

Here's a brief overview of where tourists are considered the daily sustenance for bad people.

North America/Mexico

The United States is plagued with inner-city crime. Guns are commonly used and 7-11 clerks should get combat pay. Tourists are under attack, often with more violent consequences than are found in many "uncivilized" countries.

European tourists love **Florida**. Never having seen an inner-city or rest-stop killing ground, they have little idea of what to avoid. Asian tourists love **California**. They usually stay in those fancy downtown hotels. The unsuspecting traveler can't figure out why no one else is on the streets when he staggers back to his hotel, drunk on American whisky and saki. Asian tourists carry lots of American money because it's so cheap. Crooks like rolling Asians because they don't carry guns and they're so damn polite when they fork over all that cheap American green.

Mexico is still wild and woolly. Big, bad Mexican desperadoes still exist. Mexico's frontiers are rife with mean, dusty border towns where anything can be had for a price. Corrupt *federales,* who will steal your money and piss on your shoes, abound. Cheap, dark bars still sell ammo, drugs and women. Convention hall-sized whorehouses feature nonstop knife fights. Petty crime flourishes in resort areas. Violent crime is always a threat in the boonies. And God help you if you get busted. The best advice is to stay out of the resorts and find the real Mexico. For every bad guy there are a thousand Mexicans with a heart of gold.

South America

Mexico is Disneyland compared to **Colombia**. Terrorists in **Peru**, **Bolivia** and **Guyana** await you. Pickpockets and thugs in Brazil hope that tourism will pick up before the death squads kill them all.

Africa

North Africa is still a nasty place. The Tuaregs in **Mali** and **Niger** still feed off unsuspecting travelers. Tourism is an alien concept to these nomadic warriors. Tourist groups have been robbed at gunpoint, female members raped and the victims left without transportation in the desert. Remember, in the Sahara, no one can hear you scream.

Islamic fundamentalists in **Egypt** have one of the most effective campaigns to scare away tourists. They have exploded bombs at the Great Pyramid and attacked tour buses, not to mention conducting sniper attacks on Nile river boats. Luckily the group, el-Gama'a el-Islamyia, wants to discourage tourism, not necessarily kill tourists. So there have been no major bloodbaths.

Foreigners are not so lucky in **Algeria,** where Islamic fundamentalists are killing foreigners as fast as they can. The Polisario is still raising hell in **Morocco.** Nobody even thinks of going to **Mauritania** unless they want to be kidnapped and sold off as a white slave. **Djibouti** still has rebel activity and **Ethiopia and Somalia** have the meanest bandits in the world. The **Sudan** has a very vicious war being waged in the South.

Sub-Saharan Africa

The residents of **Rwanda** and **Burundi** are still whacking each other with *pangas.* The mean deeds folks in **Zaire**, **Central Africa Republic** and **Nigeria** would make a Russian gangster blush. Desperately poor urban thieves and roving bandits plaguing **Tanzania**, **Kenya** and **Uganda** are stepping up crimes against tourists and **Madagascar** requires a cautious approach as it slides into anarchy.

Middle East/Mediterranean

The world still has a rotten core. **Bosnia** will be a mess for years to come. Ethnic and religious tensions make **Israel**, **Southern Lebanon**, **Cyprus** and the **Occupied Territories** hot spots for terrorism and violence. **Syria**, **Iraq** and **Iran** are relatively safe, in the sense that their brand of nastiness is for export only.

Turkey is a mess: The Kurdish Workers Party, or PKK, has really got this tourist- terrorism thing down pat. The PKK issued a warning that effectively broadens their battleground to hotels, beaches and other tourist attractions. They take great pleasure in ensuring that the lives of all people visiting Turkey will be in danger. There are also nasty things being done by rival Kurdish factions, Armenian terrorists, the special ops groups, drug smugglers, Hezbollah and more.

Europe

Europe is a safe haven for tourists, but petty crimes in the tourist areas and central cities are common. Skinheads are busy in **Germany,** bashing people with brown eyes and foreign accents. The Basque ETA in **Spain** likes to blow things up. **Paris** is crawling with Gypsies and petty thieves. **Sicily** is still home to bandits who like to prey on tourists. They like to use guns and rob people—and kill them, of course. Petty thievery runs rampant along the beach resorts of **Spain**, **France** and **Italy** during tourist season.

South/Western Asia

The north is a mess with separatist, ethnic and religious groups blasting each other into shreds. **Afghanistan** is a perpetual mess and no tourists dare venture there. **Pakistan** has roving bandits that will rob policemen and armed convoys for their bullets. Northern **Sri Lanka** is a bona fide war zone.

Southeast Asia

Cambodia is a free-fire zone. The Golden Triangle area of **Thailand** is controlled by drug lords and hardwood timber smugglers, although not as much as in **Laos** and **My-**

anmar. **Papua New Guinea** and **Irian Jaya** still have local tribal wars that break out around eco-trekkers.

THE STING

When traveling through Asian countries you could be the victim of overzealous law enforcement agents. In India and Thailand, there have been reports of threats of arrest on drug charges unless you give officers money. In Thailand, police officers make a monthly salary of about US$200. Thai police officers and their informants can receive a reward of 10,000 baht per kg of pure heroin recovered. It has been stated that after refusing these demands some foreign travelers were booked and charged for using heroin.

Some travelers have paid US$150-200 to get these cops off their back. If you are taken to court in Thailand, the odds are not good. No foreigner has been acquitted of an offense in more than 20 years. In India, there are 40 young Westerners serving lengthy jail sentences who claim they were sent to prison on bogus charges.

Due to the severity of sentences and the low salaries of officers, Thailand, Malaysia and India can be considered the most dangerous destinations for backpacking youngsters. Indonesia, the Philippines and Latin America are also danger spots. The only solution is to not look like a hippie, not travel alone and try to get witnesses if you feel you are being pushed into an unethical transaction.

China/Far East

China is pushing its people to desperation and, despite more executions than there are daytime Emmys in Hollywood, the crime wave is increasing. **South Korea** continually is the scene of massive anti-American demonstrations, as is **Japan** to a lesser extent. Subways in Japan should require gas masks.

How to Stay Healthy and Alive

You will hear the same advice over and over: Don't wear flashy jewelry, don't walk alone at night and stay out of bad areas. In other words, don't act like a tourist. But how the hell can a blue-eyed, six-footer wearing the latest Yuppie trekking gear look like a grizzly little Sherpa? The reality is that you can't entirely blend in anywhere but the shopping mall in Peoria—and that crime happens when you least expect it. Desperate people know exactly where to find tourists. Tourists carry money, expensive cameras and other gear that can easily be spent, fenced, torn down, worn, pawned, eaten or put to some other use. And tourists rarely put up a fight. In fact, there is an entire industry designed to ensure that tourists can be rolled and be back in the swing of things in less than a day—a new AMEX card, Traveler's cheques, and a trip to the boutique and you're back in business.

Luckily, most professional thieves won't kill you or even rough you up. In Latin American countries, it is even considered customary for the thief to give you enough money for a cab ride back to your hotel. (You have to ask nicely though.)

Most robberies can take place in broad daylight. If that's too mundane you can be also raped in your hotel suite, stabbed on the beach, mugged in an office and even illegally tossed into the joint by the cops. Many lucky people never come face to face with their predators, but simply find their hotel rooms ransacked, their backpacks slashed and their rental cars emptied. Here are some tips for travelers who don't take heed of others' tales of woe:

Know Thine Enemy

The Professionals

Understand that thieves know tourists' routines, where their valuables are usually stashed and the quickest, easiest way to get them. Kids sit up on the hills behind museum parking lots and popular beaches watching you carefully hide your video camera in the trunk and stroll nonchalantly to your destination. Women chat up conventioneers whose rooms are being ransacked. Prostitutes slip drugs into overpriced drinks and then steal your wallet. Taxi drivers tell accomplices not only where you are going to spend the evening, but when you're coming back to your hotel. Criminals spend every day maximizing their return while minimizing their risk.

Junkies and Opportunists

These guys are usually found in the sleaziest parts of town. They prey on locals, sailors and college kids who drink too much. Whether they're transvestite hookers who hang around the Moulin Rouge in Paris or the kids who crowd around you in Jakarta, they look for an opportunity and they go for it. They start with the business traveler who drinks too much or frequents questionable establishments. They hang around airports waiting for you to put your bag down to make that phone call. They prey on tour bus tourists as they rubberneck famous cathedrals. Tourists make criminals' lives a lot more lucrative than they normally would be.

The Con Men

You love to travel to meet so many interesting people. In fact, you seem to meet people easily when you travel. You're a woman and are approached by a pleasant, well-dressed man who finds you immensely attractive. He wants to show you around the city. He knows people who have the best prices. He can take you to the best restaurants, nightclubs and discos. You're back home and wonder why you have a $300,000 credit card bill.

You are flattered by a curvaceous blonde who actually offers to buy you a drink. You spend the next two days wandering around Bogota babbling to lampposts. You have been conned, drugged and rolled.

You meet a businessperson in a bar who will introduce you to potential buyers for your new widgets. He also promises that there will be "entertainment." You not only drink too much but find that your credit card has been charged up beyond the limit. You have been conned. The first rule of the con man is to never let the mark suspect he is being conned, even long after the con.

The Killers

You've just left a small bar in New Orleans and know you stayed out too late. You see a man walking quickly toward you. You know that you're in big trouble. He pulls out a piece. His hands are shaking as he screams in a pinched voice for your money. You give him your money and he pops off three rounds into your gut. You realize he was running to rob you before other thugs could reach you first. You think, "What a rotten way to die," as you pass out.

You're driving through Northern Mexico. You're stopped by a group of men that have put up a log across the road. The men calmly point rifles at you as they tell you to walk from the car into the thick brush at the side of the road. You never hear the report of the muzzle as the bullet crashes through the back of your skull and out your eye. They needed your car. They can get about $50 for your passport and maybe run your credit cards a bit before they're canceled. Don't ever take the threat of danger lightly.

Unlike domestic crime, tourist crime relies on chance. The odds are in your favor that you won't be robbed, attacked, killed, raped or even cheated. You just have to work the odds your way.

How to Beat the Odds

You can actually travel around the world and look directly into the face of danger if you follow some basic tenets of safe travel.

1. Travel Tough

Think of travel as a herd of animals roaming across a savanna. Predators watch from the sideline looking for the weary, the stragglers and the confused.

Move quickly and with conviction. Expect to be ripped off. Look suspicious people straight in the eye for a longer than normal period of time. The key to avoid becoming a victim is to not look like one in the first place. It doesn't mean getting tattoos and steel-toed boots (although it might help if you're even a kernel more corn-fed than Woody Allen). It's a look and an attitude that says, "Hey, man, I've been here before. Maybe more times than you have."

2. Travel Smart

Know real danger. Read, talk, listen and plan. Be aware of dangers and scams before you go. Understand where and what crime is most likely to occur and be alert at all times. If possible, learn and practice the art of self defense.

3. Travel Light

The more you offer to the gods of theft, the more they will cherish you and seek you out. Carry as little luggage as possible. Crooks prey on the overloaded. The less you carry, the more in control you are. Employ simple luggage pieces without outside pockets or zippers. Use a laundry marker to black out any logos or brand name colors. Buy cable locks to make thieves miserable. Mark your bags with easy-to-identify and unattractive paint or tape.Get used to sticking your leg through straps when loading luggage or waiting in line. Get in the habit of snapping your luggage straps around bus grab handles, chair legs and bedposts. Keep valuables in the center of your sleeping bag, in the door liner of your car or in hotel safes when possible. Make sure both hands are free even when you are carrying bags.

4. Think Simple

The less you look and act like a mark, the less chance you'll become a mark. Don't wear camera bags or pouches. Try to use simple and nontraditional devices for your valuables. Aluminum equipment cases advertise "steal me." Stickers bearing such names as Leica, Nikon or other high-end brands scream "steal me faster." Put electricians tape over conspicuous brand names or badges. Wear neutral or dark-colored clothing without slogans, brands or bright patterns. Do not write your address on the outside of your luggage. Put a business card inside your luggage with just your initials and fax number or office phone number on the bag. Carry plastic garbage bags to slip your luggage inside for bus rides.

5. Stay Out of Bad Places

I don't mean Florida or Afghanistan. I mean the bad places found even in good places. Don't hang around whorehouses, cheap bars, dark alleys or slum districts. This also applies to more reputable but still dangerous areas such as local markets, flea markets, bus stations, flophouses, hostels and cheap restaurants. Try, in general, to stay away from the underbelly and seams of wherever you are.

6. Avoid Having Too Good a Time

Avoid fatigue and alcohol. Travelers tend to do inane things after a 12-hour plane flight and a few Scotches. Some travelers don't even need to be robbed to be robbed. They leave their wallets in a nightclub, write down their credit card numbers on a bill, even allow others to look over their shoulder while placing calls with a phone card.

If you drink, make sure you're with someone who'll get you to your hotel. Be prepared to lose everything you take with you. Drunk tourists are easy marks. Darkness is a dangerous time, but thieves are forced to attack tourists in broad daylight for the same reason mountain lions eat joggers. They don't have a choice. Consider the city as the most dangerous place, day time as the most dangerous time and any city street as a killing field. Drive or have a driver take you around. Take a taxi and ask the driver what to look out for. Walking puts you at greater risk. Of course, there are many cases of carjacking, robbery, insurance scams, roadblocks and other attacks on mechanized tourists, but most crimes are committed against pedestrians.

7. Stay Away From Tourists

Professional criminals swarm around tourist traps like bears around salmon spawns. Famous tourist attractions like temples, *souks*, museums, fairs, churches and anywhere you see a tour bus are dangerous places for tourists. Beaches are bad. Overpriced strip clubs are bad. Airports are bad. Pickpockets, con artists, stickup men, hustlers and other petty criminals float among the throngs of distracted tourists looking for quick hits.

Additionally, and ironically, other tourists themselves may be the ones you need to fear the most. In Nha Trang, Vietnam, a rapidly burgeoning tourist destination on the Southern Vietnamese coast, local guides will often advise you against mingling with other tourists, not so that you don't set yourself up for local rip-off artists, but so that you don't become a victim of another fellow tourist's con game. There have been reports of tourists befriending other foreigners on the beach and then ripping them off.

8. Get Local

Travel with a local. Stay in small towns. Stay at B&Bs. Patronize tiny villages. On one occasion, I left my camera bag and US$3000 dollars cash in a small maze-like Andalusian village. After its discovery by a local, the entire village tracked me down and was greatly relieved when I was found and repatriated with my belongings. Stories of honesty, generosity and friendship are legion in small towns around the world. In fact, many experts, quite correctly, draw a positive correlation between the number of tourists in a particular area and the area's crime rate: the more tourists, the more crime. Any place, such as a small town or hamlet, where everyone knows each other is relatively free of crime. Large cities are the breeding grounds of crime.

9. Think Plan B

Cross the street regularly. Stop and look in shop windows to see if anyone is paying too much attention to you. If driving in rural areas, stop occasionally to let others pass to make sure you're not being stalked. Look for escape routes; avoid funny looking people. Walk fast. Keep away from doorways. Stand under bright lights. Do not stop to give people the time or directions. Carry one hand in your pocket and scowl. Look people straight in the eye and watch them until they leave. Look purposeful. Always be aware of a 100-yard circle around you.

10. Run Like Hell

In many instances, the criminals will confront you with a weapon or the threat of bodily harm. Give them what they want and create more and more distance as you complain about the fact that you are now the impoverished. When the time seems right, run like hell, yelling "Thief!" in the local tongue. The chances of the robber chasing you once he has his booty are slim to none.

If the bandit (or bandits) is armed, do not obey a command to go with him to a place more secluded than where you are standing. Instead, run in a serpentine motion toward some type of cover or refuge. This does not apply if you are stopped at a roadblock. If you come to a roadblock, remember you will be shot at if you don't stop. Your chances are better to stop first and assess the situation. Do not leave the vehicle. Do not go with your captors. If you're going to die, die on your own terms.

11. Dirty Tricks

Thieves like to hit and run. Baggage handlers like to rifle through bags quickly. Pickpockets look for easy grabs. Muggers seek weak or incapacitated victims. None of these folks really want to deal with an unknown list of sneaky tricks you might have employed to conserve your health and your cash. Any possible impediment to an expedient and successful outcome to a robbery attempt will create reservations on the part of the thief.

If you have locked your luggage together or to a strut in the trunk of your car, the thief will most likely change his plan, if not abandon the hit altogether.

I like to put dirty laundry on top of my backpack, use caribiners to secure handles to firm objects and stick razor blades in side pockets. Use zip ties to secure zippers together, gaffers' tape to seal luggage, locks to secure luggage. Even simple notes reading "Nothing of Value" or "Danger: Infectious Bacteria Samples" can deter theft.

If you expect to be robbed, carry your valuables in special pockets sewn inside your shirt and your pants. The inside ankle and thigh areas are ideal for secret pants pockets. Inside your sleeve toward the armpit is the best place for shirt stashes. Keep a small amount of money in a money belt.

Victim or Victimizer?

I was once attacked in a market in Bamako, Mali. While standing around, two men tried to steal my cameras. Finding that they were fastened rather tightly with taut straps, they tugged and tugged while a busload of onlookers gazed in fascination. Giving up their futile quest, they suddenly stood still with their heads hung low as if awaiting a beating. Half of the passengers on the bus admonished the men for trying to rob me while the other half chastised me for showing off such expensive items in their impoverished country and tempting these poor, ragged men to rob me. They were both right.

In any event, be prepared to be a victim. Crime is a reality in all countries. It's better to lose your possessions than your life. Learn from others' misfortune. It's the best teacher.

Donald...Duck!

According to the FBI, Miami-Dade County has the highest crime rate of all U.S. metropolitan areas, with 12.33 crimes committed for every 100 residents. Although Miami has all the visitors they can handle coming in on rafts from Cuba, the city's bed tax shows that tourism was down about 20% in 1994 from 1993. The most recent violent incident occurred when an Italian couple celebrated their 25th wedding anniversary by being shot and robbed outside their hotel near Walt Disney World—the second shooting of a tourist in a week.

In A Dangerous Place: East Turkey

The road is full of vehicles: tractors, horsecarts, sawed-off buses with sagging rear ends, yellow taxis, overloaded motorcycles with sidecars; some carrying entire families with their goats. Everything is square and gray. The road and sidewalks are broken, dirty and patched, more broken than straight. Unlike the deathly gray of the towns, the hills beyond are a rich chocolate brown. The water is a sickly green-blue-black. The sky is the color of slate, with one enormous white cloud stretching off into the distance like a pompadour crashing against the wall of mountains like an incoming wave. Acres of cheap boxlike social housing sprout from the plains.

DP has come to the cradle of civilization, the uppermost tip of the fertile crescent. The cradle of civilization has become a war-torn region populated by ethnic, political, tribal and religious strife. We are determined to get at the heart of this land in order to understand why so much of the world is a dangerous place.

We stop to buy gas at a new petrol station. The attendant is baffled by our credit card. I run the card and sign the bill for him.

We drive past scattered groves of figs and pistachios. Trucks carry giant pomegranates. We are following the Iraqi pipeline on a highway originally built by the U.S. It was formally known as the "Silk Road."

Cheap Iraqi diesel or *masot* sells for 10,000 TL (Turkish lira or lire) a liter. It is brought from Iraq by trucks fitted with crude, rusty tanks.

As we go east, the fertile soil becomes fields of boulders and sharp rocks. The hills are ribbed and worn by the constant foraging of goats.

At Play in the Fields of the Warlords

We drive through the nameless streets of Severik, a small town that serves as the center of the Bucak fiefdom. In this age of enlightenment, there are still dark corners in the world where ancient traditions persist. We are in the domain of the Bucaks, an age-old feudal area in war-torn southeastern Turkey.

As we drive along the cobblestones we notice that there are no doors or windows in the stone houses, only steel shutters and gates. We ask the way to the warlord's house. Men pause and then point vaguely in the general direction.

We pull up to the Turkish version of a pizza joint. Inside, two men in white smocks eye us apprehensively. The fat one recognizes Coskun and runs alongside our car when we ask for directions. The man, out of breath, chatters animatedly as he continues to run alongside our car in his apron.

We drive up a narrow cobblestone alleyway just wide enough for a car to pass. The man in the apron waves and then sprints at an even faster clip back to his store. There's a Renault blocking the way. Getting out of the car, we notice for the first time that there is a man behind a wall of sandbags pointing an AK-47 at our chests. The large house was built 200 years ago and is lost in the maze of medieval streets and stone walls.

We politely explain who we are and why we have come to visit. We had telephoned the building earlier and were told that no one was at home; an appropriate response for someone who has survived frequent assassination attempts from terrorists, bandits and the army.

Out from a side door comes a large man with a pistol stuffed into his ammunition-heavy utility vest. He flicks his head at me and looks at Coskun inquisitively. He hears our story. He recognizes Coskun from a year ago when the photojournalist stayed with the warlord for three days. He smiles and gives Coskun the double buss kiss, the traditional greeting for men in Turkey. He then grabs me by the shoulders, does the same and then welcomes us inside. We walk up one flight of stairs and are in an outside courtyard. We are joined by two more bodyguards. They're older, more grooved, hard looking. Most of one man's chin has been blown off his face; it tells us that we should probably just sit and smile until we get to know each other a little better. We sit on the typical tiny wooden stools men use in Turkey. These have the letters DYP branded into them: the name of the political party the warlord has aligned himself with.

The bodyguards stare into our eyes, say nothing and watch our hands when we reach for a cigarette. It seems that Sedat Bucak, the clan leader, is out in the fields, but his brother Ali is here. We are offered *chai* or tea and cigarettes. The bodyguards do not drink tea, or move, but they light cigarettes. One of the bodyguards sucks on his cigarette as if to suffocate it.

When Ali finally emerges, he is not at all what one would expect a warlord to look like. The men rise and bow. Ali is dressed in shiny black loafers, blue slacks, a plum-colored striped shirt and a dapper windbreaker. He looks like an Iranian USC grad. The fact that he and his brother are the absolute rulers of 100,000 people and in control of an army of 10,000 very tough men is hard to imagine. He looks like a dentist.

A Drive in the Country

Not quite sure why we're here, he offers to show us a gazelle that he was given as a gift by one of his villages. The gazelle is kept in a stone enclosure and flies around the pen, leaping through doors and windows. We ask if we can visit Sedat. Ali says, "Sure," and repeats that he is out in the fields.

Realizing they were embarking on a short drive outside of their compound, an arsenal of automatic weapons suddenly appears from another door. Ali and his bodyguards get in the Renault and drive down the streets with the barrels of their guns sticking out the windows. Strangely, nobody seems to mind or notice. Even the soldiers and police wave as they drive by.

We are brought to their fortress, an imposing black stone compound that dominates the countryside. It is a simple square structure, each wall about 100 feet long. A central house rises to about 40 feet. The walls are made from *koran*, or black stone and are hand-chiseled from the surrounding boulders into squares. The walls of the house are fashioned from brick filled with special cement to make them bulletproof. One wall is over 20 feet tall and there is still much work to do to finish this "place of last refuge."

The men appear nervous when I photograph the compound. This building is intended for combat. For now it serves as a simple storage place for tractors and grain. From the top one feels like a king overlooking his land and his subjects, which is exactly what the Bucaks do when they are up here. From this point we can only see 50 miles to the mountains in the north but we cannot see the rest of their 200 miles of land to the south and west of us.

We continue our drive along a dusty road past simple villages and houses. The people here are dirt-poor. They subsist off the arid land. The children run out into the road to wave at us as we drive by.

Ali stops near a field where men, women and children are picking cotton. Cotton needs water; there's plenty of it. It also needs cheap labor, another commodity the Bucaks have plenty of.

The people stand still while we get out of our cars. Ali tells them to continue working while we take pictures. They pick but their eyes never leave us.

The men decide this would be an opportune time to show off the capability of their arsenal. For one nauseating moment I have the impression he intends to gun down this entire village. Yet it is target practice Ali has in mind. Boys will be boys. So we then start plinking away at rocks using all sorts of automatic weapons. We aim for a pile of rocks about 400 yards away. We are only aware of little puffs of smoke and we hear the sound of ricochets as the bullets hit the black boulders. Ali is more interested in our video camera, so he plays with that while we play with his weapons.

When boredom sets in, we continue our journey in search of Sedat. We finally locate him about three miles away. We know it's him because of the small army that surrounds the man. His bodyguards are not happy at all to see us. We are instantly engulfed by his men poised in combat stances. Ali introduces us, but we still have to state our case. Sedat recognizes Coskun, but instead of the kiss we get a Western-style handshake. We introduce ourselves to his dozen or so bodyguards. They do not come forward, so we reach for their hands and shake them. It's awkward, unnerving. They never let their eyes stray from ours.

Ahmed, a chiseled sunburned man who wears green camouflage fatigues, seems to be the chief bodyguard. He likes us the least. He wanders over to our car and starts rummaging through the luggage and junk on the back seat. Luckily we deliberately put our stuff there so that it would be easy to confirm that I am a writer. He picks up a Fielding catalog and starts flipping through the pages. When he sees my picture next to one of my books he points and then looks at me.

The Feudal Lord

We chat with Sedat Bucak. He is eager to present a positive image to the outside world. We have brought a copy of an interview he had just done with a Turkish magazine. In it he suggests that he should link up with the right-wing nationalist party and, together, they could end the Kurdish problem. Coskun suggests that such a comment could be taken as a bid for civil war. Sedat says, "Hey, it's only an interview. But I'm still learning." We suggest getting some shots of him driving his tractor. He is happy driving his tractor. But even in this rural scene there are few other farmers that drive a tractor with a Glock 17 and an AK-47-armed bodyguard riding behind on the spreader.

Turkey has been at war with the PKK, or Kurdish Workers Party, since 1984. The Kurds want a separate homeland within Turkey, but Turkey insists they possess all the rights they need for now. The Turkish government is correct, but it doesn't stop the

PKK from killing, maiming, executing and torturing their own people. The Bucaks are Kurds and the sworn enemies of the PKK, who are also Kurds. The difference is that the Bucaks have essentially carved out their own kingdom and have even managed to integrate themselves into the political process in an effective, albeit primitive, way. They use votes rather than bullets to curry favor. They are also left alone by the government. They pay no taxes and have complete control over what goes on in their ancestral lands.

The Bucak family has been in Sibilek for more than 400 years. They are Kurds but more specifically, they're from the Zaza as opposed to the Commange branch of the Kurds. They also speak a different language from the Commange. They have always controlled a large part of southeastern Turkey by force and eminent domain. Their subjects give them 25 percent of the crops they grow and in return they receive services and are protected by a private army of about 10,000 men. Many other groups have tried unsuccessfully to force them off their land. In times of all-out warfare, all the subjects are expected to chip in and grab their rifles. The Bucaks have wisely aligned themselves with the current ruling political party, the DYP. Realizing that the Bucaks can deliver 100,000 votes goes a long way towards successful lobbying and handshaking in Ankara, the capital of Turkey. Sedat Bucak is head of the clan at the age of 40. A warrior and farmer by trade, he's now a sharp and shrewd politician. If he's killed, his younger brother Ali will take the helm. Ali is only 24.

Severik has long been a battleground. The city was completely closed to all outsiders, including the army, between 1970 and 1980. During this period, there was intense street-to-street fighting between the Bucaks and the PKK. Thousands of people were killed; the PKK chose easier victims. The Bucaks cannot stray eastward into PKK-held territory without facing instant death.

The countryside the Bucaks rule consists of rolling plains, similar to Montana or Alberta. This is to the benefit of the Ataturk dam project, the fifth largest dam project in the world.

Sedat can never travel without his bodyguards; neither can Ali. The bodyguards match the personalities of the brothers. Sedat's bodyguards are cold, ruthless killers. They're picked for their bravery and ferocity the last ten years of warfare. Ali's bodyguards are younger, friendlier, but just as lethal.

They pack automatic weapons: German G-3s, M-15s or AK-47s. They each also carry at least one handgun as well as four to six clips for the machine guns and three to four clips for their pistols. Ali and Sedat also carry weapons at all times. Their choice of weapons also reflects their personalities. Ali packs a decorative stainless steel 9mm Ruger and Sedat carries a drab businesslike Glock 17.

Some of the bodyguards, such as Nouri, wear the traditional Kurdish garb of checkered headpiece and baggy wool pants. The *salvars* appear to be too hot to wear on the sunburned plains. One of the guards explains that they work like a bellows and pump air when you walk, an example of something that works. Others wear cheap suits. Some wear golf shirts, still others wear military apparel.

While we are taking pictures of Sedat on his Massey Ferguson, the guards bring out the *gnass*, or sniper rifle(gnass is Arabic for sniper). It is an old Russian weapon designed to kill men at 4000 meters. When I walk down to take pictures, Ahmed, the cagey one, slides the rifle into a car and shakes his head. He knows that a sniper rifle is not for self-defense but is used for one thing only, as they explain to us, "With this rifle, you can kill a man before he knows he is dead."

Many of the men have a Turkish flag on the butts of their clips. One bodyguard offers me a rolled cigarette from an old silver tin. It tastes of the sweet, mild tobacco from Ferat. We both have a smoke. I open my khaki shirt and show him my Black Dog t-shirt, a picture of a dog doing his thing. He laughs and shakes hands: Seems as if we're finally warming up this crowd.

The younger brother of Ali's bodyguard asks me if I am licensed to use guns. He likes the way I shoot. I try to explain that in America, you need a permit to own a gun and that people are trained or licensed. He looks at me quizzically. It's no use. I doubt they would understand a society that lets you own a gun without knowing how to use it.

We blast off some more rounds. Ali's bodyguards are having fun. We then bring out the handguns. We are all bad shots. Trying to hit a Pepsi can, no one comes close. Then one of the bodyguards marches up to the can and "executes" it with a smile. It is a chilling scene and I'm glad it's only an aluminum can.

While Ali's bodyguards clown around with us, Sedat's bodyguards never move, use or even take their hands off their guns. Nouri has his AK-47 tucked so perfectly into the crook of his arm, it is hard to imagine him not sleeping with it.

After chatting with Sedat and nervously entertaining his bodyguards, we head back into town. There, we're taken to lunch at Ali Bucaks restaurant and gas station. We eat in Ali's office. The bodyguards act as waiters, serving us shepherd's salads and kabobs with yogurt to drink. They serve us quietly and respectfully. They eat with one hand on their guns. The SSB radio crackles nonstop as various people check in. We talk to Ali about life in general. Can he go anywhere without his guards? No. What about when he goes to Ankara on the plane? They have to put their guns in plastic bags and pick them up when they land. What about in Ankara? They change cars a lot. Does he like his role? He doesn't have a choice. Does he like feudalism? No, but he doesn't have a choice. The government does not provide services or protect their people, so they must do it themselves. Who would take the sick to the hospitals? Who would take care of the widows? Since power is passed along family lines, it is his duty.

As we eat, a storm comes in from Iraq. Lightening flashes and thunder cracks. We talk about politics, baseball cards and America. They are all familiar with America because every Turkish home and business has a television blaring most of the day and night. The number one show is the soap "Young and the Restless," which comes on at 6:15 every night.

Sedat is a soft-spoken man—about 5 feet 6 inches tall, sunburned and suffering from a mild thyroid condition. He wears a faded green camouflage baseball hat, Levis and running shoes. As your neighbor might, he also carries a Glock 17 in a hand-rubbed leather holster. It is unsnapped for a quicker draw. Maybe not quite like your neighbor! He is never more than 15 feet from his bodyguards. Men drawn from his army as personal bodyguards have the lean, sunburned look of cowboys. He comes from an immediate family of 500 Bucaks. They make their money by growing cotton and other crops they sell in Adana.

Severik was where the PKK began in 1978. Severik was also the site of their first military activity. For ten years all-out warfare raged in Severik as the PKK fought to wrest control from the Bucaks. It is hard to believe that this gentle, slightly nervous man is the only person in Turkey who has been able to beat the PKK at their own game.

For now, everything is well in the kingdom. The dam will bring water for crops; the PKK is defeated and now concentrates on other areas; the people are happy and Sedat is now a big-wheel politician. There is much to be said for feudalism. I offer to send him some of my books so he can read about the rest of the world. He thinks this is a great idea. But he doesn't speak or read English.

Mekap is the brand of sneakers preferred by the PKK. They can be identified by the red star on a yellow badge. If you ask at a shoe store for Mekaps you will get a very strange reaction; the merchant will assume you're from the police and testing him.

We drive from Sevirek to Diyrbakir. We will pass from a feudal kingdom to a large, bustling city that is the flashpoint for much of the violence that grips Turkey. We realize as we drive down the lonely roads that we are leaving the protection of the Bucaks and will soon be in PKK territory. If we were to be caught with Ali's address, we'd be killed. If the PKK had any knowledge of our contact with the Bucaks, we'd be instant enemies.

The PKK control the countryside and, it is said, the whole of Eastern Turkey at night. It is not a particularly large group, perhaps some 8000 soldiers trained in small camps but they're armed with small weapons; AK-47s and RPGs and a few grenade launchers. They travel in groups of 12 men and can muster a sizable force of about 200 soldiers for major ambushes. Their leader lives in the Bekáa Valley in southern Lebanon under the protection of the Syrian government. He calls for an independent Kurdistan, which Saddam Hussein has given him by default in Northern Iraq. But he wants more. He wants a sizable chunk of Iran and Turkey as well.

Despite the numerous checkpoints and military presence in the area, there has been little success in defeating the PKK. The Turkish Army has set up large special ops teams and commando units that specialize in ambushes, foot patrols and other harassment activities. But once you see the topography of Eastern Turkey, you realize that you could hide an army 1000 times the size of the PKK. The terrain is riddled with caves, redoubt-shaped cliffs, boulders, canyons and every conceivable type of nook and cranny. It is easy terrain to move in with few natural or man-made obstructions.

The PKK go into the villages at night to demand cooperation. If villagers do not cooperate they are shot. In some cases, entire families, including babies, are executed. The PKK follow a Marxist-Leninist doctrine and play out their guerrilla tactics similar to the former Viet Cong or the Khmer Rouge. The PKK also likes to kidnap foreigners for money and publicity and they like to execute school teachers and government officials. Special ops teams report to the civil authorities and to the military. Turkey considers the PKK as criminals and is reluctant to use civil law and superficial civilian forces against it.

Turkey has been in a state of war for ten years now—that being the war the military is waging within its own borders.

We decide to spend an evening with a former leader and trainer of special ops teams. Hakan is now Turkey's only test pilot. In Turkey, this doesn't mean flying new prototype planes; it means flying out to helicopters downed by the rebels, making repairs and then flying or sling-loading them out.

He lives in a high-rise building, guarded by three soldiers, barbed wire and fortifications against attack. His apartment is modern and well furnished. There are no traditional rugs, just black lacquer furniture complete with a fully stocked bar. Except for the barbed wire, we could be in Florida, which is where he trained as a *Sikorsky Blackhawk* pilot.

He has a two-month-old baby and is looking forward to being transferred back to Western Turkey. His contempt for the PKK is obvious, having killed many of its members and having many PKK rounds aimed at him. He feels that the PKK is winning in this part of the country, but there will be no victory. The PKK problem cannot be solved militarily. It must be solved economically by making the Kurds the beneficiaries of government help and giving them a stronger political voice. Killing terrorists is merely his job. He can't wait to get transferred out of Diyabakir. His wife plays with their baby on the floor. The baby never stops smiling and laughing. I think of the barbed wire and nervous soldiers downstairs. He can offer no political insights: PKK are people who he is paid to fight. When he is in Ankara he will occupy himself with other things.

Eastern Turkey is the poorest and least developed part of the nation. Most educated people come from Western Turkey. Most of the soldiers, politicians and professional classes are from Western Turkey. The government sends these people to Eastern Turkey for a minimum of two years of service. Most can't wait to get back to Istanbul or Ankara. Eastern Turkey has much closer affiliations with Armenia, Iran, Iraq, Azerbaijan, Syria and Georgia. Western Turkey has the ocean as a border. Eastern Turkey must deal with its warlike and poor neighbors. Eastern Turkey is rife with dissension. Iraqi, Iranian, Armenian and Syrian terrorists actively fight the government and each other. Hezbollah, the Iranian-backed fundamentalist group, hates the PKK. The PKK hates the government. The militia hates all rebel agitators and the army and police cleanup the messes left behind.

The Governor

I decide that we need another point of view. We go to Siirt about 40 km from the Syrian border and directly in the heart of PKK territory. We are definitely in harm's way since the PKK travel from Syria into the mountains behind us. Just down the road is the military outpost of Erub, an outpost designed to control a critical mountain road that leads down toward the Syrian border. There is another reason why we have chosen this tiny town. Coskun was born and raised in Siirt. I suggest that we should go and chat up the governor and get his point of view.

Coskun is somewhat hesitant about meeting with the governor of Siirt province because he has a natural (and well-founded) aversion to politicians. But since we will be traveling directly into and through the war zone we want to ensure that when we get stopped by the military we can drop names, flash the governor's card and ensure at least a moment of hesitation before we are shot as spies or terrorists.

As we pass the heavy security of the Siirt administration building, it seems that the governor is in. His bodyguards are quite perturbed that these strangers have walked right in and asked for an audience. They quietly talk into their walkie-talkies and stand between us and the soundproofed door that leads into the governor's office. The governor takes his time to put on his game face and finally invites us in. It is kisses all around, chocolates, tea and cigarettes. We thank him and tell him our business. We are here to see what is going on in Turkey. He is proud to have us in his region. Two of his aids sit politely on the couch. The governor speaks in long, melodious, booming soliloquies which when translated into English come out as, "We are maligned by the press" or, "There is no danger here." Finally they ask me what I have seen and what I think of their country. I tell them the truth. The people here are extraordinary in their friendship and warmth but we are in a war zone. He launches into a response that boils down to, "It's safe here and we want you to tell your readers to come to Turkey and Siirt province." He then tells us of the attractions that await the lucky traveler; canyons as deep as the Grand Canyon, white water rafting, hiking, culture, history, etc. We say great, give us a helicopter and we'll go for a spin tomorrow.

He goes one further. He invites us to dinner that night so that he can spend more time with us. Coskun wants to kick me as I accept. Later that night we are invited to the government building for dinner. Joining us for dinner will be the head of police, the head of the military, three subgovernors and a couple of aides.

We pass through security and are ushered into the dining room. Sitting uncomfortably, we make small talk while a television blares away against the wall. After an appropriate time we begin to eat. As we sit down to dinner we indicate that we are curious and ask the military commander just what is going on. Everyone is dressed in a suit and tie or uniform. Coskun and I do the best we can with our dusty khakis. Either because the room is hot or they are just being polite, they take their jackets off for dinner. The governor carries a silver 45 tucked into his waistband. His formal gun? As the men sit down to dinner, something strikes me as funny. Coskun and I are the only ones not packing a gun for dinner.

The dinner is excellent; course after course of shish kebob, salads and other delicacies washed down with *raki* (a strong anisette liquor) and water. The taste of raki brings back memories of the hard crisp taste of Cristal aquadiente, the preferred drink of the Colombian drug trade. Throughout dinner the head of police is interrupted by a walk-ie-talkie-carrying messenger who hands him a piece of paper. He makes a few comments to the side and the man disappears. Every five to 10 minutes the man returns, the police chief makes a quiet comment and he goes away.

Meanwhile, the governor continues to extol the beauty of his country—nonstop. He is the center of attention simply because no one else is speaking. The others nod, smile or laugh. Most of their attention is on the television blaring in the corner. As we move to the table, the red phone next to the television begins ringing. The call is answered by the attendant. It is for the colonel. The colonel excuses the interruption and also speaks in low tones. The police chief puts his walkie-talkie on the table. It becomes apparent that the base is under attack by a group of PKK of unknown size . Throughout dinner the conversation steers towards politics as it must. Like many countries there are two parallel worlds: the world of administrators, occupiers and government, then there is the world of the dispossessed—the people who till the soil, who build their houses with their own hands, who bury their dead in the same ground that gives them their crops. Tonight and every night, that world is ruled by the PKK, Dev Sol, Armenian terrorists, Hezbollah and bandits. At dusk the world is plunged into fear, ruled by armed bands of men that are neither chosen nor wanted by the ordinary people. At dawn the country is back in the hands of the government, the people and the light. During the conversation there is no right and no wrong, only an affirmation that each side believes it is in the right.

The red phone continues to ring and the little pieces of paper continue to be brought up to the police chief. The police chief is now speaking directly into his walk-ie-talkie. Meanwhile the governor continues to regal us with stories about Siirt. As we eat course after course I am offered cigarettes by at least three to four people at a time. Doing my best to accommodate my hosts I eat, smoke and drink the sharp *raki*, all the time keeping one ear on the governor's conversation and the constant mumbled conversations being carried out on the phone and the walkie-talkie.

The governor is very proud of the tie he wore especially for me—a pattern of Coca Cola bottles. He brings in his young daughters to meet me. They are shy, pretty and are very proud of their English. We chat about life in Siirt and I realize that they are virtually prisoners in the governor's compound. The governor tells us of a road we should take to enjoy the scenery, a winding scenic road to Lice via Kocakoy. Finally, the colonel is spending so much time on the phone that he excuses himself. The police chief is visibly agitated but is now speaking nonstop on the walkie-talkie. Messages continue to arrive.

The television is now featuring swimsuit-clad lovelies and has captured the attention of the governor's aides and his subgovernors. As the dinner winds down we retire outside to have coffee. I am presented with a soft wool blanket woven in Siirt. We have a brief exchange of speeches and I notice that the colonel and police chief have now joined us. I ask them what all the commotion was about and they mention that it was a minor incident that has been handled. The governor reminds us to tell people of the beauty of this place, the friendliness of the Turkish people and the people of Siirt.

As I prepare to go, they wrap my blanket in today's newspaper. Smack dead center is a full color photograph of a blood-soaked corpse of a man who has been executed by the Dev Sol terrorist group for being an informer.

The next day there is no helicopter waiting for us. When we inquire as to its where-abouts we are told that it was needed to do a body count from the attack the night be-fore. We ask the blue-bereted special ops soldier what the best way is to see the country side. He assumes that we must be important and instead of telling us to get lost he carefully reviews our options. As for the road we want to take into the moun-tains, he informs us that it is heavily mined and would have to be cleared before we could attempt a crossing. In any case we would need an armored car and an escort of soldiers and probably a tank. We ask about the helicopter which would be safer, but we will need to wait until he can get a gunship to accompany us.

A Place in Time

We figure the only sightseeing we are going to do today is on foot. Coskun reminisc-es with his first employer, a gentle man who puts out a tiny newspaper with a nine-teenth-century offset press and block type. He has broken his arm so he apologizes on the back page for the paper being so small. Everyday he laboriously pecks out the local news with one finger using an old Remington typewriter, he then reads his copy, marks it up and hands it to the eager teenagers who sort through the dirty trays of lead type. He has a choice between two photoengraved pictures that sit in a worn old tray. One is the governor, the other is the president of Turkey. When the type is hand set they laboriously run off a couple of hundred copies for the dwindling number of loyal readers. I leave Coskun with his old friend.

Siirt is a dusty, poor Kurdish town with a history of being occupied by everyone from Alexander to the Seljuks to the Ottomans. Some of the people are fair-skinned, blonde and blue eyed. Others have the hard Arabic look of the south, while still others have the round heads and bald spots of the Turks. Siirt is a happy town with the children contentedly playing in the muddy streets. As I walk around the town, the children begin to tag along with me. All are eager to try out their words of English. I urge them to teach me Kurdish. They point at houses, dogs, people and chatter away, "Where come you from?" and "Hello mister, what eeze your name?" I wonder where I would ever need to use Kurdish. Some visitors say Siirt looks like a poorly costumed bible sto-ry. Here and there along the broken streets are ancient houses with tapered walls; many people still use the streets as sewers. Goats, cows and chickens wander the streets. Near the mosque the less fortunate goats are sold and then slaughtered on the spot. Donkeys sit patiently. Men physically pull me over to where they are sitting and demand that we have tea. I realize it would take me years if I stopped and had tea with everyone who wanted to chat. I begin to respect the delicate but strong social web that holds this country together. Soldiers, fighters, rebels, farmers, politicians, police all offer us hospitality, tea and a cigarette. The tiny parcels of information and face-to-face encounters build and transmit an understanding of what is going on, who is going where and why.

In every shop a television blares. Western programs and news shows constantly bom-bard these people with images that do not fit into their current world. At 6:10 "The Young and the Restless," dubbed in Turkish, captures the entire population. It is typ-ically Turkish that they would treat the TV like a visitor, never shutting it up and qui-etly waiting for their turn to speak. I can only imagine that the blatant American and western European images are as familiar and comforting to the old generation as MTV's "The Grind" is to us. As with all small rural towns around the world, the young people are moving to the big cities. The future is colliding with the past.

They're Your Modern Stone Age Family

We decide not to hang around and wait for the helicopter and the helicopter gunship to be arranged. Instead we decide to drive into the countryside where the army has little control. Along the way we stop in a little-known troglodyte village called Hassankeyf. Here Coskun knows an old lady who lives in a cave. In three years this historic area will be under water when the massive hydroelectric dam is completed. Hassankeyf could be a set from "The Flintstones." A winding canyon is full of caves that go up either side creating a cave-dwellers high-rise development. Far up in the highest cave is the last resident of this area. The lady claims to be 110 years old. I guess she is closer to 80. But it probably doesn't matter since in this land—she could be older than Methuselah and have seen nothing change. We climb up to chat with her while down below the golden rays of the sun illuminate the Sassouk mosque. Across the canyon are the ruins of a Roman-era monastery.

She doesn't seem pleased to see us. In a grouchy way she invites us into her cave. The lady lives alone with a cat and her donkey. The donkey has his own cave carved cleanly and laboriously out of the soft limestone.

The outside cave where the old woman lives leads back into a rear cave where she makes her bed on straw and carpets. The roof of the cave is covered with a thick greasy layer of soot from the small fire she uses to cook on. She says she is ill and needs medicine. We have brought her a bar of chocolate but we do not have any medicine with us. We give her some money but realize she is days away from any drugstore and her only method of transport is her donkey or a ride from one of the villagers.

People from across the steep valley yell and wave at us. They do not get many visitors. We take pictures of the lady. She seems happy to have someone to talk to and after her initial grumpiness she offers us some flat bread. It crunches with the dirt and gravel baked into it. We smile and say it is good.

As the sun sets further, the ancient ambience is broken by the loud thumping and hoarse whistling scream of a Cobra gunship returning to Siirt. This was probably our escort, but we are glad to be sitting here in the cool golden dusk in a cave; in a place that will soon be erased off the map.

We have to leave. Travel at night is not safe. The PKK control this area at night. The military will fire at anything that moves on the roads at night. We must make it to the

Christian town of Mardil, or as the locals call it Asyriac, before it gets completely dark. The old lady wishes us well. The Christians who live in the town of Mardil speak the language of Jesus; Aramic. Strange that we are also in the land of the Yezidi, the religion that prays to Satan. We are told the PKK do not attack Asyriac because of their ties to Assad. Here we will spend the night with some people who hold the honor of having the most dangerous profession in East Turkey: Schoolteachers.

The Most Dangerous Job

Schoolteachers are part of the colonial oppression that the PKK is fighting against. Kurdish children are not allowed to speak the native tongue in school. Teachers in Turkey are assigned to work for four years in East Turkey before they can work in the more lucrative Eastern cities of Istanbul and Ankara. Here they are paid 8 million Turkish lira a month about $220 U.S. and about 30 percent more than they would usually make. About 30 percent never do their time in East Turkey and buy their way out of the dangerous assignment. By comparison, soldiers get paid 35–40 million Turkish lira a month.

The teachers live in simple stone houses; one room for living and one room for sleeping. There is no plumbing, the bathroom is an outhouse about 20 yards from the house. But the conditions are not what make this job dangerous. Over the last three years, 75 schoolteachers have been executed by the PKK. Schoolteachers in East Turkey are not raving political stooges of the government who spread torment and hate.They are bright college-educated people who teach reading, writing and math. Many are just starting families and enjoy the work they do. The few that are dragged out of their houses at night, sentenced and shot in the chest probably wonder what they did to deserve such a cold and uncelebrated death.

We spend the evening with two young teachers, husband and wife and their two young girls. They share their simple food and are good company. There is little to do here once the sun goes down.The inside of the simple stone house reminds me of a bomb shelter; whitewashed, cold and damp. The house is lit with a single bare lightbulb hanging down from the ceiling. After dinner we walk to the homes of the other teachers in this small village. Each family of teachers is happy to meet outsiders. There are two young female teachers who bring us cookies and tea, and there are two married couples each with a small child. We gather together in their simple homes and talk about life in the war zone. Three days ago three teachers just northwest of here were rounded up, tied hand and foot and shot the same way you would kill an old dog.

Many people feel that the teachers were shot because they had weapons in their houses. After the shootings the teachers from this village traveled to town to talk to the region's military commander and protest the arming of teachers as militia. The colonel instead greeted them as the protectors of the village. Taken aback, they explained that they thought he was the protector of the village. "No," he smiled and said, "it is much too dangerous to have troops out there at night." The colonel offered them rifles and ammunition to give them peace of mind. "After all", he said "I am surrounded by hundreds of soldiers, barbed wire and fortifications as well as over a hundred trained antiterrorist commandos for backup." He offered the teachers one of each; a "big gun" (a German G-3) for the men and a little gun (AK-47s) for the women. Not knowing how to react, the teachers abandoned their first line of attack and glumly accepted the weapons and boxes of ammunition. They admitted to us they had no idea how to use them and were terrified that the children would find the rifles under their beds. So they kept them unloaded.

As I walked back under a brilliant star-filled sky I marveled at the ridiculousness of it all. Here we were with eager, youthful young men and women—educated, enthusiastically discussing politics, life and laughter, sharing what little they have and trying to make sense of it all, while a few miles down the road was the PKK training base of Eruh and the Syrian border only 50 km away. The town has been the scene of heavy fighting between the PKK and the Turkish special forces. No one dares go out of the village at night for fear of being shot as a terrorist by the nervous militia.

The people are thankful for their stone houses as they cower below windows during the heaviest shooting. Here there is no doctor, no store, no transportation, no facilities of any kind. To think that a beautiful night like this could be interrupted by sudden death is unimaginable.

Tearing down the Silk Road

Despite our token flirtation with death, we spend a sunny morning playing with the children and then continue on our way to the Iraqi border. I am curious. Just before we leave the village we are stopped by a group of villagers. They point to a stinking swamp in the center of the village. They complain that the government came in to build a pond and now it is a sewer. They seem to think that we have some way to restore it. We smile, shrug our shoulders and drive off. Everyone has their problems, I guess.

Winding our way down to the main road we inhale the clean mountain air and stop to take pictures of the sparkling brooks and lush scenery. This can't be a war zone. Down on the main road the military checkpoints begin. At the first checkpoint 14 km from Cizre, we are quite bluntly asked, "What the hell we are doing here?" The appropriate answer seems to be the most absurd, "Just looking around." Cooling our heels and drinking tea in the commander's bunker, we are given our passports back and smugly told that we have been scooped. A television news crew from 32 GUN (a Turkish news show) had already made it into Iraq. The commander assumes that we are journalists trying to cover Saddam's big military push to the south. Apparently the television crew got special permission from the Iraqi embassy in Ankara and is the only news crew in Iraq. Not too bothered by this revelation, we share a cigarette with the sergeant and more tea is brought out. It appears that our time with the governor and the military commander of Siirt province has paid off. We ask the officer in charge if he could radio ahead and let the trigger-happy soldiers know we are coming.

We should be in the cradle of civilization between the fertile thighs of the Tigris and the Euphrates. Instead we are in a hair-trigger war zone, where every man is a potential killer and every move might be your last.

We take a few Polaroids for the officer and we hit the road again. At each blown bridge and sandbagged checkpoint we stop and chat with the soldiers. Up ahead of us is Mount Cudi where the Koran says the ark of Noah rests: It sits like a forbidden beacon 3500 meters high. We drive along the Syrian border clearly defined by eight-foot high barbed wire and 30-foot guard towers every 500 meters. We are on a beautiful piece of smooth two-lane blacktop built right smack on top of the "silk road". We are not traveling by camel today. I keep the Fiat's gas pedal pressed to the floor: the speedometer spinning like a slot machine. The only time we have to slow down is at a checkpoint or when abridge has been blown up. The heavy trucks labor toward the West as we pass burned-out hulks of gas stations. We stop in Silapi, the last Turkish town before the Iraqi border to get something to eat. Silapi is one of the dirtiest drab-best holes I have ever visited. Row after row of truck repair shops, dusty streets and grease-smeared people watch as we drive by.

We pick a restaurant where the secret police eat. You can tell the secret police by their bull necks, gold chains and walkie-talkies. The hotel next door is decorated with stickers from the world's press and relief agencies. The food is good. Outside our restaurant a retarded man with no legs sits on his stumps outside. Using blocks to get around, he is black from the soot and grime of the street. He uses an old inner tube to prevent the hot road from burning his stumps. He watches us eat. The people pass him by as he grimaces and grunts, his hand extended. I marvel that this man is still alive in this godforsaken outpost. I go outside and give him some lira. He begins to cry and tug at my leg thanking me in his tortured way. When I leave him, children begin to crowd around and start to beat him for his money. I go back outside and another man chases the children away. We tuck the money away since his spastic hands keep flailing around. When I go back into the restaurant, one of the men at a table next to us tells us that the beggar will probably be dead tonight, killed for the money he now has. I feel very sad and want to leave this place.

As we blast down the road toward the Iraqi border I notice that the big guns in the Turkish bunkers are not facing south across the road to Syria, but toward Turkey to the north and the rebel-held hills beyond.

And the Angels Fly to Heaven

Much later, back in Istanbul, I stand in front of the massive Hagia Sophia Mosque. Inside it is quiet. Two men make their prayers in the busy, serious, hurried style of Islam. The worn carpets and the vast ceiling absorb the whispering and rustling like a sponge. It feels like all the prayers of both Christian and Muslim are stored in the carpets and stones of this mosque.

Outside it is dark and the rain is cold and heavy, pushed by the sharp wind. The brilliant floodlights cut tunnels of light upward into the low clouds above the softly sculpted building. It is as if the prayers of centuries power this energy, sending the shafts of pure blue light through the clouds and into the stars above. High above are angels. In the background is a mysterious low chorus. Glowing, brilliant and white, the angels slowly circle in the pillars of light. The thrusting minarets below act like beacons seemingly radiating the illuminating shafts. The shafts of light are actually coming from the heavens and the angels are singing in chorus. But alas, the angels are just seagulls and the chorus is a distinct shiphorn. And the prayers of a thousand years are lost and rubbed to dust in the aging carpets inside the mosque.

For a brief moment it was calm and peaceful. The angels had come to answer those prayers. Instead I know that out in the rolling yellow fields of the east, there will be more death under the Eastern Turkish stars tonight.

Fielding's
The
World's
Most Dangerous
Places

Travel Tips

There is information aplenty on how to plan trips to "normal" places. Here are some sources on travel to "less than normal" places:

1) Gather Information

Travel agents: Most travel agents are useless when it comes to travel to dangerous places. Travel agents use databases provided by hotel and airline customers. Some may use State Department info or travel guides and reference books to supplement this information. Although travel agents must warn you if you are traveling to a dangerous place, they rarely follow the daily updates. If you select a travel agency that specializes in one country (Iran, India, etc.) you can expect a higher level of knowledge, but travel agents are not in the business of sending people to bad places. They also have limited access to smaller airlines, bus lines, etc. They can provide brochures and tourist information about the countries you plan to visit or. if not, put you in touch with people who can. Your travel agent should also be able to provide you with the Department of State travel advisory for any country you plan to visit, if an advisory has been issued for the country. If your travel agent cannot provide travel advisories, you can obtain them 24-hours a day by calling ☎ *(202) 647-5225.*

Newspapers: Most newspapers provide first hand coverage of dangerous areas. If a journalist is based in the area covered, chances are the information is reliable. Watch out for articles with PR-spins designed to shore up the government's position or downplay the dangers. Your best sources on international topics are the widely available *New York Times, Los Angeles Times* and local papers available at large newsstands.

Magazines: Periodicals like *The Economist, Time, Newsweek,* and *U.S. News and World Report* provide weekly updates on the world. They are good sources for overviews including maps and statistics. It is difficult to get information about regions that have fallen off the back page. Your best bet is to head to the library to find more regionalized magazines like *Asiaweek* or magazines that specialize in remote or questionable places: Magazines like *Outside, Escape* or even *Soldier of Fortune* will provide coverage of exotic regions.

Newsletters and Special Interest publications: If you plan on doing a lot of travel it may be worth investing in special interest mailings from *For Your Eyes Only, Foreign Affairs, Jane's, Pinkerton's* and other publications written for military, business and political audiences.

Public library: Probably your best single source for background information about remote areas and an excellent source for preliminary information. Be careful about outdated information.

Travel Guides: Most travel guides minimize the dangers to travelers and tend to focus on popular and proven places. In the front section of most guides there will be a note or brief warning about crime, safety, etc. Some guides like *Lonely Planet, Moon* and *Fielding* try to present a balanced opinion without the need to downplay many of the dangers that await travelers. Look for travel specialty stores. Check the copyright in the front of the book. Some publishers will copyright information one year ahead to appear more up to date. Others like Lonely Planet, will include the month the book was published.

Tourism offices: Most smaller countries will have printed information as well as brochures. If not they can be helpful if you have specific questions about your trip. In many cases the tourism office for third world countries is the same as the consulate or airline.

Foreign embassies, consulates or missions: These sources have access to up-to-date information but rarely can provide on-site, first hand confirmation of crime, war or other late breaking dangers. They can provide up-to-date information on border crossings, laws regarding travelers and other legal information. They cannot help you with items like bribes, illegal entry, drugs or even what happens when you get arrested. In putting together this book, all embassies proved to be very helpful where the home government controls the country. Countries like, Rwanda, Cambodia and Russia had no idea how to answer some of our questions. Some of the U.N. missions are staffed by local workers who have never been to the country they represent. Addresses and telephone numbers for the embassies of foreign governments are listed in the Congressional Directory, available at most public libraries. In addition to their embassies, some countries also have consulates in major U.S. cities. Look for their addresses in your local telephone directory, or find them in the publication, *Foreign Consular Offices in the United States* which is available in many public libraries.

Special interest groups and sources: A surprising source of very accurate information comes from groups like Amnesty International, journalists, local operatives, databases, hotel managers, local travel agencies and other overlooked experts. The telephone makes the world a very small place. In many cases people are happy to give you advice about travel to areas which they have expertise.

State Department Travel Advisories: We have found that the advisories, along with the incident reports issued by The Department of State, are an excellent starting point for travelers heading off to parts unknown. Faced with a daily barrage of information, it is the job of the State Department to sort out the news and developments that may affect travelers or residents. There are three types of travel advisories:

Warning: recommends deferral of travel to all or part of a country.

Caution: advises about unusual security conditions, including the potential for unexpected detention, unstable political conditions or serious health problems. It is not intended to deter travel to a country.

Notice: provides information on situations that do not present a broad scale risk, but which could result in inconvenience or difficulty for traveling Americans.

Travel advisories are posted at U.S. passport agencies, Department of Commerce field offices, and at U.S. embassies and consulates around the world. They are distributed to the travel and airline industry and can be found through airline computer reservations systems. If you plan to travel to an area or country where there is some concern about existing conditions, find out if there is a travel advisory by contacting the nearest passport agency or your travel agent or airline. You may also listen to recorded travel advisories 24-hours a day. Call the Department of State's Citizens Emergency Center at ☎ *202-647-5225.*

From the U.S. State Department

The following information is edited and expanded from U.S. State Department information and is a useful overview for travelers to the world's dangers regions. Millions of U.S. citizens travel abroad each year and use their U.S. passport. When you travel abroad, the odds are in your favor that you will have a safe and incident-free trip. Even if you do come into difficulty abroad, the odds are still in your favor that you will not be a victim of crime or violence. But crime and violence, as well as unexpected difficulties, do befall U.S. citizens in all parts of the world. No one is better able to tell you this than U.S. consular officers who work in the more than 250 U.S. embassies and consulates around the world. Every day of the year U.S. embassies and consulates receive calls from American citizens in distress. Fortunately, most problems can be solved over the telephone or by a visit of the U.S. citizen to the Consular Section of the nearest U.S. embassy or consulate. But there are less fortunate occasions when U.S. consular officers are called on to meet U.S. citizens at foreign police stations, hospitals, prisons and even at morgues. In these cases, the assistance that consular officers can offer is specific, but limited. In the hope of helping you avoid unhappy meetings when you go abroad, we have prepared the following travel tips. Please have a safe trip abroad.

What to Bring

Safety begins when you pack. To avoid being a target, dress conservatively. A flashy wardrobe or one that is too casual can mark you as a tourist. As much as possible, avoid the appearance of affluence. Always try to travel light. If you do, you can move more quickly and will be more likely to have a free hand. You will also be less tired and less likely to set your luggage down, leaving it unattended. Carry the minimum amount of valuables necessary for your trip and plan a place or places to conceal them. Your passport, cash and credit cards are safest when locked in a hotel safe. When you have to carry them on your person, you may wish to conceal them in several places rather than putting them in one wallet or pouch. Avoid handbags, fanny packs and outside pockets which are easy targets for thieves. Inside pockets and a sturdy shoulder bag with the strap worn across your chest are somewhat safer. The safest place to carry valuables is probably a pouch or money belt that you wear under your clothing. If you wear glasses, pack an extra pair. Carry them and any medicines you need in your carry-on luggage. To avoid problems when passing through customs, keep medicines in their original, labeled containers. Bring a copy of your prescriptions and the generic names for the drugs. If a medication is unusual or contains narcotics, carry a letter from your doctor attesting to your need to take the drug. If you have any doubt about the legality of carrying a certain drug into a country, consult the embassy or consulate of that country first. Bring "Traveler's cheques" and one or two major credit cards instead of cash. Pack an extra set of passport photos along with a photocopy of your passport information page to make replacement of your passport easier in case it is lost or stolen. Put your name, address and telephone numbers inside and outside of each piece of luggage. Use covered luggage tags to avoid casual observation of your identity or nationality. Last of all, lock your luggage.

What to Leave Behind

Don't bring anything you would hate to lose. Leave at home:

— expensive or expensive-looking jewelry,

— irreplaceable family objects,

— all unnecessary credit cards. Leave a copy of your itinerary with family or friends at home in case they need to contact you in an emergency.

A Few Things to Bring and Leave Behind

Make photocopies of your passport identification page, airline tickets, driver's license and the credit cards that you bring with you. Make two copies. Leave one with family or friends at home; pack the other in a place separate from where you carry your valuables. Leave a copy of the serial numbers of your "Traveler's cheques" at home. Carry your copy with you in a separate place and, as you cash the cheques, cross them off the list.

What to Learn About Before You Go

Security. The Department of State's Consular Information Sheets are available for every country of the world. They describe unusual entry or currency regulations, unusual health conditions, the crime and security situation, political disturbances, areas of instability and drug penalties. They also provide addresses and emergency telephone numbers for U.S. embassies and consulates. In general, the sheets do not give advice. Instead, they describe conditions so travelers can make informed decisions about their trips. In some dangerous situations, however, the Department of State recommends that Americans defer travel to a country. In such a case, a Travel Warning is issued for the country in addition to its Consular Information Sheet.

Consular Information Sheets and Travel Warnings are available at the 13 regional passport agencies, at U.S. embassies and consulates abroad, or by sending a self-addressed, stamped envelope to:

Overseas Citizens Services

Room 4811
Department of State
Washington, DC 20520-4818
They are also available through airline computer reservations systems when you or your travel agent make your international air reservations. In addition, you can access Consular Information Sheets and Travel Warnings 24-hours a day from three different electronic systems. To listen to them, call ☎ *(202) 647-5225* from a touchtone phone. To receive them by fax, dial ☎ *(202) 647-3000* from a fax machine and follow the prompts that you will hear on the machine's telephone receiver. To view or download the documents through a computer and modem, dial the Consular Affairs Bulletin Board (CABB) on ☎ *(202) 647-9225*, setting your software to N-8-1. There is no charge to use these systems other than normal long distance charges.

Local Laws and Customs. When you leave the United States, you are subject to the laws of the country where you are. Therefore, before you go, learn as much as you can about the local laws and customs of the places you plan to visit. Good resources are your library, your travel agent, and the embassies, consulates or tourist bureaus of the countries you will visit. In addition, keep track of what is being reported in the media about recent developments in those countries.

Things to Arrange Before You Go

Your Itinerary. As much as possible, plan to stay in larger hotels that have more elaborate security. The safest floors to book a room may be from the second to seventh floors above ground level to deter easy entrance from outside, but low enough for fire equipment to reach. Because take-off and landing are the most dangerous times of a flight, book non-stop flights when possible. When there is a choice of airport or airline, ask your travel agent about comparative safety records. There are differences.

Legal Documents. Have your affairs at home in order. If you leave an up-to-date will, insurance documents and a power of attorney with your family or a friend, you can feel secure about traveling and will be prepared for any emergency that may occur while you are away. If you have minor children, consider making guardianship arrangements for them.

Credit. Make a note of the credit limit on each credit card that you bring. Make certain not to charge over that amount on your trip. In some countries, Americans have been arrested for innocently exceeding their credit limit. Ask your credit card company how to report the loss of your card from abroad. "800" numbers do not work from abroad, but your company will have a number that you can call.

Insurance. Find out if your personal property insurance covers you for loss or theft abroad. Even more important, check if your health insurance will cover you abroad. Social Security Medicare does not provide payment for medical care outside the U.S. Even if your health insurance will reimburse you for medical care that you pay for abroad, normal health insurance does not pay for medical evacuation from a remote area or from a country where medical facilities are inadequate. Consider purchasing one of the short-term health and emergency assistance policies designed for travelers that includes medical evacuation in the event of an accident or serious illness.

Precautions To Take While Traveling

Safety on the Street

Use the same common sense traveling overseas that you would at home.

• Be especially cautious in, or avoid, areas where you are likely to be victimized. These include crowded subways, train stations, elevators, tourist sites, marketplaces, festivals and marginal areas of cities.

• Don't use short cuts, narrow alleys or poorly-lit streets.

- Try not to travel alone at night.
- Avoid public demonstrations and other civil disturbances.
- Keep a low profile and avoid loud conversations or arguments.
- Do not discuss travel plans or other personal matters with strangers.

To avoid scam artists, beware of strangers who approach you, offering bargains or to be your guide. Beware of pickpockets. They often have an accomplice who will:

— jostle you,

— ask you for directions or the time,

— point to something spilled on your clothing,

—distract you by creating a disturbance.

- A child or even a woman carrying a baby can be a pickpocket.
- Beware of groups of vagrant children.
- Wear the shoulder strap of your bag across your chest and walk with the bag away from the curb to avoid drive-by purse snatchers.
- Try to seem purposeful when you move about. Even if you are lost, act as if you know where you are going.

When possible, ask for directions only from individuals in authority. Know how to use a pay telephone and have the proper change or token on hand. Learn a few phrases in the local language so you can signal your need for help, the police or a doctor. Make note of emergency telephone numbers you may need: police, fire, your hotel and the nearest U.S. embassy or consulate. If confronted by superior force, don't fight attackers and be eager to give up your valuables.

Safety In Your Hotel
- Keep your hotel door locked at all times.
- Meet visitors in the lobby.
- Do not leave money and other valuables in your hotel room while you are out.
- Use the hotel safe.
- Let someone know when you expect to return, especially if out late at night.
- If you are alone, do not get on an elevator if there is a suspicious-looking person inside.
- Read the fire safety instructions in your hotel room.
- Know how to report a fire.
- Be sure you know where the nearest fire exit and an alternate are.
- Count the doors between your room and the nearest exit—this could be a life-saver if you have to crawl through a smoke-filled corridor.

Safety On Public Transport
In countries where there is a pattern of tourists being targeted by criminals on public transport, this information is can be found in the Consular Information Sheets for the country you will be traveling to.

Taxis. Only take taxis clearly identified with official markings. Beware of irregular cabs.

Trains. Well organized, systematic robbery of passengers on trains along popular tourist routes is a serious problem. It is more common at night and especially on overnight trains. If you see your way blocked by someone and another person is pressing you from behind, move away. This can happen in the corridor of the train or on the platform or in the station. Do not accept food or drink from strangers. Criminals have been known to drug passengers by offering them food or drink. Criminals may also spray sleeping gas in train compartments. Where possible, lock your compartment. If it cannot be locked securely, take turns with your traveling companions and sleep in shifts. If that is not possible, stay awake. If you must sleep unprotected, tie down your luggage, strap your valuables to you and sleep on top of them as much as possible.

Do not be afraid to alert authorities if you feel threatened in any way. Extra police are often assigned to ride trains on routes where crime is a serious problem.

Buses. The same type of criminal activity found on trains can be found on public buses on popular tourist routes. For example, tourists have been drugged and robbed while sleeping on buses or in bus stations. In some countries whole bus loads of passengers have been held up and robbed by gangs of bandits.

Safety When You Drive

When you rent a car, don't go for the exotic; choose a type commonly available locally. Where possible, ask that markings that identify it as a rental car be removed. Make certain it is in good repair. If available, choose a car with universal door locks and power windows, features that give the driver better control of access to the car. An air-conditioner, when available, is also a safety feature, allowing you to drive with windows closed. Thieves can and do snatch purses through open windows of moving cars. Keep car doors locked at all times. Wear seat belts. As much as possible, avoid driving at night. Don't leave valuables in the car. If you must carry things with you, keep them out of sight in the trunk. Don't park your car on the street overnight. If the hotel or municipality does not have a parking garage or other secure area, select a well-lit area. Never pick up hitchhikers. Don't get out of the car if there are suspicious individuals nearby. Drive away.

Patterns of Crime Against Motorists

In many places frequented by tourists, including areas of southern Europe, victimization of motorists has been refined to an art. Where it is a problem, U.S. embassies are aware of it and consular officers try to work with local authorities to warn the public about the dangers. In some locations, these efforts of public awareness have paid off, reducing the frequency of incidents. Ask your rental car agency for advice on avoiding robbery; where it is a problem, they are well aware of it and should tell you how best to protect yourself. Carjackers and thieves operate at gas stations, parking lots, in city traffic and along the highway. Be suspicious of anyone who hails you or tries to get your attention when you are in or near your car. Criminals use ingenious ploys. They may masquerade as good samaritans, offering to help you fix tires that they claim are flat or that they have made flat. Or they may flag down a motorist, ask for assistance and then steal the rescuer's luggage or car. Usually they work in groups, one person carrying on the pretense while the others rob you. Other criminals get your attention with abuse, either trying to drive you off the road, or causing an "accident" by rear-ending you or creating a "fender bender." In some urban areas, thieves don't waste time on ploys, they simply smash car windows at traffic lights, grab your valuables or your car and get away. In cities around the world, "defensive driving" has come to mean more than avoiding auto accidents; it means keeping an eye out for potentially criminal pedestrians, cyclists and scooter riders.

How to Handle Money Safely

To avoid carrying large amounts of cash, change your "Traveler's cheques" only as you need currency. *Counter sign* "Traveler's cheques" only in front of the person who will cash them. Do not flash large amounts of money when paying a bill. Make sure your credit card is returned to you after each transaction. Deal only with authorized agents when you exchange money, buy airline tickets or purchase souvenirs. Do not change money on the black market. If your possessions are lost or stolen, report the loss immediately to the local police. Keep a copy of the police report for insurance claims and as an explanation of your plight. After reporting lost items to the police, report the loss of:

— "Traveler's cheques" to the nearest agent of the issuing company.

— credit cards to the issuing company.

— airline tickets to the airline or travel agent.

— passport to the nearest U.S. embassy or consulate.

How to Avoid Legal Difficulties

When you are in a foreign country, you are subject to its laws and are under its protection—not the protection of the U.S. Constitution. You can be arrested overseas for actions that may be either legal or considered minor infractions in the United States. Be aware of what is considered criminal in the country where you are. Consular Information Sheets include information on unusual patterns of arrests in various countries. Some of the offenses for which U.S. citizens have been arrested abroad are:

Drug Violations. More than one third of U.S. citizens incarcerated abroad are held on drug charges. Some countries do not distinguish between possession and trafficking; many have mandatory sentences—even for a small amount of marijuana or cocaine. Although we know of no U.S. citizens who have been arrested abroad for prescription drugs purchased in the United States for personal use and carried in original labeled containers, a number of Americans have been arrested for possessing prescription drugs, particularly tranquilizers and amphetamines. They purchased these drugs legally in certain Asian countries and took them to some countries in the Middle East where they are illegal. Other U.S. citizens have been arrested for purchasing prescription drugs abroad in quantities that local authorities suspected were for commercial use. If in doubt about foreign drug laws, ask local authorities or the nearest U.S. embassy or consulate.

Possession of Firearms. The places where U.S. citizens most often come into difficulties for illegal possession of firearms are nearby—Mexico, Canada and the Caribbean. Sentences for possession of firearms in Mexico can be up to 30 years in jail. In general, firearms, even those legally registered in the U.S., cannot be brought into a country unless a permit is first obtained from the embassy or a consulate of that country. (Note: If you take firearms or ammunition to another country, you cannot bring them back into the U.S. unless you register them with U.S. Customs before you leave the U.S.)

Photography. In many countries you can be harassed or detained for photographing such things as police and military installations, government buildings, border areas and transportation facilities. If in doubt, ask permission before taking photographs.

Purchasing Antiques. Americans have been arrested for purchasing souvenirs that were, or looked like, antiques and which local customs authorities believed were national treasures. Some of the countries where this has happened were Turkey, Egypt and Mexico. In countries where antiques are important, document your purchases as reproductions if that is the case or if they are authentic, secure the necessary export permit (usually from the national museum).

Illegal Entry. Countries hostile to the United States have detained travelers on the pretense that they have entered the country illegally. Iraq has held Americans for entering illegally even though there are few border controls.

Protection Against Terrorism

Terrorist acts occur at random and unpredictably, making it impossible to protect oneself absolutely. The first and best protection is to avoid travel to unsafe areas where there has been a persistent record of terrorist attacks or kidnapping. The vast majority of foreign states have good records of maintaining public order and protecting residents and visitors within their borders from terrorism. Most terrorist attacks are the result of long and careful planning. Just as a car thief will first be attracted to an unlocked car with the key in the ignition, terrorists are looking for defenseless, easily accessible targets who follow predictable patterns. The chances that a tourist, traveling with an unpublished program or itinerary, would be the victim of terrorism are slight— no more than the random possibility of being in the wrong place at the wrong time. In addition, many terrorist groups, seeking publicity for political causes within their own country or region, are not looking for American targets. Nevertheless, the pointers below may help you avoid becoming a "target of opportunity." They should be considered as adjuncts to the tips listed in the previous sections on how to protect yourself against the far greater likelihood of being a victim of ordinary crime. These precautions may provide some degree of protection and can serve as practical and psychological deterrents to would-be terrorists.

- Schedule direct flights if possible and avoid stops in high-risk airports or areas. Consider other options for travel, such as trains.

- Be aware of what you discuss with strangers, or what may be overheard by others.

- Try to minimize the time spent in the public area of an airport, which is a less protected area. Move quickly from the check-in counter to the secured areas. On arrival, leave the airport as quickly as you can.

- As much as possible, avoid luggage tags, dress and behavior which may identify you as an American.

- Keep an eye out for suspicious abandoned packages or briefcases. Report them to airport security or other authorities and leave the area promptly.

- Avoid obvious terrorist targets such as places where Americans and Westerners are known to congregate.

Travel To Dangerous Places

If you must travel in an area where there has been a history of terrorist attacks or kidnapping, make it a habit to:

- Discuss with your family what they would do in case of an emergency, in addition to making sure your affairs are in order before leaving home.

- Register with the U.S. embassy or consulate upon arrival.

- Remain friendly but be cautious about discussing personal matters, your itinerary or program.

- Leave no personal or business papers in your hotel room.

- Watch for people following you or "loiterers" observing your comings and goings.

- Keep a mental note of safe havens such as police stations, hotels, hospitals.

- Avoid predictable times and routes of travel and report any suspicious activity to local police and the nearest U.S. embassy or consulate.

- Select your own taxi cabs at random.

- Don't take a cab that is not clearly identified as a taxi. Compare the face of the driver with the one posted on his or her license.

- If possible, travel with others.

- Be sure of the identity of visitors before opening the door of your hotel room. Don't meet strangers at unknown or remote locations.

- Refuse unexpected packages.

- Formulate a plan of action for what you will do if a bomb explodes or there is gunfire nearby.

- Check for loose wires or other suspicious activity around your car.

- Be sure your vehicle is in good operating condition in case you need to resort to high-speed or evasive driving.

- Drive with car windows closed in crowded streets; bombs can be thrown through open windows.

- If you are ever in a situation where somebody starts shooting, drop to the floor or get down as low as possible. Don't move until you are sure the danger has passed. Do not attempt to help rescuers and do not pick up a weapon. If possible, shield yourself behind or under a solid object. If you must move, crawl on your stomach.

Hijacking/Hostage Situations

The most dangerous phases of a hijacking or hostage situation are the beginning and, if there is a rescue attempt, the end. At the outset, the terrorists typically are tense, high-strung and may behave irrationally. It is extremely important that you remain calm and alert and manage your own behavior.

- Avoid resistance and sudden or threatening movements. Do not struggle or try to escape unless you are certain of being successful.

- Make a concerted effort to relax. Breathe deeply and prepare yourself mentally, physically and emotionally for the possibility of a long ordeal.

- Try to remain inconspicuous; avoid direct eye contact and the appearance of observing your captors' actions.

- Avoid alcoholic beverages. Consume little food and drink.

- Consciously put yourself in a mode of passive cooperation. Talk normally. Do not complain, avoid belligerency, and comply with all orders and instructions.

- If questioned, keep your answers short. Don't volunteer information or make unnecessary overtures.

- Don't try to be a hero, endangering yourself and others.

- Maintain your sense of personal dignity and gradually increase your requests for personal comforts. Make these requests in a reasonable low-key manner.

- If you are involved in a lengthier, drawn-out situation, try to establish a rapport with your captors, avoiding political discussions or other confrontational subjects.

- Establish a daily program of mental and physical activity. Don't be afraid to ask for anything you need or want such as, medicines, books, pencils, papers.

- Eat what they give you, even if it does not look or taste appetizing. A loss of appetite and weight is normal.

- Think positively; avoid a sense of despair. Rely on your inner resources. Remember that you are a valuable commodity to your captors. It is important to them to keep you alive and well.

Assistance Abroad

If you plan to stay more than two weeks in one place, if you are in an area experiencing civil unrest or a natural disaster or if you are planning travel to a remote area, it is advisable to register at the Consular Section of the nearest U.S. embassy or consulate. This will make it easier if someone at home needs to locate you urgently or in the unlikely event that you need to be evacuated in an emergency. It will also facilitate the issuance of a new passport should yours be lost or stolen. Another reason to contact the Consular Section is to obtain updated information on the security situation in a country. If you are ill or injured, contact the nearest U.S. embassy or consulate for a list of local physicians and medical facilities. If the illness is serious, consular officers can help you find medical assistance from this list and, at your request, will inform your family or friends. If necessary, a consul can assist in the transfer of funds from the United States. Payment of hospital and other medical expenses is your responsibility. If you become destitute overseas, consular officers can help you get in touch with your family, friends, bank or employer and inform them how to wire funds to you. Should you find yourself in legal difficulty, contact a consular officer immediately. Consular officers cannot serve as attorneys, give legal advice or get you out of jail. What they can do is provide a list of local attornies who speak English and who may have had experience in representing U.S. citizens. If you are arrested, consular officials will visit you, advise you of your rights under local laws and ensure that you are held under humane conditions and are treated fairly under local law. A consular officer will also contact your family or friends if you desire. When necessary, consuls can transfer money from home for you and will try to get relief for you, including food and clothing in countries where this is a problem. If you are detained, remember that under international agreements and practice, you have the right to talk to the U.S. consul. If you are denied this right, be persistent; try to have someone get in touch for you.

Travel to Eastern Europe

Although tourist facilities are expanding to meet the rapid increase in tourism to Eastern Europe, in most of the region they are quite limited. In many places, you will have to be patient with scarce or inadequate hotels, rental cars and other facilities. To be certain of accommodations, make reservations for hotels and transportation and make them well in advance. If you cannot get a hotel reservation, check with the country's tourist office since many cities have a bureau that arranges accommodations in small hotels or private homes.

Getting In

U.S. citizens should travel to Eastern Europe with a valid U.S. passport and with appropriate visas when necessary. Visa regulations change, so check with each embassy's consular section for current information. Remember to leave a detailed itinerary and your passport information with a friend or relative in the United States in case of an emergency. If you are a national of both the United States and an Eastern European country, see the section on dual nationality before you travel to Eastern Europe.

Customs

Customs regulations in some Eastern European countries are strict. U.S. citizens should comply fully. Generally, you should carry only those articles that you need for your trip and personal use. When obtaining your visa, declare to the country's embassy in the United States anything manufactured before 1945 (considered antique in some countries) and any precious metals, including gold jewelry, that you plan to bring with you. Ask for customs information when you apply for your visa. If you are asked to declare valuables and currency when you enter a country, include pocket calculators, digital watches or other electronic devices that may be rare or more expensive in Eastern Europe than at home. Failure to declare items could result in their confiscation upon departure. Carry a copy of your declaration with you. You may need it when you depart the country. Do not carry parcels or letters on behalf of third persons. It is highly dangerous to carry something if you do not know its contents.

Money Hassles

Some Eastern European governments restrict the import and export of their currencies. In general, do not transport these currencies across international borders. Currency regulations in Eastern Europe change frequently. Some countries have a dual exchange rate. For example, hotel bills and credit card purchases may have to be paid at a rate that is higher than a "tourist" rate. Before you go, learn the most advantageous way to handle your purchases by inquiring about exchange rates and currency regulations from your travel agent or the embassies of the countries you plan to visit. Unlimited amounts of U.S. dollars and other freely convertible or hard currencies usually may be carried into and out of Eastern European countries. Travelers may be asked to declare the amount and kind of currency they carry. Purchase currencies only at officially authorized exchange facilities in the country of issue and retain your receipts. Do not engage in private currency transactions or sell personal property. While U.S. dollars may be exchanged for Eastern European currencies, it is difficult or impossible to reconvert those currencies to dollars or another hard currency. Therefore, do not exchange more money than you plan to spend. Western travelers are frequently required to settle hotel, auto rental, train, airplane, medical and other bills in hard currency. Keep sufficient hard currency for this purpose.

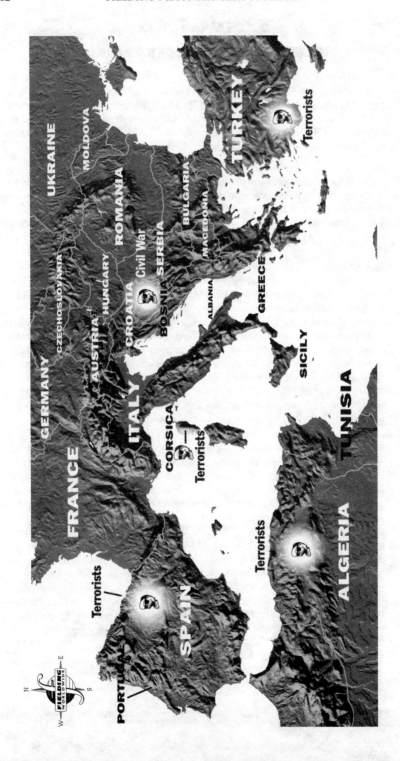

Credit Cards

Most major credit cards may be used in place of hard currency to cover purchases at major hotels or stores in Eastern Europe. However, in general, credit cards, "Traveler's cheques" and personal checks cannot be used to obtain hard currency in the region. A few major credit card companies offer services, such as cash advances in local currency and card replacement, to travelers in a few places in Eastern Europe. In addition, some "Traveler's cheques" companies offer replacement for lost or stolen travelers cheques in some places in the region. Check with your credit card company and with the company that sells you "Traveler's cheques" to learn what services they now offer in the cities you plan to visit.

Dangerous Things

Driving

Except in major cities and on super highways, avoid driving at night in Eastern Europe. Night driving can be hazardous because some roads are narrow and winding and horse-drawn vehicles and bicycles may be encountered at any time on any road. Traffic regulations, especially those related to driving under the influence of alcohol, are very strict. An international driver's license is usually accepted and, in some cases, required by Eastern European governments. You may obtain an international driver's license from an automobile association.

Political Statements or Acts

In countries where there is political unrest, refrain from political comments and activities that might be construed as interference in the internal affairs of the host country. Avoid photographing or otherwise becoming involved in demonstrations. There are restrictions on photography in Eastern Europe. In general, refrain from photographing military and police installations and personnel as well as scenes of civil disorder or other public disturbances. In some countries, also avoid photographing border areas and industrial structures including harbors, bridges, rail and airport facilities. For detailed information, consult local authorities or the U.S. embassy or consulate in the country concerned.

Crime

One result of the changes taking place in Eastern Europe is an increase in street crime in almost every major city in the region. Car break-ins have become a problem. Some cities have groups of pickpockets that use various gimmicks to distract their victims. Be especially careful on public transportation, in crowded shopping areas and in all places frequented by tourists. Watch your purse, passport, wallet, travel documents and other valuables. Loss of a passport in some locations can mean a wait of a day or more while local authorities process a new exit permit, without which it is impossible to leave the country. It is therefore strongly recommended that you make every effort to safeguard your U.S. passport from loss or theft. Carry a copy of your passport data page with you in a location separate from your passport.

Registration

Foreigners are required by the authorities in some Eastern European countries to register with the local police. This is usually taken care of by your hotel. You may have to turn your passport over to the hotel for a period of up to 24 hours. If you stay with relatives or a private family, ask your hosts or consult the U.S. embassy or consulate about how to meet the registration requirement. If you plan more than a short stay in one place or if you are in an area experiencing civil unrest or some natural disaster, you are strongly encouraged to register with the nearest U.S. embassy or consulate.

The Middle East and North Africa

Getting In

A U.S. passport is required for travel to all countries in the region. U.S. citizens are not required to have visas for tourist or business travel to Israel, Morocco or Tunisia, but may need to supply proof of sufficient funds for the trip and proof of onward or round trip travel arrangements. All other countries in the Middle East and North Africa require U.S. citizens to have visas. If you plan to travel extensively in the region, entry and exit stamps could quickly fill the pages of your passport. Before you go, you may wish to ask the nearest passport agency to add extra pages to your passport. Or, if applying for a new passport, you can request one with 48 pages instead of the usual 24. Each country has its own set of entry requirements. For authoritative visa information, contact the embassy or consulate of the country you plan to visit.

- When you make inquiries about your visas, ask about the following:

- Visa price, length of validity, number of entries.

- Financial requirements/proof of sufficient funds and proof of onward/return ticket.

- Immunization requirements. (Yellow fever immunization is often required if arriving from a yellow fever infected area.)

- Currency regulations.

- Import/export restrictions and limitations. (Several countries prohibit the import and consumption of alcoholic beverages.)

Dress and Local Customs

The Islamic religion is the pre-eminent influence on local laws and customs in much of the Middle East and North Africa. The extent of this influence varies. Some Islamic countries have secular governments, but in certain other countries, particularly those in the Arabian peninsula, Islam dictates a total way of life. It prescribes the behavior for individuals and society, codifying law, family relations, business etiquette, dress, food, personal hygiene and much more. Among the important values is a family-centered way of life, including a protected role for women and clear limits on their participation in public life. In traditional societies, Muslims believe open social relations between the sexes results in the breakdown of family life. Contact between men and women, therefore, is rigidly controlled. In the traditional societies of the region, it is considered rude to face the soles of one's feet toward other people. At traditional meals, the left hand is not used for eating. Western street clothing (except for shorts) is appropriate in most areas. In more traditional societies, however, attire for women should be more conservative, garments should have sleeves and dress length should be below the knee. On the other hand, in some areas of the region visited by many tourists Q for example, the beaches of Israel and Morocco Q, attire similar to that worn in the United States is acceptable. In many countries in the Middle East and North Africa, the weekend is either Thursday/Friday or Friday/Saturday. Workweek information is included in the list of U.S. embassies at the end of this document.

Getting Out

Be sure to keep enough local currency to be able to depart as planned. Some Arab countries will not allow travelers to enter if their passports show any evidence of previous or expected travel to Israel. This is not currently the case for Egypt, Kuwait, Morocco and Tunisia. Other Arab countries apply the ban inconsistently, sometimes refusing and at other times allowing entry when a passport shows evidence of travel to Israel. Some Arab countries also refuse to admit persons with passports indicating travel to South Africa. Several Arab countries ask visa applicants to state their religious affiliation.

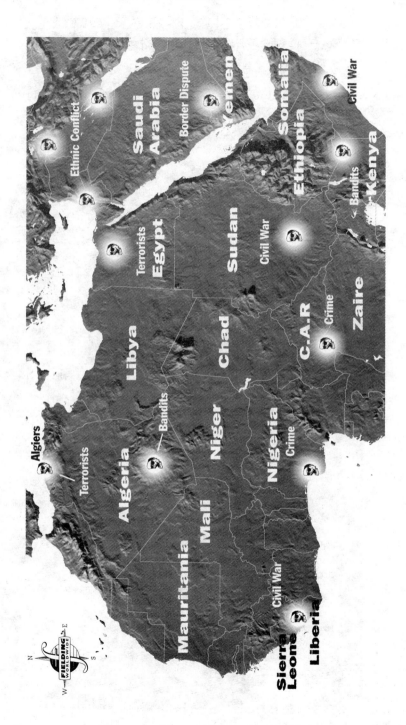

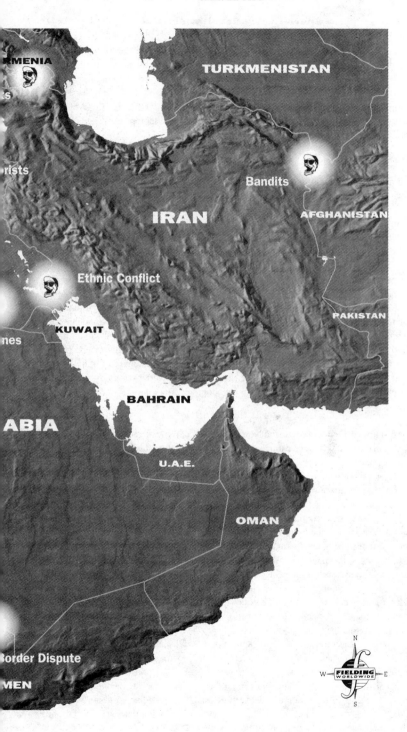

Special Entry Requirements for
Countries That Permit No Tourists

Kuwait, Oman, Qatar and Saudi Arabia do not permit tourism. (See the "Mecca" chapter for more details.) All business visitors must be sponsored by a company in the country to be visited. Private visitors must be sponsored by a relative or friend native to the country. To visit a foreigner working in a country where tourism is not permitted, you must be sponsored by the same local company that sponsors the person you are visiting. Entry is by visa or the Non-Objection Certificate (NOC) system. An NOC is obtained by a visitor's sponsor and filed with the appropriate foreign government authorities before the planned visit.

Getting Out

Countries that require visitors to be sponsored usually also require them to obtain exit permits from their sponsors. U.S. citizens can have difficulty obtaining exit permits if they are involved in business disputes. A U.S. citizen who is the wife or child of the local sponsor needs the sponsor's permission to leave the country. Do not accept sponsorship to visit a country unless you are certain you will also be able to obtain an exit permit.

U.S. Citizens Married to Foreign Nationals

In many Islamic countries, even those that give tourist visas and do not require sponsorship, a woman needs the permission of her husband and children need the permission of their father, to leave the country. If you travel or allow your children to travel, be aware of the laws of the country you plan to visit. Many children with American citizenship been abducted to, or wrongfully retained in countries of the Middle East and North Africa notwithstanding a U.S. custody order. Although some of these children were taken abroad illegally by one of their parents, many originally traveled abroad with the consent of both parents. Do not visit or allow your children to visit unless you are completely confident that you and they will be allowed to leave. Once overseas, you are subject to the laws of the country where you are; U.S. law cannot protect you.

Dual Nationality

Some countries in the Middle East and North Africa do not recognize acquisition of U.S. citizenship by their nationals. Unless the naturalized U.S. citizen renounces his or her original nationality at an embassy or consulate of the country of origin, he or she may still be considered a citizen of that country. A person born in the United States with a parent who was a citizen of another country may also be considered a citizen of that country. If arrested, a dual national may be denied the right to communicate with the U.S. embassy or consulate. Another consequence could be having to serve in the military of one's former country. If you are a naturalized U.S. citizen, a dual national or have any reason to believe another country may claim you as their national, check with the embassy of that country as to your citizenship status and any obligations you may have while visiting. Dual nationals who have not researched their citizenship status before traveling have sometimes, to their surprise, encountered difficulties such as not being allowed to depart. Even countries that recognize acquired U.S. citizenship may consider their former citizens as having resumed original citizenship if they take up residence in their country of origin. This can happen even if the embassy of the country of origin stamps a visa in the U.S. passport of its former citizen. Dual nationals may find that they are required to use a passport from their country of origin in order to enter or leave that country. The U.S. government does not object to the use of a foreign passport by a dual national to enter or depart a foreign country in compliance with the requirements of that country. U.S. regulations require, however, that U.S. citizens, including dual nationals, use a U.S. passport to depart from and enter the United States. If you have any questions about dual nationality or the use of foreign passports, contact the Office of Citizens Consular Services, *Room 4817, Department of State, Washington, D.C. 20520-4818,* (☎ *202-647-3926*) before you travel. Recorded information on dual nationality and other citizenship matters is available 24-hours a day at ☎ *202-647-3444.*

Money Hassles

Some countries in the region have no restrictions on currency imports or exports. Some prohibit Israeli currency. Most countries in the Middle East and North Africa, however, have detailed currency regulations, including a requirement to declare all currency, including "Traveler's cheques", upon entry. In those countries, the export of foreign currency is limited to the amount that was imported and declared. Be sure to make the required currency declaration, have it validated and retain it for use at departure. Buy local currency only at banks or other authorized exchange places and retain your receipts for use at departure. Currency not accounted for may be confiscated. Several countries prohibit the import and consumption of alcoholic beverages. Most countries restrict the entry of products containing pork as well as any literature, videotapes and cassette tapes deemed pornographic. Also, some countries will not permit the import of books or other goods from Israel.

Shopping

Americans have been arrested in some countries in the region for the unauthorized purchase of antiques or other important cultural artifacts. If you purchase such items, always insist that the seller provide a receipt and the official museum export certificate required by law. Travelers have also been detained at customs for possessing reproductions of antiques. The safest policy is to purchase copies of antiques from reputable stores and have them documented as such. Obtain receipts for all such purchases.

Getting Sick

Information on immunizations and health precautions for travelers can be obtained in the United States from local health departments, private doctors or travel clinics. Information is also available from the Center for Disease Control's 24-hour hotline at ☎ 404-332-4559 and from the U.S. Public Health Service book, Health Information for International Travel, available for $6.00 from the Superintendent of Documents, U.S. Government Printing Office, Washington, D.C. 20402. Depending on your destination, immunization may be recommended against diphtheria, tetanus, polio, typhoid and hepatitis A. Chloroquinine prophylaxis against malaria is recommended for travel to some areas of the region. An increasing number of countries have established regulations regarding AIDS testing, particularly for long-term residents and students. Check with the embassy or consulate of the country you plant to visit for the latest information. Review your health insurance policy. If your health insurance does not provide coverage overseas, consider buying temporary insurance that does. In addition, consider obtaining insurance to cover the exorbitant cost of medical evacuation in the event of an illness or for the return of remains in case of death. Insurance companies and some credit card and "Traveler's cheque" companies offer short-term health and emergency assistance policies designed for travelers. Medical facilities vary in the region; in some countries they are similar to U.S. standards. U.S. embassies or consulates can furnish you with a list of recommended local hospitals and English-speaking physicians. Take precautions. In the hot and dry climates that prevail in the Middle East and North Africa, it is important to avoid water depletion and heat stroke. Safe tap water is available in many areas. In some places, however, it is highly saline and should be avoided by persons on sodium-restricted diets. In many rural and some urban areas, tap water is not potable and travelers should drink only boiled or chemically treated water or bottled carbonated drinks. In these areas, avoid fresh vegetables and fruits unless they are washed in a purifying solution and peeled. Diarrhea is potentially serious. If it persists, seek medical attention. Schistosomiasis (or bilharzia) is present in the area of the Nile and in several other areas in North Africa and the Middle East. These parasites are best avoided by not swimming or wading in fresh water in endemic areas. Drug enforcement policies in the region are strict. Possession of even small amounts of narcotics, including substances such as marijuana or amphetamines, can lead to arrest. If found guilty, drug offenders are subject to lengthy prison sentences. Because what is considered to be narcotics varies from country to country, learn and obey the laws in the places you will visit. Keep all prescription drugs in their original containers clearly labeled with the doctor's name, pharmacy and contents. In addition, if you take an unusual prescription drug, carry a letter from your doctor explaining your need for the drug and a copy of the prescription.

U.S. Embassies and Consulates Abroad

Note: The workweek is Monday–Friday except where noted. For addresses in the United States see Visa Information chapter.

Algeria

American Embassy
4 Chemin Cheich Bachir
Brahimi
16000 Algiers, Algeria
☎ *(213-2) 601-425/255/186*
Workweek: Sat.–Wed.

Bahrain

American Embassy
Bldg. 979, Road No. 3119
Zinj District
(Next to Al Ahli Sports Club)
Manama, Bahrain
☎ *(973) 273-300;*
Workweek: Sat.–Wed.
after hours 275-126

Egypt

American Embassy
8 Kamal El-Din Salah Street
Cairo, EGYPT
☎ *(20-2) 355-7371*
Workweek: Sun.–Thurs.

American Consulate General

ll0 Avenue Horreya
Alexandria, EGYPT
☎ *(20-3) 482-1911*

Iran

U.S. Interests Section
Embassy of Switzerland
Bucharest Avenue &
17th Street, No. 5
Tehran, Iran
☎ *(98-21) 625-223/4,*
626-906
Workweek: Sun.–Thurs.

Iraq

U.S. Interests Section
Embassy of Poland
Hay Babil, Section 929
Lane 7, House 17, Alwiyah
Baghdad, Iraq
Workweek: Sun.–Thurs.

Israel

American Embassy
71 Hayarkon Street
Tel Aviv, Israel
☎ *(972-3) 517-4338;*
after hours ☎ *517-4347*

U.S. Consular Agency

(limited services only)
12 Jerusalem Street
Haifa 33132, Israel
☎ *(972-4) 670-615;*
after hours ☎ *246-386*

Jerusalem

American Consulate General
Consular Section

27 Nablus Road
Jerusalem 94190
☎ *(972-2) 253-288*

Jordan

American Embassy
Abdoun
Amman, Jordan
☎ *(962-6) 820-101*
Workweek: Sun.–Thurs.

Kuwait

American Embassy
13001 SAFAT
Kuwait, Kuwait
☎ *(965) 242-4151 thru 9*
Workweek: Sun.-Thurs.

Lebanon

American Embassy
Awkar
Beirut, Lebanon
☎ *(961-1) 402-200, 403-300*

Morocco

American Embassy
2 Avenue de Marrakech
Rabat, Morocco
☎ *(212-7) 762-265*

American Consulate General

8 Boulevard Moulay Youssef
Casablanca, MOROCCO
☎ *(212-2) 264-550*

Oman

American Embassy
PO Box 50202
Madinat Qaboos
Muscat, Oman
☎ *(968) 698-989*
Workweek: Sat.–Wed. 0730–1600

Qatar

American Embassy
149 Ali Bin Ahmed Street
Farig Bin Omran
Doha, Qatar
☎ *(974) 864-701/2/3*
Workweek: Sat.–Wed.

Saudi Arabia

American Embassy
Collector Road M
Riyadh Diplomatic Quarter
Riyadh, Saudi Arabia
☎ *(966-1) 488-3800*
Workweek: Sat.–Wed.

American Consulate General

Between Aramco Hqtrs. and
Dhahran Int'l. Airport
Dhahran, Saudi Arabia
☎ *(966-3) 891-3200*

American Consulate General

Palestine Road, Ruwais
Jeddah, Saudi Arabia
☎ *(966-2) 667-0080*

Syria

American Embassy
Abu Roumaneh
Al-Mansur Street No. 2
Damascus, Syria
☎ *(963-11) 333-052,*
332-557, 330-416
after hours ☎ *333-232*

Tunisia

American Embassy
144 Ave. de la Liberte
Tunis, Tunisia
☎ *(216-1) 782-566*

United Arab Emirates

American Embassy
Al-Sudan Street
Abu Dhabi, U.A.E.
☎ *(971-2) 336-691;*
after hours ☎ *338-730*
Workweek: Sat.-Wed.

American Consulate General

Dubai International Trade Center
Dubai, U.A.E.
☎ *(971-4) 313-115*

Yemen

American Embassy
Dhar Himyar Zone
Sheraton Hotel District
Sanaa, Yemen
☎ *(967-1) 238-842/52*
Workweek: Sat.–Wed.

Latin America

Travel advisories are in effect for Columbia, El Salvador, Guatemala, Honduras, Nicaragua, Panama, Peru and Suriname. Some of the dangers covered in these advisories are guerrilla or terrorist activity, banditry and areas under control of narcotics producers. If you plan travel to one of these countries, check with the Emergency Center or the nearest passport agency to see if a travel advisory is still in effect. As you travel, keep abreast of local news coverage. If you plan more than a short stay in one place, if you plan travel to an area where communications are poor or if you are in an area experiencing civil unrest or some natural disaster, you are encouraged to register with the nearest U.S. embassy or consulate. Registration takes only a few moments and it may be invaluable in case of an emergency. Remember to leave a detailed itinerary and your passport number with a friend or relative in the United States.

Getting In and Out

All Central and South American countries except Guatemala require U.S. citizens to have a valid U.S. passport. (Guatemala requires proof of U.S. citizenship, such as a birth certificate or passport.) Visa requirements for U.S. citizens vary from country to country: some countries do not require a visa for a tourist stay of 90 days or less; some only require that a tourist card be obtained at an airline office or at the destination airport; other countries require you to obtain a visa in advance from their embassy or consulate. Some countries have additional entry requirements such as proof of sufficient funds or proof of onward or return tickets. In addition, all South American countries and most Central American countries require a departure tax. If you are departing to a neighboring country, the tax may be small, but, if you are returning to the U.S., the tax could be as high as $20 per person, regardless of age. Be sure to have enough money at the end of your trip to be able to get on the plane! For authoritative information on a country's entry and exit requirements, contact its embassy or consulate. When you make your inquires, ask about:

- where to obtain a tourist card or visa
- visa price, length of validity, and number of entries
- financial requirements—proof of sufficient funds, proof of onward or return ticket
- currency regulations—how much local or dollar currency can be brought in or out
- special requirements for children traveling alone or with only one parent
- yellow fever immunization or other health requirements
- export/import restrictions
- departure tax—how much and who must pay.

Restrictions on Minors

Many countries impose restrictions on minor children who travel alone, with only one parent or with someone who is not their parent. A child must present written authorization for travel from the absent parent, parents or legal guardian. If the parent or guardian traveling with the child is the sole custodian, the court order granting custody may, in some cases, serve as the authorization document. If any of this applies to you, inquire about the following at the embassy or consulate of the country your child plans to visit.

- the age of majority at which the restriction no longer applies (e.g., age 15 in Argentina, age 18 in Brazil)
- the type of document that can overcome the restriction (e.g., court order, statement of absent parent or parents)
- whether notarizing the document is sufficient or if it must also be authenticated by the country's embassy or consulate
- whether the document must be translated.

Note: In Brazil, a child may travel with his/her father without the mother's authorization, but, if traveling alone or with his/her mother, must have notarized authorization from the father. In Brazil, a woman may authorize a child's travel only when she is the sole legal parent or guardian.

Bringing a Car

If you plan to drive to Central or South America, contact the embassy or consulate of each country you plan to visit to learn what is required for entry and exit by private car. Besides title and ownership, at most borders you will need to show insurance coverage effective for the country you are entering. If your U.S. insurance does not cover you abroad, you can usually purchase insurance when you enter a country. In some countries, if you are involved in an accident that causes injury, you will automatically be taken into police custody until it can be determined who is liable and whether you have the insurance or financial ability to pay any judgment. There may also be criminal liability assigned if the injuries or damages are serious. If you are a visitor, you will not ordinarily have to pay import duty on your car, but you may have to post a bond or otherwise satisfy customs officials that you will not sell or dispose of the vehicle in the country. To enter some countries, you must have your car documented at the embassy or consulate of the country before you leave home. Before you get behind the wheel, be sure you are in compliance with the automobile import regulations of your destination countries.

U.S. Wildlife Regulations

Endangered species and products made from them may not be brought into the United States. The penalty is confiscation and a possible fine. These items are prohibited from import: virtually all birds originating in Brazil, Ecuador, Paraguay and Venezuela; furs from spotted cats; most lizardskin products from Brazil and Paraguay; many snakeskin products from Brazil, Ecuador and Paraguay; skins from the Orinoco crocodile; and all sea turtle products.

Shopping for Antiquities

Most countries in Central and South America control the export of objects from their pre-Columbian and colonial heritage. Some countries claim ownership of all such material and consider the export of antiques, without the permission of the government, to be an act of theft. In addition, under U.S. law, importers of all pre-Columbian monumental and architectural sculpture, murals and certain archaeological and ethnological materials are required to provide proof to the U.S. Customs Service that these artifacts are legally exported from the country of origin. Beware of purchasing artifacts unless they are accompanied by an export permit issued by the government of origin.

Getting Sick

Health precautions for travelers can be obtained from local health departments, the U.S. Public Health Service, private doctors or travel clinics. Depending on your destination, immunization may be recommended against diphtheria, tetanus, hepatitis, polio, rabies, typhoid and yellow fever.

Malaria: is found in rural areas of every country in the region except Chile and Uruguay. Malaria prophylaxis and mosquito avoidance measures are recommended. If possible, avoid contact with mosquitoes from dusk to dawn by wearing long clothing, using insect repellent on exposed skin, using a flying insect spray in living and sleeping quarters and using a bed net. Prophylaxis should begin two weeks before going to an area where malaria is endemic and should continue for at least four weeks after leaving. Chloroquinine is the malaria prophylaxis most easily tolerated by humans. However, malaria resistant to chloroquinine has been reported in an area beginning east of the Panama Canal and extending through northern South America as far south as the Amazon Basin. If you plan to visit this area, consult a medical expert to work out an additional prophylaxis. Malaria may at times, however, break through any drug or drug combination. If you develop chills, fever, and headaches while taking a malaria prophylaxis, seek medical attention promptly. Early treatment of malaria can be effective, but delaying therapy could have serious consequences.

Mosquito avoidance measures, if used day and night, may also help prevent other less prevalent insect-borne diseases found in parts of Central and South America such as **Chagas' disease**, **dengue fever**, **leishmaniasis**, and **yellow fever**. Throughout most of Central and South America, fruits and vegetables should be washed with care and meats and fish thoroughly cooked. Problems of food contamination are less prevalent in Argentina, Chile and Uruguay, and tapwater is potable in those countries. Elsewhere water is generally not potable and should be boiled or chemically treated.

Diarrhea caused by contaminated food or water is potentially serious. If it persists, seek medical attention. Certain beaches in the region, including some at Lima and at Rio de Janeiro, are dangerously polluted. Avoid swimming at beaches that might be contaminated with human sewage or dog feces. Avoid swimming in fresh water in the areas where **schistosomiasis** is found: Brazil, Suriname, and north-central Venezuela. Visitors in the Andes may experience symptoms of **altitude sickness** such as insomnia, headache and nausea. If you become sick, wait until your symptoms disappear before you attempt to go higher. Mountaineers should learn about the symptoms of **high altitude pulmonary edema**, a condition that is fatal unless remedied by immediate descent. Another hazard of high altitudes is sunburn. Exposure to ultraviolet radiation increases not only as you approach the equator, but also as you ascend in altitude. Sunscreens may help prevent this.

Dangerous Things

Crime

Like many large cities throughout the world, major cities in Central and South American experience assaults, robberies and thefts. Visitors should take common sense precautions:

• Safety begins when you pack.

• Leave expensive jewelry behind.

• Dress conservatively; a flashy wardrobe or one that is too casual can mark you as a tourist.

• Use "Traveler's cheques," not cash.

• Leave photocopies of your passport personal information page and of your airline tickets with someone at home and carry an extra set with you.

• In a car, keep doors locked, windows rolled up and valuables out of sight. A common trick is for a thief to reach through a car window and grab a watch from a person's wrist or a purse or package from the seat while they are driving slowly or stopped in traffic.

• When you leave your car, try to find a guarded parking lot, lock the car and keep valuables out of sight.

• When walking, avoid marginal areas of cities, dark alleys and crowds.

• Avoid being stopped or approached on the street by strangers, including street vendors and beggars.

• Be aware that women and small children as well as men can be pickpockets or purse snatchers.

• Keep your billfold in an inner front pocket, keep your hand on your purse and wear the shoulderstrap of your camera or bag across your chest.

• To guard against thieves on motorcycles, walk away from the curb, carrying your purse away from the street.

• Do not travel alone when you can avoid it.

• If you visit an isolated area, go with a group or a reputable guide.

• Avoid travel at night.

• Do not take valuables to the beach.

Any U.S. citizen who is criminally assaulted should report the incident to the local police and to the nearest U.S. embassy or consulate.

Civil Unrest

Several countries in Central and South America have areas of instability or war zones that are off-limits to visitors without special permits. Others have similar areas that are open but surrounded by security check points where travelers must show their passport or tourist card. Always carry your papers with you, and do not overstay the validity of your visa or tourist card. Avoid public demonstrations. American citizens have been arrested when local authorities have thought they were participating in civil demonstrations.

Drugs

Most Central and South American countries strictly enforce laws against the use, possession, and sale of narcotics. Foreigners arrested for possession of even small amounts of narcotics are not deported, but are charged and tried as international traffickers. There is no bail, judicial delays are lengthy and you can spend two to four years in prison awaiting trial and sentencing. If you carry prescription drugs, keep them in their original container clearly labeled with the doctor's name, pharmacy and contents. In addition, check with the embassy of the country you plan to visit for specific customs requirements for prescription drugs.

Photography

Be cautious when taking pictures. Frequently local authorities consider all airports, police stations, military locations, oil installations, harbors, mines and bridges to be security-related. Photography of demonstrations or civil disturbances is also usually prohibited. Tourists have had their film confiscated and have been detained, so, when in doubt, ask.

Adopting a Child Abroad

Because of continuing scandals over the illegal activities of some adoption agencies and attorneys both in the United States and abroad, U.S. citizens have recently experienced difficulties when attempting to adopt children from Central or South America. Several countries in the region have either outlawed adoptions by foreigners or have passed a law requiring formal court adoption of the child in the country before the child is permitted to immigrate to the United States. Although this has resulted in adoptions less likely to be challenged from a legal standpoint, it has made the process more difficult and time-consuming. Any U.S. citizen interested in adopting a child from a country in Central or South America is encouraged to contact either the U.S. embassy in the country, United States, the Department of State's Office of Citizen Consular Services, Inter-American Division (☎ 202-647-3712) to obtain information on the adoption process in that country.

Dual Nationality

Some countries in Central and South America do not recognize acquisition of U.S. citizenship unless the naturalized U.S. citizen renounces his or her original nationality at an embassy or consulate of the country of origin. A person born in the United States of a parent or parents who were citizens of another country may also be considered by that country to be their national. If arrested, a dual national may be denied the right to communicate with the U.S. embassy or consulate. Another consequence could be having to serve in the military of one's former country. If you are a naturalized U.S. citizen, a dual national, or have any reason to believe another country may consider you its national, check with the embassy of that country as to your citizenship status and any obligations you may have while visiting. Dual nationals who have not researched their citizenship status before traveling have sometimes, to their surprise, encountered difficulties, such as not being allowed to depart or being drafted for military service. Even countries that recognize acquired U.S. citizenship may consider their former citizens as having resumed original citizenship if they take up residence in their country of origin.

This can happen even if the embassy of the country stamps a visa in the U.S. passport of its former citizen. Dual nationals should also be aware that they may be required to use a passport from their country of origin in order to enter or leave that country. The U.S. government does not object to the use of a foreign passport in such situations. U.S. citizens may not, however, use a foreign passport to enter or leave the United States. If you have any questions about dual nationality, contact the Office of Citizens Consular Services, *Room 4817, Department of State, Washington, D.C. 20520* ☎ *(202-647-3712).*

Additional Information for Certain Countries

Belize

Belize enforces a strict policy of refusing admittance to persons who an immigration officer suspects of drug use.

Brazil

Obtain your visa in advance. Brazilian immigration authorities do not hestitate to require a traveler without a visa to leave on the next available flight. Street crime can be a major problem in large cities in Brazil. Guard against it. In Sao Paulo, if you encounter difficulties or need emergency assistance, dial 1-0, radio police patrol, from any public telephone—no coin or token is needed for the call.

Chile

Anyone considering scientific, technical, or mountaineering expeditions to regions in Chile's classified as frontier areas or to Antarctica must apply for authorization to a Chilean embassy or consulate a minimum of 90 days prior to the beginning of the expedition. The application will be forwarded to the Chilean government for decision.Chilean authorities reserve the right to request Chilean participation in foreign expeditions, and require the submission of a post-expedition report on the activities undertaken and the results obtained.

U.S. Embassies and Consulates Abroad

Note: APO and FPO addresses may only be used for mail originating in the United States. When you use an APO or FPO address, do not include the local street address. For addresses in the United States see Visa Information chapter.

Argentina

American Embassy
4300 Colombia, 1425 Buenos Aires
☎ *(54) (1) 774-7611*
Telex: 18156 USICA AR
Mailing address:
American Embassy Buenos Aires
APO Miami 34034

Belize

American Embassy Gabourel Lane
Belize City
☎ *(501) 776161*
Telex: 213 AMEMBASSY BZ

Bolivia

American Embassy
Banco Popular Del Peru Bldg. Corner of Calles
Mercado and Colon La Paz
☎ *(591) (2) 350251*
Telex: AMEMB BV 3268
Mailing address:
American Embassy La Paz
APO Miami 34032

Brazil

American Embassy
Avenida das Nocoes, Lote 3
Brasilia
☎ *(55) (6) 321-7272*
Telex: 061-1091
Mailing address:
American Embassy Brasilia
APO Miami 34030

American Consulate General
Avenida Presidente Wilson 147
Rio de Janeiro
☎ *(55) (21) 292-7117*
Telex: AMCONSUL 21-22831
Mailing address:
American Consulate General Rio de Janeiro
APO Miami 34030

American Consulate General
Rua Padre Joao Manoel, 933 Sao Paulo
☎ *(55) (11) 881-6511*
Telex: 11-31574
Mailing address:
American Consulate General
Sao Paulo
APO Miami 34030

American Consulate
Rua Coronel Genuino, 421 (9th Fl.)
Porto Alegre
☎ *(55) (512) 26-4288*
Telex: 051-2292 CGEU BR
Mailing address:

American Consulate
Porto Alegre
APO Miami 34030

American Consulate

Rua Goncalves Maia, 163 Recife
☎ (55) (81) 221-1412
Telex: 081-1190
Mailing address:
American Consulate Recife
APO Miami 34030

Chile

American Embassy
Codina Bldg., 1343 Agustinas
Santiago
☎ (56) (2) 710133
Telex: 240062-USA-CL
Mailing address:
American Embassy Santiago
APO Miami 34033

Colombia

American Embassy
Calle 38, No. 8-61
Bogota
☎ (57) (1) 285-1300
Telex: 44843
Mailing address:
American Embassy Bogota
APO Miami 34038

American Consulate

Calle 77 Carrera
68 Centro Comercial Mayorista
Barranquilla
☎ (57) (5) 45-7088
Telex: 33482 AMCO CO
Mailing address:
American Consulate Barranquilla
APO Miami 34038

Costa Rica

American Embassy
Avenida 3 and Calle I
San Jose
☎ (506) 331-155
Mailing address:
American Embassy San Jose
APO Miami 34020

Ecuador

American Embassy
Avenida 12 de Octubre y Avenida Patria
Quito
☎ (593) (2) 562-890
Mailing address:
American Embassy Quito
APO Miami 34039

American Consulate General

9 de Octubre y Garcia Moreno
Guayaquil
☎ (593) (4) 323-570
Telex: 04-3452 USICAG ED
Mailing address:
American Consulate General
Guayaquil
APO Miami 34039

El Salvador

American Embassy
25 Avenida Norte No. 1230
San Salvador
☎ (503) 26-7100
Mailing Address:
American Embassy
San Salvador
APO Miami 34023

French Guiana

American Consulate General
14 Rue Blenac B.P. 561
Fort-de-France 97206
Martinique
☎ (596) 63-13-03
Telex: 912670; 912315 MR

Guatemala

American Embassy
7-01 Avenida de la Reforma, Zone 10
Guatemala
☎ (502) (2) 31-15-41
Mailing Address:
American Embassy
Guatemala
APO Miami 34024

Guyana

American Embassy
31 Main Street
Georgetown
☎ (592) (02) 54900-9
Telex: 213 AMEMSY GY

Honduras

American Embassy
Avenido La Paz Tegucigalpa
☎ (504) 32-3120
Mailing Address:
American Embassy
Tegucigalpa
APO Miami 34022

Nicaragua

American Embassy
Km. 4-1/2 Carretera Sur
Managua
☎ (505) (2) 66010
Mailing Address:
American Embassy
Managua
APO Miami 34021

Panama

American Embassy
Apartado 6959 Panama 5
Rep. de Panama
☎ (507) 27-1777
Mailing Address:
American Embassy
Panama
APO Miami 34002

Paraguay

American Embassy
1776 Mariscal Loipez Avenida
Asuncion
☎ (595) (21) 201-041
Mailing Address:
American Embassy

Asuncion
APO Miami 34036-0001

Peru

American Embassy Consular Section
Grimaldo Del Solar 346
Miraflores Lima 18
Lima
☎ *(51) (14) 44-3621*
Telex: 25028PE USCOMATT
Mailing Address:
American Embassy Lima
APO Miami 34031

Suriname

American Embassy
Dr. Sophie Redmondstraat 129
Paramaribo
☎ *(597) 72900*
Telex: 373 AMEMSU SN

Uraguay

American Embassy
Lauro Muller 1776
Montevideo
☎ *(598) (2) 40-90-51*
Mailing Address:
American Embassy Montevideo
APO Miami 34035

Venezuela

American Embassy
Avenida Francisco de Miranda y Avenida
Principal de la Floresta
Caracas
☎ *(58) (2) 284-7111*
Telex: 25501 AMEMB VE
Mailing Address:
American Embassy
Caracas
APO Miami 34037

American Consulate

Edificio Sofimara,
Piso 3 Calle 77 Con Avenida 13
Maracaibo
☎ *(58) (61) 84-253*
Telex: 62213 USCON VE
Mailing Address:
American Consulate Maracaibo
APO Miami 34037

Sub-Saharan Africa

Weather

Sub-Saharan Africa is tropical, except for the high inland plateaus and the southern part of South Africa. Within 10 degrees of the Equator, the climate seldom varies and is generally hot and rainy. Farther from the Equator, the seasons become more apparent, and if possible, you should plan your trip in the cooler months. If traveling to rural areas, avoid the rainy months which generally run from May through October, since roads may be washed out.

Getting In and Out

Visa And Other Entry Requirements

A U.S. passport is required for travel to all countries in Africa. In addition, most countries in sub-Saharan Africa require U.S. citizens to have a visa. If visas are required, obtain them before you leave home. If you decide to visit additional countries en route, it may be difficult or impossible to obtain visas. In most African countries, you will not be admitted into the country and will have to depart on the next plane if you arrive without a visa. This can be inconvenient if the next plane does not arrive for several days, the airport hotel is full and the airport has no other sleeping accommodations.

The best authority on a country's visa and other entry requirements is its embassy or consulate. The Department of State publication, "Foreign Visa Requirements," gives basic information on entry requirements and tells where and how to apply for visas. You can order a copy for $.50 from the Consumer Information Center, Dept. 438T, Pueblo, Colorado 81009.

Allow plenty of time to apply for visas. An average of two weeks for each visa is recommended. Before you apply, check the following:

- visa price, length of validity, and number of entries
- financial data required—roof of sufficient funds, proof of onward/return ticket
- immunizations required
- currency regulations
- import/export restrictions
- departure tax—if required, be sure to keep sufficient hard currency so that you may leave the country on schedule.
- AIDS clearance certification. Some countries require travelers to submit certification or be tested upon arrival for AIDS.

Some African countries will refuse to admit you if you have South African visas or entry and exit stamps in your passports. If you have such notations in your passport or plan to visit South Africa in conjunction with a trip to other countries, contact a U.S. passport agency for guidance.

Dangerous Things

Restricted Areas

A visa is good only for those parts of a country that are open to foreigners. Several countries in Africa have areas of civil unrest or war zones that are off-limits to visitors without special permits. Others have similar areas that are open but surrounded by security checkpoints where travelers must show their passport, complete with valid visa. When traveling in such a country, keep your passport with you at all times. No matter where you travel in Africa, do not overstay the validity of your visa; renew it if necessary.

If stopped at a roadblock, be courteous and responsive to questions asked by persons in authority. At night, turn on the interior light of the car. In areas of instability, however, try to avoid travel at night. For information on restricted areas and security risk areas, consult Department of State travel advisories or, if you are already in Africa, the nearest U.S. embassy or consulate.

In some areas, when U.S. citizens are arrested or detained, police or prison officials have failed to inform the U.S. embassy or consulate. If you are ever detained for any reason, ask to talk with a U.S. consular officer.

U.S. Citizens Married To Foreign Nationals

Women who travel to Africa should be aware that in some countries, either by law or by custom, a woman and her children need the permission of the husband to leave the country. If you or your children travel, be aware of the laws and customs of the places you visit. Do not visit or allow your children to visit unless you are confident that you will be permitted to leave. Once overseas, you are subject to the laws of the country you are in; U.S. law cannot protect you.

Currency Regulations

The amount of money, including "Traveler's cheques," which may be taken into or out of African countries varies. In general, visitors must declare all currency and "Traveler's cheques" upon arrival. Do not exchange money on the black market. Use only banks and other authorized foreign exchange offices and retain receipts. You may need to present the receipts as well as your original currency declaration when you depart. Currency not accounted for may be confiscated and you may be fined or detained.

Many countries require that hotel bills be paid in hard currency. Some require that a minimum amount of hard currency be changed into the local currency upon arrival. Some countries prohibit the import or export of local currency.

U.S. Wildlife Regulations

The United States prohibits the import of products from endangered species, including the furs of any spotted cats. Most African countries have enacted laws protecting wildlife, but poaching and illegal trafficking in wildlife are still commonplace. By importing products made from endangered species, you risk seizure of the product and a possible fine. African ivory can be imported legally, but much of what is offered for sale is illegal. If you do decide to buy ivory products, your chances of making legal purchases are increased if you obtain a government export permit with each purchase.

The import of some types of parrots and other wild birds from Africa is generally legal but is subject to licensing and other controls. There are also restrictions which require the birds to be placed in quarantine upon arrival to ensure they are free from disease. For further information on the import of wildlife and related products, consult TRAFFIC (U.S.A.), World Wildlife Fund U.S., *1250 24th Street, N.W., Washington, D.C. 20037.*

Photography

Africa is filled with photogenic scenery and photography is generally encouraged. However, most governments prohibit photography of military installations or locations having military significance including airports, bridges, tunnels, port facilities and public buildings. Visitors can seek guidance on restrictions from local tourist offices or from the nearest U.S. embassy or consulate. Taking photographs without prior permission can result in your arrest or the confiscation of your film.

Shortages, High Prices And Other Problems

Consumer goods, gas and food are in short supply in some African countries and prices for these commodities may be high by U.S. standards. Shortages of hotel accommodations also exist so confirm reservations well in advance. Some countries experience disruptions in electricity and water supply or in services such as mail and telecommunications.

Getting Around

Air Travel

If you are flying to places in Africa other than the major tourist destinations, you may have difficulty securing and retaining reservations and experience long waits at airports for customs and immigration processing. If stranded, you may need proof of a confirmed reservation in order to obtain food and lodging vouchers from some airlines. Flights are often overbooked, delayed or cancelled and when competing for space on a plane, you may be dealing with a surging crowd rather than a line. Traveling with a packaged tour may insulate you from some of these difficulties. All problems cannot be avoided, but you can:

Learn the reputation of the airline and the airports you will use to forestall problems and avoid any unpleasant surprises.

When possible, reserve your return passage before you go; reconfirm immediately upon arrival.

Ask for confirmation in writing, complete with file number or locator code, when you make or confirm a reservation.

Arrive at the airport earlier than required in order to put youself at the front of the line or the crowd, as the case may be.

Travel with funds sufficient for an extra week's subsistence in case you are stranded.

Local Transportation

Rental cars, where available, may be expensive. Hiring a taxi is often the easiest way to go sightseeing. Taxi fares should be negotiated in advance. Travel on rural roads can be slow and difficult in the dry season or disrupted by floods in the rainy season.

Getting Sick

Malaria is found in at least part of every country of sub-Saharan Africa except Cape Verde and Lesotho. *Falciparum*, the malignant form of malaria, is present in most sub-Saharan malaria areas. Malaria prophylaxis and mosquito avoidance measures are recommended. If possible, avoid contact with mosquitoes from dusk to dawn by wearing long clothing, using insect repellent on exposed skin and using a flying insect spray in living and sleeping quarters. Prophylaxis should begin two weeks before going to an area where malaria is endemic and should continue for at least four weeks after leaving the area. Chloroquinine is the malaria prophylaxis most easily tolerated by humans. However, in much of Africa, mosquitoes are becoming resistant to chloroquine. If you are going to an area where mosquitoes may be chloroquine-resistant, consult a medical expert for an alternate prophylactic regimen. Even if you take appropriate prophylaxis, malaria sometimes breaks through any drug or drug combination. Should you develop chills, fever and headaches while taking anti-malarial drugs, promptly seek medical attention.

Sleeping sickness, borne by the tsetse fly, is generally not a high risk for international travelers. However, you may be at risk in certain game parks and savanna regions. These insects bite in the day and are attracted by movement and bright colors. Insect repellent and long clothing that blends with the background environment are recommended. Insect repellent also provides protection against ticks. If you are going into wooded areas where ticks might be present, use repellent, wear close fitting clothes and search your body for ticks afterwards.

Schistosomiasis (or bilharzia) is found throughout sub-Saharan Africa except in Cape Verde, Lesotho and the Seychelles. These parasites can penetrate unbroken skin and are best avoided by not swimming or wading in fresh water. Safe and effective oral drugs are available to treat schistosomiasis.

Some countries have shortages of medicines; bring an adequate supply of any prescription and over-the-counter medicines that you are accustomed to taking. Keep all prescriptions in their original, labeled containers.

Medical facilities may be limited, particularly in rural areas. Should you become seriously ill or injured abroad, contact the nearest U.S. embassy or consulate. A U.S. consular officer can furnish you with a list of recommended local hospitals and English-speaking doctors. Consular officers can also inform your family or friends in the United States of your condition. Because medical coverage overseas can be quite expensive, prospective travelers should review their health insurance policies. If your policy does not provide medical coverage overseas, consider buying supplemental insurance. It is also advisable to obtain insurance to cover the exorbitant cost of medical evacuation in the event of a medical emergency.

Except in first-class hotels, drink only boiled water or bottled beverages. Avoid ice cubes. Unless you are certain they are pasteurized, avoid dairy products. Vegetables and fruits should be peeled or washed in a purifying solution. A good rule of thumb is, if you can't peel it or cook it, don't eat it. Diarrhea caused by eating contaminated food or drinking impure water is potentially very serious. If it persists, seek medical attention.

An increasing number of countries have established regulations regarding AIDS testing, particularly for long-term residents and students. Check with the embassy or consulate of the country you plan to visit for up-to-date information.

Further Information On:

Angola

Individuals arriving in Angola without a visa may be arrested. Foreigners are restricted to certain areas and should scrupulously follow Angolan laws and regulations. Shortages of medical services, food and consumer goods as well as disruptions in utilities are commonplace.

The United States does not maintain diplomatic relations with Angola. There is no U.S. embassy in Luanda, and the United States Government is not in a position to accord normal consular protective services to U.S. citizens who travel to Angola.

Travel to Angola is considered dangerous. Although travel in the capital city of Luanda is relatively safe, travel by road, rail or air within Angola is unsafe due to the possibility of guerilla attack. UNITA has publicly warned that it cannot be responsible for the safety of foreigners who live or travel in contested areas, or for the timely release of foreigners captured by UNITA.

Benin (formerly Dahomey)

Photography of the Presidential Palace and military and economic facilities is strictly prohibited. During the rainy season many roads are impassable. Credit cards are accepted at only one major hotel in Cotonou. Big game hunting must be licensed and game trophies cannot be exported without a permit. Big game hunting is sometimes suspended. Check with the Benin authorities before traveling or with the U.S. Embassy when you arrive for further details.

Botswana

No visa is needed for a visit of up to 90 days. Tap water is potable in major towns. Travelers may be stopped at roadside checkpoints. Consumables, medicines and gas are all imported from South Africa and are not in short supply.

Burkina Faso
(formerly Upper Volta)

Travelers must stop at occasional police roadblocks or other checkpoints. A government permit is required for photography, particularly in cities.

Burundi

Travelers are urged to obtain a visa in advance to avoid delays upon arrival. Because tourist accommodations are limited outside Bujumbura, make reservations well in advance. Medical facilities are also limited and some consumer goods may be in short supply.

Cameroon

Airport security is stringent and visitors may be subject to baggage searches. Cameroon has a good domestic transportation system. Roadside security checkpoints are maintained on all major roads. Be sure to carry your passport and a valid visa with you at all times in case you are stopped.

Cape Verde

These rugged volcanic islands have a dry, temperate climate. Tourist facilities are limited.

Central African Republic

Emergency medical care is inadequate. The tap water is not potable, but bottled water is available. Confirm your onward flights before you arrive because confirmation is difficult once in the country. Do not display or use photographic equipment without permission from the Ministry of Information. Roads often flood in the rainy season—from May through October.

Chad

Government permits are required for photography and for travel outside N'Djamena. Several former combat zones in the country are still heavily mined. Travel in most parts of southern Chad is safe, although the roads are poor and facilities are limited. Upon arrival, consult the U.S. Embassy for a situation report on current conditions.

Comoros

Visas are issued at the airport upon arrival, and an exit permit is required for departure. Visitors must have an onward/return ticket.

Congo

Visa applicants must show that they have a hotel reservation, an invitation from a relative or friend in the Congo, or, if visiting on business, documentation of their business status. To cross the Congo River by ferry from Brazzaville to Kinshasa, you need a visa for Zaire and a special permit issued by the Embassy of Zaire in Brazzaville. Photography of public buildings or installations is restricted.

Cote D'Ivoire

Visitors arriving without a visa are not allowed to enter the country. A good network of paved roads links all major towns. Unpaved roads are dusty in the dry season and slippery in the rainy season. Metered taxis and rental cars are available.

Djibouti

Visas must be obtained before arrival. Outside the capital, there is only one surfaced road. For travel inside the country, take an experienced guide and use a vehicle equipped for rough terrain.

Equatorial Guinea

Two photos must be submitted to airport authorities upon arrival. Visitors should carry pass-port-size photographs with them since it may be difficult to find a photographer after arrival. Visas must be obtained in advance.

Medical facilities are limited and there are no dentists or opticians in the country. Water is not potable and many visitors bring their own bottled water. Consumer goods are in short supply. Snorkeling, boating and fishing are available, but bring your own equipment. Tourist facilities are limited.

Ethiopia

Airlines and hotels do not usually accept credit cards. All bills must be paid in cash or "Trav-eler's cheques."

For travel outside Shoa province, you must have a permit from the National Tourist Organiza-tion (NTO). Permits are not always granted. Many areas of the country are off-limits to for-eigners. The NTO generally requires tourists traveling outside of Addis Ababa to take along and pay the expenses of an NTO guide. Travel within Ethiopia may involve serious inconve-nience and/or danger. The civil war between the Ethiopian regime and rebels continues in the Northern provinces. The famine in those areas and others poses problems for travelers. A mid-night to 5 a.m. curfew is in effect in Addis Ababa and most other urban areas.

Certain buildings and public places may not be photographed. Consult your NTO guide or another authority before using either a camera or binoculars in Ethiopia. To import a video camera, you must have a permit in advance and be prepared for a delay and questioning at cus-toms, up on arrival and departure. A permit is also required to export antiques and animal skins. It is not unusual for foreigners and their Ethiopian acquaintances to be stopped by government officials and questioned.

Gabon

Visas must be obtained before arrival. Travelers arriving without a visa may be detained by air-port officials or confined in an airport jail.

Taxis are plentiful along major routes in Libreville. There are roadblock checkpoints in Libre-ville and between towns. Train service is available between Libreville and Franceville and there is an extensive domestic airline network.

Gambia

Tourist facilities are good, but unpaved roads in the city and surrounding areas make travel dif-ficult, especially during the rainy season from May through September. Tap water is potable, but boiled or bottled water is recommended outside of Banjul.

Ghana

Ghana has strict laws on currency exchange, and on the import and export of gold, diamonds and other natural resources. Attempts to evade these regulations are punishable by a three to seven-year prison term. Before conducting any business transactions, visitors should contact the commercial and consular sections at the U.S. Embassy in Accra for specific advice. Smug-gling is a serious crime in Ghana and airport officials have the authority to conduct body searches. If detained for any reason, request that the American Embassy be notified. There are roadblock checkpoints where automobiles and sometimes passengers may be searched. Use cameras cautiously. Possession of a camera in some areas is considered suspicious. Individuals have been arrested for taking pictures near sensitive installations.

Prices are high and there are shortages of medicines, consumer goods and gasoline as well as disruptions in utilitiies. Hotel accommmodations are limited, so reserve well in advance. All hotel bills must be paid in hard currency.

Guinea

All travelers must surrender their passports to Guinean immigration authorities at the airport in Conakry. Visitors may reclaim their passports at the Central Immigration Office in downtown Conakry 24 hours after arrival.

Most hotels accept payment only in hard currency or by credit card. Local currency may not be imported or exported. Road travel is difficult, particularly in the rainy season from May to October. Exercise caution if taking photographs, since Guinean officials and private citizens may object even if you have a permit.

Guinea-Bissau

Visas must be obtained in advance. Local currency may not be exported or imported. Hotel bills must be paid in local currency and credit cards are not accepted. It is advisable to carry U.S. currency in small denominations of twenty dollars or less as the banks and hotels will not change large bills into local currency.

Road conditions make overland travel to Senegal difficult and to Guinea almost impossible. Water is not potable and bottled water is generally unavailable. All fruits and vegetables must be chemically treated before consumption.

Kenya

Obtain visas before arrival to avoid delays at the airport. U.S. citizens should not have trouble entering Kenya from South Africa, provided their visit there is less than three months.

Adequate medical services and potable water are available in Nairobi. Outside of Nairobi, medical facilities are limited and drinking water must be boiled. Kenya has no shortages of food and consumer goods. Most major towns are linked by scheduled air service, good passenger train service and intercity bus service. Taxis are plentiful in Nairobi.

Severe penalties are incurred for the unauthorized exchange of currency. No local currency may be imported or exported. The airport departure tax must be paid in hard currency. A permit is required to export animal skins or game trophies.

Lesotho

A visa is not required for a tourist stay of up to 3 months. Visas may be extended after arrival. Because most routes to Lesotho pass through South Africa, visitors should have a multiple-entry visa to South Africa. Tap water in Maseru is considered potable, but many foreigners boil or chemically treat their water, particularly during the rainy season.

Rental cars are available. Visitors should be especially cautious driving on mountainous roads and at night. The border crossings to South Africa are closed from 10 p.m. to 6 a.m.

Liberia

Liberia is a war zone. Use extreme caution taking photographs because restricted areas are not easily identifiable. Tourists have had their camera and film confiscated and have been detained for simply possessing a camera in areas which are off-limits for photography.

The international airport is 36 miles from Monrovia. Unpaved roads make travel difficult, particularly in the rainy season. Travelers should carry proof of identity documents at all times. Visas must be obtained in advance and exit permits are issued upon arrival.

Madagascar

International air service is limited but domestic air connections are good. Some sections of the country may be visited by train, bus or rural taxi. Four-wheel drive vehicles are recommended for travel on rural roads.

Malawi

Visas are not required for visits of up to one year. Travelers' luggage may be searched upon arrival and books and video tapes may be held for clearance by the censorship board. Visitors are subject to the government dress code which prohibits women from wearing shorts, trousers or skirts that expose the knee in public. Such attire is allowed, however, at beaches, game parks and for athletic activities. Men are prohibited from wearing hair long enough to touch their collars. Journalists and writers will be refused entry unless prior government clearance has been obtained.

Mali

Visas must be obtained before arrival. Taxis are available in Bamako. The road from Bamako to Mopti and a few other roads branching to the south are paved. Travel on other roads is difficult, particularly in the rainy season.

Mauritania

Visas must be obtained before arrival. Mauritania is a Muslim country and conservative dress is recommended; this means garments with sleeves, dress length to cover the knee and no shorts. Taxis are plentiful in Nouakchatt. Local currency may not be imported or exported.

Mauritius

Visas are not required for a stay of up to three months, provided the visitor has an onward/return ticket. Tap water is potable; avoid uncooked vegetables. Rental cars and taxis are plentiful and bus service between towns is good.

Mozambique

Due to insurgent activities of the Mozambican National Resistance (RENAMO), road and rail travel outside major cities can be hazardous. On certain highways, visitors should be careful at occasional roadblocks and searches. Keep your valid entry permit and passport with you at all times. Entry permits must be obtained before arrival in Mozambique. Obtain current security information at the U.S. Embassy, particularly if planning travel outside of Maputo.

Food is scarce, consumer goods are in short supply and there are disruptions in utilities. Bills must usually be paid in dollars or "Traveler's cheques." Bring sufficient cash for your stay as U.S. dollars are not available through local banks. Currency should be exchanged only at authorized locations.

Namibia

Several areas in Namibia have experienced bombings, mine explosions, shootings and other acts of terrorism. Most of northern Namibia should be avoided. South Africa administers Namibia, therefore your visa for South Africa is good for Namibia. Check security conditions with the U.S. Consulate in Capetown before traveling to Namibia.

Photography is not permitted at military installations, at diamond mining areas or anywhere in the north.

Niger

Visas must be obtained in advance as they are not available at the airport. Taxis are the only form of public transport easy to obtain. Roadside checkpoints should be respected. A permit is required to take pictures. Photographing the airport or government facilities is prohibited.

Nigeria

Although it is not required for a visa, yellow fever vaccinations are recommended, especially for travel outside of urban areas. All currency must be declared in writing upon arrival and a minimum of $100 must be exchanged into local currency. Currency control regulations should be strictly observed because violations are punishable by arrest, prosecution by military tribunal and prolonged detention.

Air travel is adequate for both international and domestic flights but is often overcrowded, overbooked and subject to unscheduled cancellations and delays. In Lagos and other cities, beware of high crime areas and avoid traveling at night. Export of antiquities and ceremonial objects must be approved by the Nigerian Department of Antiquities.

Rwanda

Although there are some shortages, food supplies are adequate. A permit is needed to export game trophies. Visits to the gorillas in Parc de Volcans must be booked at least a month in advance.

Sao Tome and Principe

Tourist visas are available upon arrival. There is no U.S. Embassy in this country, but the American Ambassador to Gabon is also accredited to Sao Tome and Principe. Consular services for U.S. citizens are handled through the U.S. Embassy in Libreville, Gabon.

Senegal

To avoid delays upon arrival, obtain visas in advance. Although Dakar is a major port of entry into western Africa, international air service is often overcrowded, overbooked and subject to unscheduled cancellations and delays.

Seychelles

Visas are issued upon arrival and may be extended for up to one year, provided visitors have an onward/return ticket and sufficient funds for their stay. Firearms and spearfishing equipment may not be imported.

Sierra Leone

Visitors must declare all foreign currency on an official exchange control form. This form is certified, stamped and used to record all currency exchanges while in the country. You must exchange $100 of hard currency upon arrival. Allow extra time for the river ferry on the route between the airport and Freetown.

Somalia

All foreign currency must be declared upon entering the country. Banks are the only legal place to exchange money. Private currency transactions and trading on the black market are illegal and offenders are prosecuted. Prices can be high and consumer goods are often scarce. Outside of Mogadishu, tourist accommodations are rustic. Unnecessary travel to the northern and central provinces of Somalia should be avoided because of occasional dissident activity. Check security conditions with the U.S. Embassy upon arrival.

South Africa

Obtain visas in advance. Strict government security measures are in effect and travel in regular tourist areas is generally safe. However, the security situation should be considered. The greatest unrest has been in urban black townships, although city centers and some shopping areas have experienced random terrorist bombings and sporadic unrest. Daylight muggings and robberies are also common in some areas. Avoid travel to the so-called "independent homelands" of Bophuthatswana, Venda, Ciskei and Transkei. Consult the U.S. Embassy or consulates if you plan to visit these areas.

Severe restrictions are imposed on reporting or photographing demonstrations, funerals and any incident of civil unrest. South African emergency regulations allow the arrest and indefinite detention of persons considered a threat to public order. If you are detained for any reason, ask to talk with a U.S. consular officer.

Despite security problems, air travel is efficient. You can travel throughout the country by plane, train or highway. There are no shortages or disruptions in services and utilities, and the tap water is potable.

Sudan

When visiting Khartoum exercise caution because of the potential for terrorism. Travelers should avoid Equatoria, Upper Nile and Bahr El-Ghazal, the three provinces of southern Sudan. The latter two are usually off-limits to foreigners. The U.S. Embassy is not able to provide normal consular protection and services in these areas. Visitors are required to register their place of residence with the local police within three days of arrival, to obtain police permission to change residence, and to register within 24 hours of arriving at a new location. Consult the U.S. Embassy in Khartoum on security conditions during your stay.

Travelers by air are advised to purchase round-trip tickets before traveling to Sudan. When leaving the country, arrive at the airport two hours in advance. Unforeseen circumstances, such as sandstorms and electrical outages may cause flight delays. Disruptions of water and electricity are frequent and telecommunication is slow. Because of shortages, travelers should bring adequate supplies of medicine and personal items for their stay.

The possession, sale and consumption of alcohol are strictly forbidden in Sudan. Persons with alcoholic beverages in their possession at the port of entry are subject to immediate arrest. A license to take photographs must be obtained from the Department of Hotels and Tourism. Photographing military areas, bridges, drainage stations, broadcast stations, public utilities and slum areas or beggars is prohibited.

Swaziland

No visa is needed for a visit of up to two months. For longer stays, temporary residence permits are available after arrival in Mbabane. Visitors entering from South Africa must report to Immigration authorities or the police station within 48 hours, unless lodging in a hotel. Tap water is potable in the cities.

Tanzania

Visitors must obtain visas before arrival or they may be denied entry. Travelers with a multiple-entry South African visa in their passports or other evidence of prior or planned travel to South Africa may be detained for many hours, threatened with deportation, denied entry for several days or altogether. Even tourists with new passports have been delayed at Tanzanian immigration because they were suspected of concealing second passports with South African markings.

All foreign currency must be declared upon entering the country. Undeclared currency may be confiscated. Visitors must exchange a minimum of $50 into local currency. Nonresidents must pay hotel bills and game park fees in foreign currency. Banks are the only legal place to exchange money. Private currency transactions and trading on the black market are illegal, and offenders are prosecuted. Tourists should not change more money than they will use because it may be confiscated on departure. Departure tax must be paid in hard currency.

Travel in Tanzania is generally safe. Beware of street crime, especially after dark. Be cautious at public beaches and avoid secluded areas. Consult authorities before traveling to remote regions and obtain updated information on conditions in the country from the U.S. Embassy. U.S. citizens have had problems on a number of occasions when they attracted the suspicion of authorities, violated laws, or entered the country in private aircraft without adequate notice or clearance. Police, immigration officers and prison officials are sensitive to matters that may affect national security, such as travel near the Mozambique border. If you are detained for any reason, ask to talk with a U.S. consular officer.

Visitors have been detained or had their cameras and film confiscated for taking pictures of military installations, hospitals, schools, industries, airports, harbors, railway stations, bridges, government buildings and similar facilities. These structures are often picturesque and not clearly identified as being off-limits for photography. Photography in game parks is unrestricted.

Conservative dress is recommended. Outside of Dar es Salaam, some consumer goods are in short supply.

Togo

No visa is required for a stay of up to three months; however, travel to some remote areas may require a permit.

Uganda

Visas must be obtained before arrival. Visitors must declare all currency and exchange $150 for local currency upon arrival. Travel in Kampala is generally safe. Travelers should have no difficulty at the roadblocks outside of Kampala and Entebbe if they carry their passports with them. The southern and southwestern districts of Uganda are normally safe for travel. Travel to the northern regions of the country should be avoided. Consult the U.S. Embassy for updated information on security conditions in those areas.

Zaire

Credit cards are not widely accepted. To cross the Congo River from Kinshasa to Brazzaville, you must obtain a special permit from the Immigration Department in Zaire and a visa for the country of Congo.

Most intercity roads are difficult to impassable in the rainy season. Certain mining areas are off-limits to foreigners. When driving in cities, keep windows rolled up and doors locked; at roadblocks, open your window only partially and display your passport through the window. Photography of public buildings or installations is strictly forbidden.

Zambia

Visas must be obtained in advance. Foreign currency cannot be obtained locally. If possible, carry "Traveler's cheques" since credit cards are seldom accepted outside of major hotels. Use cameras only in tourist areas or other locations specifically approved by Zambian authorities. Avoid clothing that could be mistaken as military apparel.

Visitors should be cautious when traveling in Zambia. Because several military incidents have occurred in the south, Zambian police and security forces are suspicious of foreigners. Visitors have sometimes been detained for no apparent reason and authorities have been slow in informing embassies of their citizens' detention. If you are detained, ask to talk with a U.S. consular officer.

Major roads are open but police roadblocks are common and vehicles and passengers are searched. Take precautions against crime and avoid travel at night. Also avoid driving off major roads because military restricted zones are often unmarked. In the north, be cautious in the area of the Zambia-Zaire border because of police and military actions aimed at curbing smuggling. Flying directly from Lusaka to the Luangwa Valley game park or its major attraction, Victoria Falls, is safe but travel to the west of the Zambezi River is discouraged.

Zimbabwe

No visa is required. However, you must have both an onward/return ticket and sufficient funds for the stay. Prices are high in Zimbabwe. There are no shortages of food but occasional spot shortages of consumer goods occur. All currency must be declared upon arrival. Failure to declare currency can result in confiscation and a fine. Exchange money only where authorized and save all receipts until departure. Hotel bills must be paid in hard currency.

Due to periodic unsafe security conditions, travelers should avoid certain roads and rail routes in Zimbabwe. Security conditions are particularly uncertain along the Mozambique border. The tourist destinations of Victoria Falls, the Hwange safari area and Matopos National Park have been safe, although some areas of the park have been off-limits for visitors. You should travel to unsettled areas by air. If road travel is unavoidable, stay on the main roads, travel only in daylight and avoid unnecessary stops. Consult with the U.S. Embassy and the local police before setting out. Hitchhiking or off-road travel is strongly discouraged. There are police and military roadblocks throughout the country.

Photography is off-limits in certain regions of the Zambezi Valley where anti-poaching operations are in progress. Zimbabwe authorities are also extremely sensitive about photographing certain buildings, such as government offices, official residences and embassies.

U.S. Embassies And Consulates Abroad

Note: Workweek is Monday-Friday except where noted. Mail to APO and FPO addresses must originate in the United States; the street address must not appear in an APO or FPO address. For addresses in the United States see Visa Information chapter.

Benin

American Embassy
Rue Caporal Anani Bernard
B.P. 2012
Cotonou
☎ (229) 300-650

Botswana

American Embassy
P.O. Box 90 Gaborone
☎ (267) 353-982

Burkino Faso

American Embassy
B.P. 35
Ouagadougou
☎ (226) 306-723

Burundi

American Embassy
Avenue du Zaire, B.P. 1720
Bujumbura
☎ (257) (2) 23454

Cameroon

American Embassy
Rue Nachtigal
B.P. 817
Yaounde
☎ (237) 234-014

Cape Verde

American Embassy
Rua Hojl Ya Yenna 81 C.P. 201 Praia
☎ (238) 614-363, 614-253

Central African Republic

American Embassy
Avenue President Dacko
B.P. 294 Bangui
☎ 610-200, 612-578, 614-333

Chad

American Embassy
Ave. Felix Eboue, B.P. 413
N'Djamena
☎ (235) 516-211, 516-233

Comoros

American Embassy
B.P. 1318
Moroni
☎ 731-203

Congo

American Embassy
Avenue Amilcar Cabral
B.P. 1015, Box C
Brazzaville
☎ 832-070, 832-624

Cote D'Ivoire

American Embassy
5 Rue Jesse Owens 01
B.P. 1712
Abidjan
☎ (225) 320-979

Djibouti

American Embassy
Plateau de Serpent, Blvd. Marechal Joffre
B.P. 185

Djibouti

☎ (253) 353-849, 353-995, 352-916
Workweek: Sunday-Thursday

Equatorial Guinea

American Embassy
Calle de Los Ministros
P.O. Box 597 Malabo
☎ 2406, 2507

Ethiopia

American Embassy
Entoto Street
Addis Ababa
P.O. Box 1014
☎ (251) (01) 551-002

Gabon

American Embassy
Blvd. de la Mer
B.P. 4000 Libreville
☎ (241) 762-003, 743-492

Gambia

American Embassy
Fajara, Kairaba Avenue
P.M.B. No. 19, Banjul Banjul
☎ (220) 92856, 92858, 91970

Ghana

American Embassy
Ring Road East P.O. Box 194
Accra
☎ 775-347

Guinea

American Embassy
2d Blvd. and 9th Avenue, B.P. 603
Conakry
☎ 441-520

Guinea-Bissau

American Embassy
Avenida Domingos Ramos
C.P. 297
Bissau
☎ (245) 212-816

Kenya

American Embassy
Moi/Haile Selassie Avenue
P.O. Box 30137
Nairobi
☎ (254) (2) 334-141

American Consulate

Palli House, Nyerere Avenue
P.O. Box 88079
Mombasa
☎ (254) (11) 315-101

Lesotho

American Embassy
P.O. Box 333, Maseru 100 Maseru
☎ (266) 312-666

Liberia

American Embassy
111 United Nations Drive
P.O. Box 98 Monrovia
☎ (231) 222-991

Madagascar

American Embassy
14 and 16 Rue Rainitovo, Antsahavola B.P.
620
Antananarivo
☎ (261) (2) 21257, 20956, 20089

Malawi

American Embassy
P.O. Box 30016 Lilongwe
☎ (265) 730-166

Mali

American Embassy
Rue Testard and Rue Mohamed V B.P. 34
Bamako
☎ (223) (22) 225-834

Mauritania

American Embassy
B.P. 222 Nouakchott
☎ (222) (2) 52660, 52663

Mauritius

American Embassy
Rogers Bldg. (4th Fl.) John Kennedy Street
Port Louis
☎ 082-347

Mozambique

American Embassy
Avenida Kaunda 193
P.O. Box 783
Maputo
☎ (258) (11) 742-797, 743-167, 744-163

Niger

American Embassy
B.P. 11201 Niamey
☎ (227) 722-661

Nigeria

American Embassy
2 Eleke Crescent, P.O. Box 554
Lagos
☎ (234) (1) 610-097

American Consulate General

2 Maska Rd., P.O. Box 170
Kaduna
☎ (234) (1) 201-070

Rwanda

American Embassy
Blvd. de la Revolution, B.P. 28
Kigali
☎ (205) 75601, 72126

Senegal

American Embassy
Avenue Jean XXIII
B.P. 49 Dakar
☎ (221) 214-296

Seychelles

American Embassy
Box 148
Victoria
☎ (248) 23921

Sierra Leone

American Embassy
Corner Walpole and Siaka Stevens Street
Freetown
☎ 26481

Somalia

American Embassy
Corso Primo Luglio
P.O. Box 574
Mogadishu
☎ (252) (01) 20811
Workweek: Sunday-Thursday

South Africa

American Embassy
Thibault House, 225 Pretorius Street
Pretoria
☎ (27) (12) 284-266

American Consulate General

Broadway Industries Center Heerengracht
Foreshore
Cape Town
☎ (27) (21) 214-280, 214-287

American Consulate General

Durban Bay House
29th Fl. 333 Smith Street
Durban 4001
☎ (27) (31) 304-4737

American Consulate General

Kine Center
11th Fl., Commissioner and Krulis Streets
P.O. Box 2155
Johannesburg
☎ (27) (11) 331-1681

Sudan

American Embassy
Sharia Ali Abdul Latif
P.O. Box 699 Khartoum
☎ 74700, 75680, 74611
Workweek: Sunday-Thursday

Swaziland

American Embassy
Central Bank Bldg., Warner Street
P.O. Box 199
Mbabane
☎ (268) 22281

Tanzania

American Embassy
36 Laibon Rd. (off Bagamoyo Rd.)
P.O. Box 9123
Dar Es Salaam
☎ (255) (51) 37501

Togo

American Embassy
Rue Pelletier Caventou & Rue Vauban
B.P. 852
Lome
☎ (228) (21) 212-991, 213-609

Uganda

American Embassy
Parliament Avenue, P.O. Box 7007
Kampala
☎ (256) (41) 259-791, 259-795

Zaire

American Embassy
310 Avenue des Aviateurs
Kinshasa
☎ *(243) (12) 25881*

American Consulate General

1029 Blvd. Kamanyola, B.P. 1196
Lubumbashi
☎ *(243) 222-324*

Zambia

American Embassy
Corner of Independence and United
Nations Avenue
P.O. Box 31617
Lusaka
☎ *(260) (1) 214-911*

Zimbabwe

American Embassy
172 Rhodes Avenue
P.O. Box 3340
Harare
☎ *(263) (4) 794-521*

South Asia

Getting In and Out

Visa and other Entry Requirements

A U.S. passport is required for travel to all countries in the region. India, Pakistan and most other South Asian countries also require entry visas. Travel to certain areas of many South Asian countries is restricted and special permits may be required for these areas in addition to the entry visa. Prospective travelers should contact the embassy or consulate of the country they plan to visit for specific information. All South Asian countries require travelers who have been in yellow-fever infected areas within the last six days to show valid yellow-fever immunization certificates. Yellow fever is found in some African and some Latin American countries. If you plan to travel from Africa or Latin America directly to South Asia, check with the embassy of the South Asian country where you are going to see if your itinerary makes the yellow-fever certificate required. If the certificate is required and you do not have it, you will be refused entry unless you are inoculated and kept in quarantine for up to six days.

Money Hassles

Most South Asian countries require that foreign currency and valuables be declared upon entry as a means of enforcing restrictions on the importation of items such as gold, electronic equipment, firearms and prescription drugs. Failure to make an accurate declaration or other violations of these restrictions can lead to high fines and/or imprisonment.

Dangerous Things

Shopping for Antiques

Most South Asian countries have strict regulations against the unlicensed export of antiquities. Items that are antique, or even appear to be, may be confiscated by customs officials unless the traveler has proof of authorization from the appropriate government office to export the antique, or proof that the item is not an antique.

U.S. Wildlife Regulations

The United States prohibits importation of Asian ivory because Asian elephants are an endangered species. Most lizardskin and many snakeskin products cannot be brought into the United States. The penalty for importing products derived from endangered species is seizure of the product and a substantial fine.

Getting Sick

In the United States, local health departments, the U.S. Public Health Service, private doctors and travel clinics can provide information on health precautions for travelers to South Asia. Depending on your destination, immunization is recommended against cholera, diptheria/tetanus, hepatitis, Japanese B encephalitis, meningitis, polio and typhoid. Drug prophylaxis against malaria may also be necessary. General guidance may be found in the U.S. Public Health Service booklet, *Health Information for International Travel*, which is available for $4.25 from the U.S. Government Printing Office, Washington, DC 20402, or from local and state health departments.

Travelers should be careful to drink only boiled water (or bottled drinks), to avoid ice cubes in beverages and unpeeled fruits and vegetables, to take precautions against mosquitos and to guard against overexertion at high altitudes. Trekkers and mountain climbers, in particular, should take precautions to avoid frostbite, hypothermia and altitude sickness. The latter two can be fatal if not detected in time. Modern health facilities are not always available, particularly in rural areas. Prospective travelers should review their health insurance policies to see if they provide coverage while overseas, including medical evacuation service.

Further Information on Specific Countries

Afghanistan

All of Afghanistan is effectively a "war zone" in view of the continuing conflict between various Afghan factions. All American citizens are urged to avoid travel to Afghanistan. The U.S. Embassy can provide only limited assistance to American citizens in distress in the capital city of Kabul and no assistance outside the Kabul city limits.

Bangladesh

Bangladesh is an Islamic country, and visitors should dress modestly—shorts are considered inappropriate. No visa is required for a tourist stay of up to two weeks if you have an onward ticket; all business travelers must have visas, however. Travelers should pay special attention to preventive health measures because medical facilities, especially in rural areas, are not always available. River ferries are necessary for travel throughout much of Bangladesh, but travelers should exercise caution when using them, bearing in mind that accidents frequently occur from overcrowding and from hazardous navigation during poor weather. Trekkers may not go to the Chittagong Hill Tracts, which are off-limits to foreigners.

Kingdom of Bhutan

While Bhutan and the United States do not have formal diplomatic relations, informal contact is maintained through the U.S. Embassy in New Delhi. Tourism to Bhutan is restricted; tourists are admitted only in groups by prearrangement with the Ministry of Tourism in Thimphu. Entry must be via India. For information contact the Bhutan Travel Service, *120 East 56 Street, New York, NY 10022 (☎ 212-838-6382).*

India

India is the South Asian country most frequently visited by U.S. citizens. Visas must be obtained before arrival. Persons arriving without visas must leave on the next plane. If you plan to travel from India to Nepal or another country and return to India, be sure to request a multiple entry visa. Tourist visas are issued for a maximum of 90 days. Once in India, visitors who wish to extend their stay must apply to a Foreigners Regional Registration Office. Extensions, if granted, may not bring the total visit to more than six months. Customs regulations prohibiting the importation of gold or Indian currency, and regulating importation of electronics, foreign currency and firearms are strictly enforced. Offenders of these regulations may be jailed, fined and/or charged duty at rates exceeding 300 percent of the item's value. Laws against drug smuggling carry heavy penalties, including a ten-year prison term. Due to the threat of political or ethnic violence, security conditions pose some danger in the State of Punjab and in several other areas. Whether dangerous or not, many areas of India have been declared off- limits to foreigners by the Indian authorities. Permits are required for: Punjab, Sikkim, all of India east of West Bengal, all island territories and parts of the states of Himachal Pradesh, Jammu and Kashmir, Uttar Pradesh and West Bengal. Persons of Indian origin can usually obtain permits to visit relatives in restricted areas. Other visitors may have to wait a long time for a permit or be unable to obtain one. Consult the latest Department of State travel advisory on which areas are restricted. Once in India, consult the nearest U.S. embassy or consulate for information on restricted areas and advice on obtaining permits to visit them. With the exception of the Golden Temple in the Punjab, none of the popular tourist sites in India are in restricted areas.

Republic of Maldives

The islands of the Maldives have long been popular vacation sites. Diplomatic relations are maintained and consular services are provided through the U.S. Embassy in Colombo, Sri Lanka. In emergency situations there is a U.S. consular agent on the capital island of Male (for address, ask at a resort or hotel) who can help travelers communicate with the U.S. Embassy in Colombo. A no-fee visa for a tourist visit of up to 30 days is issued upon arrival at the airport. Foreign currency may be taken in or out without restriction. Pork foodstuffs and alcohol may not be imported.

PHILIPPINES

ism

Crime

Civil Unrest

PAPUA NEW GUINEA

AUSTRALIA

Nepal

Tourism to Nepal is increasing; over 20,000 Americans visit Nepal each year. A visa valid for one week can be obtained upon arrival at the Kathmandu airport or at any authorized border-crossing point. It can be renewed for an additional three weeks at the nearest immigration office. After that, tourists may renew their month-long visa two consecutive times, allowing a total three-month visit. Departure from Nepal is mandatory at the end of a three month tourist visit. Travelers can avoid initial immigration-processing delays by obtaining a 30-day visa prior to arrival in Nepal. Nepalese customs laws, particularly those forbidding smuggling of drugs, gold and foreign currency, are strictly enforced. The penalty for smuggling is a stiff fine and/or a prison sentence. Travelers should take adequate funds in the form of "Traveler's cheques." It is difficult to obtain additional funds through bank transfers and, except at major Kathmandu hotels, credit cards are rarely accepted. Trekking is very popular in Nepal. Tourists are cautioned to obtain a trekking permit from the Central Immigration Office, to avoid trekking alone, to be alert for signs of altitude sickness and to obtain a meningococcal meningitis vaccination if trekking outside the Kathmandu Valley. Those wishing to climb the high peaks should write for permission to the Ministry of Tourism to the attention of the Mountaineering division, well in advance of planned expeditions. Travelers should note that there are no forms of international communication in rural areas. In the event of an emergency, the U.S. Embassy may assist Americans in contacting family or friends. Americans planning to travel from Nepal to Tibet should be aware that Chinese authorities strictly regulate such trips. Additional information is contained in the State Department's travel advisory on China and in "Tips for Travelers to the People's Republic of China."

Pakistan

A visa must be obtained before arrival. Pakistan is an Islamic country and visitors must respect Islamic standards of behavior. Travelers (especially women) should dress modestly, i.e., wear clothes with high necks and long sleeves; do not wear shorts. The import, manufacture and consumption of alcohol or drugs are strictly forbidden. Major hotels have special rooms where non-Islamic foreigners may buy and drink alcoholic beverages. A special permit is required for travel to the tribal areas bordering Afghanistan, including the Khyber Pass and to transit the tribal area of Darra Adam Khel. Persons traveling to restricted areas without a permit are subject to arrest. Onward overland travel to India is difficult because of border crossing restrictions. Major cities in Pakistan are safe for tourists, but travel to remote rural areas, especially in Baluchistan, Sind and the Northwest Frontier Province is not recommended. Security conditions vary; some unsafe areas are considered safe for daytime travel in groups. Because the security situation can change with little warning, visitors should check at the nearest U.S. embassy or consulate for up-to-date travel information.

Sri Lanka

The insurgency of Tamil separatists against the government in Sri Lanka (formerly Ceylon) has caused tension and violence within the country. For this reason, Americans should avoid all travel to the northern and eastern provinces. This includes the cities of Jaffna, *Batticaloa* and Trincomalee. There have been isolated incidents of violence in other parts of Sri Lanka, including Colombo. Because public transportation has often been targeted by terrorists, travel on trains and public buses should be avoided. Travel to the major tourist sites in the southern and western parts of the island has usually been safe. However, security conditions throughout the country can change quickly and travelers should get current information from the latest travel advisory or from the U.S. Embassy in Colombo. No visa is required for a tourist stay of up to 30 days.

U.S. Foreign Service Posts

For addresses in the United States see Visa Information chapter.

Afghanistan

U.S. Embassy
Wazir Akbar Khan Mina
Kabul
☎ 62230/35 or 62436
Workweek: Saturday-Wednesday Currently
closed

Bangladesh

U.S. Embassy
Adamjee Court Bldg. (5th Fl.)
Motijheel Commercial Area
GPO Box 323, Ramna
Dhaka
☎ (880) (2) 235093/9 and 235081/9
Telex: 642319 AEDKA BJ
Workweek: Sunday-Thursday

People's Republic of China (Tibet)

U.S. Consulate General
Jinjiang Hotel, 180 Renmin Road
Chengdu, Sichuan
☎ (86) (1) 24481
Telex: ACGCH CN 60128

India

New Delhi
U.S. Embassy
Shanti Path
Chanakyapuri 110021
☎ (91) (11) 600651
Telex: 031-65269

Bombay

U.S. Consulate General
Lincoln House
78 Bhulabhai Desai Rd. 400026
☎ (91) (22) 8223611/8
Telex: 011-75425

Calcutta

U.S. Consulate General
5/1 Ho Chi Minh
Sarani 700071
☎ (91) (33) 44-3611/6
Telex: 021-2483

Madras

U.S. Consulate General
Mount Rd. 600006
☎ (91) (44) 473040 or 477542

Maldives: (See Sri Lanka)

Nepal

U.S. Embassy
Pani Pokhari
Kathmandu
☎ (977) 411179, 412718, or 411601
Telex: NP 2381 AEKTM

Pakistan

Islamabad
U.S. Embassy
Diplomatic Enclave
Ramna 5
☎ (92) (51) 826161/79 Telex: 825-864
Workweek Sunday-Thursday

Karachi

U.S. Consulate General
8 Abdullah Haroon Road
☎ (009) (221) 515081 Telex: 822-611

Lahore

U.S. Consulate General
50 Zafar Ali Road
Gulberg 5
☎ (92) (42) 870221/5

Peshawar

U.S. Consulate
11 Hospital Road
☎ (92) (521) 79801/3 Telex: 52-364

Sri Lanka

U. S. Embassy
210 Galle Rd. (P.O. Box 106)
Colombo 3
☎ (94) (1) 548007 Telex: 21305

The Caribbean

Six million Americans visit the Caribbean islands every year. The number one cause of accidental death for visitors in the islands is drowning and the most common ailment is sunburn.

Getting In

Every island in the Caribbean has entry requirements. Most countries allow you to visit for up to two or three months if you show proof of citizenship and a return or onward ticket. Some countries, such as Trinidad and Tobago, require that you have a valid passport. Haiti requires children under 18 to have a valid passport. If you are arriving from an area infected with yellow fever, many Caribbean countries require you to have a certificate of vaccination against yellow fever. Some countries have an airport departure tax of up to $25. For authoritative information about a country's entry and exit requirements and its customs and currency regulations, contact its embassy, consulate or tourist office in the United States.

Getting Out

Caution! Make certain that you can return to the United States with the proof of citizenship that you take with you. Although some Caribbean countries may allow you to enter with only a voter's registration card or a birth certificate to indicate citizenship, U.S. Immigration requires that you document both your U.S. citizenship and identity when you reenter the United States. The best document to prove your U.S. citizenship is a valid U.S. passport. Other documents of U.S. citizenship include an expired U.S. passport, a certified copy of your birth certificate, a Certificate of Naturalization, a Certificate of Citizenship or a Report of Birth Abroad of a Citizen of the United States. To prove your identity, either a valid driver's license or a government identification card that includes a photo or a physical description is acceptable. The loss or theft of a U.S. passport overseas should be reported to the local police and the nearest U.S. embassy or consulate. A lost or stolen birth certificate or driver's license cannot be replaced outside of the United States. There are several countries, most notably Barbados, the Dominican Republic, Grenada and Jamaica, where airlines have refused to board American citizens with insufficient proof of U.S. citizenship. The resulting delays can be inconvenient as well as expensive.

Bringing Your Own Boat Or Plane

If you plan to arrive in the Caribbean in your own boat or plane, contact the embassy, consulate or tourist office of each country you plan to visit to learn what is required for entry and exit. Besides title of ownership, most ports of entry will require proof of insurance coverage for the country you are entering. Some countries require a temporary import permit for your boat or plane. Authorities in the Caribbean are familiar with U.S. regulations for documentation of air and sea craft. They will detain improperly documented craft that enter their territory. In some countries, authorities will confiscate firearms found on a boat or plane unless the owner or master can show proof that U.S. licensing and export procedures have been followed. In addition, some countries impose stiff prison terms for the importation of illegal firearms.

Customs, Firearms and Currency Regulations

Customs formalities are generally simple in the Caribbean. As a rule, one carton of cigarettes and one quart of liquor are permitted duty free into the islands. Most countries tax additional quantities at a high rate. In general, tourists are permitted to enter with other commodities required for personal use. If you wish to bring firearms into any country, inquire at the country's embassy or consulate about the permit required. As noted above, some countries in the Caribbean impose a stiff prison term for importing illegal firearms. Currency regulations vary. Inquire about them when you check on entry requirements. In some countries, you must declare all currency and are not allowed to take out more money than you brought in. Other countries limit the amount of their own currency that can be brought in or taken out. There may be extra fees and taxes that are overlooked in the tourist literature. Examples are hotel taxes, obligatory restaurant gratuities and airport departure taxes. When you convert your money to local currency, retain receipts. You will need to show them if you wish to reconvert money upon departure. It is usually advantageous to reconvert local currency before departure. Although U.S. currency is used along with local currency in some places, such as the Bahamas and Haiti, there may be an advantage to using local currency.

Getting Sick

Information on health precautions for travelers can be obtained from local health departments, private doctors, travel clinics or the Center for Disease Control's 24-hour hotline ☎ *(404) 332-4559*. Immunizations are recommended against diphtheria, hepatitis A, polio and tetanus. Typhoid immunization is also recommended if you go to remote areas of Haiti or Jamaica. Polio is endemic in Haiti and in the Dominican Republic. Malaria is prevalent in Haiti and in the rural, non-tourist areas of the Dominican Republic that border Haiti. If you are going to a malaria area, take a weekly dose of chloroquine, beginning two weeks before your trip. In addition, take precautions to avoid being bitten by mosquitoes because malaria can break through any preventative drug.

Review your health insurance policy to see if it covers you while out of the country. U.S. medical insurance is often not valid outside the United States. Social Security Medicare does not provide payment for medical services obtained outside the U.S. In addition to medical insurance, consider obtaining insurance to cover evacuation in the event of an accident or serious illness. Air evacuation to the United States can easily cost $15,000 if you are not insured. There are short-term health and emergency assistance policies designed for travelers. If you need medical attention during your trip, your hotel may be able to recommend the nearest clinic, hospital or doctor, or you can obtain a list of local medical services from the nearest U.S. embassy or consulate. In a medical emergency, a U.S. consul can help you locate medical treatment. Where the quality of drinking water is questionable, bottled water is recommended. Travelers to remote areas should boil or chemically treat drinking water.

Dangerous Things

Crime

Petty crime is common in large cities where there are many tourists. Thievery, purse snatching and pick-pocketing are also prevalent at some beaches. Inquire at your hotel about areas where these crimes are most common. There has also been an increase in violent crimes such as rape and assault against tourists. In some places, U.S. passports and identity documents are especially attractive to thieves. Robbery of yachts is a problem in some marinas. If you follow the these precautions you minimize, but do not eliminate, risk:

• Leave expensive jewelry, unnecessary credit cards and anything you would hate to lose at home.

• Use a concealed money pouch or belt for passports, cash and other valuables.

• To facilitate replacing a lost or stolen passport, carry two extra passport photos and a photocopy of your passport information page and other identity documents with you in a separate place from the original items.

• Do not take valuables to the beach. When possible, use the hotel safe when you go to the beach or to town.

• When you enter a marina, register with the local government authorities.

Water Safety

Make certain that sports equipment, including scuba equipment, that you rent or buy meets international safety standards. If you use a pool or beach without a lifeguard, exercise extreme caution. The surf on the Atlantic side of an island can be rough; the Caribbean side is usually calmer.

Do not dive into unknown bodies of water. Hidden rocks or shallow depths can cause serious injury or death. In some places, you may need to wear sneakers in the water for protection against punctures, cuts or lacerations from sea urchins, broken bottles, metal scrap and coral.

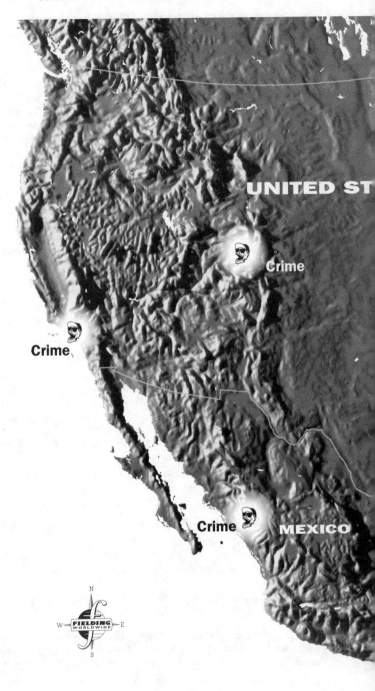

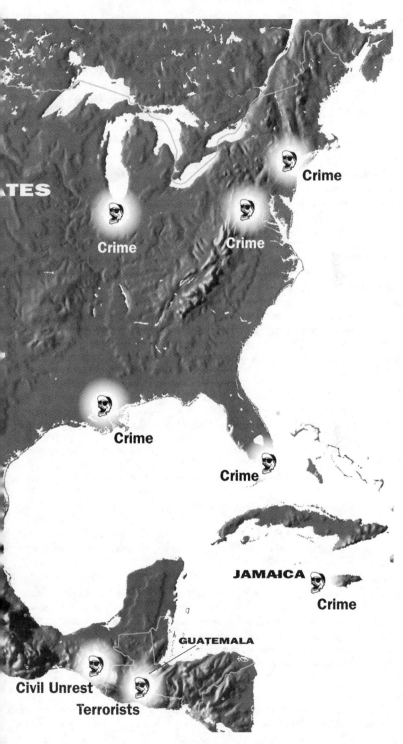

Drug Offenses

Most countries in the Caribbean have strict laws against the use, possession or sale of narcotics. Foreigners arrested for possession of even small amounts of marijuana, cocaine or other illegal drugs are often charged and tried as international traffickers. The penalty for carrying narcotics into or out of the country can be 20 years imprisonment. There are usually expensive fines as well. In some places, there is no bail and there are long judicial delays where you can spend more than two years awaiting trial. Conditions in most Caribbean prisons do not meet even minimum U.S. standards. If you carry prescription drugs, keep them in their original container, clearly labeled with the doctor's name, pharmacy and contents. Keep in mind that some drug sales by locals are set-ups designed to entrap visitors and may be run by the local police to extract high fines and bribes. Do not purchase, transport or use drugs.

Driving In The Caribbean

If you plan to rent a car, be aware that most jurisdictions of the Caribbean drive on the left. The only places where you drive on the right are Aruba, Cuba, Dominican Republic, Guadaloupe, Haiti, Martinique and the Netherlands Antilles. In the other places, if you are not used to driving on the left, proceed slowly and with utmost caution. You may wish to ride as a passenger for a while before trying to drive yourself. Driving conditions and local driving patterns are different from the U.S. Many roads are narrow or winding, signs may not be in English and in some places, domestic animals roam freely. Defensive driving is a must.

Shopping: Avoid Wildlife Products

Beware of purchasing a live animal or plant or an item made from one. Many such items are prohibited from international traffic. You risk confiscation and a possible fine by U.S. Customs if you attempt to import certain wildlife or wildlife products. In particular, watch out for and avoid:

- All products made from sea turtles, including turtle leather boots, tortoise-shell jewelry and sea turtle oil cosmetics.
- Fur from spotted cats.
- Feathers and feather products from wild birds.
- Birds, stuffed or alive, such as parrots or parakeets.
- Crocodile and leather.
- Black coral and most other coral, whether in chunks or in jewelry.

Further Information on Specific Countries

Bahamas

Criminal penalties are severe for possession of or trafficking in drugs in the Bahamas. The Bahamian court system has a heavy volume of pending cases and U.S. citizens arrested for drugs or other offenses are often held in prison for months while awaiting trial. In the Bahamas, be sure to budget for a hotel room tax, an energy surtax, a 15 percent obligatory gratuity in restaurants and a departure tax of up to $15.

Cayman Islands

Persons wearing their hair in dreadlocks have occasionally been refused entry to the Cayman Islands. Cayman authorities say they may "refuse entry to any person whose mode of dress or behavior, or unkempt appearance, may cause offense to the Caymanian community." The authorities emphasize that "this policy does not automatically exclude from entry persons wearing their hair in any particular manner. However, if such persons are also unkempt and slovenly in their attire and behavior, it is possible they could then be refused entry."

Cuba

Financial Restrictions

The Cuban Assets Control Regulations of the U.S. Department of the Treasury require that transactions incident to the travel to and within Cuba of U.S. citizens or residents be licensed.

A general license needs no application. Transactions under a general license are authorized only for the following categories of travelers:

• U.S. and foreign government officials, including representatives of international organizations of which the U.S. is a member, traveling on official business

• persons gathering news or making news or documentary films

• persons visiting close relatives who reside in Cuba

• full-time professionals engaging in full-time research in their professional areas, where the research is specifically related to Cuba, is largely academic in nature and there is substantial likelihood the product of research will be disseminated. U.S. persons whose transactions are not authorized by general or specific license may not buy goods (a meal at a hotel or restaurant, for example) or services (an airline ticket or hotel room) related to Cuban travel.

WARNING

Transactions relating to travel to Cuba for tourism or business purposes are not authorized by a general license, nor would they be authorized in response to an application for a specific license. This restriction includes transactions related to tourist and business travel from or through a third country such as Canada or Mexico. Under U.S. Treasury regulations, authorized travelers may spend no more than $100 per day for living expenses in Cuba and, except for informational materials which are not limited, may bring back to the U.S. no more than $100 total worth of Cuban goods. Failure to comply with U.S. Treasury regulations could result in prosecution upon return to the United States.

Dual Nationals

For all practical purposes, the government of Cuba considers Cuban-born U.S. citizens to be solely Cuban citizens. The Cuban government does not recognize the right or obligation of the U.S. government to protect dual U.S.-Cuban citizens. Cuban authorities have consistently denied U.S. consular officers the right to visit incarcerated dual nationals and to ascertain their welfare and proper treatment under Cuban law. Dual U.S.-Cuban nationals may be subject to a range of restrictions and obligations, including military service.

Other Information for Authorized Visitors

Street crime, including purse snatching, is a growing problem in Havana. Authorized visitors should exercise caution and keep a close eye on personal belongings while in tourist areas. Credit cards issued by U.S. financial institutions are not valid in Cuba. Hotels will not accept American Express and other U.S. "Traveler's cheques" regardless of where they are issued.

U.S. Interests Section

U.S. travelers in Cuba should register in person, in writing or by telephone during business hours at the U.S. Interests Section which is part of the Embassy of Switzerland.

Dominican Republic

Drug laws are severe and strictly enforced in the Dominican Republic. Penalties for possession of less than 20 grams of marijuana or 20 milligrams of cocaine range from six months to two years imprisonment, plus fines. For quantities of narcotic substances that meet the definition of trafficker, the penalty is a five to 20-year prison term, plus fines. No more than $5000 may be taken from the Dominican Republic upon departure. The peso is the only legal currency in the Dominican Republic, and it should be purchased only at authorized hotels and banks. In crackdowns on black market activity, U.S. tourists have sometimes been arrested for even minor illegal currency transactions. The Dominican Republic is among the places where U.S. passports and other identity documents are frequently stolen. There may be restrictions on minor children being allowed to leave the Dominican Republic without their parent(s). A child without a U.S. passport may be particularly vulnerable to being denied permission to travel alone or with only one parent. If this applies to you, check with the Embassy of the Dominican Republic about their requirements for the travel of unaccompanied children.

Haiti

Visitors to Haiti should exercise caution. Although at the time of publication there does not appear to be a specific threat to American citizens, the potential exists for civil disturbances and isolated serious criminal acts. Avoid crowds and areas of unrest. Although U.S. dollars can be used as currency in Haiti, it is usually to the traveler's advantage to use Haitian dollars. Haiti's $25 airport departure tax must be paid in cash in U.S. currency. It cannot be paid as part of the airline ticket.

Jamaica

Crime is a serious problem in and around Kingston, Jamaica's capital. Visitors should exercise prudence, not walk around at night and should use licensed taxis or hotel recommended transportation. In the north coast tourist areas, care should be taken at isolated villas and small establishments.

Trinidad and Tobago

Drug laws are severe and strictly enforced in Trinidad and Tobago. Possession of even small amounts of narcotics can result in lengthy jail sentences and expensive fines. The penalty for carrying narcotics into or out of the country is five to 15 years with no possibility of parole.

U.S. Embassies and Consulates Abroad

Note that the Bahamas, Cuba, Haiti and Jamaica are on Eastern Time. All other areas are one hour ahead. For addresses in the United States see Visa Information chapter.

Bahamas

U.S. Embassy
Mosmar Bldg. Queen Street
Nassau, Bahamas
☎ (809) 322-1181

Barbados

U.S. Embassy
Canadian Imperial Bank of Commerce
Building
Broad Street
Bridgetown, Barbados
☎ (809) 436-4950

Bermuda

U.S. Consulate General
Crown Hill 16 Middle Road
Devonshire, Hamilton HMBX, Bermuda
☎ (809) 295-1342

Cuba Swiss Embassy

(USINT) Calzada between L and M Vedado
Havana, Cuba
☎ 33-3551/9

Dominican Republic

U.S. Embassy
Calle Cesar Nicolas Penson & Calle
Leopoldo Navarro
Santo Domingo
Dominican Republic
☎ (809) 541-2171

Grenada

U.S. Embassy Point Salines
St. George's, Grenada
☎ (809) 444-1173/8

Haiti

U.S. Embassy
Harry Truman Boulevard
Port-au-Prince, Haiti
☎ (509) 22-0354, 22-0368

Jamaica

U.S. Embassy
Jamaica Mutual Life Center
2 Oxford Road, 3rd Floor
Kingston, Jamaica
☎ (809) 929-4850/9

Netherlands Antilles*

U.S. Consulate General
St. Anna Boulevard 19
Curacao, Netherlands Antilles
☎ (599-9) 61-3066

Trinidad and Tobago

U.S. Embassy
15 Queen's Park West
Port of Spain , Trinidad and Tobago
☎ (809) 622-6371 or 6176 *

DANGEROUS PLACES

We Mean Really Dangerous

Sometimes, the best way to describe our world is in the clipped, opinionated tone of a bar stool, poli-sci dropout. You could rattle off dangerous places until your chin has sunk into your beer and pretzels in total despondence. There are always reruns of "The Waltons" to cheer you up. But as of June 1, 1995 here is a short, wildly opinionated list of the world's most dangerous places:

Afghanistan Civil War between fundamentalists and ex-CIA hacks. Doesn't seem to matter who wins in the end.

Algeria Muslim fundamentalists are mad because they were cheated out of a 1992 election victory. They take it out on Westerners.

Angola A civil war between pouting egos that kills about 100,000 people a year; and to think we backed one of these wackos as a freedom fighter.

Argentina Feuding with Chile over the Beagle Channel and with Paraguay over their northeastern border. They agree that the Pilcomayo river is the boundary but the darn river keeps changing course.

Armenia The Armenians want it all and they want it now (see Azerbaijan).

Azerbaijan Squabbling with Armenia about a little 'ole chunk of land (about 20 percent of their country) that used to be theirs (see Armenia).

Bangladesh The home of Shanti Bahini, Chakma and 200,000 Royhinga refugees. Where's George Harrison when you need him? These folks are very nervous about tidal waves because they don't surf.

Bolivia Coca, Tupac (not Shakur) Katari and grinding poverty.

Bosnia-Herzegovina War in Europe. Nobody seems to care. The war to end all wars or start all wars?

Bougainville Fuzzy-haired rebels with rusty shotguns fighting for a fly-speck-size island.

Burundi Rwanda, the sequel. Same story, different location, stay tuned.

Cambodia	Land of the Khmer Rouge who don't like progress or the West despite the U.N. playing globocop.
Colombia	The nastiest place in the Western Hemisphere: drugs, terrorism and great beaches.
China	Human rights, sweat shops, occupation of Tibet, the border with Bhutan and oppression of the Muslims in the northwest. Big place, big problems, still under a firm communist grip. But dirt cheap labor ensures that Americans can get their free "Made in China" toys in their next Happy Meal.
Corsica	Swarthy men who want to have their own country of swarthy men. Unfortunately the Legion likes Corsica (its base) and killing insurgents (their job).
Cyprus	Turks versus Greeks separated by a thin blue line. The oldest U.N. mission that keeps on going and going and going...
Djibouti	The hottest, lowest place in Africa doesn't seem like it would be worth fighting over, but the Afars and the French Foreign Legion don't agree.
Ecuador	They lost a tiny sliver of land near Tiwinza to Peru in 1941 and they want it back. So its time to rumble in the jungle with tear gas, flamethrowers and artillery.
El Salvador	You thought this was over after watching the movie *Salvador*. Same place, same problem, but it never went away. Death squads and left wing insurgents seem to be a permanent fixture here.
Egypt	"Hey, send more tourists so we can take pot shots at 'em," say the fundamentalists.
Germany	Skinheads are blaming all the Middle East immigrants for their joblessness: Could it be the swastikas tattooed on their heads?
Georgia	Besieged by Armenians, Azeris, Abkazanians, South Ossetians and more. If you have a solution drop them a note.
Guatemala	With a name like URNG you'd be mad too. Indians versus the rich folks. Political killings save money on campaign donations. Belize doesn't exist on local maps. Maybe they'll want that too.
Haiti	Decades of brutal dictatorship and corruption fixed with a wave of Clinton's or rather Jimmy's hand and an old-fashioned imperialist invasion. Uh huh.
India	Seven revolts, more religions, manufacturing more people daily than China in half the space.
Indonesia	Half of East Timor used to be a Portuguese colony. Indonesia wants it to be theirs but they didn't bother asking the locals what they thought. Aceh, Irian Jaya are not happy either.
Iran	The big bad wolf for our times. Fundamentalism is the "in-thing," whether other countries like it or not. Baluchis and Kurds are not happy. Not getting along with Iraq either.

Iraq	A punch-drunk dictator who doesn't know when to retire and write his memoirs. A starving impoverished country that picks fights with the wrong people (U.S., Iran, Kuwait, Kurds, Shiites).
Israel	An occupying force that doesn't get along with the former landlords. Peace is at hand but the war is not over. Plenty of sworn enemies to keep them busy (Hamas, Hezbollah, et. al.).
Kenya	The northern border is a nasty place thanks to Somali gangs. The nomadic Masaii and agrarian Kikuyu can't get along. Lots of crime, poverty, conflict but it doesn't stop the tourists.
Laos	Too poor to really have a good knock down. Warlords still have Chao Fah rebels and a running feud with Thailand over the border.
Lebanon	Northern Lebanon welcomes tourists, southern Lebanon rockets Israel. Southern Lebanon is the nastiest place in the middle east. Home of Hezbollah.
Liberia	Dumb war, vicious leaders, no future. You need a program to follow the bit players.
Malaysia	Clean modern place surrounded by vicious seaborne pirates.
Mali	The Tuaregs are not happy. Don't go out on your camel after dark.
Mexico	Nasty place teetering between the third and first world. The Zapatistas are not happy with NAFTA. Drugs create a nasty subculture; corruption and violence are not too far beneath the surface.
Morocco	Polisario still conduct sand wars.
Mozambique	More land mines than people. All sold out of "watch your step" signs. RENAMO still exists.
Myanmar	There are eleven different uprisings, from egotistical drug lords to oppressed tribal minorities. More generals than a GMC truck dealer.
Niger	The Tuaregs are mad as hell and they aren't going to take it any more.
Northern Ireland	Keep your fingers crossed and kiss your four leaf clover.
Pakistan	Fierce mountain tribes continue to fight. So what's new?
Philippines	Communists and Muslims are fighting on the flyspeck southern islands. But for what?
Peru	The Shining Path and Tupac Amaru have lost some of their influence but none of their nastiness.
Russia	Discos, limousines, gangsters ... where is Francis Ford Coppola?
Rwanda	There is nobody left to kill anybody. They will need about 10 years to build it back to the same level of hatred so they can kill each other all over again. Will the Hutus ever get along with the Tutsis? Not likely.
Sardinia	Swarthy gangsters import drugs, kill people, make money. Sounds like Sicily or Russia.

Sierra Leone   A civil war between the ruling dictator and Revolutionary Front. The conflict in neighboring Liberia spilling over and lousy economic conditions make for a lousy vacation destination. These people are fighting over bauxite?

Somalia   Warlord central; can't keep up the political or Nielsen ratings so we are out of there. Starving people don't look so bad if they aren't on TV all the time. Greed and hatred reign.

Spain   The Basques want to be free. Free to do what?

Sri Lanka   Suicide bombers, LTTE, foreign volunteers. Screwing up one of he world's most beautiful places.

Sudan   A 20-year war with the southern animist/Christians where even aid workers are fair game for kidnapping and extortion.

Suriname   Rebels in the jungle, crime, corruption. Business as usual in the south Caribbean.

South Africa   Not everybody is happy with the new status quo: right wings, Neo-Nazis, workers in concentration camps and more: 87 rapes, 50 murders a day, great surfing and game viewing too.

Tajikistan   What are those crazy Russians up to? The muslim Tajiks don't like Russians but they don't mind using Russian weapons against them.

Turkey   The Kurds want their own country; Turkey says quit whining. The PKK like to kill people, blow things up and shoot school teachers. A full scale war in Eastern Turkey: 22,000 dead and 179 billion spent in 10 years of war. Come visit our sunny land. (The west part at least.)

Uganda   It is safe now, isn't it? Well, maybe after refugees from Rwanda, Burundi and Lord's Resistance group stop killing each other and go home.

United States   Florida still scares foreign tourists and our inner cities make south Lebanon look like a Mormon suburb.

Western Sahara/ Morocco   Imagine people fighting over sand? No, this isn't Coney Island on a long weekend. The Polisario Front, backed by Algeria wants their own sand box.

Yemen   Outside meddling by Iran caused a messy civil war. Will things calm down? Probably not. Then they start drawing lines in the sand with Saudi Arabi. Kids, there's plenty of room in this sand box.

Zaire   Dirty, nasty, corrupt, violent, but other than that not bad. Central African hellhole.

Well that's it for our barroom recap of the world's nasty places. What follows is a more in-depth view of some of these less than healthy destinations.

Afghanistan
★★★

The Rockets' Red Glare

Maybe people can get to sleep in Kabul now. The dawn was usually heralded by Hekmatyar's rockets. They swept through the sky in shallow arcs, crumbling buildings and snuffing out lives at random. Daylight was dangerous; it's when fighter aircraft made their bombing and strafing runs throughout the downtown area.

Now Hekmatyar has fled, his headquarters at Charasyab overrun by the *taliban*, a group led by militant Islamic students who originally fled Afghanistan to Pakistan to escape the war. On March 18, 1995, Rabbani, the current president, then flushed the taliban out.

If wars could be weighed on a scale of depression and misery, the ones that have ravaged Afghanistan would tip the scales. Once united by a common enemy, the Afghans fought against the Russians in what was the hardest and fiercest war of the Soviet empire.

Modern Afghan misery began in 1978, when Noor Taraki attempted to import communism into Afghanistan with the aid of the Soviet Union. His successor, Babrak Kar-

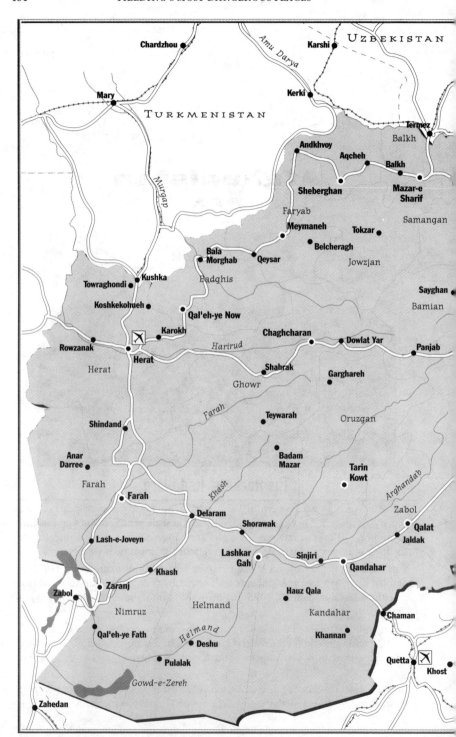

mal, asked Moscow for troops, and the war was whistled into play. Marxism was met with mortars and machine guns—and the primitive flintlock rifles of the mujahedin, or "Holy Warriors."

Eighty-five thousand Soviet soldiers invaded Afghanistan. Their pretext was that the puppet ruler, Karmal, needed help.The official demand for this intervention was sent from Kabul and signed by Karmal, who could not have been in the Afghan capital at the time because he was riding into Kabul with a Soviet army convoy.

The conservative Muslim mujahedin put up an unexpected and bitter resistance to the new government. Soviet troops, armed to the teeth with Moscow's most modern materiel, were picked apart on the ground by rebel and elusive mujahedin guerillas, employing antiquated weapons that had been state of the art when Jane's first started publishing their guide to all the world's blunderbusses. Later, the rebels, backed by the CIA, began picking Soviet gunships out of the sky with U.S.-supplied *Stingers* and other surface-to-air rockets. The fighting was bloody and both sides settled into a war of attrition, not unlike the U.S. effort in Vietnam a decade earlier.

How involved was the CIA in the conflict? When Afghanistan was invaded by the Soviets in 1979, President Jimmy Carter provided the mujahedin with US$30 million in covert aid. This manifested itself in the form of the CIA supplying the rebels with old Soviet arms procured from Egypt. As covert military aid to the mujahedin increased under the Reagan administration, so did the carnage and the number of refugees. By 1985, the Afghan rebels were receiving US$250 million a year in covert assistance. That 1985 figure was double 1984's amount. The annual amount received by the guerrillas reached a whopping US$700 million by 1988. Even after the Soviets withdrew from Afghanistan, the spook bucks kept flowing. In 1991, anywhere from US$180 million to US$300 million was funneled into Afghanistan by the CIA. In all, the CIA spent about US$3.3 billion in rebel aid over the course of the war.

An initial agreement to end outside aid was signed in April 1988 by Afghanistan, the U.S.S.R., the U.S. and Pakistan. The accords were signed on the condition that the U.S.S.R. pull out its troops by the end of the year. The Soviets' withdrawal occurred in February 1989. Another agreement, signed between the Soviet Union and the U.S. in September 1991, also sought to arrange the end of meddling into Afghanistan's affairs by the two superpowers. By the middle of April 1992, mujahedin guerrillas and other Islamic rebels moved in on Kabul and ousted President Najibullah. A 50-member ruling council comprised of guerrilla, religious and intellectual leaders was quickly established to create an Islamic republic.

Instead of peace, the rebel guerrilla factions quickly began challenging each other for control of Afghanistan. At the beginning of 1994, factional fighting broke out in earnest again in Kabul.

The Scoop

War without end, amen. As if it wasn't bad enough that 2 million Afghans died during the Russian occupation, now Muslim has set upon Muslim in a nihilistic struggle for control of this poor country. After fifteen years of take-no-prisoners warfare, there is little to recommend about this hellhole. Few travelers go into Afghanistan. Nobody comes out without a few close calls. Although nine different political or religious factions are officially warring, politicians, warlords, clans, tribes and factions are all fighting for dominance in a country that, historically, has shown that it can never be dominated by any single group. All the players are battling for an Islamic fundamentalist government. All sides believe they are fighting a jihad against the less devout. The two major factions are close enough to yell insults at each other while lobbing shells back and forth. Strangely, the attacks have lacked any cohesive ground strategy—ground assaults are rare. Instead, the shooters are subjected to the continuous, nerve-shattering crescents of mortars and shells landing indiscriminately throughout the city. The *taliban*, a group of fundamentalists (surprised?), emerged as the new player in February of 1995 descending like locusts on the killing fields. The situation is in flux.

The Players

The Taliban

The *Taliban* or "students" have been hard at work liberating Afghanistan from the bands of militia and warring factions that have choked the country and stopped transport. Their reopening of a direct route between Pakistan and Kabul has eased the blockade imposed by Hekmatyar. They have moved north from Kandahar and are now considered to be the major force in Afghanistan or at least the major enemy of Rabbani. Although they have said they will work with the U.N. to bring peace to the war-ravaged region, they have yet to control Kabul. They present themselves as students but they are reputedly backed by the Sandis and Pakistanis. Not too many student organizations can afford new tanks, rocket launchers and automatic weapons.

Prime Minister Gulbuddin Hekmatyar

Hekmatyar is the leader of the Hezb-i-islami and formerly was nurtured by the CIA in their efforts to give the Soviets a black eye. Hekmatyar is also supported by the warlord Abdul Rashid Doestam. Their former headquarters is just 15 miles from downtown Kabul in the Charasayab area of the city, comprised of the capital's southern and eastern suburbs. Hekmatyar is the quintessential pissed-off rebel who wants the current president, Burhanuddin Rabbani, to be replaced with a *loya jirga*, a revolutionary council that would organize elections. Currently he is on the run from the *taliban* and it remains to be seen where he will make his next stand.

President Burhanuddin Rabbani

Rabbani is a former professor and the official political leader of Aghanistan, although one wonders whom and what he's leading. His commander of the army, 37-year-old Syed Kadar Shah, oversees a Verdun-like battle from the Dehmazang Prison. A highly-educated man, Rabbani made an attempt to build a bridge between opposing forces when he named Hekmatyar prime minister in 1993. But there is little room for compromise in this fundamentalist country.

Ahmed Shah Massoud

The Lion of Panjr is credited with being the main reason the Russians hightailed it out of Afghanistan. Rabbani's defense minister, Commander Ahmed Shah Massoud is an old friend of *DP*'s Aral and is considered an enemy of God for his rejection of Iranian-backed fundamentalism. It remains to be seen if Massoud has political ambitions.

Mujahedin

Years of war have created an entirely new warrior caste in Afghanistan. Most mujahedin spent their young adult lives in mobile columns killing Russians and other Afghans. They have been in great demand in other parts of the world by Iran and Sudan for their absolute devotion to *jihad*. Today both mujahedin and "afghans" can be found around the world, from Bosnia to the Philippines, fighting as volunteers or mercenaries for Islamic forces.

Afghanistan - Travel Warning

January 12, 1994.

The Department of State warns all U.S. citizens against travel to Afghanistan. Fighting continues between opposing factions in the civil war and indiscriminate rocket attacks, aerial bombardments, and other violence can occur without warning. Land mines are prevalent throughout the country-side. Westerners are vulnerable to politically- and criminally-motivated attacks, including robbery, kidnapping and hostage-taking. All U.S. personnel at the U.S. Embassy in Kabul were evacuated on January 31, 1989, and no other diplomatic mission represents U.S. interests or provides consular services.

Getting In

You can get a tourist visa for 3 months for $30 per visa application. A passport and visa are required. For further information, the traveler can contact the:

Embassy of the Islamic State of Afghanistan

2341 Wyoming Avenue, NW
Washington, D.C. 20008
☎ *(202) 234-3770/1*
FAX (202) 328-3516

The Embassy told us that "in Afghanistan there are safe places to travel and there are some places (that are) unsafe." Kabul is the least safe place for travel. All border crossings are supposed to be open but the embassy recommends that travelers use the crossings from Pakistan, Iran and Tajikistan. Those entering illegally will be "put in jail for a while" and then deported; according to our embassy sources.

Getting Around

Right now there is little chance of safe travel in Afghanistan. Journalists can travel into Kabul under protection of whoever is in charge at the time. Travel outside of the city is dangerous and you will be stopped by numerous armed militias and groups. The chances are high that the majority of these groups will be happy to see you and will gladly lighten your load. Some may do you the favor of hastening your entry into the eternal kingdom. Either the *chargé d'affaires* has a sick sense of humor or he is telling it straight. In any case Yar M. Mohabbat has hit the nail on the end in his advice to *DP* readers: "Tourists must have caution and be more careful where not to go (sic) and where not to go."

Getting Out

Leaving Afghanistan is a simple matter of hoping that the people who brought you in have enough resources to get you to the airport or the Pakistan border safely.

Getting Sick

In Kabul there are medical centers which take care of the wounded and the sick. These facilities are subject to rocket attack. Even the most basic medical care is limited or nonexistent, with extreme shortages of most basic medicines. Items like syringes and bandages are reused and there is a shortage of doctors and beds. Don't get sick. To get more info, U.S. citizens who register at U.S. embassies in Pakistan, India, Tajikistan, or Uzbekistan can obtain updated information on security in Afghanistan.

Embassy Location

Because no third country represents United States' interests in Afghanistan, the United States government is unable to provide normal consular protective services to U.S. citizens in Afghanistan. The nearest U.S. embassies and consulates are in Pakistan and Tajikistan. The telephone number for the U.S. Embassy in Islamabad, Pakistan is ☎ *(92-51) 826-161/179.*

U.S. Consulate in Peshawar, Pakistan
   ☎ *(92-521) 279-801/2/3*

U.S. Embassy in Tashkent, Uzbekistan
   ☎ *(7-3712) 771-407/771-081*

U.S. Embassy in Dushanbe, Tajikistan
   ☎ *(7-3772) 21-0356/-0360/-0457*

U.S. Embassy in New Delhi, India
   ☎ *(91-11) 600-651*

Dangerous Places

Kabul

There were 30,000 known casualties (23,000 killed and 7000 wounded) from the war in Kabul in 1993. With an average Afghan life expectancy of only 44 years, maybe there is not much to look forward to in this bombed and gutted shell. A quarter million of the 1.5 million residents have fled the battered city to Jalalabad as refugees. Fighters will kill anyone who they feel is not on their side. Robbery, murder, extortion and kidnapping is an absolute guarantee for the unwary. Westerners are not welcome and even the ubiquitous Red Cross can do little with its skeleton staff. Factional fighting again closed all the roads leading into the capital in January 1995. They've been intermittently open and closed as pro-President Rabbani forces use the closures to strengthen their positions.

Everywhere Else

The Russians took great pains to make Afghanistan a dangerous place for years to come. Nearly 20,000 people have been killed in factional fighting since the mujahedin took power in Kabul from the collapsed communist government after 14 years of civil war. There are about 12 million land mines scattered by air and buried in the ground throughout Afghanistan by the Russians that have yet to be unearthed. Many of them are small, plastic mines that were scattered from Soviet planes and helicopters. Designed to blow only the foot off the unfortunate guerrilla, the mines are hard to spot and continue to maim and injure locals.

The Borders

Lawlessness and a lack of infrastructure have made Afghanistan a major drug trafficking route. Large armed convoys guard the transport of opium from Pakistan and areas within Afghanistan. When the Soviet Union stopped patrolling its Afghani border, the country became the second major conduit (the Golden Triangle in Southeast Asia is the number-one source and conduit of poppy-based drugs) of opium and heroin and the largest exporter of hashish in the world. Up to 14 metric tons of hashish have been seized by the border states of Uzbekistan, Turkmenistan, Kyrgystan, Tajikistan and Kazakastan. Badakhshan borders Russia's Tajikistan, where Russia has deployed at least 15,000 troops to help fight antigovernment Islamic guerrillas believed to have bases in Afghanistan. The border is frequently bombed by Russian planes.

Dangerous Things

Kidnapping

On January 21, 1995, the leader of the Shia political faction Hizb-i-Wahdat released a British hostage they had been holding for eight months. The hostage, Eden Paul Rollie Fernandez, who arrived in Afghanistan in 1989, had been accused by the group of being a British spy.

Stingers For Sale

Want a quick $55 million? Just round up the 300 or so aging Stinger missiles given to the Afghan rebels in the mid-1980s and send them back to Uncle Sam. The U.S. government has a standing offer to buy back the hand-held, heat-seeking, antiaircraft weapons not because they need them for defense purposes, but because of the threat they pose to commercial aviation in the Middle East. The Stingers make the perfect gift for armchair terrorists craving to take a commercial jetliner out of the sky on a Sunday afternoon. The most recent commercial victim of this effective weapon was a Tupolev Tu-154 in Georgia.

The bad news is that tribal chiefs who are trafficking in opium were outbidding the CIA for the leftover Stinger missiles now in the hands of Afghan mujahedin commanders. Recently, one tribal chief bought 105 Stingers in the Towr Kham region. Other bidders are fundamentalist groups, as well as Iranian and North Korean intelligence services.

In a Dangerous Place: Afghanistan March 1983

An expedition into war torn Afghanistan has been developed in Paris. Three French doctors from Médecins sans Frontières decide to go to the Panshir Valley headquarters of the Afghan resistance. Two other journalists will join us: Philippe Flandrin, a Frenchman, and the Iranian-born photographer Reza Deghati. Deghati wants to go to east Kabul to meet the monarchists of leader Mahaze Melli. Flandrin will continue to Baktia outside Kabul to locate the Hezb-e-Islami and their leaders, Yunus Khales and Abdul Haq.

We fly to Peshawar to meet the mujahedin organization. The Hezb-e-Islami propose to bring us into Panshir but we prefer to trust the people from Jemiaat-e-Islami because this time they control the Panshir region. The leader of this organization is Muchai Barzali. The trek will cover about 450 kilometers and is expected to last one month.

The three doctors will bring in food and medicine, and the guerrillas will provide protection. We wait until March for the snow to start melting. We will climb the 4500-meter high mountain of Hindi Kuch. On the other side, we are expecting jeeps to be waiting to provide us with transit to Peshawar. But after the long, grueling trek we will find no jeeps.

The trip begins on March 10, 1983. We dress like Afghans because we are crossing tribal country. I bring along three cameras. Flatfooted and out of shape, I am always behind.Our convoy moves at night to avoid the Russian helicopters. Despite our stealth and our altitude, the group is often attacked by Soviet gunships. I have brought along some dry fruit to supplement the meager rice rations. As our food supply dwindles, I discover there is nothing in the countryside with which to replenish our supplies. Once in a while we come across a small tea shop in the villages.

In my fatigue and hunger I make the mistake of taking a leak while standing up. An Afghan spots me and the alarm goes out. Muslims always squat to urinate. The group decides I'm a Russian spy and that I am to be shot. Our bodyguards come to my rescue and argue that Turkish Muslims always stand to piss, and that I am a true Muslim.

The argument rages on; our explanation finally prevails. It is a close call. One of our convoy is not so lucky and the cause for his execution is even more ridiculous. A young man is shot to death in the backyard of a village house because the hairs on his arms are not pointing in the correct direction. If he had been cleaning himself five times a day in preparation for prayer, the hairs on his arms would have been pointing toward his hands. The sentence is passed by the leader of our column and he is shot to death out of sight of the others.

It is frigid in the mountains. Sometimes we have to cross ice-cold rivers fully clothed. I am amazed that I do not freeze to death. I am starving. I dream of greasy hamburgers and crisp french fries.

On the last leg of the journey to the Panshir Valley we ride in a truck. The truck hits a land mine and rolls over, launching a piece of a metallic ladder into my jaw and knocking out three of my teeth. I lose a lot of blood and am saved only by the doctors.

We finally reach the Panshir Valley and set up a makeshift hospital. Wounded rebels are carried in, some from two to three days away. There is no anesthetic; bullet wounds are washed out with tea. During *Ramadan*, a Muslim fast lasting 40 days, the Afghans would not give blood so I, and the other doctors, give blood depending on the blood type necessary.

The man named Massoud, "The Lion of Panshir," is the reason for our trip. The rebel leader has asked for medical help and the doctors come at great personal risk. Massoud and I became friends. Massoud was educated in the Lycée Istiq'lal (a French high school) in Kabul. Now a resistance leader, he was considered to be very clever and was always on the move. He needed medical help because his men were dying slow, agonizing deaths from gunshot and shrapnel wounds. The doctor Gilles will accompany us. We take the injured back to Pakistan in a convoy. Since I am the least injured member of the group, I will be the leader. As a token of the rebels' appreciation, I am given a horse. I use it to help transport the wounded. When we arrive back in Pakistan, we are detained because we carry no identification papers. Finally, we are permitted entry.

I traveled back to Afghanistan two more times to cover the mujahedin. Gilles returned to Paris, and shortly afterwards committed suicide.

Algeria
★ ★ ★ ★ ★

You Can't Dance

Hey world, are you ready for Islam? Well, you'd better get ready, according to a crudely assembled and rambling four-page fax from Mohammed Said, the new leader of the Islamic Salvation Front (FIS). The FIS is calling out for the release of "martyrs" Abassi Madani, an FIS council member and Ali Belhadj, both jailed in June 1991 for 12 years. The fax goes on to claim that all singers, artists, journalists, soldiers and policemen are non believers and if you see them near the Kaaba in Mecca it's okay to kill them. They ain't kiddin' around.

Algeria has become a damned dangerous place to hang out or to do business these days. Islamic fundamentalists opposed to the Western-backed military government of President Liamine Zeroual are wreaking havoc. In the wake of cancelled elections in 1991 and 1992, the fundamentalist FIS party has chosen terrorism because the ruling government has stolen their political voice. It seems that if FIS can't talk, then the people can't dance. Foreigners in Algeria are assassinated, often quite gruesomely, to frighten Western businesses and countries supporting Zeroual's authoritarian govern-

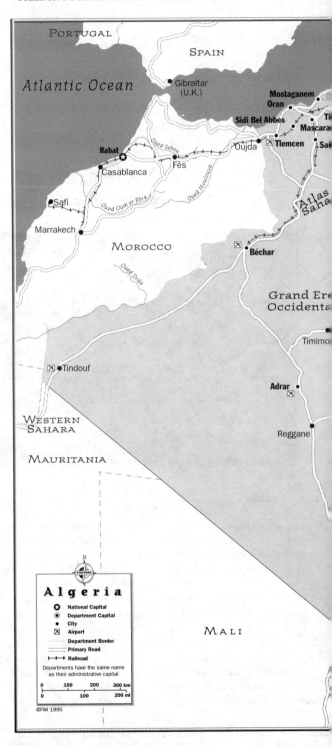

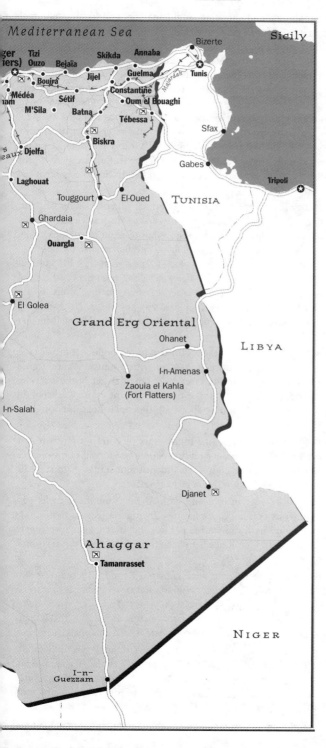

ment. When the throat-slitting and shooting of aid workers and local intellectuals stopped making foreign news the FIS decided to employ the classic bad guys PR /political leverage and fund-raising tool—hijacking. On December 24, 1994, four Algerian terrorists of the Armed Islamic Group seized an Air France *Airbus A300* jetliner in Algiers with 239 passengers and crew members aboard. Their demand, of course, was for the release of the two imprisoned FIS leaders. The gunmen killed three passengers, including a Vietnamese diplomat, before the plane was stormed by French commandos in Marseilles. The raid killed all four terrorists (the oldest was 20) and wounded 13 passengers. Since the cancelled 1992 Algerian elections, radical fundamentalists have assassinated more than 11,000 people, including 70 foreigners and 22 French nationals in an effort to topple the government. Among the victims are playwrights, artists, journalists, politicians and even school girls who refuse to don the *hejab* or traditional Muslim head covering.

These guys brag that they have sent Cheb Hasni (a popular Algerian singer who they recently shot to death) to hell. They kidnapped 38-year-old singer Lounes Matoub but then, after having second thoughts, released him. Matoub is an ethnic Berber and had recorded a satirical song about the fundamentalists. The Berbers are the country's largest ethnic minority and not a group anyone wishes to mess with. The FIS communique went on to say, "Now we will start with the journalists, the poets and the soldiers. Belly dancing is a prayer to Satan. When Satan's messengers give a direction to people, they dance." They ask that if you dance, please stay out of Algeria. Not an entirely unfair request in post-disco Africa. (The FIS has said nothing about John Travolta.)

The fundamentalists' threats are not just the rhetoric of bored bullies. Journalists are under a direct threat of immediate execution if they enter the country. Wearing glasses, Western clothes or even looking educated can make you a target of these nasties. Sounds a little like Cambodia of the 1970s. It is estimated that the entire wealth of this country of 28 million is in the hands of only about 5000 people. Reason enough for reform but not for mayhem.

Algeria is no stranger to hatred and death. Eight years of cruel warfare with the French start back in 1954 killed a quarter of a million people and forced out more than a million *pied noirs,* or white colonists. Despite its independent status, Algeria's 132-year marriage to France has made it more French than Arabic.

France has always had a love-hate relationship with Algeria, due more to its geographical proximity than to its cultural dissimilarities. In Algeria, Russia has found a major customer for its military hardware and expertise, and Italy makes sure Algeria continues to pump out the oil and gas it needs to keep those Fiats and Ferraris topped off.

In October 1993, two French technicians were kidnapped and murdered near Sidi-Bel-Abbes. In October, two Russian lieutenant colonels stationed at the air base in Laghuat (about 200 miles south of Algiers) were shot. Three days later, three Italian technicians were kidnapped and murdered. In Tiaret, merely a day after the Italians' murder, three employees of the French general consulate were kidnapped.

In 1992, at least 560 Algerian militants were training at military bases in Sudan, financially supported by Iran. Most of the trainees were veterans of the Afghan war and traveled to Sudan via Iran. These militants are trained to add to the core of the underground Islamic fundamentalist movement held responsible for the killing of more than 210 members of Algeria's security forces.The Algerian government suspended six Islamic groups: The Call and Conveyance of the Message, the Nahdha Association for

Social and Cultural Reform, the Algerian Islamic Association for Civilization and Construction, the Women's League for Adherence to God's Way, the Algerian League for Islamic Literature, and the Islamic League for Fine Arts.

The U.S. Department of State warns U.S. citizens to avoid travel to Algeria. It further recommends that Americans in Algeria whose circumstances do not afford them effective protection depart Algeria.

The Scoop

The world's most dangerous place for foreigners. A country where wacked-out fundamentalists and burned-out Algerian veterans of Afghanistan's war with Russia like to cut throats and shoot expats. Why? Algeria's military, in a ridiculous move, stupidly decided to cancel the 1992 elections which the Islamic Salvation Front was going to win handily.

The goal of FIS is to make Algeria an Islamic fundamentalist country by forcing out foreign interests and influence with Iran footing the bill. The FIS does this by deliberately murdering foreign workers and tourists. Nothing personal, but blond hair, Dockers and La Coste shirts might be your death sentence. An ultimatum was handed out in November 30, 1993 demanding all foreigners to leave the country. Since then, it's estimated that about 15 assassinations occur each day, including those of politicians, intellectuals, journalists and non-Algerians.

Of the more than 6000 victims of the insurgency, 60 have been foreigners killed in the past year. There is not much reason for thrill seekers to travel here since there is nothing visual or saleable for Western journos. Off-the-beaten-path travelers can get all the danger they need in Morocco or Egypt without being specifically targeted. Foreign workers take their chances hoping they will get transferred to a nice quiet place like Somalia or Cambodia.

The Players

FLN

The old guard revolutionaries who kicked the French out in 1962 are now the ones who have to go. They have held on to their power by simply cancelling an election that the newer and more vital Islamic Salvation Front won fair and square. The FLN tried everything from adding seats in their strongholds and arresting FIS members to finally cancelling the elections altogether. The military is directly in control of the High Security Council, with General Khaled Nezar, the leader of the Algerian military, pulling the strings.

Islamic Salvation Front (FIS)

The FIS wants to make Algeria an Islamic state with the Koran as its constitution. Some FIS members are calling for a democratic society with Muslim values. In any case, the FIS was banned by the government after being the front runner in the aborted 1992 elections. The FIS has decided to make Algeria the most dangerous place in the world for foreigners. It's hard to say whether FIS terrorist activities or the management of the current regime have more severely damaged Algeria's economy. FIS leader Shaykh Abassi Madani and his hawkish deputy Ali Belhadj were released from jail and transferred to a cushy villa under house arrest in an effort to strike a compromise with the fundamentalists. About 400 members of the FIS were sent to the Bekáa Valley in Lebanon for training in 1990. FIS members have also been trained in the Sudan by Hezbollah. The FIS is not just a bunch of crazies. The party was a grass roots political and religious movement that originally attracted the dispossessed. The party has grown to include the support of the majority of the country including intellectuals and professionals. Keep in mind that the FIS is not one cohesive party but a mish-mash of everything from tiny radical cells to large political machines, none of whom agree on much. One thing they do have in common is their collective threat to foreigners in Algeria: Leave or die.

Armed Islamic Group (GIA)

The GIA is led by probably the most heartless and cruel group of men on earth: Algerian veterans of the Afghan war or mujahedin. They're hard, brutal guys trained in Sudan and supported by Iran. The GIA views the FIS as being soft. The GIA likes to cut throats and engage in cold-blooded murder. Their leader, Cherif Gousmi, 26 and his iron-fisted deputy were shot in September of 1994, so you missed out on the US$70,000 bounty the government was offering for their heads.

President Liamine Zeroual

He's doing his best to keep the lid on, but he isn't doing a very good job. His idea of building a coalition only works when both sides want to play, which isn't often. The GIA would rather kill people.

The Army and the Death Squads

Groups of five to 10 men in plain clothes work the inner city while 35,000 troops man an "infernal arc" in the Mitidja between Algeria, Blida, Laarba and Medea. Out in the countryside, small groups of soldiers travel in helicopters and armored personnel vehicles to track down fundamentalists. It's clobbering time in Algeria.

Getting In

Passports and visas are required for U.S. citizens traveling to Algeria. Algeria does not give visas to persons whose passports indicate previous travel to Israel or South Africa. For more information concerning entry requirements, crazy travelers may contact:

Embassy of the Democratic and Popular Republic of Algeria

2137 Wyoming Avenue NW,
Washington, D.C. 20008
☎ *(202) 265-2800*

Dangerous Places

Most of Algeria (terror in the north, bandits in the south) is dangerous. The Zabarbar forest, Blida mountains and the Jijel region are frequently napalmed by the government in their quest to rid themselves of fundamentalist pockets. The favorite target of the FIS seems to be the airbase at Laghuat. *MIG-23s* regularly drop napalm on remote regions used by the terrorists for their bases of operations.

Algiers

In January 1995, a global study conducted by an international business group, Corporate Resources Group, rated Algiers the worst city in the world. The group based its findings on criteria such as quality of life, security, public services, mental and physical care and facilities and political and social stability.

Dangerous Things

Terrorists

It would be an understatement to say that political, social and economic problems have created a climate of violent unrest in Algeria. A state of emergency has been in effect since early 1992. Assassinations of foreigners, Algerian intellectuals, government officials and military officers occur frequently. Sporadic bombings, gun battles between government forces and terrorist groups and other violent acts occur almost daily.

The government of Algeria has imposed a rigorously-enforced late-night curfew in the central region around Algiers. Roadblocks are located at many major intersections. Security personnel at roadblocks and intersections expect full cooperation with their instructions. Terrorist groups have profited by this strategy by setting up false roadblocks as stages for ambushes. Not a great place for a motor holiday.

Bandits

As if the terrorists weren't enough, there are also numerous incidents of banditry and assault involving foreigners that have been reported in the far southern region of Algeria near the border with Niger. Bandits have robbed, assaulted, kidnapped and killed travelers in Algeria south of Tamanrasset.

Being a Journalist

At least 30 journalists have died in Algeria since 1993. Three were killed in January 1995 alone. Algeria's three years of civil strife has killed more than 11,000 people.

Civil Disorder

Political, social and economic problems have created a climate of unrest and uncertainty in Algeria. Sporadic bombings and assassinations continue. The most prominent victim was President Mohammed Boudiaf, who was assassinated on June 29, 1994 in the eastern city of Annaba. An estimated 100 police and security officials have been slain. These disturbances have not taken an anti-American tone with the exception of one small bomb that exploded harmlessly in the U.S. Embassy compound on January 30, 1992. Anyone living in Algiers is exposed to the risk of being inadvertently caught in the wrong place at the wrong time when violence breaks out.

Criminals

The threat of theft is increasing in Algeria. The most frequent crimes involve the theft of auto parts from parked cars. Car windows and trunk locks are frequently broken in the hope that the thief will find something of value within. Home burglary is an increasingly serious problem and most residences of foreigners are protected by alarm systems, watch dogs and/or guards. Experienced expatriot residents venture out into the city with only a minimum amount of cash carried in a carefully concealed location. Vehicles are not generally parked in unguarded locations because of theft and vandalism.

Booby Traps

Booby traps proliferate in the country. One of the less ingenious but still surprisingly effective modes is the old booby trap in the corpse trick. In January 1995, the booby-trapped corpse of a slain security force member exploded when it was picked up by two security force members killing both of them.

Buses & Trains

Crime on Algeria's trains and buses is so serious that the government has prepared newspaper articles lamenting the dangers posed by pickpockets and thieves. Baggage must never be left unattended in a public place.

Hotel Rooms

Nothing of value should be left in a hotel room. There are reports of hotel staff helping themselves to the toiletries, appliances and food of the guests. Pedestrians are not likely to encounter armed robbers, but must be alert to the danger of pickpockets and purse snatchers near the major hotels.

Hassles with Police

Armed men posing as police have entered homes of foreigners, held the occupants at gunpoint and robbed them.

Roadblocks, especially at night, are located at many major intersections and police vehicles are constantly patrolling the streets. The Algerian police are well trained and equipped. They are fully professional in their conduct and attentive to the needs of the foreign community. The types of crimes committed against foreigners (vandalism, petty theft, burglary, etc.) are difficult to solve and travelers should not have a high expectation of reclaiming stolen property. Police may be contacted in any city by dialing 17; rural areas are under the jurisdiction of the Gendarmerie Nationale.

Getting Sick

Hospitals and clinics in Algeria are available, but limited in quality. If you are seriously wounded you stand a better chance by being flown out to nearby France, Britain or Germany. Medicines can be hard to get or expensive. Don't expect much outside of the major cities.

Nuts & Bolts

The workweek in Algeria is Saturday through Wednesday, at least for those who work, 84 percent of Algerians between the ages of 15 and 30 are jobless; inflation is at 55 percent. And factories are functioning at 50 percent of capacity. Algeria has the lowest farm yield of any Mediterranean country, forcing the country to import two-thirds of its food.

"Traveler's cheques" and credit cards are acceptable in only a few establishments in urban areas. Currently, the government of Algeria requires all foreigners entering the country to exchange $200 into local currency. Documentary proof of legal exchange of currency is needed when departing Algeria.

The U.S. Embassy in Algeria is located at 4 Chemin Cheikh Bachir El-Ibrahimi, B.P. 549 (Alger-Gare) 16000, in the capital city of Algiers. The telephone number is ☎ *69-11-86, 69-18-54, 69-38-75.*

Dangerous Days	
04/20/1980	Berber spring. Berber ethnic protests held in Tizi Ouzou.
08/20/1955	Algerian independence fighters launched their first armed offensive against French forces in eastern Algeria.
11/08/1942	U.S. and British forces landed in North Africa.

Angola

When Three Tribes Go to War...

Until Rwanda set a new standard for savagery, Angola held the title of Africa's most bloody war. More than 400,000 people have been killed in the ongoing battle since its independence from Portugal in 1975. The dead may be the lucky ones. The fighting has resulted in 50,000 orphaned children and 80,000 cripples. Today, Angola has the highest percentage of amputees in the world. Nearly 40 percent of the population is estimated to be missing limbs.

The United Nations estimates that, at the war's peak, 1000 people were dying a day in this war without end. It remains to be seen whether a recent cease-fire will bring an end to Angola's civil war. Nonetheless, the 20 million explosives left buried in the soil will continue to kill and maim for years to come. There are perhaps only 10 or 11 million people left in Angola and more than enough land mines, famine, drought and pestilence to kill every one of them. At least twice.

Angola was a valued source of slaves for 300 years after the area was colonized by the Portuguese in the late 15th century. But it wasn't until after the Second World War that Portugal attempted to bring Portuguese settlers into Angola. The Portuguese in-

habitants of Angola established lucrative coffee plantations and the seeds of discontent were sewn. As the number of Portuguese increased, along with their hectares of bountiful landholdings, Angolan nationalist groups revolted in an effort to gain independence for the colony.

Bloody fighting followed for decades until Portugal agreed to grant independence to Angola, along with Portugal's other African colonies. Following to the course that most third world countries trek along after gaining independence, the insurgents didn't know what to do with their freedom. The three principal independence groups—the Popular Movement for the Liberation of Angola (MPLA), strong in central Angola; the National Union for the Total Independence of Angola (UNITA), based in the south; the National Front for the Liberation of Angola (FNLA), which had the most strength in the north and had separately carried out the rebellion— began to clash among themselves. The transitional government that was established after the Portuguese forces withdrew in 1975 soon collapsed like a house of cards. The wrath that the three groups had for the Portuguese was now being directed at each other.

The MPLA, with help from Cuba and the Soviet Union, seized the capital of Luanda and proclaimed itself the legitimate government of Angola. UNITA, with the help of South Africa, controlled the southern part of the country and waged, along with the weaker FNLA, a 16-year civil war against the MPLA. The MPLA adapted a Soviet-style governing system. Agostinho Neto, the MPLA general secretary, became president. He died in 1979 and was succeeded by Jose Eduardo dos Santos, who successfully created better ties with the West.

A 1991 cease-fire ended the civil war between the MPLA and UNITA. However, UNITA instigated renewed hostilities in October 1992 after elections resulted in an MPLA victory. The U.N. Security Council voted on September 26, 1993 for sanctions against UNITA. On October 6, 1993 UNITA accepted the 1991 cease-fire and its defeat in the 1992 elections.

Angola suffers from the myriad problems so endemic to Third World countries, including poor nutrition, education and health care. However, the most serious social problem is the antagonism between the country's tribal and ethnic groups.

Ethnic hostilities, the principal cause of the strife in Angola, resulted in a civil war that cost more than US$30 billion. The largest ethnic group, the Ovimbundu, comprises 37 percent of the population (and the essence of the UNITA forces) and lives mainly in the central and southern parts of Angola. The Kimbundu are the second largest group, comprising about a quarter of Angola's population. They are primarily found along the coast and make up most of the MPLA. Finally, the Bakong account for 13 percent of the population. They live in the north and constitute the core of the FNLA forces. About 1 percent of the population is of mixed race, many of whom control key positions in government and business, further compounding ethnic problems. Before the war, as many as 330,000 Caucasians lived in Angola; perhaps 30,000 remain.

The Angolan government has said it plans to privatize a number of state-owned groups in the hotel and tourism industry—some being companies belonging to the state-run Angohotel and Emprotel hotel groups—in line with an overall and urgent effort to liberalize its formerly Marxist economy. The Angotur tourism company would also be revitalized. Tourism has all but disappeared here in the 20 years of civil war. A significant number of residents in the capital city of Luanda live in hotels due to a severe shortage of decent housing.

Angola's ruling MPLA has promised sweeping reforms in its economy to bring it closer to a free market system. However, chaos due to the war with UNITA rebels has severely hampered these proposed moves.

The Scoop

The current bloodshed started when the Portuguese administration began to crumble in 1974. By March 1976, it had turned into a dirty, three-way war. As usual, the CIA is to blame for undermining the MPLA, whose platform was considered too radical.

Holden Roberto and the Kikongo-speaking people of the north (the FNLA) are backed by the CIA and Zaire. The Portuguese and South Africa back Jonas Savimbi's UNITA, which is comprised of Umbunda-speaking peoples and other tribes of the south and east. UNITA has also enjoyed the support of the CIA. The MPLA is backed by Cuba and is popular with urban Angolans. The MPLA technically runs the country but has been under attack from South Africa and the dissenting parties.

When the superpowers and other outside meddlers became tired of counting corpses, there were only two players left, both dazed and bloodied. It is clear that nobody has won or will win this war.

Today in Angola it is common for foreign aid to be hijacked; refugee camps are raided by soldiers and food stolen from the mouths of starving war victims. Overshadowed by the more pyrotechnic war in Bosnia and the mass slaughters in Rwanda and Somalia, Angola will continue to endure its agony into the foreseeable future.

The Players

Popular Movement for the Liberation of Angola (MPLA)

The Marxist regime held together by the soft spoken and educated José Eduardo dos Santos. He was propelled to power via a slam-dunk election masterminded by a Brazilian public relations company. Dos Santos has promised to drop the unpopular dogma of Lenin and embrace free market principles. The MPLA won the September 1992 elections, supervised by 800 outside observers—his arch rival, Jonas Savimbi, went back to his base in Huambo and continued to kill his countrymen in the name of peace.

Dos Santos' government is propped up by petroleum and diamond exports extracted and managed by foreign firms and the Angolan Armed Forces (FAA). The FAA is busy packing over 3.4 billion dollars in new weapons and deploying the 500 white mercenaries (mostly from South Africa). Also, 7000 U.N. peacekeepers are on their way to babysit the new peace agreement between UNITA and the ruling government.

National Union for the Total Independence of Angola (UNITA)

Headed by 60-year-old Jonas Savimbi. Considering the number of people his brand of socialist politics has killed, it may be surprising to learn that Savimbi was a graduate of the School of International Politics at Lausanne University in Switzerland. Educated in guerrilla tactics in China, he has vowed to topple the Cuban- and formerly Soviet-backed government. He is facing escalating pressure in terms of sanctions for his refusal to negotiate seriously with the government for peace.

UNITA controls about 70% of the country with its 40,000 troops and receives its foreign support from South Africa and Zaire. However, Savimbi is quickly losing ground. In August 1994, the government retook areas around Malanje and launched attacks in the northern diamond-producing area of Lunda Norte near Cafunfo. Savimbi's control of the diamond mines has funded his resistance movement. In 1993, UNITA pocketed about US$200 million from smuggling diamonds out of Angola. DeBeers calculates that, in 1992, about US$500 million worth of diamonds were smuggled out of Angola.

Getting In

Passport and visa required. Persons arriving without visas are subject to possible arrest or deportation. Tourist/business visas take two days and require an application form, $30, letter stating purpose of travel, and two color photos. Applications by mail require prepaid return envelope. Yellow fever and cholera immunizations are required. The embassy was quite excited about the 7000 or so UN peacekeepers heading to their country. They estimate it will be one to two years before things settle down. For now, they still welcome tourists but advise strongly that you fly directly into Luanda and do not dillydally out of Luanda, Lobito, Benguela or Namibe. The Angolan Ministry of Hotels and Tourism is the best source for people looking to book Shriner Conventions there.

Land borders may or may not be under government control. Folks caught tiptoeing in will be incarcerated if they don't hit a land mine first.

For additional information contact:

Embassy of Angola

> *1819 L Street, NW, Suite 400*
> *Washington, D.C. 20036*
> ☎ *(202) 785-1156)*
> *FAX (202) 785-1258*
> or

The Permanent Mission of the Republic of Angola to the U.N.

> *125 East 73rd Street*
> *New York, NY 10021*
> ☎ *(212) 861-5656)*

Getting Around

There is little infrastructure left in Angola. Most roads are closed or mined or both. Wandering bands of armed thugs will stop and rob any travelers found in the countryside.

Dangerous Places

Travel throughout Angola is considered unsafe because of the presence of undisciplined, armed troops and land mines, as well as the possibility of sudden outbreaks of localized combat or a direct attack by armed soldiers or civilians. Travel in many parts of the capital city is relatively safe by day, but is considered unsafe at night because of the increased incidence of armed robberies and carjackings. The presence of police checkpoints after dark, often manned by armed, poorly trained personnel, contributes to unsafe nighttime travel. Police at checkpoints actively solicit bribes and have used deadly force against vehicles for not stopping as requested.

Dangerous Things

Land Mines

> It is estimated by Human Rights Watch that there are 20 million land mines in Angola. About 120 people a day are killed. There are no figures for maimings.

Thugs

> Violent crime exists throughout the country. Armed robbery occurs in Luanda both day and night. Travel outside Luanda is not safe.

Getting Sick

Don't. Travelers are advised to purchase medical evacuation insurance. Cerebal and chloroquine-resistant malaria are endemic.

Nuts & Bolts

Angola is a developing African country which has experienced war and civil strife since its independence from Portugal in 1975. On May 19, 1993, the U.S. recognized the Government of the Republic of Angola, and a U.S. embassy was established in Luanda on June 22, 1993. Facilities for tourism are virtually nonexistent. There are severe shortages of lodging, transportation, food, water and utilities in Luanda and other cities in the country. Shortages result in a lack of sanitary conditions in many areas, including Luanda.

Per capita income in Angola was only about US$770 in 1993; 75 percent of the people are engaged in subsistence agriculture. Life expectancy is a low 44 years (1992 revision), and the infant morality rate is one of the highest in the world. More than half of the population is illiterate despite an aggressive government literacy campaign.

Registration

U.S. citizens who register at the U.S. Embassy's Consular Section, which can now extend full consular services, may obtain updated information on travel and security in Angola.

Embassy Location

U.S. Embassy

on Rua Houari Boumedienne
in the Miramar area of Luanda
P.O. Box 6468
☎ *(244-2) 34-54-81 and 34-64-18 (24-hour number)*
FAX (244-2) 34-78-84

Consular Section

Casa Inglesa, First Floor
Rua Major Kanyangunla No. 132/135
Luanda
☎ *(244-2) 39-69-27*
FAX (244-2) 39-05-15

Travel Advisories

Angola - Travel Warning
February 15, 1994.

U.S. citizens are warned against travel to Angola because of continued civil war. Travel within Angola is extremely unsafe because of the presence of armed troops, roadside bandits and unexploded land mines. U.S. government personnel in Luanda are prohibited from surface travel outside the capital.

Birds of War

One sign that there is skullduggery afoot is the sight of the ungainly aircraft with the equally ungainly name of Pilatus Porter. Designed for Short Take Off and Landing or STOL operations in remote regions, these planes are the favorite attack plane of low-budget air forces. Although the Swiss government has banned sale of the PC-P and PC-7 Pilatus plane to countries at war, the Third World has made the aircraft a familiar sight in Myanmar, Guatemala, Iraq, Angola and South Africa. Sold as trainers they are quickly converted to fighter bombers by using the six hard points under the wing to attach weapons and extra fuel tanks.

The Swiss government has banned the sale of the aircraft with more than two mounting points. Frustrated armies that don't have the time, budget or expertise to convert the newly pacified plane are said to be switching to Tucano trainers.

Armenia

★

Little Israel

Armenia has many similarities to Israel: They are both small, "ethnically pure" countries squeezed between Muslim giants. Much of Armenia's support comes from former natives who are now successful businessmen and influential people living outside their homeland. So it is not surprising that tiny (11,500 square miles) and oft-bullied Armenia has decided to defend itself by becoming the aggressor against much bigger enemies. Armenia has taken advantage of Moscow's preoccupation with its financial and political troubles and rolled through Azerbaijan into Nagorno-Karabakh, gobbling other areas along the way. During the occupation of these territories and like their twin, Armenians made sure there would be a tidy political consensus for independence and pushed out most non-Armenians. Like the Jews, Armenians have endured a holocaust equal to or greater than that suffered by the Jews at the hands of the Nazis in WWII (April 24 is the commemoration of the WWI genocide by the Turks). Given this event, it is somewhat understandable that the Armenians, like the Jews, tend to be pugnacious and feel a little boxed-in in their tiny country. One man's *Lebensraum* is

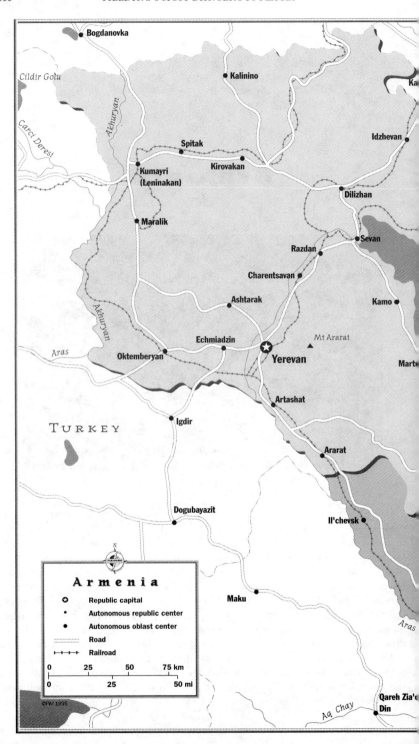

Armenia

- ✪ Republic capital
- • Autonomous republic center
- ● Autonomous oblast center
- ----- Road
- ┝━┿━┥ Railroad

0   25   50   75 km

0   25   50 mi

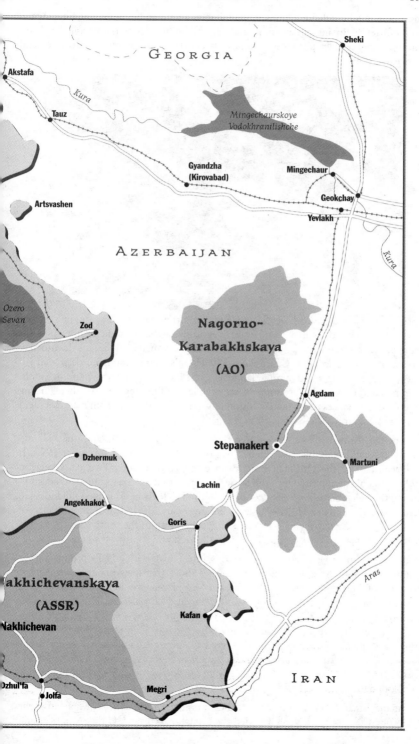

another man's homeland. However, exploitation seems to beget exploitation. Armenia is efficiently driving out all ethnic and religious minorities in its controlled regions. The ongoing conflict produces volumes of reports of indiscriminate atrocities and mass executions.

So, if you are into visiting small, struggling countries who are creating new homelands, Armenia and its new territory of Nagorno-Karabakh might be for you (just think of the low hotel rates!). Be forewarned though, Armenia can best be described as gloomy in the classic Trans-Caucasian mold. There's a lot of mud and destroyed villages, bizarre cultures and strange languages not a lot of sun and swimming pools. Fog, rain and eternal chill are some of the highlights of the region's weather. Putting on ethnic folk dances or battlefield tours are not high on their tourism's development agenda in Nagorno-Karabakh.

To be fair, Armenia has always gotten the short end of the stick. Hayastani Hanrapetutyun, or the Republic of Armenia, was originally formed in November 1920. It had been part of the Ottoman Empire since the 16th century. Two years later, in 1922, Armenia disappeared into the Soviet vortex until it gained its independence following the failed hard-line Soviet coup of August 1991. Armenia gained full independence on December 21, 1991 and became part of the Commonwealth of Independent States. Armenia is jammed in between Iran to the south, Georgia to the north, Azerbaijan to the east and Turkey to the west and southwest.

The Armenians have a bad habit of getting into brawls with equally proud, warlike and bigger neighbors so it shouldn't come as a shock that the Armenian people have lost most of their land as a result. By hook or by crook they would like it back. So there are Armenian-sponsored terrorists in Turkey, Iraq and Russia. They have been relegated to being political hotheads as opposed to serious threats. There are also large numbers of Armenians outside of the country who work to gain justice for the various injustices Armenia and its people have suffered. There are 1.6 million Armenians in the CIS in addition to the millions that live in America, Europe, Australia and the Middle East. There are actually more Armenians living outside of Armenia than within its current boundaries.

Armenia is mad about a lot of things. These range from who claims ownership of the ark (Armenia claims that Noah founded the capital of Yerevan and that Mount Ararat was originally part of Armenia) but Iraq, Turkey and Russia also lay claim to the resting place of the ancient ark. This claim has a lot more validity than the Armenian's recent real estate grab in Azerbaijan. The Christian Armenians view the Muslim Azeris as "Turks," thereby blaming them for the Turkish massacres of 200,000 Armenians in Turkey in 1895 and another million in 1915. The Azeris speak Turkish but definitely cannot be fingered for the death and destruction of the Armenian peoples during WWII.

The Scoop

Armenia is a grindingly poor but workable country that suffers from the emigration of its best and brightest. Not many people other than foreign Armenians bother visiting. Taking a lesson from Hitler and Serbia, they quickly chased out any ethnically or religiously impure folks in the occupied areas. Strangely enough, when there is no one left to complain, everything seems just peachy.

Getting In

A passport and a visa are required. Without a visa, travelers cannot register at hotels and may be required to leave the country immediately via the route by which they entered. U.S. citizens can contact the Armenian Embassy at *122 C Street, Suite 360, Washington, D.C. 20001,* ☎ *(202) 393-5983* for current information on visa requirements.

Getting Around

A natural gas and transportation blockade is causing severe food and medical supply shortages, frequent interruptions in electrical power and shortages of transportation fuel. Internal travel, especially by air, may be disrupted by fuel shortages and other problems. Tourist facilities are not highly developed, and many of the goods and services taken for granted in other countries are not yet available. Armenia's road system is surprisingly good; 6525 miles out of 7022 are paved.

Dangerous Places

Armed conflict is taking place in and around the Armenian-populated area of Nagorno-Karabakh, located in Azerbaijan, and along the Armenian-Azerbaijani border. Fighting continues on a daily basis and the front lines change frequently. The U.S. government has prohibited all U.S. officials from traveling overland between Georgia and Armenia due to the activity of bandits.

Getting Sick

Medical care in Armenia is limited. There are 43 doctors and 91 hospital beds per 10,000 people as of 1989. The U.S. Embassy maintains a list of English speaking physicians in the area. There is a severe shortage of basic medical supplies, including disposable needles, anesthetics and antibiotics. Elderly travelers and those with existing health problems may be at risk due to inadequate medical facilities. Doctors and hospitals often expect immediate cash payment for health services. U.S. medical insurance is not always valid outside the United States. Travelers have found that in some cases, supplemental medical insurance with specific overseas coverage has proved to be useful.

Nuts & Bolts

Armenia is a cash only economy. "Traveler's cheques" and credit cards are not accepted anywhere except as fuel and for lock-picks.

Currency in Armenia is the ruble, with 100 kopeks to 1 ruble. Yerevan is the country's commerce center. An ethnically and religiously pure country in contrast to its neighbors (Armenian 94 percent or 93.3 percent; Kurdish: 1.7 percent; Russian - 1.5 percent; other - 3.5 percent.), Armenia is virtually entirely Christian, with 94 percent being practicing Armenian Orthodox. Armenian is the "official" tongue, but you can find people who speak Russian. The Kurds speak Kurdish. English is not common except among business professionals. Armenia has cold winters and hot summers. The average temperature during the winter in Yerevan is 26 degrees F, while summer enjoys a comfortable average of 77 degrees F. Annual rainfall in Yerevan averages 13 inches but is much higher in the mountainous regions, which also have cooler temperatures. Mud and drab characterizes the Nagorno and Karabak regions.

Americans who register at the Consular Section of the U.S. Embassy may obtain updated information on travel and security within Armenia.

Embassy Locations

Armenian Embassy in the United States
1660 L Street, N.W.
11th Floor
Washington D.C. 20036
☎ *(202) 628-5766*

The U.S. Embassy
18 General Bagramian Street
Yerevan, Armenia
☎ *(7-8852) 15-11-44*

Dangerous Days

03/16/1921	Signing of the Soviet-Turkish border treaty that ended Armenian hopes of establishing an independent state.
04/01/1915	April is designated a "month of remembrance" to commemorate the anniversary of the claimed Turkish massacre of 1915.

Azerbaijan

★

The Russians' First "Wars 'R Us" Store

Oil rich and sparsely populated Azerbaijan finds itself in the crosshairs of Russia, Georgia, Iran and Armenia. The region of Nagorno-Karabakh is now controlled by invading Armenians who want to grab back a predominantly Armenian region now inside Azerbaijan. The fact that Armenia is also the landlord of large tracts of Azeri and Kurdish regions doesn't seem to bother the Armenians.

At least 2500 people have been killed in seven years of fighting over the disputed 1700-square-mile mountain region of Nagorno-Karabakh, a part of Azerbaijan populated by Armenians but under Azeri control since 1923. The relative dominance of a single ethnicity in the country (Azerbaijani - 82.7 percent; Russian - 5.6 percent; Armenian - 5.6 percent; others, including Daghestani - 6.1 percent) normally wouldn't be a predicator of civil war, as the Muslim Azeris vastly outnumber the Armenians. The Azerbaijan Republic was a former province of Persia that was annexed by Russia in 1828. It gained its independence in 1917 but was invaded by the Soviet Army in 1920 and became a Soviet republic in 1936.

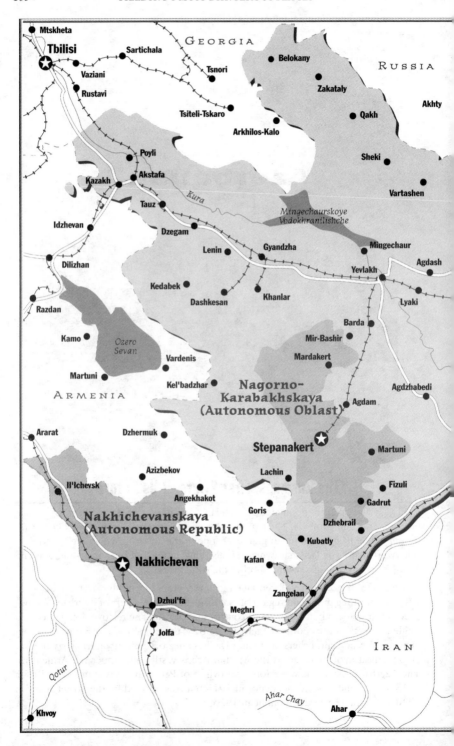

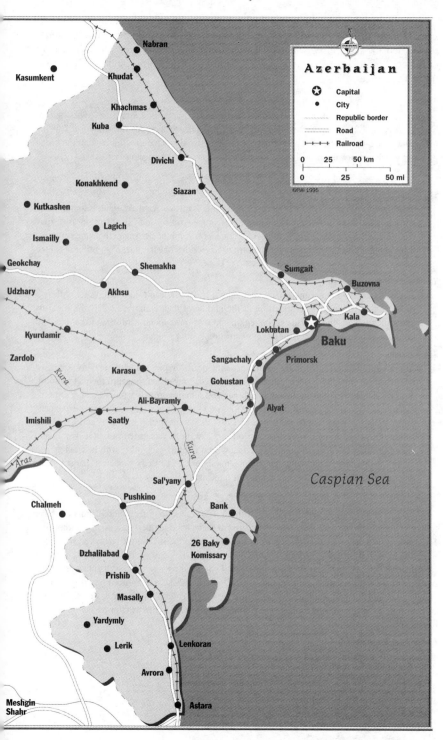

Azerbaijan

⊗ Capital
● City
---- Republic border
==== Road
+-+-+ Railroad

0   25   50 km
0   25   50 mi

©RWI 1995

Nabran
Kasumkent
Khudat
Khachmas
Kuba
Divichi
Konakhkend
Siazan
Kutkashen
Lagich
Ismailly
Geokchay
Shemakha
Sumgait
Buzovna
Udzhary
Akhsu
Kala
Kyurdamir
Lokbatan
Baku
Zardob
Sangachaly
Primorsk
Karasu
Gobustan
Ali-Bayramly
Alyat
Imishili
Saatly
Kura
Aras
Kura
Sal'yany
Chalmeh
Pushkino
Bank
Caspian Sea
26 Baky
Komissary
Dzhalilabad
Prishib
Masally
Yardymly
Lerik
Lenkoran
Avrora
Meshgin
Shahr
Astara

Azerbaijan has been a member of the Commonwealth of Independent States (CIS) since Dec. 21, 1991. Militarily weak, Azerbaijan stands to lose 25 percent of its land to the Armenians and will start marching backwards as Armenia strengthens its grip on occupied territories, and as refugees swell the rest of the country straining Azerbaijan's meager resources.

The Scoop

The Armenians have made an old-fashioned land grab for Nagorno "Carry-back." The Russians have dropped an old-style Politburo member into Azerbaijan to kick out the Armenians. In the meantime, thousands of innocent people have been slaughtered and millions displaced in the brutal fighting, which features an unusual scenario of Russian army soldiers battling each other.

The Players

The Armenians

The Armenians have about 50,000 troops occupying Nagorno-Karabakh. Unless someone big and ugly—and disciplined, unlike Moscow's troops—comes along to throw'em out, they won't be leaving. In the meantime, they've done a good job of cleansing ethnic impurities by driving out all non-Armenians, not only from Nagorno-Karabakh but, from other occupied areas.

The Azeris

The little guys with an army the size of a church choir who can't do a helluva lot with two thirds of the Armenian army squatting in the middle of their country. Luckily the Russians know the value of the oil fields in the region and rent out enough hardware to the Azeris to keep the Armenians shelling their way into attrition.

The Russians

About 62,000 Russian troops are waiting patiently nearby, representing the only real threat to the Armenian army. Both sides accuse the former Red Army of acting against them. The 366th motorized infantry regiment, bored, poorly run and suffering from low morale and desertions, was ordered out of Nagorno-Karabakh by Moscow. Originally utilized to help expel Armenians out of Nagorno-Karabakh in the spring of 1991, they went freelance of sorts and have been aiding both sides in the conflict. Russian officers have gone renegade in the war, with many choosing sides, and Russian units have actually been fighting each other with helicopters and tanks. The officers rent out tanks to both sides for about US$400 a day and even charge for soldiers, as the Russian Army opened up its first franchise of Wars'R Us.

Getting in

A passport and visa are required. Travelers without a visa cannot register at hotels and are subject to hassles and expensive (read that as bribes) treatment at the hands of local visa issuance authorities. Business travelers will need an invitation from someone in Azerbaijan and travelers need telex confirmation from the hotel in Azerbaijan. There is no fee for the visa but there is a $20 express handling (less than 10 days) charge. You will be dinged $75 if you need your visa in less than five days. The border with Armenia is closed and the region of Nagorno-Karabakh is considered unsafe due to the Armenian occupation and ongoing conflict. If you are caught entering the country illegally you will be deported. U.S. citizens can contact the Azerbaijan Embassy for current information on visa requirements.

Embassy of Azerbaijan

927 15th St., NW, Suite 700
Washington DC 20005
☎ *(202) 842-0001*
FAX (202) 842-0001
In Azerbaijan the U.S. Embassy is in the:

Szadliq Prospect 83
☎ *[7] (8922) 96-00-19 or [7] (8922) 98-03-35*

FAX [7] (8922) 98-37-55

Getting Around

Of the total 22,805 miles of roadway in Azerbaijan, 19,760 of them are paved (1990). If that was anywhere else, it might mean smooth sailing—but not here. Vehicles aren't available. There are 1299 railway track miles in Azerbaijan. Take a train and count on it being rocketed or bombed on. The major seaport is at Baku. There is virtually no civil aviation in Azerbaijan. Buses, those that are still running, have no spare parts. Nagorno-Karabakh is currently occupied by the Armenians.

Dangerous Places

Armed conflict and ethnic cleansing is taking place in and around the Armenian-populated area of Nagorno-Karabakh located inside Azerbaijan and along the border areas of Armenia and Iran. Travelers are frequently stopped at roadblocks while vehicles and travel documents are inspected.

Nagorno-Karabakh

The obscure and mildly unpronounceable regions of Nagorno and Karabakh have been the locations of dirty and hate-filled fighting in Azerbaijan. Armenia has simply grabbed a quarter of Azerbaijan under the pretext that it wants to bring the predominantly Armenian region of Nagorno-Karabakh back into the fold. Formerly 94.4 percent of Nagorno-Karabakh's population was Armenian. Now the area is 100 percent Armenian. Armenia maintains that the Armenians of Nagorno-Karabakh voted for secession in a December 1991 referendum. They forget to mention that the Armenians cast 40,000 votes from a region of 160,000 people in a country of 7 million. Think of it as a small Cajun bayou town in Louisiana asking France to liberate them.

In the Armenians' enthusiasm to liberate their fellow Armenians, they have managed to also occupy non-Armenian areas in Azerbaijan, such as the 4741 sq km regions of Lachin, Shusha, Agdam and Kelbajar, which just happen to lie between the Armenians and Nagorno-Karabakh. The fact that there are 131,197 sq kms of Azerbaijan under foreign occupation has not seemed to interest the world's press other than to create little sidebars in annual roundups of small wars. Since the Armenians are on a roll, they also are busy cleansing themselves of Kurds. In 1992, after forcing the 25,000 Kurdish residents out of Armenian-occupied areas, the historic Kurdish capital of Lachin was looted and burned. Kurdish monuments, libraries and cultural sites were razed. Armenia has also expelled Kurds in the occupied regions into Iran and what little of Azerbaijan still exists. All told, the war between the Armenians and Azeris has spawned more than 1 million Azeri refugees, 300,000 Armenians, tens of thousands of Kurds and countless other tribal and ethnic factions. In 1989, Nagorno-Karabakh was run by a committee in Moscow. Gorbachev proposed a six-mile buffer zone around the enclave but he resigned as the Soviet president before any action was taken.

The local Russian Army has been backing both sides depending upon the financial arrangement or ethnic alignment of the officers. The president of Azerbaijan, Abulfez Elchibey, fled the country on June 18, 1993, leaving the parliament leader—an old Brezhnev-era-former-head-of-the-Azeri-branch-of-the-KGB-boss named Heydar Aliyev—to run the show. Technically the CIS is an autonomous group of independent countries. But they usually go running to mother Russia when there is trouble. The Russian Army has bolstered the scrawny 5000-man Azeri army but has been losing in magnificent form to the Armenians.

Nakhichevan

Alikram Gumbatov and his supporters made a grab for power in seven southern areas of Talysh-Mugan. This area, also known as Nakhichevan, is a minuscule region in southeast Azerbaijan. Shoehorned between Armenia, Iran and Nagorno-Karabakh, it is not surprising that it declared its independence in August of 1993. The Nakhichevan People's Front has not announced when a new McDonalds will open or when postage stamps will go on sale. It remains to be seen whether the Azeris, Armenians or Iranians will remember to set up an embassy.

Dangerous Things

Money Hassles

Azerbaijan is a "cash only" economy. "Traveler's cheques" and credit cards are not accepted. While the local currency is the manat, the Russian ruble is in circulation and prices are often confusingly quoted in manats and rubles. U.S. dollars are required in most hotels and preferred in many restaurants. .

Drug Penalties

U.S. citizens are subject to the laws of the country in which they are traveling. Penalties for possession, use or trafficking in illegal drugs are strict and convicted offenders can expect jail sentences and fines.Azerbaijan dabbles in the cultivation of marijuana and opium, which are lucrative exports.

Getting Sick

Medical care in Azerbaijan is dangerously limited. There were 40 doctors and 101 hospital beds per 10,000 people before the war. The U.S. embassy maintains a list of English-speaking physicians in the area. There is a severe shortage of basic medical supplies, including disposable needles, anesthetics and vaccines against communicable diseases. Doctors and hospitals often expect immediate cash payment for health services. Some recent health problems include cases of cholera in Baku and cases of anthrax in Nakhichevan. Malaria is found in some southern border areas near Iran.

Nuts & Bolts

The currency is the manat with a hundred gopik to the manat.The port city of Baku is the capital and major business center. It has a population of just over a million and not much else.

Many of Azerbaijan's people live in geographically isolated, ethnically pure pockets of topography, the result of years of wars, migrations and dubious, short-lived peace settlements. The 1828 Russo-Persian carved up a much larger Azerbaijan into two slices. Half went to Persia (about nine million Turkish-speaking Azerbaijanis comprise one-fifth of the Iranian population) and the rest went to Russia.

The country is 87 percent Muslim, 5.6 percent Russian Orthodox and 5.6 percent Armenian Orthodox. The language is Azeri (82 percent) with a smattering of Russian (7 percent) and Armenian (11 percent.) Azerbaijan has the same lousy weather that the rest of Caucasus enjoys: cold in the winter (average January temperature in the plains area is 34 degrees F) and baking in the summer (average 80 degrees F). There's a lot of rain and mud in the spring and fall. The Lenkoran plains area has an average rainfall of between 39 and 68.9 inches. The average annual rainfall in low-lying areas varies between 7.9 and 11.8 inches.

Embassy Location

Prospect Azadling 83
Baku, Azerbaijan
☎ *(7-8922) 96-36-21, 96-00-19 or 91-79-57 (from outside Azerbaijan)*
☎ *96-36-21 or 96-00-19 (from within the country)*
FAX (7-8922) 98-37-55.

In a Dangerous Place

March 1991 Azerbaijan

The war had just begun in Azerbaijan. We caught an early morning flight into Baku on a beat up old *TU-154*. I was with three other journalists and figured we could get past the Russian border guards with a minor bribe. The Aeroflot logo had been crudely painted over and the plane now was called Azerbaijan Airways. On board was a motley crew: doctors and nurses on their way to the war zone, businessmen looking to set up import-export contracts and men on their way to the cheap sex vacations Baku was famous for.

When we arrived, $50 each was all it took to get our passports stamped. We found a driver outside the airport who would make the 200km trip to Gendje southeast of Baku. This would take us close to the war zone on the Karabakh border. Along the way we passed hundreds of Russian-made trucks carrying soldiers and tanks. Whatever the Russians had left behind after Azerbaijan declared its independence was now the official property of the Azeris. Despite Gendje's proximity to the war, the only complaint the people seemed to have was how the prices had been driven up by the visiting soldiers and short supplies. That night we found another driver who would take us into the war area. We arrived in Agdam by midnight. The road was rough but the ever increasing check points made the journey tedious at best. The fact that we were Turkish meant that we were among friends. Of all the Central Asian Turkic languages, the Azeri's is the closest to that of the Turks. Our arrival in Agdam looked like a Hollywood director's version of a war zone. It seemed that every building was in flames or exploding.We were welcomed by a heavy barrage of Katusha rockets. Our driver was a volunteer member of "the Popular Front" and took us to their local HQ. a large house in the center of the besieged town. The place was teeming with soldiers and volunteers. They were talking anxiously on Russian-made walkie-talkies, counting, unpacking and distributing weapons for the front, and what made it all unusual was that they were all speaking Russian. Even the older Azeris were using Russian, though they spoke Azeri amongst themselves.

We were given beds on the upper floor of the headquarters. The fact that we were surrounded on all sides by burning buildings didn't help us get to sleep. When we found out that the headquarters also doubled as the ammunition depot, sleep was soon forgotten. We listened to each explosion to hear if we would be next. We looked at what was in the crates that held up our mattresses and found that they were packed with grenades and rockets. Though we were worried, we fell to sleep and woke a few hours later when a large explosion blew up a sawmill outside our window. We got up and walked the 200 meters to the sawmill to take photos. There was not much to photograph and the intense heat kept us back. When we went back to our room to try to catch up on our sleep we found a club-footed soldier in our room setting up a radio and fiddling with the dial. We watched as he listened to the radio at full volume while we had our sweet tea and Russian biscuits.

Wanting to get to the front to get some photographs, we arranged for two soldiers to take us to the front in a Russian jeep about 4.5 kms away. We joined a tedious parade of trucks carrying ammunition, rations, men and other journalists. We arrived during an artillery barrage. The Azeris were positioned just below the summit of a hill that faced the Armenian position on another hilltop. The equipment they were using to fight this war was cast off by the Russians and it was obvious why they didn't take it with them. The volunteers that manned the artillery were surprisingly young, about

15 or 16; most of them had little idea how to properly utilize the decrepit tanks and artillery. I remember watching the teenagers playing around with the colored rings of the mortar shells. Each ring sends the mortar 100mm towards the target, but if the kids undid the knots that held the explosive rings around the narrow tails of the mortar shells they would go off like Chinese Crackers. They played with these deadly toys around the bodies of their wounded and dead comrades.

I also noticed what made the tanks and artillery look so ridiculous. The Azeris had bent the barrels of the tanks into "S" shapes by improperly loading their tanks. The shortage of skilled soldiers and operational equipment had created a market for entrepreneurs. The Russians had kept their presence in Azerbaijan unofficial but there was an ominous force that looked markedly different. These were the tanks manned by soldiers for hire. These were Russian soldiers who rented out their tanks for $100 a day; the crew cost $50 extra. The white Russian ID number was covered in mud. The comical part is that the same tank would show up on the opposite side a day or two later and shell their former employers.

We stayed in our deadly accommodations, becoming indifferent to the explosions around us and the fact that we would be instantly atomized if a shell landed on our building. The deaf and club-footed radio operator never returned, and his radio sat in the corner of our room untouched.

The next day we went to the cemetery to see the fighting that raged where the Azeri cemetery butted up to the Armenian cemetery. We rented a minibus and when we arrived the fighting was fierce and hand-to-hand. Both sides used the tombstones as cover as they shot at each other and charged each others position. We got out of the minibus some distance away and crawled toward the cemetery wall. We tried to capture the fighting while keeping our heads down behind the wall.

We were surprised by the arrival of the local Armenian commander. Middle-aged with snow white hair, Allahverdi (which translated means "God given") whipped out a megaphone and began shouting orders to his men in Russian. The fighting stopped and one of the soldiers with him explained that he was negotiating for the release of 15 prisoners captured the day before. The Azeris were 250 meters away on the other side of the cemetery. The deal was a tanker full of gas in exchange for the prisoners. The answer came back: "No. We want a tanker full of gas and 12 hours of electricity." A deal was cut and the prisoners were released the next day. We saw the prisoners when they arrived at the HQ building where we were staying. Most were old; they had their gold teeth yanked out and their toes had been broken when they were tortured. The women had been raped, while the young teenagers seemed to be in shock and would not talk. The people that had done this had been their neighbors only 15 days before. Now they were sworn enemies.

We had seen enough. This was a dirty, stupid war. We hitchhiked our way back to Gendje. We found a plane flying to Baku and asked the fare. It was the cheapest flight I have ever taken—$1. The plane was another ex-Aeroflot junk heap. We counted over 80 passengers not including goats, chickens and luggage. There was standing room only as they shoved more passengers on board. When the plane was well past capacity we took off. Just before take-off the pilot, mistaking us for Russians, turned to us and said "For $20 I will fly us all to Moscow, Do you want to go now?" We passed.

Bolivia
★

The Lure of Easy Money

Butch Cassidy and the Sundance Kid hung out here. So did other outlaws and bandits. It was a great place to hide, with rugged, inaccessible terrain. Police and the army were easy to pay off to ensure some protection and anonymity. Today, it's much the same.

Bolivia is undoubtedly the poorest country in South America with a per capital annual income of a little over US$600. That's the official figure. If you include the amount thousands are making picking coca leaves, chewing coca leaves and turning them into white powder, then moving it to North America to be tooted, toked and mainlined by high school kids, gold-encased ghetto gangsters, sleazy Hollywood movie moguls and a few million decent people who've gotten caught up in a bad thing, then you'll see a huge number of wealthy Bolivians.

In the 1980s, Bolivia's economy took a nose-dive. Surging unemployment (nearly 20 percent) forced a large segment of the population into the drug trade, and coca was an easy cash crop. Four crops can be harvested a year. It's easier to grow than grass.

Bolivia

✪ National capital
● Department capital
Department border
Road
┝━┿━┿━┥ Railroad

0 50 100 150 200 km
0 50 100 150 mi

©FWI 1995

Ariquemes

Ji-Paraná

Vilhena

Guaporé

Paraguá

BRAZIL

Mato Grosso

Cáceres

Santa Cruz

San Miguel

ntero

Santa Cruz

San José de Chiquitos

Roboré

Puerto Suárez

Corumbá

General Eugenio A. Garay

Capitán Pablo Lagerenza

montes

ja

PARAGUAY

Paraguay

Mariscal Estigarribia

Bolivia's cocaine industry is a US$2 billion a year business. Who wants to go back to slashing sugar cane and picking cotton? Throw in a virtually lawless and uninhabitable terrain along with a turbulent political history rooted in racial, ethnic and geographic strife and you've got the fodder for rock & roll anthems. Not to mention a lot of death.

What else would you expect from the land of Ché?

Bolivia was sliced up and much of it divided by three neighboring countries. Bolivia lost several thousand square miles, and its outlet to the Pacific, to Chile after the War of the Pacific in 1884. Brazil annexed Bolivia's rubber-rich Acre province in 1903. In 1938 after a war between those two countries nearly 100,000 miles of the Gran Chaco was swallowed up by Paraguay.

Then in 1965, Ché (Ernesto) Guevara was dispatched from Cuba by Uncle Fidel—not one to miss an opportunity to start an insurrection—to the revolutionary-fertile soil of Bolivia to off some fascists, wreak havoc and recruit anyone with a pop gun. The CIA—not one to miss an opportunity to quell an insurrection—smashed Ché's little red tag sale and executed the guerrilla on October 9, 1967.

Bolivia took a serpentine course toward democracy, but an attempt at a civilian government was quickly snuffed in 1980 when General Luis Garcia Meza Tejada wrested power. In 1982, the military moved to restore civilian rule to Bolivia after a succession of cigar-chomping generals followed Tejada. However, under President Hernán Siles Zuazo's rule, the country became paralyzed by strikes and work stoppages, including the processing of the nation's natural resources, such as gold, natural gas, lithium, tungsten and potassium. Inflation soared to 3000 percent. Enter the coca leaf.

The Scoop

Bolivia is a recovering country, its economy improving at a snail's pace. Although inflation has come down to 10–20 percent, unemployment continues at alarming rates, making tourists the frequent targets of petty crime, particularly in La Paz. Bolivia's acute poverty problem, along with widespread corruption, continues to create unrest. Although terrorist incidents are infrequent in comparison with Andean neighbors of Chile, Peru and Colombia, it should be noted that U.S citizens are the primary targets of Bolivian terrorist groups.

The Players

Nestor Paz Zamora Commission (CNPZ)

A radical leftist terrorist organization that first appeared in October 1990. It is named after the deceased brother of President Paz Zamora. It currently operates under the umbrella of the ELN (Bolivia) and is a violent, extremely anti-U.S., Marxist-Leninist organization. In June 1990, the Bolivian owner of the La Paz Coca-Cola Bottling Company was kidnapped by the CNPZ while he was being driven to work in downtown La Paz. The victim was murdered by his captors on December 5, 1990 during a rescue attempt by Bolivian police. In October 1990, the group attacked the residence of the U.S. embassy's marine security guard detachment in La Paz with automatic weapons and explosives. One Bolivian police officer standing guard at the marine house was killed and another officer was seriously wounded. None of the marines were injured. The same month, the CNPZ bombed a monument to U.S. President John F. Kennedy in La Paz.Today, the group is probably operating with fewer than 100 guerrillas. Peru's MTRA (Tupac Amaru) has provided training, limited funding and logistic support.

General Luis Garcia Meza Tejada

A former military dictator of Bolivia, Garcia Meza was sentenced to 30 years imprisonment for humans rights offenses at the end of Jaime Paz Zamora's presidential term. Although Garcia Meza was jailed, along with a number of convicted accomplices, he managed to escape from custody during his trial. He was recaptured in Brazil during early 1994.

Gonzalo Sanchez de Lozada

He became president of Bolivia in June 1993 despite accruing the necessary 51 percent majority votes needed to become president. A half-dozen other candidates for a short time rejected his ascendancy to the presidency but eventually conceded.

Dangerous Places

Santa Cruz and Vicinity

Up to the present time, there has been no major problem with terrorism or civil disorder in Santa Cruz. Although a number of major narco-traffickers consider Santa Cruz their home, there has been only one act of retaliation against the DEA personnel stationed there. Crime in Santa Cruz is both more prevalent and more violent than in any other Bolivian city. Armed robbery has become commonplace in certain areas and taxi drivers have even been murdered for their money. Vehicles traveling from Paraguay to Santa Cruz have been robbed by armed bandits. Large amounts of cocaine have been smuggled out of both Santa Cruz and Cochabamba. It is strongly advised that you not hitchhike or accept rides from strangers. Various sectors of Santa Cruz, Cochabamba and Beni regions are under the control of narco traffickers. Travelers should contact the consular agents for specific information.

Cochabamba and Vicinity

There has been a perceptible shift in public opinion and a rise in anti-American sentiment in Cochabamba during the last two years. This can be explained by the fact that drug-related interests have acquired access to mass media and leftist politicians have begun to organize the coca leaf growers. Furthermore, there is growing evidence of radical leftists linking up with the coca growers. As the COB (Bolivian Workers Central) membership has dwindled (due to lay-offs in the miners' and factory workers, unions), radical organizers and union leaders increasingly organize and advise the coca growers. Leftist university students have consistently demonstrated in support of coca growers demands. A few years ago (1987-1988) Cochabamba businessmen were being kidnapped for varying periods of time and later released after paying substantial ransoms. The criminals responsible for these kidnappings have been imprisoned and no other kidnappings have been reported since then. As far as drug-related violence is concerned, the press recently reported the forcible break-in to the house of a former Bolivian police colonel. Aside from that, all residents and foreign visitors are vulnerable to purse snatching and pilfering of objects. Burglaries are common and there are continual reports of wallets and documentation being stolen at bus terminals, airports and hotels. Pickpockets are, of course, common in the open-air markets.

Dangerous Things

Street Crime

Street crime, such as pickpocketing and theft from parked vehicles, is common. Violent crimes or crimes involving weapons are rare, especially in La Paz, although there are indications of an increased incidence of such crimes in Santa Cruz. In downtown La Paz and the Calacoto region most frequented by Americans, crime consists of pickpocketing, vehicular break-ins and burglary. Robbery, assault and other violent crimes are almost unheard of in these areas. In the poorer areas of the city, especially the sprawling suburbs of El Alto, assault, rape and robbery are much more common. Americans are cautioned against staying in these areas at night.

Civil disorder and terrorism

All terrorist acts directed against U.S. citizens over the last five years have occurred in La Paz. Although terrorist incidents are infrequent in comparison with the Andean neighbors of Chile, Peru and Colombia, it should be noted that U.S citizens are the primary targets of Bolivian terrorist groups. Of the Americans targeted, those at the most risk are the ambassador, military and DEA personnel. Some local employees have also been subject to harassment. U.S. corporations are also at risk, although not as high profile as U.S. government personnel. Most U.S. businesses have contractual relations with the Bolivian national police to provide physical security for their buildings. There have been isolated terrorist incidents against American officials, installations and resident missionaries over the past three years. There have been two incidents in 1993, one involving a low-level bombing of a U.S. Agency for International Development (USAID) facility in La Paz and another against a Mormon Church in El Alto.

Since January 1991, there have been numerous bomb placements and bomb threats throughout La Paz. The La Paz bomb squad has been receiving at least three bomb threats a day for the last six months. The great majority of these threats are false; however, a dozen or so bombs have been found throughout La Paz's commercial centers and three were found at the La Paz airport. To date, no one has been killed or wounded by a bomb blast. Demonstrations or strikes occur on an almost weekly basis in La Paz. The majority of these demonstrations are peaceful and not anti-U.S. in nature. All travelers are cautioned to stay away from these marches due to the frequent detonation of small dynamite charges and rockets by protesters. For the most part, tourists and business travelers are not targeted in terrorist acts or civil disorders.

Bogus Cops

Bolivian law holds that police may only search your belongings at a police station. If you are asked to be searched, demand to be taken to a police station. If you're detained by an individual in plain clothes claiming to be a cop, insist on seeing an identity card or badge and note the date on it. There are numerous instances of tourists being robbed by bandits posing as police officers, particularly in La Paz and Sucre. If you are robbed, go to the nearest Departamento de Criminalistica.

Hassles with Police

There is police resentment in some Bolivian cities and towns toward Americans because of U.S. involvement in Bolivia's drug eradication efforts. Some police officers don't appreciate gringos messing with Bolivia's internal affairs. Their animosity may be taken out on you; however, not violently, but in the form of laxadaisical assistance.

Drugs

U.S. citizens are subject to the laws of the country in which they are traveling. Penalties in Bolivia for possession, use and trafficking in illegal drugs are strict, and convicted offenders can expect lengthy jail sentences and fines.

Police response capability

U.S. Government employees are protected by the embassy's 300-man local guard force because the Bolivian police force cannot provide adequate security. The police do not possess sufficient manpower, communication equipment or vehicles to be able to quickly react to any ongoing crime. The lack of good police response capability is the same throughout Bolivia.

The recently instituted roving patrol has proven to be very responsive to official American needs. Local businessmen have received visits from and visited Bolivian police commanders who have shown themselves pleasant and cooperative. Emergency telephone numbers in Bolivia:

Embassy La Paz: ☎ *430251*
Roving Patrol La Paz: ☎ *342723, 323035*
Bolivian National Police La Paz: 110 Cmdo.
Departmental De Cochabamba: ☎ *25550*
Roving Patrol Cochabamba: ☎ *22793*
Consular Agency Cochabamba: ☎ *44775*
Cmdo. Departmental De Santa Cruz: ☎ *321826, 345677*
Roving Patrol Santa Cruz: ☎ *40937*
Consular Agency Santa Cruz: ☎ *330725*
Cmdo. Departmental De Trinidad/Beni: ☎ *21090*
Sub. Comando: ☎ *20466*
Transito: ☎ *20933*
Cmdo. Departmental De Cobija/Pando: ☎ *2242*
Transito: ☎ *2328*
Criminalistica: ☎ *2287*

Cmdo. Departmental De La Paz: ☎ *377384*
Cmdte De Criminalistica: ☎ *377317, 375333*

Extortion

There is a perceptible increase in extortions practiced on visitors and foreign tourists by Bolivian government officials. Typically, Bolivian males who identify themselves as immigration or customs officers will extort 10 to 20 U.S. dollars from tourists who have not "registered" their video cameras or other equipment in their passports. Routinely, tourists are forced to pay bribes to expedite the issuance of visas or other permits by Bolivian government agencies.

Narcotics Activities

Because of anti-narcotics activities in the Chapare region between Santa Cruz and Cochabamba, the potential for security risks exists in this area. Travelers to this area may consult with the Consular Section of the U.S. Embassy prior to travel.

Demonstrations

La Paz and other cities have been the scene of frequent demonstrations by various local groups. Although there has been no violence specifically directed at foreigners during these demonstrations, there are occasional confrontations between police and demonstrators.

Getting Sick

Medical care in large cities is adequate but of varying quality. Doctors and hospitals usually expect immediate cash payment for health services. U.S. medical insurance is not valid in Bolivia. In some cases, supplemental medical insurance with specific overseas coverage has proved to be useful.

Cholera is present in Bolivia. Visitors who follow proper precautions about food and drink are not usually at risk. For additional health information and information on high altitude travel, travelers may contact the Centers for Disease Control's international travelers hotline at ☎ *(404) 332-4559.*

Nuts & Bolts

Bolivia is a developing nation with a slowly growing economy. Facilities for tourism are adequate, but vary in quality. The country is about the size of California and Texas combined. It's bordered by Chile and Peru to the west, and by Paraguay and Argentina to the south. The western part of Bolivia is a great plateau—the Altiplano, enclosed by two chains of the Andes—with an average altitude of 12,000 feet (3658 m). The area is home to 80 percent of the population as well as the administrative capital of La Paz. Lake Titicaca, at 3812 meters, is one of the largest high lakes in the world. Ancient Inca ruins can be found on islands in the lake. The eastern portion of the country is a low alluvial plain drained by the Amazon and Plata river systems.

The principal language is Spanish, however, Quechua and Aymara are widely spoken. Roman Catholics comprise 95 percent of the country. The monetary unit is the boliviano (Bs). It's divided into 100 centavos. The local time is four hours behind GMT.

Business hours are normally between 9 a.m. and 12 p.m. (11:30 a.m. in La Paz) and between 2 p.m. and 6 p.m. Monday-Friday; 9 a.m.–12 p.m. on Saturdays. In the provinces, businesses generally open and close later. Banks are open from 9 a.m. to 12 p.m. Monday-Friday and closed on Saturdays. Government offices are open during normal business hours but are closed Saturdays.

The best time of the year to visit Bolivia is during the dry season from May to November. Keep in mind however, May, June and July are the coldest months.

Embassy Location

Americans who register with the Consular Section of the U.S. Embassy in La Paz, located one block from the Embassy on the second floor of the Tobia building on Calle Potosi near the corner with Calle Colon, ☎ *(591-2) 356-685*, can obtain updated information on travel and security within Bolivia.

U.S. Embassy

Avenida Arce No. 2780
San Jorge
☎ *(591-2) 430-251*

FAX (591-2) 433-560

Consular Agents:

in Santa Cruz

Marilyn J. McKenney (acting)
in the Edificio Oriente
on Calle Bolivian, corner of Chuquisaca, Room 313
☎ *(591) 33-30725 (office)*
☎ *(591) 33-23467 (home)*
in Cochabamba

William Scarborough
1724 Libertador Bolivar Ave.
☎ *(591) 42-43216 (office)*
☎ *(591) 42-44775 (home)*
The Consular Agencies are open mornings Monday through Friday.

This replaces the Consular Information Sheet of October 27, 1992 to provide updated information on crime, terrorist activities and to add information on reporting the loss or theft abroad of a U.S. passport.

Important Phone Numbers:

Banco Popular Del Peru Building

Calle Colon No. 280 (Cor. Calle Mercado)
La Paz
☎ *(591) (2) 350-120 Or 350-251*

Comando General De La Policia Boliviana

☎ *(591) (2) 378-280*

Entry Requirements

A passport is required. U.S. citizens do not need a visa for a one-month stay. For current information concerning entry and customs requirements for Bolivia, travelers can contact the Bolivian Embassy at *3014 Massachusetts Avenue NW, Washington, D.C. 20008,* ☎ *(202) 483-4410* or the nearest consulate in Los Angeles, Miami, New York or Houston.

Dangerous Days

07/04/1991   The Tupac Katari Guerrilla Army (EGTK) carried out its first terrorist act—blowing up two electric power pylons in the city of El Alto—on this date.

Bosnia-Herzegovina

The Balkanization of the Balkans

When the Soviet tablecloth was yanked out from under the Communist Bloc, regimes smashed into pieces. One of these was Yugoslavia. Yugoslavia had been bound
in the big bear hug of Tito for more than 45 years, but now it is a patchwork of religious and ethnic groups—all harboring long standing grudges that go back to the
Middle Ages.

Bosnia-Herzegovina is not one country, but two regions glued together. Without
"Big Brother" around to settle disputes, the country erupted into a land grab for in-
dependence.The Serb minority called up the Serbian-run Yugoslav Peoples Army to
wage an old-fashioned blood feud. The Muslims, found primarily in the cities of Bosnia, found themselves under siege. Serbian snipers took great pride in gut shots over
head shots; they enabled the gutless gunners to watch their victims squirm to death.
Children were worth more points because they were harder to hit. Atrocities and mass
executions were *de rigueur*. Television reporters tried to make sense of the sickening
carnage; viewers watched shoppers try to sort which leg they should take to the hospital. We preferred "Beavis and Butthead." At least that made sense.

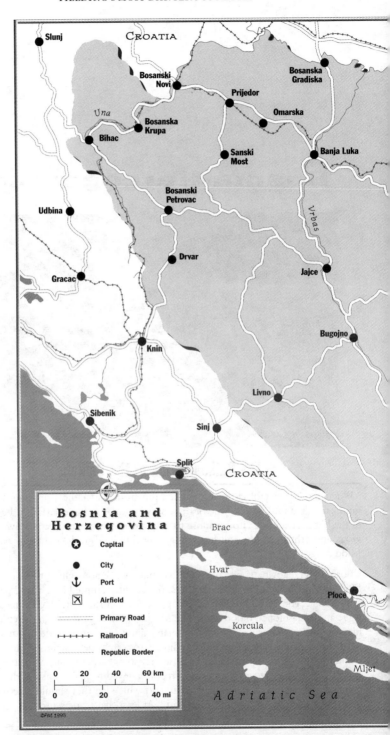

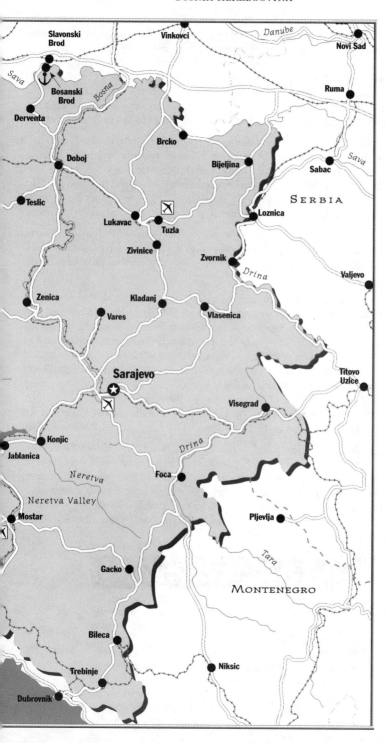

Bosnia has continued to be a seesaw battle zone. The foes in this bitter, three-year-old conflict aren't sure what to do. Battering and reeling, they don't quite know how to kiss and make up. The odds are they never will. Former U.S. President Jimmy Carter brokered a superficial cease-fire that has reduced the body count, but not the hatred. This beleaguered ex-Yugoslav republic agreed to end all hostilities between rebel Bosnian Serbs and the Croats for four months. But, as usual, the Serbs use these "time outs" to do a little spring ethnic cleansing in the Bihac region while the world press turns to more important matters like O.J.'s trial and the glut of music award shows.

The five-nation Contact Group has drawn up a plan for dividing Bosnia-Herzegovina. It involves ceding 49 percent of the former Yugoslav republic's land to Bosnian Serb leader Radovan Karadzic and 51 percent to the internationally-recognized government. Although the Muslim-led government initially balked and then accepted the plan, the Serbs have held out, demanding more territory. However, they have started opening up besieged roads in Sarajevo for civilian transportation and supply purposes.

The Serbs continue to lay claim to the government-held area of Mt. Igman. The area is supposed to be demilitarized, but the Serbs claim government forces have occupied areas in the region illegally. Nonetheless, the Serbs say, they have no plans of scuttling the cease-fire.

High in the mountains above embattled Sarajevo, once—seemingly in a fairy tale—the pristine, majestic site of the winter olympics, is Pale, the capital of the self-proclaimed Republika Srpska, or Republic of the Bosnian Serbians. Even though atrocities have been committed by all sides in the war, the Serbs have been getting most of the blame. There have been death camps run by the Serbs, examples of savagery and systematic barbarism that hasn't been seen on the continent since the Nazis of World War II. Karadzic's Serbs, under the military leadership of Ratko Mladic, have been strangling Sarajevo's 300,000 or so residents for three years. The Serbs, in 1992, began their ethnic cleansing campaign, forcing hundreds of thousands of Muslims out of the region. Thousands died in the Drina River Valley campaigns of 1992 and 1993.

Mladic doesn't seem at all prepared to give back anything he and his 80,000 soldiers have taken in the last three years. He's gone on the record saying he'll never retreat. The Serbs hold about 70 percent of the country, more than 800 miles of front lines, meaning they'll have to cede nearly a quarter of the territory they've gained since 1992. They claim they have enough oil reserves to fight a full-scale war for months to come, in spite of Serbian President Slobodan Milosevic's moves toward blocking oil, arms and food shipments to the rebels.

Sniper Alley: Rapid transit in Sarajevo

The streetcars in Sarajevo may be old but they are never dull. They were shut down by shelling when war broke out in April 1992. The tram system reopened in March 1994 after a local cease-fire ended the daily bombardment of Sarajevo. The trams have become a daily target for Serbian snipers. They travel only 300 meters from Grbavica, a Serb-held district where snipers fire from high-rise apartment buildings. But they're a healthier alternative to running or walking the same distance. U.N. anti-sniper teams have been deployed along the tram line and are firing back to deter the shooters. The line's most dangerous stretch passes between the Bosnian parliament building and the Holiday Inn, a base for foreign diplomats and journalists.

The Scoop

Starting in 1991, war in Yugoslavia spread like a cancer from the northwest to the southeast. The rest of the world has since seen children murdered, concentration camps, atrocities and sniper-stricken Sunday shoppers sliding around in their own blood. The armies of NATO are a two-hour drive away but they choose to keep practicing for a Soviet invasion. Most politicians don't remember much Balkan history, but they do recall that this region has been the crucible of many a European and world war. Bill, John, Helmut and Boris do not want to be remembered as the next Neville Chamberlain. So, they leave the dirty work to the world's lowest paid referees: the U.N.

Balkanization is the term used to describe insurmountable factionalism. So, the U.N. acts like a chaperon at a high school dance, scolding, but turning its backs when the kids start goosing each other.

Now Bosnia burns while the Western world fiddles. While the politico boys live it up on their expense accounts in Paris (in between "vital" negotiations), the Muslim population seems to decrease in proportion to Serbian land gains. The insurgent Serbs want to annex the ground they've gained to Serbia. The Muslim Croats just want the damn war to end.

This conflict is arguably on par with the last great noble war: the Spanish Civil War. Mercs and volunteers from Great Britain, Russia, Iran, Iraq, Afghanistan, Egypt, Turkey, Canada, Greece and the U.S. put in a few days in-country until they realized there was little glory and even less money. War photographers, who initially covered Bosnia like flies on dog dung when newspapers gave a damn about it, headed for Somalia where there was more sun and they didn't have to get so damn muddy.

The U.S. State Department warns U.S. citizens not to travel to Bosnia-Herzegovina because of the ongoing war. Due to the limited number of staff and the need for heightened security, the U.S. Embassy in Sarajevo is unable to perform consular functions except in extreme emergencies.

The Players

The Serbs

The bad guys. The Serbs have made fools of the international community and the U.N. They had their hands slapped through token U.N. airstrikes. They continue to expand their control of Muslim regions and to lay siege to Sarajevo. The Serbs control about a third of Croatia and two thirds of Bosnia. They are not giving it up.

General Ratko Mladik

The Serb rebel commander. Ruthless but loved by his soldiers. Has said that only an army that is defeated retreats. "Smash, don't sprinkle!" he proclaims. Although Srpska Republic President Radovan Karadzic is in charge, Mladik calls the shots on the ground, where most of the "peace process" is taking place. He eats and sleeps with his soldiers, and leads them into combat in an armored personnel carrier. In June 1994, a Bosnian government offensive took the southern slopes of Mt. Ozren. The Serbs counterattacked, retaking the area and killing approximately 1000 soldiers. Such ingenuity is countered by his constant pounding of innocents in Sarajevo, not a difficult tactic. Mladik said he would send terrorist bombers to London and New York after the U.S. and Great Britain announced in 1993 they were considering airstrikes against Serb positions.

Srpska Republic President Radovan Karadzic

Not as fanatical as Mladik; the president called Mladik's terrorist threats "idiotic and irresponsible."

Croat-Muslims

Croatians and the mostly Muslim Bosnians, who comprise about 75 percent of Bosnia's population, formed a federation to try to counter the Serb juggernaut. They tend to elicit sympathy from both the West and the Islamic world, but still generally get their asses kicked on the battlefield. Supported by Iranian-backed mujahedin and Hezbollah fighters, as well as mercenaries and volunteers from a number of countries.

The U.N.

Bosnia has been the worst PR disaster in its history for the U.N. Ineffective, insulted and frustrated, the U.N. soldiers have watched as the Serbs mercilessly pound Sarajevo, as well as their own soldiers. U.N. troops have been the frequent targets of Serb snipers and other attacks.

Mercenaries/Volunteers

Some countries such as Iran view the conflict as a Muslim-Christian thing and have sent in mujahedin guerrillas and members of Hezbollah. Others see it as a Serb-Croat fight, and volunteers from the U.S., Canada and Europe have come in to take some potshots. Still others simply see Bosnia-Herzegovina as a great place to kill someone.

Getting In

A passport is required. Permission to enter Bosnia and Herzegovina is currently granted at the border on a case-by-case basis. Journalists have a good chance. Looky-loos create grief for the U.N. forces. Without press credentials, forget it.

Getting Around

Journalists are the only ones trying these days and they need tanks to do it. Sygma, one of the world's top photo news agencies, acquired an armored personnel carrier in 1993 to protect its under-fire shooters in Bosnia, and to get them around. However, there isn't yet regularly-scheduled armored personnel carrier service in Bosnia. Women journalists seem to be better able to get around in Bosnia than their male counterparts. Alain Mingnam, editorial manager of Sygma's Paris office, said that women were preferable to men in many instances because they'll go "where no man will ever go."

There are checkpoints throughout the country which are manned generally by militia personnel, but occasionally by undisciplined, untrained reserve militia groups. These militia groups frequently confiscate relief goods and trucks, and may otherwise behave unprofessionally. Travelers are expected to provide identification and cooperate fully at these checkpoints. Travelers should refrain from photographing police, buildings under police or military guard, border crossings, demonstrations, riots, and military personnel, convoys, maneuvers and bases.

Dangerous Places

The Entire Country

The ongoing civil war has completely ruined the tourist industry in Bosnia-Herzegovina. The cultural heritage of Bosnia's Muslim cities is no longer accessible. The unabated fighting between the Serbs and the Croats has created massive social and economic problems, including mass homelessness and chronic unemployment. All plans for modernization and industrial growth have been shelved for at least the next decade.

Eastern Bosnia and Sarajevo

Travel to Eastern Bosnia and the capital city of Sarajevo is particularly dangerous. The popular religious shrine at Medjugorje is located within Bosnia-Herzegovina's borders, but not a lot of tourists get a chance to see it these days.

The Border with Serbia

The ongoing war in Bosnia-Herzegovina makes this area very dangerous. The danger is especially acute in the Drina River Valley of both Bosnia-Herzegovina and Serbia.

Dangerous Things

Kidnapping

Hostages are often taken by all the warring factions with the aim to swap them for imprisoned compatriots in the future.

Crime

General lawlessness and deteriorating economic conditions have brought an increase in crime. Adequate police response in the event of an emergency is doubtful. Murder has increased dramatically with many incidents in broad daylight and some at popular public places. Crime has increased markedly in the cities, particularly near railroad and bus stations and on trains. The possession of firearms has proliferated greatly. Effective police protection is almost nonexistent.

Being an American

Anti-American sentiments run high in many parts of the country, particularly in Serb-dominated areas. The loss or theft abroad of a U.S. passport should be reported immediately to the local police and the nearest U.S. embassy or consulate.

Being a Charter Pilot

Britain's Overseas Development Administration halted its airlift of supplies into Sarajevo after its aircraft were fired on at the airport. An official of the agency stated, "it's really the cumulative effect of having been shot at too many times in Sarajevo. The owner refuses to continue leasing the aircraft to us under the circumstances." United Nations relief airlifts are continually interrupted by small arms fire.

Shopping in Sarajevo

Forget about that Versace suit, and about everything else for that matter. Stay at home. Rebel Serbs find civilians great target practice. For gunmen, Sniper Alley is like Pac Man.

Getting Sick

Health facilities are minimal or nonexistent. Many medicines and basic medical supplies as well as x-ray film often are unavailable. Hospitals usually require payment in hard currency for all services. Further information on health matters can be obtained from the Center for Disease Control's international traveler's hotline at ☎ *(404) 332-4559.*

Nuts & Bolts

Bosnia-Herzegovina declared its independence from the former Yugoslavia in October 1991 and was subsequently invaded by the Federal Army, comprised primarily of Serbs. Bosnia is bordered by Serbia to the east, Croatia to the north and west, and Montenegro to the south.

The official language is Serbo-Croat, or Bosnian, written in Latin and Cyrillic. Ethnically, Bosnian Muslims comprise 44 percent of the population; Serbs, 31 percent; and Croats, 17 percent. Religiously, Slavic Muslims make up 40 percent of the population; Orthodox, 31 percent; Catholics, 15 percent; and Protestants, 4 percent.

The monetary unit is the dinar, with 100 paras to the dinar..It is impossible to use credit cards or to cash "Traveler's cheques". German deutsche marks are the currency of favor at present.

The small coastal area of Bosnia enjoys a mild, Mediterranean climate with a mean temperature of 27 C (80 F) in summer. The interior has a moderate, continental climate with warm summers and frigid winters.

Embassy Location

The U.S. Embassy in Sarajevo opened in July 1994, but due to extremely limited staffing, the Embassy is unable to provide consular services except in extreme emergencies. U.S. citizens seeking assistance while in Bosnia can contact the U.S. Embassies in Belgrade or Zagreb. The U.S. Embassy in Belgrade's ability to assist is limited, however, because of conflict in the area, lack of communications and reduced Embassy staffing.

The U.S. Embassy

Djure Djakovica 43
Sarajevo, Republic of Bosnia and Herzegovina
☎ *(387-71) 659-992.*
Until the security situation stabilizes, the U.S. Embassy in Sarajevo may not be staffed at all times. When no personnel are in Sarajevo, U.S. officials accredited to the Government of Bosnia and Herzegovina will be available in Vienna, where they have resided since the establishment of relations between the Government of Bosnia and Herzegovina and the United States. They cannot provide consular services in Vienna. The address of the Vienna office of U.S. Embassy Bosnia is c/o U.S.

Embassy Vienna, Boltzmanngasse 16, Vienna, Austria. The telephone number is ☎ *(43-1) 31-339, extension 2173, FAX [43] (1) 310-0682.*

U.S. Embassy
> *Kneza Milosa 50*
> *Belgrade, Serbia*
> ☎ *(381-11) 645-655*

U.S. Embassy
> *Andrije Hebranga 2*
> *Zagreb, Croatia*
> ☎ *(385-41) 456-000*

Dangerous Days	
	New Years Day
05/01-02	May Day
07/04	Fighter's Day
09/06/94	Pope cancels visit
11/29-30/91	Day of the Republic (Nov. 29–30)

In a Dangerous Place: Yugoslavia

It is odd for me to have to cover a war in Europe. I left Paris with my ears full of the noise made by the French about the need to preserve Dubrovnik's architectural marvels. Nobody seems to care for the Serbs and the Croats, but talk about the ancient city of Dubrovnik and everybody yells about how it belongs to mankind's culture and should be preserved at all costs.

I spent only a week in Yugoslavia, enough to see a horrible war. In Belgrade everything seemed normal. Then things started to change as we approached the frontier with Hungary in Zagreb and even more in Ossiek.

I traveled to the war with a friend, American journalist Chris Morris. He took me in his car to Vukovar. We spent three days there amidst the battles. We met a Canadian mercenary known only as John, the commander of the place. That's one of the features of this war: there are lots of mercenaries. John is a Croatian by origin and commanded the Croats.

Our biggest fear was the number of snipers here. John brought us to a mortar position. It was teatime first, then the bombing of the Serbs' position resumed, followed by an offensive with mortars made in Germany. The night came. The situation became hellish. It was like the end of the world. We spent three nights in cellars with a Croatian family. The son kept entertaining his girlfriend who lived nearby, through a walkie-talkie. The girl asked him to give her some cassettes to play on her walkman. The boy turned towards me and I agreed to lend him two cassettes. He then proceeded to walk out in the middle of the night under the bombs, but did not come back. Everybody started worrying. Some people went out to look for him, but they did not come back either.

The next morning we were awakened by shouting and loud sobs. We got out of the cellar. Here they were—dead bodies. I recognized the boy to whom I had loaned the tapes, and not far from him lay the headless body of his girl friend. Her head had rolled away after it had been chopped off, either by shrapnel or by some other means.

We left Vukovar to go to Ossiek. We saw prisoners. Lots of them were to be executed.

We received the news a few hours after our departure that Vukovar had just fallen. There was no story here, just killing and atrocities. The news magazines aren't interested in running more dull grey shots of people being killed. It will be Europe's dirty little secret.

Burundi
★★★

Unsafe Conduct

Burundi—which suffers the geographic misfortune of being Rwanda's closest neighbor—has never quite been the same since enduring one of Africa's worst tribal wars in 1972. War is not the right word. Genocide fits better. It all happened after King Ntaré V returned in April of that year. Usually, when the president of the country promises safe conduct to a returning monarch, the chances are pretty good the red carpet will be rolled out. Well, that wasn't exactly what Burundi President Michel Micombero had in mind for the return of the man he overthrew. Not even a party. No sooner had Ntaré V stepped off the plane than he was judged and executed by Micombero. Hell of a homecoming. What happened afterward defies explanation.

Thousands of invading exiled Hutus attending Ntare V's return to Burundi were slaughtered by the rival Tutsis. But the Tutsis didn't stop there. Over the next eight weeks, nearly a quarter of a million native Burundi Hutus were massacred by the Tutsis. The genocide was followed by coup after coup after coup, until Burundi's first democratically-elected leader, Melchior Ndadaye, assumed the presidency in June 1993.

All's well that ends well? Hardly.

Tutsi paratroops overthrew Hutu President Ndadaye on October 21, 1993, abruptly ending the three-month experiment with democracy in the central African state. The predawn coup was led by army chief of staff Colonel Jean Bikomagu and former President Jean Baptiste Bagaza, who was himself overthrown in 1987. The paratroops arrested Ndadaye and detained him at the Muha barracks on the outskirts of the capital city of Bujumbura before executing him. The coup was the fifth since the country's independence in 1962, and led to unprecedented violence and death in that year of Burundi's history. More than 200,000 deaths were caused by the unrest, equaling if not exceeding the casualties that occurred in the 1972 genocide that swept the country. Tribal massacres drove nearly a million Burundians into neighboring countries to escape the slaughter.

The coup collapsed, but it hardly made any difference. Burundi had already collapsed. Ethnic fighting between the Hutu tribe, which Ndadye came from, and the minority Tutsis, who controlled the military and have dominated politics for generations, continued to ravage the country. Pictures revealed hundreds of bodies, devastated towns, destroyed farms and a countryside that had been set on fire. Corpses littered the countryside after the army stood by and watched as Tutsis and Hutu slaughtered each other. Thousands of Burundians marched through the streets of Bujumbura urging the remnants of Ndadaye's government to emerge from hiding and lead the country from the chaos caused by the military revolt: 500,000 refugees have fled to Rwanda alone.

The Trash War

The morning was foggy and we had driven up the slippery slopes from Tanzania. When we camped for the night we saw no one. Now we were surrounded by a circular wall of people. They pressed in slowly, curious to see what these visitors might have. They began to touch at first, and then grab. Fighting back, we chased them off. As they ran and tripped, they grabbed anything they could pry loose—empty water bottles, scraps of paper. As the bolder ones tried to grab and run back into the crowd, they were immediately pounced upon by other Hutus, who ripped and tore whatever meager trophy they had retrieved until they possessed minuscule scraps in their hands. The Hutus were stealing trash, fighting for trash. As we quickly jumped in our vehicles and drove off, we watched them continue to beat and fight each other for trash until, finally, the battle was lost in the fog.

But even the foiled coup failed to bring stability to Burundi. The presidents of both Burundi and Rwanda were aboard a plane that was blasted out of the sky by rocket and gun fire as it was landing at Kigali airport in Rwanda on April 6, 1994. Intense fighting broke out in neighboring Rwanda. During the ensuing 14-week civil war in Rwanda, Tutsi rebels swept across the country, decimating the mainly Hutu government.

On April 29, 1994, hundreds of people fled shelling in Bujumbura, after the expiration of a government ultimatum to militants to turn in their weapons. Although Burundi has escaped much of the latest round of fighting between the two ethnic groups, Hutu militants of the "People's Army" have declined to comply and surrender their weapons.

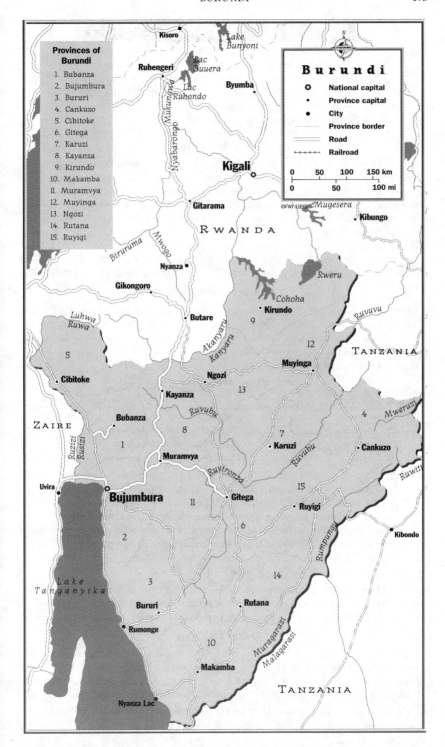

Provinces of Burundi

1. Bubanza
2. Bujumbura
3. Bururi
4. Cankuzo
5. Cibitoke
6. Gitega
7. Karuzi
8. Kayanza
9. Kirundo
10. Makamba
11. Muramvya
12. Muyinga
13. Ngozi
14. Rutana
15. Ruyigi

Burundi

⊕ National capital
• Province capital
● City
---- Province border
— Road
+++ Railroad

0   50   100   150 km
0   50   100 mi

©FWi 1995

The 1:30 to Paris

Our arrival was not an important event, but reason enough for lunch at the embassy. After a brief tour, including meeting the grizzled marine security officer, we had lunch high up in the hills overlooking Bujumbura. In between polite conversation, a silence would fall as an airliner took off from the airport. Without looking, our hosts would rattle off the flight and carrier as if repeating a religious chant. We had a wonderfully meaningless lunch.

The Scoop

Some half a million people are reported to have been killed and one million more have fled abroad as a result of ethnic violence between the Hutus, who control the military, and the minority Tutsis. The airport in Bujumbura opens and closes like a an L.A. rave club. A per capita annual income of around US$210 makes the country perhaps the poorest in Africa, even more impoverished than neighboring Rwanda. The nation suffered one of Africa's worst genocides—a duck shoot that continues to this day. Burundi is arguably one of the most dangerous places in Africa. Looting, raping, pillaging and murder are the norm. Gangs of youths from the minority Tutsi tribe occasionally paralyze the capital, encountering brutal resistance by the military. The tourist infrastructure is all but nonexistent. Few travelers stay long in Burundi. Most are in transit between Tanzania and Rwanda.

Travel Advisory

Warning: The Department of State warns U.S. citizens to defer all travel to Burundi at this time. The U.S. Department of State has ordered the temporary departure of all U.S. government dependents and nonessential employees from Burundi because of security concerns following the deaths of the presidents of Burundi and Rwanda in Kigali, Rwanda on April 6, 1994. U.S. citizens in Burundi are advised to depart immediately.

The Players

The Hutu

Hutus comprise about 85 percent of Burundi's population and were the victims of a Tutsi-led mass genocide campaign in 1972. After President Ndadaye was overthrown and executed in an abandoned coup effort in October 1993, the Hutu went on a stampede. When it was over, nearly a quarter million corpses were left in the wake.

The Tutsi

The Tutsi-led military junta purged the military and bureaucracy of Hutus from 1964-1972. In 1972, a large-scale revolt by the Hutus killed more than 100 Tutsis. The Tutsi machine followed with the mass extermination of selected and unselected Hutus. Any Hutu with an education, a decent job or any degree of wealth was arrested and murdered, most in a horrifying fashion. More than 200,000 Hutus were slaughtered in the ensuing three months. Tutsi army vehicles could be seen in the streets packed with the mutilated corpses of Hutu victims.

Party for the Reconciliation of the People (PRP)

Led by Mathias Hitimana, now under house arrest, the Hutu dissident group opposes the oppression of the Hutu people by the government. The group, a champion of Hutu dissidents, is a frequent instigator of street clashes with government security forces.

Getting In

You can get into Burundi by air, road or lake ferry. By land from Rwanda, you can get in from Butare as well as Bujumbura. Expect to have your belongings searched on both sides of the border. From Zaire, you can get into Burundi from Bakavu via Uvira. You can also get to Bujumbura from Bakavu via Cyangugu in Rwanda. On Lake Tanganyika, you can get in from Tanzania.

A passport and a visa are required. Only those travelers resident in countries where there is no Burundian embassy are eligible for entry stamps, without a visa, at the airport upon arrival. These entry stamps are not a substitute for a visa which must subsequently be obtained from the immigration service within 24 hours of arrival. Visas cost from US$30 to US$60, depending on anticipated length of stay. Travelers who have failed to obtain a visa will not be permitted to leave the country. Multiple entry visas valid for three months are available in Burundian embassies abroad for US$11. Evidence of yellow fever immunization must be presented. Also, visitors are required to show proof of vaccination against meningococcal meningitis. Additional information may be obtained from the,

Embassy of the Republic of Burundi
2233 Wisconsin Avenue, NW, Suite 212
Washington, D.C. 20007
☎ *(202) 342-2574*
or the

Permanent Mission of Burundi to the United Nations in
New York
☎ *(212) 687-1180.*

Getting Around

Burundi has a good network of roads between the major towns and border posts. Travel on other roads is difficult, particularly in the rainy season. Public transportation to border points is often difficult and frequently unavailable, but it is improving. There has been a proliferation of modern Japanese-made minibuses in recent years. They're usually not terribly crowded and are far less expensive than taxis. These buses leave terminals (gare routière) in every town in the early morning through the early afternoon, and depart when they are full. They display their destinations on the windshield. The government-owned OTRACO buses are mainly found in and around the capital of Bujumbura. Total road miles are 3666; 249 of them are paved. There are six airfields in the country, only one with a permanent surface.

Dangerous Places

In light of the October 1993 coup attempt and the 1994 assassinations of the presidents of both Burundi and Rwanda, all areas of the country should be considered potentially unstable. Sporadic violence remains a problem in Bujumbura, as well as in the interior where large numbers of displaced persons are encamped or in hiding. Renewed warfare in neighboring Rwanda has caused thousands of Rwandans to flee to Burundi and other countries in the region. The U.S. Embassy has reiterated the importance of using extreme caution, with no travel to the troubled neighborhoods of the capital and none but essential travel in the city after dark. Burundi periodically has closed its land borders without notice and suspended air travel and telephone service, in response to political disturbances.

Dangerous Things

Crime

Street crime in Burundi poses a high risk for visitors. Crime involves muggings, purse-snatching, pickpocketing, burglary and auto break-ins. Criminals operate individually or in small groups. There have been reports of muggings of persons jogging or walking alone in all sections of Bujumbura, especially on public roads bordering Lake Tanganyika.

Bujumbura U.S. embassy sources report that dangerous areas for criminal activity in Bujumbura are the downtown section, the vicinity of the Novotel and the Source du Nil hotels, and along the shore of Lake Tanganyika. The majority of the criminal incidents in the Burundian capital consist of muggings, purse snatching, and breaking into autos (to steal the contents). A non-American expatriate was stabbed in September 1993, when he tried to fight off a gang of robbers. He was hospitalized for his injuries.

Street Demonstrations and Clashes

Minority Tutsi youths regularly engage with the military and police in street protests in Bujumbura. Although the protests are not anti-U.S. in nature and Americans and other foreigners are rarely targeted, stay off the streets during any public rally. Relatively peaceful demonstrations can turn violent at the drop of a clip.

Getting Sick

There are 14 hospital beds and 0.5 doctors for every 10,000 people. Yellow fever and cholera immunizations are required. Inoculations for tetanus, typhoid and polio are also recommended, as are gamma globulin shots and malaria suppressants. Doctors and hospitals often expect immediate cash payment for health care services. U.S. medical insurance is not always valid outside the United States. Supplemental medical insurance with specific overseas coverage, including medical evacuation coverage, has proved to be useful. The Center for Disease Control recommends that travelers to Burundi receive the meningococcal polysaccharide vaccine before traveling to the area.

Nuts & Bolts

Burundi is a small, inland African nation (about the size of Maryland) passing through a period of instability following a coup attempt in October 1993. Facilities for tourism, particularly in the interior, are limited. The country is divided into 15 provinces, each administered by a civilian governor. The provinces are subdivided into 114 communes with elected councils in charge of local affairs.

Burundi's climate varies from hot and humid in the area of Lake Tanganyika, with temperatures around 30 degrees C, to cool in the mountainous north, about 20 degrees C. The long rainy season runs from October through May.

Hutus comprise about 85 percent of the population. About 14 percent are Tutsi. Kirundi and French are the official languages; Swahili is also spoken; English is rare. Indigenous religions are held by 34 percent of the population; Roman Catholics make up 61 percent of the population; Protestants account for 5 percent. The literacy rate is about 50 percent.

The currency in Burundi is the Burundi franc (BFr): 100 centimes are to the BFr. Approximately

Embassy Locations

U.S. Embassy

on the Avenue des Etats-Unis
B.P. 34, 1720
Bujumbura, Burundi
☎ *(257) 223-454*

Canadian Embassy in Burundi

None

U.S. Embassy in Burundi

Ave des Etats-Unis
BP 1720, Bujumbura
☎ *(257) 22-34-54*
FAX (257) 22-29-26

Burundian Embassy in Canada

151 Slater Street, Suite 800
Ottawa, ONT. K1P 5H3
☎ *(613) 741-7458*
Telex: (369) 053-3393
FAX (613) 741-2424

Burundian Embassy in United States

2233 Wisconsin Avenue, NW, Suite 212
Washington, D.C. 20007
☎ *(202) 342-2574*

Dangerous Days

04/25/94	Failed coup. A military coup in Burundi failed when soldiers, fearing the triggering of a tribal bloodbath similar to the one in neighboring Rwanda, refused to participate in the military mutiny.
04/06/94	A plane carrying the presidents of both Rwanda and Burundi was shot out of the sky as it attempted to land in Rwanda.

Dangerous Days

10/28/93	Evacuations to Bujumbura. Foreigners in Burundi were being evacuated to the country's capital, Bujumbura, as concern over tribal violence associated with a failed military coup grew.
10/28/93	Six government ministers were confirmed murdered during a failed coup in Burundi.
10/21/93	Paratroops overthrew President Melchior Ndadaye and executed him.
06/02/93	Melchior Ndadaye became Burundi's first democratically-elected president.
11/06/1976	Lt. Col. Jean Baptiste Bagaye led a coup and assumed the presidency, suspending Burundi's constitution.
04/19/72	Natré V returns to Burundi and is executed by President Micombero, sparking one of the bloodiest wars in African history.

Cambodia
★★★★★

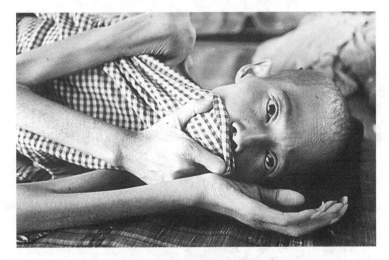

Hell in a Hand Basket

Perhaps no country on earth has so brutally suffered from as many forms of conflict over the past 30 years as has Cambodia. Civil wars, border wars, massive bombardment via a superpower's *B-52s*, a deforestation rate considered unparalleled anywhere in the world and an autogenicide unprecedented in its savagery—effectively eliminating a full seventh of the country's population—have ravaged this once proud and culturally influential empire.

In 1993, with the help of the United Nations, Cambodia began crawling back into the world on its knees, literally, as so many of the country's citizens are missing limbs after accidental encounters with one of the perhaps six million land mines still buried beneath the surface of the countryside's topsoil. And those not missing arms or legs are most assuredly missing relatives, victims of Pol Pot's murderous Khmer Rouge regime of the mid- and late-1970s. The Khmer Rouge were responsible for more than a million deaths between 1975 and 1979 alone.

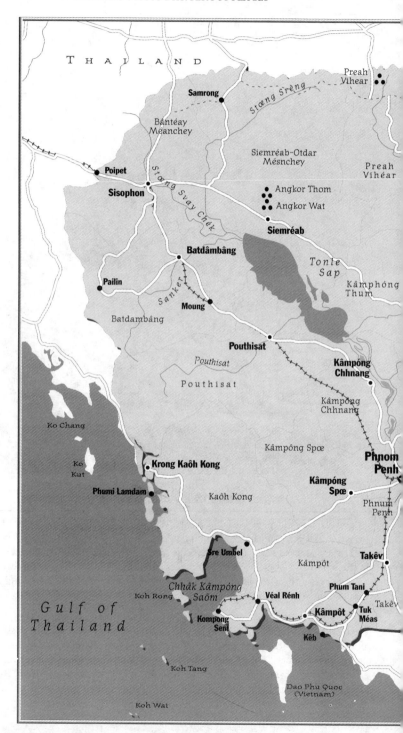

LAOS

Siem Pang

Rótânôkiri

Virachei

Tônlé Kong

Phnum Tbêng Méanchey

Stœng Trêng

Boung Long

Tônlé San

Lomphat

Stœng Trêng

Tônlé

Srêpôk

Rovieng

Stœng Sên

Stœng Chinit

Mekong

Sâmbor

Móndól Kiri

Chbar

âmpóng Thum

Sandan

Krâchéh

Senmonorom

Krâchéh

Prêk Kák

Srê Rônéam

Chhlong

Srê Khtum

Kâmpóng Cham

Snuol

Kâmpóng Cham

Tônlé Bet

Mimot

andal

Prey Vêng

Svay Rieng

VIETNAM

a hmau

Prey Vêng

Mekong

Svay Rieng

Kâmpóng Trâbêk

Ho Chi Minh City (Saigon)

Song Tien Giang

Cambodia

⊙	Province boundary
⊙	National capital
•	Province capital
●	Secondary City
++++++	Railroad
	Primary Road
- - -	Trail
••	Ruins

0   25   50   75 km
0   25   50 mi

N

©FW 1995

However, peace didn't last long after UNTAC (United Nations Transitional Authority in Cambodia) peacekeepers left the country in November 1993. In the wake of their departure, the Khmer Rouge stepped up their attacks on the Cambodian People's Armed Forces (CPAF) and gained decisive battlefield victories against an army that one Western analyst characterized as the "most ill-equipped, mal-trained, undisciplined, officer-heavy and corrupt in the world."

The Khmer Rouge attacks didn't stop with the CPAF. In 1994, six Western hostages were kidnapped and subsequently executed by KR guerrillas. Their crime: being tourists.

Khmer Rouge 82mm mortars are felt daily today by Cambodians, by Westerners, but mainly by the hundreds of thousands of ethnic-Vietnamese who have called Cambodia home for generations. It seems a weekly occurrence for entire villages to be wiped out overnight by Khmer Rouge guerrillas launching rocket-propelled grenades from the backs of motorbikes at frightened townspeople. In one attack, in October 1994, 46 Cambodians were slaughtered by KR marauders in Battambang. Ethnic Vietnamese villages, especially those along the banks of the Tonle Sap River and the Great Lake of Tonle Sap, are routinely ransacked, their inhabitants usually bludgeoned to death; the guerrillas choose to save their bullets for the Cambodian army.

Even the spectacular and once relatively highly-touristed ruins at Angkor are in constant danger of attacks by Khmer Rouge guerrillas who, despite U.N.-supervised elections in May of 1993, still control fully 20 percent of Cambodia's landscape. Shortly before the polls that spring, armed guerrillas attacked a U.N. garrison at Siem Reap and injured a Portuguese tourist. A Japanese tourist fled the area on a motorcycle and streaked all the way to the Thai border, nearly 100 miles away.

In Siem Reap province itself, not more than 10 km from the temple complex, Khmer Rouge guerrillas are busy "recruiting" soldiers and murdering ethnic Vietnamese.

In many areas across this lush countryside, bones spring from the earth like desert cactus, still shrouded with the tattered garments their owners were clothed in on the day they were slaughtered—a testament to Pol Pot's demonic wrath of the mid- and late-1970s. Human teeth can be found among the rocks and grass like pebbles in an old parking lot. And many of these locations are not named, not enshrined by glass and concrete and tour guides and ticket booths. They're just there, baking in the same sun as the resin harvesters dotting the rutted, muddy roads nearby, toting Chinese-made AK-47 rifles and readying to enter the fog-thick encasement of dark green jungle for another day's toil.

Red signs depicting skulls and crossbones are tacked to trees, sharing the bark with bullet holes, warning of land mines. Barrages of tracers being traded back and forth between government forces and the Khmer Rouge can regularly be witnessed in the night sky by the rare visitor to this exotic land. To the uninitiated, the orange tracers streaking in a large arc across the Asian twilight appear to be a display of grand fireworks that simply aren't functioning properly, some sort of defused celebration—which is in fact what Cambodia is.

Cambodia's most significant offering to the world in the mid 1990s is not its art, its dancing, nor its culture; it is its own testament to the country's horrific past. Cambodia's most popular attractions, apart from its magnificent ancient *wats*, are museums and fields that depict the mass genocide of its people so vividly that many simply don't have the stomach to visit the blood-stained walls of schoolrooms turned-torture chambers, or of longan fields-turned-open graves.

Many of Pol Pot's victims unlucky enough to have survived the genocide today roam Phnom Penh's trash-laden boulevards like zombies out of a George Romero film. Some are hideously disfigured; nearly all are penniless and they follow Western tourists around like gulls behind a shrimper, begging for handouts.

Cambodia belies itself; it's perhaps the greatest paradox on the planet in its contrast of human warmth and vile indignity. Its people are arguably the gentlest on the globe, sentenced by circumstance to an environment that's utterly raw and entirely untamed. They are struggling to enter the modern world by investing salaries that average as little as US$4 a month on English lessons along Phnom Penh's English Street. (It's English now—not French. The majority of people who were versed in French either fled the country or were executed by the Khmer Rouge.)

To the adventure tourists who don't heed King Norodom Sihanouk's recent call for Western tourists to stay out of his country, Cambodia is one of the last frontiers, the Wild West of East Asia, where one can hitchhike from Phnom Penh to Angkor Wat with a relatively high likelihood of being stopped and detained at rifle point by Maoist guerrillas; where one can share a ferry ride in a raging storm across the Great Lake of Tonlé Sap on a dilapidated, rusted barge with a dozen sows, cockroaches the size of plums and a few soldiers and joke about the ferry that sank over the same reef last night during a monsoon, killing 50; where one can sneak across the border from Thailand aboard a speed boat manned by smugglers bound for Kompong Som, harboring a cache of Singaporean VCRs; where one can ride a train from Phnom Penh to Sihanoukville with a virtual guarantee of being abducted and executed.

With the UNTAC presence in Cambodia, tourism boomed. Whereas only 2000 tourists visited Cambodia in 1988, 1991 saw 25,000 foreign visitors to the country. And that figure more than tripled in 1992—to 87,000. And why not? Under the M-16 umbrella of UNTAC, foreigners could take relative comfort in visiting Cambodia's more than 200 miles of pristine, virgin coastline, from Krong Koh Kong to Kampot, save for the periodic intrusion of a few Chinese-made shell casings that sprout from the sandlike snail shells. However, by the end of 1994, with UNTAC gone, and Cambodia with a ragtag army, a government cabinet with its cups and plates falling to the floor like those in an earthquake and an abortive July 1994 coup against the ruling coalition, analysts were saying that tourism was down as much as 90 percent over the same period in 1993.

Cambodia's Interior Ministry had been completing plans to introduce tourist police units in Phnom Penh, Siem Reap and the seaside resort, Sihanoukville. Secretary of State for Tourism, Veng Sereyvuth, said the units would be on call 24 hours a day and trained to help tourists in situations ranging from emergencies and crime to simple requests for information. The one problem, of course, is that there aren't any tourists.

In a Dangerous Place: Cambodia

In Bangkok, in October 1994 (shortly after the deaths of three Westerners at Vine Mountain), while visiting perhaps the best tour agent specializing in Indochina tours, several urgent (panicked, actually) faxes were sent by a Colorado-based Southeastern Asian tour company who had two groups of clients (one in Laos and the other in Vietnam) who were to proceed into Phnom Penh the next day and then to the temples at Angkor:

URGENT…URGENT…URGENT!

We have learned the Khmer Rouge (sic) have massacred a village in Siem Reap. At least 7 killed. Ethnic Vietnamese. We are scheduled to have our groups in there in two days! Our guides won't do it! Will only proceed with a military escort. Can you provide this for us?!!! Can this be done? Need ASAP! Rusty.

The Bangkok agent, although adept at speaking English, was less so in reading and writing the language. I read him the fax. After rubbing his palms, pacing the floor and moaning a few moments, he told me, "Sure I can get them a military escort, but it's damned expensive." Then he looked me in the eyes. "You've just been there," he said. "What would you do?"

"Seriously?" I asked. He nodded.

"I'd tell them to stay the hell out of there," I said.

"You write the fax for me," he said.

"What do I tell him?" I said, bemused.

"Don't tell him what I'd say," he sighed. "Tell him what you'd say." Then he stood over my shoulder as I keyed in the fax to Rusty.

Rusty—Can provide you with a military escort on your visit to Angkor. You'll have to absorb the cost. But I cannot guarantee the safety of your group even with an escort. In fact, an escort may even further endanger your clients' safety. Cambodian military not the hunters. They're the hunted. In exchange for Cambodia, we'll give you 5 days and 4 nights in the Central Highlands (Vietnam). Somnuk.

"Send it!" the Thai demanded.

In the wake of the deaths of three Western backpackers at the hands of the Khmer Rouge in September 1994, King Norodom Sihanouk advised foreign tourists, especially Westerners, against visiting Cambodia.

Briton Mark Slater, Frenchman Jean-Michel Braquet, and Australian David Wilson were taken hostage by the Khmer Rouge on July 26, 1994 as they traveled by train from the capital to the seaside "resort" of Sihanoukville. The train was ambushed by the Khmer Rouge in southern Cambodia. At least 13 innocent travelers were killed in the ambush. The three Westerners, three ethnic Vietnamese, and an unknown number of Cambodians were marched into the forest. The ethnic Vietnamese are suspected to have been executed a short time later. Although hopes lingered into November that the three foreigners were still alive at the Khmer Rouge camp at Vine Mountain (150 km south of Phnom Penh), as KR leaders in the area continued to demand first a ransom and then a political role (including an end to a ban on the guerilla group) in Cambodia's government as a condition for their release, it was subsequently learned that the three Westerners had been summarily bound and shot or bludgeoned to death execution-style by KR soldiers at the command of KR General Nuon Paet near the end of September.

King Sihanouk said that "Cambodia is clearly insecure," and joined foreign embassies in advising tourists to avoid Cambodia entirely, including the capital of Phnom Penh. The governments of France, Great Britain and Australia called on its nationals not to visit the country. The king said that he couldn't fathom why anyone would be foolish enough to tour a country still clearly in a state of war, and chastised foreigners foolish enough to visit the country as ignorant, naive or just plain stupid. He wrung his hands at the numbers of ignorant Westerners who insisted on visiting Cambodia despite the vast and clearly-evident dangers.

"I cannot continue to assume responsibility for the accidents that could happen to travelers in Cambodia," the king said, "because I have repeatedly warned that my country can provide no safety guarantee to travelers without a big escort."

(Apparently, neither will Western governments assume responsibility for procuring the release of their citizens once they are seized by KR bandits. Many Australians condemned their government's lack of effort in obtaining Wilson's release, which was believed entirely plausible by sending Australian commandos and chemical weapons into the Vine Mountain area. It was argued that the government was too "pussyfoot" in the crisis, by putting its long-term trade interests in Cambodia ahead of the lives of its citizens).

Earlier in the year, two young Britons—on their way to Sihanoukville to explore the opportunity of opening a restaurant in the area—and an Australian were executed after their car was stopped at a Khmer Rouge roadblock.

Sihanouk's warning actually had little effect on tourism to Cambodia, as it had primarily stopped altogether since that previous summer, as the Khmer Rouge notched significant and decisive battlefield victories against the government army.

According to travel agencies I spoke with in Bangkok and elsewhere, tourism to Cambodia beginning in September 1994 slowed to, at best, a trickle. One agency, N.S. Travel & Tours, which had previously sent at least 10 clients a month to Cambodia, revealed in November that it hadn't booked a single tourist since August of that year. Another agent, who booked an average of 40–50 people a month to Cambodia while UNTAC administered the country, stopped sending tourists to Cambodia after the U.N. body's withdrawal in November 1993.

Bangkok Airways cancelled all its daily flights to Phnom Penh in August 1994, citing the worsening political situation, including an attempted but failed coup on the government in July 1994 that involved at least 14 Thai nationals. Investigations are still ongoing as to whether Thai government officials and businessmen were involved in the attempt to overthrow the FUNCINPEC-led coalition. Cambodian Second Prime Minister Hun Sen has continued to assert that Thai government officials were involved in the coup attempt. The Vietnamese government has denied any involvement.

While as recently as July 1994, Cambodian Tourism Minister Veng Sereyvuth outlined an ambitious plan—"Millions of Visitors and Billions of Dollars" was the tagline—to turn Cambodia into a nation where jumbo jets would glide from the sky onto the tarmacs of numerous Khmer international airports, where visitors would wine and dine at lavish hotel complexes, play golf on a number of pristine golf courses, or try their luck at the card tables of a US$500 million casino and marina, the murders of the Western hostages in September tolled a death knell for Cambodian tourism.

The government had earlier gone so far as to pronounce Cambodia "100 percent safe. As safe as London, Paris and New York."

London, Paris and New York are hardly "100 percent safe." But what can be safely said at the time of this writing is that Cambodia is 100 percent unsafe.

As unsafe as Bosnia, Somalia and Iraq.

Cambodia's Train to Hell

After one leaves Pochentung by train heading south for Sihanoukville, the track cuts a swath through scenic rice fields accented by towering sugar palms before winding its way through the mountainous areas of the south. The route offers some of the most magnificent scenery in Cambodia. Rice farmers toil in the fields, coaxing their oxen to pull wooden ploughs. Bright Buddhist pagodas can be seen in the fields and on the hillsides, set far away from the track.

But this same route, one formerly popular with adventure tourists and the curious alike, today is less than affectionately known as "The Death Railway," or, "The Train to Hell."

"Safety features" on the Cambodian railway system include 1960s French-built locomotives sporting steel plates in front of the cab and two up-front "mine clearing" cars where passengers with enough balls can ride for about 1500 riel (US$.60).

Brackets welded into the plates are made from railway iron and resemble the "cow-catchers" on 19th-century U.S. locomotives—all this to protect passengers and crew from mines laid on the tracks by the Khmer Rouge and corrupt army soldiers and police, not to mention rocket attacks spawned by one or more of the above.

Sixty cents seems like a small life insurance policy, and it is. But Cambodian trains are the only means rural Khmer farmers and other poor Cambodians have to get their produce, animals and other goods to markets from Sihanoukville to Phnom Penh.

On July 26, 1994, a Khmer Rouge attack on one such train left 13 people dead, with three Westerners taken hostage and ultimately executed two months later.

This certainly wasn't an isolated occurrence. More than one Cambodian railroad engineer has survived at least 10 train ambushes since the early 1980s, when the KR began their efforts in earnest to create anarchy in Cambodia after Pol Pot's fall to the Vietnamese in January 1979. But their numbers are diminishing rapidly.

On the day prior to the May 1993 elections, KR marauders formed a gauntlet on both sides of the track and rocketed a train, resulting in the deaths of at least 30 people.

On paper, at least, the trains aren't as defenseless as you might think. Usually, a "railway militia" team consisting of about two dozen government soldiers is on board each train. Their job? To repel bandits and raiders, typically KR guerrillas. For the initial leg of the journey from Phnom Penh southward, the guardian force can usually be found asleep or playing cards. But by the time the train reaches Kompong Trach (an area under marginal KR control), it's lock 'n load. But, typically, when a firefight breaks out, the "militia" is the first to abandon their positions aboard the train and flee into the forest. Crew members tend to follow suit. Some crew members on board are heavily armed with assault rifles and grenades. But it's a lot to ask of a man who makes about US$20 a month to defend a Cambodian train against a disciplined and ruthless KR unit. Under attack, the forest is mighty appealing to even the toughest-skinned Cambodian railroader.

Many Cambodian engineers who were trained in the 1960s on steam trains aren't around anymore to recount their adventures, having either been slain in the mid-1970s during Pol Pot's regime, or by subsequent KR ambushes on their trains during the '80s and '90s.

So skip Sihanoukville, you say. The train to Battambang has got to be a lot safer.

Maybe. Maybe not.

Kiss the ground when you get there, if you can find some between the corpses. KR marauders slaughtered 46 Khmer villagers there last November.

It takes a lot of nerve and bravery to crew a Cambodian train, and, these days, even more stupidity to buy a ticket to ride one.

Phnom Penh: Caught Between Empty Baskets

I had been to Phnom Penh and Cambodia for the first time in 1992, when tens of thousands of UNTAC (United Nations Transitional Authority in Cambodia) troops from dozens of nations across the globe—from the U.S. to Indonesia, from Bangladesh to Bulgaria—roamed in queues about the streets of the capital in their white Toyota Land Cruisers like uniformed, multihued aliens from another planet toward their mecca, the magnificent French colonial UNTAC headquarters building next to the Wat Phnom Pagoda. These were the new protectors of a nation shrouded by a quarter of a century of perpetual siege, fright and death, a country that has endured civil war for 30 years—perhaps the bitterest and most deadly internal conflict ever fought in modern times. And it could easily continue for another 30 more in Cambodia.

History has enveloped the horrors of the Nazi concentration camps, the Armenian massacre, the American massacre in Vietnam at My Lai, the rape and pillaging of Bosnia—but few individuals in the world today understand what has happened (and what continues to occur) in this neglected, forgotten limbo in Southeast Asia. Phnom Penh and Cambodia are the skunks of the Far East.

For those few in the know, it is no secret that the regime of Pol Pot and the Khmer Rouge were responsible for more than a million Cambodian deaths between 1975 and 1979. The Killing Fields outside Phnom Penh (and other mass grave sites sprinkled across the countryside) are a grisly and horrifying testament to an autogenocide unparalleled in modern times. The Khmer Rouge eliminated a full seventh of the population of Cambodia during its horrific reign. Today, you will not meet a single individual in the entire country of Cambodia who has not lost at least one nuclear family member to the isolationist wrath of Pol Pot. The bitterly sad truth is that the "rain" of the Khmer Rouge continues to this moment.

Shortly before arriving in Phnom Penh on a recent trip in the summer of 1994, I was in Ha Tien, Vietnam (on the southwest border with Cambodia). I happened to come across a man drenched in a deep, glazy, rust-colored sweat digging a hole in the sun-packed, clay earth beside a rutted remote path. His name was Khan. I thought perhaps he was digging a well. Children surrounded Khan as if they were on an Easter egg hunt, and Khan had found a cache of chocolate bunnies.

I stopped to watch.

Fifteen minutes later, he pulled from the earth a large, frayed plastic bag which he sliced open with a dull knife. Perhaps some buried treasure, I thought. Maybe fermented rice for Vietnamese whisky. Hell, maybe even chocolate bunnies.

Instead, he pulled from the bag the remains of his mother and sister, who had been murdered by the Khmer Rouge in 1979. They both had been torn apart limb by limb while alive, he told me. I helped him remove the remains from the bag and place them in a large lacquered urn. We separated the clothes from the crumbling corpses and burned the garments in the grave. Khan sifted through his mother's fingers and found a gold ring which his father had given her some years earlier. Without a trace of emotion, he placed it in his pocket and continued separating the earth from the bone, the dust from the dust.

We lifted the urn onto a cart and he drove off as if he were hauling a water drum to a hotel in this water-starved Vietnamese port town. I stood for many minutes to watch the pyre in the grave, a meaningless and solitary moment in history—I was the only witness—yet one engraved into my memory for the rest of my days. Meaningless in its anonymity, meaningless in its impact on how human beings continue to treat one another in this lawless corner of the earth, but I had witnessed the raising of two spirits, free of their underground prison, and free to be worshipped as ancestors by their poor, humble descendants on small shrines built in the living areas of their dilapidated hootches.

I came to Cambodia and Phnom Penh on this trip with tremendous expectations of prosperity and happiness. The first free elections had been held in May 1993 and brought with them a chance for peace and relative prosperity that no living Cambodian has ever witnessed. Luxurious hotels and guesthouses had been built. New office buildings pierced the black clouds of the northwest monsoon (more than 100 such structures by many estimates) in anticipation of the wave of foreign investment that would bring wealth to the relatively prosperous and food to the millions of Cambodians who are hideously malnourished.

UNTAC had departed in November 1993 (to that point, the largest peacekeeping operation ever staged by the United Nations, involving more than 22,000 soldiers), leaving with droves of white doves sent into the humid, thick tropical sky to signify a new era of peace in this perpetually beleaguered landscape. Of course, many foreign soldiers were killed to bring peace to Cambodia. But their mission of peace was "accomplished."

It was about as "accomplished" as a platonic relationship between Adam and Eve.

Instead, in the summer of 1994—a full year-plus after "peace in Cambodia"—I found in Phnom Penh the same naked children sleeping and urinating on the garbage-strewn sidewalks, the same rutted-faced amputees pulling on my shirtsleeves for handouts, the same grimy metropolis that was thought to become the new Singapore, the new Bangkok, the new Kuala Lumpur. Yes, many Phnom Penhoise are now driving cars—there were perhaps a handful of privately-owned cars before the elections. And there are considerably more motorbikes on the streets that have created congestion problems that rival Ho Chi Minh City. Was this a sign of the new wealth and prosperity that had come to Cambodia after the May 1993 elections?

Hardly; the new money was simply being pulled from the rapidly drying well of cash the UNTAC soldiers left behind when they departed late in 1993. Conspicuous consumption had arrived in Phnom Penh.

But perhaps my arrival at Phnom Penh's Pochentong Airport signified more than anything else the instability that remains here, a reaffirmation of the pessimism all Phnom Penhoise possess that nothing in Cambodia has changed since UNTAC's efforts to unify the country, that nothing will change, and that life will become far more difficult before it gets even an iota better.

As I got off the plane, a massive entourage of expensive German passenger cars, flanked by dozens of police cars and motorcycles, paraded through a gauntlet of saluting soldiers in khaki uniforms onto the airport's tarmac. From the largest Mercedes emerged an ailing Norodom Sihanouk, Cambodia's king. Unbelievably, the customs officer, as I was having my passport stamped, allowed me back onto the tarmac unescorted to photograph the king and the dozens of military and political officials and press helping him up the stairs to a North Korean jetliner. He was bound for the North Korean capital of Pyongyang to hold, yet again, more roundtable discussions with the leaders of the Khmer Rouge, a roundtable—like all previous ones—that would ultimately end up in more rounds being fired, near tables and far from them.

When UNTAC was in Cambodia, soldiers from many nations were living on daily allowances of US$150. Hotel prices in the capital skyrocketed. Rents increased fivefold. Asian companies eagerly opened construction and finance institutions. Many Cambodians made a wad of cash from the peacekeepers. They bought cars and motorbikes and VCRs and TVs. But when the peacekeepers left Phnom Penh, they took with them two important items: their money...

And peace.

Of the 100 or so new structures built in the city, perhaps only 20 are still occupied. New, tinted glass high-rises are covered with dust and boarded up. Hotel and restaurant rates have plummeted. (Whereas, where I stayed in 1992 at the Capitol Hotel the room rates were US$10-20, they now hover around the US$5 range). Land prices, although an official at the American embassy here told me otherwise, have bottomed out. But most importantly, tourism to Cambodia, and Phnom Penh in particular, has dropped by as much as 90 percent since April 1994 according to Phnom Penh Tourism, mainly because of the fear of violence. The Khmer Rouge still occupy much of the countryside (see the U.S. Consular Sheet sidebar) and banditry in both Phnom Penh and the countryside is becoming more prevalent and violent.

Banditry is becoming particularly more acute among Phnom Penhoise youths, which some local officials have termed as "anarchy." Lawlessness among youths in Phnom Penh is on the rise. It's difficult to determine the increase of violent incidents because so many offenders aren't arrested or are released immediately, local police sources told me. Currently, there about 20 students in Phnom Penh prisons for robberies, usually involving weapons, although the assaults appear to be directed at Phnom Penhoise rather than foreign tourists, who outnumber only polar bears in Cambodia.

"The problem of juvenile delinquency in the capital has reached a state of anarchy, " said Peou Samy of the Youth Rehabilitation Center in Phnom Penh. Children who have never known stability and have not received an education begin to beg and steal at a young age. And the children of wealthier families can afford guns. "The problem has increased in 1993 and 1994," Peou Samy said. "These children are quite different from other generations."

Whether, for foreigners, the fear of visiting Phnom Penh is justified is open to judgement. Most of the descent of Cambodian tourism is due to the decreasing amount of Europeans visiting Phnom Penh. Publications in Europe are comparing Cambodia with Bosnia. The government of Belgium has reportedly mandated all its citizens currently in Cambodia to leave the country immediately and has imposed stringent guidelines for travel to Cambodia (usually for business purposes solely). Australia, France and Great Britain have issued their most extreme travel advisories to citizens wishing to visit Cambodia. On April 11, a pair of British citizens and an Australian were abducted from their taxi en route to Sihanoukville along National Route 4 by the Khmer Rouge, taken into the forest, and haven't been heard from since. An American relief worker, Melissa Himes, was released on May 11, after 41 days of captivity by the Khmer Rouge. She was released in exchange for three tons of rice, 100 bags of cement, 100 aluminum roofing sheets, medicines and 1500 cans of fish to be delivered to the KR-occupied village where she was being held. At one point, a KR soldier came to her hut and told her she was going to be killed, as Royal Government troops were closing in on the village. When they abandoned their efforts to take the village, the death threat against her was lifted. Her only words were, "I really didn't want to think about it, only that 'God, if it's my time, it's my time.'"

Three Westerners were abducted in July 1994 and executed by the Khmer Rouge in September.

During my most recent stay in Phnom Penh, the Malaysian Embassy was attacked by a grenade. Some here in the capital, myself included, believe the attack was a case of mistaken identity, and that the American Embassy next door was to have been the actual target of the assault in response to President Bill Clinton's recent commitment to the Cambodian government of technical aid to fight the Khmer Rouge. (The two embassies are side-by-side, and the flags of each country are virtually identical.)

Yesterday, a police colonel was killed by an assault rifle and his motorcycle stolen. Bandits and KR living in Phnom Penh have no qualms about killing, simply because they realize its insignificance. Cambodia and Phnom Penh lie in an impenetrable pocket of ice, despite the extreme, bone permeating heat. On numerous occasions, I heard the reports of automatic weapons fire on Phnom Penh streets. The locals say that, in many instances, policemen (who all carry assault rifles) fire their weapons into the air to test them. On other occasions, the gunfire can be attributed to enraged motorists who have gotten into an accident.

Phnom Penh has most definitely changed. Whereas during my previous visit while UNTAC occupied the nation (or much of it), I ran into a number of independent tourists traveling individually, these days, those few remaining are traveling in pairs or groups. The American embassy official, who asked not be named, said that the busloads of European tourists he used to see traversing the capital's streets to Phnom Penh's attractions have all but disappeared since the beginning of the year. Yeah, there are Westerners here. A lot of them, in fact. But they're all lugging around pounds of photographic equipment and Reuters, AFP, and AP calling cards.

"Frankly, we're puzzled why so many people are so scared," the U.S. embassy officer told me. "Particularly in Europe, where the media is creating the most panic concerning visiting Cambodia. Phnom Penh is safe for foreigners. But in Europe, the press has created an exaggerated impression of the amount of fighting here."

However he also admitted to me that just a few days earlier he was driving behind a car on the streets of the capital that was traversing the road erratically—braking suddenly and hard for no apparent reason and then speeding up again as if to intimidate the American official driving behind. This so incensed the diplomat that he had his driver pull up alongside the weaving car to confront its driver—until he noticed an AK-47 assault rifle hanging from the passenger side's seat. The American backed off like a fleeing gecko. "You don't flip anybody the bird in Cambodia," he said.

Phnom Penhoise and visitors alike might consider that comment a little understated.

Phann Sok Pip, who runs a Phnom Penh restaurant, is haunted by his past and skeptical of the future of the capital city and a government that's held together by dental floss. Patronage by foreigners in his eatery has dropped by at least 80 percent, he told me. And he, too, is scared of the Khmer Rouge. A large man in his late 40s, with thinning black hair and eyes that vacillate from cold steel to a warm cup of tea in an eyeblink, was a young man when the Khmer Rouge seized his village near Battambang in 1975. Those who could speak a foreign language (as Pip could) or who were formerly in the army or currently students had a red "X" placed next to their names. The Khmer Rouge separated his family and killed his two brothers-in-law. "I was sent far off into the country with groups of other young people, who had also been separated from their families," he said. "I had to work in the fields from 5 in the morning until 11 a.m., and then again from 1 to 5 p.m. and then from 6 p.m. to 11 o'clock. We were able to eat only one small bowl of rice soup a day. My two brothers-in-law were killed through malnourishment, as were many thousands of others. During the middle of the night, three or four Khmer Rouge soldiers would enter our huts in the fields and take people away. I wasn't taken away because they had not yet discovered I could speak English, but I knew they would find out soon. They might speak to someone in English or French to catch them off guard. If a man unwittingly acknowledged the question, the Khmer Rouge would then know the man could speak a foreign language. They would take these people into the forest and make them dig their own graves. Then they would make these people kneel down in front of the hole. They used large bamboo sticks to strike the backs of their necks. The corpses would then fall into the holes. I lost many friends."

"I knew I had to escape, so one night, I left the camp and swam across the Sanke River. I was able to draw up a fake travel permit, which was actually quite easy at the time. I changed my name to Pham Heng. I was stopped all the time by Khmer Rouge soldiers, who asked to see my permit. I told them I was an ice cream salesman. In the villages, in order to stay, I had to give the soldiers my watch and my clothes. To survive, I went out into the fields everyday and hid."

Pip said that things have changed in Phnom Penh since the departure of UNTAC. "The future here is very dark for the Cambodian people," he said. "Now there is little investment, whereas there used to be a lot of investment here, especially by the Japanese; now there is none. The new buildings are empty. We thought after the elections, the economy would improve and that there would be peace in Cambodia. Now I forecast no peace in Cambodia."

As well, the Phnom Penhoise have changed. They seemed more jaded, more reluctant to converse with foreigners. There were fewer smiles and tighter jaws. No children followed me with the cheerful, youthful curiosity of seeing what a strange, white-skinned man was up to. Whereas two years ago I would ride my bicycle through a gauntlet of "hellos" and "What's your name?," instead I was met with a disappointing indifference. UNTAC changed Phnom Penh. They arrived and left on their golden calf. And believe me, they took that damned calf with them.

I ran into a very confused young American tourist from Boston named Jay Bourbon. He was leaning over the railing of the Capitol Hotel during an electric purple sunset pondering his next move. He'd fallen in love with Phnom Penh and was considering staying awhile to teach English. He'd been on the road 10 months and admitted to me that he had never seen a country like Cambodia, nor a city like Phnom Penh. His desire was to visit Angkor Wat, arguably the most spectacular ancient temple in the world. He wanted to take the 24-hour ferry journey up the Tonle Sap river to Siem Reap. When I informed him that foreigners making the journey by ferry had dwindled to a trickle due to security concerns and the marked increase of banditry on the ferries, his eyes narrowed to slits, and he threw the butt of his Lucky Strike out onto the street. Then darkness shrouded the city, as if it was an omen. It may not have been lost on him, either. "I don't want to talk about travel anymore," he said. He went back to his room.

Two days later, he left by himself for Angkor by ferry. The day after he left, 600 government troops were ordered immediately to the Siem Reap area in anticipation of a massive KR assault on the Siem Reap and the Angkor complex.

The biggest problem in Phnom Penh is obtaining accurate information. While I was in Saigon, I saw television reports that Jacques Cousteau's *Calypso* had been fired upon along the Mekong River after crossing into Cambodia from Vietnam. The assailants were unknown, but were presumed to be Khmer Rouge. I figured most assuredly press sources in Phnom Penh would have the scoop, so I paid the offices of the *Cambodia Times* a visit. There, journalist Umej Bhatia said that he was unaware of any such incident. I asked him whether he might be interested in the story if I did some digging for him.

"Even if it did occur," he said, "we probably wouldn't print such an article because it would hurt tourism to Cambodia."

Khmer Edition Editor Ouk Kimseng was also unaware of the incident and dismissed it as a rumor fabricated in Saigon. "Prosperity in Phnom Penh has gone down," he said. I wasn't sure why he made that statement. But I had an idea.

Visits to *Le Mekong*, the French Indochina periodical, gleaned the same results. The American embassy here was also unaware of such an attack, as was the Cambodian Ministry of Information. Finally, an AFP reporter, Kevin Barrington—whom I'd met two years earlier when he was with the *Cambodian Times*—said simply, "Even if the ship had been fired upon, what would the news be? All the ships are fired upon out there. That's not news."

When the Malaysian embassy was grenaded, officials there wouldn't allow photographers from the *Cambodia Times* nor from the *Phnom Penh Post* to enter the compound to photograph the damage. My visit to the embassy enabled me to speak with Mohan, an embassy official who would only say, "If someone had thrown a grenade into a house, it wouldn't have made the news because it happens all the time. But because it was an embassy, it makes all the headlines."

French photojournalist Franck Nolot had been in Phnom Penh for 18 months. Only an hour before these words, he left Cambodia for "home" in Paris. Despite his youth, he looked tired and thin. He had been covering the civil war in Cambodia for nearly two years, and his photographs of the struggle between Royal Government and KR troops were horrifying. He'd covered the skirmishes between UNTAC and KR forces as well as bitter fighting between the Khmer Rouge and government forces. His photos went on exhibition in Paris during the summer of 1994. I asked him how Cambodia had changed in the last two years, especially after the withdrawal of UNTAC.

"The situation has deteriorated, absolutely," he said. "What the government does with the money it allocates to fighting the Khmer Rouge, no one knows (but it doesn't appear to me that it's going to the Army). The government had their chance last month when they attacked Pailin (the KR headquarters city in far-western Cambodia). But the assault failed. It was their only chance (to defeat the Khmer Rouge). As long as Pailin remains under the control of the Khmer Rouge, they will continue to be financed. The government has no chance of taking Pailin."

British photojournalist Martin Flitman, a middle aged man with nervous, alert eyes and hair not unlike Larry of the Three Stooges, who had also been in Cambodia for nearly two years, agreed. "In the army, there is no leadership, there is no training, and there is no morale," he said. "But this a beautiful city," he continued, as we photographed a bustling local market amidst a brilliant copper sunset. "Look at the faces of these people! There are no people on earth like the Cambodians."

Consequently, the Khmer Rouge survive, despite a purported dwindling of their numbers due to defections. Estimates of their troop strength range from between 10,000 to 50,000 soldiers. But they continue to be financed primarily through trade in hardwood and gems with Thai businessmen and corrupt elements of the Thai military, despite a United Nations ban on this commerce and the fact the Thai government's well-intentioned but dataless claim that trade between Thais and the Khmer Rouge has ended. The Khmer Rouge have made, by conservative estimates, hundreds of millions of dollars in dealings with the Thais. The 700 km-plus border with Thailand is essentially lawless and is riddled with corrupt Thai army officials that freely permit the crossing of Cambodian (i.e., KR) hardwood and gems into Thailand—for a price, of course.

The late 1993 discovery by Royal Cambodian troops of a well-maintained dirt road leading from Ta Phraya, on the border of Thailand, a mile into the Khmer Rouge-controlled Cambodian town of Phnom Prak, revealed a massive, elaborate compound of spacious wooden homes and warehouses built by Thai contractors for none other than Pol Pot himself. Khmer Rouge defectors reported that one of the largest houses, hidden on a densely-foliaged hillside with a small garden was Pol Pot's own home during his sojourns into Cambodia from his base in Thailand. He brought along both his wife and daughter during his frequent visits there. Even more shocking was the nearby discovery, within Cambodian territory, of offices belonging to the Royal Thai Army's Task Force 838, a military unit that worked secretly with the Khmer Rouge and acted as intermediaries between the KR and the Thai Army.

Although the compound was overrun by Cambodian troops, it only serves as further evidence of the Khmer Rouge-Thai connection, a thriving relationship that continues to this day.

Essentially the Thais and the Khmer Rouge forged their relationship after the Vietnamese overthrow of Pol Pot's Phnom Penh regime in January 1979, in mutual antagonism toward the Vietnamese, a traditional enemy of both countries. Failed assaults on both nearby Anlong Veng and the Khmer Rouge capital at Pailin in May 1994 have nothing but strengthened the guerillas' resolve—and strength.

And there have been recent accusations in Phnom Penh that the Khmer Rouge are acquiring outside military aid. *The Cambodia Daily* reported that the KR has started receiving tanks and other armored equipment from China, a country that once vigorously supported the Khmer Rouge with arms and financing until the Paris Peace Accords and subsequent attacks on Chinese UNTAC soldiers by KR units. But the Khmer Rouge contends they obtained their new tanks after the government's assaults on both Pailin and Anlong Veng (another strategic KR stronghold in the west) failed.

A Khmer Rouge radio message monitored in Bangkok said that when the government troops withdrew from Pailin and Anlong Veng, the Royal Army "abandoned dozens of their tanks on the battlefield. Khmer Rouge forces captured them like crabs and then used them to attack government positions."

No one seems to know for sure why the strength of the Khmer Rouge continues and where this muscle is coming from. Perhaps most confused are government officials themselves. "The Khmer Rouge are using Chinese tanks," said Cambodian Co-Premier Prince Norodom Ranariddh, "the tanks that UNTAC, with all its helicopters and photographs, did not manage to discover. I want to know, where do all of these tanks come from?"

Although many sources say that the Khmer Rouge control only the Thai border regions (and indeed most of the fiercest fighting is occurring in Pailin, Battambang and the northwest) this information cannot be considered to be entirely reliable. Tourists have been abducted south of Phnom Penh by KR units, such as the July 1994 abductions at Vine Mountain, and the Vietnamese border guards at the crossing at Ha Tien in the extreme southwest of Vietnam told me that the Khmer Rouge controls areas just across the border, which, if true, contradicts accounts given to me by the American embassy in Phnom Penh as well as Phnom Penh Tourism sources. But again, who to believe?

At the time of this writing, Angkor is only marginally safe to visit from Phnom Penh, but only by air. Only the foolish try it any other way.

Ian and Cale had just gotten back to the capital from Angkor yesterday, where they had visited the temples for two days. They were glad to be back in Phnom Penh, and astounded by what they had seen and heard in and around the complex. Ian, a lanky young Englishman in his late 20s, had heard the complex was safe to visit, but, nonetheless teamed up with Cale, a body builder, to make the journey, first by truck and then by boat.

"I had heard the place was safe," Ian said, "but hundreds of government troops had just arrived," he said. "There was shelling going on outside the complex. One round landed not more than 20 meters from me (outside Angkor). For the first time in my life I was really frightened. The Khmer Rouge, from what I could best tell, is preparing an assault on Siem Reap. They're all around the temple complex, a ring of them, within 10 km, and a number more in Siem Reap dressed in civilian clothes. I was riding my motorbike around the perimeter of the complex and I came upon a well dressed and well groomed Cambodian who I was convinced was a Khmer Rouge. You can just tell when you see these guys. There's a look about them. As I passed by him I sped up because I was afraid; he lifted his t-shirt and moved closer to the road. I know he was pulling a pistol from his pants. I don't know how I made it by him, perhaps because I was driving so fast. The shelling I heard was amazing. People who say that it's safe to visit Angkor are crazy, and how tourism officials can say it's safe to visit this place, I can't figure out. If I were to go back, it would be only by plane. And even then, the security seems minimal at best."

"If I had known in Bangkok how unsafe Angkor was, I would never have come," said Cale, a strapping Dane with a long ponytail and who seemed to epitomize fearlessness. "The Khmer Rouge I think are surrounding the city (Siem Reap) and I know they're getting stronger. The trip there scared the shit out of me. If I had known the situation there was like it was, I would never have gone. We traveled by truck over roads I know had been mined. The craters in the road weren't the result of road neglect. You could just tell. They had been caused by mines. I'm absolutely convinced of it. And the worst part was traveling by road at night. The jungle closed in on both sides. I was convinced the truck was going to be stopped."

Other excursions from the capital are also dangerous. "Many tourists wish to visit Sihanoukville on the south coast (a magnificently beautiful beach area with some of Southeast Asia's best diving and snorkeling)," said Yo Sakhan, an official with Phnom Penh Tourism. "But National Highway 4 to Sihanoukville is extremely dangerous. At Kompong Speu, there is, at many times, a roadblock set up by the police. You'll need to pay US$50 to the police in order to pass, even if you are in a taxi. Further south, at Sre Ambel, you'll very likely run into another roadblock set up by the Khmer Rouge. They will demand anything of value you possess, including watches, jewelry, and even your clothes before allowing you to proceed. But they will allow you to proceed (in most cases)."

So you end up in Sihanoukville naked and without cash. "If you have no money or items of any value to the Khmer Rouge," he continued, "there is the possibility they will shoot you. They will most certainly take your clothes." Yo, a man in his 50s—and also with the ability to speak both French and English during the KR's reign of terror—had also survived the wrath of Pol Pot by obtaining a bogus permit. He worked in the fields for five years. His teeth fell out and his weight dropped to that of a raisin, which, indeed, he resembled.

But in all honesty, there remains some optimism in Phnom Penh—albeit guarded—at least among tourism officials.

"Hey, some of the roads are paved now," said Yo. But he, too, admitted that life in Phnom Penh has reverted to its former pre-UNTAC condition. "Life is difficult now," he said. "Admittedly, peace is not stable, and there is fighting everyday in the countryside. There are attacks in the city. The fighting will, I fear, continue for a long time."

The few travelers I met in Phnom Penh were simply using the city as a springboard for visiting Angkor. Most left the capital disheartened within a few days of arrival and indeed the country itself, not believing in the optimism of tourism officials, but instead in the reports given to them by their hardy colleagues recently returned from a tourist mecca that is becoming once again a war zone.

Phnom Penh is accessible and generally safe to visit. The principal point here is that travelers to Phnom Penh and Cambodia should not rely on guidebooks that were created while UNTAC had established what was essentially a colony here in Cambodia, making much of the countryside safe to visit. Nor should they rely on travelers' reports of their visits here while UNTAC had established some degree of stability. That stability simply no longer exists at present. The current presence of UNTAC personnel in Cambodia is estimated to be about the size of a Sri Lankan high school history class.

Phnom Penh remains caught between empty fruitbaskets, a city in perpetual limbo in a besieged nation landlocked by adversaries within and outside its borders. Phnom Penh is like a bee, and no one wants to get stung. And worse yet, Indochina is a dirty word in the West, whose reluctant governments are perhaps the only solution to ending the civil war in Cambodia.

Phnom Penh remains a marginally safe destination in my opinion. But the situation here is deteriorating. Even after 30 years of civil war, the first chapter of modern Cambodian history has not been completed. It will take many authors and many, many years to write this book, a book that will confuse its readers as much as its authors—as well as the Cambodian people. Life in Phnom Penh continues. And our exposure to and interaction with this life can continue. For how long, I cannot say. But many here say it won't last long.

Julian's the type of guy out of a Rambo movie. He's 44 years old and a Vietnam War vet with a thick toothbrush mustache. He dresses in military fatigues and gets around Phnom Penh astride an old Indian motorcycle with a sidecar, usually occupied by his Thai wife. He's lived in Phnom Penh for five years and gets by meagerly shooting photos the local rags occasionally publish. He's a guy with a face forged from steel who couldn't ever adjust to life back in the States after the war. He moved to Thailand first, then Cambodia in 1989 because Thailand wasn't dangerous enough.

"Anyone who comes to Cambodia now is just' crazy," he said. "I wouldn't have said that a couple of years ago. This place is a war zone. You see these tourists and they're damn' crazy, man. I'd never come here as a tourist. The situation here is warfare, and it won't end. Bringing in American troops won't necessarily solve the situation. Phnom Penh isn't safe and I'd say anyone considering to come to Cambodia is a fool. There's so much shit going on around Phnom Penh, that you'd have to have a death wish to come here. Everyone has assault rifles and they aren't scared to use them. You'd be damn' crazy to come to this country now. So you hear about the fear of

Cambodia the European press is generating. The stories are all true. I'd tell people to stay away from Cambodia, even Phnom Penh. You're freakin" crazy to put this place on a Southeast Asian itinerary. Cambodia and Phnom Penh are irrefutably more dangerous than it's ever been around here."

Is Phnom Penh safe for foreign travelers?

Phnom Penh Tourism official Yo Sakhan had two requests for me: 1) Could I possibly send him reading glasses from the United States so that he could read his maps better; 2) Could I possibly help him emigrate to the United States?

I made a deal with him. I'd send him the reading glasses and help him try to emigrate to the U.S.—but in exchange for reading glasses of my own to help me better understand Cambodia.

Obviously, Yo, whose job it is to encourage tourists to witness the cultural bounty of his city and nation, wanted to get the hell out from between the empty baskets.

What Will Save Tourism In Cambodia?

Tourism as a goal in Cambodia diminishes on a criteria scale given the nation's 30-year murderous, heinous past, which continues into the present. The fact that at least six Western tourists were slain by the Khmer Rouge in 1994 only demands that tourism to Cambodia be addressed on a far deeper level than is applicable to any other country Fielding covers for our readers. Only a few short years ago, there was a precious (albeit precarious) window of relative peace in the country, where tourists and adventure travelers alike could marvel at such wonders as Angkor Wat in relative safety. That window was UNTAC, and when the peacekeepers left in November of 1993, the window was slammed shut for tourists, of course, but, more importantly, for 8 million innocent Cambodians, the vast majority of whom live in fear, poverty and squalor. The few tourists that continue to risk a Cambodian visit will not be met with the broad smiles that once were there. Many Cambodians no longer delight in white skin and blue eyes. They are now fully aware of the West's impotence. Foreigners are no longer a novelty, but a nuisance and a reminder of the Cambodian epiphany—a revelation that other developing peoples of the world have long since discovered—that exploitation is a larger goal than the benefits of cultural discovery and mutual respect and corroboration.

Cambodians are fully aware that the Khmer Rouge have not deviated an inch from the policies and activities that characterized the group during their reign of terror in the mid to late 1970s. Despite the urging of many Western analysts that the Khmer Rouge solution still ultimately rests on "political inclusion," Cambodians know otherwise. The recent shunning of the guerrillas by other Western politicians and diplomats for continuing to use deadly, indiscriminate tactics against foreigners and their own people alike in the wake of the May 1993 elections rings hollow in the ears of the Cambodian people. What Western nation, as well as Cambodia's own Asian neighbors, could be naive enough to believe the bloodshed would stop? It isn't naivete at all. Rather, it's stuffing Cambodia's core problems under the mattress of trade interests. It just might explain Britain's, France's and Australia's lethargy in procuring the release of their nationals held hostage and subsequently executed in September 1994. These nations' lame excuse, of course, was not wanting to infringe upon the "sovereignty" of the Cambodian government.

Cambodian Second Prime Minister Hun Sen, himself a turncoat Khmer Rouge, instead of blaming the Khmer Rouge (or his own government, for that matter) for the

September 1994 KR slayings of three Westerners and the failed efforts to procure their release, directed his wrath toward the press for causing the killings.

The press.

Right.

A Khmer Rouge unit rockets a train in southern Cambodia, killing 13, then executes three ethnic-Vietnamese (a given under any circumstances) and then three Western tourists—and the press is to blame for it.

Blame for the killings has been tossed around like a plastic salad, with no one willing to eat it.

Shortly after the discovery of the September slayings and just prior to the October 1994 APEC summit in Indonesia, Australian Foreign Minister Garth Evans blamed the Thai Government for the killings, alleging that corrupt elements of the Thai military were freely allowing the Khmer Rouge to trade hardwood and gems to Thai interests. A furious Thai Prime Minister Chuan Leekpai challenged Evans to substantiate the allegations or face a severing of bilateral trade between the two nations (ironically, the principal Australian export to Thailand being arms). Evans subsequently toned down his allegations, embarrassingly "admitting" that his claims were based on "outdated" satellite intelligence of the Thai-Cambodian border gathered in July 1994. Chuan self-righteously cooled down. Less than a week after Evans' retraction, Cambodia's new defense minister supported Evans' original claims. Chuan scoffed, dismissing the renewal of the charges as essentially the squealing of a voice from a set of impotent bleachers. Of course, two days later, a truckload of Cambodian (i.e., Khmer Rouge) hardwood was confiscated by honest elements of the Thai military—kilometers inside the Thai border.

A *Bangkok Post* editorial shortly after the Khmer Rouge tourist killings of September 1994 was headlined "Tourist Killings Expose Menace of Khmer Rouge." Another recent headline in the same paper announced, "Tougher Khmer Policies Urged Against Khmer Rouge." It was like reading a time capsule. These were the same headlines in every paper across the globe in the mid-1970s.

Tourism in Cambodia? It's on the back of the bus compared to lives and livelihoods of the millions of Cambodians up front near the blind driver. The solution to the tourist plunge in Cambodia is the same solution to the human plunge in Cambodia.

The bumbling ASEAN nations (also a group united virtually solely for the motive of profit) of Brunei, Indonesia, Malaysia, Singapore, Thailand and the Philippines has to formulate a Cambodian policy—one doesn't exist. ASEAN member Thailand must more thoroughly tighten its border with Cambodia, as most of the billions of dollars the outlaw group "earns" is through illegal gem and hardwood trading with Thai businessmen via corrupt current and former Thai military officers. On the record and in policy, Thailand does not support the Khmer Rouge. Yet the government is curiously reluctant to see any external power provide aid to the Cambodian government. When Thailand balks, people listen.

Hmmm.

This further compounds the divergences and confusion within ASEAN, as Indonesia is actively training Cambodian troops.

Cambodia itself doesn't possess a Cambodian policy. The government, reluctant to sacrifice its impotent armed forces, most of whose numbers are on paper only, is saying the Khmer Rouge will simply self-dissolve through rebel desertions. Sure, there were a few hundred guerrillas who turned to the other side after their defeat at Vine Mountain. But when the Cambodian army can only accrue a handful of victories in the battlefield against the Khmer Rouge, it means only a handful of desertions. And only the government is calling them "desertions." Semantics. Whose to say the guerrillas aren't merely prisoners?

As hard as Southeast Asian nations want to continue to be under the illusion that the Khmer Rouge is a pesky little Cambodian internal problem, the capture and murder of foreigners is the best illustration that it is not, but instead it is one of international proportions—and one with only an international solution.

If anything positive emerges from tourist deaths in Cambodia, it will be a multilateral world effort to isolate and cut the Khmer Rouge movement to pieces.

At the time of this writing, at least 50 U.S. Special Forces "advisors" are in Cambodia, "confined" to Phnom Penh.

Also at the time of this writing, a number of these "confined advisors" have been spotted on the front lines.

In 1941, the French made Prince Sihanouk king of Cambodia, believing they had installed another loyal puppet on the throne who'd do anything the French asked of him for the price of a lavish existence.

Instead, King Sihanouk moved in the direction of Cambodian independence. In 1953, he declared martial law and dissolved the parliament. On November 9, he proclaimed Cambodia an independent state. But internal divisions continued to hamper the solidarity among the nation's leaders. In 1955, Sihanouk abdicated the throne in favor of politics. His People's Socialist Community party was hugely successful and, in fact, captured every seat in parliament in elections held in 1955. His father, who had gained ascendancy to the throne after Nordom stepped down five years earlier, died in 1960. Sihanouk simply assumed both roles, bannered under the title of chief-of-state.

Sihanouk's traits as a politician emerged and became evident. First, he slowly began drifting Cambodia toward the clutches of China and North Vietnam in the early 1960s in the fear that Cambodia's biggest problems would come from the U.S., Thailand and South Vietnam, even so far as cutting ties with the U.S. and permitting North Vietnamese and Viet Cong to use Cambodia for bases of operation during the Vietnam War.

Then, when a conservative and peasant backlash erupted internally, Sihanouk began aligning Cambodia with U.S. efforts to dispose of the communists in Vietnam, an effort that was backed by the army. In 1969, the U.S. initiated the first of what would become four years of merciless B-52 bombing strikes of eastern Cambodia, thoroughly decimating vast areas of land and killing thousands of people.

In 1970, an apparently U.S.-backed coup deposed Sihanouk and made Prince Sisowath Matak and Army General Lon Nol the leaders of Cambodia. Sihanouk himself fled to Beijing, where he still maintains his primary residence today. It was in Beijing where Sihanouk, acting as a leader in exile, nominally held the strings of the newly formed Khmer Rouge.

Lon Nol's troubles, in the meantime, were just beginning. The U.S. invaded Cambodia in 1970, driving North Vietnamese forces further inside Cambodia. Peasants fled en masse to Phnom Penh to escape the fighting. Civil war raged in the countryside. Cambodia's troubles were further compounded by mainly substantiated charges of deep corruption within the government. Hundreds of thousands of people died in the senseless fighting of the early 1970s.

It was this anarchy that played such a formidable role in the ascendancy of the Khmer Rouge. The Maoist guerrillas, amply supplied by the Chinese, were too formidable a force for Lon to suitably suppress, despite heavy U.S. aid. The Khmer Rouge rolled into Phnom Penh on April 17, 1975. Two weeks later, Saigon fell to the communists.

On that day in April in Cambodia, everything changed. It was the start of Year Zero.

Pol Pot evacuated the capital; the entire urban populace was force-marched into the countryside where individuals were assigned to state-run collective farms. Phnom Penh became a ghost town overnight. It was Pol's objective to reinvent Cambodia, to transform the society into a single vast agrarian collective. Between 1975 and the end of 1978, these efforts had reduced cities and towns and ancient pagodas to rubble. But even more ghastly, more than a million Cambodians had lost their lives at the hands of the Khmer Rouge. Many hundreds of thousands were tortured and executed. Others simply collapsed and died in the fields from exhaustion and malnourishment. All travel was prohibited, currency abolished. Citizens were executed for merely having the ability to speak a foreign language.

The savagery continued for nearly four years. Although Sihanouk returned to Cambodia in 1975 as chief of state, he was kept in Phnom Penh under house arrest until 1978—the year Vietnam invaded Cambodia.

The Vietnamese ousted Pol in just two short weeks and took control of the capital on January 7, 1979—installing Hun Sen and Heng Samrin as leaders. The Khmer Rouge fled into the jungles of western Cambodia, to areas near and beyond the Thai border, leaving behind hectares of burning rice fields in their wake. The ensuing famine forced hundreds of thousands of Cambodians to take refuge in camps across the border in Thailand, camps they have only recently returned from.

Meanwhile, Sihanouk, with China's backing, formed a loose opposition coalition dominated by the Khmer Rouge. Although Pol Pot reportedly handed down the reins of his leadership in 1985, he still remains the group's leader, basing his operations over the border in Thailand's Trat Province.

From 1980 through 1989, government forces engaged in frequent and fierce battles with Khmer Rouge units which, operating out of their base in Pailin, continued to terrorize the Cambodian countryside, using civilians as human shields and planting millions of land mines across the country. And not to discriminate, Hun Sen's troops were equally guilty of turning the countryside into one big jar of nitroglycerine, by double- and even triple-booby trapping their own mines.

Although China ceased its quasi-official support of the guerrillas, the Khmer Rouge continued to finance themselves through hardwood logging and gem concessions to Thai businessmen; concessions that have netted the Khmer Rouge more than US$100 million to date. The resultant damage to the environment has been catastrophic; only about seven million of the country's 16 million hectares of tropical forests remain today. The Thai military, which controls all the checkpoints along the 500 mile border, had—and still has, many charge—a finger in the Khmer Rouge pie. Thailand's historical tacit support of the guerrillas has stemmed mainly from its traditional hatred of the Vietnamese.

Finally, in Paris in October of 1991, after years of intractable negotiations, an agreement was reached to end the civil war in Cambodia, an accord that also called for free elections to be held in May 1993.

More than 22,000 troops and civilian officials descended upon Cambodia, from Japanese policemen and Australian land mine disposal experts, to crack Indonesian and

Malaysian combat units. More than US$2.6 billion was spent. Phnom Penh, as it was transformed so suddenly in 1975, was reborn again. But this time with discos and video stores and hamburger joints and international soldiers with US$100 a day allowances, an amount inconceivable to the vast majority of Cambodians—in a year much less a day.

But, despite the massive presence, the fighting continued. At first, it was still contained between the Khmer Rouge and CPAF troops. But by the beginning of 1993, UNTAC soldiers themselves had become the targets of Khmer Rouge ordnance, including the first Japanese to have been killed on a foreign military mission since World War II. A Bulgarian peacekeeping unit was gunned down by Khmer Rouge guerrillas they had invited to lunch. UNTAC helicopters were being shot out of the sky regularly, their passengers being "detained" by Khmer Rouge units. Pol Pot's soldiers attacked Siem Reap, near the site of Angkor Wat. The Khmer Rouge refused to disarm, as the Paris accord required them to do, or to participate in the political process at all.

It seemed that the peace process was doomed, that the elections wouldn't be held at all. The *Los Angeles Times* reported that the "celebratory clinking of champagne glasses in Paris is being mocked by events on the ground."

But, surprisingly, the Khmer Rouge did not follow through on their threats to disrupt the elections, perhaps because of UNTAC's overestimation of their numbers and military capabilities. Polling stations remained relatively violence-free as nearly 90 percent of the Cambodians registered to vote by UNTAC registration teams cast their ballots. The big winner was Norodum Ranariddh, Sihanouk's son and leader of the FUNCINPEC (Cambodian National Front for an Independent, Neutral, Peaceful and Cooperative Cambodia) party. He overcame what at first were heavy odds in favor of incumbent Cambodian Premier Hun Sen to win the May elections. Hun Sen seemed a shoo-in for many months, but Cambodians became disillusioned as more reports surfaced implicating the government in political violence.

But the margin of victory was narrow enough that Sihanouk, still considered by most Cambodians as the nation's leader and battling health problems, flew to Phnom Penh from Beijing, where he announced that a coalition between FUNCEINPEC and Hun Sen would rule Cambodia.

In October 1993 the U.S., satisfied the U.N. had accomplished its objective in Cambodia, formally recognized the new Phnom Penh government and established full diplomatic relations with Cambodia. Today the country is referred to as Cambodia.

Death of the Dove

In January of 1992, Cambodia cautiously opened its doors to tourists. In April 1994, they were slammed shut—not by the government, but by prospective visitors themselves. After UNTAC's departure in November 1993, the Khmer Rouge stepped up their attacks on both government troops and foreign tourists alike. In 1994, six Western tourists were abducted and subsequently executed by the Khmer Rouge. A number of unsuccessful peace talks were held between the Khmer Rouge, leaders of the elected Cambodian government and an ailing King Sihanouk in Pyongyang, North Korea. Because of the Khmer Rouge's continued refusal to disarm under the banner of national reconciliation, the group was outlawed in early 1994. Fierce fighting rages between government troops and Khmer Rouge units in western, northwestern, northern and southern Cambodia. American military advisors have been committed to the Phnom Penh government by President Bill Clinton. Although supposedly confined to Phnom Penh, there have been reported sightings of U.S. Special Forces soldiers on the front lines.

Tourism has dropped as much as 90 percent over 1992, according to some officials. There had been 50 flights a week to Phnom Penh from Bangkok in 1992. The number has dropped to about 14.

Banditry is at an all-time high in the capital of Phnom Penh.

On July 2, 1994 a coup attempt was led by the former regime's interior ministry chief Sin Song and Prince Norodom Chakrapong, King Norodom Sihanouk's son.

Nineteen armored personnel carriers (APCs) with approximately 200 soldiers moved from the eastern Cambodian province of Prey Veng toward Phnom Penh. The vehicles were stopped by government troops 20 km from the capital. There was no fighting, and the soldiers in the vehicles were set free and not charged.

The coup attempt also involved 14 Thai nationals, who were later repatriated after being given suspended sentences. With the aid of his father, Prince Chakrapong fled Cambodia. Sin Song suspiciously "escaped" from military detention in September, illegally entered Thailand and was subsequently arrested by Thai immigration police in Bangkok. As Thailand has no extradition treaty with Cambodia, at the time of this writing, Sin Song's fate hasn't been sealed. France and the United States are among several countries that turned down his request for political asylum. Thai judges are mulling over returning the former Cambodian official, who has been sentenced to 20 years imprisonment in absentia. Thai-Cambodian relations have been seriously compromised by the Thais' involvement in the abortive coup attempt.

There are still questions about the possible involvement of Cambodian Second Prime Minister Hun Sen in the coup attempt. According to statements to his lawyer by senior Cambodian interior ministry official Sin Sen (who received an 18-year sentence for his role in the coup attempt) Hun Sen ordered the APCs to be moved from Prey Veng to the southern province of Kampot to secure the area against the Khmer Rouge. These allegations were also supported by another convicted coup conspirator, Cambodian defense department police chief Tea Choy. However, these claims were not admissible in court. One legal expert described the courtroom like this: "The judge did not allow questions to be asked. He asked questions to each of the (defendants), then he dismissed them. Neither the prosecution nor the defense had any opportunity to question the witnesses, nothing like any trial that I know."

The coup case today is still shrouded in mystery. In October 1994, the government performed a major housecleaning of its cabinet, including the firing of popular finance minister Sam Rainsy, a brilliant, French-educated free market reformer and ardent anti-corruptionist.

The Scoop

In September 1993, a democratically elected government took office in Cambodia, following a two-year United Nations peacekeeping program. The country has enormous economic needs and faces a strengthening Khmer Rouge insurgency in several provinces. High levels of crime and banditry remain a persistent problem in Cambodia. On July 2, 1994 a coup attempt, led by King Sihanouk's son Prince Norodom Chakrapong and the former government's interior ministry chief Sin Song, was aborted after 19 armored personnel carriers moving toward Phnom Penh were intercepted by troops loyal to the government. On May 18, the Malaysian embassy in Phnom Penh was grenaded. It's suspected the attack was a case of mistaken identity, and that the U.S. embassy next-door was the intended target. President Bill Clinton had recently committed "nonlethal" military assistance to Cambodia's military. After the execution of three Western tourists in September 1994, King

Norodom Sihanouk advised that all Western tourists avoid visiting any part of Cambodia. On December 29, 1994, the U.S. government said it was satisfied that the Cambodian government had distanced itself from the Khmer Rouge and would provide increased military aid. There have been some reports, none confirmed, of sightings of U.S. Special Forces personnel on the front lines with Cambodian troops battling the Khmer Rouge.

The Players

The Khmer Rouge

With a firm power base in northern and western Cambodia. The Khmer Rouge number between 10,000 and 50,000 soldiers (according to which source you talk to) and control approximately 20 percent of the country, primarily in the north, the northwest, the west along the Thai border and pockets in the south (particularly in Kompot province) between Phnom Penh and the coastal port city of Sihanoukville.

United Nations Transitional Authority in Cambodia (UNTAC)

Numbering at its peak more than 22,000 soldiers and support personnel from May 1992 through November 1993 in the largest U.N. peacekeeping mission to date (one costing more than US$2 billion), UNTAC began its withdrawal from Cambodia after the May 1993 elections. During the summer of 1994, there were an estimated 50 UNTAC administrators remaining in Cambodia, primarily in Phnom Penh. UNTAC no longer has a role in maintaining political and military stability in Cambodia.

NADK (National Army of Democratic Kampuchea or Khmer Rouge)

Outlawed in 1994 by the FUNCINPEC-led coalition Cambodian government, the Khmer Rouge are Maoists. The communist Khmer Rouge refuses to allow the disarmament of its fighters until certain conditions are met, including a prominent role in the coalition government. But most of these demands are rhetoric, as its real aims are apparently creating its own provisional government in as much of Cambodia as it can seize. Khmer Rouge leader is Pol Pot, who, although based across the border in Thailand, makes frequent forays to a new home he has had built inside the Cambodian border. Khieu Samphan is the nominal leader of the Khmer Rouge. Headquartered in Pailin, a power center that remains despite a spring 1994 government siege of the city. The Khmer Rouge is supported by oil, timber and gem trade with Thai businessmen and corrupt elements of the Thai Army and is backed by the Thai generals, using Chinese weapons. They are striving to create a self -sustaining economy in the Cambodge Profound. Their attempts to create a completely agrarian community in the 70s resulted in the genocide of more than 1 million Cambodians.

King Norodom Sihanouk

In 1941, the French made Prince Sihanouk king of Cambodia, believing they had installed another loyal puppet on the throne who'd do anything the French asked of him for the price of a lavish existence. Instead, King Sihanouk moved in the direction of Cambodian independence. In 1953, he declared martial law and dissolved the parliament. On November 9, he proclaimed Cambodia an independent state. But internal divisions continued to hamper the solidarity among the nation's leaders. In 1955, Sihanouk abdicated the throne in favor of politics. Politically, Sihanouk has vacillated between the right and the left throughout his career (intermittently supporting the Khmer Rouge and its foes alike). Known for bending with the wind, he is nonetheless still worshipped by the core of the Cambodian people. Ill with cancer, he resides primarily in Peking and Pyongyang, North Korea. His relationship with the late North Korean leader Kim Il Sung was deep and lasted for decades.

Getting In

A passport is required. An airport visa valid for a 14-day stay is available upon arrival at Phnom Penh's Pochentong Airport from the Ministry of National Security for US$20. Various Saigon tour operators run boats up the Mekong River from Vietnam to Phnom Penh. However, most of these excursions have been curtailed due to lawlessness and Khmer Rouge attacks on river-going vessels. Entry by land from Thailand is illegal.

Getting Around

See "In a Dangerous Place: Cambodia."

Dangerous Places

Southeast Cambodia has seen an upsurge in banditry and military activity. On March 31, 1994 an American employee of an international relief organization was abducted in Kampot Province, and on April 11, 1994 three Western tourists were abducted at a daylight roadblock on National Route 4, the main route to the coast, and later executed. On July 26, 1994, three other Westerners were abducted after a Khmer Rouge rocket attack on a train traveling from Phnom Penh to Sihanoukville. They were executed two months later near Vine Mountain. Lawlessness has also increased along National Route 3 in Kampot Province and on the road that links Kep to the provincial capital of Kampot.In the first direct attack against foreign tourists since the opening of Angkor in 1990, an American woman was killed by robbers in Siem Reap province and her husband seriously injured on January 14, 1995. The American Embassy in Phnom Penh has advised Americans in Cambodia to avoid travel to Sihanoukville and Kampot province at this time. Several other areas in Cambodia, such as parts of Battambang Province, are also insecure. The temples at Angkor are only marginally safe to visit and the security of the site changes daily. Travel in other areas of Siem Reap province is also highly dangerous, as the Khmer Rouge control large parcels of the province. Americans traveling outside urban areas are urged by the U.S. Embassy to exercise caution and restrict travel to daylight hours and to travel only in vehicle convoys to enhance security. Crime, including armed vehicle theft, is a serious problem in areas including the capital city, Phnom Penh. Travelers can register and obtain updated security information from the U.S. Embassy upon their arrival in Phnom Penh.

Dangerous Things

Land Mines

UNTAC officials estimate between two and ten million mines are scattered around the country. The Russian PMN2 antipersonnel mine is the most common mine in Cambodia. Three hundred people are killed or maimed every month. It is estimated that one person in 236 in Cambodia is an amputee because of an injury from land mines.

Crime

There are frequent armed thefts of vehicles, armed extortion attempts and numerous incidents of petty crimes, such as hotel theft and purse snatching. In October 1994, armed bandits, dressed as police officers, robbed an armored courier truck of about US$100,000 that was en route to Pochentong Airport for transfer of the funds to a Bangkok bank. In May 1994, a police colonel was slain by armed bandits for his motorbike. Automatic weapons abound in Cambodia, and are possessed and used by numerous citizens, even within Phnom Penh.

Car- and Motorbike-jackings

There's been a surge in armed carjackings and forcible ripoffs of motorbikes in Phnom Penh. Even the police themselves are not immune to becoming victims. In many instances, the victims are shot.

Trains

Western tourists traveling by railroad have a better chance of being robbed and/or abducted than not. The Cambodian railway system may be the most lethal stretch of tracks in the world. In addition to the Westerners that have been abducted off trains by the Khmer Rouge, the guerrillas often target ethnic Vietnamese as well as other Cambodians. On New Year's day in 1995, KR guerrillas ambushed a train 60 km northwest of Phnom Penh, killing eight and injuring 36. Among the dead were four women. The rebels stopped the train by blowing up the tracks in front of it and then spraying the railway cars with machine gun fire and B-40 rockets.

Buses

Western tourists are prohibited from traveling aboard local buses. Only the bus to Saigon is open to foreigners.

Getting Sick

Medical facilities are not widely available and do not meet U.S. standards of hygiene and caregiving. Doctors and hospitals often expect immediate cash payment for health services. U.S. medical insurance is not always valid outside the United States. Supplemental medical insurance with specific overseas coverage has proved helpful in some instances.

Nuts & Bolts

Americans can register at the U.S. Embassy in Phnom Penh and obtain updated information on travel and security within Cambodia. *Fieldings Southeast Asia* by Robert Young Pelton and Wink Dulles provides up-to-the-minute coverage of travel in Cambodia for adventurous travelers.

Embassy Location

On September 24, 1993, the U.S. Mission was upgraded to an Embassy.

The U.S. Embassy

27 Eo Street 240
Phnom Penh, Cambodia
☎ (855) 23-26436 or 23-26438

The consular entrance to the U.S. Embassy is located at *16 Street 228 (between Street 51 and Street 63)*. The embassy is able to offer essential consular services.

Cambodia is in the process of putting together an embassy in the U.S.

Cambodian U.N. Section

866 U.N. Plaza, Suite 420
New York, NY 10017
☎ (212) 421-7626

Dangerous Days	
10/09/1970	Cambodian monarchy abolished. The country subsequently was named the Khmer Republic.
11/09/1953	Independence Day
06/19/1951	Army-people solidarity day celebrates the founding of the Cambodian People's Armed Forces.
02/03/1930	Founding of the ICP, the Indochinese Communist Party (ICP). The origin of the communist party of Vietnam, the Kampuchean People's Revolutionary Party, and the Lao People's Revolutionary Party, was founded.
05/19/1928	Pol Pot's birthdate. Pol Pot, the leader of the Khmer Rouge was born on May 19, 1928.
05/24/0000	Birth of Buddha.

Colombia
★★★★★

Coca Loco Land

Each hour someone is killed in Bogota, the capital city of Colombia. The 8600 cadavers that pass through the morgue pile up at an average of 23 a day. Violent death is so ingrained in Colombian life that the health department has listed violence as the leading cause of death for individuals over 10 years old. To date, there isn't a known vaccine for a bullet to the head. The victims fit a neat pattern: male, one or more bullet holes and very dead; 61.2 percent are under 34. Firearms account for nearly 37 percent of the deaths (traffic accidents account for 14 percent of all deaths and 30 percent were from "unknown causes").

The only saving grace in these morbid stats is that 75 percent of the 27,000 murder victims in Colombia last year were classified as "common criminals." Colombia has a murder rate of 65 per 100,000 inhabitants making it among the most violent countries in the world.

After soccer, murder is the national pastime. After a recent soccer victory for Venezuela in Bogota, 27 people were killed and the police outpost was dynamited.

These National Statistics Office figures do little to tell the entire story of what is happening in Colombia. Colombia is turning into a lawless nation that functions on the edge, barely keeping the lid on anarchy. Colombia's wealthy, its intellectuals, and the educated have fled to escape kidnapping, extortion and murder threats. The drug lords, criminals, revolutionaries and terrorists not only wage war against the government and infrastructure but among themselves.

Attacks against "American interests" are expected to increase with the U.S. occupation of Haiti and its continued hard-line against Cuba. Attacking "American interests" can cover anything from bombing a local travel agency displaying an American Express logo to kidnapping Mormon missionaries for being "agents of the U.S. government."

The Scoop

Colombia is currently the most dangerous place in the Western Hemisphere. The drug lords, terrorist groups, very active engagement by government forces against both these groups, and general lawlessness make Colombia a must-see for anyone planning a vacation in hell. If you travel to Colombia you will be the target of thieves, kidnappers or murderers.

How bad is it? Civilians and soldiers are stopped at roadblocks, dragged out of their cars and summarily executed in the *Antioquia* department. Tourists are drugged in bars and discos, then robbed and murdered. Expats, missionaries and other foreigners are favorite targets of terrorist groups, who kidnap them for outrageous ransom amounts that climb into the millions of dollars.

Wealthy rightwingers employ about 100 or so paid killers to systematically murder left-wingers. Left-wingers attempt to kidnap every freckle-faced foreigner they can get their hands on. Drug dealers are knocking off police at the rate of about one a day. The survivors are those who stay away from office buildings, bus stops, police stations and travel agents displaying American Express logos on their windows. However, tourists and other travelers are way down on the list of people who have any protection in this cocaine-fueled free-for-all.

Should you be victimized or seek revenge due to a misfortune, expect little comfort or sympathy from the police, military, judicial or diplomatic folks; they're busy covering their own asses from the threat of terrorism, drug cartels and crime lords. Only 12 percent of the crimes committed in Colombia ever reach the judicial system.

If you get into trouble and can't afford the ransom, hire a death squad. The price is lower.

Any good news? Some. Violent and terrorist incidents were slightly down in 1994 compared to 1993, due namely to the snuffing of Escobar by security forces December 2, 1993. The other bright spot is the "regulator" approach of the military; the death squads have forced many drug traffickers to move into neighboring Brazil for "health" reasons.

Colombia - Travel Warning

Note: As of October 24, 1994 U.S. citizens are warned against travel to Colombia by the U.S. government until further notice. With the exception of several popular tourist areas, violence continues to affect a significant portion of the country and recent attacks have been targeted against American citizens and institutions.

The Players

The Government

Liberal Ernesto Samper Pizano squeaked into power June 19, 1993 in a dead heat with Conservative Andres Pastrana Arango. Considering that only one of every three Colombians voted, it doesn't seem to make any difference who runs the country. Samper has been accused as being a stooge of the Cali drug cartel, despite his public calls for the extermination of Columbia's drug problem. A recent investigation into his alleged ties with drug lords concluded that he was offered backing but didn't accept it.

Colombia

- ✪ National Capital
- ● Department Capital
- ● Secondary City
- ☒ Airport
- ⚓ Port
- — Province Border
- --- Road
- ++++ Railroad

| 0 | 100 | 200 km |
| 0 | 100 mi | |

©FWI 1995

Caribbean Sea

Guajira

Riohacha

Santa Marta
Barranquilla
Atlantico
Ciénaga
Valledupar
Cartagena
Maracaibo

PANAMA

Magdalena
César

Tolú
Sincelejo
Montería
Sucre
Bolívar
Norte de Santander
Cúcuta

Turbo
Córdoba
Pamplona

Chocó
Antioquia
Bucaramanga
Arauca

Pacific Ocean

Quibdó
Medellín
Santander
Barbosa
Paz de Río
Casanare

Arauca

VENEZUELA

Meta
Puerto Carreño

Pereira
Manizales
Boyacá
Tunja
Yopal

Armenia
Bogotá
Vichada

Valle del Cauca
Ibagué
Girardot
Puerto López
Puerto Inírida

Buenaventura
Cali
Villavicencio
Guaviare

Cauca
Neiva
Meta
Guainía

Popayán
Guaviare
San José del Guaviare
San Felipe

Nariño
Huila
Florencia
Mitú

Tumaco
Pasto
Mocoa
Vaupés

Putumayo
Caquetá
Vaupés

Quito

ECUADOR

Amazonas

BRAZIL

PERU

Central Provinces
1. Risaralda
2. Caldas
3. Cundinamarca
4. Quindío
5. Tolima
6. Districto Especial

Iquitos

Leticia

The government is actively but unsuccessfully trying to negotiate peace with various rebel factions, but for now is trying to figure out how to find jobs for the 5200 ex-guerrillas left over from the EPL and the M-19 groups.

The Simon Bolivar Guerrilla Coordinator (CGSB)

This is an unholy triumvirate of three terrorist groups: FARC, ELN, and the EPL/D. They claim about 8000 effective members among all three. The military has said that it managed to diminish that number in 1993 by killing 993 guerrillas and capturing another 1873. They also nabbed five tons of explosives and 1863 weapons in over 2000 armed engagements. Not as high a count as fowl during the duck hunting season in Minnesota, but not bad.

Revolutionary Armed Forces of Colombia
(Fuerzas Armadas Revolucionarias de Colombia (FARC))

FARC was established in 1966 as the military wing of the Colombian Communist Party; it is the largest guerrilla group operating in Colombia. FARC is organized along military lines, is strongly anti-U.S., and may have at least one urban commando element. They adhere to a Marxist-Leninist ideology that once aligned them with the former Soviet Union and now with Cuba.

The group specializes in armed attacks against Colombian targets, bombings of U.S. businesses, kidnappings of Colombians and foreigners for ransom, and assassinations. Their funding comes from extortion (ransom payments) and income from the trafficking of drugs (predominantly cocaine). FARC has well-documented ties to drug traffickers and Cuba. It is assumed that any drug transportation from Colombia to Cuba and beyond is controlled by FARC, and with the blessing of Fidel Castro. The dope bucks provide much needed hard currency for Cuba, whose economy has been in tatters since the collapse of the Soviet Union. Peace talks between the government of Colombia and FARC have proved unsuccessful.

There are an estimated 4500 to 5500 armed combatants and 10,000 supporters of FARC.

FARC likes to be cruel to be kind. They mainly target the wealthy, but off a couple of peasants once in awhile to keep their attention. The Patriotic Union (UP) is FARC's political arm, seeking change through old-fashioned rhetoric and arm twisting.

In a perfect world, FARC would overthrow established order in Colombia and replace it with a leftist and anti-American regime, in the process creating a broad antimonopoly, anti-imperialist front while uniting left-wing parties and organizations into a single political movement.

On the scarier side, FARC is the largest, best trained, best equipped, and most effective insurgent organization in Colombia, and perhaps in all of South America—the one Western terrorist group voted "most likely to succeed" by U.S. intelligence services. Many consider FARC to be the "military" arm of the Communist Party of Colombia (PCC).The leadership of FARC is composed largely of disaffected middle- and upper-class intellectuals, although it recruits from the peasant population in an effort to maintain a popular base. FARC also draws support from traditional left-wingers, workers, students and radical priests. The popularity of FARC has been undermined by the questionable practice of kidnapping peasants and murdering them as "collaborators" and "traitors" if they're not cooperative.

FARC is the principal force behind National Simon Bolivar Guerrilla Coordinator (SBGC), which includes all major Colombian insurgent groups. FARC was able to muster this coalition due to its closer ties with Colombian narcotics traffickers than the other insurgent groups. The relationship appears to be the strongest in those areas where coca cultivation and production, and FARC operational strongholds overlap. In exchange for FARC protection of narcotics interests, the guerrillas have received money to purchase weapons and supplies.

There is evidence that various FARC fronts have actually been involved in processing cocaine. Money from the narcotics trade has supplemented FARC revenues from kidnappings, extortion and robberies.

National Liberation Army (Ejercito de Liberacion Nacional or ELN)

A rural-based, anti-U.S., Maoist-Marxist-Leninist guerrilla group formed in July 1964. The ELN raises funds by kidnapping foreign employees of large corporations and holding them for ambitious ransom payments. The ELN conducts extortion and bombing operations against U.S. and other foreign businesses in Colombia, particularly the deep-pocketed petroleum industry. The group has inflicted major damage on oil pipelines since 1986.

They boast up to 2000 members, many of whom have been trained and armed by Nicaragua and Cuba. The ELN seeks "...the conquest of power for the popular classes..." along with nationalizations, expropriations, and agrarian reform.

The ELN is a political-military organization that draws its support from among students, intellectuals, peasants and, surprisingly, the middle-class workers of Colombia. Operations include the kidnapping of wealthy ranchers and industrialists, assassinations of military officers, offing of labor leaders and peasants, multiple armed robberies, various bombings, raids on isolated villages, weapons grabs on police posts and army patrols and occupations of radio stations and newspaper offices. The ELN is currently perfecting attacks on petroleum pipelines and facilities, seeking to damage Colombia's economic infrastructure and investment climate.

Popular Liberation Army (EPL/D)

This dissident former affiliate of the Popular Liberation Army can't seem to get ahead. The PLA signed a peace treaty several years ago with the government but these Maoist EPL/D sad sacks won't quit. The EPL/D leaders are followed and arrested on a regular basis (probably due to informants from the PLA). Members enjoy killing each other. They are currently busy murdering, stealing, kidnapping and being nasty primarily in the Uraba region.

The U.S. Military

The U.S. government has unofficially declared war on the drug trade in Colombia and therefore, FARC. Currently there are nine U.S. advisors in Colombia training troops; 62 military technicians are installing radar bases; 32 members of a navy construction battalion in Meta province are building a military base on the Meta River, a heavily used artery for drug transport; one hundred and fifty-six U.S. Army engineers northwest of Cali are building a school, clinic and a road. Although overt U.S. involvement in Columbia is low-key presently, further disintegration of Colombia's infrastructure could lead to escalation.

Death Squads

More than a hundred groups of teams made up of five -10 members each are paid by wealthy and influential Colombians to kill former and current left-wingers and communists on an ongoing basis, and to act as a more effective deterrent to kidnapping, murder and extortion threat than the police or military. The death squads are primarily active in Medellin and Bogota, and around the Antioquia Department. One of the principal players is the Macetos paramilitary group, which is centered in the San Martin municipality. This group has performed numerous massacres against leftist guerrilla groups and their sympathizers.

Drug Lords

Pablo Escobar is gone; however, cocaine is still the biggest covert industry in Colombia. Coca is grown in the country, processed in labs and then shipped or flown out to various ports in the Caribbean. The headquarters for the drug trade is in Cali and Medellin. The drug folks are very tight with both left and right-wing terrorist groups. So be nice when you talk to anybody about drugs.

Getting In

A passport and a return/onward ticket are required for stays up to three months. Minors (under 18) traveling alone, with one parent, or with a third party must present written authorization from the absent parent(s) or legal guardian, specifically granting permission to travel alone, with one parent or with a third party. This authorization must be notarized, authenticated by a Colombian embassy or consulate, and translated into Spanish. For up-to-the minute information regarding entry and customs requirements for Colombia, contact the Colombian Embassy at *2118 Leroy Place NW, Washington, D.C. 20008,* ☎ *(202) 387-8338* or the nearest consulate in Los Angeles, Miami, Chicago, New Orleans, New York, Houston or San Juan.

An onward ticket is not always asked for at land crossings. But you may be asked to prove that you have at least US$20 for each day of your stay in Columbia. Thirty-day extensions can be applied for at the DAS (security police) office in any city.

By air, Avianca and American Airlines fly regularly to Bogota from the U.S., Cali and Barranquilla. There is an airport tax of US$18.

Entering Columbia by land usually presents no problems at the frontiers. But note that when leaving Columbia by land, you'll need to have an exit stamp from the DAS. You may not be able to get this stamp at the smaller frontier towns. Get the stamp in a city. Otherwise, you may be detained.

Getting Around

Cities within Columbia are served by Avianca, Aces, SAM, Intercontinental, Satena and Aires airlines. The bigger cities are reached on a daily basis, the smaller ones less frequently, sometimes once a week. Prices are higher in the high season (June–August, December). Purchase intra-Columbia tickets inside the country.

Buses are a great way to get around, but incidents of thefts are increasing. The air-conditioned buses are often quite frigid when the air conditioning is working. When it isn't they're quite hot, since the windows don't open. Bring your own food, as rest stops are infrequent. Additionally, expect the bus to be periodically stopped and boarded by police. Your identity will most likely be checked. Occasionally, a photocopy of your passport will be sufficient. Make one and have it notarized anyhow. Buses leave according to schedule, rather than when they are full. Columbia's VELO-TAX minibuses are efficient. However, other buses experience frequent breakdowns (see "Dangerous Things").

Taxis are plentiful. Take only metered taxis. But if one cannot be found, bargain and set a fixed price before you enter the taxi. Women should not take taxis alone at night (see "Dangerous Things").

The roads in Columbia are often dilapidated and unmarked. Avoid driving at night; Colombian drivers are careless and often reckless.

Dangerous Places

Bogata Airport and Environs

Where do we start? How about at the airport. Theft of hand luggage and travel documents at airports is common and should be expected. Use the well-marked taxis, do not share a ride or enter a cab with more than one person even though many cab drivers will tell you that your travel mate is for protection; you only need to be wrong once. Lock the doors and be prepared to have Scopolamine sprayed in your face by keeping alert and a window cracked (not enough to let people reach in).

Taking the bus is worse. Here, taking a rural bus is asking for a close encounter of the wrong kind. Theft, druggings, extortion and kidnapping occur frequently on buses in both the city and rural areas.

If you survive the 7.5 mile ride into Bogota be forewarned that crime is prevalent in cities, especially in the vicinity of hotels and airports. Large hotels, travel agencies, corporate headquarters and other institutions that display U.S. corporate IDs are targeted by terrorists for bombing attacks.

Santa Marta

The north end of town and the Rodadero Beach areas are extremely dangerous. Do not travel alone into these areas. Daylight armed robberies of tourists are commonplace. Thieves will often relieve their victims of their clothes as well as all other valuables.

Cartagena

Professional pickpockets abound, especially at the beaches. They especially like to strike in crowded areas. Cameras are a favorite trophy for thieves here. Scams in Cartagena are numerous. Other crooks pose as tour guides. Some of them can be rather touchy if you turn down their expensive excursion offers. If you're offered a job on a ship bound for the U.S. or other parts of South America, this is most assuredly a con.

Medellin

Despite being a major drug traffickers' center, the city is a remarkably friendly place. However, it's not the drug lords you should be afraid of here. Rather it's petty thieves and street thugs.

Valle Department

Everywhere off the main roads in Valle Department is extremely unsafe due to guerrilla activities. Beware particularly Cauca Department E off the Pan-American Highway. Tourists should avoid this area entirely. Areas of Cra 6 are also extremely dangerous, including Parque Bolivar and the market. There has also been guerrilla activity in the Purace National Park area, particularly near the Popayan-La Plata road. In Inza, women should not be on the streets unaccompanied.

Other Guerrilla Areas

The Departments of Boyaca, Norte de Santander, Casanare, Caqueta, Huila, Putumayo, Cesar, Guajira, Arauka, Meta, as well as the Turbo/Uraba region.

The Upper Magdalena

You'll constantly encounter riffraff here touting everything from drugs, gold and emeralds to pre-Columbian art. The items are always fake, except for the drugs.

Antioquia Department and Medellin

Medellin was the focus of much of the shoot 'em outs and wars between Escobar and PEPES. There are roadblocks throughout the countryside and there have been executions of military, civilians and locals without provocation. This is a very nasty area and the most dangerous place in Colombia.

Bogota

Narco-traffickers/guerrillas have threatened and carried out terrorist attacks against Colombian officials, foreign embassies, and other targets. Expect to travel in fear of violent crime, particularly in the south of Bogota. Tourist areas are infested with thieves, pickpockets and opportunists. The richer, northern suburbs of Bogota have experienced a rash of car bombings.

Colombia East of the Andes

This area can be hazardous to your health with the exception of the city of Leticia in the Amazonas Department and adjacent tourist areas in Amazonas.

North Coast

Cali is the home of two of the major drug cartels. Expect plenty of fighting between the two rival groups. San Andres is a major drug shipment area. Cartagena is considered somewhat safe due to the increased presence of police protecting the lucrative tourist trade. Expect "tourist" crime.

Baranguilla is the site of guerilla attacks on businesses and government centers. The busy port is a major center for drug traffickers. Guerrillas like to regularly attack the Navy base near the airport at night. Outside the city limits is the domain of bad people, particularly at night.

Rural Valle de Cauca Department

As well as most of the Cauca River Valley including the cities of Cali and Buenaventura, and the road between Cali and Buenaventura.

The Northern Half of Choco Department

Particularly the Uraba region, except for the tourist area of Capurgana.

The Magdelena Medio Region

The Magdalena River Valley south to Tolima, including western Boyaca, eastern Caldas, and northwestern Cundinamarca.

Tolima Department South of Espinal

Especially if traveling after dark.

Road Travel in Huila and Cauca Departments

The cities of Neiva and Popayan are considered to be safe if reached by air.

U.S. Companies

Several terrorist or guerrilla groups are active in Colombia; U.S. interests are among their targets. Kidnapping for ransom or political purposes, including U.S. citizens, is increasingly common in Colombia. In early 1994 bombs destroyed a Mormon temple in Medellin, damaged another in Bucaramanga, and damaged a Coca-Cola bottling plant in Bucaramanga. Additionally, two American missionaries were kidnapped, apparently for political reasons, by guerrillas. It is believed that U.S. citizens are targets of this latest wave of violence.

Dangerous Things

"War"

Paramilitary and guerrilla members of Uraba and Cordoba declared an all-out "war" between the two factions. The war began in Antioquia's Uraba region and Cordoba in January 1995. Guerrilla and paramilitary groups have forced peasants and cattlemen, who won land concessions from alleged drug trafficker Fidel Castano, into the middle of the crossfire. Hundreds of peasants have been forced to migrate to the cities as a result of the fighting.

Kidnapping

Remember the last time you asked your boss how much you were really worth? Well you may find out on your next trip to Colombia. About 121 kidnappings occur a month in Colombia, or about four a day. Kidnapping has become a US$350 million industry in Colombia. Sixty-four foreigners have been abducted in the last three years, each for huge ransoms. Fewer than one in 30 kidnappers are ever caught and sentenced. Although kidnappings in Colombia fell 23 percent between 1992 and 1993, in 1994 they shot up nearly 35 percent to 1378 abductions. Fewer than half the kidnappings that actually take place are ever reported. Luckily Colombians make up the bulk of the victims. Most never report the abductions fearing it would just advertise their culpability. There were believed to be 10 Americans being held captive in Colombia as of February 1995. A splinter group of the Popular Liberation Army (EPL) took responsibility for the January 1995 abduction of Edward Gravowsky. Although the EPL was disbanded in March 1991, a group of about 150 diehards remains. Gravowski was the fourth foreigner kidnapped by Colombian guerrillas in a four-month period. In the past few years, only one in 10 of the reported victims have been rescued by security forces. Many others are murdered by the kidnappers, who often demand large ransoms and then return a corpse.

Power Blackouts

When the lights go out, make sure you are nowhere to be found by street criminals. Common street crime increases exponentially during blackouts in major cities.

Phony Cops

A common scam is an approach to an obvious tourist by an alleged "policeman" who says that he is checking for counterfeit U.S. dollars and wants to "check" the foreigner's money. The person gives the criminal his/her money, receives a receipt, and the "policeman" disappears. Others request that the victim accompany him "downtown." You have just been kidnapped.

Strolling Through the Country

You may want to save the rain forests, but coca growers and processing labs would prefer that you stay at the beach. Two French tourists were snatched by FARC in the La Macarena nature preserve south of Bogota. The countryside is effectively controlled by rebel groups who view you as a source of income.

Bombs

Bombs don't come from the sky here. Bombing is a deliberate attempt to capture publicity and strike fear into the populace. The victims are incidental. Car bombs are deliberately detonated in crowded central locations. Buses are bombed, as well as oil pipelines, refineries, hotels and office buildings.

Driving

Columbia's roads are in poor condition. Many routes aren't marked. Avoid driving at night. Many vehicles have dim headlights, if any at all. Other drivers are reckless. Cattle is unwitting as they pause to pee in the middle of the road at midnight.

Taxis

Women should never travel alone at night in taxis. Both sexes are subject to popular scams where the driver feigns a mechanical breakdown. The passenger is asked to get out of the car and help push the taxi to a "jump-start," which separates passengers from their luggage. The driver will then start the car and drive off.

Buses

Bus travel in the south of Columbia can be hazardous. Thieves haunt buses in this area waiting for passengers to fall asleep. Then, guess what they do. Buses between Bogata and Ipiales and between San Augustin and Popayan are frequented by scam artists/thieves who offer doped chewing gum, cigarettes, food and sweets before taking everything you've got.

Hotel Rooms: Hotel rooms of foreigners are not infrequently raided by the police looking for drugs. Having a witness around may prevent them from planting drugs in the room. But, then again, it may not.

Booze

Beware brand-label liquor that appears to be expensive and imported, such as Johnnie Walker scotch. In many instances, the labels are fake and the booze is a potentially lethal spirit. Drink only beer if you need to catch a buzz.

Packages

Never carry a package for a stranger. We don't need to tell you why.

Drugs

Despite what we said about the few criminals that get to justice in Colombia, if you get arrested for any drug-related crime expect at least threats of lifelong incarceration and spending a few thousand bucks bribing your way out of jail. The government will do little to help. Any foreigner who wants to cut out the middle men and go into competition with the Colombian drug dealers should watch the movie *Scarface* a few times. Strangely enough, every year some yahoo ends up in a Colombian jail for doing exactly that.

Burundanga comes from a fairly common plant found in many countries, including areas in the Andes Mountains. In Colombia they brew burundanga by extracting it using alcohol or sulfuric acid from el borrachero (the intoxicator in Spanish). El borrachero is a tree with trumpet-shaped flowers that grows wild in Colombia. Scopolamine is used in small Band-Aid-like round patches to prevent motion sickness and to treat Parkinson's disease. The most common form in Colombia is white powder that is mixed into drinks, food or even innocuous chewing gum.

Hassles with Police

Watch out for police that aren't. Many police officers and soldiers will shake you down for doing everything from taking pictures to walking on the beach at night. The best bluff is to demand to see their supervisor and walk quickly in the direction that takes you farthest away from them. If the police really do arrest you, get on the horn to the consulate ASAP. They can't do much if you really screwed up, but they're all you've got.

Firearms

Colombian law prohibits tourists and business travelers from importing or bringing firearms into Colombia. The penalty for illegal importation and/or possession of firearms is three to 10 years in prison.

Getting Sick

Medical care is adequate in major cities, but varies in quality elsewhere. Health problems in Colombia include the presence of cholera, though cholera is found largely in areas outside the cities and usual tourist areas. Visitors who follow proper precautions regarding food and drink are not generally at risk. Doctors and hospitals often expect immediate cash payment for health services. U.S. medical insurance is not always valid outside the United States. In some cases, supplemental medical insurance with specific overseas coverage is considered useful. If you are the victim of a Scopolamine attack remember to seek medical assistance immediately. Scopolamine is usually mixed with other narcotics and can cause brain damage.

Scopolamine

You probably thought it was something Nazis injected brave Allied spies with to make them talk. When you get hit with Scopolamine, or Burundanga as it is called locally, you will just get stupid. Colombian criminals use the drug "Scopolamine" to incapacitate tourists, rob them, and then leave them unconscious, often for over 24 hours. The drug is administered in drinks (in bars), through cigarette smoke (in taxis), and in powder form (tourists are approached by someone asking directions, with the drug concealed in a piece of paper). The drug renders the person disoriented and powerless to resist the criminal's orders. Scopolamine takes effect in two to three seconds and causes stupor, blurred vision, disorientation, incoherence, and other narcotic effects. It can also cause brain damage. If you think you have been a victim, you only have two to three seconds to attach yourself to a hopefully helpful bystander and yell for help. If you like to bar-crawl late at night, and alone, expect to wake-up naked or dead.

Nuts & Bolts

Spanish is the official language. English is common in major cities and tourist centers. The Colombians like to party, so expect massive crowds and price hikes during local holidays. Electricity is 110V/60hz. Local time is the same as New York. The local currency is the peso, about 837 to the U.S. dollar at press time.

Temperatures are fairly high throughout the year. It gets cooler and wetter the higher you go. Seaside areas are muggy. Heavy rain falls between April and October.

Business hours are from 8 a.m.–12 p.m. and from 2 p.m.–6 p.m, Monday-Friday. Bank hours in Bogata are from 9 a.m.–3 p.m. Monday–Thursday, and from 9 a.m.–3:30 p.m. on Fridays, except the last Friday of the month, when they close at 12 p.m. In other major cities, they're open from 8 a.m.–11:30 a.m. and from 2 p.m.–4 p.m. Monday–Thursday. On Friday, they're open until 4:30 p.m., except the last Friday of the month, when they close at 11:30 a.m.

Embassy Location/Registration

Upon arrival U.S. citizens are urged to register with the Consular Section of the U.S. Embassy in Bogota at *Calle 38 No. 8-61*, ☎ *(57-1) 320-1300* or at the U.S. Consulate in Barranquilla at *Calle 77, Carrera 68, Centro Comercial Mayorista*, ☎ *(57-58) 45-8480 or 45-9067*, and to obtain updated information on travel and security within Colombia.

Dangerous Days

Anniversaries are bad days for a stroll in the country or shopping downtown in Colombia. Rebel groups like to remind people by blowing things up.

10/08/1987 The Simon Bolivar Guerrilla Coordinating Board (CNG) is an umbrella organization under which the Revolutionary Armed Forces of Colombia (FARC), the National Liberation Army (ELN) and a dissident faction of the Popular Liberation Army (EPL) coordinate political positions and organize joint terrorist operations.

08/28/1985 April 19 movement (M-19); leader Ivan Marino Ospina was killed in a clash with government troops.

11/20/1983 Legalization of the M-19. The April 19 movement (M-19), a leftist terrorist organization, was legalized by an amnesty law after the group had made peace with the government. The M-19 is now a legitimate political party.

04/29/1967 Founding of the EPL (Popular Liberation Army).

08/15/1964 The National Liberation Army (ELN) begins its armed struggle.

05/27/1964 On this date, government troops attacked the "independent republic" that communist peasant groups had set up at Marquetalia, Caldas Department.

11/11/1957 The Popular Liberation Army (EPL), a leftist terrorist organization, has since made peace with the government and become a legitimate political party. However, a dissident faction continues the armed struggle against the government.

07/17/1930 Communist Party founded.

07/20/1810 Independence Day.

08/07/0000 Battle Of Boyacas.

"El Jefe"

I had agreed to go out with the official's daughter. She was coming into San Andreas tomorrow from Cali for Holy Week. I watched in amazement as this distinguished gentleman was able to piss in the sink at the same time he was washing his hands. We were in his hotel suite which served as his full-time home. He was a very high level government official on the island. Instead of wallpaper he had cases of Mumm's stacked up from floor to ceiling, creating a pleasing but somewhat industrial pattern. His choice of music was limited to the one or two AM radio stations on the island—he used a state of the art quadraphonic stereo system to blast out Julio Iglesias. Like most of his possessions, they were "gifts" or leftovers from customs inspections of travelers.

"El Jefe"

He explained how he makes his money. He has a group of three to five "beach boys" who sell coconut oil on the beach to tourists. Along with the golden fragrant oil in old beer bottles, they offer hash or marijuana to unsuspecting tourists. As the sun goes down, they turn in the money they've made and carefully point out each and every person who bought drugs that day. During the night, the doors of the surprised victims are crashed down and they're trotted off to jail at gunpoint. They then pay the judge, the lawyer, the DAS, the F2 and of course the Aduana dearly for their freedom. In fact they even have to pay for meals while they are in jail. As he adjusted his evening clothes and carefully combed his hair I thought he looked rather dashing for a thug.

Egypt
★★★

The Temples of Doom

Egypt has long thrived on the income tourists spend to visit its ancient monuments. Even during the most intense moments of the Arab-Israeli conflict, trips to the pyramids could be arranged for a minor fee for passengers in transit through Cairo. Today, Islamic fundamentalists furious over Egypt's pact with Israel have decided to attack Egypt where it hurts most: the tourist industry. Sporadic attacks on tourist boats, buses and trains traveling to the great temples are designed to scare away Western tourists.

Since American travel agents must warn their clients of any known dangers before sending them on trips, the policy has worked in reducing the flow of tourism dollars to Egypt. About 150,000 Americans visit Egypt every year.

Egypt's response has been tough and far ranging. Terrorists have been tried in absentia and have been tracked down as far away as Pakistan. It is well known that the al-Gama'a al-Islamiya is based out of Sudan and is backed by Iran in their ongoing campaign to spread their own brand of Islam to the Arab world. Most of the attacks target

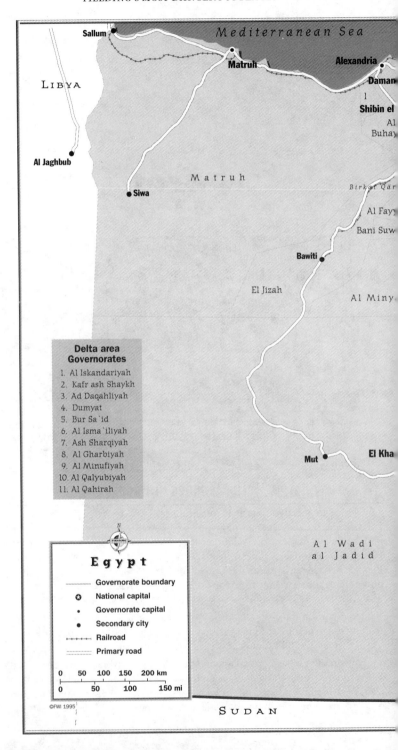

Sallum

Mediterranean Sea

Matruh

Alexandria

Daman

LIBYA

Shibin el

Al
Buhay

Al Jaghbub

M a t r u h

Birkot Qar

Siwa

Al Fay

Bani Suw

Bawiti

El Jizah

Al Miny

**Delta area
Governorates**

1. Al Iskandariyah
2. Kafr ash Shaykh
3. Ad Daqahliyah
4. Dumyat
5. Bur Sa`id
6. Al Isma`iliyah
7. Ash Sharqiyah
8. Al Gharbiyah
9. Al Minufiyah
10. Al Qalyubiyah
11. Al Qahirah

Mut

El Kha

Al Wadi
al Jadid

Egypt

——— Governorate boundary

⊕   National capital

·   Governorate capital

●   Secondary city

+--+--+ Railroad

------ Primary road

0   50 100 150 200 km

0   50   100   150 mi

©FWI 1995

S U D A N

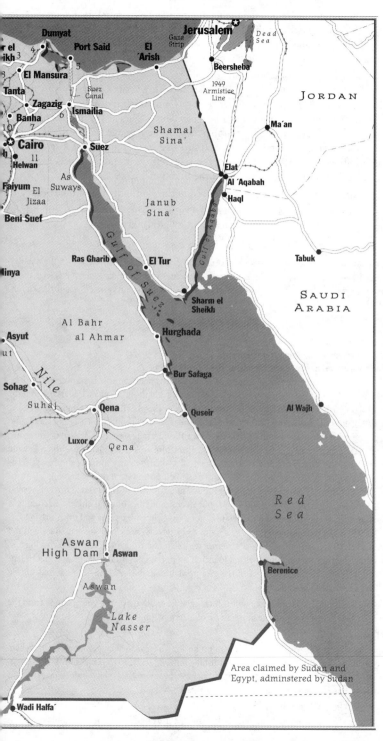

Area claimed by Sudan and
Egypt, adminstered by Sudan

Egyptian government officials, with the tourist attacks being more for PR reasons. In February 1994, the extremists threatened to step-up their terrorist campaign against the government and called on all foreigners to leave Egypt. They declared that foreign investors and tourists would be the targets of this stepped-up campaign.

Since February 16, 1994, eight foreign tourists have been injured in attacks on trains. A Nile River cruise ship, with 17 tourists aboard, was fired upon with an assault rifle. On February 18, a southbound train from Cairo was fired upon, injuring four people. The attack on the overnight train occurred at about 1:30 in the morning just south of Assiyut. On February 23, a bomb placed in the luggage rack of the first-class section exploded on a train traveling from Cairo to Aswan, injuring six foreign tourists. The bomb went off 30 minutes after the train left the station in Assiyut and was placed onboard by a food vendor who hid the bomb in a Coca Cola case.

Attacks continue to be sporadic and centered in the southern area of the country.

Fundamentalism is blamed as the root of all evil here. There are over 70,000 private mosques that stir the witches' brew of hate and religious intolerance.

The Scoop

The militant al-Gama'a al-Islamiyas seek to overthrow Egypt's government and turn the country into a strict Islamic state. Minya province has been the center of the conflict, which has seen about 675 people killed in political violence in Egypt since the Gama'a began its guerrilla campaign of terror in 1992.

The Players

al-Gama'a al-Islamiya
(El-Gama'a El Islamiyya, al-Gama'a al-Islamiyya,
Al Gam'a Al Islamiyya, El Gama'a El Islamiyya, The Islamic Group)

This Egyptian Islamic extremist group has been staging attacks against the government since the late 1970s. They began in 1928 with the Muslim Brotherhood. Gama'a leaders have a tight control on business and religion in the Assiyut region of Egypt. Their attacks on tourists began in 1992. Sheikh Omar Abdul Rahman (Abd al Rahman) is the group's spiritual leader and came to fame for his role in the bombing of New York's World Trade Center. The goal of the group is to overthrow the government of President Hosni Mubarak and replace it with an Islamic state. The group carries out armed attacks against Egyptian security forces and other government officials. Their targets are Coptic Christians, Western tourist and Egyptian opponents of Islamic extremism. The actual size of the group isn't known but it's estimated to be several thousand hard-core members along with about an equal number of sympathizers. Recruiting is done around the mosques and poor neighborhoods in Cairo, Alexandria and other urban locations. They also recruit unemployed graduates and students. Activities are focused around the areas of al Minya, Assiyut, and Qina governorates of southern Egypt. There are recruiting and training bases in Pakistan. Financial and logistical support comes from Iran and Sudan. On January 11, 1995, a leading member of the group, Mahmud abd-al-Mahud, committed suicide when police raided his hideout.

Today, the group hides out in the bullrush-clogged fields alongside the Nile, eluding from the police who are making headway in their task of exterminating the group.

Naguib Mafouz

Another reluctant player. An old man with no business at play in a dangerous arena. But there are those who would argue that Salman Rushdie must be reckoned a player in this arena, representing the Muslim who stands heroically against the awful tide, which indeed he does, but much more so to us than to those in the arena itself.

Which is where Mafouz sits as a representative figure there. No idealogue, just a writer of popular novels, a practicing Muslim himself, but under threat of death from the righteous and for that representative there, in the dangerous place itself, of the secular man who stands against the Islamic tide. It is fair to say he is not only known but read by more devout Muslims in the Sudan than he is by secular Americans.

Which isn't to deny that America is where he should probably be right now, but there he continues to sit, positively inviting the knife, which positively finds him, and still, he just won't go abroad or stay home. All his adult life he has hung out with his cronies in the dusty sidewalk cafes of Alexandria and Cairo and he refuses to cease his regular visits, even though that was where the man with the knife found him.

Reaching for something to say when Mafouz won the Nobel Prize, the highbrow world characterized the kudos as a slap at the many Egyptian writers who are closer to literature's leading edge (whatever that is). Mafouz, they informed us, may have been little known in the west but in Egypt he was simply a popular novelist who wrote about and for the masses, "Charles Dickens, if you will."

Yes. Very much Charles Dickens. Nor does he look down his nose at commercial survival. He knows his customers. He serves them, as surely as Gangsta Rap serves rich white kids who like to be scandalized and Salman Rushdie serves rich white adults who like to be scandalized. As a popular writer his audience is as broad as the sweep of Egyptian characters in his books, from the Alexandrine professor with broken glasses to the crowds who go to see the movies made from his books, chewing sunflower seeds and spitting the husks at each other.

Writing almost exclusively for them and about them, he has little need to leave Egypt. Besides, travel at his age is not so easy, and in truth, by standing his ground in Egypt and just going to the cafe and facing the dangerous music of the Kalatchnikov as it splits the air in celebration of a wedding (and in warning of fate), this old man in a worn sweater flies closer to the sun than Rushdie, who flits in dramatic secrecy from cosmopolitan market to cosmopolitan market.

Getting In

A passport and visa are required. For those arriving by air, a renewable 30-day tourist visa can be obtained at airport points of entry. Those arriving overland and by sea, or those previously experiencing difficulty with their visa status in Egypt, must obtain a visa prior to arrival. Military personnel arriving on commercial flights are not exempt from passport and visa requirements. Proof of yellow fever and cholera immunization is required if arriving from an infected area. Evidence of an AIDS test is required for everyone staying over 30 days. Tourists must register with local authorities (either through their hotels, at local police stations, or at the central passport office) within seven days of arrival. For additional entry information, U.S. citizens can contact:

Embassy of the Arab Republic of Egypt
3521 International Court, NW
Washington, D.C. 20008
☎ *(202) 895-5400*
or the Egyptian consulates in San Francisco, Chicago, New York or Houston.

Everyone entering Egypt must declare items such as jewelry, electronic equipment and other valuables. This requirement is strictly enforced. Any valuables not accounted for may be confiscated. For those staying in Egypt less than one month, there are no currency exchange requirements. For each month thereafter, U.S. citizens must present proof, in the form of bank receipts, that they have converted US$180 per month per person into Egyptian pounds. A maximum of 100 Egyptian pounds may be carried into or out of Egypt.

Getting Around

Egypt borders some of the world's most dangerous places. If you want to explore the remote border regions, including oases near Libya and off-road areas in the Sinai, you must obtain permission from the Travel Permits Department of the Ministry of the Interior, located at the corner of Sheikh Rihan and Nubar Streets in downtown Cairo. Remember that the attraction of traveling by camel should be tempered by the reality of debilitating heat and the potential for injury; it makes this mode of transportation dicey at best. Attacks on tourists occur while traveling on buses, trains and river-boats between Cairo and Luxor. The attacks tend to be random.

Dangerous Places

Cairo

There have been attacks on obvious tourist facilities and tourist transportation vehicles. Avoid the large hotels and do not travel via tour bus.

The South (Assiyut Province)

Assiyut is the center of Islamic fundamentalism in Egypt. Assiyut is the country's third largest city with 14,000 government troops trying to keep a lid on it. You can hire professional assassins here. Anwar Sadat was a major supporter of the Muslim Brotherhood in an effort to keep out communist influences. It may not surprise some that Anwar Sadat was killed by a member of the Muslim Brotherhood and army officer, Khalid Islambuli after he was enraged at what had happened to his brother who was beaten and tortured in an Assiyut prison two months earlier. Most attacks on tourists have occurred in the southern governorates of Assiyut, Minya and Qena, which lie between Cairo and Luxor. Travel via tourist buses, Nile River boats, car and trains from Cairo (first-class sections) in this area through those southern governorates is considered dangerous.

The towns of Dayrut, Assiyut and Abu Tig along the Nile River are centers for fundamentalists. The attacks seem to be targeted on the transportation links to the famous monuments of the south.

Dangerous Things

Bilharzia

The Nile and its canals are carriers of the bilharzia parasite. It'll get ya when swimming in the Nile or canals, walking barefoot along the river or drinking untreated river water. Bilharzia can cause extensive tissue damage, kidney failure and blindness.

Rift Valley Fever (RVF)

This disease exists throughout Egypt, having spread from its original concentration along a 60-mile stretch of the Nile in the Kom Ombo area of the Aswan governorate. RVF is primarily a disease of domestic animals, but it can readily infect humans. The vast majority of cases of RVF in humans results in only fever and flu-like symptoms, with complete recovery in a few days. In two-to-three percent of cases, however, RVF leads to liver necrosis, encephalitis and blindness. Preventive measures include avoiding farm animals (particularly those that appear ill), camels, freshly slaughtered meat, mosquitos, raw milk and locally prepared cheese products.

Crime

Crime is confined to pickpockets, purse snatching, and other petty crime. (U.S. visitors are rarely targeted because of nationality.)

Tourists are fair game in Egypt for scams. Travelers may find themselves being overcharged for everything from taxi rides to cheap *hookahs*. In many of the tourist areas, visitors can find special "tourist police" to assist them. The telephone numbers for the tourist police in Cairo are: ☎ *926-027, 984-750* and *847-611.* Outside of Cairo, tourists and business travelers should consult with their hotel for guidance.

Drug Penalties

Travelers are subject to the laws and legal practices of the country in which they travel. Drug enforcement policies in Egypt are very strict. The death penalty may be imposed on anyone convicted of smuggling or selling marijuana, hashish, opium, LSD or other narcotics. Law enforcement authorities prosecute and seek fines and imprisonment in cases of possession of even small quantities of drugs.

Photography Hassles

Egypt has strict duties on the importation of expensive photographic and video equipment, including all video cameras, autofocus cameras, etc. They may try to charge you the standard duty for importing these items, so you can either have the equipment stored, an unlikely scenario, or you can ask that the Egyptian customs official inventory the equipment and list it by model and serial number in your passports. Your equipment will be checked upon your departure, in which case no duty will be collected. As in most African or Middle East countries, there are restrictions on photographing military personnel and sites, as well as bridges and canals.

Getting Sick

Access to medical help and professionals is good in Cairo, Luxor and Aswan. The U.S. embassy in Cairo can provide a list of local hospitals and English-speaking physicians. Medical facilities are adequate for non-emergency matters, particularly in the areas where most tourists visit. Emergency and intensive care facilities are limited. Many Nile cruise boats employ a medical practitioner with the equivalent of a U.S. Bachelor's degree in medicine.

Nuts & Bolts

Egypt can be visited without many restrictions. Terrorists target trains and riverboats with little or no regularity to their attacks. The workweek in Egypt is Sunday through Thursday. The emergency number for local police assistance in Cairo is ☎ *122.*

Embassy Location

The U.S. Embassy in Cairo is on Lazoghli Street, Garden City, near downtown Cairo. The mailing address from the U.S. is:

American Embassy Cairo

APO AE 09839-4900
from Egypt, it is
8 Kamal El-Din Salah Street, Cairo
☎ (20-2) 355-7371 (24-hour switchboard)
FAX (20-2) 357-3200

The Consular Section of the American embassy is located at the embassy, but has a separate entrance on Lazoghli Street. The consular mailing address from the United States is:

American Embassy Cairo

Consular Section, Unit 64900
Box 15, APO AE 09839-4900
☎ (20-2) 355-7371
FAX (20-2) 357-2472.

Dangerous Days

01/07/1994	Coptic Christians in Egypt celebrate Christmas on January 7.
07/02/1993	Sheikh Omar Abdul Rahman, the radical Egyptian cleric, surrendered to U.S. Justice Department officials in Brooklyn, New York.
11/23/1985	An Egyptian jet was hijacked to Malta. Fifty-nine passengers, including one American, were killed when Egyptian troops stormed the plane in Malta on November 24.
10/07/1985	Hijacking of the *Achille Lauro.* Four Palestinian gunmen hijacked the Italian cruise ship *Achille Lauro* off Alexandria, Egypt. While off the Syrian port of Tartus, the terrorists killed a wheelchair-bound American. Egypt and Italy negotiated the return of the ship and the remaining passengers. U.S. fighters intercepted an Egyptian jet carrying the hijackers and forced it down at a NATO base in Italy.

Dangerous Days

09/15/1982	Black September terrorists seized the Egyptian embassy in Madrid, demanding that Egypt renounce the Sinai agreement with Israel. The ambassador signed a renunciation, which was later dismissed.
04/15/1982	The assassins of Anwar Sadat were publicly executed in Cairo.
10/06/1981	Anwar Sadat assassinated.
02/19/1980	Israel sends first ambassador.
03/26/1979	Egyptian-Israeli peace treaty.
09/17/1978	Camp David Accords signed.
06/05/1975	Suez Canal reopened.
10/06/1973	Armed Forces Day.
10/06/1973	Yom Kippur War begins.
03/09/1968	Day of The War Dead.
06/05/1967	Six Day War.
05/25/1963	OAU—Africa Freedom Day. The Organization Of African Unity was founded on May 25, 1963. The day is celebrated as Africa Freedom Day. The OAU was organized to promote unity and cooperation among African states.
02/22/1958	Unity Day.
12/23/1956	Victory Day. Celebrates the withdrawal of British, French and Israeli Forces from Port Said and the Suez Canal Zone.
10/29/1956	Invasion of the Sinai. Israeli, French and British forces invaded the Sinai and seized control of the Suez Canal following its nationalization by Egypt.
10/24/1956	Popular Resistance Day.
07/26/1956	Nationalization of Suez Canal.
06/18/1953	The monarchy was abolished and Egypt was declared a republic following the coup led by Gamal Abdel Nasser.
07/23/1952	Egyptian Revolution celebrated.
01/07/1949	First Arab-Israeli war ended.
02/28/1922	Britain unilaterally declared Egypt independent in deference to growing nationalism.
01/15/1918	Former Egyptian President Gamel Abd el Nasser was born.
12/18/1914	Britain declared a formal protectorate over Egypt that lasted until February 28, 1922, when Britain unilaterally declared Egypt independent in deference to growing nationalist sentiment.
04/25/0000	Sinai liberation day.

El Salvador

U.N.der Fire

It's hard to fathom how such a small place geographically, is so prominent on the globe, and how so much killing has happened in such idyllic surroundings. El Salvador is a tiny country of only 8124 square miles, of which 30 percent is mostly mountainous.

El Salvador (Republica de El Salvador, or Republic of El Salvador) gained independence from Spain in 1839. Instability and frequent coups have marked the country's political history. In this century, the army has dominated political affairs. From 1960 until recently, this domination was met with increased resistance, with underground opposition groups proliferating, and violent conflict and terrorism by rightist and leftist extremists escalating—especially in connection with the insurgent Farabundo Marti National Liberation Front (FMLN).

The most violent opposition to El Salvador's government was centered in the leftist FMLN. However, the group is now an active force in the post-civil war government. Its long fight against the ARENA-led government caused thousands of deaths, but fi-

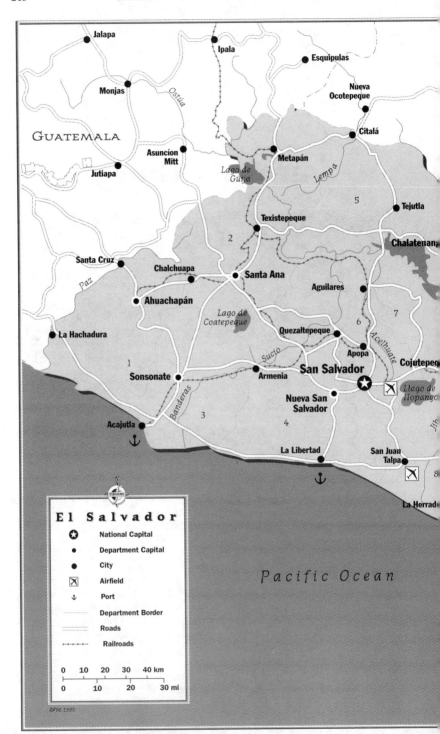

El Salvador

- ⊗ National Capital
- ● Department Capital
- ● City
- ☒ Airfield
- ⚓ Port
- ─── Department Border
- ----- Roads
- +--+--+ Railroads

0 10 20 30 40 km
0 10 20 30 mi

Pacific Ocean

©FWI 1995

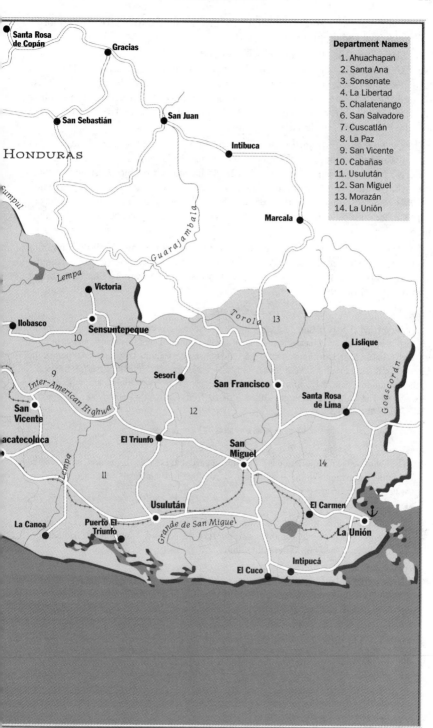

Department Names

1. Ahuachapan
2. Santa Ana
3. Sonsonate
4. La Libertad
5. Chalatenango
6. San Salvadore
7. Cuscatlán
8. La Paz
9. San Vicente
10. Cabañas
11. Usulután
12. San Miguel
13. Morazán
14. La Unión

Santa Rosa de Copán

Gracias

San Sebastián

San Juan

Intibuca

HONDURAS

Marcala

Sumpul

Guarajambala

Lempa

Victoria

Ilobasco

Sensuntepeque

10

Torola

13

Lislique

9

Inter-American Highway

Sesori

San Francisco

Santa Rosa de Lima

Goascorán

San Vicente

12

acatecoluca

Lempa

El Triunfo

San Miguel

14

11

Usulután

La Canoa

Puerto El Triunfo

Grande de San Miguel

El Carmen

La Unión

Intipucá

El Cuco

nally resulted in major constitutional reform that has started to improve the country's political, social and economic conditions.

On September 25, 1991, the government and FMLN leaders signed an accord in New York City that set the stage for final negotiations in late December 1991. The talks resulted in a formal cease-fire that came into effect on February 1, 1992. Although there was some delay on behalf of both sides of the civil conflict in fulfilling the terms of the pact, on December 15, 1992 the civil war was declared formally over, and the FMLN was registered as a legitimate political party.

Most people pass through El Salvador as they travel through Central America. The main reasons for stopping include beaches, volcanoes, lakes and Mayan ruins. El Salvador's 12-year civil war, which ended in 1992, had a catastrophic effect on the country's tourist industry. Of the country's 6214 miles of roads, only 932 are paved. There are 374 miles of railroad. Of the 105 airfields, only 74 are usable; five have a permanent surface, and only the major airport in San Salvador is serviceable for international flights.

The total armed forces in El Salvador number 30,500: Army, 28,000; Navy, 500 (110 marines, 10 special forces); Air Force, 2000. There are also 34 (current strength) United Nations observer troops currently stationed in El Salvador. The U.N. operation began in July 1991.

Getting In

A passport and visa are required for entry into El Salvador. Travelers may be asked to present evidence of employment and finances at the time of visa application. There are no airport visas or tourist cards available for last-minute entry. For additional information, travelers may contact the Embassy of El Salvador at *2308 California St., NW, Washington, D.C. 20008;* ☎ *(202) 265-9671,* or the nearest consulate in Houston, Los Angeles, San Francisco, New Orleans, Miami, New York or Chicago. The address for Consular Affairs is *1010 16th Street NW, Third Floor, Washington, D.C. 20036;* ☎ *(202) 331-4032.*

Dangerous Places

Buses

The use of public transportation is highly discouraged, but taxis may be used. The road to and from the international airport is considered safe during the daytime, but traveling on it at night is strongly discouraged.

The Mountains

Travel to the northern and eastern parts of the country should be restricted to hard surface roads only. This physically comprises two-thirds of the country. Travel outside San Salvador between cities should not be done after sunset.

Eastern San Salvador

Travel to the eastern side of San Salvador should also not be attempted after sunset. Twenty-fifth Street (calle) is the north/south line of demarcation used to make this distinction.

The following are emergency contact numbers for visitors to San Salvador. Travelers to other regions should note that the respective emergency telephone numbers are different and are encouraged to obtain them prior to departure from San Salvador.

National Police
☎ *(503) 271-44-22*

Civilian National Police
☎ *(503) 298-18-49 and 298-18-56*

San Salvador Fire Department
☎ *(503) 271-22-27*

Ambulance Service from San Salvador's Diagnostico Hospital
☎ *(503) 226-51-11 and 225-05-19*

Dangerous Things

Crime

Violent, as well as petty crimes are prevalent throughout El Salvador. There were 75 homicides in San Salvador in the first 15 days of January 1995 alone. This was nearly a 100 percent increase over the same period in 1994. Most of the murders in El Salvador are related to carjackings.

U.S. citizens are often victims. Visitors should avoid carrying valuables in public places. Armed assaults and carjackings take place both in El Salvador, the capital, and in the interior of the country, but are especially frequent on roads outside the capital where police patrols are infrequent. Criminals have been known to follow travelers from the international airport to private residences, where they carry out assaults and robberies and other dirty deeds. Criminals often become violent quickly, especially when victims fail to cooperate immediately in surrendering valuables. Frequently, victims who argue with assailants or refuse to give up their valuables are shot.

The Peace Accords signed in 1992 between the government of El Salvador and the FMLN have brought a halt to fighting in El Salvador. Areas formerly considered conflicted zones or zones of concentration for demobilizing guerrillas are now open for travel. The U.S. Embassy warns its personnel to drive with their doors locked and windows raised, to avoid travel after dark, and to avoid travel on unpaved roads at all times because of random banditry, carjackings, criminal assaults and lack of police and road service facilities. Most fatal accidents or robberies and assaults occur during the evening or early morning hours. Travelers with conspicuous amounts of luggage, late-model cars and foreign license plates are particularly vulnerable, even in the capital. Many Salvadorans are armed and shootouts are not infrequent. Travelers, from the United States however, may not carry guns, even for their own protection or for use on the road without first procuring a gun license from Salvadoran officials. Failure to do so will result in detention and confiscation of the traveler's firearm even if it is licensed in the U.S.

After a 12-year-old civil war, however, some resentment toward "gringos" and anti-U.S. sentiment remains. The primary threat to U.S. citizens comes from the explosion of criminal activity. The consular section of the embassy sees approximately two to three Americans per week who claim to be victims of assaults and robberies. The theft of personal documents and effects, passports, money and vehicles is typical of these incidents. Within the past year, there have been no reports of violence against U.S. Citizens for reasons of anti-American sentiment nor have there been organized acts of terrorism against U.S. citizens. A significant element of the rising crime rate is the surge in crimes of violence.

Politics

The Salvadoran constitution prohibits foreigners from participating in domestic political activities, including public demonstrations. The government of El Salvador considers such involvement to be a violation of the participant's tourist visa status.

Land Mines

Mine removal efforts are underway, but land mines in back country regions have caused numerous unintended casualties and pose a threat to off-road tourists, backpackers and campers.

The Maras

During the first six months of 1993, an average of 56 sexual assaults, 671 unspecified violent acts and 245 homicides were committed each month in the metropolitan area of San Salvador. Increased drug trafficking and use, displaced workers, unemployment and criminal gangs provide the impetus for this continued growth. The gangs, known as "maras," are extremely violent and use weapons to commit their crimes. Using armed roadblocks, they rob victims and then carjack their vehicles. Due to the prevalence of combat weapons, the arms used in many of the assaults are M-16s, AK-47s and grenade launchers. The crimes take place in private residences, public streets, businesses, markets and the beach areas. Since it is generally accepted that many Salvadoran males are armed, many of these crimes become fatalities. The daily news media carry stories of gunfights and shootouts.

Given the prevailing violence, the people exercise their right to self-defense. Wealthy Salvadorans hire security guards to protect themselves, their families and personal property. All visitors are encouraged to cooperate and surrender personal effects in the event of a robbery. The legacy of the 12-year war has led many to place a low value on human life.

Death Squads

A number of rightwing terrorist groups and "death squads" continue to exist. The ruling Alianza Republicana Nacionalista (ARENA—National Republican Alliance) is an extreme rightwing party founded in 1981. It now works with the FMLN to preserve the integrity of the 1992 peace agreement that ended the long, bloody war between them.

Getting Sick

Medical care is limited. There are about 12 hospital beds and four doctors per 10,000 people (1990). Doctors and hospitals often expect immediate cash payment for health services. U.S. medical insurance is not always valid outside the United States. Most hospitals accept credit cards for hospital charges, but not for doctors fees. Tap water is generally not considered safe to drink in El Salvador. There have also been numerous incidents of cholera in recent months. The U.S. embassy advises its personnel to avoid shellfish and other food sold by streetside vendors or in establishments where hygiene may be questionable.

Nuts & Bolts

The Central American nation has a tropical climate on the coastal plain which changes to cooler and wetter weather in the mountainous inland regions. The average temperature for the city of San Salvador is 73 degrees F. The rainy season is between May and November, and the average annual rainfall is 66 inches in San Salvador.

Currency is the colon, with 100 cents or centavos to the Salvadorean colon.

The people of El Salvador are predominantly Mestizo (94 percent) and Roman Catholic (88 percent). Indians comprise 5 percent of the population, while whites make up only 1 percent. Spanish is the predominant language, while some Indians speak Nahua.

Embassy Location

Americans who register with the Consular Section of the U.S. embassy in San Salvador may obtain updated information on travel and security within El Salvador.

The U.S. embassy in El Salvador is located at *Final Boulevard Station, Antigua Cuscatlan, Unit 3116, San Salvador, El Salvador* ☎ *(503) 78-4444.*

Dangerous Days	
10/10/1980	Founding of the Farabundo Marti National Liberation Front (FMLN), the umbrella organization of the five main leftist guerrilla groups in El Salvador.
03/02/1980	Archbishop Oscar Arnulfo Romero assassinated by a presumed right-wing death squad. The anniversary has been marked in succeeding years by leftist terrorist attacks, including attacks on American interests.
02/28/1977	Founding of the Popular League Of 28 February (LP-28), a leftist guerrilla group.
06/14/1975	Founding of the Armed Forces Of National Resistance (FARN), a leftist guerrilla group.

Dangerous Days

04/01/1970   Founding of the Popular Liberation Forces (FPL), a leftist guerrilla organization.

09/15/1821   Independence Day.

Georgia
★

Rebel Yell

Georgia seems to suffer more from the spillover of the Armenian-Azeri conflict than it does from its own internal problems which, in their own right, are profound.

The Scoop

Boris Yeltsin thought that he would turn up the heat by having his soldiers and local tribes raise a little hell. When Georgia yelled "uncle" he turned the heat down..

The Players

Although things have quieted down in Georgia there still is a simmering discontent among special interest groups who want to take advantage of Georgia's poverty and confusion.

The Mkhedrioni (knights)

The personal militia loyal to Jaba Iosseliani, president of the Georgian Emergency Committee. This militia contains some criminal elements. The current Georgian government has been trying to disband the *mkhedrioni* and absorb them into regular army units.

Georgia

Georgia

✪	Republic capital
★	Autonomous republic center
•	Autonomous oblast center
●	City
⊠	Airport
———	Road
＋＋＋＋	Railroad

0   25   50   75 km

0   25   50 mi

©FWI 1995

Zviadists

These rebels are fighting for former president Zviad Gamsakhurdi, who returned from exile and is fighting to regain control of Georgia. They are in cahoots with the Confederation of Mountain Peoples. The Zviadists are also opposed to the stationing of Russian troops at three military bases in Georgia.The Zviadists are engaged in a low-key civil war with the Shevard-nadze government.

Abkhazians

The Abkhazians demanded more autonomy and Georgia responded by sending in troops in August of 1992, resulting in the deaths of hundreds of people. The Abkhazians were supported by Russian units.

The Government

Led by Georgian leader Eduard Shevardnadze.

The Mafia

There is little the mafia does not control in Georgia, so it really doesn't matter who is in power.

Getting In

A passport is required. A visa is not required before arrival. Visitors who enter at the Tbilisi airport receive a temporary stamp at passport control and are instructed to obtain a visa from the consular division of the Ministry of Foreign Affairs. Visas are usually granted within three days. Fees vary from US$30 to US$90 depending on the duration of the visa. Travelers arriving from and returning to another country of the former Soviet Union are not required to obtain a Georgian visa. Those arriving from the former Soviet Union and departing to countries outside the former Soviet Union must obtain a visa in order to leave. On an exceptional basis, the Georgian Ministry of Foreign Affairs can assist travelers in obtaining visas for Georgia through the checkpoint at Sarpi on the border with Turkey.

Dangerous Places

The U.S. government has prohibited U.S. officials from traveling overland between Georgia and Armenia due to the activity of bandits on the Georgian side of the border. Sporadic violence occurs in the western regions of Georgia and South Ossetia. In Abkhazia, extensive fighting has occurred. Georgia has become the battlefield for Armenian and Azerbaijani terrorists. There have also been numerous bombings of trains destined for both Armenian and Azerbaijani territory. Oil and gas pipelines have also been sabotaged. The prime suspects are Armenian terrorists. The railway line between Tbilisi and Yerevan, is the frequent target of Azeri and Armenian saboteurs. The oil and gas pipelines in the area have also been hit some 12 times in the last year. All this is "spillover" from the Nagorno-Karabakh conflict.

Recently, a bomb was detonated in an Armenian drama theatre in Tbilisi. As long as the conflict over Nagorno-Karabakh continues, there will be ongoing terrorist attacks against both Armenian and Azerbaijani-related targets in Georgia.

Between February 25 and March 3, 1995, 38 people were killed and 138 wounded in fighting in Ochamchire Rayon. As of March 1993 the number of people killed in the Abkhaz region alone stood at 781 and the number of wounded totaled 2565. A significant percentage of this figure were civilian casualties.

A number of aircraft have been lost in the fighting, including civilian airliners, also resulting in numerous civilian deaths and injuries.The U.S. government has prohibited any travel to Sukhumi by U.S. officials for the foreseeable future.

Nighttime

Georgia has a high rate of crime; the risk is especially high at night. Georgian citizens in uniform or civilian clothes openly carry firearms. Criminals are often armed. Gunfire in the capital city of Tbilisi is fairly common. Outside Tbilisi, unescorted travel is difficult and dangerous.

Police authority in many cities in western and central Georgia has collapsed. Foreigners have been the targets of criminal activity.

Getting Sick

Medical care in Georgia is limited. The U.S. embassy maintains a list of English-speaking physicians in the area. There is a severe shortage of basic medical supplies, including disposable needles, anesthetics and antibiotics. Elderly travelers and those with existing health problems may be at risk due to inadequate medical facilities. Doctors and hospitals often expect immediate cash payment for health services. U.S. medical insurance is not always valid outside the United States. Travelers have found that in some cases, supplemental medical insurance with specific overseas coverage has proved to be useful.

Nuts & Bolts

Georgia is a "cash only" economy. "Traveler's cheques" and credit cards are rarely accepted.

Americans who register at the Consular Section of the U.S. Embassy may obtain updated information on travel and security within Georgia.

Embassy Location

In Georgia:

The U.S. Embassy

> *25 Atoneli Street*
> *Tbilisi, Georgia*
> ☎ *(7-8832) 98-99-67 or 93-38-03*
> *Telex: 212210 AMEMB SU*
> *FAX (7-8832) 93-37-59*

In the U.S.:

Embassy of the Republic of Georgia

> *1511 K St., NW, Suite 424*
> *Washington, D.C. 20005*
> ☎ *(202) 393-5959*
> *FAX (202) 393-6060*

Dangerous Days

12/25/1991	U.S. Recognition of Georgia. President George Bush formally recognized Georgia and eleven other former Soviet republics on December 25, 1991. On that occasion, he also stated that formal diplomatic relations would be established with six of the republics as soon as possible and that diplomatic relations would be established with the other six (Georgia was one of them) when certain political conditions were met.
12/21/1991	Commonwealth formed at a meeting in Alma-Ata, Kazakhstan. On December 21, 1991, 11 former republics of the Soviet Union (which ceased to exist on December 25, 1991) established the Commonwealth of Independent States (CIS). Georgia sent an observer but did not join the CIS, which is expected to have military and economic coordinating functions and be headquartered in Mensk, Byelarus.

The G3

Heckler & Koch are known for high precision German weapons. A relative newcomer to the arms trade (they were formed in 1949 by three partners; Seidel is the modest one). Originally the post-war German army used old M1 Garands and the FAL rifle. The G3 was adopted in 1959 and was the first entirely German designed and made rifle (based on the Spanish CETME). The G3 used the standard 7.62 X51 NATO cartridge and its accuracy and durability led it to being adopted by more than 50 other countries. The basic rifle design was made in everything from sniper versions to .22 calibre versions.

The ultimate H&K version is the PSG1 a $5000 sniper version for military and police use.

India
★★★★

Kashmir Sweat

It is a miracle that India even exists. Being a nation of so many ethnicities and religions, it should have ripped itself into a bunch of dinky fiefdoms long ago, each with hundreds of years of history, separate religions, dialects and customs. Instead, 866 million Indians and their government hobble painfully forward—burdened not only with poverty, skin-and-bones hunger and sickness, but also with an alarming birthrate.

Like a terminally ill patient, India deals with the ugliest boils and rashes first. Its big problems are in the extreme south with the Tamil Tigers, and in the north with Sikh separatists. The Hindu majority can't get along with the Muslim minority. If simmering disdain for each other wasn't enough, on December 6, 1992, militant Hindus, intent on aggravating the Muslims, demolished a mosque in Ayodha in Uttar Pradesh state. They then intended to build their own temple on the grounds, but the government wisely stepped in and stopped them. By the time the dust had settled, 1200 people had died throughout India. This gave the Islamic fundamentalist nasties in Iran and Pakistan a good reason to stir things up in India. The fallout has been felt as far

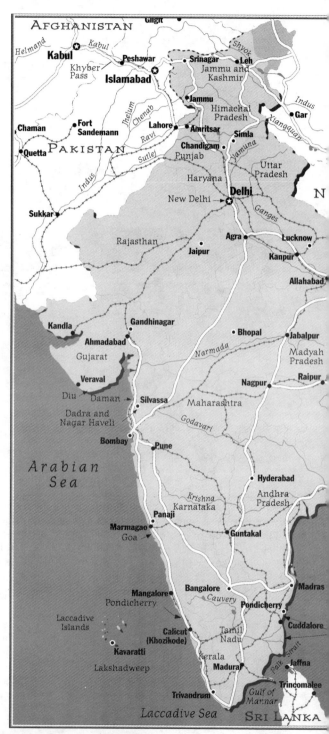

India

India

- ✪ National Capital
- • State or Union Territory Capital
- • City
- ▨ Disputed Territory
- —— State or Union Territory Border
- ═══ Primary Road
- ┼┼┼ Railroad
- ▪ ▪ ▪ Disputed Border

0 100 200 300 400 km
0 100 200 300 mi

©FWI 1995

CHINA

NEPAL

Tongtran
(Yangtze)

Mekong

Kathmandu

Sikkim

Gangtok

Siliguri

BHUTAN

Arunachal Pradesh

Itanagar

Ledo

Assam

Nagaland

Sillong

Meghalaya

Kohima

Manipur

Imphal

Gandak

Varanasi

BANGLADESH

Ganges

Agartala

Aizawl

Bihar

West Bengal

Dhaka

Tripura

Mizoram

Jamshedpur

Calcutta

Jessore

Mandalay

Mahanadi

Cuttack

Mouths of the Ganges

MYANMAR
(BURMA)

Bhubaneshwar

Orissa

Puri

Irrawaddy

Vishakhapatnam

Pondicherry

Yangon
(Rangoon)

Bay of Bengal

Mouths of the
Irrawaddy

Andaman
Islands
(India)

Pondicherry

Andaman Sea

Port
Blair

Andaman
and
Nicobar
Island

Nicobar Islands
(India)

away as Great Britain, where a large Indian community lives. Every time a bomb goes off, and they go off a lot, the suspects include Indians, Pakistani agents, Kashmiri separatists, Sikh terrorists, Maoist rebels, Sri Lankan Liberation Tigers of Tamil Eelam guerrillas, Muslim militants, drug traffickers and even gangsters. Mother Theresa is the only one exempt from suspicion.

India is rattling its sabre at Pakistan and Sri Lanka and also having a go-at-it with Bangladesh, who they've also charged with providing aid to Indian rebels, including allowing Pakistan to instigate terrorist activities on Bangladeshi soil. Nepal is another nasty neighbor. India can't seem to get along with anyone. However, it's trade and transit issues that dominate relations between India and Nepal.

Not one to miss out on ideological rocket attacks, China is also part of India's multi-front diplomatic fray. Just to keep China honest, India fought a brief border war with the Sinos back in 1962. Since then, though, the two countries' relations have improved—if for no other reason than their mutual respect for the size of each others' populations, and the realization that a conventional ground war might take a few hundred years to fight, and still leave each country with populations the size of the U.S. Although India is furious over closer Sino-Pakistani ties, it has withdrawn most of the troops deployed to the border area with China.

With so many enemies, who do you call? Why Russia, of course. Everyone else who needs arms does. Motherlode Russia, the Office Depot of weapons systems.

India actually enjoyed smooth relations with the U.S. when George Bush called the shots, literally—but they've deteriorated since President Bill Clinton took office. Time will only tell if the Republicans' new Contract with America will include a new contract with India as well.

The Scoop

What we have here is a failure to communicate. Language, religion, history, politics and fear collide like a dark room full of drunks with chainsaws. A hefty 249 terrorist incidents have put India at the top of the list for individuals injured in terrorist attacks—2546 people. Their tiny teardrop neighbor to the south, Sri Lanka, still has the record for terrorist-related fatalities. Its interconnected agony with India gives Sri Lanka the dubious DP Award for being the World's Most Dangerous Place—Terrorism Category (WMDP—TC), —with 1268 deaths. The get-tough policy of the Indian army and police has been somewhat effective combating Sikh militants in the Punjab. The rising incidents of rape, torture and murder attributed to the Indian security forces are creating a furor with human rights groups outside of India.

The Players

Hizbul Mujahedin, or Fighters for the Party of God

In 1990, the Muslims became violent in opposing Indian rule. There are 6 million people in Kashmir; 4 million of them are Muslim. Since 1990, about 18,000 people, mostly Muslims, have been killed. Half the toll has been civilians. Most of the casualties have been in the Kashmir Valley area around Srinagar. Kashmir is currently divided, with some parts under the control of Pakistan rebels and others under the auspices of the Indian Army.

Syeed Salahuddin, whose real name is Syeed Mohammed Yusuf Shah, is the commander of the Hizbul Mujahedin. They receive financial backing and support from Pakistan. Pakistan's Prime Minister Benazir Bhutto, wants the Muslim majority states of Jammu and Kashmir out of Hindu-dominated India and aligned with Pakistan. The rebels claim they are fighting for *azad* Kashmir, or free Kashmir. Currently there are about 15,000 active rebel fighters with several subfactions among them. The rebels operate in small, hit-and-run groups in cities like Srinagar, or from remote bases in Kashmir. Pakistan has fought two out of three of its last wars over Kashmir and the situation is expected to remain tense for years to come. The geopolitical volleyball started when Britain sliced up India and Pakistan in 1947 based on geographic divisions rather than religious ones. At the time, India promised to hold a plebiscite among all Kashmiris to determine whether the territory should be part of India or Pakistan. They backed down and the conflict has been going on ever since.

The Indian Army

Governor K. V. Krishna Rao, the 72-year-old former chief of staff of the Indian Army, has about 400,000 soldiers, border troops and police at his service to keep the peace in Kashmir. It is the largest force India has ever fielded against a secessionist rebellion. Governor Rao subscribes to the Domino Theory: If Kashmir is allowed to break away from India, other parts of the country with separatist groups would follow and India would exist no longer.

All-Party Hurriyat Conference

This is an alliance formed by the numerous guerrillas who use secession from India as a common rallying point. Maulvi Omar Farooq, 21, is chairman of the All-Party Hurriyat Conference; the umbrella group formed of 32 rebel organizations. Farooq is also the hereditary Mir Waiz of Kashmir, the religious leader of the region's Muslims. The losers seem to be the Hindus of the region. At last count there were about 400,000 Hindu refugees from the Kashmir Valley in refugee camps around the state's winter capital of Jammu.

United Liberation Front of Assam (ULFA)

The ULFA was supposed to cede their fight for a socialist state in Assam when they signed a peace deal with the government in January 1992. The hard-liners said "screw that" and began a campaign of kidnapping and extortion against the rich tea growers. The Indian Tea Association quickly put together a 7000-man private army to protect themselves from ULFA thugs.

There have been reports of large-scale extortion and attacks on police stations throughout Assam by both ULFA and the Bodo Security Force (BSF). ULFA murdered the chairman of Assam Frontier Tea in 1990 and continued gunning for more high-level executives. Another tea executive, working for the Tata Tea Company, has been held for ransom by militants since April 1993. His kidnappers are demanding a US$5 million ransom. The executives are Indian nationals. Security forces have stepped-up their operations against the militants and have rounded up large numbers of both suspects and weapons. Assam state officials, however, are hoping that the government in New Delhi will send in a paramilitary force to end the rebels' kidnappings. For now Assam is an especially dangerous place if you grow tea. Crumpets, anyone?

The Sikhs

The Sikhs want their own turf and India doesn't want them to have it. They are led by Sohan Singh, a 76-year-old doctor who was captured by the Indian government in November of 1993. Typically proud and bellicose, a small segment of Sikhs want to establish an independent homeland called Khalistan, or Land of the Pure. The Sikhs target security forces and other government symbols in their bomb attacks. The problem is that the bombs, although they may lean left or right, don't have political affiliations—and kill a lot of innocent people. Sikhs comprise only 2 percent of India's population, but they are a majority in Punjab state. The center of the Sikh terrorist movement is in the capital of Punjab, Chandigarh. Pakistan is sympathetic to the Sikh movement. Although the Indian government claims that the movement has been shrinking since its leader was captured, there are still a lot of angry bad boys in turbans with the last name of Singh (all Sikhs are named Singh). Journalist Peter Hillmore described the Sikhs: "Let us get one thing clear. The bands of Sikh gunmen who rampage around here, regularly and randomly shooting people in cold-blood are not, repeat not, a bunch of mean and vicious terrorists. They are in fact dedicated and idealistic militants who are simply misunderstood. Actually, that is a load of nonsense. Of course, they are terrorists; they certainly seem to enjoy creating terror. They are barbaric and vicious killers, murdering at random. They appear to be totally without moral scruples and, by now, are devoid of even political logic. Too many people are being killed every week for there to be any restraining influence at work. There are too many different gangs at work for there to be any grand scheme. Punjab, quite simply, is out of control."

Sri Lankan Liberation Tigers of Tamil Eelam (LTTE)

The Tigers bagged their biggest victim when a suicide bomber killed former Indian Prime Minister Rajiv Ghandi. Ghandi sent 50,000 troops to put down the Tamil insurrection in 1987. These guys know how to carry a grudge. The Tamil Tigers may be too effective; India's Tamil population provides little sympathy or support to the overly violent Tigers. See "The Players" section in the Sri Lanka chapter for a wider description.

Naxalites

Operate out of Andrah Pradesh. The Peoples War Guerrillas; a Maoist insurgent group that continues the plight of the Naxalites; a 1960s revolutionary group.

Getting In

A passport and visa (which must be obtained in advance) are required for entry into India for tourism or business. Evidence of yellow fever immunization is needed if the traveler is arriving from an infected area. Convicted drug offenders in India can expect a minimum jail sentence of 10 years and heavy fines. Indian customs authorities strictly enforce the laws and regulations governing the declaration, importation or possession of gold and gold objects. Travelers have sometimes been detained for possession of undeclared gold objects. For further entry information, the traveler can contact:

Embassy of India

2536 Massachusetts Avenue
NW, Washington, D.C. 20008
☎ *(202) 939-9839 or 939-9850*

Or contact the Indian consulates in Chicago, New York and San Francisco.

Bombay International Airport is a 45–60 minute ride from Bombay and about 23 miles Northwest of the city. There is a departure tax of 100 rupees for international flights, 50 rupees for Southwest Asian flights.

Getting Around

A taxi from the airport to the center of New Delhi runs about Rs150. In Bombay it will cost you Rs170 and takes about an hour.; in Calcutta, about Rs120. You can prepay in New Delhi and Bombay but drivers will haggle a fixed price with tourists.

There are about 2 million km (1.2 million miles) of roads in India; 33,112 km of which are the national highways. While this constitutes only 2 percent of total road length, they carry around 35 percent of the traffic. According to the National Transportation Research Centre, Indian roads are the most dangerous in the world. With 1 percent of the total vehicles in the world, India accounted for 6 percent of total road accidents and has the highest accident rate in the world at 34.6 per 10,000 people.

The size of the railway network was estimated at approximately 63,900 km (37,850 miles) in 1990. India's railway network is the largest in Asia and the second largest in the world. India has four major international airports—Bombay, Calcutta, Madras and Delhi—and 115 other airports serving domestic routes.

Travel by road after dark is not recommended and train passengers have been subjected to robberies and schedule disruptions due to protest actions.

Restricted Areas

Permission from the Indian government (from Indian diplomatic missions abroad, or in some cases, from the Ministry of Home Affairs) is required to visit the states of Mizoram, Manipur, Nagaland, Meghalaya, Assam, Tripura, Arunachal Pradesh, Sikkim, parts of Kulu district and Spiti district of Himachal Pradesh, border areas of Jammu and Kashmir, areas of Uttar Pradesh, the area west of National Highway 15 running from Ganganagar to Sanchar in Rajasthan, the Andaman and Nicobar islands and the Union Territory of the Laccadive islands.

Dangerous Places

Countrywide

Serious communal violence and riots erupted in India following the destruction of an Ayodhya mosque in December 1992. There continue to be major civil disturbances. These riots pose risks to a traveler's personal safety and can disrupt transportation systems and city services. In response to communal violence, Indian authorities may occasionally impose curfews. In addition, political rallies and demonstrations in India have the potential for violence and bomb attacks.

Kashmir

Terrorist activities and violent civil disturbances continue in the Kashmir Valley in the states of Jammu and Kashmir. There have been incidents in which terrorists have threatened and kidnapped foreigners.Undoubtedly, though, Pakistan is the biggest influence on India's foreign relations. India and Pakistan have duked it out on the battlefield three times since World War II— in 1947, 1965 and 1971. Relations between the two became less strained only after Rajiv Gandhi replaced his mother as India's prime minister. In December 1985, Rajiv Gandhi and Pakistan President Mohammed Zia ul-Haq each pledged not to throw the first punch, particularly jabs aimed at the nations' nuke sites. But the increased violence in Kashmir, the one Indian state where Muslims comprise a majority, has brought about a greater likelihood the two countries will again go to war. India claims that Pakistan is fueling the flames by encouraging and supporting Kashmir secession from India. Of course, rather than Kashmir becoming an independent entity, Pakistan would like to be the sponge that absorbs it. In December 1992, Hindu extremists turned the Muslim mosque at Ayodhya into rubble. The Indian governor of Kashmir charged Pakistan in January 1994 with hiring more than 10,000 Afghan mercenaries to help Kashmiri rebels in their efforts against the government.

Assam

Terrorist groups in Assam have bombed trains, buses and bridges. The government of India has declared Assam to be a "disturbed area."

Punjab and Uttar Pradesh

Significant separatist violence continues in the Punjab and nearby regions outside Punjab state. Gangs have kidnapped and held for ransom foreign company executives. All areas of Punjab state have been affected to some extent over the past year. Violent incidents also occurred in 1992 at various places in Uttar Pradesh state in the northwestern foothills and north-central Terai region. Militants and robber gangs operate in the area in and around Jim Corbett National Park and Dudhwa National Park, as well as on roads leading to Hardwar, Rishikesh, Dehra Dun and Mussoorie.

India-Pakistan Border/Kashmir

Pakistan wants Kashmir and India won't let them have it. Some groups want to glue together the Indian and Pakistani controlled sections of Kashmir and create a separate country; other militants want Kashmir to annex with Pakistan. You can guess which group is backed by the government of Pakistan. All groups have managed to cause the deaths of about 17,000 people since January of 1990 when the tiff began.The Kashmiri separatist groups keep their squabbling and killing confined to the predominantly Muslim states of Jammu and Kashmir.

Tensions run high between India and Pakistan, particularly over Kashmir, resulting in frequent clashes. There are stringent security checks, travel restrictions and curfews. The only official India-Pakistan border crossing point for foreigners is at Attari, Punjab/Wagah, Pakistan. A Pakistani visa is required.

Delhi and Northern India

In Delhi, there have been several bombings that have resulted in casualties and property damage. The targets are areas of public access such as public transportation facilities, bazaars and shopping areas, and restaurants. Americans are not specifically targeted. The potential always exists that Americans, particularly in these public areas, might inadvertently be caught up in an incident just by being in the wrong place at the wrong time. In the states of Jammu and Kashmir, and Punjab in northern India, the terrorist threat is considerably higher. Bombings, kidnappings and assassinations are common occurrences in these regions. Two American tourists were kidnapped in Kashmir for several days. Two Swedes were taken hostage and held for more than three months by Kashmiri militants. The State Department is advising American citizens not to travel to Kashmir and to avoid nonessential travel to Punjab.

In Delhi there were over 700 homicides reported for the month of July 1991. Foreign residents throughout India usually employ *chawkidars* (residential guards) outside their homes. Police assistance throughout northern India can be requested by dialing 100 from any public phone; 100 connects to the nearest police control room which can usually dispatch a patrol vehicle.

Karakoram Mountain Range

Both India and Pakistan claim an area of the Karakoram mountain range which includes the Siachen glacier. The two countries have established military outposts in the region and armed clashes have occurred. Because of this situation, U.S. citizens traveling to or climbing peaks anywhere in the disputed area face significant risk of injury and death. The disputed area includes the following peaks: Rimo Peak, Apsarasas I, II and III, Tegam Kangri I, II, and III, Suingri Kangri, Ghaint I and Ii, Indira Col and Sia Kangri.

Bombay

There has been a dramatic increase in the number of organized criminal gangs operating in Bombay and police confirm that the problem exists throughout Maharashtra state. Drug gangs have proliferated in the larger cities and police report these gangs have moved into some of the most affluent areas of Bombay. In 1994, there were three drive-by shootings in the Malabar hill area of Bombay. Home burglary still remains the most prevalent crime in Bombay, often committed by servants or other persons with easy access to the residence involved.

Police emergency numbers:

Deputy Commissioner of Police (Bombay)
☎ *262-1763*

Assistant Commissioner of Police (Bombay)
☎ *822-0431*

Commissioner of Police (Pune)
☎ *(0212) 666396*

Inspector General of Police (Goa)
☎ *5360*

Commissioner of Police (Ahmedabad)
☎ *333959*

Director General of Police (Ahmedabad)
☎ *377-301l*

Director General of Police (Bhopal)
☎ *540880*

Calcutta

Insurgent activities, including killings and kidnappings by the United Liberation Front of Assam (ULFA) continue in the northeast. Despite army intervention, violent dissidence continues in parts of Assam. Local ULFA militants have carried out coordinated kidnappings throughout the state. A Soviet mining engineer was killed and a number of Indian hostages taken, including several high ranking officials. Political clashes occur sporadically in different parts of west Bengal and Bihar. Americans who are members of the Ananda Marg have been victims of mob violence in some areas of west Bengal and Bihar states (especially Calcutta and Purulia district) and are not welcome by state government authorities, who, upon locating such individuals, usually detain and deport them.

The crime situation in west Bengal and Orissa relates to petty thefts, etc. However, in Bihar, there have been killings and other violence stemming from caste and tribal differences. Travel by road after dark is not recommended and train passengers have been subjected to robberies and schedule disruptions due to protest actions.

Emergency numbers:

Police Headquarters in Calcutta
☎ *25-5900, 25-5762*
Control Room (24 Hours)
25-3340

Bhavani Bhavan
☎ *45-1761*

The South

Sri Lanka is a thorn in India's side because of the ethnic conflict between Sri Lanka's Sinhalese majority and the island's Tamil minority. India withdrew the last of the 70,000 troops it had sent to Sri Lanka to combat violence between the two groups on March 24, 1990. The nearly three-year presence of the Indian army in Sri Lanka didn't go over well in either of the two nations. After the withdrawal, Indian-Sri Lankan relations improved to a degree, especially with Sri Lankan cooperation in the investigation of Rajiv Gandhi's assassination. And, Sri Lanka was thankful for the additional pressure India put on Sri Lankan Tamil terrorists in India after the May 1993 assassination of Sri Lankan President Premadasa.

In May 1994, Prime Minister Rajiv Gandhi was killed in Tamil Nadu by a suicide bomber. Members of the Sri Lankan Tamil terrorist group, Liberation Tigers of Tamil Eelam (LTTE), commit acts of terrorism and violence throughout Southern India. To the north in Andhra Pradesh, the Peoples' War Group, popularly known as Naxalites, kidnaps and/or murders politicians and bureaucrats.

Emergency telephone numbers:

Police Headquarters (State Of Tamil Nadu)
☎ *84-45-50*

24 Hour Control Room
☎ *84-41-23*

Police Commissioner's Office (City Of Madras)
☎ *825-21-76*

24 Hour Control Room
☎ *825-33-75*

Police Commissioner's Office (Coimbatore)
☎ *30-898*

Police Commissioner's Office (Madurai)
☎ *30-579*

Police Headquarters (State Of Karnataka)
☎ *21-18-03*

Police Commissioner's Office (City Of Bangalore)
☎ *26-45-01 & 20-01-73*

Police Commissioner's Office (Hubli & Dharwar)
☎ *72800*

Police Commissioner's Office (Mysore)
☎ *28301*

Police Headquarters (Union Territory Of Pondicherry)
☎ *27243 or 26791*

Police Headquarters (State Of Kerala)
☎ *61601*

Police Commissioner's Office (Tribandrum)
☎ *60555*

Police Commissioner's Office (Cochin)
☎ *36-77-40*

Police Commissioners Office (Calicut)
☎ *77116*

Police Headquarters (State Of Andhra Pradesh)
☎ *23-01-91 or 23-01-67*

Police Commissioner's Office (Hyderabad)
☎ *52-53-49*

Police Commissioner's Office (Vijaywada)
☎ *47-62-82 or 47-31-12*

Police Commissioner's Office (Vizag)
☎ *62-763 or 62-709*

Dangerous Things

The Roads

According to the National Transportation Research Centre, Trivendrum, Indian roads are the most dangerous in the world. With one percent of the total vehicles in the world, India accounted for six percent of total road accidents and had the highest accident rate in the world at 34.6 per 10,000 people in 1988/89. In October 1989 there were about 2 million km of roads in India, 33,112 km of which were National Highway. While this constitutes only two percent of total road length, it carries around 35 percent of the traffic.

Bombay Train Stations

There have been many bombs defused or detonated at Bombay's crowded rail stations. It is not known exactly who the perpetrators are but it is a safe guess that you wouldn't care who blew you up. A rash of thirteen car and suitcase bombs in Bombay caused almost half the injuries in one day, March 12. Luckily police defused three more bombs.

When Bombay police filed charges against 189 people in connection with the bombings they had to use canvas sacks to haul in the 9392 criminal charges. Bombay's chief of police claims the Pakistani Government was behind the attacks and that they provided cash and arms for the bomb attacks.

Political Rallies

Various separatist groups love to blow up politicians using suicide bombers. These bombs usually contain way too much explosive material and nasty things like ball bearings. Needless to say they bury what's left of the politician in a sandwich bag and a lot of people die. Political rallies in India are much safer on TV.

Terrorism

In the month of March 1993, a series of bombings in several major cities resulted in over 300 deaths and 1000 people injured. The principal targets were public buildings, hotels and transportation centers. Foreigners have not been specifically targeted and none were reported injured. As a precaution against further terrorist acts, the government of India has enhanced security measures considerably in New Delhi and other major Indian cities.

Terrorism is a significant problem in widely separated geographic regions. Arising from tensions between religious groups, it is deliberately employed against specific targets. Muslim terrorism against the Indian authorities in Indian-ruled Kashmir dates from the rioting in Kashmir that led to the 1947 war between India and Pakistan and the partition of that area between the two nations. In January 1990, tensions between Hindus and Muslims in Indian Kashmir rose to their highest level since the 1971 war between India and Pakistan. Although the central government has placed the state under direct control and has deployed troops there to keep order, Muslim terrorism is still high. A similar situation exists in the Punjab as the result of Sikh terrorism aimed at the establishment of an independent Sikh nation. As in Kashmir, the state has been placed under direct presidential rule and the military deployed to keep order. Violence in the Punjab annually causes thousands of deaths. Kashmir and the Punjab are India's two most troubled regions, but occasional terrorist incidents occur elsewhere. Bombings in Delhi and throughout northern India are believed to be the work of Sikh terrorists. Smaller ethnic groups occasionally engage in terrorism in order to obtain greater autonomy or independence.

Getting Sick

Adequate medical care is available in the major population centers, but is limited in the rural areas of the country. Travelers to India should take preventive measures against malaria, hepatitis, meningitis and Japanese encephalitis (if arriving during the monsoon season). Travelers arriving from countries where outbreaks of yellow fever have occurred will be required to furnish a certificate for yellow fever vaccination. Cholera and gastroenteritis occur during the summer monsoon months, mostly in the poorer areas of India. The best protection includes eating only at better-quality restaurants or hotels, drinking only boiled or bottled mineral water and avoiding ice.

Nuts and Bolts

India has three main regions: the mountainous Himalayas in the north; the Indo-Gangetic Plain, a flat, hot plain south of the Himalayas; and the Peninsular Shield in the south, where India neighbors Sri Lanka and the Maldives are located. The coldest months are January and February, with sweltering heat between March and May. The southwestern monsoon is from June to September. The post monsoon, or northeast monsoon in the southern peninsula occurs from October to December.

India is hot, dirty and humid throughout most of the year. If you are looking to latch onto some bacteria, India is the place to do it. A 1994 outbreak of pneumonic (not bubonic) plague, a deadly disease spread by breathing, didn't help the tourist business much. Bombay may be the dirtiest city on earth. The hottest months are April to July; the wettest months from June to August.

There are more than 900 million people crammed into India's 3.3 million square kilometers (1.3 million square miles). About 26 percent of India's people live below the poverty line, defined as the resources needed to provide 2100-2400 calories per person per day. About 70 percent of the population lives in the countryside. The official language is Hindi, but English is the second language and is widely spoken. All official documents are in English. In keeping with India's diverse makeup, there are 18 languages recognized for official use in regional areas, of which the most widely spoken are Telugu, Bengali, Marathi, Tamil, Urdu and Gujarati, each with its own script. Hindus do not eat beef. Muslims avoid pork. Sikhs do not smoke. Strict Hindus are also vegetarian and do not drink.

Vegetarian dishes and rice are popular in the south. In the north, meat dishes with unleavened breads are the standard. Popular dishes are *rogan josh* (curried lamb), *gushtaba* (spiced meatballs in yogurt) and *biryani* (chicken or lamb in orange-flavored rice, sprinkled with rose water). *Tandoori*, a marinated meat or fish cooked in a clay tandoori oven is a northern speciality.

Banking Hours: 10:30 a.m.–2:30 p.m., Monday to Friday; 10:30 a.m.–12:30 p.m., Saturday. Business hours: 9:00 a.m.–12:00 p.m., 1:00 p.m.–5:00 p.m., Monday to Friday. Stores are open 9:30 a.m.–6:00 p.m., Monday to Saturday. The workweek is Monday through Friday.

The Rupee (about 31 to the U.S. dollar) is the currency and should be changed only through banks and authorized money changers. Electricity is 220v/50hz.

Embassy Location

The U.S. Embassy is located in the capital city of New Delhi on Shanti Path, Chanakyapuri 110021
☎ *((91-11) 600651*

U.S. Consulates General

In Bombay

U.S. Consulate General
Lincoln House
78 Bhulabhai Desai Road, Bombay 400026
☎ *(91-22) 363-3611*

In Calcutta

U.S. Consulate General

5/1 Ho Chi Minh Sarani, Calcutta 700071
☎ *(91-033) 22-3611 through 22-3615 and 22-2335 through 22-2337*

In Madras

U.S. Consulate General
Mount Road, Madras 600006
☎ *(91-44) 473-040/477-542*

Other useful numbers are

Ministry of Communications

Sanchar Bhawan, New Delhi 110 003
☎ *383600*

Ministry of External Affairs

South Block, New Delhi 110 011
☎ *301-1813*

Ministry of Tourism and Civil Aviation

Parivahan Bhawan, Sansad Marg, New Delhi 100 001
☎ *351700*

Dangerous Days

12/06/1992 Hindu extremists destroyed the 16th-century Muslim mosque at Ayodhya in India's Uttar Pradesh state. The subsequent rioting and Muslim-Hindu clashes that engulfed India, Pakistan, Bangladesh and other nations resulted in over 1000 deaths. Hindus claim the mosque was built on the birth site of the Hindu god Rama, a claim disputed by Muslims.

12/06/1992 Dr. B.R. Ambedkar, revered leader of India's Dalits (untouchables), died and was cremated in Bombay.

05/21/1991 Former prime minister Rajiv Gandhi was assassinated during a campaign rally in Tamil Nadu state.

01/06/1989 Two of Prime Minister Indira Gandhi's Sikh bodyguards were hanged for her assassination on October 31, 1984.

01/03/1989 Muslim Kashmiri militants began their campaign for independence from India.

07/06/1987 Seventy-two Hindus were killed in an attack by Sikh militants on a bus in the Punjab.

04/29/1986 Sikh militants seized the Golden Temple of Amritsar in Punjab and declared the independent state of Khalistan. Expelled by government of India forces the next day.

06/23/1985 A bomb exploded on an Air India flight over the North Atlantic following its departure from Canada, killing all 329 passengers on board. A second bomb exploded at Narita airport in Japan, killing two people. Sikh extremists claimed responsibility for both bombings.

12/03/1984 A chemical leak at Union Carbide's Bhopal plant resulted in 2000 deaths and nearly 150,000 injuries.

10/31/1984 Indian Prime Minister Indira Gandhi was assassinated by her Sikh bodyguards. Anti-Sikh rioting following the assassination resulted in thousands of Sikh deaths throughout India.

08/09/1984 The head of the Indian security forces that stormed the Sikh golden temple of Amritsar was assassinated by Sikh terrorists.

Dangerous Days

06/06/1984   Indian troops stormed the golden temple of Amritsar, killing three hundred Sikhs in the attack.

02/11/1984   Maqbool Butt, founder of the Jammu-Kashmir Liberation Front, was hanged in a New Delhi jail for the 1965 murder of an Indian intelligence agent in Kashmir. Militant Muslims have marked the anniversary of his death with sometimes violent demonstrations in Jammu and Kashmir.

01/26/1950   India's constitution was promulgated and India became a republic within the Commonwealth. (Republic Day is also called Constitution Day.)

01/30/1948   Mahatma Gandhi was assassinated.

08/15/1947   Independence Day.

04/13/1699   Sikh religion was founded in 1699 by Guru Gobind Singh.

07/13/0000   Martyr's day in Kashmir. It commemorates the deaths of Kashmiri nationalists during the British raj.

05/24/0000   Birth of Buddha.

Israel
★★★★

Eye For An Eye

Despite the Israelis need and demand for a homeland, their Arab brethren don't see eye to eye, more like eye for an eye. Despite the peace agreement reached with the PLO, the trading of eyes and teeth between Israel and its numerous enemies continues at unprecedented levels. The increase in terrorist threats against Israel, particularly in the wake of the historic Israeli-Palestinian pact, has turned out to be more than merely the holy smoke of bored car bombers. Since 1988, there has been an upward trend in the number of terrorist incidents: 50 in 1988; 203 in 1989; 197 in 1990; 152 in 1991; 215 in 1992; 240 in 1993; 142 in the first half of 1994. The 1994 quarterly average of 71 incidents is 54 percent higher than the average of 46 incidents per quarter compiled since 1988.

America's checkbook diplomacy convinced Israel and the Palestine Liberation Organization (PLO) to recognize each other's right to exist on September 9, 1994, with the historic signing of a Declaration of Principles by Prime Minister Yitzhak Rabin and PLO Chairman Yasir Arafat. And, it would be fair to say that the increase in attacks, deaths and political violence is escalating due to the intense opposition to the agreement by extremist Palestinian groups such as Hamas.

While most of the world has lauded the pact as the most significant peace agreement in decades, enemies of Israel and Israeli settlers in the Occupied Territories, believing they'd been bought out by the U.S.—which essentially they were—have nothing but revenge in mind for Arafat. These "enemies" include some heavy hitters. Both Abu Nidal of the Fatah Revolutionary Council and Ahmed Jibril, leader of the Popular Front for the Liberation of Palestine–General Command (PFLP-GC), have threatened to assassinate Arafat for treason. George Habash, head of the Damascus-based Popular Front for the Liberation of Palestine (PFLP), said the agreement would, ironically, increase *intifada*, the uprising on the West Bank and the Gaza Strip. So far, he's been right. Right-wing Jewish settlers and Hamas alike have launched terrorist attacks in an attempt to discredit and dissolve the agreement.

Earlier that year, on May 4, 1994, Rabin and Arafat signed a long-awaited pact allowing Palestinians limited self-rule in the Gaza Strip and Jericho. Under the agreement, Israeli forces were withdrawn from designated areas, turning enforcement over to a Palestinian police force. A week later, the first contingent of nearly 150 Palestinian police officers entered the Gaza Strip from Egypt. (The agreement calls for an eventual force of 9000 officers to police what is to become Palestine.) The new cops were greeted with flowers by inhabitants in the Strip. Not so by Hamas and other radical factions.

Watch for an increase in violence in the area—commensurate with the increase since the accords were signed—as these groups are not likely to abandon their opposition to any agreement between Israel and anyone even remotely connected with Islam.

The Scoop

Israel was carved out of Palestine by the British after World War II to provide a home for the Jews. The Arabs who had inhabited the region for hundreds of years were not happy. Not happy at all. Like most colonial border carvings, both sides are still arguing about it. What complicates the situation is that Jerusalem is a holy site for Christians, Jews and Muslims. It's a stew pot, filled with just the right spices and garnishes for one helluva long war. The Israelis' land grabs in Egypt, Jordan, Syria and Lebanon have not made them very popular with their neighbors. Peace agreements with their once bellicose neighbors have cooled things down but Hamas, *Hezbollah*, and their hometown supporters of Iran, Syria and Lebanon aren't just going to forgive and forget. Despite the cultural and scenic attractions of the Holy Land you could end your vacation as a puff of holy smoke. You stand a better chance of being caught in a terrorist attack in Tel Aviv than in most cities of the world.

The Players

The Israeli Military

Without the Israeli army, Israel would cease to exist. A tiny nation with a reputation for striking first, Israel has been on the offensive rather that the defensive for most of its short life. The armed forces total 141,000 personnel including 110,000 conscripts. The army consists of 104,000 personnel including 88,000 conscripts and 598,000 reservists. The navy has 9000 personnel including 3000 conscripts and 300 naval commandos and a further 10,000 reservists. Naval bases are at Haifa, Ashdod and Eilat. The air force totals 28,000 including 19,000 conscripts and a further 37,000 reservists.

The Israelis spent IS15 billion in 1992 (about 20 percent of their entire budget) on defense. Uncle Sam kicks in another US$1.8 billion a year in military aid. Troops are stationed in the occupied zones, throughout the country and along the border with Lebanon, where a security zone is controlled by the South Lebanese Army (SLA); a militia funded by Israel. The military is a big part of any Israeli's life in Israel (unless you are an Arab, Christian or Circassian). Mili-

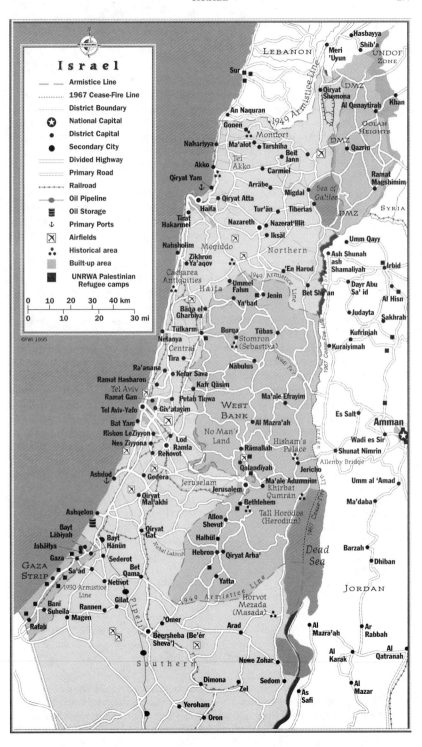

Israel

- —— —— Armistice Line
- ·········· 1967 Cease-Fire Line
- ·········· District Boundary
- ✪ National Capital
- • District Capital
- ● Secondary City
- Divided Highway
- Primary Road
- ⊶⊶⊶⊶⊶ Railroad
- ⊶⊙⊶ Oil Pipeline
- 🗄 Oil Storage
- ↓ Primary Ports
- ⊠ Airfields
- ⁖ Historical area
- Built-up area
- ■ UNRWA Palestinian Refugee camps

0 10 20 30 40 km
0   10   20   30 mi

©FWI 1995

tary service is four years for officers, three years for men and two years for unmarried women. Annual compulsory reserve duty continues up to the age of 54 for men, 24 for single women. Because of the Palestinian *intifada* or uprising, annual compulsory reserve duty was increased to 62 days from 42 days in 1988. Jewish and Druze citizens are conscripted, but Christian, Circassian and Muslim citizens are exempt. However, they're permitted to volunteer.

The military budget was IS12.43 billion in 1990 and IS11.54 billion in 1989. This includes an allocation to cover the Palestinian *intifada* in the Occupied Territories. Troops are also stationed along the border with Lebanon where a security zone is controlled by the South Lebanese Army (SLA). The security zone is designed to prevent guerrilla attacks on the country. In addition, troops are stationed on the Golan Heights. The navy patrols the eastern Mediterranean and the Red Sea. Israel has a strategic cooperation agreement with the U.S.A., signed in 1982.

The fear of an Arab chemical or missile attack has prompted the Israeli government to research and develop increasingly sophisticated weapons. It was the largest foreign participant in the U.S.A.'s Strategic Defence Initiative (SDI). The U.S. paid 80 percent of the cost of the Arrow antimissile system which Israel can use for its own defense. In addition, the navy is developing an interceptor system capable of destroying missiles, ships and aircraft within a 12 km range. An intelligence gathering satellite is being developed and was expected to be operational. The aim of this is to reduce dependence on U.S. intelligence sources. Although it has never been confirmed, Israel is believed to have the capacity to manufacture nuclear weapons.

Hezbollah

The most dangerous terrorist group for Israel is *Hezbollah*, the Iranian backed Shia group that continually battles Israel on their northern border. Under the religious guidance of Sheikh Fadlallah, the most senior cleric in Lebanon, *Hezbollah* members were originally Shiites in the various Palestinian refugee camps. The Israelis conduct numerous retaliatory attacks against these camps in revenge for their shelling and rocketing of Israel.

Shortly after the revolution in Iran, the country began recruiting the most fanatical Shiites to setup its first major military base outside Iran, at Zabadani in Syria. The Iranians sent in about 5000 Pasadaran to Lebanon to help the fight against Israel. A thousand of these troops fought the Israelis in the Shouf mountains. After the fighting ended, 500 Iranians stayed behind in the Bekáa (or Biqáa) Valley under the protection of Syrian forces. The Baalbak area became something of a Silicon Valley for terrorism, where a number of special interest groups lived and trained; from Abu Nidal's headhunters to the Libyans. The Bekáa Valley became the world headquarters for terrorism in 1982. Supplied from Damascus and supported by Iran, these Iranians quickly consolidated their dominance of *Hezbollah*. Soon, *Hezbollah* would become a federation of 13 Islamic terrorist movements (11 Shiite and 2 Sunni). Decisions are made by a religious council. Although Sheikh Sayyid Muhammad Hussein Fadlallah says he is not the movement's leader, it's known that his authority is absolute, even if not secured with a title. He was born in 1943 or 1944 in Najaf, Iraq to a family originally from Lebanon. He rose to prominence after the Iranian revolution. He is an author of two books on Islam: *Islam and the Concept of Power* and *Dialogue in the Koran*. His religious preachings and his political beliefs are one and the same: Jihad is absolute and all encompassing and the war must be fought by whatever means necessary.

Hezbollah's Sayyid Abbas al-Mussawi has vowed that the terrorist group will continue its struggle until the city of Quds (Jerusalem) is liberated.

For more information, see "The Players" section in the Lebanon chapter.

Hamas

Hamas was formed in 1987 in the West Bank as competition to al-Fatah (Arafat's group) for political leadership of the 1.8 million Palestinians in the occupied zones. Currently the group is supported by about 30 percent of the Palestinians in the Gaza Strip and is the second most powerful organization behind Fatah, the PLO's military wing. The *intifada* (which began in the summer of 1988) hardened Hamas into the most ardent and powerful group defending the Palestinians' perceived right to not only self-determination, but to the destruction of Israel. Part of their success strategy is a decentralized structure based on the Muslim Brotherhood, a popular Islamic fundamentalist group, and their ability to work cohesively with the PLO instead of creating internal turmoil as the Israelis had hoped.

One of the leaders of Hamas is Musa Abu Marzuk who is hiding out in Teheran, riding out a shoot to kill order given by Israel after the Tel Aviv bus bombing.

Hamas is short for Harakat al-Muqaama al-Islamiya (Islamic Resistance Movement) but also means zeal or enthusiasm in Arabic. Hamas members are not the well-trained military terrorists of al-Fatah but a youthful cadre of young Palestinians mostly enlisted from the poorest parts of the Occupied Territories. Most believe that they will find salvation and martyrdom by destroying Israel. Every member is sworn to destroy Israel and to create a new Islamic state based on the Koran. Initially their campaign of rock throwing turned to stabbing Israeli citizens, including teenage school children. After Hamas killed five Israeli Defence Force members, 415 Hamas members were exiled to Southern Lebanon by the Israelis, provoking an international outcry. In the seven years of *intifada*, Israelis have killed more than 2000 Palestinians. Hamas has slain more than 575 collaborators and more than 160 Israelis. The attacks have escalated in their frequency and nature, including the recent bombing of a Tel Aviv bus. Hamas is expected to continue to terrorize Israelis into the foreseeable future, and Yasir Arafat and his Palestinian police will be expected to control Hamas, thereby pitting Muslim against Muslim to protect Jews.

Hamas, however, is more of a political party than a military structure. The military wing (Izz ad-Din al Qassam Brigade) is the smallest section of the group, numbering only a few hundred young men. But the group's political followers number in the tens of thousands. Hamas, like *Hezbollah*, has created schools, clinics, mosques and financial support systems for the poor, widows and orphans. The group even sponsors a soccer team. Because of Hamas' political strength and the support it receives from Palestinians, it finds a ready source of financing from Muslim and non-Muslim wallets alike. America is an important source of funding for Hamas. It is alleged by the Israelis that the leadership and central control of Hamas is actually in the United States, an accusation once dismissed by the FBI but now being studied very seriously.

Organizations considered supportive of Hamas in the U.S. are:

The United Association for Studies and Research in Springfield, Virginia.

The Islamic Association for Palestine in Dallas, Texas.

The Monitor and the Al-Zaituni (Olive Tree in Arabic).

The Islamic Committee for Palestine.

Muslim Youth League.

Mostazafan Foundation in New York.

Muslim Students' Association in U.S. and Canada.

Al-Da'wa (the Call).

Jundulah (Soldiers of God)

It is important to note that the Qassam Brigade and militant Palestinians will continue to attack, murder and terrorize Israelis while the political structuring continues. Volunteers to the Qassam Brigade are trained in Sudanese camps and in Southern Lebanon by *Hezbollah*. The Iranians provide over US$30 million a year, including use of a radio station in southern Lebanon which broadcasts messages of revolution into Israel. The Hamas base of power is in the West Bank and Gaza Strip. They have managed to create an alliance of the 10 Palestinian groups including the PLFP and the DFLP. The leadership of Hamas is young and highly educated. Hamas runs information offices out of Amman, Jordan (Ibrahim Ghosha and Mohammed Nazzal); Teheran; Lebanon(Mustapha Kanua), and Khartoum(Mohammed Siam). Their U.S. rep (Moussa Abu Marzouk) operates out of Damascus.

Yasir Arafat and The PLO (Palestine Liberation Organization)

The PLO began in 1964 as a Palestinian nationalist umbrella organization dedicated to the establishment of an independent Palestinian state. After the 1967 Arab-Israeli war, control of the PLO went to the most dominant of the various *fedayeen* militia groups, the most dominant of which was Yasir Arafat's al-Fatah. In 1969, Arafat became chairman of the PLO's executive committee, a position he still holds. In the early 1980s, the PLO became fragmented into several contending groups but remains the preeminent Palestinian organization. The United States considers the Palestine Liberation Organization to be an umbrella organization that includes several constituent groups and individuals holding differing views on terrorism. At the same time, U.S. policy accepts that elements of the PLO have advocated, carried out, or accepted responsibility for acts of terrorism. PLO chairman Arafat publicly renounced terrorism in December 1988 on behalf of the PLO. The United States considers that all PLO groups, including al-Fatah, Force 17, Hawari Group, PLF and the PFLP, are bound by Arafat's renunciation of terrorism. The U.S.-PLO dialogue was suspended after the PLO failed to condemn the May 30, 1990 PLF attack on Israeli beaches. PLF head Abu Abbas left the PLO executive committee in September 1991; his seat was filled by another PLF member.

In the early 1970s several groups affiliated with the PLO carried out numerous international terrorist attacks. By the mid-1970s, under international pressure, the PLO claimed it would restrict attacks to Israel and the Occupied Territories. Several terrorist attacks were later performed by groups affiliated with the PLO/al-Fatah—including the Hawari group, the Palestine Liberation Front (PLF) and Force 17—against targets inside and outside of Israel.

Formerly the number one bad boy of terrorism, Yasir Arafat and his fashion-conscious wife have gone mainstream. It remains to be seen whether he can be as powerful in peace as he was in war. Arafat's group al-Fatah trained more terrorists and freedom fighters than any other group in the 1960s and 1970s. Running the government of the West Bank, Gaza and Jericho may be more of a challenge than the terrorist battle he fought to get to this position. As Israel withdraws its occupying troops, it will be up to Arafat's group to provide security and management of these impoverished, undeveloped and primitive areas. More importantly, he will be expected to protect the Jewish settlers (or occupiers from the Palestinian point of view) from Hamas.

Perhaps wishful thinking, Arafat feels that economic aid will undermine the Hamas' zeal and build a lasting peace. He doesn't have much choice; a forceful attempt to restrain Hamas will plunge Gaza and Jericho into civil war.

Popular Front for the Liberation of Palestine (PFLP)

George Habash's group of about 800 Palestinians follows a Marxist-Leninist doctrine and disagrees with Arafat's deal with the Israelis. The PFLP lost a lot of steam when Wadi Haddad was taken out in 1978. Qaddafi and Assad provide most of the green for this hard-line group. For more information, see "The Players" section in the Lebanon chapter.

Popular Front for the Liberation of Palestine-General Command (PFLP-GC)

PFLP-GC's leader Ahmad Jabril regarded, and still does, Habash's PFLP as a bunch of wimps, so he and his men split in 1968 to focus on killing and maiming while Habash employed just a little less violence to achieve his ends. Because Jabril was a captain in the Syrian army when Assad was minister of defense at the time Israel took the Golan Heights, it's understandable why the PFLP-GC is tighter with Syria than latex on an aerobics instructor. The PFLP-GC is headquartered in Damascus. Iran chips in when they run short of funds.

The group's sensationalist suicide attacks, employing everything from hang gliders to hot-air balloons, has given its "airline" the fewest number of members of any frequent flyer program found in Palestine. Although not as large as the vanilla-flavored PFLP, the PFLP-GC is still a major threat to Israelis. For more information, see "The Players" section in the Lebanon chapter.

Palestine Liberation Front

This is a break-away faction of the PFLP-GC (which is a break-away faction of the PFLP, which is a break-away faction of the PLO). If this sounds like a scene from Monty Python's *Life of Brian* you're not far off. The PLF is led by Abu Abbas, or Muhammad Abbas, who is either hanging out in Libya with his buddy Qaddafi or in Iraq with Hussein. Abbas' group is tiny, possibly nonexistent. Their most famous job was the attack on the *Achille Lauro* and the less than admirable killing of wheelchair-bound Leon Klinghoffer. For more information, see "The Players" section in the Lebanon chapter.

Democratic Front for the Liberation of Palestine (DFLP)

The Hawatmeh faction does not go along with the Arafat-brokered peace and continues their opportunistic attacks and raids. For more information, see "The Players" section in the Lebanon chapter.

Israeli Extremists

There are random incidents of far right-wing Israelis and external Jewish groups such as the Kahane Chai and Kach, as well as individuals striking against Palestinians. These groups present little danger to Americans.

Getting In

Warning

The Department of State advises all American citizens to avoid travel to East Jerusalem, the West Bank and the Gaza Strip at this time due to the violence stemming from the murders of Palestinians in Hebron on February 25, 1994. However, current security conditions do not preclude the travel of U.S. citizens to the immediate vicinity of the U.S. Consulate General facility at 27 Nablus Road, East Jerusalem, for the purpose of obtaining consular services. For detailed information on areas of instability in Israel, as well as the West Bank, Gaza Strip and East Jerusalem, refer to the appropriate paragraphs in this chapter.

Ben Gurion International Airport is 20 km from the center of Tel Aviv. Taxis are common and a bus service runs every 15 minutes. A passport, an onward or return ticket and proof of sufficient funds are required. A three-month visa may be issued for no charge upon arrival and may be renewed. Anyone who has been refused entry or experienced difficulties with his/her visa status during a previous visit can obtain information from the Israeli embassy or nearest consulate regarding the advisability of attempting to return to Israel. Arab-Americans who have overstayed their tourist visas during previous visits to Israel or in the Occupied Territories can expect, at a minimum, delays at ports of entry (including Ben Gurion airport) and the possibility of being denied entry. To avoid these problems, such persons may apply for permission to enter at the nearest Israeli embassy or consulate before traveling. For further entry information, travelers may contact:

Embassy of Israel

3514 International Drive, NW
Washington, D.C. 20008
☎ *(202) 364-5500*

Contact the nearest Israeli Consulate General in Los Angeles, San Francisco, Miami, Atlanta, Chicago, New Orleans, Boston, New York, Philadelphia or Houston.

Getting Around

The major airport is Ben Gurion International Airport with a smaller civilian airport in Tel Aviv. There are also airports in Jerusalem, Haifa, Eilat, Herzlya, Mahanayim and Sodom. A new airport at Eilat is under construction and will replace the old one. National airline El Al operates international flights to Europe, North America and some African countries. Its fleet consists of five *Boeing 747-200B*, two *B747-200B Combi*, one *B747-200F*, one *B747-100F*, three *B757-200*, two *B737-200* and four *B767-200* aircraft.

Israel has a modern road system although it abounds with crazy drivers. In 1988 the paved road network was 12,980 km, including 3995 km of intercity roads of which 284 km were motorways. Road accidents have been on the increase in the last decade, due mainly to deteriorating road conditions. The Israeli cabinet has, on several occasions, pledged to improve road safety. There are approximately three fatalities for every 100 million km traveled.

The rail system is operated by Israel State Railways under the supervision of the Israel Ports and Railways Authority. The length of the main lines is 528 km and secondary lines and sidings total 337 km. The main passenger service is between Tel Aviv and Haifa, with some trains continuing to Nahariya in the north. The government has been building a rapid railway service between Netanya and Tel Aviv to solve the traffic congestion in northern Tel Aviv. In addition, the railway line south is being extended to the Red Sea port of Eilat.

Hassles with Police

Israel has strict security measures that may affect visitors. Prolonged questioning and detailed searches may take place at the time of entry and/or departure at all points of entry to Israel or the Occupied Territories. American citizens with Arab surnames may expect close scrutiny at Ben Gurion airport and the Allenby Bridge from Jordan. For security reasons, delays or obstacles in bringing in or departing with cameras or electronics equipment are not unusual. Items commonly carried by travelers such as toothpaste, shaving cream and cosmetics may be confiscated or destroyed for security reasons, especially at the Allenby Bridge. During searches and questioning, access may be denied to U.S. consular officers, lawyers or family members. Should questions arise at the Allenby Bridge, U.S. citizens can telephone the U.S. Consulate General in Jerusalem for assistance at ☎ *(02) 253-288.* If questions arise at Ben Gurion Airport, U.S. citizens can phone the U.S. Embassy in Tel Aviv at ☎ *(03) 517-4338.*

Broadcasting and the Press

Under the military censorship system covering defense and security matters, journalists are required at all times to submit all relevant items to the censor's office for approval before transmitting them abroad or issuing them in the local media. The occupied territories are officially open to media coverage, except that local commanders may close specific areas for a limited period "for operational reasons." Since the *intifada* began in the occupied West Bank and Gaza Strip in 1988, censorship, closures, arrests, detentions and distribution restrictions have muzzled Palestinian newspapers; those that can still publish are virtually unable to use original material. Various measures were also enforced on newspapers in Israel and on foreign media correspondents, most of whom are Israeli citizens. The army has sometimes imposed a virtual news blackout. The media has regularly complained about security forces personnel impersonating journalists in order to obtain information about the Palestinian *intifada* and journalists claim it puts their lives at risk.

Israel Television and Israel Radio are owned by the government and run by the Israel Broadcasting Authority (IBA). Its central committee members oversee programming. Israel TV broadcasts on one national channel in Hebrew and Arabic, funded by viewer license fees and, more recently, by commercial sponsorship. The government plans to set up an independent commercial second channel. The IBA is a member of the European Broadcasting Union (EBU) and receives its satellite feeds. There were 1.18 million television sets and 2.07 million radio receivers in use in 1988.

Israel Radio broadcasts nationally on five stations, one of which is in Arabic. External Services broadcast in Hebrew, easy Hebrew, Arabic, Moghrabi, English, French, Russian, Spanish, Portuguese, Amharic, Bukharian, Georgian, Persian, Hungarian, Romanian, Yiddish and Ladino. The Soviet Union used to jam Israel Radio's international broadcasts, especially the Russian language service, but this stopped in November 1988.

Dangerous Places

The Occupied Territories

Following the killings of Palestinians in Hebron on February 25, 1994, the Israeli government closed the West Bank and Gaza Strip. The West Bank has since been partially reopened. Travel restrictions may be reimposed with little or no advance notification, and curfews placed on cities or towns in the occupied territories may be extended or, if lifted, reimposed. Palestinian demonstrations in the West Bank and the Gaza Strip have led to violent confrontations between the demonstrators and Israeli authorities, resulting in the wounding or death of some participants. Demonstrations and similar incidents can occur without warning. Stone-throwing and other forms of protest can escalate. Violent incidents such as stabbings have occurred. Vehicles are regularly damaged.

Northern Israel

See "Rocket Attacks."

East Jerusalem

Although the Department of State has warned all U.S. citizens against traveling to East Jerusalem, the West Bank and Gaza, the Consular Section of the U.S. Consulate General at 27 Nablus Road, East Jerusalem, remains open. While conditions in parts of East Jerusalem have been volatile, the Consular Section of the U.S. Consulate General is only one block from the major north/south highway. The facility is easily accessible by taxi or private vehicle and is guarded both by private security guards and Israeli police. Current security conditions in the immediate vicinity of the Consular Section do not preclude the travel of U.S. citizens to the Nablus Road facility for the purpose of obtaining consular services. Traveling by public or private transportation in parts of East Jerusalem less frequented by tourists, however, remains dangerous. If, despite the above warnings against such travel, persons must travel to other areas of East Jerusalem, including the Old City, or to the West Bank, they may consult with the U.S. Consulate General in Jerusalem, and in the case of travel to the Gaza Strip, with the U.S. Embassy in Tel Aviv, for current information on the advisability of such travel.

Dangerous Things

Buses

In the past, several violent incidents have involved buses and bus stops. For this reason, the U.S. Embassy is advising its employees and American citizens in Israel to avoid use of public transportation, especially buses and bus stops. This restriction does not apply to tour buses. It is useful for U.S. citizens to carry their U.S. passport at all times.

Driving

Traffic fatalities increased from 387 in 1985 to 415 in 1986 and to about 500 in 1987. In 1986 there were 1.5 motor vehicles involved in road accidents per 1 million km travelled. There are 3.2 fatalities for every 100 million km traveled.

Rocket Attacks

Rocket attacks from *Hezbollah* positions in Lebanese territory can occur without warning close to the northern border of Israel.

Land Mines

In the Golan Heights, there are live land mines in many areas and some minefields have not been clearly marked or fenced. Visitors who walk only on established roads or trails reduce the risk of injury from mines.

Being arrested in the West Bank and Gaza Strip

U.S. citizens arrested or detained in the West Bank or Gaza Strip on suspicion of security offenses often are not permitted to communicate with consular officials, lawyers or family members in a timely manner during the interrogation period of their case. Youths who are over the age of fourteen have been detained and tried as adults. The U.S. Embassy is not normally notified of the arrests of Americans in the West Bank by Israeli authorities and access to detainees is frequently delayed.

Getting Sick

Medical care and facilities throughout Israel are generally excellent. In 1987, there were 153 hospitals, including 60 private hospitals, with 27,500 beds. Israel has one of the highest doctor/patient ratios in the world, about one doctor for every 339 patients. Travelers can find information in English about emergency medical facilities and after-hours pharmacies in the *Jerusalem Post* newspaper. Doctors and hospitals often expect immediate cash payment for services. U.S. medical insurance is not always valid outside the United States. Supplemental medical insurance with specific overseas coverage has proved useful. Water is normally safe to drink but bottled water is a better choice for the cautious. Tap water outside the main towns is not safe for drinking.

Nuts & Bolts

Israel is a small country, about 20,700 square km (7992 square miles), that forcibly occupies the Golan Heights (annexed from Syria in 1981; 1150 square km, 444 square miles), the West Bank (annexed from Jordan; 5878 square km, 2270 square miles) and the Gaza Strip (363 square km, 140 square miles). The territories currently occupied and administered by Israel are the West Bank, Gaza Strip, Golan Heights and East Jerusalem. The Israeli Ministry of Defense administers the Occupied Territories of the West Bank and Gaza Strip. In 1993, 65 Israelis were killed and 390 wounded; 14 Palestinians were killed by Israeli citizens; 83 Palestinians were killed by other Palestinians. In 1992, Fatah and Hamas were going at it and managed to kill 200 Palestinians between them.

The population includes 635,000 Muslims, 105,000 Christians (almost all Arabs) and 78,000 Druze. Mass immigration of Jews from the former Soviet Union since late 1989 has swelled the population. Although Israel claims Jerusalem as its capital, the claim—especially to East Jerusalem, annexed in 1967—is disputed by most countries. The currency is the new shekel (IS), with 100 agorot to the shekel. The weather is arid, warm and mild most of the year with hot days and cool evenings. Because of its higher elevation, Jerusalem is quite cool, and even cold in the winter. In Tel Aviv and along the coast the weather is more humid with warmer nights.

The Jewish Sabbath, from Friday dusk until Saturday dusk, is rigorously observed. Stores close on Friday by 2 p.m. and do not open again until Sunday morning. Most cinemas and restaurants are closed on Friday night. In most cities during the Sabbath there is no public transport (except for taxis), postal service or banking service. It is considered a violation of the Sabbath (Saturdays) to smoke in public places such as restaurants and hotels. The same is true on the six main Jewish religious holidays.

Jewish religious laws (*Kashrut*) prohibit the mixing of milk products and meat at the same meal. Kashrut is strictly enforced in hotels. Because of this, some restaurants serve only fish and dairy dishes while others serve only meat dishes. Pork is banned under religious laws, but some restaurants serve it, listing it euphemistically as white steak.

Banks are open from 8:30 a.m. to 12:30 p.m., and from 2:00 p.m. to 6:30 p.m. on Sunday, Tuesday and Thursday, and from 8:30 a.m. to 12:30 p.m. on Monday, Wednesday and Friday. Businesses are open from 8:30 a.m. to 7:30 p.m. Sunday to Thursday; some are open 8:30 a.m. to 2:30 p.m. on Fridays. Government offices are open from 7:30 a.m. to 4:00 p.m. Sunday through Thursday.

Registration

U.S. citizens who register at the U.S. Embassy in Tel Aviv or the U.S. Consulate General in Jerusalem can obtain updated information on travel and security within Israel and the Occupied Territories.

Embassy and Consulate Location

U.S. Embassy
> *71 Hayarkon Street*
> *Tel Aviv, Israel*
> *U.S. mailing address*

PSC 98, Box 100
APO AE 09830
☎ *(972-3) 517-4338*

U.S. Consulate General

27 Nablus Road
Jerusalem
U.S. mailing address
PSC 98, Box 100
APO AE 09830
☎ *(972-2) 253-288 (via Israel)*
☎ *(972-2) 253-201 (after hours)*

U.S. Consular Agent, Jonathan Friedland, in Haifa

12 Jerusalem Street
Haifa 33132
☎ *(972-4) 670-615*

Useful Addresses

Central Bureau of Statistics

Hakirya, Romema, Jerusalem
☎ *2-553553*
FAX 2-553325

Federation of Israeli Chambers of Commerce

PO Box 20027, 84 Hahashmonaim Street
Tel Aviv 67011
☎ *5612444*
FAX 5612614

Ministry of Communications

PO Box 29515
Tel Aviv
☎ *3-5198247*
FAX 2-5198109

Ministry of Trade and Industry

Palace Buildings
PO Box 299, 30 Agron Boulevard
Jerusalem 91002
☎ *2-750111*
FAX 2-253407

Ministry of Tourism

24 King George Street
PO Box 1018
Jerusalem 91000
☎ *2-754811*
FAX 2-253407 or 2-250890

Dangerous Days

10/11/1994	The Palestine Liberation Organization (PLO) Central Council approved Chairman Yasir Arafat's peace deal with Israel by a vote of 63 to eight, with 11 members abstaining or absent.
09/23/1994	Yom Kippur.
09/13/1994	Israel and the Palestinian Liberation Organization signed a peace agreement in Washington, D.C., outlining a plan for Palestinian self-rule in the Israeli Occupied Territories.
09/09/1993	The PLO and Israel signed a mutual recognition agreement.

Dangerous Days

12/17/1992	More than 400 suspected members of Hamas were forcibly expelled from Israel into Lebanon following the kidnap-murder of an Israeli border policeman. The expellees were refused entry into Lebanon and were forced to camp in the Israeli controlled security zone in south Lebanon.
12/16/1991	The United Nations General Assembly repealed the 1975 resolution which said Zionism is a form of racism.
10/30/1991	The first round of Arab-Israeli peace talks began in Madrid, Spain.
05/15/1991	Palestinian Struggle Day.
01/15/1991	Abu Iyad, the second ranking PLO leader, and two other high ranking PLO officials were assassinated by a guard suspected of working for the Abu Nidal Organization (ANO).
10/08/1990	Eighteen Arabs died during clashes with police at the Temple Mount religious site.
05/20/1990	A lone Israeli gunman killed eight Arab laborers in Rishon le Ziyyon, south of Tel Aviv. Nine workers were injured. The gunman was identified as a discharged Israeli soldier.
07/28/1989	Israeli commandos seized Shaykh Obeid from a village in southern Lebanon and detained him in Israel on allegations of involvement in terrorist activity on behalf of *Hezbollah*.
12/09/1987	Date used to mark the beginning of the *intifada* or uprising on the West Bank and the Gaza Strip.
10/01/1985	The Israeli Air Force bombed the headquarters of the Palestinian Liberation Organization (PLO) in Tunis.
05/17/1983	Israel signed an accord with Lebanon for the withdrawal of Israeli troops from most of south Lebanon.
06/06/1982	Israel invaded Lebanon.
06/04/1982	Israeli planes bombed Beirut.
06/03/1982	Abu Nidal terrorists critically injured the Israeli ambassador to the United Kingdom in an attack in London. The government of Israel used the incident as a pretext for launching the invasion of Lebanon in the "Peace for Galilee" operation.
06/06/1981	Israeli warplanes attacked an Iraqi nuclear power plant near Baghdad.
02/19/1980	Egypt sends first ambassador to Israel.
05/15/1979	The Arab 15 May Organization under Muhammad al-Umari was founded from the remnants of Wadi Haddad's Popular Front for the Liberation of Palestine-Special Operations Group (PFLP-SOG). The group was headquartered in Baghdad until it disbanded in 1984-1985.
03/26/1979	Egyptian-Israeli peace treaty.
09/17/1978	Camp David accords signed.
03/16/1978	Israel forces invade Lebanon.

Dangerous Days

07/04/1976	The Israeli raid on Entebbe airport in Uganda freed 103 hostages from a hijacked Israeli airliner.
03/30/1976	Land day protests by Israeli Arabs against alleged expropriation of Arab property.
12/21/1973	Geneva Peace Conference opens.
10/06/1973	The Yom Kippur War begins.
12/28/1972	Black September terrorists took hostages after seizing the Israeli embassy in Bangkok. The hostages were released in exchange for safe conduct.
09/06/1972	Palestinian Black September terrorists massacred Israeli athletes at the Munich Olympics.
05/30/1972	Members of the Japanese Red Army (JRA) killed 26 people in a massacre at Lod Airport.
02/21/1970	Suspected members of the PFLP-GC placed a bomb on a Swissair passenger jet enroute from Zurich to Tel Aviv resulting in the death of all 47 passengers.
07/22/1968	Members of the Popular Front for the Liberation of Palestine (PFLP) hijacked an El Al flight enroute to Tel Aviv and forced it to land in Algiers. The attack marked the first aircraft hijacking by a Palestinian group. The hijackers were said to have believed Israeli General Ariel Sharon was on the flight. The passengers and crew were detained by Algeria for six weeks.
06/05/1967	The Six Day War ends.
05/31/1967	Israeli troops captured East Jerusalem in the Six Day War.
01/01/1964	Fatah Day. The Palestine Liberation Organization (PLO) was founded at a meeting in Jerusalem.
04/14/1949	Holocaust Memorial Day.
03/21/1949	Palestinian Solidarity Day. Arab solidarity day with the Palestinian people against Israel.
01/07/1949	A cease-fire was signed by the major combatants ending the first Arab-Israeli war.
05/14/1948	Israel was proclaimed a state as the British mandate in Palestine expired. Arab armies launched attacks on Israel immediately following the proclamation.
05/14/1948	The first Arab-Israeli war began shortly after the State of Israel was proclaimed.
05/07/1948	Israeli Independence Day as observed by Arabs in the Occupied Territories.
11/02/1917	Anniversary of the Balfour Declaration which promised a Jewish homeland in Palestine. Demonstrations in the Occupied Territories and the Gaza Strip area have occurred on this date.

The UZI

The UZI is the brainchild of Israeli designer Major Uziel Gal, borrowing heavily from Czech Model 23 and 25. The Uzi is designed to spray a room with bullets or be used as an infantry weapon. The 9mm version has a rate of fire of 10 bullets per second. The magazine inserts through the pistol grip and the UZI comes in 16"-long barrel or ultra-compact machine pistol size. The UZI is also a favorite of the Secret Service. Originally designed for 9mm NATO standard ammunition, the UZI was manufactured in a more powerful .45 calibre format for the U.S. market. Magazines come in 20-, 25-, and 32-round capacity (the .45 calibre version comes in a meager 16-round capacity).

Lebanon
★★

Hell's Boot Camp

If God created a training ground for the Armageddon, Beirut would be the stage. Once called the Paris of the Mediterranean, it's more like bullet-riddled plaster of Paris. No longer vibrant but tired, the shattered ruins of Western development and Eastern tradition stand broken, sad and dead.

Populated and run by tribes of fanatical gangs, the realities of Beirut would challenge even the most creative scriptwriter. Religion, drugs, war, love and death all interact in this biblical epic of death and destruction. Beirut has been incinerated by the heat of Judeo/Arabic hate. The one true god has surfaced and has remained unshakable: The U.S. dollar, now the formal currency of this land with no people. Beirut is trying to shake itself off and evolve from its 12th-century feudalism into the 20th century. Someone, though, needs to inform the fanatics.

For 15 years, from 1975 to 1990, Lebanon was plunged into a civil war that violently divided the country into regions controlled by religious and ethnic factions, including Sunni, Shiite and Druse Muslims and Maronite Christians. A central government in Lebanon was one in name only.

The war was fueled by the belief that the 1943 National Pact that had determined the distribution of power between Christians and Muslims and among the different Muslim sects, no longer reflected the nation's ethnic and religious demographics. The presence of foreign soldiers and militias from such countries as Syria, with territorial ambitions in Lebanon, only made the situation worse, not to mention those whose real ambitions were to slash Israel's throat at the jugular.

Introduced by Muslim leaders and Syrian officials and approved by the surviving members of the legislature, the 1989 Taif Agreement reestablished a central and legitimate government in Lebanon. The larger Muslim population was reflected in an increased number of seats in the National Assembly. De facto leader General Michel Aoun, however, refused to accept the Taif agreement and remained in power until he was ousted by factional Lebanese Army units and Syrian forces in October 1990.

Although a number of Maronite Christians boycotted the polls, Lebanon conducted its first legislative elections in 20 years in the Fall of 1992. The assembly has 128 members. The Taif accord stipulated that half the membership of the National Assembly chamber should be Muslim and the other half Christian, altering the 5:6 ratio that had existed previously.

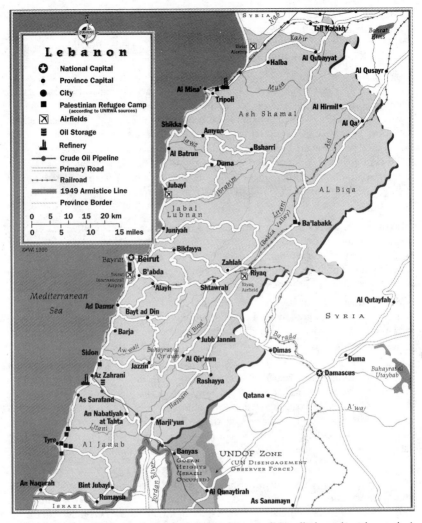

The majority of Lebanon's political parties have traditionally been based on ethnic and denominational differences, namely because seats in the National Assembly are distributed on the basis of religion as opposed to politics. For instance, the al-Amal (Movement of the Deprived) is a Shiite Muslim party that was allied with left-wing Palestinian forces during the civil war. It now spends a good portion of its time protecting the position of Shiite Muslims forced out of their homes by fighting among rival pro-Palestinian forces and between those forces and Israeli-backed forces in the south. And Hizb al-Ahrar al-Watani—Parti National Liberal (NLP, or National Liberal Party) refuses to join with any Muslim groups that are linked to Palestinians or Palestinian independence. Of course, the militant Shiite group, al Jihad al-Islami (Islamic Jihad or Holy War) has claimed responsibility for a number of kidnappings of foreigners in Lebanon, as well as other terrorist acts, including the 1983 Beirut bombings in which 300 U.S. Marines and French troops were killed.

In all, there were 330 attacks on Israeli and South Lebanon Army (ASL) troops in 1993 compared to 170 in 1992. Iran, especially, likes to recruit terrorists from among the Lebanese. Prime for the picking are the Hamade, Tleiss, Bdreddine, Kassem, Yazbeck, Berjaoui and Ammar. They are then sent to the Iman Ali school north of Teheran.

However, Beirut, as is much of Lebanon, is again reaching out to the world—and Western tourists and business people are beginning to trickle back in. Lebanon's rebirth can be evidenced by the opening of tourist offices in London and other Western European capital cities. Some estimates reveal that more than US$400 million has been raised by billionaire businessman and Lebanese prime minister Rafik Hariri to rebuild central Beirut. Some major hotel chains, including Marriott and Inter-Continental, are exploring either opening or reopening hotels in Beirut. There's even mention of Beirut hosting the Arab Tourist Year conference.

We'll see.

Lebanon has indeed made progress toward rebuilding. In Lebanon, armed militias are slowly disappearing and the dreaded *Hezbollah* now limit their activities mainly to the southern part of the country.Under the Taif accord, the Lebanese have created a more equitable political scheme, particularly by giving Muslims a greater say in the political process. Most of the militias are gone or they've become phenomenally weak.

Massive quantities of arms used by the militias and terrorist groups during the civil war have been confiscated by the Lebanese Armed Forces (LAF). Government authority actually extends over about half the country, although nearly 30,000 Syrian troops still refuse to move from Beirut. Damascus says this is due to the weakness of the LAF.

Israel continues to support a proxy militia, the SLA (Southern Lebanese Army), near its border. About 1000 Israeli soldiers and 3000 ASL militiamen patrol the 15-km wide security zone established in 1985 against anti-Israeli guerrillas as Israel withdrew the bulk of its 1982 Lebanon invasion force. But they're still playing rocket volleyball in the south on a weekly basis. Syrian troops are based principally in Beirut, North Lebanon and the Bekaa Valley. Syria's deployment was legitimized by the Arab League early in Lebanon's civil war and also in the Taif accord.

Lebanon—Travel Warning: August 31, 1993

The United States Department of State warns all U.S. citizens against travel to Lebanon. The situation in Lebanon is so dangerous that no U.S. citizen can be considered safe from terrorist acts. While all known American hostages have been released, the organizations which abducted them continue to operate within the country. U.S. passports are not valid for travel to, in or through Lebanon unless special validation has been obtained. Due to an extremely limited staff and heightened security, the U.S. Embassy in Beirut cannot perform normal consular functions. In addition, local telephone service is highly unreliable and it is extremely difficult to contact the embassy by phone or to place a local call from most of the country.

Intermediate Stops in Beirut

Several international air carriers are now making intermediate stops in Beirut. U.S. citizens are advised not to board such flights because of the danger of traveling to, or transiting through Lebanon. Such stops are not always announced. Travelers should therefore inquire, before making travel arrangements in the region, whether a flight will make a stop in Beirut. U.S. passports are not valid for travel to, in or through Lebanon, which includes landing at the Beirut airport, unless specifically endorsed by the Secretary of State.

The Scoop

The Republic of Lebanon is getting back to normal. However, the south remains a war zone. The country is emerging from two decades of civil war which has seriously damaged the economy and the social fabric. The population is composed of both Christians and Muslims from a variety of sects.

The Players

Few screenwriters or playwrights could create a cast of characters and dramas as complex as the terrorist groups in Lebanon. Forged by a lawless society, nurtured by Syria and Iran, supported by drug and oil money and hardened by Israeli intolerance, the terrorist factions in Lebanon have worldwide reach and are responsible for much of the pain, death and suffering caused by terrorist acts since the early '80s.

Hezbollah

Founded in Lebanon in 1982. *Hezbollah* means Party of God or Army of God depending on how militant you are. The name comes from the torture/murder of a young *mullah* in Qom, Iran in 1973. His last words were that there is only one party, the party of God. They are an Iranian-backed organization that polarizes the plight of Muslims into Muslim versus The Great Satan. The Great Satan can be Israel or America depending on expediency. *Hezbollah* is a political machine as well as a terrorist organization. This group has been responsible for some of the most well-known acts of terrorism in the last 15 years, including the bombing of the U.S. Marine barracks in 1983, the hijacking of the TWA flights, the frequent kidnapping of Western hostages in Beirut and the car bombing of the Israeli embassy in Buenos Aires, Argentina in 1992 that killed 56 people.

Probably the most dangerous and most widespread terrorist organization in the world. Under the direct control of Teheran *Hezbollah*, the group seems to be the most successful in following in the steps of Mohammed by combining religious, political and military fanaticism to spread the cause of fundamentalist Islamic belief. Not content with waging war with the world, *Hezbollah* is undergoing some serious infighting. In February, two rival *Hezbollah* clans shot it out in the Baalbeck, reflecting the differing beliefs of hard-liner Nasrallah and pro-Syrian Sobhi el -Tufaili. The Syrian army intervened before they could kill each other off. There is a move to replace the Secretary General Hassan Nasrallah with *Hezbollah's* spiritual leader, Mohammed Hussein Fadlallah, as well as moves to replace others who believe that the less militant Sheikh Ibrahi Assayed is better suited to the political role the group is gradually adopting.

Today, *Hezbollah* limits its campaign of terror to the very southern part of Lebanon. Recent events in Brazil and Argentina, and recruitment drives among Algerians in Europe lead us to believe that they are directing their activities toward a more global scale where there is little fear of direct retaliation.

Hezbollah has been involved in numerous anti-U.S. terrorist attacks, including the suicide truck bombing of the U.S. Marine barracks in Beirut in October, 1983 and the U.S. Embassy annex in September 1984. Elements of the group are responsible for the kidnapping of most, if not all,U.S. and other Western hostages in Lebanon. The military wing is estimated to have 5000 members.

Hezbollah operates in the Bekáa Valley, the southern suburbs of Beirut and in southern Lebanon and has established cells in western Europe, Africa and elsewhere. The group has claimed responsibility for attacks as far afield as Argentina. It receives substantial amounts of training, financial aid, weapons, explosives, as well as political, diplomatic and organizational assistance from the Islamic Republic of Iran.

They want to establish a revolutionary Shi'a state in Lebanon, modeled after Iran, eliminate non-Islamic influences, force Western interests out of the region and of course become Lebanon's principal Islamic movement with close ties to Iran.

The *Hezbollah* is a political, social and military organization that seeks to achieve in Lebanon what the Muslims achieved in Iran. It espouses an intense hatred of any influence that does not support its views of Shi'a ideology. The movement was born from the merger of Sheikh Husayn Musawi's Islamic Amal and the Lebanese branch of the Da'wa party in 1982-83. It should be noted that Sheikh Musawi was killed in early 1992 in southern Lebanon in an Israeli attack on his motorcade. Three area councils—Beirut, the Bekáa Valley, and southern Lebanon—oversee activities in their respective regions. A series of functional committees play roles in policy recommendation and execution. A consultative council (*shura*) functions as the principal governing body on day-to-day matters but actually exists to advise Iran on the unique situation of the Islamic movement in Lebanon. *Hezbollah* elements receive training in the Bekáa Valley of eastern Lebanon. Through this connection, Iranian revolutionary guardsmen provide political indoctrination, financing and material support. The *Hezbollah* and the revolutionary guards work together on terrorist operations. The group itself seldom claims responsibility for specific acts, but does so under a variety of aliases.

Unlike most terrorist groups that come and go like Midwest thunderstorms, *Hezbollah* is a real and long-term political force in the Middle East. A list of their attacks is enough to convince anyone that they are not juvenile delinquents bent on revenge.

Date	Action
April 1983	Carried out suicide car-bomb attack on the U.S. Embassy in Beirut, killing 49 and wounding 120. Islamic Jihad claimed responsibility.
October 1983	Suicide drivers drove two trucks carrying high explosives into the U.S. Marine and French military barracks in Beirut, killing 241 U.S. and 56 French soldiers. Islamic Jihad claimed responsibility.
November 1983	A *Hezbollah* operative drove a car bomb into the Israeli headquarters in Tyre, causing numerous casualties.
December 1983	Staged a series of car bomb attacks against the U.S. and French embassies in Kuwait.
January 1984	Murdered American University of Beirut President Malcolm Kerr, a U.S. citizen. Islamic Jihad claimed responsibility.
January 1984	Kidnapped a Saudi diplomat; released him in May 1985.
February 1984	Believed responsible for the assassination of former Iranian General Gholam Reza Oveisi (martial law administrator for Teheran under the Shah) and his brother in Paris.
February 1984	Kidnapped U.S. Professor Frank Reiger; rescued April 1984.
March 1984	Kidnapped U.S. journalist Jeremy Levin; escaped February 1985.
March 1984	Kidnapped William Buckley, a U.S. diplomat stationed in Beirut. He was reported killed in 1985. Islamic Jihad claimed responsibility. Buckley's remains were returned to the U.S. Embassy in December 1991.
May 1984	Kidnapped Reverend Benjamin Weir, a U.S. citizen; released him in September 1985.
September 1984	Carried out suicide truck-bombing of the U.S. Embassy annex in east Beirut. Twenty three persons, including two Americans, were killed. Islamic Jihad claimed responsibility.

Date	Action
December 1984	Hijacked Kuwait Air flight #221 to Teheran. Murdered two officials of the U.S. Agency for International Development.
January 1985	Kidnapped Father Lawrence Jenco, U.S. citizen; released him in July 1986. Islamic Jihad claimed responsibility.
March 1985	Kidnapped Geoffrey Nash, a UK citizen; released him shortly thereafter.
March 1985	Kidnapped Brian Levick, a UK citizen; released him shortly thereafter.
March 1985	Kidnapped AP journalist Terry Anderson, a U.S. citizen. Released him in December 1991.
May 1985	Kidnapped two French citizens; one was killed in March 1986 and the other was subsequently released.
May 1985	Kidnapped David Jacobson, a U.S. citizen and official at American University of Beirut; released him November 1986. Islamic Jihad claimed responsibility.
May 1985	Murder of Dennis Hill, a U.K. Citizen. *Hezbollah* suspected.
June 1985	Kidnapped Thomas Sutherland, a U.S. citizen and official at American University of Beirut; released him in November 1991. Islamic Jihad claimed responsibility.
June 1985	Hijacked TWA flight #847 en route to Athens. U.S. Navy diver Robert Stethem was murdered. *Hezbollah* and Amal held 39 U.S. citizens hostage for 17 days in Beirut before they were released.
July 1985	Islamic Jihad claimed responsibility for the bombings of an airline office and a synagogue in Copenhagen. One person was killed and 26 were injured.
December 1985	Implicated in a series of bombings in Paris.
March 1986	Kidnapped four French television news team members. They were released between June 1986 and November 1987.
September 1986	Kidnapped Frank Reed, U.S. citizen; released April, 1990.
September 1986	Kidnapped U.S. citizen Joseph Cicippio. Released him December 1991.
September 1986	*Hezbollah* suspected in the murder of Colonel Christian Goutierre, French military attache in Beirut.
September 1986	Suspected in a series of Paris bombings.
October 1986	Kidnapped Edward Austin Tracy, a U.S. citizen. Released him August 1991. Revolutionary Justice Organization claimed responsibility.
January 1987	Kidnapped Anglican church envoy Terry Waite. Released him November 1991.

Date	Action
January 1987	Kidnapped Beirut university professors Jesse Turner, Alan Steen, Robert Polhill—U.S. citizens—and M. Singh. Singh was released in October 1988. Turner was released in October 1991, Steen was released in December 1991 and Polhill was released in April 1990. The Organization of the Oppressed of the Earth claimed responsibility.
July 1987	A suspected *Hezbollah* member hijacked an Air Afrique flight between Rome and Paris. The suspect had boarded the flight in Brazzaville. One French citizen was murdered before the hijacker was overpowered by a member of the cabin crew.
February 1988	Kidnapped United Nations military observer and U.S. Marine Lt.Colonel Richard Higgins. Lt. Col. Higgins was subsequently murdered (date unknown). His remains were handed over to the American embassy in Beirut in December 1991.
April 1988	Hijacked Kuwaiti Airways flight #422 en route from Bangkok to Kuwait. Plane initially diverted to Mashad, Iran, then to Cyprus and finally to Algiers. Two hostages were murdered during the incident. The hijackers escaped in Algiers.
October 1990	Islamic Jihad claimed responsibility for a car bombing in Ankara, Turkey which seriously wounded a Saudi diplomat.
November 1990	Islamic Jihad claimed responsibility for the murder of a Saudi diplomat in Beirut.
March 1991	Islamic Jihad claimed responsibility for a car bombing in Ankara, Turkey in which an Iraqi diplomat was injured.
March 1992	Islamic Jihad claimed responsibility for the bombing of the Israeli embassy in Buenos Aires in which 29 people were killed and 252 injured.

Hamas (Islamic Resistance Movement)

Hamas was formed in late 1987 as an outgrowth of the Palestinian branch of the Muslim Brotherhood and has become Fatah's principal political rival in the Occupied Territories. Various elements of Hamas have used both political and violent means, including terrorism, to pursue the goal of establishing an Islamic Palestinian state in place of Israel. Hamas is loosely structured, with some elements working openly through mosques and social service institutions to recruit members, raise money, organize activities, and distribute propaganda. Other elements, operating clandestinely, have advocated and used violence to advance their goals. Hamas' strength is concentrated in the Gaza Strip and in a few areas of the West Bank. It has also engaged in peaceful political activity, such as running candidates in West Bank chamber of commerce elections.

Hamas activists—especially those in the Izz Al-Din Al-Qassem forces—have conducted many attacks against Israeli military and civilian targets, suspected Palestinian collaborators, and Fatah rivals. During 1992, elements of Hamas were responsible for several prominent anti-Israeli attacks, including ambushes of military units in the West Bank and the murder of a member of the Israeli border police in December 1992. Hamas elements increasingly use lethal weapons and tactics—such as firearms, roadside explosive charges and car bombs—in their operations.

It is estimated that there are tens of thousands of supporters and sympathizers. Funding is received from Palestinian expatriates, Iran and private benefactors in Saudi Arabia and other moderate Arab states. Some fund raising and propaganda activity takes place in Western Europe and North America.

Democratic Front for the Liberation of Palestine (DFLP)

The DFLP is a Marxist group that split from the Popular Front for the Liberation of Palestine (PFLP) in 1969. The group is currently led by Nayifhawatmeh. It believes Palestinian goals can only be achieved through a popular revolution. In the early 1980s, the group occupied a political stance midway between Yasir Arafat's and that of the more radical rejectionist groups.

In the 1970s the DFLP carried out numerous small-scale bombings and assaults, and other more spectacular operations, in Israel and the OccupiedTerritories. The group has historically concentrated on striking Israeli targets, such as the 1974 massacre in Ma'alot in which 27 Israelis were killed and more than 100 wounded. Since 1988, the DFLP has been involved in small-scale border raids into Israel and the Occupied Territories. The membership is small (current strength is estimated at only 500). This group seeks revolutionary change in the Arab world, especially in the conservative monarchies, as a necessary precursor to the achievement of Palestinian objectives.

The DFLP is a Marxist-Leninist historically pro-Soviet group and believes that the Palestine national goal cannot be achieved without a revolution of the working class; elite members of the movement should not be separated from the masses, and lower classes first should be educated in true socialism to carry on the battle. At the spring 1977 Palestine National Council meeting, the DFLP gave its full support to the Palestine national program, seeking creation of a Palestinian state from any territory liberated from Israel. In mid-1979, the DFLP reportedly experienced a surge in its membership and an accompanying increase in influence. Although it remained a member of the Executive Committee of the PLO, the DFLP cooperated increasingly with anti-Arafat Palestinian extremists. DFLP terrorist operations have always taken place inside Israel or the Occupied Territories. Typical acts are minor bombings and grenade attacks, as well as spectacular operations intended to seize hostages and negotiate for the return of Israeli-held Palestinian prisoners.

Palestine Liberation Front (PLF)

The PLF is a terrorist group that broke away from the Popular Front for the Liberation of Palestine–General Command (PFLP-GC), in the mid-1970s. It later split again into three factions: one pro-PLO, another pro-Syrian, and the last pro-Libyan. The pro-PLO faction is led by Mohammed Abbas (Abu Abbas), who became a member of the PLO executive committee in 1984, but left the executive committee in 1991.

The Abu Abbas faction of the PLF carried out an abortive seaborne attack staged from Libya against Israel on May 30, 1990. The same group was also responsible for the October 1985 attack on the cruise ship *Achille Lauro* and the murder of U.S. citizen Leon Klinghoffer. A warrant for the arrest of Abu Abbas is outstanding in Italy. The PLF openly supported Iraq during the Persian Gulf War.

There are at least 50 members within the Abu Abbas faction. Other two factions have between 200-250 members. They receive logistic and military support mainly from the PLO, but also from Libya and Iraq. They are working to destroy Israel.

Although originally a part of the Popular Front for the Liberation of Palestine—General Command (PFLP-GC), the PLF was established under Mohammed Abu al Abbas in opposition to PFLP-GC leader Ahmed Jibril's support for the Syrian incursion into Lebanon in June 1976. After unsuccessfully attempting to gain control of the PFLP-GC in September 1976, the PLF was split from the PFLP-GC officially by PLO chairman Yasir Arafat in April 1977. The PLF was established with Iraqi support, and its existence as an independent group was recognized when it obtained seats on the Palestine National Council in 1981 with its headquarters in Damascus. Near the end of 1983, the PLF itself split into factions when Abu Abbas felt that his organization had become too close to Syria. Leaving Damascus, along with many supporters, Abu Abbas went to Tunis to align himself with Arafat and the mainstream Fatah organization. Following the *Achille Lauro* incident, the Abu Abbas faction relocated to Baghdad at the request of the government of Tunisia.The parts of the PLF remaining in Damascus were further split in January 1984 when Abd al-Fatah Ghanem attempted a takeover of the PLF offices and held Tal'at Yaqub, secretary general of the PLF, hostage. Through Syrian intervention, Yaqub was released and Ghanem formed his own faction with ties to Libya. Yaqub's faction joined the Palestine National Salvation Front and is generally aligned with Syria.Operationally, the Abu Abbas faction of the PLF has demonstrated creativity and technical acumen. The group has employed hot air-balloons and hang gliders for airborne operations, and a civilian passenger ship for mounting a seaborne infiltration operation.The *Achille Lauro* hijacking in October 1985—followed by the murder of an elderly American citizen, Leon Klinghoffer—contributed to the international condemnation of Abu Abbas and the PLF. In 1988, the PLF and Yasir Arafat feuded over the PLO's moderating stance on Israel and on the use of terror against Israel. The differences appear to have been overcome when the PLO refused to condemn an attempted attack by the PLF on a Tel Aviv beach.

Popular Front for the Liberation of Palestine-General Command (PFLP-GC)

This group split from the Popular Front for the Liberation of Palestine (PFLP) in 1968, claiming that it wanted to focus more on fighting and less on politics.Violently opposed to Arafat's PLO and led by Ahmed Jibril, a former captain in the Syrian army, this group is closely allied with, supported by, and probably directed by Syria.

The group specializes in suicide operations and has carried out numerous cross-border attacks into Israel, using unusual means, such as hot-air balloons and motorized hang gliders. Hafiz Kassem Dalkamoni, a ranking PFLP-GC official, was convicted in Germany in June 1991 for bombing U.S. troop trains. He faces additional charges in Germany for other terrorist offenses, including manslaughter. It is not known how many current members there are but the more radical factions tend to attract young volunteers at a greater rate than the more moderate.

The PFLP-GC receives logistic and military support from Syria and Iran as well as financial support from Libya. The group is given safe haven in Syria.

Ahmed Jibril formed the Popular Front for the Liberation of Palestine-General Command in 1968 when he became disenchanted with George Habash's leadership of the Popular Front for the Liberation of Palestine (PFLP). An officer in the Syrian army, Jibril was initially interested in developing conventional military capabilities to complement PFLP-GC terrorist activities. As a result, the PFLP-GC has always been known for its military expertise. In addition to ground infiltration capabilities, the PFLP-GC has worked toward developing air and naval striking capabilities as well. PFLP-GC terrorist activities have included the use of letter bombs and conducting major cross-border operations directed at Israeli targets. The PFLP-GC has also shared its terrorist expertise with other international terrorist groups, such as the Armenian Secret Army for the Liberation of Armenia, as well as European groups which have sent members to Lebanon for training.The PFLP-GC arsenal includes sophisticated weaponry such as Soviet SA-7 anti-aircraft missiles, heavy artillery and light aircraft such as motorized hang gliders and ultralights. The Communist Bloc countries provided small arms such as Kalashnikov assault rifles and RPG-7 anti-tank rockets, but Syria and Libya may have served as conduits for such support.The PFLP-GC actively participated in the Lebanese conflict, including sniping attacks that injured U.S. marines who were members of the peacekeeping forces in Beirut in 1982–83. In addition, the group attacked Israeli citizens and interests through operations launched from Lebanon. The PFLP-GC has also occasionally recruited West Bank Palestinians to conduct terrorist operations inside Israel.

Popular Front for the Liberation of Palestine (PFLP)

Marxist-Leninist group that was a member of the Palestine Liberation Organization (PLO). Founded in 1967 by George Habash. After Fatah, the PFLP is the most important political and military organization in the Palestinian movement. The PFLP has spawned several dangerous terrorist groups.

The group committed numerous acts of international terrorism between 1970 and 1977. Since the death in 1978 of Wadi Haddad, the PFLP's operational planner of terrorism, the group has carried out less frequent but continued attacks against Israeli and moderate Arab targets.

The group of about 800 men receives most of its financial and military aid from Syria and Libya. The PFLP is trying to create a Palestine in the manner of a Marxist-Leninist revolution. The PFLP was formed after the Arab defeat in the 1967 Arab-Israeli war. George Habash created the PFLP as a merger of three formerly autonomous groups—the Arab Nationalist Movement's Heroes of the Return, the National Front for the Liberation of Palestine and the Independent Palestine Liberation Front (to be distinguished from the present Palestine Liberation Front—PLF). Referred to by his followers as *al-Hakim* (the "wise one" or "the physician"), Habash has remained consistent in his position towards solving the Palestinian problem—the total liberation of Palestine. The PFLP established itself early as one of the most violent Palestinian terrorist groups. It concurrently sought to establish strong ties to other Marxist revolutionary organizations. Those links facilitated PFLP operations in Europe which gave the group much of its notoriety. Habash strongly favors well-publicized attacks on civilian targets and the PFLP reputation for ruthlessness was built on that strategy. As a result of ideological inflexibility, internal disputes and personality conflicts, the PFLP has spawned several splinter groups, including the PFLP-General Command (PFLP-GC) and the Democratic Front for the Liberation of Palestine (DFLP). The PFLP was one of the most active terrorist organizations in the early 1970s. As a result of publicity that attracted condemnation even from Communist Bloc countries, the PFLP curtailed international operations and concentrated on developing conventional and guerrilla forces for use against targets in Israel.

South Lebanese Army (SLA)

The SLA is Israel's early warning system. A remnant of the 1982 invasion of Lebanon. After the Israelis were pushed out of the country by Syrian and Iranian-backed militia in 1985 they left behind a little pocket protected by Lebanese General, Antoine Lahd.

The SLA controls about 8 percent of Lebanese territory. Although no one believes that the moniker Lebanese is correct, these are essentially occupation forces paid for, trained and supported by Israel. The SLA is about 2500 strong and manned by Christian and Shiites. They also have backup from about a thousand Israeli Defence Forces (IDF) forces. The SLA occupies a string of hilltop bunkers that parallel the Israeli-Lebanese border. They are well armed but no match for the hardened *Hezbollah* fighters who control the region. Many of the SLA soldiers are inducted without their consent and the constant boredom and stress has taken its toll on discipline. There are about 160,000 Palestinian refugees in Southern Lebanon. They provide a fertile recruiting ground for *Hezbollah*. The various Palestinian groups such as the PFLP, PRLP-PC, DFLP and Abu Nidal's FRC also recruit from these camps. True to Middle East politics though, the refugee camps have their own small cliques and groups that often create violent confrontations without outside agitation. *Hezbollah's* main source of support comes from the Bekáa valley and squalid camps in southern Beirut.

The United Nations Peacekeeping Mission (UNIFIL)

The United Nations Interim Force in Lebanon is kept away from the border so its 6500-person task force gets to twiddle its thumbs in Naqoura on the coast. They operate checkpoints inland from Tyre and throughout the area. They can only try to keep carloads of machine gun-toting Palestinians from wiping each other out. They also create a human barrier that Israel has to think about if they roll tanks back into Lebanon.

The Lebanese Army

The Lebanese army prefers to let the Israelis and Palestinians duke it out while they look the other way. Since the Lebanese army is under the direct influence of Syria, they are not about to fire on Islamic elements to please their bellicose neighbor to the south. On the other hand, they feel a slight obligation to bring some law and order to the south, but so far there is little indication that they will replace the SLA or the United Nations.

The Syrians

Lebanon is a vassal state of Syria. Syria has 30,000 troops deployed in eastern Lebanon. Syria uses *Hezbollah* to carry out its dirty work against Israel: a charge that Israel has always echoed. That's why Israel considers Lebanon to be a merely a buffer zone between itself and Syria. Syria is still angered that the Israelis stole the strategically important Golan Heights from them during the 1967 Arab-Israeli war.

The Israelis

The Israelis had 21 killed and 18 wounded in south Lebanon in 1994. Although the number seems low, it is a constant reminder that Israel is still at war with *Hezbollah*, which is backed and directed by Syria and Iran. Israel is not foolish enough to take on Syria or Iran directly, therefore each side has created its pawns to judge the strength and commitment of the other without resorting to total warfare. Israel has the SLA and Syria has Hezbollah. Israel may decide to invade Lebanon again to push back Hezbollah fighters and clear out the Palestinian refugee camps, but each side remembers the lingering and vicious war that was triggered by Israel's invasion of Lebanon in June of 1982 which has lasted in various forms to this day. Rabin is very aware that Hezbollah was the spawn of that war and that any invasion could create a bigger monster.

For now, Israel is content to wage an eye for an eye war. When Hezbollah sends shells and rockets into Israeli outposts, the Israelis are content to send in their Cobra gunships and take out preannounced villages, cars or buildings.

Getting In

Passports and visas are required. Without the requisite validation, use of a U.S. passport for travel to, in or through Lebanon may constitute a violation of U.S. law and may be punishable by a fine and/or imprisonment.

The categories of individuals eligible for consideration for a special passport validation are set forth in 22 C.F.R. 51.74. Passport validation requests for Lebanon should be forwarded in writing to the following address:

U.S. Department of State
11 19th St., NW, Suite 300
Washington, D.C. 20522
☎ *(202) 955-0518*

The request must be accompanied by supporting documentation according to the category under which validation is sought. Currently, the four categories of persons specified in 22 C.F.R. 51.74 as being eligible for consideration for passport validation are as follows:

[a] Professional reporters: Includes full-time members of the reporting or writing staff of a newspaper, magazine or broadcasting network whose purpose for travel is to gather information about Lebanon for dissemination to the general public.

[b] American Red Cross: Applicant establishes that he or she is a representative of the American Red Cross or International Red Cross traveling pursuant to an officially sponsored Red Cross mission.

[c] Humanitarian considerations: Applicant must establish that his or her trip is justified by compelling humanitarian considerations or for family unification. At this time, "compelling humanitarian considerations" include situations where the applicant can document that an immediate family member is critically ill in Lebanon. Documentation concerning family illness must include the name and address of the relative, and be from that relative's physician attesting to the nature and gravity of the illness. "Family unification" situations may include cases in which spouses or minor children are residing in Lebanon, with and dependent on, a Lebanese national spouse or parent for their support.

[d] National interest: The applicant's request is otherwise found to be in the national interest.

In all requests for passport validation for travel to Lebanon, the name, date and place of birth for all concerned persons must be given, as well as the U.S. passport numbers. Documentation as outlined above should accompany all requests. Additional information may be obtained by writing to the Department of State (see above) or by calling the Office of Citizenship Appeals and Legal Assistance at ☎ *(202) 326-6168 or 326-6182.*

Dangerous Places

Southern Lebanon

South Lebanon was the base for the PLO in the early '70s and now it is *Hezbollah* and SLA territory. It is a no man's land, 850 kilometers square, that protects Israel's border. The area south of the Awwali River is known as southern Lebanon. To the east is Mount Hermon and in the Syrian-Lebanese border and to the west are the ancient cities of Tyre and Sidon. The landscape is rough with small villages and wadis connected by poorly maintained roads. The area has predominately Shiite Muslims who eke out a living growing oranges and olives.

The best way to find out what the hot zone of the day is, is to listen to Voice of the South Radio operated by the SLA which will broadcast areas to be attacked by Israeli jets or helicopters.

The entire area is under curfew at night and few SLA or IDF soldiers venture out after dark. It is at night that *Hezbollah* will mine the roads with remote control bombs. The terrorists will also use rockets against bases and missiles, usually Saggers or SA-7s, against helicopters. *Hezbollah* strongholds are at Mlita, Jebel Safi, Ain Busswar, Mach Gara and Saghbine.

Dangerous Things

Prisons

Israeli-controlled prisons in Lebanon are notorious for torture and brutality. A young Lebanese prisoner, held for 10 years without a trial, died in January 1995. He died of torture. He was the third prisoner, from the Khiam Detention Camp in Israel's south Lebanon occupation zone, to die in less than two months. Israel and the South Lebanese Army have refused to allow prisoners' families to visit them, as well as refusing international humanitarian agencies access. Perhaps 250 Lebanese and 100 Palestinians are held at Khiam. One human rights agency estimates that 80 percent of the inmate population has heart, pulmonary or nervous disorders due to the extreme dampness of their cells. It is also believed the prisoners are allowed outside only once every three days.

Drugs

During the civil war the Bekáa Valley became a major center of opium cultivation. Controlled by the warlords in Beirut, the poppy flourished until recent pressure by the U.S. on Syria, which began to replace the poppy with less dangerous cash crops.

Consular Services

Although registration records are maintained at the consular section, the tight security under which the U.S. embassy operates means that assistance is available only in cases of extreme emergency such as arrest or death. The Consular Section is not able to replace lost, stolen or expired passports. Because of unreliable telephone service in Lebanon, contacting the embassy can be difficult. Access to the Consular Section is not possible unless prior arrangements have been made.

Embassy Location

U.S. Embassy

P.O. Box 70-840
Antelias
Beirut, Lebanon
☎ *(961-1) 402-200, 416-502, 426-183, 417-774*

In the U.S.

Embassy of Lebanon

2560 28th Street, NW
Washington, D.C. 20008
☎ *(202) 939-6300*

Arrival

Kidnapping is a fine art in Beirut. The most dangerous place is the airport and the road leading into town. These areas were easy pickings for Americans during the glory days of hostage-taking. Have a driver meet you at the airport with a prearranged signal or sign. If not, take the official airport taxis. If you take a taxi, officials will write down your name and destination so the news media can get it right after you're abducted. The many bombed, shelled and abandoned buildings are being reclaimed by squatters. The U.S. embassy, destroyed in a 1983 suicide attack, is a modest but comfortable home for a few ragged families. Most of the downtown area is being bulldozed and will be rebuilt. Many corporations have setup headquarters in Jouneih (Juniyah), about 45 minutes north of Beirut.

The government has evolved from resolving issues in the streets to arguing in parliament, but don't think for a moment of Beirut as a sunny Mediterranean beach destination.

Currency

The U.S. dollar is the official currency.

Hotels

Most travelers stay in Muslim West Beirut. There are frequent power outages.

Summerland

Jnah
☎ *(961-1)304830*
$160 single
On the beach with pool and restaurants. You must pass a Syrian checkpoint.

Cavalier

Hamra
☎ *(961-1) 515920*
No pool, but cheaper and closer to the action in Hamra.

Montemar

Jounieh
☎ *931996*
$60 single
Telephone service can be spotty to nonexistent. This should change as Beirut replaces its antiquated and damaged system with new technology. Many calls are routed through Cyprus or through satellite systems found in some hotels.

Nightlife

You can actually party in Beirut. Charley's Bar at the Cavalier is a favorite.

People like to take sunset or evening strolls along the corniche and eat at the food stalls.

You can rent cars but it is advisable that you hire taxis. This also facilitates passing the numerous Syrian or Lebanese checkpoints throughout the region.

Getting Sick

In Beirut and the surrounding areas, basic modern medical care and medicines are widely available. Such facilities are not always available in outlying areas. Doctors and hospitals often expect immediate cash payment for services. U.S. medical insurance is not always valid outside the United States. Supplemental medical insurance with specific overseas coverage has proved useful. The international travelers hotline at the Centers for Disease Control, ☎ *(404) 332-4559*, has additional useful health information.

Dangerous Days

04/20/1993	Russia and the United States issued invitations to Israel, Lebanon, Jordan, Syria and the Palestinians to meet in Washington, D.C. on April 20, 1993 to resume peace talks stalled by the Israeli's expulsion of 400 suspected Hamas activists to Lebanon.
12/17/1992	The government of Israel deported more than 400 suspected members of Hamas, however, the government of Lebanon refused to allow the deportees to enter and they were sent "camping" in the Israeli "security zone" in southern Lebanon.
02/16/1992	General Secretary Abbas Musawi was killed in an Israeli helicopter ambush near the village of Jibsheet in southern Lebanon.
10/30/1991	The first round of Arab-Israeli peace talks began in Madrid, Spain.
07/28/1989	Israeli commandos seized Shaykh Obeid from a village in southern Lebanon and detained him in Israel on allegations of involvement in terrorist activity on behalf of *Hezbollah*.
02/28/1987	Georges Ibrahim Abdallah, a principal figure in the Lebanese Armed Revolutionary Faction, was sentenced to life in prison for murder.
01/28/1987	U.S. bans travel to Lebanon.
06/14/1985	TWA flight 847 was hijacked from Athens to Lebanon. The hijackers shot and killed U.S. Navy diver Robert Stetham in Beirut on June 16 and dispersed the remaining passengers throughout the city. Thirty-nine American citizens were released on June 30 in Damascus, Syria.
09/20/1984	Fourteen people were killed and 70 were wounded when a van loaded with four hundred pounds of explosives drove past the checkpoint in front of the U.S. Embassy annex in Awkar and exploded. The driver of the van was shot and killed by British security guards. Islamic Jihad claimed responsibility for the bombing in a call to the media.
02/06/1984	West Beirut fell to Muslim militias.
10/23/1983	Islamic Jihad (read that as *Hezbollah*) bombings in Beirut killed more than 200 U.S. Marines and more than 50 French paratroopers.
04/18/1983	A car bomb exploded in front of the U.S. Embassy in Beirut, killing 63 people, including 17 Americans. More than 100 others were wounded. Islamic Jihad claimed responsibility, calling the bombing "part of the Islamic Revolution." Iran subsequently denied having any role in the attack.
09/15/1982	Israel invaded West Beirut.
09/15/1982	Lebanese Christian Phalangists killed hundreds of Palestinian refugees in a camp near Beirut.
09/14/1982	President-elect Bashir Gemayel was assassinated.
07/19/1982	David Dodge, president of the American University of Beirut, was kidnapped. He was subsequently released on July 19, 1983.
06/06/1982	Israel invaded Lebanon.
06/04/1982	Israeli planes bombed Beirut.
03/16/1978	Invasion by Israeli forces.

Dangerous Days

06/01/1976 During this month, Syria entered the civil war in Lebanon on the side of the Christian Phalange and against the Palestinians and their Muslim allies. In response, Abu Nidal renamed his terrorist group, then based in Iraq, the Black June Organization and began attacking Syrian targets.

04/13/1975 Phalangist militiamen attack Shia Muslim targets sparking the first round of fighting in the Lebanese civil war.

04/11/1968 The Popular Front for the Liberation of Palestine (PFLP-GC) split from the PFLP under the leadership of Ahmad Jabril.

07/15/1958 U.S. Marines were sent to Lebanon in order to thwart the overthrow of the government.

11/22/1943 Independence Day.

05/06/1915 Martyr's Day.

In a Dangerous Place: Lebanon

For more than fifteen years, the war in Lebanon was the compulsory and compulsive topic of headlines and television news throughout the world. It replaced Vietnam in our consciences. A hopeless quagmire of death and destruction. A place where we could never figure out who was killing whom or why.

With its seventeen different religious communities and an obsolete political system, Lebanon was, and still is, the ideal battlefield for warlords who have wanted control of this ancient region. Lebanon also became the best place for marketing and testing weaponry coming from all corners of the planet.

The war began in Ayn er-Remmane (a suburb east of Beirut), on April 13, 1975, with a massacre: During the inauguration of a church, by the leader of the Katayeb party, four people were shot dead from an unidentified car. The retaliation was immediate. A few hours later, in the same place, Christian militants machine-gunned a coach transporting Palestinians from the camp of Sabra to the one at Tall ez-Zatar. Twenty-seven people died in this coach and three more in the crowd. The answer was prompt: One hundred Christians were killed the very next day. Massacres and revenge became a common feature of this war.

Unlike the wars that make good movies or backgrounds for spy novels, Lebanon was not black and white, good and bad. Lebanon was and still is a nest of wars. It is a civil war between several of the seventeen religious communities. It is a national war in which Lebanese fight Palestinians, Lebanese (or at least some of them) fight against Syrians, Lebanese (or the majority of them) fight against Israelis. It is a religious war between Christians—the majority group when the state was created in 1920. It is a war of sects between Sunnites and Shiites, the latter of whom constituted the majority, and within the Shiite community, between Amal, pro-Syrian and *Hezbollah*, pro-Iranian. It is a war between militias of all fractions, but more particularly, from the Christian group. It is a social war pitching the poor (Christians and Muslims) against the rich (Christians and Muslims).

What made this new medieval hierarchy so bizarre was the fact that a few months prior, Lebanon was called the Switzerland of the East, an affluent population of just under three million in 1975, it comprised a comfortable, tolerant, harmonious and beautiful place, and was an important seaport, a banking center and a holiday resort.

The war in Lebanon was my home for many years. I became acquainted with a lot of different people, learned about their difficulties, saw many of them wounded or dead. I saw history first hand. The new war of terror was fraught with booby-trapped vehicles, suicide commandos, kidnappings, and so on. I would like to think that in later years people will look at my photos and examine the faces of the people who fought this war. I hope they will try to understand why humans can do these things. As with any war, a recollection of the years I covered in Lebanon would not make sense if viewed as a whole. I flew in and out depending on the level of activity at the time. Like drifting in and out of a bad dream there are certain incidents that capture the war in Lebanon and will explain the unique people, places and activities that shape this turbulent region.

1980

The history of Lebanon is best left to scholars and philosophers since, like the rest of the Middle East, it is like a mass of knots that once untied, bears no resemblance to the original structure. When I first came to Lebanon the war had been raging for five years. Eager to earn my spurs as a war correspondent I went to visit the Druses, an ancient heretic sect born in Egypt around the year A.D. 986, and later classified as Muslim. I was there on a short assignment to take photos of SAM-106 missiles being secretly deployed in the Bekáa Valley by the Syrians who (at that time) backed and actually controlled the Druses. Along the road I saw hashish plantations that kept the militiamen loyal and well paid. Drugs were an important source of income for all the militiamen controlled by the Syrians.

It is not surprising that in a war-torn country with a dismembered economy, the people try to make the quickest profits possible. The missiles were there all right, amidst the hashish fields.

1982

I flew into Cyprus (the Greek side) from Paris because the airport in Lebanon was closed. We then waited for two days before taking a cargo-boat transporting wood to the Lebanese port of Jounieh. The Israelis had crossed their common frontier with Lebanon and were moving forward towards West Beirut. Their ultimate target was to be the headquarters of the Feddayins of the Palestinian Liberation Organization, PLO, led by the ever elusive Yasir Arafat, and other Palestinian groups. Around the same time the Israeli Air Force launched heavy bombing raids using American-made fighters and Israeli-made KFIRS.

It is hot and sunny out but the black smoke has turned everything to grey. From time to time, I can hear small explosions accompanied by bursts of flames.

The journalists are all staying at the Hotel Commodore off Hamra street. This is where the journalists usually gathered to watch the war. Today, I have decided to set-up my observation from the terrace of the Hotel Carlton, a cheaper place but an equally cinematic vista of Beirut under the bombs. The Carlton Hotel is situated in the residential quarter of West Beirut in Raoucheh, by the coast. I spend the time with an Algerian journalist named Sadri. The streets below are empty. Everybody is seeking refuge underground. For the first time in my life I am watching the heavy bombing of a modern city. We stare in amazement at the jets hurling down in 'piqué' dangerously close to the ground (100 to 200 m). At the same time, warships launch their shells from the Mediterranean sea, shooting missiles of 150 to 240 mm caliber. The noise and destruction is overwhelming—30,000 people die during those terrible days, most of them civilians buried in the rubble of collapsing and burning buildings. I am struck by the fact that the Israelis are deliberately killing innocent people—people who are not attacking them but who are easy to kill. I do not know whether to be angry or appalled.

We decide to climb down from our "watch tower", on the 13th story's terrace, to take pictures of the destruction. There are two armed men ahead of us. Suddenly the two of them turn toward Sadri and myself, abruptly asking us to hand over our cameras. I thought at first they were going to take all the cameras, but I soon understood that they only wanted mine because I have got the latest Nikon cameras whereas Sadri has only got old Leicas. Our two aggressors then shoot around our feet and start shouting at us to freeze. Then they frantically run away holding our cameras tightly in their hands. A young Palestinian man, wearing a *keffieh* and a sash, who has been watching from a nearby balcony comes down to the street and asks us for details, then starts making a call on his walkie-talkie. Soon jeeps and military vehicles arrive on the scene. They ask us, "Which direction did the thieves run?" After indicating the way, I am told that this way leads to the headquarters of the Panarab party; the Mourabitoun, which follows Nasser's ideology.

The bombing is still going on but the Palestinians seem to ignore it, they surround the Mourabitoun building and one of them, using a megaphone, requests the cameras as well as the surrender of the thieves. Their answer does not come in words but in bullets. The Palestinians reply in kind. During the shootout we take cover under a car. The car explodes from a grenade thrown by a Mourabitoun and we are dragged out by a Palestinian fighter. The shootout lasts about 30 minutes. Finally the men inside the building send out our cameras. The cost for their return has been three men killed and ten people wounded.

July 1982

I knew a young man, a Christian Maronite, during those turbulent days in Lebanon. He told me about his education at the Sorbonne (he spoke perfect French) and his refined taste for arts and culture. The next day he was involved in a shootout against another faction. I was there to cover the event, confident in my friend's desire to protect me from harm. But under fire the blood lust came. He became another person; shouting, firing, demonstrating his joy at killing other people. In the massacre which followed it was obvious that he was deriving great pleasure at cutting off the heads and ears of his victims. He even tried to kill me, after having declared his friendship the very day before, when he saw me taking pictures of what he was doing.

———

I had planned to go to Khalde, near the front, with my friend Reza, an Iranian photographer working, like me, for SIPA. We decided to leave in the very early morning and on foot since nobody wanted to take the risk of driving us there due to the intense gunfire. We wanted to see for ourselves how far the Israelis had advanced and to take some pictures.

Khalde is a small town facing the Mediterranean Sea about ten kilometers away from Beirut and about eight kilometers from Baabda; the inland town where the Lebanese presidential palace stands. The Israelis had been progressing very quickly in the past few days using the coastal highway across Israel and Lebanon. Baabda was about to fall and soon afterwards so would Beirut.

We walked in the rising heat towards the white smoke in the distance and listened to the sound of the gunnery, we were also aware of the brisk clattering noise made by the bursts of machine guns and the isolated shots of automatic weapons. We came across two soldiers walking slowly in the heat. One was helping the other who was obviously terminally wounded. They did not utter a word as we passed them and did not even acknowledge our presence when I took a picture of them.

Nothing unusual perhaps, but enough to force us to breathe a little faster and to feel a little edgy.

The tension and mounting fear got to us because Reza stopped and said he would not go any further because it was too trying to do anything in such adverse conditions.

I do not know for what reason I decided to carry on alone, but there I was walking and getting tired when I saw a group of people near a petrol station. It was on the front. I was stopped by one of them who was carrying a Kalashnikov. He asked who I was, listening carefully to my answer. Then he told me that he and his friends belonged to the SAIKA, a pro-Syrian organization fighting against the Israelis. As soon as he understood I was Turkish and that I spoke a little Arabic he befriended me, telling me his name, Saleh, and offering me some tea and sandwiches.

We all sat around an improvised table made from an oil drum. I took some pictures of him. One shot is still my favorite, a portrait in classic warrior pose, ready to shoot on sight, looking through the hole left by a shell in the inner wall of an abandoned house. All the while the bombardment was going on around us.

Then it happens: first a giant flash of white light, followed by a shock ... around me everything seems to be rocking and I lose consciousness for a minute... When I wake-up again I can see nothing but dust. I remember thinking only then that it must have been the explosion of a shell. Everything is so silent that I think I have lost my sense of hearing.

The dust settles and I realize that I am surrounded by the pieces of hacked bodies. Perhaps you can imagine my reaction... I panic. The next thing I remember is that I can hear again, people are shouting and running in every direction. Around me nothing is the same anymore: tables upturned, glass broken, dust, rubble...blood, torn limbs...and so on. I look at myself frantically. I have been lucky. I am complete, without even a bruise, but I am trembling. Then I see them: Saleh's eyes, wide open, transfixed, staring at me. The explosion had instantly killed most of the people who were drinking tea around us. Only Saleh, the Syrians and I were spared.

All of a sudden a man comes to the scene from the burning petrol station, brandishing his Kalashnikov. He starts yelling that I am a spy, responsible for the bombings and that I ought to die. He shoots in my direction. For a second I am petrified. Saleh understands the danger faster than I and he shouts at me to run away to a safer place. Thanks to his intervention, I realize that my life is at stake and I start running away as fast as I can leaving the burning petrol station behind me.

Nobody has followed me. I shut myself in a bath cabin. And I cry and cry and cry...

I stayed in the bath cabin for a few hours till the end of the bombardment. In the evening I got out and walked back to Beirut. I was still in a state of shock when I met my fellow photographer, Patrick Chauvel, who worked for Sygma at that time.

As I told him my story I realized that in the panic, I had left all my cameras behind near the petrol station. Chauvel cheered me up and told me not to worry. His words could not calm me since I realize that without my cameras I am just an idiot wandering through a war zone.

The next morning I started asking everybody how I could go back to Khalde to fetch my cameras.

I found an Italian nurse working, like Saleh, for the SAIKA organization. She drove me in her ambulance to look for the leaders of the SAIKA. We found them just as the bombardment was resuming.

We went inside a grocery store to feel the illusory but comforting presence of a ceiling above our heads. The gunnery was intense. We had nothing to do but wait anxiously. I felt useless without my cameras. Suddenly, as if answering my silent prayers, one of the combatants came smiling like a politician, proudly handing me a video camera. I explained to him that it was not mine since I only worked with still cameras; he said I could have that one as a replacement. I agreed to take it anyway to prevent an argument.I could tell by the stickers that it belonged to the CBC (Canadian Broadcasting Company) who were staying at the same hotel as I.

Back at the hotel, I returned the videocamera to the Canadian television crew who had lost it the day before.

I was so anguished not to be able to take pictures. Luckily, Robin Moyer, a *Time* Correspondent, let me borrow one of his cameras.

Two days later, the Italian nurse came to tell me that my cameras had been found among the corpses of Palestinians in the morgue of Sabra in West Beirut. One of my cameras was broken but the other one was still usable. As in a tale, I was happy to retrieve them but sad to do so on corpses. I could not help thinking that a piece of these people was inside my bashed cameras, along with their joy when they took pictures of each other with my cameras and how their happiness had been stopped stupidly and so suddenly.

––––––

Sipa Press, the photo agency I work for, covered only half of my expenses while in Lebanon. To stay one night in Beirut costs as much as US$400 in a big hotel, so I decided to stay in a hotel inside a refugee camp opposite the Hotel Commodore. The other journalists can afford to be driven around in armored vehicles and stay in the Commodore. A Palestinian named Mahmud has become my driver and he provides me with all sorts of information and help.

––––––

Recently, I took an interesting shot, in East Beirut, of a woman carrying a child in her arms running away from the explosions. She is surrounded by soldiers carrying machine guns who seem to protect her amidst cars and rubble and smoke, composing a very dramatic picture. One can see how the people had to move from house to house during the bombing in order to avoid getting killed. This picture has been taken with a broken camera (that's why it is blurry) because of the bombings.

The other journalists could not go out of their hotel. I managed to snap this shot and others because I am close to the action. But it was impossible to send my film out because of the siege. The American television crews organize 'shippings' but the print journalists who want to use this system have to pay $10,000 per package. I only have $100 but my friend Reza proposes to put my film with his own in an envelope to be given to the American newspaper men.

I was most surprised when I got a telegram of congratulations a few days later. The pictures had reached Paris via New York and I was told that this very picture (only the part with the woman) had been chosen to become the cover of *Time* magazine, *Paris Match, VSD* (French) and other magazines around the world.

————

Being a war correspondent, I can say that I was there when it happened. Unlike other journalists or viewers I cannot describe or do a voice-over. My photos are silent witness to war. Most of the people see these scenes on TV during their evening meal, they are very moved for a short while, then they flip the channel to something else. But a magazine photo can haunt you for a long time.

I was in a street not far from the Hotel Commodore, the general headquarters for the Red Cross, when a booby-trapped car exploded. Usually journalists arrive with the police and the military too late to capture anything but the confusion and wet blood.

For once I was there right on time and I had the reflexes to take photos during the panic scene which followed the explosion. Everybody was running, desperately looking for shelter or just to get away, as most humans do.

I noticed a young man start running who was wearing only a white singlet and carrying his pajama-clad son. He was followed by his wife. He was holding a silver pistol in his right hand. I started taking pictures of the three, rapidly running along with them as they rushed in my direction. I was quite excited with my eye glued to the viewfinder and the pictures came out a little blurry. I saw him leveling his pistol at me, taking aim and shooting but I didn't connect his actions with reality. And he kept shooting as he ran by me. All around me everyone was screaming and yelling. The explosion had blown out all the windowpanes around us and the noise of the glass crunching and shattering under the feet of the passersby added to the cacophony. Then the sirens took over, first those of the ambulances, very quickly and on the spot, as usual in Beirut, then those of the vehicles of the civil protection.

After the scene had calmed down I walked back to my hotel and it was only then, in the lobby, that I realized what had happened. The hotel attendants and the clients were all watching me with a look half disgusted, half concerned. I looked at my clothes trying to understand what was wrong, then I put my hand on my head. When I removed my hand, it was smeared with blood. The man's bullet had grazed my scalp.

1985

In Beirut a massacre always follows another massacre. The chain is impeccable and implacable. This time it is the Druzes who are responsible for the deaths of some three hundred Christian combatants of the Kataeb party and of the Lebanese Forces. The Druzes have lived for centuries in the mountains of the Shuf and have been considered to be ferocious warriors. Their leader is Wallid Jumblatt (the son of Kamal Jumblatt, founder of the PSP; Progressive Socialist Party).

The Druzes have just finished a merciless battle in the mountains overlooking Beirut, in the southeast of the city, which they won against the Phalangists. Once their victory was assured, they immediately perpetrated a massacre in order to avenge another massacre perpetrated against them (so they claim) by the Christian Phalangists.

I went to Bhamdoun, about twenty kilometers southeast of Beirut with two other journalists to visit Wallid Jumblatt and see the situation. The two other journalists were Samy Ketz of the AFP (*Agence France Presse* - French Press Agency) and David Hirst of the *Guardian*. We had been blindfolded to prevent us from seeing the exact location of the Headquarters.

We met with Wallid Jumblatt, then we went to see firsthand the extent of the damage inflicted upon Bhamdoun and its defenders. Although we were forbidden from taking pictures, we were not blindfolded and I was able to take some photos with an autofocus camera. I counted approximately three hundred dead. Most of them had been killed after having been captured, hanged with electrical wires and dragged through the streets, where they were abandoned like trash. It is hard to understand that to kill, and to kill cruelly, can be a very joyful activity.

I was able to photograph the gaiety of the Muslim combatants after they had massacred their enemies. Some of them had discovered some mannequins in a shop and amused themselves with one of these, transporting it to the street in front of me, then hanging it with a cable. A placard was attached under its strangled neck on which they hastily wrote the name: Amin Gemaye (the Christian president of Lebanon at the time). One of the Muslim militia kisses a dummy dressed in a grey flannel three-piece suit. The whole scene was surrealistic. They did it because they were aware I was recording their actions. It was not much different from what soccer supporters can do after a match or what happens during a carnival. The camera is a tease.

———

Today, we went out to take some particularly disgusting shots. The Muslim militiamen of the AMAL movement had asked some photojournalists to accompany them. The sky, usually bright blue, was evenly grey-white, very shiny and quite disturbing for the eyes; not very good for pictures either. The militants wanted us to come to the vicinity of an ancient well situated ten kilometers north of Sidon, in a region which was recently under the control of the Lebanese Forces and which has fallen into the hands of the Shiites of the AMAL movement and the Druses of Wallid Jumblatt's PSP. They had just made a horrible discovery.

Hunters had signaled the presence of corpses in the bottom of an ancient well, to the militiamen. The militiamen had to go down wearing gas masks. When we arrived, they showed us the decomposed bodies of Muslim militants killed a year before on a beach near Sidon during a massacre by the Christians.

Later I learned that there was some doubt about the identity of the corpses I had photographed yesterday near Sidon. Some people claim that they were not Shiite Muslims but perhaps even Christians.

Like a bullet, I pride myself on my lack of alignment or cause but I am becoming a tool for killers, a weapon to be used by whomever wants to cause damage.

A few weeks ago, I did a photo-souvenir of a very special sort. It was in Jieh, a Christian village set along the road to Sidon. This village had been besieged by Wallid Jumblatt forces. They eventually managed to break the resistance of the villagers and at the joy of their victory they allowed the photographers to take pictures of their rejoicing. They looked like the famous hunters of the safari days in the African savanna, proudly posing with one foot on the slaughtered lion. The difference is that the lion had been replaced this time by an unlucky and very dead enemy soldier.

The men were proudly posing, lifting their weapons high above their heads in a victory gesture, while stepping joyfully on the corpse of their enemy, as if they were walking on a carpet.

Without this picture the world might seem saner, cleaner and fairer but now that this picture is recorded people know how low humanity can sink.

———

Weapons and soldiers. That's what the war is about, no? I have taken countless shots of both. It is always a surprise for me to see how the soldier identifies himself with his weapon. Everybody knows that there is something sensual about holding a weapon. In the case of men holding a gun or a machine gun it has also got something to do with male pride. I have never encountered a soldier who refused to be photographed, and in every case the rifle or gun is raised upward like an erection.

In Lebanon, stereotypes are falling apart. There is a clash of cultures and images. In past wars soldiers were like football players. One red, one green. One good, one bad. Here everyone is evil, everyone is righteous. There is no regular army to speak of. The militiamen are usually dressed in a hodgepodge of half civilian, half military clothing. They choose freely the fashion they want to follow after their favorite mythology. It gives an incredible mixture of western and oriental influences. Some of these men wear big cowboy hats, or t-shirts with the picture of Ayatollah Ruhollah Khomeini on them, or hairbands and ammunition bands crossing on their chest like Mexican revolutionaries in Zapata's time.

All the world's a stage and we are just actors upon it.

These past days I have accompanied the Druses militia close to the demarcation line in the Shuf mountains in southeast Beirut. They are fighting against the Christian Phalangists using Soviet-built tanks which they received from their Syrian allies. With these weapons the fight will be fierce and not likely to last very long. I was lucky not to get killed. I managed to get close to what was happening. I always have to remember that I only have a still camera, not a movie camera. I have to take shots with continuity so as to make my "story" understandable. Sometimes I wish I could just watch and direct what is happening to tell the entire story. I am allowed 36 pictures for each camera body I carry, then I must reload.

I try to capture the essential moments even though I have no idea of the outcome of each battle. The dust flying, the oblique light of the sun contrasting with the silhouettes of the soldiers, the sudden movement of a tank, the bursting of a shell, the assault of the infantry, the last moments of a soldier brought on a stretcher to an ambulance. I am able to take these pictures because I follow the militiamen everywhere instead of staying in a downtown hotel with the rest of the journalists.

I am becoming biased because I am learning too much.

1986

Snipers get their kicks shooting at isolated and unarmed people. Many snipers are mercenaries hiding out in apartments on top of buildings.

I met a sniper today, a Frenchman, who used a rifle specially designed for his line of work; made in the U.S.A. He would shoot people, then play the piano, mostly Mozart, then resume his watch, waiting for the next target to come along. He killed children or old ladies without remorse or hesitation. Dozens of deaths have been attributed to him but he has never expressed the slightest regret because, as he explained to me, he was on the demarcation line, the line that separates Beirut into two parts, East and West, and it was not to be crossed at any time. Therefore, he had every right to do what he did.

Special rifles are available for conscientious snipers: For example, the American M-16 with a field glass and the Soviet-made Brejnev. I took many pictures of people trying to pass the demarcation line; one of them is particularly significant.

My advice about snipers is to never be number three. The first one across the street has a 90 percent chance, the second has got a 50 percent chance, but the third has no chance at all because the sniper has had ample time to adjust his aim and tracking.

I am beginning to remember rules that should never be needed.

The main contradiction of a war is its perpetual hesitation between lawlessness and obeyance to strict and strange rules. To kill at random whatever comes in front of your rifle does not mean there are no situations where some sort of rules are followed. In the past, for example, the soldiers were not supposed to go about killing each other during certain periods of the day, during nights, and on Sundays. In Beirut there was a reminiscence of this long forgotten period as we can see in the following letter.

In Beirut there is an unwritten tradition, somewhat bizarre, probably inherited from the Middle Ages and respected by all parties: Start shooting from 5 a.m. till 8 a.m. then stop for breakfast, and resume shooting up to lunch time, stop again for lunch and a siesta, and resume shooting until sundown.

1986

The influence of Muslim fundamentalism is felt more and more in Lebanon. It comes from Iran whose leaders have always said they wanted to export their Islamic Revolution to all the Arab countries first and then to the rest of the world. Islam being the second most important religion in Lebanon, it was normal that the new ideology would provoke a tremor in the diverse Muslim communities. Things would have been complicated enough that way but the Iranians infiltrated the country and trained the people to the new ideas so that many turned to Iran as a model to follow. A movement was born which was soon going to be well-known throughout the world for the expediency of its methods and for its extremism. This movement is the *Hezbollah*, the Party of God.

The Shiites have been influenced by Khomeini like the AMAL militia. I have taken many photos which show the extent of the personality cult to which the famous Ayatollah is subjected in the various Muslim communities and factions.

Fanaticism is an indispensable feature of many wars, especially those fought for religious reasons. Everybody remembers the kamikaze of the second World War who gladly gave their lives for their Emperor-God. The same thing happened in Iran during its eight-year long war against Iraq, and in Lebanon. Sana, the young Palestinian girl who blew herself up in the explosion of a truck she had loaded with explosives, was a modern kamikaze. She took the time to explain her gesture to journalists (including myself) and had taped a message which was distributed to the press after the success of the operation.

Looting and robbing became very commonplace in Lebanon. People actually went shopping with a weapon.

I came across the body of an old man who had been murdered for the plastic bag full of goods he had just bought in Beirut.

I could imagine him, just moments before, walking peacefully under the bright blue sky feeling the warm sun on his back and the heat bouncing off the hot road. The shining light is difficult to bear, so he lowers his head. Suddenly everything seems to blur, the world around him stops, the light diminishes, and a pain digs into his belly. He has dropped his bags; blood is gushing out of his bowels. He dies wondering what he has done to deserve such an ending...

Why am I taking a picture of this?

I had heard that the young Lebanese militants had taken up Russian roulette as a badge of courage. I introduced myself to a group of militants averaging nineteen years of age. I gained their trust slowly and I eventually asked them how they feel about the war and how they cope with anxiety, fear of death and the like. I also talked to them about my own fear of death, then I switched from this topic to war being a big lottery, and what did they think of games, gambling, etc. At last I was able to ask them about Russian roulette, saying only that I had been told it was common practice for the militants but that I had never seen proof.

They remained mute for a while, then one of them nodded in a silent acquiescence. He explained to me that almost all the militants, whatever the party, played this game, that he himself had played it often and that it was quite an enthralling experience; quite addictive in fact. I then asked him to permit me to photograph them during a game, but they quickly replied that it was not possible because all this was done clandestinely and that if their chiefs heard about it they would be punished. I eventually managed to photograph them , but due to my subjects' suspicion of being jinxed I was barred from taking pictures of the real game of death.

The first picture shows us how the table is set with a white tablecloth. The bets have already been taken. The game is for money and for the thrill. The rules of the game are simple and well-known. Everybody bets on the chances of the shooter surviving and the game starts. The game must be played with a six-shot revolver, usually a small Smith & Wesson or Colt Detective. One bullet is loaded into the chamber and the cylinder is spun around. Without looking, the player must hold the pistol to his temple and pull the trigger.

If he survives, the gun is passed, the barrel spun and the trigger pulled again.

The game can stop at any time or start anew. In Lebanon, some men have taken to playing this game alone.

This nihilistic game is perfect for Lebanon, where life is worth little and drugs and death provide the entertainment. In the beginning of the war they were content with smoking hashish or marijuana to pass the time. Now it is cocaine and heroin. Death is the ultimate high.

The young bearded man has put a gun on his right temple. He is now facing his possible immediate death. The others watch him in awe. For a brief moment he is a superior being, a true hero, in a second he might become a true zero...Like a powerful drug every drop of adrenaline surges to his brain, he pulls the trigger slowly, his testicles tighten, and then...click. Today he was lucky, after all, it was but a mock game. Two days after having posed for these photos, he tried his luck once more, with a loaded pistol this time (the very one in these pictures), and died. There was no click.

How can young men kill themselves for no reason? Russians invented this game when they were bored on the battlefield. These photos were taken in 1985, ten years after the beginning of the war. These young men have known nothing but war, death and violence during the crucial years of their adolescence.

I have heard that sound before. Click is the sound my shutter makes when I push the button. With that click comes the same rush of adrenaline, the feeling of omnipotence. As long as I click that shutter I am immortal, free from death, separated from the horror on the other side of my lens. But someday I will not hear the click.

The incident happened during Terry Waite's press conference at the Hotel Commodore, the headquarters for the French press. An Anglican minister from England, Waite had come to Beirut to help find a solution to free the hostages and ended up kidnapped and remaining as a hostage for more than three years himself.

A car with three passengers inside was the target of a shootout probably just aimed at scaring Terry Waite. When the car stopped in the middle of the street I realized that the driver had been hit by a bullet. I rushed to help the driver, forgetting about taking pictures, and tried pulling him out. An American journalist (working for *U.S. News*) came to our rescue but we both arrived too late. The driver of the car was dead.

Later on, the driver was considered a hero by the militiamen and other witnesses of the simple violent event. The shooting was filmed by the cameramen who had come for the press conference and was shown around the world by the TV networks.

Just another death, no pictures, another nameless victim.

I was traveling in and out of the main Palestinian camps of Beirut, Sabra and Chatila and Borj el Barajneh. They are all situated in the south of Beirut, not far from the city of sports. The war interzones had burst out again, more violent than ever. The leader of Shiite militia AMAL, Nabih Berri, who is also the Minister of State for South Lebanon and who proclaimed himself Minister of National Resistance to fight against the Israelis, received his orders from Syria and had the camps attacked.

The AMAL and the Lebanese Forces militiamen can be organized like search and destroy teams and go from one house to the other to accomplish their task, or they surround a quarter and wait patiently for the end, cutting all the roads and blockading the supply of food and water. The people inside are starving and some have already died of hunger and thirst. Those who are daring enough to get out are killed instantly by the militiamen standing outside.

The women and the children are of course suffering more than the men because they cannot fight and must wait anxiously for the outcome of all this. They already know by instinct that the worst is always guaranteed. I also tried to record their suffering for their history. Sometimes the women come to me begging me to stop this nightmare as if I could do something about it. My so-called neutral position makes me interesting enough and everybody believes I can become a go-between.

Some Palestinians manage to sneak out of the camps but the militiamen are waiting outside and whenever they have a doubt about the identity of one person or another they apply what is known around here as the "tomato test." It consists of asking the person caught to pronounce the Arabic word for "tomato." A Palestinian will denounce himself immediately by pronouncing this word as 'panadora' instead of 'ponadora' which is the way the other Arabs pronounce it around here. Once a Palestinian is found he is usually taken aside and executed. Hundreds of people have already died that way, or another, since the reawakening of intercommunal feuds.

Today I followed and photographed a child who has probably become half crazy because of the bombings. He was hanging around in the camp of Sabra, wearing only his underwear and a pair of grotesque pink slippers, far too big for him. As soon as he saw me he started behaving like a clown, dancing, chanting, making faces amidst the rubble and the ruins of the camp. I took many pictures of him because he seemed to me the epitome of what has happened to the people here. Being very young he represents the future of this world without a future. His hopeless behavior reminds us sarcastically about the hopeless world that humankind is proposing for the young generation of this country who were born with the war. Next to him is seen a young man wearing a funny straw hat, his face covered by a yellow handkerchief like a bandit set out to attack the stagecoach in the western movies, but this one has given it a personal touch, he has poked three holes in his mask in order to breathe and see. This young man was following the kid; he is probably his brother or a relative. I found the contrast between the two very weird.

———

I did something unusual, even for me, a few days ago. Something which has left a bitter taste in my mouth. Photojournalists are sometimes like vultures hovering above and around those who are going to die or who have already met their demise, in the vulgar expectation of a spectacular shot.

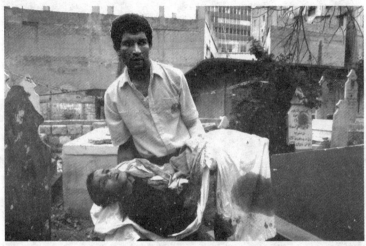

The light was bright as usual in this "blessed" country, but the sky was uniformly white. I went to a Palestinian camp near Sidon during a heavy attack. The camp had been bombed nonstop for many days. The shells kept exploding around us damaging only the walls of the houses, until one, guided by I don't know which force, burst out very close to a group of people. A child happened to be there... Badly injured in the chest and belly, he died almost immediately.

I then saw his father, a man in his late twenties, coming to his side, in a very dignified way. He covered the frail dead body, still dripping blood, with a white sheet in the false hope to stop the draining and to resuscitate his son.

He quickly understood that the task was beyond his limited powers and he lifted his child in his arms, unaware of his weight, and directed his steps toward the cemetery. I decided to follow him. We were alone. No one else had come. I was taking photos all the while. I remember the gaze in his eyes.

In a universal gesture of love, devotion and pity, he was looking for the proper place to bury his child.

There are human feelings in Lebanon. I am thankful I still have mine.

Liberia
★★★★★

Smell No Taste

In Liberia, there's a small town called Smell No Taste. One legend has it the town was named because of its proximity to the former Robertsfield International Airport. Locals gazed longingly at well-heeled passengers hopping on planes bound for Paris, London and New York. The Liberians could only fantasize about such a way of life. They were close enough to smell, but not close enough to taste: As it's been with peace in Liberia.

Peace has been a carrot dangled in front of Liberians' noses more than 10 times during the six-year-old civil war here, but not achieved. "Close" only matters in horseshoes and hand grenades.

Founded in 1822, Liberia was an attempt—an experiment, actually—by the American Colonization Society to create a homeland in West Africa for freed slaves from the United States. It became the Free and Independent Republic of Liberia in 1847.

It's interesting that a group of individuals so jaded by the racial strata system of 19th-century America chose to recreate the United States constitution on the other side of

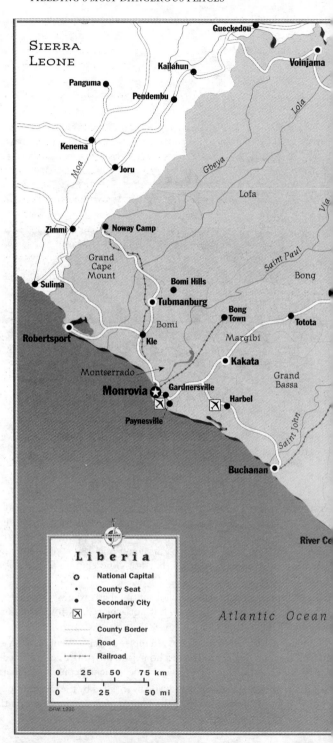

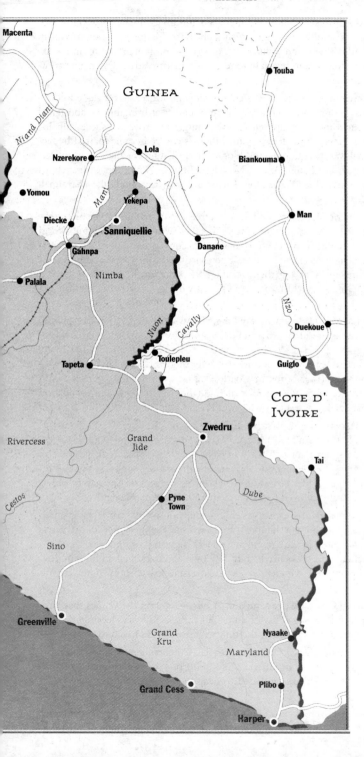

the Atlantic. As Africa's first "republic," Liberia's debut government was modeled directly after the one it sought to escape. With names like Joseph J. Roberts, William V.S. Tubman, Charles Taylor and William R. Tolbert, Jr., prominent figures in Liberian history read more like a Palm Beach polo team roster than a struggling ragtag community of displaced slaves.

The attempt at creating a duplicate America in Africa, however, never came full-circle, namely because more than a century's worth of efforts at bringing the aboriginal population onto the same "playing field" as the emigrants proved unsuccessful. Instead of democracy, liberty and all that stuff, Liberia's course became marred by factional fighting, civil war, partitioning and bloody coups led not by men with sinister, nasty-sounding names like Stalin, Arafat, Noriega, Hitler or Amin, but with such innocuous, landed-gentryish handles as Doe, Taylor and Sawyer. Sounds like a Savannah law firm.

Instead of freedom for all, Liberia has become a free-for-all, reduced to primal clashes among rival clans randomly slaughtering each other with old machine guns from the back of ancient, dented jeeps. Bands of marauders cut swaths across the rain forest plateau, donning Halloween masks and bolt-action rifles as they rape and pillage in small villages before finally razing them. Calling the situation in modern Liberia a "civil war" is giving it too much status—crediting it with too much organization and purpose.

One of the few Liberian leaders with any longevity was William V.S. Tubman, who was in his sixth term as president when he died during surgery in 1971. He was replaced by his longtime associate, William R. Tolbert, Jr. Tolbert actually lasted nine years in office before he was ousted by a mere master sergeant, Samuel Doe, in 1980. Yet another coup attempt was borne by Charles Taylor, a former Doe aide, in 1989. Leaving a bloody wake in capturing most of the nation's economic and population centers, Taylor managed to wrestle power from Doe by mid-July 1990.

Shortly afterwards, a six-nation West African peacekeeping force called the Economic Community of West African States Cease-Fire Monitoring Group (ECOMOG) essentially partitioned Liberia into two zones. The first encompasses the capital of Monrovia and is led by President Amos Sawyer. The other half, run by Taylor and his National Patriotic Front (NPFL), amounts to about 95 percent of Liberian territory; world support is generally enjoyed by Sawyer's marginal slice of the apple pie.

Reconciliation and peace agreements were signed like journalists' bar tabs. A March 1991 conference failed to get anything accomplished but the reelection of Sawyer as interim president. Despite a peace agreement in 1991, fighting continued to flare. Another peace agreement and cease-fire in July 1993 which established an interim government and setup general democratic elections crumbled a short time later in November.

Gambia, Mali, Ivory Coast, Switzerland and Benin are among the venues that have hosted Liberian peace talks since Taylor launched the civil war in December 1989. Some ended with agreements hailed at the time as historic. All proved to be failures.

The current agreement, signed in Benin with U.N. guarantees, seemed the most likely to succeed. Today it lies in tatters. Only 3000 of Liberia's estimated 60,000 fighters—many of them teenagers addicted to drugs and killing civilians—have been disarmed.

In August 1994, there were accusations by ECOMOG in Liberia that Cote d'Ivoire was supplying arms and ammunition to Taylor's NPFL in violation of a United Nations embargo. The embargo on shipping arms to Liberia was imposed by the United Nations in August 1992 following repeated accusations by ECOMOG and the former Liberian Interim Government that Cote d'Ivoire and neighboring Burkina Faso (formerly Upper Volta) were openly supporting Taylor's forces.

ECOMOG's COS General Femi Williams claimed that a dozen lorries from Cote d'Ivoire had delivered arms and ammunition to the headquarters of the NPFL in Gbarnga 120 kilometers (75 miles) west of the Liberian-Cote d'Ivoire border. A charge the Cote d'Ivoire Foreign Ministry vehemently denied, citing that its 340-mile border with Liberia isn't entirely manageable and part of ECOMOG's responsibility to monitor it. ECOMOG has also claimed links in arms trafficking between Burkina Faso and the NPLF, the principal Liberian Army. In July 1994, the Liberian transition government charged that 3000 Burkinabe mercenaries were operating in the ranks of the NPFL troops.

Regardless, Taylor has continued to put up a fight. In 1990, his forces sat opposite the presidential mansion in Monrovia for a month, but were never able to take the city because ECOMOG arrived and put an end to the fighting.

At least a third of Liberia's prewar population of 2.4 million fled the country after fighting broke out on December 24, 1989 when Taylor invaded Liberia from the Ivory Coast. Since then, the fighting has forced tens of thousands to flee areas in central, southeastern and northwestern Liberia, including nearly 20,000 who recently crossed the border into Guinea. Forty percent of the population is living in accessible areas, reflecting the huge number displaced. It has become nearly impossible for relief workers to operate in rebel-controlled areas. Military structure and law and order have broken down since the latest peace agreement fell apart shortly after disarmament began in March.

September 7, 1994 was slated to have been the date for democratic elections in Liberia, as determined in a 1993 peace agreement signed by the NPFL, Kromah and the former government of Amos Sawyer. It would've ended nearly five years of conflict in which the U.N. estimates 150,000 people have died and close to half of Liberia's estimated 2.5 million people have fled the country. But instead of voting for a president in free elections, Liberians were still fighting and there are now more armed factions than there were when the peace treaty was signed.

And what about Smell No Taste? Today, as many as 200 people flee from battles in central Liberia to Smell No Taste everyday, bringing the number of displaced people living here to more than 40,000. However, they're no longer drooling over arriving and departing jet-setters.

The Scoop

Liberia was once the most Americanized country in Africa. Created by former slaves who brought American surnames and American-style politics to Africa, Liberia no longer functions as a country. Prolonged civil war has reduced the country to a subsistence economy.

The country is terrorized by up to 60,000 mostly young (sometimes under 15) but always brutal, armed thugs who use rusty guns and vicious tempers to steal food.

The Players

There have been attempts at peace talks that united all three leaders in a triumvirate but the last peace accord lasted only a few hours until fighting broke out again. It is safe to say that none of the players have any following outside of the people on their immediate payroll.

Liberian National Transitional Government

The only shred of normal government left has a tenuous grip on Monrovia. These folks are keeping their bags packed and cashing their checks before the ink dries.

Charles Taylor

The leader of the National Patriotic Front of Liberia (NPFL). Originally from Gbarnga in central Liberia, he's the warlord who started this mess in 1989 and, today, can't even control his hometown. Known for videotaping his torture and murder of former President Doe. In 1992, the NPFL, the largest rival faction in the civil war, had a combat strength of approximately 15,000.

Alhaji Kromah

Leader of the United Liberation Movement (ULIMO), an unstable coalition of ethnic Krahns and Mandingos. The ULIMO Krahns, led by Chief of Staff Roosevelt Johnson, like to war with the ULIMO Mandingos when things get slow. The Krahns usually win.

Liberia's Armed Forces (AFL)

Also known as Liberia Peace Council, is led by the Reverend George Boley, a Krahn, and Chief Hezekiah Bowen. They control the coastal areas east of Monrovia with a total force of about 5000 men. Boley may be supported and armed by Nigerian soldiers from ECOMOG. By 1992, as a result of the civil war, the AFL maintained only limited authority and most of its equipment had been destroyed or rendered useless.

ECOMOG

A six-nation peacekeeping force, the Economic Community of West African States Monitoring Group (ECOMOG), has maintained a presence in Liberia since 1990. It consists of approximately 2600 troops from Nigeria, Senegal, Ghana, Guinea, Sierra Leone and Gambia. The only source of stability in Liberia comes from intervention by this West African peacekeeping force.

General Julue (a.k.a Rock One)

He was once the security chief for President Samuel Doe and now claims to be the leader of Liberia with a pathetic army of about 100 men. Brutal, cruel and now in captivity for his brief attempt at wresting power.

Ghana President

President Jerry Rawlings has accomplished a lot more than Liberian politicians in bringing the various Liberian factions together for peace talks, as well as U.N. officials and West African diplomats.

Political Parties

Founded in 1878, the True Whig Party ran the country until the 1980 coup, after which it was banned. It was revived in 1991. The National Patriotic Party (NPP), formed in December 1991, is the political wing of the National Patriotic Front of Liberia. The Independent Democratic Party was created as the political branch of the breakaway Independent National Patriotic Front of Liberia (INPFL) in 1991. Formed in 1991, the United Liberation Movement of Liberia for Democracy (ULIMO) was organized by supporters of the late President Samuel Doe. It split into two factions in November 1992, one being based in Tubmanburg, Liberia and the other in Freetown, Sierra Leone. Former members of the pan-African Movement for Justice in Africa founded the Liberian People's Party (LPP), a significant factor prior to the 1980 coup that brought Doe to power. The party's leader is former interim President Amos Sawyer.

Getting In

The roads leading from Monrovia are closed except for limited preapproved travel. U.S. Embassy employees are not allowed to travel outside Monrovia except for official business. Roberts International Airport outside of Monrovia is closed. Limited air service exists only between Spriggs Payne Airfield in Monrovia and Abidjan, Cote d'Ivoire and Freetown, Sierra Leone. No major international air carrier serves Spriggs Payne Airfield. Overland routes to other West African countries are not open. Travelers who plan a trip to Liberia are required to have a passport and a visa prior to arrival. Additionally, in order to be granted a visa, you must present to a Liberian embassy a letter stating the purpose of your visit and another from a doctor confirming you have no communicable diseases. Evidence of yellow fever vaccination is required. An exit permit must be obtained from Liberian immigration authorities upon arrival. There is no charge for a tourist visa.

The embassy tells us that the only area considered safe is inside the capital of Monrovia, since the Liberian National Transitional Government does not control areas outside of town. If you are caught entering illegally you will be arrested and tried, at which point you will be imprisoned or deported.

Further information on entry requirements for Liberia can be obtained from the:

Embassy of the Republic of Liberia
> *5201 16th Street, NW*
> *Washington, D.C. 20011*
> ☎ *(202) 723-0437 to 723-0440*
> This building is currently closed because of fire. The temporary address is:

> *5303 Colorado Avenue, NW*
> *Washington, D.C. 20011*

Getting Around

Total road mileage in Liberia is 6268; 1818 miles are paved. Total railroad track miles are 298. There are four ports, the three major ones at Buchanan, Greenville and Monrovia. There are 66 total airfields in Liberia; 49 with a permanent surface.

Roads leading out from Monrovia are not open for travel except for limited preapproved trips. Travelers to the interior of Liberia may be in danger of being detained, harassed, delayed, injured or killed. Since the onset of the civil war, travel to many parts of the country is simply impossible.

Warning

Although a Peace Accord was signed on July 25, 1993, U.S. citizens are warned against travel to Liberia because of continuing unsettled conditions. A security buffer, made-up of forces of the West African Peace Monitoring Group (ECOMOG), surrounds Monrovia.

Dangerous Places

Anywhere outside of Monrovia

Essentially the entire country is a free fire zone. The situation in Liberia changes virtually daily. Although a security buffer exists around Monrovia, tensions remain high in much of the country. There have been incidents of violence against civilians by partisans of Liberia's several warring factions. Travelers, including U.S. citizens, have been detained, harassed, delayed, injured or killed. A curfew is strictly enforced in Monrovia. Monrovia's crime rate is high. Foreigners, including U.S. citizens, have been targets of street crime. Residential break-ins are common. The police are largely incapable of providing effective protection.

The Firestone Rubber Plantation

Militia groups have been battling at the Firestone Rubber Plantation, the world's largest rubber estate, about 30 miles (48 km) east of the capital. Krahn fighters and their clansmen in the Liberia Peace Council (LPC) militia have been attacking Taylor's men at Firestone. Gun-toting marauders have also hijacked United Nations vehicles on the city's northwestern outskirts. ULIMO's Mandingo tribesmen have been fighting Krahn dissidents since March 1994, sending nearly 40,000 people fleeing the battle zone northwest of Monrovia.

Dangerous Things

Red Cross Vehicles

Red Cross operations in territory controlled by Charles Taylor's National Patriotic Front of Liberia (NPFL) were suspended in response to the confiscation of Red Cross vehicles and harassment of its staff by Taylor's soldiers.

Getting Sick

All visitors more than one year old must have a yellow fever vaccination certificate. Malaria and Hepatitis B are widespread and such arthropod-borne diseases as river blindness and sleeping sickness can also be a hazard. There are 15 hospital beds and one doctor for every 10,000 people. Medical facilities have been disrupted. Medicines are scarce. Information on health matters may be obtained from the Centers for Disease Control's international travelers hotline at ☎ *(404) 332-4559.*

Nuts & Bolts

Liberia, 37,743 square miles, is situated on the west coast of Africa, bounded by Guinea and Sierra Leone on the north and Cote d'Ivoire on the east. Monrovia, with a population of about half a million, is the capital. Liberia's total population is estimated at 2,839,000 with about half the inhabitants living in urban areas. Currency is the Liberian dollar, with 100 cents to the dollar.

Liberia has a tropical climate, with temperatures ranging from 65 degrees F to 120 degrees F. The rainy period extends from May through November and is characterized by frequent, prolonged and often torrential rainfall. Humidity is high, usually between 70 percent and 80 percent.

Indigenous Africans (including Kpelle, Bassa, Gio, Kru, Grebo, Mano, Krahn, Gola, Gbandi, Loma, Kissi, Vai and Bella) makeup 95 percent of the population; Americo-Liberians (descendants of black American settlers) account for 5 percent. Liberia is officially a Christian state, although indigenous beliefs are held by 70 percent of the population. Muslims comprise 20 percent and Christians only 10 percent of the population. English is the official language. There are close to 20 local languages derived from the Niger-Congo language. About 20 percent of the population uses English. Illiteracy stands at about 60 percent.

Lodging, water, electricity, fuel, transportation, telephone and postal services continue to be uneven in Monrovia. Such services are nonexistent or severely limited in rural areas. Mail delivery is erratic. Parcel delivery service is available to Monrovia. Courier mail services are available in Monrovia.

U.S. citizens who register at the U.S. Embassy in Monrovia may obtain updated information on travel and security in Liberia. Consular assistance may be limited by the unrest in the country.

Embassy Locations

The U.S. Embassy is located in the capital of Monrovia

111 United Nations Drive, Mamba Point
☎ *(231) 222991 through 222-994*
FAX (231) 223-710
The U.S. Embassy's mailing address is:

P.O. Box 10-0098
Mamba Point, Monrovia
or APO AE 09813
or PO Box 98.

Canadian Embassy in Liberia

None.

Liberian Consulate in Canada

1080 Beaver Hall Hill, Suite 1720
Montreal, Quebec H2Z 158
☎ *(514) 871-4741*
FAX (514) 397-0816

Dangerous Days

01/06/1986	New constitution inaugurated.
04/12/1980	President William Tolbert was overthrown in a coup led by Sgt. Samuel K. Doe, who subsequently suspended the constitution and imposed martial law.
05/25/1963	OAU - Africa Freedom Day.

Dangerous Days

07/26/1847	Independence Day.
02/11/0000	Armed Forces Day.

Pakistan
★★

Dodge City with Skiing

There are still a few places where the world is free of eco-tourists and hordes of yuppies corrupting indigenous cultures with Reeboks and R.E.M cassettes.

Pakistan, like its neighbor Afghanistan, has been surprisingly effective in resisting the influences of the outside world. Some areas of Pakistan have never felt the presence of their own government. There are areas where tribes and clans maintain their own basic social, political and military structures. Many view travelers and visitors as walking CARE packages. You're simply shot and relieved of your worldly goods. British adventurers such as Rudyard Kipling and Sir Richard Burton maintained a healthy respect for the "wily Pathans," who have always controlled the remote mountainous regions of Pakistan.

Today, Pakistan is an angry jigsaw puzzle of four semiautonomous provinces—Punjab, Sind, North-West Frontier Province (NWFP) and Baluchistan. It also encompasses federally administered tribal and northern areas (FATA/FANA) and lays claim to the Indian states of Jammu and Kashmir. The teeming population of Pakistan is as diverse as it is large. Its 115.59 million people are comprised of Punjabi (56 percent), Sindi (23 percent), Pashtun (13 percent), Baluchi (5 percent) and others, including Mohajirs; Muslim emigres from India.

Pakistan is dirt poor even by African standards. The per capita annual income in 1992 was US$410. Thirty percent of the population lives below the poverty line and only 35 percent of the population can read and write. Only 20 percent of Pakistani females can read and write and barely 40 percent of children of primary school age were actually enrolled in schools.

Pakistan is another country heading toward Muslim fundamentalism. By law, the country's president must be a Muslim. The legal system follows the Islamic code of justice, or *Sharia*. Even the banking system must abide by Koran dictates which say it is improper to charge or pay interest. Bank customers actually share the profits and losses with the institutions where they do business. However, fiscal common sense still supercedes religious zeal when, every year, just prior to Ramadan, customers withdraw their entire bank accounts to avoid the Zakat tax, a 2.5 percent levy on certain bank accounts charged annually on the eve of Ramadan.

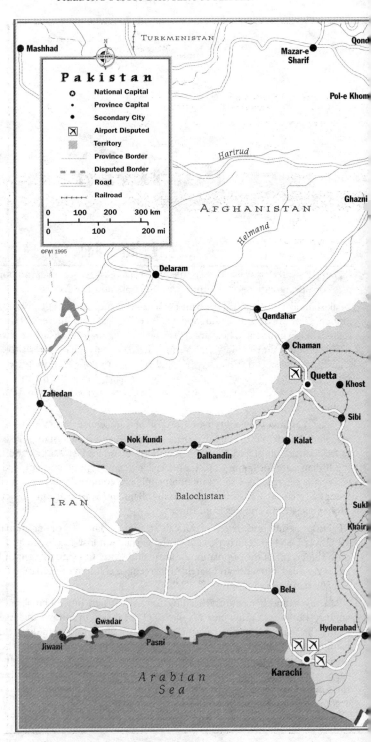

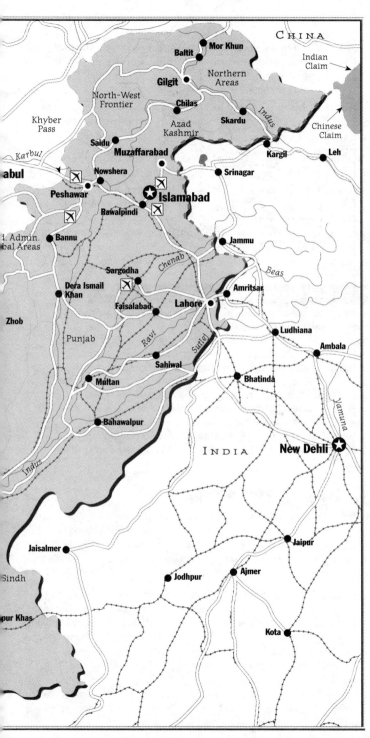

Pakistan's lifeline and major export is raw cotton; most of it goes to Europe and Japan. As with many other former British colonies, Pakistan was built around its railway system. The country is linked by the north-south railway between the southern port of Karachi and the city of Peshawar in the North-West Frontier Province. The line runs through most major population centers. Today, Pakistan is busy spending the millions appropriated to it by the World Bank to upgrade its highways. Unfortunately, no one has been taught to drive. If you're injured in Pakistan the chances are you'll end up splattered like a pancake, on freshly-laid pavement, by an overloaded bus or truck listing on the roadway like a dinghy in a squall.

Pakistan (Islami Jamhuria-e-Pakistan or the Islamic Republic of Pakistan) became independent on August 15, 1947 when Britain sliced up India in response to public pressure to create a separate Muslim state. East Pakistan seceded and became the separate country of Bangladesh in March 1971. Pakistan aligns itself with the U.S. and was a vital supply line for anti-Communist Afghan insurgents. Population growth is among the world's highest, the literacy rate is low and deteriorating, and the unofficial unemployment rate is greater than 25 percent. Agriculture still accounts for about 70 percent of total exports.

The Evils of Pork, Booze & Smack

As in most Muslim countries, pork is not available in Pakistan and all public eating is banned during Ramadan. Strangely, illegal drugs (even heroin) are easily found. Foreigners are expected to eat in the Western hotels or in private during the time of Muslim fasting. If you want a drink, you can order cocktails through room service (after signing that you need alcohol for "medical purposes"). But don't think you're doing the locals a favor by sneaking them a drink. Officials will search for drugs at Karachi airport. Despite the ease of procuring large amounts of hashish, opium and heroin, Pakistan has tough penalties for drug traffickers. Address your hosts as (last name) "sahib," and women as "begum sahiba" without the use of a personal name which is considered too familiar or informal. Pakistanis you meet will serve you tea and cakes, if not a large meal.

The Scoop

Pakistan is the classic adventurer's paradise, a wild mountainous region inhabited by fierce warring tribes. The countryside features dramatic alpine scenery and cultures unchanged for 2000 years. Pakistan offers natural, archeological and historical sites, as well as a wealth of interesting backwaters. Some of the planet's best mountaineering, hiking and photography are set against a backdrop of constant warfare and banditry.

There have been major ethnic tensions in Pakistan since the country became independent. Pakistan has been pushed closer to the edge by the massive influx of weapons and refugees. There are a lot of guns in Pakistan with a lot of people who use them on a regular basis. Tourists are kidnapped for ransom but have not been harmed or executed.(A Swede was killed in 1991 in a messy government rescue attempt.) Your health is definitely at risk; everything from cobras to dengue-carrying mosquitoes can end it all rather suddenly. Mountainous highways and insane drivers make Pakistan's roads a killing ground. Population growth is among the world's highest, the literacy rate is low and deteriorating, and the unofficial unemployment rate is greater than 25 percent. Much of the country is not under the control of the government but ruled by tribes. Professional bandits prey on poor and rich alike. What better place for a stroll through the countryside?

The Players

Islamic Jihad

Islamic Jihad is led by Mohammed Shawky Islambuli. He's supposedly hiding out in Meched, Iran. (See "*Hezbollah*" in "The Players" section in the Lebanon chapter.)

The Government

The government, bolstered by total armed forces of 580,000 (513,000 reservists), is actively stirring up revolt in Jammu and Kashmir. In June 1990, the Pakistan army had a total strength of over 500,000 soldiers. The navy has a total force of 20,000 men (including naval air personnel). The Pakistan air force (PAF) has 30,000 servicemen. Pakistan supplies much of the Middle East's cheap labor and is a low-cost supplier of military troops. About 30,000 military contract personnel from Pakistan were serving in Saudi Arabia, Libya, Oman, the United Arab Emirates and Kuwait in mid-1989, mainly in an advisory capacity. There have been complaints that the government actually makes money by renting out its poorly-paid troops to serve in U.N. peacekeeping missions. The U.N. compensates Pakistan at a higher rate of pay and the government allegedly pockets the difference. The government is actively trying to stir up the Muslim peoples of Jammu and Kashmir. They hope that both states will join Pakistan rather than seeking independence.

The "Afghans"

Hundreds of "Arab Afghans" from Libya, Egypt, Yemen, Jordan, Palestine, Algeria and Tunisia based in Peshawar and the border region between Pakistan and Afghanistan are being tracked by Mukhabarat al-Amat (political police), the Egyptian intelligence service.

The inner circle of the Afghans consists of 300 Egyptians. The Afghan branch of the Islamic Jihad is directed by Mohammed Shawky Islambuli, brother of the assassin of President Anar el-Sadat. Some 30 Egyptian "Afghans" work directly with the Iranian Pasdarans. Eight of these Egyptians constitute the central command of the Islamic Legion; a terrorist and political group active in Egypt, Eritrea, Kenya, Tanzania, Sudan, Algeria, Libya and Lebanon.

Some of the "Afghan" leaders have fled to Jalalabad from Peshawar. Jalalabad is controlled by the Gulbuddin Hekmatyar's fundamentalist Hezb al-Islami. Most filter back and end up in terrorist training camps in Iran or Sudan.

The "Arab Afghans" have ties with fundamentalist Muslims in the United States. Ramzi Ahmed Yussef, a suspect in the bombing of the World Trade Center in New York is an Egyptian "Afghan" now in hiding. Yussef was trained from 1987 to 1990 in Peshawar camps in the ranks of the Islamic Jihad groups under the orders of Dr. Ayman al-Zawahiri. Pakistan is winding down in its training of Muslim radicals from Indonesia, the Philippines and Morocco, and has reduced its support for Islamic fundamentalists in the Muslim Central Asian republics.

Getting In

A passport and visa are required. The visa must be obtained from a Pakistani embassy or consulate before arrival at the point of entry. Information on entry requirements can be obtained from the Embassy of Pakistan or the Pakistani Consulate General. There is a $20 fee for the visa and a $10 fee for rush delivery. Business visitors and tourists are required to carry a valid Pakistan visa in their passports which must be obtained prior to entry. Pakistani requirements to legally cross the country's borders are different for each nationality. U.S. citizens must have a visa issued by a Pakistani consulate as well as a valid U.S. passport.

Embassy of Pakistan

2315 Massachusetts Avenue, NW
Washington, D.C. 20008
☎ *(202) 939-6200*

Travelers may also contact the

Pakistani Consulate General

12 East 65th Street

New York, NY 10021
☎ *(212) 879-5800*

Do not bring in alcohol; it will be confiscated and given back to you upon your departure. Crossing from Afghanistan officially is forbidden for foreigners, although many of the remote tribal areas do not observe any immigration formalities. Currently the Afghanistan-Pakistan border is closed. Only U.N. personnel and locals are allowed to cross the border officially. The Iranian border can be crossed using weekly train service (Zahedan–Quetta), or by a painfully slow 22-hour bus trip (Taftan–Quetta). Folks who like avoiding those messy passport stamps can expect to be arrested and tried in court which can result in deportation, fines and/or imprisonment.

You can enter from China via the efficient, but weather-sensitive, Karakoram Highway. The road is open from May 1–November 30 if "mother nature" obliges. The route continues to the famous trading town of Kashgar (see "Forbidden Places"), but the bus ride will test the stamina and intestines of any traveler. Coming in from India is via train (Lahore–Wagh) or a four-hour bus ride (Lahore–Amritsar) but subject to closure due to Sikh attacks. Check with the government or the embassy for exact restrictions and closures.

Getting Around

Safe travel inside Pakistan is subject to regional idiosyncracies and plain luck. Bandits prey on buses and trains; the roads are makeshift, and if the robbers don't get you, the dilapidated buses might. Pakistan is a patchwork of tribal and government controlled areas sprinkled liberally with bandits who couldn't care less who "rules" the area.

Substantial areas within North-West Frontier Province are designated tribal areas, outside the normal jurisdiction of government law enforcement authorities. Travel within these areas is particularly hazardous. Tribal feuds or conflicts between smuggling factions may incidentally involve foreigners. Even in the settled areas, ethnic, political or sectarian violence may target foreigners. Car hijackings and the abduction of foreigners are occasionally reported from the tribal areas. If visitors must enter the tribal areas, a permit must be obtained from the Home Department, which may require that an armed escort accompany the visitor.

Driving

Despite all the press about *dacoits* and civil unrest, the greatest potential for injury while visiting Pakistan is from being involved in a bus or car crash. The aging Bedfords are adorned with loud horns, extensive murals, miniature disco systems, tassels and other bric-à-brac. Prayers to Allah, bucolic scenes, dingleberries, doo-dads and mascots glued like African fetishes are just some of the advance safety techniques designed to ensure the longevity of the driver (but not necessarily their passengers). The decorations are actually designed to ward off danger but, apparently, are ineffective in stopping the carnage.

Of a total 35,258 miles of roads in Pakistan, 24,952 (a generous 70 percent) are paved. The torturous terrain requires major engineering feats to put in roads. Most of the country can only be traversed via pack-trails and footpaths. The main highway is the Grand Trunk Road between Karachi and Peshawar.The multilane highway linking Karachi with Hyderabad is also a major route, permitting crazed drivers to get more out of their sheet-metal buckets than Isaac Newton would ever advise. The Indus Highway, the other north-south artery, is being improved, and there will eventually be a highway connecting Peshawar with Karachi, via Islamabad and Lahore.

Daewoo is busy building a 340-kilometer, six-lane toll road from Islamabad to Lahore. The 1200 km Karakoram Highway was built over a 20-year period to link the remote far north and China with the tribal areas to the south. The road is a mind-blower and is frequently closed due to landslides, snowstorms, floods and other topographical afflictions.

On paper, Pakistan borrows the British rule of driving on the left. In reality, Pakistani drivers have accidents in lanes that seem convenient, adhere more closely to the German fundamentals of operating motor vehicles with the pedal to the floor and the Asian custom of ignoring the fact that the roads are designed for camels and oxen and not Indy racers. If you want some control over your destiny you might want to hire your own driver and car from the Pakistan Tourism folks. A 4-WD jeep is preferable for more rugged trips in the north. Suzukis and Jeeps are popular. You will need a large security deposit and will be dinged about eight rupees per km and 200 rupees per day. Or, you can negotiate a fixed rate if you know your itinerary.

In the cities, taxis are cheap and should be hired round trip since they tend to gravitate to hotels and are hard to find elsewhere. The highway system is extensive but the drivers are a lot rougher than the roads. Pakistanis are notorious for their disregard of proper and safe driving techniques. Use a seatbelt at all times. Timid travelers should also refrain from traveling via public transportation such as buses, trains and taxis. Private taxi service supplied by the major hotels is your best bet in town.

The taxi fare from the airport to the centers of both Islamabad and Karachi is approximately 150 rupees. Negotiate the fare since, in the past, foreigners have traditionally been charged what the market will bear. If you want to see the country by bus, stick to the more comfortable "Flying Coach" buses rather than the brightly decorated but deadly local buses. For some amusement, try the horse-drawn "tonga" carriages and cheap motor "rickshaws."

Air travel is the recommended means of transportation between the major cities in Pakistan. Air travel, particularly to the northern areas is, however, often disrupted due to weather conditions. Caution is in order if traveling overland into remote areas of the country as foreigners increasingly have been the victims of armed robberies and vehicle theft. The greatest potential for injury while visiting Pakistan is from vehicular accidents.

By Rail

Pakistan Railways offers 8775 km of track, 907 stations, 78 train stops, 714 locomotives, 2926 passenger coaches and 32,440 freight wagons. Sixty percent of Pakistan's track and 30 percent of its rolling stock are supposed to be scrapped, but are in use every day. Express trains have been held up by *dacoits* (local bandits) on the link between Karachi port and Lahore. You'll have a choice between 2nd, Economy, 1st and Air-Conditioned classes. Go for the Air-Con class since rail travel is cheap. Bedding, toilet paper, soap and towels are not supplied on first-class couchettes but can be rented from the reservations office.

By Air

Islamabad/Rawalpindi International Airport is five miles northwest of Islamabad and a 20-minute drive by taxi. State-run Pakistan International Airlines (PIA) maintains service to 41 international and 33 domestic destinations. There are 112 airfields of which 104 are usable, 75 have a permanent surface. There are 31 runways over 8000 feet. Domestic tickets are cheaper when bought inside Pakistan. You must pay in rupees. International flights should be bought in major European or Asian bucket shops. Pakistan International Airways has the dubious task of flying aged equipment around the world's most hostile flying environments. Soaring mountains, dust, high winds, turbulence, down- and updrafts and the extra maintenance required to keep planes airborne may be the reason why the landing announcement is a Muslim prayer: "God willing, we will be landing in Karachi." The feeling of flying heavily loaded turboprops well below many of the world's highest mountains is, quite frankly, a thrill. Despite the white-knuckle flights, air travel is still the recommended means of transportation between major cities in Pakistan. Keep in mind that flights in the northern areas are often canceled due to weather conditions and are subject to overbooking.

Trekking

Pakistan realizes that most of the tourism is related to its spectacular mountain scenery. To facilitate understanding and access, tourism officials have divided the country into Open, Restricted and Closed zones for trekkers. Open zones go up to only 6000 meters. Travel above that point is classified as mountaineering and requires a separate permit. The best source for information and permits is through the various trekking packagers well in advance of your trip (permits can take months). **Pakistan Tours** (*Flashman's Hotel, The Mall, Rawalpindi;* ☎ *64811*) or **Adventure Pakistan** (*10 Kahayaban-e-Suharawardy, Aapara Market, Islamabad;* ☎ *28324*) are good sources for information, permits, guides and porters.

Getting Out

You will need an exit visa to leave the country. Although you may adhere to the paper chain faithfully, expect to get a quizzical look as the immigration official notes certain "irregularities" and requires additional funds to let you catch your plane out. If you are carrying anything that can be interpreted as being an antiquity, you are in trouble again. You'll need an export permit for rugs; and don't think for a moment that nifty pen-gun you bought in Darra Adam Khel is not going to be spotted and confiscated. If you're bringing some smoking green back with you, expect to be discovered by sniffer dogs at Karachi and Lahore airports.

Dangerous Places

Karachi

Sectarian violence killed more than 1000 people in 1994, compared to 75 in 1993. Even the army left in December saying it was too "hot" for them. In 1993, 88 soldiers and police officers were killed in ambushes and shootings. No one has been convicted or even charged with the murders. More than 170 people were killed in sectarian and ethnic violence in December 1994 in this southern port city. Police killed six kidnappers holding a businessman captive for ransom in January 1995. As of the beginning of 1995, the *Mohajirs* are the principal rebel group in the area. The *Mohajirs* are Urdu-speaking Muslim immigrants who came here from India after the partition between Pakistan and India. Their political/military group, the Mohajir National Movement (MQM), has opened peace talks with the government. There are six major political and religious groups in Karachi. In total they have 1000 armed guerrillas and snipers operating at any one time.

The Jali Rabhat Area

This area is frequently used by heroin smugglers moving drugs to Europe via Turkey. Here, bad men hide out in relative safety. Among them are the Egyptian "Afghans" sentenced to death in absentia. Here they work closely with the Iranian Pasadaran. Among the Egyptian "Afghans" are the central command of the Islamic Legion, which maintains "branch offices" in Egypt, Eritrea, Kenya, Tanzania, Sudan, Algeria, Libya and Lebanon. Those the Pakistani government are forced to deport usually end up traveling to Iran via Jallalabad, Afghanistan. The other favored destination is Sudan.

The North-West Frontier Province

An area created by the British in 1901, the NWFP is the land of *badal*, or revenge. It is one of the oldest continuously lawless areas in the world. Home to the "wily Pathans," the land of valleys and rivers has never been fully conquered by Moghuls, Afghans, Sikhs, Brits or even the

Russians. The North-West Frontier Province has an affinity with Afghanistan in the west rather than India, and is known for its well-armed populace. Weapons are carried and sold openly on the streets. Peshawar, the largest city and capital of the province, has been described as Dodge City without Wyatt Earp. Peshawar has been the scene of numerous terrorist incidents, many relating to the unsettled Afghan situation. Americans and Western interests have been specifically targeted in the recent past. Travelers should be keenly aware of the current political climate and should check with the American consulate before traveling to Peshawar.

Khyber Pass

It is dangerous to travel overland through the tribal areas to the Khyber Pass. The North-West Frontier areas are ruled by militant tribes and are not under the control of the Pakistani government or police. Tribal feuds or conflicts between smuggling factions may involve foreigners. Even in the settled areas, ethnic, political or sectarian violence may target foreigners. Car hijackings and the abduction of foreigners are occasionally reported from the tribal areas. If visitors must enter the tribal areas, a permit must be obtained from the Home Department, which may require that an armed escort accompany the visitor.

Sind Province

Hundreds of years ago travelers called Sind the "Unhappy Valley" because of its burning deserts, freezing mountain peaks, dust, lack of water and general fear of the predatory tribes. Today in rural Sind Province, the weather has not improved and the security situation is still hazardous, especially for overland travelers. Foreigners have occasionally been kidnapped, and in one incident in 1991, a Swedish kidnap victim was killed in a rescue attempt that turned into a battle between police and bandits. The home of the ancient Indus culture was known for its total lack of warfare or warlike activity. Naturally the civilization disappeared in 1700 B.C. Today, Sind province is in turmoil due to friction between the political factions based out of Karachi. Drug smugglers and *dacoits* also make the rural areas unsafe for travel. Smugglers use the local beaches of Karachi to move drugs and contraband at night. Sinds, Pathans and Mohajirs are jostling for political supremacy in the region. The result is frequent assassinations, firefights, bomb attacks, murders and overall mayhem. Travel outside of Karachi into the Sind interior must have prior approval of the government of Pakistan. The interior of Sind is experiencing severe law and order problems. Crimes such as robbery and kidnapping have escalated in recent years, particularly attacks on foreigners. These robbers (known as *dacoits*) are well armed and have, at times, attacked travelers even under police escort. Travel by land, whether by car or train is not advised. Bandits have been known to stop entire trains or vehicle caravans, often kidnapping and killing passengers. Anyone contemplating travel into the Sind interior should first contact the American Consulate, 8 Abdullah Haroon Road, Karachi, ☎ 515081 for advisability. If travel is subsequently approved, a Pakistan police escort would normally be provided.

The Pakistan government has recommended that travelers limit their movements in Sind Province to the city of Karachi. If visitors must go into the interior of Sind Province, the Pakistan government requests that travelers inform police authorities well in advance of the trip so that necessary police security arrangements can be made. Bodyguards can be hired from travel groups or on the street (not advised) for about 4000 rupees a day. You will have to pay for bodyguards' room and board. The best place to start is the U.S. embassy in Karachi. Sind province once had a fairly healthy kidnappings-for-ransom business, the number of which went from 45 in 1990 to 79 in 1991, then dropped to 16 in 1992 because of the increased military presence in the area.

Karachi

Karachi is a dirty bustling city with a population of more than 5 million people and, like most large cities, has a serious problem with crime, as well as periodic incidents of ethnic and sectarian violence. Demonstrations, rallies and processions (footnotes anti-American) occur frequently throughout the city; although individual Americans have not been targeted. Politically-motivated crimes such as robbery and kidnapping are often carried out with the intention of creating a sense of instability among the populace. More recently, bombings have occurred at Pakistan government facilities and public utility sites. Vehicular hijacking and theft by armed individuals are common occurrences. Persons resisting have very often been shot and killed.

Hyderabad

In Hyderabad, there have been recurring outbreaks of ethnic and sectarian violence which have been characterized by random bombings, shootings and mass demonstrations. Recent incidents have resulted in several deaths and the unofficial imposition of curfews. There have also been numerous incidents of kidnapping for ransom.

Punjab Province/Islamabad and Rawalpindi

Islamabad, the capital of Pakistan, is not officially a part of the Punjab province but does lie within its borders. It is considered a sister city to Rawalpindi; they are located only 10 kilometers apart. Islamabad and Rawalpindi are frequently the scenes of demonstrations, rallies and processions. These events are often anti-American in nature and have at times become violent. Violent demonstrations have been directed at American facilities in the past, but fortunately individual Americans are not usually specifically targeted. Travelers should be aware of planned or unplanned demonstrations and leave or avoid the area. Although the crime rate in Islamabad is lower than in many parts of Pakistan, it is on the rise. In the recent past, Americans have been the victim of armed robberies and assaults although these types of incidents are not frequent. Thefts from residences are common. However, most incidents experienced by the American community are committed by servants employed in the household. In the past year, the area has been the scene of several bombings. Most of the incidents have occurred in Rawalpindi in public areas such as markets, cinemas and parks. Generally, the government of Pakistan attributes responsibility for these acts to the intelligence services of neighboring countries. In the past, foreigners have not been the target of the bombing incidents, but could be victimized by being in the wrong place at the wrong time.

Punjab Province/Lahore

The Punjab Province has been the site of numerous bomb blasts occurring at cinemas, marketplaces and other public areas. A professional criminal element exists in the Punjab (operating mainly in the interior) with kidnapping for ransom, robbery and burglaries all being carried out by gangs of professional criminals. There are frequent reports of Pak-Indo conflicts along the border area and in east Punjab and in the disputed territory of Kashmir. Since the creation of Pakistan in 1947, this region has been the focal point of an intense dispute between Pakistan and India. Travel to the border areas of eastern Punjab is not recommended. Violent confrontations have also occurred in this region between the Pakistan security forces and individuals supporting the liberation of the Jammu and Kashmir region (disputed territory) from India. Travel to these eastern interior locations should first be cleared by the U.S. Embassy in Islamabad or the U.S. Consulate in Lahore.

Kashmir

The Kashmir dispute, which caused the 1948 and 1965 wars with India, remains unresolved. Kashmir was one of India's largest princely states but has turned into a war zone with both sides owning large chunks of land. The Simla Agreement after the 1971 Bangladesh war adjusted the boundary between the Indian state of Jammu and Kashmir and the Pakistani state of Azad and Kashmir. The Muslims in the Indian state of Jammu and Kashmir demand greater autonomy from Hindu and somewhat colonial India. Since an active insurgency began in January 1990, estimates of the numbers who have died range from a low of 7000 to a high of 13,000.

The separatist elements within Jammu and Kashmir, particularly the Jammu and Kashmir Liberation Front (JKLF), receive training and military equipment from Pakistan. China is also aligning itself with Pakistan against India. A December 1993 meeting resulted in agreements to provide increased economic and military cooperation.

Dangerous Things

Crime

In Karachi, armed robberies are common and drivers resisting the theft of their motor vehicles are often shot. In addition, petty crime, especially theft of personal property, is common throughout Pakistan.

North-West Frontier Province/Peshawar

The North-West Frontier Province borders Afghanistan on the west and is known for its well-armed populace. Weapons are carried and sold openly on the streets. Americans and Western interests have been specifically targeted in the recent past. Travelers should be keenly aware of the current political climate and should check with the American Consulate before traveling to Peshawar. Where the level of crime is high, with armed robberies and politically motivated kidnappings topping the list. Most criminal acts have been attributed to the large number of Afghan refugees living in Peshawar and the NWFP area. The police have generally demonstrated an unwillingness or inability to address crimes committed by Afghans. Foreign travelers should maintain a low profile and contact the consulate for information on areas to avoid. Travel outside of Peshawar and into the North-West Frontier tribal areas is extremely dangerous and not recommended. Kidnapping, vehicular hijacking and robbery occur frequently. Although Pakistan has a limited law enforcement presence, the area is governed mainly by tribal laws. Travel outside of Peshawar should not be undertaken without first contacting the U.S. Consulate and obtaining approval from the government of Pakistan. This includes trips to the Khyber Pass region.

Sind Province/Karachi

Travel outside of Karachi and into the Sind interior must have prior approval of the government of Pakistan. Interior Sind is experiencing severe law and order problems. Crimes such as robbery and kidnapping have escalated in recent years, particularly attacks on foreigners. These robbers (known as *dacoits*) are well-armed and have at times attacked travelers even under police escort. Travel by land, whether by car or train is not advised. Bandits have been known to stop entire trains or vehicle caravans frequently kidnapping and killing passengers. Anyone contemplating travel into the Sind interior should first contact the American Consulate in Karachi for advisability. If travel is subsequently approved by the GOP, a Pakistan police escort would normally be provided.

Baluchistan/Quetta

The province of Baluchistan which borders both Iran and Afghanistan is notorious for cross-border smuggling operations. This region also has a high occurrence of armed robberies. Terrorist bombings have occurred frequently in the region, primarily concentrated among those districts along the Afghanistan border. As there is limited provincial police presence and influence, those persons considering travel into the interior should first notify the province's home secretary, travel in a group and limit travel to daylight hours. Permission from the provincial authorities is required for travel into some interior locations. Quetta, the capital city of the province, has experienced outbreaks of serious ethnic violence. Police have in the past used deadly force and imposed curfews in response to these ethnic clashes. Information regarding current conditions may be obtained by contacting either the American Consulate in Karachi or the U.S. Embassy in Islamabad. Crimes such as robbery and vehicular hijacking have also been on the rise in Quetta. Western organizations have been targeted and travelers should be alert as to what areas of the city to avoid.

Terrorist Camps

In the town of Peshawar there are a number of terrorist training camps under the banner of Islamic Jihad. Here Algerians, Tunisians, Yemenis, Jordanians and others train for Holy War. There are no tours, and visitors are not welcome.

Dacoits

Possibly the most lucrative night job in Pakistan. Many *dacoits* are professional bandits aligned along tribal lines who hold normal day jobs and then head out into the country for a little extra cash at night. Unlike the greasy thugs of Russia or the gold-toothed banditos of Mexico, *dacoits* are usually bad guys for hire led by educated or civil service-level young men. They cannot find employment so they use their organizing and planning skills to support political parties, back up rebel units, raise operating funds and to expand operations areas. Despite the genteel background of the leaders, the actions of their members are bloody and crude. *Dacoits* will stop buses and trains, rob, rape and murder, and generally create a bloody mess. They also use kidnapping as a way to generate funds and "flip the bird" to the local government. Expect to be a well-treated but powerless pawn as the *dacoits* negotiate with the local government (not your home government) for payment for your release. Your biggest problem may be a heavy-handed (but fiscally efficient) rescue attempt staged by the government on your behalf.

Ethnic Clashes

Pakistan is a country that really shouldn't hold together. Artificially carved up by Sir Cyril Radcliffe in 1947 in an effort to separate warring Muslims from the Hindus, the hastily created border caused instant riots and violence sending 6 million people from each region fleeing across the new border. It is estimated that up to a million people were killed. Today, with 60 million Muslims in India and more than 10 million Hindus in Pakistan, there is little hope for peace. Demonstrations often get ugly in Karachi and Hyderabad where Sindhis and immigrant groups in Karachi and Hyderabad duke it out. Between January 1990 and October 1992, Pakistan-trained militants killed 1585 men and women; including 981 Muslims, 218 Hindus, 23 Sikhs, and 363 security men. In three years, over 7000 Kalashnikov rifles, 400 machine guns, 400 rocket launchers, 1000 rockets, 7000 grenades, 2000 pistols and revolvers, and thousands of mines were seized. One of the keys to staying alive in heavily-armed areas is to not bring a knife to a gun fight. If you visit Pakistan, you might want to bring your own army.

Cheap Guns

Pakistan is (and traditionally has been) a Wild West region with most tribal, ethnic and criminal groups being well-armed with cheap weapons brought in from Afghanistan. There are few tribes that don't possess large arsenals and fierce rivalries against one another. Crime is becoming a problem in Karachi and other areas where theft, burglary and kidnappings of businessmen are becoming endemic. Most urban residents employ *chowkidaars* or private guards for protection. If you are not caught in the middle of a firefight you may be worse off at a wedding or party. Pathans have a bad habit of using their AK-47s as firecrackers and shoot bursts into the air, ignorant of Newtonian physics.

Bandits

The remote areas of Sind province have traditionally been an ideal place to get held up and killed by armed tribes who take great pride in their stealth and brutality.

The Pathans

Pakistan's Pathan community still wants to unite with the Pathans in Afghanistan. The nearly 3 million Afghan refugees in Pakistan constitute a drag on the economy and are the cause for ethnic conflict. Afghans have played a significant role in disputes between Shiite and Sunni Muslims, and provide a scapegoat for ethnic conflict in Sind.

Mountain Climbing

Bandits and bugs may be the last of your worries as you wait out a sudden blizzard, clinging to the icy face of one of the world's highest mountains. Make sure you are hooked up with an experienced guide and spend some time getting acclimatized to the thin air.

Getting Sick

Adequate medical care is available in major cities in Pakistan, but may be limited in rural areas. U.S. medical insurance is not always valid outside the United States. Doctors and hospitals often expect immediate payment in cash for treatment. Supplemental health insurance which specifically covers overseas treatment has proved to be useful. You need proof of a cholera vaccination if arriving from infected areas. You should get a typhoid shot and take malaria prophylaxis. Yellow fever vaccination and certificate is required if you have visited a country in the endemic zone recently.

Inoculations against yellow fever and cholera are required for visitors arriving in Pakistan within five days after leaving or transiting infected areas. In addition, immunization against typhoid, polio and meningitis is recommended, as are prophylactic anti-malarial drugs. Hepatitis and tetanus are further health risks in Pakistan, as are amoebic dysentery and worms. Bilharzia (schistosomiasis) and elephantiasis (filariasis) are also endemic diseases, although not widespread. Follow the usual precautions for countries with poor sanitation. Military hospitals, frequently open to fee-paying local civilians and foreigners, often provide the best facilities.

Nuts & Bolts

Pakistan is a land of hard extremes. The climate is generally arid and hot, except in the northern mountains, where the winters are very cold. The best time to visit Pakistan is between October and April. Karachi and Lahore are pleasant; Islamabad can get cool. The average annual temperatures in the southern city of Karachi are between 55 degrees F and 93 degrees F. Summer brings the monsoon season, but rainfall is negligible at other times of the year. After April, the temperatures climb from mid-July through September during the monsoon season, which can dump up to 16 cm of rain. North of Islamabad is mountainous, with a temperate climate. Summers are cool, winters cold, and the average annual rainfall is 120 cm. The world's second-highest mountain, the famed 8611-meter-high K-2 (Mount Godwin Austen), is the star of the Karakoram Range: K-2 has been the site of several notable climbing expeditions since 1909.

The currency is the rupee, about 30 rupees to the U.S.dollar. You can only bring into Pakistan up to 100 rupees. The rupee is best purchased at a bank, not at your hotel. Many money changers will try to foist off the faded dirty notes, but don't take them. They will be tough to exchange back. You will need to carry around the paperwork you get when you swap dollars for rupees. Credit cards are worthless outside the major cities but good old AMEX has offices in Islamabad, Rawalpindi, Lahore and Karachi. The best exchange rates are on the black market. Merchants will give you a better exchange rate if you pay in U.S. dollars. You will not get a receipt for the transaction, since the transaction is illegal. *Baksheesh* is the Pakistani version of tipping. When people help you it's normal and expected that you will drop a few *paisa's* or rupees in their palm.

You can bring in as much foreign currency as you want, but it must be declared upon arrival. Electricity is 220V/50Hz.

If you hate crowds and crave danger, Pakistan provides excellent opportunities for winter sports, including mountaineering and hiking in the Himalayan hill stations, as well as magnificent scenery. The AK-47s, pistols and 50-caliber machine guns are dirt cheap in Peshawar but a bitch to bring home. There is a departure tax of 100 rupees for international flights and 10 rupees for domestic hops.

Down below, where the Indus River makes the Punjab and Sind fertile, temperatures are more moderate, with an average of 15 degrees Centigrade in January to an average of 37 degrees C in the summer. Baluchistan consists of deserts and low bare hills. Here and in northern Sind, temperatures can climb over 50 degrees Centigrade in the summer.

Normal office hours from Saturday to Wednesday are from 9 a.m. to 2 p.m., with at least one hour for lunch. Offices close earlier on Thursdays, usually at lunchtime. Friday is the weekly holiday. Banks are open from 9 a.m. to 1:30 p.m. from Saturday to Wednesday, and until 11a.m. on Thursday. Urdu (the national language) and English are the official languages of Pakistan. Punjabi, Sindi, Pashtu, Baluchi, Seraiki and other languages and dialects are also spoken.

Pakistani cuisine is what many people confuse here as Indian food. *Kebabs*, *tikkas* (spiced-grilled meats) and curries are the staples; they're served with *naan* (flat bread). The most popular drinks are tea (black or green), *lassi* (a milk drink) and Western-style soft drinks, which are widely available.

Useful Addresses

Associated Press of Pakistan (APP)

House 1, Street 56
F 6/3 POB 1258, Istanbul
☎ *(51) 826158*
FAX (51) 813225

Government Publications, Central Publications Branch, Government of Pakistan

Block University Road, Karachi
Habib Bank Ltd. Habib Bank Plaza
Karachi 75650
☎ *219111*
FAX: 2414191

Ministry of Commerce

Block A, Pakistan Secretariat
Islamabad
☎ *825078*

Ministry of Communications

Block D, Pakistan Secretariat
Islamabad
☎ *826277*
FAX 828724

Pakistan International Airlines Corp. (PIA)

Head Office Building, Quaid-i-Azam International Airport
Karachi
☎ *(21) 4572011*
FAX (21) 4572754

Pakistan Publishers' and Booksellers' Association

YMCA Building
Shahrah-e-Qaid-e-Azam
Lahore

Pakistan Tourism Development Corp. Ltd.

House No. 2, St. 61, F-7/4
Islamabad
☎ *811001*

UK Embassy

Diplomatic Enclave, Ramna 5
P.O. Box 1122
Islamabad
☎ *822131*
FAX 823439

Canadian Embassy in Pakistan

Diplomatic Enclave, Sector G-5
P.O. Box 1042
Islamabad
☎ *(92) (51) 211101*

U.S. Embassy in Pakistan

Diplomatic Enclave, Ramna 5
P.O. Box 1048
Islamabad
☎ *(51) 826161*
FAX (92) (51) 214222

Pakistani Embassy in Canada

151 Slater Street, Suite 608
Ottawa, ONT. K1P 5H3
☎ *(613) 238-7881*
FAX (613) 238-7296

Pakistani Embassy in United States

2315 Massachusetts Avenue, NW
Washington, D.C. 20008
☎ *(202) 939-6200*
FAX (202) 387-0484

Embassy Location

The U.S. Embassy
Diplomatic Enclave, Ramna 5; ☎ *826 161, Islamabad,*

The Consular Section
Located separately in the USAID building, 18 Sixth Avenue, Ramna 5.

The Consulate General
8 Abdullah Haroon Road; ☎ *568-5170, Karachi.*

The U.S. Consulate General
Sharah-E-Abdul Hamid Bin Badees (50 Empress Road), New Simla Hills; ☎ *636-5530, Lahore.*

The U.S. Consulate
11 Hospital Road, Peshawar Cantonment; ☎ *279-801, 279-802, 279-803, Peshawar.*

Dangerous Days

04/07/1991	Shia Muslims mark the death of Hazrat Ali, fourth caliph of Islam.
08/05/1988	Arif Hussain al-Hussaini, a leading Shiite religious and political leader in Pakistan, was shot to death in Peshawar.
07/17/1988	An airplane carrying President Zia Ul-Haq and U.S. Ambassador Arnold Raphel crashed, killing everyone aboard.
09/05/1986	Twenty-one persons, including two Americans, were killed in an abortive hijacking of Pan Am flight 73 by four Arab gunmen.
04/10/1986	The daughter of former President Bhutto, Benazir Bhutto, returned from exile in Europe.
07/18/1985	Shahnawaz Bhutto, son of executed President Zulfikar Bhutto and older brother of Pakistani People's Party Leader Benazir Bhutto, died under mysterious circumstances in France.
07/14/1985	Bombing of Pan Am office.
11/22/1979	The U.S. Embassy in Islamabad was attacked and burned by Islamic militants following rumors that the U.S. was involved in the violent takeover of the Grand Mosque in Mecca, Saudi Arabia.
04/04/1979	Former president of Pakistan Zulfikar 'Ali Bhutto was executed by the Pakistani government under President Zia. The terrorist group al-Zulfikar, founded by his two sons, is named after him.
07/05/1977	Army Chief of Staff Mohammad Zia leads an army coup to seize power and becomes chief martial law administrator.
06/08/1962	Martial law, which was imposed in 1958, was lifted and the national assembly convened.
03/23/1962	A new constitution was promulgated by President Ayub Khan.
10/07/1958	President Iskander Mirza, supported by senior military officers, seized power and imposed martial law.
09/06/1957	Defense of Pakistan Day.
03/23/1956	The national assembly adopted a new constitution which rejected Pakistan's status as a dominion and became an "Islamic Republic" within the commonwealth. Also known as "Pakistan Day."
08/14/1947	Independence Day. Pakistan became a self-governing dominion within the British commonwealth.

Peru
★★

Shadow and Light

When Francisco Pizarro and the Spaniards "discovered" Peru in 1531, the Incan empire was already past its zenith. The Incas were licking the wounds of a nasty civil war and were easily thumped by their uninvited guests.

The Spanish weren't the first or the last conquerors to impose a military dictatorship on Peru. But the nation's destiny was reflected in a historical strobe light as it vacillated between despotism and democracy, continuing to this day, nearly 500 years later.

After almost 300 years of Spanish rule, it took more outsiders—Jose de San Martin of Argentina and Simon Bolivar of Venezuela, to finally break Spain's grip on the country. Peru announced its independence in 1821, but it took a few more years to purge the Spanish. In December 1824, General Antonio Jose de Sucre defeated the Spanish troops at Ayacucho, ending Spanish rule in South America. Spain recognized Peru's independence in 1879 after yet another war with Peru between 1864 and 1866.

Today, the ruling class is a tossed salad of predominantly white-bread landed gentry hailing from families of global origins, with a sizable garnishing of East Asians. It's quite the norm in Peru to have a surname of German, Spanish, English, Japanese or French lineage. But that hasn't enhanced the "civility" of Peru. Modern Peru is the world's leading producer of coca and perhaps its largest concealer of citizens killed, tortured or abducted. In 1993, a Peruvian human rights group estimated that 28,809 people had been killed in 12 years of political violence. The government fessed up to only 53 of the deaths (leaving at least 2660 people unaccounted for). The Maoist rebel group Shining Path (SL) seems proud to admit that nearly half the body count came at their hands.

Peru's a basketball game of body counts. In 1992, 3101 people were killed in violent actions; 60 percent died in battles, 30 percent were murdered. Two hundred and eighty-six people were abducted in the same year; 178 weren't heard from again. The balance were summarily executed. Torture is the favored, and a routine, mode of interrogation employed by Peru's armed forces, and is employed even during investigations of petty crime.

The U.N., the Red Cross and the U.S. Department of State all agree that, in Peru, human rights are human wrongs. Executions by the military, the disappearance and murder of students and the torture of arrested persons and missing people are simply everyday life in Peru. The only good news is that deaths by terrorism were down in 1993 and 1994—almost by half. Only 1692 people died in guerrilla wars in 1993, compared to 3101 in 1992.

The country has been under emergency rule for more than two years, permitting President Alberto Fujimori to put some heavy-duty dents into terrorist itineraries. And, he did some serious name-dropping. Literally, the names dropped. Victor Polay Campos, head of the Tupac Amaru Revolutionary Movement (MRTA), was recaptured (he had escaped from custody in 1990) after he was recognized in a Lima bar. Peter Cardenas Shulze, MRTA's second-in-command, was busted in a raid by security forces on a safe house in Lima. Government forces snatched Abimael Guzman Reynoso, the SL founder, along with seven other SL members. His personal diary and plans for an upcoming SL offensive were also found.

Now that Fujimori has Guzman and Campos wearing stripes and is singing for peace like a lonely finch (with a little prodding from the head of the secret police), you'd think he could relax. Fujimori also brags that he has convicted more than 1000 terrorists, reformed another 1500 and captured thousands. The fact that he thinks he's David Copperfield by making students, political opponents and journalists disappear doesn't seem to bother hard-working Peruvians, who are sick and tired of the terrorists actions. Fujimori received a 67 percent approval rate in 1993.

Well, dictators can never relax.

Fujimori fled his Lima palace the night of November 13, 1992 after being tipped-off about a coup attempt. Not to a television station did he dash to plead for calm or reassure a frightened nation, nor to a military base to bravely lead his troops on a counter-assault. Instead, Fujimori high-tailed it to the Japanese embassy to save his own butt. Safe, sound and sushi-satiated, he then directed his crush against the insurrection by calling coup leader General Jaime Salinas from his cellular phone. Finally, after a predawn shoot-out with Salinas' rogues, the coup was put down; thank Vladimiro Montesinos for saving his bacon. Montesinos is the man who runs the military; he's got direct connections to the CIA and the drug mafia. Montesinos is alleg-

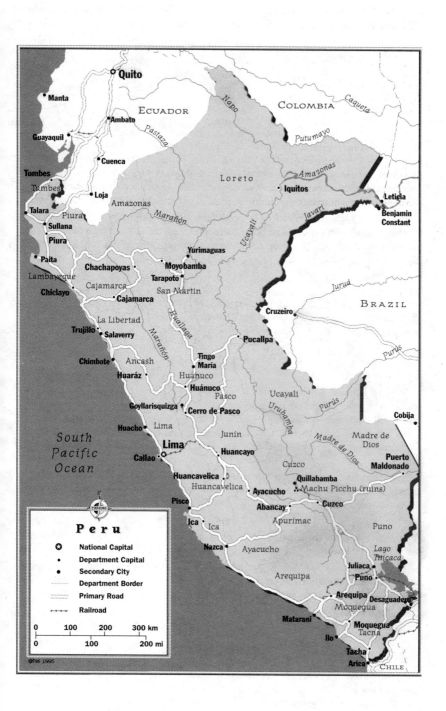

edly the man who directs death squads, bullies the military with his secret files and put Fujimori in to power. He apparently intends to keep him there.

The Scoop

Among the more than six million dispossessed, homeless and impoverished souls in Lima, hides, arguably, the most apocalyptic group of terrorists on earth. The squalid, nameless shantytowns dotted across the Peruvian landscape are where The Shining Path (Sendero Luminoso) recruits its legions.

With the exception of certain tourist areas (Arequipa, Cuzco, Ica, Iquitos, Paracas, Puerto Maldonado, Puno and Trujillo), many regions of the country are designated as "emergency zone" areas. These are areas under terrorist threat and governed under martial law by well-armed soldiers who rip off a couple of clips on full automatic first and ask questions later. Despite the arrest of key leaders in 1992, two insurgent organizations—the Shining Path (SL) and the Tupac Amaru Revolutionary Movement (MRTA)—continue to carry out bombings and other terrorist attacks against a range of targets in Peru; principally Peruvian nationals, government installations, banks and foreign interests.

The unofficial headquarters of terrorism is the city of Lima, a designated "emergency zone". Bombings and terrorist incidents have been frequent in the city, and violent crime is common. There are power outages during the day due to the drought conditions affecting the hydroelectric plants. This is important to know when choosing a high-rise hotel. Ask if the hotel has its own generator. Hotel rooms are favorite targets of burglars. The lack of tourists means that you will be particularly conspicuous.

Banks do not normally cash "Traveler's cheques," but money changers will come to your room to exchange soles into U.S. dollars. Credit cards are accepted. There is a black market in soles, but don't be scummed by trading U.S. dollars for old notes.

Police augment their meager paychecks by setting up checkpoints on Thursday and Friday evenings to finance their weekends. Use air transportation when possible, and don't trust reports claiming that certain areas are safe.

Junk-yard locos like the Shining Path have deliberately killed governors, mayors, tourists, schoolteachers, civil servants, hundreds of campesinos, entire villages, journalists, elderly people, children, presidential candidates, British ornithologists, Mormon missionaries, an agronomist, nuns and priests from various countries, mine workers and their wives, American helicopter crew members and a helluva lot more. They have bombed embassies, power lines, police vans, police stations, even public parks.

If by some miracle you don't run into the military or terrorists, there are always the hard working farmers who live off the land. The fruits of their labor generate about US$1 billion in sales. What is the favorite cash crop of Peru? Why coca, of course.

Tips:

Arrange to be met at the airport by someone you can identify. Hire only taxis from inside the airport. Unlicensed taxi drivers have been known to drive victims into the barrios and rob them.

The streets are not safe at night despite vehicle curfews. Inside major hotels, there is a generally decent level of security. Hotels are usually empty so don't be shy about negotiating a good rate. For security, DP recommends the following establishments:

Central Lima Hotels
    Grand Bolivar ☎ 14-276400
    Crillon ☎ 14-283290
    Lima Sheraton ☎ 14-333320

Lima Restaurant
    Rosa Nautica ☎ 14-470057 on the Miraflores oceanfront

Miraflores Hotels
    Las Americas ☎ 14-459494
    Miraflores Cesar ☎ 14-441212

El Pardo ☎ *14-470283*

San Isidro

Country Club ☎ *14-404060*

The Players

Alberto Fujimori

The current ruler is President Alberto Fujimori. Fujimori is Peruvian of Japanese descent. In two years, he managed to dissolve parliament and assume the role of dictator. His stated goal was to deal with political corruption, and he bestowed upon himself absolute, unimpeachable authority in destroying the terrorist elements within Peru. Fujimori deftly constructed a new congress completely under his control, albeit behind a facade of democracy.

A tough talking, power hungry leader who is criticized for his abuses of human rights, Fujimori was elected in July of 1990 and took absolute power in an *auto-golpe* or self-coup in April of 1992. He is also applauded by the ruling classes for his success against the two main terrorist groups, the MRTA and the SL, but despised by others for his brutality towards opposition groups, elimination of human rights and elimination of the democratic process. The first acts of Fujimori's new government were to have the army spend two days and nights destroying over 10,000 judicial files on active cases in the Palace of Justice. Not only did the most incriminating evidence disappear on all legal files on Fujimori and his family; those of his trusted confidant Vladimiro Montesinos magically disappeared, as well. This act took place the same day Fujimori dissolved parliament and became a dictator.

Vladimiro Montesinos

Presidential advisor and unofficial director of the National Intelligence Service. Montesinos has had ill-defined connections with the drug kingpins, Peruvian military, intelligence community and, since 1990, the direct support of the CIA. Called Rasputin by one local paper, Montesinos is considered the power behind the throne. Born in Arequipa, the same neighborhood as the SL's Guzman, he has had a rocky and convoluted climb to the top. A former court-martialed soldier, fugitive and legal fixer for the corrupt members of the Peruvian military, Montesinos is considered instrumental in helping Fujimori climb to his position of power. Montesinos is accused of directing death squads and being responsible for ordering various massacres and disappearances. He is also in charge of the eradication of drugs in Peru using Peruvians trained and equipped by the CIA. Much like similar programs in Haiti, their efforts were diverted from drug eradication into private activities that helped overthrow the democratic leadership.

Coca

What a lot of the killings are about. The White Stuff, nose candy, rails, speedballs and crack. The Upper Huallaga Valley near the provincial city of Tingo Maria is one of the world's biggest coca-producing centers. In May 1991, Peru was the producer of 60 percent of the world's supply of raw coca leaf.

The Military

Emergency legislation has permitted the military special autonomous powers in fighting terrorist and politically subversive elements. The military administers and tightly controls emergency zones comprising over one-quarter of the country's territory. People arrested by the military are subject to the dreaded military courts. Many are not seen again afterwards.

The military appreciates its new power, but continues to be antagonistic toward the government. Fujimori still does a lot of personal promoting of buddies and demoting of fast-trackers. Any soldier opposed to his policies is relieved of duty, sometimes of bodily functions as well.

In 1992, 286 people were reported abducted, 178 of whom were subsequently reported missing. Responsibility for almost 90 percent of missing detainees was believed attributable to the armed forces. The same year, there were 114 extrajudicial executions, including 50 people who were captured by security forces and later found dead.

Since 1983 Peru has managed to win the grand prize or the runner-up trophy for the "Country with the Highest Number of Missing Detainees," a dubious and oft-sought distinction awarded by the United Nations work group on missing people. In 1992, the Red Cross counted 3330 arbitrary arrests; the State Department counted 654 bodies attributed to the Sendero Luminoso and 95 as the work of the government, the result of victims being executed without trial. In that same year 30 students disappeared, 11 of whom turned up dead.

Armed forces personnel number about 80,000 conscripts in the army, 25,000 in the navy and 22,000 in the air force. If you want to make it in politics in Peru, you've got to join the army first. Then stage a coup.

Sendero Luminoso (Shining Path, or SL)

Jose Carlos Mariategui was the founder of the first communist party in Peru and called Marxism "a shining path to the future." The group was led by Manuel Ruben Abimael Guzman Reynoso, a pudgy, bearded ex-philosophy professor who now will spend the rest of his life in San Lorenzo naval base on an island just off Callao. Guzman follows the teaching of Mao and was a Student in the Chinese Communist Party's cadre school. The Shining Path began its armed struggle in 1980 and has been responsible for numerous bombings and assassinations. It has vowed to pursue "total war" until the government is overthrown. The group hopes to create a peasant-worker state along Maoist lines. The group's ideology is a strange hybrid of Maoism, Marxist-Leninism and the religious beliefs of the highland Quechua Indians of Peru. What began as a rural following in the remote highlands around Ayacucho spread along the mountainous rural areas towards the south and the east until the Shining Path included rural revolutionaries, urban terrorists and the coca-growing farmers of Upper Huallaga Valley.

The Shining Path became famous for its Viet Cong tactics of intimidation of villagers. Villagers would be tried, the victims publicly tortured, mutilated, executed and left on display.

In urban areas, car bombs have been another successful terror weapon. Using a simple mixture of ammonium nitrate, diesel and dynamite, these car bombs bore the strength of hundreds of pounds of explosives.

Most of its leaders are college-educated, middle-class Peruvians from Lima who command Indian peasant armies. Their approximately 10,000 attacks since 1980 against the government and innocent villagers have killed 27,000 people and cost the country more than US$24 billion. The SL likes to bomb symbols of bourgeois power: banks, police stations, political party headquarters and factories in Lima. Before the arrest of their leaders, the SL was estimated to comprise 5000–10,000 armed members.

Shining Path leader Guzman has issued a number of government-sponsored communiques from prison that call for an end to the guerrilla war, alienating about half its membership in the year following his bust. Prior to Guzman's arrest, the SL controlled an impressive 40 percent of Peru's territory.

The group is self-sustaining, with some fund raising done in Europe. It has access to the lucrative drug trade, which it uses to procure weapons and supplies. The group controls large portions of the Upper Huallaga Valley, the center of Peru's coca plantations, and taxes drug traffickers near their base in the southern highlands around Ayacucho.

Despite numerous attempts to win the hearts and minds of the rural poor and disenfranchised, the SL are finding little support and have started to seek cadres in the shantytowns of the larger cities. With Guzman's demise, the group is weakening.

Movimiento Revolucionario Nuevo Peru
(New Peru Revolutionary Movement)

These boys don't like holidays. The movement is a new, hard-line group of radicals once part of the Shining Path and based in the highland provinces of Huancavelica and Puno. The group has carried out attacks in the highlands and detonated bombs in the capital over holiday weekends, including an attack on an army post late one Christmas day that wounded eight people in Lima's impoverished El Agustino section. The group apparently split from Shining Path after its jailed leader Abimael Guzman called for peace.The leader is Oscar Ramirez or "Comrade Feliciano." Comrade Feliciano says those who support any peace process with Fujimori's government are servants of Yankee imperialism and terms such pacts as "revisionist bitches' excrement." The man's got a way with words.

Tupac Amaru Revolutionary Movement (MRTA)

The current MRTA groups are the ragged remnants of a traditional Marxist-Leninist revolutionary movement formed in 1983 in Peru. Led by Nestor Serpa and Victor Polay—now in prison—its objective is to rid Peru of its imperialist influence and establish a Marxist regime. Their chances are slim at this point but, in their heyday, they were responsible for more anti-U.S. attacks than any other group in Latin America. Originally 1000 to 2000 combatants strong, it has dwindled to less than a hundred, which has split into unorganized criminal bands. But they aren't simple thugs. Most have received training in Cuba. And, at one time, the MRTA enjoyed close ties to Libya.

If you are detained by MRTA cadres, remember that most are former college students who may have lived in Russia or Cuba in the 1970s who like to kick Yanquis' asses. So you may get a lecture, a whopping and told to go on your way. If you are stopped by a xenophobic Maoist of the SL, bend over and kiss it adios.

The MRTA is not as violent or unpredictable as the Shining Path. Founded in 1984 and based in Lima, the MRTA has links to Colombia's M-19 guerrillas, Ecuador's Alfaro Vive and the Cuban government. Using publicity as its major weapon, the MRTA likes to attack the news media and U.S. related businesses.

The MRTA tried to wrest control of the coca traffic from the SL but lost. And their battles with the government ended with the capture of their leader. With most of their leaders behind bars (Victor Polay Campos studied in France and Spain in the 1970s, was captured in 1989, escaped and then was recaptured in 1992), the MRTA has broken down into small bands of criminals with little or no coordinated political agenda. They continue their financially, (if not politically) successful M.O. of kidnapping and extortion.

The Alianza Popular Revolucionaria Americana (APRA–American Popular Revolutionary Alliance)

A democratic left-wing party. A middle-class party with strong worker support and led by former President Alan Garcia Perez, the APRA did not get along with the military during the party's rule.

The Frente Democratico (FREDEMO–Democratic Front)

A right-of-center coalition with three main partners: the liberal, pro-U.S. Accion Popular (AP–Popular Action); the Partido Liberal (Liberal Party), a right-wing group led by former presidential candidate Mario Vargas Lhosa; and the conservative Partido Popular Cristiano (PPC–Christian Popular Party).

Izquierda Unida (IU–United Left)

A mishmash of left-wing groups including the Partido Comunista Peruano (PCP–Peruvian Communist Party), the Frente Obrero, Campesino, Estudantil y Popular (FOCEP–Popular-Front of Workers, Peasants and Students), the Partido Comunista Revolucionario (PCR–Revolutionary Communist Party), the Partido Integracion Nacional (PADIN–National Integration Party), the Partido Socialista Revolucionario (PSR–Revolutionary Socialist Party), and the Partido Unificado Mariatequista (PUM–Unified Marietaguista Party).

The Izquierda Socialista (IS–Socialist Left)

Way, way left. Toward the dateline. A coalition of left-wing groups that broke away from the IU before the April 1990 elections.

Getting In

A passport is required. U.S. citizens do not need a visa for a one-month stay. A visa is not required for a tourist stays up to 90 days, extendable after arrival. Tourists may need an onward/return ticket. For official or diplomatic passport and other travel, visas are required and must be obtained in advance. A business visa requires a company letter stating purpose of trip and US$27 fee. For current information concerning entry and customs requirements for Peru, travelers can contact the:

Embassy of Peru

1700 Massachusetts Avenue, N.W.
Washington, D.C. 20036
☎ *(202) 833-9860*
For further information, contact the Embassy of Peru or nearest Consulate:

Los Angeles, California

☎ *(213) 383-9896/5*

San Francisco, California

☎ *(415) 362-5185 or 7136/2716*

Miami, Florida

☎ *(305) 374-1407*

Chicago, Illinois

☎ *(312) 853-6173*

New York, New York

☎ *(212) 481-7410*

San Juan, Puerto Rico

☎ *(809) 250-0391*

Houston, Texas

☎ *(713) 781-6145/5000*

U.S. Embassy

Corner Avenidas Inca Garcilaso de la Vega and Espana
Box 1995, Lima 1
☎ *(51) (14) 33-8000*

Consular Section

Grimaldo del Solar 346
Miraflores, Lima 18
☎ *[51] (14) 44-3621 or 44-312*

Getting Around

Peru is a tough place to get around via land travel. Internal air services link a number of cities that, via other modes of transit, are difficult to get to. A number of new airlines have sprung up in recent years, causing domestic prices to go down somewhat. The four principal carriers are AeroPerú, Cia de Aviacion Faucett, Aero Continente and Americana. The two most dangerous airlines are Expreso Aéreo—which connects with some of the isolated burgs in the jungles and the mountains—and Aero Tumi, which hauls a few passengers aboard its cargo routes. Hang on. Schedule changes and delays are frequent. Cancellations are common during the rainy season. The main airport is Jorge Chavez International about 10 miles northwest of Lima; about 35 minutes by cab. A trip between the center of Lima and the airport costs about US$5. In 1991 AeroPerú ran five *DC-8s*, three *Boeing 727s* and two *Fokker 28s*. Faucett had five *Boeing 737s*, two *Boeing 727s* and one *DC-8*.

Very few roads in Peru are paved, the major routes of the Pan-American and Central Highways being the exceptions. The roads connecting Pacasmayo with Cajamarca and Pativilca with Caraz and Huaraz are also paved. The road to Bolivia from Puno-Desaguadero has been completed. There are also numerous toll roads in Peru. Outside the cities travel can be a mess. Roads are dusty when they're dry and impassable when they're wet. The roads have been falling apart since 1985 when the government stopped maintaining them. Some work has begun rebuilding the south section of the Pan-American Highway. In 1987 there were 69,942 km of roads, of which 7459 km were paved and more than 13,538 km surfaced. The South American Explorers Club is a good source for maps, as well as the Touring y Automóvil Club del Peru (Av César Vallejo 699, Lince, Lima; ☎ *403270; FAX: 419652*). As throughout most of the world, green and red are merely pretty colors, hardly incentives to brake or accelerate. Be wary of drivers everywhere in Peru.

Trains are more comfortable than buses, although many routes are cut back or even cancelled in the rainy season. Trains link virtually all the major cities in Peru. There are two major rail lines. One runs inland from the capital, Lima, and reaches the highest point of any standard gauge railway in the world at 4780 meters. The other major line runs inland from the port of Matarani in the south, linking the Altiplano to the sea. This line stretches in the Altiplano from Puno on Lake Titicaca to Cuzco, and extends from Cuzco to the Quillabamba on the Urubamba River; the main waterway to the jungle region. It passes the Inca city of Machu Picchu, Peru's most famous tourist attraction. The Cuzco-Machu Picchu route accounts for about 30 percent of all rail traffic.

Bus service is generally good, but exceedingly uncomfortable. Avoid bus travel at night. Bandits prey on tourists dozing on nighttime bus rides.

Taxis, identified by a small red and white windshield sticker, are plentiful and cheap. Taxis have no meters and fares are negotiated in advance. A map is useful, as few drivers know specific streets in the sprawling suburbs where many businesses and ministries are located.

U.S State Department Travel Warning: May 27, 1993
Warning: U.S. citizens are warned against all travel to Peru until further notice. With the exception of certain tourist areas, terrorist violence continues to affect a large part of the country.

Dangerous Places

Military or "Emergency Zones"
More than 25 percent of Peru's land and 50 percent of its population are situated in "emergency zones;" areas where terrorist groups still control large parts of the country. Here, the "military-political commander," usually an army general, is the supreme authority. Elected civilian representatives have little or no real roles in local affairs. The military has also acquired wide powers in the administration of justice. Leading terrorists charged with "treason to the fatherland" are tried by secret military courts. They regularly receive summary life prison sentences from what critics describe as "faceless" judges. Travel to, and within emergency zones outside Lima subjects one to extraordinary risk. These zones are extremely dangerous regions where both terrorism and violent crime are common. Overland travel to, or through, the emergency zones outside the capital city of Lima is particularly dangerous.

The following areas have been designated as "emergency zones" by the Peruvian government:

Apurimac Department

Ayacucho Department

Huanacavelica Department

Huanuco Department

Junin Department

Lima Department (except the city of Lima)

Pasco Department

San Martin Department

Ucayali Department (except for air travel to the city of Pucallpa)

La Convencion and Calco Provinces within Cuzco Department

Ucayali and Alto Amazonas Provinces within Loreto Department

The military has started arming peasants in an effort to make the SL's job of intimidation a little more risky. This, in turn, prompts the SL to execute entire villages as punishment for bearing arms. Guerrillas can expect speedy and one-sided military trials, and there are plenty of stool pigeons fluttering about to put away their former cohorts. Villagers can look forward to a few more centuries of oppression and brutality.

Cuzco and Iquitos

Pickpocketing and armed robbery in or near hotels is common. Foreigners, unarmed and cash rich, are sitting ducks for thieves. The police are too busy sniffing out terrorists, so don't expect a team of detectives to be put on the trail of your missing camera case or AMEX card.

Police or Military Facilities

If you haven't guessed by now that the Peruvian zanies have a thing for bombs and government facilities, hang around and find out for yourself.

Lima

Despite the setbacks suffered by Sendero Luminoso during 1993, the terrorism that occurred in the capital last year helped certify Lima as one of the most violent cities in the hemisphere. While the number of attacks and deaths in Lima during 1993 were down significantly compared to 1992, nearly 60 percent of the total number of attacks nationwide were carried out in the capital last year, comprising 20 percent of the total number of deaths. According to statistics issued by a political violence monitoring group, at least 153 persons were killed in some 639 terrorist-related incidents in Lima's metropolitan area last year. Lima's central district (where the U.S. embassy is located) accounted for some 25 percent of all incidents and close to 40 percent of related deaths in Lima, making it decidedly the most dangerous part of the city. (Incidents in the outlying shantytowns are sometimes underreported.)

The western districts, including Lima's port city of Callao and the international airport sector, were the next most dangerous areas, with some 16 percent of Lima's terrorist incidents and deaths reported in these areas. Residential districts accounted for only 12 percent of the incidents and 5 percent of the deaths, but were the target of 13 of Sendero's 33 car bombs in 1993. At least 12 bystanders were killed by car bombs in 1993, a brutal example of being in the wrong place at the wrong time. The 33 Lima car bombs last year, however, do not include at least eight other car bombs (three in residential districts) that were defused or did not explode. For a brief comparison, there were 62 car bombs in Lima during 1992, with 19 in the residential districts. While the overall number of car bombs dropped by almost half in 1993 (33 versus 62), it is important to note that the number of car bombs in the residential districts remained almost the same (13 in 1993 versus 19 in 1992).

The city of Lima is located in Lima Department, a designated emergency zone. Bombings and terrorist incidents have been frequent in the city and violent crime is common. Most acts of terrorism occur in Lima. The targets are police stations, banks and commercial areas. Terrorist activities are shifting from the rural areas (which require money to support) to urban areas (which make money). Although many of the threats are for extortion, some robberies result in goods being confiscated and then distributed in the shantytowns. The SL continues to murder villagers and assassinate high level government and military officials.

The group known as "Los Destructores" are knocking-off banks and armored cars with continued success. There are problems with petty theft of auto parts taken from parked cars. Lima's airport and American Airlines have been the targets of terrorist attacks. On January 22, 1993, an AA flight from Miami was hit by three bullets while taxiing shortly after landing. The shots were assumed to have come from the Villa El Salvador shantytowns bordering the airport. No one was hurt. Four days later, a small bomb went off in the duty-free shop. Again, no injuries were reported.

If you need police assistance in Lima (don't hold your breath), the Policia de Turismo (Tourism Police) is located at *Avenida Salavarry 1158, Jesus Maria;* ☎ *71-4313 or 71- 4579.*

American Businesses

The SL continues to target high profile American businesses such as IBM, Coca-Cola and American Airlines along with bomb attacks against the U.S. embassy. The Japanese have also been targeted.

Arequipa Region

Many mines in the central and southern highlands as well as the Arequipa region are attacked for their cache of explosives.

Dangerous Things

Drugs

In January 1995, three tons of pure cocaine and 500 kg of cocaine paste was seized and 20 traffickers were busted in northern Peru in what was to date the greatest amount of hydrochloride confiscated in the 1990s. Among those arrested were the leaders of the notorious Los Nortenos cartel. The cocaine empire covers one-fifth of Peru's territory and the lives and activities of 1.2 million people inhabiting 60 percent of the Peruvian Amazon. The "empire" handles nearly 300 tons of cocaine per year and receives US$1 billion annually. Additionally, the cartel controls 241 clandestine airstrips.

Money Changers

Tourists have been ripped off while changing money with street money exchangers called *cambistas*. Counterfeit U.S. dollars are exchanged or slipped in during the transaction. These counterfeit bills are of very high quality and most people do not realize they are counterfeit until they try to pass them, or compare them to real bills in bright sunlight.

Power Outages

When the towns go black, the crooks grow hair on their palms and howl at the moon. Get inside a hotel or business during a power outage. Ahooooooo!

Getting Sick

Medical care does not meet U.S. standards. Cholera is present in Peru. However, visitors who follow proper precautions about food and drink are not generally at risk. U.S. medical insurance is not always valid outside the United States. In some instances, supplemental medical insurance with specific overseas coverage has proved useful. Malaria and yellow fever are present in Peru.

Nuts & Bolts

The official language is Spanish, the mother tongue of around 70 percent of the population. Quechua and Aymara are also official in some regions. Numerous other languages are spoken by Indian tribes in the Amazon basin. Phone calls are very expensive from the hotels in Lima.

Peru's three distinct geographic regions present significant difficulties for economic development. Offshore and coastal areas in the northwest contain oil deposits but the width of the arid Pacific coast that runs the length of the country averages less than 160 kilometers, and rivers flowing from the Andes irrigate only a few valleys. Major traditional agricultural exports include fish products, cotton and fruit grown on the coast, and coffee grown in the Andean foothills.

The Andean highlands rise sharply from the coast to a height of more than 4000 meters, and much of the country's mineral wealth comes from mines in the Andes. Coffee and coca are the major cash crops of the foothills of the east Andes. The real agricultural export is coca (The U.S. of A is the biggest customer). More than US$1 billion is generated in coca sales to the United States of America. Half the country lies in tropical lowlands. The northern jungle is a wealthy oil-producing area that used to cause friction with Peru's neighbors.

The coastal population is primarily *mestizo*, with a small percentage of whites of European descent. The Quechuan highlanders are direct descendants of the Incas, and the Amerinds are related to the jungle tribes of the Amazon.

The currency is the Nuevo Sol which fetches about 2.1 to the U.S. dollar. Electricity is 220V/60Hz. Any time of the year is best to visit Lima, since it's dry with temperatures ranging from an average high of 82° F in January to lows of 66° F in August. Lima is arid with an annual rainfall around 48 mm; the marine layer is a common factor, with long periods of overcast skies, *garua* between June and September. Higher up in the Andes and the Amazon, the rainy season is from December to March. Remember, the summer and winter are reversed. There are also fertile valleys, such as those of Cuzco and Cajamarca. Lake Titicaca in the south, at an altitude of 3815 meters, is the highest navigable lake in the world. About 60 percent of Peru's area is covered by the triple canopy rainforest in the Amazon basin. The Andes, of course, with some peaks as high as 7000 meters, can get quite frigid.

The informal "*tu*" form is commonly used with younger Spanish-speaking business visitors. While Peruvians are sometimes inclined to be late for appointments, visitors are expected to be punctual.

Useful Addresses

Aeroperu

Avda Jose Pardo 601
Miraflores, Lima 18
☎ 322995

Aeropuerto Internacional Jorge Chavez

Avda Elmer Faucett
Lima
☎ 529570

Empresa Nacional de Ferrocarriles, del Peru

Ancash 207
Apdo 1379, Lima
☎ 289440

Foptur (tourist promotion)

Jiron de la Union 1066
Belen, Lima
☎ 323559
FAX 429280

Ministry of Industry, Commerce, Tourism and Integration

Calle 1 Oeste, Corpac
San Isidro, Lima 27
☎ 407120

UK Embassy

Edif El Pacifico Washington
Piso 12, Plaza Washington
Esq Avda Arequipa
Casilla 854, Lima 100
☎ 334738
FAX 334735

U.S. Embassy

Avda Garcilaso de la Vega 1400
Apdo 1995, Lima 100
☎ 338000
FAX 316682

Embassy Location/Registration

Upon arrival, U.S. citizens are requested to register with the Consular Section of the U.S. Embassy in Lima at *Grimaldo del Solar 346, Miraflores;* ☎ *(51-14) 44-3621 or 44-3121* to obtain the latest travel and security information within Peru.

Dangerous Days

10/07/1992   Abimael Guzman, the founder and leader of Sendero Luminoso, was sentenced to life imprisonment by a military court.

04/05/1992   President Alberto Fujimori, with military cooperation, closed the congress and courts and set aside portions of the constitution in an action that concentrated extraordinary powers in his hands. The Organization of American States (OAS) has demanded that Fujimori restore the constitution. Opposition parties and leftist insurgents oppose Fujimori's takeover.

Dangerous Days

06/18/1986	Security forces killed more than 200 jailed members of the Sendero Luminoso (SL) guerrilla organization during a riot at Lima's Canto Grande prison. The event is marked by the guerrillas as "Heroes Day."
07/28/1985	President Alan Garcia Perez succeeded Fernando Belaunde Terry as president, the first transfer of power from one democratically-elected Peruvian President to another in forty years.
11/04/1982	MRTA founded the Tupac Amaru Revolutionary Movement (MRTA), a Cuban-inspired Marxist guerrilla organization.
05/18/1980	The Maoist Sendero Luminoso (Shining Path) guerrilla organization began its armed struggle 12 years ago with an attack on a rural polling station; it has since grown into the largest and most active insurgent group in the country.
12/03/1934	Birthday of Abimael Guzman, also known as "President Gonzalo," the founder and leader of the Sendero Luminoso guerrilla organization. Guzman's followers often "celebrate" his birthday by carrying out attacks or murdering soldiers, public servants and municipal authorities.
12/26/1893	The birthday of Chinese communist leader Mao Zedong has been "celebrated" by the Sendero Luminoso (SL) guerrilla organization reveling in terrorist attacks.
07/28/1821	Independence Day.
10/07/0000	Communist Party founded.
02/21/0000	Birthday of Haya de la Torre Victor, the founder of the "American Popular Revolutionary Alliance (APRA)," the former ruling party of Peru. Date is also celebrated in Peru as the "Day of Fraternity."

In a Dangerous Place: Central Africa

The less literate might define Central Africa as the anus of the world. From this tiny, fetid spot comes Ebola fever; a hemorrhagic disease that would give Steven King nightmares; AIDS, the scourge of the West, and other dark horrors. Few historians or scholars of African history could have predicted the depths to which the tribal war would escalate this year but most people knew that the tiny lands of Rwanda and Burundi are similar to the tiny fuses that are used to set off dynamite. Excuse us if we dwell too long on these foreign lands. In fact if you stretch each word end to end you may find that this chapter may be larger than the actual countries it covers. The authors have all found themselves in these regions at one time or another. RYP has fended off attackers in downtown Burundi and narrowly escaped a raging mob, Aral was with the first group of journalists into an eerily silent Rwanda this year to cover the rotting corpses, and Jack Kramer's expertise in making sense of East African politics and people gave us some unusual brain power in the region. We'll let Jack start this one off.

Hell In A High Place

The hill country of the high mountain chain which is the spine of Africa is best seen through the eyes of a vulture. Nubian, Egyptian or griffin, she loops out high in 200-mile arcs, drops suddenly into deep green ravines, careens through rock defiles, cants and catches thermal drafts on which to climb a thousand feet above crystalline lakes, and even flat dry savanna set among the wet hills.

Beneath is some of the most densely populated land on earth, terraced plantations lightly brushed with wisps of smoke from cooking fires, and here and there, the drifting puffs of an artillery barrage. The hills begin amid the downs of Malawi, as soft as County Kildare, rise swiftly to alpine forest, and alternately plunge and soar right up the long finger of Lake Tanganyika, at the end of which steamers and broad colonial boulevards at the foot of a sheer mountain face mark the port of Bujumbura, the beginning of Burundi. Here the mountains are terraced even more intensely, and then Rwanda, more intensely still, terraces punctuated by volcanic peaks in swirling mists of cloud and snow, well into Uganda, until at last these Mountains of the Moon yield to scrub and a vast swamp in the haze. The terraces are so crowded with humans, their crops and their animals, that there should be barely room for a vulture's wild meal to die, yet she need nevermind. For starters, interlaced amid all this are some barely accessible gullies, chilly hill tops (where leopards, monkeys, mountain gorillas die), and even (though beset by poachers and armies gone bad in the heat) open game country: Zebra, buffalo, red river hog, warthog, duiker, bushbuck, eland; not as much these days, but enough that there is the competition of the hyena, jackal, even those aloof cats who wouldn't want you to know it, but are as able as the next carnivore to recognize the virtue of dead meat. Hyenas can spot a diving vulture from three miles, then shoot off at a dogged thirty miles an hour for all three miles, eyes like slits, wet black maws to the wind. But another vulture, spotting the dive at the same time, from the same distance, can cruise off, flap down among her kind and stick her head and naked neck into the fly-thick miasma a good five minutes before the hyena even gets there.

This is indeed her country. And for more reason than the game. Often enough, even those densely peopled hillsides provide some variety for her diet, as the pressures of population erupt in agony.

When the first European explorers arrived here in the middle of the nineteenth century, the population of Buganda (a domain much smaller than its offspring, today's Uganda) was already a million and a half. In tiny Rwanda, right next door but totally unknown to the west, there was a kingdom of two million souls. It had been building for perhaps a millennium, this population density so uncharacteristic of Africa before Curie and Pasteur. Bantu yeomen—people like the Hutu and Hima who still retain their identities— already crowded parts of the best land when an exceptionally tall, exceptionally black race, people with long, calfless legs, aquiline features and a tendency for the teeth to protrude, showed up in clouds of dust with their great longhorn cattle, looking for pasture. They found some glades, but soon enough they had to clear more, and not long after that, they needed yet more for their grass-hungry herds. They took land from the Bantu, then they took the Bantu themselves to clear yet more land. They came from a region to the north whose identity scholars still debate. All we know for sure is who they are now, in Uganda, people like the Baganda and the Ankole, in Tanzania, Karagwe, in Rwanda and Burundi, the Watutsi, who were apparently the last of the waves of migrants from the north, people seven, even seven and a half feet tall, whose warriors had to jump their own height.

Is their origin Somali? Their faces show it, and this was a pet-conviction of race-conscious Europeans who admired the Watutsi and were convinced that the fierce, handsome Somalis could not possibly be African.

Likely the Watutsi were Nilotes. The Kushitic Somalis are tall, but not this tall. Only the blue-black Nilotes of the Sudan, Dinka, Nuer, loom so high. Or does the Watutsi's highly developed social order reveal an origin somewhere between Nilote and Somali country Ethiopians also have fine features, and the feudal order they developed is much like the feudal empire the Watutsi ruled here in Central Africa; so eerily like the secret kingdoms of fiction which suddenly appear deep in some African wilderness. Isolated for centuries by geography and by tribes as predatory as the big cats, all the kingdoms of these heavily populated highlands, not just those ruled by the Watutsi, had complex hierarchies, at the top of which were those tall, dark people who had come down in waves from somewhere between the Old Testament lands of Kush in the Sudan and Punt on the Somali coast, waves which began in Old Testament days, 2500 years before the wave of Watutsi.

It's still a great mystery. There is no doubt there were established orders in the lands from which the invaders came. Not just the Old Testament, but Egyptian sarcophagi, Homer and Herodotus talk about Kush, Punt and Ethiopia—and not as realms of savages. Every year, more evidence turns up that deep in the wilderness which the invaders penetrated, in the very heart of Africa, among tribes distinctly primitive, there were other tribes distinctly developed. Indeed, fledgling Bantu kingdoms.

In the kingdoms visited by the European explorers of the nineteenth century (kingdoms like Buganda, which gave Uganda its name), the invaders had intermarried to such an extent that while the royal families are often fine of feature, the ruling castes were much less physically distinct. In Rwanda, and to a somewhat lesser extent in Burundi, a physically distinct caste was maintained. The lords of the land were Watutsi, and the feudal order they developed has been called the most structured in Africa outside Ethiopia. Which certainly suggests that Ethiopia was the country from which they came—except that Ethiopians are short. And, except for a conundrum which further confounds this already mysterious story.

The origin of the most obscure groups can often be traced through the meticulous detective work of linguists. These sleuths can trace the language of Amazon headhunters back across the Bering land bridge, and they can place Kinyarwanda—the Bantu language of Rwanda's Bantu Bahutu—within the pattern of the great Bantu migrations which began in West Africa and swept south and then north up the eastern flank of these mountains. You'd think, then, that the language of the ruling Watutsi people who came down from regions anciently civilized, would be even richer in cues.

Alas, it is not. The Watutsi of Rwanda, the overlords who kept themselves so arrogantly distinct from their Bantu serfs, abandoned their own language in favor of Kinyarwanda, the Bantu language of the Bantu Bahutu they conquered. Likewise, the Watutsi of Burundi speak Kirundi, the Bantu tongue of the Bantu Bahutu they conquered.

Even their name has been made Bantu. In Bantu languages, prefixes are added to a word to shift its meaning. The prefix "ki" means "language." A Swahili speaks "Kiswahili;" in Burundi it's "Kirundi." In the Bantu languages of East Africa, the prefix "wa" means "people," so that in Kenya, Kamba people are "Wakamba;" Kikuyu people, "Wakikuyu." There is even a new tribe—and a prolific one, at that—called Wabenzi. They're Africa's new tribe of prosperous bureaucrats, and they take their name from the cars they favor. The Tutsi people, Bantu fashion, are "Watutsi." It's always plural, that prefix "wa"—"people." There are different prefixes for individuals. So saying something like "Didier is a Watutsi" (translation: "Didier is a Watutsi people") is like saying "Jose is a Mexicanos." Saying "the Watutsi people" is both clumsy and redundant. ("The Mexicanos people.") As a practical matter, though, non-Africans seldom use the prefixes for individuals; an individual is generally a Hutu, a Tutsi, a Kikuyu; forms which work well enough as adjectives also, "a Hutu girl." In other Bantu languages, "wa" is often "ba;" thus "Bahutu;" so, the Watutsi do at least retain some linguistic distinction from their Hutu serfs. But it's a small difference. They speak the same language, and language as much as geography is what holds together this forever fractious and now thoroughly fractured world. From the Victoria Nile in the north to Lake Tanganyika, linguists classify the languages of this lake region together in a distinct Bantu subgroup they call "interlacustrine;" distinct, of course, from the Nilotic and Kushitic languages to the north, distinct also from other groups of Bantu tongues. But what do vultures care of language.

Of the ties which bind the people of Central Africa, the one that matters to the vulture is cruelty. When John Haning Speke gave Mutesa, King of Buganda, a pistol, and told him what it did and how it worked, Mutesa gave the novelty to a young page and told him to try it out on one of his assembled subjects. The lad did. Laughter filled the court as the man fell dead, and it has never really stopped since then.

Barely a century later it was still echoing a few miles away in a torture chamber Idi Amini called "the State Research Bureau."

Vultures never got the first man shot dead in Central Africa, but better pickings were to follow. Arab slavers, already at work, were about to mine this people-rich lode in earnest. Just beginning was the career of Central Africa's great slaver and explorer, the Zanzibari Arab, Tipu Tib. His slaving safaris would clutter the tracks of Central Africa with the bodies of the weak, especially children, some still living, who couldn't keep up, whose fate would be the vulture's beak, the jaw and maw of the hyena. Today their misery is disease and war. Today the crowded countryside means fertile ground for the AIDS virus; infection rates hover at an average 20 percent, worse than anywhere else in the world. But then, too, there was disease, sleeping sickness spread by the slavers (as late as 1901, it stupefied 300,000 villagers on the southern shores of Lake Victoria, then killed 200,000 of them), and soon after, missionaries.

With so many heathen souls to save, Christians were soon killing Muslims and Muslims were killing Christians in the name of the great monotheistic tradition they shared. By the time Protestants began killing Catholics and Catholics began killing Protestants in the name of the same God, the undertakers just couldn't keep up anymore. It was the vulture's day, as it was to be again in this century. The Watutsi, warriors that they were, kept the slavers out, and while they couldn't keep the Germans out, nor the Belgians who grabbed German spoils after the Great War, they could use their administrative grip to make it impossible for the Europeans to rule without them. They remained privileged, African Mandarins for the Germans and Belgians. But, with the end of World War II, they began to see what was coming.

In 1959, a faction intent on maintaining Tutsi privilege in Rwanda assassinated several Hutu leaders. Hutu rage slaughtered 100,000 Rwandan Watutsi, and the carnage was on; a 22-year pogrom which in 1994 alone wiped out half of the two million Watutsi in Rwanda. When the Belgians pulled out of the two countries in 1962, Bahutu ruled Rwanda. In Burundi, Watutsi were hanging on to power, and still were a decade later, when Hutu frustration exploded in Burundi's landmark revolt of 1972. A thousand Watutsi died in the outburst. Having witnessed the 1962 killing of 100,000 Watutsi in Rwanda, this 1972 rampage by Burundi's Bahutu was all Burundi's ruling Watutsi needed. They killed 100,000 Bahutu, and chased out another 200,000. Then the pickings got a little less abundant for the vultures. As the rest of the world saw it, an equilibrium of sorts had been struck. In Burundi, where the mass murderers were Watutsi, the Watutsi ruled. In Rwanda, where the mass murderers were Bahutu, Bahutu ruled. But the equation was inherently volatile. For one, the Bahutu remained the overwhelming majority in both countries. For another, if the Watutsi ruled anywhere, it made more historic sense in Rwanda; historically, Rwanda's Watutsi were a stronger group than Burundi's. In a way, this was why they had become the victims of genocide, the failed pre-emptive strike by one of their clans.

But this hardly justified the genocide, and it hardly made the quarter million Rwandan Watutsi in exile any less talented or disciplined a people. Amidst the horror of Idi Amin's Uganda, they hung on. When Uganda's horror was finally brought to an end, it was the work of an obscure, disciplined guerrilla army made up in good part of adolescent orphans of the horror, very much a latter-day children's crusade, with a 'security chief' still in his twenties. His name was Paul Kagame, and he was a Rwandan Tutsi.

Inevitably, Paul Kagame went home. With about 8000 of his friends. In front of them was a Hutu army 30,000-strong, but like Idi Amin's army, it was corrupt. Unfortunately, what French and Belgian papers saw as all this unfolded in the fall of 1990 was not resistance against an army which had committed genocide. It saw an evil bouillabaisse boiling over, a stew in the creation of which France and Belgium had been no mere sous-chefs. It saw the minority Tutsi overlords, already in power in Burundi, about to regain power in Rwanda. They were beginning to feel guilty. Some, also saw opportunity. The tide, through Africa, has been with the majority, and in any case it's always easier to find room in a European budget for financing neocolonial clients who are a 'democratic' (read: a majority). France, Belgium and Zaire rushed in to stop Kagame's army.

More later of Mr. Kagame, the troubles which were to come, and the further trouble yet brewing in Central Africa. Suffice it to say for this overview that once again, the victors were the vultures.

Nowadays, air safaris are becoming especially popular. The planes can soar above the tangled geography, the volcanic Virungas, the snow-dashed Mountains of the Moon, whose lakes and foaming white waters are the source of both of Africa's two great rivers; the Zaire and the Nile. Beneath them is all the wonder which spreads beneath the soaring buzzard, but the grim acuity of her gimlet eye must see so much more.

The Scoop

The most important player on the Central African stage is brutality. It is there. Not only a player in its own right, but to one extent or another, at play in the personalities of all the others, and whatever the crimes of the colonists, it was there for centuries before they arrived. (When Germany claimed Rwanda and Burundi in 1885, no European had ever seen either of these kingdoms, and there was no substantial colonial administration until 1910.) There is no way it can be ignored as a key aspect of what makes Central Africa a dangerous place. But it is also a highly charged subject, easy to misunderstand when you hear about it, easy to be misunderstood when you ask about it, in short, not a subject to waltz into without some thought.

Consider, for example, these two ancient courts: Having ordered wild game for a show, he found butcher's meat cost too much and decided on prisoners instead. Ignoring the charges against the men, he just gave them a quick look over and ordered: "All of them between that bald head there and the other one there; kill them all." Aristocrats bore serious obligations to the peasants, who wore simple white togas. Every boy went to court to learn history (they'd recite by heart the names and deeds of 40 emperors), the arts of both war and poetry, polite conversation, grace under stress. Self-control was their sine qua non. Showing the slightest distemper was vulgar. Now consider this: The first court, with its prisoners killed for fodder, was neither barbaric nor primitive. The second, with its blue bloods schooled in responsibility and the arts of poetry, was depraved—and not because of its art of war.

In the second court, dinner was followed by poetic recitations, then torture; the more novel, the better. One of their heraldic legends tells of a peasant who suggested a man be roasted alive on a white-hot slab. The emperor pronounced it a capital idea and had that very peasant roasted. So much for the young men in togas. But by what logic is that first court anything but primitive and barbaric? By the logic that both are worse than that; they're depraved. The first passage is from Suetonius, the coyly frugal monster is Caligula. The refined young men in the second passage are Watutsi. If there is anything which both ancient Rome and these young Watutsi are not, it's primitive, nor the variant of primitive, barbaric. "They are civilized to the marrow of their bones," said the German ethnologist, Leo Frobenius, of all the lacustrine kingdoms. It's tempting to dismiss the entire subject of brutality among the civilized as fit only for fools or saints. But you don't wade into the sort of danger Central Africa presents without at least some idea of what you're getting into. Meantime, hey, ever since Alcoholics Anonymous was organized with its several-step program, there have been six-step, four-step and ten-step programs to deal with everything from gingivitis to schizophrenia, so here it is, at no extra charge:

Learning to Live with Total Depravity
Four Step Program

Step one

Say some communal mea culpas and throw in a couple of maxima culpas. The Watutsi have nothing on our man Caligula, not to speak of Adolf, and...

Step two

If recognizing Caligula with a mea culpa is a good first step to understanding this depravity, a good second step is recognizing that it can never be understood.

Step three

Ponder the difference between depraved and barbaric. The depraved and the merely barbaric have lived side-by-side here for centuries, and still do. There seems to be a lot they share—and a lot they don't. The likes of Caligula, for whom civilization is no thin veneer, frighten me more than men merely primitive or barbaric. They are not simply brutal, they are deliberately cruel, and the skills of civilization leverage enormously their power to be deliberately cruel. But actually separating the merely barbaric from the more dangerously depraved has required getting through the humbug of tooth and claw, which Jack London fashioned 'the law of tooth and claw.' He must have had good reason for picturing the primitive world that way, but he did such a good job with pictures that we're induced to feel there could be nothing worse. In fact, primitive tribes like the Samburu, the Karamajong and the Masai, distantly related to the Watutsi, can be exceptionally brutal. For years, their cold, deadly skill as warriors stymied commerce between the coast and the great kingdoms of Central Africa. On top of this, the practices of some of them, like moving their dying children and parents to the edge of their settlements, to be finished off by hyenas and vultures, are repulsive.

But they never seem brutal for the sake of brutality, or for cruel amusement. Their brutality appears to be adaptive, harsh contortions of the spirit required for life in a punishing, dry environment. The ferocity of the Samburu morale springs from the same cultural resources which permit a reed-slender Samburu teenager, armed with nothing but a spear, to face down a charging lion. They are often warm, even with strangers, and most crucially, their brutality is not leveraged by the power of a highly organized society.

In fact, many call these pastoral peoples to the east and north of the Central African kingdoms victims of their own success. So well have the centuries adapted them, that they see no need to change. As societies around them developed, they have been left behind. Not so the Watutsi, who share much with their distant cousins: cattle, a ferocity as warriors which springs from cultural adaptation to a harsh world. But the Watutsi, the Ankole, and similar herdsmen, did not sit back as primarily agricultural Bantu tribes developed. They took over, became the aristocracy, developed a highly structured world and with it, powerful social leverage, and somewhere along the way, perhaps because of the pressure of population, perhaps because of the absolute corruption which results from absolute power, became depraved.

Step four

Just say no when you hear that it's Africa that makes men do what they do here. Aside from rank racism, which can be easily dismissed, this luridly attractive notion seems to owe its power to Joseph Conrad, who used a journey to Africa's interior as a metaphor for a journey into the evil in all of us. In that universal sense, he probably has as much to say about the evil of the realms of Central Africa as he does about the evil in you and me. But using his imagery to picture the heart of Africa as the heart of darkness reverses and subverts the man's metaphor; it also flies in the face of Suetonius and any number of other documentarians (not least, the documentarians of the Holocaust) who show us civilized depravity outside Africa. Perhaps worst of all, those deluded by the notion that Africa makes its monsters do what they do, soon find a continent full of wonder, an unbearable place to be.

The Players

Yoweri Museveni and Uganda's National Resistance Army (NRA)

When word of Museveni and his guerrillas began popping up in the mid-eighties, they were the most obscure of players. In Kampala, moderates of various stripes had been at work trying to pull Uganda from the pit into which Amin had shoved it. At most, this reputed Maoist with no visible Mao for support (indeed, North Korea was helping Kampala's moderates deal with him) would be a spoiler, making Uganda's slow recovery all the slower. It didn't work out that way. We'll see why.

Uganda, under Museveni as its president, is today still struggling to recover. Large portions remain insecure. Its military (still the NRA, now with a political wing, the National Resistance Movement) is poorly armed. But Museveni, without seeking the role, has become the most powerful man in Central and East Africa today, more powerful inside and outside Uganda than the well- armed, well-financed (though ultimately bankrupt) Amin could ever have hoped to be.

Paul Kagame and the Rwandan Patriotic Front (RPF)

A Rwandan Tutsi, and under age 40, he is the most powerful man in the Tutsi homelands. for more background information on Kagame, see "Players" in the Rwanda chapter.

Mwalimu Julius Nyerere

Retired from Tanzanian rule, he is still very influential in local politics. For more background information on Nyerere, see "Players" in the Rwanda chapter.

Ghosts

Mutesa, Kabaka of Buganda

The first ruler of Uganda's namesake to have been seen by a European, Mutesa was the skillful leader of an ancient and highly structured kingdom. About the right age to have been Woodrow Wilson's father, he appears on stage as something of a Woodrow Wilson of Central Africa's inverted statecraft by terror. He began his career by killing sixty of his brothers, an elegant move successfully designed not only to win him the top spot, but to cow his 1-1/2 million subjects into craven subservience.

Artfully playing off European against Arab, Muslim against Protestant against Catholic, he pronounced his power with drums consecrated with blood drawn from the necks of human victims. When the first white man came to his royal compound on Rubaga Hill near Lake Victoria (a compound in which grass *rondavels* soared 70 feet in the air), the visitor presented Mutesa with a carbine, which Mutesa then gave to a page, instructing the boy to shoot a subject in the courtyard to see if the firearm worked. It did, to the great delight of page and king alike. Today, you don't have to go to Rwanda or Burundi to see evidence of how ghosts like Mutesa, 60-some generations of ghosts teaching brutality, haunt Central Africa. Just a few blocks from Mutesa's royal compound on Rubaga Hill, now part of the city of Kampala, is Nile Mansions, which once housed an organization known as the "State Research Bureau." That was the euphemism for Idi Amin's secret police. They say you could hear the screams as you walked by.

Henry Morton Stanley and John Haning Speke

These two ghosts of white men past tell a tale whose unlikely turn shows how dangerously easy it is for the most substantial of western personalities to get thrown off balance by Africa, while Europeans awkward and discounted at home may be better at navigating its perils. Stanley was not just an accomplished explorer, he was also an accomplished man among men, raising thousands of pounds from newspaper lords for his expeditions. Speke was stiff-necked, awkward, often obtuse.

The outgoing Stanley met Mutesa in 1875, during his landmark expedition to settle the debate over the source of the Nile.

The introverted Speke met Mutesa a dozen years earlier, on his own landmark journey touching off the debate. On that expedition, he'd discovered Lake Victoria, and claimed it was the Nile's source. Sir Richard Burton, an explorer both learned and intrepid, said no. Humiliated during the dispute (some suggested he was a fake), Speke died of a self-inflicted shotgun wound (possibly accidental, possibly not) just before he was scheduled to debate the facile and erudite Burton before the Royal Geographical Society.

Yet the barely social Speke did a better job than the socially adept Stanley at taking the measure of Mutesa. Stanley, whose expedition established that Speke was right and Burton wrong about the source of the Nile, found Mutesa charming. Speke saw him for the danger he was.

Patrice Lumumba and the Central Intelligence Agency

Martyred by his murder after a coup brought down his presidency of Zaire, Lumumba is still remembered for his socialist agenda. For more information on Lumumba, see "Players" in the Rwanda chapter.

Stooges
(Of which, of course, there are three.)

General de divison/Augustin Bizimungu

Reportedly on the lam in Zaire, this general without an army or staff bears watching. Fore more background information of Bizimungu, see "Players" in the Rwanda chapter.

President and Field Marshal El Hadji Idi Amin Dada, VC, DSO, MC, CV

Still alive, a breathing reminder of how things can go wrong in Central Africa.

At least he's a self-made man. Those initials after his name are all self-conferred, save the final initials, CV, which are an editor's mark indicating that yes, correct version, this really is what the man called himself. Still calls himself, for all we know; plaguing the harsh scrub where the frontier of Uganda meets the frontier of the Sudan, there are several companies of thugs, a twilight army for which he serves as a sort of warlord in absentia.

Does he matter? Do they matter? Does cancer matter, once it's in remission? Regardless, stooges aren't so important for what they can actually do. (It was Amin the monster, not the stooge, who did the doing.) They're important for the role they play, how they make people feel. Amin alive, his men still lurking out there somewhere beyond the distant and dangerous town of Nimule, is like a cancer in remission, a gargoyle ghoulishly reminding the afflicted how they may well die, if not by this cancer, then by another, if not by this Amin...

When he escaped to Libya, he was a man of enormous interest in the west, a personality—a stooge become monster. When he disappeared, there was enormous interest in what happened to him. Bumped off. Shanghaied to East Germany. Shanghai sightings were reported everywhere, but scrambling reporters could never confirm them. Soon enough, though, it became a matter of the public's shrinking attention span. One month, he was the center of speculation; the next he was, Idi Who?

On assignment in Jiddah in 1980, I noticed a large group of African children eating breakfast in the dining room of my hotel in the outskirts. About ten minutes later, another group of African children came down for breakfast. Next morning, the same thing. The third morning, a huge man came in, had breakfast with one of the groups, finished, and went over to the second group for a second breakfast. After making sure I was seeing what I thought I was seeing, I wired my editors that the missing Idi Amin was in Saudi Arabia with two of his wives and lots of his kids. A few months later there would be a report confirming rumors that Saudi Arabia had granted Amin asylum, an inside item, virtually a filler, so I guess my bosses were right. They were business editors; if it wasn't a business development, it had to be pretty lively stuff, and Amin wasn't lively anymore, he was old news. Well, old news is still alive and maybe even kicking. Outside Uganda, much of Africa enjoyed his buffoonery. Now that Africans, and especially his Central African neighbors, know how bad it became, there's something like a morbid fascination with the moment the cells, which confer buffoonery, exploded in malignant growth and the clown they loved turned into a monster. It's almost as if they're concerned it might happen to someone they know and they need to learn the symptoms.

Everyone has their pet theory. For me it was the Begaya incident, Amin as stooge becoming monster. Elizabeth Begaya was a princess of one of the old realms whose regal beauty won her several contracts as a fashion model in London. But then she became serious, read law, was admitted to the bar, and at one improbable point, actually served as Amin's Foreign Minister. But not for long. She must have done something to annoy him. He publicly accused her of having sex in a toilet at Charles de Gaulle airport.

Joseph Mobutu, aka, President-For-Life Mobutu Sese Seko

By what reasoning, you may well ask, is a man who puts together a $5 billion fortune, safely socked away in Switzerland, a stooge.

Well, maybe Mobutu isn't a stooge at home. But there's no need to invade the poor man's privacy. We're talking about the role he plays on the Central African stage. Larry, Curly and Moe probably weren't stooges at home either. It was a role they were paid to play. Likewise, Mobutu; and you've got to say this for the guy: however overpaid he might be, he gives that role all he's got, throwing around hundreds of millions on palaces and Swiss dairy farms recreated in the jungle, even as his mineral-rich nation slips more deeply into squalor, with streets so heavy with desperation that you drive through them with every window of your vehicle tightly rolled. Overhead banners proclaim, MOBUTU POUR TOUS, TOUS POUR MOBUTU.

Meantime, a private Disneyland goes up in his distant hometown; and even as such outrages to social justice are played out, one after another, he instructs his people to address each other, in the egalitarian tones of the French Revolution, as "citoyen," which, incredibly, they do, even though they consider him (as does much of Central Africa) a stooge. More specifically, he's considered a stooge for the west, paid to frustrate their aspirations whenever they conflict with western interests. For this reason, paying him is getting to be an increasingly dangerous game, short-term advantage at the cost of trouble down the pike.

Getting Around

From Murchison Falls on the Albert Nile to the shire downs of Malawi, the hills of Central Africa are often cool. Where they are not terraced and planted with richly rolling cash crops of coffee or tea, the bush is deep green; here a grove of hardwood, higher up, thickets of bamboo, all of it punctuated with almost orgiastic profusions of wildflower. The Mountains of the Moon were first plotted with startling accuracy in the second century A.D. by the Greek geographer Ptolemy, who appropriately enough, lived in Alexandria. From Homeric times, the Greeks were fascinated with both Egypt and the African lands beyond it. These mountains include both the Ruwenzoris, non-volcanic peaks between Lake Albert (aka Mobutu Sese Seko) in the north and Lake Edward (aka, Idi Amin Dada; aka, Rwitanzige) to the south, and the volcanic Virungas between Lake Edward and Lake Kivu, further south. Both are lashed, high up, with swirling mists of snow and freezing rain.

But this is high ground which even gung-ho generals aren't too crazy about seizing; so far and so steep for the dragging of big guns, so often socked in, so hard to supply. So that freezing hell way up there serves us down here mostly as a heavenly grace note, a visual cue that however hot it may sometimes get (you are, after all, nearly on the equator), it's a lot cooler than it would be were it not for the elevation and those frigid gales you can see swirling way off in the blue distance. Banana and coconut palms grow up here, higher than palms grow anywhere, the end of a long climb they began vague centuries ago when they showed up on the coast from Madagascar, to which they had been brought by ancient Indonesian colonists. At one turn, orchids fill your vision; at another, the smell of eucalyptus, also a settler from abroad.

It is country more deceptively pleasant even than the bush of the foothills and table land, and it's deceptive enough. The foothills and table land are open country, often washed with a soft green which gives its punishing thornbush (hot, dry, bug-ridden and abrading as you scratch through it), the look (as at last you rest on a hillock) of a dreamy deer park on some rolling Irish estate. In fact, all this can be genuinely pleasant for those blessed with four-wheel drive, fuel (never to be taken for granted), a modest first-aid kit and a tent, with bed and roof reachable in no more than a week. For a body exposed to the elements day after day, the nights can be bone-chillingly cold. Nor are the miseries of heat unknown, especially during the dry season on the savannas, where game and armies tend to collect, to the great detriment of the former. Savanna does exist west of Lake Victoria. You find it in Tanzania between the lake and the tumbling Kagera River, ambling off to far mountains. In Rwanda, on the other side of the Kagera, it suddenly appears laced among the hills of the Parc National de l'Akagera; it's laced also among the hills of southern Uganda. It is not good country for the cheetah, which is threatened everywhere in Africa, but can nonetheless be spied easily enough on the vast open lands to the east, thanks to its daylight hunts. In recent years, this hasn't been good country for any big game, with vast tracts poached out. But for one big cat this has always been, and to an extent, still is, good country. It's not often seen; it's not often seen anywhere in Africa. But that's because of its craft and its nocturnal hunting habits. In fact, it is almost everywhere more numerous than the much more easily found cheetah. For the leopard hidden in the thickets, this was once ideal country, and even as it is sorely pressed, its territory taken over by *shambas*, its prey poached daily, poached itself, it may be the predator best-equipped to hang on. Best able to lurk among human settlement, it has much less prey to hunt these days, but less competition, too. Sometimes (and especially during the heat of the dry season) you see acres of palms without fronds. It isn't disease which has attacked them. Natives have lopped off their tops to force the sap out from which they make palm wine. Regenerative fires burn at the end of the dry seasons; regenerative, even beautiful in their way, a powerful, ghastly beauty. When the burn is the work of poachers' flushing game, or of incendiary shell fire, it's just ghastly.

Getting Sick

Mosquitoes bite year-round. The tsetse fly which brings sleeping sickness is not common, but the other tsetse, the one which kills domestic cattle, likes to chew on humans, too, and just because it won't kill you doesn't mean it's fun. *Siafu*, safari ants, aren't much fun either, crawling up your leg, biting furiously en masse.

Surprise: shell fire doesn't seem to bother these bugs. In any case, add it to the list of beasties; sometimes, it is almost as much a feature of the bush as the tsetse and the mosquitoes, both of which appear more subject to human control.

They say the Crimean War was Europe's first evil whiff of industrial-strength weapons. In that sense, World War I, in which Europe first felt the full force of those weapons, was the first whiff for this part of Africa, the first hint of the full force which would set ablaze the bush of Uganda and Rwanda in the last quarter of the century. When Germany went to war with Britain in the century's first quarter, the gentleman farmers of Britain's Kenya Colony marched into the bush of German East Africa and were decimated. As for the Germans, there were hardly any left when it was over. German East Africa split in three: Rwanda and Burundi were grabbed by Belgium as spoils of war; bush-covered Tanganyika territory fell to the British, who somehow conquered it without ever winning a battle against the German commander, Count Paul von Lettow Vorbeck, mythic leader of a largely black army.

For Africans conscripted to fight for both sides, and especially for those who made up almost all the troops of young von Lettow Vorbeck, it was more of a horror than it was for either the British or the Germans. They were conscripted in greater numbers, slept in filthier quarters, pulled more taxing duty and died at a greater rate, victims of the bush as much as combat.

It wasn't just modern weapons which made life a quantum measure more dangerous, but a deadly equation: modern weapons squared by the bush and its beasties, then squared again by the climate squared by drought, flood, heat, the diseases and disease-bearing insects which breed in heat. It was the trenches of World War I (in which men slept for months with rats) which served as a petri dish for the great influenza epidemic of 1917, which killed not only troops (more by far than were killed by rifle-fire) but thousands of civilians in Europe and America. Thanks to tetracycline and any number of cheap antibiotics exported by China and India and massively dispensed without prescription throughout Central Africa (thereby cultivating a generation of bugs immune to them), the bush, for now, is not the killer the trenches were then. But it's still a killer. Even cheap antibiotics are expensive for a post cold war army without visible means of support in Peking, Teheran, Paris, Washington. It was expensive for Yoweri Museveni's National Resistance Army in Uganda, and even after that army won its war, it became no rich patron which could make antibiotics any less expensive for its cousins-in-arms, Kagame's Tutsi-led Rwandan Patriotic Front.

The Bush and the Watutsi

Outnumbered six to one, Kagame studies the terrain

The miseries of the bush in which the Watutsi operated in the first half of the nineties are much the same as the miseries which in this last half of the decade plague the newer outlaw armies of Central Africa—Hutu in the south, Karamajong and other Nilotic tribes in the non-Bantu bush north of Uganda's Lake Kyoga…which is more a shifting, amorphous marsh than a lake with a distinct shore.

Kagame's Tutsi-led force briefly made headlines when it engaged Rwanda's army in mid-1994; what never even made the inside pages was their struggle to survive in the bush. Before that '94 offensive, they had found themselves stalled by a cease-fire during which they began to hear rumors of organized rampages against Tutsi civilians. But all they could battle was the bush. Frustrated, they moldered alternately in the damp cold of night in the high hills and the bake of the savanna.

These were men who still carried themselves with a certain assured arrogance. They were famed through the centuries as great warriors and great hunters, but 'great hunter' meant the skill, courage and self-control to face down big game with a spear. Never in memory had they been aboriginal denizens of the bush.

By '94, the bush was a misery they had already been living with since they first invaded their old homeland in '90. It was under these conditions that the Watutsi had executed their first offensive, the one thrown back by the French, Belgians, Zairois. And it was under these conditions, that much of the '94 campaign was planned, and planned again.

Outnumbered six to one, at least as badly as von Lettow Vorbeck, Kagame went over the potential battlefield from every perspective, from thornbush to fogged-in high ground, as his men, picking at their sores, nursing their infections, patching their cheap sneakers, fought the bugs, the heat, the cold.

The Bush Fights Back

It was the dry season that saw the Watutsi stranded, the period of those regenerative fires which make the savanna, so rich in game just twenty-five years ago, seem all the more empty, especially in Rwanda's Kagera, and the neighboring savannas of Tanzania and Uganda. There is no way to exaggerate the decimation of wildlife during the years of Amin and the little Amins. An exaggeration here simply balances an untold horror there. But the regenerative power of the land is impressive. Wildlife creeps out of forgotten thickets, bush takes over houses only briefly abandoned. After the fires, rains are not even required to bring a dead land back. After a few days of nothing but morning dew in early July, the green creeps back and wildflowers bloom.

The liberation armies seem at times to hate the bush as intensely as they must love it. Many Africans see no reason not to develop as rapaciously as America did, and the bush be damned. At the same time, the successful liberation armies know the bush so intimately, can so easily recognize a small rock after a seemingly wild chase over trackless savanna, that more must be at work within them than the simple need to know the bush this well to survive. The intimacy with which they can know the land is beyond anything a mortal soul could force himself to acquire just because somebody tells him it's important. You may hate the bush, but you have to love it, as well, to get to know it so intimately.

Cultural Crib Sheet

The Bush and its Mythic German

On this subject of the terrain and its afflictions, one foreign term jumps from my notes, to the exclusion of all others, a term neither French, Arabic nor Swahili, but German: *bundu*, bush, as it was before the word was debased by overuse. In military and aid compounds these days, the bush can be anything beyond the gate which isn't a street. The *bundu* is where you find those military units which have no gates—anywhere. It's the bush truly beyond the gate, the perimeter, the pale. FRELIMO in the bundu of Mozambique under the Portuguese. Contra-FRELIMO in the bundu of Mozambique under FRELIMO. UNITA in Angola. The Watutsi after they were thrown from power in Rwanda. The Bahutu now. The Simba Rebels in the Ituri Forest. Bundu is also a term for the distant bush which a few of your sources will use if they aren't all American or British, and it is the term used by the Germans who opened up Tanganyika and laid claim to Rwanda and Burundi in 1885. As the bundu was and is a test of mettle for the Watutsi, it was a test for many a German who came here, and never more so than during the Great War, when von Lettow Vorbeck and a few German officers led a black army against the British.

They were, as well, at least halfway decent men and one way or another, they set a certain standard for the outlaw armies of today's Africa. Witnessing those armies, it is hard to imagine anything so sorry as their poorly clothed, barely shod, blistered and cankered troops. In fact, they're formidable souls, those troops; they have to be. Their life is a misery which can find company only in the likes of what von Lettow Vorbeck and his troops suffered.

Like Kagame today, von Lettow Vorbeck was a brilliant strategist, especially under pressure; like Kagame he had little with which to work. The count and his troops left Kenyans dead in the thousands even as the German force melted deeper into the wild, virtually without resupply. He was driven all the way to the Rufiji River, in the wilds of what is now the world's largest and perhaps most inaccessible game reserve, the vast Selous, named in 1922 for Frederick Courtney Selous who was one of the great white hunters of East and Central Africa. (Among his clients: Theodore Roosevelt.) Selous was shot to death in battle with von Lettow Vorbeck, in one of the many battles in which the count drew the British ever more deeply into the bundu he knew so well. The German tied up a huge force—and never lost a battle. Military men whose skin is white are fond of calling him the greatest guerrilla fighter of modern times. What seems worth remembering amidst today's dangers is not the invidious superlative, but the guerrilla part. When circumstances forced him to become a guerrilla, he was able to command the loyalty which guerrilla leaders require more than any other sort of military commander—and he was able to command it from black troops who had no love for Germany. To this day, the Germans have a beastly reputation east of the Virungas, much worse than that of the British in Kenya. And they were loyal to him because of the most traditional of reasons: they respected him as a soldier and knew that he was as loyal to them as they were to him. The best of today's African armies draw above all on their own African legacies. But if the colonials aren't off the hook for what's going wrong here, they're probably responsible as well for a little of what's right. So let us now praise von Lettow Vorbeck and his black troops. They fought for a lost cause which today few mourn, even in Germany, but they were lords of the bundu.

The Scoop

A Sweaty Pas De Deux For Two Master Races

Who is to say what part of the danger which hangs over Central Africa today is a legacy of its colonists? Who is to say what part is a legacy of its own tribal past?

All that's for sure is that nobody's off this hook, and as this question of guilt hangs in the air, the bush seems to play a strangely compelling role. For Europeans as well as Africans, it seems to present itself as a sort of trial by fire in which strength is tested and either guilt or virtue revealed. British, Gallic, Dutch and Deutsch; Von Lettow Vorbeck is but one example.

The Germans, though, do seem to have had a particular appreciation for those masochistic enough to let the bush rip them up. Not incidentally, they were also the first Europeans to sing the glories of the Watutsi, and here we see the flip side of the coin represented by von Lettow Vorbeck, a fuzzy sort of hero-worship the Watutsi could again inspire this generation, now that their underdog force has seized the day in Rwanda.

So strong, so tall, so courageous, so commanding of lesser men; as the German colonials saw things, the Watussi (as they spelled the word) must certainly have come from some place beyond Africa, quite possibly someplace Aryan. But similarity between the Watutsi and the Germans is almost too obvious: both self-described master races. In a way, even their dissimilarity is too obvious: the Watutsi, like the Jews of German-speaking lands, are an educated, persecuted minority. More to the point is a dangerous unpredictability which seems to lurk about prewar Germans and Watutsi alike, a sense of culturally inherited moral confusion, von Lettow Vorbeck without the strong moral rudder that empowered him. Perhaps better than anyone else, an acute observer of many things African, the Afrikaaner, Laurens van der Post, captured that underside of the legacy the German left behind. Van der Post tells of a passage he booked aboard the Hamburg-Afrika line between the wars. At first, he was charmed. The food was excellent, and after perfunctory renderings of the Strauss waltzes favored by Germany's new Nazi rulers, the ship's string quartet, "beneath stars on tiptoe," played inspired chamber music. But then van der Post struck up a friendship with an American couple, Jim and Elsie Williamson. For years, they had invested in Germany and even lived there. Though British-born, Jim Williamson seems to have acquired the American habit of blunt talk. As he saw them, the Nazis were cancer. Then van der Post met a German who eventually confided that his grandmother was Jewish; with his family, he was fleeing. He and other Germans warned Williamson to keep his peace. They said there was a Nazi cell among the crew. The ship's captain, van der Post noticed, had an eternally dour expression. One night, Jim Williamson failed to return to his cabin. Elsie searched for him everywhere. He had disappeared on a night of perfectly calm seas, perhaps with the string quartet playing Bach.

The next day, van der Post learned that the ship was under the control of the Nazi cell; the doleful ship's captain was under the command of his own personal steward. Their liner was named The Watussi.

Getting Around with Gupta and Alihussein

There you are, you took your chance, you went into the bush. A few unpleasant checkpoints, but the gamble paid off. (The gamble with your company's time, not with your neck.) You got the story, and now you're easing back in the comparative comfort of the control shack at some provincial airport, waiting for the flight back. Phones are out, and your report doesn't have a real long shelf-life, but the schedule gets you in with time to burn. The shack is empty, flies buzz, you pop a lomotil and doze on a torn vinyl bench. You're not sure what time it is when you wake-up, but you are sure there's a crowd. You stroll over to the ticket agent. Where are they headed? Same as me. Must be a big plane. It isn't. Must be landing empty. It isn't. Poor devils. How could they turn up with all this stuff, all these chickens, and no reservations. What do you mean, 'hapana jambo,' they have reservations but that doesn't matter. What if you were these people, coming all the way out here, with all this heavy stuff? How would you like it if some ticket agent told you your reservations don't matter?

Your reservations matter.

My reservations matter.

What do you mean, my reservations don't matter?

Where's the queue?

I just see pushing.

I just see shoving.

This is the queue?

When's the next flight?

Next week!

Planes, Trains and Matatus

Flights do work, but often they do not, real time arrivals and departures are only somewhat similar to printed schedules, and if Central Africa does nothing else, it has its way of bringing us down to earth. So let's start with transport on the ground.

On assignment in the mid-nineties, I scanned the horizons of East and Central Africa from this vantage and that. I was plied with advice to the point of overload. None had the dutch uncle savvy of the homely scoop two young Asians offered in the mid- seventies, almost twenty years earlier. Often pedantic, sometimes overbearing, occasionally modest, what Gupta and Alihussein had to offer has checked out on assignment after assignment, which means something to a reporter. We're hit daily, hourly, with the latest news, most of it hopelessly dated in a month. Until then, my picture of Asians was one of tight-fisted shopkeepers (*duka wallas*) abusing their African help. Gupta was a short, fat Gujarati, a smooth-skinned Buddha in aviator glasses and a powder-blue safari suit with those huge collars that were trendy a decade earlier; he was about 22. Alihussein was a Valentino look-alike in a tailormade suit of khaki drill (the only tailored cotton suit I've ever seen) and a white shirt, open at the neck; he was about 25. Thoroughly African (both fourth generation Ugandans; both from families expelled by Amin), thoroughly Asian (right down to the nodding lilt so easily mimicked), and of course more British than the Brits (right down to Wordsworth), the two shared a mahogany-paneled second-class cabin with me aboard East African Railway's morning express from Nairobi, west up the viaducts of the great Mau escarpment, to the port of Kisumu on the near shore of Lake Victoria.

From there, we would take the steamer M.V. Victoria across the yawning 200-mile expanse of the lake. On the other side lay the foothills of the mountains which rise at the center of Africa, and for me, a question: I had never liked the idea of a fixed, planned route through country I'd never seen before. I liked making choices along the way. And I was beginning to wonder what sense this made this time. Nerves were frayed throughout East and Central Africa. I could no longer drive into Tanzania from Kenya as I once had. Amin was in power in Kampala. Advice was welcome, and so what if these two agreed on hardly a thing

"It's all beginning with those blighters, the Watusi," said Alihussein, pronouncing the word fifties-style, like the dance.

"The killing, Amin..."

"Buganda," said Gupta. "Old Buganda. That's where it's beginning. Before Uganda, the old *kabakas*." To which Alihussein retorted, "Not Buganda," and so it went. At one point Alihussein talked about a hardware broker he'd met in Kigali who showed him Polaroid shots of "hands, long thin hands, Watusi hands; a great mound of severed Watusi hands." To which Gupta retorted, "and just who would be playing the blighter in this load of cod's wallop? First you're telling us the blame is falling on the Watusi, and now it's appearing the Watusi are on the wrong end of your *panga*."

"Details," said Alihussein. "You've got to be seeing the big picture. It's beginning with the ruddy Watusi..."

"With Buganda."

"Rwanda." Should I have expected a Pakistani to agree with an Indian? What mattered is that these two dedicated students of getting around, both Uganda-born, both living a life on the move (Gupta as a reporter, Alihussein as an accountant for a collection agent) were earnestly debating the virtue of this mode of transport, the vice of that, and not incidentally, whether it was even the train we should have been taking to the center of Africa.

Trains

"Locomotives," said Gupta. "Not up to standard." "Roadbed," said Alihussein. "New '90s class diesels pulling on this run. Best in the Commonwealth. But no proper roadbed, and even the best diesel isn't picking up speed."

The conductor, a crisply uniformed Masai with one eye clouded with trachoma and his long, pierced earlobes looped trimly up over the tops of his ears, came around to punch our 40 shilling tickets, and Alihussein was so deferential ("*tafadhal, bwana, tafadhal*") that it made me think of the Asians' reputation for treating Africans rudely.

"Locomotives," said Gupta. "And no rail at all in Rwanda or Burundi," said Alihussein.

Nor, these days, in Uganda. Terror is largely gone from the roads here. Checkpoints are mostly polite. But Amin's legacy lives on, so totally did infrastructure break down. The trains now are all third class and so slow they're not worth taking. Alihussein told us of a young woman he met while she was on holiday from a university in Australia, a student of photography on scholarship. "A railway conductor accused her of wearing shorts" which apparently she was doing, they were, what is it is calling them, culottes, that's it, and as shorts are forbidden, he's pulling her along to the constable's desk at the next station, which I'm recalling was Jinja. A real fright she's had. Then she's getting jolly well angry, demanding the chief constable, when along comes the bloke himself, swagger stick, cocked hat, reeking he is of *waraki*! A crowd's collecting, egging the boss on, and right off, he's accusing her of trafficking in contraband and confiscating all her camera gear."

Gupta had a story, too, about a student from Ankole country in Uganda's south, not at all political, studying veterinary medicine at Makerere University. "The chap just disappeared. One day he's there; one day he's gone." They seemed to be giving me the barest inkling. Mayhem, sometimes planned but often random, killed up to half a million Ugandans. The extended families of both Gupta and Alihussein had been among 50,000 Asians expelled. The backbone of a robust economy, but thoroughly resented, Uganda's Asians had to leave everything or sell in a lopsided buyers' market. Amin's cronies divied up the spoils, milked businesses dry. But this the world knew. What was hard to know was what it was like up close. They told no stories of what had happened to them, nor to their families, and I didn't push. Ruddy racialist," said Gupta. "Amin?" I asked. "No, old man, not Amin," said Gupta. Nonplussed, I looked at Gupta. Nothing. At Alihussein. Nothing. "Us," said Gupta. Alihussein didn't argue.

Buses

"Crowding," said Alihussein. "Value for money," said Gupta. "Slow." "But getting you there."

Matatus

Both were partisans of the matatu, that pickup with a wooden bench which proliferates throughout East and Central Africa. But for different reasons. For Gupta, ever the progressive, they were truly democratic transport. Gupta "drew his salary" in Kenya, but seemed to wish there were a decent salary for him to draw in Tanzania. He was an *ujamaa* man. For Alihussein, they were "value for money. It can be ruddy dear, getting around country all bollixed up like this. I'm wagering there's a whole blooming lot of these places a *matatu* will be getting you." "You're asking where they muster," said Gupta. "Then you're asking for one going your way. You're negotiating the fare." "Making yourself as comfortable as possible," said Alihussein. "The driver, he won't be leaving until he's been shoving in fares enough to make you as uncomfortable as possible."

"This is how the Bantu is living everyday," said Gupta.

"And we must be considering as well the matter of mental health policy," said Alihussein. "The policy of deinsitutionalizing facilities. For that is most assuredly where these matatu drivers are coming from. The looney bin in Pangani."

"Speeding insanely," nodded Gupta, "taking insane chances," and Alihussein, who had begun by urging matatus on me, ended it all with a flourish. "These maniacs. They are no sooner deinstitutionalized than they are institutionalizing their clients. For some it's hospital. For others, the morgue."

Planes

"Disgraceful," said Alihussein.

"Deplorable," said Gupta.

"But in a real pinch," said Alihussein, "when they're telling you there's nothing scheduled, that's when you're sitting on the tarmac, thumb out for anything unscheduled."

"Not possible," said Gupta.

"Not possible if the pilot's Gujarati," said Alihussein. "If he's Pakistani, he'll be piping you aboard."

The first time I tried this, it took forever, but a plane finally landed, and the pilot agreed to take us aboard. He was Gujarati.

Fellow Travelers

I'm old enough to remember, however vaguely, the way Joe McCarthy and Roy Cohen carried on about "fellow travelers" of the Communist Party infiltrating the government. Alihussein is the only man I know who used this phrase as much. Of course, he wasn't talking pinkos. He was talking opportunity, finding literal "fellow travelers" to leverage your way out of a tight spot.

"Two of you could be hiring a Peugeot. Three of you could most definitely be hiring a Peugeot. Perhaps even a driver."

Gupta and I got the hint. We resolved to hire a car when we got to Tanzania's far-western port of Bukoba, on the other side of the lake.

Trucks

"I'm just not remembering that bloke, the one on the telly always combing his hair," said Gupta. "Kooky," said Alihussein absently as he stared out the window at a troop of baboons walking as if they were villagers along one of those ubiquitous footpaths which crisscross Africa from the Cape to Cairo. We were finishing supper, Nile Perch, nicely poached, oversized brown bottles of Tusker lager. At a table at the other end of the dining car, the waiters, having finished the last sitting, were pulled up around a big communal plate of *ugali*, a staple gruel of corn which they would scoop up with their right hands, dipping the fresh, bland stuff into a fiery *piripiri* sauce. "Route 66," said Gupta. "We had our own Route 66 until that blighter Amin came along, and will have again someday." Indeed, after Amin fell, that route did open up again, then closed again with the '91 troubles in Rwanda, then opened again. As Gupta put it, eyes closed: "Mombasa, Nairobi, Nakuru, Jinja, Kampala, Kigali, Butare, Usumbura. Route 66 through Africa. Port to port. Indian Ocean to Lake Tanganyika. There was always something moving up and down that pipeline."

Disease for one, but more on that later. Gupta was right. Trucks are always on the move along that route, now open again, and all along the route there are *dukas* (country stores), cheap motels and petrol stations where drivers stop for beans, women, gas. Sometimes they'll give you a ride, and it can't hurt to have a friend in the U.S. military. Over the past few years, in fact well before the Somali crisis, the U.S. has been building a substantial military presence in Mombasa. The shots on TV showed huge C-130s landing U.S. relief supplies in the Rwandan theater, but that's an expensive way to ship, and it's not how most of the relief gets there. Most is trucked in U.S. military eight-bys out of Mombasa. The military is doing its best to do the least, and doing pretty well at it: by year-end 1994, convoys had been cut way back, but there were still some scheduled for 1995.

Cars

I woke the next morning to the sound of a *muzzein* calling the faithful to prayer. The train was at a halt in Kisumu station. Outside, a troop of dark blue, smartly waxed Land Rovers were mustered. I mulled what sort of four-wheel-drive vehicle we would rent on the western side of the lake. Alihussein was on his knees on a prayer mat, genuflecting. The air was dank, still, but it didn't have the oppressive torpor I had anticipated. Something was in the air; was it frangipani or jasmine?

Kisumu had just begun its decline. Trade with Uganda had just recently reached the point of virtually complete collapse. These days Kisumu itself seems in complete collapse. For the very reason of its dependence on trade with Uganda, this third largest city in Kenya seems at first a special case, a unique depression due to Uganda's collapse. But these days 'special cases' of this sort are the rule rather than the exception in Africa, and especially in Central Africa.

I liked Kisumu then and wondered whether I would like it when depression took its inevitable toll. I still like it.

"This is not Kenya," said Gupta.

"Jamia Mosque," said Alihussein. "The imam is Pakistani."

"Central Africa is beginning here," said Dilip.

Outside, the Land Rovers beckoned. They say you can take a nap crossing Lake Victoria in a plane and wake up still surrounded by water. The story is credible enough after crossing it by ferry. It is an inland sea. Tanzania's far west on the far side appeared as a welcome dash of green through the humid haze. Likewise the whitewashed face of Bukoba.

But no four-wheel-drive vehicles (let alone a nicely waxed dark blue Land Rover). Bukoba is considerably bigger than Rwanda's capital of Kigali, a little further west, but no four-wheel-drive vehicles. Not even something with a limited slip differential.

For an accountant, Alihussein had a real weakness for turning off the road, which wouldn't have been so bad if we hadn't rented a seven-year-old Toyota Corolla.

We were on the high planes near the Rwandan frontier, along the tumbling Kagera River which brings bodies down to Tanzania from Rwanda. This river was once called the Alexander Nile, and is in fact a true source of the Nile, for it empties into Lake Victoria.

"You must be remembering, speed kills," Gupta would say whenever Alihussein was at the wheel. Gupta drove so nicely we'd fall asleep, even off the road, and it was very much a reverie, driving through the scrub in these foothills. We were near the Rumanyika Game Reserve on the Tanzania side of Rwanda's Kagera Park, but we weren't in the reserve, and for me the thrill of it was waking fitfully and seeing game; antelope, elephant that was truly wild, off a reserve.

Once Gupta hit something and both Alihussein and I awoke at once. Forty yards in front of us lay a thin screed of water at least 100 yards wide.

"You must be remembering, speed can save a lot of time," said Alihussein, and Gupta got the message quickly. This studious lad who had been driving so carefully suddenly put pedal to metal, extracting as much speed as he could from that sorely abused four cylinder engine, anything to maintain momentum. The rear end fishtailed madly, throwing great sprays of rufous clay into an electric blue sky, and somehow he slewed through the muck.

Gupta was feeling okay. "You're getting stuck, that's also the way out," he said. "You're giving it everything it's got."

"Wishful driving, chappy," said Alihussein. "Once you're stuck, you can't speed anymore."

"Must do," said Gupta.

"Must not," said Alihussein. "You're finding yourself stuck and it's pole-pole, slowly, slowly, oh so proper, with the gear box in second, not first, second. If you're showing sufficient contrition by doing what good little drivers are supposed to, then perhaps, just perhaps, the *juju* will be with you."

He was right, of course, and I might add that if you don't show proper contrition, if you just spin your wheels and manage to get unstuck anyway, then you better watch out for the pits they dig in Rwanda to trap gazelle. Very well camouflaged, and at the bottom are sharpened sticks like those punji stakes of VC fame.

Sightseeing

Gupta put it this way, "take in the scenery before you're on the road." It was another of the few things on which the two agreed, perhaps because it gave them a chance to lecture an American. Seems we take borders too seriously. Obviously things change as you cross one, they said. Askaris wear different uniforms. Roads paid for by state treasuries get better or worse. But governments can't draw borders around danger. That's how it was then; that's pretty much how it is now: the '94 war in Rwanda was surrounded by war zones in Zaire, Burundi, Tanzania and Uganda, and now the roads of these cross-border war zones are more dangerous than Rwanda proper.

Hutu refugees, many of them killers who can't go home, clog the Tanzania side of the Kagera. It was through this country that Nyerere's poorly equipped, poorly trained army crossed into Uganda to end, at last, the Amin terror.

Safest of the border crossings is the Rwanda/Uganda frontier which was not long ago the most dangerous.

This is the region along Uganda's Kisororo-Kabale-Mbarara Road from which Paul Kagame came with his 5000 men on October 1, 1990. And it's the region to which his Tutsi-led Rwandan Patriotic Front was thrown back when France, Belgium and Zaire jumped in on the side of the Hutu, the region to which his troops repaired to wrap their wounds, set their bones, bury their dead; the region from which they had to watch as Hutu and even Zairois troops went on pogroms against civilian Watutsi in Rwanda.

The Word On Words

As Gupta saw it, getting around turf which is both literally and figuratively a minefield is not just a function of transport. It was a function of language. Things change fast, he said. "You've got to talk, use words, speak up." I could almost hear his father lecturing him with the same words.

Alihussein never agreed, but he didn't disagree. Once I asked in frustration, "how do you get around this place," and he gave me a pocket grammar of the Swahili language. When I stared, he gave me an Arabic grammar.

Schedules are subject to remorseless change in the best of African worlds. In a war zone, all you can depend on not to change are the crucial words you need to find out how to get where you want, and more importantly, how to get out of there.

In Central Africa, that means either a few words of French or a little Swahili, preferably a little of both and why not a dollop of Arabic Right, it's hardly used at all, and besides, anyone in East or Central Africa who speaks Arabic is going to have no trouble understanding your smattering of Swahili; the two are just that *sawa-sawa* (which in both Swahili and Arabic means cheek by jowl). But for one, all we're talking about is a shot, and for another, speaking up, using words, is not something you do just like that. Face it: you're dropping into a dangerous place 11 time zones away, in fact a place where time is kept by a clock that's totally unfamiliar, and where street news—often wrong, often crucial, sometimes all you've got—isn't spoken in any language vaguely related to high school Spanish II. This demands at the very least a couple of weeks of the time you put into your morning shower. In short, it's a conditioning exercise. Fifteen minutes of Arabic now and then amounts to cross training, and while you're pumping up, it helps to think about how ignorant we are about the extent to which Islamic culture, for good, for evil and forever, influenced Africa. A glimpse at the language of the Koran is a good exercise, sort of mental push-ups to get ready for a tough day on the road. At least you won't gush "weird" when you see the King Faisal Hospital in Kigali, or the huge new mosque in Bujumbura, or any number of other signs that Abdul was here, is here. You may even have a sharper ear for misinformation. One widely read book, for example, tells us that Idi Amin converted to Islam during his presidency in order to get Arab money. Having just a smattering of Arabic, this yarn will have you wondering. A convert. A man who's name was already "Amin." (A fairly common name in the Muslim world, and particularly in the Muslim tribes of Uganda, among which are the Kakwa of West Nile Province to whom Idi Amin Dada belongs.

Swahili

Talking the Talk

Linguistic overviews show Swahili used less as a lingua franca as you get further off the old Swahili tracks from the coast into Central Africa, less in Kampala than Nairobi, less in Kigali than Kampala, a lot less in eastern Zaire. In fact, you may find yourself using it more in Rwanda, Burundi and Zaire than in Uganda. It probably has something to do with the limited utility of French with the many foreigners who don't really speak it. Many foreigners do speak some English, though, so Ugandans taught English in school are better off using it than Swahili. Just the opposite with the Francophones of Central Africa who don't have much English; they're more likely to fall back on Swahili.

All of which is by way of saying that no matter what the books tell you, when it comes to getting around, the word for that all- important vehicle is the same in Bujumbura and Kigali as it is in Dar and Mombasa, *matatu*.

Anyone who hasn't learned that fundamental bit of Swahili is lost. Where the crump of artillery is heard in the land, and making tracks could be crucial, the traveller unfamiliar with the word matatu could be lost indeed.

Here are some words which jump out from notes taken over a few years of struggling to get around East and Central Africa. Where Arabic words appear after Swahili ones, it's not to show origin. There are lots of Arabic loan-words in Swahili. Where an Arabic word appears, it's because it seems to add some dimension to the comedies, tragedies and soap operas in which the Swahili word might be used. Also, these few random words are no mini-lesson on the language. They're offered only as shoehorns into language, and out of trouble:

alf	A thousand; a lot. From Arabic.
asante sana	The first word means "thanks," and I just can't remember it being used alone (though the books all show it that way). It seems always to be asante sana, "thanks a lot", and the phrase never seems to be offered sarcastically, as we so often do. It's an important phrase. People are either nice to each other or dreadful, and in this part of the world, you never know when getting off on the right foot is going to turn out to have been a terrific idea.
askari	Soldier. Same in Arabic. Often just a guard, or anyone riding shotgun, and if that's what you need, you can ask for an askari without wondering whether you will be misunderstood to be asking whether the Chief of Staff can be hired out.
baadaye	After; in Arabic, baada.
barabara kuu	Paved road. Most aren't. Unpaved, they can be slow- going. There may be something worse than driving miles through ruts so deep you expect the undercarriage to hang up on the hump running mid-track, wheels spinning in midair. Offhand, though, the only thing worse I can think of is driving that way for hours, then discovering that this sorry imitation of a road has been paralleling, for the past 50 miles, a nice new arbara kuu, which you would have been on, had you but known the words.
baridi	Cold. An important word if you like pombe, which means beer. Baridi also means cold in Arabic.
basi	Bus. Not as important a word as matatu. Also handy is the Arabic, sayara; car.
bwana	How you'll be addressed if you're a man. If you're an unmarried woman, it will be bibi; if you're a married woman, mama. If you don't like these, you could be lucky and get m'em saab.
dahab	Gold, both languages.
habari	Information, news, in many senses. An information office may be marked habari ofisi, or quite commonly someone will greet you, habari, bwana, literally, what's new with you, but more like, how do you do.

hakuna

There isn't any; there aren't any; we haven't got any; it's all gone; no pills; no morphine; no diapers; no cab; no matatu ; you can't get there from here; yes, we have no bananas. Same as the Arabic, mafeesh. Often expressed with an exclamation point. Both languages make different words, even sentences, by adding prefixes, suffixes, infixes. The root here is kuna, which means both "there is" and "there are." In country where a lot of people have plenty of nothin', you hear hakuna a lot more often. Sometimes, though, it can be upbeat, as in the refrain hakuna matata; no problem, from *The Lion King* ("it's our problem-free/ phil-o-so-phy..."). See also, hapana jambo; No sweat.

haraka!

Fast!

hashish

Grass. That's the literal meaning in Arabic, as well as the word for the drug. In Swahili, it's just the drug. The hashishim (assassins) were killers high on grass.

hatari

Danger.

hatari ya mauti

Danger of Death.

ita polisi

Call the police.

jali hapo

Look out!

kiasi gani

How much?

kitabu

Book; Arabic, kitab. Also, maktoob, literally, it is written, it is fated, more like, shit happens.

la

No; same as Arabic.

leila

Evening; same as Arabic. (Alf Leila Wa Leila; A Thousand Nights and a Night.)

leila salama

Good night.

msaada!

Help!

nafahamu

I understand, from an Arabic root, fahem, for understanding; useful in varied circumstances. An Arab may say gruffly fahem much as a mafioso might say capish ("You're not welcome here, capish ") Either "I understand"—na fahamu—or "I don't understand,"—sifa hamu—could be the button to push. Sifa is Swahili for zero, a word directly borrowed from the Arabs, from whom we also got the sifa, cipher, zero, and not just the word, but the mathematical concept. Sifahamu is literally "'zero understanding," a nicely emphatic expression if you come down hard on the sifa. Though both sifa and hamu are from Arabic, the Arabs say mishfahem when they don't understand. In fact both sifa and mish are useful prefixes, letting you reverse the meaning of any number of words you may already know, in a way that's almost always understood even if it's not always correct. (Good can become no good; pretty, no pretty; danger, no danger.)

nimepotea

I'm lost.

nungunungu

Porcupine; more likely to do you harm than any mammal in the bush.

ondoka!

Scram! Arabic, emshee.

pikpiki

Nothing close to "picky picky;" it means "motorcycle"

pole-pole

Slowly, carefully, dismount .

saah	Hour, directly from the Arabic. A apropos of which, in the Swahili world, as in much of the Muslim world, hours are not counted from noon and midnight, but from a dawn of 6:00 A.M., and a dusk of 6:00 P.M., which works out pretty well smack on the equator where days get quickly light and quickly dark at just those times month-in and month-out. The Swahili words for half-hour and a quarter of an hour also come directly from Arabic, nus (half) saah, and rob (quarter) saah. Rob itself is a usefully memorable word. In Swahili and Arabic, just as in English, "quarter" can mean either the numeric fraction or a region, as in "The Latin Quarter," or Arabia's "Rob al Khali," the Empty Quarter. Another convenient variation: nus wa nus, half and half, comme ci, comme ca; often usefully noncommittal.
safari	Trip, directly from Arabic.
safari-moja	One way trip. Moja is Swahili for one; kwanza for first.
salamu	Hello, from the Arabic salamat, from the Arabic, salaam, peace. If you want to show directly cordial respect, you can approach someone with the formal Arabic expression, salaam alayikum (peace be with you), and you'll be surprised how often you'll get the proper reply, alayikum salaam, even in Bujumbura.
samahani	I'm sorry. Also good for "excuse me" when you're trying to get someone's attention.
shaba	Copper, as in Zaire's Shaba province, from Arabic safa.
shamba	Farm; sometimes it means a thatched rondavel.
sielewie	Also means, "I don't understand." It's pronounced something like "seeya, lewie," which is especially easy to remember when you've had enough.
simama!	Stop! (More emphatic.)
simama mwizi!	Stop thief!
simu	Phone
tafadhal	Please; Arabs say the same. Formal Arabic is min fadlik.
tumekatiwa simu	We were cut off, which is what you tell the operator (remember, simu is "phone") when your line has been cut.
twende sinema	Want to go to a movie?
tusismame	Don't move.
wa	And. From the Arabic. (Alf Leila Wa Leila)

Aches, Pains and Deadly Humors

Hepatitis kills more people in Central Africa than AIDS. That doesn't mean AIDS is any less a problem here. It's just a measure of how bad hepatitis is, and how underreported. In fact, the AIDS pandemic may be worse here than anywhere. At what may be the epicenter of AIDS along Uganda's montane border with Rwanda, entire villages have been wiped out. But death is only one face of AIDS. Hysteria is another. At the epicenter, the desperate are turning to false messiahs. The hysteria is not uniquely African. In the western world, studies suggesting that the human immunodeficiency virus (HIV) may have begun with vervet monkeys in West Africa led quickly to muted hysteria about how HIV spread to humans. Scientists rushed to print with less-than-scientific articles on how some tribes might be smoking monkey meat; the more hysterical spread stories about sex with animals which the tellers swore was a traditional African practice. Somewhat less baseless, but nonetheless wrong, were stories that the disease was spread by certain rural practices, in particular circumcision and infibulation (a still-common rural practice in which a young wife's vaginal opening is sewn in a way that makes sex painful); science has long known that AIDS in Africa spreads from urban, not rural areas. African students, HIV positive or not, were suddenly expelled from countries like India.

A mortified Africa at first pretended it had no AIDS. To a real extent, the pretense lives on. Almost alone among African heads of state, Uganda's Mouseveni, whose resistance army was notably straitlaced, openly allows medical professionals to study and treat the disease. As with so many calamities, the victim cries out not just for relief, but for someone to blame, and that's something you have to experience firsthand. For me, it came unexpectedly at a bar alive with Bob Marley off the courtyard of a pleasantly unassuming hotel called The Lotus in Mombasa. A young Luo from Kisumu in town on trade union business was treating me to a couple beers. Philip had a commercial degree and was knowledgeable; he saw big trouble coming in Rwanda a year before the 1994 eruption. "You'll see Waranda here," he said, and eventually he talked about AIDS. "I can't help asking: how do you know what they'll do next?" I asked what he meant by 'they.' "The government, the C.I.A.," he said, then began to apologize. "You know, we really do know the difference. Everybody likes the American people. We don't confuse you with the government."

For example "Well, Tom Hanks," he said. "We love Tom Hanks, and Clint..."No," I said, "for example, our government..." "And your C.I.A., your army," he said. A shower was suddenly washing through the palms in the small courtyard, the breeze bringing with it the smell of frangipani and the perfume of an attractive young woman who had just run in. We both glanced over at her. "Especially your army," he said, still looking away at her, "Your army and that business at Camp Detrick." Was he sure he didn't mean the Marine Corps? The army doesn't have camps. "No, it was the army." "Could he mean Fort De..." "Yes of course, old man, Fort Detrick. So perhaps you have heard of it then..." All I knew was the difference between a camp and a fort. "It's in Maryland; must be right next to you." "Must be," I said, a little embarrassed. At least he didn't know I covered the military and was still barely aware of this fort next door to Washington. "It's where they developed the AIDS virus." The bell finally rang. It's an old story but I'd missed it or forgotten the Fort Detrick angle; again, his knowledgeability had become apparent. He hadn't just heard the story; he had absorbed the verisimilitude of its detail, knew the Fort Detrick part; knew Fort Detrick is in Maryland. According to the C.I.A., this story—that the U.S. Army developed the AIDS virus to wipe out black people—began with the old Soviet KGB, and has now taken on a life of its own. "So finally you recall," he said, leaning forward over his beaker of stout. "My friend, we are real people. You shouldn't forget so easily what some people are willing to do to us." So he believed it, then. "And why not?" "Well, according to the C.I.A..." He sat back and looked at me: "According to the C.I.A..." I said reporters had looked into it; that they'd filed requests under the Freedom Of Information Act (a law he plainly had trouble taking seriously); that they found no basis for the story. "So you Americans, you're ready to believe the C.I.A." "Not always, but..." "Another beer?" he asked, and our conversation turned to football. We both had nine-year old sons playing football. Not a few of those Rwandans he spoke of in Kenya are Tutsi girls forced by the cost of urban living into prostitution. Mostly to reassure nervous johns, they almost all carry condoms these days; young as they are, many seem to realize that they are beyond the point that protection can do much good for them. AIDS is an urban disease, and both Rwanda and Burundi, as well as surrounding regions of Zaire, Uganda, Tanzania, are notably rural, not urban. Towns are small. At independence in 1962, the population of Rwanda's capital was 5000. But the countryside is heavily populated, and it flanks "Route 66," that trunk road about which Gupta had rhapsodized. Long distance truck routes have turned out to be the primary agent for spreading the disease in Africa. Studies show that almost a third of the drivers on the Mombasa-Kigali-Bujumbura haul are HIV positive. Another major carrier—and a major victim—of AIDS are the professional classes. It wasn't long ago that Central Africa's professionals, that is, its professional men, joked openly about how they were able to carry on, what with their government salaries. Now AIDS appears poised to devastate Central Africa's professional classes with nearly the fury Amin loosed on Kampala's professionals. Washington-based Africa specialist Sandy Unger recounts having dinner with an M.D. in one of the best restaurants in one of Africa's most prosperous cities. As they entered, the owner, the maitre d', the headwaiter, the wine steward, and patron after patron, at table after table, rose to greet the man, as if he were a celebrity. As they were seated, Unger gave a perplexed look to the physician, who leaned forward and explained. "These people. I'm treating them all for AIDS."

Flying, War and Tortured Logic as Public Health Hazards

Of course, planes do crash, not the least in Central Africa, and not the least in Rwanda, but the logic by which flying is a public health problem is tortured. However, tortured logic may itself be a public health hazard here. (An official once explained to me how "linguistics demonstrates the relationship between the peoples of France and Scotland: you'll notice they both use the word, 'wee'".) So the fear of flying given me by one Rwandan informant may be telling in its own way. "You know," she said. "Takeoff and landing are the most dangerous moments. In fact, we had a terrible incident at Kigali Airport very recently. An airliner crashed just as it took off." Actually, what she was talking about has a lot to do with what makes Central Africa hazardous to health, but not until you hear the rest of her story: She was talking about the plane carrying the presidents of Rwanda and Burundi which was shot down in April of '94. In fact, the greatest public health problem in Central Africa may well be politics, general bloody mindedness, war. This is no rhetorical flight. In America, public health officials commonly reckon gunshot wounds a health hazard right along with AIDS, drugs and Alzheimer's disease. In Central Africa, you simply add shell fire, assault by *panga*, assault by blunt instrument, and the inevitable companion of these categories, blood poisoning, gangrene. After that July takeoff which killed two presidents, the Rwandan generals who controlled the entire airport zone blamed the Watutsi, and another pogrom was underway. Paul Kagame was watching a football video when a runner rushed the news to his tent near Biumba just south of the Uganda border, and it presented him with a dilemma: All his planning for renewed combat hinged on the fact that with his 5000 poorly armed troops against 30,000 well-armed troops, supported by a militia and by foreign advisers, it would be crucial for him to concentrate his forces, to avoid distraction. And now there was a powerful distraction; the health of his countrymen. Watutsi managing to escape slaughter on the spot were fleeing, often wounded, into the bush, especially the higher mountains where the nights were cold and wet, and where they faced gangrene, starvation, disease. Meantime, the killing wouldn't stop.

These are not dangers faced simply by the locals. Beyond Kisumu, Western travelers are few, but those with reason enough to go are generally resourceful enough to make sure their health insurance covers them here, and that they are covered for evacuation. Insurance outfits seem to know this; some are given to packaging prudent medical coverage for this sort of travel with what is generally considered a lousy deal, coverage of air crashes.

The Scoop

As a deadly but long-term killer, AIDS doesn't grab the sort of attention as other diseases during emergencies like the Rwanda crisis. But it keeps on working all the same, especially in crowded camps. As does hepatitis, dysentery. And then there are swarms of lesser but nonetheless maddening beasties of prey: mosquitoes, boils, heat rash, spider bites, snake bites, food poisoning, fleas, ticks, and bed bugs—which is another half-baked theory about how AIDS is spread in Africa: bed bugs. Hepatitis may kill more than AIDS, but the full force of AIDS, given gestation periods, is yet to be felt. When it is felt, it is hard to imagine a way it will be felt more sorely than in the loss of educated leaders by a continent already in desperate need of direction. Meantime, an economic crisis sending Africa backward in time is devastating what is left of once wonderful universities, like Kampala's Makere. Testimony from some more Swahili: *choo*, Toilet; *daktari*, Doctor; *hospitali*, Hospital; *inyenzi*, Cockroach. Two very different varieties pose a danger. First there are the insects. Then there are the young Watutsi who call themselves *inyenzi*. They first appeared after the first pogrom against the Watutsi in Rwanda. Small bands of Tutsi refugees in Burundi or Uganda would organize for a raid on a Rwandan military base, almost invariably they would overrun the base, and then they would be virtually wiped out themselves when reinforcements came in vastly superior numbers. In the aftermath of each inyenzi attack, Watutsi still in Rwanda, most of whom had nothing to do with the inyenzi, would be slaughtered: *jeraha*, Wound; *jipu*, Boil; *kichwa*, Headache; *kuhara*, The runs; *mwiba*, Sting; *mwite daktari*! Call a doctor! (*haraka*! Fast!) *ninata pika*, I've been throwing up. I'm sure the circumstance is purely coincidental, but it was at about the time I began using words like these that I realized how fundamentally Bantu Swahili is, for all it's Arabic words. One reason Arabic may have meshed so smoothly with whatever Bantu languages became Swahili is that the grammatical structure of both Bantu tongues and Arabic pivot on prefixes, suffixes and infixes. But it's also here that Swahili's fundamentally Bantu character asserts itself: Arabic and Bantu prefixes, suffixes, infixes are completely different, and in Swahili, the fundamental ones are Bantu, not Arabic.

Uganda

Where Danger Still Hangs Out

Realms Beyond Death and Beyond Borders

Return to Central Africa after four or five years and you court disorientation. A place once decent is deadly, a place once deadly has settled down; you wonder which decent place today will be dangerous tomorrow.

We seem always taken by surprise. Yet there seem always to be people, quietly out of the way, who will tell you that the changes are driven by beliefs, habits, traditions which are as much a part of the landscape as the green banana and the marabou stork.

Problem is, these quiet sources are seldom sufficiently "authoritative." Rank in a news outfit can be as precarious as life and death in one of those royal courts of the old Watutsi, and everyone wants to be a correspondent. It is not a climate which encourages risk-taking. If someone authoritative back in New York or Washington questions the quality of your source, your source had best be authoritative himself.

One week back in January '71 correspondents came out of State Department backgrounders in more than one capital reporting "this new guy Amin might be okay." ("Establishment military," authoritative sources had said; "we've dealt with him.")

Alas, when Yoweri Museveni's outlaw army began showing up on a distant bush-horizon fifteen years later, it wasn't so easy to get the scoop. He just wasn't the State Department's type. All we could tell was that authoritative sources were uneasy. So we were uneasy, too.

We fancied ourselves detached and independent, but after all, that was the news. Without putting it in so many words, important sources were uneasy, and absent of much more to go on, what else could we write? In our correctly objective voice, correctly throwing in easily missed qualifiers like "unconfirmed," we speculated about Museveni the radical, about reports he'd been with FRELIMO in Mozambique, among Maoist Chinese on the Tanzanian island of Pemba. We heard reports that this renegade off in the shadows of the bush was even sending children into battle…and, hey, the reports checked out. He was.

We pictured a gang of bush-hard cultural revolutionaries, armed with AKs and simpleminded slogans, about to drag Uganda right back into chaos, just as new and moderate leaders were at last in place to nurse that sorry realm back to life.

During his long march on Kampala through a shell-shattered free-fire zone in Buganda known as the "Lowery Triangle" (shattered largely by the government's North Korean shells), Museveni had slipped out to London. In fact, he was there duirng a period when any practical leader (and he is a practical man) could see his cause was lost; he had virtually no financial resources, no trained military resources, the triangle was hamburger, it was over, guile with reporters was pointless.

Alas, we paid slight attention to him then, just as we failed fully to appreciate until too late that Uganda's "moderates" were crooks who killed more Ugandans than Amin. A little more attention to quiet voices and we might not have evoked such foolish dismay as we relayed third-hand reports about a bullet-riddled beast (so rudely subhuman in its ability to live after such punishment), slouching toward Kampala.

This beast, as we now know, was an army of some 20,000 adolescents and twenty-somethings; the kids the despairing Museveni had left behind. On their own, they had hung on; and at last, slowly, pushed on. Less dependent on authoritative sources, we might even have provided some modest inspiration in dispatches about a true children's crusade, about orphans left with no choice but combat, their families and their lands having been trashed first by Amin, then by the undisciplined, unpaid and rapaciously angry soldiers of Tanzania, and then again by Amin's old military, now led by corrupt "moderates."

We didn't deliver that story until Museveni's kids were on the cusp of victory in mid-'85. To this day, many are surprised to learn that Julius Nyerere's protege, the school teacher Apollo Milton Obote, killed more Ugandans than Amin.

All this matters now because all of Central Africa is dangerous. Danger here is almost always tied to danger there, and wherever you land, sooner or later somebody shows up to say don't count on the news to keep you out of trouble.

In fact, Museveni has succeeded in removing most of Uganda from the world's most dangerous places. The State Department reports that snatch and grabs from cars stalled in Kampala traffic are common, but security in Kampala and Entebbe is by no stretch frightful. Uganda's frontier with Rwanda is notably less dangerous than the refugee-ridden frontiers which Tanzania, Burundi and Zaire share with Rwanda. But throughout East and Central Africa, you hear that we ignore Uganda at the risk of getting taken by surprise yet again...and not just in Uganda. Ask why, and here's what they say:

Dangerous Places

Restless Watutsi, Restless Bahutu, Restless Border

Mbarara and Ankole Country

The maxim for most dangerous places is, don't go unless you have to. That's not what you hear about the town of Mbarara and Ankole country just north of Rwanda and Tanzania, where you still find, after years of the white man's devastating rinderpest, longhorn Ankole cattle. Not unlike Tutsi cattle, they are owned by a tall, dark aristocracy, descended like the Watutsi from northern invaders who seized a Bantu-speaking kingdom. Here the serfs are the Hima people, the aristocrats, the Ankole.

This is the region through which Henry Morton Stanley (the explorer who presumed to discover Dr. Livingstone) passed in 1875 on his way to meet Mutesa, king of Buganda, and what you hear about it is don't let the danger keep you away.

For one, it's beautiful, often the spare, dry beauty of the savanna rather than the ever-lush beauty of Buganda just to the north. (Buganda's deep green light filtering through banana groves colors the Uganda of our imagination.) For another, there is both the human and animal population. Mbarara is not an unusual African town, but then you begin to realize how combat tore the place up, and how other towns, similarly battered, still languish in a decrepit state. It's bracing to experience the resilience of this much patched place. Gusty *jambos* in a town with cheap hotels sporting names like, The Super Tip Top Lodge Bar & Restaurant; this is Africa? Talk of poached-out Uganda is not to be discounted, but here it is: accounts even of a tom leopard playing with a warthog like a house cat with a house mouse, in a sense, Uganda's cat and mouse game with fate. Wildlife is in fact devastated, but just when you think it is utterly gone, there it is, and seeing it in such circumstances, the sudden appearance, for example, of a bull eland, big and blue, brings a melancholy rush.

Then there is the actual downside risk, possibly severe for the unlucky, but to all appearances, placid enough. Snatch and grabs in Mbrara are probably less likely than in Kampala. Since well before the '94 mess in Rwanda, rumors of trouble, of refugees streaming through this Ankole region, were everywhere, but travelers enough came through, well aware of the rumors, and encountered only pleasant Ankole, a thorn-rough Eden which keeps you awake, healthy country in which all nastiness is forgotten, or shoved to the back of the mind.

Which in Ankole is nasty enough so that it can never really be forgotten, nagging always from the back the of the mind. Oh yeah, this is the place where the neighbors went nuts not long ago.

Which is what wins Ankole's place in this gallery; not any mission to include even moderately dangerous places, but something much more critical—Ankole sits cheek by jowl with Rwanda. This place which is itself not unknown for the swing of the panga, sits right next to a place where the panga swung with force never before known in Africa.

After it was over, seasoned correspondents sent to cover fleeing Hutu refugees, found it almost impossible to face for more than a few hours the stinking misery in which tens of thousands, many of them children and mothers, died of disease. Because there were no "visuals," in fact no print reporters to witness it, the horror in which a million Watutsi, many children, many mothers, were hacked to death by panga, got much less attention in living rooms. But here in Ankole, something rare seems to happen: For once, the notorious inability of mere numbers ("quake kills dozens") to compete with individual anecdotes ("firemen rescue spaniel buried six days") is overcome by sheer force of numbers. The sheer force of that million-killer panga slashing unseen so close to the ear of Ankole is impossible to ignore. Not simply next to Rwanda, Ankole is a tightly dovetailed part of the Rwandan theater. In fact, its Rwanda frontier is secure largely because it is freest of Hutu refugees, and it is freest of refugees because it's the base from which Tutsi refugees launched their attack.

The North

Kampala, Entebbe, the Uganda of repute, is a place of enveloping warmth, pineapple-sweet, lush-green, coffee-rich, a rush of bluebells, crested cranes, a jacaranda breeze. The far north of Uganda is nothing like this. The country north of the Victoria Nile and Lake Kyoga is drier than the savanna in the far south, wide open land, often trackless, which even before the days of Idi Amin, travelers were warned to enter with no less than two four-wheel drive vehicles. Today, you're warned to shun it altogether unless you can rent a light plane to get in and out of secure redoubts like the army base on the Kidepo River frontier with the Sudan, a region whose land, people and animals are so close to the Pleistocene, and so palpably distant from the rest of the world, that you find yourself hypnotized.

This is Nilote country. Amin came from the Nilotic tribes which populate this harsh country; likewise, Obote. Meantime, Museveni's crusade came from the green south and west, the heartland of the old Bantu kingdoms.

The far north has always been a rough place, a place where men can still be seen with chest scars toting their kills (left breast for women, right for men), and cattle rustling has long been both a routine way of life and a routine way of death. Today it's especially dangerous. Remnants of Amin's army are about, as well as outright *shiftas*. In this territory more than any I know of, the term shifta, meaning "bandit," is likely to be used honestly, and not as a euphemism for guerrillas your source would prefer to think of as bandits.

One expedient in spots like this is to travel with army or U.N. convoys, but the government hasn't got resources to patrol the north frequently, and in recent months, even U.N. convoys have been hit.

The Scoop

Even after a fairly brief safari through the towns and lore of Central Africa, the likes of these three monsters, Mutesa, Amin and Bizimungu, begins to hint at a monumental lending library of malevolence accumulated in the old realms of the great lakes. Like the English Constitution, it's an unwritten inheritance. Like the English Constitution, its influence is felt beyond the borders of the mother country. And a little like England, Uganda is something of a mother country, home to all the great lake kingdoms save Rwanda and Burundi, and something of a cultural home to their shared brand of statecraft whose most distinctive feature is terror.

What seems to matter most now is that this brand of statecraft is becoming dangerously influential beyond the ruling classes of the old realms who developed it.

Take these three faces behind the danger—Mutesa, Amin, Bizimungu. All three learned from lore passed down generation to generation that murder and terror are the twin arts of Central African rule. But such is the growing reach of this lore that two of the three, Amin and Bizimungu, don't even come from the ruling clans which long had a mandarin lock on these princely arts.

Amin is from Uganda's primitive far north, and general de division, Augustin Bizimungu is neither princely nor Ugandan. A Rwandan Hutu, he was chief of staff of Rwanda's military in early '94 when the military there began its pogrom. Mutesa, by sharp contrast, represents the unalloyed essence of the tradition, the source of the trouble. After killing sixty of his brothers to win power, he carried Buganda's centuries-old tradition of brutality into the modern age with assagais aloft, exercising the power to kill (casually, randomly, often) for both enjoyment and statecraft, to frighten subservience from his court. As the Watutsi sang the praises of an ancient emperor who roasted a Hutu serf alive, Mutesa thought nothing of executing a dozen subjects to celebrate some middling event, who minced about in tiptoe imitation of a lion, and never bothered to look where he sat because he knew implicitly that a peon would be on hands and knees to receive his backside.

In a narrow but important sense, Paul Kagame, the "parfit gentle knight" of the Rwandan Watutsi, a man with a largely unblemished record, is closer to Mutesa, a brutal creature from another country and another century, than he is to his countryman and contemporary Bizimungu. Unlike Bizimungu and Amin, both Kagame and Mutesa were spawned by the ruling classes which cultivated statecraft by terror. Two more quick and random examples of how interwoven the people of Central Africa are, regardless of today's borders:

First, the word "*saza.*" On both sides of what is today the Rwanda, Uganda border, it meant one of the king's sub-chiefs, and on both sides of the border today, the word is still used as an official title for someone resembling a district commissioner. And then there is Kagame's recent past: Before he lead the Watutsi back to their homeland from Uganda, he was not simply a refugee there, totally out of his element. He was Uganda's chief of intelligence

Cultural Crib Sheet

Much of Uganda is somewhat dangerous, but most of it is not. These listings cover the far north, which is especially dangerous, and the far south, which is not especially dangerous just now, but is an integral part of the dangerous Rwandan theater.

Consulates

There are of course no embassies in the dangerous parts of Uganda. There may be a Sudanese consul in Gulu, but this is no place to count on getting a visa for the Sudan. For that matter, neither is Kampala. All visas must go to Khartoum for approval and in any case, the Sudan is one of those places you can't get to from here. The civil war in the Sudan has effectively closed the border.

Medical Assistance

You're on your own, friend. Any number of western embassies in Kampala can of course advise where to get competent medical attention in Kampala, but Kampala isn't a dangerous place, nor for that matter are the actual towns of Gulu and Moroto, where there are also adequate (not to speak of inadequate) medical facilities.

In the best of times, driving into the country north of the Victoria Nile has entailed the sense of entering country so open and vacant that once you're off the track and in trouble, it could be weeks before you're found. Check the "Nairobi Dossier."

Legal Assistance

Legal trouble is usually a danger in those African countries where an antagonistic regime is in power or exchange rates are totally skewed and you're totally screwed if you don't trade on the black market. Mouseveni hasn't let exchange rates get out of hand, and Uganda under his leadership is not a place which encourages antagonism. Even in those dangerous parts where government control is loose, you are unlikely to run into an antagonistic Ugandan ready to charge you with some trumped up legal infraction, something quite common during the Amin years. Highway robbery, even death, is a danger now, but not legal trouble.

Camera, Video, Computer Sources

What exists in the dangerous parts of Uganda is skimpy. In fact what exists in Kampala is skimpy. Hotel shops there have the usual complement of overpriced film; you can be sure that if you need print, all they will have is slide; if you need slide, all they will have is print. One good source by Kampala's poor standards: The Camera Centre in Africa House at 42 Kampala Road. Much better, in fact indispensible if you have any serious need for camera, computer, video or business services: Nairobi. Check the "Nairobi Dossier."

Contacts, Emergencies, Evacuation

At least one Kampala safari outfit, **Hot Ice, Ltd.** (*P.O. Box 151, Kampala; FAX 230008*) maintains radio contact with its safaris, and it has a tented camp at Lake Mburo near Mbarara in the Rwandan theater. Should things get hot, they'd likely get their clients out fast; there's a chance they could get you out aboard a light plane with an extra seat. A minor problem is that you might have to kiss your gear goodbye. A major problem is the word "fast." Safari outfits are not in the business of getting their clients killed, which means that once a place gets dangerous in any clear and present way, they are out of there, good only for the first couple days at best. After that you're on your own, and the best bet, if you can find a radio phone, are charter outfits. Depending on distance and danger, count on paying anywhere from US$750 to $10,000. If there is anyone flying out of Entebbe or any other field, the best way to find out would be through Wilson Airport (not Embakazi, out of which the commercial airlines fly) north of Nairobi. **Z. Boskovic Air Charters** (☎ *501210*) is one possibility; **Air Kenya Aviation** (☎ *501421*) is another. Whether or not they are flying, they are in as good a position as anyone to know who might be. If you can't get through, and even if you can, you should either have a car and driver available or be looking for one. The best bet is a group of two or three who hire a four-wheel drive vehicle and a driver. Self-drive rental cars are not easily available in Kampala, let alone out of town. Check "Getting Around" in the "Nairobi Dossier."

Getting Around

There is something to be said for the third-class train. There is a branch line to Gulu, and if it is running, it could be a reasonably safe way to get to Gulu and see the country. Driving to Gulu is discouraged; there have been numerous incidents. Hitching is even less advisable, but you may end up hitching if you decide to drive.

Where To Stay

The Dangerous North

I can only vouch for two towns, Gulu and Moroto, and one outpost, the National Resistance Army Camp on the Kidepo River frontier with the Sudan. Moroto is a lovely place in this sere wilderness. There are even some decaying colonial structures surrounded by green, and a huge green mountain rises due east of the town. But as far as I know, this has always been the sort of African town where you sleep on the floor of the police post.

Gulu, on the road to the Sudanese frontier town of Nimule to the north, and the rail line to Pakwach on the Albert Nile to the west, offers considerably more, but outside of town, this country is just as dangerous. There's the proper, if faded, Acholi Inn (a reminder that this is the country of the Acholi, many of whom were killed en masse by Amin), and a notch down, the Luxxor Lodge (a reminder, perhaps, that the Khedive, through his agents in the Sudan, once claimed all Uganda as Egyptian territory). These days it's unlikely that either of these hotels would require reservations, but even if they do, it's not a police-post town: both the Church of Uganda and the Red Cross Society are said to offer accommodation.

Meantime, if you've got business on the Sudanese frontier on which the National Resistance Army does not frown, and you come with a letter from Kampala, chances are you can bivouac with them along the wonderfully wild Kidepo River frontier. They may even tell you where you can hire a Karamajong driver, guide and cook.

The Rwandan Theater

Mbarara is a good base for business here. Somebody should really try The Super Tip Top Lodge Bar & Restaurant, if only for its name. Meantime, the town is equally characterized by a couple of the old Edwardian inns which the English used to run throughout Uganda; threadbare but hardly decrepit, both the Buhumuriro Guest House and the University Inn (university, anyone see a university?) are surrounded by the requisite gardens, and feature the requisite pub and dartboard. They should have vanished before Amin; walking into their bars these days, after all Uganda has been through, is like encountering a bewhiskered pub crawler placidly enjoying his pint of bitter in the burned out hulk of an oil rig fire.

Rwanda

Watutsi-1/French-0

Three Roads South from Uganda

Maps don't often show Merama Hill, but it's the border post on the main road from Uganda to Kigali. The land (scrub, candelabra trees), and what game you can see (fine impala), and the longhorn cattle, look much the same on both sides. But the minute you're in Rwanda, you know things are getting treacherous.

Traffic, for one, is running on the right, not the left, as it had in Uganda, and if it takes more profound dangers to unsettle you, there's the genocide which seems to have stopped at a million, but may merely have paused. In three months of 1994, the Hutu hard-liners killed as many people as the Khmer Rouge did in three years.

Rwandans like to remind visitors whose cars have the steering wheel on the wrong side what it was like when Sweden switched its traffic from the left to the right; an experience not unlike driving from Uganda into Rwanda. The Swedes' transport ministry put together a giant educational campaign, alerting drivers to the date and the dangers. Signs and police were everywhere, yet minds wandered. Six or seven were killed.

If those figures sound outrageous side-by-side, a million murdered Rwandans next to the six or seven Swedes killed in the big switch which now tries your nerves as you cross from Uganda to Rwanda, well, this is a pretty outrageous place. Just outside the window on the left you can see the tumbling Kagera River, aka, the Alexander Nile, rushing on to Lake Victoria, from whence its waters will spill into the Albert Nile, from whence they will find the Mediterranean. It tumbles fast, there are white caps; you can almost see the bodies of children in white togas rushing with the river down to Tanzania, to which their killers have fled in fear of retribution.

You can skip the Merama Hill crossing and drive west up the Virungas to a point just before Uganda's border with Zaire. From there you can take the road from the Ugandan mountain village and gorilla station of Kisoro to the Rwandan mountain village and gorilla station of Ruhengeri. Both towns can be charmers.

Just above Kisoro is where you'll find Traveler's Rest. Always a patchwork place and now especially patched (against the ravages of rot, not war), Traveler's Rest is the inn which a pioneer of gorilla research, George Schaller, called "Africa's unofficial gorilla headquarters." Often it was a base for the late Dian Fossey.

Across the border, Ruhengeri is charming as only a mountain town anchored by a grass air strip can be. Then again, you have to give some thought to what's up in the hills due northwest of town, hills which present themselves in misty blues and purples to travelers enjoying a cold lager at the air strip. It was into the bracken of those hills that a few peasants retreated a decade ago, mad as hell at Fossey for making it so tough to poach gorillas, even madder that they were being chased for having put an end to such a nag and nuisance.

None too pleasant, either, was the event which made Ruhengeri one of the first datelines inside Rwanda after the '94 war. It was through Ruhengeri that the largest exodus of Bahutu trekked on their way to death in the cholera-choked wallows of Zaire.

And if you stick around, you'll find that there's even more, and worse, hanging about this pleasant place, something the reporters who came here seem never to have noticed: ghosts. Not figments of some quack's imagination but real ghosts, as only Africa can produce them, ghosts so evident they're invisible perhaps only to western reporters, insensate as many are to anything which can't be discussed at a current events club.

Of course, one thing reporters never saw, and couldn't report nearly as much as the exodus, was the slaughter. Just from what we know about how many people died from what causes, it's now evident that for every Hutu child whose death from cholera was reported by western news outfits, at least a thousand Tutsi children died unreported deaths by hoe, club and panga. The World Council of Churches in Geneva says it's investigating credible reports that both Protestant and Catholic pastors turned over parishioners to be shot by the Guarde Nationale. The Council is even investigating a Kigali priest charged with shooting ten of his own parishioners with a pistol he longboasted of carrying.

But these are recent horrors, which doctors of medicine tell us the human mind has a healthy tendency to deny until it can deal with such magnitude, and which doctors of *juju* tell us have not yet ripened in the spirit world. What haunts Ruhengeri are fully developed ghosts, in particular a group of about 100 Tutsi mothers caught in the Christmas season pogroms of 1962-63. On a road just out of town, they found themselves trapped between two mobs of Bahutu. Beneath them flowed the Nywarungu River, alive with crocodiles. They threw their children in, then jumped in after them.

This was not an isolated incident. It echoed from the past, it echoed again in 1994, and even as those women jumped, it was echoing throughout Rwanda. Another 100 Tutsi women in the town of Shgira jumped into the river after their husbands were rounded up and they knew they'd never see them again. Children were skewered alive and left to die, buried alive, thrown into rivers, heads tied to knees. Tutsi men were left to bleed to death after having had their legs cut off at the knees, 'to bring them down to our size.' After 10,000 Watutsi were killed near Gikongoro, a thousand women and children there gathered and committed collective suicide.

There's a third way into Rwanda from Uganda. Half way between Merama Hill in the east and Kisoro in the west is the road from the Ugandan town of Kabale to Biumba, just over the border, and here the story turns from genocide to war. We've already seen how Paul Kagame, head of a force of 5000 mostly Tutsi insurgents, was watching a soccer video in a tent near Biumba when a runner brought news that a burst of shellfire had brought down the president's plane as it took off from Kigali airport, killing the president, the chief of staff of the armed forces, plus Burundi's president, and how this confronted him with a dilemma. He could concentrate his forces, as sound doctrine dictates for outnumbered forces. Or, he could split his men up in an attempt to stop the genocide which was now beginning in earnest. Hutu hard-liners blamed the Watutsi for the attack, and the Hutu Radio Des Milles Collines explicitly incited the population to slaughter Watutsi. But this was only one aspect of his bind.

For one, under the cease-fire which preceded the outburst, he was permitted to barrack 600 troops in Kigali; now they were stranded and under heavy attack. More fundamental was the strategic position of his main force in the north. As the press put it, his forces "controlled" this corner of Rwanda. It would be accurate to say that the heavily armed, French-trained, 25,000-man Rwandan Army, backed by Guarde Nationale troops everywhere, had him cornered here. When the news of the crash came, he was in a tent near Biumba, not in the town. Based in Biumba were seven battalions of the Rwandan Army, backed up with heavy weapons, armored personnel carriers, paratroops, and helicopter gunships. Kagame's troops with no such weaponry, were scattered out of harm's way, entirely afoot, carrying all their materiel on their backs. (If nothing else, being forced to carry everything on your back has a salutary impact on fire discipline, which was to become important after the United Nations imposed an arms embargo.) Now that was something of a blessing. He immediately sent orders for them to gather at pre-planned assembly points, but it would take them a little time, which gave him a little time to think what to do with them when they got there.

Reporters didn't write much about the war itself. It was not easily accessible, and at that point, the French-Canadian officers running the United Nations contingent in Rwanda had little to say about what little they knew. Off the record, there was speculation aplenty. All agree that whatever Kagame's numbers, he must and will take the offensive, and to be successful in any way, he must concentrate his limited forces for a focussed attack. But beyond that, they split into two camps.

Camp one keeps it simple: Find a weak spot, concentrate forces, attack it for a doable big victory in one battle, certainly no more than a few, then use the Hutu pogroms to call for a cease-fire that the United Nations might actually enforce, then negotiate.

Camp two says negotiations with the less-extreme government of the late president were barely working. Negotiations with the extremists who killed him just weren't really promising. Concentrate, yes, they said, but in a bold strike at Kigali.

Camp one said, impossible, since a major force was defending the capital. Assuming he could get around the major force cornering him in Biumba, Kagame's small, ill-equipped force would be ground up in a frontal assault on Kigali, even if it won. Meantime, on its rear would be the heavily armed Biumba force it had earlier bypassed. There would be virtually no Watutsi left to negotiate anything.

Kagame knew camp one was right. Both the force cornering him in the northwest and the force defending Kigali were too strong to attack frontally. And meantime, all over the country, Watutsi were being slaughtered, a powerful inducement to split up his forces rather than concentrate them to win a significant battle. For years, he had planned for this moment, but now that it was at hand, and his forces were assembling, he didn't know what to do.

Gupta's Tale: Gatwa, Gahutu and Gatusi

Reporters strive for economy, but digging into the making of this fight, and the danger which hangs over Central Africa, I fear that a quick telling of the Watutsi's swift victory over the Bahutu can make what must have been a monumentally difficult and dangerous undertaking seem downright easy. My mind keeps being drawn back to the miseries of guerrillas under heavy packs afoot in the bush, remembrances I must resist because that was in other African countries (and besides, those wenches of war are dead), and we do know that Kagame's strategy pivoted on mobility. Without vehicles, that meant moving at night—fast. If you caught a glimpse of them, it would be in those same hours that Africa's great predators are about, amid the fog and smoke of dusk and dawn, phantoms, maybe it's them, maybe it isn't, and I well remember our friend Gupta as we sat in this gray light sipping piping hot tea from chipped enamelware cups on the Tanzania side of the Kagera. Peering into the mists, he would wonder not just about the identity of shifting shadows they shrouded, but at the nature of the shroud itself: fog, mist, smoke from a cooking fire, from a land-clearing fire, from a dry-season fire set by lightening, from fire set by poachers to flush game.

This was Karagwe country; a long day, a decent meal, a plastic Listerine bottle full of *waraki*, and the spell of the old empires hereabouts. Karagwe, Ankole, Tutsi, had Gupta conjuring punch-drunkenly, straining to glimpse Lord knows what through the mists as he told us that an ancient iron-age city had recently been excavated on the flanks of the Ngorongoro crater on the Serengeti Plain, a highly developed place whose people and whose collapse remains a mystery. He said they had buildings made of brick, which required firing in kilns, which in turn required charcoal. "That mist over there," he said, gesturing toward a cloud which looked like fog to me, "I'm reckoning it's a charcoal mound. What they're doing, you see, is they're digging a pit, lining the bottom with damp leaves and hot coals, filling it with timber, then covering it with dirt and you're walking about and you're seeing this mound of earth with smoke rising from it, as if the earth itself were smouldering. Well, soon enough they're coming along and uncovering it all, and there you have your charcoal." He told us it was also done that way in an ancient empire on the Indian subcontinent called Mohenjo-Davo, and apropos of nothing charcoal, he told us one of the primal legends of the Watutsi. "As Rwanda's first king lay dying, he summoned his sons, Gatwa, Gahutu and Gatusi. Here's a jug of milk for each of you, he told them. Guard it all night. But Gatwa drank all his, and Gahutu fell asleep, spilling half his jug as he rolled over. Only Gatusi sat up the night, presenting his father with the full jug, and thus Watusi came to rule the land, Bahutu became serfs, and Batwa were driven from mankind to live in the forests."

The Watutsi Strike

To this day, there are a few of the pygmoid Batwa living amidst the smokes and mist of the forests around Lake Kivu west of Biumba, but mostly the country to the west is heavily cultivated and thick with Bahutu. In fact, in early '94 it was a stronghold of hard-line Bahutu, and with Kagame unlikely to strike in this inhospitable direction, the strong blocking force of the Hutu based in Biumba was positioned to keep him from slipping to the east in an attempt to bypass the blocking force and strike at Kigali, due south.

Not long after the president's plane crashed, the Presidential Guard assassinated Prime Minister Agathe Uwilingiyimana (cv), Kagame struck, and every observer who knew about the assassination (no news reports) was nonplussed. First surprise: he struck west into that inhospitable country thick with Bahutu, which struck some terror even though he had no designs here at all. The strike to the west finessed the Hutu force deployed mostly to block an attempt to bypass them on the east. Having passed them on the west, he moved south toward Kigali. That surprise, however, seemed almost natural in retrospect. The second surprise didn't. Having bypassed the blocking force in Biumba, Kagame split his forces in two, sending one in a wide sweeping arc to the savannas of the east, and sending barely half his men, now doubly vulnerable, to strike at Kigali.

How an Antique Ceremony Brought on a Modern War

Belgian tourists loved Rwanda, but it made others uncomfortable. Alan Moorehead, whose books, *The White Nile* and *The Blue Nile*, were landmark accounts of exploration, limned the scene in *No Room in the Ark*, a travel book about East and Central Africa which is sadly out of print...where the Belgians have encouraged [Africans] to cling to their ancient habits a weird kind of surrealism sets in. You notice this particularly among the Watutsi tribe at Lake Kivu. The Watutsi are celebrated hunters, very tall and lithe and energetic, and for a sum...they can be induced to perform their war dance. A party of about twenty of us went out to see them one day, and it was an odd experience. The performance was given in the open among a grove of young trees that looked absurdly like the Bois de Boulogne in Paris in the spring. We sat on wooden benches with our cameras in hand. Presently the warriors arrived in their war paint with a drummer at their head, and for the next half-hour they waved their assagais and in formation, thumped their hard feet on the ground.

It was wonderful timing, and the rhythmic movement of their feathered headdresses was a remarkable thing to see; yet it was not real. It had neither the vicarious reality of the theater, nor any reality in life. There had been no war to justify this war dance, nothing to inspire them except their professional skill and perhaps the thought of the L25...

Traditional warriors mocked by the tame reality of the present, tourists clicking cameras; Moorehead wouldn't be the last to lament a scene like that. But then Africa has a bedeviling way of playing games with surface and substance, substance and surface. The gross national products of most African nations have been falling for years now. Highways return to the bush. From today's perspective in the hell which surrounds Lake Kivu, those 1956 tourists look at least as quaint as the spear-wielding Watutsi, in some ways more so.

Witness this scene three years after Moorehead pictured those Watutsi as emblems of a relict past.

July 1959; Belgium is preparing Rwanda for independence. In the past, Brussels would let the Watutsi rule unless it seriously disliked what was going on, in which case it deposed the king, and chose an agreeable *mwami*. But now democracy is in the air. The Watutsi fear the Belgians will leave Rwanda to the Hutu majority. On July 24, the king, 46-year-old Mwami Mutare, suddenly dies, and his European doctors won't say why. In fact, it was an overdose of penicillin administered in a last-ditch attempt at saving his excellency from intractable venereal disease. But the Watutsi blame the Belgians and the Catholic Church.

At the funeral, Rwanda's Belgian rulers, in suits and ties, find themselves ringed by Watutsi warriors in traditional garb. At spear-point, the warriors force the Belgians to name Jean-Baptiste Ndahindurwa, Mwami Kigeri V.

Lest their spears be taken as mere symbolism, the Watutsi begin assassinating one Hutu leader after another, one week after another. The long subservient Bahutu rise up. Before 1959 is over, 10,000 Watutsi die, 120,000 flee, and Rwanda's Watutsi are powerless victims of mass murder until 1994.

The Importance of Focus

Afoot, Kagame's Kigali-bound force cut through 40 miles of enemy-held turf in four April days. As they approached the city, U.N. staffers in town were reporting widespread slaughter of noncombatant Watutsi by the Army and the Guarde Nationale, both of which often fired large volumes of ammunition wildly. But Kagame didn't attack. The city was defended all around by heavily armed Hutu forces with ambushes prepared along street after street.

Instead, Kagame focused on three more modest objectives. First, he organized an advance to link up with his force of 600 men in Kigali as they tried to break out of their compound which was under heavy attack. The Bahutu were intent on those 600, and many showed exceptional courage attacking the compound. But the Watutsi inside were at least as intent; they broke out, joined up with Kagame's Kigali force, and Hutu morale was hit hard.

Then, as the Hutu generals redeployed to defend a city Kagame had no intention of taking at that point, the Tutsi leader wheeled his strengthened Kigali force on his second objective, the airport. By mid-April, his mortar fire had shut it down, and hard fighting for limited targets filled the next month, with no sign of a concerted attack on the city whose streets were seeing the slaughter of more and more Watutsi civilians. Then, on one day, May 22, these tactics paid off. Both the airport, and Kagame's third limited objective, the Rwandan Army's Kanombe barracks, fell to the Watutsi.

Reporters and the Hutu population are stunned. But military observers knew Kagame had still not won a major pitched battle with a heavily armed Hutu force. His enemy in Kigali is still more numerous and better armed, and his force is split, with half of it off somewhere to the east. But those are just military observations. Everyone else expects Kagame to join a battle for Kigali, and as days pass without an attack, reporters wonder in print why he is taking so long, as Watutsi in Kigali are butchered. Kagame answers, "we have to do this methodically; we can't rush in."

Bait and Switch

What reporters don't know—but the Hutu military does—is that even as Kagame is explaining why he is proceeding so slowly, his Kigali force is wheeling rapidly away from Kigali and toward a new target: the heartland of the hard-line Bahutu in the hills to the west. Their core constituency threatened, the Hutu generals move reinforcements to defend this heartland.

What they don't know is that Kagame has no intention of seeing his troops chewed up in this Hutu heartland, where the largely untouched Biumba force is still based. Instead, he turns again, all the way around to the east, again ignoring Kigali, even though some of its defenders have been drawn off for the defense of the western heartland. He leaves just enough forces to keep the Hutu generals pinned down and wondering, and links up with the eastern spearhead he had launched at the beginning of April. Now at last his forces are rejoined, concentrated, as they sweep around Kigali from the north to the south and then to the west, nearly enveloping the capital, but carefully leaving the government one avenue of escape, and an attractive one at that: west to the Hutu heartland.

Panicked, the Hutu leadership takes the bait and quits its capital for the town of Gisenyi. At the time, it sounded much more like a retreat to the bush, with a government representing the vast majority fighting with its people from the countryside. But Gisenyi is a resort on Lake Kivu, not far from the resort where Alan Moorhead watched his Watutsi folklorique, a lighthearted place where steep lawns sweep in extravagant expanse around equally extravagant villas. A place with expensive hotels, a 'Palm Beach' and a Meridien. It's a place spread out along a plage dotted with bright Martini sun umbrellas, with lots of action at nightspots sporting names like the 'Club Loisirs,' the 'Club Time Off,' where doubtless many a Hutu officer wished he could call time out. Nonetheless, it was surrounded by heavily Hutu country, and now the Hutu armed forces, still unhurt by any major defeat in battle, were deployed to defend a much more compact area, backed by a friendly border with Zaire—when Kagame's force first invaded in 1990, Zairois troops had joined the French and Belgians to fight the Watutsi. In an arc from Biumba to Ruhengeri to Gisenyi, strong points were set-up. On high ground dominating all three key towns, paratroops, regular army troops and militiamen from the Guarde Nationale manned armored personnel carriers, heavy artillery, and an array of other weapons Kagame didn't have.

A Face-Off With the Bahutu

Thanks to a U.N. weapons boycott, the Hutu forces were running low on ammunition, lower than the Watutsi who had greater fire discipline (in fact, greater discipline in almost every category). But the Bahutu still had heavy weapons, armor and aircraft, none of which Kagame had, and its forces still had not lost a major pitched battle. The way the elusive Watutsi had fought, there had been no major pitched battles. But now, at last, that day was at hand, and the Hutu hard-liners had the weapons.

Come the end of the day, who would be the victor? That was the question as Kagame's force headed from southeast to northwest. But it was never really answered. The rulers of Hutu Rwanda's rump government in carefree Gisenyi took one look at the Watutsi headed their way, and they were out of there.

The Scoop

How French Skill May be the Real Measure of Kagame

What moment in this war tells most about the danger Kagame now poses to those who fate (or the Quai d'Orsay) pits against him in the months and years ahead? It may be that neither the battle for the airport, nor the assault on the Kanombe barracks, nor the drive on Gisenyi, but a minor skirmish in which neither side lost a man and the adversary was not even the Bahutu but French naval commandos. It may be that Kagame's real enemy—as belligerent Watutsi charged so unconvincingly—was France. It must be remembered that just three and a half years earlier, Paul Kagame's close friend and comrade-in-arms, Fred Rwigyema, was killed in combat when the French put together a four- nation force (France, Belgium, Rwanda, Zaire) to throw the refugee army out of Rwanda. For two years Kagame had been stymied by what amounted to a talk and stall strategy refined and perfected at the Quai d'Orsay for France's Hutu clients.

As France publicly deliberated putting together a force to rescue civilian Watutsi from slaughter, belligerent members of Kagame's front charged that France was actually planning to join the war on behalf of the Bahutu. True, the Bahutu were still French clients, and true, the French had fought against the Watutsi. But it was clear this time that with the slaughter of the Watutsi so horrible, no French government could survive actually going to war for the Bahutu against the Watutsi. This was surely clear to Kagame, as well. But that was just his dilemma. With the French public aware that the government would not possibly fly in to fight the Watutsi, the government could comfortably fly in to rescue civilian Watutsi, and in so doing, secure strategic ground for their Hutu clients. In short, unless Kagame played this dangerous game just right, the French could again defeat the Watutsi, this time without firing a shot.

Specifically, the French could fly in to the uncaptured south of Rwanda in order to stop the slaughter there, and not incidentally, to keep the south out of Kagame's hands. And that's pretty much how it developed. With the world calling for an end to the butchery, French President Francois Mitterand announced "Operation Turquoise," a short-term rescue mission to demilitarize the south and southwest. On July 3, as the world heard of Kagame's troops moving into a largely deserted Kigali, France choppered paratroops and naval commandos to a lower profile, political prize—Rwanda's second largest city, Butare, far to the south on the Burundi border, a city bursting with Bahutu who had chosen French protection in the south to protection by their own army in the north. France would not battle Kagame for turf. Having proclaimed neutrality, they couldn't. But they would occupy turf like Butare in the far south that he had not yet reached. What they didn't realize as they flew in was how fast Kagame's foot soldiers were moving, and now there were nearly 25,000 of them.

What the French found as they landed in far-southern Butare July 4 was Kagame's army just 500 yards from the city line. They pulled out, and Bahutu driving everything from Peugeots to backhoes followed them. Their license plates were from all over Rwanda, not just the CB plates of Butare, but ABs from Kigali, and even IBs and HBs from Ruhengeri and Biumba. At one point, there was even that skirmish between the naval commandos and the Watutsi; minor, but with widespread charges that their motives were more than just humanitarian. The last thing the French needed was combat with the Watutsi, who were now proclaiming they were quite prepared for it (though of course they were not).

The French had to make a deal, and after the hot words of his cohorts, Kagame proposed one which was very tough for them to refuse. Essentially it was a deal which would make certain that the French "rescue mission" was indeed just that, terms confining the French to a small refuge they would briefly protect on Zaire's border.

On paper—and in the papers—this looked like no big deal, basically it was just getting the French to affirm their benign intent. But a big deal it was. France's deputy commander in Rwanda, Col. Jacques Rosier, frankly acknowledged that the agreement amounted to a retreat. "This is not what we thought two days ago," he said as he pulled his force back, virtually *hors de combat*, to positions along the edge of the Nyungwa Forest (a primeval place where the forest elephant, with its small, hard tusks, has long dwelled, and where six of them may yet dwell). I remember hearing a few miles from here in the mid-seventies of a young American naturalist, Lee Lyon, who had just been killed by an elephant in this forest while she was photographing a capture program.

As the Bahutu in Gisenyi watched the French pullback, they knew the French wouldn't be choppering here and there as a "humanitarian" blocking force between them and the Watutsi. Meantime, Kagame could ignore the far southwest, temporarily secured for him by his French friends, and drive his entire, concentrated, strengthened force to a foregone conclusion in Gisenyi.

A Nairobi Dossier for Travelers to Central Africa

So much is so easily available in Nairobi, and so little is available in Central Africa's dangerous places, that there is really no substitute for operating out of Nairobi before, after and during any travel to any dangerous place in East or Central Africa. Mombasa is often overlooked as a good provisioner of services, but from a strictly practical point of view, Nairobi is indispensible.

U.S. Embassy in Burundi
  Ave des Etats-Unis, BP 1720
  Bujumbura
  ☎ *(2) 3454,*
  FAX (2) 22926

Burundian Embassy in Canada
  151 Slater Street, Suite 800

Ottawa, ON K1P 5H3,
☎ (613) 236-8483
Telex: 053-3393
FAX (613) 563-1827

Burundian Embassy in United States

2233 Wisconsin Avenue, NW, Suite 212,
Washington, DC 20007
☎ (202) 342-2574

Burundi 2
April 7, 1994

Warning: The Department of State warns U.S. citizens to defer all travel to Burundi at this time. The U.S. Department of State has ordered the temporary departure of all U.S. government dependents and nonessential employees from Burundi because of security concerns following the deaths of the presidents of Burundi and Rwanda in Kigali, Rwanda, on April 6, 1994. U.S. citizens in Burundi are advised to depart immediately.

The Scoop

Burundi is a small, inland African nation passing through a period of instability following a coup attempt in October 1993. Facilities for tourism, particularly in the interior, are limited.

Getting In

A passport and a visa are required. Only those travelers resident in countries where there is no Burundian embassy are eligible for entry stamps, without a visa, at the airport upon arrival.

These entry stamps are not a substitute for a visa which must subsequently be obtained from the immigration service within 24 hours of arrival. Visas cost from $30 (U.S.) to $60 (U.S.), depending on anticipated length of stay. Travelers who have failed to obtain a visa will not be permitted to leave the country. Multiple entry visas valid for three months are available in Burundian embassies abroad for $11 (U.S.). Evidence of yellow fever immunization must be presented. Also, visitors are required to show proof of vaccination against meningococcal meningitis.

Additional information may be obtained from:

Embassy of the Republic of Burundi

Suite 212, 2233 Wisconsin Avenue, N.W.,
Washington, D.C. 20007,
☎ (202) 342-2574; or the

Permanent Mission of Burundi to the United Nations in New York,
☎ (212) 687-1180.

Dangerous Places

In light of the October 1993 coup attempt, all areas of the country should be considered potentially unstable. Sporadic violence remains a problem, in Bujumbura as well as in the interior where large numbers of displaced persons are encamped or in hiding. Renewed warfare in neighboring Rwanda has caused several thousand Rwandans to flee to Burundi and other countries in the region. The U.S. Embassy has reiterated the importance of using extreme caution, with no travel to the troubled neighborhoods of the capital and none but essential travel in the city after dark. Burundi periodically has closed its land borders without notice and suspended air travel and telephone service, in response to political disturbances.

Getting Sick

Medical facilities are limited in Burundi. Doctors and hospitals often expect immediate cash payment for health care services. U.S. medical insurance is not always valid outside the United States.

Supplemental medical insurance with specific overseas coverage, including medical evacuation coverage, has proved to be useful. The Centers for Disease Control recommend that travelers to Burundi receive the meningococcal polysaccharide vaccine before traveling to the area.

Crime

Street crime in Burundi poses a high risk for visitors. Crime involves muggings, purse-snatching, pickpocketing, burglary, and auto break-ins. Criminals operate individually or in small groups. There have been reports of muggings of persons jogging or walking alone in all sections of Bujumbura, and especially on public roads bordering Lake Tanganyike.

In-Country Travel

Burundi has a good network of roads between the major towns and border posts. Travel on other roads is difficult, particularly in the rainy season. Public transportation to border points is often difficult and frequently unavailable.

Embassy Location:

The U.S. Embassy
Avenue des Etats-Unis
B.P. 34, 1720
Bujumbura, Burundi
☎ *(257) 223-454.*

Women's lib the hard way— or why the Afro is back

When the Eritrean Peoples Liberation Front (EPLF) won its hard fought 30-year battle for independence in 1992, Mangiest Hailed Marram ran Ethiopia as a dictatorship with help from the Soviets. Hatred of him and his policies forged an alliance between Christian and Muslim, poor and wealthy and between men and women. The EPLF made use of women fighters and lifted them out of the Stone Age burden of dowry, circumcision and corn row hairdos. When the women fighters marched into the capital of Asmara on May 24, 1991, the teenage girls began to imitate the Afros and men's trousers worn by the female freedom fighters.

Rwanda
★ ★

Radio Panic

The heat has been building since 1990. Rwandans now must carry identity cards to reveal their tribal affiliation. The government of President Habyarimana has expanded the army to 30,000, has bought weapons from France, Egypt and South Africa, and trained Hutu extremist militia to massacre Tutsis.

The black cloak of fear hung over the country while Radio Mille Collines broadcast anti-Tutsi messages calling for total extermination of the Tutsi tribe, even broadcasting names of specific people to be targeted once the killing started.

On April 6, 1994, a plane carrying Rwanda President Juvenal Habyarimana was shot down just before landing and each side blamed the other. The largest slaughter since WWII began. Drug-crazed rebel soldiers looted, murdered and raped without any resistance. When it was all over there were 500,000 dead (almost all Tutsis killed by Hutus), one million refugees, 114,000 orphaned children and a hollow empty little country remained.

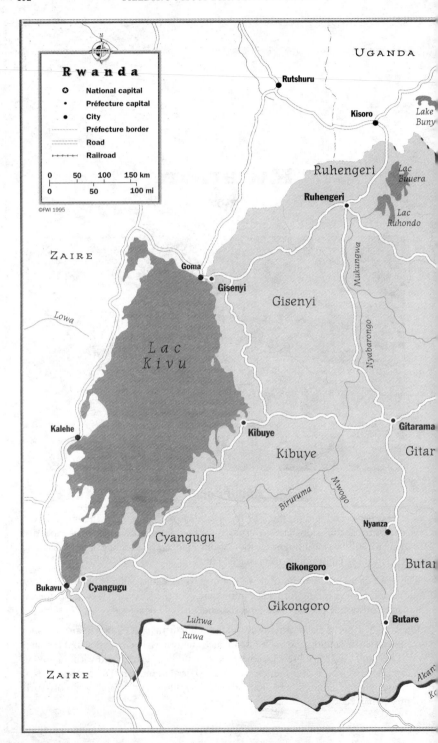

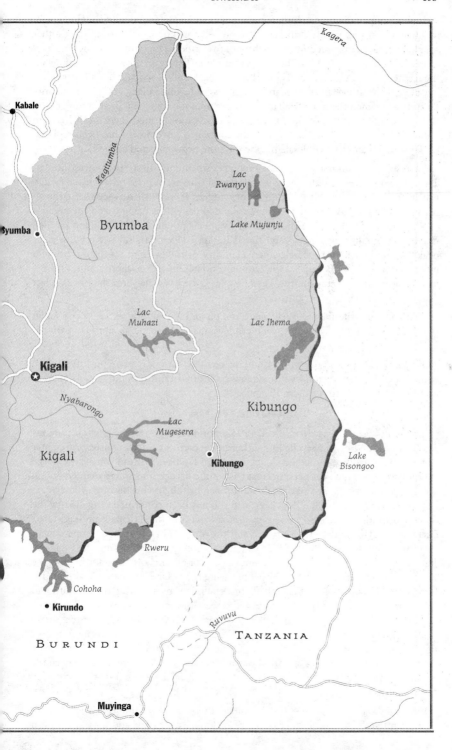

How can one of the tiniest, lushest countries in Africa become one of the largest killing grounds in the world? Tribalism. Rwanda, like neighboring Burundi, is a rather simple (for most African countries) hybrid of two tribes: The Hutus and the Tutsis. A four-year uprising made minor headlines every time Tutsi guerrillas would infringe on the territory of Rwanda's famous silverback gorilla families. When full-scale war broke out after the death of Burundi's and Rwanda's leaders in a plane crash, the majority Hutu tribe blamed the minority Tutsis and began indiscriminately slaughtering them. But the surprise success of the ragtag Tutsi rebels transformed them from freedom fighters into outright butchers. The Hutu-controlled government has been replaced by Tutsi rebels and the wholesale massacre is now being directed at the Hutus.

The result has been massive waves of refugees streaming toward the nearest border. The number of dead and displaced is countless. Estimates at press time put the fatality toll at nearly a million and the number of refugees at more than twice that figure—perhaps three times—with hundreds being added daily. It is being called the greatest exodus in modern history. Almost half of Rwanda's population of 8 million has fled since the beginning of renewed hostilities in April 1993; 10,000 per minute at its peak. What is in store for the beleaguered country? If you listen to official government intentions, there is no talk about the economy, no talk about social programs, only the intention to totally annihilate the Tutsi people—a barbaric platform that would elect governments in few other countries.

What's fanning the flames? Well, there is a pirate radio station called, "The Radio that Speaks the Truth," based in southern Rwanda that broadcasts anti-Tutsi propaganda.

Of course, there's also overpopulation, deep ethnic hatred, massive poverty, disease and hunger that can only get worse, thanks to Brother Hutus, as the displacement of millions continues into northern Rwanda.

Guns 'R Us

The Indian Ocean Newsletter, July 2, 1994 reported that part of the arms and ammunition confiscated by the Seychellois authorities aboard the Greek-registered freighter *Malo* last year had been sold and shipped by air to Goma, a Zairean town close to the Rwanda frontier which has been the rear base of the French humanitarian intervention force since last week. News of the sale was broken by the Seychellois opposition weekly *Regar* on June 17 but ten days later, had still not been confirmed or denied by the Seychellois authorities. *The Indian Ocean Newsletter* confirmed that a Zaire-registered aircraft made two flights to Goma to airlift the arms and ammunition (in particular, more than 500 boxes of antitank and fragmentation grenades) during the nights of June 16-17 and 18-19. The unusual movement of Seychellois army lorries and the Zaire aircraft was seen and noted by people living near Mahe international airport. Information available included aircraft flight details (given as AZR 3024 outward and AZR 4032 inward), and the flight plan indicated Goma as the destination. This town in Zaire is barely more than a stone's throw from Gisenyi in Rwanda, the temporary seat of the Rwandan interim government set up by Hutu extremists to fight against the Rwanda Patriotic Front after head of state Juvenal Habyarimana died in a plane crash in April. The real customer for the arms shipments could therefore have been the Rwandan interim government, in flagrant defiance of the United Nations Security Council arms embargo.

According to the information ION obtained, the arms transaction is believed to have been negotiated by several intermediaries including a Zairean and a South African businessman. In connection with the affair, three persons arrived in Mahe on June 4 on an Air Seychelles flight from South Africa: Themeste Bagasora (a Rwandan national), Willem Ehlers (a South African) and Hunda Nzambo (a Zairean citizen). Ehlers and Nzambo returned to South Africa on June 11, still flying Air Seychelles, but Bagasora stayed on in Victoria where he was joined by another Rwandan, Jean Bosco Ruhorahoza. The intermediaries had meetings with several Seychellois officials including the transport and tourism ministry's principal permanent secretary, Maurice Lousteau-Lalanne, and head of state France Albert Rene's counsellor for public relations, Gilbert Pool. It was learned that the civil aviation authorities in charge of Mahe international airport had been very reluctant to allow the loading of arms and ammunition on civil airport premises. President Rene is understood to have intervened personally to remove this hurdle.

The Seychelles government was extremely embarrassed by the untoward revelations since a number of flights to Goma had been planned to ship further arms and ammunitions, and it is hard to see how these could have been effected discreetly enough. It could have been in connection with this arms deal that the chief of staff of the Seychelles Defence Forces, colonel Leopold Payet, flew to France, thus feeding speculation that was rife on the role that certain French circles may have played in facilitating the arms sales.

About the middle of May, the Rwandan interim government's foreign minister, Jerome Bicamunpaka, sent the French government an impressive order for military hardware which included thousands of rounds of mortar bombs of various calibres, 10,000 hand grenades, 200 rockets, two million rounds of rifle ammunition, mortars, transmission equipment, and also 20,000 military uniforms for its soldiers.

At the time, the reply to the Rwandan order was a diplomatic negative and the Rwandans went to other suppliers. It must be said that the arms confiscated by the Seychelles authorities on the Greek freighter would certainly correspond with Rwanda's order.

When the *Malo* was intercepted by the Seychelles navy in March 1993, it was carrying 10,542 boxes of ammunition and 389 boxes of various arms consigned to Somalia. Apart from the rifles, pistols and light machine guns and more than 7,000 boxes of ammunition, the cargo comprised 2,500 boxes of mortar bombs (of calibre 60 mm, 82 mm, and 106 mm), 300 boxes of ammunition for rocket launchers, 150 boxes of antitank grenades, and 383 boxes of fragmentation grenades. The master, first officer and chief engineer of the *Malo* were charged with "illegally importing military arms and ammunition into the Seychelles" and the cargo was impounded and placed under seal in a Seychelles Defence Forces building for the duration of the officers' trial. At the end of the six-month trial, however, only the master of the Greek freighter was found guilty and was sentenced to one year. The Seychelles authorities were then able to recuperate both the ship and the precious cargo (estimated to be worth about US$40 million).

The master appealed the sentence but died in prison in March 1994 after a short illness, just before the case came before the appeal court. The ship's owners took over the appeal in a bid to recover the vessel but lost, although the appeal court judge did not publish his judgement. After the Seychelles government announced its intention of selling the arms cargo, several international organizations including the International Committee of the Red Cross called on the island's authorities to act with the highest sense of responsibility.

Reacting tardily to reports of the Seychellois government's sale of part of the arms cargo seized on the Greek freighter Malo (ION No. 629 and 630), defence minister James Michel said on July 5 that the transaction was carried out to the advantage of Zaire. As proof, he revealed that the Kinshasa government had produced an end-user certificate, without naming the minister who had signed it. He claimed Zaire was also interested in a third delivery of arms and ammunition.

Meanwhile, the *Sunday Tribune* of Durban (South Africa) has identified the South African national who was named by *The Indian Ocean Newsletter*; he is named as captain Willem (Ters) Ehlers, a naval officer who had been private secretary to former South African head of state P. W. Botha. Captain Ehlers later worked with an ex-member of South African secret services named as Craig Williamson when the latter was employed in South Africa by the GMR group of Italian businessman Mario Ricci. Ricci was for a long time in contact with the Seychelles' head of state France Albert Rene and still has interests in The Seychelles. According to GMR, Ehlers and Williamson are no longer working for that company.

The second go-between in the arms sale appears in all probability to be a Rwanda army colonel named as Theoneste Bagossora, the chef de cabinet of the Rwandan defence minister and notorious as the most heavily implicated officer in the anti-Tutsi genocide carried out since the death of former head of state Juvenal Habyarimana on April 6. Bagossora is believed to be the principal person ordering arms purchases for the Rwandan army and was already compromised in an aborted transaction organized from Belgium. The name of the Zairean businessman who went to The Seychelles for this arms transaction is very similar to the

Zairean head of state Mobutu Sese Seko's special counsellor, ex-defence minister Ngbanda Nzambo, better known under the touching nickname of "Terminator" and who is persona non grata in Belgium.

I.O.N.- The Seychelles' government's theory that the arms and ammunition it sold were not intended for the Rwandan government army which was fighting the Rwandan Patriotic Front does not really hold water. First, because the arms consignments were off-loaded at Goma, a Zairean town very close to the Rwandan frontier through which pass all arms shipments for the army and the Rwandan interim government located only 4 km away, in the Rwandan border town of Gisenyi. Secondly, because end-user certificates for arms shipment are traded like other commodities and are very frequently cover-ups to conceal the real destination of the shipments. For example, on May 27, the second secretary of the Rwandan embassy in Cairo announced that 35 tons of arms worth some 765,000 US dollars had been delivered to the Rwandan army and mentioned end-user certificates prepared in Kinshasa for a transaction concluded in Paris. Finally, Seychellois go-betweens of the arms sales were themselves very explicit on the shipments' final destination.

The Scoop

In 1959, a faction intent on maintaining Tutsi privilege in Rwanda assassinated several Hutu leaders. Hutu rage slaughtered 100,000 Rwandan Watutsi, and the carnage was on—a 22-year program which, in 1994 alone, would wipe out half of the two million Watutsi in Rwanda.

When the Belgians pulled out of the two countries in 1962, Bahutu ruled Rwanda. In Burundi, Watutsi were hanging on to power and still were, a decade later, when Hutu frustration exploded in Burundi's landmark revolt of 1972. A thousand Watutsi died in the outburst. Having witnessed the 1962 killing of 100,000 Watutsi in Rwanda, this 1972 rampage by Burundi's Bahutu was all Burundi's ruling Watutsi needed. They killed 100,000 Bahutu and chased out another 200,000. Then the pickings got a little less abundant for the vultures. As the rest of the world saw it, an equilibrium, of sorts, had been struck. In Burundi, where the mass murderers were Watutsi, the Watutsi ruled. In Rwanda, where the mass murderers were Bahutu, Bahutu ruled. But the equation was inherently volatile. For one thing, the Bahutu remained the overwhelming majority in both countries. For another, if the Watutsi were to rule anywhere, it made more sense in Rwanda since historically, Rwanda's Watutsi were a stronger group than Burundi's. In a way, this was the reason they had become the victims of genocide, the failed preemptive strike by one of their clans.

But this hardly justified the genocide, and it hardly made the quarter-million Rwandan Watutsi in exile any less talented or disciplined a people. Amidst the horror of Idi Amin's Uganda, they hung on. When Uganda's agony was finally brought to an end, it was the work of an obscure, disciplined guerrilla army made up in good part of adolescent orphans of the horror, very much a latter-day children's crusade, with a "security chief" still in his twenties. His name was Paul Kagame, a Rwandan Tutsi.

Inevitably, Paul Kagame went home with about 8000 of his friends. In front of them was a Hutu army 30,000-strong, but like Idi Amin's army, it was corrupt. Unfortunately, what French and Belgian papers saw as all this unfolded in the fall of 1990 was not resistance against an army which had committed genocide. What it saw was an evil bouillabaisse boiling over; a stew in the creation of which France and Belgium had been no mere sous-chefs. It saw the minority Tutsi overlords, already in power in Burundi, about to regain power in Rwanda. They were beginning to feel guilty. Some, also saw opportunity. The tide, through Africa, has been with the majority. In any case it's always easier to find room in a European budget for financing neocolonial clients who are "democratic" (read: a majority). France, Belgium and Zaire rushed in to stop Kagame's army.

More later of Mr. Kagame, the troubles which were to come and the further trouble yet brewing in Central Africa. Suffice it to say for this overview that once again, the victors were the vultures.

Nowadays, air safaris are becoming especially popular. The planes can soar above the tangled geography, the volcanic Virungas, the snow-dashed Mountains of the Moon whose lakes and foaming white waters are the source of both of Africa's two great rivers: the Zaire and the Nile. Beneath them is all the wonder which spreads beneath the soaring buzzard, but the grim acuity of her gimlet eye must see so much more.

The Players

Paul Kagame and the Rwandan Patriotic Front (RPF)

The man is a Rwandan Tutsi, born in Rwanda, and residing there today, not yet 40. He is the most powerful man in the Tutsi homelands of Rwanda and Burundi and probably the most powerful man that either of those two precarious states have known since they both became independent in 1962. But most of his life he lived in Uganda, during that country's most wretched years—and there's the twist. The very wretchedness of that period helped bring the Watutsi and their son Kagame back to Rwanda.

The Uganda in which Kagame matured was a nether world, a place of attenuated pain, both psychological and physical. This the Watutsi shared with their Ugandan hosts and helped them bear, first the nightmare of Amin, then two more nightmares, as bad or worse, of which we'll learn more later. With little more outside help than refugee Watutsi could provide, the people of Uganda finally ended those nightmare years, and when they did, the Watutsi were not without influence.

First among these influentials was young Paul Kagame, Rwandan refugee, intelligence chief for all of Uganda...and a key organizer of the RPF. The Tutsi front was formed by the guerrilla years its leadership had spent with Museveni's National Resistance Army, which drew its strength from popular support. This meant, above all, discipline. Rape was punishable by death, and a summary execution for just such an offense was meted out to a Tutsi fighter in the midst of 1994's 14-week war for Rwanda. The front demanded no privileges for the Watutsi, though there was little rhetorical nonsense, either: It was clear that majority rule would be balanced by minority rights. And there was clearly a danger that with meager resources, it could not control the climate of terror.

As a member of Uganda's military, Kagame was able to apply for a course in tactics given by the U.S. Army Command and General Staff College at Fort Leavenworth, Kansas. In fact (and reflecting in part Tutsi chutzpah), Kagame was in Kansas in October, 1990, the very month he and a close comrade-in-arms, Fred Rwigyema, had planned to invade Rwanda. The invasion went ahead anyway, and it went well, until France put together a combined force of French troops, Zairois troops, Belgian troops and French-trained Hutu paras. The Watutsi were thrown back, Kagame's old friend Fred Rwigyema was killed in combat, and like many a college student with trouble at home, Kagame had to drop out.

In 1991, his movement launched its last, frustrated invasion. Again, it went well, but with the prospect of intervention again hanging on the horizon, he stopped short in the north and agreed to talks. These were to drag on for two years in the Tanzanian town of Arusha at the foot of Mt. Kilimanjaro. At last, late in 1993, Rwanda's hard-line president agreed in priniciple to terms which called for a moderate Hutu to be installed as President and another as Prime Minister. The hard-line president signed a formal cease-fire, Rwanda's even harder line military was enraged, and a large question began to loom as to whether Rwanda's government would or could fulfill the terms to which it had agreed. As he watched from his camps along the Biumba road, this was the chessboard upon which Kagame had to focus all his strategic faculties: French armor in Hutu hands; French heavy weapons; a Hutu military for which France and Belgium had successfully bought time for a huge build up—Hutu airborne troops and 30,000 regulars, all trained by the French. Against this he had no armor and no heavy weapons, just mortars and rocket-propelled grenades which Uganda had to pretend it didn't supply. As for training, it's basically the homegrown discipline of Museveni's children's crusade, plus Kagame's course, which was in tactics, not strategy, as American reporters were wont to boast.

Mwalimu Julius Nyerere

A great teacher of lessons, not all of which should be taught. Tanzania's soft-spoken leader, now retired, is influential still: For Africans, he remains Mwalimu, the teacher. In fact, without portfolio, he is more influential than most African heads of state. His suasion has declined distinctly, but this has little to do with his retirement. What he retired from, the presidency of backward, resource-poor Tanzania, was never the prime source of his influence. The decline is due almost entirely to the failure of his most ambitious ideas.

They are powerfully attractive ideas, even after their failure, and he is an attractive figure: the very image of intelligence, unblemished by greed, stirred by the responsibilities of leadership, an intellectual who did not merely adopt ideas, but tried to craft them to fit Africa. Alas, for all the shrewd pragmatism that implies, he is not a practical man. He is known, will long be known, for a magnificent idea which has failed magnificently. Nyerere tried to craft, from the Swahili word for family, *ujamaa*, something between a voluntary Israeli kibbutz and a compulsory Chinese commune.

It rarely worked. It cost millions. Whole villages were uprooted. Labor was forced. It never came close to paying its way. Today, the effort is largely abandoned.

Regardless, he's a man of integrity, remains a powerful teacher of integrity and many believe Africa needs more leaders like him. For awhile, they saw Nyerere's Ugandan protege, Apollo Milton Obote, a schoolteacher become prime minister, as a good example. We'll see how he became an example of something much different.

Patrice Lumumba and the Central Intelligence Agency

No, the CIA isn't dead, but you might want to check its pulse. More to the point here in Central Africa (from which the CIA was pulling back well before its recent self-induced troubles), the agency plays the role of a ghost, which is to say that what matters is not what it's actually doing (about as much as most ghosts), but what people are afraid it's doing.

How appropriate then, that it should live (inasmuch as ghosts live) in symbiotic partnership with a real ghost, the late Patrice Lumumba, an elected president of the Congo (now Zaire) who was overthrown in a CIA-financed coup and murdered purportedly while in the custody of men on the CIA payroll.

People who despise the CIA and what it did to Lumumba, describe the man as "a big mouth." Clearly, he was a passionate socialist. In any case, many Congolese loved him and now in his martyrdom he's a ghostly icon for much of Africa. Who is to say what would have happened had he not been beaten to death. Would the Congo have become the first Soviet satellite in Africa?

It's all moot. What matters today and tomorrow is that the CIA lives as a ghost haunting both talk and action in Central Africa largely because so many Central Africans believe the agency killed Patrice Lumumba. This is not merely a twist of passing interest. It's dangerous, giving people a powerful reason to see America and the CIA behind everything bad that happens.

General de Divison/Augustin Bizimungu

The Hutu general, now a Hutu renegade, is not to be confused with Hutu moderate Pasteur Bizimungu, who was slated to become Rwanda's president under terms of a peace agreement signed by Kagame's Tutsi front and Rwanda's Hutu government. The agreement was violently resisted by military leaders like Augustin Bizimungu, who itched to turn their French heavy weapons on the Watutsi in a military showdown. Augustin Bizimungu thus became, quite unintentionally, the man most responsible for the success of Pasteur Bizimungu. When the showdown came and the Watutsi licked the Rwandan Army, Kagame's front simply let the previously signed peace treaty kick in and Pasteur Bizimungu became president.

When Rwanda's military collapsed, Augustin Bizimungu was its chief of staff. As he sees it, he's still its chief of staff, and a chief he most certainly is. He's ensconced at this resort hotel or that, commander of an army without a country, at large in Zaire.

According to various sources it is speculated that Bizimungu and his cronies blew up at Rwanda's longtime, hard-line Hutu president, Juvenal Habyarimana, for not being hard-line enough when he initialed the agreement with the Watutsi calling for Hutu moderates as President and Prime Minister. Also, if you found it irritating to read, in the background graph of one Rwandan news item after another, that the country's president had been "killed in a suspicious plane crash," Bizimungu and his buddies are the suspects.

It's been widely reported that the president of Burundi was also on that plane; less widely reported was news that Rwanda's chief of staff was aboard, which is how Bizimungu became chief of staff. (Chew on that, Tom Peters.) But the promotion didn't come right away. The prime minister didn't want Bizimungu in the slot and she was under the protection of the Presidential Guard. As jockeying for the leadership of the military went on, Bizimungu and his cronies told the rank and file that their president had been shot down by the Watutsi. The military (army and militia) then went on its infamous *pogrom* and, in the meantime, Bizimungu's appointment as chief of staff was iced by the Presidential Guard killing the prime minister it was supposed to be protecting.

The Parti Liberation du Peuple Hutu (PALIPHUTU)

This is the Hutu People's Liberation Party, formed in 1980 as a tiny Hutu opposition group of exiles in Rwanda and Tanzania.

Getting In

Diplomatic ties were severed with Rwanda in July 1993. Diplomats were expelled and the embassy closed. Passport and visa are required. Multiple-entry visa for a stay of up to three months requires a US$30 fee (cash, check or money order), two application forms, two photos and immunization for yellow fever. Exact date of entry into Rwanda is required with application. Include prepaid envelope or $1.50 postage for return of passport by certified mail.

Although President Clinton has declared that the Rwandans are not welcome on our soil, the embassy staff does not know exactly when they will be leaving. Embassy staff recommends applying to Brussels, Belgium for visa information:

Embassade du Rwanda

> *1 Avenue de Fleurs*
> *(coin Avenue de Terzuren)*
> *1150 Bruxelles*
> ☎ *(322) 763 07 21 or 763 07 02*
> *FAX (322) 763-0753*

At the height of the hostilities when *DP* asked about entry, permission or other questions regarding entry. A spokesperson replied, "We know nothing." Later, after things had calmed down it seemed the embassy staff had developed a sense of bureaucratic humor. When we asked if there were any Americans currently in jail in Rwanda we were told that "we have none; they have been behaving so far." You should know the first of the 12 conditions for entry and stay in Rwanda is that "proper attire and conduct are required of persons staying in Rwanda." The embassy maintains that as of March 1995 it is safe to travel in Rwanda.

Former addresses:

U.S. Embassy in Rwanda

> *Boulevard de la Revolution*
> *BP 28, Kigali*
> ☎ *(250) 75601/2/3*
> *FAX (250) 72128*

Embassy of the Republic of Rwanda

> *1714 New Hampshire Avenue, N.W.*
> *Washington, D.C. 20009*
> ☎ *(202) 232-2882*

Permanent Mission of Rwanda to the U.N.

> *336 East 45th Street*
> *New York, NY 10017*
> ☎ *(212) 808-9330*

Consulate General in Chicago

> ☎ *(708) 205-1188*

Consulate General in Denver

> ☎ *(303) 321-2400*

Canadian Embassy in Rwanda

> *Rue Akagera, BP 1177*
> *Kigali*
> ☎ *73210*
> *FAX 72719*

Rwandan Embassy in Canada

> *121 Sherwood Drive*
> *Ottawa, ONT. K1Y 3V1*
> ☎ *(613) 722-5835/722-7921*
> *FAX (613) 729-3291*

Getting Around

Rwanda has a total road length of 3036 miles; 286 of them are paved. There are neither railways nor ports. There are eight airfields in the country, three of them with a permanent surface.

Air Rwanda flies internally from Kigali to Gisenyi and Kamembe. Occasionally you can fly between Gisenyi and Kamembe. Due to the amount of foreign aid into the country, Rwanda's road system isn't too bad. As in neighboring Burundi, the roadways are served by a fleet of relatively late-model Japanese minibuses. The buses leave most towns when they are full. Larger government buses also traverse Rwanda's roads, although they are fewer and farther between. They cost less than the minibuses, but take longer to get to their destinations.

Dangerous Places

The Entire Country

The entire country of Rwanda can be considered extremely unsafe. Travelers are regularly the victims of theft, petty crime and murder. Sporadic violence is a problem in Kigali as well as in the interior. Fighting has caused thousands of refugees to flee into neighboring Burundi as well as other countries in the region. Travelers should use extreme caution everywhere in Rwanda. Do not travel into the troubled areas of Kigali or anywhere in or near Gisenyi. Do not travel after dark.

Dangerous Things

The Rwandan Government

The Rwandan interim government has conspired in the massacre of hundreds of thousands of civilians in Rwanda's civil war.

Gun Running

Arms have been brought into Rwanda in defiance of a U.N. Security Council arms embargo. The Seychelles have been embarrassed by their participation as an unwitting (perhaps conspiring) conduit in running guns into Rwanda. France was abashed when one shipment reached Goma, in Zaire near the Rwandan frontier, unimpeded. The agreement had been consummated on French soil. Part of an arms and ammunition cache originally meant to go to Somalia was confiscated by the Seychellois authorities aboard the Greek freighter *Malo* in 1993. This was sold and shipped by air on June 16 and 18, 1994 to Goma, a Zairean town close to the Rwanda frontier which had been the rear base of the French humanitarian intervention force. Goma is right next to Gisenyi in Rwanda, the temporary seat of the Rwandan interim government setup by Hutu extremists to fight against the Rwanda Patriotic Front after Rwanda President Habyarimana died in the April 1994 plane crash. The customer for the arms shipments was the Rwandan interim government, in defiance of the embargo. The arms transaction was negotiated by a Zairean and a South African businessman and concluded in Paris.

Volcanoes

Near Goma, Zaire, two active volcanoes threaten more than 800,000 refugees. In January 1995, U.N. officials made arrangements for a quarter of the threatened Rwandan refugees to be moved to new camps. The two volcanoes, Nyamuragira and Nyiragongo, have been leaking lava toward a massive camp at Mugunga, home to 200,000 refugees.

Getting Sick

Medical facilities, doctors and supplies are dangerously scarce in Rwanda. There are 0.3 doctors and 15 hospital beds for every 10,000 people in the country. Cholera and yellow fever inoculations are required. Tetanus, polio, typhoid and gamma globulin vaccines are advised, as are antimalarial prophylaxes: DPT, measles and mumps vaccines are recommended for children. Tap water is not potable.

Nuts & Bolts

About the size of Vermont and located in east central Africa, Rwanda (the capital is Kigali) is a landlocked country just south of the Equator bordering Uganda to the north, Burundi to the south, Tanzania to the east, and Zaire to the west. There were estimated to be over 8 million people in Rwanda before the holocaust. They live packed in 789 per square mile: 90 percent are Hutu, 9 percent Tutis. Today, almost half of the Tutsi have been murdered.

The country is divided into 10 prefectures, each headed by a centrally appointed prefect. There are 143 communes and municipalities, each administered by a presidentially appointed governor who is assisted by an elected council of local citizens.

Rwanda (Republika y'u Rwanda—Republique Rwandaise—Republic of Rwanda) was originally a feudal monarchy ruled by the Tutsi tribes. From 1899–1916, the country was a German protectorate before it came under the administration of Belgium in 1920 as part of Ruanda-Urundi. Rwanda became an independent state on July 1, 1962. Strife between the majority Hutu tribe and the Tutsi resulted in a bloodless coup on July 5, 1973, led by the head of the National Guard and Minister of Defense, Major General Juvenal Habyarimana. A civilian-military government was established. All legislative processes were banned until 1975, when the Mouvement Revolutionnaire National pour le Developement (MRND—National Revolutionary Movement for Development) was formed and later recognized in the December 17, 1978 Constitution as the sole legal party. Recognizing the need for reform, on June 2, 1991, Habyarimana announced the legalization of multiparty politics, and on June 10, 1991 a revised Constitution was adopted.

In 1988, 36,000 people made the trek to Rwanda. Many went to visit its population of rare mountain gorillas and the bizarre topography and plant life of its montane forests found in Parc National des Volcans. Visitors to Rwanda are attracted to the country's beautiful mountain scenery, national parks, and recreation offerings at Lake Kivu. Tourism provides Rwanda with its second largest source of foreign funds. Found in Parc National des Volcans, as of July 1994, the gorillas have been unharmed due to the remoteness and the fact that the Rwandan park guards have remained on duty. The World Wildlife Fund reports that foreign researchers and scientists were evacuated in April. At last count there were only 650 mountain gorillas left on the planet of which 320 live in the 125-sq. kilometer Parc National des Volcans in Rwanda's northern mountains.

The 1991 Constitution introduced a multiparty system and a separation of powers between the executive, legislature and judiciary. It also mandates that although political party formations may be established along tribal or ethnic lines, they must remain open to all. The Constitution also guarantees freedom of the press and awards civil servants the right to strike.

The currency is the Rwanda franc (RFr). There are 100 centimes to the RFr. Local time is two hours later than GMT, seven hours later than U.S. EST. Hutu comprise 90 percent of the population; the Tutsi account for 9 percent. Sixty-five percent of the population is Roman Catholic. Protestants make up 9 percent, Muslim 1 percent and indigenous beliefs 25 percent.

Kinyarwanda and French are the official languages, and Kiswahili is used commercially. Illiteracy stands at 50 percent (1990). In 1989, there were 1671 primary schools with 1,058,529 students; 65,323 students enrolled at secondary schools; and 3389 students enrolled at institutions of higher education.

Rwanda has a tropical climate which varies slightly with altitude. The major rainy seasons are February through May and November through December, with an average annual rainfall of 31 inches.

Total armed forces number 5200. Rwanda also maintains a 200-member parachute company. Military service is voluntary in Rwanda.

Dangerous Days

08/12/94	Thousands of Rwandan refugees began moving toward Zaire from southwest Rwanda.
08/03/94	Rwandan president, Pasteur Bizimungu warned that his government was prepared to go to war if France refused to grant access to its self-declared safety zone in the southwest of the country.
07/19/94	Rwanda's new president, Pasteur Bizimungu, was sworn in as president at a ceremony at the parliament building in the capital Kigali. Rebel commander Major General Paul Kagame was named vice president and defence minister.
07/18/94	The rebel Rwandan Patriotic Front (RPF) claimed it had won Rwanda's civil war.
07/15/94	A tidal wave of Rwandan refugees poured into neighboring Zaire.

Dangerous Days

07/04/94	Rwandan rebels captured the capital Kigali and the last major government-held southern town of Butare.
06/19/94	A Red Cross worker was killed when a mortar round exploded in a hospital complex in the city center of Kigali.
04/06/94	President Juvenal Habyarimana was killed in a plane crash, sparking nationwide fighting.
01/28	Democracy Day.
07/01	Anniversary of Independence.
07/05	National Peace and Unity Day.
10/26	Armed Forces Day.

In a Dangerous Place: Rwanda

The apocalypse in Rwanda was too dark and compelling to ignore. In the 20th century an entire nation was being murdered while the world sat by and refused to believe it. If any story needed to be captured it was this one. We flew to Nairobi. On our arrival we discovered that the jeep we had reserved was not available. It was the height of safari season and they had rented out four-wheel-drive vehicles for the $250–$500 a day they could get.

My cameraman Gokhan Acun took local transport. For $20 a head we took a five-hour minibus ride to Arusha just south of Nairobi. Seeing our massive professional camera the locals just assumed we were tourists. For $5 we could take still photos and for $20 all the video we wanted. We passed. We found a 4x4 and driver that would take us on the 13-hour trip to Mvamza, a major staging area for the relief effort in Rwanda. The price was $100 but we had to squeeze in all the locals who wanted to go along as well. We went through some of the more dramatic scenery of East Africa, but the rough road and long trip made it an ordeal.

We treated ourselves to a three-star hotel when we arrived in Mvanza. There was a U.N. crew and wherever there are U.N. people there are usually pilots around. Naturally we went straight to the hotel bar to find them. Strangely, not a pilot to be found. The next day we found the pilots eating breakfast. I went to the oldest and asked him if he would fly us to the Ngara Refugee camp. The answer was a definite no. We worked on them until finally they agreed to take us on. When we let people know that our footage and coverage will support the relief effort, they have a greater desire to help us. As we climbed into the Spanish-built *CASA* we made ourselves comfortable among the crates of medicine and food destined for the refugees.

The 90-minute flight was uneventful except for the trip over Lake Victoria. From our altitude I could see tiny islands floating in the turquoise water—they were clumps of bloated bodies. We landed on the dusty runway surrounded by a tent city that seemed to stretch for miles. A fleet of Land Rovers came to collect the supplies and take us to the U.N. headquarters for the camp. There was a veritable United Nations of relief organizations here—the U.N., the Red Cross, MSF, CARE and the Red Crescent. All of them told us that they had no room for us. The Tanzanian branch of the Red Cross gave us some simple mats to sleep on and a hot meal.

There were endless lines of Hutus and Tutsi waiting for their daily handout of milk, flour and rice. We shot some photos and interviewed the people. There were clusters of children, newly orphaned and wandering around with blank expressions on their faces. There was not much to capture here other than a sea of gaunt faces. We found a Tutsi chauffeur who, for $100, will take us as far as the headquarters of the "Rwandese Patriotic Front" about 10–15km inside the border. We didn't bother with a visa since we doubted there was much of a government left. It took us an hour to get as far as the Tanzanian border post on the eastern shore of the Kagera River. It should have only taken 15 minutes but we were like salmon swimming upstream as we tried to make our way through the river of refugees streaming out of Rwanda. The people were carrying the last of their possessions; even the children carried bundles. Old men carried firewood, now a valuable commodity. At this rate it would take us all day just to get to the HQ in Rwanda where there were no basic commodities and where terror reigned at night.

We decided to try to cross the border the next morning. Our hunch was right. All the refugees were sleeping by the side of the road and the going was easy. We were waved across the Tanzanian border with little fuss. Our exit visa was simply gifts of pens and Camel Trophy stickers, a strangely powerful international currency. As we crossed the bridge high above the Kagera River we could see bodies floating down-stream. It is strange how their dark skin turns white. One cadaver is caught between two rocks and bobs up and down in the fast moving water.

At the other side there is no one manning the border posts. Our relief was short-lived. About 50 meters past the bridge we are stopped by armed members of the RPF. They asked for ID, questioned our purpose here and treated us like celebrities when they saw our press cards.

Our Tutsi driver did not fare as well. The guards treated him as a deserter and ques-tioned his ownership of the vehicle. They took him away to a nearby building despite our desperate protests. We never saw him again. Distraught, we came across two old friends—fellow journalists Luc Delahey and James Natchway. We hugged each other and exchanged information. They had come from Kigali to report on the recently dis-covered massacre in the village of Nyarubuye 115 kms away. They never got there, having all the tires on their vehicles blown when they ran over sabotage spikes laid across the road. They had spent two days trying to find a way out. They had flown in from Uganda, and then were stuck in Kigali by the fierce fighting. They had seen our vehicle and were disappointed that it was no longer there.

We hung around the bridge pondering our situation. When a truck crossed the bor-der we flagged it down and cut a deal on the spot. For $400 we now had wheels. A guard from the RPF rode shotgun in the front with Jim Natchway. Our first dramatic sight was thousands and thousands of rusty, bloodstained machetes confiscated by the RPF from captured Hutus. I immediately thought of the piles of glasses, shoes and clothing photographed in the concentration camps in WWII. We drove through burned out villages and by rows of bodies—most killed with machetes. Among the bodies were stunned survivors searching for relatives. I will never forget the look in these people's eyes. I have seen many, many wars but never one that created so much fear and horror.

The 115 km of horror brought us to Nyarubuye where we had heard a dark tale from the refugees inside Tanzania. They told us of hundreds of men, women and children herded into a church and slaughtered like pigs. We smelled the heavy stench of rotting flesh long before we came upon the scene. We tried to inhale the scent of the eucalyp-tus trees but all we could smell was the revolting odor of decay. There were pieces of humans strewn everywhere. Wild dogs had probably been feasting on the corpses. None of us had ever seen anything like this before. Even Luc, Jim and I, who had seen so much, could not comprehend the horror that we beheld. The monastery was sur-rounded by a brick wall. Inside the wall was a flower-filled garden. Among the flowers were the rotting bodies of hundreds of women and children. The building was a low brick building built during the Belgian colonial period. There was a simple church ad-joining the monastery.

We had all emptied our stomachs when the stench first hit us—a natural and healthy reaction to human decay—but I continued to wretch as nausea came over me in waves. The people had fled to the church afraid for their lives. They had been taught that the church was the place of last refuge. They were wrong. Men armed with ma-chetes ordered them into the garden and began to slash and cut them. Some tried to escape. One man's upper torso was halfway up the metal ladder on the church steeple. His lower torso and legs hung half a meter below.

Inside the church a man lay hacked to death at the altar. Piles of bodies lay among the pews. My other memories are bizarre. I remember being covered in fleas and the dark shadows that dead bodies leave on the ground long after the dogs have dragged them into the bushes and I remember the strange grimacing expressions of their contorted faces as they putrefy.

We returned the way we came, knowing that we had captured mankind at its most base. The perverse irony of this sin being committed in a church made it even more surreal.

Sri Lanka

Island Popping

The bitter, 12-year-old conflict in Sri Lanka has left 34,000 Sri Lankans dead, including the president, the Navy commander, the government's opposition leader and the husband of new President Chandrika Kumaratunga, not to mention India's Prime Minister, Rajiv Gandhi. The major conflict is in the north and eastern Jaffna Peninsula.

Known as Serindip in ancient times and then as Ceylon, Sri Lanka is made up of a teardrop-shaped main island and groups of smaller islands 50 miles off the southern coast of India. Sri Lanka has been called one of the most beautiful islands in the world with its gentle people, lush jungles and dramatic interior. Thirty-one percent of the island is mountainous jungle and nestling ancient cities such as Polonnaruwa and Anuradhapura. The 833 miles of coastline are primarily pristine, coral-fringed beaches basking in the sun beneath towering and jutting coconut palms, caressed by the lapping azure waters of the Indian Ocean and the Bay of Bengal—a beautiful destination for you to put on your island-hopping itinerary. Unfortunately, the Tamil Tigers have put this enchanted isle on their island-popping itinerary. And they take no prisoners.

The majority of the island's population are Sinhalese Buddhists, the troublesome minority being the ethnic Tamil, who comprise about 20 percent of the population. The ethnic Tamils, virtually indistinguishable from the Sinhalese, save for different languages, are seeking independence. Muslims make up the difference at about 7 percent.

Although many (namely the Sinhalese and Tamils) claim the Sinhalese and the Tamils have been fighting each other for more than 2000 years there's actually been little tension between the groups historically. Much of the tension and fighting that has gripped the island has occurred only in recent years. The fighting began in earnest after a Tamil Tiger ambush of an army patrol in the Jaffna area in 1983. Sinhalese all over the island then went on a rampage for the next three days, murdering and looting Tamils and burning down their villages. Perhaps 2000 Tamils were killed in the uprising.

The north and the east of the island have been war zones for the better part of 10 years. Although fighting and terrorism cooled around 1990, and tourists had written Sri Lanka off as a battlefield in the mid-1980s, tourism is surging once again. Although areas in the south are still relatively safe, nowhere on the island is 100 percent secure. Even visiting the ruins at Anuradhapura and Polonnaruwa is damned risky. The Batticaloa region remains the Tamil Tigers' principal area for staging operations in the south. In July 1992, a train on the Colombo-Batticaloa line was ambushed and some 40 people were killed.

Police are attempting to register all the island's 17,890,000 inhabitants to keep track of their movements and political/religious sympathies. The figure of 719 inhabitants per square mile does not reflect the immense density of the nation's larger cities, including the capital of Colombo and Moratuwa in the south and Jaffna in the far north.

The Scoop

The Sinhalese Buddhists are the majority. The minority Tamils want independence. The two groups have been massacring each other since 1983. By 1988, the entire country was in turmoil and the economy was crippled. The tourist doors began opening up again in 1990. But the hatches were battened down soon afterwards, as terrorism and renewed fighting resumed again. The government army doubled in size to 75,000 from 1983 to 1992 in order to fight the Liberation Tigers of Tamil Eelam (Tamil Tigers, or LTTE). More than 30,000 people have died in the 12-year-old conflict.

Sri Lanka

- ⊕ National capital
- • District capital
- ● Secondary City
- ┼┼┼ Railroad
- ─── Primary Road
- ─── Province boundary
- --- District boundary

District names are the same as their capitals.

0 20 40 km
0 20 40 60 mi

©AM 1995

Kankesanturai
Point Pedro
Jaffna

Delft Island
Palk Bay
Kilinochchi
Mullaittivu

Ferry
Talaimannar
Mankulam

Mannar
Northern
Pulmoddai

Gulf of Mannar
Vavuniya

Horowupotana
Yan Oya
Trincomalee
Medawachchiya
Kinniya
Mutur
Anuradhapura
Mihintale
North Central

Kalpitiya
Kala Oya
Kekirawa
Hingurakgoda

Puttalam
Habarane
Polonnaruwa
Valachchenai
Mampuri
Maho
Dambulla
Eravur
Batticaloa

Nikaweratiya
North Western
Central
Mahaweli Ganga
Kattankudi

Chilaw
Maha Oya

Kurunegala
Matale
Kalmunai

Kandy
Amparai
Gal Oya
Negombo
Kegalla
Ja-ela
Gampola
Ragama
Nuwara Eliya
Badulla
Colombo
Kelani Ganga
Pottuvil
Dehiwala-Mt. Lavina
Hatton-Dikoya
Uva
Moneragala
Moratuwa
Panadura
Ratnapura
Opanake
Wellawaya
Kalutara
Matugama
Balangoda
Beruwala
Sabaragamuwa

Bentota
Deniyaya
Walawe Ganga
Ambalangoda
Elpitiya
Hambantota
Southern
Galle
Ambalantota
Ahangama
Tangalle
Matara

Indian Ocean

The Players

The Tamil Tigers

The Liberation Tigers of Tamil Eelam (LTTE) are the largest and most active secessionist group in Sri Lanka. The LTTE began in 1972 and today it is the largest Tamil separatist guerrilla group. The Tigers have maintained their hard-line position on separatism and have conducted numerous military and terrorist acts to further their cause. They are most famous for their suicide attacks on prominent politicians. These attacks not only snuff their intended victims but, because of the type of bomb employed (usually a very powerful explosive unleashing a volley of shrapnel or metal pellets) they usually take out a couple of dozen innocents as well. It is believed that LTTE members were responsible for the 1993 assassination of President Ranasinghe Premadasa. The Tigers are experiencing an internal rift between leader Velupiliia Prabhakaran and his top deputy Gopalaswamy Mahendrarajah. (Mahendrarajah was accused by Prabhakaran of plotting with the Indian government against him. Prabhakaran has fled into the jungle to avoid reprisals after trying to arrest Mahendrarajah in a surprise raid on April 23, 1994.)

In 1992, 1157 members of Sri Lanka's security forces and 2876 members of the Liberation Tigers were killed in clashes. Another 2004 soldiers were injured. In 1991, 1111 soldiers and 4374 LTTE rebels died.

The LTTE maintains their own navy, called "Sea Tigers." Operating in the Jaffna Lagoon, each light boat carries five or six guerrillas who attack Indian Navy ships or make landings to attack Sri Lankan army units.

Bombs are the favored method of Tamil suicide bombers. One does not know if this is due to the lack of timing devices or just old-fashioned bravado. In any case, the suicide bombers are revered among the Tamils. Their pictures are defiantly and proudly displayed along the road and in the houses of their families. Their families are accorded a distinction equal to the mothers of saints. How do you spot a suicide bomber or Black Tiger? Despite the fact that an average Tamil lives until he is over 70, most suicide bombers are young, in their early 20s; they wear a pendant around their necks with a cyanide capsule dangling from the end.

A favorite mode of assassination is for the bomber to drive right up to the victim on a scooter and detonate the bomb. If the Tiger is caught, he gulps down the cyanide tablet, resulting in a painful death usually within five minutes.

The Government

The new president and daughter of two former Sri Lankan prime ministers, Chandrika Kumaratunga, 49, is not letting the assassination of her husband by the LTTE get in the way of the peace process. In November 1994, she sent delegates to begin discussions on ending the 12-year-old civil war.

The Sri Lankan military is small and has required help from the Indian Army to control the LTTE. The total strength of the armed forces is 105,900 including recalled reservists. The breakdown is 89,000 army; 8900 navy and 8000 air force (including 2000 active reservists).

TULF

The Tamil United Liberation Front (TULF) is an alliance of a number of Tamil groups. They were formed shortly after the LTTE (1974). Originally named the Tamil Liberation Front, the TULF is working for (as opposed to killing for) the creation of an autonomous Tamil region. They are moderates and are criticized by other Tamil groups for being too complacent in light of the Indian Army militant crackdown on Tamils.

EROS

Organized in 1985, the Eelam Revolutionary Organization of Students (EROS) is a smaller Tamil separatist group that became the third largest group in Parliament following the 1989 elections. In 1990, all 13 of the EROS members in Parliament resigned their seats, stating that they "do not want to be dormant spectators who witness the torment of our people."

The little-known group Ellalan Force of Tamil rebels has threatened to attack tourist hotels in southern Sri Lanka. There are also other groups like the Maoist JVP, who want all foreign-owned estates returned to the people. Sri Lanka's return to normalcy which followed the apparent decimation of the JVP and the ensuing negotiations with the LTTE was short-lived, when, on June 11, 1990, the LTTE initiated hostilities against the GSL in the eastern district of Amparai and Batticaloa; the fighting quickly spread to the north.

Getting In

A passport, onward/return ticket and proof of sufficient funds (US$15 per day) are required. A tourist visa can be granted at the time of entry into Sri Lanka, and may be valid for a maximum period of 90 days. For business travel or travel on an official or diplomatic passport, visas are required and must be obtained in advance.

Business visas are valid for one month and require an application form, two photos, a company letter, a letter from a sponsoring agency in Sri Lanka, a copy of an onward/return ticket, and a US$5 fee. Include US$6 postage for return of your passport by registered mail.

Yellow fever and cholera immunizations are needed if arriving from an infected area.

Embassy of the Democratic Socialist Republic of Sri Lanka

2148 Wyoming Ave., NW
Washington, D.C. 20008
☎ *(202) 483-4025*
or nearest Consulate:

California
☎ *(805) 873-7224*
Hawaii
☎ *(808) 735-1622*
New Jersey
☎ *(201) 627-7855*
New York
☎ *(212) 986-7040*

or the Sri Lankan Consulate in New York. There are also honorary Sri Lankan consulates in Los Angeles, Honolulu, New Orleans and Newark.

Getting Around

About a third of Sri Lanka's 47,070 miles of road are paved. There are 1210 miles of heavily traveled railroad and 14 airfields; the only major airport is in Colombo. There aren't any internal flights in Sri Lanka, so the traveler is limited to buses and trains. Trains are arguably more comfortable than buses, but are slower and don't service as many areas of the island as do buses. The train stations, although dilapidated, aren't nearly as crowded as those in India, where rail travel is the lifeblood of Indians. However, don't fall asleep on the trains. You'll more than likely get ripped off by a thief.

Dangerous Places

There is a long-standing armed conflict between the Sri Lankan government and a Tamil extremist group, the Liberation Tigers of Tamil Eelam (LTTE). Fighting between government security forces and the LTTE continues in northern and eastern areas of the island. Sri Lankan defense regulations restrict travel to much of the island's northern area.

National Parks

Remote forested areas such as Wilpattu and Galoya National Parks are considered especially unsafe.Rebels like the peace and quiet and may take exception to your need to explore and save their rain forest. They're doing just fine beneath their blanket of triple canopy forest hidden in deep bunkers—excellent cover from air force helicopter and bomb attacks.

Jaffna Lagoon

The lagoon has been declared a shoot-on-sight zone by the Sri Lankan government. The Sea Tigers (the marine version of the LTTE) operate small gunboats to conduct naval- and marine-style raids. Each boat usually carries five or six guerrillas. When DP used these boats to visit the Tigers, the boat in front of us was blown from the water by a naval shell. Usually, though, the high speed boats manage to outrun the slower naval gunners.

Political Rallies

The Black Tigers, or suicide bombers, cast their votes by blowing themselves and anyone else in a 50-yard radius, into small fleshy pieces. Using massive explosives packed around ball bearings, pellets and other homemade shrapnel, they can kill up to 60 people at a time. Prominent national leaders and senior military personnel have been targets and/or victims of terrorist violence which, of course, makes anyone else in the neighborhood a target, as well.

Bathrooms in Large Hotels

The Tigers give new meaning to taking a shower. In April 1994, four bombs exploded in Colombo hotels. While U.S. citizens have not been singled out as targets, a group calling itself "Ellalan Force" threatened to target foreigners after the April bombings.

Road Blocks

Travelers who encounter roadblocks staffed by security personnel are wise to follow closely and heed any instructions given.

North and East

Currently, fighting between the government forces and the LTTE continues in much of the north and east. Although the current situation appears to be contained in these regions, security checkpoints have become the norm along major crossroads in and around Colombo as a result of the March 1991 bombing assassination of Deputy Defense Minister Ranjan Wijertaine, and the June 1991 bombing of the Ministry of Defenses Joint Operations Command. (The LTTE is believed to be responsible for both incidents.) Although no foreigners were killed in these incidents, several were injured. Travelers should be alert to the continuing threat of terrorism in Colombo.

Colombo

In general, the level of criminal activity in Colombo is moderate in relation to other cities of the world. Nonetheless, visitors should be aware that petty "street" crimes are not uncommon. Although pickpocketing and purse snatchings do occur with some frequency, violent crimes such as armed robberies are rare, particularly among the expatriot and tourist population. Residential crime, historically a problem in the city, has been on the decline. The Sri Lankan police, though limited in resources, generally make every effort to provide assistance to foreign visitors. This is particularly so within the confines of Colombo. Police coverage tends to be less reliable outside of the city. Important police emergency telephone numbers for the greater Colombo area:

Police Emergency (24 hours daily)
☎ 433333

Cinnamon Gardens Police Station
☎ 693377

Colpetty Police Station
☎ 20131

Bambalapitiya Police Station
☎ 593208

Getting Sick

Medical facilities are limited—you'll find one doctor and 27 hospital beds for every 10,000 people. Doctors and hospitals often expect immediate cash payment for health services. Malaria is prevalent in many areas outside of Colombo. Visitors must take precautions against malaria, hepatitis and yellow fever prior to arriving in Sri Lanka. Rabies is common in many animals in Sri Lanka; take some comfort that the painful injections against rabies can be obtained locally. Tap water is laced with everything from amoebas to horses and should not be ingested unless boiled for a couple of decades, strained through an offset press and carpet-bombed with iodine.

Nuts & Bolts

The major ethnic group is the Sinhalese (74 percent) followed by the Tamils (18 percent) and Moors (7 percent). Burghers, Malays and Veddhas comprise the last 1 percent. The Sinhalese are predominantly Buddhist and the Tamils are Hindu. Christians and Muslims make up only about 8 percent of the religious pie, each.

English is widely spoken in this former British colony. Sinhala is the official language, but Tamil is recognized as a national language. As one would expect in the Indian Ocean, the heat and humidity can wring you out like a wet sponge in a boxing match. Since the British were fond of colonizing tropical destinations with cooler hill stations you can expect cool, moist weather up high. The average temperature along the coast is a sweltering 81 degrees F with little change all year.There are two cooling monsoon seasons, the southwest and the northeast monsoons, which dump about 100 inches of rain every year.

Embassy Location and Registration

Updated information on travel and security within Sri Lanka is available at the U.S. Embassy.

U.S. Embassy

P.O. Box 106
210 Galle Road
Colombo
☎ *(94-1) 448007*
FAX (94-1) 437345
U.S. citizens are encouraged to register at the U.S. Embassy upon arrival in Sri Lanka.

Embassies

Canadian Embassy in Sri Lanka

6 Gregory's Road
Cinnamon Gardens
Colombo 7
☎ *(94-1) 695841*
Postal address:

P.O. Box 1006
Columbo, Sri Lanka

Sri Lankan Embassy in Canada

85 Range Road, Suites 102–104
Ottawa, ONT. K1N 8J6
☎ *(613) 233-8440/8449*
FAX (613) 238-8448

Dangerous Days	
09/04/1992	Dasain Festival. Hindu Festival.
06/13/1990	LTTE offensive launched. The Liberation Tigers of Tamil Eelam (LTTE) launched a renewed offensive against Sri Lankan government forces by storming at least 24 police stations in northern and eastern Sri Lanka. Several hundred police officers were taken hostage and a number of them later killed.
08/18/1987	Grenade attack on parliament. One legislator was killed in a grenade attack on the Sri Lankan parliament.
07/29/1987	Indo-Sri Lankan peace accords.
07/20/1986	Sinhalese rioting.

Dangerous Days

05/14/1985	Separatists attack shrine. Tamil separatists killed more than 150 people in an attack on a Buddhist shrine at Anuradhapura.
07/23/1983	Widespread violence begins. The killing of 13 Sri Lankan soldiers in an ambush by Tamil militants touched off widespread anti-Tamil violence that left as many as 2000 Tamils dead and 100,000 homeless.
05/22/1972	Republic Day. Also known as National Heroes' Day.
11/24/1954	LTTE founders birthday. The Liberation Tigers of Tamil Eelam's (LTTE) founder and leader was born. His birthday is marked by the LTTE as "heroes week" which also commemorates LTTE members who have died in battle.
02/04/1948	Independence Day.
05/24/0000	Birth of Buddha.
01/14/0000	Tamil Thai Pongal Day.

The Horn of Africa

In a Dangerous Place: The Sudan

For my part I would as soon be descended...from the old baboon, who, descending from the mountains, carried away in triumph his young comrade from a crowd of astonished dogs...

-Charles Darwin
The Descent of Man, chapter 21

Looking down from the C-5A, the Sudan and Africa's Horn look heroic. The Great Rift runs down from the Siberian waters of Lake Baikal to Lake Nyasa and passes the Mountains of the Moon. Below, in harsh contrast is the brilliant blue of the incorrectly named Red Sea against the tan of desert and steppe. There is also the green ribbon of the Nile, the pale green of the savanna and the deep green of Abyssinian highland.

At Malakal, Dinka warriors, blue-black and seven feet tall, meet our plane, after which there were sundowners on a verandah overlooking the wilder expanses of the White Nile in the twilight of the Anglo-Egyptian Sudan. Malakal, they say, was a favored stop on an itinerary of the old pontoon plane which included a landing at dusk on the vast cobalt of Lake Victoria and the next morning, a low, slow all-day flight south to Victoria Falls on the Zambezi. This was long ago. Today, transportation is a matter of life and death here. Things change. No longer a quaint rest stop, Malakal today is known for its rats and their fleas, in a district quarantined for plague.

The Technical

But no need to wax nostalgic about old planes that made this arid place romantic. The camel comes easily to mind as the land transportation of choice. There are more of them on the Somali steppe than in all of Arabia, more still in the Sudan. This is their country and a journey atop them is no holiday. But their genius has been to make badlands easier for humans than we have any natural right. At times, so far up there, as you lope along in deep hypnotic strides, desert, savanna, thornbush, even intense heat, can seem a dream.

Today, the Sudan has a new form of transportation. Slower and lower still, cheap, battered, reliable, it's the Toyota FJ-40 and its cousin the FJ-45 pickup. In constant and coughing, but seldom vital, need of a rebuilt carb, it bangs through wadis, sluices across mud plains and whips dust devils through villages of mud and wattle. At Baidoa and Bardera in the furthest of Somali reaches, at el Fasher in the far west of the Sudan, at Harrer in the far east of Ethiopia, on the salt plains of the Danakil desert in the new nation of Eritrea, the Range Rover is the emblem of power and the FJ-40 is power.

It rules: a car so cheap and simple that in itself it represents a dangerous development in industrial history, permitting what Somalis call a 'technical' to become the center-piece of a form of desert war in which jeeps can take on tanks. The true equalizer of haves and have-nots. Tough and mean.

Great Sucker of Maggots

Let's get down and dirty, where the bugs are, among the thorns, moving through parched steppe to the wet uplands and shivering cold at 10,000 feet to meet the new symbol of Somalia: the baboon. As vindictive and mean a beast as you'll ever meet and capable of great cowardice. The baboon is the most numerous on the margins of this scarp which is a tough climb for humans and even mules and mountain camels (a smaller beast the color of pale rust); it seems purpose-built for the baboon. But he is to be found throughout the table land, even here and there, wind whipped and shivering, atop Abyssinia's highest place, the Sembian plateau. Creased with deep rock defiles and studded with peaks rising to as much as 13,000 feet, the Sembian floats some-where above our real world, a place where frigid mists and thunderclaps are the order of the day, virtually every day.

This is country where getting anything done demands a capacity for just hanging out, sometimes for days, so sooner or later, you're hanging out with baboons. With nothing to do but watch them, you get a little used to them, and the magnificence of a great chief does become recognizable as he struts about grabbing food and females from his lessers, then lounging with a rotten twig from which he sucks maggots.

The comeliness of the females, though, is another thing, not even with their flaming purple bums. In fact, often as not that magnificent male, strutting so arrogantly, will soon strut across the path of a similarly magnificent male, whereupon there will be much baring of fangs, the briefest of fights, and just like that, one of these gallant young men will run for dear life until he's finally cornered. At this point, the magnifi-cent male suddenly begins pretending he's a comely female, presenting his own flam-ing purple bum in an act of submission which positively implores the other beast to mount. This, we're told, is the loser's way of getting the winner to say "no hard feel-ings." The winner complies, mounts, pretends to copulate for a couple of seconds, his dog-face the picture of boredom.

Mean and tough. In Gojjam, shepherds complain baboons rip open the stomachs of nursing lambs just to drink the milk.

He does not, however, scavenge everywhere. He still ranges in scattered troops through the Yemens but never northwest of Khartoum, and only in scattered high-lands in the Sahel to the southwest.

It was in the Sudan that I first heard a story I've since heard transmuted to one awful place after another:

A frog is about to cross the Nile. A scorpion shows up who also wants to cross. He asks the frog to let him climb on his back and carry him over.

"Do I look crazy?" says the frog. "I let you on my back. You sting. I'm dead."

"Come on," says the scorpion. "You die, I drown."

"Ta'ib," says the frog (that's frog for "ok"), the scorpion climbs on, they get half way across the great river and the scorpion stings.

"Why?" gasps the frog with his last dying breath.
"This is the Sudan, man," says the scorpion.

Mean and Tough. Scavengers with shifting loyalties. Populated with desperadoes, guerrillas from battered tribes, lost nations, clans, all called *shiftas* (bandits in Arabic) These are the most simple and detached of bandits, unsmiling men who won't even bother to watch you twitch to death in the sun while they fight over Maria Theresa dollars (yes, they still circulate) and a 20 pound traveler's cheque.

Bandits can also wear tailored safari suits in air-conditioned government offices. They walk the walk and talk the talk with sublime authority, sometimes sporting, like Zaire's Mobutu Sese Seko, a pillbox hat of fake leopard. They are the Lions of Judah. And as the lion and the leopard are the terror of the baboon, they are the terror of desperado populations.

Here in the Horn of Africa the baboons use deception and artifice to survive. They creep up on your camp at night, charging en masse when you don't retire early enough for them to get on with their all-important scavenging, beating an unseemly retreat as a lone, unarmed human chases them off, then barking and charging again.

The baboons love to eat scorpions and tarantulas; their expertise is defanging these beasties. Feinting with one hand, the baboon bluffs the scorpion into bringing his tail up in that threatening arch, then instantly he grabs from behind with the other hand, snapping off the venomous tail, popping the rest in his mouth.

The Baboon and the Scorpion

Haile Selassie, using U.S. money to bankroll Africa's largest standing army, brought his heel down on anybody he could, and when he was overthrown, the Marxists who overthrew him did the same, using Soviet money. The victims were the largely Somali Ogaden, the heavily Coptic but non-Amharic Tigre, the Oromo southeast of Addis (most populous of all Abyssinians), and (big mistake) the Eritreans.

Hardly the most numerous group, the Eritreans (unlike Ethiopia's ruling Amharas) had been unable to preserve their independence from the Italians during the grab for Africa, and on top of this, they weren't even a single ethnic or confessional group like the Somalis. Something less than half were Muslim; something less than half were Copt; the rest were pagan. But for all that, this non-state, Eritrea, had one quality in greater measure than any East African government: that crucial polity of a nation-state.

Britain took Eritrea from Italy in 1941 and after the war, the U.N. scheduled a plebiscite. Selassie marched in, called the plebiscite off, and during the next decade and a half, he made desperadoes of the wrong people. In 1961, the Eritrean Liberation Front went to war.

Reduced to ranging among the rock defiles of the Eritrean steppe like the baboons who watched from just a little higher up, they crafted from among their variety an outlaw nation that would take on Africa's largest standing army in Africa's longest war and make it pay.

Haile Selassie

In the west he was a gallant, exotic hero. To Rastafarian makers of wonderful reggae, he was God. In this part of the world Haile Selassie was the premier practitioner of the "politics of exclusion" recorded in the Oxford Companion to World Politics.

With U.S. money he put together Africa's largest standing army, used it to build an empire until finally he was overthrown by the Marxist *Dergue* (the word means committee in Amharinya). The Dergue then did the same thing using Soviet money to bankroll Africa's largest standing army. The largely Somali Ogaden, the largely Coptic but non-Amharic Tigre, the Oromo people were all secured within Selassie's Empire and then excluded from all but meager power.

The Technicals

The vehicle is a a scabby yellow FJ-45 four-wheel drive pickup mounted with a fifty caliber machine gun. You wouldn't want to call it a welcome wagon, but it is painted a pretty lively color. (Hand-painted; you can see the brush strokes.) And don't miss that lively fringe stretched across the windshield, not to speak of the ingratiating way the kid behind the wheel asks if he can be of help.

He'll look after you and Allah knows you'll need looking after in this lawless place. People have been known to lose their transportation because there were a couple of characters up the wadi who needed a fresh battery. But with him and his friends, you're in safe hands. By the way, have you met his friends?

Mahmud is the fine-featured lad with a dirty '49ers T-shirt, a madras skirt and a wad of kat in his left cheek; the kid sitting in the back with an AK-47 in his lap. Ali is the fine-featured lad with a dirty Cowboys t-shirt, a madras skirt and a wad of kat in his right cheek; the kid behind the 50-caliber.

The reason you wouldn't call this a welcome wagon is that they want lots of *dinero* for their services, and if you're not hiring today, you might find out they were the ones with the dead battery.

But don't jump to conclusions. The vehicle is not called a "technical" (*arabeya* will do) the way it is in Mogadischu and any number of other Somali tourist spots. That's because this isn't Mogadischu. It's the Yemen. In fact, only one of the kids is even Somali.

You look at them. Their fine features seem just a little darker than those of the fine-featured lads in the Yemen, but then you're all pretty dirty. The wastes which stretch in all directions are called, *Arabia Petrea* or stoney Arabia. In the late twentieth century, the phrase *Arabia Felix*, which is what the Romans called Sheba to distinguish it from stoney *Arabia Petrea*, conjures a rough place. Like *Arabia Deserta*, it's a fuzzy name on old maps of wild and dangerous places.

They're Africans, what Homer called "Aethiop's faultless men" and more specifically, what the Arabs call *Habashat*, Abyssinians. It is an army of Abyssinnians which stands over Mecca, preparing to conquer it. Their real home isn't the realm of Sheba which they once ruled in *Arabia Felix*, but the kingdom of Axum, across the Red Sea.

Here on the shores of the Red or Eritrean (in Greek for Red) Sea things have not changed much.

The Sudan

In the course of a chequered career, I have seen many unwholesome spots; but for godforsaken, dry-sucked, flyblown wilderness, commend me to the Upper Nile. A desolation of desolations, an infernal region, a howling waste of weed, mosquitoes, flies and fever, backed by a groaning waste of thorns and stones— waterless and waterlogged. I have passed through it, and have now no fear for the hereafter.

-Ewart S. Grogan
one of the first westerners
to cross the Sudan, c. 1875

The North

The Sudan today, or at least the Muslim two-thirds of it which rules the rest, is so thoroughly Muslim, that it is hard to imagine that after the decline of Ancient Egypt (one of whose dynasties was Sudanese) and while Britain was still untouched by the Church, Nubia, from what is now Aswan to what is now Khartoum, was a Christian kingdom.

Late into the Roman occupation of Egypt, well after Egypt had abandoned the last of its gods for Greek gods and then Roman, in fact well after Rome itself had turned from Mars and Jupiter to Christ, all the known-Nile, from the delta up to the sixth cataract at Wad Ben Naga, was thoroughly

Christian. Rome's proconsul in Upper Egypt was shocked by the appearance of warlike tribes out of the Sudanese desert.

These weren't Nubians. The proconsul lived with Nubians, knew these tall and stately Africans as among the first Christians. Indeed, some of them, well into the Sudan, would cling to Christianity almost 1000 years after the birth of Muhammad. To this day, ruins of their monasteries are still crumbling in far Darfur, near what is now the Saharan state of Chad.

These were warlike nomads, out of the desert, men of a fierce faith which wasn't even faintly Christian. But what faith?

If it pleased his excellency, they wished to worship at the Temple of Isis in Thebes.

They were the last known people to worship the old Egyptian gods. Today they are the most militant of Muslims.

The Mahdi

Much of Sudan's identity today can be traced to the Mahdi. His father was a ship chandler, he received his early religious training along the Nile, and it was along the river that he began cultivating the image of ascetic humility that we see today in Islam's sidewalk preachers. The Sudanese of this time were not a happy people. They didn't like the taxes increasingly imposed by the foreign agents of the Anglo-Egyptian Khedive—bureaucrats universally labeled "Turks" by the Sudanese, backed up by the Khedive's notorious horsemen, the *bashi bazooks*. They didn't like what the infidel British, who bankrolled the Khedive, were doing to their slave trade.

Becoming ever more ascetic, the thin young man who was to become the Mahdi took to living in a cave on the river's bank. Word went around. Steamers began blowing their whistles whenever they passed that spot which by now every believer knew by heart. When he decided the moment had come for the revolt, the word went out quickly.

But that's when he left the Nile and rode far into the Kordofan desert to lead the Beggara bedouin. He needed fierce desert zeal crucially, and it didn't hurt that they needed him, too. The Beggara were the greatest slavers in all the Sudan.

Whenever reports surface these days of slaving by the Sudanese Army, the government denies it, and usually they're right. For the most part, it's not the regular army which goes on slave raids, it's the Popular Defence Forces, which on paper means a force something like our National Guard, but in the bush means the Beggara.

The Nubi

These ancient people of Upper Egypt and the Sudan are well-known as the great *bowabs* of Cairo, tending their jobs as doormen with an alert efficiency much less evident in Egyptian fellahin, and making the lowly post of doorman into one of some power, commanding the respect of diplomats from Berlin. Likewise, these same Nubians, with deep roots along the Nile, have become the bowabs of the Sudan; master gatekeepers of power, intrigue and resurgent Islam.

But it's in the bush, dry-sucked and fly-blown, that the desert wellsprings of Sudanese fanaticism gurgle beneath the sand.

Khartoum and Omdurman

Khartoum is still very much the town where Lord Gordon was beheaded in hand-to-hand combat with the *ansars* of the Mahdi. It is surrounded now by huge refugee settlements, originally a mix of Eritreans from the war in Ethiopia and Nilotes from the horror in the south, now just hundreds of thousands of Nilotes languishing in squalor. But Khartoum itself, and Omdurman, were never big cities and they still aren't.

The twin cities are at the junction of the White and Blue Niles; it is from the loop the rivers take here that Khartoum got its name from the Egyptians who were sent down by Muhammad Ali to build it in the 1820s. In Arabic it means "the Elephants trunk." Omdurman is the Sudanese city. In Khartoum, there's Gordon's palace and in its image, the Grand Hotel and myriad churches reflecting the soldiers and merchants who have come here: Roman Catholic, Greek Orthodox, Coptic, Armenian, Maronite. The last time I was through, I even saw an old synagogue, which was shuttered and locked, but not deserted. In Omudurman there's the Mahdi's tomb, and the suq.

Khartoum is a grim place these days. Sudan's hard liquor was always distilled in secret, and probably still is, but beer is gone and Khartoum without its big brown bottles of chilled Camel Beer is like Yankee Stadium without hotdogs.

All that seems left of more congenial days is the nags and they're not doing too well. Jockeys get a dollar a race but betting is now illegal which just seems to add to the thrill in a country in desperate need of some cheap thrills.

In fact the crowd at the Friday afternoon races may be the best look you'll get at the spectrum of Sudanese politics. They hate each other, but they love nags and they're all here: Dinka and Nuer stable hands, followers of Sadiq el Mahdi to followers of his brother-in-law, Hassan Turabi, godfather of the coup which deposed Sadiq. There's even a smattering of Brits in faint shadow of their countrymen who brought racing to Khartoum in 1929...the same years the Muslim Brothers came together.

You'll even find the brothers here. To be sure, betting is *haram*, but that's all right, because the secret police are here too, making sure no one bets.

The Wanderers

When Ethiopia's dictator Mengistu Haile Mariam fled to Zimbabwe in 1991, the Nilote armies lost refuge there. Since then they have lost all the towns they held: Juba, Torit, Kapoeta and Pochala between the Nile and the Kenya frontier, and far to the west, near the Central African Republic, the settlement of Wau, forever in and out of rebel hands. When I landed there it was in Sudanese hands, but just barely. In fact we only went to Wau because disaffection had forced the cancellation of all regular flights in and out of Malakal. The only way we could get back to Khartoum was by hitching an unscheduled flight and the only unscheduled flight that came through was an old Dakota flying five hundred miles the other way, to Wau. The pilot never would tell us who had chartered him, but the very fact of the charter was telling.

Wherever we went through the Sudd, we were told that people were burying gasoline. Somebody had chartered this old Dakota just to get one single fifty-gallon drum of *avgas* from Khartoum to Wau, some 800 miles southeast, a round trip of at least 2000 miles, airfield to airfield.

The boys who grow older in the towns instead of leaving seem to never grow out of the pain. Not long ago, as word of fracture within the rebel movement was spreading, a soccer game between the boys turned nasty. Relief workers say there is virtually no crime among these boys, no theft; these are not Britain's football goons. The game ended with a hundred children seriously hurt and one of them dead.

Today, many towns are inhabited by ghosts. On the outskirts, haggard Sudanese troops peer nervously out of shot-up quarters; in town, living corpses, flacid flesh hanging limply on bones, drag themselves through the streets. No males older than nine or younger than 60. Holes dug to hide scraps. A lithe 12-year-old girl, starving, wanders the streets at 3:00 a.m., woken by the smell of bread secretly baked: Bread is now baked in secret, long before dawn.

Here are the wanderers. They had families. They were pastoralists. The boy, as young as five or six, no older than eleven, was likely out in the halfa grass tending his father's great long horned cattle when there was a sudden deafening concussion, a flash of orange from over where the village was, and then he watched as the village disappeared.

These wandering populations are made up exclusively of boys between five and eleven because boys older than that are killed and the women and girls are taken as slaves.

To the Muslims of the North, they are *kaffirs* living a primitive life in the malarial vastness. Indeed these impossibly tall, blue-black Nilotes live a primitive life.

Standing on the edge of a precarious pirogue, a Dinka can keep his buck-naked body so perfectly still, aim his spear so precisely, that when just the right shadow passes through the muddy water seven and a half feet beneath his intently focused gaze, the family has lunch. But his real pride is his cattle: After puberty, the boys live in cattle camps which are themselves an apparition. Coming out of hot, thorny scrub, you are suddenly in a realm of smoke about which tall gaunt wraiths wander totally naked, white as ghosts.

In fact, the smoke is to drive off mosquitoes, and the boys are white from ash which likewise discourages bugs. On closer inspection you notice that the boys keep the camp immaculate, even down to the dirt on which it stands, swept almost as clean as they sweep their mud-floored *ronadavels*, and they sweep these immaculately indeed. But it is a ghostly sight nonetheless, and all the more so as bits and strands of the unraveling horror drift into Kenya and Uganda.

There are entire villages now of motherless boys who have wandered for months across hundreds of miles of the south, eventually coming together, then drifting across a border. Many are convinced they are being punished by God. A relief worker tells of a boy who draws a gayly colored picture of a woman on the wall of his hut. "It's his mother," his friend explains. "She isn't here."

Somalia

How do you describe the difference today between the two largely lawless Somalias? Only one makes the news—the southern half, which is to say that part of Siad Barre's defunct Somali Republic which was formerly Italian Somaliland. The northern half, formerly British Somaliland, barely makes the news and is sometimes portrayed as considerably more peaceful.

Well...it has been able to get itself sufficiently together to call itself something, namely 'Somaliland.' For some reason, the world continues to refer to "Somalia," as if there is actually a country by that name. The south is simply lawless territory inhabited by Somalis. Unlike the south, the north has had something of a government—the government of Somaliland—since the fall of Barre's republic, and even, at times, a head-of-state.

That said, it must be noted that while there is something of a country that calls itself Somaliland, it's the sort of country where the head-of-state has been held up by bandits, and not too many other countries are rushing to recognize it. But at least its strife seems marginally less insane than the strife in the south, its clans at least marginally more committed to working things out.

The guerrilla force which overthrew Siad Barre in Mogadishu—the Somali National Movement—got its start in the north, and having seen to Barre's overthrow, it has long since gone back to the north. The problem in the north is that the victorious guerrillas turned the government over to an interim president—Abdirahman Tour—who at worst was bent on destroying his own government because he wanted to see a reunited Somali Republic (he has ties to the old Barre regime and to Egypt, which supported Barre) and at best was simply unable to contain clan warfare. In fact, clan warfare began in the north when the president sent armed men from his own clan, the Habre Younis, to seize Berbera, the north's chief port and the turf of the Issa Musa. Already ensconced in the capital at Hargeisa, it now appeared as if he were set. At least for a few months.

Along came an old man now commonly acknowledged to be brilliant, Ibrahim Dhega Weyne. Under his direction, the Issa regrouped and took Berbera back. With that, the two clans repaired to a mountain village where for 17 days they argued fiercely, illustrating their points with long passages of the lyric poetry for which the Somali language is known. When it was all over, they kissed and hugged.

The Dr. Schweizer's of lore live in isolated compounds of sanity at the far ends of rivers along whose fevered courses the quality of mercy has been strained so thin it can swim with the crocodiles and the E. coli. The compounds of the aid outfits still struggling in Mogadishu don't really defy the cliche. It's dry here, not dank, and it isn't a river at the end of which you find your compound, just a dust-choked street. But it's Africa with a vengeance: On this street, abstract forces like evil meld quickly into less abstract forces like greed and instantly into totally nonabstract forces like Belgian assault rifles: As you approach the compound's high white walls, a teenager's eyes challenge, demand and insult all at once. A rifle slips from his shoulder, then slips back.

Nowhere in the world have I felt the predatory menace you feel on these streets.

On paper, the property in the particular neighborhood I was visiting belonged to a once-privileged clan, the Murusade. By the terms of *force majeure*, it belongs to a heavily bandoleered clan named the Habr Gedir. A couple of weeks before I approached the compound on this street, a gunman had slipped in the gate, pulled a mechanic out from under the Land Cruiser on which he was working, and shot the man in the head. Now a visitor must bang on the heavy steel plate of the gate. A peephole slides open and you slip through a small gate within the gate.

The Scoop

All is not well. Somaliland's primary problem is not getting recognized. Jockeying still goes on. The clans have resolved to stop fighting, but the country is bankrupt, people sometimes get desperate, there is little money to run their shadow of a government and under these circumstances, it is not always easy to control the kids in technicals. But it is not Mogadishu. It appears much more governable, and at some point, the world's government, which has an ingrained resistance to sanctioning devolution, may have to recognize Somaliland.

The Players

Muhammed Farah Aideed

Muhammad Siad Barre, the President of the Somali Republic whose excesses finally undid him, was a protege of Egypt and of Boutros Ghali when Boutros Ghali was in Egypt's Foreign Ministry. When Barre's man Aideed became Barre's enemy Aideed, Boutros Ghali, understanding the exercise of power, targeted Aideed. He worked against him before the U.N. intervention, and it was during his tenure as Secretary General, with his men ensconced in Mogadishu, that he allowed the U.S. functionaries to get so worked up over Aideed that they shifted the focus of the U.N. mission there. As Boutros Ghali looked on, the U.S. went after Aideed, with results whose disastrous character can only be compared to those of the old Khedive during the grab for Africa.

The U.S. never got Aideed, and when on March 2, 1995 the Somali walked onto the airstrip as U.S. Marines did rear-guard duty for the retreating U.N., Boutros Ghali was in Vienna, speaking to military scholars. His message, as it was rendered in the next day's *New York Times*: "...the hopes for a new international order that blossomed at the end of the cold war [have] evaporated."

His latter-day Khedive, you can be sure, will not evaporate so easily.

The Habr Gedir

The Habr Gedir are only one Somali clan and not necessarily the most important, even though they are the clan of Muhammad Farah Aideed. They are players only because they represent the extent to which clans in general, and the past in general, can be such powerful players throughout the northeast of Africa. Aideed is a smart, powerful warlord.

Aideed's driving ambition is to forge a Somali state. When his U.S. pursuers boasted of getting so close to catching him that his bed was still warm, reporters invited into that 'still warm' sanctum found Thomas Jefferson on the bedside table. But this is not merely a man who as head of the Habr Gedir clan is unable to accommodate other clans. Within his own Habr Gedir, vicious infighting has erupted between extended families.

Djibouti

The port of Djibouti lies irretrievably midstream in the Great Rift Valley through whose narrow channels humanity has rushed since its very beginning with such highly channeled pressure that even today it's easy to see. To the northwest of Djibouti, the rift is marked by a hellhole of bleach-white salt and jagged black basalt called the Danakil Depression, dropping to 200 feet below sea level, routinely hitting 120 degrees Fahrenheit, the sort of turf which anywhere else on earth would be uninhabited but is in fact inhabited by a people whose nastiness is the land's equal. One measure: The Danakil, also known as the Afars, are Muslims, with their own sultans, yet the simple fact of their existence, at the foot of the Abyssinnian highlands, was a major factor in protecting the Copts of the Ethiopian Empire as successive waves of *jihad* swept out of Arabia and across the Sahara.

It could be that their only match in nastiness are the Somalis on the opposite bank of the rift.

The Republic of Djibouti, formerly the French Territory of the Afars and the Issas, formerly French Somaliland, is a state whose original reason was for no more than the colonial convenience and ambition of the French. So far from being a true nation, it is a state which bottles up in a boiler maker these two terminally nasty people, the Danakil and the Somalis, and more specifically, those Danakil known as the Afars and those Somalis known as the Issa.

Earlier in the century, French Somaliland seemed a sorry wannabe; a vestpocket of desert which wasn't even Somali compared with the vastness of the British and Italian Somalilands. But the very national homogeneity of the British and Italian colonies made them natural candidates for decolonization. Meantime, the very weaknesses of Djibouti, it's size (who was going to make a big issue out of this little place?), its lack of national homogeneity (grant independence? to whom? Afars? Issas?) and its lack of any reason for being (aside from French strategic and commercial interests) have come together to make the third-place French the only-place French.

Pro forma independence was granted and on paper, it doesn't even look so bad. Those to whom rule was conceded can win elections.

But most of this territory was and remains the desert turf of the Danakil. The Issas here have become mostly urban people and therefore more numerous than the Danakil who rule most of the surrounding desert.

The result? The supposedly ruling Issas are dependent on the French Foreign Legion for protection from ambitious foreign powers and from the territory's own Afars, and on French capital to finance the French enterprise which is its sole reason for being. So guess who really runs Djibouti.

And what do you think the likelihood is that today's Danakil are any less intransigent than the Danakil of history?

The year before American newspapers were reporting the dispatch of U.S. Marines on their mission to rescue tens of thousands left starving in what was once Italian Somaliland, Reuters was reporting that the President of Djibouti was flying to Ethiopia to discuss border clashes with 'Ethiopians' who had cut the rail link between Addis Ababa and the port of Djibouti.

Translation: This was not and is not a conflict with the new government in Addis. The Afars live in Eritrea and Ethiopia as well as Djibouti and the diplo-speak which constricts both diplomacy and news reporting renders the Afars who cut the line as

'Ethiopians.' The fairly routine diplo-trick in play here is the effort of a ruling regime (in this case the Franco-Issa rulers of Djibouti) to portray an internal problem as an external problem.

As the president flies off to speak diplomatically with the foreign power he's blaming, the French chopper's off to squash the Afars.

For several months it works as it has always worked. In other words, things are bad enough that the U.S. State Department must issue travel advisories warning Americans to "defer nonessential travel due to guerrilla activity." There's a grenade attack in the city that kills a French child, there are reports filtering into town of nearly a quarter million refugees stranded in the desert by fighting and facing starvation, crime in town gets bad. But nothing that threatens French control.

Then starvation in the countryside around Mogadishu gets so bad it attracts world attention. Both the Foreign Legion and the force of French Marines in Djibouti dispatch troops south to help the Americans. And it starts to become clear that the French forces left in Djibouti are stretched thin—and to expose the danger which lies just under the surface here. There is fighting almost everywhere outside the city and inside town, crime gets so bad that police sweeps round up as many as a thousand at a time. At one point, seaborne Danakil sent rocket-propelled grenades raining down on the city and out of town the government admits it is having trouble securing the road to Tadjourah in the north. At last the French return from humanitarian work they relish among the starving Somalis far to the south and get back to their grim task in Djibouti.

Things return to normal. Roads are more or less secured, but government ministers are attacked when they visit Tadjourah and police are regularly killed on the road.

The Scoop

A lot of spooking comes out of this part of the world. It's easy to believe that both the Somalis and the Afars are terminally vicious, and there is no doubt that this is dangerous country. That said, talk gets out of hand and that is itself dangerous. For example: early explorers made much of the vicious reputation these people had before they arrived and it remains an attention getter. Reporters and travel writers still routinely describe the Danakil as those people who must present their brides with the gonads of an adversary recently killed in combat. The Afar themselves are never quoted denying this yet they do deny it. This doesn't mean Afar brides don't ever get nicely wrapped gifts of gonads, but it does mean that among other dangers to watch out for here is exaggerated talk. And never mind that this is exactly how the French would describe our account of Djibouti.

Ethiopia

Beginning with the end of World War II, one Abyssinnian tribe after another revolted against the ancient rule of the Amhara ensconced in Addis Ababa. Many of these revolts, if not most, eventually fashioned themselves Marxist, but the victory of the Marxist Dergue over Haile Selassie in 1974 was no victory for these peoples. The Dergue was largely Amharic. It was a continuation of Amharic tyranny in Marxist garb.

Real victory didn't come until the Eritreans defeated the Ethiopian Army south of Asmara in 1991, sending their revolutionary protoges in the province of Tigre on a march to Addis which could have only one result. With their arrival at the city gates and with the fall of the Dergue, came a euphoria in which all things seemed possible...quickly followed by the frightened distrust of all, even slightly alien peoples, which is shot through each of the many peoples of this land, each deeply distinct, deeply traditional, anciently, rigidly structured.

For a true outsider, the human array is downright bewildering, but there is less chaos than first meets the eye. For a traveler in such dangerous parts, there's grief to be sidestepped and reward to be won, in taking a closer look.

Ethiopia's Tigre people come from a northern province named Tigre, there are many Tigre in Eritrea, as well, and in both Tigre province and Eritrea, Tigre people are characteristically Coptic Christian. That in itself shouldn't be hard to keep straight except that there's a wrinkle which makes all of this hard to keep straight: The Tigre people of both Tigre province and Eritrea have a language of their own, and there is a language called Tigre, but the language, Tigre, is not the language of the Tigre people.

The Tigre people of Tigre province and most of the Tigre of Eritrea, are native speakers of a language called *Tigrinya*. Tigrinya's relative, Tigre, is the native tongue of most of Eritrea's Muslim tribes...and a few of its Tigre Copts.

It's only confusing at first. There are so many tribes, peoples and religions in Ethiopia, that at first the picture seems so crowded with detail that nothing stands out in relief. These linguistic differences add the shading which provides the relief. Tribes who seem at first distinctly similar are revealed to have distinctly dissimilar tongues, and most likely dissimilar roots. Tribes which seem distinctly different are revealed as not so distinctly different after all.

The panoply of nomadic Muslim tribes from Port Sudan through Eritrea, Djibouti and the Somali steppe share so much besides religion, from food to music to their handsome mocha features that, at first it's hard not to picture them as variations on a single people. Likewise, the customs of Abyssinia's highland Copts in Tigre and Eritrea are highly similar to those of the highland Copts further south around Addis, their Christian faith virtually identical.

The Afar language spoken by the fierce Afar Muslims of southern Eritrea, northeastern Ethiopia and Djibouti (which was once called the territory of the Afars and the Issas) belongs to the linguistic group called Hamitic. Likewise, the language of the Afars' enemy, the Somali Issa, and of all the other Somali tribes, and of the virtually Somali Galla of Ethiopia, is Hamitic. Likewise the language spoken by the ancient Egyptians was Hamitic.

Without drawing any conclusions at all (a dangerous business indeed), it's worth recalling all those mellow, Somali-looking faces limned on the walls deep within the pyramids of ancient Egypt, and the ancient Egyptian tales of Punt, a land which could have been either the Somali coast, the Eritrean coast or both. It's worth recalling, as well, the reason linguists call these tongues "Hamitic."

Ham was the son of Noah; the Bible tells us it was Ham who begat the people of Africa. The most recent linguistic research challenges the old concept that Hamitic languages are strictly African; they're now lumped in a group called "Afro-Asiatic." But Africa is where you go to find Hamitic languages.

Noah's son Shem, by contrast, was the father of all Semites. Hebrew, Arabic and Amharic are all Semitic languages; Amharic is the language of the Coptic Christians whose long rule of Ethiopia came to a momentous end in 1991. The Coptic Tigre who led the revolution, also have ancient roots as rulers in Abyssinnia, but they are nonetheless distinct from the Amhara, with their own Semitic language, Tigrinya.

Meantime, among the seemingly similar Muslim nomads of Eritrea, only the Afar, sprawling across three countries, speak a Hamitic language. Only one small tribe claims Arabic (the lingua franca through much of the Horn) as its native tongue. A few share Tigrinya with the Coptic Christians of Eritrea and Tigre. And the first language of most of the rest of Eritrea's Muslims is Tigrinya's relative, Tigre. In short, these Semitic-speaking Muslim tribes have more in common with the Copts of Eritrea and Ethiopia than at first meets the eye and less in common with the Hamitic-speaking Muslims of Ethiopia and the Somali steppe.

The Scoop

This is not combat as usual in Ethiopia. Ethiopia could actually come out worse, virtually destroyed as a nation. But there seems a genuine effort by almost everyone to arrive at a consensus for all Ethiopians and meantime, trouble has not gotten out of hand. Ethiopia today is a dangerous place, but hardly the most dangerous place in the Horn. If it survives the struggle, it will emerge a stronger nation than the brittle empire held together by Haile Selassie and the Dergue.

Meles Zenawi

The man who lead the revolution which overthrew centuries of Amharic rule in 1991, Meles Zenawi, is Tigre. Tigreans, with the help of heavily Tigre Eritrea, had spearheaded the revolution. There was fear among other peoples that Amharic tyranny would simply be replaced with Tigrean tyranny.

The Amhara were especially apprehensive. To the outside world—indeed to most Ethiopians— Tigreans and Amharas are a picture in similarities: both, anciently, the rulers of Abyssinnia, both Coptic, both speakers of Semitic tongues. The Amhara knew differently. Arabic and Hebrew are also Semitic tongues; after years of war, Ethiopians who spoke the Tigrinya of Tigre were getting along with those who spoke Amharic about as well as Arabs get along with Israelis.

Fortunately, Zenawi had credentials which impressed the other groups. He even managed to win the confidence of at least some Amharas.

Having been plucked from Tigre to board at the Brit's Wingate School in Addis, where he won honors both as a student and a card shark, he spoke Amharic. During the war in Tigre he had challenged the dictatorial chief of his own Tigrinya-speaking front, took over the front and eventually formed coalitions with other ethnic groups, especially the Oromo.

When Zenawi was a kid at the Wingate School, a volleyball game with Oromo students had turned into a brawl which didn't end until leftist students from Haile Selassie University rushed over, broke it up and delivered a stern lecture on the evils of tribal fighting. Zenawi was impressed and later, as a pre-med student at the university, he was impressed by Meles Tekle, the editor of the student journal, *Tigil*; in English, *Struggle*.

Before he could complete his studies, he was 'in the field,' as the Eritreans say, a guerrilla back home in Tigre province. He hadn't been there long before the leftist Dergue back in Addis killed his leftist hero, Meles Tekle. Until then, Zenawi's name had been Legesse Zenawi. From then on it was Meles Zenawi. All that mattered, on June 21, 1992, the date the victorious revolutionaries had set for national elections. International observers hadn't been especially happy with procedures leading up to the election. But they were highly impressed at the turn out; it was in the tens of thousands Zenawi himself had gone from *kebele* to *kebele*—poll booth to poll booth—disguised as an ordinary citizen to gauge the mood.

The observers were convinced of the authenticity of Zenawi's victory. They were impressed with his performance at a press conference afterwards, confidently answering tough questions which would have landed reporters in jail had they been asked during any previous regime. And since then, Ethiopia's government, heavily composed of former Marxists, has put members of the Marxist Dergue on trial for the murder of Haile Selassie, the enemy against whom they both had fought.

But the euphoria is long over. The days in which everything seemed possible have shifted to days in which it sometimes seems as if nothing is possible, trying even the nerves of a card shark.

Does Zenawi address reporters in Amharic? So what, say many Amhara, who fear that his emphasis on self-determination is destroying Ethiopia's sense of nationhood.

Had he once fought side-by-side with Oromo? So what, say members of the Oromo Liberation Front who feel he is not granting enough self-determination.

It has gotten so bad that under terms of a treaty penned by the winners after the revolution, the Eritreans (who desperately want to sell their war materiel to raise cash for reconstruction) have had to send armed brigades into Ethiopia to intervene as peacemakers in outbreaks of frustrated combat between the new Ethiopian Army and the Oromo. In a few instances, they have actually had to fire on the Oromo—a choice so uncomfortable for both parties that the Oromo leadership barely complained about it to the Eritreans.

Eritrea

Sharifa's Story

The first time I heard of Sharifa, I wondered if she were real. Her tale was so perfect. She couldn't be. She had to be.

Then I heard the story again, and then again. Three sources; real story. And then months later I heard it yet again. The ring of myth was beginning to attend Sharifa. Sometimes her name wasn't even Sharifa, and with each telling her beauty became more storied. As if the women of Abyssinnia are not beautiful enough as is and as if her story would be any the less were she not beautiful.

Regardless, a story with a life of it's own is a reality in its own right and this one is Eritrea, through and through.

When I was there, way back in 1968, she must have been about three. Twelve years later, she was her father's pride, about 15, with an ability to maintain her modesty and flash her eyes at the same time, dressed always in the gauzy folds of brilliant white and brilliant color, turquoise, yellow, orange; colors characteristic of Muslim women in this part of the world. Tattoos graced her forehead; she was laden always with hand-hammered jewelry, some of it washed in gold, some of it 14 karat.

Her father, a widower, was not a vastly wealthy man, but he was a merchant in a part of the world which is anciently mercantile and where, anciently, women have been walking banks, wearing much of the family's wealth as jewelry. Of course, it's a man's world. Sons, especially first sons, are what count. But Sharifa's big brother had frustrated, even humiliated, their father. He'd rejected his family responsibilities, his inheritance, had run off to fight a war that was clearly unwinnable.

At least he had Sharifa. Second only to a father's pride in his eldest son was his pride in a beautiful, marriageable daughter, bedecked in jewels which spoke of family status, of a father's accomplishment, of security.

Unmarried daughters may have been seen as burdens for some; for Sharifa's father, she represented security even more than her jewels. She stood for home and family as much as impetuous young sons stood for the insecurity which was everywhere. Sharifa was a daughter of substance, exhibiting with schooled perfection the well-known modesty of Muslim women in public, exhibiting just as clearly (at least for her father), the less well-known power a strong woman can wield within the family. His male world, after all, was itself largely one of competing, bargaining, feuding families. Fathers put themselves at the center of those families, but in each one, it is a woman who is the essential element.

Sharifa was an astute questioner of the details of her father's all-male palavers, an active mind focused always on the family; she had in effect replaced her brother as her father's point of pride.

It was a scene full of timeless qualities, set in a part of the world which often seems timeless. The proud, well-to-do but vulnerable merchant father, the almost predictably rebellious son, the female as an anchor in a sea of troubles.

The one element that isn't timeless, of course, is the specifics of the prodigal son's defection. There's nothing timeless about Soviet tanks.

Of course, he put it all in what he called "revolutionist" terms...which don't quite stand the test of time. The reader would recognize it for the propaganda it was and likewise, my callow gullibility for what it was. In fact, it's probably best to leave the arguable details of their war with Ethiopia to the Oxford Companion to World Politics, whose entry on the subject was written by an Ethiopian scholar:

> *With its defeat in World War II, Italy relinquished its legal right to its colonies to...France, the United Kingdom, the United States and the Soviet Union [to] dispose of...by agreement, failing which they would submit the matter to the UN General Assembly. Libya's and Somalia's cases were determined without much ado at the UN; Eritrea proved to be difficult, principally because of Emperor Haile Selassie's interest in acquiring it, and U.S. strategic and geopolitical interest in the Red Sea region. The convergence of these two interests and the dominant U.S. position sealed the fate of Eritrean self-determination.*
>
> *Instead of gaining independence, as demanded by the majority of its inhabitants, Eritrea was joined with Ethiopia in a lopsided federation...imposed by a U.S.-engineered resolution. Eritrean protests were ignored by the UN, which bore responsibility for the integrity of the federation. Finally, emboldened by the impunity with which he had violated the UN arrangement, Emperor Haile Selassie abolished the federation in 1962...*

Sharifa's Story II

I've never seen a massacre, and with luck I'll never see one: in Vietnam, Eritrea, the western Sahara, Iran, Lebanon and the southern Sudan, I've seen mute evidence, heard stories, but I'm reluctant to repeat them. What can I really know of them? Talk is cheap. Suffice it to say that sometime near the end of the seventies, when Sharifa was fifteen and her father's pride, her village suffered a massacre.

We don't know who they lost. We just know that while her father kept functioning, he apparently went days unable to talk. He must at some point have felt rage as well as grief but when he did speak, he saw the war no differently. It was foolishness. This was Ethiopia. Even counting Eritrea's Christians, they were at best three million barely armed men, women and children against the tanks and bombers of a nation of 58 million.

And beautiful Sharifa? She witnessed her father's grief, but showed none, and then one day her father came home and she was gone. Where? "We're not sure," her sisters said. "She left most of her jewelry."

"Where?" her father repeated.

"To join the revolution."

In a rage, he gathered up two men, three camels and galloped into country he'd never dared enter and found her at a training camp, about to be inducted. He insisted she return. She refused. He raged that this was no fit enterprise for a woman; it was indecent. He grabbed her. She pulled back. He called her a whore. He said she was no longer any daughter of his. He demanded her remaining jewels. She ripped them off and threw them at him. For the past fifteen years, they had spent every day of their lives together. They were not to see each other again for another fifteen years.

Sharifa's Story III

By the time young Sharifa reached the field at the end of the seventies, a lot had happened. The Muslim-led Eritrean Liberation Front I found in Kassala had become the Eritrean People's Liberation Front. After barely surviving a spate of internecine bloodletting, it was now run primarily by Tigrinya-speaking revolutionaries like Kidane, but with Muslim recruits like Sharifa joining, as she would put it, "by the tens."

In the year after Haile Selassie was deposed, the Front had virtually won the war, with its troops occupying major towns and even entering the capital. Then again it had suffered brutal losses as the Soviets and Cubans intervened massively for the Dergue. Then came hunger as the Ethiopians pursued a scorched earth policy which international aid agencies, in need of Ethiopian approval to move relief supplies, felt constrained to portray as "drought." Then came famine, as the Ethiopians used food as a weapon, refusing to let relief through to Eritrea.

But they survived and now they were rebuilding, yet again, but this time they were building something more.

No longer heavily Muslim, the Front no longer had the appeal it once did for Arab backers, but it still had some. Meantime, the force it was fighting was fat with Soviet hardware, which meant that after most engagements, more Soviet hardware was carefully inventoried in the bush warehouses of the Eritrean Peoples Liberation Front.

The likes of Kidane Kiflu are now credited with enormous organizational and logistic talent. To Ethiopian pilots flying Northrup F5s, MiGs and Antonov bombers, the ground below looked barren; deserted by a population on the run. When I was with them, it was indeed barren. But this was Sharifa's time. Laboriously hidden from view in country with virtually none of Vietnam's notorious jungle cover was all this:

Machine shops.

Munitions factories.

Motor works.

Fuel depots.

Truck yards for tractor-trailers and tanker trucks whose drivers made routine nightly runs cross-country, off the road, over hostile turf.

Hidden warehouses of stolen materiel, artfully inventoried for efficient access.

Hospitals in caves, staffed by young Eritrean surgeons and internists trained largely in the U.S. and Italy. Hospitals complete with operating theaters, intensive care wards, maternity wards, infectious disease wards, rehabilitation wards in which amputees were forever busy making artificial limbs, processing paperwork, issuing orders.

But more than all that, in a part of the world long-maligned for its bloody-mindedness, home of the baboon, the hyena, the cutthroat clan-bandit, and after a trying contest that had pitted Muslim Eritrean against Christian Eritrean, they were forging some wildly diverse people into a unified nation.

Right through the war, western intelligence experts who were convinced that Eritrea's Copts wanted to be part of Coptic Ethiopia and that its Muslims wanted to be part of the Sudan, simply refused to believe what was happening, and they can't be blamed. Here indeed was a people ready to die for their God, their tribe, their clan, their family, maybe even for the ancient Empire of Ethiopia. But for Eritrea? What was Eritrea besides a short-lived Italian colony, populated by dozens of tribes anciently antagonistic to each other, with virtually no national or religious coherence?

In fact, tiny Eritrea is so diverse that it may be more representative of the Horn of Africa than any other country. In the vastness of the Somali steppe and along the Somali coast virtually everyone is Somali, save a few Bantu who are farmers…and for that matter can be found farming along the Red Sea coast of Arabia. The Sudan, of course, is richly diverse, and in the south has a large population of blue-black Nilotes, many of whom have given up their river gods for Christianity. But the Sudan's diversity is spread over yawning territories and it is an indelibly Muslim state. Likewise Ethiopia has many Muslims, but is an indelibly Christian place. Eritrea has all the variety of these much larger places, even a few Nilotes who worship river gods and it sits perched between the Horn's Muslim and Christian worlds.

This makes for an interesting place to write about, but it does not make for a nation; some argue it makes for everything a nation is not.

Go tell it to the Eritreans.

They made Sharifa a forward observer for a mortar crew. It was a shock. She thought maybe she'd be a nurse. She didn't complain.

In all my time in Eritrea, nearly a month from west to east, I saw just one female guerrilla. But nearly a dozen years had passed since then and Sharifa wasn't unique. There were thousands like her.

Part of the reason was vision; leaders like Kidane Kiflu who had made the revolution. Another reason was the men, the rank and file troops, the brothers, uncles, cousins, fathers of these young women, men who would ordinarily never tolerate such disgrace to their women, but now had a special reason not to protest.

They were dead.

This is not the United States, where every year feminists break new ground, but women still do not serve in combat. This is a part of the world where women are confined not just by ancient religious stricture, Christian and Muslim, but are often circumcised, which means considerably more for a young bride than a young boy; it means that her clitoris is cut off. It's a part of the world where it is not rare for a woman to be infibulated, which means her vaginal cleft is sewn tight; pleasure for her man, excruciating pain for her.

When Sharifa joined the Front, the Ethiopian Army was a quarter million strong. There were at best 90,000 Eritreans wearing the uniform of the Front, and so many men had died that almost 30,000 of those troops were young women like Sharifa.

Were most spared combat? Every guerrilla is a combat guerrilla. Every square foot of Eritrea was contested. She must have been stunned: all around her, women, pious young Muslim women, sweating with men, amputating limbs, loading trucks, loading shells into the breeches of heavy artillery, locking and loading in combat.

She was wounded, recovered in an underground hospital, was wounded again, married a guerrilla named Osman, the commander of a squadron of captured Soviet tanks, gave birth to a daughter in the same underground hospital, got a letter from her brother on another front, got a letter that her brother was dead.

Did her father know? She did not even try to write. The 'field' was another world. For most of the guerrillas, there could be no communication with that world back in the villages. These boys and girls did not march off to war. They simply slipped away. In the hearts of their parents each was given a funeral, and she knew that her father was no different. You do not send a child off to serve the duration of a thirty-year guerrilla war and expect him to return; few did. After the war did finally end, there was story after story of elderly mothers and fathers suffering heart attacks when unannounced, their long-dead child showed up at the door. Sharifa knew that she was as much in the world of the dead as her brother.

Still, there were victories. Eritreans in tanks meant a war with front lines, trenches. Liberated zones. She dug trenches and helped administer liberated zones, and here she could see more clearly how the men were responding. There was no shame. They called their young women in uniform "our backbone."

But yet there was an undercurrent. She had lost her long beautiful hair, gone off to war, and everywhere, the men respected her, but it seemed so much the respect they paid the infirm who had gone off to war and lost a leg. In the villages the beautiful young girls in their robes and jewelry looked up with awe at these young women with cropped hair. In this world where girls began losing their marriageability at nineteen, these young women were delaying marriage to serve. Some like Sharifa would marry guerrillas. More often the men she fought with would marry the pretty young things with long hair. Now and then, a guerrilla married to a female guerrilla would divorce her for the genuine article. In one village there was a father so proud of his short-haired daughter in uniform, but he would not let her near his other daughters.

Sharifa's Story IV

The three million souls of Eritrea never enjoyed the support of a great, or even second-rank power. Ethiopia, a nation of 58 million, enjoyed the support first of the U.S. and then of the Soviet Union. As the Soviet Union imploded, the largest standing army in sub-Saharan Africa began to weave like a punch-drunk fighter.

Methodically, the Eritreans closed in. Again, Sharifa was wounded. Again she was in a hospital in a cave, but this time her husband Osman was able to visit. It was spring, 1991. A huge Ethiopian garrison held both Asmara and its U.S.-built airbase, out of which the Ethiopian Air Force was now flying constant bombing runs. An Eritrean force swung around to the south of Asmara and cut the garrison off, virtually inviting the Ethiopians to commit yet more troops to relieve their men in Asmara.

The Ethiopians accepted the invitation. The full force of the Ethiopian Army, heavy artillery, self-propelled guns, troops in armored personnel carriers, tank brigades deployed on either side of the Asmara Road rolled north, supported by Ethiopian fighter-bombers flying out of both Addis and Asmara.

Osman's squadron of captured, jealously maintained Soviet tanks was called to join the battle.

On May 26, 1991, the battle was joined. Ethiopian fighter-bombers out of Asmara and Addis hit the Eritrean force with air to ground missiles and napalm. The tanks closed in. Inside Asmara, the Ethiopian force deployed to break out and link up with the relief force. It was not to be. When it was finished, more than a battle was over. A 31-year war was over.

The Ethiopian Army was in the midst of a panicked retreat from which it would never recover. Eritrea was free. Osman was dead. Sharifa went home.

There was no way she could call ahead. Outside of Asmara, Eritrea still doesn't have much in the way of phone service. She could only show up, the prodigal daughter, old and tired, with short hair, a daughter and no husband. She told herself she had nothing to be ashamed of. If she was still disowned, so be it.

He was stunned, of course. He didn't say a thing. But as it began to get dark, he moved his belongings out of his bedroom and into the mud courtyard in the back. He said the house was hers. She was the head of the family now. "I was wrong," he said.

In a Dangerous Place: Eritrea

One evening, without prelude and so unexpectedly that for a minute I thought he was joking, Kidane said, "Would you like to meet the freedom fighters in the mountains?" As if he were inviting me to dinner. "A squad could cross the border tomorrow night and be back in three days."

I said I'd really like to but unfortunately, I had this prior engagement...

Years later, considerable numbers of reporters, documentarians and writers were to go behind the lines with the Eritreans, not least the Australian novelist Thomas Kineally, who wrote Schindler's List and who wrote an emotional novel about Eritrea, *To Asmara*. But it would be years before that would happen, years in which the Eritreans would acquire not just tanks and heavy artillery, but much more importantly, jeeps in which to carry we frail vessels called journalists. Meantime, I had just arrived in this distant Sudanese town, barely aware there was a place called Eritrea, which in any case was most decidedly not my objective. Addis was my objective. If I were to go with these people at all, it couldn't just be across the border and back. Back in Kassala, I'd be in the same fix. It would have to be all the way across the territory to its capital, Asmara, from which I could then get to Addis on my own. Which was of course a totally hypothetical notion: I was not about to disappear into some trackless hills with an off-the-wall band of African guerrillas.

Kassala is a backwater town on the Atbara River in the Sudan, a few dry miles from the Abyssinnian frontier. By Kassala the vegetation has begun to get thick. But the town is suffused with the atmosphere of the desert. The train station is out of town. I'd just dragged myself off the slow train from Haiya Junction when suddenly a band of camel-mounted *Bedj* came galloping at breakneck speed across the river and into the town.

In town, along with a clutch of Yoruba pilgrims bound for Mecca, I slept on the floor of one of the outbuildings of the police post; a single-room building devoid of any appointment, save a few straw mats upon which duty officers slept and prayed. A single bald electric bulb burned constantly. And constantly asleep in one corner was Yacoub, trustee and servant, a half-breed with a huge head for which he was nicknamed, an Ethiopian, or at least, they told me, in the pay of the Ethiopians. He was serving a sentence for bomb-tossing. "At who?" I asked. "At the Eritreans," he said. "At the Communists."

I was in no mood to understand. Eritrea was not my objective. My objective was Addis Ababa, and I had a headache: That goes with travel in these parts. It had been hard to get a visa for the Sudan. Americans were being turned down out of hand. Finally, I got a two week overland permit. Now it was virtually expired. In London, the Ethiopian Embassy said I wouldn't need a visa for Ethiopia. They reminded me what an ally we had in Ethiopia; indeed, almost all the military aid we were sending to sub-Saharan Africa was going to the Emperor, commander of black Africa's largest standing army. "You're an American," they'd said; "A visa for Ethiopia is just a matter of picking one up at the border." Now I was at the border. My Sudanese visa was expiring. His Excellency's Consul was hemming and hawing.

It was dangerous to cross there. "*Shiftas*," he said. "Bandits." But just to show what a good chap he was, he'd wire Addis.

It was Thursday. The next day, everything would be shut for the Muslim sabbath. I dealt with the tension by pretending to create options should the answer come back as no.

I met an Indian, a *Hendi*, in Arabic. Did he know the Eritreans? No, he said over instant coffee at this radio shop, but would I photograph his infant daughter? We bicycled through Kassala's suk to his house on some suburban mud flats. I waited in the sitting room as his mother prepared Japanese Kool-Aid and his wife prepared the baby. The sitting room was dominated by a single ornament: a blinking neon 'Sankyo' sign. As I waited, I saw a young Bedj approach the yard with a wooden bowl of fresh milk. At the door he glanced about nervously, almost, it seemed, like a wolf in a kennel, set the bowl down and hurried off without a word. The Hendi's wife appeared with the infant. The child's face had been powdered almost geisha white, her lips and cheeks were rouged and her eyes were made up like the eyes of houris in ancient illuminations from the Sind. I took the photos, drank the Kool-Aid, the Hendi said thank you, and as I was leaving, he said that although he did not know the Eritreans, he did know Hassan mi Jack, and Hassan mi Jack knew the Eritreans.

Hassan mi Jack rented and repaired bicycles, refrigerators and Waring blenders. On the wall of his storefront office, which was also his repair shop, there were two pictures; one of Mao as a young scholar in Kiangsi, another of a female Chinese guerrilla about to pitch a grenade. The man was dark, imposing, heavy, gregarious. On his head he wore a fake leopard turban.

"My name is Hassan mi Jack," he said. "They call me Jack Palance. The Man Without A Gun. Only I have a gun." And he pulled a .38 revolver from the top drawer of his desk.

Did I want to meet the Eritreans? I would meet the Eritreans. Unfortunately, he could not be there to make the introductions, but if I took a table in the central gardens about 9:30 in the evening, they would approach.

The central gardens of Kassala are an overgrown, ragged place, lit at night by lurid yellow neon bulbs, buzzing loudly with the electric hum and whine of nocturnal insects. The great Egyptian diva, Um Kalsoum, hoarse with static, moaned soulfully over two loudspeakers. Small, circular metal tables were scattered about. A small stand served fruit juices and tea. I came early and sat alone with a hot glass of tea. At 9:30 promptly, a young man in a crisp white shirt and black trousers approached. I stood, we shook hands.

"I am Kidane Kiflu," he said in a clear but exotic English, the sort of English you hear from those who seldom hear our difficult language spoken but are especially intelligent and study hard, the English of a bright but provincial Japanese schoolboy. "I am of the Eritrean Liberation Front." Years later, when I learned he'd become more than something of a figure, it wasn't surprising.

We talked of this and that for most of that evening and most of several following evenings. He spoke of how Italian influence was heavier in Eritrea than it was in the rest of Ethiopia; his native province had been an Italian colony since the grab for Africa in the nineteenth century; the Italians hadn't marched into Ethiopia proper until the eve of World War II. On the question of independence, he offered the party line. He asked to see what I'd written.

In those days, the Eritrean insurgency was dominated by Muslim Bedouin like those camel-mounted Bedj I'd just seen galloping into Kassala. Kidane Kiflu was a Copt from the densely populated highlands. His native language was Tigrinya, but he also spoke the Amharic of Ethiopia's rulers in Addis Ababa, and well enough to have been accepted at the University in Addis on a scholarship. Like a fellow-Copt and native-speaker of Tigrinya, Meles Zenawi, now the president of Ethiopia, he'd dropped out to join the revolution. But Zenawi, the man who leads all of Ethiopia in the nineties, was a native of Tigre province just south of Eritrea, and dropped out to fight for the overthrow of the government. Kidane was a native of Eritrea, and for the sake of a distinct and independent Eritrea, this Tigrinya-speaking Copt had made common cause with Eritrea's Muslim tribes.

Six of us left Kassala at dusk, squeezed with a driver and all our gear in an old Peugeot taxi that took off straight out over the desert. There were three scouts—Ismail, Ibrahim and Ali—and two cadres, Abdullah and Abara. We all wore cheap muslin robes over khaki uniforms; the robes to be discarded when we crossed the border. The robes of the scouts also covered AK-47s, what they called Kalatchnikovs.

The cadre Abdullah was slight, just seventeen, a quiet zealot. Abara was a heavy, 30-year-old Copt, a former schoolmaster who seemed to be leaving the meager comforts of Kassala with great reluctance. Neither carried a weapon, save a single suicide hand grenade apiece.

Soon enough the old Peugeot could go no further and we got out and began walking toward the barren mountains of the border. We walked well into the night. Eventually the sound of domestic animals (agitated at our approach, braying mules, bleating goats, the unloved yapping dogs of Islamic countries) indicated a Bedouin settlement ahead. The Bedouin fed us and we slept in their huts. For several hours in the morning, we waited for someone to come with a camel, but he never came. At 5:00 a.m., we left the settlement and climbed further into the foothills until finally we came to a deep wadi. Here we camped, still waiting for the camel. We waited all that day and all the next, changing camps only once, rough muslin robes still over our uniforms.

Abdullah, the young Muslim cadre, dug into the sand of the wadi for water, but found none. Our supply, kept in goat hides and tasting of goat hide, was running low. He and Abara tried to reassure me. They kept repeating the instructions I'd received from Kidane: If anybody asked me who I was, I was to reply simply that I was a student; "Ana talib."

I'd fall asleep in the heat, hallucinate a little, wake-up disoriented, a face in my face asking, who are you?

"*Ana talib.*"

"Who are you!"

"*Ana talib.*" The camel never came. Finally, at dusk on the third day we began climbing on foot. It was hard. We had to hurry. "Hurry," they kept saying. We had to get to the border before dawn. When at last we got to the border it was just dawn. My feet were swollen. Just over the crest of the last mountain of the border chain, Ibrahim took out his binoculars, scanned the great flat Eritrean plain spread beneath us. At first it looked greener than the Sudan behind us. It was studded with green acacia trees. In the dawn light, it even looked cool. The dew was heavy. But on second glance, you could see how flattened the acacia trees were, as if bent to the desert wind. Their branches were stiff and thorny. They were almost miniature trees growing close to the ground and I was to discover beneath them more thorns, barbed ones, that would pierce our shoes and stick to our legs as we walked, so that periodically we'd have to stop and pick them out. And beyond the plain, faint but evident even in the half-light of dawn, you could see another chain. And there would be another, they told me, and another...

It took a day and a half to reach the second chain; still we'd met no one. The whole trip was to take seven days. Four and a half days had passed. We'd barely penetrated Eritrea. The evening of the fifth day, the scout Ibrahim came running back, gesturing, "*Yacoub. Wahid sanaf b'il Abu Shanab.*"

Yacoub, was what he called me, *wahid sanaf* was one squad; soon enough, from just over a rise at the horizon, there they were, seven men, widely dispersed, at the extremities, uniformed riflemen with Enfields, just left of center a man with a Bren gun, slightly to the rear, a native leading a camel.

Neither group quickened pace, though we could see each other long before we met. In our group, only Ibrahim, the joker, was vibrant, the rest betrayed no emotion, though surely they were glad finally to have made contact. Nor did any sign come from the advancing squad, no shouts, no waves. When we were within talking distance, Abara, the older cadre, said "*salaam alaiykum,*" "peace be with you" to which the leader of the advancing squad (older than the rest, middle-aged, moustached, a .45 strapped to his hip, a camel crop in his hand) said "*alaiykum salaam*" "with you be peace." When finally they reached each other, they embraced in a long and formalistic ritual and then we all did the same with each member of the squad, in the same long and formalistic ritual we were to repeat across the breadth of Eritrea, a ritual characteristic of all the Horn and Arabia and to a lesser extent, Arab and Islamic cities; ritualistically repeating questions about the well-being of mothers, fathers, brothers, sisters, uncles, aunts and cousins, all of whom we'd hear were well (whether they were or not). And our mother, father, brothers, sisters? Well indeed, we'd say. And theirs? Well indeed. And again they'd ask of ours. And again, we'd ask of theirs.

Little emotion was shown, but our collective sentiment was close to true joy. It was evening. We built a fire and rested for the night, drinking rancid but wonderful water from whole, untanned hides of goats.

The next morning we set out for the camp of Abu Shanab, this time with a camel to share. As we moved, the scouts fanned out and came back with reports: many people, they said, had heard that a white man was coming. I couldn't imagine where in this barren country 'many people' might be and the notion of a man uniquely white rang as archaic as being called Mr. Jack by Abdullah and Abara. But the next morning, two native runners caught up with us to find out if it was true. Abdullah told me we'd soon be in the camp of Abu Shanab and the day after that, just before we reached the camp, we passed through a Bedouin settlement, fenced by thornbush against unseen predators: jackal, wild dog, leopard. From atop the camel, I could just barely make out the forms of black-robed women as they peered out at us from the shadows of the doorways of their huts.

There were many more natives at the camp than uniformed guerrillas and many camels. Some of the natives wore crude muslin robes but others were dressed like those wild Bedj back in the Sudan, Kipling's fuzzy-wuzzies, with elaborate gold and orange and turquoise robes with leather girdles, leather-sheathed sabres, knives and elaborately saddled camels. All wore their hair in those great fuzzy-wuzzy dos, all carried stout staves. The guerrillas wore uniforms like us, khaki shorts, khaki shirts. All mingled together, in assemblies under trees.

Abu Shanab was a big man with a sergeant-major moustache and a sergeant-major's booming voice. The natives argued loudly among themselves and one had to be led from the meeting by a guerrilla sergeant-at-arms. At this, a nine- or ten-year-old boy in guerrilla uniform and carrying a small Italian carbine, jumped to his feet and began shouting, apparently in defense of the native. Abu Shanab waved for him to be quiet, but he went on. Abu Shanab waved again and the same guerilla sergeant-at-arms dragged the young boy—screaming and in tears—from the assembly. The assembly, which had been laughing lightly, laughed aloud and went back to its dispute.

The boy, it turned out, was Abu Shanab's recalcitrant son, sent to the field with his father by a mother who couldn't handle him.

The next day we left Abu Shanab's camp with a fresh camel and fresh scouts, but things did not go well. We all got sick, and all around us was sickness and death. The twentieth day out of Kassala, thirteen days past schedule, it began to seem we were traveling in broad circles. Abdullah was offended by the question. Abara rubbed his feet and brushed his hair and said something about a battle somewhere, something about helicopters. It was hot.

There are many Ethiopians who honestly believe Eritrea is part of Ethiopia and Americans who see Haile Selassie as a heroic figure who was right to want Eritrea.

There were many knowledgeable Americans who saw the war here as the stuff of devious Levantine politics, clandestine factions, sinister games of cell versus cell. It was hard to argue with all that went on. In one nearly self-defeating episode of internecine killing, the original Eritrean Liberation Front, heavily Muslim, Arab-financed, was subsumed by the breakaway Eritrean People's Liberation Front, led primarily by Tigrinya-speaking Copts like Kidane; in fact, by Tigrinya-speaking Copts inspired by Kidane.

To Americans knowledgeable of all this, I was hopelessly naive. Exasperated, one once looked at me and asked, "Do you really think what you've got here is Emiliano Zapata and his boys?"

I didn't have anything to say so he filled the awkward silence; "Of course, that's reducing it to the absurd, but do you really think…"

In fact, I hadn't taken it as a reduction to the absurd at all. Zapata and his boys was exactly how I saw them and never mind the Levantine moments.

On the evening of that twentieth day, as our latest compliment of scouts (at each guerrilla encampment, a new set would take over) genuflected deeply in the evening prayer (a white spot of sand on their dark foreheads as they rose), it became suddenly and frighteningly clear: We had been traveling in circles. We were supposed to be traveling the northeast, almost precisely in the direction of Mecca. But if the direction we were traveling was truly northeast, then Meccaa would have to be due south, for the guerrillas were facing due south from the direction they had told me was northeast.

Abdullah, the zealot, himself suffering disease, refusing comfort, pushing himself, said nothing. Abara admitted it. "Just trust us," he said.

Within the span of the following week entire lifetimes were lived and ended. Somewhere out there, something vague was happening, and then something not so vague, a battle we didn't even hear, and then its backlash, forever and unexpectedly raking past us. We traveled almost entirely by night.

One evening they told me a runner had brought orders for them to leave me. They introduced me to Hassan, an Arabic-speaking young cadre who would take me to the other side of the town of Keren. Down the slope, by two wounded guerrillas, a female guerrilla, the only one I'd ever seen with them, was helping to pack and saddle a mule. They asked me to give them all my tape, all my 35mm film, all my notes. It was supposedly for my protection, and again they put me through the drill: If I were picked up and they asked me who I was, what was I to say?

"*Ana talib.* I'm a student."

"Just trust us," they said. But they did not watch closely and it was possible to wrap one roll of 35 mm in a sock and to stick the sock in a hip pocket. Leaving the bivouac with Hassan, I turned in the saddle to wave good-bye. The pressure of the 35 mm cartridge in my hip pocket spiked any tendency toward excessive sentiment.

From then on, said Hassan, we'd move exclusively by night. Hassan was a different sort of cadre than Abdullah and Abara. He spoke English hardly at all, only Tigre, a Semitic language close to Tigrinya but more characteristic of Eritrea's Muslims, and Arabic, long the lingua franca here, and that was how we used it. He was quiet, confident, and with the scouts (there were now three), much more the combat commander. And yet, for all that, he carried no weapon, only that single hand grenade.

The first morning out, Hassan led the way up a short pass to an escarpment high above a valley. The valley was vast and much different from the valleys behind. The countryside was green and I could see farms plotted out to a far horizon. From the hell behind; it looked like some fairyland ahead. The descent into the valley was very nearly precipitous. The mule was sure-footed, but often I had to dismount as the trail wound down along ledges that kept disappearing into the face of the cliff.

At the bottom, we were in high grass country. We stopped briefly by a village. The village structures were more permanent here. A delegation came out, there was some nervous negotiation, and one of the village men came along with us as a guide. He led us at a quick pace to a wadi with high grass growing on either side, so that I could not be seen, even atop the mule. We proceeded single file down the wadi, one man behind me, Hassan just in front, the others in front of him, the point man way ahead. We moved about half an hour, when suddenly shots cracked. Hassan spun, waving me back, shouting "Ethiopi! Ethiopi!" My blood left my head, I wheeled about on my mule and galloped back up the wadi. Then, just as suddenly, there were more shouts. "*Agif! Agif!*" ("Stop. Stop.") I pulled up my mule and looked back. Hassan, kneeling, was looking back as well. The shots had stopped. There were still shouts from back down the wadi. It turned out that it was not Ethiopians at all, but another guerrilla squad that had mistaken us for Ethiopians as we had them, and opened fire. We had been approaching each other at the junction of two wadis. As I reached the junction, I saw our point man genuflecting deeply in prayer. Each time he rose, I could see that white patch of sand on his dark forehead.

The night was cold. At the next village there was more nervous negotiation and finally a new guide. As we were about to leave, the new guide refused and we had to wait for another. At least he came, there were some hurried whispers in the dark and we took off so quickly that there was no time to explain, myself atop the mule, galloping up the wadi while (to my total astonishment) the others ran along on foot beside me, keeping right up. As I galloped, the black, thorny branches whipped and cut my face. We were moving fast, too fast, it seemed to me for even these tough men to last. There was no actual panic, but the heavy breathing of the running men, and of my galloping mule, and the quiet rushing slap of plastic sandals on the sand of the wadi, struck a distinct note of hysteria held in hard check.

The branches whipping out from the embankment of the wadi got thicker, the shadows ever more black. There was no moon, hardly any sky to be seen above the suddenly dense vegetation in this near-desert country. Eventually it crowded in so close that there was barely room to move single file and at last we were forced to slow down. Just as I thought the vegetation could get no thicker, we suddenly broke into a large clearing which turned out to be the soggy bed of the Anseba River.

"Halhal," Hassan whispered, "Halhal min Anseba." It was all he needed to say, for he knew that I had learned well enough of Halhal, an Ethiopian combat base, and the name of a major battle that had been fought during the worst of the miseries with Abdullah and Abara, and aside from disease and infection, the reason for those miseries. As we moved through country the Ethiopian Second Division was scouring to find the guerrillas who had attacked Halhal. Though it was the dry season, in the middle of the bed the river still ran, black and deep.

Twice we followed promontories that seemed to lead to the other side, wading up to our chests. It was cold, dark. Both times we had to turn back. The water rushed about my feet as I rode the mule toward the other side. The guide, the guerrillas and Hassan cut in front of me, crossed and scouted up the river. Just over half way, the mule suddenly began sinking into the sandy bottom. She panicked and threw me into the river. I was up and after her, but her panic was compounded as she struggled to pull herself free and sank ever more deeply into the sucking bottom. I was into it myself nearly to my ankles, the water about my waist. She was down to her rear haunches. The others were in front of me, out of sight. I pulled at the mule's saddle. Her eyes bulged. She heaved against the sucking sand. She seemed to be coming out of it. In the cold I began to sweat, and to sweat more. I felt somewhere near panic myself, but looked at that panicked, stupid mule, eyes bulging, inviting disaster even as she was slowly coming free and thought I couldn't be that stupid. In the midst of our mutual sweat and pulling this mountain-nimble animal lurched free with an awkward heave and stumble. Afoot, I dragged her up the Anseba, toward the men, remembered Hassan's whispered, "Halhal min Anseba..." and found relief from the fear and tension in anger. "The idiots!" I fumed silently at my betters. All that noise. Then I discovered the reason for their slight commotion in the dark. They had discovered an orange grove and were delightedly picking oranges. Oranges! The first fresh thing I'd had in twenty-one days; a steady diet of sour milk and gruel finally broken. Sweating, soaking wet, shivering in the cold, we sucked on oranges one after another.

Leaving Anseba and its little jungle, we began once again to climb. Unlike Abdullah and Abara, they were able to tell me what was happening. Now, at last, we were due north of the town of Keren. We'd begun southwest of it. The plan was to circle the town, ending up southeast of it. We couldn't move directly from the point southwest to the point southeast because the turf in between was securely in the hands of reinforced Ethiopian brigades, as was the town. A trip that might have taken a few minutes by car, a few hours by foot, was taking three or four days. Fatigue hit hard at three in the morning. Once again we were very high up. Just before dawn one of the scouts pulled on my sleeve and bid me look back. I looked back, twisting in the saddle. Beneath us, I could see, quite clearly, the lights of enemy-held Keren, the first electric light I'd seen in twenty-one days. Dawn was just breaking as we collapsed, still soaked, on a cold mountain hillside.

The next day was pleasant. It was warm. We spent all day just lying about the hills, a lot like the foothills around San Francisco. We joked, ate some more Anseba oranges. A goat was brought up to us from one of the villages below and we slaughtered it. One of the guerrillas slung his Kalatchnikov over the branch of a tree, and straight-faced I pretended to reprimand him for something every recruit in every decent army is disciplined not to do; if we were surprised, he'd have to stand up to get it. I never imagined myself their superior, but I'd put on their uniform and should have been. He took me seriously. Hassan chewed him out. They'd all been trained not to do that, he said and he told me of his training in Syria, how fortunate he was to have been sent there, how much he'd learned. For example, he said, he'd never before known that eighty percent of the U.S. population was Jewish and that the war in Vietnam was being fought to make money for Jewish millionaires. "And I know it's true," he said. "I've seen pictures of their houses."

In the late afternoon a headman, a copt, came up from one of the villages. We talked, ate another meal and he offered me his daughter in marriage if I settled in his village.

In the evening, I went down to the village to prepare for the night's march. I'd taken off my uniform. I was to leave Hassan and his squad, the last of the guerrillas. From then on the headman would lead me. From then on, Hassan reminded me, I could tell no one who I was or where I'd been. "Who are you?" he smiled.

"*Ana talib*. I'm a student."

The squad followed me down. All day we'd been joking. Now they were silent.

Near the edge of the village, the headman saddled my new mule. It was a nasty beast. It bucked and kicked as he rode it, but finally it settled down. He got off, I got on, and again it began to buck and kick. Finally it settled down and I was about to ride around a hut when Hassan stopped me.

"Not yet," he said. "The men are preparing."

I got down off the mule. Hassan looked around the corner of the hut. "OK. Now." I followed him around.

The squad was standing at attention, their ragged uniforms squared away to the best of all possible efforts. Hassan came to position before them. He called them to present-arms and they brought their rifles up in snappy British manual. Hassan executed an about face and hand saluted. Not knowing quite how to respond, awkwardly, I returned his salute. He called the men to port-arms. I shook his hand and thanked him and we embraced as we had in the desert. With each of the men I did the same. The headman came forward with the mule, I mounted and we left. Just once, I twisted in the wooden saddle to wave back; it was a different wave than it had been a few days before, with that 35mm cartridge in my pocket. It was dusk. They were the last guerrillas I was to see.

As night came, time began alternately to rush at me and slow down to excruciatingly long hours. I lost all sense of it. He moved relentlessly, this old headman. We moved upward through narrow corridors, dark cathedrals of rock that rose forever, echoing every pebble drop. I was barely able to stay awake. I kept slipping from the saddle, waking in rude starts. It was cold, silken webs spread from tree to tree brushing across my face and I was constantly hallucinating—old friends waited for me, perched in trees just ahead; old loves lay dead on the boulders beneath me; jackals barked accusations, howled of my guilt; Ethiopians lay in wait. We moved on, slipping over rocks, through unseen thorned branches that whipped at our faces, down gullies, over boulders, up narrow rock defiles that bruised our ribs as we smashed against them. Up and up, again to high mountains. Finally we stumbled into a village. Dogs yapped. The headman led me to a hut and called out by the thorn fence that surrounded the hut. Two adolescent boys came out. The headman spoke with them and we entered the mud hut, warming ourselves at a small coal fire. The headman was exhausted. He spoke briefly with the boys and then suddenly there was a fight. The headman sprang at one of them and began beating him with his fists. The second boy stepped in and we settled back down by the fire. I was confused, but without the strength to meet my confusion. I just wanted to sleep. For the first time I noticed how much this second boy looked like Kidane Kiflu.

In gentle textbook English, he asked me who I was, why I had come.

"I'm a student," I mumbled, "Ana talib."

"No," he said. "I know who you are. I know why you come. You come for freedom."

The headman disappeared. Just before dawn this boy with the face of Kidane Kiflu woke me up, led me down, down, down to the Asmara road and said good-bye. I stuck my thumb out. Within forty minutes I was atop a semi loaded with tractor tires. An easy hour after that I was in Asmara; high, cool and Italian, where congenial Neapolitans prepared cappuccino with the latest machines.

True to their word, the Eritreans returned all my tape, notes, film. They hadn't even bothered to develop the film. Kidane sent the package, and with it a letter in long hand, in the same exotic English: "Allow me please to convey to you my heartfelt greetings. I hope you have had an enjoyable and not agonizing experience...due to the terranian nature of Eritrea and due to circumstances. I hope to write to you of the latest developments. I saw your article on a Lebanese Newspaper and our people here are startled by your presentation. Please convey Greetings to all members of your Family."

I have said that in the years after I met him in Kassala, Kidane Kiflu became something of a figure. I've also said that Eritrea never commanded much attention in the U.S. Kidane Kiflu became a figure in the small world of the Eritreans and I only learned of his prominence in the course of dry research.

Poring over a propaganda tract mimeographed on pink paper in which the Eritrean People's Liberation Front attempted to explain in dialectic terms why it had been forced to move against the Muslim leadership of the Eritrean Liberation Front, I came at last to the middle of the last graph of the thirteenth page:

"...they placed six members in prison and subjected them to harsh treatment. Further, right in the heart of Kassela they murdered the two revolutionary fighters, comrades Kidane Kiflu and Welday Gidey, who for many years had energetically worked to redirect the course of the struggle. They were under the impression that if they killed these valiant and insightful leaders, the rest could hardly accomplish anything. The dead bodies were placed in sacks and put on a taxi to be transported to a trash dump called Hafera. On the way, however, as if to plead their case to the world-public, the corpses of the two martyrs fell out in the middle of the street."

The Players

Melawes Zenawi

President of Ethiopia since May 1991, Zenawi represents the Tigre-led revolution which overthrew years of Amharic rule. Ethiopia's Tigre people come from a northern province named Tigre, and there are many Tigre in Eritrea, as well. Neither the Tigre nor the Amhara are Ethiopia's largest ethnic group (the Oromo southwest of Addis claim that distinction), but these two groups have traditionally led the country.

The original Abyssinnian empire of Axum was centered in what is today the Ethiopian province of Tigre and the newly independent state of Eritrea. Eritrea's Tigre never wanted to take over Ethiopia. They wanted the independence they have finally achieved. But once they began fighting the Amharic regime in Addis in the sixties, they had good reason to help the unhappy Tigre to their immediate south, who focused not on independence but on getting rid of the tyrants in Addis. Most obviously, trouble in Tigre would make it all the harder for Addis to fight the Eritreans. But there was also a less obvious, more important reason: The Eritreans came to insist on total independence as the only answer for them (a conviction which Addis faithfully fertilized by refusing them any real autonomy) but they knew that under any formula, they would be living in close quarters with Ethiopia, with a vital interest in who ran Ethiopia.

They got what they wanted, and with a vengeance. They not only defeated the Ethiopians on the battlefield and secured the independence they wanted, but they were then able to sit back and watch their protoges from Tigre march on Addis and take it.

Given the skills which these two groups—the diverse Eritreans and the much more homogenous Tigre—developed during their years of jointly organizing themselves against Addis, they could enjoy considerable regional power. Among the Somalis and others, the Eritreans have clearly won prestige as a dividend. Meantime, by sheer force of numbers, Ethiopia is a power house. Eritrea has a population of 3.2 million. Ethiopia's is 58.7 million.

But there's a lot to be done before that happens: Both groups rule countries wrecked by war and they're not getting a lot of help bringing them back. The Tigre's of Ethiopia, having led a revolution whose watchword was freedom must now negotiate and mediate the demands of group after group. On top of this, the Tigre's may have been the protoges of the Eritreans, but Zenawi and his Tigre-led Ethiopian leadership recognize that they and the Eritreans do not have identical interests, and these unsettled days were made for whatever differences they have getting out of hand.

Majid Kamal

When I was working in Lebanon, Majid Kamal was Iran's charge in Beirut; this was during the months that saw the U.S. and French barracks blown up, Hezbollah emerge as a Lebanese party, and the first kidnappings of Americans. There's been a lot of speculation about what role Iran played in all this and little about the role Majid Kamal played.

I have no forestland knowledge except that in the Lebanon I knew before Kamal got there, particularly the civil war years of '78 and '79, the country's Shia were strongly united behind a party called *Amal*, hope in Arabic. *Hezbollah* was a name I never heard in Lebanon until I returned at the end of '83.

Even then, it wasn't yet the prominent capital 'h' party it was to become, had not yet openly challenged Amal as insufficiently righteous in its Shia faith. Often as not it wasn't even *Hezbollah*, literally Party of God, I'd hear pop up in talk, but something like *hezbollahi*, partisan of God. Often it seemed simply a way of describing someone as a diehard, and as the party became more formally identifiable in the months that followed, I did a little start everytime I heard someone identify it as a 'Lebanese' party, because, in fact, I had heard the word *hezbollahi* before 1983, I just hadn't heard it in Lebanon.

Where I'd heard it had been on the streets of Teheran, Ahwaz and Abadan, in the midst of the Iranian revolution.

As it happened, the day the Shah actually left Teheran, I wasn't there. I was in Khartoum, and I remember the day distinctly because the streets exploded in celebration. I'd been coming to the Sudan on and off for almost twenty years, knew what a deeply Muslim place it was, but I was surprised. Source after source had been telling me what a difference there was between Shia and Sunni Muslims, how much more towheaded the Shia were, how much enmity there was between these two prime branches of Islam. The Muslims of the Sudan are virtually all Sunni; those crowds deliriously cheering Khomeini were entirely Sunni.

Majid Kamal stayed on as Iran's charge in Beirut for some time after the bombing of the French and Marine barracks, and the combat in which the Shia militias drove the Muslim brigades of the Lebanese Army out of West Beirut. Eventually, however, he was given another posting—Khartoum.

Sheikh Abd el-Rahman and the Sidewalk Faithful of Islam

The literal meaning of Muslim is one who prostrates himself before God. For all the divisions within Islam, what that means for all Muslims is not so much the craven submission it suggests to Westerners, but humility before the wonder of God, and for the truly faithful, it is a humility which characterizes how they live and deal with people, Muslim and non-Muslim.

By "the truly faithful," I do not mean those who practice a form of the religion inoffensive to us. I mean the intolerant, the planters of bombs and assassins of Sadat. They are at once enormously dangerous and very nice people.

I flew home once from Amman to Cairo and got quarantined at the airport. There was cholera in Amman and I didn't have the shot on my card. It's something you shouldn't let happen. The next time I discovered an expired shot on my card, I broke a ball point pen, inked a quarter, stamped the card, and presto, Thomas Jefferson had pronounced me immune. But not that day. With a clutch of itinerant laborers, I was sent for 24 hours to an isolated camp on the long straight road to the airport. We were each assigned a cement cubicle, eight-by-eight, three or four to a cubicle, then issued tongue depressors. "For feces, for feces, for feces..." said the health official, as he passed them out.

How should I describe our mood the next morning as they began to release us? Grumpy? And that was before we discovered the deal with the cabs.

I was used to paying two or three pounds for a ride to the airport. At this point, we were almost half way into town. I approached a cab, got a big smiling *salaam*, returned a big smiling *salaam*, and asked *bikam*, how much, which really isn't a question so much as a routine precaution against getting taken for a ride in more ways than one. "Den Bounds," the cabby enunciated with great, distinct consonants. With less than a consummate show of cool, I harumphed over to another cab. "Den Bounds." And another. There were no other cabs to be hailed on this isolated stretch of highway. There was only this drift of swine who had come out to snuggle at our pockets.

Then I spotted the cabby with a white skull cap. It was like finding an old friend. In fact, I didn't know him at all. I just knew the skull cap. I didn't even have to bargain. The correct fare and a pleasant ride.

I think it is fair to say they grace Cairo, and they are everywhere. That sort of humility does not respect huge mosques and religious hierarchies dressed out in fancy vestments. A Jew needs just nine other Jews and he has a *minyan*, all that is needed for full, formal worship. All a Muslim needs is a circle of stones in the desert, which you see everywhere in the desert, or a rug on the sidewalk, and you see them everywhere on the sidewalk. Especially on Fridays, you see the faithful and their rugs collected about simple sidewalk preachers, railing against corruption, In particular, they rail against "the Gang of Sons," yet more particularly, against the sons of Hosni Mubarak. If you think Newt's Contract With America was a sweet maneuver, you should see the gang's multiple contracts with Egypt, and with Libya, for that matter. Of course, not too many folks have seen those contracts, but they are said to be sweet indeed, sweet enough to buy the silence of Egypt whenever anyone suggests trial for the killers who brought down PanAm 107. Silence, and off the record, wounded pride; do you really think your $2 billion a year can buy us?

And before the Gang of Sons there was Jihan Sadat, living like Cleopatra on the meager salary of an Egyptian head-of-state.

Just one of those curbside *qadis*, but one who got a little more play in the papers, perhaps because his words bit harder, perhaps because he was blind, and young, was Abd el Rahman. At kiosks all over Egypt, his cassettes sold like the cassettes of the latest pop stars, his blind, homely visage inside the case, so much the humble Egyptian *fellah*. In fact what the Egyptian public was buying was a sort of gangsta rap, but in much deadlier earnest, marketed not to reap profits from thrill-seeking rich kids with marginal wealth to spare, but in simple earnest, to galvanize the street.

It is surprising he was tolerated as long as he was. The acts of terror he inspired in Egypt were at least as clearly incited by him as the World Trade Center bombing, and eventually he did become a wanted man, a distinct and apparent threat to the government of Egypt.

It was the Sudan which took him in, it was the Sudan from which he emigrated to the United States, and when he was indicted for the bombing of the World Trade Center, an official of the Sudanese government was jailed along with him for participating in the plot.

The sheikh, of course, is Sunni. Majid Kamal is a Persian Shia. Nonetheless there is speculation about Iran's role in all of this, speculation easily discounted because we are so used to hearing established powers with homegrown headaches who blame it all on outside meddling, and Hosni Mubarak is forever blaming his woes on Iran and the Sudan and on Iranians in the Sudan.

Without indulging false syllogisms, it's worth noting that Majid Kamal was in Khartoum when Khartoum welcomed the sheikh; that he and those who lead the Sudan look at the west, see decadence, and are equally repelled; and finally, that the Sudan is broke. It owes considerably more than $10 billion. It needs oil desperately.

It isn't easy to say with precision what Majid Kamal has wrought in the Sudan. They say he has chaperoned a massive influx of Persian oil and money into the country, and figured in the organizing of training camps run by Revolutionary Guards, though what this means is also wide open to question. The Revolutionary Guards I saw on their home turf were distinguished more by intemperance than any discipline or training. When we went to Ahwaz on the Iraqi border to look into trouble with the Arabs there, they rammed the back of our cab out of sheer bloody mindedness. When we went to their mosque, we saw a platoon of them leaping from a truck with their Kalatchnikovs hanging loose. Used to seeing trained troops jump with their rifles held firmly in both hands, I looked at their safeties. Half were off.

Issaias Afwerki

Eritrea's head of state is a former military commander much in the mold of Museveni and Kagame, except that his Eritreans were in the business of building a disciplined grass-roots force well before the other two. Indeed, he would be stage center rather than a godfather were it not for, a) Eritrea's preoccupation with reconstruction and, b) the limits which the size of Eritrea's population—just 3.2 million souls—puts on the influence it has won with its victory over the old Amharic regime in Addis Ababa.

However, the moral suasion it won with that victory is considerable, reconstruction is proceeding apace and just one thing seems to stand in the way of Eritrea becoming influential far beyond what its size suggests: the wave of Islamic fire sweeping the entire area, and in particular, Islamic extremists infiltrating Eritrea from the Sudan.

Nuts & Bolts

At various times, Khartoum has been something of a practical jumping-off point, more comfortable even than Cairo, though with hardly the banking, business, diplomatic, wire and photographic services of either Cairo or Nairobi. Today, it might be described at best as a forward jumping-off point. Cairo and Nairobi have always been jumping-off points for the Horn, and today there is no real alternative anywhere within the Horn; though Khartoum could come back, Addis is quite cosmopolitan and Asmara has great potential as a clean, small city with a developed infrastructure and a skilled population.

Elsewhere in this volume will be found a dossier for Cairo and a Nairobi dossier for travelers to Central Africa. This will serve travelers to the Horn almost as well. What follows is practical information on destinations within the Horn. One caution: Recently published material purports to list facilities for travelers in Mogadishu. According to the best available information, these facilities have been out of commission for years. At one point, a businessman closely associated with the warlord, General Mohammed Farah Aideed, opened a hotel for reporters but booking was all done locally and informally and while reporters can keep a hotel in a dangerous place alive, they are notorious for traveling to places like Mogadishu either in droves or not at all, so that any hotel which depended upon them would be alternately overbooked or out of business. Anyone traveling to Mogadishu would best do so under the auspices of a private aid organization with a floor to sleep on, or under the auspices of a warlord.

Khartoum

The level of tension in Khartoum can be measured by the hour of the curfew. Currently it is midnight, which is not as relaxed as it may seem. In most dangerous places with curfews, stragglers are still racing home at least 30 minutes after the witching hour. In Beirut our press passes allowed us to walk home at three in the morning. In Khartoum, the streets are virtually deserted by 11:00 p.m., an hour before curfew.

Hotels

The Grand Hotel, on the Nile corniche, regardless of its state of repair, is just that; grand, with thick, cool walls, fans, high windows, high ceilings, solid floors, starched white tablecloths. With its broad terraces, it sits grandly facing the Blue Nile, at the west end of the complex of the ministries anchored by Gordon's palace.

In marked contrast, its top-of-the-line competitor, the **Hilton** is isolated far out on the Corniche in what seems intended as aloof luxury but is just isolation.

Likewise, the **Meridien**, on Sayed Abdel Rahman, is about as grand as the Fresno Holiday Inn.

Built in the same tedious manner, but a little cheaper and a lot more Sudanese is the **Arak** at the top of Zulfu Street near the meat market, which is about half way between the hotel and the ministries on the Nile.

Tip:

*Like Saigon, Khartoum is one of those towns with open sewers. In such a dry, sunny climate, this is not so bad. But walking from the **Arak** to a ministry, you must remember that the creamy slurry of offal which runs from the market's abbatoir can fill the sewers virtually even with the road, making their surface appear continuous with the road, and if you fail to notice this, as I failed to notice it, you may well sink into this offal, as I did, to mid-calf, showing up for your interview with the minister, as I did, much too redolent of Khartoum.*

Reporters often put in at the **Acropole**, run by an informative Greek on Zubir Pasha Street. At one point, it was bombed by Abu Nidal, but it hangs on.

Given the fact that inflation has been running upwards of 200 percent a year, and a lot of business is done at some risk on the black market (see "Money Trouble"), prices don't mean much.

Food

Most Westerners eat at the hotels, but juice bars and outdoor garden restaurants patronized by Sudanese are good and enjoyable.

The **Grand** serves good standard fare.

The **Meridien** serves bad French fare.

The **Hilton** serves airplane food.

All offer some Sudanese dishes like *bamia* (okra), and *ful*, the mashed red beans which are a staple throughout Egypt and almost everywhere in the Horn. The hotel with the best Sudanese food is the **Arak**.

Tip: Sudanese consulates are given to issuing visas as brief as two weeks. If you don't offer your waitress at the **Arak** a healthy portion of baksheesh up front, before the meal, your visa may expire before your meal comes.

The Arak usually has a supply of *karkedeh*, a cold drink made from red flower petals which is also one of the delights of Egypt but is more common in the Sudan. It has an astringency which is especially bracing in the Sudanese heat.

Beer, of course, is no more in Khartoum. You'll find lots of pleasant juice bars and ice cream parlors with names like **Casablanca** and **Bimbo**.

Getting Around

I have traveled by train from Alexandria to Cairo to Aswan, thence by boat to Wadi Halfa, and from there by train again to Atbara, Port Sudan, Kassala, Khartoum. In fact, there are trains to distant Bahr El Gazal in the west, and schedules...which mean nothing. If you are interested, go to the station in Khartoum North and hang out.

Sometimes it's hard to get a cab, especially during one of Khartoum's many financial crises, when gas is scarce. If it makes you feel any better, outside of Khartoum the situation is incomparably worse. In Khartoum, *matatus* (see "Central Africa") are called **box taxis**.

Photography

Shooting photos in Khartoum has always been socially difficult; now it is especially difficult. For starters, you will need to get a license at the Ministry of Information. There is a photo processor with a lab beneath the Arak.

Embassies

Call first, get directions, then take a cab.

U.S.A.	UK	France
☎ 74611	☎ 70760	☎ 77619
Italy	**Egypt**	**Iran**
☎ 45270	☎ 77646	☎ 78861
Germany	**Lebanon**	**Greece**
☎ 77995	☎ 45057	☎ 73155
Uganda		
☎ 43049		

Visas

Required. Technically, foreigners who stay more than three days must register with the police, and must register with the police whenever they enter a town. In many towns, the floor of the police post is a good place to sleep if there's nowhere else.

Office Hours

Banks

8:30 a.m. to Noon (Note: always closed in the afternoon.)

Ministries

7:30 a.m. to 2:30 p.m.

Post Offices

8:30 a.m. to 1:00 p.m.; 5:30 p.m. to 6:30 p.m.

Addis Ababa

Addis is struggling to recover from the war with Eritrea, but it was always incomparably more the tourist destination than Eritrea's Asmara, and it retains most all of its well-known venues, however seedy some may have become. It can be cheap. More often, for foreigners, it is expensive.

Hotels

The Hilton on Menelik Avenue. A Hilton. $100 plus.

Ghion also on Menelik Avenue. This hotel features bungalows, though hardly of the standard of the bungalows at Nairobi's Norfolk. $20–$40.

The Ethiopia on Yohananes Avenue. Same.

The Waba Shebelle on Ras Abebe Avenue. Same.

Food

Ethiopian food is by now well-known, but Addis offers many options. **Four Corners** is an Armenian restaurant on Desta Demtew Avenue.

Visas

Required. Easily available at Ethiopian embassies.

Daily Life

Addis was always more colorful than efficient, and now it has a war to recover from, so it's not much of a competitor as a jumping-off point. Nor is it a poorly known place with features like Khartoum's alcohol ban, or Asmara's tank-park. It may not hold much promise as a jumping-off point, but it remains the long-established tourist destination it's always been (with a few time-outs for combat). In the past, tourism has earned a lot for Ethiopia. The new regime does not want to lose it and knows that 'no surprises' is key to keeping the goose laying its eggs. Addis is not a frontier.

Asmara

Eritrea harbors much that is exotic, but there is little exotic about this capital. Many of the towns the Brits built in Africa during the late nineteenth and early twentieth century have an uncanny way of looking and even feeling like bucolic midwestern towns built in America during the same period. Broad, clean streets laid out in grids, an agricultural economy, quiet sidewalks, a sense not of the Happy Valley high jinks that made Kenya notorious, but of solid, even stolid middle class prosperity?

Can Italians possibly be solid and stolid? No need to explore that one too far. What matters is that while there has always been a settlement here, not the least a settlement built by the Ottomans, it was the Italians who built most all of this efficient, cleanly plotted little city, and they built it around an agricultural economy which they also built.

Overflowing bougainvillea and espresso machines grace its sidewalks, making Asmara a good deal more pleasant than, say, Lusaka. Asmara, with its sidewalk cafes and flowers and clean streets may be the most simply pleasant city in all of Africa. And with its population of lively, variegated Eritreans, it is hardly a sleepy Kansas town in mid-summer. In fact, before World War II, Asmara's Italian population ran an annual sports car rally that was second only to Nairobi's East Africa Rally.

But it is decidedly not what Zanzibar was like before a later generation of Italians turned that genuinely exotic backwater into an exotic holiday destination. Asmara was not built by those sort of Italians, and fortuitously or not, Eritreans tend to share their no-nonsense approach to life.

It is a city built on business and looks it. Its National Avenue is gracefully palm lined, but it's pretty much a straight, broad avenue. It has an impressive grand Mosque and a Catholic Cathedral, but nothing to draw travelers; they're more visual cues that this quiet little place is no backwater. The nature of the war ruined much of the Eritrean countryside, but the war never really came to Asmara. It deteriorated some but it never fell apart and it always had an excellent infrastructure of sewers, water, phones. And on top of that, it has a population whose skills don't need a lot more demonstration. It could become an efficient jumping-off point.

But it needs work, and what it doesn't have is money. It has a decent airport, but roads in and out are fair to poor to rotten. A rail line which the Turks built from the coast to Asmara to Agordat in the far west is in such disrepair that it may never be rebuilt...and that would be a true pity as it cost a lot to build and traverses spectacular topography.

Something else it doesn't have is class A hotels—and it doesn't need them. To see why, consider two extremes, Egypt and Switzerland. For travelers, Egypt is a cheap country where you pretty much have to stay at a class A or B hotel. Switzerland is an expensive country where standards are so high you can stay in a class C or D hotel that's cheaper than your class A room in Egypt, and would be better as well if it were just a little bigger. Asmara combines the best of both. Quality is hardly up to Swiss standards, but it is very good indeed, and the city is as cheap or cheaper than Cairo.

Hotels

The **Ambasoira** on Dejatch Hailu Street costs $20 to $40 a night. Nothing exceptionally fancy, quality service, bright, pleasant, clean.

Likewise the **Nyala** on Col. belay Haibeab Street.

The Karen is Asmara's answer to Khartoum's Grand. Not nearly as grand, and going to seed, but the city's old colonial landmark nonetheless, and comfortable enough. Price: $5 to $7 a night. I've actually heard of rooms there going for $2, but it's hard to believe. And there are other hotels offering equal value. Naturally, hotels this cheap aren't booked internationally. You have to go, wander around, enjoy. The **Karen** is on Victory Street.

Food

Ful followed the Khedive, but when it got to Eritrea, it achieved its apotheosis. If anything demands the discipline of a chef, it's beans. Egypt's fellah is so dirt poor, what comes in the tin bowl (from a huge, heavy copper urn over a low, slow flame) seems nothing but mashed fava beans, but while he may be poor, he is demanding. No screw-ups. No burned beans.

Just the right seasoning. It's good food. Ascetic as they are, the Sudanese tend to eat ful the same as the Egyptians, and in Eritrea, the *ful* itself is in fact the same, carefully prepared *ful*.

But Abyssinnians are ancient makers of yogurt, and the Abyssinnians of Eritrea have the same fondness for something fresh and green as their cousins across the Red Sea; meantime, they weren't beyond picking up a little of this and that from the Italians. The little enamel-ware bowl of Eritrean *ful* comes with four extras, neatly and distinctly dolloped on top. A little yogurt, some fresh chopped tomatoes, some chopped, fresh, sweet onion, and a little mound of fresh green hot pepper.

It can be had for less than a dollar. And then of course there is all the wonderful food of Abyssinnia with which Americans have become familiar in the last few years. In particular, Eritrea produces major crops of tef, the wheat which is required for the best *injera*. And of course Italian fare. A number of Eritrean restaurants in the U.S. serve mostly Italian food, many Eritrean restaurants in Asmara serve Italian food, and there are still Italians in Asmara preparing Italian fare. One example: the **Cafe Alba**.

Nightlife

Sudanese fundamentalists are said to be infiltrating zealots and Asmara was never known for the prostitution for which Addis is notorious. But this is not Khartoum. There are two night spots: The Mocambo Club and Caravelle Disco.

Getting Around

Cars can be rented. It's hard to say what difficulties there might be. Visit the **Casa d'Italiano**. Somebody there is bound to know what you need to know.

Embassies

Eritrea's constitution isn't even written yet. Many foreign governments are represented there, but the process of setting up embassies is still in flux. Once again, the **Casa d'Italiano** is a good place to check. The U.S. used to have a huge presence here. There was even a U.S. military base, Kagnew Station, whose prime reason for being was a satellite dish which spied on telecommunications throughout this strategic region. U.S. advisors helping Haile Selassie fight the Eritreans were also based here and U.S. Air Force pilots flew transport and training flights out of the air base. Kagnew is now a huge tank-park for war materiel, mostly Soviet gear captured from the Ethiopian Army, that the Eritreans want to sell.

Know anybody looking for a nice, low-mileage T-55 tank?

Photography

Casa d'Italiano. There could be some sensitivity about picture-taking here, too, but nothing like the Sudan. Once some capital gets invested, Asmara is the sort of place which will almost certainly have the skilled labor to offer quick, quality photo-processing.

Visas

Required. Available, for the time being, at Ethiopian Embassies.

Office Hours

Banks

8:30 a.m. to Noon; 3:00 p.m. to 6:30 p.m.

Ministries

What do you say about the office hours of a government whose army still serves without pay? Somebody is always at work.

Djibouti

Don't expect Asmara. For one thing (and most superficially), while Asmara is high, dry and temperate, even cool, Djibouti is one of the hottest, wettest places on the globe and more appropriately compared to the Eritrean ports of Assab and Massawa, which compete for that dubious honor.

More significantly, the mood bears no comparison to the mood in Eritrea and Djibouti is expensive. It is Ethiopian port traffic to Assab, which is ironic since one reason Selassie wanted Eritrea was that without it, he would lose Assab and be cut off from the sea, dependent on French Djibouti. Now Ethiopia has lost Assab...and is using it more.

Hotels

The Djibouti Sheraton. A Sheraton. Expensive: $100 plus.

La Siesta on the Plateau du Serpent. A little cheaper.

Plein Ciel on the Boulevard Bonheure. Same.

The Continental on the Place Menelik. Same.

The Djibouti Palace overlooking the rail yards and the bay. A little cheaper.

Food

There are two Vietnamese restaurants: **Hanoi** and **Vietnam**.

Getting Around

Djibouti is important because this is where you can charter a short flight to that non-country, the Somali republic whose capital is Hargeisa. Check with the Aero Club at the airport. Flights can be chartered to either Hargeisa or Berbera.

Hargeisa

You're on your own, but this is not Mogadishu. The old British Club (this was British, not Italian Somaliland) is now the **Hargeisa Club** and takes guests. Likewise the **Somali Club**.

Berbera

You're also on your own in the officially ungoverned port, but again, the north has not suffered nearly the internecine blood letting, even though the war against Mohammed Siad Barre began up here. The old Khedive is especially palpable in Berbera. There's an Egyptian mosque and an Egyptian fort. Three cheap hotels: **Wabera, Sahel, Saaxil**.

Sudan
★★

The Cauldron of Hate

There is a great seething cauldron of hate fired by the two-headed monster—Love of Allah and Hatred of the Great Satan (the West). Its nexus is in Sudan. Here, young men and women from third-world countries learn how to love the purity of Allah and how to further the cause of Islam by killing, maiming and terrorizing the corrupted servants of Satan. What that means is the moment you decide to get on a plane to Sudan you've become the enemy and are taking a vacation behind enemy lines.

Sudan is cursed not only by its poverty (a per capita income of only US$330), its size (it is the largest country in Africa) and its history of fundamentalist leaders who declare holy war on the West, but it is also crippled by its dubious distinction of straddling the uneasy and unmarked border between the arid, Islamic Arab north and the lush, animistic Black south. These two cultures have never dwelled in harmony and in Sudan they never will. The two tribes continue to battle as the north persists in imposing its political will on the tribal south. The U.N. estimates that the war has caused five million refugees of which one million have starved to death.

Sudan is 70 percent Muslim, 20 percent animist and 5 percent Christian; a bad mix on any continent. Ethnically, it's an even a nastier brew: Sudan is 52 percent Black, 39 percent Arab and 6 percent Beja. The hatred between the north and south has killed more than 500,000 people and driven 4.5 million others from their homes. Even the rebel factions are known for their intolerance of each other. They wage siege warfare against each other, using starvation and terror as weapons of war. The SPLA (Sudan People's Liberation Army) rebel factions have been known to murder international aid workers and will not even guarantee safe passage for relief aircraft in case they may be providing food or medicine for the enemy. The north, with its equally zealous adherence to Islam, threw every Christian missionary out of the southern city of Juba in 1992.

Since Iran has 23 years left on its leases of bases in Port Sudan and Suakin, there are thousands of Iranian soldiers stationed and training in Sudan. There is also an Iranian-funded radio station based in Port Sudan that broadcasts Islamic and Iranian propaganda to Egypt and other Arab countries. Sudan's strategic position and its holy alliance with Iran gives it a powerful presence in the Red Sea and the Horn of Africa. Iran's recent meddling and the resultant civil war in nearby Yemen, might provide a good reason to dust off the Domino Theory formerly applied to Southeast Asia. Iran pays its new friend with oil and military supplies while it receives strategic real estate and full cooperation from Sudan. Sudan also has new lethal exports to pay its militant friend: murder and mayhem.

Some side effects of this new export business include the terrorist attack on the World Trade Center, the murders of more than 210 of the Algerian defense forces by Algerian fundamentalist groups and the continuing attacks on tourists and officials in Egypt. Although a Muslim country, Egypt is considered too soft on Israel and becoming too Westernized.

Sudan is a country known for its unrelenting heat and sandstorms, and its inability to create a stable government or a unified country. Sudan (Jamhuryat es-Sudan—The Republic of the Sudan) was conquered by Egypt in 1820–1821 and was ruled from Cairo until 1881 when a revolt led by the Mahdi, a charismatic self-proclaimed prophet began. The Mahdist revolt succeeded in 1885 and its leaders controlled the region until an Anglo-Egyptian force invaded in 1898. The nation was ruled jointly by Britain and Egypt until 1954, when it became an independent state.

Since then, there has been a succession of military leaders and little relief from overwhelming poverty. In 1972, the Addis Ababa accord gave the south limited autonomy (an oxymoron) that ended the war against the Anyana guerrilla movement. But in the early 1980s, the SPLA was born to fight the same battle. In 1984, Islamic law was introduced and the SPLA began fighting in earnest. The SPLA was supported by Cuba, Ethiopia, Libya and, strangely, by Israel. In 1985 Nimeiri's regime was overthrown in a coup and democratic elections were held. "Democracy" lasted until yet another coup in 1989 brought in the current ruler, General Omar Hassan Ahmad Al-Bashir, in June of that year.

The Ethiopians have had their hands in the pie since November of 1987. Khartoum has also sought the assistance of Iran and Libya, including MIG-25s flown by Libyans. Even Iraqi and PLO (Palestine Liberation Organization) lent a hand by flying bombing missions over the south.

Ethiopia hasn't meddled in Sudan's affairs since the ouster of Mengistu, allowing the SPLA to go on a roll. They almost took the city of Juba in the spring of 1989 when a factional group led by Garang's second in command, Riek Machar, created SPLA/

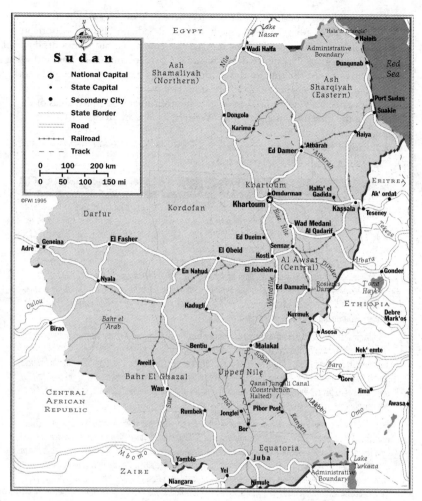

United. The two southern factions began to battle each other. In 1993, the two southern SPLA groups called a truce after killing thousands of each other's members. The CIA is busy working to get the two sides to kiss and make up.

Today, the Southern Sudan is controlled by the SPLA, with the exception of the city of Juba, which is still a garrison town. The Islamic fundamentalist military government of General Omar al-Bashir finally launched its long-awaited offensive against the rebel Sudan People's Liberation Army (SPLA) in February 1994 in an effort to end the 25-year civil war. Tens of thousands of refugees have fled to the Ugandan border.

The government garrisons at Juba, Wau and Torit were beefed up as the offensive began against SPLA positions along the Kit River, the ultimate goal being the capture of the rebel supply base of Nimule on the Ugandan border. The border routes are also used by the international relief efforts to feed millions of starving Sudanese.

The government launched previous offensives in the dry season when troops and heavy equipment can be moved more easily across southern Sudan's marshy terrain. This tactic protects the rebels from major land-based offenses during the wet season.

Sudan was formerly, perhaps the largest recipient of Western aid, but most of that was cut off in 1991 after the government supported Saddam Hussein's efforts in the Gulf War. The Sudanese people now only receive emergency aid from outside relief agencies. Aid workers experience delays regarding travel permits and visas, and sometimes are arrested. At the time of this writing, Oxfam's personnel officer and another senior administrator have been under arrest for two weeks.

Only Islamic agencies are allowed to operate in government-occupied areas of the south since the government claims many Western groups are fronts for Christian missionary work or intelligence-gathering. Dawa Islamia, the largest Islamic aid agency, with close links to the government, withholds food from Christian and animist Southerners until they convert to Islam.

Hard times for El Gordo

Illich Ramirez Sanchez or El Gordo (The Fat One in Spanish) has hit lean times. El Gordo alias Carlos alias The Jackal is officially yesterday's news. The terrorist of the '90s is grassroots, hardened and committed. He will pull the detonator or immolate himself in the name of Allah, not for money. But '80s terrorists, upper class kids who kill, maim and terrorize for fun and profit are thankfully out of style. Just as Sanchez has sold his services for self-interest, he was recently offered as a downpayment from the government of Sudan hoping that the U.S. would see their action as positive and take them off the list of countries that support terrorism. Apparently the U.S. was unimpressed by the importance of Carlos, and the gesture, and continues to deny Sudan international aid due to its continued involvement and support of world terrorism. El Gordo didn't carry any weight after all.

It appears that the most famous terrorist in the world is out of business, a cocky but washed up symbol of the post Soviet world of terrorism. He even managed to outrage his employers when in 1975 instead of executing kidnapped OPEC ministers as planned, he ransomed them for US$20 million. Illich Ramirez Sanchez sits in a Paris jail awaiting what will probably result in a life sentence. Having taken credit for the deaths of 83 people and causing thousands of injuries, it is unlikely that Illich will see the light of day. Many countries would like it that way.

Served up as a pawn by the Sudanese government which asked that they be removed from the list of countries that support terrorism, Carlos was arrested in Sudan on August 14th and sent to France to stand trial. Balding, fat and described as a cigar-smoking alcoholic who liked Johnny Walker, he was arrested after being anesthetized preparing to undergo liposuction (some say a hernia operation) at a military clinic. On the way home he was met by a Sudanese officer who offered to take him to a safe house. There he was bound and tranquilized and flown six-and-a-half hours in a French government Mystere' Falcon 900 to Paris. His nemesis, Brigadier Philippe Rondot, had single-handedly convinced the Sudanese government as to the uselessness of the Jackal.

He left behind his most recent flame, Lana, a Lebanese belly dancer at a local Armenian nightclub. Lana begged to be taken with Carlos and after being denied she flew to his side with US$30,000 in cash. At the time of his arrest Carlos was still married to Magdalena Kopp, a former terrorist with the Red Army faction.

There has been little glamor in Carlos' life. Unremorseful, violent and known as a master of disguise, Carlos was a terrorist for hire with little conscience. Carlos demanded cash and cared little for his client's political rhetoric. His clients included Armenians, the Baader-Meinhof group, the Japanese Red Army, the IRA, Basque separatists and The Popular Front for the Liberation of Palestine. The surrender of goods exchanged for Carlos were French satellite reconnaissance photos of rebel SPLA positions in the south and safe passage of Sudanese troops through the French Allied territory of Central African Republic.

Hard times for El Gordo

Carlos fits in perfectly with the '70s and '80s. Spoiled, rich and almost politically correct, he was able to combine capitalism with Marxism and make money at both. He may have learned how to blend these two bipolar philosophies from his father. Born in Venezuela on October 12, 1949, he was the son of a wealthy real estate developer and lawyer. His father was a Marxist-Leninist who named his three sons Illich, Vladimir and Lenny after Vladimir Illich Lenin. Carlos sought the respect of his Marxist father and his father still rants on about how dedicated, smart and idealistic his son is.

Carlos learned his terrorist trade while training for guerrilla warfare in Cuba in the '60s and then moved to London in 1970 with his mother. He showed his easy grasp of both ends of the philosophical spectrum by gaining a reputation as a free spending playboy while attending the London School of Economics.

Some say Illich picked up the name "Carlos the Jackal" from a Scotland Yard agent who picked the name from Frederick Forsyth's book Day of the Jackal. Others say it was because Forsyth's book was found in Carlos' apartment. Sanchez's known terrorist acts are planning the takeover of the French Embassy in Den Hague in 1974, holding 11 OPEC oil ministers hostage in Vienna in 1975, murdering two unarmed French Secret Service agents and murdering his top aid who he thought was an informer. A third Secret Service agent was shot but survived.

Carlos really didn't get personal until his girlfriend Magdalena Kopp, a member of the Baader-Meinhof gang, was arrested and sentenced to four years in prison in France on weapons charges. He then began a series of bombings on trains and train stations in Europe. When his girlfriend was released the bombings ceased.

Although he has lived in East Germany, Libya, Hungary, Czeckoslovakia, Iraq, Syria and finally Sudan, Sanchez has managed to live well. He was forced to move to Sudan in 1993 after being ousted from Syria. Although he did some work for the Yemenis, he was booted out of Yemen (where he ran training camps) and ended up in Iraq. The Sudanese blamed Sanchez for trying to set up attacks against foreign targets in Sudan without their knowledge. French intelligence sources asked Syria for his arrest specifically to bring him to trial for killing two of their agents and wounding a third in 1975. After a brief stop in Yemen, Carlos, along with a group of other people, entered Sudan using false passports and false names. Sanchez and his group were arrested by Sudanese authorities because "they were not conducting any activity that would justify their presence in the Sudan." The reality is that Sanchez or the Jackal had one more role to play in the world of terrorism: A worthless poker chip played and lost by the Sudan. The lack of customers for his services and the systematic removal of sponsors of terrorism have led to his decline. He even tried to retire and write his autobiography, but no publisher took him up on it. He will have plenty of time to finish his memoirs now.

Actions linked to Sanchez:

1973 Botched assassination of Joseph Sieff, Jewish owner of Marks & Spencer department stores in London

1974 Bombing of a Paris drugstore.

1975 Murder of two French intelligence officers.

1975 Murder of three people and kidnap of 11 OPEC ministers who, after flying to Algeria, netted Carlos 20 million in ransom money

1982 Bombing of Paris–Toulouse train killing five people.

1983 Bombing in Marseille train station killing eight people and wounding 80.

Total of 83 killed and over 1000 wounded.

Sudan has been expelled from the World Bank, suspended from the IMF (and likely to become the first country to be thrown out of the International Monetary Fund entirely since the fund was created) and kicked out of both the Arab Monetary Fund and

Arab Fund for Economic and Social Development. Sudanese experience 300 percent inflation per year.

The Scoop

Sudan is a large underdeveloped country in northeastern Africa. Tourism facilities are minimal. U.S. Citizens are warned against all travel to Sudan because of potential violence within the country. Due to continuing security concerns, the U.S. Department of State has determined that dependents may not accompany employees assigned to the U.S. Embassy in Khartoum. Travel anywhere outside the capital city of Khartoum requires the permission of the government of Sudan.

The Players

Lt. General Omar Hassan Ahmad al-Bashir

This is the leader of the 15-member National Salvation Revolutionary Council, comprised entirely of military officers. Reigning in a state of emergency and with a suspending constitution, al-Bashir has brought Sudan into the swelling ranks of despot-ruled countries in Africa. The people get their news from the daily newspaper of the armed forces. There have been only three periods of civilian rule since 1955. He continues to appoint National Islamic Front (NIF) loyalists who are appointed more for their religious zeal than for political skills. The NIF leader Dr. Hassan Abdullah al-Turabi was the minister of justice and attorney general under Nimeiri and was the architect of both the 1983 and 1991 versions of *Sharia* law. Before the new federal structure was introduced, the *Sharia* laws only applied to administrative and civil cases and not to criminal cases. The first victim of the new *Sharia* law was a Christian southern Sudanese petty thief whose punishment was the "cross-amputation" of his right hand and left foot. Nimeira was said to have fainted while attending his first amputation. Al-Bashir is not so squeamish about carrying out the wishes of al-Turabi's NIF. He is busy battling the 55,000 or so armed Southerners with his 68,000 soldiers.

Dr. Hassan Abdullah al-Turabi

The man pulling the strings. Intelligent, well educated and determined to be the first fundamentalist on his block to have a fundamentalist state. He has described himself as being the symbol of a new movement that will change the history of humanity. His goal is to unify the billion or so Muslims under one guiding theocratic government. He was educated in London and earned his doctorate at Sorbonne in 1964. Five years later, he became leader of what was then a small and fanatical group of religious nuts. Turabi became the head of the Muslim Brotherhood only to be banished from Sudan less than a month later when General Nimeiri's Marxist coup made Turabi's style of religion out of style. Saudi Arabia took him in and the Brotherhood took hold among the 350,000 professional Sudanese working in oil-rich but skills-poor Saudia Arabia. They provided a source of funds which Turabi used to send the brightest Sudanese to Western universities to get their Ph.D.s. The Brotherhood was busy turning out doctors, lawyers, writers and teachers who would then take the message of Islam back to other Muslim countries. They created the Islamic African Relief Fund (now the Islamic Relief Association) to help with the millions of African refugees in sub-Saharan Africa. In the mid 1970s, they created Faisal Islamic Bank to handle the deposits of ex-pat workers in the Gulf States. Islamic banks charge no interest, pay no interest and share profits with their depositors. The bank made loans to small businessmen, taxi drivers and shopkeepers.

After building a strong financial and political base from Saudi Arabia, Turabi returned to Sudan in 1977 as attorney general under Nimeiri's program of national reconciliation with former enemies. In 1983 Nimeiri declared *Sharia*, or Islamic law, after a particularly vivid dream. Turabi was not the force behind the change. Although Turabi is extreme in his long-term plans, he is a moderate in affecting change.

The dramatic changeover did not affect the political climate as much as it affected the financial health of Sudan. Nimeiri instituted the 354-day year; taxes were abolished and replaced with voluntary tithing. Interest was abolished, and the resultant loss of revenue and fiscal chaos plunged Sudan into bankruptcy. Sudan was US$8 billion in the hole and sinking fast. When the government couldn't cut a check for US$250 million, they went into default with the IMF. By March of 1985, Nimeiri blamed the country's slide into debt on the Islamic laws now ostensibly enforced by Turabi. Leaders of the Muslim Brotherhood were removed from political office and Turabi was put in jail. Three months later, Nimeiri was ousted in a coup, and the first thing General Siwar el-Dahab did was dispatch a plane to fly Turabi back from prison to Khartoum. By then, Turabi was head of the National Islamic Front, originally an opposition party. But Turabi, once again, became attorney general. The Muslim Brotherhood was welcomed back into politics. It ran most of the newspapers and businesses and began to build a strong base in the military.

In 1989, the end of the war in Afghanistan released upon the world thousands of hardened war veterans. The Mujahedin were well-trained volunteers from various Muslim countries who had little chance of employment but were well-armed and tempered to a hard fanatic edge by years of hardship in Afghanistan. The warehouses of Afghanistan and Pakistan overflowed with weapons and ammunition the U.S. had sent in to be used against the Russians.

This surplus of Muslim warriors was ready-made for the Muslim Brotherhood. Turabi realized that God had sent him the tools of his next great project. Sudan became a provisioning and training point for the Mujahedin. In August and September of 1993 alone, four plane-loads of weapons were flown in from Kabul. The Arab-Sunni Muslim Brothers even bit the bullet and forged a link with their traditional enemies, the Shia Muslims of Iran. The Brothers began sending men to Iran for training as security officers even though they had sent men to fight Iran in the Iran-Iraq war. Turabi also invited Iran to play in his backyard. This includes use of seaports and training bases for terrorists.

Sudan, like Iraq and Libya, is now an outcast, not only financially (Sudan was removed from the support of the IMF in 1987). Western pressure is actually strengthening the fundamentalist movement. Meanwhile, Turabi has taken up the mantle of the Ayatollah Khomeini; he continues to give lectures, write books and spread the concept of a world Islamic union free from Western corruption. Today, the Muslim Brotherhood has strong membership in Algeria, Egypt, the Israeli Occupied Territories, Jordan, Tunisia and Yemen. It has members in all Islamic countries. Total armed forces in mid-1990 numbered more than 75,700 men in active service.

The Sudanese

Sudanese heads-of-state come and go. You'd think that in the midst of the current Islamic tide, at least Sadiq el Mahdi, leader of the Umma Party (in Arabic *umma* means the Muslim community), grandson of the zealot who took Khartoum from Gordon, could maintain power. He could not. The state seems inherently unstable.

But short of violent revolution in Khartoum, Hassan Turabi and his National Islamic Front will be the Sudan's most focused, coherent power. Not the most popular. Turabi's currency is popular will and public sentiment but he is not the master of a majority, and if he represents anything it is this: The fact, often lost in the west, that Islamic fundamentalism has many faces, and the fact that the Sudan is far from the simple place it is thought to be.

Politics goes back a long way here. The Sudanese were among the first pharoahs. The Sudanese were among the first Christians. The Sudanese were among the first Muslims and to this day they adhere to such a pure and fundamental Islam, and speak its language with such pure distinction (an Arabic which may be closer to Muhammad's than the Arabic spoken in Arabia) that they are commonly reckoned to be Arabs. Indeed, they are an immensely handsome people, tall and grand in their deliberately simple white *jelabas*. But to this imperfect eye they look less Arab, with darker skin and heavier features, than the Bedj tribes of the Red Sea Hills, Kipling's forbidding fuzzie-wuzzies. Regardless, they regard themselves as Arab, they're recognized as Arab, this pleases them to no end, and in the complexity of their feelings toward the *kaffir* (there's another Arabic word; in South Africa today the equivalent of nigger, but coined by the Arabs) can perhaps be found their predisposition for complex politics.

Not long ago in the Sudan there were basically three parties, two of which were religious. Followers of the *khatmiya* sect made up the one which demanded independence most insistently from the Brits and Egyptians. Followers of the Mahdi made up the other; Sudanese just as eager for independence, but with baggage that made foreign governments a little nervous. The secular party was simply a creature of the army that took over the government by force in 1956 because the two Islamic parties were locked in what amounted to Islamic gridlock. Eventually, they were overthrown, but not punished, so in a few years they took over again, yielded again, took over again...

During the sixties, as Marxism swept the Third World and often toppled military dictatorships, in the Sudan it was the other way around. Military governments, swayed by Nasser, moved steadily left, and meantime, in command of the state's propaganda apparatus, they set about cultivating a new generation of Sudanese leaders in their own leftist image.

Often on the outside looking in, the two Islamic parties continued to command electorates, but once elected, they just couldn't govern. The last time around, it was a coalition of the two Islamic parties, star-crossed from the beginning, and once again, the military took over.

This time, though, the military is taking over in the name of rising Islamic sentiment, and backed by a civilian party, the new, highly focused Islamic Front, so militantly religious that Turabi has been virtually able to position the two Islamic parties as secular. This is not an outlandish notion. The Front is militantly Islamic, and though Sadiq el Mahdi is a Muslim through and through, and the grandson of the greatest firebrand of them all, he is nonetheless a couple of comfortable generations removed from the Khalifa's backcountry fervor; and an Oxbridge man, to boot.

But this is the Sudan, and anything this complicated is bound to get even more complicated. While Turabi's Muslim credentials go way back, those of many in his Islamic Front are a lot more suspect than Sadiq el Mahdi's. The reason is that more than a few of these guys are simply the constituency developed by the old military governments, Islamic partisans who were not so long ago leftist, Arab-Socialist, the most secular of Muslim Sudanese, Jerry Rubin in drag as Jerry Falwell.

The Sudan could provide a great case-in-point for proponents of displacement theories. Denied alcohol, constrained to behave with great dignity in the male world, and with even greater reserve should he find himself among proper females, the devout Muslim seems to have developed an incomparable sweet tooth (*helweh, helweh,* sweet, is among the finest of compliments) and along with it, a considerable appetite, sanctioned by Islam, for buying concubines, or seizing them as a prize of holy war. Among the Baggara of Kordofan and the Bedouin tribes of Darfur, raids on the south have always been and still are, part of the year's rhythm; like calving and harvest. The Khedive (as if he cared, it was Britain calling the shots) sent Chinese Gordon, fresh from the Boxer Rebellion to stop it and to raise some taxes while he was at it. With heroic effort he had some modest success, which is to say he made a hell on earth for the Sudanese who love their harems. Throughout history, whenever hell has descended upon the Islamic world, a mahdi would come to redeem the faithful, and so he did, killing Gordon and restoring slavery while he was at it.

Mustafa Mashur and the Iqhwan

The Muslim Brothers, the *Iqhwan*, in conversation simply *aqhi*, "brothers," the Arab world's oldest Islamic party, were founded in Egypt in 1928 and today are a force in Syria, Jordan, the Sudan. Trying to use his riveting personality to transform Egypt, Nasser banned them as reactionaries. Under fire from the Nasserite left, Sadat brought them back to legal life as a counterweight. Today, Hosni Mubarak uses them as a foil to parry the Islamic radicals bearing down on his regime; he pressures them to renounce terror, he makes sure the favors due Islam either go their way or the way they favor.

SPLA (Sudanese People's Liberation Army)

Like the Shilluk and the Nuer, the Dinka are Nilotes, perhaps the tallest, blackest people in the world. For centuries, the Muslim north raided them for slaves, concubines, wives. For decades, they have been so ravaged by venereal disease that many clans are almost totally barren. When we drove overland from Malakal to the heart of the Sudd at Bor in 1979, warriors from a barren Nuer village raided a Shilluk village, carrying off several girls.

The minimum demands of the SPLA are for the abolition of Islamic Sharia law, introduced by Bashir, and the creation of a new constitution. The breakaway faction of the SPLA is calling for the complete independence of southern Sudan. The SPLA is headed by Dr. John Garang de Mabior, a former Sudanese army colonel. He is a graduate of the Infantry Officers Advanced Course at Fort Benning, Georgia and has a Ph.D. earned while Stateside.

Garang's original job was to fight the rebels but he ended up joining them instead. He worked his way to the top of the SPLA mostly because he was on very close terms with Ethiopia's Lieutenant General Haile Mengistu Mariam. He feels that the simplistic principle of Muslim against Christian and Black against Arab is too Western in concept. It is simply a matter of discrimination, which gets in the way of economic development and political power—a raison d'etre echoed by German mercenary Rolf Steiner, who helped the Anya in the 1970s and was tortured, tried and imprisoned for his troubles. The current war is about life for the south not about death for the north. Iran is pushing Sudan relentlessy to create a fundamentalist Islamic state. The fact that the black Africans of the south predate the Muslims of the north is immaterial. The SPLA armed forces are estimated to number 55,000. Support, even clandestine training in the bush, came from Israel and Ethiopia.

Nafi Osman Nafeh

The powerful intelligence chief of the National Islamic Front (NIF, directed by Hassan al-Turabi). He was trained in intelligence in Pakistan and the United States after becoming a member of the fundamentalist movement in the 1960s. Using Saudi money, he created a clandestine fundamentalist intelligence network inside the Sudanese army. He was one of the brains behind the June 1989 military coup which brought al-Bashir to power.

General al-Fateh Orawa

Security advisor to the Sudanese president, Orawa is a member of the powerful Orawa clan. Trained in the United States, Turkey and Pakistan, he worked closely with the CIA in 1985 during the Nimeiri regime to organize the transfer of Falashas from Ethiopia to Israel via Sudan.

General Hachim Abu Said

The director of Sudan's foreign intelligence service. CIA trained, Abu Said served as a senior Sudanese intelligence officer during the regime of Gaafar Nimeiri. He was later employed by Saudi intelligence before taking up service with the new fundamentalist government of Sudan.

Spies

The Horn of Africa is buzzing with spies from the French DGSE, the American Defense Intelligence Agency (DIA) and the British MI6. Regardless of the latest political makeover of this war, there is no denying that a war for liberation between the south and the north has been fought since 1956 when Sudan gained its independence. The SPLA is the latest name under which the south has been fighting. It has undergone a power struggle and the north is content to let the two subfactions try to kill each other.

The government of the north has little jurisdiction in the south. The provinces of Upper Nile, Equatoria and Bahr el Ghazal are controlled by the SPLA.

Sudan is trying to distance itself from Iran. With the recent serving up of Carlos and the flurry of media interviews al-Turabi has given, things may be changing.

Charles Pasqua and the Deuzieme Bureau in the Horn of Africa

This back-slapping Corsican has made good use of his aggressive cultivation of contacts in the Arab and African world. Even before nabbing Carlos, Pasqua was riding a wave of popularity for ordering nightly ID checks of the immigrants surging into France from dangerous places throughout the community, and especially from Algeria. There was even talk of him succeeding Francois Mitterrand as president, and even if that was a long shot for a one-time salesman for the Marseilles pastis, Ricard, it was clear he was boosting the presidential stock of his boss, Premier Edouard Balladur.

Pasqua is most famous for nabbing Carlos, the press hinted that this was a swap—The Jackal for the passage of Northern armored units to the south. Drawing on deep French influence in two of the most corrupt states in Africa, Zaire and the Central African Republic (where de Gaulle's 'noble idiot' practiced cannibalism in the Presidential Palace), Pasqua persuaded these governments to permit the Sudanese Army to cross into their territory with entire mechanized brigades.

The move permitted the Sudanese to deploy for a climactic push on the beleaguered Southerners, and it promised to internationalize the war even beyond Zaire and the Central African Republic. Squeezed from these two directions, many of the Southerners would be cornered in the Nimule theatre at the Sudan's far southern extremity, thus making a player of a man who didn't need the headache, but to whom France was glad to give it. The man who made the man who made France a fool in Rwanda.

The French have a charming capacity to be as frank about politics as they are about sex. We find it hard to believe that in the post-Cold War world, something as craven and pointless as the grab for Africa is on again. Who needs the Sudan? *Beau geste* imperialists out of French West Africa once faced-off against Edwardian Brits down from Cairo over these badlands that neither could ever control, bring peace to, or make any decent use of. Are we still that nuts?

In a dictated memoir published late in the winter of 1995, he confirmed everyone's worst fears about the French in Africa: Indeed, when Felix Mumie, a leader of the opposition in Cameroon, was assassinated in Geneva, it was on French orders. Indeed, many French ambassadors to many a state in France's African sphere have a hotline to the head of state's bedroom. Indeed, many such heads of state have signed blank communiques authorizing French intervention. Indeed, Omar Bongo, president of Gabon, literally had to audition for the job before he got it; in fact, Foccart conducted the interview. Indeed, America is as much a predator in Africa as the leopard. Indeed, France installed Jean-Bedel Bokassa as dictator of the Central African Republic. Indeed, Bokassa called Charles de Gaulle, "papa." Indeed, de Gaulle called Bokassa, "a noble idiot."

Is Foccart the last of his kind? Is that sort of thinking gone from the French Foreign Office? From the Deuzieme Bureau? Have the French spent all these years cultivating that Gallic shrug for nothing? But to be fair, this cynicism is not totally unrelieved. Sometimes they even insist they value common decency and to demonstrate their's, they participate when they feel we're doing something right.

Yoweri Museveni

A reluctant player indeed in this arena. We have already met Museveni as the man who led the epic effort to make a safe place of Uganda. He has his hands full keeping it that way, given the ruin left by Idi Amin and his corrupt successors, and the danger which has always inhabited the dry, sparsely populated badlands which stretch across the north of Uganda.

But that was not the only reason he is a player in Central Africa. He is a player throughout that region because of the disciplined movement he has been able to put together; so unique among the armies of Africa, both insurgent and regular. And so uniquely effective. Paul Kagame, who shocked the world with his lightening victory in Rwanda (even as Muhammad Farah Aideed struggled to control his own clan), was both a product and then a practitioner of that discipline.

If you were a visionary, you could say that Museveni's hand is just what the fractured resistance in the southern Sudan needed as it tried desperately to fight off slave raids and the heavy artillery of the Sudanese Army. The problem with that is that part of the discipline is resisting such visionary excesses. The U.S. government can do so little about the monstrosities going on in the wilderness within a wilderness which is the Sudan, that it seems to cringe every time the subject of the horror there comes up. What could Museveni do about a war taking place on the other side of Ugandan badlands he was already having trouble keeping at peace?

The problem with that problem is that the French are such great visionaries.

Nimule was already a prime venue for western relief to the south. Pasqua was an improbable figure in this role of helping Hassan Turabi, the most powerful Islamic extremist in the Arab and African world, bring his *jihad* against the south to Nimule and Uganda. Pasqua, after all, had roundly criticized the U.S. for giving insufficient support to Algeria's secular government as it tries desperately not to drown in the tide of Islamic passion. Now here he was shaking hands on a deal with Hassan Turabi whose faithful drove tanks. But then isn't that what makes an idea visionary?

France had spent billions on the Hutu regime in Rwanda. Thanks to Museveni and his man Kagame, it was all wasted. The exercise of power requires making people who treat you that way understand that there is a price to be paid.

Getting In

A passport and a visa are required to enter Sudan. The visa will cost Americans $50 and is good for eight days to three months.The Sudanese government recommends that malarial suppressants be taken, and that yellow fever, cholera and meningitis vaccinations be administered. Visas are not issued to those who have previously traveled to Israel. Business visa's require a letter from a sponsoring company in Sudan with full details on length of stay, financial responsibility and references in Sudan. All borders are open but questionable people who enter in the South may experience problems. Expect three to four weeks to process your visa.

Journalists have been known to enter Sudan from the village of Periang, 500 miles northwest of the Kenyan border. From there it is about 100 miles into the Nuba Mountains and SPLA-controlled territory.

Others enter from Uganda to interview pro-SPLA groups and leaders without a passport or visa. Rides can be hitched for little or no money. Bring cigarettes, small gifts and be prepared to meet starvation and disease head-on. There is little to help you tell the difference between freedom fighters and bandits. Both may happily shoot you for your boots or supplies. The trip to the center of Khartoum from the airport is about 4 km. Negotiate and write down the agreed upon taxi fare on a piece of paper before you get into the cab. There is a surcharge after 10:00 p.m. Remember, before you use our taxi tip, 73 percent of the population is illiterate, according to the World Bank.

Those travelers who enter illegally will be prosecuted under Sudanese laws.

Contact the Sudanese embassy for more information:

Embassy of the Republic of the Sudan
2210 Massachusetts Avenue NW
Washington, D.C. 20008
☎ *(202) 338-8565*

Getting Around

Unforeseen circumstances such as sandstorms (April and September) and electrical outages may cause flight delays. The Khartoum Airport arrival and departure procedures are lengthy. Passengers should allow three hours for predeparture security and other processing procedures at the airport.

Only 994 of Sudan's 12,428 miles of roads are paved. The main paved routes are from Port Sudan through Kassala to Shavak, and from Khartoum through Sennar to Malakal. Most rural roads are simple tracks. In the northern part of the country most of the roads are impassable during the July to September rainy season.There is an ancient rail system (with only 40 out of 150 locomotives working) with 3418 miles of track. The rail system links Khartoum with Port Sudan, Kassala, Wau, Nyala, and Wadi Halfa. The Sudan Railways Corporation operates a three-class service including air-conditioned cars as well as sleeping and dining cars. There are 66 airfields, eight with permanent surfaces and four runways over 8000 ft. The main international airport is Khartoum International Airport.

Major airlines flying to Khartoum include: Aeroflot, Air France, British Airways, Egypt Air, Ethiopian Airways, Gulf Air, KLM, Kuwait Airways, Lufthansa, Saudia. Other less attractive carriers include Iraqi Airways, Libyan Arab Airlines, Kenya Airways, Middle East Airlines,Tunis Air and Yemenia. The national airline is Sudan Airways.

In the north, the major attractions are ancient temples and pyramids, and the ruins at Shendi and Karima.

Dangerous Places

Travel in all parts of Sudan is considered hazardous.

The South

Civil war persists in southern Sudan in the three provinces of Upper Nile, Bahr El Ghazal and Equatoria. The most recent phase of the civil war has killed 259,000 people and driven three million from their homes. In 1988, 250,000 died and over four million fled their homes. Sudan is anti-Christian and Zionophobic to the point of psychosis. Iran and Sudan have joined together in declaring *jihad* on the Great Satan, so consider yourself Satan's Fuller Brush salesman.

The West

Banditry and incursions by southern Sudanese rebels are common in western Sudan, particularly in Darfur province along the Chadian and Libyan borders, and in southern Kordofan province.

Khartoum

Western interests in Khartoum have been the target of terrorist acts several times in recent years.

Iraqi Military Sites

Iraqi missiles and fighter planes were positioned in Sudan to threaten the Saudi Arabian Port of Jeddah and Egypt's Aswan High Dam.

Dangerous Things

Fighting

Renewed fighting between Sudanese and rebel forces in southern Sudan is sending 500 refugees a day into Uganda. The bombing and firefights between the Sudanese forces and members of the SPLA can be heard well into northern Uganda.

Terrorist Training Camps

Sudan is considered very dangerous for Western travelers because of the large number of terrorist training bases here. There are Islamic fundamentalist and terrorist training camps outside Khartoum, along the coast and in other nameless places.

Curfews

The government of Sudan has ordered a curfew that is strictly enforced. Persons who are outside during curfew hours without authorization are subject to arrest. Curfew hours change frequently. The U.S. embassy's Consular Section, some hotel officials and local police can inform visitors of current curfew hours.

Hassles with Local Police

Travelers are required to register with police headquarters within three days of arrival. Travelers must obtain police permission before moving to another location in Sudan and must register with police within 24 hours of arrival at the new location. These regulations are strictly enforced. Even with proper documentation, travelers in Sudan have been subjected to delays and detentions by Sudan's security forces, especially when traveling outside Khartoum. Authorities expect roadblocks to be heeded.

Getting Sick

Medical facilities are as scarce as literate Sudanese outside Khartoum. In 1981, the country had 158 hospitals with a total capacity of 17,205 beds. There were 220 health centers, 887 dispensaries, 1619 dressing stations and 1095 primary health care units. Despite the fact that there were 2122 physicians and 12,871 nurses working in the country, you can expect less than one doctor and nine hospital beds per 10,000 people. Don't expect squat in the rebel-held south. Some health care is provided free of charge but your best bet is to have repatriation insurance should you get truly ill. Visitors traveling to the south of the country will need a valid certificate of vaccination against yellow fever. Travelers entering Egypt from Sudan will need to produce either a certificate of vaccination against yellow fever or a location certificate showing that they have not been in a yellow fever area. A valid cholera certificate is required of travelers arriving from infected areas. Malaria, typhoid, rabies and polio are endemic. Bilharzia is also present, and visitors should stay out of slow-moving fresh water.

Nuts & Bolts

The arid north of Sudan is mainly desert with greener, agricultural areas on the banks of the Nile. Crops can only be grown during the rainy season (July to September). The south is mainly swamp and tropical jungle. The most important features are the White and the Blue Nile. The Blue Nile is prone to severe flooding. Mid-April to the end of June is the hot, dry season with temperatures well above 40 degrees centigrade.

The official language is Arabic but English is widely understood. The government is trying to eradicate the use of colonial-tainted English as part of its Islamification. Ta Bedawie and Nubian are also spoken, as are dialects of the Nilotic, Nilo-Hamitic, and Sudanic languages. Evening meals are served around 10:00 p.m. The staple diet is *fool* (beans or *dura*) eaten with vegetables.

Disruptions of water and electricity are frequent. Telecommunications are slow and often impossible.

Banks are open from 8:30 a.m. to 12:00 noon Sunday to Thursday. Businesses are open 8:30 a.m. until 2.30 p.m.. Government offices are open in Khartoum 8:00 a.m. to 2:00 p.m. Sunday to Thursday, and other centers are open 6:30 a.m. to 2:00 p.m. with a break for breakfast. Shops are open 8:30 a.m. to 1:30 p.m. then 5:30 p.m. to 8:00 p.m. Saturday through Thursday.

Note:

Government offices and businesses have been closing on Sundays since 1991 in an effort to conserve energy. The strict Islamic code (the *Sharia*) has been in force since 1991. There is no gambling or alcohol allowed in the north. Individuals who exchange money anywhere other than an authorized banking institution risk arrest and loss of funds through unscrupulous black marketeers. The dinar is the official currency. The new dinar (introduced May 18, 1992) is equal to 10 Sudanese pounds.

Photography Restrictions

A permit must be obtained before taking photographs anywhere in Khartoum, as well as in the interior of the country. Photographing military areas, bridges, drainage stations, broadcast stations, public utilities, slum areas and beggars is prohibited. Sudanese are reluctant to be photographed without their permission.

Registration

U.S. citizens who visit or remain in Sudan, despite the warning, may register at the U.S. Embassy and obtain updated information on travel and security.

Embassy Location

The U.S. Embassy is located at *Sharia Ali Abdul Latif* in the capital city of Khartoum. The mailing address is *P.O. Box 699, or APO AE 09829.* ☎ *74700 and 74611.* The workweek is Sunday through Thursday.

Addresses

U.S. Embassy in Sudan

P.O. Box 699
Sharia Ali Abdul Latif
Khartoum
☎ *74700/74611*

UK Embassy

St 10, off Baladia St
P.O. Box 801
Khartoum
☎ *249-11-70760*
FAX 873-1445 605 ext 239

Sudanese Embassy in Canada

85 Range Road, Suite 407
Ottawa, ONT. K1N 8J6
☎ *(613) 235-4000*
FAX (613) 235-6880

Embassy of the Republic of Sudan

2210 Massachusetts Avenue, NW
Washington, DC 20008
☎ *(202) 338-8565/6/7/8*

Bank of Sudan

Gamaa Ave
P.O. Box 313
Khartoum
☎ *78064*

Ministry of Trade, Cooperation and Finance

Khartoum
☎ *730030*

Sudan Airways Co. Ltd.

SDC Bldg Complex, Amarat St 19
P.O. Box 253
Khartoum
☎ *47953*

Sudan Chamber of Commerce

P.O. Box 81
Khartoum

Dangerous Days

The following days are good days to stay inside due to the proclivity of terrorist groups to generate lethal publicity on media spin days (i.e., anniversary dates).

06/30/1989	A group of officers led by general Omar al-Bashir overthrew the government of Sadiq Mahdi.
04/15/1986	A U.S. embassy communicator was shot and wounded while riding home from the embassy in Khartoum. The shooting was believed to be in retaliation for U.S. air raids on Libya earlier in the day.
05/16/1983	Founding of the SPLM/SPLA (The Sudanese People's Liberation Movement/Army).
03/01/1973	U.S. Ambassador Cleo Noel and Deputy Chief Of Mission George Moore were assassinated in Khartoum during the seizure of the Saudi Embassy.

Dangerous Days

03/03/1972	Anniversary of the Addis Ababa accords that ended the insurgency against the central government and granted southern Sudan wide regional autonomy on internal matters.
07/22/1971	Anti-communist military elements loyal to Gaafar Nimeiri led a successful counter-coup and brought him to power several days after a coup by the Sudan Communist Party.
06/09/1969	The South declared independence.
05/25/1963	The Organization Of African Unity was founded on May 25, 1963. The day is celebrated as Africa Freedom Day. The OAU is organized to promote unity and cooperation among African states.
01/01/1956	Independence Day.

Money Man

Money makes the world go 'round. One of the people who allegedly keeps the fundamentalist merry-go-rounds spinning is forty-something Ussama ibn Laden. Laden is the banker for Muslim fighters in Bosnia, bankrolls Jamaa Islamiya and picks up the tab for Egyptian, Jordanian and Tunisian fighters in the Hassan al-Tourabi's Sudanese militia, as well as for the National Islamic Front (NIF) centered in Lobiod and in the countryside around Khartoum.

Laden apparently made his fortune the hard way, he inherited it. Not content to work with his brothers, he set up a drug trafficking business with the Afghan veterans (the Hisb al-Islami of Gulbuddin Hekmatyar).

He was stripped of his Saudi nationality by the Saudi government in retaliation for his backing of Islamic fundamentalist groups in Egypt and his alleged support of an attack against a Saudi aircraft and the Saudi ambassador to Pakistan.

He previously worked with Saudi intelligence until 1988, organizing and financing the Afghan militants who passed through Jeddah on the way to Peshawar in Pakistan. Having been trained by Egyptian officers, their goal was to fight the Russians with the help of the CIA.

Laden is worth around seven billion dollars. He lives in Omdurman in Sudan.

Tajikistan

Persian Rogues

Tajikistan, after long rules by the former Soviet Union, Persia and Afghanistan, joined with 10 other former Soviet republics to form the Commonwealth of Independent States in December 1991, although it had formally declared its independence in August 1990. In 1991, the republic's communist leadership supported the failed coup against then-Soviet President Mikhail Gorbachev.

However, Tajikistan president, Makhkamov, a communist, was ousted via pressure from pro-democracy groups and the Tajikistan parliament outlawed the Communist Party. But the elections of November 1991 were won by pro-communist Nabiev, who was once head of the local communist party. Communists made-up the core of the new government and began to purge the anticommunist coalition, which was comprised principally of Muslims and Western-influenced intellectuals. The four opposition groups were banned by the government in 1993 and a clamp was put on the press.

Today, the republic is in a state of anarchy. Bitter fighting, lost in the more media-popular wars in Chicane and Bosnia-Herzegovina, continues today between Afghan-

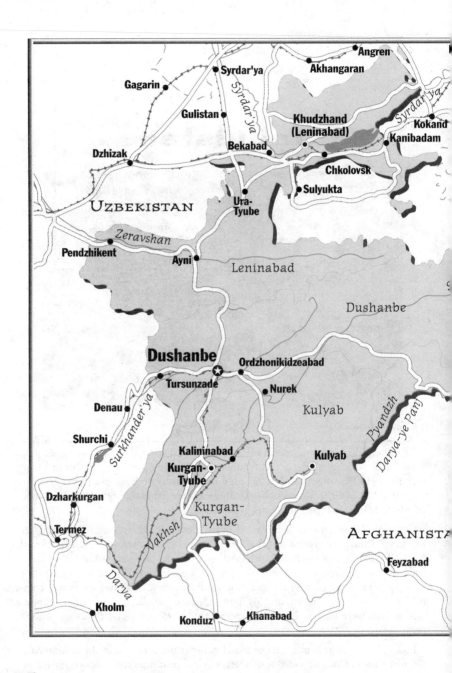

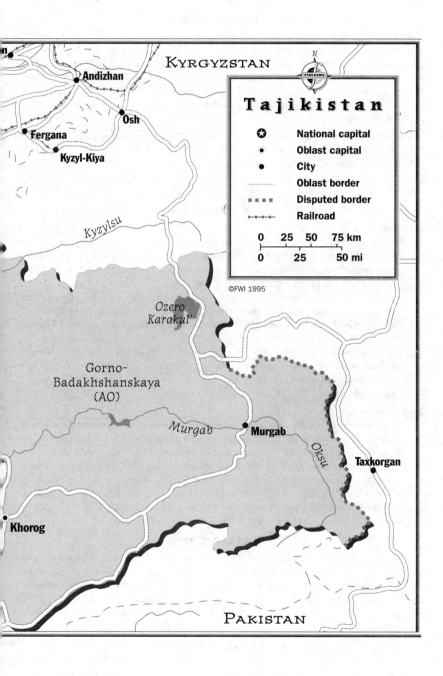

based Tajik Muslim rebels, with the help of Arab mercenaries who are battling Russian troops and taking shelter from the bombs of Russian warplanes inside Afghanistan.

The Scoop

Tajikistan is a nation undergoing profound political and economic change. It is a newly independent nation still in the process of stabilizing its relations with neighboring states. Tourist facilities are not developed, and many of the goods and services taken for granted in other countries are not yet available. There is a curfew in parts of Tajikistan, including the capital, Dushanbe. In Dushanbe, the 10 p.m. until 6 a.m. curfew is strictly enforced at checkpoints staffed by personnel who fire on vehicles that fail to obey orders to stop. These checkpoints operate round-the-clock, and expect adherence to their instructions.

U.S. citizens are warned against travel to Tajikistan. There are terrorist actions in the capital, sporadic fighting along borders, and unsettled conditions in many areas of the country. U.S. citizens presently in Tajikistan are advised to exercise extreme caution and to consider departing because of the deteriorating security situation. The U.S. Embassy in Dushanbe is providing only emergency consular services. The potential for terrorist actions against Americans exists in Dushanbe.

The Players

The Islamic Party

The Islamic Party was overturned in a bloody coup late in October 1992. It continues to battle with Russian troops from its bases in Afghanistan with the help of Arab mercenaries sporting land mines and Stinger missiles. Periodically, the rebels raid Russian border crossings and patrol posts. Seven Russian border guards were killed on August 19, 1994 and 13 were injured in Tajikistan when rebels launched a raid on the frontier with Afghanistan. The Afghan rebels used mainly light arms, but also shelled the border posts with missiles. Russian media quoted the Russian border guards commander in Dushanbe as saying the attack was preceded by two days of shelling from Tajik territory, and from Afghanistan, where the rebels found refuge following the loss in the civil war in 1992. Sources advised that about 500 rebels were involved in the attack and that rebels were stepping up their aggression in order to seize a strip of Tajik territory to announce the creation of a rebel government. The Kremlin has protested formally to Afghanistan.

The Russian Army

There are currently 25,000 Russian troops in Tajikistan, most of them guarding the southern border against attacks from rebels based in northern Afghanistan. Prior to 1994, attacks on Russian officers in Dushanbe were rare. Most of the casualties suffered by Russian forces in Tajikistan have been on the Tajik-Afghan border, where, since 1993, over 40 Russian border guards have been killed. Within a week, four ethnic Russian officers were killed in Dushanbe. While some of these incidents may have been carried out by criminal elements, others could be attributed to the Tajik opposition element who are trying to sabotage Russian-engineered negotiations between the government of Tajikistan and the opposition.

Getting In

A passport and visa are required. Without a visa, travelers cannot register at hotels and will be required to leave the country immediately via the route by which they entered. Visas for Tajikistan are issued by a Russian embassy or consulate. U.S. citizens can contact the Russian Embassy, Consular Division, *1825 Phelps Place, NW, Washington, D.C. 20008;* ☎ *(202) 939-8907, 8911, 8913, 8918* or the Russian Consulates in New York, San Francisco or Seattle for current information on visa requirements.

Getting Around

Travel to, from and within Tajikistan is difficult and unreliable. Currently, the only regular international air travel to and from Dushanbe is a four times weekly connection with Moscow. There are infrequent and irregular charter flights to other destinations. International train connections can be dangerous because of criminals who operate on-board. Travelers to Uzbekistan must have an Uzbek visa, which cannot be obtained in Tajikistan. There is no tourism infrastructure.

Dangerous Places

The Entire Country

Travelers can expect to find checkpoints and, periodically, unsettled conditions in all parts of the country, with the possible exception of the northern region of Leninabad which was spared the civil/communal fighting that engulfed most of Tajikistan in 1992. Travel within 25 kilometers of the Tajikistan-Afghanistan border remains tightly controlled and extremely dangerous due to armed clashes.

Dangerous Things

Crime

There have been serious attacks against foreign diplomats and individuals on main thoroughfares, in broad daylight. Cars have been stolen and houses robbed. The disintegration of local economic conditions, widespread unemployment in Tajikistan, and a less than effective police force are in large part to blame.

Getting Sick

There has been a significant deterioration in the medical infrastructure in Tajikistan with many trained personnel having fled the country. There is a general scarcity of medical equipment and medicines. There is a potential for significant disease outbreaks because of massive population displacement and a partial breakdown in immunization activities. U.S. medical insurance is not always valid outside the United States. Travelers have found that supplemental medical insurance with specific overseas coverage has proved to be useful. Further information on health matters can be obtained from the Centers for Disease Control's international travelers hotline; ☎ *(404) 332-4559.*

Nuts & Bolts

Almost the entire country is mountainous and earthquake-prone, its rivers are sourced in mountain glaciers. But not a lot of helicopter skiing here, folks. More like helicopter gunships. Tajikistan, about the size of Illinois, is bordered by Afghanistan to the south, China to the east, and by Uzbekistan and Kirghizia to the west and north.

Dushanbe, with a population of slightly more than half a million, is the capital. Sunni Muslims comprise perhaps 80 percent of the population. The official and most widely spoken language is Tajik. Currency is the Russian ruble, although American dollars are preferred when they can be found.

Tajikistan is a cash-only economy. International banking services are not available. Major credit cards and "Traveler's cheques" are rarely accepted. Traveling in Tajikistan with large amounts of cash can be dangerous.

Embassy Location

The U.S. Embassy resumed operation in April, but is providing only emergency consular services.

Oktyabrskaya Hotel
#39 Ainii Street
☎ *(7) (3772) 21-03-56*

Dangerous Days

09/10/1992   Declaration of Independence.

09/07/1992   President Rakhmon Nabiyev resigned after Islamic rebels forcefully
took control of the government. The Islamic Party was overturned in a
bloody coup late in October 1992. September 10 is recognized as the
date of Tajikistan's declaration of independence. Islamic rebels have
continued fighting since early September 1992.

12/25/1991   President Bush formally recognized Tajikistan and 11 other former
Soviet republics. On that occasion, he also stated that formal
diplomatic relations would be established with six of the republics as
soon as possible and that diplomatic relations would be established with
the other six (Tajikistan was one of them) when they met certain
political conditions.

12/21/1991   Tajikistan joined with 10 other former republics of the Soviet Union
(which ceased to exist on December 25, 1991) in establishing the
Commonwealth of Independent States. The commonwealth expected
to have military and economic coordinating functions and be
headquartered in Mensk, Byelarus.

02/12/1990   Twenty-five persons died as Interior Ministry troops fired on
demonstrators massed outside the Tajikistan communist party
headquarters in Dushanbe, the capital of Tajikistan. February 12 now is
celebrated as "Memory Day" and an obelisk was unveiled on February
12, 1992 to commemorate the persons who died in February 1990.

Turkey
★★★

The Devil's Thanksgiving

Turkey is a lot like the bird it wasn't named after. There's white meat and dark meat. It's where East meets West. Turkey can be as cosmopolitan as Paris and as depressingly medieval as Iran. Americans know little about this country. Most of our impressions have been formed through Hollywood, particularly by the dark, disturbing movie *Midnight Express*, the harrowing story of a young American arrested for drugs and tortured by his Turkish captors. To many others, Turkey is simply some God-forsaken, giant landing strip for American *F-18s*—a land-based aircraft carrier—a convenient place for allowing us to periodically blow the hell out of Baghdad.

The truth covers a much wider spectrum. Turkey is waging an all-out war against the terrorist Kurdistan Workers Party (PKK), the stated representatives of the ethnic Kurds. Turkey's Marxist guerrillas of the PKK have declared war on the country and attack tourist targets as well as teachers, government workers and other innocent bystanders. They believe that by destroying the infrastructure and hard currency earners of Turkey, they will be ceded their own homeland. The PKK operates primarily in

Black Sea

GEORGIA

...sun
Carsamba
Ordu
Giresun
Trabzon
Rize
Artvin
Kura
Kars
ARMENIA
Vesilirmak
Coruh
Aras
Tokat
Gümüshane
Erzincan
Karaköse
...zilirmak
Sivas
Euphrates
Erzurum
IRAN
Murat
Bingöl
Tuncell
Van
Gölü
Elâzig
Mus
Tatvan
Malatya
Bitlis
Van
Diyarbakir
Tigris
Siirt
Ferr
Adiyaman
Batman
Kurtalan
Maras
Mardin
Hakkâri
Gaziantep
Urfa
...erun
Akcakale
...ya
Euphrates
SYRIA
...NON

Turkey

⭐ National Capital

⦿ Region Capital

● Secondary City

━━━ Primary Road

✜✜✜ Railroad

─── Administrative Border

0	100	200 km
0	100	200 mi

©FWI 1995

Turkey and Western Europe. Its targets also include civilians and government forces in the southeastern portion of the country. They began taking Western hostages in 1991.

Perhaps Turkey's biggest problem has been its long denial of even the existence of the Kurds. Whereas the Kurds' demands as recently as the 1970s had been limited to the government's recognition of their language in culture, rising Kurdish pride and a recognition of their resources turned into vehement nationalism and moves toward independence. Although the Kurdish political parties that formed in the late '70s were illegal, they nonetheless brought huge parcels of Kurdistan under their own control until another period of assimilation began after the Turkish military coup of 1980. Enter the PKK, which, in 1984, not only forced the government to open its eyes to the Kurdish problem, but also the eyes of innocent people who began finding themselves staring down the barrels of AKs.

But not for long.

Incest Is Best

An enraged mob of 200 Alawite demonstrators attacked the Istanbul headquarters of a private Turkish television channel, Interstar, with stones, sticks and shovels after a game show host had suggested that Alawites–an esoteric branch of Islam–practiced incest regularly. The host later apologized and admitted his allegation was merely an uneducated guess.

The Scoop

Although you will hear about "terrorist" activity in Turkey, it would be more accurate to say that—with more than 12,000 people killed since 1984 in violent encounters with the PKK—the situation would be better classified as a civil war. The problem is figuring out who's killing whom. First with a bullet is the PKK, perhaps the most ruthless terrorist group in the world after the FIS in Algeria and the Khmer Rouge in Cambodia. In one five-month period, the army killed more than 1700 Kurdistan Workers Party members and captured 2000 others. In southeastern Turkey, the government troops used to quell the Kurd uprising numbered more than 150,000.

There has essentially been a state of war in southeastern Turkey since the PKK opted for a guerrilla war in early 1984. The conflict became agitated even further by other players getting involved in the fray: the Iranians, Iraqis, Syrians, Armenians, regional warlords, police, private militias and the military joined in the fun. Southeastern Turkey may be the most dangerous place in the world because of its warring neighbors and attempts by the government to portray the problem as less significant than it is.

Although the source of discontent is in the east of Turkey, the most visible terrorist acts have been in the west. The PKK likes to target tourist sites and tourist-oriented facilities in western and Aegean Turkey in an effort to scare away tourists. In 1993, there were seven attacks against tourist facilities by the PKK, injuring 27 tourists. The PKK also kidnapped 19 foreigners (one American) in southeast and eastern Turkey in 1993. During the summer of 1993, a series of bomb attacks in Antalya wounded 26 persons; in Istanbul, a grenade was thrown under a tour bus, injuring eight persons, and a bomb was thrown at a group of tourists as they were sightseeing around the city walls, resulting in six injuries. A hand grenade was found buried on a beach southeast of Izmir, and there were reports of similar incidents in other areas along the west coast. In 1994, PKK bomb attacks were conducted on some of Istanbul's most popular tourist attractions, including St. Sophia and the Covered Bazaar, resulting in the deaths of two foreign tourists. Intermittent terrorist bombings have also occurred elsewhere, including Ankara, the state capital, causing damage to property and loss of life. Some parts of Turkey are currently under the control of the PKK.

The Players

Kurdistan Workers Party (PKK)

The Kurds want their own homeland. Turkey says the Kurds will enjoy the same rights as any other ethnic minority in the country. So the PKK has taken it upon itself to blow people to bits until it gets its dream home. But, considering that Turkey is proud of its long record of assimilating diverse cultures into the Turkish social and political mainstream, Ed MacMahon is unlikely to be knocking on the PKK's door anytime soon. Out of this endless philosophical quagmire comes the largest, best organized and most active terrorist group in Turkey, the PKK. Founded in 1974, the PKK does not represent all 20 million Kurds in the Middle East, but is the best known and most violent advocate of Kurdish independence. Many nonsupporters are marginal sympathizers, though—most Kurds are still miffed that their language was once outlawed in Turkey, and that many were displaced from their traditional homelands in the east to new settlements in the west.

The PKK has declared war on a formidable foe—the tourists—since it feels that income from tourism (US$7 billion a year) funds the Turkish government's war against the Kurds. Despite their tough talk, the 20 or so tourists that have been kidnapped have all been released unharmed. Why? Because frightened tourists make for better interviews on CNN than dead ones.

In southeast Turkey, the PKK is very active, setting up roadblocks, placing land mines and kidnapping foreign tourists. Although, geographically, the PKK should be fighting in Iraq, Iran and Syria, it does most of its warring in eastern Turkey and carries out most of its terrorist activities along the Aegean resort towns and in Europe. In Germany alone, there are more than 450,000 Kurds, about a quarter of the total Turkish population in Germany. The PKK, along with 35 other organizations, was banned by the German government in November 1993.

Westerners can relax slightly because, unlike the Algerian fundamentalists, most assassination victims of the PKK are locals—typically, Kurds suspected of informing on the organization or of not complying with PKK decrees. The PKK has also reportedly extorted money from businesses and professionals not only in Turkey, but from Turkish businesses in Europe. They threaten to kill those who do not contribute "taxes" to their cause. The PKK is a Marxist group now controlled from Syria, where its leader, Abdullah Ocalan, fled when the PKK was outlawed in 1980. Their major source of income is from extorting money from Turkish expats in Europe and fees for safeguarding drug shipments from Lebanon into Afghanistan, Iran and Russia.

Recently, one of the PKK's favorite targets has been electrical transformers. In the latest transformer bombing, which took place in October 1994 in the back of the four-star Buyuk Surmeli Hotel, two people were killed and several injured. The PKK has also bombed Havi supermarkets, which are owned by the Adana municipal government. The city of Adana is divided socially, economically and ethnically in two. In the prosperous and orderly northern half, unrest or disturbance is extremely rare compared to terrorist activity in the poorer, largely Kurdish southern half. Unrest at times is considerable, sometimes escalating into major battles.

There are estimated to be about 8000 armed PKK members. They currently control areas of Eastern Turkey, 3000 of them in mountainous Tunceli province. At press time, elite Turkish commandos were preparing a winter assault on the rebels in the region, using armored vehicles and even dogs.

Dev Sol (Devrimci Dol or Revolutionary Left)

This isn't a surf reverb rock group out of California, but a splinter faction of the Turkish People's Liberation Party/Front formed in 1978. They espouse a Marxist ideology and are intensely xenophobic, virulently anti-U.S. and anti-NATO. Dev Sol seeks to unify the proletariat to stage a national revolution. The group finances its activities largely through armed robberies and extortion. Their symbol is a yellow star with hammer and sickle against a red background.

Dev Sol has conducted attacks against U.S., Turkish and NATO targets but was weakened by massive arrests from 1981-83. Five members, including one of its leaders, were shot and killed in Istanbul on March 6, 1993. Types of attacks include handgun assassinations and bombings, including execution of informers and collaborators. Since its reemergence during the late 1980s, it has concentrated its strikes against current and retired Turkish security and military officials and was responsible for the murders of four generals and nearly 30 police officers in 1991. The police are usually shot while sitting in their patrol cars. Dev Sol also claims responsibility for assassinating two American contractors and one British businessman, an attempt to murder a U.S. Air Force officer, and conducting over 30 bombings against Western diplomatic, cultural and commercial facilities.

Dev Sol is down to several hundred hard-core radicals with several dozen armed militants. Its support comes from Lebanon, with training and logistical support from Palestinian radicals.

While other groups have concentrated their actions in Adana in recent years, only Dev Sol has attacked Americans. In February 1991, the group assassinated an American employee of a Department of Defense contractor outside his home in downtown Adana. The same year, the group bombed the American consulate and other U.S. affiliated organizations.

Despite these attacks, the main targets of these groups are Turkish officials and Turkish government property. In its most recent attack in Adana in August 1993, Dev Sol assassinated the former medical director of a state hospital. Local state banks are a favorite target and have been bombed numerous times. Dev Sol is led by Karatas.

IBDA-C/IKK (Islamic Great East Raiders-Front/ Islamic Retaliation Detachments)

This is the Iranian-backed fundamentalist group that attacks the PKK as well as the Turkish establishment. Their goal is to create a more rigid Islamic state.

Hezbollah

This is where things get complicated. Iranian-supported *Hezbollah* (based in the Bekáa Valley in southern Lebanon) has unleashed a scourge on the Marxist PKK. Imagine a terrorist group that preys on another terrorist group. You would think the Turkish government would be ecstatic, but *Hezbollah* is gunning down Islamic fundamentalists as fast as the Marxist rebels. Thirty-five *Hezbollah* are on trial in a state security court in the southeast on charges ranging from supporting separatism to killing 25 people and wounding 32 others in 39 attacks in recent years around Diyarbakir and Batman. The *Hezbollah* calls on its followers to kill PKK members on sight and is believed to be behind many street murders in the southeast. For a more complete description, see "The Players" section in the Lebanon chapter.

Turkish Workers Peasants Liberation Party (TIKKO)

A small group with a fetish for blowing up automatic teller machines and banks (everyone's enemy) in major cities. What fun.

Kawa

Kawa is a legendary folk hero among the Kurds. The Kawa group was established in 1976 after breaking away from the Revolutionary Culture Association (DDKD), a pro-Soviet Kurdish group advocating uniting all the Kurdish people under the Marxist banner. Kawa's anti-Soviet stance was the reason for the break with the DDKD. Kawa also fell victim to dissension within its own ranks over the teachings of Mao Zedong.

The Army

Turkish military forces (there are over 150,000 troops in the southeastern region) have killed 1700 Kurdish rebels and have captured 2000. A special ops unit under the control of the local governor conducts raids against the PKK. Their utilization of the latest American military hardware (i.e., Cobra helicopter gunships) against the PKK's guerrilla tactics and small arms (AK-47 rifles) gives the conflict a neoVietnam aura.

INSIDER TIP

Stay inside during the PKK's two anniversary dates: August 15 and November 27, as well as on March 21 (Now Ruz, or New Year celebrations). Or get shot.

Getting In

A passport is required. A visa is not required for tourist or business visits of up to three months. For information on entry requirements to Turkey, travelers can contact the Embassy of the Republic of Turkey at *1714 Massachusetts Avenue, NW, Washington, D.C. 20036;* ☎ *(202) 659-8200,* or the nearest Turkish Consulate in Chicago, Houston, Los Angeles or New York. When you get off the plane in Istanbul you need to proceed to the line to the left of the longer lines. You'll know what we're talking about.

If you wish to travel to eastern Turkey, your request may be refused. There are numerous police, militia, army and special ops roadblocks in the area. DP visited the area (see "At Play in the Fields of the Warlords") and can confirm that Turkey is at war with the PKK and is conducting major operations on an almost daily basis. Do not believe any tourism hype about a minor problem with rebels. Certain areas and roads around southeast Turkey are under the control of the PKK.

Getting Around

The authors have traveled extensively in eastern Turkey, both alone and with an armed military escort consisting of armored personnel carriers and commandos using Land Rovers. We consider traveling with a military escort to be the most dangerous way to travel since the PKK regularly ambushes the military. Travel by road after dark is hazardous throughout Turkey. There are currently four groups fighting at night and any one of them will shoot you dead without asking a question. When we were staying in a small village, we were told about a man who set out to fetch his cow on a recent evening. Hearing noises in the dark, the entire town militia began firing their AK-47s and G3s into the dark on full automatic. Luckily, the man was only injured. Road and driving conditions off the main highways and in remote areas are particularly dangerous. A curfew exists from dusk to dawn, so plan your itinerary accordingly. Turkish drivers drive fast but are generally considerate. Buses are common but are subject to lengthy searches at all checkpoints. Turkish authorities expect travelers to cooperate with travel restrictions and other security measures imposed in the east—which means you should get plenty of permission and paperwork before you go.

Ataturk Airport, near Istanbul, is the main international entry and exit point. Turkish air carriers are modern and safe. Ankara's airport is the hub for domestic flights and is about 20 miles from downtown.

Dangerous Places

Eastern Provinces

With the exception of the Mediterranean and Black Sea coasts, travel in Turkey is hazardous—particularly eastern Turkey. Terrorist acts by the PKK continue throughout the eastern provinces. These attacks are not only against Turkish police and military installations but also against civilian targets including public ground transportation. While most attacks have been at night, daytime attacks are increasingly frequent. Over the past nine years, several thousand Turkish civilians and security personnel have been killed in terrorist attacks. In 1991, the PKK began kidnapping foreigners in eastern Turkey to generate media attention for their separatist cause. Over the past two years, a number of foreigners, including Americans, have been held by the PKK and eventually released. As recently as October 9, 1993, an American tourist was abducted by the PKK while traveling by bus on the main highway between Erzurum and Erzincan. Due to the tense security situation, the climbing of Mt. Ararat in eastern Turkey is extremely dangerous, even with the required Turkish government permits. In light of these dangerous security conditions for travelers in eastern Turkey, the U.S. military has advised its personnel to avoid all tourist travel to this region. U.S. embassy and consulate personnel travel to eastern Turkey only for essential U.S. government business, and only with prior approval. In instances where travel to cities in eastern Turkey is essential, air travel is considered safer than other forms of public transportation. As stated above, travel to this part of Turkey should not be undertaken without first consulting the American embassy in Ankara; ☎ *(90) (312) 468-6110* or the American consulate in Adana; ☎ *(90) (322) 454-3774.*

Istanbul

Police presence is heavy at historic sites to guard against any major terrorist incident. However, during August 1994, there were two incidents of terrorism directed at tourists in Istanbul. One group of German tourists was attacked by a young man with a small incendiary device. The other attack involved a hand grenade being tossed under a parked Hungarian tourist bus. In both cases, tourists suffered minor injuries. Istanbul does not have a major crime problem. Typical street crimes (i.e., purse snatchings, pickpocketings and thefts) have been reported in the major shopping areas, tourist sites and around many hotels. The U.S. consulate warns visitors to stay away from nightclubs in the Beyoglu section of the city. Frequently, visitors to these clubs have been subjected to scams that have resulted in a loss of money and, in some instances, physical assault.

Ankara

While Americans living in Ankara on a permanent basis are at some risk of being involved in a terrorist incident, visiting Americans are at significantly less risk. Some minor bomb attacks have occurred at American business offices in Ankara and a U.S. military member was killed in late October 1991 by a car bomb. The climate toward Americans in Ankara is generally positive. Heavily-armed police are a common sight throughout the city. Young Turkish males like to hassle American women. Americans living in Ankara on a permanent basis are more at risk from crime, burglaries to some American residences have been reported.

Western Turkey/Mediterranean and Aegean areas

Expats are at some risk of being involved in a terrorist incident, although visiting Americans are at significantly less risk. However, during the summer of 1994, the PKK conducted a series of hand grenade attacks against establishments frequented by tourists in Antalya, and planted at least six hand grenades in beaches around Izmir and Kusdasi. The Antalya attacks injured both Turkish nationals and tourists, as well as causing extensive property damage. These attacks apparently were directed at financially damaging Turkey's tourist industry rather than causing tourist casualties. Crime against Americans is rare in western Turkey. However, there are continuing reports of pickpocketing and petty theft occurring among the large number of European tourists visiting the Turkish coast every summer.

The Black Sea Coast

The safety and security situation along the Black Sea coast is identical to conditions found in western Turkey.

Dangerous Things

Crime, Muggings and Bar Brawls

There is the usual petty crime against tourists, including pickpocketing, purse snatching and mugging. In Istanbul, incidents have been reported of tourists who have been drugged and robbed in nightclubs and bars, usually by other foreigners who speak English and French.

Americans have been involved in fights at discos, and bar scams involving girls ordering drinks at inflated costs have been reported.

Pavions

There is a certain style of clipjoint in Istanbul and Ankara called a glitter bar, or *pavion*. Many are found around Taksim Square in Istanbul. The pretty ladies you meet will order enough drinks to melt your VISA card. Even if you drink yourself into a coma without the help of a local lass, your eyeballs will roll back in your head when you see the bill. Owners of pavions do not take kindly to debt restructuring or threats of recrimination. Many patrons have been robbed of watches or rings to meet payment with little sympathy from the local cops.

Newspaper Publishing

Don't publish anything advocating separatism in Turkey. Turkish police seized two days' editions of the pro-Kurdish journal *Ozgur Ulke* and accused it of publishing separatist propaganda. On orders from an antiterrorism court, police seized about 13,000 copies of the daily. Turkey maintains strict laws against advocating separatism.

Police Hassles

Dual U.S.-Turkish citizens may be subject to compulsory military service and other aspects of Turkish law while in Turkey. Those who may be affected can inquire at a Turkish embassy or consulate to determine status. In some instances, dual nationality may hamper U.S. government efforts to provide protection abroad.

Unauthorized purchase or removal from Turkey of antiquities or other important cultural artifacts is strictly forbidden. Violation of this law may result in imprisonment. At the time of departure, travelers who purchase such items may be asked to present a receipt from the seller as well as the official museum export certificate required by law.

Ankara

Police presence throughout Ankara is high. The Turkish National Police are headquartered in Ankara and the quality of service they provide is adequate by American standards. However, response time in some cases can be significantly slower than that of their U.S. counterparts. Plainclothes policemen are used extensively. Although responsive, few Turkish policemen speak English and communicating with them can be difficult. American citizens having a need to communicate with the police should contact the U.S. Embassy for assistance. The U.S. Embassy security office can be reached at ☎ *(90) (312) 426-5470, extension 354* and the Air Force Office of Special Investigations at ☎ *(90) (312) 287-9957.*

Western Turkey/Mediterranean and Aegean areas

Turkish National Police response to accidents and crime scenes in this part of Turkey is similar to that found in Ankara except the uniformed police presence is not as heavy.

Eastern Turkey and the Black Sea Coast

Turkish National Police response along the Black Sea coast is exactly the same as that found in western Turkey. Turkish National Police/Jandarma response in eastern Turkey is significantly slower than their counterparts in western Turkey due to the hazardous security situation and roadway quality outside of major cities.

Istanbul

There are numerous police stations throughout the city, along with a large uniformed police presence around the major tourist areas. Police assistance is generally good. All Americans involved in a criminal incident are urged to contact the Consulate ☎ *(90) (212) 251-3602* for immediate assistance.

Istanbul Specific

In Istanbul street crime occurs more often due to the large number of tourists. Travelers should exercise caution and beware of pickpockets while shopping and sightseeing.

Some tourists have been drugged and robbed in Istanbul. Normally this occurs to persons traveling alone. Again, if at all possible, travel with a companion and avoid overly-friendly tour guides or people offering free drinks or assistance.

There have been incidents reported where tourists, usually traveling alone, have been drugged and robbed by criminals, some posing as taxi drivers. Visitors must only ride in taxis with meters and should note the license plate in case there is a problem.

Getting Sick

Medical facilities are available, but may be limited outside urban areas. Doctors and hospitals often expect immediate cash payment for health services. In the southeastern city of Diyarbakir, there are recurring outbreaks of dysentery, typhoid fever, meningitis and other contagious diseases.

Nuts & Bolts

The local currency is the Turkish lira, a limp currency that makes you an instant millionaire each time you change about 15 bucks. Turkey has high plateaus and Mediterranean coastal areas. The plateau areas in the east get very cold in the winter and very hot in the summer. The fall and spring are quite pleasant. Istanbul has moderate temperatures year-round, with summer temps in the 80s (F) and winter lows in the mid 40s (F). Istanbul gets about four inches of rain a month in the winter.

The bulk of tourists in Turkey are Russians, attracted by the proximity, beaches and cheap goods. Germans comprise the second largest block, followed by tourists from England, Romania and Israel.

Drug Penalties

In Turkey, the penalties for possession, use, and dealing in illegal drugs are extremely strict, and convicted offenders can expect lengthy jail sentences and fines. Turkey is subject to smuggling of drugs due to its proximity to Syria and activity in the eastern states. Do not get involved.

Registration

U.S. citizens who register at the Consular Section of the U.S. Embassy or Consulate may obtain updated information on travel and security in Turkey.

Embassy and Consulate Locations

The U.S. Embassy in Ankara
> *110 Ataturk Boulevard*
> ☎ *(90) (312) 468-6110*

The U.S. Consulate in Istanbul
> *104-108 Mesrutiyet Caddesi*
> *Tepebasl*
> ☎ *(90) (212) 251-3602*

The U.S. Consulate in Adana
> *at the corner of Vali Yolu and AtaTurk Caddesi*
> ☎ *(90) (322) 453-9106*

The Adana local police emergency number
> ☎ *(322) 435-3195*

Americans who are victims of crimes may also call the consulate
> ☎ *(322) 454-2145*

Dangerous Days

04/17/1992	Turkish police killed 11 suspected Kurdish guerrillas in a series of raids in Istanbul. Kurds undertook several terrorist attacks in 1992 in Germany and Turkey citing this date.
08/30/1991	August 30, 1991 was celebrated as Victory Day and made an official Turkish holiday.
05/27/1991	May 27, 1991 was celebrated as Constitution Day and made an official Turkish holiday.

Dangerous Days

04/25/1988	Hagop Hagopian, leader of the Armenian Secret Army for the Liberation of Armenia (ASALA)—a.k.a. the Orly group, 3rd October Organization—was shot dead in his home in Athens by two gunmen. No group claimed responsibility for his murder.
09/06/1986	Twenty-one Jewish worshippers were killed in Istanbul during an attack on a synagogue by an Abu Nidal terrorist team.
08/15/1986	Turkish troops raided Kurdish rebel camps in Iraq.
08/15/1984	The day that Kurdish Workers Party (PKK) elements first launched an attack against Turkish government installations.
08/27/1982	The Turkish military attache in Canada was assassinated by Armenian extremists.
08/07/1982	Nine people, including one American, were killed, and more than 70 were wounded in an attack on the Ankara airport by the Armenian Secret Army for the Liberation of Armenia.
01/28/1982	The Turkish consul general to the U.S. was assassinated in Los Angeles by members of a group calling itself the Justice Commandos for the Armenian Genocide.
03/10/1979	The death of Kurdish leader Mullah Mustafa Barzani (Kurdish regions only).
11/27/1978	Considered to be the date on which the Kurdish Workers Party (PKK) was founded. PKK guerrillas may engage in terrorist attacks in connection with this date.
05/01/1977	More than 30 leftists were killed during clashes with security forces in Istanbul.
10/24/1975	The Turkish ambassador to France and his driver were shot and killed in Paris by members of the Armenian Secret Army for the Liberation of Armenia (ASALA).
01/22/1946	Kurdish Republic Day.
11/10/1938	Death of Kemal Ataturk.
10/29/1923	Turkish National Day. The date commemorates the declaration of Turkey as a republic by Mustafa Kemal Ataturk and his inauguration as its first president.
03/16/1921	Signing of the Soviet-Turkish border treaty that ended Armenian hopes of establishing an independent state.
04/24/1915	Armenians observe this date as the anniversary of the alleged 1915 Turkish genocide of Armenians.
03/12/1880	Birthday of Kemal Ataturk, founder of the modern Turkish state.
06/16	June 16 is the anniversary date of the founding of the Turkish leftist terrorist group, 16 June. Until 1987, the group acted under the name Partisan Yolu. Since 1987, the group has claimed responsibility for numerous acts of terrorism, including the December 1989 firebombing in Istanbul of the Hiawatha, a U.S. Government-owned yacht.
03/21	Kurdish New Year.

In a Dangerous Place: Hijacked over Turkey

In October of 1980 I was 23 and a beginning war correspondent. I was returning from my first trip to Iran, where Iraq had just launched what was to be a long, deadly war of attrition. I went to the front but my film was developed and the best shots confiscated by Iranian censors. I was left with useless shots of people, smiling soldiers and not much else. After I checked in with SIPA, my photo agency in Paris, I was told to try the other side—Iraq. On my way I decide to cover the military maneuvers of the Turkish army near Diyarbakir in the southeast of Turkey. First I would stop in at Ankara to get my visa for Iraq.

Our Turkish Airlines *Boeing 727* took off as scheduled around 5:30 p.m. for its 35-minute-long flight. But, one hour later we still had not landed. The other passengers and I started feeling uneasy. I remember wondering if the wheels of the plane were blocked. Suddenly the voice of the pilot broke through the tension: "Ladies and gentlemen we might be obliged to land in Diyarbakir. Otherwise we will head toward Iran. I now give the microphone to a Muslim brother." Instantly the entire plane knew we had been hijacked.

Yilmaz Yalciner, the leader of the hijackers, carried on with his statement given in the most imperative intonation:

"Islam takes over the plane. Long live the Divine Ayatollah Ruhollah Khomeini... Shariat, the unique sure way to bring happiness to the entire human race, is the name of our mission. We are changing the route of this plane so as to go to Teheran, the cradle of the Islamic Revolution. Then, my three Muslim brothers and I will proceed to Afghanistan where we will fight alongside the brothers who are leading a *Jihad* (Holy War) against the Russian atheists. For this reason I am now going to pass around the hat. Whatever you give, make sure to give with your heart."

The passengers, still in a state of shock after this announcement, search their pockets for some money. The collection began. The passengers, afraid of the reprisals, give as much as they could to the militant who is passing a bag. Yilmaz Yalciner counted the money and got back to the microphone: "89.000 Turkish Lira (US$100)," he says, "it's really too little for people like you, but thanks anyway. Don't forget that we are going to fight with this money against the atheist Soviets."

For the passengers, the unbearable wait, starts.

Nobody moves anymore; there is little to talk about and everyone knows the gravity of the situation. All of us are probably thinking of the same thing—fanatics are unpredictable. All we can do is wait anxiously for their next move. Once more the voice of the hijacker breaks the heavy silence, "All women on board must cover their hair, it is a rule of Islam. And Islam only constrains you to do good things." The 28 female passengers quickly cover their hair with whatever is available including the white cotton cloth of the headrests of their seats. Some women, short of anything looking like a *chador*, shroud themselves under their husband's jackets.

Being a photojournalist first and a terrified passenger second, I pulled out my camera and started taking photos. I was more concerned about running out of film since I did not know how long the ordeal would last. I found myself elated that I was at the center of what would be an international story, but scared out of my wits that the usual *laissez passer* accorded to the press would not be observed by the Muslim fanatics. The hijackers were just as terrified as the passengers but found comfort in carrying out this simpleminded and dangerous act.

At first I photographed the passengers clandestinely, but this was not the story. Then I had an idea. I informed my fellow passenger and friend Osman, a radio journalist sitting next to me, about my intentions to talk to the hijackers and ask their permission to take photos of the whole event. He quickly dismissed the idea as insane and advised me to adopt a low profile instead, so as not to attract their attention.

My hunch was that the hijackers were Iranian. I figured that if I showed them the recent stamps in my passport and some of the recent Iranian photos I had with me they might allow me to document the hijacking. I headed toward the first-class compartment where three of the militants had gathered, and told them I was a journalist and asked permission to take photos. One of them, Omer Yorulmaz (I learned his name later), calmly told me to wait and he would check with the leader in the cockpit. In the meantime I went back to my seat to get my cameras. He comes out and told me I could enter. I was elated.

As I quickly took photos of the crowded cockpit, I noticed the contrast between the tense but efficient crew, and the theatrical laughter of the hijacker (Yilmaz Yalciner) as he held a gun close to the right temple of someone sitting behind the pilot. I was even more elated with the fact that this was the first time a hijacking had ever been photographed in the air.

Suddenly, Yalciner commanded me to stop. I realized his smile was a natural schoolboy's reaction to the camera and not indicative of the tension in the cockpit. Ignoring me, he resume his negotiations with the pilot. I was being watched carefully by another hijacker. The pilot, Ilhan Akdeniz, was trying to convince Yalciner once and for all: "It was impossible," he said, "to violate Iran's airspace. There is a war going on! They are going to shoot us down with missiles! They won't want to know whether we've been hijacked."

Yalciner's answer surprised everyone, "Don't worry, the Muslim world knows me very well. Khomeini knows me too. Stop worrying we'll make it to Teheran."

Even with this as a given, the pilot explained the need for the long trip to Teheran. There would not be enough fuel. He asked if the plane land in Dyabakir to refuel. The hijackers, convinced, agreed. That issue resolved, the lead hijacker seemed to relax and resumed his casual demeanor.

He turned toward me and told me abruptly, "I am not a mean terrorist. I am a good terrorist. So you're a journalist? " "Yes." "So am I and the three brothers, too," he explained. "You can take more pictures of me, you know, but I must admit I don't know how to pose," he added before bursting out laughing.

They were all working for a banned publication called *Shariat*. Hence, the name of the "mission" they were undertaking. They were religious terrorists belonging to the "Akincilar group" (independent Sunni Muslims linked with the National Salvation Party).

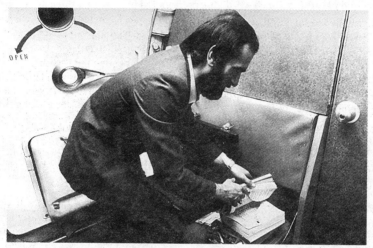

I resumed taking pictures of the scene, and of the passengers. The passengers still had no idea what fate had in store for them. These hijackers were unusually calm. They were obviously fanatics to the point of candidness; they seemed to be absolutely confident that they were going to get to Teheran. But I could feel their tension. I lied to them pretending I understood their motivation and wanted to provide them oodles with publicity. They were quite willing to talk. I asked them how they managed to smuggle their guns onto the *Boeing* inspite of the tight security control. Yalciner pulled out a book which he opened to show me that it had been hollowed to make room for a pistol. He laughed heartily about the clever trick he had played on the security guards. Another showed me an attache case filled with Turkish Lires so they could survive in their new country, Iran. In times like this it was hard to understand whether I was in the presence of childish stupidity or enormous confidence.

We made small talk until the plane landed at Diyarbakir. The passengers were worried since they didn't know what city or country they were landing in. Most passengers knew that bad things start to happen once hijacked planes touch down.

I became self-conscious realizing that I was the only one who did not have the fear. The passengers looked at me with hatred and fear. Was I a hijacker? The confusion made them suspicious. I found myself in a no man's land between the passengers and the terrorists. Because of my decision to document this criminal act, the terrorists have made me part of their drama. By not intervening, I have become a coconspirator in the minds of the passengers. The camera has given me a special passport.

The hijackers also treated the cowering passengers differently. The burning light in the hijackers' eyes looked nothing but ominous.

We waited on the ground. The stewardesses attended to the people quietly and efficiently. The air in the plane was hot and stale. There was no more water or food. The plane felt like a tomb or a submarine that had sunk to the bottom of the ocean. Outside our plastic windows the ground crews, the vehicles and the world seemed a thousand miles away. Time was irrelevant.

It was not hard to figure out what was going through the minds of the 148 people aboard. The hijackers were also getting tense and I sensed it is time to stop taking pictures.

It was now 8:30 at night. We had only been aboard the plane for three hours but no one on this plane would forget this day. Given the time for reflection, I remembered why I had come to Diyarbakir in the first place. I realized that the hijackers had made a fatal mistake: They had landed in the center of a major military base and smack in the middle of preparations for showy military maneuvers. I was supposed to cover the strength and power of the Turkish Army. I was about to be center stage. To make matters worse, the Turkish and European press was there in full force. Faced with the tedious coverage of a nonevent, they were delighted to be at the scene of a hijacking. The worst part was that the new hard-liner president of Turkey himself, Kevan Evren, was at the airport and had taken charge of the event. He declared "No concession." The negotiations between the hijackers and the Airport Authority were going on with no apparent progress. The hijackers made a concession—they would free the women and the children. But it really didn't matter what they agreed to, since their fate was being decided for them in the smoke-filled meeting rooms inside the airport.

At 10:00 p.m., 19 *Celik Kuvvet* (Steel Force) commandos were flown in from Ankara and Adana. Their planes landed at Diyarbakir at 11:00 p.m. At midnight the airport was blacked out and the plane was by itself on the tarmac. The fear could be felt.

It was now Tuesday. We had lived another day. At 1:00 a.m. electronic listening devices were installed on the body of the plane to locate the hijackers. Four more hours were necessary to prepare the rescue operation. Inside the grounded plane the passengers were aware of, and could see, nothing.

At 5:00 a.m., the commandos split in to two groups. One group silently cut open the rear door while the front group create a minor diversion near the cockpit. The commandos burst through the back of the plane, yelling: "Lie down everybody," followed by a shoot-out. The sound of the firefight in the small enclosed space was deafening.

The passenger I photographed in the cockpit was wounded and later died in the hospital. I ducked under my seat, afraid that my camera might be mistaken for a gun. I regret not taking pictures but realistically I knew I would have been killed instantly.

Crammed below the seat I had just enough time to hide some film in my underpants and to give some rolls to Osman, the radio journalist sitting next to me. The three surviving hijackers surrendered quite easily as if all was in good fun.

The passengers were asked to lie down on the tarmac and later we were driven to an army barracks. I was pointed out by some of the passengers as one of the hijackers. In fact the news wire reports included me in the list of hijackers arrested in the assault. I was taken into custody for interrogation.

After some minutes most of the passengers were freed and brought to the barracks. Five passengers and I were kept behind. The three hijackers were taken away in a truck. Then the police threw the six of us in a second truck which followed the first one. My cameras had been confiscated. I still felt confident that the whole situation was soon going to be clarified.

There were six of us crammed into the same jail cell. We were still tired, dirty and thirsty from the 12-hour ordeal—two engineers, one Italian and two Turkish customs officers who usually control the passports on board, Osman, the radio-journalist, and myself are detained. The police suspected the customs officers of complicity. They want to confirm the identity of the foreign engineers. Osman was detained because he was a journalist and I, because I was a suspected terrorist. The hijackers were put in another cell not far from ours.

My interrogation was a lot tougher than I imagined. I was bullied by the policemen when they discovered that I worked for SIPA PRESS (SIPA means donkey in Turkish). When I told them that I was born in Siirt they realized that I was a Kurd. They found my story hard to believe—that I would simply ask permission to take photos because it was my job. They did not believe I was only a journalist and I was sent back to my cell. During the entire night we couldn't sleep very much as we were disturbed by the comings and goings of our jailkeepers accompanying the hijackers to their interrogations. We could hear a lot of their yells. We were very uneasy about all this. We could also hear the news on a radio set. I gathered that everybody believed I was the fifth terrorist and I therefore should not expect any mercy.

The next day Osman was freed and I had time to give him some film to take to SIPA. I was left alone in the cell. Later on, the terrorists and I were sent to another jail well-known as a torture center for prisoners captured by the military.

Luckily this time my interrogation was shorter. I was told I would be released because they checked my identity and they understood I had told the truth. It seemed also that some people (journalists and politicians) had vouched for me. Never underestimate the usefulness of political contacts.

I was very surprised when I was finally released. I rushed back to SIPA's headquarters in Istanbul just in time to learn that only a handful of photos had been published in Turkey as well as around the world. Most of them had been lost due to Osman's mishandling of the developing process. There were more rolls of film that I had hidden under the aircraft seats that had still not been recovered.

1985: Hijacking No. 2

Five years (1985) later I was involved in another hijacking. This time I was not inside the plane, a *TWA-727*, but on the tarmac in Beirut.

The plane was coming from Athens, Greece and going to Rome, Italy. Two Shiite Lebanese ordered the pilot to divert the flight to Beirut. Other hijackers joined them at Beirut. They demanded the discharge of more than 700 Shiite prisoners and others detained in Israel. One passenger, a member of the Mexican Navy, was killed. Between June 14 and 26, 111 passengers were released, as well as five crewmen. The 36 other passengers and three other crewmen were detained until June 30. The plane was prevented from leaving Beirut by the Lebanese authorities.

So it became a long wait with pictures few and far between.

The hijacking was a comic opera. The hijackers were able to roam about outside the plane and even go back home to sleep at night, thanks to the complicity of the AMAL militia. I was a little wiser, tougher and cynical. I decided to leave the dull, monotony of the airport and cover the more salable action in town. I negotiated a deal with one of the hijackers for him to cover the event from inside the plane. The hijacker agreed and I gave him an automatic camera. My reward for my ingenuity was that I was run over by an armored vehicle which crushed one of my legs. I assume the hijacker showed up with the film to get his payment, but he did not know that I was in the hospital with a crushed leg. So I could not get the photos. *C'est la Guerre.*

CRIMINAL PLACES

Brazil

Street Kids Named Desire

Brazil is a bad place for its own people. And the guys you gotta watch out for are the cops, anyone who ever was a cop, and anyone who's ever thought of becoming a cop—not to mention all off-duty cops. Four policemen and the brother-in-law of one of the officers, were arrested in August 1994 for the murders of eight young boys (the youngest was eight) outside the Candelaria Church, a popular Rio tourist attraction.

Rio de Janeiro is a continuing source of petty crimes committed by street kids barely out of pajamas. Most people believe shopkeepers pay the police to pick off the toddler thieves like coyotes on a Wyoming sheep farm. The murders of street children account for five homicides a day, according to the University of São Paulo. Treated like vermin, most street urchins have a short life span. Many work for drug dealers; they sniff glue and gasoline to kill their hunger pangs. There is little sympathy on behalf of Rio's citizenry for these prepubescent dope peddlers, and it's unlikely the police will be convicted for what is generally viewed as a socially beneficial act.

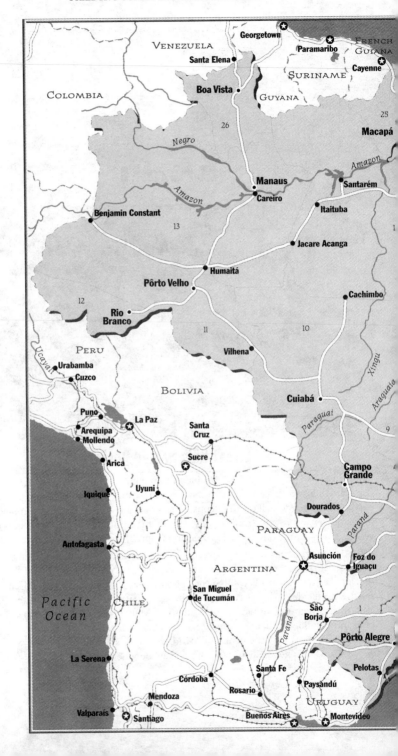

Atlantic Ocean

Brazil

⊕	National Capital	=====	Primary Road
•	State Capital	-----	Secondary Road
●	Secondary City	+++++	Railroad
----	State Border		

0	250	500	750 km
0		250	500 mi

©FW 1995

Belém
São Luís
Santa Inês
24
Fortaleza
Teresina
Pôrto Franco
22
21
Natal
20
Picos
João Pessoa
Miracema do Norte
23
19
Recife
Juázeiro
18
17
Maceió
15
Aracaju
Barreiras
16
Ibotirama
Salvador
Brasilia
São Francisco
Vitória de Conquista
oiânia
Pirapora
Montes Claros
Pôrto Seguro
erlândia
8
7
5
Belo Horizonte
Vitória
Volta Redonda
Niterói
o Paulo
Rio de Janeiro
ritiba
Santos
Florianópolis
0
Tocantins
upi

States of Brazil

1. Rio Grande do Sul
2. Santa Catarina
3. Paraná
4. Mato Grosso do Sul
5. São Paulo
6. Rio de Janeiro
7. Espírito Santo
8. Minas Gerais
9. Goiás
10. Mato Grosso
11. Rondônia
12. Acre
13. Amazonas
14. Pará
15. Tocantins
16. Bahia
17. Sergipe
18. Alagoas
19. Pernambuco
20. Paraíba
21. Rio Grande do Norte
22. Ceara
23. Piauí
24. Marnahão
25. Amapa
26. Roraima

Note: Brasilia is surrounded by a federal district

Is is estimated that there are 7 million kids living on the streets in Brazil. Hunted by death squads like rats in a sewer, they subsist by begging, stealing and deionizing themselves on petrol-based solvents. Are they a threat? You bet.

Other criminals in Brazil fall under the umbrella of nebulous quasi-terrorists. Since 1988, 92 incidents of terrorism and other forms of political violence have been reported, an average of slightly more than 3.5 per quarter. This average increased to just over six incidents per quarter during the last three years of the period. However, only five incidents were reported during the first half of 1994. No indigenous terrorist group is known to operate within the country, although leftist guerrillas from Peru and Colombia occasionally cross Brazil's western frontier. A street gang with visions of sugarplums and Abu Nidal menacingly calls itself the Commando Vermelho (Red Command). The "terrorist" group strikes from time to time but its actions are essentially criminal activities, such as the January 2, 1994, brief armed abduction and robbery of an American business executive and his wife in Rio de Janeiro. The Red Command may be no more than a gang operating under a *nom de guerre*. The responsibility for many incidents goes unclaimed (real terrorists love the media more than machine guns), as does the motive behind them. And the absence of any identifiable pattern in the crimes suggests most are the work of individuals rather than any organized group.

There's a huge difference in living standards between the developed south of Brazil and the northeast. Consequently, there has been massive migration to Rio's slums. This has caused a sharp increase in urban violence. The poverty-stricken lower classes have essentially seen zero benefits from the past growth of the economy. In Brazil, nearly one-fifth of the population is illiterate. The country can be embarrassed by having one of the world's most disparate income distributions; 60 percent of the national wealth is possessed by 1 percent of the population. Perhaps 20 percent of the population lives in poverty. Since World War II, the purchasing power of Brazil's minimum wage has been cut in half. Because of widespread inefficiency and corruption, only 8 percent of the government's social spending reaches the poorest 20 percent of the population. In Rio, poor families have become squatters on empty lots and in abandoned and partially-completed housing complexes. Brazil's underbelly is also being corroded by the spread of drug abuse and such diseases as AIDS, bubonic plague and cholera—a few good reasons for a lot of crime.

Getting In

A passport and visa are required. Tourist visas are valid for 90 days and must be obtained in advance and are free of charge. Minors (under 18) traveling alone, with one parent or with a third party must present written authorization by the absent parent(s) or legal guardian, specifically granting permission to travel alone, with one parent or with a third party. This authorization must be notarized, authenticated by the Brazilian Embassy or Consulate, and translated into Portuguese. If you are caught entering illegally you must leave the country voluntarily within three to eight days. The Ministry of Justice can hold you for 90 days before deporting you.

For current information concerning entry and customs requirements for Brazil, travelers can contact the

Brazilian Embassy
3006 Massachusetts Avenue N.W.
Washington, D.C. 20008
☎ *(202) 745-2700*
FAX (202) 745-2827
Brazil has consulates in Los Angeles, San Francisco, Houston, Miami, New York, Chicago or San Juan.

Dangerous Places

Rio

Rio likes to party, so its no surprise that the areas surrounding beaches, discos, bars, nightclubs and other similar establishments are dangerous, especially at dusk and during the evening hours. Prime targets in Rio are the popular beaches and neighborhoods of Copacabana and Leme.

São Paulo

On the weekend of June 11-12, 1994, 42 people were murdered in the city; 21 of them shot execution-style. However, crimes of opportunity, such as larceny, purse snatching, armed street robbery, car theft and carjackings pose the greatest threat to foreign visitors in São Paulo. Most foreign visitors dress differently and do not speak the local language. This increases the chance of being recognized as a foreigner, and therefore perceived as an easier target for criminals.

Dangerous Things

Hit Squads

Don't expect much help from the police. They have their hands full running after glue sniffing kids who plague the tourist areas.

Despite their reputation for tardiness and diffidence in daytime law enforcement, the Military Police are famous for off-hours over-zealousness. Human rights groups estimate there are two police-committed such killings a day on average in Brazil. About 200 police officers are fired every year for their participation in organized kidnapping, corruption and death squads. The Vigario Geral shantytown massacre on August 30, 1994 is probably the most famous example of their devotion to cleaning up the streets. That night 21 men, women and children were murdered by at least 30 masked gunmen believed to be police officers acting in vengeance for four officers killed two days earlier in the shantytown.

But while the Policia Militar (usually retired or off-duty police officers) spend their off hours in hit squads eliminating street kids, the hit squads are being hunted by each other less violent but equally eager hit squads. In August 1994, Brazil's justice minister announced the creation of a police force to police the police force: A federal police unit that would investigate and eliminate death squads all over the country.

Death squads and drug traffickers are considered major contributors to Rio's murder rate of more than 60 per every 100,000 people. In 1993, 3255 individuals were murdered in Rio alone. Instances of multiple executions and murders are not uncommon here. Many are the result of gun battles between rival gangs. Bodies of the victims are usually located later by police in the trunks of cars.

Rather then retaining attorneys to handle legal matters, Brazilians prefer hitmen. The menu reads like the clown at Jack-in-the-Box. Want to off an impoverished peasant? This week's special is only US$70. But if you want to take out a prominent politician, expect to pay for the caviar: about US$20,000. Although foreigners are rarely targeted, about 10 killings a day in São Paulo—half the daily total—are contract killings. Read that as nearly 4000 assassinations every year executed by hired executioners.

Kidnapping

Kidnapping in Rio and São Paulo has become a pastime in the last few years. And it's as easy as stealing an apple off a produce cart. More than 150 people were kidnapped in Rio in 1992. That figure is almost double what it had been the year before. Both figures were records. Authorities believe the actual number was far greater. Many in Brazil have no faith in the police to handle kidnapping situations competently and successfully. It's part of a vicious cycle, giving kidnappers the confidence for carrying out their activities.

Carnival

About US$24 million gets injected into Rio's economy during Carnival week. In addition, the 80,000 tourists who attended the Carnival (a new record) in 1994 represented an increase of

20 percent over last year boosting hotel occupancy rates to between 90–100 percent. Most revelers come to Rio from São Paulo and from around Brazil; many from Argentina.

If you do find yourself one of the statistics, contact the Rio tourist police. Don't worry, they won't execute you and stuff you in a trunk.

Emergency Numbers

Local "911-type" police numbers include:

Rio tourist police
☎ 511-5112

Military police (patrol)
☎ 190

Fire
☎ 193

Civil police (investigations)
☎ 147

The U.S. Embassy is located in Brasilia
Avenida das Nacoes, Lote 3
☎ (55-61) 321-7272

There are consulates in:

Rio de Janeiro
Avenida Presidente Wilson 147
☎ (55-21) 292-7117

São Paulo
Rua Padre Joao Manoel 933
☎ (55-11) 881-6511

Porto Alegre
Rua Coronel Genuino 421 (9th flr.)
☎ (55-51) 226-4288

Recife
Rua Goncalves Maia 163
☎ (55-81) 221-1412

There are also consular agencies in:

Belem
Avenida Oswaldo Cruz 165
☎ (55-91) 223-0800/0413

Manaus
Rua Recife 1010, Adrianopolis
☎ (55-92) 234-4546

Salvador de Bahia
Avenida Antonio Carlos Magalhaes S/N Edificio Cidadella Center, Suite 410
Candeal
☎ (55-71) 358-9195

Fortaleza
Instituto Brasil-Estados Unidos (IBEU
Rua Nogueira Acioly, 891
Aldeota
☎ (55-85) 252-1539.

Getting Sick

Medical care varies in quality, particularly in remote areas. Cholera has been reported in the Amazon Basin region and northeastern Brazil. Some cholera outbreaks have also been reported in major cities. However, visitors who follow proper precautions about food and drink are not usually at risk. Doctors and hospitals often expect immediate cash payment for health services. U.S. medical insurance is not always valid outside the United States. In some cases, supplemental medical insurance with specific overseas coverage has been found to be useful.

Chechnya
★★★★★

Boris Badenough

It seemed only a matter of time before the fiercely independent Chechen people would rise up against "Mother Moscow." Banished to Northern Kazakhstan by Stalin for being German collaborators, accordingly, the Chechens have a mean streak as wide as the mountainous border that divides their country. After they were repatriated, the Chechens, hardened and mean, set about forming the largest criminal gangs in the former Soviet Union. For centuries they have been considered by Russians as the toughest, baddest people in the former Union. It didn't help that Chechens like to raise money by kidnapping airlines and schoolbuses and then hot-footing it back to Chechnya to hide out.

It is strange that the news media was so quick to recast the ornery Chechens as the underdog/heroic-defenders-of-their-homeland in the West. Outnumbered by five- or 10-to-one according to some estimates, the Chechen irregulars, along with volunteers and highly paid mercenaries, (some brag they get paid the equivalent of $2000 a day, the reality is about one tenth of that) resigned to waging a guerrilla war from the mountains. The Russians seemed happy to oblige as they built forts along the major highways. In Grozny nervous Russian troops stop and check papers endlessly and regularly arrest any male Chechens they find hiding in their homes just to be sure.

It was a story the Western media loved—peasants armed with sticks and shovels defiantly dancing around bonfires in central Grozny seemingly holding off the entire might of the Russian army and air force. Chechen fighters, unshaven and dirty, waving their flag while strafing fighters soar overhead and turn their parliament into Swiss cheese. Meanwhile, the most feared army in the world turned out to be shivering, confused and mostly prepubescent.

Just prior to Russia's intercession into the rebellion, Russian Defense Minister Pavel S. Grachev bombastically boasted that a single paratroop regiment would need only a couple of hours to wipe out the rebellion. Boy, was he wrong. A December 1994 attempt to take Grozny revealed, in a rebel rout of the Russian forces, precisely how weak the Russian war machine is. Yeltsin was seemingly out of control of his own army. Renegade commanders refused to follow orders or never received them. Russian soldiers captured by the insurgent Chechens revealed that they were without food and maps—essentially that they had no direction nor any idea of what the hell they were doing. Russian corpses littered Grozny like dead worms after a heavy rain. Although the vastly superior forces were eventually to take the Chechen capital in January 1995, they face a repeat of Afghanistan. The Chechen insurgents—many of them former Soviet soldiers trained in mountain guerrilla fighting—have dug into the hills, prepared for a long and fierce battle of attrition against an undisciplined, underage band of Boris' best. And, in true Afghanistan form, the Russian army is setting up a puppet government while the rebels regroup in the hills. Since the Russians have decided to exterminate any and all Chechen fighters, there is little for the Chechens to lose. Although the daytime is ruled by Russian APCs and soldiers, the night belongs to the Chechens.

By most estimates there are about 1500–3000 Chechen fighters in three groups waiting to strike back—and the Russian command concedes that guerrilla raids staged by rebels in the mountains will, in all likelihood, continue for years to come. In typical Chechen style, the crisis has been more Moscow's than Grozny's. The Chechens bitter resistance, along with low morale, poorly dropped bombs (resulting in untold civilian casualties) and incompetence in the Russian ranks, turned world support against the Russians. Of course, few in the world realize that the Chechen's principal natural resource is organized crime. The Russian mafia (i.e., Chechen) has spread throughout Russia and is now flexing its muscles in Western Europe. Chechen terrorists have adopted banditry as a form of social protest. They specialize in the large-scale kidnapping of schoolbuses and passenger airplanes, many ending in Wild West shootouts that have left hostages dead.

In February 1995, the Russian army had 38,000 troops in Chechnya, the Interior Ministry another 15,500. Russian sources insist Chechen strength is far greater than what's being reported in the media. The general leading the Interior Ministry troops, Gen. Anatoly S. Kulikov, said the Chechens began the conflict with a regular army of 15,000 men and perhaps 30,000–40,000 in the militia, which put the troop strength about equal—if you are to believe the Russians. The Chechens now are estimated to have 30,000 men of various quality on tap. They range from highly trained soldiers (courtesy of the Soviet Army) to clan gunmen. They can put about 2 helicopters in the air and possibly about 10 L-15 trainers. Most of the air force was destroyed by the Russian army. There are about 1000 men in the National Guard and about 900 men

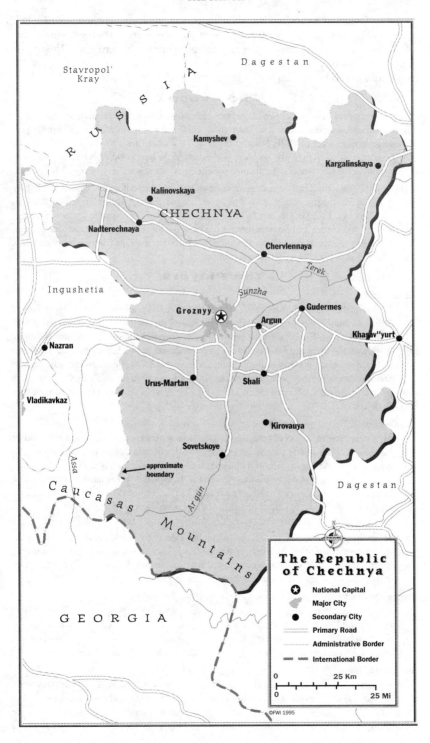

Stavropol'
Kray

Dagestan

RUSSIA

Kamyshev

Kargalinskaya

Kalinovskaya

CHECHNYA

Nadterechnaya

Chervlennaya

Terek

Ingushetia

Sunzha

Groznyy

Gudermes

Argun

Khasav''yurt

Nazran

Urus-Martan

Shali

Vladikavkaz

Kirovauya

Assa

Sovetskoye

approximate
boundary

Dagestan

Caucasas
Mountains

Argun

GEORGIA

**The Republic
of Chechnya**

⭐ National Capital

Major City

● Secondary City

Primary Road

Administrative Border

International Border

0   25 Km

0   25 Mi

©FWI 1995

in the armored and motorized brigades. The Chechens started the war with 15 T-72 tanks and 219 aircraft. All aircraft and most tanks were destroyed in the opening hours of the Russian bombing attacks. Regardless, air superiority has given the Russians the only advantage they have. But should the rebels get a hold of enough Stingers, this could turn out to be an even nastier conflict than it's been already.

The Scoop

The looters, drug runners, pimps and gangsters that are the Chechens have given Moscow the ultimate headache: another Afghanistan. Only about 1000 miles south of Moscow, Chechnya proclaimed its independence in 1991. Boris let'em alone for a while (not a bad idea, considering the Chechens seem to have a tight grip on Moscow) but sent in the heat in December 1994. (For more information on the Chechen organized crime presence in Moscow, see the chapter on "Russia.")

How'd the war start? The best reason we've heard was that the conflict was ignited by a big oil deal struck by Azerbaijan, which needed to export the oil through Russian pipelines that pass through Chechnya. Both Grozny and Moscow wanted a piece of the action, in terms of transport fees. Moscow and Grozny had been rhetorically duking it out for three years over the Moscow control of Chechen oil exports. Since Yeltsin pays the military by the week, he construed a meaner deal. The death toll as of June '95 is 20,000 and climbing.

The Players

Boris Yeltsin

Boris is mad as hell and he isn't going to take it anymore. Boris forgot that the massive army of Stalin and Breshnev is long gone. When Boris pushed the button, all he got was a bunch of sparks and fizzles. Finally, when he sent in the few generals who would obey him, the entire world saw the ineptitude and deceit on television every night. For a guy who has to get reelected soon he's no George Bush. In the meantime most of his generals and state governments do whatever they please and the people of Russia have a justifiably healthy distrust of politicians. An early 1995 poll gleaned that fully 72 percent of the Russian people do not trust Boris Yeltsin.

The Chechens

Mountain bred and mean as polecats, the Chechens are traditionally fierce and independent Caucasians. They adhere to a Sufi mysticism branch of Sunni Islam called Muridism. This branch of Islam divides its followers into sects led by local feudal leaders. They are united only in their opposition of domination by Christians. In fact, they break all the fundamentalist Islamic laws. The men smoke and booze it up, while the women do not cover their heads, as they're required to do in stricter branches of the religion. Instead of praying five times a day, Chechens may pray only once or twice a day. They're too busy battling with Boris.

Militarily, the Chechens' chain of command is like a dime-store necklace. If units of irregulars meet up with each other, its purely by happenstance. They go out and fight, then come back to eat and sleep. They're about as coordinated as a demolition derby, but equally as destructive. If they end up bringing the battle to the hills, pull up a chair.

Ruslan Khasbulatov

Chechen home boy. Former speaker of the Russian Parliament and leader of the October 1993 coup against Yeltsin. Khasbulatov has aligned himself with a powerful Chechen warlord to oust Chechen leader Dudayev. The motive seems to be market control as opposed to political idealism. The village of Tolstoy-Yurt serves as headquarters for Khasbulatov's supporters.

Dzhokhar Dudayev

Looking and acting surprisingly like Boris Badenov of "Rocky & Bullwinkle" fame, Dudayev is Muslim and a former general in the Soviet air force. His principal enemy—aside from the Russians—is the Russian-backed Provisional Council, headed by Umar Avturkhanov. Dudayev has delivered on his promise of a *jihad*, or holy war, if Moscow invades his tiny gangster kingdom.

Dudayev hates Russians. In once instance, Russian Federal Counterintelligence Service (FSK) officer Stanislav Krylov was captured while on a reconnaissance mission to Chechnya. Dudayev did not mess around with diplomatic negotiations. Krylow was given the choice of signing a confession detailing his mission, or his daughter living in Moscow would be kidnapped and executed. Krylow was rescued by two masked men during an attack on the military camp where he was being held.

Dudayev hates Russian journalists. In September 1994, he ordered all Russian journalists to leave Chechnya within 24 hours.

Unlike some pocket dictators who talk tough and then split for Monaco, Dudayev has the men, the money, the guns and the cojones to play hardball with the Russians for some time to come. Dudayev's men are veterans of the war in Abkhazia and are backed up by mercenaries (who can be identified by their hooded masks in battle). In September 1994, Dudayev's army wrestled control of the city of Argun (about 15 km from Grozny) from the Russian-backed forces of Ruslan Labazanov.

Dudayev has paid a high price for Chechen freedom. His son was killed during the Russian assault on Grozny. It is assumed that Dudayev is in hiding outside Grozny.

The Provisional Council

A group of ex-soldiers and "paid volunteers" led by Russian Umar Avturkhanov. Funded by Moscow and gaining in popularity, the "volunteers" are actually bored Russian soldiers, usually from idle units based around the Moscow area, and soldiers on the payroll of the Federal Counterintelligence Service, the reincarnation of the KGB. Volunteers are paid between US$1500-2000 a month. If they are killed in battle, their families are compensated 25 times the monthly pay of the dead soldier, a payoff—remarkably high by Russian standards—ensuring a widow a short mourning period.

Russian Defense Minister Pavel S. Grachev: Winner of the DP Vodka Voice Award. Grachev proclaimed the war would be won in two hours by a single parachute regiment. After the Russian parliament demanded that Yeltsin fire Grachev, the DM responded by firing "six or seven" generals for insubordination. Last seen checking into a Moscow hospital for a "routine checkup." Read that as heading out to his summer home in Siberia.

Getting In

Chechnya is a state within Russia. A passport and Russian visa are required for all U.S. citizens traveling to or transiting through Russia by any means of transportation, including train, car or airplane. While under certain circumstances travelers who hold valid visas to some countries of the former Soviet Union may not need a visa to transit Russia, such exceptions are inconsistently applied. Travelers who arrive without an entry visa may be subject to large fines, days of processing requirements by Russian officials, and/or immediate departure by route of entry (at the traveler's expense). Carrying a photocopy of your passport and visas will facilitate replacement should either be stolen.

All Russian visas, except transit visas, are issued on the basis of support from a Russian individual or organization, known as the sponsor. It is important to know who your sponsor is and how they can be contacted, as Russian law requires that your sponsor apply on your behalf for replacement, extension or changes to your visa. The U.S. Embassy cannot act as your sponsor. Tourists should contact, in advance, their tour company or hotel for information on visa sponsorship.

U.S. citizens can contact the

Russian Embassy

Consular Division
1825 Phelps Place NW
Washington, D.C. 20008
☎ *(202) 939-8918, 939-8907, or 939-8913*
or the Russian Consulates in New York, San Francisco or Seattle for current information on visa requirements.

All foreigners must have an exit visa in order to depart Russia. For short stays, the exit visa is issued together with the entry visa; for longer stays, the exit visa must be obtained by the sponsor after the traveler's arrival. Russian law requires that all travelers who spend more than three days in Russia register their visas, through their hotel or sponsor. Visitors who stay in Russia for a period of weeks may be prevented from leaving if they have not registered their visas. Errors in the dates or other information on the visa can occur, and it is helpful to have someone who reads Russian check the visa before departing the United States.

The Southern borders are not manned and checkpoints are only on main roads. Most Russian soldiers can be bribed due to their low pay and acceptance of side income. Do not expect any assistance if you are detained by soldiers or Chechens.

Entry into Chechnya should only be attempted by journalists or aid groups. The republic of Chechnya, as a state in Russia, isn't, at this writing, technically closed. Journalists can enter Chechnya on the ground with the Russian Army after flying from Moscow to Ordzonikidze. Journalists covering the conflict from the rebel side can either contact Chechen elements in Moscow or fly from Moscow to Kizljar in Dagestan and make their way to the mountains near Gudermes to make contact with the insurgents. It may take hanging around for awhile, but you'll get in. DP has arranged for the Chechen mafia to transport us into Grozny for about US$10,000. It includes a meeting in Istanbul with a Chechen representative, a flight to Moscow to meet with the Chechen mafia and then a long flight into Dagestan. From then we would be met by fighters and hike into the area around Grozny. It is not recommended that our readers duplicate this method since Russian troops shoot first and ask questions later. Secondly, the Chechens do not hold any specific part of Chechnya and are subject to air and ground attacks at all times.

Getting Around

There is no way to safely get around Chechnya. At press time, the only mechanized means of getting around the republic were via military convoys and occasionally by passenger cars. Fighting has spread to areas outside Grozny. The entire republic is considered extremely hazardous for travel.

Dangerous Places

The Entire Country

At press time, the Russians claimed they controlled all of provincial Chechnya except the town of Gudermes to the east of Grozny and towns in the plains and Caucasus Mountains to the south. Russian shelling is a continuing problem in the towns of Samashki, to the west, and Argun, to the east.

Grozny

At press time, the Russians have control of Grozny and have checkpoints on all major roads. The situation seems to be stable during the day with sporadic small arms fire and shelling during the night.

On January 31, 1995, Russian president Boris Yeltsin issued a decree authorizing the military to disarm militias in both North Ossetia and Ingushetia.

Dangerous Things

You Name It

Travelers can expect all conditions and dangers found in a confused war zone.

Unidentified Tanks

In this war, it's not easy to tell who's who—especially whose side the tanks are on. One day, in Grozny, about five dozen Chechen rebels were kicking back and taking a dinner break near the presidential palace. They noticed a tank heading in their direction, glanced casually at it, and went back to their feast. The Russian tank swiveled its turret and blasted them, killing five and wounding two. Whoops.

Being a Russian Pilot

The Chechens have brought down numerous helicopters, and even a Russian jet fighter, using modified rockets. But if a truckload of Stinger antiaircraft missiles bound for the Chechens and seized by Russian troops in neighboring Dagestan is any indication, the flyboys won't have it nearly as easy in the future.

Being a Russian Soldier

Without adequate food and maps, Russian infantrymen have been sitting ducks. At the end of January 1995, the Russians put their dead at 608, and their wounded at 2250. The actual number turns out to be 1146 killed and 5000 sick or wounded as of March 95.

Being a Civilian

So far 25,000–35,000 civilians have been killed or missing. Over 450,000 are refugees. Either Russian pilots are bad shots or they feel the odds are better at snuffing unarmed civilians. Markets (bazaars), medical facilities and civilian cars on the roadways, some sites hit multiple times, seem to be the Russians' favorite targets. The Russians even attacked a funeral procession in Samashki, killing three.

Smaller Cities

The Chechens like to fight in the towns and cities, terrain they know and the Russians don't. If the Chechen fighters possess any fear, it is fear of open fields and the countryside. Chechen rebels even intentionally left the way into the strategic town of Argun open, hoping to lure Russian soldiers into an urban front. Evidently, Grozny taught them a lesson and they stayed away. The Russians are currently bombing and shelling towns held by Chechen rebels. The situation changes day to day.

Getting Sick

You're SOL if you catch a nasty bug here. What little medical care remains in Chechnya is provided to casualties of war. The few remaining doctors here are more concerned with sewing up a guy's stump than with your queasy stomach.

In a Dangerous Place: Chechnya

One can never live a normal life as a war photographer. As soon as the words "hostilities have broken out in." are heard on CNN it is expected that there will be a flow of videotapes and photographs that cover and explain the conflict. Most journalists are dispatched on a hunch and get in-country before the borders are closed and the infrastructure seizes up. Other must make their way in by what ever means necessary.

The large networks and news gathering organizations pay extraordinary amounts of money not only to send in news teams but also to charter airplanes, couriers and even military planes to get their dispatches out of the country. Satellite telephones and transmitters make it easy to send reports now but the units are expensive and heavy to pack in.

When Russia sent its troops into Grozny there were plenty of journalists and reporters. As the situation became embarrassing, the Russians began to simply round up and send journalists out of the country. Previously Dudayev had sent out all Russian reporters because of their inflammatory articles. When the Russian and western press began to highlight the Russian incompetence and division, the Russians rounded up the western press. Unlike major conflicts where the press is carefully clothed, fed, housed and "spun" by briefings, press releases and carefully prepared interviews, Chechnya was the opposite. Russian troops couldn't care less if they shot at the glint of a camera lens or a sniper's telescopic sight. Mortars, bombs and shells dropped by the Russians care even less.

We wanted to see for ourselves so we sent in a correspondent to understand the situation first hand. The story of just what it takes to get into a war zone like Chechnya will give readers some idea of the new face of reporting war.

We made the our preliminary arrangements before leaving Istanbul with the "Caucasus Peoples Federation," a group that was supporting Dudayev's fight in Chechnya, or Chechenstan as it locally known. The plan was to allow us to go in with a group of "volunteers" or mercenaries via Baku in Azerbaijan through Dagestan and then on to Grozny. Although they could provide some forms of transportation to the border, from Hasalyurt we would have to walk for about three days through the mountains in the middle of winter to reach Grozny. Although we were being sent in under the protection of the Chechen forces, there was no guarantee who would be in charge once we arrived.

We set off the day before Christmas with minimal survival gear; our cameras, a stove, some tins of fish and warm clothing. We flew to Baku, in Azerbaijan, to meet the people who would take us into Grozny. The "friends" turned out to be members of the Lezgi Mafia, one of the toughest groups in Russia and the Trans-caucasus region. The Lezgi number about 1.5 million and live in the North of Azerbaijan and in south and central Dagestan. Our goal was to fly 1800 kms east to Baku and then travel 400 kms north along the Caspian Sea through Dagestan and then west 50 kms over the border into Grozny.

These entrepreneurial bandits had decided that since things were heating up and they didn't know the difference between DP and NBC they would need a $5000 transportation fee. Now normally when you make a business transaction in any country, you have some basic understanding of the value of money, intentions and general cost of a service. When you are dealing with the Mafia in Azerbaijan there is no guarantee that you would not end up a frozen cadaver with a slit throat two miles out of Baku.

Seeing how we had a plan "B" we had nothing to lose by negotiating this fee down to a paltry $1,000 which included transportation, food, lodging but no cable TV.

Plan "B" was the official Russian tour of Chechnya. Most Westerners are not aware of Moscow's new entrepreneurial spirit. Journalists who are accepted can arrange a $4,000 junket into Chechnya from Moscow via military transport. We opted for the lower-priced more adventurous ground operator version via the locals.

We made our deal over tea and cigarettes and once down we were as good as kinfolk with these tough characters. Although we were kissing cousins we also agreed to pay our fee once we were over the border in Hasalyurt. The man who was to take us there told us we would have company. He was bringing in 10 mercenaries and volunteers from Iran, Uzbekistan and Tadjikistan who would be joining us 10 kms short of the Azerbaijan-Dagestan border. Oh, he mentioned casually, a load of antitank missiles as well. We didn't ask him how much money this one trip would clear but it is obvious that war is good for business in these parts.

One of his men drove us two hours north to Quba in a Lada complete with reflective tinted windows. The mafia may have money but they sure don't have taste. We stayed at an old Russian farm house surrounded by apple orchards as far as the eye could see. Now abandoned, it was a way station and safe house for the Lezgi mafia. In the courtyard were two tractors with the antitank rockets. The men were packing oranges, apples, flour and other agrarian items to camouflage the clearly labeled crates.

We were awakened early the next morning and set off north towards Qusar a town about 25 kms short of the Dagestan border. We were now traveling in three groups. The first group consisted of two Lezgi who would travel ahead us to meet with the local officials, grease the border guards and ensure our safe passage into Dagestan. Behind us came the volunteers, now happy farmers bringing in foodstuffs. The border is officially closed but the guards just stared dispassionately at us and never bothered to even wave us down or check our passports. We thought the mirrored windows were bad taste; now we know their function. Inside Dagestan, we stayed in the car until we reached an old Lenin Pioneer Camp, a relic of the Russian regime where primary and high school kids learned the ways of the revolution. It was the Soviet version of our Boy Scout Camps.

That night we had a typical Azeri meal—smoked meat, and smoked fish, washed down with homemade vodka strong enough to remove paint. Tonight would be cold and the fire from the vodka made us warm.

After our feast we set off down a small side road that leads to the official checkpoint at the border. The cart track is used by the local farmers and is too bumpy to allow large trucks. There is little reason for a 24-hour border patrol and by "coincidence" there was no border patrol that night. As we traveled along the grey Caspian sea into Derbent we learned some unsettling news. Moscow had replaced the local police and border guards with special security team members known as "Omon". This was indeed a bad "omen." Security was tight because one of Dudayev's assistants had made a visit to Turkey and asked for the Turks to send assistance to Chechnya via Azerbaijan. The sudden heavy presence of the Russian military was to cut off any aid coming to the embattled capital of Grozny.

We were told this by a Lezgi mafia customs official. The fellow who held this oxy-moronic post advised us that in order for us to continue through Dagestan we would need to become citizens of the Dagestan Autonomous Region.

That night a man from the local police force brought two blank passports and we be-came Dagestanis for $300 each. It was a busy night as we filled out forms, and com-pleted the passports. Before dawn the next morning it seems that our new status was to be rewarded. Our transport was a brand new BMW bought (or stolen) in Germany. We left our old passports behind as partial payment and to avoid being searched and arrested as spies. Dagestan is a war zone with a penalty of two years in jail for crossing the border illegally. The Russian soldiers are also empowered to detain and/or exe-cute people who they suspect as volunteers or spies.

I always wondered who Sefail Musayev was but I carried his passport thankfully. The fact that we could not speak a word of Russian made every border crossing a gut wrencher. The Russians were not in any mood for levity but our Azeri driver/guide managed to chat and joke our way through a total of seven checkpoints. At each tense checkpoint my hair turned a little greyer, the lines on my face were etched deeper and I wondered what the hell I was doing here. When we reached the bustling city of Mo-hachkale (or Makhachkala) we finally could breathe. From here it was 170 kms to the border of Chechnya. From this point on our driver knew nothing of the conditions ahead.

We drove on in our beautiful new BMW feeling like royalty, although we were the last people the Russians wanted in this area. We came to Kizlar and our driver stopped to talk with a Chechen contact family who worked as a link between the Chechen mafia and the Lezgi. We asked about the Reuters journalists who were based in Hasa-lyurt. We had made an earlier deal to use their transmitter and satellite phone. The news was not good. The day before the Russians had severely bombed the Hasalyurt-Grozny road, knocking out a number of bridges. The journalists who were staying in the local sports stadium and using it as a base for their forays into Grozny were round-ed up and sent back to Moscow.

After coming this far we had no way to send out our information, no one to take us across the border and all that lay ahead of us was a bombed-out wasteland.

After much discussion with the Chechen family we learned there was one chance. If we could make it to Babayurt, another border town, we could try to contact a group of Chechen volunteers who were to cross the border soon. They mentioned that we would be safer in Chechnya since the Russians were increasing their crackdown on for-eigners and volunteers in Dagestan daily.

Kizlar is about 40 kms north of Hasalyurt and Babayurt is half way in between, hard along the Chechen border. One of the refugees from Kizlar staying in the house of-fered to come with us to help us get into Chechnya and to ease our way past the checkpoints that awaited us. Our luck held because the Russians had concentrated their Omon special forces south of Hasalyurt and the checkpoints to the north were manned by local Dagestanis. We met up with a group of 20–30 Chechen volunteers who were preparing to cross the border that night. We discussed the various ways into the country. Most agreed that to try to walk over the mountains into Grozny was fu-tile since the snow was now 4–5 meters deep. The 130 km trip would take at least a full week with an excellent chance of being attacked by jets or helicopters during the day.

We decided to tag along with the heavily armed volunteers. We began our trip in a convoy of cars and crossed the empty border post. At around midnight, the drivers of the cars dropped us off and returned. We would continue on foot. We walked for six or seven hours covering 20 km of frozen lowland impeded only by a slight snow cover. We let the main group of armed volunteers go on ahead of us. Our group was not armed but if they met up with Russians we were close enough to hear the sound of gunfire before we stumbled into the same trap.

The cold was numbing and we plodded on through the night like zombies. The wind whipped and slapped our faces making icicles on my mustache. The moon was our only light. After a while we came upon a dirt track that led to the village ahead. The wind not only brought cold and pain; it now brought the sound of heavy gunfire, fading and building as it slapped our numb faces. Our temperatures began to rise as we went through in the fields leading down to the village. The sound of rockets and automatic weapons cracked and thumped in the crystal clear night. As we crunched our way down to the village, the light of the dull blue sky began to rise like a curtain at the start of a movie. The sound of Russian helicopters rose up from a muted drumroll to a thunderous chorus.

My cold hands reached for my frozen cameras in anticipation. This was the play we had come for, the drama that we had fought so hard for admission to. Now on with the show.

AK-47 (Avtomat Kalishnikova obrazets 1947g)

If there is one visual symbol or prop that symbolizes the Soviet/revolutionary influence, it is the unmistakable profile of the AK-47. Once it was the hammer and sickle, now it is the banana shaped clip and pointed barrel of the world's most dangerous weapon.

Why is the AK-47 the most dangerous rifle? They're cheap (between $50–$350) available around the world and rock hard reliable, and in use from Afghanistan to Zaire. It is estimated that there are about 30–50 million copies of the rugged rifle in existence. They can pour out 600 rounds a minute and are designed to be manufactured and repaired in primitive conditions.

In 1941, the 23-year-old tank commander Mikhail T. Kalishnikov was wounded in the battle of Bryansk by the German invaders. While recuperating he listened to the complaints of Russian soldiers about their archaic bolt action rifles. Kalishnikov made use of his down-time to copy the current German machine pistol. The pistol never made it into the arsenal of the Russian army, but in 1943 it got him an entry to compete with other Russian gun designers to create the first Soviet assault rifle. An assault rifle is designed to be light, possess high rates of fire and do double duty as an accurate defensive rifle.

AK-47 (Avtomat Kalishnikova obrazets 1947g)

His design was chosen based on its durability and simplicity. The AK-47 and variants thereof have been manufactured in 12 countries from Bulgaria to Yugoslavia. The AK-47 and the AKM (a simpler to make variant) are sighted in to about 1000 meters, field strips down to 6 parts, fires 30 rounds of the 7.62 X 39mm cartridge and will deliver three-inch patterns at 25 meters. The rifle is accurate to about 200 meters when fired from the shoulder at rest, and accurate to about 50 yards fired from the hip. The newest version of the classic assault rifle is the AK-74 (adopted in 1974 by the Soviets), which uses a lighter but more accurate 5.45 X 39mm cartridge.

Kalishnikov was born in the Siberian town of Izhevsk, west of the Ural mountains. Today, Izhevsk is home to Izhmash, a former major arms manufacturing company that exports hunting rifles under the name The Kalishnikov Joint Stock Co.

Kalishnikov still designs hunting rifles and has never received a royalty for his design. He has received many medals for his innovative design.

Mexico

Run for the Border

Walking through the barrios of Tijuana overlooking the suburban sprawl of San Diego and the United States, it is hard to imagine that half a mile could make such a difference. Here is where the third world runs smack into the first world—like putting Mogadishu next to Santa Barbara. Stick any red-blooded American in this barrio for more than a week and they'd be scrambling across the chain-link fence and dashing for the promised land. Although the contrast between these two countries is obvious, Mexico itself is a land of contrasts and turmoil.

Imagine a bunch of armed Texans in ski masks in 100-degree heat rallying around a statue of Sam Houston and declaring the state an "autonomous region." On second thought, it isn't that difficult to imagine at all. On New Year's Day 1994, hundreds of armed peasants in ski masks—brandishing bolt-action rifles and sticks—declared their autonomy. They called themselves the Zapatista Army of National Liberation, after Emilio Zapata, one of the leaders of the 1910 Mexican Revolution. They stormed a number of Chiapas communities, including San Cristobal, Ocosingo, Altamira and Las Margaritas. The uprising came with the January 1, 1994 implementation of the North American Free Trade Agreement. The Zapatistas said, and continue to say, that

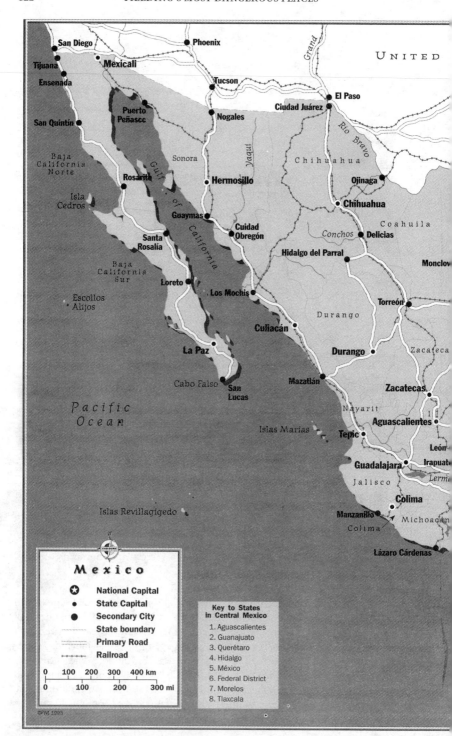

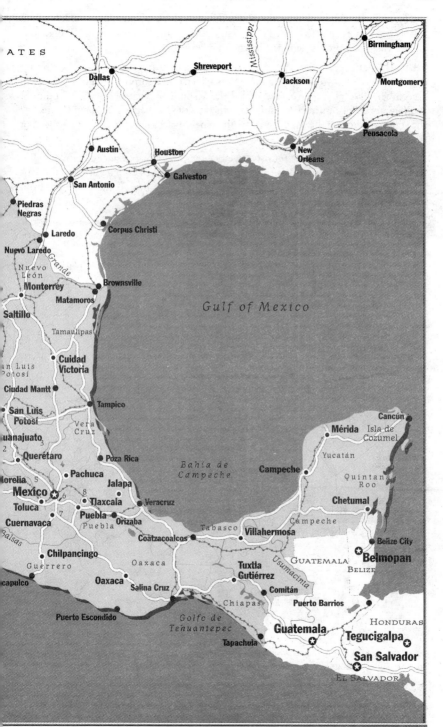

the agreement will essentially strip the *indigenes* of claims to their ancestral land. The tour buses that usually descended upon San Cristobal and the surrounding indigenous Indian villages in droves slammed on their brakes.

After a lengthy cease-fire, the rascals were back at it. Armed Zapatista rebels set up countless roadblocks and checkpoints across Chiapas in a surprise "military action" in December 1994. They virtually doubled the amount of territory they seized during the January 1994 insurrection. But, as with the last occupation, once confronted by the superior forces of the Mexican army, the rebels melted into the rain forest ahead of advancing troops, leaving 145 people dead.

Adventure and "daredevil" tourists have been visiting Chiapas since February 1994, with no incidents reported. It's the rare tourist who catches even a glimpse of a Zapatista rebel, as Zapatista camps are set deep in the jungle near Toluca, far away from even off-the-beaten-track destinations.

Zedillo has been faced with a double-whammy. Not only have the Chiapas rebels been a thorn in his side, but, while he wasn't looking, the peso crashed. Investors began makin' a run for the border in droves in January 1995—but in the other direction, away from Mexico. As the national solvency has continued to dissolve, with the peso so low against the dollar that Mexicans have stopped robbing other Mexicans entirely, with armed insurgent highlanders brandishing black flags emblazoned with a red star stalking the southern rain forests, it's a wonder so many still venture to this part of the world.

One thing is for sure, for the traveler Mexico is filled with extremes. It's where you can live the life-style of the rich and famous on the Mexican Riviera, or still shop for ammo behind the saloon in Sonora.

The Scoop

Mexico has one foot in the first world and the other in the third world. Depending on where you are you can be perfectly safe or in mortal danger. Sounds like America.

The Players

Rafael Sebastin Guillen Vicente (a.k.a. Subcommander Marcos)

(Starring in Che for a Day, or The Adventures of Subcomedian Marcos)

The image of the intellectual revolutionary is an appealing one in Latin America. There are few who are willing to pay the price of catapulting the brave into the heroic. Che Guevara did and now it seems like the 37-year-old son of a furniture store owner in Tampico is going for it. Rafael Sebastin Guillen Vicente, or Subcommander Marcos, is a former college professor (with a degree in sociology) from a well-off family in the state of Tamaulipas.

The pipe smoking, balaclava wearing Marcos appeared two years ago when the rebels suddenly said they were mad as hell and not going to take it anymore. What attracted the world's press was the 60s' aura of a group of peasants led by a charming, wisecracking mystery man who never appeared without his trademark disguise, shotgun bandoleer, pistol and pipe. He communicated with the press via video press release, satellite phone, fax machine and word processor. Adventurous types beat a path to his jungle doorway for an in-depth interview. He was long on rhetoric and short on results. His methodology was to "capture" a town with his ragtag army (some armed with sticks carved to look like rifles), then hightail back into the bush before the troops arrived. Most of the victims were innocent villagers killed by bombs or wild cross fire when the rebels didn't move fast enough.

Alas, his revolution will never match "Uncle Fidel's" nor Mao's nor even that of his real ideal, Sandino. Vincente was born on June 19, 1957, and was educated at the National Autonomous University of Mexico. He left in 1980 with a degree in sociology, earned a graduate degree and became an associate professor at Xochimilco south of Mexico City.

In 1984 he left for Managua where he taught and learned about revolution. He returned to Mexico in the late '80s to begin the Zapatista National Liberation Army. The revolution began on January 1, 1994.

President Ernesto Zedillo

Accused of being weak and indecisive and smarting from his recent trashing of the peso, Zedillo ordered the Boris Yeltsin's Manual on "How to Stamp Out Insurrections." He initially bombed the hell out of the region and ended up with truckloads of dead peasants. He then adopted a conciliatory stance, and after the peso was lower than a cucaracha's belly button he sent the troops in again. This time the stock market went up and the white ruling class applauded while the working class protested. The bottom line is that Zedillo has the tanks, men and helicopters; Marcos doesn't.

Getting In

Tourist Cards

All U.S. citizens visiting Mexico for tourism or study for up to 180 days need a tourist card to enter and leave Mexico. The tourist card is free and may be obtained from Mexican consulates, Mexican tourism offices, Mexican border crossing points and from most airlines serving Mexico. If you fly to Mexico, you must obtain your tourist card before boarding your flight; it cannot be obtained upon arrival at an airport in Mexico. The tourist card is issued upon presentation of proof of citizenship such as a U.S. passport or a U.S. birth certificate, plus a photo I.D. such as a driver's license. Tourist cards are issued for up to 90 days with a single entry, or if you present proof of sufficient funds, for 180 days with multiple entries. Upon entering Mexico, retain and safeguard the pink copy of your tourist card so you may surrender it to Mexican immigration when you depart. You must leave Mexico before your tourist card expires or you are subject to a fine. A tourist card for less than 180 days may be revalidated in Mexico by the Mexican immigration service

Visas

If you wish to stay longer than 180 days, or if you wish to do business or perform religious work in Mexico, contact the Mexican Embassy or the nearest Mexican consulate to obtain a visa or permit. Persons performing religious work on a tourist card are subject to deportation.

Residing or Retiring in Mexico

If you plan to live or retire in Mexico, consult a Mexican consulate on the type of long-term visa you will need. As soon as possible after you arrive in the place you will live, it is a good idea to register with the U.S. Embassy or nearest U.S. consulate or consular agent. Bring your passport or other identification with you. Registration makes it easier to contact you in an emergency. (Registration information is confidential and will not be released to inquirers without your express authorization.

Travel Requirements for Persons under 18

A person under age 18 traveling with only one parent must have written, notarized consent from the other parent to travel, or must carry, if applicable, a decree of sole custody for the accompanying parent or a death certificate for the other parent. A child traveling alone or in someone else's custody must have notarized consent from both parents to travel, or if applicable, notarized consent from a single parent plus documentation that parent is the only custodial parent.

Short Stays near the Border

U.S. citizens visiting Mexico for no more than 72 hours and remaining within 20 kilometers of the border do not need a permit to enter. Those transiting Mexico to another country need a transit visa which costs a nominal fee and is valid for up to 30 days.

Driving Your Car to Mexico

Once you cross the border things change dramatically. When you drive to Mexico, you must obtain a temporary vehicle import permit. You must show: your proof of ownership or notarized authorization from the owner to bring the car into Mexico, a valid driver's license, proof of auto liability insurance, and current registration and plates. The permit is issued free at border entry points and is generally valid for the same period of time as your tourist card (up to 180 days). You must remove your motor vehicle from Mexico before the permit expires or have the permit extended by the Temporary Importation Department of a Mexican customs office. If you do not do so, your motor vehicle may be confiscated. You may not sell, transfer or otherwise dispose of a motor vehicle brought into Mexico on a temporary importation permit, nor may you leave Mexico without the vehicle. In case of emergency, or following an accident where the vehicle cannot be removed, the owner may request permission to depart Mexico without the vehicle from the Mexican Customs Office in Mexico City, or the local office of the Treasury Department (Hacienda) in other cities.

If you bring spare auto parts to Mexico, declare them when you enter the country. When you leave, be prepared to show that you are taking the unused parts with you or that you have had them installed in Mexico. Save your repair receipts for this purpose. If you wish to authorize another person to drive your car, record the authorization with Mexican officials when you enter Mexico—even if you expect to be a passenger when the other person drives. Do not, under any circumstances, allow an unauthorized person to drive your vehicle when you are not in the car. Such a person could have to pay a fine amounting to a substantial percentage of the vehicles's value, or your vehicle could be confiscated.

Car Insurance

Mexican auto insurance is sold in most cities and towns on both sides of the border. U.S. automobile liability insurance is not valid in Mexico nor is most collision and comprehensive coverage issued by U.S. companies. Therefore, when you cross the border, purchase auto insurance adequate for your needs in Mexico. A good rule of thumb is to buy coverage equivalent to that which you carry in the U.S. Motor vehicle insurance is invalid in Mexico if the driver is found to be under the influence of alcohol or drugs. Regardless of whether you have insurance, if you are involved in an accident, you will be taken into police custody until it can be determined who is liable and whether you have the ability to pay any judgment. If you do not have Mexican liability insurance, you are almost certain to spend some time in jail until all parties are satisfied that responsibility has been assigned and adequate financial satisfaction has been received. There may also be criminal liability assigned if the injuries or damages are serious.

Tourists should enter Mexico with only the items needed for their trip. Entering with large quantities of an item a tourist might not normally be expected to have, particularly expensive appliances, such as televisions, stereos or other items, may lead to suspicion of smuggling and possible confiscation of the items and arrest of the individual.

Bringing in Expensive Items

You may have difficulty bringing computers or other expensive electronic equipment into Mexico for your personal use. To prevent being charged an import tax, write a statement about your intention to use the equipment for personal use and to remove it from Mexico when you leave. Have this statement signed and certified at a Mexican consulate in the United States and present it to Mexican customs as you enter Mexico. Land travelers should verify with Mexican customs at the border that all items in their possession may be legally brought into Mexico. You will be subject to a second immigration and customs inspection south of the Mexican border where unlawful items may be seized, and you could be prosecuted regardless of whether or not the items passed through the initial customs inspection.

Firearms

Do not bring firearms or ammunition into Mexico without first obtaining a permit from a Mexican consulate in the United States.

If you are caught entering Mexico illegally you will typically be expelled to your point of entry. The Mexican authorities can fine you between 300–5000 pesos and put you in jail for up to two years.

For further information concerning entry requirements, travelers may contact the

Embassy of Mexico

1911 Pennsylvania Avenue NW
Washington, D.C. 20006
☎ *(202) 728-1600, or any of the Mexican consulates in major U.S. cities.*

Getting Around

Mexico has an extensive road, rail and air system. Travelers in the remote areas should be very careful at night or when stopped outside of town. Robbery is common. Roads may seem well paved but large potholes, animals, people and large objects can be found around blind corners. There are numerous guidebooks about Mexico including *Fieldings Mexico* by Larry and Lynn Foster.

During heavy seasonal rains (January–March), road conditions can become difficult and travelers can become stranded. For current Mexican road conditions between Ensenada and El Rosario, Mexico, travelers can contact the nearest Mexican consulate or tourism office or the U.S. Consulate General in Tijuana.

Between 4 and 6 million U.S. citizens visit Mexico each year, while more than 300,000 Americans reside there. Although Mexico is "just across the border" it could not be compared to Canada in terms of safety, health and crime threats. Remember that you are entering a country struggling to leave its third world status. All tourists (both Mexican and American) are the best targets for criminal acts simply because they routinely carry cash and expensive goods. Plan on being viewed as a robbery suspect whenever and wherever you travel to major cities and tourist areas in Mexico.

Driving in Mexico

Poor roads, infrequent repairs and lack of repair stations make motoring in Mexico a true adventure. It is not uncommon to be driving for 50 miles along a newly paved highway only to find a four-foot-wide chasm marked by a single branch. You have more to fear from cows than rattlesnakes since livestock like to sleep on the warm asphalt at night. Many routes have heavy truck and bus traffic, some have poor or nonexistent shoulders and many have animals on the loose. Also, some of the newer roads have very few restaurants, motels, gas stations or auto repair shops. If you have an accident you will be assumed to be guilty and since you are a "wealthy foreigner" all efforts will be made to detain you until satisfaction for the victim is received.

For your safety, have your vehicle serviced and in optimum condition before you leave for Mexico. Pack a basic first-aid kit and carry an emergency water supply in your vehicle.

Bad Gas

Unleaded gasoline will not be available away from the main highways.Even if the gasoline is dispensed from a pump marked as unleaded there is still no guarantee. This means you will destroy your catalytic converter and will require replacement upon return. Auto shops at the border can construct a replacement pipe for long trips in Mexico. Remember that American auto repair shops are prohibited by law from doing this so have your converter put back on before you come home. The gas you end up getting may contain water and other contaminants. Bring a flexible funnel and a crude filter (a handkerchief or coffee filter) to fill your gas tank because some gas stations have nozzles too large to fit unleaded gas tanks. Also be aware of kids who pump gas but nary a drop reaches your tank. Fuel your car with the key on to monitor how much gas you're getting. Be aware of rigged pumps.

Do not drive at night. Loose livestock and mufflers can appear at any time. Mexicans not only drive fast but seem to be unfazed by the lack of lights or sobriety at night. Construction sites or stranded vehicles are often unmarked by flares or other warning signals. Major dropoffs are sometimes marked with bent tires and other resultant pieces of detritus. Sometimes cars have only one headlight; bicycles seldom have lights or reflectors. Be prepared for a sudden stop at any time. Mexican driving conditions are such that, for your safety, you must drive more slowly than you do at home. In Mexico, a blinking left turn signal on the vehicle in front of you could mean that it is clear ahead and you may pass, or it could mean the driver is making a left turn. An outstretched left arm may mean an invitation for you to pass. When in doubt, do not pass. An oncoming vehicle flashing its headlights is a warning for you to slow down or pull over because you are both approaching a narrow bridge or place in the road. The custom is that the first vehicle to flash has the right of way and the other must yield. Freshly wet roads are dangerous because oil and road dust mix with water and form a lubricant. Until this mixture washes away, driving is extremely hazardous. Beware of sudden rains. Stop, or go extremely slowly, until conditions improve.

Driving Information

U.S. driver's licenses are valid in Mexico. Mexican insurance is required. All vehicular traffic is restricted in Mexico City in order to reduce air pollution. The restriction is based on the last digit of the vehicle license plate. (There is no specific provision regarding license plates with letters only.)

Monday: No driving if license plate ends with 5 or 6.

Tuesday: No driving if license plate ends with 7 or 8.

Wednesday: No driving if license plate ends with 3 or 4.

Thursday: No driving if license plate ends with 1 or 2.

Friday: No driving if license plate ends with 9 or 0.

Also, no driving of vehicles with temporary license plates or any other plate that does not conform with the above.

Saturday and Sunday: All vehicles may be driven.

Rental Cars

Many car rental companies in the U.S. have clauses in their contracts which prohibit drivers from traveling out of the country. The Mexican police are aware of these regulations, and will sometimes impound rental vehicles driven from the United States. When renting a vehicle in the United States, check with the company to see if your contract allows you to drive it into Mexico.

Renting a Car in Mexico

The standard insurance included with many car rental contracts in Mexico provides only nominal liability coverage, often as little as the equivalent of US$200. Because Mexican law permits the jailing of drivers after an accident until they have met their obligations to third parties and to the rental company, renters should read their contracts carefully and purchase additional liability and comprehensive insurance if necessary.

Bringing Your Own Plane or Boat to Mexico

Private aircraft and boats are subject to the same Mexican customs regulations as are motor vehicles. When you arrive at a Mexican port in your private boat, you can obtain a temporary import permit for it similar to the one given for motor vehicles. Flying your own plane to Mexico, however, is more complicated. Well before your trip, inquire about private aircraft regulations and procedures from a Mexican consulate or Mexican Government Tourist Office.

Operation of Citizen's Band (CB) Equipment

American tourists are permitted to operate CB radios in Mexico. You may obtain a 180-day permit for a nominal fee by presenting your U.S. citizen's band radio authorization at a Mexican consulate or Mexican Government Tourist Office. This permit cannot be obtained at the border. Transmissions on CB equipment are allowed only on channels nine, 10, and 11, and only for personal communication and emergency road assistance. Any device which increases transmission power to over five watts is prohibited. CB equipment may not be used near radio installations of the aeronautical and marine services.

Getting Out

Mexican authorities require that all international transit of persons (transmigrants) and merchandise through Mexico destined for Central America from the area of Ciudad Acuna to Matamoros, be handled by the Lucio Blanco-Los Indios customs office and by the Colombia, Nuevo Laredo customs office. Transmigrants entering Mexico from areas other than the Ciudad Acuna-Matamoros zone will continue to use their regular ports of entry. Mexican authorities require that a customs broker handle the temporary entry into Mexico of all nonpersonal property of travelers destined for Central American countries. Fees will be processed through the customs broker. For more detailed information, travelers can contact the nearest Mexican consulate or tourism office or the U.S. Consulate in Matamoros prior to departing the U.S.

Residents of the U.S. returning to the U.S can expect long lines and waits in Tijuana and other major gateways.

Exporting Gold or Silver Currency

In 1982, the Mexican government lifted currency controls and modified its exchange rate system, permitting tourists to exchange dollars for pesos at the fluctuating free market rate. There are no restrictions on the import or export of bank notes and none on the export of reasonable quantities of ordinary Mexican coins. However, gold or silver Mexican coins may not be exported. Take "Traveler's cheques" with you because personal U.S. checks are rarely accepted by Mexican hotels or banks. Major credit cards are accepted in many hotels, shops, and restaurants. An exchange office (*casa de cambios*) usually gives a better rate of exchange than do stores, hotels or restaurants.

Wildlife or Products Made from Wild Animals

You risk confiscation and a possible fine by U.S. Customs if you attempt to import virtually any wildlife or products made from wild animals from Mexico. In particular, watch out for and avoid: all products made from sea turtles, including such items as turtle leather boots, tortoiseshell jewelry and sea turtle oil cosmetics; fur from spotted cats; Mexican birds, stuffed or alive, such as parrots, parakeets, or birds of prey; crocodile and caiman leather; black coral jewelry; wildlife curios, such as stuffed iguanas. When driving across state lines within Mexico, you can expect to be stopped at agricultural livestock inspection stations.

Antiques

Mexico considers all pre-Columbian objects to be the "inalienable property of the Nation" and considers the unauthorized export of such objects as theft which is punishable by arrest, detention and judicial prosecution. Under U.S. law, to import pre-Columbian monumental and architectural sculpture and murals, you must present proof that they were legally exported from the country of origin. U.S. law does not prohibit the import of nonmonumental or nonarchitectural artifacts from Mexico.

Glazed Ceramics

According to the U.S. Food and Drug Administration, it is possible to suffer **lead poisoning** if you consume food or beverages that have been stored in or served on improperly glazed ceramicware. Analysis of many ceramic pieces from Mexico has shown them to contain dangerous levels of lead. Unless you have proof of their safety, use glazed ceramics purchased in Mexico for decorative purposes only.

Returning to the United States

You must present the pink copy of your tourist card at your point of departure from Mexico.

Dangerous Places

Chiapas

Travel throughout Chiapas, Mexico's southernmost state, may be delayed due to security checks while the government cleans up the civil unrest. Chances of meeting a rebel roadblock are reduced after the recent military crackdown. Sometimes you may run into a roadblock put up by locals. Roadblocks in the Chiapas region can be as simple as a piece of string held up across the road. Many times rebels or locals will ask for articles of clothing. There have been no reports of attacks on travelers in this region. Travelers should exercise caution, and obey requests by Mexican military personnel. Journalists are also restricted in their movements. Interviews with subcommander Marcos, although fairly easy to obtain, frequently involved long waits (up to a week or more) and a late night rendezvous in a remote location. Now that he is on the run it is not known if he will resurface.

The town of San Cristobal in the state of Chiapas is relatively quiet after the disturbances in early January and December of 1994. The situation could become unstable in areas of Chiapas state outside of San Cristobal. U.S. citizens residing or traveling in Mexico may contact the U.S. embassy or consulates for further security information.

Bad Highways

Beware of Highway 15 in the state of Sinaloa and of Highway 40 between the city of Durango and the Pacific coast areas. These are particularly dangerous and are where a number of criminal assaults have occurred. Avoid express Highway 1 (limited access) in Sinaloa altogether—even in daytime—because it is remote and subject to bandits.

To avoid highway crime, try not to drive at night and never drive alone at night. Never sleep in vehicles along the road. If your vehicle breaks down, stay with it and wait for the police or the "Green Angels." Do not, under any circumstances, pick up hitchhikers; not only do they pose a threat to your physical safety, but they also put you in danger of being arrested for unwittingly transporting narcotics or narcotics traffickers in your vehicle. Your vehicle can be confiscated if you are transporting marijuana or other narcotics. There are checkpoints and temporary roadblocks where vehicles are examined.

On Public Transport

Be vigilant in bus and train stations and on public transport. Do not accept beverages from other passengers. On occasion, tourists have been drugged and robbed while they slept.

On the Street

Street crime is common, especially in urban areas. Persons driving on some Mexican roads, particularly in isolated regions, have been targeted by bandits who operate primarily after dark. Criminals, particularly in Sinaloa, sometimes represent themselves as Mexican police or other local officials. Any U.S. citizens who become a victim of crime in Mexico are encouraged to report the incident to local police authorities and to the nearest U.S. consular office.

On the Road

The U.S. Embassy advises its personnel not to travel on Mexican highways after dark. Highway 15 and Express Highway 1 (limited access) in the state of Sinaloa are particularly dangerous areas where criminal assaults and murders have occurred, during the day and at night.

Dangerous Things

Being Drunk

Despite every stereotype of the unshaven drunken *muchachos* firing their rusty guns into the air on Friday nights, drunkenness is a no-no south of the border. Certain border towns have become impatient with teenaged (and older) Americans who cross the border to drink and carouse. This behavior usually leads to fights, arrests, traffic accidents and even death, not to mention those nasty mescal hangovers. Cops do crack down on drunks and the chances of you retaining your wallet and your teeth are not high.

Dining and Dashing

Failure to pay hotel bills or failure to pay for other services rendered is considered fraud under Mexican law. Those accused of these offenses are subject to arrest and conviction with stiff fines and jail sentences.

Drugs

Sentences for possession of drugs in Mexico can be as long as 25 years plus fines. Just as in the U.S., purchase of controlled medication requires a doctor's prescription. The Mexican list of controlled medication differs from the U.S. list, and Mexican public health laws concerning controlled medication are unclear. Possession of excessive amounts of a psychotropic drug such as Valium can result in arrest if the authorities suspect abuse.

Drugs are a major part of Mexican life. Some areas are considered to be run by narcotics dealers. Drug dealers can be spotted by their love for Chevy Suburbans and Jeep Cherokees, Ray Bans and AK- 47's. The sport-utility vehicles are usually stolen, and some even display California license plates. About 10 percent of the stolen vehicles in San Diego county end up in Mexico. The recovery rate for sport-utilities is only 20 percent compared to 82 percent for stolen cars. Ideal for the rough roads of Tijuana and the Baja peninsula, the sturdy, swiped vehicles are also the favorites of Mexican officials, who keep the trucks once they are recovered from *aspirinas*, or paid enforcers, who control the theft rings in California. In San Diego, thefts of Jeeps jumped to 88 during May 1994 alone, up from an average of 34 a month. The explanation was that officials who were sent in to investigate the death of Luis Donaldo Colosio were taking advantage of the situation to place their own orders for the shiny but stolen California cars.

Earthquakes

Earthquakes pose a major danger in Mexico due to the lack of earthquake standards in buildings and the frequency of earthquakes and tremors.

Firearms

Do not bring firearms or ammunition of any kind into Mexico unless you have first obtained a consular firearms certificate from a Mexican consulate. To hunt in Mexico, you must obtain a hunting permit, also available from the consulate. Travelers carrying guns or ammunition into Mexico without a Mexican certificate have been arrested, detained and sentenced to stiff fines and lengthy prison terms. The sentence for clandestine importation of firearms is from six months to six years. If the weapon is greater than .38 caliber, it is considered of military type, and the sentence is from five to 30 years. When you enter Mexico, make certain that Mexican customs officials check both the firearms and your certificate. When you reach your destination, register your firearms with the appropriate military zone headquarters. If you enter Mexican waters on a private boat, you are still subject to the ban on importing firearms. Remember that before you leave the States, you must also register your firearms and ammunition with U.S. Customs or they will assume you picked them up from a kid in a bar. In some areas of Mexico, it is not wise to carry anything that might be construed as a weapon. Some cities, such as Nuevo Laredo, have ordinances prohibiting the possession of knives and similar weapons. Tourists have even been arrested for possessing souvenir knives. Most arrests for knife possession occur in connection with some other infraction, such as drunk and disorderly behavior.

Kidnapping

There have been cases of kidnapping of wealthy Mexican businessmen.

Mexican Legal System

Tourists who commit illegal acts have no special privileges and are subject to full prosecution under the Mexican judicial system. Mexico rigorously prosecutes drug cases. Under Mexican law, possession of and trafficking in illegal drugs are federal offenses. For drug trafficking, bail does not exist. Mexican law does not differentiate between types of narcotics: heroin, marijuana and amphetamines, for example, are treated the same. Offenders found guilty of possessing more than a token amount of any narcotic substance are subject to a minimum sentence of seven years, and it is not uncommon for persons charged with drug offenses to be detained for up to one year before a verdict is reached. Remember, if narcotics are found in your vehicle, you are subject to arrest and your vehicle can be confiscated.

Mexican Jails

Mexico has the highest number of arrests of Americans abroad—over 2000 per year—and the highest prison population of U.S. citizens outside of the United States—about 425 at any one time. If you find yourself in serious difficulty while in Mexico, contact a consular officer at the U.S. Embassy or the nearest U.S. Consulate for assistance. U.S. consular officers cannot serve as attorneys or give legal assistance. They can, however, provide lists of local attorneys and advise you of your rights under Mexican law. If you are arrested, ask permission to notify the U.S. Embassy or nearest U.S. Consulate. Under international agreements and practice, you have the right to contact an American consul. Although U.S. consuls are restricted by Mexican law as to what they can do to assist you in legal difficulties, they can monitor the status of detained U.S. citizens and make sure they are treated fairly under local laws. They will also notify your relatives or friends upon request. An individual is guaranteed certain rights under the Mexican constitution, but those rights differ significantly from U.S. constitutional guarantees.

The Mexican judicial system is based on Roman and Napoleonic law and presumes a person accused of a crime to be guilty until proven innocent. There is no trial by jury nor writ of habeas corpus in the Anglo-American sense. Trial under the Mexican system is a prolonged process based largely on documents examined on a fixed date in court by prosecution and defense counsel. Sentencing usually takes six to 10 months. Bail can be granted after sentencing if the sentence is less than five years. Pre-trial bail exists but is never granted when the possible sentence upon conviction is greater than five years.

Phony Cops

Be aware of persons representing themselves as Mexican police or other local officials. Some Americans have been the victims of harassment, mistreatment and extortion by criminals masquerading as officials. Mexican authorities are concerned about these incidents and have cooperated in investigating such cases. You must, however, have the officer's name, badge number and patrol car number to pursue a complaint. Make a note of this information if you are ever involved with police or other officials. Do not be surprised if you encounter several types of police in Mexico. The Preventive Police, the Transit Police and the Federal Highway Police all wear uniforms. The Judicial Police who work for the public prosecutor are not uniformed.

Truck Hijackings

Truck hijackings have become a growing problem in Guadalajara, San Luis Potosi, Estado de Mexico, southern Tamaulipas and along the Laredo-Monterrey highway corridor. Both American and Mexican trucking companies have been hit. Nearly 80 trailers were taken in 1994, resulting in a US$5 million loss. The principal targets are trucks carrying electronic equipment. Corrupt PGR and PGF inspectors may be behind many of the incidents, as they are able to see manifests and inspect trucks at the border.

Volcanos

Popocatepetl volcano, about 40 miles south of Mexico City, has been active. Villages in the area were evacuated in December 1994, and travelers in the region should avoid areas near the mountain's base. Popocatepetl, which means "smoking mountain" in the local Nahuatl language, had its last major eruption in 1921. Mexico City is not considered to be in danger.

Watersports

Many people are injured having fun in Mexico. Sports equipment that you rent or buy may not meet the safety standards to which you are accustomed. Critical equipment used for scuba diving or parasailing, jet-skis or motor boats may not be properly maintained or defective. Inexperienced scuba divers should beware of dive shops that promise to "certify" you after a few hours of instruction. On a recent trip to Acapulco we were separated into two groups: experienced divers and people who had never been underwater. The neophytes had their equipment strapped on, a brief explanation about how to breathe using the regulator, a warning not to go too deep and within five minutes they had become certified scuba divers.

Getting Sick

Adequate medical care can be found in all major cities and most drugs can be found over-the-counter. Most major hotels have a doctor on call who can treat everything from venereal diseases to drug addiction. Health facilities in Mexico City are excellent, and are generally quite good in the major tourist and expat cities, including Cancun, Acapulco, Puerto Vallarta, Mazatlan, Merida, Manzanillo, Guadalajara, etc. Care in more remote areas is limited.

In some places, particularly at resorts, medical costs can be as high as or higher than in the United States. If your health insurance policy does not cover you in Mexico, it is strongly recommended that you purchase a policy that does. There are short-term health policies designed specifically to cover travel. Medical facilities in Mexico differ from those in the United States, and treatment for some types of illnesses or injuries may be only remedial. Some remote areas or coastal islands may have few or no medical facilities. For these reasons, in addition to medical insurance that you can use in Mexico, consider obtaining insurance or joining a membership organization that will cover the exorbitant cost of medical evacuation in the event of an accident or serious illness. As part of the coverage, medical evacuation companies usually offer emergency consultation by telephone. They may refer you to the nearest hospital or call directly for help for you; they may translate your instructions to a health care worker on the scene. The cost of medical evacuation coverage can be as low as $50 for a trip of 30 days. On the other hand, escorted medical evacuation can cost in the tens of thousands of dollars. If your travel agent cannot direct you to a medical evacuation company, look for information on them in travel magazines. The U.S. government cannot pay to have you medically evacuated to the United States.

Immunizations are recommended against diphtheria, tetanus, polio, typhoid, and hepatitis A. For visitors coming directly from the United States, no vaccinations are required to enter Mexico. If you are traveling from an area known to be infected with yellow fever, a vaccination certificate is required. Malaria is found in some rural areas of Mexico, particularly those near the southwest coast. Travelers to malarial areas should consult their physician or the U.S. Public Health Service and take the recommended dosage of chloroquine. Although chloroquine is not considered necessary for travelers to the major resort areas on the Pacific and Gulf coasts, travelers to those areas should use insect repellent and take other personal protection measures to reduce contact with mosquitoes, particularly from dusk to dawn when malaria transmission is most likely.

Montezuma's revenge is as sure as hangovers from cheap tequila. Drink only bottled water or water that has been boiled for 20 minutes. Avoid ice cubes. Vegetables and fruits should be peeled or washed in a purifying solution. A good rule of thumb is, if you can't peel it or cook it, don't eat it. Medication to prevent travelers' diarrhea is not recommended. If symptoms present themselves and persist, seek medical attention because diarrhea is potentially dangerous. Air pollution in Mexico City is severe. It is the most dangerous during thermal inversions which occur the most from December to May. Air pollution plus Mexico City's high altitude are a particular health risk for the elderly and persons with high blood pressure, anemia, or respiratory or cardiac problems. If this applies to you, consult your doctor before traveling to Mexico City. In high altitude areas, such as Mexico City, most people need a short adjustment period. Spend the first few days in a leisurely manner, with a light diet and reduced intake of alcohol. Avoid strenuous activity— this includes everything from sports to rushing up the stairs. Reaction signs to high altitude are lack of energy, a tendency to tire easily, shortness of breath, occasional dizziness and insomnia.

Nuts and Bolts

Shopping

Make sure the goods you buy are in good condition and always get a receipt. There is a federal consumer protection office, the Procuraduria Federal del Consumidor, to assist you if you have a major problem with a faulty product or service. However, if the problem is with a service of the tourist industry, you should bring the matter to the Mexican Government Tourist Office (Secretaria de Turismo).You may obtain a list of Mexican lawyers from the U.S. Embassy or a U.S. Consulate or from the Office of Citizens Consular Services, Inter-American Division, *Room 4817, Department of State, Washington, DC 20520,* ☎ *(202) 647-3712.* To avoid disputes with merchants, ba a careful shopper.

Emergency Help

In an emergency, call ☎ *[91] (5) 250-0123,* the 24-hour hotline of the Mexican Ministry of Tourism. The hotline is for immediate assistance, but it can give you general, nonemergency guidance as well. In Mexico City, dial 06 for police assistance.

If you have problems filling out a police report or if you have difficulty filing a report, you can call the "Silver Angels." This group helps tourists who are victims of crime file a police report.

If you have an emergency while driving, call the Ministry of Tourism's hotline to obtain help from the "Green Angels," a fleet of radio-dispatched trucks with bilingual crews that operate daily. Services include protection, medical first aid, mechanical aid for your car and basic supplies. You will not be charged for services, only for parts, gas and oil. The Green Angels patrol daily, from dawn until sunset. If you are unable to call them, pull well off the road and lift the hood of your car; chances are good that they will find you.

Embassy and Consulate Locations

American Embassy

> *Paseo de la Reforma 305*
> *Mexico 06500, D.F.*
> ☎ *[52] (5) 211-0042*
> *Telex 017-73-091 and 017-75-685*
> *FAX [52] (5) 511-9980U*

U.S. Export Development Office/U.S. Trade Center

> *31 Liverpool*
> *Mexico 06600, D.F.*
> ☎ *[52] (5) 591-0155*
> *Telex 017-73-471*

American Consulate General

Avenue Lopez Mateos 924-N
Ciudad Juarez, Chihuahua
☎ [52] (16) 134-048
After Hours (emergencies) ☎ (915) 525-
6066
Telex 033-840
FAX [52] (161) 34048 ext. 210 or [52]
(161) 34050 ext. 210

American Consulate General

Progreso 175
Guadalajara, Jalisco
☎ [52] (36) 25-2998, [52] (36) 25-2700
Telex 068-2-860 ACDMC
FAX [52] (36) 26-6549

American Consulate

Calle Monterrey 141, Poniente
Hermosillo, Sonora
Tel [52] (621) 723-75
After Hours (emergencies) ☎ [52] (621)
725-85
Telex 058-829 ACHEME
FAX [52] (62) 172375 ext. 49

American Consulate

Ave. Primera No. 2002
Matamoros, Tamaulipas
☎ [52] (891) 2-52-50 or [52] (891) 2-52-
51
Telex 035-827 ACMTME
FAX [52] (89) 138048

American Consulate

Circunvalacion No. 120 Centro
Mazatlan, Sinaloa
☎ [52] (678) 5-22-05
Telex 066-883 ACMZME
FAX [52] (678) 2-1775

American Consulate

Paseo Montejo 453
Merida, Yucatan
☎ [52] (99) 25-5011
After Hours (emergencies) ☎ [52] (99) 25-
5409
Telex 0753885 ACMEME
FAX [52] (99) 25-6219

American Consulate General

Avenida Constitucion 411 Poniente
Monterrey, Nuevo Leon
☎ [52] (83) 45-2120
Telex 0382853 ACMYME
FAX [52] (83) 42-0177

American Consulate

Avenida Allende 3330, Col. Jardin
Nuevo Laredo, Tamaulipas
☎ [52] (871) 4-0696 or [52] (871) 4-9616
After Hours (emergencies) ☎ (512) 727-
9661
Telex 036-849 ACMLME
FAX [52] (871) 4-0696 ext. 128

American Consulate General

Tapachula 96
Tijuana, Baja California
☎ [52] (66) 81-7400 or (706) 681-7400
After Hours (emergencies) ☎ (619) 585-
2000
Telex 056-6836 ACTJMEX
FAX [52] (66) 81-8016

Dangerous Days

05/05/1867   Archduke Maximilian of Austria, who was established as emperor of
Mexico in 1864 by Napolean III of France, was deposed by Benito
Juarez and executed in 1867.

12/06/1822   Establishment of the Republic.

09/16/1810   Independence from Spain was declared by Father Miguel Hidalgo. The
war for independence continued until 1822, when the Mexican
Republic was established.

Russia

Big Red

Russia has an affinity for red. If it isn't the red blood of its people that is being spilled it is the red ink that Russia seems to be drowning in. Their new flag is too cutesy to really represent the bloody and financial woes this country is going through. Strangely enough the red blood and red ink seem to go hand in hand as Russia tries to rebuild its economy while rebuilding its empire. The recent brutal crackdown on Chechnya and its resultant costs (in lives, bad PR and money) is likely to derail Russia's attempt to revive its economy. Communism doesn't look so bad anymore. With Russia's woes kept in the background, snappy marching soldiers are seen on TV instead of frozen cadavers, and manly portraits of great leaders who seemed to know what they were doing. Poverty was a lot easier when you could blame it on the U.S. imperialist aggressors.

The bricks that hold Russia together are the stoic, proud people who seem to endure any injustice, survive any hardship and still maintain a sense of cynical humor throughout their Darwinian trials. Russia is a tough place, but then again its people have always been tough and are getting tougher.

How tough is it? In August 1994, in the grubby town of Nizhini Tagil in the Ural Mountains, Russian criminals hijacked (or rented) a T-90 tank from the local military base, drove it back to town and shot it out with Muslims who had tried to strongarm control of their market stalls. Makes our Wild West look like a sorority pillow fight.

Despite the debacle in Chechnya, Russians are famous for their bullheaded achievement of objectives against all odds. When the Russians lose, as in Eastern Europe and Afghanistan, there is little for the other side to gloat about owning.

In December 1991, the Cold War ended when the Soviet Union collapsed.The high-flying Russian revolution had finally run out of gas and crashed. The jagged pieces totalled 12: Armenia, Azerbaijan, Belarus, Georgia, Kazakhstan, Kyrgyzstan, Moldova, Russia, Tajikistan, Turkmenistan, Ukraine and Uzbekistan. And most of these states are going through a secondary breakup as ethnic and religious factions fight for sovereignty, usually with the help or antagonism of "Mother Russia," Iran or gangsters. After their brief taste of independence (and financial insolvency) many of these independent states are thinking about realigning themselves with Moscow.

Russia is the largest country that emerged from the former U.S.S.R. In 1992, Russia introduced an array of economic reforms which not only freed the prices on most goods and services, but set the course for a downward economic spiral which continues today. Although President Boris Yeltsin survived a national referendum on his ability to lead the country in April 1993, he dissolved the legislative bodies still left dangling from the Soviet era in September of that year, a move that paralyzed his presidency. On October 3, 1993, tensions between the executive and legislative branches of the government escalated into armed conflict. Again, with the help of the military, Boris survived, as he did against another foe, arch-conservative Vladimir Zhirinovsky.

But Boris' boys are crippled, the military in tatters. A December 1994 attempt to take Grozny in the rebel republic of Chechnya revealed in a rebel rout of the Russian forces precisely how weak the Russian war machine has become. Yeltsin may think he is in charge, but it became apparent that when push comes to shove, the army will decide. Renegade commanders refused to follow orders or never received them. Russian soldiers captured by the insurgent Chechens revealed that they were without food and maps—essentially that they had no direction nor any idea of what the hell they were doing. Russian corpses littered Grozny like dead worms after a heavy rain. Although the vastly superior forces eventually took the Chechen capital in January 1995, they face a repeat of Afghanistan. The Chechen insurgents—many of them former Soviet soldiers trained in mountain guerilla fighting—have dug into the hills, prepared for a long and fierce battle of attrition against an undisciplined, underage band of Boris' best. It may be a while, a long while, before any of us know how this will play out.

However, crime may be Russia's biggest export in the next decade. The brutal control of a central government has been reborn in the form of Russian Mafias. In the first five months of 1994, there were 664 crimes committed with firearms and explosives, 118 cases of hostage-taking, and an average of 84 murders a day. The ominous part is that the majority of the murders were contract killings, according to the Ministry of the Interior. Compare the rate of 16 murders per 100,000 in Russia to the U.S. rate of 9 per 100,000 and you can see why even trigger-happy Americans look like Buddhist monks next to the Russians.

There is more afoot than just thuggery in Russia. Tired of polishing their ICBM's and rotating their nuclear weapons, some army units have decided to strip them down into more economically attractive components and by doing so generate a little cash. In 1993 there were 6430 cases of stolen weapons ranging from assault rifles to tanks.

To date there have been over 700 cases of nuclear material being sold to various buyers outside and inside Russia. On the black market a kilo of chromium-50 can go for US$25,000, cesium-137 for US$1 million and lithium-6 for US$10 million. Prospective customers for these goodies are Iran, North Korea, Libya and other nations looking for a big bang for their money.

Future civil disturbances and uprisings are inevitable as the economy continues its slippery slide and the standard of living continues to drop.

There's not a lot of anti-American sentiment in Russia, although some Russians despise foreigners, particularly Americans and Western Europeans who remind them of all they don't and will never possess. Occasionally, there are protests against U.S. policy. But Americans aren't targets because of their nationality, however, but because Russians perceive all Americans as rich. Americans aren't hard to spot in their Levis and Nikes, toting camcorders and wearing bulging fanny packs. As social and economic conditions in Russia deteriorate and there are more unemployed and low-salaried individuals, crimes against monied foreigners will rise. Americans who possess hard currency and imported goods have increasingly become attractive targets.

Instability in the social-political sphere, deteriorating economic processes, a falling standard of living and an absence of specific programs to combat crime are all contributing to a general and steady increase in crime. The entire former Soviet region is a patchwork of government and private organizations that may or may not be functioning when you get there.Some are being replaced by new governments or are withering away without replacement. Intourist (☎ *212-757-3884*) is a good source of local information for prospective visitors to this beleaguered land. Intourist is now a non-governmental body and is still the largest tour operator in Russia and the other 11 former Soviet republics. Other Russian tour operators include Sputnik and Intratours.

But, do you really wanna go there?

The Scoop

Russia is still red, blood red. Someone is murdered in Russia every 18 minutes. Sixty percent of the murders are for material gain and 20 percent are thought to be murders of gangsters by rival gangs. In fact, there are more gangsters than there are police in Russia. Less than half of all perpetrators are ever brought to justice. Russians based in Moscow put much of the blame for this crime wave on southern foreigners, people who come from Armenia, Azerbaijan, Chechnya and Georgia. Crimes against foreigners jumped 44 percent in 1993.

The Players

The Russian Mafia (*Organizatsiya*)

The Russian Interior Ministry says that in 1993, police uncovered 5700 organized crime groups and brought charges against 11,400 people. One-sixth of these groups were working in more than one region while 300 were operating outside Russia's borders. The report also claimed that 150 major criminal societies controlled 35,000 enterprises. Most crime in Russia is controlled by eight "families," such as the Chechens, the most powerful group and descendants of a centuries-old tribe who still control the Caucasus Mountains. The Chechens specialize in bank fraud and extortion.

The Government

What government?

The Army

The army is slowly building back its power base in Russia and the CIS. The army finds itself the target of organized criminals. In some areas army commanders rent out weapons and men are hired out as mercenaries to the highest bidder.

Perestrelka

No, not *perestroika*, a word used by Mikhail Gorbachev to symbolize reforms. *Perestrelka* means "shoot out" in Russian and is a better description of what is going on in Russia today.

The military vacuum in Russia has allowed the rise of the *vory v zzakone*, or "thieves in law." A class of thugs created before the revolution and toughened in Soviet gulags, these gangsters are enamored with pomp and circumstance and even possess private jets. The government estimates that there are 289 "thieves in law" operating in Russia and 28 other countries around the world. Below these very wealthy and powerful mafia figures are the gangs. There are about 20 criminal brigades, or gangs, that control Moscow with LA-style monikers for their neighborhoods. There are estimated to be 5800 gang members in Russia. The gangs aren't quick or smart enough to control the country, so it's left to the *vory v zzakone* to reap the profits of absolute control.

There are four levels of Mafia in Russia. The lowest stratum consists of shopkeepers who sell goods at inflated prices to afford protection money. The enforcers are burly, loud men with a fancy for imported cars (usually stolen). They'll also double as pimps, gunrunners and drug dealers. The businessmen are unfettered capitalists who steer most of the lucrative deals the Mafia's way.

Finally, at the top of the food chain, is the "state Mafia." They are the controllers of a large percentage of the moneys earned by the lesser Mafia. These politician/gangsters allow the lower echelons to operate in peace and without fear of prosecution. They have driven away a lot of Western investment and businessmen who find themselves forced to retain a local "partner" in their enterprises.

Getting In

A passport and Russian visa are required for all U.S. citizens traveling to or transiting through Russia by any means of transportation, including train, car or airplane. While under certain circumstances travelers who hold valid visas to some countries of the former Soviet Union may not need a visa to transit Russia, such exceptions are inconsistently applied. Travelers who arrive without an entry visa may be subject to large fines, days of processing requirements by Russian officials and/or immediate departure by route of entry (at the traveler's expense). Carrying a photocopy of passports and visas will facilitate replacement should either be stolen.

All Russian visas, except transit visas, are issued on the basis of support from a Russian individual or organization, known as the sponsor. It is important to know who your sponsor is and how they can be contacted, as Russian law requires that your sponsor apply on your behalf for replacement, extension or changes to your visa. The U.S. Embassy cannot act as your sponsor. Tourists should contact their tour company or hotel in advance for information on visa sponsorship.

U.S. citizens can contact the

Russian Embassy

Consular Division
1825 Phelps Place, NW
Washington, D.C. 20008
☎ *(202) 939-8918, 939-8907, or 939-8913*
or the Russian Consulates in New York, San Francisco or Seattle for current information on visa requirements.

All foreigners must have an exit visa in order to depart Russia. For short stays, the exit visa is issued together with the entry visa; for longer stays, the exit visa must be obtained by the sponsor after the traveler's arrival. Russian law requires that all travelers who spend more than three days in Russia register their visas, through their hotel or sponsor. Visitors who stay in Russia for a period of weeks may be prevented from leaving if they have not registered their visas. Errors in the dates or other information on the visa can occur, and it is helpful to have someone who reads Russian check the visa before you depart the United States.

The Southern borders are not manned and checkpoints are only on main roads. Most Russian soldiers can be bribed due to their low pay and acceptance of side income.

Getting Around

Internal travel, especially by air, can be erratic and may be disrupted by fuel shortages, overcrowding of flights and various other problems. Travelers may need to cross great distances, especially in Siberia and the Far East, to obtain services from Russian government organizations or from the U.S. Embassy or its consulates.

Unlike during Soviet times, you can go just about anywhere you want these days. You don't even need to use Intourist to get around. The cheapest way into Moscow from the airport is via the regular bus. You can use rubles. Taxis usually require long waits and cost about 1000 rubles. You can also pick up a private car from one of the many people who will try to offer you one. Expect to pay US$50 in real money (not rubles) or the equivalent amount in cigarettes. You run the risk of getting waylaid or robbed if you take the wrong car. For about the same price you can arrange a car in the arrivals section. You must use a credit card. In Moscow most taxis demand U.S. dollars, or one to three packs of cigarettes or R10 to R20.

Russia stretches over 6000 miles east to west and 2500 miles north to south. Winter can last a long time.

About half the roads in Russia are paved. The worst time to traverse Russian roads is during the spring when the rural roads become muddy rivers. About 20 percent of the roads are simple tracks. The railways are the major means of transport, with most routes spreading out from Moscow on 11 major trunk lines. There are 32 railway subsystems within the Soviet Union. The main route is the passenger artery through Russia along the Trans-Siberian Railway, which travels east from Moscow across Siberia to the Pacific and China, Mongolia and Korea.

The main entry rail route to the West is the Moscow-Smolensk-Minsk-Brest -Warsaw and Berlin line. The new Baikal-Amur Mainline (BAM) follows a more northerly route than the Trans-Siberian route. The lines south from Moscow run through Kharkov to the Caucasus and the Crimea.

Traveling by sea is also an efficient way to get around Russia, particularly in the Baltic. Twenty-seven former Soviet passenger ships form the largest such fleet in the world.

Russian airlines service 3600 population centers inside Russia. The severe winters affect schedules. The major airports with scheduled flights are: Moscow (Sheremetyevo I and II, International), Domodedovo, Vnukovo, St Petersburg (Pulkovo), Kiev (Borispol International and Iuliany), Tashkent (Yuzhny), Omsk, Odessa, Vladivostok, Novosibirsk, Alma Ata, Astrakhan (north-west), Frunze, Karaganda, Samarkand, Baku (Bina), Tallinn (Ulemistu), Sukhumi (west), Kherson, Kharkov, Tbilisi (Novoalekseevka), Kuibyshev, Lvov, Zaporozhe, Kishenev, Krasnodar, Mineralye Vody, Minsk (Loshitsa), Riga, Simferopol (north), Yerevan, Riga, Uralsk, Vladivostok and Sverdlovsk.

Keep in mind that Russian airlines have dubious safety records; you may prefer to go by rail.

The telecommunications infrastructure remains underdeveloped. Only 30 percent of urban and 9 percent of rural families have telephones. More than 17 million customers have ordered telephones, but are still waiting (sometimes for years) to have them installed.

Dangerous Places

The political situation remains unsettled in Russia's north Caucasus area, which is located in Southern Russia along its border with Georgia. Travel to this area is considered dangerous. The regions of the Chechen Republic, the Ingush Republic and the North Ossetian Republic have experienced continued armed violence and have a state of emergency and curfew in effect.

The Caucasus

In Nagorno Karabakh Armenians have been fighting for independence from Azerbaijan since 1988. Over 3000 people have died according to the latest figure from 1992.

Georgia

In Georgia, fighting in the South Ossetia region and the Mingrelia area has killed hundreds since 1989. In May of 1991, Zvaid Gamsakhurdia was elected president of Georgia with an overwhelming majority of the popular vote (86.5 percent). Not content with popular support, Zvaid began to conceive and implement very undemocratic statutes such as, "making fun of the president gets you six years in the slammer." He also put his money on the wrong ponies when he backed the coup plotters who failed to overthrow Yeltsin. He cracked down on the southern Muslim state of Ossetia, which instigated a revolt effective enough to force him to flee on January 6, 1992. The opposition, which consisted of his prime minister and foreign minister (who had backed Yeltsin), invited Eduard Shevardnadze, the former Soviet foreign minister and first secretary of the Georgian Communist Party to be chairman of the state council.

The return of old hard-line communist hacks did not satisfy the Muslim Abkhazian separatists who, feeling their oats, had taken over the Abkhazian region along the Black Sea.

The Russians meddled and brokered a cease-fire which was quickly broken on September 16, 1993. Despite a pistol-waving Shevardnadze, the rebels took over the strategic Black Sea port of Sukhumi. The bizarre twist is that Shevardnadze blames the Russians for setting him up by brokering a phony cease-fire and then letting the rebels take over the country. The fact that the "rebels" were using Russian-supplied weapons and equipment confirmed the perception that the Russians were backing the Abkhazians.

Additionally, there is the continual threat of Zvaid Gamsakhurdia and his efforts to setup his own republic in Mingrelia.

Eduard Shevardnadze is a busy boy these days. (See the "Georgia" chapter.)

Moscow

In Moscow alone, in 1993, there were 5000 murders and 20,000 incidents of violent crime. The local population easily recognizes U.S. tourists and business travelers as foreigners because of their clothing, accessories and behavior. American visitors tend to experience a relatively high incidence of certain types of crime, such as physical assaults and pickpocketing of wallets, money "Traveler's cheques," passports and cameras on the street, in hotels, in restaurants and in high-density tourist areas.

St. Petersburg

St. Petersburg has a crime rate 30 percent higher than Moscow's. The area around Gostiniy Dvor and the underground passage on Nevsky Prospekt, train stations, the food markets, the flea markets and the so-called "art park" are frequent stages for street crime against foreigners. It is estimated that 20 percent of the foreign businesses are controlled by the Russian Mafia. Most groups who try to set up businesses in the city find they are hit up for a US$10,000 fee to arrange the "necessary contacts." If you are edgy, bodyguards can be hired for about $600 a month (U.S. dollars only). Not bad when you figure that the average monthly wage is about US$20. Most crimes are committed in broad daylight since the police will do little, if anything, to help or track down your assailants. If you are staying in one of the better hotels in St. Petersburg have them send a car for you at the airport. If not, you can take a taxi into town for about US$30. If you want a car for the entire day figure on spending about double that.

Emergency Numbers

Fire
☎ *01*

Police
☎ *02*

Ambulance
☎ *03*

U.S. Consulate
☎ *274-8692*

Taxi
☎ *312-0022*

Hard Currency Taxi
☎ *298-6804, 298-3648*

Western Style Medical Care
☎ *310-9611*

American Express
☎ *311-5215*

Delta Airlines
☎ *311-5819/20/22*

Chechnya

A remote Transcaucasian region just north of Georgia, the republic of Chechnya is home to Russia's largest and most powerful crime families. In fact, they have a friendly neighborhood branch in your town (Boston, Philadelphia, Chicago, Los Angeles and New York). The Chechens told Yeltsin to get stuffed during the winter of 1991 and they've never looked back. Boris turned his eyes away for a while, but then launched one of the most embarrassing military attacks in Russian history.

There were, at last report, about 1500 Chechens living in Moscow. Many came back to Chechnya after the outbreak of hostilities to fight Yeltsin's army. The Chechens are an old-line crime family, one extremely difficult to infiltrate or join unless you are a member of the family.

The Chechens are split into three main criminal factions. The most powerful is the "Central," followed by the "Ostankinsky" and the "Automobile." Finding these groups used to be easy, as they operated from plush Moscow hotels until the war. The Centrals could be found in the Hotel Belgrade, the Golden Ring and the Russia Hotel. Here they controlled drugs, prostitution, restaurants, Moscow markets and the retail trade. The Ostankinsky takes its name from the Ostankinsky Hotel. The group has also headquartered in the Voskhod and Baikal hotels. Their specialty is the transfer and shipment of all types of goods (including drugs) between Moscow and their home base of Chechnya. The "Automobile" group brings in cars from Western Europe and looks after seven gas stations.

The transport and sale of drugs are a major source of income for the Chechens. They also employ the time-honored method of extortion to supplement their income. Everyone from street vendors to major international corporations have to cough up about 10 percent of their gross or face the music. The Chechens are linked to the three main Italian mafia families as well as members of the former Soviet government, the KGB and former Soviet Communist Party Members. See the "Chechnya" chapter.

Tajikistan

Afghanistan-based Tadjik guerrillas continue their attacks against Russian border posts. Russian planes have been bombing rebel positions inside Afghanistan. During New Year's celebrations in 1995, champagne laced with cyanide was sold at stalls near the Russian Embassy, killing 10. The Russians have tracked dozens of Arab mercenaries on their way to aid the insurgents, armed with Stinger missiles and mines.

Train and Metro Stations

Many attacks against tourists take place on trains (both city and national) and in the subways. The Trans-Siberian Railway is a common target of organized gangs of criminals who rob, rape and murder passengers. Russian businesses have stopped sending any valuable commodities through Chechnya.

Dangerous Things

Airlines

Airline passengers are more likely to be killed in Russia than anywhere else in the world. The number of fatalities per million passengers has risen from one in 1990 to 5.5 in 1993. The breakup of Aeroflot into hundreds of regional carriers who cannot afford to properly maintain their planes has a lot to do with it. The pilots, who make an average of $21 a month, are threatening to strike unless maintenance is improved.

Drinking, Eating and Smoking

If murder doesn't take out most Russians, vodka will. Russian deaths as a result of disease caused by toxins such as alcohol and nicotine are rising at an alarming rate. There was a 20 percent increase in alcohol poisoning between 1993 and 1994, and a 17.9 percent increase in infectious disease in the same period. Russians are famous for their love of vodka, heavy, greasy foods and smoking. Stress, leading to cardiovascular disease, is another big killer. One disease not commonly reported as a cause of death is cancer. Russia produces 75 million tonnes of toxic waste each year. It also does not have a single toxic waste treatment center.

Business

More than 90 people classified as entrepreneurs were murdered in Russia last year—a very convincing reason why 80 percent of the businesses pay protection money to the Russian Mafia. It ranges between 10 percent and 20 percent of gross revenues. It is estimated that 40,000 private and state run businesses are already controlled by the Mafia.

Banking

The second most dangerous job in Russia may be that of a banker. Banks are the most common target of the Mafia. In 1993, 30 bankers were murdered across Russia, 10 in Moscow.

Crime

In a place where hiring a hit man to kill someone costs only US$200, you had better watch your step. Foreigners are targets of crime in Russia, especially in major cities. Pickpocketing and muggings occur both day and night. Street crimes are most frequent in train stations, airports and open markets; on the Moscow-St. Petersburg overnight train; and when hailing taxis or traveling by the Metro late at night. Groups of children who beg for money sometimes pickpocket and assault tourists. Foreigners' hotel rooms and residences have also been targeted. Some victims have been seriously assaulted during robberies. If you receive a replacement for your lost or stolen U.S. passport from the U.S. Embassy or a consulate in Russia, your exit visa must also be replaced, with assistance from your sponsor, so that the passport number written on the visa matches your new passport. This normally requires a Russian police report.

Older people are also targets of crime in Russia. In addition, there has been a sharp rise in the number of taxi drivers killed while on duty. Policemen have been killed at their posts. And, to make matters worse, Russian jails are becoming overcrowded. An expected 40,000 prisoners in Russian jails have been, or are expected to be, released earlier than scheduled, much earlier. The government has been calling it amnesty. Keep up your guard.

Overnight Trains

Thieves routinely rob the sleeping berths in overnight trains throughout Russia. The problem is most acute along the Moscow-St. Petersburg route. The common M.O. is for the thief to drug victims before robbing them.

Americans

Yep, you read that right.There have been reports of Americans creating a distraction while a local rips you off.

Deaf Mutes

There are scams in Russia where deaf mutes feign illness and seek the aid of an American. While you're helping the ailing, a bunch of his buddies will rip you off.

Prostitutes

Prostitution is a bane the world over. But in Russia, particularly the larger cities, the hookers are controlled by Mafia-style bosses. Guests at many hotels can expect to be solicited at any time of the day. Hookers, as in Southeast Asia, are known to even knock on guests' doors.

Kids

Crimes by kids pose a unique threat to the population. Adolescents, often unemployed, travel and operate criminally in groups. One may also find younger boys of ages 10-12 operating in small groups or as individuals. The groups may have an adult ringleader for whom the kids work. If you're a victim of youth crime in Russia, especially in the cities, contact the police and fill out a report. In many instances, youths strike in the same place employing similar methods, making them easier to catch. Some foreigners have also reported successes in catching thieves by advertising on local TV stations.

The Police

An alarming trend in Russia is the growing police involvement in crimes against fellow Russians and foreigners. This is particularly worrisome in Moscow and St. Petersburg. In other instances, the police may not come to the aid of a crime victim, even if the crime is being committed before their eyes.

Crime Against Foreign Businesses

Extortion and corruption permeate the business environment in Russia. Organized criminal groups target foreign businesses in many Russian cities and reportedly demand protection money under threat of serious consequences. Many Western companies hire security services, but this has not always proven effective in thwarting armed extortion attempts.

Some Useful Advice on Crime

A booklet entitled, *How Not to Become a Crime Victim/Advice of Professionals*, published by the Leningrad Association of Workers, offers advice to citizens on avoiding crime. Here's some of it:

— Make purchases at reputable outlets.

— Count your change carefully before leaving the cashier or the seller. Recount your change if the seller has recounted it a second time because of a problem to make sure you have not been tricked during the recounting.

— Check to make sure that the article you believe you have purchased is the one that is packed for you.

— Do not invite people you do not know well into your living quarters, or drink alcohol with them to avoid the possibility of being drugged.

— Do not open the door to your quarters to unknown individuals.

— If you feel you are being followed, apply to the police for help.

— Do not get into an elevator alone with a stranger.

— If you are in trouble, yell *pozhar* (fire) to attract attention for aid.

— Be constantly aware and on the alert.

St. Petersburg security office recommendations:

— Dress down and do not flash cash or jewelry.

— Do not tell strangers where you are staying or your travel plans.

— Avoid crowds. Although this is difficult to do, do not let your curiosity get the better of you. Leave the area as soon as you can.

— When deciding when and where to make your purchases or to change money do not place convenience over your personal security. Street vendors are certainly more convenient, but dealing with them necessitates that you subject yourself to the scrutiny of bystanders who will make note of the location of your passport, money and other valuables. In many instances shortly after making a purchase, the customer falls victim to street thieves. Do not purchase drinks from already-opened bottles; i.e., in bars.

— When out on the town leave hard-to-replace, nonessential items such as passports, credit cards, driver's licenses and family pictures with the hotel security office or at home. Disperse your money throughout your garments. Remember the amounts in each location and when making purchases retrieve only the amount of money needed for that purchase. Never display large sums of money.

— Do not believe that you are getting a bargain. When you believe this, watch out; chances are that you are being setup. Thieves understand and utilize human emotions such as greed and lust. Situations in which these emotions are most commonly played upon include dealings with vendors of so-called antiquities, with prostitutes and in currency exchanges.

— Never patronize unmarked taxis or enter any taxi carrying unfamiliar passengers. Agree upon the price and destination prior to entering the vehicle.

— If you have a car with you, do not leave any items inside the vehicle when it is parked. These items will be attractive to thieves and will encourage break-ins. Also remove windshield wiper blades when parked. Do not park in dark and isolated places.

— Never drink alcoholic beverages without having a trusted friend along who has agreed to remain sober. Even slight intoxication is noted by professional thieves.

— When a victim of a crime, be it a violent act or general trickery, do not let your vanity or apathy prevent you from immediately making a report to the police and U.S. Embassy or Consulate. Others will benefit. In addition, stolen items are routinely retrieved.

Getting Sick

Medical care in Russia is usually far below Western standards, with severe shortages of basic medical supplies. Access to the few quality facilities that exist in major cities usually requires cash dollar payment at Western rates upon admission. The U.S. Embassy and consulates maintain lists of such facilities and of English-speaking doctors. Many resident Americans travel to the West for virtually all their medical needs; such travel can be very expensive if undertaken under emergency conditions. Travelers may wish to check their insurance coverage and consider supplemental coverage for medical evacuation. Elderly travelers and those with existing health problems may be at particular risk.

An outbreak of diphtheria continues in Moscow, St. Petersburg, and other parts of Russia. Although only a small number of cases have been reported, up-to-date diphtheria immunizations are recommended. Typhoid can be a concern for those who plan to travel extensively in Russia. Drinking only boiled or bottled water will help to guard against cholera, which has been reported, as well as other diseases. More complete and updated information on health matters can be obtained from the Centers for Disease Control's international travelers' hotline, ☎ *(404) 332-4559.*

Nuts and Bolts

The Russian Federation is the largest republic of the CIS; it's almost twice the size of the U.S. Moscow, with nearly nine million residents, is the largest city.

The Russian Federation officially came into existence in December 1991. Russia is a presidential republic containing 22 autonomous republics that maintain an uneasy balance between the Russian president and the Congress of People's Deputies (parliament). In practice the power base is much more complex. Russia's vast size (10.5 million square km) and small population (148 million) make the region ripe for exploitation by Western investors; the military-laden infrastructure makes business profits unlikely for years to come.

One curious effect of the Soviet regime has been the disappearance of religion in Russia. Official Soviet estimates indicated that about 10 percent of city dwellers and 25–30 percent of rurals followed a formal religion. Estimates of religious populations put Russian Orthodox at 35–40 million, Roman Catholics at 5 million, Muslims at 40–45 million, Uniate (banned) counting 3–4 million, Baptists at 500,000 and Jews at 2 million.

Russian is the official language although there are many local ethnic languages. English is widely read but not yet fluently spoken. Translators, of varying abilities, will be found in all sizeable organizations. The country boasts a nearly 100 percent literacy rate.

Business hours are from 9 a.m. to 1 p.m., with a break for the typical heavy Russian lunch between 1 and 2 p.m. Some stores close from 2 p.m. to 3 p.m. Banks are open from 9:30 a.m. to 12:30 p.m., with currency exchanges open longer. You can change money at Sheremeytevo II International Airport in Moscow 24 hours a day. Also, the American Express office in Moscow can cash your Amex "Traveler's cheques" into dollars.

Russia owes US$80 billion in debt but still manages to keep finding major oil fields such as the Tenghiz field in Kazakhstan The field is estimated to contain between seven and 25 billion barrels of oil. The Azeri oil field in the Caspian Sea and the Timan Pechora basin in the north Russian Archangels province will help to pay off that debt.The former U.S.S.R. had about 6.4 percent of the world's oil reserves and was the world's largest producer and exporter of natural gas. However, poor management has led to annual decreases each year since the 1980s.

Gas comes from Western Siberia; the largest areas are Urengoi and Yamburg. New fields on the Yamal peninsula are waiting for development. The former U.S.S.R. was the world's third largest coal producer in 1990 (after China and the United States). Russia possesses the world's largest explored reserves of copper, lead, zinc, nickel, mercury and tungsten.It also has about 40 percent of the world's reserves of iron ore and manganese. Figures released in September 1990 show confirmed iron reserves of 33.1 billion *tonnes*. The world's largest gold deposits at the Sukhoi Log reserves are estimated at more than 1000 *tonnes*, much of which is smuggled out of Russia through the Baltic States. Russia is also trying to retain more control over its diamond reserves. The government created the Federal Diamond Centre, granting parliament more control over the industry. The intent is to weaken control over Russia's diamonds by DeBeers, which has operated a supply cartel and maintained Russia's output at 7,500,000 carats per year.

Russia will be a net food importer for some time to come. In 1990, though there were record harvests, a shortage of labor caused the crops to rot in the fields.

Arms sales continue to be an important part of Russia's exports, although there is worldwide concern that a lot of hi-tech systems are getting into the wrong hands. In 1992, Russia sold more than US$2 billion worth of weapons through contracts with China, India, Iran and Syria.

In 1992, the former Soviet Union had more than 3 million men in its armed forces, over 60% of them conscripted for a two-year period. About 1 million conscripts perform essentially civilian jobs, such as construction. All men are subject to conscription, although in the past, many students have received exemption. There were between 2 and 2.5 million members of the military by 1994. Today, there is a reserve force numbering 55 million.

Addresses

British-Russian Chamber of Commerce

60a Pembroke Road
London W8 6NX
☎ *071-602-7692*
(services for members: Moscow office, group visits to Russia, seminars in conjunction with Oxford University scholars and others)

Consulate of Russia

Kensington Palace Gardens
London W8 4QS
☎ *071-229-3215/6*

Department of Trade and Industry, Russia Desk

Overseas Trade Division
1Victoria Street
London SW1 0ET
☎ *071-215-5265/4268*
Tx: 881-1074 DTHQ G
FAX 071-222-2531/2629

East European Trade Council

Suite 10, Westminster Palace Gardens
Artillery Row

London SW1P 1RL
☎ *071-222-7522*
Tx: *071-290-1018*

EETC GUS-Russia Trade and Economic Council

805 Third Avenue
New York 10022
☎ *212 644 4550*

The official currency is the ruble; it's pointless to post its rate against the U.S. dollar since it changes as frequently as most people change their underwear. There are 100 kopeks to the ruble.

Goods that are purchased from street vendors can be problematic and expensive to export. Russian customs laws state that any item for export valued at more than 300 rubles (value is established by customs officials at the time of export; for example, just prior to a traveler's departing flight) is subject to a 600 percent export tax. Items purchased from government licensed shops, where prices are openly marked in hard-currency, are not subject to the tax. Request a receipt when making any purchase.

Money Hassles

"Traveler's cheques" and credit cards are not widely accepted in Russia; in many cities credit cards are only accepted at establishments catering to Westerners; Old, or very worn dollar bills are often not accepted, even at banks. Major hotels or the American Express offices in Moscow or St. Petersburg may be able to suggest locations for cashing "Traveler's cheques" or obtaining cash advances on credit cards. Western Union has agents in Moscow, St. Petersburg and some other large cities which can disburse money wired from the United States.

Getting Out

Russian customs laws and regulations are in a state of flux and are not consistently enforced. A 600 percent duty is required to export any item with a value greater than 300,000 rubles. All items which may appear to have historical or cultural value—icons, art, rugs, antiques, etc.—may be taken out of Russia only with prior written approval of the Ministry of Culture and payment of a 100 percent duty. Caviar may only be taken out of Russia with a receipt indicating it was bought in a store licensed to sell to foreigners. Failure to follow the customs regulations may result in temporary or permanent confiscation of the property in question.

Embassy and Consulate Locations

Moscow: *Novinskiy Bulvar 19/23;* ☎ *(7- 095) 252-2451.*

After hours duty officer: ☎ *(7-095) 230-2001/2601.*

The U.S. Consulate General in St. Petersburg is located at *Ulitsa Furshtadskaya 15;* ☎ *(7-812) 275-1701.* After hours duty officer: ☎ *(7-812) 274-8692.*

The U.S. Consulate General in Vladivostok is located at *12 Mordovtseva;* ☎ *(7-4232) 268-458/554 or 266-820.*

The Consulate General in Yekaterinburg provides emergency services for American citizens; ☎ *(7-3432) 601-143, FAX (7-3432) 601-181*

Better Living Through Chemistry

Russia's drug addicts already number 1.5 million (or one percent of the entire population), and the figure keeps growing. Illegal hemp fields in Russia cover an area exceeding 40 million hectares. In an eight-month period in 1994, Russian law enforcement bodies made arrests in connection with 40,000 drug-related crimes, seizing 13.3 tons of various drugs. Police have busted 3300 gangs engaged in drug trafficking and sale. From 30 percent to 35 percent of the drugs are imported. In Moscow and St. Petersburg, however, the figure reaches 80-90 percent.

Better Living Through Chemistry

The price of one gram of cocaine in Moscow is from 400 percent to 900 percent higher than in New York, for which reason the Russian drug market looks very attractive to the international Mafia. Nearly US$100 million were involved in the drug trade in Russia in late 1993. The police force fighting drug dealers today numbers as few as 3500 men. Police are especially concerned that a new synthetic drug–trinisilsyntholin–is being produced in Russia. It had formerly only been produced in the U.S. The substance is so strong that one gram of it is enough to make ten liters of narcotics more powerful than heroin or cocaine. Imported drugs, such as heroin and cocaine, are now sold everywhere in this country. In Moscow, for instance, the price of one gram of heroin ranges fromUS$200 to US$300 dollars. The government is taking urgent measures to stamp out the social malady. A comprehensive federal antidrug program for 1995-1997 is being worked out by a special government commission.

Dangerous Days

09/18/1993 The last 24 former Soviet soldiers stationed in Poland returned to Russia, ending a presence which helped fortify Moscow's military and political domination for almost half a century.

12/31/1991 President Bush recognized the independence of all 12 former Soviet republics and proposed the establishment of full diplomatic relations with six of them, including Russia. Russian President Yeltsin responded formally and positively on December 31, 1991, the date officially considered to be when the U.S. established formal diplomatic relations with Russia.

12/25/1991 Mikhail Gorbachev resigned as president of the Soviet Union and transferred control of the Soviet nuclear arsenal to Russian President Boris Yeltsin. A few hours later, the United States recognized Russia as the successor state to the Soviet Union. These actions marked the end of the Soviet Union, 74 years after the Bolshevik revolution.

12/21/1991 Russia joined with ten other former republics of the Soviet Union (which ceased to exist on December 25, 1991) in establishing the Commonwealth of Independent States. The Commonwealth was expected to have military and economic coordinating functions and would be headquartered in Mensk, Byelarus.

08/19/1991 Failed coup attempt which symbolized the end of communism in Russia and the break up of the Soviet Union. Violent demonstrations occurred in Moscow in August 1992 resulting in several deaths.

05/02/1945 Berlin falls to the Soviets.

02/01/1943 Germany's 6th Army surrendered to Soviet forces in Stalingrad.

06/22/1941 German invasion of U.S.S.R.

11/07/17 Revolution Day, considered the most sacred day by Russian Communists.

Nukes for Sale

There are 80,000 nuclear weapons in the former Soviet Union waiting to be sold, destroyed or left as a bargaining chip in upcoming disputes. Many of the warheads' whereabouts are unknown. There are estimated to be between 19,000 to 40,000 in Russia alone. Iran and Kazakhstan have already offered to take some of these weapons off the cash-strapped Russians hands. Three grams of radioactive mercury can bring in a thousand US, so it is only a matter of time before materiel begins to slip out with the help of the Russian mafias.

North Korea's embryonic nuclear program has produced enough plutonium for two warheads in its 25 megawatt reactor at Yongbyon and may be able to produce enough for five more if they continue the current program.

It is assumed that current customers for the medium-range missiles (Syria, Iran and allegedly Libya) would be interested in the deluxe nuclear version. Col. Mohamar Kadafi is reportedly negotiating to buy ballistic missiles from North Korea.

The Ukraine is expected to dismantle the 1656 nuclear missiles it owns within seven years.

The nuclear club includes the US (1945), the Soviets (1949), China (1964) and Iraq was on the verge of joining the club within a year of the Gulf War. Other countries such as Japan, Brazil, Argentina and South Africa either have built or have the ability to build nuclear weapons but have decided not to continue their programs. Israel continues to deny its abilities in this arena.

Potential hot spots for future nuke-fests include the Middle East, Iran vs. Iraq, India vs. China, Japan vs. China, China vs. Taiwan, the two Koreas and the Russian steppes.

The Nuke Club

USA	Kazakhstan
Britain	Russia
France	India
Belarus	Pakistan
Ukraine	China

The United States

How the West Was Stunned

Land of the free and home of the brave. You'd better be damned brave here, because people are free to do pretty much anything they feel like. Behind white picket fences and two-car garages, husbands clobber their wives silly while their kids make crack deals over the phone with "Scarface."

In L.A., inner city toddlers catch stray bullets from drive-by shooters while in New York, Islamic whackos use a rented van full of fertilizer makings to blow up the World Trade Center. In San Diego a despondent plumber hot wires a tank, flattens some cars and is shot to death after high-centering on a freeway divider. What would Ozzie and Harriet Nelson say?

Doctors kiss their wives goodbye and later lose their lives outside burning abortion clinics in Massachusetts, Virginia, Florida, Oregon, Ohio, Minnesota and California—the victims of preachers, former altar boys and women who look more like manicurists than terrorists.

In Idaho, Alabama, Louisiana, Georgia and Utah, young white-trash punks, parading under the lofty and pontifical banner of white supremacy, stash a couple of years'

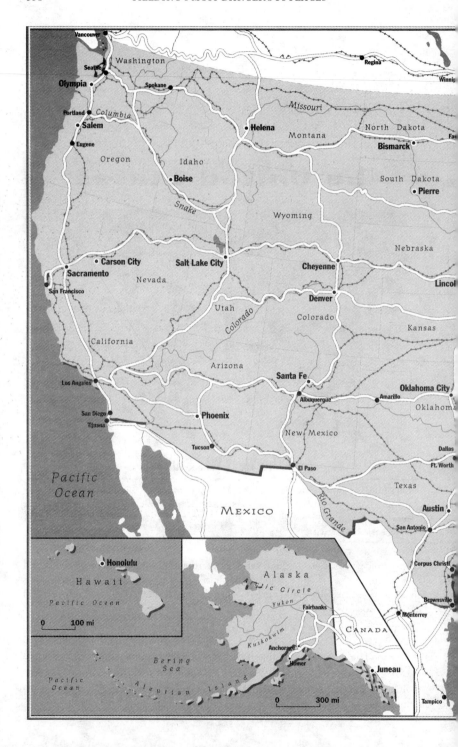

THE UNITED STATES

United States

✪ National capital
• State capital
● Secondary city
Primary road
Railroad
State border

| 0 | | | 800 km |
| 0 | | | 500 mi |

worth of Spam into a cave in the hills, run around in the forest with paint guns and plot the demise of every "nigger" and "kike" west of Bethesda. Fear not because in this land of equality and free speech, the JDL and Nation of Islam do their part to keep the hate at a fever pitch.

In Florida, penniless, HIV-positive heroin addicts from Haiti stalk the streets near Miami Airport looking for Chrysler convertible Lebarons and Ford Aerostars sporting Hertz stickers, whose occupants they strip-rob before perforating them with 9 mm blobs of molten lead and tossing the corpses into a drainage ditch.

Throughout the U.S., selected business executives and university professors open up packages that come in the mail, only to be blown into orbit.

In New York, Muslim extremists led by a blind man blow up the World Trade Center. In Wisconsin and Illinois, deranged cannibals lure 14-year-old gay hookers into their homes, decapitate and disembowel them, boil their heads and consume their viscera for dinner. In jail, they get stuck by nasties who can't live with a guy who's munched on some dead dude's brains.

A recent Gallup poll discovered that 40% of the American people think that "the federal government has become so large and powerful that it poses an immediate threat to rights and freedoms of ordinary citizens."

In Oklahoma, the Alfred P. Murrah Building is blown up. The nondescript building has no significance other than the headquarters for the DEA, Secret Service and the ATF. The aftermath is a nine story hole, a crater 30 feet wide by 8 feet deep and 168 innocent people killed. The methodology is very similar to that used in the World Trade Center bombing. A 1000–1200 pound fertilizer- and diesel-based bomb packed into a rented Ryder truck and detonated by remote control or timer.

The press is quick to blame "Muslim fundamentalists" but the real horror starts to sink in. According to the FBI, the worst terrorist attack on American soil is the reputed handiwork of two pissed off rednecks. Trained by Uncle Sam, fired up by hatred of the government, they provide singularly unproductive and deadly solution. The message is clear; the dispossessed are amongst us. We no longer have to worry about Egyptian clerics, Sudanese cab drivers or Palestinian tourists.

Farther south, some 300 miles away in Waco Texas, the site of the Branch Davidian compound is becoming a popular local tourist attraction. The bomb blast occurred two years to the day of the attack by the ATF on the cult's compound.

Mayhem, Tabloid Style

We used to chuckle at the tabloids as we bought our groceries. Now we can't figure out if its news we're watching or promos for sick B movies.

Hey America... what time is it?	
every 2 seconds	a criminal offense
every 11 seconds	a burglary
every 16 seconds	a violent crime
every 20 seconds	a vehicle is stolen
every 48 seconds	a robbery
ever 5 minutes	a rape

Hey America... what time is it?

every 21 minutes	a murder
every 30 minutes	news, sports & weather

Source: 1993 FBI Reports

In all 50 states, plumbers, carpenters, politicians, real estate agents, movie moguls and cops get into their cars after a fifth of gin at Sam's Bar and later plow into a family of six on the interstate, ending up with some scratches while killing all six.

In America everywhere, 12-year-old kids playing on the railroad tracks stumble across one of their classmates—who was sodomized and strangled to death...a month ago.

In California, fires ravage the hills of Berkeley and Malibu. Tremors, measuring 7.1 on the Richter scale rattle hills that later disappear entirely—along with the houses on them—after 10 inches of rain fall in a 14-hour period.

In Texas, in a town appropriately named Waco, a brainwashed prophet with an arms cache the size of the Serbs' has his followers blow their brains out as he torches his compound—and their children—during an ATF raid backed up by tanks.

The corpses of Central American would-be illegal immigrants float like logs down the Rio Grande. Those who make it to the other side of the river are looted, beaten and raped by sinister "coyotes."

Criminals As Superstars

Hard times breed strange heroes. The hardscrabble days of early America bred the outlaws of the Wild West. Jesse James and Billy the Kid were popularized in East Coast dime novels. The great Depression gave us Dillinger and Al Capone. Today in down-on-its-luck L.A. we are hatching a new breed of famous ne'er do wells. In Los Angeles, the land of "three strikes you're out" has become "do a crime, do the prime time." Here random violence and thoughtless pain take on plot, character and movie deals, as two rich kids splatter their parents' brains against a wall with a 12-gauge for a couple of Rolexes. In Los Angeles, a former football hero and movie star is accused of nearly severing his ex-wife's head and brutally stabbing to death her acquaintance. Meanwhile, during his "getaway," traffic on plagued L.A. freeways comes to a halt; motorists emerge from their cars waving banners urging, "Go O.J.!" and "Save the Juice!"

Here crime needs a subplot and linkage. A mother tosses her kids off a bridge and jumps in afterward. The news media immediately links it to a woman in the south who rolled her two kids to their watery end—a woman who played the media like a fiddle in her search for her "kidnapped" children.

Crime also needs a surprise ending, a payback. Rodney King gets the crap beaten out of him, sues and gets millions. Reginald Denny gets the crap beaten out of him and hugs and kisses the mother of one of his attacker's. We like our crime. Keep it fresh, surprising and very brutal.

200 Grand, Free Housing and All the Bullets You Can Dodge

In Washington D.C., a convicted crack freak is reelected mayor. In Louisiana, an admitted KKK leader and affirmed racist nearly gets elected to the U.S. Senate. In South Carolina, an already-elected and longtime U.S. senator warns the president of the United States that he had better have a lot of bodyguards if he's going to visit a military base in that state. America is the land of the tough guy, people who don't take any crap, and will gun you down if you give them any lip. In New York, Goetz Bernard dinged for gunning down thugs (while Bronson makes millions in movies doing the same thing). Meanwhile, on the other coast, L.A. taggers get gunned down by irate citizens who are considered heroes. Go figure.

Being the boss man of the land of the free is no picnic. In America, four presidents have been assassinated. Two others have been shot. There have been nearly successful assassination attempts on three others. Three serious contenders for the presidency have been critically shot, two dead.

The White House may even consider opening up a shooting range to give irate voters an outlet for their violent tendencies. The venerable building has been riddled with the bullets of drive-by shootings, bad snipers, even a crashed airplane. America is not Kathy Lee Gifford lip-synching the National Anthem at the Super Bowl game. America is no longer the sipping ice tea on the front porch swing. America was never a Diet Pepsi commercial. America is a dangerous place.

President Bill Clinton has called crime "the great crisis of the spirit that is gripping America today." The number of crimes recorded by police in the U.S. has risen by more than 60 percent since 1973. Violent crime, by the most conservative estimates, has risen by nearly 25 percent during that same period. The Statue of Liberty may well want to pull her arm down and take in the welcoming mat. Four out of 10 violent crimes in the U.S. are committed by relations or acquaintances of the victims. In the U.S. nearly 10 of every 100,000 people are the victims of a homicide. In 1900, only one person in every 100,000 could expect to become a murder victim.

Fear of Islam, People Who Wear Bedsheets and Other Bad People

And if crime isn't enough, the denizens of Irvine, Greenwich, Newport and Palm Beach, Westchester County, the Main Line and Skokie now have a new kid in town—terrorism. Islamic terrorism is on the rise. There's Qadaffi, Khomeini, Hezbollah, Hussein and Hassad. The U.S. is the Great Satan, whose demise is the ultimate objective and goal of all Islamic terrorism movements. For countries such as Syria, Iran and Libya, terrorism is state policy and the obese, limp-wristed and pantywaisted U.S. of A is the kid these bullies like to pick on.

The U.S. is more vulnerable than it's ever been. We can't follow rules of engagement with terrorism because then we would look like the bullies. We can't send America's sons and daughters to patrol the mean streets of the world because their parents back in Iowa want to know why they keep coming back dead, murdered by people they have never heard of and for reasons that are as alien to them as the IRS's taxation laws.

When acts of foreign terrorism creep onto American shores as with the World Trade Center bombing, the heartland calls out for revenge against the "ragheads, sand niggers, A-rabs, Eye-raqis" and every other xenophobic and naive stereotype. The new enemy does not have a face or even a press agent. We now cast the entire Muslim, Arab and red world trying to remember if the Arabs were our friends (the Gulf War) or our enemies (the fuel crisis). Burning questions like, "Wasn't Yasar Arafat a bad guy?" and "Why are Palestinians still blowing up Israelis?, or "What's the difference between Iran and Iraq, they are all ragheads?" still make for cocktail chatter. The truth is that O.J. (guilty or not guilty) and "Baywatch" (real or plastic) are a lot more interesting than the political situation in the Middle East.

The traditional threats of terrorism in the U.S. have been perceived to originate from countries such as the former Soviet Union, Cuba and the former eastern bloc countries. Evidently we were all too busy preparing for "The Big One" to consider such rustic and petty acts as car bomb attacks and assassinations. Islamic fundamentalists are less confined to territorialism than were the former communists. The war against America is not one of soil, but of theology. While Moscow and Washington were playing geographical dominoes, Damascus, Tripoli and Tehran had something far different in mind. And they don't mind paying the price.

Qadaffi, with the help of North Korea and Cuba, is busy establishing a terrorist infrastructure in the U.S. It's no secret. One only has to go back to the 1982 International Conference of the World Center for Resistance of Imperialism, Zionism, Racism, Reaction and Facism (we wonder how they got all that on the hotel's marquee) held in Tripoli to glean that Libya, Iran, Syria, Cuba and Benin established an executive committee to organize concerted efforts at exporting terrorism inside U.S. borders. In 1983, Qadaffi sponsored another symposium to devise a coordinated effort to bring the Islamic struggle into the U.S. In attendance was a U.S. delegation, comprised of elements from the American Indian Movement, the Nation of Islam, Black Argus and the Afro-Arab Foundation, among other groups. The Colonel must have been impressed by what he saw. The Americans met privately with the Libyan leader at least twice while he assessed their capabilities of fermenting torment among the dispossessed of America.

Soon, the cash began flowing and cells were established. A friend of Qadaffi established a front company in Panama. In 1980, the Manara Travel Agency opened in Washington, D.C. A Manara branch was opened in 1987 in Ontario, Canada. Manara was a cover for an umbrella of Libyan-run companies attempting to illegally procure hi-tech goodies from the U.S.

The export of terrorism into the U.S. is running along two other channels: drugs and arms.

The drug trade is helping to bring terrorism to America. Terrorist organizations such as *Hezbollah* and M-19 have been establishing closer ties with drug lords in an effort to get into America's veins. As *Hezbollah* announced: "If we can't kill 'em with guns, we'll kill 'em with drugs." A deal was struck between Syria and Pablo Escobar's Medellin cartel in the mid-1980s. It called for the Colombians to help establish Syria's fledgling Lebanon cocaine factories in exchange for terrorist training and military supplies that would be (and still are) used to fight local governments and drug enforcement agencies in Colombia and elsewhere. Coca paste is sent to Syrian labs in Lebanon's Shouf mountains, processed and then moved into Western Europe.

In 1992, the weapons really began moving into Colombia, with some US$20 million worth in one shipment alone that reached the eager paws of the Colombian insurgent groups FARC and the ELN. Guns are being gobbled up by Syrian and Iranian purchasers in Eastern Europe and funneled into the Colombian cartels. And if that's not enough, they're being bought with devastatingly authentic counterfeit U.S. bills printed at Iran's state currency mint in Tehran.

Tehran is one of the possible suspected supporters behind the Pan Am explosion over Lockerbie, Scotland on December 21, 1988, killing 270. On March 10, 1989, pro-Iranian terrorists exploded a pipe bomb in the van of Sharon Lee Rogers in San Diego, California. Rogers was the wife of the captain of the U.S.S. Vincennes, which had accidentally shot an Iranian airliner from the sky on July 3, 1988. On March 26, 1992 in Franklin Lakes, New Jersey, Mrs. Parivash Rafizadeh, the wife of a senior officer in the Shah's SAVAC, was shot at close range in the stomach and died. Her assailants vanished without a trace. On January 25, 1993, an Iranian-planted Pakistani terrorist blew away two CIA employees and injured three more with an AK-47 outside the agency's headquarters in Langley, Virginia. Although the shootings took place in broad daylight, in front of dozens of witnesses on a crowded street, the shooter, 28-year-old Mir Aimal Kansi, turned up a week later munching *mughlai* with his mom in Pakistan. It was subsequently learned that Kansi's uncle was assassinated in 1984, in all likelihood by the CIA.

The Rogers' bombing in particular revealed that Iran had established a viable terrorist infrastructure within the U.S. Among the 30,000 Iranian students in the U.S., at least 1000 can be counted upon by Tehran to carry-out some form of terrorism. In 1991, Iran sent assassination teams into Canada, one of which is believed to have been responsible for the Rafizadeh attack. These teams remain buried in both Canada and the U.S. Mir Aimal Kansi could only have vanished the way he did through the support of an entrenched Tehran-backed terrorist network within the U.S.

Which is Meaner? Our Army of God or Their Army of God? Or, the Adventures of the Anti-Coat Hanger Squad.

Have we got you scared yet? Don't be—at least not of these bad boys. Because it's Betty Boop next door, an accountant's secretary married to her high school halfback sweetheart, who is more likely to be versed in hexogene and combustible fuses than guys who go by Mohammed, Ahmad or Abdul.

Take Shelley Shannon, for instance. She's a regular Betty Boop, but a Betty Boop who's shot a man and allegedly injected toxic acid into or burned to the ground nine abortion clinics in four states. A Florida jury needed less than 30 minutes to convict Paul Hill of the murders of an abortionist and his aide. The list goes on. There is an ongoing investigation into pro-life (save a baby, kill a doctor) groups to see if there is a national conspiracy going on.

Over the past 10 years in the U.S., there have been at least 154 attacks on abortion clinics, including bombings and arson, costing more than US$14 million. The National Right to Life Committee, to which most of these homebred terrorists belong, has 3000 chapters in all 50 states. Although this "pro-life" organization doesn't sanction the violence, its numbers suggest that a significant percentage of its zany membership does. The offshoots sound like delegations at a Middle Eastern terrorism conference: the Pro-Life Action League, Defensive Action, Christian Action Group,

Operation Rescue, Rescue America and the American Coalition of Life Activists. And these folks are about as likely to abandon their bombs as the Libyans are to serve cocktails at the end of a symposium.

To pin the correlation further between these American terrorists and the Middle Eastern groups they so emulate, radical anti-abortionists adhere to a doctrine spelled out in their bible, *The Army of God*. Now, if we're not mistaken, in Arabic, that translates into *Hezbollah*. Seems to me we might have some trademark or copyright infringement here.

Some samplings from our home grown *The Army of God* manual:

- If terminally ill, use your final months to torch clinics; by the time the authorities identify you, you will have gone to your reward.

- Use a high-powered rifle to fire bullets into the engine block of a doctor's car.

- Never make a bomb threat from anywhere but a pay phone.

- Hot-wire a bulldozer at a construction site, drive it to a clinic, jump-off and let the bulldozer crash through the clinic wall.

- Drop butyric acid into dumpsters or boxes of trash when people are in the building.

- Put holes through clinic windows. The problem with .22-caliber weapons is the noise—the Fourth of July and New Year's Eve are great times for gunshots.

- Why get out of the way of an abortionist's car? The current lawsuit-crazy attitude can be used against baby-killers, and many awards have been received.

- Look up survivalist magazines such as *Soldier of Fortune* or *Survivalist*. Guaranteed that you'll be amazed, if not shocked, by the materials available.

We live in the land of the free, the home of the brave where everyone has a right to do something, to speak his mind, to 15 minutes of fame, to a guest appearance on the Ricky Lake show. What is wrong with this picture? It seems that Americans are punctuating their angry sentences with bullets.

Great advice for groups with slogans like, "If you think abortion is murder, act like it!" You gotta ask yourself: Do you know where your nearest abortion clinic is?

The Scoop

The United States is a large modern country with devolving inner cities. There are more than 200 million guns in the possession of Americans. Most violent acts in the States are the result of robberies and drug-related violence. Terrorist acts ranging from killing of abortionist doctors to the bombing of the World Trade Center are highly publicized but not considered a real threat to travelers. The threat of robbery or violent crime in inner cities and some tourist areas is real and should be taken seriously. Travel in American is considered safe and danger is confined to random violence and inner cities. Those seeking adventure can find it in a New Orleans bar at five in the morning or strolling through South Central L.A. after midnight.

North America ranks lowest in the number of incidents of terrorism and political violence among the regions of the world averaging only 10 incidents per year over the last six years.

In 1993, there were 28 attacks in the U.S., up from six in 1992, and well above the six year average of eight. The increased numbers of incidents was driven for the most part by several spectacular terrorist attacks in the U.S. by Islamic fundamentalists.

The Players

Aryan Nation, the KKK and Hate Groups

These are right wing belligerent groups that specialize in pipe bombs and the intimidation of blacks, Jews and immigrants. Although not considered a threat to the social structure, they constitute a growing menace. On July 30, 1994, two skinhead thugs of the white supremacist group Aryan Nations Brotherhood were busted on charges that they offered to kill a federal drug agent in exchange for US$120,000 in cash, weapons and cocaine. One of the men allegedly said he would kill a Drug Enforcement Agency (DEA) agent by bombing his home. On July 29, 1994, two whackos from Washington—members of the white supremacist group known as the American Front—who were in possession of three metal pipe bombs, four rifles, military-type clothing, wigs and white supremacist literature, were busted by the FBI in Salinas, California. The men were allegedly behind a pipe bomb explosion on July 20, 1994 at the Tacoma chapter of the National Association for the Advancement of Colored People (NAACP). In a twist on the hate thing, a black male shot 23 whites and Asians, killing five and wounding 18, on a Long Island commuter train in mid-December 1993. Klanwatch Project, the rights group, called the incident a "shocking reversal" in the pattern of hate crime.

Rights Groups

Activities by rights groups are centered around the abortion issue, but certainly aren't confined to it. Animal rights activists have been out doing dirty deeds, but their acts go largely unnoticed. The Animal Liberation Front (ALF), an underground animal rights group, claimed responsibility for a number of fires that caused damage in downtown Chicago department stores in November 1993. Five of eight incendiary devices ignited, causing fires in Marshall Field's, Carson Pirie Scott and Saks Fifth Avenue stores. While death is not an objective in the actions of most rights groups—as it undermines their causes—each possesses its crazies, and terror and death are the tools. In August 1994, an anti-abortion activist tried to kill Dr. George Tiller in Wichita, Kansas, and in March of the same year, Dr. David Gunn was killed in Florida.

Islamic Terrorists

Islamic terrorists were behind the February 26, 1993 bombing of the New York World Trade Center (WTC), which killed six and wounded more than 1000 others. The FBI and local authorities busted eight suspected Islamic terrorists associated with the bombing as well as other plots to bomb targets in New York, including the UN building and the Lincoln and Holland tunnels beneath the Hudson River. They also are alleged to have put plans together to assassinate both prominent American and Egyptian politicians. FBI agents and immigration authorities also nabbed a blind Egyptian cleric named Sheikh Omar Abdel-Rahman on felony charges in connection with the WTC bombing and the other proposed terrorist activities. Additionally, the indictment named El Sayyid Nosair as aiding in the planning of the bombings. Nosair, a close associate of Abdel-Rahman, had been in prison on a weapons possession conviction at the time and an assault rap in connection with the killing of Rabbi Meir Kahane in New York City in 1990. The charges also accused the group of planning to bomb bridges and U.S. military facilities.

Office Workers

There's an alarming trend of murder in the workplace. More than 1000 Americans are murdered on the job every year. The U.S. Postal Service has had 34 employees gunned down since 1986. Last year there were 214 assaults at post offices.

Gangs

America's willingness to absorb large masses of refugees resulted in the growth of some of the nastiest and hardest groups of street gangs in any Western country. In New York rival gangs of Puerto Ricans, Irish or blacks don't actually break out into spontaneous choreography when they want to settle a dispute. *West Side Story* has become *Apocalypse Now*. In L.A. fast cars and even faster weapons have elevated gangs into small armies. The weapons of choice are full automatic weapons with semiautomatics reserved for rookies. Assault weapons like the AK-47,

Tec 9, MAC, UZI or shot guns are preferred. Most gangs are created along ethnic and neighborhood lines. Bloods and Crips are the new Hatfields and McCoys. The *gangsta* look has become big business now. Baggy pants, work shirts, short hair, and that unique gangsta *lean* have all been adopted by freckle faced kids from Iowa. Gangsta music has towheaded kids reciting tales of inner city woes just as their parents were able to recite *Ittsy Bittsy Teeny Weenie Yellow Polka Dot Bikini.* The new proponents of this violent/hip misogynistic culture seem to live life a little too close to their lyrics. Rappers Tupac Shakur and Snoop Doggy Dog both probably wish they were singing Barney's theme of *I love you, you love me.* In Los Angeles there are over 200 gangs with 30,000 members. There are at least 1000 homicides every year and well over 1000 drive-by shootings. In 1993 L.A. officers were involved in 700 officer-involved shootings, 21 of them fatal.

But gangsterism in America is not black, white and Hispanic. Gangbangers come in all flavors. The most dangerous gangs in America are the new Asian gangs, groups of Cambodian, Vietnamese, Laotian and Filipino youth who came from the refugee camps, killing fields and dung heaps of South East Asia.

Your Next Door Neighbor

Four out of 10 violent crimes in the U.S. are committed by relations or acquaintances of the victims.

President Bill Clinton

Responding to what Clinton termed "a wave of crime and violence" in America, the Senate passed a modified version of the president's crime bill in September 1994. It's difficult to say whether politicians are echoing public anger over crime or fueling it. Although most Americans believe the levels of crime have increased in recent years, some statistics say that they have indeed dropped. Whereas police statistics show that violent crime affects more than 180 Americans for every 100,000—up from 100 people in 1973—a recent National Crime Victimization Survey has shown the actual level to be slightly lower than 100 people per every 100,000.

UNABOM

There is a whacko code-named UNABOM (University and Airline Bomber) who has been sending out letter bombs since 1978. The 15 incidents have killed two people and injured 23. The bombs are usually disguised as books and road hazards. The mysterious UNABOM has been striking his victims over a number of years and his motive is still unknown. On June 22, 1993, a professor of pediatrics at the University of California at San Francisco was maimed when he opened a parcel bomb sent through the mail to his home in a Marin County suburb. Two days later, on June 24, 1993, a Yale University associate professor of computer science was critically injured when a parcel bomb exploded in a fifth-floor computer center at the university campus in New Haven, Connecticut. Seven of the bombs were parcel bombs sent through the mail and seven were placed on the road. Two more similar incidents resulting in two deaths have occurred in 1995. The U.S. attorney general has established a joint task force consisting of investigators from the FBI, Bureau of Alcohol, Tobacco and Firearms (ATF), and the U.S. Postal Inspection Service to investigate and capture the person(s) responsible for these bombings. There is a US$1 million dollar reward for the capture and conviction of the bomber. ☎ *1-800-701-2662* if you have information.

Mir Amial Kansi

Kansi is the Pakistani citizen who killed two CIA employees and wounded three others on January 25, 1993 outside CIA headquarters in Northern Virginia. The State Department is offering US$100,000 for information leading to the arrest of Kansi. He is believed to be in Pakistan, Afghanistan, Iran or Iraq.

Militias

Militias were once social centers for good 'ole boys with a strong sense of gun love. Ignored by the mainstream press until the Oklahoma bombing, they were free to dress in army surplus gear and shoot off guns in the swamps of Florida. The Branch Davidians created a dangerous mix of Jesus and gunpowder and became targets for their insolence.

Now militias are in the spotlight and they don't quite know what to do with their political notoriety. Given a few more longnecks and a couple of pinches of Skoal, it won't be long before they come up with a coherent political agenda.

Currently, there are 24 states where militias are in operation. California, Arizona, Nevada and Colorado make up the South/Western area while the Southeastern area includes Florida, Alabama, Georgia, Tennessee, Arkansas, Missouri, North Carolina and Virginia. There is also a Northeastern area that is composed of New York, New Hampshire, Ohio, Pennsylvania, Indiana and Wisconsin.

It is interesting to note that many of the militia groups are growing in popularity thanks to Janet Reno and massive television coverage of the immolation of the Branch Davidians. The most well-known militias in the good 'ole USA are:

Florida State Militia

A right wing, Christian group with about 500 members led by Robert Pummer.

Guardians of American Liberties (GOAL)

This Colorado-based group wants to be the mouthpiece for militias everywhere (probably in direct competition with the Unorganized Militia based in Indianapolis).

James Gritz

Although Gritz is not a militia, he is very active in the militia business giving commando training and survival courses. James "Bo" Gritz, a famous icon of the right wing set and former Green Beret "bring 'em back alive" war hero, has done much to advance the cause of the MIA because he was convinced that there were still live POWs in Southeast Asia. None ever were brought back alive or were positively identified. He does so well as the poster boy and role model for the ultra-right wing that he ran as vice presidential candidate in 1988 with David Dukes.

Lone Star Militia

Leader Robert Spence (who bills himself as an Imperial Wizard of the True Knights of the Klu Klux Klan) says he heads up 11,000 militia members.

Militia of Montana (MOM)

John Trochman heads a little family-run militia in the wide open, "negro free" lands of Montana. This white supremacy group is reported to be working closely with the Aryan Nations Church in Hayden Lake, Idaho.

Northern Michigan Militia

It's cold in Michigan, so cold that it can freeze the rational parts of most folks brains. Considering the inclement weather and "band together or freeze" syndrome, it seems that joining a militia is the next favorite activity after ice fishing. Commander Norm Olsen manages to combine his skills as minister, gun store owner and former air force officer to lead his flock of 12,000 NMMS (Numbs?).

Police Against the New World Order

Although we couldn't find a *Yellow Pages* listing for the New World Order (we couldn't figure out if it was chinese restaurant or a church) apparently this group thinks "it's" out there. Probably the most famous and visible of the groups, PANWO(?) is captained by former Phoenix police officer Jack McLamb. McLamb was last seen nationally doing some expostulating and mugging for the camera with Bo Gritz at the ill fated Waco Compound.

Texas Constitutional Militia

Once headed by Jon Roland, the group claims 1500 members in 30 separate groups.

Unorganized Militia of the United States

Created by Linda Thompson, a lawyer from Indianapolis whose specialty seems to be suing the Federal government. The only nationally organized militia with far, far less members than the 3 million their PR claims.

Getting In

Passport required. The United States has over 20 different types of visas indicating different reasons for travel. Visa type and length varies by country. Travelers from selected countries can stay for up to 90 days without a visa. New Zealand and Australian nationals need visas, not necessary for British citizens. Contact the nearest U.S. embassy or consulate to obtain visa information and requirements.

Getting Around

However you want to. The United States possesses perhaps the most modern and comprehensive transportation systems in the world, both private and public. As public transportation in the U.S. is not nationalized, you can expect different levels of service in different areas. Whereas New York City possesses an intricate public transit infrastructure, public transit in Los Angeles is still in the development stage. However, intercity and interstate transportation links in the U.S. are considered excellent. Problem areas are principally inner city areas at night. Avoid late-night trips in these areas, due to the increased probability of crime.

Dangerous Places

Atlanta

1996 Olympians beware. This southern city has the dubious distinction of possessing the highest crime rate in North America.

Miami

Metro-Dade statistics show that tourist robberies dropped 56 percent between January and April 1994, compared to the same period in 1993. However, Miami is still considered the nation's second most dangerous city with 4022 crimes for every 100,000 residents. A *Money* magazine poll used FBI statistics and its own polling of 1000 adults in 187 cities. It found Florida had the highest crime rate of all 50 states. Dade County ranked number one among 79 metropolitan areas in aggravated assault, burglary and larceny. The county ranked second in robbery and auto theft and eleventh in murder. Miami has surpassed Orlando in tourism, and has become the third most popular destination in the U.S. among international visitors. Only New York and Los Angeles see more foreign visitors.

New Orleans

It's not the bad guys here that make the Big Easy so damn uneasy. It's the cops. The New Orleans Police Department is considered the most corrupt and brutal major city force in the U.S. Currently, an FBI investigation is ongoing into police abuses of civil liberties and overall corruption in the department. A few years ago, the week before Rodney King was clobbered by the cops in L.A., I was arrested and beaten by the police in New Orleans—I was hauled in on drug trafficking and prostitution charges after I'd been seen giving an impoverished black guy (I'm white) a few dollars for directing me to an ATM in the French Quarter. But the good-ole-boy attorney network in N.O. went to work for me. My attorney played golf with a prominent judge a few days later and got the charges dropped—and it only cost me five grand. During a subsequent attempt to sue the department and the city, I was informed that the highest damages I'd receive would total no more than US$3000, that the city was bankrupt and that any damage award would be paid over 18 years. If you're planning a trip to New Orleans, call DP first, and I'll give you the names of the bad badge and the cheesy counselor. Come and get me, boys. Am I bitter? Naaawww.

The South

The southern states lead the U.S. in per capita murder rates. Seven of the 10 states with the highest murder rates are in the south. The U.S. is the most murder-prone country in the developed world.

Abortion clinics

There have been three murders, 28 bombings and 61 cases arson of over the last few years. In 1993, 70 clinics were attacked by persons who have thrown or spread butyric acid, a noxious compound. Attacks on abortion clinics include harassment by picketers, mailed and verbal death threats, arson, vandalism, bombings and chemical attacks.

BBs

The Daisy BB Rifle Factory in Rogers, Arkansas turns out 65 million BBs a day.

The Most Dangerous Cities in the U.S.

Although Uniform Crime Report (UCR) statistics released by the FBI show a slight decrease in overall crime, the report found that minorities remain in the grasp of a major crime wave. Black teens between 16 and 19 years old are becoming victims of serious crimes at nearly seven times the national rate. Blacks in America are three times more likely than whites to be victims of violent crimes. Cities with the highest populations do not necessarily possess the highest crime rates.

	Most Dangerous	Safest
1.	Atlanta, GA	Irvine, CA
2.	Miami, FL	Amherst, NY
3.	St. Louis, MO	Livonia, MI
4.	Tampa, FL	Simi Valley, CA
5.	Little Rock, AK	Sunnyvalle, CA
6.	San Bernardino, CA	Virginia Beach, VA
7.	Baltimore, MD	Sterling Heights, MI
8.	Baton Rouge, LA	Madison, WI
9.	Detroit, MI	Scottsdale, AZ
10.	Flint, MI	Thousand Oaks, CA
11.	Chicago, IL	Rancho Cucamonga, CA
12.	Washington, DC	Plano, TX
13.	Oakland, CA	Salem, OR
14.	Birmingham, AL	Arlington, VA
15.	Kansas City, MO	Glendale, CA

Dangerous Things

Murder

About 70 people are murdered each day in the U.S. The U.S. homicide rate is 17 times greater than Japan's, and 10 times the rate in Germany, France and Greece. Louisiana has the highest homicide rate in the country, with 18.5 murders per every 100,000 people. Anywhere in the south is dangerous; the southern states possess the highest rates in the country. But the place where you're most likely to be snuffed is in the nation's capital; a whopping 66.5 people are murdered in Washington, D.C. for every 100,000 people. Males between the ages 15–24 are most likely to commit murder. Men commit 91 percent of the murders in the U.S.

Being Black

African-Americans make up about half of the murder victims in the U.S. Young African-Americans are more likely to be killed than any other segment in the country.

Terrorism

The number of terrorist incidents in the United States has declined each year since 1982 except for 1986 according to an FBI intelligence division report issued in late August. From a high point of 51 incidents in 1982 the count dropped to four in 1992 for a total of 165 over the entire 11-year period, according to the division's counterterrorism section. In addition, there were 44 suspected terrorist incidents in the U.S. during the same period, with most in 1989. The 165 incidents included 77 involving Puerto Rico, 23 by left wing groups, 16 by Jewish extremists, 12 by anti-Castro Cubans, six by right wing groups, and 31 by various other groups. The preferred targets were commercial establishments (60 incidents), followed by military targets (33), state and federal property (31), private property (18) and diplomatic establishments (17). The preferred regions were Puerto Rico (65), northeastern U.S. (53), western states (20) and southern states (19). Also according to the FBI, 74 terrorist incidents were prevented in the U.S. during the same period.

Although the State Department's annual report on incidents of "international" terrorism (as distinct from the "domestic" U.S. terrorism as described by the FBI) showed a 17-year low (361 incidents), officials spoke of "ominous signs" of escalation.

AIDS

According to the U.S. Centers for Disease Control, in 1993, AIDS surpassed accidents as the leading cause of death for Americans between 24–44 years old. For every 100,000 people, about 35 die of AIDS, about 32 die in accidents.

Small Aircraft

Over the past five years, regional airlines, flying mostly turboprops, have averaged 5.1 accidents per million departures. Commuter carriers, flying planes with 30 seats or fewer, have averaged 6.6 accidents. The big carriers, flying jets, have averaged 2.9 accidents.

Driving a Car

Driving a car is 20 times more dangerous than flying, the statistics say. Half of all traffic-related fatalities involve alcohol.

The Top States with Fatalities per 100,000 Drivers (1993)	
Mississippi	49.15
New Mexico	37.67
Kentucky	34.90
South Carolina	34.70
Wyoming	34.48
Alabama	34.45
Arkansas	33.53
Louisiana & Tennessee	33.07
Montana & West Virginia	32.12
Arizona	31.46

Rental Cars

Tourists driving rental cars are easy marks for thieves, muggers, rapists and murderers. Although the car rental firms have pulled their identifying badges off their cars in most areas of the country, cunning criminals can still ascertain a vehicle belonging to a rental firm through its license plate numbers. Confused tourists doing circles around the airport looking for the beach or the hotel are plum pickin's for carjackings and other crimes. Particularly dangerous areas are the urban sun-spots, such as Miami, Ft. Lauderdale and Los Angeles.

Handguns

Americans own more than 6.7 million handguns (200 million of all types of guns), and aren't afraid to use them. In 1993, 13,252 people were killed by handguns (16,189 by all types of firearms).

Assault Rifles

A U.S. ban on private ownership of assault rifles hasn't stopped the thousands of kooks already in possession of them from letting their fingers do the walking and picking up mail-order full-auto kits. And the ban hasn't decreased their numbers. In fact, the ban has become a boon for gunmakers. Gun dealers report that business has never been more brisk. Loopholes in the law allowed assault rifle manufacturers to simply change their muzzles and redesign the stocks so they no longer featured a "pistol grip." But, essentially, they're the same damn things. Gunmakers, in anticipation of the law, went into an assault rifle-building frenzy. Anything built and stamped before the date the ban went into effect is perfectly legal to sell on the street today: new guns, but stamped before the law went into effect. And what about the clips? Can you still buy those 32-round magazines? You bet. Police supply companies, who can legally sell new clips to police departments, take back their old ones in exchange for clips that were built before the ban. Where do they end up? Back out on the street. Legally. A cop may soon be shot by rounds from his old magazine. Despite all the brouhaha about assault rifles, very few people are killed each year by them. Hand guns do the most damage.

Getting Sick

Excellent health care is available throughout the U.S. Medical facilities and supplies, including medicines, are in abundance. The level of medical training of U.S. doctors is considered excellent. Foreign visitors without medical insurance will be expected to pay in cash or by credit card where accepted. No special precautions are required.

Hassles with the Police

The U.S. features one of the most disciplined and honest police structures in the world. However, there are the bad apples. Prejudiced detainment of travelers is frequent. Use of excessive force, particularly in the inner cities, occurs frequently. False arrest occurs less frequently but is also common in the inner cities. Police response time in most areas of the U.S. is considered excellent. Police in rural areas are known to stop speeders and demand immediate payment for traffic violations. Refusal to pay will result in free room and board.

Dangerous Days	
11/22/1963	President John F. Kennedy assassinated.
06/05/1968	Robert F. Kennedy assassinated.
04/05/1968	Martin Luther King assassinated.
04/14/1865	President Abraham Lincoln assassinated.
07/02/1881	President James A. Garfield assassinated.
09/06/1901	President William McKinley assassinated.

In a Dangerous Place:
Los Angeles

Above Los Angeles, aboard a Delta jetliner that's had to deviate from its approach due to zero visibility, the result of thick, black plumes of smoke billowing into the sky, the captain announces to the passenger cabin: "Ladies and gentlemen, the city of Los Angeles is in a state of civil unrest. We will be landing. However, we must urge you in no uncertain terms to use extreme caution in reaching your final destination. Lawlessness and violence exist in many areas of the metropolitan region. A Delta representative will be at the gate to advise you about which sections of the city should not be traveled through under any circumstances."

A petite dental hygienist in 26B turns and says to a long-haired record store manager from Van Nuys in 26A: "So? What else is new?"

The scene is pure Beirut. Pillars of thick black smoke rise straight up in the hot windless afternoon. Looking down from the hill where I live, I see dozens (I counted at least 120) of puffy dark columns rising up from Long Beach in the south to the Valley to the north. Down there people are looting, burning, killing, maiming and beating each other. Up in the air over twenty helicopters circle and swooped like hawks. Onboard are video cameras with new image stabilizers that made your living room feel like the cockpit of a Huey going into a hot LZ. The cameras are in tight. Kids look up and make victory signs as they hustle six packs, clothes, backyard toys, 19-inch televisions and even mattresses out of shattered storefront windows. Ostensibly, the black community is angered at the "not guilty" verdict in the Rodney King trial. King, a known criminal, was stopped, detained and beaten into submission. Had a neighbor not captured the scene on video tape, Rodney would have been just like any one of L.A.'s petty hoodlums. Today he is a lucky man. His violated civil rights have elevated him to the level of celebrity and wealthy icon of America's need to punish itself for not doing the right thing.

Because the television viewers can see the expressions of joy on the faces of the looters we know this is payback time. These folks are tired of paying retail for the American Dream and they are going straight for that Friday night, Smith & Wesson discount. This isn't about race and it wasn't about anger; it's about maximizing the one benefit of being forced to live in the foul, wasted bowels of one of America's wealthiest cities. It's payback time. Poverty means not being able to buy all the things they sell incessantly on TV. The poor man's heroin. Well, now every looter in South Central L.A. is rich.

Normally the merchants of the inner city have iron bars, security guards, video cameras, buzzers, 911 autodialers, shotguns taped under counters and fast-draw waist holsters to enforce compliance with their usurious prices. Anyone who tries for a five finger discount or a stickup is either gunned down, picked up or chased down with police helicopters, dogs and car patrols. This day the balance was out of whack, big time.

Although the police try to put a lid on the initial drunken violence, they are quickly outnumbered. Fearing for their safety, the police try driving by to scare off the first malcontents. When the spectators start throwing beer cans and rocks at the cop cars they beat a hasty retreat. The police are reigned in by politics and overly sensitive to the violence that must be dealt out to contain the looters. They are prisoners in their stations. When the word goes out over the news that the police are not going in, all hell breaks loose. For the first time since the '60s, America looks straight into the face of its dispossessed and blinks.

Business stops, people dash to their cars and head home. Along with most residents of L.A., the police watch the mayhem live on television and wonder how it will end.

On the street looters are methodically knocking off first liquor stores, then the big chain stores. The Koreans, the only people tough enough to run these inner city five-and-dimes waited a long time for this day. They finally have a chance to use all that German and American firepower they have been practicing with and oiling for years.

Any visitor to L.A.'s shooting ranges can't help but notice the Asian shooters with their black cordura bags full of expensive and well oiled weapons. They range from riot shot guns to 9mm handguns to MAC 10s and AKs, many with full automatic capability.

As the riot rages, the Koreans break out the ammo and the weapons. The looters think twice and focus on the national chain electronics and camera stores. The 911 lines are jammed with terrified people who have spotted cars full of "black" men or "Hispanics" in their white neighborhoods. The police inform the people that they are responsible for the safety of the neighborhood, not for the safety of individuals or their private property. Suddenly people start rummaging in the attic for their old WWII-era Garand, hunting rifles, even BB guns. Gun stores quickly sell out of ammunition and the city works fast to ban gun sales as they hit record highs. People now sat in their Barca Loungers watching the news waiting for the first sign of looters heading into their neighborhood. The looters wisely opt for new electronic goods and continue their looting of stores.

As in *War of the Worlds*, people sit glued to their television screens and radios tracking the spread of the violence. Reports come in from Beverly Hills, Orange County and Newport Beach; some false, all inflated, but ominous just the same. The rioters move to the north like locusts. Along the way business owners, tired of eking out a miserable existence, clean out their cash registers and torch their own businesses.

Coskun calls me from Istanbul. What's it like, are you getting pictures? The world has learned that L.A is in flames and its black population has risen up. I tell him that years of hard knocks have taught me that driving my nice new car into a maelstrom of fire, smoke, bullets, looters and thugs is probably not a wise idea.

Into the night coverage from helicopters gives us all the amazing sight of hundreds of glowing fires over the Los Angeles Basin.

Once the beer and the drugs flame out and the National Guard rolls in, the riots subside. Many proud new owners of ironing boards, car stereos and toasters can't wait to try them out. Driving through the worst hit area is no different from visiting Groxny, Beirut or any other burned-out war zone except there are no bodies on the street and the curious splatter marks from RPGs and 50 caliber bullets are absent. In the aftermath the civic leaders pledge to rebuild L.A and a committee is formed to do absolutely nothing. Most inner city business owners decide that the snow in Iowa looks a lot more inviting than the white soot that gently falls on their burned out lot.

After the media is done analyzing and proselytizing they move on to other more mundane matters. Life goes on.

In a Dangerous Place: New York City

There are Americans who have never heard of either Fort Apache or the Bronx. Even more draw a blank when they hear the conceit which forever links the two in Paul Newman's faded hit, *Fort Apache, the Bronx*, now too dated for the late, late show.

As it happens, there really is and still is a precinct house in the Bronx dubbed, for good reason, Fort Apache. Nor has the movie faded without leaving a trace. However unfamiliar they are with either the Bronx or Fort Apache, the image, *Fort Apache, the Bronx*, seems to have become part of America's shared image of New York City.

Badlands of broken glass, rats, smack and crack cocaine. Cars stripped and abandoned, buildings abandoned, buildings seemingly abandoned but actually housing *homo sapiens* (translation: 'species doubly wise'). Decaying blocks of ten-story tenements yawning on, block after gray, treeless block—police besieged.

Entering the zone now, we find ourselves cruising into a vision of life as we know it falling apart. Rotting garbage, gangs, men, women too, passed out on the street (junkie or just wino?), resurgent TB, methadone clinics reeking of urine, dank subways, death by AIDs, hepatitis, mugging. There have been attempts at rehabilitation and one going on right now has done a lot, but the South Bronx is still the South Bronx.

In better neighborhoods, steel bars and clanking tambours protect bodegas and botanicas. Here they protect nothing. The bodegas and botanicas are gone. There used to be do-wop and salsa groups on the corners. In other neighborhoods, street corners showcase salsa and rap. Here, it's just sullen kids with baggy shorts pulled low. They give you directions in New Yorican, that vibrant patois of Rosie Perez, with vowels sometimes Brooklyn, sometimes Latin. Here the Spanish accent is especially heavy, but when you ask directions in Spanish, you realize that New Yorican is their native language. They can't speak Spanish.

As for the South Bronx, yesterday's bad memory is today's bad trip. A bad place, with little reason to linger. But by itself, it's not what makes New York a dangerous place. Badlands as grim as this are not exactly rare, but neither do they blanket the city.

In a way, what makes New York dangerous is what makes it one of the world's great places.

The Players

The Thugs

Akbar Community Services has been around for awhile. It's got offices in a storefront on Livonia Avenue in the Bedford-Stuyvesant section of Brooklyn. Next year it could be gone. But the likes of Akbar Community Services are unlikely to be gone. It's the right time and the right place for playing the Akbar game.

It goes like this: For years, the skilled construction trades were a tough nut to crack for minority workers. To some extent, they still are. While mid-level white collar jobs, and especially government jobs have enormously increased minority staff, progress has been real but slower in the skilled blue collar trades which should be a more practical rung up for populations trapped in poverty. But mix residual (and often not so residual) blue class prejudice, with modest hiring progress their skilled trade-unions have made, with the fact that many minorities don't have the skills, and the bottom line has been that while middle class minorities have leaped ahead, the skilled trades have not offered nearly the same opportunity for the minorities who have by far the most critical need for help...and who make for the danger in New York's most dangerous places.

Enter Akbar Community Services. Any major construction contract, and they organize the community to make sure minorities are hired. Makes perfect sense. Makes a perfect scam.

For one thing, big contractors in New York City have been filling their unskilled ranks with minority labor for years. For another, unless he's got a sweetheart deal, which is not unheard of, the contractor is in a competitive business. When it comes to skilled jobs, he can't afford to hire more less-qualified minorities than the competition does, which is to say what the law makes them hire, and they do hire, not out of the goodness of their hearts but because they can't offer competitive bids if they have to figure the cost of going to court into the price.

In fact, court is what Akbar, for the record, threatens; lots of minority hiring suits have been brought, and with some success. But these suits, at least not the successful ones, weren't brought by Akbar or the 55 to 65 outfits like Akbar in virtually all the boroughs but Staten Island. In fact, court is not their real threat. Their real threat, as their front man hands the manager of the construction site his business card, is the van full of guys looking bored, some with boom boxes, some with ball bats, some with box-cutters and foot-long lengths of 3/4 inch galvanized pipe. Likewise, jobs are not what they really want. They have to insist on a few, but what they really want, and not just a few, are dollars.

It's such a lucrative business that there are between 55 and 65 outfits like Akbar heavily represented in virtually every borough except Staten Island.

In early '95, a major brawl broke out at a construction site in the center of Manhattan, just as few blocks from the New York Police Department's Midtown South Precinct. Major rehabilitation work is being done to the Times Square area, and at first it seemed the brawl was between workers at the site and one of the minority coalitions demanding work. And not just a little dust-up. As tourists and business people looked on, men jumped out of vans, rushing up 42nd Street, pipes raised. Then as tourists and business people dove for cover, shots cracked through the normal din of traffic, followed by sirens, and bleeding men were carried away in ambulances, one of them from a gunshot wound.

In fact, workers at the site weren't involved at all. The battle was between two of the minority coalitions, in open combat in mid-Manhattan over which one got the payoff.

In the Bronx, East Harlem and sections of Brooklyn like Crown Heights, Bedford-Stuyvesant, Red Hook, it's distinctly worse. Here the contractors are often minority and negotiations with minority contractors in particular can be particularly short, running something like this:

"We don't think enough of your work-force is minority."

"My work-force is a hundred percent minority."

And that's it. For those who pay up, the cost on a small to medium-size contract is $4000 to $7000 a week. Those who don't pay up come home each day, check their answering machines for messages, listen to the death threats, and then like you and me, they routinely erase them.

Both local and federal prosecutors are doing what they can, but this business has become so common that for cops, listening to yet another series of death threats on a yet another contractor's answering machine is not altogether unlike wasting time on paperwork for a fender bender.

The Organizations

On their own, tough New York cops like Robert Morgenthau, Rudolph Giuliani and William Bratton have put the squeeze on crime. Meantime, the Medelin cartel's Jaime Escobar has been smoked, a boon to the Cali cartel, but even as they reap this windfall it proves too much for their most crucial staffers, i.e., the ones who do the laundry. One after another, compromised U.S. bankers and businessmen, a couple of them Chassidic rabbis, have been caught by the Maytag repairmen of the FBI. And above all, the RICO statutes, which permit the Feds to go after criminal organizations rather than individual criminals, has been acting a little like the

Sherman antitrust act of the criminal world. This is what makes the drug trade these days such a dangerous one: None of the events just recited has done a thing to dampen the market for drugs, but as it corners the big boys, it opens worlds of dangerous opportunity for upstarts.

This does not mean that one-time street dealers in Manhattan's notorious Washington Heights are the capos of the future. Nor does it mean that the *organizatsiyas*, the new mobs from the Ukraine and Russia are going to take over. Drugs are in fact among their rackets, but they have many more going, from running bootleg gasoline to bootleg cigarettes to insurance fraud to murder for hire, and in any case, they do not have the easiest access to the drug market.

The Brighton Beach Bath and Racquet Club will close soon and that has more than nostalgic meaning. The *organizatsiyas* really sort of liked Brighton Beach and put their stamp on it. Where else in America can you sit down in a restaurant where they serve vodka by the carafe? But they were starting to get around anyway, looking at the bigger picture, and with the baths closing, that just puts the clincher on it. New York City's Russian mafia is already going nation-wide.

Specifically, the New York *organizatsiya* is now operating in Boston, Philadelphia and Los Angeles. A Los Angeles grand jury has already indicted one *kapusta*, Michael Smushkevich for a billion dollar insurance fraud in which Americans were offered free medical exams over the phone. Those who took up the offer ended up signing forms which surrendered their medical benefits to the *organizatsiya*, which then collected from insurance companies for the "free exams."

We can only hope the restaurants last. The carafes of vodka are the least of it. Where else can you get an assortment of cold cuts that includes smoked chubb, jellied beef feet, fat veal and that *basterma* advertised by halal butchers over on Eighth Avenue? Where else can you enjoy all this while the band goes wild and the patrons jump up in spontaneous dance? Even if you come early, they'll have "Family Feud" on TV, and for desert there's something only a Russian could come up with: Chocolate Potatoes.

To go with it, a full cup of Turkish coffee. Brighton Beach is the only place in the world that I've seen Turkish coffee served in a full, American-sized cup.

The Odessa Mafia has made Brighton Beach their new world neighborhood. There are occasional shootouts in its string of new restaurants, where fastidiously prepared Georgian, Ukrainean and Russian delights are served beneath those decorative basketball-sized balls of bluish cut-glass that were popular in the fifties. As you get off the subway, a blond-haired man once Soviet and now drunk stumbles on in a Road Runner T-Shirt.

Brighton Beach and its boardwalk show every sign of seedy health, a Georgian Black Sea resort transported to the Atlantic, girls, comely girls, beefy and true *babushkas*, which is what Russians call their doughy little grandmothers, after the scarves, the *babushkas*, they forever wrap around their heads.

Only these *babushkas* wouldn't be caught dead in a babushka. One was wearing a tight Calvin Klein T-shirt that said "Paris." Behind her, on the landward side of the boardwalk, was a big sign, nicely executed, with the professional gloss of the forties.

But that's just what you can see. What's out of sight is the organizatsiya with ties to the Columbo and Lucchese families. These boys call their capo *kapusta*, and their core business is bootleg gasoline, jewel robberies, and murder for hire. Needless, to say, in this sort of world, no one is created equal, least of all kapustas. Vyacheslav Lyubarsky was a kapusta of sorts, making pretty good money, they say. In fact his son Alexei was something of a kapusta himself. Until January 12, 1992, when they were both murdered.

Right now two *organizatsiya* are jockeying for power in Brighton Beach. The Brooklyn DA's office says they're importing hit men from Russia, which is having its own crime boom. Hit men from Russia work cheap—contracts run in the $2000 to $3000 range. On the black market back home that can bring a half million rubles, which for now is a fortune.

That's a problem, but the fundamental problem is the U.S.-based *organizatsiyas* that put out the contracts. Just one in Brighton Beach, known on the street as Monya's Brigada, has handled volume drug traffic and extortion rackets, but they have competition, and some other headaches, too.

In mid-March of '95, in the Adriatic town of Fano, Italian police arrested Monya Elson, the Brigada's 44-year-old kapusta. In Manhattan, he was indicted on a laundry list of charges, among them, contracting the murders of Vyacheslav Lyubarsky and his son Alexander.

The Mob

No metaphorical pun intended. In the dangerous places of the New York of lore, the mob is stage center. The New York of lore, however, does not exist. What exists is a reality both less sensational and less pat. New York is unfathomable.

Right now the mob is tired. Some strong prosecutors, federal and local, lawyers like Robert Morgenthau and Rudolf Giuliani, have put the squeeze on outfits whose vaunted traditions of silence and honor have commanded so much frightened respect, thereby winning such notoriety, that notoriety has led to familiarity, which as we all know, breeds contempt. What better targets. Dapper John Gotti is dapper as ever in prison (that kind of dapper is more than threads), but Gotti had been untouchable. The direction in which he had been trying to move, some twenty years ago, was that of rackets run with such businesslike skill that fronts wouldn't be just fronts, they'd be smart, conservative investments, at once more credible as generators of income that really came from rackets, profit-centers themselves, and in the complexity of their genuine business dealings, not just more credible as fronts, but with greater opportunity for deception in their books. On top of that, more money for good accountants and good lawyers who know no businessman with his head on straight would ever call consigliere. And on top of that, RICO.

Where do you find the silk-suited vipers with the razor cut hairdo? Along with similarly isolated neighborhoods like Bensonhurst in Brooklyn, Arthur Avenue has a reputation of being more the redoubt these days of the mob than shrinking Little Italy where Umberto's Clam House used to draw mobsters with its reputation for seafood oreganato; it now draws tourists with its reputation as the place where Joey Gallo met his maker in a tabloid burst of small arms fire.

The salumerias are moving to Arthur Avenue, as are the osterias and the mob.

On Arthur Avenue, you can even get *pasta fazool*. Only that's not what they'll call it on the menu. Physically, Arthur Avenue is vintage Italian-American. A lot more salumerias and osterias than you'd find in your average Italian-American neighborhood, but neither is this Gore Vidal's Rome. It's restaurants are dark and ornate with floral carpets, gold leaf, dark paneling (don't look too close, it's four-by-eight sheets of Masonite), a foam-cast replica of Michelangelo's David staring over your shoulder as you stuff your face. Or maybe it's the master's rendering of Perseus holding up the head of Medusa by the snakes which grew out of her scalp; from his perch on top of the cigarette machine, he stares down at the perfectly prepared calamari before you.

However, as those robustly stocked salumerias suggest, Arthur Avenue is more than spaghetti and meatballs. Nevermind the kitsch; white coated waiters speak real Italian, and if it's a steaming bowl of pasta fazool you want on a frigid winter day, you'll find it on the menu as *pasta e fagiole*. (An echo of America's dangerous places past, when Sicilians were sometimes called A-rabs by seemingly ignorant American rubes: For six hundred years, Sicily was in fact Arab, the Mafia has roots in Arab resistance to the conquering Papacy, and to this day, what Italians call beans—*fagiole*—both Sicilians and Arabs call *fazooli*. Pasta fazool!)

Given the direction organized crime was going when it was enacted, this federal statute may be working better than the wizards who mixed this brew ever hoped. It may well be dangerous itself, but in being able to go after a bad guy just because he can be proven to be a member of a criminal enterprise, rather that for committing any individual crime, prosecutors were handed one wicked weapon. Meantime, dovetailing with RICO, the FBI has shifted from a focus on tracing crimes back to criminals to a focus on criminal organizations.

For years, New York's Coliseum on Columbus Circle at the southwest corner of Central Park, was famous as the venue for a national convention, and then, for years it was infamous as the place not to book a convention. The mob had seized control of its union, turning it into such a craven patronage mill that the Coliseum priced itself out of the market.

Then along with RICO came New York State with the Javits Center, purpose-built to upstage the Coliseum and its mob-controlled union. Then aggressive prosecutors. Competition from the Cali and Medellin drug cartels. Gotti put away. Bloody noses as they tried to hang onto the Fulton Street Fish market.

But then they haven't exactly retreated to Bensonhurst and Arthur Avenue.

While all this was going on, mob interests were taking control of the Teamsters local at—you guessed it—the Javits Center, which has become such a craven patronage mill that it has virtually priced itself, and New York, out of the convention market. In February 1995, under fire for rank corruption at its local, the International seized control. But nobody claims the last chapter has been written. Meantime the mob is working out relationships with the likes of New York's Columbian drug traffickers and Russian racketeers that focus more on a role as godfather than competition.

Dangerous Places

The Subway

Much of the best of hidden New York is outside Manhattan, and even Manhattan is gridlocked most of the day. Meantime, the subway *is* New York. Not too pretty; this isn't the Moscow underground. Nor does it have that fast, almost silent whoosh of the Paris Metro with its rubber wheels. High decibel squeals is all you get here, the screech and whine of metal against metal, a perfect compliment to the headache the city has already given you, and those things are dangerous to boot.

Real improvements have been made over the past few years. The subways aren't as dirty as they used to be. But things could get worse. Every day the city's books look worse. And meantime, at its best, the subway has never been a joy ride.

But then what did you come to New York for? This is not a pretty city. It's big, powerful, rich in just about every category you can think of, but pretty it's not. Least of all the subway. There is not a more extensive system in the world, and it's combination of express trains and locals (way too ambitious for Paris or London) can make for some nimble block-hopping. It also makes for a complex system, so complex it seems designed to madden; a maze with treasures at the end of the ride…and like a maze, it's designed with such delicious complexity that its true purpose can only be to protect those treasures rather than get you to them.

Uptown

Vast stretches of New York City are turf which prudent strangers simply don't wander into, and in most cases, there's not much reason to wander in anyway.

Rolling into the city toward Grand Central Station on the old York Central tracks, you can see great dismal stretches of back street Harlem and East Harlem which fall thus beyond the pale.

La Marqueta, the Latin market in East Harlem, has long been a cynosure for Puerto Ricans from up and down the coast, and East Harlem is still the place to find Santeria. Of course, any of the tiny New York shops Latinos call botanicas will have the requisite candles, oils, spiritual unguents and plastic figurines. Some may even dispense advice on how, why, when and where to stick the needles. But Santeria is one of those things you encounter on successive levels, as nerve, inclination and access permit.

Should you be of a mind, when the bars close, to go sit on the floor of a half-lit basement apartment, on the walls of which hang black velvet tapestries of Jesus, Mary, Joseph and Jack

Kennedy, and in the air of which *cannabis sativa* hangs thickly sweet, and should you happen to have a hard-to-get fifth of Ron Jave (harsh stuff, but the rum closest to Puerto Rican hearts), *and* you know where to go, then your hostess just might take the Ron Jave as a sign you understand that she can't be bought for the $75 you offer. You'll trade a few shots, she'll invite you back, you'll proffer another bottle, another $75, and there will be a ceremony, during which the fuller lore of Santeria is brought to bear.

Spirits consulted, spirits shouted down, spirits invited, spirits most certainly consumed; eventually a spirit invades the body of the chubby lady puffing a cigar with a gaze that penetrates right through you, the basement wall and whatever lies beyond that, until at last with a suddenly violent flapping of wings, raking of claws, squawks and spurting blood, a living oven-stuffer-roaster looses her life in this effort to reach the spirits controlling your destiny as a midtown lawyer/uptown gambler/aspiring beautician/besieged publisher.

For this, East Harlem is as good a place as any. But there aren't a lot of Puerto Rican (or as they often describe themselves, from a relict Indian tribe, "Borinquen") restaurants in New York generally. Back home, they say, there was a long tradition of street chefs who delivered if you didn't want to cook. On top of this, many New York Puerto Ricans are working class people without the business skills to run restaurants. And meantime, the gaunt, gray, bombed out *alleys* of East Harlem do not invite.

Washington Heights

Washington Heights, the Dominican barrio north of Harlem, has had an even worse rep. Here danger doesn't merely lurk; it attacks. In 1994, this nethermost tip of Manhattan north of 155th Street registered 8608 arrests (20 percent jump from '93), 81 rapes, 56 murders, 1330 robberies, 794 felony assaults. Drug-dealing on the street has been so blatant that in 1986, Al D'Amato (then as now New York's Republican senator) and Rudy Giuliani (then the U.S. Attorney for Manhattan) donned sunglasses, leather vests and old army caps, went up to 160th Street and quickly scored crack cocaine on the street.

In fact, dealers in Washington Heights come as young as 12, a free clinic run by Columbia-Presbyterian Hospital, which sits in the middle of all this, draws long lines of teenagers seeking treatment for VD, and at night gunfire echoes through alabaster caverns.

But Dominicans seem an immensely complex people, and as with all such people, all is not what it seems.

Take even the neighborhood's worst feature: assertive crime, unwilling merely to lurk. These are indeed assertive people. But that doesn't mean raw brutality; it means a real skill for political assertion. When a politically active young Dominican named Jose Garcia—'Kiko' to the community—was shot to death by a cop one July night in 1990, there were five days of riots, angry editorials, sermons on brutality, and with some dispatch, the cop, one Michael O'Keefe, was relieved of duty and hauled before a grand jury.

Which made some interesting findings:

Kiko Garcia, to whatever extent he might have been a community organizer, spent a lot more time pushing drugs. Because they simply couldn't control the drug traffic, Washington Heights' 34th Precinct had instead focused on controlling the mayhem. Cops on patrol learned how to spot men with concealed weapons. O'Keefe and his partner had spotted Garcia, Garcia had noticed and he had run. Anticipating the sort of slip they expected Garcia to give them, they split up, but it didn't work and O'Keefe found himself trapped in a dark hallway with this known, armed drug dealer, unable to radio his location to his partner. Garcia pulled his weapon; so did O'Keefe.

It turned out the entire flap was a hustle by Dominican drug dealers trying to pressure the cops off their turf. They had almost destroyed the careers of young Michael O'Keefe, sitting dazed at home with his wife and kids.

So now you know the worst. It's time for the reason it's worth the danger:

For one, a *media noche*. In fact, this sandwich called the middle of the night is Cuban, but consumed in a Dominican restaurant, with Dominican Broadway still alive in the media noche, it's a great little meal.

And *mofongo*, which is really Puerto Rican, a ball of mashed pork and plantains, but Dominicans eat it *con queso* for breakfast, which makes for a breakfast as substantial as American ones.

And *mondongo*; whoever can make something this tasty out of tripe has to know how to cook.

And *merengue, merengue, merengue*, which is not something they put on your pie for desert. It's the beat to which Dominican Broadway jumps, both a style of Latin music and a dance. Before it was a Dominican neighborhood, Washington Heights was populated heavily by Greeks and German Jews who came over after World War II, and remnants remain on the street, a Kosher butcher, a Greek diner, and other living, resonant echoes: the Audobon Ballroom; St. Nick's Arena. Everywhere there are signs touting international phone calls, "*Pronto Telefonica*." It's a sign that hints of more going on: Dominican families are tight. Money raised in Washington Heights often courses straight back to the island where peasants then live like dukes.

You gotta make a living somehow. Ask some residents of neighborhoods where drugs are rife what it's like and they draw their thumbs across their throats. Ask a Dominican about Washington Heights and he's more likely to rub his fingers together. Money. About the same time Jellybean Benitez struck his deal, the U.S. Attorney arraigned a 64 year-old gambler called Spanish Raymond whose business does $30 million a year.

Yes, that's in the present tense. Do you really think that kind of volume goes away just because the boss gets arraigned? Sold maybe. Or franchised. Or merged. But go away? In fact, this was the second time in a few months the heat had come down on Spanish Raymond. Released on bail on condition he refrained from gambling, Raymondo tried to go the merger route, but the deal doesn't seem to have had nearly the finesse it needed. For one, the other half of this merger was run by a gaming entrepreneur named Spanish Bob who the police were bound to be watching pretty closely because of the relationship the two already had. (In fact, Roberto is Raymond's nephew.) For another, he did a lot of his business on a cellular phone, which $30 million a year doesn't seem to have taught him isn't exactly a secure means of communication. The NYPD was listening and the U.S. Attorney was real peeved.

As for drugs, police can boast that the mayhem on the street is down. Those crime figures, the stuff of Washington Heights' image, are especially misleading. Compared to the 56 murders in 1994, there were 119 in 1991. A prime reason for the drop is that drug dealing has moved off the street.

But not out of Washington Heights. Nowadays, customers from Jersey still drive across the George Washington Bridge, which carries drivers to the heart of the Washington Heights barrio. But they don't make many buys on the street anymore. Instead, they get steered to a bare apartment with little but a desk, scales, video cameras trained on the street outside, and young men with CBs talking to other young men on the street with CBs.

Harlem Heights and Harlem Hollows

A few blocks south of this bridge, on high ground overlooking the Apollo Theater down on 125 Street, George Washington challenged the British camped down in Harlem Hollows. When it was over, George had won what became known as The Battle of Harlem Heights and Harlem Hollows.

The whiff of cordite seems never to have gone away, though Harlem is not and never has been the South Bronx or Red Hook or for that matter, largely Puerto Rican East Harlem. Even during its days as a step up for immigrant Jews and Italians, East Harlem didn't boast buildings as solidly substantial as those of Harlem proper. The elegant brownstones of Harlem Heights still stand; still elegant.

Early in 1995, New Yorkers were enjoying a film made about a single photograph taken in front of one of those brownstones. It was taken for the January 1959 issue of *Esquire* and it featured on the stoop of that Harlem brownstone, Sonny Rollins, Dizzy Gillespie, Maxine Sullivan, Coleman Hawkins (in his trademark pork pie hat), Gene Krupa, Lou Williams, Charlie Mingus, Jimmy Rushing, Mary Lou Williams, Lester Young, Gerry Mulligan and Count Basie and Thelonious Monk, most of whom are now dead and only the last of whom I ever heard in person, at a club in San Francisco that same year, 1959, about the only place an 18 year-old college kid could get into without an ID. Harlem today is known more for crime than for the days of the Harlem Renaissance and the Cotton Club, but charm of those days is at least painted in part with the air brush of nostalgia while today's crime obscures resilient talent. New York watched the film with some nostalgia, but the music they made was notably intellectual and unsentimental, and just as the brownstones are still there, the music is still there, with good young musicians like the Marsalis brothers playing jazz not because it's a nostalgic kick but because they love it and have chosen it as their profession.

The dashing old Hotel Theresa is now an office building. At the indelibly Harlem Theresa, notables from Adam Clayton Powell to Fidel Castro let the Scotch flow. Nkita Khruschev once made a great show of visiting Castro there and when he came to New York immediately after his release from prison in 1990, Nelson Mandela chose the street in front of the Theresa to give his speech. But the Apollo is still alive, and not all the changes are for the worse. Up where the best brownstones are clustered, that one-time bastion of poor, determined Jewish students, CCNY, now has a heavily black student body, and throughout Harlem are stories that defy the stereotype.

Just one small example of this cause as that *Esquire* photo was being taken. Just a few blocks away a single mother was just beginning the upbringing of two young sons who would spend virtually all of their years in or near Harlem until the eldest, Jonah, went off to Cornell, and his younger brother Eddie went off to Phillips Exeter Academy, where he graduated with honors in 1985.

Sadly, they must appear again in this picture of the dangerous place which is New York City, but the fact is, they did it.

The Upper East and West Sides: The Happy Hunting Grounds

These neighborhoods have distinctly different personalities. The East Side matron would sniff at the sight of them lumped together. The West Side TV producer would implore, "pleeeze."

Tailored WASPS, whose breeding over the generations has tended to lock their jaws ever more rigidly, still set the tone on the Upper East Side. In their way, these quiet, wealthy blocks are as variegated as the rest of New York. There aren't many poor Jewish tailors, but plenty of tailored Jews; their jaws, too, have begun to lock over the generations. And now there are the tailored, connected expats, Hong Kong Chinese, Japanese, Brits, French, Northern Italians and at expensive private primary schools like Dalton, the lockjaw children of Bombay bankers, Arab diplomats, tribal Arabian dealseekers and wealthy Persians chased out by the mullahs.

On the West Side, pretensions are more ambitious, more intellectual, more artistic.

For the thief, there's not a lot of difference. More furs on the East Side, but otherwise... Out to eat on an East Side evening, you wear worn jeans with your well-cut blazer; it shows you're not as stuffy as the rest. On the West Side, you wear a well-cut blazer with your worn jeans; it shows you're civilized. The West Side producer is the only child of the East Side matron.

East Side, West Side and all across the park, this is rich game country for those sportsmen whose gear of choice is a four inch, flat bladed screwdriver whose short shafts they bend to a nearly precise thirty degree angle in a bench vice.

This is all they need for their prey, which sits enticingly within East Side BMWs and West Side VWs, the last of whose drivers, they know, are anything but just plain folks. Just plain folks don't park with baggies full of dried herbs and powdered chemicals in the glove compartment.

On the city's many drug markets, a stash ripped off from a glove compartment, or from under the dash, or the passenger seat, or the rug, is fungible, like cash.

For the thief, this is where the money is. Here the prey is abundant, secure in its wealth. The prey here does not show nearly the caution of other New York quarry. In Washington Heights, the block watches the block, or at least it watches a lot closer than the blocks do on the East and West sides. A junkie breaks into a car in Washington Heights, he runs a bigger risk for a smaller reward.

Upscale New Yorkers are a little like high strung Wildebeest. As danger lurks, there is a general unease, but once the jackal picks its prey and runs it down, the herd goes on browsing.

It's not quite the Kitty Genovese scene—that infamous case in which a young woman was murdered on a New York street even as her neighbors heard her scream for help and did nothing. It's more like this: The well-schooled are educated to question everything. The West Side gent's no fool. He sees a stranger fiddling with a car, then nosing inside, and he does question whether this is legit…and then he questions the easy conclusion that it's a break-in. If he opens his mouth, it's likely to be something along the lines of, "excuse me…"

Brooklyn

In Manhattan, corridors of danger interlace some of the world's rougher stretches of earthly delight. In the outer boroughs, it's often the other way round; islands of earthly delight surrounded by seas of danger.

Adonis Matthews, as befits his name, was a handsome 17-year-old, the pride and center of Wanda Matthews' life in the projects in Bedford-Stuyvesant, which is one of the names by which danger goes in Brooklyn. The zip codes here are not heavily targeted by direct marketers. Incomes are marginal, and that doesn't mean high marginal income. Nonetheless, Wanda Matthews put together $600 for Christmas. Which meant Christmas for her Adonis and something that was all the rage among his friends: A set of gold caps for his teeth, each one studded with little diamonds. Needless to say, Adonis had no problem with his teeth.

Four days after Christmas, 1994, Adonis Matthews was shot to death on a Bed-Stuy subway platform. His killers were spotted before they could get anything, but Wanda Matthews is convinced they were after those caps.

Red Hook is another name for danger in Brooklyn. Like the South Bronx and another Brooklyn neighborhood, Crown Heights, this is where the 'minority coalitions' recruit the crews to intimidate contractors into paying them off.

Just Another Mugging

Another prime hunting ground of this sort, not quite as abundant but closer at hand, is Morning Side Heights, further up on the West Side, overlooking Harlem from the south. It looks like most seedy New York neighborhoods, but it is also the home of Columbia University and the Juilliard School of Music. In short, bookbags and rich kids with lots of things on their mind besides the streets. Cars full of goodies.

One way the NYPD deals with this is undercover. Undercover cops dress like easy marks for muggers, and up here, that means like Columbia kids. Often as not, though, they're not acting as bait for muggers. What they have on their mind is bad guys breaking into cars.

That was Lee Van Houten's job one muggy summer night. He was 24, and looked even younger as he walked down Morning Side Drive between 113th and 114th streets, wearing sneakers, a sweatshirt and jeans, focused on cars. Maybe that was part of the problem; he might have been so focused on his job, those cars, that he had that distracted look which invites muggers. Or maybe it was just that he looked so young. Around the precinct house, they called him "the kid"…he was so intent on watching the cars that he didn't notice the muggers.

Specifically, the two teenagers, both over six feet tall. The first thing he knew, one of them had grabbed him around the neck from behind, yanking him backwards. Then the other kid started throwing punches until he went down, then began stomping. "Give it up!" they yelled. "Give it up!"

Van Houten had a radio, hidden in a brown paper bag, but it had gone flying. There was no way he could call for help. "I'm a police officer," he shouted, or tried to shout. He was losing it. He tried to get up, but each time the blows came again and he went down again. He could feel one of the kids starting to go through his pockets; he still had a pistol in an ankle holster, but it wouldn't be long before one of the kids had it; meantime the blows kept coming and the world was starting to swim.

He grabbed for the pistol, shot three times and blacked out.

Considering what might have happened, Van Houten came out okay. When his partners found him he was on the sidewalk, next to one of the muggers. The mugger was bleeding badly from the stomach. The cops were not in a really good mood. They handcuffed the kid anyway.

Van Houten didn't suffer professionally, either, though he might have. The case went before a grand jury, which cleared him of any wrongdoing, and meantime, the other mugger had been caught and was indicted for assault and attempted robbery.

In fact, the case would probably never have gone before a grand jury at all if it weren't for the identity of those two kids, both of whom we've also met before, in Harlem, where they were raised. The one who was indicted was Jonah Perry, on summer vacation from Cornell. He was later acquitted and went to work for the City of New York. His younger brother Eddie, who had just graduated with honors from Phillips Exeter Academy, was never even indicted. He died in the emergency room of St. Lukes Hospital.

For the Love of Money

Danger breeds opportunity. Just as Russian soldiers rent tanks and terrorists have day rates, the mean streets of New York have created legions of entrepreneurs.

Need the latest film on video? Can you believe $2.50 for the latest Walt Disney release? Can you believe the guy actually shot it himself? From his seat in the theater? He had to. How else could it be so blurred and jerky, with all those voices going shhh, and popcorn crunching!

Did you know that foreign nationals can't collect on lottery tickets? Well if you didn't that's not surprising because they don't like it to get around. If they did they'd lose a lot of sales to illegal immigrants. Just think what it's like for those people when they win and then find out they aren't allowed to collect! In fact you don't have to think about it. See that nice lady over there, the one who looks a little upset. She's doing a pretty good job of hiding it, but you can tell. She's upset. And why? I just heard why. That piece of paper in her hand. The one she keeps balling up. God forbid she should ruin it. A winning lottery ticket. A winning ticket. And she can't collect a dime. Makes you feel so rotten. Maybe we could do a little something for her. Like buy it for half what the prize is. But first let's check if she really won. Maybe she just read the numbers wrong. Hey lady...

A number of people come to New York with hotel reservations and the problem isn't so much that there's really no reservations. The problem is there's really no hotel.

Did you know that people make a powder out of bread crumbs and sell it as crack cocaine? It's a crime how some people abuse the public.

By the way, do you want to know how people get real Rolexes on 42nd Street? They steal them. A Dutch prince recently entered the NY marathon; lost his Rolex at Times Square.

Scams are so routine in New York, you've got to sell the Brooklyn Bridge to get noticed. Which happens. Not the Brooklyn Bridge, but some real estate which is nevertheless choice.

Not long ago, there was a homeless guy living in an Amana refrigerator box by the U.N. on the East River drive. These buses would always come up full of Japanese businessmen, and he began to notice how they were admiring this parcel and that. So he freshened up a little and the next time one of those buses came, he began offering options to buy.

And then there was David Caba. Now there was a hard working civil servant. New York is an expensive town. For two years he'd been working for the Department of General Services, doing responsible work, locating city properties, leasing them out, the sort of thing that people in private business make big bucks at. And what did he make? $24,647 a year. So the next time he located some city property for the city that the city didn't even know it had, he leased it himself. In his own name. Not the Brooklyn Bridge, but there's nice money in parking lots.

In February of '95, he got caught.

In a Dangerous Place: Midtown South

A Night in the Life of Midtown South

The Boys at Smith's. Midtown South at 357 West 35th Street, near Eighth Avenue, is the largest precinct house in New York City. For officers Gene Giogio and Charlie Edmond, on the four to midnight shift, the routine this summer night starts with a swing right up Eighth. Both are young and trim, Edmond with light hair; Giorgio, dark.

Some heavy real estate money is betting on Eighth Avenue and the entire Times Square area, which, in fits and starts, is improving. Forty Second street has drifted upward from total decrepitude marked by child pornography to moderate decrepitude marked by sex shops which provide shopping carts for men in suits to push through aisles marked 'TICKLING,' 'SHOES,' 'SPANKING,' 'SLAVES'…

Eighth Avenue has never been pretty, but beneath its grime there's always been real life and still is. As Giorgio and Edmond cruise north, they pass an Italian pork store with a 62-cent-a-pound special on pig's toes, a kosher meat market featuring the world's best pastrami, a halal meat market featuring the world's best basterma (which not only sounds but tastes like a distant cousin of pastrami), and further up some totally different meat markets, lounges with three gold chain minimums where wise guys from the union go to pickup broads.

At 44th and Eighth is Smith's Restaurant, one of those long-established operations that's open 24 hours for a neighborhood that works 24 hours: a take out counter, a bar the length of a bowling alley, booths, the kind of place where you can get your pleasure at 4:00 a.m., breakfast or a tumbler of Irish whiskey and a steak. They get a lot of trade from Midtown South.

"You see those prostitutes over there," says Charlie Edmond to his backseat guest.

"Men," says Giorgio. "Over here on Eighth, most of the prostitutes are men."

The Seventh and Eighth Avenue corridor is not the most dangerous in New York, but it is periodically plagued, and in the weeks ahead, it will be plagued. Rapper Tupac Shakur will be shot in a lobby on Seventh, and as summer fades to autumn, a rash of knifings will overtake Eighth Avenue. A victim will be knifed, a few hours later a uniform just coming on duty will scan the report, look into space a second, then inform himself out loud: "I think we got a prior, aggrieved party." Finally in October, a rookie cop, Timothy Torres, will make a collar.

As they cruise slowly past what might be a nascent game of three card monte, an order in the indecipherable language called static breaks over the radio and suddenly we're shooting east across town on 42nd Street a lot faster than I'm used to. The siren wails on, and I look around to see where it's coming from.

"Mugging," says Edmond. "Grand Central. Right in front." By then we're there. Another squad car had squealed up even earlier and a large, muscular man, so dirty you can't tell what color he is, wearing hardly any clothes, is lying face down on the sidewalk, handcuffed. The cops from the other car had just finished stringing their yellow tape, outside of which a crowd was gathering and inside of which there was just "the perp," the other two cops, and two college kids in shorts, looking like they're on the wrong side of the yellow tape. But nobody's asking them to leave.

The victim, an elderly woman who only spoke Spanish has just been taken away, shivering, they said, in the heat.

The kids look mildly stunned. The front of Grand Central Station, just after dark on a pleasant summer evening, right on Park Avenue, should not be among New York's most dangerous places.

"We were coming out of the restaurant," says one. "And right there we see this guy jumping the old lady. So my buddy here grabs him…"

"No way. You grabbed him," says the buddy.

"And you didn't?"

"OK, but you grabbed first."

"Didn't."

"Did."

Carlos Sam. Just like that it was over, the street was returning to normal, and as we were getting back into the squad car, through the New York cacophony of honks, shouts and distant sirens, I caught snatches of a conversation a black man in a smartly tailored business suit was having with a liveried black doorman. "*Le probleme aujourd'hui est…*" Haitien, you think to yourself, then wonder why this casually incidental detail in a brutal picture has jumped out and induced you to jump to a conclusion. To impress on you that this is New York? Haitians are in the news, and Haitien refugees are everywhere. But here, these men could be from Martinique, Senegal, the Ivory Coast…

Thus mulling as the lights twinkle by, there's a sudden lurch and I realize we're violating the speed limit again. Back to the West Side. A silent alarm on an office building in one of the side streets between Eighth, and Seventh.

"This time of day over there or I should better put it, this time of night over there, it's real closed up. Dark." It's the driver talking as we shoot toward the intersection of 42nd Street and Sixth Avenue, the light's red ahead and I'm hoping that at this time of night up there, drivers pay attention to sirens. "Not long ago, we're just driving around, checking things out, and up ahead we see bales of dresses getting thrown out of a window, maybe six, seven stories up, must have been thousands of 'em. Later we here it's been going on. Perps ran, but two weeks later they're collared."

"Thing is, you never know what you're going to run into there," says Giorgio. By now we're coming up on the block and the siren goes off, we roll down the narrow, deserted side street; in a city where a parking place is a valued commodity, there are more dumpsters strewn along the curb than parked cars. Way ahead, a homeless guy is rooting through one of them. We pull to a stop. One light is on in the lobby, but that's it. We get out. I make a point to stay out of the way (or if you prefer, harm's way.) "Generally it's a false alarm," says Giorgio, *soto voce*, and generally perps in this line of business don't give you trouble."

"Unless sometimes. When they get surprised." says Edmond. It comes back to me: this was a silent alarm.

"Problem building," says Giorgio.

They already have keys. They draw their .38s. After the first floor, the building is dark. At a control panel, they snap on lights, push the elevator button. From above, there's a noise. Floor to floor, along the corridor walls; if there's no one there, it's faintly ridiculous, but then how do you know when it's for real?

A couple more sounds, along with brief starts as we hear them, but this is a real night in the life of Midtown South, not highlights of the day in sports. False alarm. No actual danger. Just the daily drumbeat of tension.

There are homeless wherever we go, not in great droves, but they're here, thanks to a byzantine system of aid that parks some of New York's poorest people on some of New York's most expensive real estate. In the theater district, they come because the pickings are good. Virtually next door to the Algonquin Hotel where the legendary round table once regularly held forth, a 300 pound woman with an amputated foot now regularly holds forth with a sweet eight-year-old son who lives there with her. They've got an address at the distant end of some subway line, but it's clearly not much, it's hard for her to get around, and this is where the money is. The conversation with Edmond and Giorgio is professional. They're just checking. She knows they can't move her. They know they can't move her.

One of the homeless of Midtown South, Carlos Sam, by name, is a computer repairman. Not a former computer repairman fallen on hard times, but a computer repairman now, on the street, with no prior training beyond electronics picked up in an uncle's TV repair shop. He's illiterate, periodically delusional, crippled. He owns a jealously guarded tool box and three canvas mail carts. From discarded computer parts rummaged out of dumpsters he's taught himself computer repair. Nowadays, he's not only a repairman, he's in the business. For $15 to $45, you can get a repaired monitor or keyboard. His shop is on the 43rd Street sidewalk between Seventh and Eighth.

Badge 4049. By this hour, Carlos Sam is off the street, but this is when the porn shops, now run largely by Indians and Pakistanis, bring in their biggest bucks. "Stuff they sell isn't as rank as it used to be, and on top of that, they're mostly cheap copies, but these guys rake it in."

The porn store is, above all, a business struggle. Landlords who rent to porn shops between 40th and 53rd get $90 to $125 a square foot. If it isn't porn, it only commands $60 to $90. Meantime other landlords are trying to light a fire under the redevelopment which slowly proceeds, anticipating a boom which may already be getting underway...if they can finally get rid of the porn. Disney is spending $34 million to renovate the extravagant, dilapidated New Amsterdam Theatre on 42nd, a 92 year-old landmark that was home to the Ziegfeld Follies. But still there's those rents that can be had from porn shops. They say one group of landlords actually went to the rabbi of a wavering colleague to help him resist.

There are other ways in which this midtown corridor is less impersonal than it seems. Timothy Torres, the Midtown South cop who collared the Eighth Avenue stabber a couple of months after our cruise through the precinct, was a college dropout, on the force barely two years, wearing the same badge, No. 4049, that his dad, Cesar, had worn as a New York cop before he resigned. Young Torres was on foot patrol the October night he saw the suspect racing up Eighth Avenue on a bike, knife in hand. He jumped the guy, and came out of it bloodied, but with considerable pride for father and son.

Smith's again. Another rapid fire set of directions over the radio, again indecipherable. Edmond talks into the mike. "Can you ascertain what you got us out on?" More static; more speed.

"A heavy bleeder," says Giorgio. "Group therapy session at this hotel, a welfare hotel, a welfare hotel for guys with AIDS actually. Terminal cases. Looks like the group therapy got out of hand and we got a heavy bleeder."

The dispatcher's voice cracks over the radio, at last decipherable: "All units. Stay off the air unless you have priority. All units."

We brake to a stop with squad cars from every direction. Cops are all over the place. They're up there fifteen minutes, a half hour; gaunt, unshaven men in stocking hats stand about in the grim light; beefy young men in stocking caps, also unshaven, come out; an undercover team. There's tension but when Giorgio and Edmond return, they don't make a big deal out of it.

"If it was serious they would have had a sergeant over here."

A few minutes later, cruising up Seventh Avenue, we're flagged by a cabbie, Indian or Pakistani. His fare won't pay. Fare is out of the cab by now, a little stocky, substantial, middle-aged guy in a suit, maybe a little tight but not obviously drunk, and meantime he's quiet, even sort of fatherly with the cops, who ask him what the trouble is. He doesn't have the money? Come on, he says. A wad is discreetly flashed. He's getting a little more fatherly. So what's the trouble, sir? Again, fatherly, but no answer, and then some discreet advice: for their own good, they should drop it.

"So sir, like what's the beef?"

"Look, son, this is not how you want to spend your beat."

"No sir, it's not. So just tell us your beef and..."

"Son..."

It was going nowhere, except from fatherly to patronizing to abusive. Once they got him to pay they let it be, but of all the low to medium grade tension, the mugging, the silent alarm, the 300 pound amputee living on the street with her eight-year-old son, the heavy bleeder at the AIDS hotel, this seemed to get under their skin the most, this, the least potentially serious, the ordinary, garden variety jerk who for the very reason of his ordinariness represented the drum beat of tension.

Across the country, about 300 cops killed themselves in 1994; that's more than twice as many as the 137 who died in the line of duty. Over the past decade in New York City, 20 cops have been killed in the line of duty; 64 killed themselves.

Columbia University released a study in '94 that showed NYPD officers killing themselves at a rate of 29 for every 100,000. Among the general population the rate is 12. The cops are almost always young, with clean records. The study notes that a virtually standard feature of every suicide is a statement from the department or the family or both that the suicide was personal, the job had nothing to do with it.

Christmas Eve, Timothy Torres, who had brought down the stabber in October and wore his father's badge, pulled the midnight to eight in the morning shift at Midtown South, foot patrol. A little after midnight he responded to a call on West 43rd, where a man was distraught and raving in the lobby. Torres got him to Bellevue for treatment.

At four, he met up with another cop on foot patrol, and they went to Smith's, the landmark on Eighth Avenue, for breakfast. It was now Christmas Day. Torres shot himself in the head in a booth.

"My understanding was that he went through a divorce six months ago," said a police spokesman.

On the same street Torres responded to the call about the man raving in a lobby, Carlos Sam is still doing business. He melts plastic spoons to solder the innards of keyboards and monitors. If you want to know if he's really fixed the thing, he uses the swivel chair which is among his few possessions to squeak over to a light pole, at the base of which is an electrical outlet. In fact, every light pole in New York City has an outlet at its base, usually sealed. Carlos Sam swears he only uses the ones that are already open.

Guns & Rifles

There are more than 200 million guns in the United States. It is estimated that firearm injuries in the states cost about $20 billion in medical costs and lost wages.

The most dangerous hand held weapons are rifles. Handguns require short ranges and careful aim to be lethal. Handguns tend to be the weapons of choice for domestic violence and robberies. Most handguns lose any effectiveness after 25 yards. In fact, the western movies where men bang away from across the street without hitting anyone are not too far from reality.

On the other hand, if someone is shooting a rifle at you, you will probably end up dead.

In the 1850s, rifles were called muskets. They were smooth bore, long barreled (about 4–5 feet in length) and could kill a man at 100 meters. Loading slowed down the killing process to about 8 shots a minute.

In 1855, the Crimean War introduced the rifled bullet, a major advance that pushed the killing range out to 600 yards. The French invention meant that armies could now battle without the standard volley, advance and hand-to-hand combat. Armies were slow to adapt the deadly new Minié ball and the Civil War still saw armies facing each other 50 to 100 yards apart, firing at point blank range and then charging.

The next big advances were in the late 1800s when breech-loading weapons like the Mauser rifle and metal cased bullets were introduced. The next step was the 1903 Springfield rifle and the later 1917 Enfield. These rifles were deadly out to 1200 yards and could be loaded and fired quickly.

WWI trenches were typically spaced 300 to 1200 feet apart and dictated rifle design. The ideal weapon was one that fired accurately, from rest with a minimum of maintenance and training. The focus was on careful killing of fleeting targets. When fighting got close, bayonets and pistols were the choice. Machine guns were heavy and water-cooled and used for withering fire during assaults or attacks. In 1917 came the introduction of the first semi-automatic weapon that could fire 20 rounds as fast as the trigger could be pulled. The simple Pedersen-device modification to the 1903 Springfield rifle was ordered too late to make a difference in the Great War but changed the use of rifles in warfare.

Guns & Rifles

WWII introduced the idea of rapid fire, portable weapons that could intimidate rather than kill. The MI Garand (designed by John C. Garand) was a semiautomatic, gas operated rifle that could fire 30-06 cartridges in 8-round clips. Later, it would be found that the number of rounds fired for every person actually killed was 15,000 rounds, even though the range of engagement closed to half WWI distances. Heavy bolt action rifles were still the infantry weapon of choice but the Germans and Russians used machine guns and infantry attacks to good effect. The Germans were the first nation to create the Sturmgewehr (assault rifle) but the first successful version was the post-war Russian AK47.

Assault weapons provide killing power out to about 600 meters although battlefield results showed that 350 meters was the maximum practical range in combat. Most firefights occurred with opponents 200 to 300 yards apart.

Vietnam and a host of other dirty bush wars introduced the ambush concept of very high rates of fire, light ammunition and firepower. Ammunition had to be light, weapons cheap and easy to fix and general tactics dictated spraying thousands of rounds during short fire fights. The number of rounds per kill tripled from WWII levels to a staggering 50,000 rounds for each kill. In Vietnam the light and deadly M16 became the overwhelming choice of ground troops.

The future of rifle design is anyone's guess. Everything from all-plastic bullets to nonlethal ammunition is being developed. In the meantime, it seems to take a major war to change the face of battle and eventually the use of weapons.

M-16

The M-16, or the civilian version called the AR-15, was introduced in 1965. By this time, the light and powerful AK47 was the best weapon available. In Vietnam, the light and deadly M16 suffered initially because of ammunition that caused fouling. After the problem was sorted out it became the standard issue for all ground troops (replacing the M-14). The M16 used a lighter (5.56) bullet compared to the Viet Cong 7.62 used in the AK-47. The M16 round had just as much impact at 200 yards as the AK47 round.

The M-16 lays down 700 rounds per minute with a muzzle velocity of 3250 feet per second. It comes with 20 or 30 round clips. With a weight of 6.6 pounds, it has been adopted by Asian armies as the weapon of choice.

Zaire
★★★★

Heart of Darkness

There is no other country on the continent that more typifies the deep, festering core of darkest Africa. Joseph Conrad based his famous tale of depravity and corruption on this dying, diseased land, formerly the Belgian Congo.

Zaire, a little larger than a quarter of the U.S., is mostly a vast drainage pan for its mountains in the east. Its neighbors are no shining examples of humanitarianism. Sudan, Uganda, Tanzania, Angola, Burundi, Rwanda, Central African Republic and the Congo all compete for the title of "Horror Capital of Africa." Like the decay that quickly turns vegetation and animals into rot, the economy and social structure of Zaire are slowly disintegrating. The local currency has lost all value. Most families live off subsistence farming. A barter economy has returned; all this while Zaire sits on some of the world's largest reserves of mineral and agricultural resources.

Life is tough in Zaire. There are no permanent crops. Only three percent of the land is arable; 78 percent of the country is covered in dense tropical forest. Life expectancy is a depressing 45.5 years of age. Within this steaming bowl of vegetation exist more

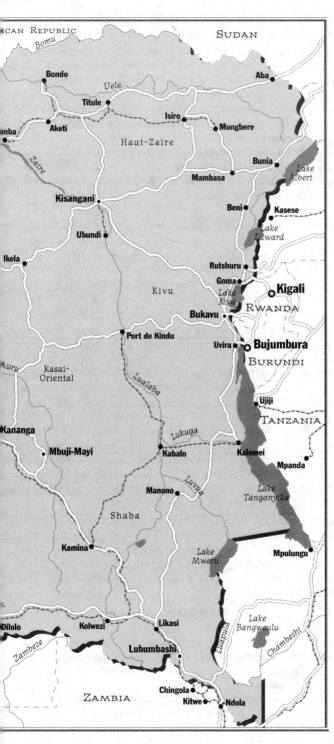

than 200 tribes. The most prominent one is the Bantu. Four tribes—the Mongo, Luba, Kongo and the Mangbetu Azande—comprise 47 percent of the population.

Blame much of the pestilence on the CIA and its puppet, General Joseph Mobutu Sese Seko, who seized power in Zaire in a CIA-backed coup in November 1965. Although the Mobutu regime started out democratically enough—by African standards—as a military dictatorship with a junta comprised entirely of the military's high command, Mobutu soon assumed the standard role of his neighboring compatriots—that of a one-man-controlled, single-party, authoritarian dictatorship. All small and medium expat-owned businesses were seized and distributed among the nation's elite. Mobutu personally plundered the treasury and state-owned businesses. The word "kleptocracy" sneaks into any conversation about Zaire. However, his banditry of the nation's resources pale in comparison with Mobutu's record for murder, assassination, extrajudicial executions, kidnapping, torture, massacres of civilians and unfounded arrests.

In line with the dictator motif, Mobutu has maintained his grip on power through brutal repression of any opposition. He appointed educated cronies to key ministerial positions. To keep them happy, they were made board chairmen of seized companies, allowing them to milk these companies as Mobutu was doing Zaire. He reshuffled the cabinet constantly in order to allow more and more lackeys the opportunity to pick cookies from the jar. Mobutu had five different prime ministers in 1991 alone.

With the breakup of the Eastern Bloc in the late 1980s, the CIA saw no further reason to support Mobutu's crimes, and opposition in Zaire began to take a recognizable shape. In 1990, Mobutu began a series of "political reforms," including abolishing the one-party system. Given an inch, dissidents wanted a mile. Mass demonstrations against the government led to another crackdown. On May 11–12, 1990, Mobutu's personal commandos, Division Spéciale Présidentielle (DSP), massacred unarmed university students, provoking a world outcry. The Union Sacrée was formed in 1991 as a coalition of Zaire's major opposition groups. The group's principal demand was to organize a conference bringing together representatives from all sectors of Zaire's society. Because this would do nothing more then expose the horrors of Mobutu's regime, the president used all of his might to crush the conference. At least 30 people were killed by government troops in February 1992 as they were peacefully demonstrating for the reformation of the conference. Again, world revulsion to the brutal act forced Mobutu to allow the conference to reconvene in April 1992.

But good 'ole George Bush and France's Mitterrand regime continued to give enough support to Mobutu to prevent the reformers in Zaire from achieving anything but marginal gains. Zaire continued, and continues, to plunge into deeper and deeper squalor, as the entire political, social and economic infrastructures have been looted and pillaged to the bare bones—reducing the government to a loose clan of petty street thugs and thieves.

The Scoop

Zaire is the largest sub-Saharan African country. It has substantial human and natural resources, but for the past several years the country has suffered a profound political and economic crisis which has resulted in the dramatic deterioration of the physical infrastructure of the country; insecurity and an increase in crime in urban areas (including occasional episodes of looting and murder in Kinshasa's streets); occasional official hostility to U.S. citizens and nationals of European countries; periodic shortages of basic needs such as gasoline; chronic shortages of medicine and supplies for some basic medical care; hyperinflation; corruption; and in some urban areas, malnutrition of the local population to the point of starvation. Tourism facilities are minimal.

The Players

General Joseph Mobutu Sese Seko

Yet another "President-for-Life," Mobutu is really the only player in Zaire. Thrust into power via a 1965 CIA-backed coup, Mobutu is the Idi Amin of Zaire and a stooge of Uncle Sam. He's known best for his massacres, executions and assassinations of political opponents. His brutal, despotic regime has weakened in recent years, but, as all of Zaire has crumbled, so have his opponents.

By what reasoning, you may well ask, is a man who puts together a US$5 billion fortune, safely socked away in Switzerland, a stooge?

Well, maybe Mobutu isn't a stooge at home. But there's no need to invade the poor man's privacy. We're talking about the role he plays on the Central African stage. Larry, Curly and Moe probably weren't stooges at home either. It was a role they were paid to play. Likewise Mobutu; and you've got to say this for the guy: however overpaid he might be, he gives that role all he's got, throwing around hundreds of millions on palaces and Swiss dairy farms recreated in the jungle, even as his mineral-rich nation slips more deeply into squalor, with streets so heavy with desperation that you drive through them with every window of your vehicle tightly rolled. Overhead, banners proclaim, MOBUTU POUR TOUS, TOUS POUR MOBUTU.

Meantime, a private Disneyland goes up in his distant hometown; and even as such outrages to social justice are played out, one after another, he instructs his people to address each other, in the egalitarian tones of the French Revolution, as 'citoyen', which, incredibly, they do, even though they consider him (as does much of Central Africa) a stooge. More specifically, he's considered a stooge for the west, paid to frustrate their aspirations whenever they conflict with western interests. For this reason, paying him is getting to be an increasingly dangerous game, short-term advantage at the cost of trouble down the pike.

Union Sacrée

The opposition coalition Union Sacrée was formed in July 1991 under the leadership of the Union pour la Démocratie et le Progrés Social (UDPS) and Joseph Ileo's Parti Démocrate Social Chrétien. The UDPS was formed in 1982 after a 1980 rebellion by 13 parliamentarians. This "Group of 13" was tormented and brutally treated by the government. They formed the UDPS in response to Mobutu's outlawing of opposition parties. Also in the coalition is the former Parti Lumumbiste Unifé (PALU), led by the "Iron Lady of Zaire," Thérèse Pakasa. The PALU also was able to organize mass demonstrations against Mobutu's regime.

Getting In

A passport, visa and vaccination certificate showing valid yellow fever and cholera immunizations are required for entry into Zaire. Intending travelers are advised that the government of Zaire announced in 1993 that visas would not be issued to nationals of countries practicing "discriminatory" visa policies toward Zairians. Although the government did not name the countries to which this edict would be applied, it is presumed that Zairian visas will become more difficult for U.S. citizens to obtain. In addition, some travelers are currently obliged to transit the Congo to reach Kinshasa which means a Congo visa may also be necessary. U.S. citizens may not be able to obtain a visa at Zairian embassies in neighboring countries; it is suggested that travelers apply at the Zairian Embassy in Washington well in advance of any planned trip. Visa fees range from US$45 for a transit visa to US$360 for a six month multiple entry visa. Most visitors will opt for the one entry, one month visa for US$75 or US$125 for multiple entries for the same period.

You will need a valid passport, proof of inoculation against yellow fever, a copy of your return ticket as well as application forms and passport photos in triplicate.If you show up in person it takes 48 hours for a visa to be issued or 24 hours if you are a diplomat.

For more information, the traveler may contact the

Embassy of the Republic of Zaire

1800 New Hampshire Avenue N.W.
Washington, D.C. 20009
☎ *(202) 234-7690, 91*
Travelers may also contact

Zaire's Permanent Mission to the U.N.

747 Third Avenue
New York, NY 10017
☎ *(212) 754-1966.*

Air Zaire flies into Kinshasa and, within Zaire, to Goma and Kinsangani. Within Zaire, the plane may be appropriated by Mobutu on a whim for his own purposes, so schedules are not always maintained. By land, from Burundi, you can get into Bukavu via Cyangugu in Rwanda, and into Bakavu via Uvira. From Uganda, the two routes are from Kasese to Rotshuru and from Kisoro to Rotshuru. From Rwanda, the two main arteries are between Gisenyi and Goma and Cyangugu to Bakavu. See the "Getting Around" section for more details.

Getting Around

Of the 146,500 km of local roads, only 2800 km are paved. Most intercity roads are difficult or impassable in the rainy season. When driving in cities, individuals often keep windows rolled up and doors locked. At roadblocks or checkpoints, documents are displayed through closed windows. A government "mining permit" may be required to travel to large areas of the country, regardless of the visitor's purpose in going there. This permit must be obtained before entering the "mining zone."

Border Crossings

A special exit permit from Zaire's immigration department and a visa from an embassy of the Congo are required to cross the Congo River from Kinshasa to Brazzaville, in the Congo.

There are three ferry crossing points for overland traffic between Zaire and The Central African Republic. They are located at Bangui, Mobaye and Bangassou. Beginning in the summer of 1993, the crossing points at Bangui and Mobaye have been closed to overland tourist traffic on the direct order of President Mobutu of Zaire for security reasons. The ferry crossing point at Bangassou is not affected and remains open. The ferry serving that crossing point has, however, a history of breaking and can be down for weeks at a time, waiting for someone to pay for repairs. In the event it is not functioning, overland groups will be stranded on either side of the border, unable to use the other working, but restricted, ferry crossing points. Local citizens are not affected by these orders, but may also be temporarily stranded at times.

Taxis

There is a fixed rate for taxis from the airport. The rate is posted at the airport. In town it is wise to agree on the price prior to getting into the taxi, or you may be overcharged.

Dangerous Places

The Entire Country

Although there are several flights each week between Kinshasa and European cities, schedules are often disrupted by security problems in Kinshasa or neighboring Brazzaville. There have been instances of shooting into Kinshasa from Brazzaville and of shell fragments falling on Kinshasa from fighting in Brazzaville. In the past, during these occasions, the U.S. Embassy in Kinshasa has alerted U.S. citizens to the precautions to be observed. In September 1991 and January 1993, there were major episodes of military mutiny in Kinshasa, resulting in many deaths and major property theft, damage and destruction. Similar events occurred in late November 1993 in the provincial capital of Kananga. The underlying cause of these mutinies—the inability of the government to pay the military sufficiently to enable them to support themselves and their families—has not been resolved. Civil disturbances, including looting and the possibility of physical harm, can occur without warning in all urban areas of Zaire. Zairian security personnel are increasingly suspicious of foreigners and sometimes stop them on the street for proof of immigration status. Some foreigners, especially journalists, have been arrested for contacting members of the Zairian opposition parties. Border control personnel scrutinize passports, visas, and vaccination certificates for any possible irregularity and sometimes seek bribes to perform their official functions. Travelers are requested to be cautious and polite if confronted with these situations.

Dangerous Things

Crime

In a country where there is little law or the police are the major criminals, you have to park your moral indignation when visiting. Morality, legality and right/wrong issues have been sidelined in the interest of survival. It is estimated that customs officials have an unwritten law of extracting about US$100 from all Western travelers that enter Zaire. All border officials will hit you up for some type of *cadeau* or bribe. Once inside you may wish you were being jacked up by a uniformed border guard rather than the street criminals who will continually hit on you. The continued deterioration of Zaire's economy has led to an increase in armed street crime, especially in Kinshasa, where violent crime is commonplace. Vehicle thefts, including hijackings at gunpoint, are on the increase.

Zaire is quickly reverting to an agrarian or barter economy. Most visitors will tell you that it is a predatory environment where the use of deadly weapons has led to the deaths or serious injury of several expatriate citizens. As the economy continues to collapse, crimes such as armed robbery, vehicle theft and house break-ins increase accordingly, with the foreign community and travelers expected to become more frequent targets. If you find yourself looking to the police for help, you may find yourself in worse hands. Police officials are often corrupt and demand bribes for their services. If you think you can appeal to the U.S embassy for help, think again. There is no U.S. government representation in Zaire.

Walking

Walking through Serrekunda and Half-Die in Banjul is not considered safe day or night. You should not walk alone at night and not walk alone on the beach day or night.

Taking Photos

Photography of public buildings and/or military installations is forbidden, including photography of the banks of the Congo River. Offenders can expect to be arrested, held for a minimum of several hours and fined.

Carrying Money

The Foreign Exchange Office at N'djili Airport in Kinshasa closed in September 1991. While U.S. dollars and "Traveler's cheques" can, in theory, be exchanged for local currency (Zaires) at banks in Kinshasa, banks often do not have sufficient Zaire cash on hand to make transactions. Visitors may be given an unfavorable rate of exchange, making any daily necessities extremely expensive. Participating in the unofficial, "parallel" money exchanges that flourish in some areas is illegal. Some foreigners have been picked up for infractions of this type and had their money confiscated. Credit cards are accepted at a few major hotels and restaurants. It is illegal to take Zairian currency out of the country. When you consider that you need 2,000,000 (two million) zaire to buy one U.S. dollar there is little incentive to smuggle the local currency for anything but gerbil nesting.

The Police

Zaire's Gendarme Force fired nearly 100 patrolmen in January 1995 and said it would reorganize the force after a public outcry over police corruption and abuse. The complaints were made to Prime Minister Kengo Wa Dondo about the Gendarme patrols who demand money to let drivers pass. The police and government soldiers are responsible for much of the crime in Zaire, especially violent crime—from street holdups to periodic mass rampages of looting, rape and murder.

Getting Sick

Getting sick in Zaire is as inevitable as it is debilitating. Zaire is famous for being the incubator of some of the world's nastiest diseases. If you come down with anything, try to get on the next plane out to Europe. Medical facilities are extremely limited. Medicine is in short supply. Doctors and hospitals expect immediate cash payment in full for health services. Not all U.S. medical insurance is valid outside the United States.

Nuts & Bolts

Zaire was formerly called the Belgian Congo until 1971 and was inhabited principally by the Pygmies until they were driven into the mountains by the Bantus and the Nilotics. Zaire is located in west central Africa. The main rivers are the Ubangi, the Bomu (both in the north) and the Congo in the west. Lake Tanganyika forms Zaire's eastern border.

Zaire is hot and fetid, with little relief except in the southern and eastern highlands. The wet season north of the equator is from April to October; the dry season is December to February. Below the equator the wet season is November to March with the dry season April to October.

The influence of the former Belgian colonists is evident in Zaire, as half the population is Roman Catholic. Protestants make up 20 percent, Kimbanguist 10 percent, Muslim 10 percent, and indigenous 10 percent. The official language of Zaire is French. However, English is also spoken, as is Swahili, Lingala, Ishiluba and Kikongo. Zaire is made up primarily of Bantu, Sudanese, Nilotics, Hamites and Pygmies. The literacy rate stands at about 72 percent.

The official worthless currency in Zaire is not ironically called the Zaire.

Embassies

U.S. Embassy in Zaire
310 Avenue des Aviateurs, Unit 31550
APO 09828
☎ *[243] (12) 21532/21628*

Dangerous Days

11/24/1965	Revolution Day commemorates the establishment of the Second Congolese Republic by General Joseph Mobutu (now Mobutu Sese Seko) following his seizure of control of the government on this date.
05/25/1963	OAU - Africa Freedom Day. The Organization of African Unity was founded on May 25, 1963. The day is celebrated as Africa Freedom Day. The OAU was organized to promote unity and cooperation among African states.
06/30/1960	Independence Day.
10/14/1930	Birthday of President Mobutu.

FORBIDDEN PLACES

Albania

Oil and Water

What do you get when you throw into a bowl a bunch of Albanians and a garnish of fanatical separatist Greeks? Oil and Water. Add in some nasty drug traffickers using Albania as a transshipment point for Southwest Asian heroin transiting the Balkan route and you've got a regular lead salad.

A battlefield during World War II, Albania has been one of the poorest countries in Europe and has vacillated between communism, democracy and anarchy since it proclaimed independence on November 28, 1912 after a history of Roman, Byzantine and Turkish domination. Located in southeastern Europe on the Balkan Peninsula, Albania's got some nasty neighbors, the likes of Serbia and Greece.

March 1991 elections gave the communists in Albania a decisive victory. But soon after, strikes and demonstrations broke out and the entire communist government hightailed it out of the capital of Tirana in the spring of that year. The Communist Party of Labor was reborn as the Socialist Party and abandoned its former communist principles. However, the opposition Democratic Party won a landslide victory in elections held in 1992. The economy improved slightly, but relations with Greece continued to be the bane of Albania. And Albania continues to get its tentacles caught up in the Bosnia-Herzegovina conflict. Its two primary disputes are the Kosovo question with Serbia and Montenegro and the Northern Epirus question with Greece.

On May 20, 1994, Albanian authorities charged six ethnic Greek Albanians with espionage, fomenting separatism, possessing weapons without a license and maintaining links with the Greek secret service. The six were all ranking members of the ethnic Greek organization Omonia. The accused were residents of an area some ethnic Greeks claim as Northern Epirus—linking it by name to a neighboring Greek province. Greece cancelled ministerial talks with Albania in protest of the detention of six ethnic Greeks, severing hopes that the two Balkan countries could patch up their shaky relations, caused by the killing of two Albanian soldiers on April 10, 1994, by what Albania believed were ethnic-Greek separatist gunmen.

On that day, six or seven gunmen, wearing Greek military uniforms and shouting "This is for Vorio Epirus (Northern Epirus)! Don't think we have forgotten!" opened fire on sleeping Albanian border guards in their dormitory. One was killed and three seriously injured. The gunmen had previously killed another border guard before reaching the dormitory. A group calling itself the Northern Epirus Liberation Front (MAVI) claimed responsibility for the attack. Vorio Epirus is a term used by Greeks to refer to southern Albania, and seen by Albanians as a foundless territorial claim to the region, which borders Greece's province of Southern Epirus and contains either a large or small ethnic Greek minority, depending on who you talk to. Many ethnic Greek leaders in southern Albania have called for autonomy or unification with Greece, which has been the basis of poor and heated relations between the two countries. Albania maintains some 60,000 ethnic Greeks live in the south, while Greece claims there are 400,000 ethnic Greeks there.

No matter the number, Albania is ethnically quite pure; 90 percent of all Albanians are of Albanian descent. Greeks comprise 8 percent of the population, while the Vlach, Serbs, Gypsies and Bulgarians make up the last 2 percent. The country is 70 percent-Muslim. Greek Orthodox make up 20 percent of the population and Roman Catholic 10 percent. The official Albanian dialect is Tosk. Greek is also widely spoken, but obviously, not understood very well.

Getting In

The Albanian government no longer requires visas of U.S. citizens. A passport is required. A US$10 airport fee must be paid to Albanian customs officials upon departure. Americans planning to travel to Albania can contact, for specific entry/exit requirements, the Embassy of the Republic of Albania at *1511 K Street, NW, Suite 1000, Washington, D.C. 20005,* ☎ *(202) 223-4942, FAX (202) 628-7342,* or an Albanian mission abroad.

Getting Around

Albania has undergone profound political change and continues to see significant economic change. For the most part, the government has restored stability and public order. Facilities for tourism are not highly developed, and many of the goods and services taken for granted in other European countries are not yet available.

Albania has a low rate of crime. However, crimes against tourists (robbery, mugging, and pickpocketing) do occur, especially on city streets after dark. Credit cards, personal checks and "Traveler's cheques" are rarely accepted in Albania. In addition, hotel accommodations are very limited, and even confirmed reservations are sometimes not honored.

The U.S. Embassy in Tirana, Albania is located at Rruga E Elbasanit 103; ☎ *(355-42) 32875.* Although the U.S. Embassy in Tirana is open, routine consular assistance to U.S. citizens in Albania is

SERBIA

Valbonë

Han i Hotit

Bajzë

Koplik

Lake Scutari

Shkodër

2

Drin

Bajram Curri

Laq i Koman

Ligeni i Fierzës

1

4

Pukë

Kukës

Laq i të Dejës

Drini zi

3

Adriatic Sea

Buenë

Shëngjin

Lezhë

Rrëshen

Zall-Reç

6

Milot

Rubik

7

Peshkopi

Laç

Burrel

8

5

Krujë

Klos

9

Mat

Shijak

10

Durrës

Tiranë ✪

MACEDONIA

Kavajë

11

Librazhd

Rrogozhinë

Elbasan

12

Shkumbin

Cërrik

Lake Ohrid

13

Lushnjë

Gramsh

Pogradec

Lake Prespa

Seman

Qyteti Stalin (Kuçovë)

16

Fier

Berat

Devoll

14

15

Maliq

Osum

19

18

Korçë

Vjosë

Ballësh

Çorovodë

Selenicë

Vlorë

21

Mavrovë

Këlcyrë

2

Ersekë

25

22

Tepelenë

Përmet

24

Gjirokastër

Delvinë

Sarandë

23

GREECE

Disricts (rreth) of Albanli

1. Shkodër
2. Tropojë
3. Kukës
4. Pukë
5. Krujë
6. Mirditë
7. Mat
8. Dibrë
9. Durrës
10. Tiranë
11. Librazhd
12. Elbasan
13. Lushnjë
14. Fier
15. Berat
16. Gramsh
17. Pogradec
18. Korçë
19. Skrapar
20. Përmet
21. Tepelenë
22. Vlorë
23. Sarandë
24. Gjirokastër
25. Kolonjë

Albania

✪ National Capital

● Region Capital

● Secondary City

Primary Road

Railroad

Administrative Border

0   25 km

0   25 mi

©FWI 1995

limited by the difficult environment and a small staff. U.S. citizens who register at the U.S. Embassy can obtain updated information on travel and security within Albania. Medical facilities are limited and medicine is in short supply. Doctors and hospitals often expect immediate cash payment for health services.

Cuba

The Sinking Island

Fidel Castro is still numero uno in Cuba. After 36 years of socialism and dictatorship—a dictatorship which itself replaced the seven-year, brutal authoritarian reign of Fulgencio Baptista—Castro retains an undaunted defiance against the United States; an antagonism which seems to grow ever more resolved with each act by the U.S to choke Cuba into democracy.

However, the 36-year U.S. embargo on Cuba, tightened with the Cuban Democracy Act of 1992 and again by President Bill Clinton in August 1994, is now taking its toll on the island nation. The Cuban economy is in tatters, and the signs are visible everywhere. The cars are gone—the result of the reduced availability of oil—having been replaced by Chinese-made bicycles. Everything from shampoo and paper to medicine and eyeglasses is in short supply. There are few medical supplies. Sutures, syringes and even surgical gloves are in such demand that those that exist are reused time and time again. The shortage of eyeglasses has hampered the ability of schoolchildren to learn.

There is little food. With the U.S. embargo, Cuba simply doesn't have access to food as it once did. U.S. foreign subsidy trade with Cuba is now prohibited with the passage

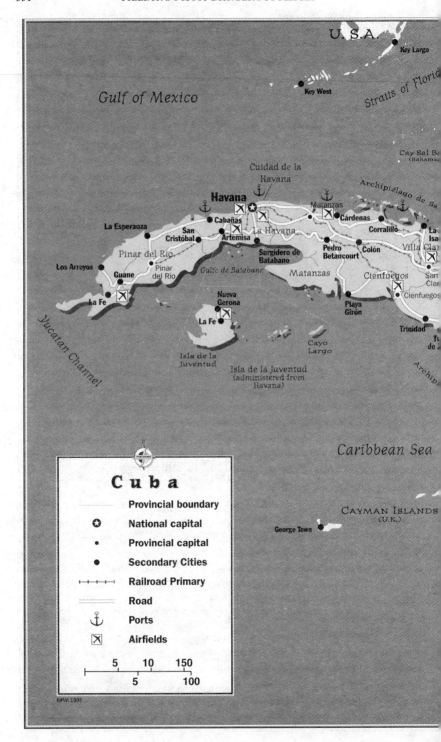

U.S.A.

Key Largo

Gulf of Mexico

Key West

Straits of Florida

Cay Sal Bank
(Bahamas)

Cuidad de la
Havana

Archipiélago de Sa

Havana

Matanzas

Cárdenas

La Esperanza

Cabañas

San
Cristóbal

Artemisa

La Havana

Corralillo

La
Isa

Pinar del Río

Surgidero de
Batabano

Pedro
Betancourt

Colón

Villa Clar

Los Arroyos

Guane

Pinar
del Río

Gulfo de Batabano

Matanzas

San
Clar

La Fe

Cienfuegos

Nueva
Gerona

Cienfuegos

Yucatan Channel

La Fe

Playa
Girón

Isla de la
Juventud

Cayo
Largo

Trinidad

Tu
de 2

Isla de la Juventud
(administered from
Havana)

Archip

Caribbean Sea

Cuba

....	Provincial boundary
✪	National capital
•	Provincial capital
●	Secondary Cities
⊢•⊢•⊣	Railroad Primary
═══	Road
⚓	Ports
⊠	Airfields

CAYMAN ISLANDS
(U.K.)

George Town

5   10   150

5   100

©RW 1995

of the Cuban democracy Act. Ninety percent of this trade included food, medicines and medical supplies. Before the act, Cuba had virtually purged itself of the communicable diseases so endemic to developing countries and was primarily plagued with those found in advanced countries, chronic diseases such as cancer, diabetes and heart disease. Cuba's infant and child mortality rates rivaled those of any industrialized nation. Even though they still currently do, new diseases such as neuropathy—a debilitating eye disease—have mushroomed all over the country. Venereal diseases, hepatitis A, anemia in young children and pregnant women and stomach disorders are on a marked rise. Much of Cuba's diagnostic equipment is under U.S. patent, making the procuring of replacement parts virtually impossible. With a decrease in access to such vital minerals as iron, as well as protein-rich food, malnutrition is also on the rise.

Yet, after 36 years, the embargo has still failed to bring democracy to Cuba. Castro remains in power, despite suffering the loss of Soviet subsidies and enduring Cuba's worst sugar harvest and most destructive tropical storm in years (the March 1993 storm caused more than US$1 billion in damage). For 36 years, defenders of the embargo have argued that by cutting Castro off from the rest of the world and by strangling the Cuban economy, the U.S. will eventually force Castro to capitulate—or at least incite a deprived Cuban people to stage an uprising to overthrow the dictator.

But, to date, the embargo has yet to accomplish either goal and has essentially only reinforced nationalism in Cuba and provided a common anti-U.S. stand that all Cubans can rally behind. Castro's continued resiliency in defying U.S. pressure seems to only strengthen with each tightening of the noose around his neck.

Another of the reasons for the continued U.S. embargo on trade with Cuba surrounds the human rights issue. Whereas the U.S. policy has been designed to champion the human rights cause on the island, it's apparently backfiring and, instead, creating a justification for Cuba's silencing of political opponents. A 1994 U.N. report to the U.N. commissioner on human rights stated that the embargo is "totally counterproductive" to improving human rights. The embargo, rather than unifying the masses against the regime, has permitted the suppression of anyone advocating reform.

In the post-Cold War world, Fidel Castro's near bankrupt island is no longer a security threat to the U.S. The prospects for a peaceful transition to democracy through the embargo are diminishing, many experts argue. If anything arises from the economic sanctions, it will be such hardship as to incite mass political violence on the island, resulting in an unparalleled mass exodus of the nation and the consequent intervention by the U.S. military—on a scale that will make the Haiti intervention seem like running down a purse snatcher on the Bonneville Salt Flats.

Cuba is no longer exporting liberation and Marxism because it cannot afford to. Cuba used to import US$8 billion worth of goods during its Soviet marriage. Now it has a hard time exporting US$1.7 billion to anywhere.

Tourism has been generating hard dollars and creating jobs. According to a March 1993 report by Cuba's Tourism Group, the number of visitors per year more than doubled from 289,000 in 1987 to more than 600,000 in 1993. The industry generated US$530 million in gross hard currency in 1992 and directly accounted for 62,000 jobs.

The downside? Economists say Cuban tourism would be four or five times more profitable if it had access to the U.S. market, which traditionally accounted for 60 percent of Caribbean tourism. Due to the U.S. economic embargo, American tourists cannot legally visit the island. Yet many still do, and return back home to Peoria and Fresno to tell their friends about it.

The Scoop

More than 5000 Cuban boat people were picked up by U.S. Coast Guard boats in 1994, far exceeding the total of 3,656 picked up in 1993. The 1993 total was the highest since Mariel. The recent tightening of the 30-year-old U.S. embargo, which Cuba claims has cost it US$40 billion, also is contributing to the country's economic crisis. In a major speech on July 26, 1993, President Fidel Castro spoke of the need to postpone the construction of socialism and to take some steps leading to a market economy, making "concessions" because of the extremely grave economic situation the nation was facing. He announced plans to legalize the possession of foreign currency and create an alternative market to the present hard currency market. Authorities disclosed the country closed 1993 with foreign currency revenues of only $1.719 billion in comparison with US$2.236 billion in 1992 and US$8.139 billion in 1989, before the collapse of the "Eastern European socialist community," with which the country carried out 85 percent of its foreign trade.

The Players

Uncle Fidel

After a bitter and often heroic three-year struggle against the government of dictator Fulgencio Batista (at one point Castro's guerrilla force had been whittled down to a dozen or so men), Fidel Castro came to power in 1959 and led Cuba down the path of communism as he experienced increased hostility to his new regime from the U.S. Castro's government seized all farms greater than 67 hectares, and all American businesses, including banks, were nationalized. The subsequent U.S. embargo and severing of diplomatic ties with Cuba only began to choke the island nation after the fall of the Soviet Union and Eastern Bloc. Castro maintains a Stalinistic grip on Cuba's people, although the economy is in tatters.

Uncle Sam

After the revolution of 1959, the United States placed a trade embargo on Cuba. At the time, the U.S. had an estimated US$1 billion invested in the island nation, primarily in agriculture, oil and mining. The U.S. had been the recipient of more than 65 percent of Cuba's exports and responsible for more than 70 percent of the nation's imports. The embargo had relatively minimal impact until the collapse of the Eastern Bloc and the Soviet Union in the late 1980s and early 1990s. Although trade between Cuba and the former U.S.S.R. continued and continues today, the U.S. has put pressure on the Boris Yeltsin government to end oil shipments to the island as a means of receiving U.S. aid. President George Bush, prior to the 1992 elections, signed the Torricelli Bill (the Cuban Democracy Act), which further tightened the embargo by prohibiting all U.S. subsidiary firms in other countries from doing business with the Castro government. Another recent tightening of the 30-year-old U.S. embargo, which Cuba claims has cost it US$40 billion, was enacted by President Bill Clinton in August 1994.

Half of Miami

Almost half the population of Miami today is Hispanic, the vast majority Cubans, or families of Cubans, who fled their homeland after the communist takeover in 1959. Virtually the entire Miami Cuban community is ardently anti-Castro. In 1980 alone, more than 125,000 Cubans fled Cuba, most ending up in Miami. As they constitute a large voting block—and a "door jam"—infuriating the hard-line Miami emigres by softening the embargo may have profound political consequences for Clinton's reelection chances in 1996.

Getting In

According to a consular information sheet May 1993, travel to Cuba in the form of "tourist and business travel is not licensable. This restriction includes tourist or business travel from or through a third country such as Mexico and Canada. Visitors who attempt to enter Cuba without the proper documentation are subject to detention and arrest.Transactions are authorized by general license for the following categories of travelers: U.S. and foreign government officials, including representatives of international organizations of which the United States is a member, traveling on official business; persons gathering news or making news or documentary films; persons visiting close relatives residing in Cuba; and, full-time professionals engaging in full-time research in their professional areas where the research is specifically related to Cuba, is largely academic in nature, and there is substantial likelihood the product of research will be disseminated."

In August 1994, President Clinton further tightened restrictions on travel by Americans to Cuba, by essentially saying "forget about it" unless you have a direct relative in Cuba in a "grave emergency" situation and can prove it. A DP call to the U.S. Treasury Department gleaned that a letter of request to the Office of Foreign Assets Control isn't enough. The letter must clearly describe the relative's condition and be accompanied by a medical certificate describing in detail the medical condition.

"It is absolutely illegal for an American tourist to visit Cuba," a representative of New York-and Miami-based Marazul tours told DP from Miami. "How about from Mexico?" we asked. "I'm not in position to answer that," she said. "How about from Canada?" "I cannot comment on that either," she said and hung up. A representative of the company's New York office echoed much the same but added an American tourist in Cuba "would be in defiance of the U.S. Trading with the Enemy Act." Those actually permitted to travel to Cuba on a visa must report to the immigration office at the corner of Calle 22 and Av. 3 within 24 hours of arrival in Havana.

So is it impossible to get into Cuba without meeting the above criteria? "Of course not," said a representative with Bureau de Tourisme de Cuba in Montreal who gave her name only as Veronica. "U.S. tourists are not refused in Cuba. There aren't any flights from the U.S., but the Cubans haven't been stamping passports since 1990, regardless of your nationality. As an American tourist you can get to Cuba either on a package tour or independently from either Canada or Mexico."

The key is obtaining a tourist card. These can be had through a number of travel wholesalers, including Cuban Holidays in Montreal (☎ *(514) 382-9785)*, perhaps the best-contacted wholesaler in the Americas regarding tourism to Cuba. The wholesalers can provide American tourists with Cuban tourist cards without any questions asked by the Cuban embassy or consulate issuing the cards. If you attempt to procure the card yourself through a Cuban embassy or consulate, there's a good chance you'll be turned down for being an American. But no such problems have been reported through the wholesalers. You can obtain a tourist card for either package or independent travel in Cuba for US$15.40 (CAN$20). You must first have a reservation for at least three nights in a Cuban hotel and an airline ticket showing your departure date. A U.S. citizen cannot enter Cuba with an open airline ticket. And when making your hotel reservations, do so from either Mexico or Canada. Do not place the call to Cuba from the U.S. "If, by chance, you're an American and have arrived in Havana without a hotel reservation, you'll be required to immediately make one before you'll be permitted to leave the airport," Veronica said. "If a Canadian is in the same predicament, he'll be given preference over an American, especially if there is a shortage of hotel space. It's a nationalism thing."

Round-trip airline fares on Cubana from Montreal to Havana range from approximately US$300 during the low tourist season to US$400 during the high season. The tourist card is actually valid for one month and can be renewed twice, for a stay of up to three months.

Although entry by Americans into Cuba can be handled in a similar way from Mexico, it's more easily accomplished from Canada, where travel wholesalers have better connections in Havana regarding accommodations, tour packages, and—yes—food (tough to find in the island country). "We simply have better contacts in Cuba," said a rep from Cuban Holidays. "We get travelers into the better hotels than our Mexican counterparts. A lot more people come to Cuba from Canada than from Mexico. There's much more of a demand from Montreal than from Cancun. The biggest reason is the climate. Hell, Mexico has the same climate as Cuba." Entry into Cuba, according to San Francisco-based Freedom to Travel Campaign, is possible from any nation outside the U.S. where travel to Cuba is possible. The major springboards for Americans are Montreal, Mexico City and Cancun, Mexico and Nassau, the Bahamas.

"Although it's tempting to go to Cuba as an independent tourist, especially since you can travel the country relatively freely once inside, we suggest going in as part of a package tour," Veronica said. "The main reason is food, or a lack of it. On a package tour, you're guaranteed at least three international-standard meals a day. On your own, it will be quite difficult to find food and keep yourself properly nourished. Additionally, accommodations are more difficult to procure. If you travel independently, bring food."

For more information, to book tours, or to acquire a tourist card, contact:

Freedom to Travel Campaign

P.O. Box 40116
San Francisco, CA 94140
☎ *(415) 558-9490*

Global Exchange

2017 Mission Street, Ste. 303
San Francisco, CA 94110
☎ *(415) 255-7296*

Cuban Information Project

198 Broadway, Ste. 800
New York, New York 10038
☎ *(212) 227-3422*

Getting Around

Getting around Cuba is remarkably cheap. Cubana de Aviación offers fares as low as US$38 to Camagüey, US$44 to Holguín, US$58 to Baracoa, US$44 to Manzanillo, US$54 to Guantánamo, US$54 to Moa, US$44 to Bayamo, US$50 to Santiago, US$42 to Las Tunas, US$32 to Ciego de Avila, and US$12 to Nueva Gerona/Isla de Juventud. Cubana is located at the seaward end of Calle 23. Payment is usually preferred, if not required, in U.S. dollars.

Trains offer the best way to get around Cuba. Buses often won't accept foreigners and, when they do, usually require payment in U.S. dollars. Rail tickets will also have to be paid for in U.S. dollars. Car rentals are scarce, but are available at the Capri, Triton and Riviera hotels in Havana, as well as at the airport. The minimum fee is US$40 per day (US$45 for air conditioning) and US$.30 for every kilometer after 100. You'll need to purchase petrol coupons in 20-liter amounts. Tack on another US$5 a day for insurance and you're looking that US$70 a day range. Peso taxis, once a popular form of tourist transit before the fuel crunch, are seen about as frequently these days on the streets of Cuba's cities as a state visit by George Bush.

Getting Out

Getting out of Cuba is as simple as getting in—as long as you get back to the point where you left before returning to the States. Certainly do not attempt to return directly to the U.S. from Cuba. Since your passport hasn't been stamped by the Cuban authorities, getting back into the U.S. will pose no problem from either Mexico or Canada, as you've left behind no "passport trail." Expect to pay a US$11 airport departure tax. Many American visitors to Cuba go in protest of the travel ban and have their passports stamped as badges of crusade. Some go in groups that leave and return through Mexico. American customs and other authorities will know who you are, no matter where you arrive back in the States from. If you get your passport stamped, expect some trouble once Stateside.

Dangerous Places

Tourists frequenting beaches, hotels and historic sites are prime targets for petty theft and other crimes. Most tourists are hit at beaches, parks, hotels and historic sites. Some of the beaches include Miramar, Playa de Marianao, El Mégano, Santa María del Mar, Bacuranao, Arena Blanca and Bahía Honda. Areas around museums are also frequented by muggers.

Dangerous Things

Crime

Crime is rising steadily and tourists increasingly are targeted, especially by Cubans desperate to find the money to build or buy a raft to float to Key West. The Cuban raft exodus and the associated crime are beginning to bite large chunks out of Cuba's last hard currency earner: tourism. Robberies, including those resulting in injuries, are increasing. Even low-budget travelers find they have many items, including currency, that are attractive to thieves. Tourists frequenting beaches, hotels and historic sites are prime targets. The country's worsening shortages and living conditions are attributable to an economic crisis reaching critical proportions. The government of Cuba does not publish crime statistics. However, according to informal reports, thefts and burglaries are high in the diplomatic community and among tourists. Clothing, passports, and food items are most likely to be stolen. Robberies, especially purse snatching, are frequently accompanied by assault. Visitors, in general, are easily identifiable in this environment with all tourists being especially attractive targets. Since U.S. credit cards are not valid in Cuba and most expenses must be paid in dollars, American visitors can be counted on to have large amounts of cash on hand. Police and security forces are visible throughout the country. However, criminal investigations are often slow. Police seldom capture criminals or recover stolen goods. At the Havanauto car rental office at Havana's international airport, the company offers two insurance policies to cope with the theft of car tires used ultimately for raft-building. The cheaper US$10-a-day policy provides no coverage against tire theft, while for US$18 a day partial coverage can be obtained. Even backpackers and other low-budget tourists have become targets in recent years—simply because even they possess more of value than would-be assailants and most other Cubans, for that matter. Many tour packagers and travel agents have reported a surge in cancellations to Cuba. There have been reports of tourists discovering the corpses of rafters on Cuba's beaches, although this is rare. Many women have been forced into prostitution, making the island a burgeoning destination for sex tourists.

Terrorism

There is no specific threat to Americans traveling to, or doing business in, Cuba. There is no known terrorist organization operating on a continuing basis within the country, although it suffers from occasional forays by anti-Castro emigres based in Florida. Only 11 incidents of terrorism and other forms of political violence have been reported since 1988 but the trend is up as all but one of the 11 incidents occurred during the past 30 months. This increase is most likely tied to the deteriorating state of the economy which has befallen the country since the disintegration of its major trading partners. In early November 1993, Andres Nazario Sargen, head of the paramilitary anti-Castro group Alpha 66, affirmed threats to kidnap foreigners in Cuba beginning November 27 of that year. He acknowledged such kidnappings would "constitute a terrorist action," but vehemently denied characterization of Alpha 66 as a terrorist group. In addition, he averred, Alpha 66 "cannot be accused in Miami of what occurs in Cuba." According to Nazario, one of the 66 Cuban exiles who founded the organization in 1961, current membership totaled approximately 6000 members in the U.S., plus a network of 45,000 "collaborators" in Cuba. He stated that for the past 20 years, Alpha 66 had "underground cells" in place that were "now preparing for an irregular struggle" by staging attacks against tourism centers, government enterprises and sugar plantations in Cuba. The U.S. Government subsequently strongly urged the Cuban community in the United States to discard the use of violence against Cuba and threatened legal action against those who attacked or conspired to attack U.S. citizens with links to Cuba. To date, no such attacks have occurred.

Government Harassment

Private U.S. citizens the government judges to oppose the regime have been harassed and followed, but since so few come to Cuba, it is difficult to make a general statement.

Anti-U.S. Demonstrations

In the past, the government has encouraged anti-U.S. demonstrations, sometimes staged at the U.S. interests section. In addition, U.S. diplomats have previously been targeted for harassment. While there is no credible evidence of significant in-country opposition to the Castro regime, the growing economic stress leads some observers to predict an end to the communist system once the charismatic but aging leader passes from the scene.

Blackouts

Nighttime blackouts in Havana (and other locations) have provoked unprecedented vandalism and anger against Cuba's communist government, sources report. Cubans already putting up with drastic cutbacks in public transport and entertainment facilities and severe consumer shortages of everything from fresh meat to toothpaste, now are enduring daily electricity cuts lasting between 12 and 20 hours. The blackouts plunge whole sectors of the city into darkness at night, leaving pedestrians, cyclists and property vulnerable to attack and robbery. Numerous apparently spontaneous and unrelated incidents have occurred in which individuals or groups have damaged state and private property and shouted antigovernment slogans over the last few weeks. Foreign diplomats and local residents say crime and vandalism, especially at night, have reached unprecedented levels in a city previously known for safe streets. Although major tourist hotels and hospitals are spared power cuts, foreign consular officials in Havana have reported an upsurge in muggings and purse-snatchings against foreign visitors, even in daylight.

Getting Sick

Despite being only 90 miles from the U.S., Cuba is one of the last places on earth where you'll want to become ill enough to have to enter a hospital. Once having been a showcase of socialized medical care—on par with Sweden's system—the loss of billions of Soviet rubles for health care in the wake of the collapse of the Eastern Bloc has left Cuban hospitals unsanitized and suffering from a severe shortage of even the most rudimentary medical supplies and medicines. For example, in Havana itself, syringes and needles are in such demand that they are routinely reused on multiple patients. They're supposed to be sterilized, but it's a crap shoot if you have to be injected with anything. Antibiotics and other medicines and vaccines imported from the former Soviet Union are all but nonexistent. The only medicines available are those which are produced in Cuba itself—and these consist of only a limited number of vaccines. And, again, Americans will not receive preferential treatment in Cuban hospitals. In other words: get sick, get out.

Dangerous Days

10/08/1967	Che Guevara was killed by security forces in eastern Bolivia while trying, unsuccessfully, to spark an uprising. Celebrated as "heroic guerrilla" day.
01/08/1959	President Fulgencio Batista flew to exile in the Dominican Republic and Fidel Castro marched into the capital, Havana, on this date to take power.
12/04/1956	Revolutionary Armed Forces Day.
07/26/1953	Castro led a group of revolutionaries in an attack on the Moncada army barracks in Santiago de Cuba. The attack failed and Castro was imprisoned for two years before being allowed to go into exile in Mexico. Castro slipped back into Cuba in 1956 to begin his final drive for power.
08/13/1927	Fidel Castro's birthday.
05/10/1902	Independence Day. Cuba achieved independence as a U.S. Protectorate in 1899. This date marks the end of U.S. Protection.
10/28/1492	Discovery of Cuba by Columbus.

Iran

★

Terror's Backbone

Ronald Reagan had it easy. When he thought the world was being overrun by zealots, controlled by subversives, bullied by foreign-controlled thugs or just getting too full of fanatics, lunatics, heretics, zombies, crazed clerics, guerrillas, psychotics and brainwashed bandits, all he had to do was call up Moscow and threaten to push the button, drop the "big one" or send in the Marines. The former Soviet Union policy of guns for butter demanded that countries like Libya, Cuba, Bulgaria and East Germany export death and fear to feed their people. Today, there is a new sugar daddy who asks only that its people strike at the heart of the Great Satan in exchange for a paycheck.

Their M.O. is surprisingly similar to the old fashioned brand of communism: Find the oppressed, teach them to respect themselves, give them pride and then give them a gun. The commies screwed up by tossing out religion. The Iranians know that adding their interpretation of the Koran to this classic revolutionary format is like adding nitro to gasoline. It burns brighter and goes faster.

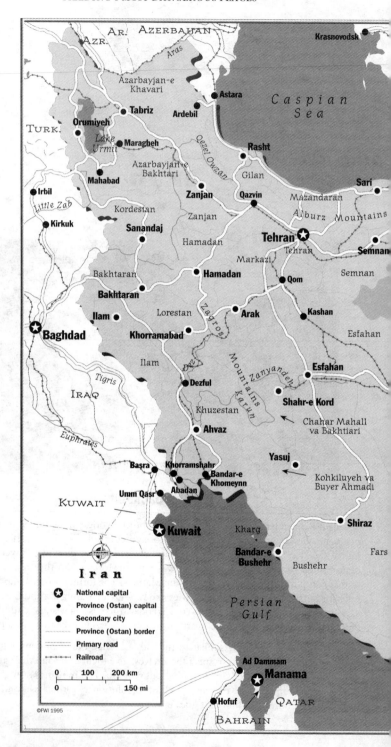

Iran

⊛ National capital

• Province (Ostan) capital

⬤ Secondary city

⋯⋯ Province (Ostan) border

--- Primary road

+++ Railroad

0   100   200 km

0   150 mi

©FWI 1995

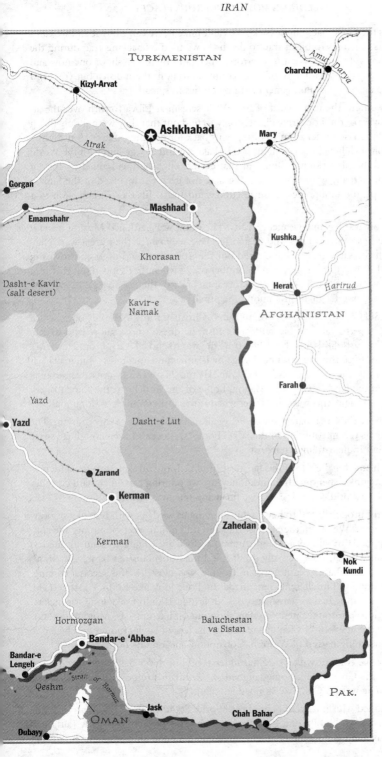

How does the Great Satan fight back? We can't nuke it, we can't buy it and we can't pay our worst enemies to bleed Iran to death (as we tried by backing Iraq during the eight-year war with Iran). We arrest terrorists here and there, we shoot one now and then and we pay the bill for a lot of other countries to hunt them down but you can't use a gun against a virus. Fundamentalism continues to spread.

How do we fight the new sword of Islam? We scream at Libya to turn over the alleged destroyers of the Lockerbie disaster only to find out that they were simply filling out an evil Purchase Order from Iran to pay us back for downing one of *their* flights. We snatch one evil henchman from his bed in Pakistan and charge him with the World Trade Center bombing only to find out that even though he was trained by Iran, it was Iraq who actually wrote the check. We dare not even get involved in the Sudan, Algeria, Egypt, the Philippines, Bosnia, Turkey and India. Jihad is coming soon to a country near you.

Jihad or holy war has many eager recruits. The poor, war hardened Muslim teenagers from the dusty cities of the Middle and Far East see *jihad* as their great war. They sign up with the same fervor that cleared out the iron mines and dead end towns in World War I. It was not surprising in December of '94 when they slipped out that Iran had spent over US$10 billion dollars on weapons just in the last five years—all that money and not one B1 or ICBM among the purchases.

Pity poor Bill Clinton and his Southern Judeo-Christian roots. Not only does he not have a red phone to call or a big button to push, he doesn't even know who to call. Worse yet, this just may be the big one—truly the war to end all wars. From New York City to Zamboango the world is under siege by Islamic fundamentalists. Bill may be at the helm during the apocalypse, World War III, the 21st-century crusade, the final showdown in the land of Gog and Magog, home of the Antichrist, the fomentors of Armageddon. Whew, this was a lot easier when it was just commies or dominoes.

To Iran we are the Great Satan, the defiler of all that is pure, the enemy of Islam. The U.S., despite its recent roundup of the WTC bombers, doesn't have enough jail space to house every Iranian-trained terrorist.

Who is to blame for the rise of this fanatical empire? Is our addiction to fossil fuels to blame? Like a junkie spending his rent money, are we pouring too much hard currency into dusty third world countries? Are we financing our own downfall?

In our (and Europe's) need to have stable oil supplies we dealt with Iran like an overprotective parent. We put in the Shah of Iran and told him to keep pumping. We continue to support a tribal clan in Saudi Arabia, and we are willing to send in one less Stealth bomber because we actually don't mind mad dog Hussien barking at Iran's Western border. What we got for our trouble was close to the second coming. Khomeini a dour and intelligent cleric made the Pope look like Rodney Dangerfield. Iran for the first time had a charismatic, devout leader. It didn't take long for the *fatwa*'s or religious pronouncements to start shooting off like missiles. More importantly, Iran used the new power vacuum created by the loss of Soviet money and began to harness the seething hatred of Western "corruption" beyond its borders.

Muslims, once content with being misunderstood but never bellicose, were told to strike down the Great Satan. Some laughed at Khomeini's return to the biblical era. But when *jihad* was on CNN we stopped laughing.

Iranian-trained Muslims were behind the World Trade Center bombing (although some say Iraq paid the bill) and the Pan Am flight 103 Lockerbie tragedy (although some still say Libyan governement was involved). (A Scottish newspaper in January

1995 quoted U.S. Air Force Intelligence Agency files as saying that Iranian diplomat Ayatollah Ali Akbar Mohtashami paid US$10 million to a Libyan terrorist group to down the jetliner.) Iran operates terrorist training bases in Lebanon and Sudan and supports the annihilation of the Christian/Animists in southern Sudan, Israel, beating back the Serbs in Yugoslavia, the recent civil war in Southern Yemen and maintains fanatic cells of trained Islamic terrorists in the United States.

Iran was the principal supporter of Somali warlord Mohammad Aidid. Iran has sent 10,000 troops into Azerbaijan against the Armenians. Iran has sent 60 tons of weapons and 400 Revolutionary Guards into Bosnia. Iran supports fundamentalist insurgent groups in Algeria and Egypt. Iran caused the Yemeni civil war by creating the fundamentalist party in Northern Yemen which unbalanced the ruling coalition. Iran supplies 19,000 barrels of oil a day to North Korea and receives Scud missiles and weapons in exchange; which they exchange with all the above for their souls. Iran has disputes over no fewer than three islands—Abu Musa and the Greater and Lesser Tumb Islands. Iran was undoubtedly responsible for the assassination of well-known Turkish journalist Ugur Mumcu in a car bomb attack.The 200,000 persons who participated in a demonstration in Ankara during the burial shouted a clear slogan: "Turkey will never be Iran." At Bursa, the Turkish police found the mutilated remains of a former bodyguard of the Shah of Iran, Abbas Golezadeh, 45, who was kidnapped on December 28, 1992 in Istanbul. The list of killings, subversive activities, insurrection and general mayhem attributed to Iran is impressive. Intelligence agencies keep monstrous dossiers on the convoluted connections between the religious leaders in Iran and the skinny, badly shaven men who pull the trigger. The problem is that the religious leaders are not politicians, and wield absolute control over their military and political leaders. Unlike Western law, the Koran spells out very clearly what is right and what is wrong. Western leaders do so much to affront the Iranian view of Islam that it does not take much more than a brief discussion and a nod of the head for the next terrorist attack to be launched. They will go so far as to issue a *fatwa* identifying someone as an enemy of Islam to make them a target for life. Salmon Rushdie has switched to children's tales, but there is no court of appeals for him.

Like showbiz agents from Hell, the Iranians orchestrate the creation and success of some very scary groups. To cover its tracks, Tehran is using members of the Lebanese *Hezbollah* to do its dirty deeds. The Iranians have enlisted dozens, perhaps hundreds, of Lebanese Shiites in Beirut, in the Baalbeck region and particularly among specific clans such as the Hamade, Tleiss, Bdreddine, Kassem, Yazbeck, Berjaoui and Ammar. The recruits are trained at the Imam Ali school north of Tehran. Using Turkey as a base, Iranian intelligence and terrorist "services" have extended their reaches into Germany, where a significant Turkish community lives. In a land where many young teens have known nothing but war and killing, *Hezbollah* or army of God is a well funded political group that seeks to lift up the social and mental status of all its members. Their tone is a bit strident to Western ears, but anyone who has spent their childhood in Afghanistan or Palestine could do with a bit of uplifting. These are dangerous times and these are dangerous people.

Since the Islamic Republic was formed in 1979, Iran has had two goals: to become the dominant power in the Persian Gulf and to further the efforts of Islamic fundamentalism around the world, without regard for human life. Because bullet-buddy Saddam Hussein in Iraq has sort of the same idea in mind for his crumbling "fiefdom," it became "all Muslims for themselves" as Iran became embroiled with Iraq in a lengthy and bloody eight-year war in the 1980s. Relations are still hair-triggered at best. After Iraq's withdrawal from Kuwait in 1991, Iran backed the failed effort of Iraqi Shiites to dump Saddam. Iran has also refused to return Iraqi war planes that fled to Iran during the Persian Gulf war.

Iran has seemed to make partial amends with some of its other neighbors, though. Iran and Saudi Arabia normalized their relations in 1991 (perhaps because of their mutual disdain for Hussein). Tehran's support of the return to power of the Kuwaiti government after the Iraqi invasion of Kuwait in August 1990 has led to improved relations with Kuwait, but the United Arab Emirates continues to be pesky. Iran claims total sovereignty over the small Persian Gulf island of Abu Musa, but the UAE has been like a tick you just can't pull off.

You got the wrong one baby, uh huh

In January 1995, the Ayatollah Ali Khamenei issued a religious decree apparently banning the consumption of both Coca-Cola and Pepsi-Cola, American soft drinks that had recently been reintroduced into Iran. Khamenei was asked by a local paper, "Assuming drinking Coca-Cola and Pepsi politically strengthens world arrogance and financially helps Zionist circles, what would the Islamic decree on the issue be?" Khamenei replied: "Anything that strengthens world arrogance and Zionist circles in itself is forbidden." Only time will tell which real thing Iranians consume, Islamic dogma or the right one, baby.

You probably won't be surprised to learn that satellite dishes are also banned.

Iranian relations with some other Islamic countries have gone to hell in a handbasket, because of generally well-founded allegations that Iran is supporting Islamic terrorists. In March 1993, Algeria broke diplomatic relations with Iran, citing Tehran's aid to over-the-edge fundamentalist rebels. This has forced Iran to seek closer ties with more xenophobic Islamic states, although it periodically makes conciliatory overtures to the West, especially concerning the reform of its economy. Iran is also sticking its nose in the new breakaway Islamic states that helped comprise the former Soviet Union in Central Asia. Iran has offered to aid Azerbaijan in its conflict with Armenia over the Nagorno-Karabakh enclave. Even though Iran has criticized Russia for helping Tajikistan battle Islamic fundamentalist insurgents, no reactionary third world country in its right mind puts too much distance between itself and the "Moscow Machine Gun & Missile Market's" weekly specials. In March 1993, Iran and the Market reached an agreement for economic and military cooperation.

What does the future hold for better relations between Magog (the home of the biblical Antichrist) and The Great Satan (me and you)? Iran doesn't like our opposition to fundamentalist states, especially those backed by Iran. We haven't got a hope in hell of infiltrating them or buying them off so we just have to chase them around the world like international Keystone cops. When we catch 'em they have to have done something pretty direct (like pulled a trigger) or preached violence (we have to tape them) or tried to sell/buy something nasty from a government informant. Bottom line is we don't get around enough to figure out who's who and chances are slim we will send in the Marines again after they scared us off with just two car bombs in Beirut. We hauled ass out of Somalia when we ended up looking like bad guys and I doubt you will see America's youth in Algeria, Pakistan, Sudan or any other place where they don't have McDonald's. So Iran will be out stalking us. They're still that we supported Saddam in the Iran-Iraq war and they are not happy that we are sitting on US$5 billion in Iranian assets that we froze in 1979. Our efforts to prevent the ayatollah from buying anything deadlier than firecrackers or muskets keeps a lot of their Shah-era hardware in mothballs.

As for Europe, Iran's relations with the EU world have become more distant since 1993, reflecting a decision of spiritual leader Ali Khamenei to exercise a greater control over foreign relations and to revise what he considered Rafsanjani's excessive friendship with non-Islamic nations. Negotiations are under way with Germany and Japan over foreign aid and debt renegotiation.

Islamic fundamentalists in Europe are just an *Iran Air 747* ride from Teheran. The Mufti Jamal Eddine Kabalan and his Union of Muslim Associations and Communities is the most sympathetic and powerful to the Iranian cause. In Cologne, the association with its 5000 members uses the name of Islamic Groups and Communities and publishes a journal, *Ummet Mahomed (Nation of the Prophet)*. The House of Iran is not a new MTV political affairs show but a command center for fundamentalist operations in Europe. Located in a quiet suburb of Cologne, the House of Iran is suspected of being where the assassinations of Abdul Rahman Ghasemlou, secretary general of the PDKI in 1989 in Vienna, and that of four Iranian Kurd leaders on September 17, 1992 in Berlin (I.N. n. 201) were organized and carried out. Massud Hendi, second nephew of imam Khomeini and involved in the assassination of the former prime minister of the Shah of Iran, Chapour Bakhtiar, in August 1991 in Paris, visited the House of Iran frequently. Once again no one can place direct blame, but the evidence points in their direction.

Iran takes full advantage of the refugees that have streamed into Germany and sends many of the disillusioned back to Turkey to join the Turkish *Hezbollah*. Germany is home to an extreme right-wing Islamic movement, many of them followers of the former mufti of Adana, Jamal Eddine Kabalan, founder of the Turkish *Hezbollah* who sought refuge in Cologne in 1984.

The hub of Iranian intelligence activity in Turkey is now in Istanbul. Within the Iranian community (estimated at over one million people) Iran has established or supports organizations, restaurants, book stores, hotels, Koranic associations, youth organizations, journals and other public institutions. The Turkish *Hezbollah*, a new organization which the Iranians are setting up by recruiting among clandestine networks of Islamic revolutionaries such as the anti-Kemalist brotherhoods and the Suleymanci, the Nurgiu and the Nakshibandi, is important because of the connections it provides to Europe.

Reach Out and Touch Someone

Iran conducts a lot of its dirty business the old fashioned Soviet way, by using embassies and embassy staff (who are immune from prosecution) to gather information and do dirty deeds. The Iranian Ministry of Intelligence and Security (MOIS) operates out of Iranian embassies in Europe and is known to be responsible for assassinations of Kurdish leaders in Germany.

The largest center of Iranian fundamentalist activities is reputedly in Bonn, Germany. Here at least 20 people man an operations station that takes up a full floor in, where else, the Iranian embassy. The station was setup between 1986 and 1987 and is just one of the bases Iran set up in its embassies in Berlin, Frankfurt, Hamburg and Munich. Their job is to provide secure communications and support within Europe for activities supported and authorized from within Iran.

Terrorism on a Budget

The low-budget but far more terrible arm of Iran is Hezbollah. The foreign operations sections of the Lebanese Hezbollah is busy recruiting, training and arming the worlds dispossessed. Nobody joins Hezbollah to see the world and have an expense account—probably one good reason why CIA operatives are not lining up to infiltrate this group. Hezbollah stirs it up in the world's cesspools; the destitute and war-torn regions of Iraq, Turkey, Afghanistan, Pakistan and the occupied territories in Israel.

They are busy recruiting folks to beef up their opposition party in Iraq (definitely a short tenure, high risk political profession). *Hezbollah's* goal is to combine all the fundamentalist groups in Iraq and setup a single "Supreme Council for the Islamic Revolution in Iraq.

They have tagged Ali Aka Mohammedi, in Hamadan (the Iraqi affairs writer for the somewhat biased rag *Guide of the Revolution, Ali Khamenei.* His first step was to send the top guns of the opposition's elite to Lebanon for training. Naturally they traveled via Damascus to *Hezbollah* bases in Lebanon's Bekaa Valley—Baalbeck and Hermel. If you would like to be on the short list to run Iraq, there is a recruitment office in Bir al-Abed in the southern suburbs of Beirut (ask for Abu Haidar or his assistant Abu Maysam). If you think it is you who they want to run Iraq, think again. Fundamentalist Iraqi groups seek to reestablish *hodjatoleslam* Mohammad Bakr al-Hakim who now lives in Iran. They believe he is the moral and spiritual authority as well as the founder of the Supreme Council for the Islamic Revolution in Iraq which now gives its name to an organization uniting pro-Iranian Shiite and Kurd movements in the Iraqi opposition. If you thought American politics were complicated, the groups belonging to this organization are as follows:

- the Islamic Movement of Iraqi Kurdistan of mullah Osman Ali Abdulaziz
- the Iraqi Islamic Association of hadjatoleslam Bahr al-Ulum
- the Al-Dawa party founded by Mohamed Bakr al-Sadr and headed by Abdul Hamid Kachani (its representative in Lebanon is Abu Maysan)
- the Al-Amal al-Islami organization of ayatollah Mohamed Taki al-Mudarissi (who lives in Iran and Syria), represented in Lebanon by ayatollah Taghi
- the Jund al-Imam group headed by Sami al-Badri
- the Islamic Movement in Iraq of sheikh Jawad al-Khales
- the Jamaa al-Ulema al Moujahedin group of hadjatoleslam Mohamed Bakr al
- Nasiri
- the Popular Democratic Party of Kurdistan (PDPK) of Mohamed Mahmud Abdul Rahman (nicknamed "Sami")
- the Socialist Party of Iraqi Kurdistan (SPIK) of Rassul Mahmand.

Now you know why George didn't nuke Saddam in his curly bedroom slippers or sling-load him out on the next Blackhawk. Hussein will be begging for a lifetime in San Quentin once this group starts knocking on his door.

Savak, the Iranian intelligence network, is also busy spinning its web. They now work out of Cyprus using a dozen shell companies. They have extended their network to Barcelona and Rome where they seek out Algerian immigrants to carry out terrorist operations. The Savak suffered a major setback in the early nineties when their intelligence networks in Switzerland, France and Germany were destroyed. Their recruitment of Algerians is also a switch from their normal recruitment of Tunisians in the 80s.

The Iranians are more than a little concerned about Israel's new peace with the PLO. Despite being a quick sortie away from Israel, Iran has decided not only to keep, but to expand and beef up their bases in Lebanon, which will be used as the principal station for Syria and Israel as well as Lebanon.

The Iranian Ambassador to Beirut has been instructed by Tehran to begin strategic study centers and to promote publication of favorable periodicals, journals, articles and books. Many of the journalists or workers on these publications are exported to Europe using passports from Kuwait, Bahrein and other Gulf countries.

The Scoop

Iran is going nowhere fast and taking the rest of the Muslim world with it. It's also hurting because of the long drop in world oil prices. The rial fluctuates on the free market as much as 15 percent a day. Inflation is between 60–100 percent a year, and a thriving black market takes advantage of outrageous official rates. Government employees make the equivalent of US$60 a month and many Iranians are forced to take two jobs to get by. Iran is home to more refugees than any other country in the world. There are an estimated 2.2 million Afghans, 1.2 million Iraqis and 1.2 million others who have fled the strife in Pakistan, Azerbaijan and Tajikistan. The country is held together by a wide net of informers. But give Iran credit. Like most exporters of terror, it's a peaceful country.

The Players

Ayatollah Mohammed Ali Khamenei

The ayatollah is Iran's spiritual leader and commander in chief. A hard-liner and a fundamentalist to the max, he is viewed as the most likely successor to Rafsanjani.

President Ali Akbar Hashemi Rafsanjani

The president has tried to resign three times, and three times has been told no. The fact that he has narrowly escaped seven assassination attempts might be the source of his on-the-job dissatisfaction. He is viewed as a moderate, and has the support of the middle class. He gathered 63 percent of the 1993 presidential election vote and 94 percent a year later. Regarded as the most pragmatic of the Iranian leaders, Rafsanjani is credited with persuading Khomeini to finally agree to a cease-fire in the war with Iraq in August 1988.

Rafsanjani has attended primarily to the economy and repairing the damage left by the war with Iraq. He has strived to get Iran acquainted with the international community by expanding world ties and by arranging the release of hostages held by terrorist groups with ties to Iran. The defeat of the Mulim extremists in the 1992 parliamentary elections strengthened Rafsanjani's stance in his pursuit of moderate policies. However, Rafsanjani's position has weakened because he has been blamed by hard-liners for the country's continuing economic struggle. Additionally, Rafsanjani's grip on the country's economic and foreign policies has also been loosened by Khamenei's pronouncement that he was taking more personal responsibility in those areas.Rafsanjani may be replaced by the parliamentary speaker, Ali Akbar Nateq-Nouri, a conservative mullah favored by local businessmen because he wants to return to a centrally-controlled economy.

Ali Akbar Mohtashemi

The leading Islamic fundamentalist critic of the Rafsanjani government. The leader of the Muslim extremists in the previous Majlis, Mohtashemi could play a critical role as an ally of Khamenei, should Khamenei try to oust Rafsanjani. It's agreed Mohtashemi has enough political support to become president or supreme ayatollah if the Muslim extremists pick up some steam in Iran. After the start of the war with Iraq, Khomeini made him ambassador to Syria. He helped obtain Syrian support for Iran and strengthened Iranian ties with sympathetic terrorist groups in Lebanon. His service in the key post of minister of the interior ended when Rafsanjani was elected president. More than 100 members of the Majlis asked Rafsanjani to retain Mohtashemi. Nonetheless, the president excluded him during the reorganization of the Cabinet. Politically, Mohtashemi has become stronger as Rafsanjani has weakened.

Ali Mohammed Besharati

He's the influential interior minister. A former student and Revolutionary Guard, Besharati was one of the students who seized the American Embassy in 1979. His latest action was to unsuccessfully ban Iran's embarrassingly popular satellite dishes—which he views as instruments of Western filth—when he learned that "Star Trek" and "Baywatch" were getting better ratings than "Modern Muslim! Live From Mahabad!" and "Good Morning, Tehran—with Ali Mohammed Besharati."

The Mujahedeen-e-Khalq

Founded in 1980, this is an armed group based in Iraq. Its ideology is a combination of Islam and Marxist babbling. The group is headed by Masud Rajavi. The Iranian government insists that the Mujahedeen is supported by England and France. The government may be looking for an excuse to conduct a full-scale attack on Mujahedeen forces in Iraq, where the time seems appropriate for Saddam Hussein to look the other way. Iran's top judge accused the Mujahedeen-e-Khalq of conducting a campaign of bombings and assassinations aimed at igniting sectarian tensions. Although government repression has significantly curtailed the effectiveness of the Mujahedeen-e-Khalq, the guerrillas still conduct operations inside Iran and remain vocal in the opposition to the government of Iran. The organization was 50,000-strong after the Islamic revolution, with nearly half-a-million supporters. About 5000 activists have been executed in the government's crackdown and more than 25,000 imprisoned. After the cease-fire in the Iran-Iraq war, the Mujahedeen invaded Iran but were crushed by the Iranian armed forces.

The organization abandoned much of its leftist diatribe in order to gain support from the U.S. and have stepped-up their attacks on government targets, including a February 1994 attack at the tomb of the Ayatollah Khomeini on the anniversary of the establishment of the Islamic government. There was also an unsuccessful assassination attempt against the ayatollah during the Friday sermon at the Meshad mosque.

The Iranian Military

Rafsanjani has raised the prestige of the regular army, navy and air force since becoming president. The military's support could be decisive in determining which political faction gains control should economic and political conditions deteriorate. The military is a large player despite desertions, the imprisonment or execution of a number of soldiers who had served under the shah, and the huge losses it suffered in the Iran-Iraq war. The balance of the purging occurred during the war. The army is the most important branch of the military. However, the Revolutionary Guards Corps, numbering 250,000 soldiers, is considered more reliable by the government as it is dedicated to the Islamic Republic.

Iran continues to spend a large percentage of its budget on defense (or offense, some might argue). Mostly in the search and procurement of expensive weapons systems. Iran still doesn't trust Iraq. And what would a Middle East superpower be without some Scuds and Sidewinders?

The Sunnis

The Sunni Muslims comprise about 4 percent of Iran's population and are regularly gunned down by their enemies, the Shiites.

Getting In

Travel Warning August 31, 1993

The Department of State warns all U.S. citizens against travel to Iran, where danger continues to exist because of the generally anti-American atmosphere and Iranian government hostility to the

U.S. U.S. citizens traveling to Iran have been detained without charge, arrested and harassed by Iranian authorities. There are restrictions on both import and export of goods from Iran to the United States.

The U.S. government does not currently have diplomatic or consular relations with the Islamic Republic of Iran. The Swiss government, acting through its embassy in Tehran, serves as the protecting power for U.S. interests in Iran and provides only very limited consular services. Neither U.S. passports nor visas to the U.S. are issued in Tehran.

Visa and passport are required. The Iranian government maintains an Interests Section through the

Embassy of Pakistan
2209 Wisconsin Avenue, N.W.
Washington D.C. 20007
☎ *(202) 965-4990*

U.S. passports are valid for travel to Iran. However, U.S./Iranian dual nationals have often had their U.S. passports confiscated upon arrival and have been denied permission to depart the country documented as U.S. citizens. To prevent the confiscation of U.S. passports, the Department of State suggests that Americans leave their U.S. passports at a U.S. Embassy or Consulate overseas for safekeeping before entering Iran. To facilitate their travel in the event of the confiscation of a U.S. passport, dual nationals may obtain in their Iranian passports the necessary visas for countries which they will transit on their return to the U.S., and where they may apply for a new U.S. passport. Dual nationals must enter and leave the United States on U.S. passports.

Getting Around

Mehrabad International Airport is seven miles west of Tehran, about a 30-minute drive. Airport facilities include a 24-hour bank, 24-hour post office, 24-hour restaurant, snack bar, 24-hour duty-free shop, gift shops, 24-hour tourist information and first aid/vaccination facilities. Airline buses are available to the city for a fare of RL10 (travel time-30 minutes). Taxis also are available to the city center for approximately RL1200-1500. There is a departure tax of RL1500. Transiting passengers remaining in the airport are exempt from the departure tax.

Once inside Iran transportation by private car (with driver) or with a guide (who will be assigned to keep tabs on you) is recommended.

Dangerous Places

Travel throughout Iran continues to be dangerous because of the generally anti-American atmosphere and Iranian government hostility toward the U.S. government. U.S. citizens traveling in Iran have been detained without charge, arrested and harassed by Iranian authorities. Persons in Iran who violate Iranian laws, including laws which are unfamiliar to Westerners (such as laws regarding proper attire), may face penalties which can be severe.

The eastern and southern portions of Iran are major weapons and drug smuggling routes from Pakistan and Afghanistan. Drug and arms smuggling convoys may include columns with tanks, armored personnel carriers and heavily-armed soldiers. Miami Vice doesn't have a prayer against these guys.

Dangerous Things

The Iranian people, being an American, the Vavak and Savama (secret police), disease, pestilence, drugs, Washington Redskins ballcaps, your opinion, speaking at all, getting off the plane, trying to get back on.

Drugs
Three pieces of advice: Don't do 'em, don't bring 'em in, and don't bring 'em out. Iran has executed well over 1000 people since 1989 when it made possession of 30 grammes (slightly over an ounce) of heroin or five kg (11 lbs.) of opium a capital crime. Read that as death. The Golden Crescent—Pakistan and Afghanistan, has become the world's second biggest source of

heroin after the Golden Triangle of southeast Asia. Opium is grown mostly in Afghanistan, processed in the tribal areas of Pakistan where Pakistani law doesn't reach, and smuggled to Iran for shipment to the West. About 10 percent of the drugs which enter Iran are destined for consumption in Iran and the rest for other world destinations, including London, Paris and New York. There are approximately one million addicts among Iran's 60 million people.

Dual Citizenship

U.S. citizens who were born in Iran or who were at one time citizens of Iran, and the children of such persons, may be considered Iranian nationals by Iranian authorities, and may be subject to Iranian laws which impose special obligations upon Iranian nationals, such as military service or taxes. Exit permits for departure from Iran for such persons may be denied until such obligations are met. Dual nationals often have their U.S. passports confiscated and may be denied permission to leave Iran, or encounter other problems with Iranian authorities. Specific questions on dual nationality may be directed to the Office of Citizens Consular Services, *Department of State, Washington, D.C. 20520,* ☎ *(202) 647-7899.*

Imported Goods

The United States prohibits the importation of all Iranian-origin goods or services into the United States without authorization. This authorization may be obtained for qualifying goods from either of two sources: the Treasury Department's Office of Foreign Assets Control ("FAC") *(*☎ *202-622-2480)* or the U.S. Customs Service ("Customs") in the port where the goods arrive.

FAC issues licenses only for goods which were located outside of Iran prior to imposition of these sanctions on October 29, 1987. Goods in Iran after that do not qualify for authorization from Customs criteria for authorization: Iranian-origin goods, including those that were in Iran after October 29, 1987, may enter the United States if they qualify for entry under the following provisions administered solely by Customs:

(1) gifts valued at US$100 or less,

(2) goods for personal use contained in the accompanied baggage of persons traveling from Iran valued at US$400 or less, or

(3) goods qualifying for duty-free treatment as "household goods" or "personal effects" (as defined by U.S. law and subject to quantity limitations). Inquiries about these provisions should be directed to Customs in the U.S. port where the goods would arrive.

Doing Business

While there is no blanket prohibition against U.S. companies doing business with companies in Iran, there are restrictions on U.S. exports to Iran as well as on the importation of Iranian-origin goods and services into the U.S. Questions concerning exports to Iran may be addressed to the Department of Commerce, Office of Export Licensing at ☎ *(202) 482-4811.*

Getting Sick

A yellow fever vaccination is required for travelers over the age of one year coming from infected areas. Arthropod-borne diseases and Hepatitis B are endemic. Malaria is a risk in some provinces from March through November. Food- and water-borne diseases, including cholera, are common, as is trachoma. (Snakes and rabid animals can also pose a threat.) Basic medical care and medicines are available in the principal cities of Iran, but may not be available in outlying areas. There are three doctors and 14 hospital beds for every 10,000 people. The international travelers' hotline at the Centers for Disease Control, ☎ *(404) 332-4559,* has additional useful health information.

Nuts & Bolts

Iran, about three times the size of Arizona, is a constitutional Islamic Republic, governed by executive and legislative branches that derive national leadership primarily through the Muslim clergy. Shia Islam is the official religion of Iran, and Islamic law is the basis of the authority of the state. Islamic ideals and beliefs provide the conservative foundation of the country's customs, laws and practices. Shiites comprise about 95 percent of the country. Sunnis make up about 4 percent. The literacy rate is at about 75 percent. Iran is a developing country.

The workweek in Iran is Sunday through Thursday. The rial is about 1800 to the dollar. Electricity is 220V/50hz. Languages are Farsi, Turkish, Kurdish Arabic and scattered English.

Temperatures for Tehran can be very hot in the summer and just above freezing in the winter. The nothern part of the country can experience quite bitter winters. Iran has a mostly desert climate with unusual extremes in temperature. Temperatures exceeding 130 degrees F occasionally occur in the summer, while in the winter the high elevation of most of the country often results in temperatures of 0 degrees F and lower.

There is no U.S. Embassy or Consulate in Iran. The U.S. Interests Section of the **Swiss Embassy** in Tehran is located at *Bucharest Ave., 17th street, No. 5, Tehran*. The local telephone numbers are ☎ *(98-21) 625-223/224 and 626-906.*

Dangerous Days

06/04/1989	Day the Ayatollah Khomeini died.
02/14/1989	Khomeini announced a death decree on *Satanic Verses* author Salman Rushdie, an Indian national, resident in the United Kingdom.
07/03/1988	The USS Vincennes mistakenly shot down an Iranian Airbus airliner over the Persian Gulf.
12/04/1984	Four Islamic Jihad terrorists hijacked a Kuwaiti airliner bound for Pakistan from Kuwait and ordered it flown to Tehran. Two U.S. aid personnel were killed during the hijacking, while two others, another U.S. aid official and an American businessman, were tortured during the ordeal. Iranian troops stormed the aircraft on December 9, retaking it from the hijackers.
06/28/1981	The prime minister and 74 others were killed in the bombing of the legislature.
01/20/1981	U.S. Embassy hostages released. Fifty-two American hostages were released after 444 days in captivity following an agreement between the U.S. and Iran arranged by Algeria.
09/19/1980	Iran-Iraq war began.
07/27/1980	Death of the Shah of Iran.
04/25/1980	The day operations to rescue American hostages failed in the desert of Iran due to operational shortfalls and an aircraft accident. The hostages remained in captivity for 444 days until released by the government of Iran.
11/04/1979	The U.S. embassy was seized and sixty-three people were taken hostage.
04/01/1979	Islamic Republic Day commemorates riots by Islamic fundamentalists in Isfahan.
03/10/1979	Death of Kurdish leader Mullah Mustafa Barzani. (Kurdish regions)
02/11/1979	Revolution Day. Celebration of the victory of the Islamic revolution.
02/04/1979	Iranian revolution began. Iran's Shiite clerics begin their takeover of the government.

Dangerous Days

02/01/1979	Khomeini returned from exile and called the start of the "ten days of dawn," commemorating the ten days of unrest ending with Khomeini taking power on February 11 (the "Day of Victory").
01/16/1979	The Shah departed Iran.
11/04/1978	Student uprising against the Shah.
09/09/1978	The Shah's troops opened fire on protesters in Tehran, killing several hundred demonstrators.
11/04/1964	The Ayatollah Khomeini was exiled to Turkey.
06/05/1963	The arrest of the Ayatollah Khomeini by the Shah's police. Also the Day of Mourning and Revolution Day.
01/22/1946	Kurdish Republic Day.
02/07/1902	Birth date of the Ayatollah Ruhollah Khomeini.
06/28	Revolutionary Guard's Day.
03/21	Persian New Year. Kurdish New Year celebrated.

In a Dangerous Place: Iran

I traveled to Iran many times during the eight-year-long war against Iraq.

I was sent to Iran by SIPA press, as a very fresh journalist, just to retrieve film made by other photographers working for SIPA and to bring the film back. In time this would illustrate the headlines and articles of magazines and newspapers around the world.

My entire trip lasted only a few days. I traveled around the war front through cities under fire: Bassorah, Esdouf, Abadan, Koramchar to collect film. I got back to Tehran and from there rushed to the frontier with Turkey but soon discovered that in the countryside, almost every type of transport was forbidden or simply not available. Cars were scarce, the people were prevented from using them and the curfew was severely imposed.

Despite the ban on travel I managed to hire a car and an Armenian driver. Off I went in the middle of the night, using only the light of a flashlight instead of the headlights so we wouldn't be attacked or stopped. When we came to checkpoints I would produce a polaroid photo of myself being welcomed by the Iranian president of the time—Bani Sadr (now an exile in France). It worked every time. The officers were very impressed, and I was passed on, eventually arriving at Bazargan.

At Bazargan all journalists had to be searched and all film had to be surrendered. By pure chance I was not searched. I jumped into two successive taxis and rushed towards an airfield out of Erzewon, inside what was then known as the Soviet Union where I knew a plane was waiting. The plane was especially chartered by SIPA. From there I took another plane to Ankara, in Turkey, where I took a regular Lufthansa flight to Frankfurt, Germany, and then another one to Paris. From there I took a taxi to the offices of SIPA PRESS. The film from the trip was developed immediately and sent to New York the same day via the Concorde; one of the photos was chosen to become a cover for *Time* magazine. The whole trip lasted only thirty hours.

Islam

Islam is the religion of more than a billion people on this planet. Long viewed as the Arab religion, it is just as likely that a Muslim is Indonesian, Chinese, Russian or even an American black.

Islam is based on some very simple premises. It could be said it is a shade more intolerant (regarding the hatred of Jews and non-believers) and a shade more merciful that Christian (in charity towards orphans and widows). Muslims have dietary and health laws (no pork or alcohol), they have a period of fasting (the ninth Muslim month of Ramadan) and are encouraged to make a pilgrimage to Mecca at least once in their lifetime (the haj).

Muslims' adherence to the Koran (a holy book revealed to Mohammed by God) and the tenets of Islam range from tolerant to fanatic. The two main sects of Islam are the mostly-Arab Sunnis (85%) and the mostly-Persian Shi'ites (15%). The Iranian Shi'ites are the most evangelistic of the two branches.

Islam

Are there really any major differences between Christianity and Islam? First, Muslims believe that both Christians and Jews have it all wrong since they worship untrue gods. Second, Muslims see decadence as a sign of Westerners being infidels.

Terrorism has been linked with Islam—an unfair connection since Christian anti-abortion groups are just as reprehensible in this practice as Islamic fundamentalists from a legal sense. There is no denying that Iran has encouraged the development and activities of fundamentalist groups around the world. The one area where Islam scares Westerners is that there is no promise of material happiness or personal gain from terrorist activities. More important, Islam has not lost a war since the Crusades. The real enemy of Islam is factionalism. Warring Islamic groups in Afghanistan, Iraq, Turkey and Iran show that any ideology loses its momentum once a common enemy (in this case, Russia) is removed.

Iraq

★

Let's Make a Deal

After Saddam Hussein's recent efforts to turn the Persian Gulf deserts into Mr. Boffo's hell, people were surprised to learn that not only did Saddam still have an army, but he was willing to use it and lose it. Saddam doesn't have a whole lot of options these days. His people are hungry, the country is in shambles and he still eludes one or two assassination attempts a year. His next door neighbor, Iran, is busy destabilizing his country and organizing the disparate opposition groups into one central party. Iran's long-term goal is to erase the border between the two countries.

Iraq's plummet into the depths began in earnest in 1980. That year, Saddam launched the war against Iran, which lasted until August 1988. Iraq had long-standing border disputes with Iran and Kuwait and a fierce animosity toward Israel. In addition to this, the ruling Iraqi Ba'ath Party had a 20-year rivalry with the ruling Ba'ath Party of Syria. After the August 1988 cease-fire with Iran, Iraq supplied arms and money to the Christian forces in Lebanon to relaunch the war there against the Syrian army and Islamic Lebanese forces. It invaded and annexed Kuwait in August 1990, with the ap-

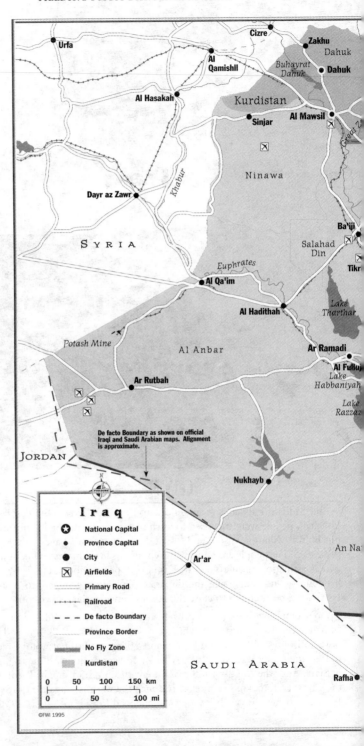

Urfa

Cizre

Zakhu

Dahuk

Al Qamishll

Buhayrat Dahuk

Dahuk

Al Hasakah

Kurdistan

Sinjar

Al Mawsil

Great Z

Khabur

Ninawa

Dayr az Zawr

Ba'iji

SYRIA

Salahad Din

Euphrates

Tikr

Al Qa'im

Lake Tharthar

Al Hadithah

Potash Mine

Al Anbar

Ar Ramadi

Al Fullu

Lake Habbaniyah

Ar Rutbah

Lake Razzaz

De facto Boundary as shown on official Iraqi and Saudi Arabian maps. Alignment is approximate.

JORDAN

N

Nukhayb

Iraq

⭐ National Capital

● Province Capital

● City

☒ Airfields

——— Primary Road

••••• Railroad

– – – De facto Boundary

——— Province Border

▬▬▬ No Fly Zone

Kurdistan

An Na

Ar'ar

0   50   100   150 km

0   50   100 mi

©FWI 1995

SAUDI ARABIA

Rafha

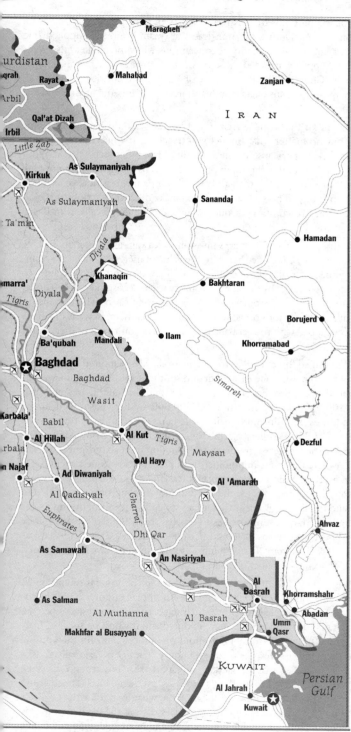

parent intention of seizing funds from Kuwait's banks and investment companies for the reconstruction of Iraq. During the Iran-Iraq war, many countries supplied Iraq with arms in contravention of international conventions which preclude arms supply to countries at war. Suppliers included the U.S.A., the former Soviet Union, France, Germany, UK, Italy, China, Chile, Brazil and east European countries. Iraq was accused of using chemical weapons against Iranian forces and subsequently against the Kurds in northern Iraq.

For now, Iraq is one of the world's great travel bargains. You'd have a hard time finding things to buy no matter what budget you travel on. If you want to top your tank off, you're in luck. The collapse of the Iraqi dinar from its official rate at about US$3.20 to its real rate of about a thousand times less, means that when you buy a full tank of gas using dinars, you pay less than an Uncle Sam's penny. Gasoline costs .0009 cents a gallon and costs 0.07 dinars a liter. But if you make other transactions at the official rate, beware. Don't reach out and touch someone. Telephone calls from Baghdad to the U.S. can cost US$158 a minute.

The embargo on Iraq imposed after Iraq's invasion of Kuwait, and a scarcity of U.S. dollars, is pulling the value of Iraq's currency to the value of used Charmin. In a country where educated people make about 2000–3000 dinars a month, there is little to buy and even less to buy with it. Just imagine a country where a crisp, U.S. $100 dollar bill will bring you a thousand 25 dinar notes. It's positively retro! The currency is worth so little that people pay for goods, where they can find them, in wads of a hundred 25-dinar bills wrapped with rubber bands. Shopkeepers don't even bother counting the notes.

After the Gulf War, Allied forces had destroyed, neutralized or captured 41 of the 42 Iraqi army divisions in the war zone of Kuwait and southern Iraq. The coalition estimated the number of Iraqi prisoners of war at 175,000 and the number of Iraqi casualties at 85,000–100,000, out of an estimated 500,000 soldiers positioned in the combat area. Iraq lost 3700 of its 5500 main battle tanks, 1857 of its 7500 armored vehicles and 2140 of its 3500 artillery pieces. Ninety-seven of Iraq's 689 combat aircraft and six of its 489 helicopters were destroyed. One-hundred-sixty combat aircraft were flown to Iran where they were impounded as war reparations. Nine airfields were destroyed, as well as 16 chemical weapons plants, 10 biological weapons plants and three nuclear weapons facilities. Yet Baghdad continues holding onto thousands of pieces of civilian and military equipment that it had stolen from Kuwait during its occupation of the country. Iraq currently possesses approximately 9000 pieces of military equipment, including trucks, jeeps, armored personnel carriers, Grog-7 missiles, as well as perhaps 6000 civilian items. These items were supposed to have been returned under the 1991 UN Security Council Resolution.

Since Iraq's devastating defeat in the 1991 Gulf War, the country has rebuilt much of its infrastucture, including the phone system, electrical plants, government buildings and bridges. The Iraqi people have shown themselves to be a very resilient people. Saddam's is not the first dictatorship they have endured and it won't be the last. Economic embargoes tend to have greater ramifications on innocent citizens than on the dictators who led them into it. Despots rarely go hungry. They're occasionally assassinated, but usually with full stomachs. Saddam still sports that tire around his waist while his people are being starved to death by the West. Just a single well-aimed cruise missile could dramatically change things for the better in what used to be the cradle of civilization. Saddam's effectiveness in eliminating successors was the main reason he is still in power. He seems to be somewhat confident of a long reign despite the U.S.'s claim that its embargo will ensure his demise within six to eight months. Why do we know he is confident? Well, since the Gulf War, he has spent $1.2 billion building or rebuilding more than 40 palaces in Iraq. In April 1995, Saddam threw a big 58th birthday bash to remind everyone he was still alive. Meanwhile things get worse for the common folk. As of April 95, Iraqis needed 6000 rials to get one American dollar.

The UN reports that most of Iraq's population is experiencing mass deprivation, chronic hunger, endemic malnutrition, along with the collapse of personal incomes and a rapidly increasing number of destitute, jobless and homeless people. Sounds like a great place for a bargain vacation.

The Scoop

Considering that Baghdad used to be the Garden of Eden, the breadbasket of the ancient world and part of the fertile crescent, the boys from Baghdad have done a good job of screwing it up. This, despite enough oil to make Saudi Arabia look like a dry sump in Lubbock. Instead of basking in its riches, Iraq is poor, the consequence of Saddam's maniacal insistence on becoming the superpower of the Middle East. The Gulf War was a laughable attempt by Hussein to shun international diplomacy and snatch back oil-rich Kuwait. Either Saddam didn't pay attention during history class or he just likes expensive fireworks, because he plunged his country into the third-world club in a mere three months.

There are lots of reasons to travel to Iraq—its history, people, culture, etc. But you can't if you are an American. You can if you are a journalist or aid worker, but that's it.

The Players

President Saddam Hussein al-Tikriti

He's still the man. Hussein has managed to remain in power since 1979, despite questionable and ill-fated foreign policy moves that have caused the impoverishment of his country and the deaths of more than 100,000 Iraqis in the Gulf War. But the man still retains a respectable following. He is president and chairman of the Revolutionary Command Council (RCC), regional secretary of the ruling Ba'ath Party and head of the 100,000-strong Popular Militia. When he needs help running the country, he hires good old boys from his home town of Tikrit, north of Baghdad.

Hussein's absolute rule rests with his status in the RCC. The chairman of the RCC is, ex-officio, president of the republic. The president appoints ministers and judges, and laws are enacted by presidential decree. Routine governing of the country is carried out by an appointed council of ministers.

Saddam is swiftly using up his nine lives. He survived a failed military coup in May 1991, and he offed 18 senior army officers just to make sure he could get a good night's sleep. It isn't known how many times the U.S. tried to take him out during the Gulf War. In June 1991, he fired 1500 senior army officers and 180 senior police officers as a reward for following his orders during the Gulf War. Since then, there have been at least three coup attempts against Saddam's rule. Recently, more than 200 current and former officers and civilians were arrested, including the commander of the Republican Guard's tank battalion, Brig Sufiyan al-Ghurairi and former parliamentarian Jasser al-Tikriti. All the plotters hailed from Saddam's hometown of Tikrit, as well as from Mosul and Ramadi. The attempt appears to have been the first in which members of the Tikrit clan played an important role in removing the despot. There were at least two unsuccessful assassination attempts against Saddam in late December 1993 and January 1994. Hussein's recent misguided sabre rattling in the fall of 1994 managed to anger more troops just itching to deliver some high-priced ballistics directly into his place of residence.

Hussein also leans on the loyalty of his security services and the Republican Guard divisions of the army to put down any uprisings. The Republican Guard suppressed the Shiite uprising in the south of the country and the Kurdish rebellion in the north. Saddam's paranoia is well-founded.

The Kurds

Only a few days after the Gulf War ended, major insurrections broke out in both the south of Iran and particularly in Kurdistan, where Kurd rebels seized large areas of territory by the first week of March 1991. Iraq's "elite" Republican Guards used repugnant brutality in suppressing the Kurd rebellion. Kurd refugees fleeing the wrath of the Republican Guard numbered 2 million or more along the Iraqi borders with both Turkey and Iran. The U.S. and Great Britain dispatched troops to northern Iraq on a short-lived effort to entice the Kurds to return home.

When the Iraqi army pulled out of the north they left a political vacuum. The U.S.-controlled area is now called Kurdistan. Of the 19.2 million people in Iraq, 21.6 percent are Kurds (73.5 percent are Arabs). There is a legitimate argument for the state of Kurdistan since the Kurds were left out of any postcolonial country-carving. The Iraqi army has been doing bad things to the Kurds while away from the scrutiny of the world. They have been engaged in using a variety of methods to exterminate the Kurds, including, bombing, starvation and even employing chemical weapons in an effort to reduce the population. Hussein is less interested in being nasty to the Kurdish people than he is in keeping the oil their new country would sit on—especially the oil fields in the Kirkuk area.

Potatoes for diesel

Despite the embargo on Iraq, when DP visited Northern Iraq in October of 1994 during Hussein's military feint to the south, we passed a line of trucks three kms long and in rows of three waiting to bring basic foodstuffs into northern Iraq. The truckdrivers were rewarded for their three-day waits with homemade rusty tanks bolted below the trucks full of crude diesel fuel that would later sell in Turkish gas stations for around 10,000 Turkish lira a liter.

Money Hassles

The Iraqi dinar is virtually worthless. The shortage of foreign currency has created a thriving black market, although the penalties for its use are severe, with heavy fines and possible imprisonment. The difference in exchange rates is vast between the black market and the official rates. The official exchange rate to the U.S. dollar has remained unchanged at US$3.2169:ID1 since 1982. You must declare your funds on entry, but few people do. It is legal to bring only ID25 into Iraq and take out ID5. Any amount of hard currency may be imported but this must be declared on entry and receipts must be obtained for any expenditure in Iraq. The balance and receipts must be shown upon leaving the country. Credit cards are not generally accepted and traveler's cheques are virtually useless. Iraqis traveling abroad may take out ID100.

Getting In

Iraq - Travel Warning August 31, 1993

The Department of State warns all U.S. citizens against traveling to Iraq. Conditions within the country remain unsettled and dangerous. The United States does not maintain diplomatic relations with Iraq and cannot provide normal consular protective services to U.S. citizens. U.S. passports are not valid for travel to, in or through Iraq, unless they are specially endorsed by the U.S. Government. There is a U.S. trade embargo which severely restricts financial and economic activities with Iraq, including travel-related transactions.

The Iraqi embassy considers Iraq safe for travel and they are probably about 80 percent right. It's the 20 percent you have to worry about. Border crossings between Jordan and Iraq are closed; all others are open. Crossings from Turkey are backed up but are orderly and efficient.

You have to be a reporter or use a foreign passport. Passports and visas are required. On February 8, 1991, U.S. passports ceased to be valid for travel to, in or through Iraq and may not be used for that purpose unless a special validation has been obtained. Without the requisite validation, use of a U.S. passport for travel to, in or through Iraq may constitute a violation of 18 U.S.C. 1544, and may be punishable by a fine and/or imprisonment. An exemption to the above restriction is granted to Americans residing in Iraq as of February 8, 1991 who continue to reside there, and to American professional reporters or journalists on assignment there.

In addition, the Department of the Treasury prohibits all travel-related transactions by U.S. persons intending to visit Iraq, unless specifically licensed by the Office of Foreign Assets Control. The only exceptions to this licensing requirement are for journalistic activity or for U.S. government or United Nations business. The categories of individuals eligible for consideration for a special passport validation are set forth in 22 C.F.R. 51.74. Passport validation requests for Iraq should be forwarded in writing to the following address:

The Iraqi Interests Section in the U.S. is located at:

1801 P St., NW
Washington, D.C. 20036
☎ (202) 483-7500

Deputy Assistant Secretary for Passport Services

U.S. Department of State, 1425 K Street, N.W.
Washington, D.C. 20522-1705
Attn: Office of Citizenship Appeals and Legal Assistance (Rm. 300)
☎ (202) 326-6168 or 326-6182

The request must be accompanied by supporting documentation according to the category under which validation is sought. Currently, the four categories of persons specified in 22 C.F.R. 51.74 as being eligible for consideration for passport validation are as follows:

[a] Professional reporters: Includes full-time members of the reporting or writing staff of a newspaper, magazine or broadcasting network whose purpose for travel is to gather information about Iraq for dissemination to the general public.

[b] American Red Cross: Applicant establishes that he or she is a representative of the American Red Cross or International Red Cross traveling pursuant to an officially-sponsored Red Cross mission.

[c] Humanitarian Considerations: Applicant must establish that his or her trip is justified by compelling humanitarian considerations or for family unification. At this time, "compelling humanitarian considerations" include situations where the applicant can document that an immediate family member is critically ill in Iraq. Documentation concerning family illness must include the name and address of the relative, and be from that relative's physician attesting to the nature and gravity of the illness. "Family unification" situations may include cases in which spouses or minor children are residing in Iraq, with and dependent on, an Iraqi national spouse or parent for their support.

[d] National Interest: The applicant's request is otherwise found to be in the national interest.

In all requests for passport validation for travel to Iraq, the name, date and place of birth for all concerned persons must be given, as well as the U.S. passport numbers. Documentation as outlined above should accompany all requests. Additional information may be obtained by writing to the above address or by calling the Office of Citizenship Appeals and Legal Assistance at ☎ *(202) 326-6168 or 326-6182.*

U.S. Treasury Restrictions

In August 1990 President Bush issued Executive Orders 12722 and 12724, imposing economic sanctions against Iraq including a complete trade embargo. The U.S. Treasury Department's Office of Foreign Assets Control administers the regulations related to these sanctions, which include restrictions on all financial transactions related to travel to Iraq. These regulations prohibit all travel-related transactions, except as specifically licensed. The only exceptions to this licensing requirement are for persons engaged in journalism or in official U.S. government or UN business. Questions concerning these restrictions should be addressed directly to:

Chief of Licensing Section, Office of Foreign Assets Control
U.S. Department of the Treasury
Washington, D.C. 20220
☎ *(202) 622-2480*
FAX (202) 622-1657

In the past year, most foreigners detained at the Kuwait-Iraq border, regardless of nationality, have been sentenced to jail terms of seven to 10 years for illegally entering Iraq.

During 1992 and 1993 Iraq detained nine Westerners: three Swedes, three Britons, a U.S. national, a German and a Frenchman on charges of illegally entering Iraq. They were released by late 1993 after much diplomatic energy. In March, 1995, two Americans were held and sentenced to eight years in prison. Tom Jerrold and an ABC news crew were also detained but were released after the UN intervened. Brent Sadler who interviewed the two Americans in the Iraq jail was asked for his written permission to be in the jail even when accompanied by Polish diplomat negotiating a hold on the U.S. State department!

There have been attacks against foreigners and antagonism is still high in the Western world. Many Egyptians and other Arab expatriates were killed by disgruntled, unemployed Iraqi ex-soldiers. Don't forget that expats were held hostage by Hussein from mid- to late-1990 during the Mexican standoff between Iraqi and allied forces over the Iraqi annexation of Kuwait. All travelers and foreigners in Iraq run the risk of being detained, harassed and questioned, particularly in the south near the Kuwaiti border. The Iraqi embassy referred us to Mr. Ganji at Babylon travel ☎ *(312) 478-9000;* for readers who want more details about travel to Iraq.

AIDS test

Iraqi government officials have seemingly watched so many soap operas and pay-for-view dirty movies while out of the country that they think all Westerners are sex-crazed adulterers, fornicators and deviants.

Therefore, all visitors aged over 12 and under 65 who plan to stay in Iraq for longer than five days (official visitors have 15 days) must call on the Central Public Health Laboratory in Al Tayhariyat al Fennia Square between 8 a.m. and 2 p.m. to either present HIV and Syphilis (VDRL) certificates or arrange for a local test at a cost of ID100. HIV and VDRL certificates valid for Iraq may be obtained in the UK by arranging a blood test with a general practitioner. The sample should then be tested by a Public Health Laboratory Service listed on the blank certificate and attested by the Foreign Office and the Iraqi Embassy in London. Failing to comply with these requirements carries a fine of ID500 or six months imprisonment. A yellow fever vaccination certificate is required for all visitors arriving from an infected area.

Getting Around

Iraq has 33,238-km of roads, most of them improved during the 1980s. Expressway No. 1 (a 1200-km, six-lane freeway connecting Baghdad to Kuwait in the south and to Jordan and Syria in the west) was damaged by the bombing raids during the Gulf War. A 630-km freeway (Expressway No. 2) is being built to run north from Baghdad to the Turkish border where it will link up with the modern freeway connecting southeast Turkey to Ankara and Istanbul. Another Baghdad-Basra route is planned via Kut and Amarah and will be known as Expressway No. 3.

There are 2035 kms of rail network, including the 461-km Baghdad-Kirkuk-Arbil line, the 528-km Baghdad-Mosul-Yurubiyah standard line and the 582-km Baghdad-Maaqal-Umm Qasr standard line. The 516-km line between Baghdad and al-Qaim and Qusaybah on the Syrian border was opened this year. The 252-km northern line between Kirkuk, Baiji and Haditha,which connects the Baiji oil refinery with the al-Qaim fertilizer plant, was opened in 1988.

Iraq's main port of Basra is inoperative because of the closure of the Shatt al-Arab waterway during the war with Iran. Several Iraqi naval vessels were sunk in the waterway during the Gulf War.

Iraq has one functioning international airport, at Bamerni, 17 km south of Baghdad. The airport at Basra reopened in May 1991 following repairs. A third international airport was planned for Mosul with a 4000-meter runway capable of handling 30 landings and takeoffs a day. Domestic regional airports at Arbil (3000-meter runway), Amara and Najaf (for small 50-seater aircraft) were also planned. Iraqi Airways has a fleet of four Boeing 747s, two Boeing 737s, six Boeing 727s and two Boeing 707s.

You can rent a car from the airport. You will need both national and international driving licences. You can also take the bus service for the 17-km trip from the city center to the airport. In Baghdad, the double-decker buses are cheap and can take you just about anywhere you want to go; don't forget to buy your tickets at the kiosks first. There are also private minibuses and shared taxis. There is a train service that operates three times a day from Baghdad to Basra; don't plan on comfort or air conditioning unless you're lucky. You can choose from three class services with sleeping accommodations, restaurant cars and air conditioning. You can take the train between most of Iraq's major centers (Baghdad-Mosul, Baghdad-Arbil and Baghdad-Basra).There is also regular bus service from Baghdad to other major cities and regular flights between Baghdad, Basra and Mosul.There are domestic airports at Mosul, Kirkuk and Basra, as well as Bagdad.

Taxis must be negotiated in advance. During the war, DP paid US$1200 to get out of Baghdad, but we didn't have to tip. Taxis have meters but it is legal to charge twice the amount shown on the meter. After 10:00 p.m. there is a surcharge.

Dangerous Places

Baghdad

Baghdad is the location for periodic bombings against state targets and occasional unsuccessful coup attempts against the regime of Saddam Hussein. Passersby occasionally sustain injuries in such incidents.

The North (Kurdistan)

There have been uprisings against the government by Kurds in the north as well as fighting between Kurdish factions. Since May 1991, Kurdistan has been an autonomous state, home to large numbers of Kurdish refugees in Iran and Turkey in the north.

The South

Shia refugees have fled to the marshlands bordering Iran, to Iran itself and to Kuwait and Saudi Arabia. The Iraqi government is currently busy draining the marshes to deprive the Shia's of their homeland.There have been uprisings against the government by Shias in the south.

The Kuwaiti Border

U.S. citizens and other foreigners working near the Kuwait-Iraq border have been detained by Iraqi authorities for lengthy periods under harsh conditions. Travelers to that area, whether in Kuwait or not, are in immediate jeopardy of detention by Iraqi security personnel.

Everywhere Else

Hostilities in the Gulf region ceased on February 27, 1991. United Nations Security Council Resolution 687, adopted on April 3, 1991, set terms for a permanent cease-fire, but conditions in Iraq remain unsettled. Travel in Iraq is extremely hazardous for U.S. citizens. Iraq is crawling with informants who report any movements of foreigners and dealings with locals. Because of Iraq's "Big Brother" environment, do not try to bribe police or military personnel.

Getting Sick

The diseases you should be vaccinated against are typhoid, cholera and hepatitis. Tap water should be sterilized before drinking and visitors should avoid consuming ice. Milk is unpasteurized and should be boiled. Comprehensive medical insurance covering repatriation is essential unless you want to get even sicker in an Iraqi hospital. Health and sanitary conditions weren't too good before the war and they are worse now in all the major cities. Water, refuse and sanitation services are nonexistent, especially in the south, where outbreaks of typhoid, hepatitis, meningitis and gastroenteritis had reached epidemic proportions by late,1993. An outbreak of cholera was contained. Hospitals and other medical facilities were also damaged during the war and vital electricity supplies disrupted. Many expatriate doctors and hospital staff left the country. Stocks of pharmaceuticals have been depleted and there are severe shortages of even nonprescription drugs. Essential drugs are almost nonexistent. If you need or think you may need medication or drugs, bring plenty with you. You can always donate or sell what you don't need on your way out.

Nuts & Bolts

The Iraqi currency, for what little it's worth, is the Iraqi dinar (ID). One ID=1000 files. Banks are open from 8 a.m.–noon (Sat.–Wed.); 8 a.m.–11 a.m. (Thurs.); 8 a.m.–10 a.m. during Ramadan. Government offices are open 8:30 a.m.–2:30 p.m. (Sat –Wed); 8:30 a.m.–1:30 p.m. (Thurs., winter); 8 a.m.–noon (Sat.–Wed.); 8 a.m.–11 a.m. (Thurs., summer). Businesses are open 8 a.m.–2 p.m. (Sat–Wed); 8 a.m.–1 p.m.(Thurs.). Shops, when they have anything to sell, don't follow the clock, opening at dawn, closing for lunch when the sun is high and reopening when the day cools off around 4 p.m. Small shops tend to open very early, close during the middle of the day and then reopen from around 4 p.m. till 7 p.m. or later. Food markets open around 9 a.m. and close at midday, or when supplies are exhausted. The Islamic year contains 354 or 355 days, meaning that Muslim feasts advance by 10–12 days against the Gregorian calendar each year. Dates of feasts vary according to the sighting of the new moon, so they cannot be forecast precisely.

During January and February in 1991, Iraq became a testing ground for much of America's high-tech aviation and missile technology. Why Iraq thought its second-rate Soviet junk had even a chance against stealth bombers, cruise missiles and high-tech weapons is still a mystery to military analysts. Iraq lost most of its oil refineries, petrochemicals plants, munitions factories, the al-Qaim fertilizer complex (uranium is a by-product of phosphates) and almost all heavy and light industry in Baghdad (everything from textiles factories to the notorious baby formula plant) during the Gulf War. Most of these sites have been rebuilt.

There is a neutral zone between Iraq and Saudi Arabia administered jointly by the two countries with Iraq's portion covering 3522 square km. The country's most fertile area is the centuries old flood plain of the Tigris and Euphrates rivers from Turkey and Syria to the Gulf. The northeast of Iraq is mountainous, while the large western desert area is sparsely populated and undeveloped. The northern mountainous region experiences severe winters, but the southern plains have warm winters with little rain and very hot, dry summers. The temperatures in Baghdad are between 4 degrees Centigrade (C) and 16 degrees C in January, and between 24 degrees C and 33 degrees C in July and August. The average annual rainfall is 28 mm.

Iraqi dishes provide the usual range of Middle Eastern and Turkish offerings: *tikka* (shish ke bab) *kubba* (cracked wheat mixed with minced meat and molded around nuts, sultanas, spices, parsley and onion); *dolma* (vine leaves or other vegetables stuffed with rice, meat and spices); *quozi* (small lamb stuffed with rice, minced meat and spices and served on rice); and *masgouf* (fish from the Tigris cooked on the river bank). Alcohol is available only in international hotels.During the Ramadan fasting month, both smoking and drinking in public are forbidden.

Although 53.5 percent of the population are Shia Muslims, the minority Sunni Muslims (41.5 percent) are politically dominant.

Embassy Location

There is no U.S. embassy or consulate in Iraq. The U.S. government is not in a position to accord normal consular protective services to U.S. citizens who are in Iraq. U.S. government interests are represented by the government of Poland, which, as a protecting power, is able to provide only limited emergency services to U.S. citizens.The U.S. Interests Section of the Embassy of Poland is located opposite the Foreign Ministry Club (Masbah Quarter); *P.O. Box 2447 Alwiyah, Baghdad, Iraq.* The telephone number is ☎ *(964-1) 719-6138, 719-6139, 719-3791, 718-1840.*

Dangerous Days	
04/16/1991	U.S. President George Bush announced that U.S. Troops would enter northern Iraq to create a safe haven for displaced Kurds around Zakhu.
03/02/1991	Iraq signed a cease-fire agreement with allied forces ending the Persian Gulf War.
02/27/1991	Allied forces in Kuwait and Iraq suspended military operations against Iraq.
02/24/1991	Allied forces launched the ground assault against Iraqi forces occupying Kuwait.
01/30/1991	Iraqi and multinational force elements had their first combat engagement in Khafji in the Persian Gulf War.
01/17/1991	The start of hostilities between the multi national forces and Iraqi forces. The beginning of Operation Desert Storm.
08/02/1990	Iraqi forces invaded Kuwait and seized control of the country.
08/15/1986	Turkish troops raided Kurdish rebel camps in Iraq.
11/26/1984	Relations with the U.S. restored.
06/07/1981	Israeli warplanes attacked an Iraqi nuclear power plant near Baghdad.
09/19/1980	Iran-Iraq war began.
03/10/1979	Death of Kurdish leader Mullah Mustafa Barzani (Kurdish regions).
06/01/1976	During this month, Syria entered the civil war in Lebanon on the side of the Christian Phalange and against the Palestinians and their Muslim allies. In response, Abu Nidal renamed his terrorist group then based in Iraq the Black June Organization and began attacking Syrian targets.
07/17/1968	Ba'ath party seized power.
02/08/1963	Revolution Day.
02/03/1963	The Ba'ath party took power in a popular revolt.
07/14/1958	Republic Day. Celebrates the coup by General Abdul Karim Qasim during which King Faysal iI and Prime Minister Nuri as-Said were killed.

Dangerous Days

04/08/1947	Iraqi Ba'ath party was founded in 1947.
01/22/1946	Kurdish Republic Day.
04/28/1937	Saddam Hussein's birthday.
03/21	Kurdish New Year celebrated.

In a Dangerous Place: The Gulf War

The Gulf War, as it was known even during the six months of its preparation by the allied forces (led by the U.S.A.), began on August 2, 1990. I was on holiday and by chance was headed back to Istanbul just before the beginning of the war. I was told to go to Habur in Turkey, the gateway to Iraq, a very important entrance during the eight-year long Iran-Iraq war. I was being sent there to take photos of people fleeing the country. The Kerkuk-yumurtalik pipeline had just been closed by the Turks at the request of the international community for a boycott of Iraqi oil. The boycott was imposed by the UN as retaliation against the invasion of Kuwait by Saddam Hussein's Iraq.

The frontier was only open to the refugees during the preparation of the war.

After the ultimatum of the UN to Iraq, I went to Amman in Jordan in order to get a visa to go to Baghdad. I was not alone, 1500 journalists came from all over the world for the same reason. Everybody was anxious to be the first and only, and the street in front of the embassy of Iraq was vibrant with rumors and stories of the "media circus." The Iraqis were not willing to allow such a mass of people into their country and they wanted to use them if possible for their own propaganda.

There was a real battle to get the precious visas. The Iraqi authorities allowed the first batch of fifteen journalists to get in. I was not taken in at that time, but was accepted in the second batch.

I soon discovered that it was a mistake to try and get in because we were going to be trapped in the world-famous hotel Al Rachid where all the journalists were to stay under heavy surveillance and without any opportunity to get out. We were like prisoners, but prisoners who have to pay tremendous amounts in U.S. dollars...for everything.

I was to stay in this hotel for two and a half weeks prior to being expelled like the others. Food was scarce. Electricity was soon cut because of the American bombs. Water was not readily available. We had to climb seven stories by foot because the lifts were no longer working.

We had little to do apart from listening to the radio. The Iraqis were not allowed to listen to western radios but some did so anyway. The journalists do too, of course, and made interesting comparisons between the propaganda from Iraq and the absence of concrete news from the West. The Iraqis began feeling that they had been fooled, but none would dare say so. The soldiers coming back from the front looked exhausted, and the triumphant communiqués of near-complete victory against the "forces of evil" sounded more and more dubious to more and more people.

But the society was too much under the tight control of agents faithful to Saddam Hussein, so that nothing could really happen inside the country. It did happen, though, with the rebellion of the Kurds and of the Shiite Muslims.

Saddam Hussein is still in power; most of his ministers are too. The same old system rules the country. Saddam Hussein managed to defeat two rebellions (the Kurds and the Shiites) in his usual bloody way after having officially lost the war against the UN coalition.

There is not much to be said about the effect of the Gulf War. The U.S. did an infomercial for its new military technology. Saddam Hussein, the dictator, runs the country exactly as he did before the war. The only difference is that the Kuwaitis can now continue to dance in their discos and fly back and forth to London to go shopping.

Barbie jihad

Kuwait issued a Fatwah against the Barbie doll. Insisting that it would affect the cultural stereotype of Kuwaiti women, a religious cleric has asked that all Barbie toys and accessories be banned from the country of Kuwait. It is not known whether all Barbies must go into hiding or whether Mattel is coming up with a chador to pacify the Islamic world.

Kashgar

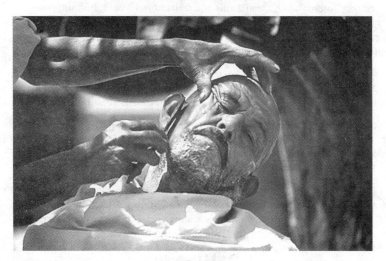

Red Tag Sale

DP has been in Kashgar three times, once during the Paris to Beijing rally, once with a guide and once illegally. The forbidden pearl lies in a land inhabited by the "ugly men," or Vun-Suns. Far from civilization on the southwest corner of China's Taidamakan Desert, this is one of the most exotic and remote trading centers in the world; although it's lost some of its mythical quality since the communists took China. (A large statue of Chairman Mao pierces the sky like a monolith in the center of town, letting you know who's in charge.) But each Sunday, perhaps 100,000 people descend upon the market to sell and buy everything from cows to camcorders in a scene that looks the way the L.A. riots would have appeared had they occurred in the 14th century. This is the scene of the largest open market under communist control, making it, in a sense, the world's biggest red tag sale.

Kashgar was first settled by the fair-haired Vun-Suns almost 2000 years before Christ. The language spoken here is Uygur, a tongue entirely unrelated to Chinese. Marco Polo was the first Westerner to set eyes upon the market at Kashgar and it would be fair to say that little has changed since his last visit.

Kashgar, or Kash-i (meaning shining pearl), is the most exotic stop along the Silk Road. Travelers and traders have stopped in this oasis town along the Kyzyl Derya, or Shule River, to rest and ply their wares for thousands of years. The waters of the river come from the snowy, rugged Tien Shan mountains in the north, rising to 3795 meters above sea level. This city of 200,000 inhabitants swells by another third on market days.

Every Saturday evening and into the dawn hours of Sunday morning, the men prepare their tents and stalls for the Sunday bazaar while children sleep on their horse-drawn carts. To this remote place come salt traders from Tibet with their gray blocks of salt, silk traders from Manchuria and spice sellers from India and Pakistan. However, the most eagerly awaited merchants are the "ice men." These entrepreneurial souls bring ice down on horseback from high in the mountains into the north. They make ice cream by adding sugar, vanilla, milk and cinnamon. Here in this mud-brick city can be found every conceivable item of desire. Goats and horses are offered by livestock traders. Also on the fare are Siberian bear paws, monkey teeth from Shaman, silk and cloth garments, shish kebob and other exotic fast food from the street hawkers.

Tinkerers are in great supply and demand here, employing ancient, handmade tools. The Maytag man here can fix any nonelectrical item the same day, usually in a matter of minutes. It had better be that way, as he won't be back until the following week.

The market's also a good place for a haircut, medieval style. The barbers use ancient but effective razors to shave your head as clean as a cue ball. Then you'll get a scalp massage with walnut oil. Ahhhh.

Then take the new you in for a game of billiards. Pick any of the numerous faded, dusty tables—but don't bet any money. These joints may take yuan, rupees, paisas, rubles and patacas—but they don't take American Express. And children begin playing pool at the market from the age of six. Kashgar may be the farthest place of anywhere on earth from the ocean, but with a teeming shark population.

Getting In

Kashgar is in Xinjiang, the most northern and westerly region of China. Xinjiang borders Pakistan, Russia and Mongolia and is seldom visited by outsiders. Kashgar sits about 1300 meters above sea level and is situated about halfway along the ancient Silk Road between Istanbul and China, and can be reached by flying from Beijing to Urumqi. Daily flights are now scheduled between Urumqi and Kashgar. The road journey from Urumqi to Kashgar is a grueling 1473 km.

At last count, only about 20,000 travelers visit this remote region a year, most of them Chinese. Kashgar can only be visited with direct permission from the tourist ministry in Beijing. You cannot reach Kashgar from the European side of the continent unless you drive overland along Karakoram Highway through Pakistan. Border rules change as frequently as the weather so check with the embassy and be prepared to get bogged down in blizzards. From Beijing, you may be required to bring a guide along. You'll be expected to pay all the guide's expenses, including airfare for the TU-154 flight from the capital. The return fare from Beijing to Kashgar is about US$700.

Once in Kashgar, you must stay in the massive but depressingly drab, 294-room, government-run Kashgar Hotel (or Kashgar Guesthouse) outside of town. *Way* outside of town. Your guide will shoo off any local who approaches you for a conversation. If you can get in from Pakistan, you've got more of a choice: the Seman Hotel (the former Soviet consulate, with 120 beds) and the Qiluowake Hotel (100 beds). Kashgar can also be reached by crossing the Taldamakan desert on a three-day drive from the border of Kazakhstan.

Getting Around

Donkey carts have been banned. The bus system is useless. Essentially, you've got a choice between your feet and a bicycle. The Seman Hotel may have bikes for rent, depending on whether they've got any bikes. The better-heeled may also be able to rent a jeep at the Kashgar Hotel.

The best time to go is in the spring or fall. In January, the temperatures drop to -65 degrees F. The summers aren't hot, but they can be comfortable, with temperatures around 81 degrees F.

Getting Out

The same way you got in.

Libya

The Future's So Bright I Gotta Wear Shades

Libya, or as the locals abbreviate it, al-Jamahiriya al-'Arabiyah al-Libiya al-Sha'biya al-Ishtirakiya (The Great Socialist People's Libyan Arab Jamahiriya), has a bright future.

In fact it's so bright, Libyan leader Colonel Muammar Qaddafi needs shades—even at night. And with that toothy, earlobe-to-earlobe grin, the man could get a job on the side of a Close Up toothpaste box (most in the West would like to see him close up to a Tomahawk). In fact, times are so good in that garden oasis of his, he threw a big Marxist bash in the fall of 1994 to celebrate the 25th anniversary of the military coup that plopped him into Tripoli's driver's seat. The evening's feature: all brand-new, uncensored, anti-Western rhetoric! Must've been one hell of a party.

He gassed up about a thousand of his rusty old Soviet-era tanks, greased up a whole parade-load of mechanized vehicles and had an old-time, Marxist-style dictator birthday bash for the benefit of his North African guests.

Among the honored visitors was a former enemy, Chad's President Debi. (Qaddafi invaded Chad's Aouzou Strip in 1987.) Other folks, seemingly in need of a free meal

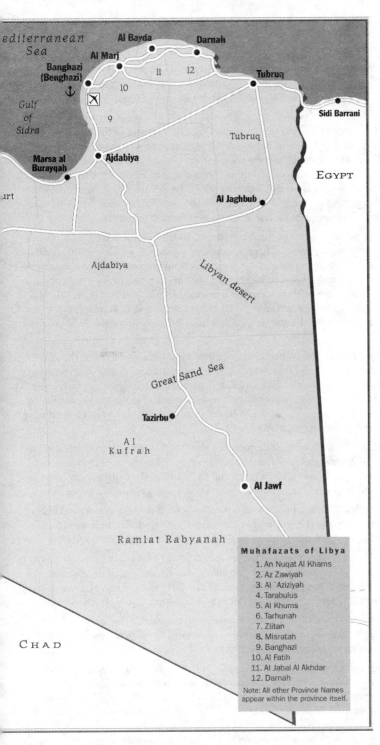

Muhafazats of Libya

1. An Nuqat Al Khams
2. Az Zawiyah
3. Al `Aziziyah
4. Tarabulus
5. Al Khums
6. Tarhunah
7. Zlitan
8. Misratah
9. Banghazi
10. Al Fatih
11. Al Jabal Al Akhdar
12. Darnah

Note: All other Province Names appear within the province itself.

and the chance to wear their dime store medals, were the presidents of Algeria, Sudan, Tunisia, Maurtania and Morocco and the secretary-general of the Arab League. A regular terrorist tea and toast party.

In his self-imposed quarantine and chicken wire chain of command, Qaddafi is still a colonel—it's anyone's guess who the general is—and he's truly focused on the goodwill of his people. Three years of UN sanctions and isolation from the rest of the world doesn't seem to phase him.

He still refuses to surrender two men accused in the bombing of the 1988 Pan Am jet over Lockerbie. The U.S. and Europe don't like the shades or the smile. Qaddafi's assets are frozen abroad; travel imports are restricted. Inflation runs at about 100 percent and the Libyan dinar is worth 10 times more on the black market than its official rate. The chances of a McDonald's opening up in Tripoli are slim—anorexic—since the sanctions against Libya are reviewed every 120 days. Think Uncle Sam's worried about Saddam? The sanctions on Iraq are reviewed every 60 days.

What are you missing by not being able to tour Qaddafi's Corner? Well, a lot of sand and some of the most exquisite Roman ruins in the world, including the ancient Roman city of Leptis Magna, built in the first and second centuries A.D. and the once-buried city of Sabratha—preserved by entombment in desert sands for a millennium. But getting a chance to see the sites in the foreseeable future will be tough. The U.S. State Department warns against travel for all U.S. citizens, and U.S. passports are not valid in Libya unless special authorization has been obtained from the U.S. government.

The Libyans are resigned to being out of circulation for a while. Even though air travel is banned to and from Libya, travelers find few restrictions once inside the country.There is a good road system. Resourceful travelers can hire taxis to nearby Tunisia. The road from Libya to Tunisia is one of the few overland routes those wishing to enter or leave the Jamahariya must use. And the ferry to and from Malta is a good way to slide into and out of the country.

Education in Libya is now widespread. The tiny but propagating population (4,212,000 and counting: There should be a big digital billboard at Tripoli's airport.) still benefits from the US$8 billion a year in oil income. But the embargo has taken its toll. Oil revenue is down US$23 billion a year since the sanctions were imposed.

The *mukhabarat,* security police, along with hundreds of paid informants and thugs, make sure that everyone is happy and in agreement with Qaddafi's policies. The media, or Muammar's Minions, march in step with Qaddafi's bombastic diatribes.

There aren't a lot of decent jobs in Libya, so that leaves a lot of time for idle chatter in coffee shops (chatter more cerebral than idle is illegal), praying in the mosque and watching the cheaper foreign labor do most of the dirty work. Libya is a major employer of contract laborers from Egypt, Mali, Sudan, Morocco and South Korea.

Despite the tight controls on speech, printed communications and politics, Libyans can watch European and American television shows on their satellite dishes and there are few restrictions on communications by fax and telephone.

Libya was an independent monarchy until 1969. Qaddafi and some army buddies changed that by turfing out the anachronistic government and setting up a Revolutionary Command Council (RCC), with Qaddafi as Chairperson. He proclaimed Libya the Libyan Arab Republic. In March 1977, he fine-tuned the country's name by calling it the more popular word Jamahiriya, or state of the masses.

He also took the title of Revolutionary Leader. He continues to be Libya's dominant political force, wielding final and total authority. The government is based on Islamic law derived from the Koran, and local authority rests with a variety of socialist groups: people's committees, trade unions, vocational syndicates, and people's congresses.

Qaddafi permits the Arab Socialist Union (ASU) to exist as Libya's sole political party. The ASU began in Sudan in 1981. The National Front for the Salvation of Libya (NFSL) was the country's principal opposition group, but is now in exile. The NFSL's modest goal is to establish a democratically-elected government. There are a number of political parties outside the tent, so to speak. Other exiled political parties include the Libyan National Democratic Front, the Libyan National Association, the Libyan Democratic Movement and the Libyan Liberation Organization.

Libya is 91 percent desert with only 1 percent usable for growing food. Qaddafi's 2000 miles of coastline once attracted European tourists (about 100,000 of them every year used to pump money into the economy in better days), and his oil once allowed him to buy secondhand Russian and East German weapons. In fact, he made so much money, he spent a lot of it on terrorist groups and picking fights with his neighbor to the south.

But Libya got its butt kicked by the Chadians and the French between November 1986 and March 1987 when the Chadian army evicted Libyan and pro-Libyan forces from their strongholds of Fada, Ouadi Doum and Faya Largeau. The Libyans retreated to the Aouzou Strip, basing its ownership of the area on a 1935 treaty between Italy (which controlled Libya) and France (which controlled Chad).

A cease-fire was signed with Chad on September 11, 1987, and it was agreed that the border dispute would be arbitrated. Libya had also settled previous disputes with Tunisia and Malta through arbitration. In October 1988, Libya and Chad restored diplomatic relations. Historically, Libya has shied away from full-blown hostilities and settled its disputes amiably. But that hasn't stopped the U.S. from taunting its enemy and periodically teasing it into cat-and-mouse exchanges of rockets. In January 1989, the U.S. concocted a silly story alleging Qaddafi had built a chemical weapons (mustard gas) factory at Rabta. After enough finger poking and name calling, Libya threw the first punch when one of its Mig-23s attacked a U.S. Navy task force mockingly positioned off the Libyan coast. The aircraft was blasted from the sky. The U.S. bombing of Tripoli and Benghazi in April 1986 didn't do much for Uncle Sam's image, either.

U.S. economic sanctions introduced in June 1986 forced five U.S. oil companies out of Libya, forcing them to kiss away US$4 billion in equipment and oil. The companies lose an estimated US$120 million a year in revenue.

Libya has provided military supplies to the Islamic fundamentalist military junta in Khartoum, Sudan in its civil war against the rebel SPLA, but denies responsibility for the bombing raids against SPLA positions. During the Gulf War, Libya did not support President Saddam Hussein. Qaddafi insisted upon a complete Iraqi withdrawal from Kuwait and the return of its legitimate government. He wasn't pulling for Western forces; he just hates Saddam Hussien more than George Bush.

The Egyptian government imposed new travel restrictions on Egyptians crossing the border into and from Libya and Sudan in 1993. Egyptians are now required to show passports rather than identity cards (which are easily forged). The new rules were imposed to make it harder for militant fundamentalists to cross the borders. The opening of the border with Egypt has, however, led to a boom in the smuggling of electrical goods, clothing and other merchandise. Egyptians travel to Libya to procure goods because of the cheap Libyan dinar on the black market. Libyan customs officials no longer make vigorous inspections at the border.

Although Qaddafi relies on foreign workers, he is still xenophobic. Between two and four years of military service is mandatory for men and women between the ages of 18 and 35. Qaddafi is a fan of Rommel, Patton and Stalin and owns more than 2300 Russian tanks (mostly T-54s, 55s and 62s). He boasts an impressive 38 tank battalions and 54 mechanized infantry battalions, and more than 1000 military aircraft if he wants to pick a fight again. Currently, most of the equipment is gathering dust in storage.

Flying the deadly skies and other programs

Libya's biggest wrench in the spokes of global acceptance is not coming clean on the December 1988 bombing of Pan Am flight 103 over Lockerbie, Scotland. It still refuses to hand over two members of its security force accused by the U.S. of carrying out the catastrophic deed. The strongest evidence suggests that nongovernment elements in Iran hired the Palestinian Syrian-based PFLP General Command to blow up an American aircraft in revenge for an earlier accidental U.S. downing of an Iranian passenger aircraft. The Libyan Security Service is assumed to have acted as the hired guns, however, the real culprits are still in Tehran. The U.S., having little or no intelligence capabilities in Iran, apparently prefers the bird-in-the-hand solution to the bird-in-the-bush problem.

Not that the Libyans are completely innocent. Tripoli is also accused of blowing up a UTA flight over the Sahara in 1989, killing 171 people. The plane exploded over Niger after making a stopover in Chad during a flight from Brazzaville to Paris. The French have warrants out on four Libyans, including the deputy head of Libya's Security Service, Abdullah Senoussi, who is Qaddafi's brother-in-law.

Qaddafi, in a PR effort to mend his ways, cut off support for the IRA. He told the Chief of Intelligence Services, Colonel Youssef Abdel-Qader al-Dabri, to work on cleaning up his image abroad. Although the 1986 freezing of Libyan assets in the U.S. (estimated to be between US$1–$2.5 billion) hurt Qaddafi, Tripoli has plenty of liquid money (about US$6 billion) in Switzerland and the Gulf States as well as significant holdings in other European countries.

To show how bright the future is for Libya, Qaddafi is blowing US$25 billion on the Great Manmade River, a program designed to suck water from the deep underground in the Sahara and carry it to irrigate coastal farmlands.

The Great Manmade River (GMR) project alone employs 10,000 Asian workers. It's estimated that there are about 6000 Americans, 4500 Britons, 4000 Italians, 2000 Germans, 25,000 Eastern Europeans and around 10,000 South Koreans in the country working on the project. The GMR is considered to be the Middle East's largest irrigation project, providing a flow rate of two million cubic meters a day and enough water for 400 years. Environmentalists have raised concern about the effects of siphoning off underground water from desert well fields, but GMR authorities insist that environmental consequences of the project will only affect areas within 50 kms of the individual wells. It is expected that phase two will be completed in 1997; the principal contractor, Dong Ah, has already completed the transport roads.

Qaddafi has pledged up to 25 percent of all Libyan oil sales to debt repayment and barter deals. So the country has about US$6 billion left to subsist on. Senators in Washington thought that the oil companies should be paid through Libya's frozen assets in the U.S. About US$2 billion—leaving enough left for a postage stamp and a letter to let Muammar know where his money went.

But greed seems to have prevailed, as American oil companies would rather be friends with Qaddafi, considering oil exploration experts believe that the barren sands of Libya will be one of the top three oil discovery sites in the world. They believe multiple fields exist that will yield 100 million barrels or more each. For example, in July of 1991 the Sirte Oil Company discovered a field with reserves of 250 million barrels in the Ghadames Basin.

Travel notes

Needless to say Libya is hot, cooler along the coast, and hot enough to melt the treads on your Nikes down south. Temperatures normally range from 55 degrees F to 100 degrees F. Bus and taxi services are quite good, and the road system excellent (14,914 miles out of Libya's 20,195 miles of road are paved). Local air transportation is also good and airfields are in abundance (122 at last count, with 53 paved and 37 over 8000 ft.). Don't expect to fly anywhere outside of Libya's borders. Just to show how tough Libyans are, a group of pilgrims to Mecca rode camels to protest Libya's lack of an international air transportation system. In May 1994, 110 pilgrims rode 60 camels from the Libyan border to Suez where they took a ship to Jeddah.

The Scoop

The Socialist People's Libyan Arab Jamahiriya considers itself an Islamic Arab Socialist "Mass-State" (i.e., a state run by the masses). Libya has a developing economy. Islamic ideals and beliefs provide the conservative foundation of the country's customs, laws and practices. The country is virtually ethnically pure. Berber, Arab and Sunni Muslim comprise 97 percent of the population. Arabic is the official language but Italian and English are spoken in the main urban centers. About half the people are illiterate although the situation is improving rapidly.

The Players

Col. Muammar abu Minyar al-Qaddafi

After losing his crown as the "West's most despised Arabic ruler" to Saddam (who inherited it from Yasir Arafat), Qaddafi still refuses to hand over the two Libyan intelligence officers who are accused of being responsible for the bombing of two aircraft. U.S. President Ronald Reagan's April 1986 attempt to "wax his ass" while he was sleeping has toned down Qaddafi's troublemaking.

Internally, he has lost little popularity. There is no denying who is in charge of the Jamahiriyya. The "People's Committees" and "General People's Congress" know that the equally powerful and less democratic "Revolutionary Committees" call the shots.

There has not been and is unlikely to be a viable alternative to Qaddafi in the foreseeable future. A member of the Qadhafa tribe and born in 1941, Muammar was an early Arab activist when he joined the Army after being educated in Britain. He formed the Free Officers Movement, a group of military officers who believed in Arab nationalism. He made it as far as captain. When King Idris was away on vacation in September 1969, the Free Officers Movement took control of the government of Libya. Qaddafi became head of state in 1970. Born in Arab nationalist times, and influenced by Communist successes, he created the Green Book, a three volume collection of his personal ideology. Regarded as a comical figure and buffoon in the Western press, he has managed to shape the political and ideological future of Libya over the last 25 years through both good and bad times—a feat his Western political counterparts cannot claim. Only Fidel Castro can claim more longevity.

Libyan National Salvation Committee

In 1987, the dissident groups merged to form the Libyan National Salvation Committee under the leadership of Abdel Moneim al-Houni, a former Revolutionary Command Council member and Interior Minister. The group has accomplished little.

National Front for the Salvation of Libya (Inqat)

The largest opposition group, formed in 1980 by Mohamed Megharief, the former auditor-general and Libyan ambassador to India. They have found support from the Saudis and the U.S., but there is a slim chance of any power changes soon.

The CIA and Israel

Who else are you gonna call to train hundreds of anti-Qaddafi Libyans in an effort to insert a Reagan-style "contra" army designed to infiltrate southern Libya and start a general uprising?

The Muslim Brotherhood (Ikhwan)

This and other fundamentalist groups do not support the Qaddafi regime since Qaddafi has suppressed fundamentalist groups like the puritan Wahabis (an ancient sect that once dominated Saudi Arabian society for more than 100 years).

Abu Nidal

Kicked out of Syria in March 1994, terrorist for hire Abu Nidal returned to Libya via Sudan and is now living in Suk Sabat in the Tripoli suburbs near the airport.

Getting In

Warning: The United States Department of State warns all U.S. citizens to avoid travel to Libya and to depart the country immediately if resident or visiting there. The U.S. Government has determined that due to Libya's long history of flouting international law and directing terrorist attacks against U.S. citizens, it is unsafe for Americans to travel there. U.S. passports are not valid for travel to, in or through Libya unless a special validation is obtained from the Department of State. All financial and commercial transactions with Libya are prohibited, unless licensed by the U.S. Treasury Department. There is no U.S. Embassy in Libya. U.S. Government interests are represented by the Government of Belgium, which as a protecting power can provide only limited emergency services to U.S. citizens.

Passports and visas are required. On December 11, 1981, U.S. passports ceased to be valid for travel to, in or through Libya and may not be used for that purpose without a special validation. Without this requisite validation, use of a U.S. passport for travel to, in or through Libya may constitute a violation of 18 U.S.C. 1544, and may be punishable by a fine and/or imprisonment. In addition, the Department of the Treasury prohibits all travel-related transactions by U.S. persons intending to visit Libya, unless specifically licensed by the Office of Foreign Assets Control. There are limited exceptions to this licensing requirement for Libyan nationals' family members, and for journalists. The categories of individuals eligible for consideration for a special passport validation are set forth in 22 C.F.R. 51.74. Passport validation requests for Libya can be forwarded in writing to the following address:

Deputy Assistant Secretary for Passport Services

U.S. Department of State
1111 19th Street, NW, Suite 260
Washington, D.C. 20522-1705
Attn: Office of Citizenship Appeals and Legal Assistance
☎ *(202) 955-0232*

The request must be accompanied by supporting documentation according to the category under which validation is sought. Currently, the four categories of persons specified in 22 C.F.R. 51.74 as being eligible for consideration for passport validation are as follows:

[1] Professional reporters: Includes full-time members of the reporting or writing staff of a newspaper, magazine or broadcasting network whose purpose for travel is to gather information about Libya for dissemination to the general public.

[2] American Red Cross: Applicant establishes that he or she is a representative of the American Red Cross or International Red Cross traveling pursuant to an officially sponsored Red Cross mission.

[3] Humanitarian considerations: Applicant must establish that his or her trip is justified by compelling humanitarian considerations or for family unification. At this time, "compelling humanitarian considerations" include situations where the applicant can document that an immediate family member is critically ill in Libya. Documentation concerning family illness must include the name and address of the relative, and be from that relative's physician attesting to the nature and gravity of the illness. "Family unification" situations may include cases in which spouses or minor children are residing in Libya, with and dependent on, a Libyan national spouse or parent for their support.

[4] National interest: The applicant's request is otherwise found to be in the national interest.

In all requests for passport validation for travel to Libya, the name, date and place of birth for all concerned persons must be given, as well as the U.S. passport numbers. Documentation as outlined above should accompany all requests. Additional information may be obtained by writing to the above address or by calling the Office of Citizenship Appeals and Legal Assistance at ☎ *(202) 663-1184.*

U.S. Treasury Restrictions

In addition to the passport validation, U.S. Treasury requirements must be met. Travelers may contact the Treasury Department at the following address and phone number:

Chief of Licensing Office of Foreign Assets Control

U.S. Department of the Treasury
1500 Pennsylvania Avenue, NW
Washington, D.C. 20220
☎ *(202) 622-2480*
FAX (202) 622-1657

U.S. Treasury Sanctions

On January 7, 1986, the United States imposed sanctions against Libya, which are administered by the U.S. Treasury Department, prohibiting all travel-related transactions with respect to Libya for U.S. citizens and permanent resident aliens. There are limited exceptions for Libyan nationals' family members who register with the Treasury Department's Office of Foreign Assets Control or with the Embassy of Belgium in Tripoli, and for full-time journalists. As of February 1, 1986, the President further prohibited transactions by U.S. persons relating to transportation to or from Libya. Additionally, all financial and commercial transactions by U.S. persons anywhere in the world with Libya are prohibited. This includes working in Libya, providing a service of any nature to Libya, or participating in an unauthorized transaction of any kind involving property in which Libya has an interest. Violations of the Libyan sanctions may result in penalties, fines and/or imprisonment.

Under the Libyan Sanctions Regulations and in addition to any passport validation issued by the Department of State, the U.S. Treasury Department requires that U.S. citizens and legal permanent residents who wish to travel to Libya to visit immediate family members in Libya are authorized to visit Libya only if they file a registration letter prior to their trip with the Office of Foreign Assets Control or with the Embassy of Belgium in Tripoli. The registration must contain the following information:

(1) Name, date and place of birth of the person registering (including the name under which a registrant's most recent U.S. passport was issued, if that is different);

(2) If applicable, place and date of the registrant's naturalization as a U.S. citizen, and the number of the registrant's naturalization certificate, or, for permanent resident aliens, the alien registration number of the registrant's alien registration receipt card;

(3) The name, relationship, and address of the immediate family member in Libya whose relationship forms the basis for the registrant's eligibility; and

(4) The number and issue date of the registrant's current U.S. passport, and the most recent date on which the passport was validated by the U.S. Department of State for travel to Libya.

U.N. Sanctions

U.N. Security Council sanctions against Libya, including an air embargo, took effect on April 15, 1992. U.N. Security Council Resolution 748, passed on March 31, 1992, imposed sanctions on Libya until Libya fully complies with the provisions of U.N. Resolution 731 and 748, adopted on

January 21, 1992. U.N. Security Council Resolutions 731 and 748 were adopted in response to Libya's alleged responsibility for the bombings of Pan Am flight 103 and UTA flight 772. The U.S. cannot predict if or when Libya will comply with the U.N. demands. Since April 15, 1992, when air links were discontinued, it has become difficult to leave Libya. The sale in the United States of air transportation including any stop in Libya became illegal under the International Emergency Economic Powers Act, 50 U.S.C. 1701.

Getting Sick

Basic modern medical care and medicines may not be available in Libya. There are 14 doctors and 53 hospital beds per 10,000 population.

Nuts & Bolts

The currency value is 1000 dirhams = 1 Libyan dinar. There are no Canadian or American embassies in Libya. The U.S. Government is not in a position to accord normal consular protective services to U.S. citizens in Libya. U.S. Government interests are represented by the Government of Belgium, which as a protecting power can provide only limited emergency services to U.S. citizens. The U.S. Interests Section of the Embassy of Belgium is located at Tower 4, That al Imad complex, in the capital city of Tripoli. The Belgian Embassy's mailing address is *P.O. 91650, Tripoli, Libya*. The telephone number is ☎ *(218-21) 37797, FAX (218-21) 75618*.

Dangerous Days	
04/15/1992	United Nations security council sanctions, approved on March 31, 1992, went into effect. The sanctions sever air links, ban arms sales and significantly reduce the staffs of Libyan embassies and consulates abroad.
03/31/1992	The United Nations Security Council voted to impose wide sweeping sanctions on Libya for its refusal to surrender two suspects in the 1988 bombing of Pan American flight 103. Under the sanctions all countries must bar flights to or from Libya, prohibit any arms deals and significantly reduce the staff of Libyan embassies and consulates. The sanctions take effect on 4/15/92.
11/14/1991	The United Kingdom issued indictments against two Libyans for the bombing of Pan Am flight 103 in December 1988.
08/13/1987	Libyan forces routed by Chad.
04/15/1986	U.S. bombs Tripoli and Benghazi in retaliation for terrorist attacks against American targets. Several terrorist operations commemorating the raid have occurred on this date.
03/24/1986	U.S. sinks Libyan patrol boats. The U.S. Navy forces crossed the "line of death" in the Gulf of Sidra and engaged Libyan patrol boats. Four Libyan vessels were sunk or damaged and an SA-5 radar site was crippled.
01/04/1986	Two Libyan planes shot down. U.S. warplanes shot down two Libyan warplanes over the Gulf of Sidra.
08/13/1984	Temporary union with Morocco.
08/19/1981	U.S. shoots down two Libyan jet fighters over the Gulf of Sidra.
03/02/1977	People's state established. The official name of Libya was changed to the "Socialist People's Libyan Arab Jamahiriya."

Dangerous Days

10/07/1970	Fascist Evacuation Day. Celebrates the departure of the last Italian settlers from Libya. (Also called Revenge Day.)
06/11/1970	U.S. bases were turned over to Libya. Also known as Evacuation Day.
09/01/1969	Qaddafi seizes power in a coup
05/25/1963	OAU - Africa Freedom Day. The Organization of African Unity was founded on May 25, 1963. The day is celebrated as Africa Freedom Day. The OAU is organized to promote unity and cooperation among African states.
12/24/1951	Independence Day.
11/21/1949	Proclamation Day. Commemorates the United Nations resolution on Libyan independence.
10/26/1943	Day of Mourning. Day to commemorate Libyan suffering and the deportation of Libyans to Italy during Italian colonial rule.

In a Dangerous Place: Chad, June 1983

In 1979 Chad plunged into a civil war pitting Goukkouni Oueddei and Hissène Habré, the two northern leaders, against each other. In 1982, Hissène Habré seized power and installed his government in N'djamenah, but Goukkouni Oueddei signed a pact with Lybia's leader, Muammar Qaddafi, who sent an army to Chad.

Lybia occupied the north of the country in 1983 causing France to intervene. The country was neatly split in two: the Islamic North (above the 19th parallel), was placed under the control of the GUNT of Goukkouni Oueddei and Lybia, while the animist South was placed under the control of Hissène Habré supported by France and the U.S.A.

In 1986, the rallying of Goukkouni Oueddei helped Hissène Habré fight against the Lybians. In 1987, a cease-fire was decided and in May 1988 the Lybians officially recognized Hissène Habré's government. Diplomatic relations were restored in October and Libya agreed with Chad to evacuate the Aouzou Strip, a piece of land between the two countries which it had occupied since 1972. Are you with us so far?

The political situation was not stable for long, though, because of the rebellion of Idriss Deby, former commander-in-chief of the Armed forces, and companion of Hissène Habré, in 1990. One more time France was asked to intervene. On December 2, 1990, Idriss Deby, at the head of his FPS (Forces Patriotiques du Salut-Salvation Patriotic Forces) entered N'Djamenah and forced Hissène Habré's National Army (FANT) out. Habré took refuge in Senegal. France eventually decided to let things go and intervene less in Chad.

I flew into Chad from Tripoli. I negotiated a trip into the combat zone and we are taken in aboard a *C-130* plane along with other journalists and military. We took-off from Faya-Largeau and head toward Oumchalloulah and Abeche where the battle was raging. The heat on the ground was intolerable but the unpressurized, unheated plane soon dropped below freezing as we gained in altitude.

As we were on final approach into the airport at Abeche, the cold was the least of my worries. There were strange movements on the tarmac. I climbed up to the cockpit to grab some photos in case anything happened. While in the cockpit the pilots figured out that Hissene Habre's troops had taken the town and the airport, and we are landing in enemy territory.

The strange movements we saw were men shooting up at the plane. In the clear air I could see the bullets and rockets arc toward our plane.

The pilots pulled the nose up and gave it full power. Slipping and sliding, they tried to dodge the bullets as they made the long trip out of range of the soldiers on the ground.

We landed without any damage twenty minutes later, not far from Abeche.

Once on the ground we realized that we had no plans to spend more than an hour in the desert and here we were in the middle of the Sahara with only some soup, rotten camel meal that we bought from a local and dirty water.

We spent the night hoping the enemy soldiers would not find us. The next morning, a Libyan picked us up and returned us to Faya Largeau.

Five years later in Kuwait for a summit of African heads of state, I told this story to a soldier from Chad. He recognized the incident and told me he was the leader of the soldiers on the ground that were trying to shoot down the plane. C'ést la Guerre.

Mecca and the Impenetrables

Olé

If you're afraid of bulls, but still love a good stampede, this is your place. In 1990, 1426 people were killed in a stampede inside the al-Muaissem tunnel leading from Mecca to Mina in Saudi Arabia. In May 1994, 270 died in a stampede in Mina.

The pilgrims were trampled to death during a ritual known as stoning the devil. It takes place in Mina, a town 10 km east of Mecca. It's the Middle East's version of the Ickey Shuffle, the Sack Dance, Australian Rules football and the Iditarod thrown into one. The hell with Barcelona. Forget Cuba. Tecate's boring. Mina is where the real action is.

During the ritual, the pilgrims throw pebbles at three stone pillars surrounded by low walls to symbolize man purging himself of evil. The ritual must be performed at specific times of the day. The tragedies usually occur when large crowds surge toward the pillars.

Stoning the devil can be performed at two levels, from an overhead bridge and from a tunnel beneath the bridge. The slightly less devout (in other words, the more practical) perform the ritual within the tunnel, where there are fewer people, and where you are less likely to end up covered with Nike and Timberland treadmarks.

Religious leaders and hajj travel agents (known particularly for their economy desert-crossing packages and discount round trip camel fares) have even gone so far as to offer pamphlets providing tips on what hajj pilgrims should do in a stampede.

In the event of a stampede, they suggest, stay calm and head straight for the nearest post of your nationality. The posts are setup at prominent places by general sales agents for the hajj and can be spotted flying the flag of your nationality. People who are lost should also head for one of these posts.

Try not to panic. Remaining calm will help in such a situation, say the travel agents. That's authoritative.

But there's plenty of reason for panic. Each year, enough hajj pilgrims converge on Mecca to make the Super Bowl seem like a cockfight in a bookie's basement. More than 2 million of them show up every year. In 1994, 2.5 million Muslim pilgrims descended upon Mecca during hajj in May—certainly the largest gathering in history where beer wasn't served.

The stampedes happen mainly on the bridge, where masses of pilgrims hang out and camp out, setting themselves up to become pancakes during the Zuhur, the midday peak period for performing the ritual. The crushes begin for a number of reasons. In some instances, people fall from overhead bridges, sparking panic and, ultimately, a human sunami. Others allege impatience and physical discomfort among those in the long lines at the limited number of port-a-johns. Those suspicions have yet to be confirmed.

At any rate, Saudi authorities have spent millions of dollars to widen roads and to build tunnels and overhead passes so that the large crowds can be handled more easily.

The number of pilgrims who travel to Mecca for hajj every year number more than 2 million. They come from all over the world, however, mainly from the Middle East, Asia and Africa. Most, today, travel via modern conveniences such as planes, trains and automobiles. Others caravan through baking deserts astride camels. In 1994, a number of Libyan hajjis traveled by these "ships of the desert" to Mecca in protest of the U.N. embargo on Libya. At least two of the Libyans died en route due to the scorching conditions. Others, as well, use hajj as a vehicle to voice their discontent of and hatred for the West, especially the U.S. In 1993, Libyan pilgrims took a detour from Mecca, where they ended up in Israel in an attempt to encourage Israel to put pressure on the U.S. to drop the embargo against Qaddafi. Iranian pilgrims use hajj as a stage for anti-American protests.

After Iran's Islamic revolution of 1979, the Ayatollah Khomeini began utilizing the hajj as a venue to stage anti-U.S., anti-Western, anti-Israel and sometimes anti-Saudi protests. Saudi security forces and Iranian pilgrims clashed in 1987, resulting in 250 Iranian deaths, a breaking of diplomatic relations between the two countries and a three-year Iranian boycott of the pilgrimage. In the last few years the Saudi government has tolerated the Iranian protests, but has insisted they only take place in segregated areas. But they put the clamp down in 1994. In the early 1990s, the scene was circus-like, or resembled some type of surreal consumer electronics convention. In one booth, you'd find a Jordanian exhibiting his footwear, and in another, yapping Iranians torching American flags.

Hajj, indeed, is the Disneyland of the Middle East. Surrounding the mosques and the perimeter of the Mecca itself, vendors pack the alleys and streets, hawking everything, it seems, from Ayatollah Khomeini T-shirts to Qaddafi Cream for Younger Skin. Attendees are arbitrarily pulled aside by security personnel and hussled into makeshift booths, where they are demanded to recite passages from the Koran to prove they're truly Muslim and not an M15 or NSC operative.

Camels have been largely replaced by beat-up automobiles as the principal means of getting to Mecca. In the past, travelers often lost their way because of a lack of road signs, or they became incapacitated in narrow mountain passes or on boulder-strewn routes. Travelers have been known to show up for hajj as late as Christmas, which isn't good.

In the past, in Mina, Arafat and Muzdalifah, water was generally unavailable and food in short supply. There was a scarcity of hospitals, doctors, hotels and bathrooms. Pilgrims wrote down their wills before going on hajj, quite sure they wouldn't be coming back. Today, residents of the Eastern Province of Saudi Arabia can complete the pilgrimage in five days, in what used to take nearly a month.

These days, pilgrims travel in comfortable vehicles on sweeping expressways and stay in air-conditioned tents. They're even known to rush out for 99-cent Big Macs.

The Impenetrables:
Countries We'll Get to After We Visit Disney World
One More Time

My stepfather had it all figured out: Who were the richest people on earth and what would they pay the most for? Time's up! The answer is, of course: The Saudi Royal family and water. Having a country all to yourself and being king makes for some very unusual dress codes (head to toe) and tourism policies (no no.).

Of course, the people of the desert regions do not suffer from Oprah reruns, drive-by shooting, Beavis and Butthead marathons and other cultural treasures. They take their guardianship of the Mecca and Medina very seriously and are on one hand the most welcoming country to the true believers and the most forbidding to the rest of us. If you truly want to visit Saudi Arabia it pays to know a member of the Saudi royal family, convert to Islam, work in the oil patch, be a journalist or join the air force during the next Gulf War. Otherwise, a couple of weeks in Northern Mexico or Namibia will produce the same experience.

Saudi Arabia

Getting In

The Saudi government does not issue tourist visas. It issues two types of entry visas: one for temporary business visits or to visit relatives, the other for individuals entering Saudi Arabia on an employment contract.

One problem—the Saudis don't like tourists. Can't stand them. Even though the Saudis are the Americans' buddies and they revere George Bush just slightly less than Mohammed, the country has banned tourists, even satellite dishes. They don't want any part of the West. Neither do pilgrims to hajj. Anti-West and particularly anti-U.S. demonstrations break out like a high school kid with a skin problem. With no Americans around to kill, the gatherings usually end up as—yeah, you got it—stampedes. Saudi Arabia possesses the two holiest sites in Islam: Mecca and Medina. It features public beheadings and perhaps the most breathtaking deserts on earth—two great reasons for making the country your family's next vacation destination. Forget about exploring the lore of the Bedouin. Saudi Arabia is closed. The country does not issue visas for tourism. The only way to get in is to have bona fide business in the country and a Saudi sponsor.

Customs Clearance

Customs clearance procedures in Saudi Arabia are formal, thorough and lengthy and may involve a full search of every piece of luggage. Transit passengers who wish to leave the transit area of the airport are subject to the same strict searches as arriving passengers.

Vaccinations

Travelers to Saudi Arabia may wish to get a meningococcal vaccine prior to departure. Before traveling, consult the Centers for Disease Control for updated recommendations on this and other vaccines.

AIDS Clearance

All persons going to Saudi Arabia for purposes of employment are required to present a certificate stating that they are free of the Acquired Immune Deficiency Syndrome virus. The test should be included as part of the global medical examination which is given to those who enter Saudi Arabia on a work permit. It is not required of travelers entering Saudi Arabia on a temporary visitor visa.

Temporary Visits

All applicants for temporary visitor visas for the purpose of business consultations must have a Saudi company or individual sponsor their applications. Individuals who wish to visit non-Saudi relatives must have their relatives or a Saudi sponsor request authorization of their applications through the Saudi Foreign Ministry. Persons present in Saudi Arabia on temporary visitor visas should not surrender their passports to the Saudi sponsor. The passport and visa are the only evidence of the bearer's legal right to be present in the country. If an individual is present in the kingdom on a temporary visitor visa and has obtained Saudi sponsorship for employment, he or she must exit Saudi Arabia to obtain an entry visa for employment. This visa need not be issued in the individual's country of origin, but the applicant must be physically present to apply for the visa.

Employment and Residence

Visas for employment and residence are obtained the same way as visas for temporary visits. Documentation, such as a letter from the sponsoring company, a copy of your signed contract or a notarized copy of the your university degree may also be required.

Before you sign a contract with a Saudi company, it is extremely important you obtain an independent English translation of the contract. The official and binding version of the contract that you sign is the Arabic text. Some Americans have signed contracts that in fact did not include all of the benefits they believed they were acquiring. The employee's dependents (spouse and children under the age of 18) may be brought into Saudi Arabia only with the concurrence of the Saudi sponsor and authorization of the Foreign Ministry. Ordinarily, only managers and professionals (holders of college degrees) may bring their families. Children over age 18 are likely to be refused residence.

Visas

Persons entering Saudi Arabia for the purpose of employment are issued residence permits (*iqamas*). These permits are evidence of legal residence in Saudi Arabia and must be retained at all times. Foreign residents are not permitted to travel between different major regions of Saudi Arabia unless permission is noted in their permits.

Getting Around

The passport offices have introduced a new law controlling the travel of foreigners legally in the country, within Saudi Arabia. The new law requires sponsors to provide reasons for their employees' travel within the country. They may also be asked to submit details or documents of commercial registration or contracts of the sponsor's establishment in the city, or cities, where the employee is traveling to. Previously, sponsors could get travel permits without specifying reasons for the movement of their employees within Saudi Arabia. The residential permit (*iqama*) rules in Saudi Arabia require expat workers to stick to the area where they work. When they travel within the kingdom, they have to carry a letter from the sponsor certified by the passport authority.

If an employer doesn't possess commercial registration or a contract in the city where his employee is visiting, the employer is required to submit an application specifying the reasons for the employee's travel. The only exceptions are for travel to Mecca or Medina. Visits are not to last longer than 10 days. Additionally, employees may be permitted to visit family and relatives within Saudi Arabia if they can substantiate their existence and provide proof of the relationship. Travel within Saudi Arabia by expat workers has dropped significantly since the implementation of the new regulation, according to Saudi sources.

Getting Out

A resident in Saudi Arabia may not depart the country under any circumstances, however exigent, without obtaining an exit visa. Exit visas are issued only upon request of the Saudi sponsor. U.S. consular officials are not able to 'sponsor' exit visas for Americans resident in Saudi Arabia under any circumstances. In a genuine emergency, however, consular officials will attempt to facilitate the Saudi sponsor's request for the exit visa. Residents in Saudi Arabia are almost always required to surrender their passports, and those of their dependents, to the Saudi sponsor. This practice is specifically authorized in the Saudi employment law. If an urgent need for travel exists and if the Saudi sponsor will not release the first passport, the U.S. Embassy or Consulate can issue a replacement passport. The issuance of a replacement passport does not guarantee, however, that a person will be able to depart, since the replacement passport would not contain a Saudi residence permit or exit visa.

A woman married to a Muslim should be aware that she must have her husband's permission to depart or have their children depart from Saudi Arabia. This is true even if the woman or children are U.S. citizens. The husband is the sponsor of his foreign wife and of his children, and is, as such, the only individual who can request an exit visa for the wife or children.

Dangerous Things

Booze

Import, manufacture, possession and consumption of alcoholic beverages are strictly forbidden. Saudi officials make no exceptions. Americans have spent up to a year in Saudi prisons for alcohol-related offenses. Americans have also been sentenced to receive 75 lashes in lieu of prison for failing a blood test for alcohol. Travelers should also exercise extreme care and discretion when consuming alcohol on flights landing in the kingdom. Persons obviously inebriated are subject to arrest or deportation.

Drugs

Laws regarding the importation, manufacture, possession and consumption of drugs are just as nasty. Many drugs sold with or without prescription in other countries may be illegal in Saudi Arabia. For instance, captagon (fenetylline hydrochloride), a drug used to treat exhaustion which is available without a prescription in some countries in Asia, is considered an illegal substance in Saudi Arabia. Americans in Saudi Arabia have received prison sentences of up to two and one half months and 70 lashes for possession of captagon. The attempted importation of drugs or controlled substances, even in very small amounts, is a serious offense under Saudi law. The traveler will be arrested and tried for carrying drugs into the country. Some Americans are currently in Saudi prisons serving sentences for drug possession or use. The death penalty for drug smugglers and traffickers convicted of a second offense underscores the gravity with which authorities treat drug offenses in the kingdom. Customs authorities are now using dogs to detect drugs at Saudi airports. Prescription drugs in small quantities, clearly labeled with the traveler's name, doctor's name, pharmacy, and contents on the original container, should cause no problem. It is wise to carry a copy of the prescription as well. The importation of drugs in large amounts, however, can be done legally only through the Ministry of Health.

Being a Woman (or just dressing like one)

Females are prohibited from driving vehicles or riding bicycles on public roads, or in places where they might be observed. Males and females beyond childhood are not free to congregate together in most public places, and a man may be arrested for being seen with, walking with, traveling with, or driving a woman other than his wife or immediate relative. In Saudi Arabia, playing of music or dancing in public, mixed bathing, public showing of movies and consumption of alcoholic beverages are forbidden. Saudi religious police, know as *Mutawwa*, enforce female dress standards in public places and may rebuke or harass women who do not cover their heads or whose clothing is insufficiently concealing. In addition, in more conservative areas, there have been incidents of private Saudi citizens stoning, accosting, or pursuing foreigners, including U.S. citizens, for perceived dress code or other infractions. While most such incidents have resulted in little more than inconvenience or embarrassment for the individual targeted, the potential exists for persons to be physically harmed. U.S. citizens in Saudi Arabia should be aware of Saudi social practices, and that any infractions may be dealt with aggressively. If you are accosted by Saudi authorities, cooperate fully in accordance with local customs and regulations. U.S. citizens who are harassed by private Saudi citizens should report the incidents immediately to the U.S. Embassy in Riyadh or the U.S. Consulate General either in Dhahran or in Jeddah.

Pornography, etc.

Items considered pornographic by Saudi standards, including magazines and videocassettes, are strictly forbidden. It is also illegal to import firearms of any type, ammunition, related items such as gunsights and gun magazines, food items and banned books. Personal religious items such as a Bible or a rosary are usually permitted, but travelers should be aware that on occasion, these items have been seized at entry and not returned to the traveler.

Commercial and Business Disputes

If you get into a tiff don't plan on leaving anytime soon. Disputes between parties who do not have a signed formal contract must be settled through mutual agreement or through an appeal to the local governor (*amir*) for judgment. Such disputes usually involve business representatives on temporary visit visas. Some Saudi business sponsors have gained possession of the passports of their visitors to use as leverage in disputes, but this is not authorized under Saudi law. Commercial disputes between parties who have a formal contract can be brought to the Commercial Arbitration Board of the Saudi Chamber of Commerce or to the Committee for the Settlement of Commercial Disputes in the Ministry of Commerce. Disputes involving a government agency may be brought before the Grievance Board, an autonomous court body under the Office of the King. Employer/employee disputes may be brought before the Committee for the Settlement of Labor Disputes in the Ministry of Labor. An amicable out-of-court settlement is always the best and least expensive way to resolve a dispute, since referring matters to commercial or labor tribunals can be costly and time-consuming. Ultimate responsibility for obtaining private legal counsel and resolving a dispute through the Saudi legal system lies with the parties involved. Consular officers will offer lists of local attorneys to help settle such disputes. Business visitors should be aware that if the Saudi party in a commercial dispute files a complaint with the authorities, Saudi law permits barring the exit of the foreign party until the dispute is completely settled, including payment of any damages. Saudi law is applied exclusively in all commercial and contract dispute cases, even if the contract was drawn up and/or signed outside Saudi Arabia. Remember that the Arabic text of the contract or agreement is the text that is considered binding.

Photography

Visitors should not photograph mosques, people who are praying, military or government installations and key industrial, communications or transportation facilities. If you have any doubts about what you may photograph, request permission first.

Dogs

Most pets, except dogs, may be brought into the country provided they are accompanied by a health certificate authenticated by the Saudi consulate in the country of origin. Dogs are banned with the exception of guard dogs, hunting dogs and seeing-eye dogs. Dogs in these excepted categories must be accompanied by a health certificate and a certificate authenticated by the Saudi consulate in the country of origin that attests that the dog fits into one of the exempt categories.

Nuts & Bolts

Nearly 36 percent of the inhabitants of Saudi Arabia are resident foreigners. This includes approximately 30,000 American citizens. English is acknowledged as a second language and is taught in the secondary schools. Islam dominates all aspects of life in Saudi Arabia; government policy, cultural norms and social behavior. Islam is the only official religion of the country, and public observance of any other religion is forbidden. The Saudi government considers it a sacred duty to safeguard two of the greatest shrines of Islam—the holy mosques located in the cities of Mecca and Medina. Travel to Mecca and Medina is forbidden to non-Muslims. Muslims throughout the world turn to Mecca five times a day for prayer. Restaurants, stores and other public places close for approximately a half-hour upon hearing the call to prayer, and Muslims stop their activities to pray during that time. Government and business activities are noticeably curtailed during the month of Ramadan, during the celebrations at the end of Ramadan, and during the time of the annual pilgrimage to Mecca, the *hajj*. Travel facilities into, out of and within Saudi Arabia are crowded during these periods.

Saudi Arabian Social Norms

U.S. citizens are advised that Saudi Arabia is a conservative country with a rigorous code of public behavior that everyone, including foreigners, is fully expected to observe. In particular, Westerners need to be aware of the standards of appropriate attire and the prohibition of mingling of the sexes.

Dress

Although Westerners have some leeway in dress and social contacts within company compounds, both men and women should dress conservatively in public. Women's clothing should be loose fitting and concealing, with high necks, skirts worn well below the knee and sleeves below the elbow. It is recommended that women not wear pants.

Other Middle Eastern Countries Not Likely to Be Chosen as a Site By the Walt Disney Corporation for a Major Theme Park

Ok, so a trip to Saudi Arabia or a job with Aramco is out of the question. Just where can you go to get your fill of sand dunes, camels, cold starry nights and all the lamb you can eat? Well, how's this for spiffy ad copy for tourist ads straight from the State Department and DP:

Algeria

Travelers to Algeria should be aware of the crime situation. Crimes include car break-ins, theft of auto parts from parked cars, theft of items (even those of moderate value) left in hotel rooms, home burglary and pickpocketing and purse snatching near hotels and on trains and buses. Some tactics that residents of Algeria use to avoid being victimized include carrying only a minimum amount of cash and concealing it well and parking only in guarded locations. The police can be reached in Algerian cities by dialing 17. In rural areas, contact the gendarmerie nationale. Algeria does not give visas to persons whose passports indicate travel to Israel or South Africa. Hotel shortages in the city of Algiers are chronic; confirm reservations in advance. Some hotels accept some credit cards. Before traveling, ask your credit card company if your card will be accepted in Algeria, and if not, bring "Traveler's cheques" to cover your expenses. Algerian currency and customs regulations are strictly enforced. All currency must be declared upon entering the country, and completely accounted for when departing. Nonresidents are required to change the equivalent of approximately US$200 into Algerian dinars at the official exchange rate while in Algeria. You will need to present evidence of this currency exchange before you are allowed to depart the country. All hotel bills must be paid in hard currency such as U.S. dollars. Paid hotel receipts may be used as evidence of currency exchange.

Bahrain

Bahrain is getting a little miffed at all the fundamentalists Iran keeps sending in to stir things up. Tourism is still possible with some fairly major restrictions. Business representatives, conference and exhibition delegates, and holders of diplomatic and official passports may obtain a visitors visa, valid for up to three months, from the Bahrain Embassy in Washington, D.C. or the U.N. Mission for Bahrain in New York. Persons in the above categories may also be able to obtain either a seven-day visa or a 72-hour transit visa at the Bahrain airport upon arrival if they present a confirmed return or onward air ticket.

Single women who have no sponsor or family ties in Barain may have difficulty in obtaining an airport visa. In addition to an onward ticket, they may need to secure in advance a sponsorship from a hotel that will arrange to have an airport visa waiting for them. The 72-hour airport visa can be extended, on a case by case basis, for up to one week if a Bahraini sponsor applies to the Immigration Director stating the purpose for the extension.

A seven-day visa is possible for members of tourist groups, provided arrangements are made with the Directorate of Tourism and Archaeology in the Ministry of Information or through a private agency in Bahrain, such as a hotel, travel agent or tour group organizer. Journalists planning travel to Bahrain should contact the Ministry of Information providing travel details at least one week in advance of arrival. The Ministry will then authorize airport officials to issue a 72-hour or a seven-day visa upon arrival. Failure to notify the Ministry may result in delay at the airport or denial of permission to enter the country.

The Ministry's address is: *P.O. Box 253, State of Bahrain;* ☎ *(973) 689-099; FAX (973) 780-345; telex: 8399* inform BN. Office hours: 7:00 a.m.–2:00 p.m. Saturday through Wednesday. Water is drinkable though often highly saline. Conservative dress is recommended. Bahrain prohibits the import of pornography, firearms, ammunition or of items such as knives, swords or daggers that are capable of being used as weapons. Videotapes may be screened by customs in Bahrain and either confiscated or held until the traveler departs the country. Consumption of alcohol is allowed in most bars and restaurants, except during the month of Ramadan. If there is any indication that a driver has consumed alcohol, authorities will regard that as evidence of driving under the influence of alcohol. The penalty for drunken driving may be incarceration or a fine of 500 Bahraini dinars, the equivalent of US$1300. This fine can be increased up to double that amount, depending on the circumstances of the case and the judge's decision. Under Bahraini law, convicted drug traffickers may receive the death penalty.

Egypt

Egypt has a thriving tourism industry with most of the news coming from the area south of Cairo. Currency declaration procedures are strictly enforced in Egypt. In addition to cash and "Traveler's cheques," jewelry and other valuables must be declared upon entry. Retain your declaration form for use at departure. Any currency or valuables not accounted for may be confiscated. Travelers who bring expensive photographic and video equipment to Egypt may have to pay a fee to Egyptian customs that can be refunded upon departure. For more information, check with an Egyptian embassy or consulate.

All persons entering Egypt from cholera or yellow fever areas must produce evidence of up-to-date immunizations. Immunization must have been administered before arrival; cholera at least six days before arrival and yellow fever at least 10 days. Travelers without evidence of required immunizations may not enter unless they are vaccinated and detained in quarantine for six or 10 days, respectively.

Foreigners are required to register with the police within seven days of arrival. Hotels usually take care of this. All hotel bills must be paid in foreign currency or in Egyptian pounds exchanged at the official bank rate, as evidenced by a bank receipt. All travelers to Egypt should be aware that Egyptian authorities strictly enforce drug laws. The death penalty may be imposed on anyone convicted of smuggling or selling marijuana, hashish, opium or other narcotics.

Iran

U.S. citizens are advised to avoid all travel to Iran. Travel to Iran continues to be dangerous because of the generally anti-American atmosphere and Iranian government hostility to the U.S. government. U.S. citizens traveling to Iran have been detained without charge, arrested and harassed by Iranian authorities. Persons who violate Iranian laws, such as those concerning proper dress, may face penalties that are, at times, severe. U.S./Iranian dual nationals often have their U.S. passports confiscated, have been denied permission to leave Iran, have been compelled to serve in the Iranian armed forces, or have encountered other problems while in Iran. U.S. citizens who are the spouse or child of an Iranian citizen are also considered Iranian citizens and may be required to enter Iran using an Iranian passport. The wife and minor children of an Iranian citizen will not be allowed to leave Iran without the written permission of the husband or father. Before planning a trip to Iran, Americans who also possess Iranian nationality are advised to contact the Office of Citizens Consular Services at ☎ *(202) 647-3926.* The United States does not have diplomatic relations with Iran. U.S. interests in Iran are currently served by the Embassy of Switzerland. Iranian officials have often prevented Swiss officials from providing even minimal protective services to U.S. citizens.

Iraq

U.S. citizens are warned to avoid all travel to Iraq. Conditions in Iraq remain unsettled and dangerous and travel is extremely hazardous, particularly for U.S. citizens. On February 8, 1991, U.S. passports ceased to be valid for travel to, in or through Iraq unless a special validation has been obtained. An automatic exemption to the restriction is granted to Americans residing in Iraq as of February 8, 1991 and to professional journalists on assignment. The categories of individuals eligible for consideration for special passport validation are representatives of the American or International Red Cross, persons with compelling humanitarian considerations or applicants whose travel is determined to be in the national interest. Exceptions will be scrutinized carefully on a case-by-case basis. Requests for exceptions should be forwarded in writing to: Office of Citizenship Appeals and Legal Assistance, U.S. Department of State, *1425 K Street, N.W., Room 300, Washington, DC,* ☎ *(202) 522-1705.* The request must be accompanied by substantiating documentation according to the category under which an exception is sought. It must also include the prospective traveler's name, date and place of birth, and passport number. In addition, the Department of the Treasury prohibits all travel-related transactions by U.S. persons intending to visit Iraq, unless specifically licensed by the Office of Foreign Assets Control. The only exceptions are for persons engaged in journalism or in official U.S. government or U.N. business. Questions about U.S. Treasury restrictions should be directed:

Licensing Section Office of Foreign Assets Control, *U.S. Department of the Treasury, Washington, DC 20220* ☎ *(202) 566-2701.* Travelers granted exceptions to travel to Iraq should be aware that normal protection by U.S. diplomatic and consular representatives cannot be provided. U.S. interests in Iraq are represented by the government of Poland which can provide only limited emergency services to U.S. citizens. All travelers to Iraq are required to submit certification or be tested upon arrival for AIDS.

Israel

And the Territories Occupied and Administered by Israel

Israel wants you to come home; just make sure it is not in a box or a pile of Baggies. Hamas and other Islamic and Palestinian groups are working overtime to show their displeasure of Arafat's deal. Some days it seems that there are more martyrs than there are bedsheets to go around. They are actively recruiting young Palestinian men to blow themselves up on the crowded streets of Tel Aviv and other urban centers, so be careful who you help with that heavy backpack.

U.S. citizens do not need a visa to visit Israel or the territories occupied and administered by Israel (the West Bank, Golan Heights and Gaza Strip). Upon arrival, a U.S. citizen is issued a tourist visa that is valid for three months and is renewable. Anyone, however, who has been refused entry to Israel or experienced difficulties with their visa status during a previous visit should contact the nearest Israeli embassy or consulate before attempting to return to Israel. At ports of entry, Israeli officials determine a U.S. citizen's eligibility to enter Israel. Applicants may be questioned in detail and/or required to post a departure bond. Western dress is appropriate in Israel. At religious sites, attire should be modest. Religious holidays in Israel and Jerusalem are determined according to the Hebrew calendar and fall on different dates each year. Because hotels are usually heavily booked before and during religious holidays, tourists should check holiday schedules with their travel agent or with the Embassy of Israel in Washington, DC.

Travelers should make reservations for holiday periods well in advance.

Entering Israel

Visitors to Israel will experience strict security screening. They may be subject to prolonged questioning, detailed searches of their personal effects and, in some cases, body searches. Anything that cannot be readily examined, such as tubes of toothpaste, cans of shaving cream, computers, cameras and other electronic or video equipment may be refused entry and may be confiscated and destroyed. If you plan to bring electronic, video or other high-tech equipment to Israel, check with an Israeli embassy or consulate as to whether it could pass through security. Cameras should be empty when going through security so they can be opened for inspection. American citizens with Arab surnames, and in particular those seeking to enter Israel at the Allenby Bridge from Jordan, may encounter extra delays, including greater difficulty in bringing cameras and electronic equipment into the country. American citizens have, on occasion, had their U.S. passports taken as a guarantee of their departure. If this should happen to you, contact a U.S. consular officer and report the seizure of your passport.

Any U.S. citizen experiencing difficulties at points of entry, except from Jordan, should ask to telephone the U.S. Embassy in Tel Aviv at ☎ *03-517- 4338 (weekends: 03-517-4347).* Those experiencing difficulties attempting to enter from Jordan should ask to contact the U.S. Consulate General in Jerusalem at ☎ *02-253-288.* Although they will be pleased to assist you, neither the U.S. Embassy nor the Consulate General can guarantee the admission into Israel of any traveler.

Departing Israel

Persons leaving Israel by air are subjected to lengthy and detailed security questioning. Travelers should arrive at the airport several hours before flight time. In recent years, the government of Israel has imposed a departure tax on all Israeli citizens (including dual nationals normally resident abroad) and on all residents of Israel regardless of nationality. The tax applies to temporary residents, including students, as well as to permanent residents. The amount of the tax varies with the exchange rate, but it has been as much as the equivalent of US$160. Check on the current amount with your airline or travel agent.

A few areas in Israel are off-limits to unauthorized persons for military reasons, and American visitors are expected to observe those off-limits restrictions. Conditions along Israel's cease-fire lines, including the Lebanese border, change frequently, and U.S. travelers planning a visit close to the lines should first consult the U.S. Embassy in Tel Aviv. At the time of publication, the Department of State advises U.S. citizens to avoid travel to the West Bank and Gaza because of continuing disturbances in those areas. Popular tourist destinations in the West Bank include Bethlehem, Hebron, Ramallah and Nablus. Should you decide to travel to the West Bank despite this warning, register with the U.S. Consulate General in Jerusalem. In the case of travel to Gaza or the Golan Heights, register with the U.S. Embassy in Tel Aviv.

The situation in East Jerusalem, including the old city, is unpredictable and Americans should check with the U.S. Consulate General in Jerusalem for an update on conditions. Avoid demonstrations and other situations that have the potential to lead to violence and remember to carry your U.S. passport with you at all times. Persons who, despite the West Bank travel warning, need to cross from the West Bank to Jordan, should keep in mind that the Allenby-King Hussein Bridge crossing the Jordan River is the only land entry between the West Bank and Jordan. Tourists crossing from Israel and the occupied territories to Jordan via the bridge must have a valid Jordanian visa, and are not permitted to return to Israel or the territories via the bridge. Those tourists who wish to return must go by way of a third country.

Dual Nationality

It is our understanding that Israeli citizens who are naturalized in the United States retain their Israeli citizenship, and their children are considered Israeli citizens as well. In addition, children born in the United States to Israeli parents acquire both U.S. citizenship and Israeli nationality at birth. Israeli citizens, including dual nationals, are subject to Israeli laws requiring service in Israel's armed forces. Dual nationals of military age who do not wish to serve in the Israeli armed forces should contact the Israeli Embassy to obtain proof of exemption or deferment from Israeli military service before traveling to Israel.

Kuwait

Visitors to Kuwait should be aware of the danger of unexploded land mines, bombs and shells throughout the country courtesy of the Iraqi Tourist Bureau. We couldn't come up with many tourist attractions so we assume that if you want to retrace the road to victory you'd better watch where you step.

Stay on main roads, do not travel on unpaved roads and avoid open areas and beaches. A large amount of weaponry left in Kuwait by the Iraqis after the August 1990 invasion remains in private hands and may be used in committing crimes. The crime rate in Kuwait has increased from prewar levels. Women have been the object of an unusual amount of harassment and should take precautions as they would in any large city. Women should be alert to the possibility of being followed, should not respond to the approaches of strangers and should avoid travel alone in unfamiliar or isolated parts of the city, especially at night. Conservative dress is recommended, particularly for women. Garments should cover elbows and knees. No alcohol may be imported or consumed in Kuwait. If customs officials discover alcoholic beverages in a traveler's personal effects, the traveler may be arrested and prosecuted for smuggling. U.S. citizens should avoid the Iraq border and surrounding areas because of the risk of detention by Iraqi authorities. Be extremely careful when traveling north of Kuwait City because the border is not well marked. Persons near the border have been taken into custody by Iraqi officials and convicted of violations of Iraqi law. Some have received lengthy prison sentences. Anyone who must travel near the demilitarized zone is strongly advised to notify family, friends, colleagues and the U.S. Embassy in Kuwait of their intention.

Lebanon

Yes, Virginia, there is a Beirut Marriott. After the Holiday Inn became swiss cheese during the civil war, the hotel industry felt there was a need for a new watering hole for the world's press. This year the Marriott will open up a 175-room hotel in the Jnah District, considered to be the center of the "New Beirut." The new hotel is about three miles south of the airport and on a good day you can probably hear the Israeli jets bombing the *Hezbollah* training camps outside the airport. For reservations ☎ *(800) 228-9290.*

As of January 31, 1987, U.S. passports became invalid for travel to, in or through Lebanon. U.S. citizens are advised to avoid all travel to Lebanon. This is expected to ease up over the next few years.

The situation in the country is considered to be so dangerous that the State Department feels no U.S. citizen can be considered safe from terrorist acts. To avoid the possibility of transiting Lebanon, U.S. citizens should make certain that any international flight they book in the region does not make an intermediate stop in Beirut. Such stops are not always announced. Individuals in the following categories are eligible for consideration for special passport validation: professional journalists, representatives of the American or International Red Cross, persons with compelling humanitarian considerations, or persons whose travel is determined to be in the national interest. Applications for exceptions to the U.S. passport restriction may be made following the procedures outlined in the section on Iraq. U.S. dual nationals do not violate U.S. law if they use a foreign passport for travel to Lebanon, but they are required to use their U.S. passport when they depart from and return to the United States. There are no U.S. Treasury restrictions on travel to Lebanon. Travelers who are granted passport exceptions to travel to Lebanon should be aware that normal protection of U.S. diplomatic and consular representatives cannot be provided. The U.S. Embassy in Beirut is not fully staffed and its personnel operate under exceptionally tight security conditions. Local telephone service is unreliable, and it is extremely difficult to contact the U.S. Embassy or place a local call from most of the country.

Libya

On December 10, 1981, U.S. passports ceased to be valid for travel to, in or through Libya unless a special validation has been obtained, and on January 8, 1986, U.S. economic sanctions were imposed on Libya. In addition, on March 31, 1992, United Nations sanctions were imposed. These sanctions include an air embargo which took effect April 15, 1992. The categories of individuals eligible for consideration for special passport validation are professional journalists, representatives of the American or International Red Cross, persons with compelling humanitarian considerations or persons whose travel is determined to be in the national interest. All financial and commercial transactions with Libya are prohibited, unless licensed by the Office of Foreign Assets Control, U.S. Treasury Department. Those persons granted exceptions to travel to Libya should be aware that there is no U.S. mission in Libya and U.S. interests are represented by the government of Belgium which can provide only limited protection for U.S. citizens.

Morocco

U.S. citizens do not require a visa for a tourist or business visit of up to three months. The regular route in for visitors is via ferry from Malta.

Syria

Syria being the eye of the storm is a very calm, quiet place. Damascus also provides one-stop shopping for people who like to collect brochures on terrorist organizations from the PKK to *Hezbollah*. Syrian law does not recognize the U.S. citizenship of a naturalized Syrian unless the Syrian government has given that person permission to renounce Syrian nationality. U.S.-Syrian dual nationals who have not received that permission are considered Syrian when they enter Syria even when they enter on their U.S. passports. A Syrian male cannot leave the country until he has satisfied the requirement for military service. This does not apply to a man who is the only son in a family, but it applies to all other men of normal military service age or older. Any person, male or female, who is considered Syrian may take no more than US$2000 worth of convertible currency out of Syria, no matter how much they may have brought into the country. U.S. citizens of Syrian origin may experience difficulties if they remain in Syria after the expiration of their visas. If you are a dual national, check with the Syrian Embassy on the obligations of Syrian citizenship before you visit Syria. Travelers may bring any amount of currency into Syria. Syrian law does not require currency to be declared unless the total is more than US$5000. It is wise, however, to declare any currency you have, because you can not take currency out of Syria unless it has been declared upon arrival. There are two rates of exchange in Syria. In addition to the official rate, Syrian pounds may be purchased at the more favorable 'neighboring country rate' at the Syrian Commercial Bank or at a major hotel if you have convertible currency in cash or "Traveler's cheques." Hotel bills must be paid in convertible currency or with Syrian pounds obtained at the official rate from the Commercial Bank of Syria (receipt required). Meals and all other purchases can be paid for with Syrian pounds and do not require official rate certification. Credit card charges are figured at the official rate. Syrian pounds cannot be taken out of Syria. Travelers cannot convert Syrian pounds back into convertible currency, and should therefore not purchase more of the currency than they expect to spend in Syria. Conservative dress is recommended for Syria. Travelers should exercise caution when photographing historic sites. Photographs may be taken of regular tourist attractions, such as ancient ruins and temples, but warnings are issued against photographing anything other than tourist sites.

United Arab Emirates

The United Arab Emirates (U.A.E.) is a federation of seven independent emirates. Visitors to the U.A.E. must obtain a sponsored visa before arrival. The sponsor can be a business associate, a relative or friend, or the hotel where the visitor has a reservation. Non-Muslims may consume alcohol in licensed bars or restaurants.

Yemen

U.S. citizens should exercise caution in Yemen and avoid travel in remote areas. Local tribal disputes in remote parts of Yemen have occasionally led to violence. Westerners, including U.S. citizens, have been kidnapped as a result of such local disputes, and vehicles have been hijacked. Because of the 7200 feet altitude of Sanaa and the lack of adequate medical facilities, travelers may wish to consult their physicians before visiting Yemen. Independent travel in Yemen is difficult; it is advisable to arrange your trip though a travel agent. Specific written permission from the Yemen General Tourism Corporation must be obtained for any travel outside the cities of Sanaa and Aden. Specific permission is also required to use a video camera. Photography of military installations, equipment or troops is forbidden. Although the civil war is over there are rumblings of new hostilities between the Saudis and the Yemenis. There is little, if any, fixed border between the two countries leading each country to do a little "fudge" on where to build a nice picket fence.

Oman

There are no tourist visas to Oman, and visa requirements for business travelers are stringent. Anyone arriving in Oman without a visa is subject to arrest. A business visitor must contact an Omani sponsor, either a businessman or firm, for assistance in procuring a nonobjection certificate (NOC). The sponsor should begin application procedures several weeks ahead of expected travel. American firms new to Oman may receive guidance on Omani sponsorship from the commercial office of the U.S. Embassy in Muscat. They should send a telex (TLX 3785 AMEMBMUS ON) describing their company's activities and what they expect to accomplish in Oman. Relatives of Omanis may be sponsored for a short visit using the NOC procedure. Although Oman imposes stringent entry requirements for all visitors, it does not require exit permits. Conservative dress is recommended for Oman. No alcohol, firearms, pornography or fresh food may be imported.

Qatar

Visitors to Qatar must have a business or personal sponsor. Passengers may transit Qatar without a visa if they continue their journey within 24 hours, have confirmed reservations on the same or the next available flight, and do not leave the transit lounge of Doha Airport. Conservative dress is recommended for Qatar. No alcohol may be imported.

That's about it for places that you will never want to visit and many that don't care if you ever do. For more information on dangerous places see their respective chapter.

Information supplied by the United States State Department.

Mount Athos

Just Slightly Behind Our Time

The Byzantine Empire lives on. Mount Athos, a time machine in Macedonian Greece pointing toward the Aegean Sea, is an ancient and semiautonomous republic governed by Greek Orthodox monks. I mean, this place is lost. The 1700 or so monks that live on this isolated peninsula in eastern Greece use the old Julian calendar to measure time. That means right now, these folks live about 13 days behind the rest of us. That's by the clock. By the cloak, they live 13 centuries behind the rest of us.

You can only get to Mount Athos by boat, and you need a separate visa (obtained in Thessaloniki) to do it. The land border to Mount Athos is closed; the whole place is really closed, especially if you're a woman. If you want to visit, forget it. The monks, take this quite seriously. Even female domesticated animals are prohibited to be on the island. We hope this is for a reason other than the obvious.

The only two women purported to have gotten into the place were the Virgin Mary herself and the Queen of England.

Founded in A.D. 963, the religious community has remained essentially unchanged after more than a millennium. It receives less contact with the outside world than the stone-age Sentinel islanders in the Andaman Sea. Only 10 pilgrims are permitted to visit this Eastern Orthodox enclave each day. You can cruise around the area by boat from Halkidiki but you can't get in unless you have received permission from God.

Mount Athos is a promontory about 12 km wide and 50 km long. In the southern end of the peninsula rises a 2200-meter mountain carved from limestone and marble, traversed by wild boar, jackals, wolves and eagles. From the earth springs chestnut, pine and oak forests. Fir and cypress abound, as well as maples and aspens—a cornucopia of rugged bounty.

On the "island" itself, there are scores of onion-domed monasteries (20 in all), reachable by long, rugged, uneven paths that wind their way though olive orchards. Inside the monasteries are hidden the treasures of the Byzantine era, silver and gold relics that are rarely seen by anyone. Many of these were brought to Mount Athos when the Byzantine capital of Constantinople fell in 1453. Around the balconied temples are aqueducts. Simonopetra is the magnificent seven-story tower originally built in the 14th century and destroyed in both the 16th and 17th centuries, and again in the 19th. It clings precariously to a rock outcropping. There is also the enormous 10th-century Vatopedi citadel.

Hermits, those who can't accept a monastic life shared with others, live isolated in the cliffs and the mountains surrounding the area. Some are fortifying or rebuilding old mills, olive mills and distilleries.

Mount Athos continues frozen in time beneath a searing Aegean sun. Unless you're a Greek Orthodox monk, however, the likelihood of visiting it is about the same as being able to turn back the clock 13 days.

Getting In

Passport and visa required. Although Mount Athos is in Greece, a separate visa is required. It can be had in the Greek city of Thessaloniki. But if you're not a monk, or haven't been invited to the promontory by pretty high-up cleric types, forget it. You'll have to settle for a boat ride around Mount Athos.

Olympic Airways flies to Thessaloniki four times a week from London Heathrow. Tour operators offering inclusive holidays to Halkidiki include Amathus (☎ *071-636 9873*), Portland (☎ *071-388 5111*), and Tjaereborg (☎ *0293 554444*). No one offers tours of Mount Athos.

People wishing to visit Mount Athos should contact Christos SengouIis, Athos City Travel, *63075 Ouranoupolis, Halkidiki, Greece*. He can arrange boat trips around the peninsula and one- and four-day trips (men only) to Mount Athos under special circumstances. Very special circumstances.

Getting Around

If you can actually get in, you'll get around on foot with the companionship of a very old man with a very long and very gray beard.

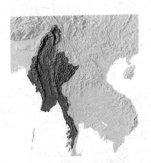

Myanmar (Burma)

Politically Incorrect

Visit Myanmar Year is 1996. Think it's a joke? Wrong! Watching tourism surge (and hard currency) in its Southeast Asia neighbors such as Thailand, Malaysia, Vietnam and Indonesia, good old SLORC (the State Law & Order Restoration Council) has said "Why the hell not?"

The most politically incorrect destination on earth has to be Myanmar. While its buddies along the Pacific Rim sponsor tourism years and award lucrative contracts to companies to build up the infrastructure and create tourist attractions, Myanmar saves a few bucks by having its general population do it—at gunpoint.

Then there are the drug lords. The most famous, the notorious Khun Sa, now supplements his income with a line of ladies' shoes. Between SLORC and the Karl Lagerfeld of opium, Myanmar makes for a bad soap opera.

But let's go back a bit.

In keeping with the trend among developing and newly independent states to throw off the stigma of their colonial past, Burma became Myanmar in 1989. (Burma has always been called Myanmar in the Burmese language.) Rudyard Kipling turned in his grave when Rangoon became Yangon and the Irrawaddy became Ayeyarwady.

Myanmar has been a nation of bellicose rulers and brutal suppression since 2500 B.C. when the Yunnan enslaved the Pyus along the upper Ayeyarwady river. Throughout its various occupations by the Mons, the Arakanese, the British and the Japanese, there have been tales of ruthless excess and exotic splendor. Unlike the nepotistic concept of royal hierarchy in Western countries, it was considered normal for Burmese rulers to exterminate heirs, rivals or the offspring of rivals. Up until the mid-1800s Burmese rulers burned, beat and drowned not only any potential claimants to the throne but also their children and servants. Hey, so what's the big deal about enslaving a few thousand peasants to build a road?

Today, the despotism continues. It's called something right out of a "Get Smart" episode: SLORC. A foreboding name in a forbidding land.

Myanmar was cocooned from the world by General Ne Win, who seized power in 1962. His 26-year reign plunged Myanmar backwards. He ruled until 1988, when pro-democracy demonstrators won and Ne Win stepped down. But the military refused to honor the results of an election it itself organized. Over 3000 Burmese protestors were killed when SLORC wrestled control of the government in a military crackdown. The 80-something Ne Win lives in the shadows and is a close friend of current intelligence chief Maj.-Gen Khin Nyunt.

Although the 21-member military junta of General Than Shwe (Saw Maung was removed due to mental problems, according to the new regime) continues to violently suppress any dissidents or uprisings, it controls only about 35 percent–50 percent of the country at any one time. There are about 1000 political prisoners in about 20 "detention" centers around the country.

Whether by blowing up a student union building the day after a large student protest or executing members of its own army for insurrections, the government continues to keep a tight grip on this dirt-poor but culturally-rich country. The current boy's club government hasn't lured a steady stream of eager investors, so the bulk of the 42 million Myanmarese are condemned to grovel on an average per capita income of

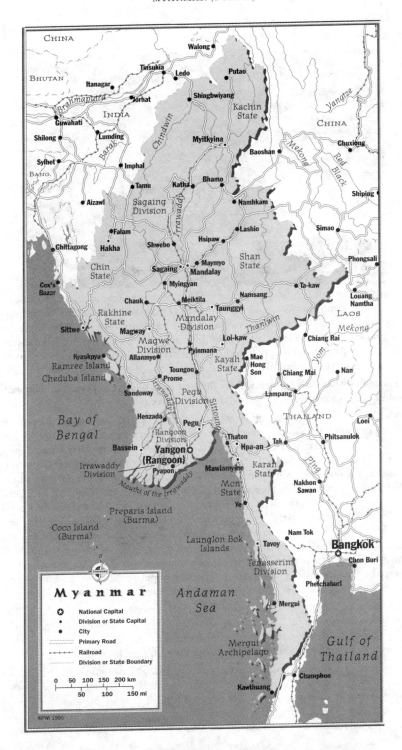

US$200. Even the normally idealistic causes of insurgent groups have been replaced by the need for profits from opium production.

This year, Myanmar is busy preparing for Visit Myanmar Year in 1996, and true to form, the government has chain-ganged not only criminals and dissidents, but regular folks to help rebuild monuments, palaces, temples and attractions. In Mandalay, the junta ordered that each family must contribute at least three days of free labor. Mandalayans can pay US$6 a month to be exempted from this drudgery. The average wage is about $6 a week in Mandalay.

The military regularly abducts villagers in rural areas to serve as porters in their wars against the insurgents, and to build roads to get there.

Myanmar is one of the more ethnically segmented countries in the world. 68 percent of the population is Burmese, however, there are 5 major ethnic groups (Shan, 11 percent; Karen, 7 percent; Kachin, 6 percent; Arakanese, 4 percent; and Chin, 2 percent.). There are an estimated 26,000 insurgents in Myanmar fighting for various causes at any one time. But figuring out who's fighting who is like unraveling an urchin stuck in a gill net. The Shans, found also in China, Loas and Thailand, have been waging a battle with China. The Karens straddle northern Thailand and eastern Burma and pay little attention to the border between the two countries. The Burmese live primarily in the central plains along the Ayeyarwady River and are the builders of the great monuments at Bagan. The Shan are found in the north or Myanmar and along the Myanmar/Thai border. They are fiercely independent, speak Tai and are represented by the Shan State Progress Party. The Mon populate the same fertile area as the Karen and are ethnically related to both the Khmers and Burmese.

Burma is unique for its dusty, worn but largely intact historical monuments. The country is famous for its Buddhist pagodas, especially the huge Shwedagon Pagoda, the plains of Bagan, its gentle people and colonial ambience. It is one of the best countries in the world to visit hill tribes and bask in unvarnished history.

The lure of forbidden zones and the Golden Triangle may lure adventurers, but there is little to see or do in these mostly rural and deforested zones. As the government creates an uneasy but profitable peace with rebel groups, more and more areas will open up to camcorder-toting, tour bus-bottomed "adventurers." In all cases you are expected to have an MTT guide, who's very uninterested in anything adventurous.

Myanmar experiences the typically Southeast Asian tropical monsoon climate, with hot, humid lowlands and cool highlands. The wet monsoon season is from June through September, the cool dry season from November to April.

The official language of Myanmar is Burmese (Myanmar); a number of ethnic languages are also spoken. Buddhists comprise 85 percent of the population, while animists, Muslims, Christians and other indigenous religion followers comprise the rest. The literacy rate stands at 81 percent. The monetary unit is the kyat.

Telephone calls can be made from hotels and the Central Telegraph office in Yangon. International calls go through operators (watch what you say and who you call). There is no guarantee of a phone line being available or even usable. Telexes can be sent from major hotels as well as the telegraph office.

It costs six kyat to post an airmail letter but don't count on it getting there anytime soon. Buy the stamps and mail your postcards or letters from Bangkok. *MTT, 77-79 Sule Pagoda Road*, is the main source for travel info in Yangon. There are also offices in Mandalay, Bagan and Taunggyi.

Voltage is 220/50 cycles when it works.

The Players

Ksar el Hirane, SLORC and the Generals

With a 265,000-man army, the 21-member junta comprised of the ruling families and selected investors holds most of the marbles here, at least in the majority of the country. However, the real and future wealth of the country is in the rich but remote regions ruled by ethnic tribes. Timber, jade, precious stones and, of course, opium are all under the control of the ethnic minorities, many of whom are wealthy enough to support affluent civic centers, tax collectors, customs, public services and their own private armies. The government is similar to the coalition of generals in Thailand and Indonesia.

Recent announcements of peace between insurgents and the government are assumed to be "live and let live" agreements which allow the rebels to concentrate on the more lucrative business of raising and exporting opium rather than vying for political power.

Although vast parcels of Myanmar are controlled by insurgent groups, there exist tacit agreements between SLORC generals and Thai logging companies permitting rebel factions to smuggle hardwood and gems out of the country into Thailand. In turn, the logging roads created by this lucrative trade provide the government an expedient route to send in troops during the dry season to pressure-play the insurgents. Myanmar possesses about of 75% of the tropical teak left in the world. The government, the Karens and the Shans, along with about 20 Thai logging companies are rapidly sawing everything down before the political winds shift direction. According to some estimates, in 10–15 years, there won't be enough teak left to put together a decent deck chair.

The Karen National Liberation Army

The largest insurgent group is the Karen National Liberation Army of the Karen National Union (KNU), based in Manerplaw and headed by Saw Bo Mya. Converted to Christianity by missionaries at the turn of the century and allied with the British during WWII, they have been fighting for their own independence since Burma was granted its independence without provision for a Karen homeland. The Karen battle for sovereignty has been ongoing since 1948, one of the longest struggles for freedom in Asia. They are funded through their control of the smuggling routes between Myanmar and Thailand.

The Arakan Rohingya Islamic Front and the Rohingya Solidarity Organization

The Arakan Rohingya Islamic Front and the smaller Rohingya Solidarity Organization represent theRohingyas, Muslim refugees from Arakan state now based in camps in Eastern Bangladesh. About 280,000 Myanmarese Muslims fled from Arakan state to southern Bangladesh in early 1992. In a century-old tradition since the days of King Bodawpaya, the refugees are persecuted by the Myanmarese military. In the past, the Rohingyas have been armed and trained by Afghan mujahedeen and Filipino Moros.

The Kachin Independent Organization

This is a group of 5000 rebels also known as the Kachin Independence Army (KIA). The Kachins are animists and Christians of Tibeto-Burman descent who originally migrated from China. Found in northern Myanmar, they are funded in part through the mining of rich jade deposits in the area. Jade is then sold to China. At one time this group was the primary organizer of opium transportation to the Thai border.

The National League for Democracy

The National League for Democracy is an opposition party, whose rarely-seen dissidents have allegedly hidden in the jungle since 1988, when the Myanmarese military suppressed a nationwide uprising for democracy.

The Shan State Army

Another group, the Shan State Army, was given large timber concessions along the Thai border and also benefit from trade in gemstones and opium. Their relationship with the Thai military has led to massive deforestation of the region.

The Shan United Army

The Shan United Army is the private play-toy of ruthless drug lord Chang Chi Fu, also known by the theatrical title Khun Sa (the Prince of Death). The U.S. government credits Khun Sa with providing a full two-thirds of the world's heroin supply.

Khun Sa is a self-styled "freedom fighter" who's been duking it out with the government as well as equally notorious enemy, drug lord Chao Yelaiin, an ethnic Wa. A peace agreement the two signed in October 1993 resulted in an unabated surge in heroin flowing through the Golden Triangle area. Khun Sa, who's wanted by the U.S. government on narcotics smuggling charges, agreed to the settlement with his traditional rival as it became more apparent that the heroin factories in the Shan state were becoming increasing dependent on raw opium produced in Wa-controlled areas. The Myanmar government accuses Khun Sa of dozens of massacres, including the slaughter of 122 villagers in Shan state in March 1993.

Khun Sa Takes on a Sole

Drug lord Khun Sa is stepping into another role; he's going legit. Well, sorta. The rebel/heroin cartel leader now has his own line of ladies' designer shoes. He imports them from England and redesigns the shoes using precious and rare Burmese rubies and gems. The shoes are then sold to well-heeled Westerners in Sydney and London for about US$20,000 a pair.

Getting In

To get in legally you have to book a tour through an MTT-approved travel company. The timid can book the entire trip, or the more adventurous can buy the required minimum tour (usually 5–6 days) and then use the balance of the visa of 10 days to wander around. Journalists and writers are automatically refused entry.

Passport and visa are required. Single-entry visas, for stay up to 14 days, require a US$16 fee for a tourist visa and a US$30 fee for a business visa. You'll need two application forms, three photos and an itinerary. Tourists visas are issued for package or group tours as well as Foreign Independent Travelers (FITs). Burma offers an FIT visa that allows visitors to wander within the approved areas. FITs holding tourist visas must change a minimum of US$200 upon arrival. Business visas require company letter and invitation from a Myanmarian company, extendable after arrival. Overland travel into and out of Myanmar is only permitted at certain points (check with embassy). Enclose prepaid envelope for return of passport by registered/certified mail. Allow two to three weeks for processing. Minimum of US$100 must be changed for local currency on arrival. For further information contact a Myanmar embassy.

There is little incentive to try to sneak into Myanmar since it can be easily done by hiking over land or along logging roads into the country from Thailand. Troubles you encounter won't be with the government but with the various ethnic and rebel groups, who will have no qualms about shooting you and leaving you to rot. You can try contacting the various groups through expat sympathizers; however, don't try this from inside the country.

The northern and eastern border areas are technically closed. But since the government is in control of so few of these areas, it raises the question of who will stop you first, the government or the rebels. If you are a caught you will be deported and may magically lose most of your valuables

Arakan province is technically closed but there are flights to Sittwe and two attractive beach resorts in Ngapali. This is the favorite getaway of the rich and famous and the area is sprinkled with their homes away from home.

You have a choice of seven air carriers into Myanmar, the best choice being Silk Air (an arm of Singapore Airlines), and the worst being Myanmar Airways. You can buy a ticket outside the country but you will not be guaranteed a seat. Even if you make a reservation inside Myanmar, there still is still no guarantee that the plane will leave, or that an unsmiling gentleman with a military uniform and Louis Vuitton luggage won't be given your seat.

When you leave you will need US$6 for the airport tax. They never have change.

Embassies/Consulates

American Embassy

> 581 Merchant Street
> Box B
> Yangon
> ☎ [95] (1) 82055 or 82181

Directorate Of Defense Services (DDSI)

> ☎ 60611 Ext. 145

Embassy of the Union of Myanmar

> 2300 S St., NW
> Washington, D.C. 20008
> ☎ (202) 332-9044-5
> or the

Permanent Mission of Myanmar to the U.N.

> 10 East 77th St.
> New York, NY 10021
> ☎ (212) 535-1311/0/1716
> FAX (212) 737-2421

Getting Around

Myanmar would like to get half a million well-heeled gawkers a year, but ends up attracting only about 20,000–50,000 curious visitors each year. Those who do go are on two-week visas that whisk them around the old favorites: Yangon, Bagan, Mandalay and maybe a quick glimpse of the Shan state. Before you can bang off a roll of Velvia, your are back on the bus and back in Bangkok.

Most tours start in Bangkok and most tour companies are based in Bangkok. You can fly in from Chiang Mai to Mandalay and Bagan. Pwin Ol Lwin, or Maymyo as it was formerly known, is an old British hill station that still has153 horse-drawn carriages left over from colonial times. The Burma Road in the Shan hills is the major trade route with Yunnan in China. The old Candacraig Inn, now a government rest house, was built in 1906 and, at US$30 a night, is one of the best bargains in the world.

The Golden Triangle area in Myanmar can be reached by train from Mandalay. You can also make the arduous 160-km trip from Kengtung to Tachileik. Additionally, you can travel from Kengtung to Mai Sai in Thailand's Chiang Rai province.

Lashio is a mecca for adventurers, for this is where the Burma Road begins its long, winding path into China. Mogok is 115 km from Mandalay and is the site of jade and ruby mines controlled by rebels on odd days, and the government on even days. You can see (and purchase) the fruits of their labors by posing as a buyer at the annual gem auction each February in Yangon.

Good maps are not available. Bartholomew, Nelles and Hildebrand are the best brands for maps of the country. The local MTT office in Athenian and Mandalay can provide street maps.

Money Hassles

You can change money at the airport in Yangon. Avoid the many black market touts unless you're a damn good negotiator. You will probably be approached by someone offering to exchange kyats for bucks before you even get to the check-in desk at your hotel. Also, you can head for the Bogyoke Zay market (Yangon) and bring your smokes and booze. Haggle, haggle, haggle—and remember that big U.S. bills are worthless if you flash the Johnnie Walker whiskey and 555 cigarettes you bought duty-free from Bangkok. Two hundred cigarettes can bring in up to 2,500 kyat. The kyat is posted at about six kyat per U.S. dollar but can be fetched at 100 for the dollar on the black market. If you use kyat, become accustomed to 45- and 90-kyat bills based on Ne Win's love for the number nine.

FEC, or Federal Exchange Currency, is gaining in popularity as the preferred tender for tourist services such as taxis, hotels, train and domestic air transportation. It is issued in U.S. denominations of 1-, 5- and 10-dollar bills. Away from the tourist areas they are worthless.

Big Brother

The military rulers of Myanmar keep a very close watch on their own people and particularly "hnakaung shays" or long noses. That means you. Do not converse freely with strangers.It can be safely assumed that anyone who loiters near you or reappears often in your travels is a paid intelligence operative.

February and March is a bad time to visit due to the influx of gem buyers into yangon for the annual auction.

North Korea

Il or Illin?

At Pyongyang's Mansudae Hill, a line of street cleaners who look more like housewives (which, of course, they actually double as), armed with straw brooms, march stooped over like a bad ensemble at Pasadena's Doo-Dah Parade. Like a 17th-century Zamboni machine, they clear what little soil has accumulated on the walkway in front of the Korean Revolution Museum before a giant bronze statue of the late North Korean leader Kim Il Sung. Kim's massive right arm is eternally locked forward in a handshake with the clouds, which was about all he was able to shake hands with during his neurotically xenophobic, despotic and frequently brutal 46 years of rule of a country that may as well be on Mars.

Shaking hands with nothing. The image lingers with you, even after reading the romantic, campy description in the city's official guidebook: The statue of Kim portrays his sublime figure looking far ahead, with his left hand akimbo and his right raised to indicate the road for the people to advance.

Oh.

That's what he's doing.

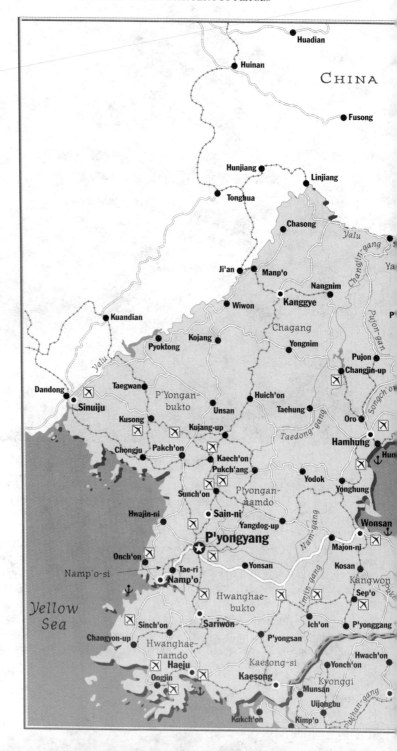

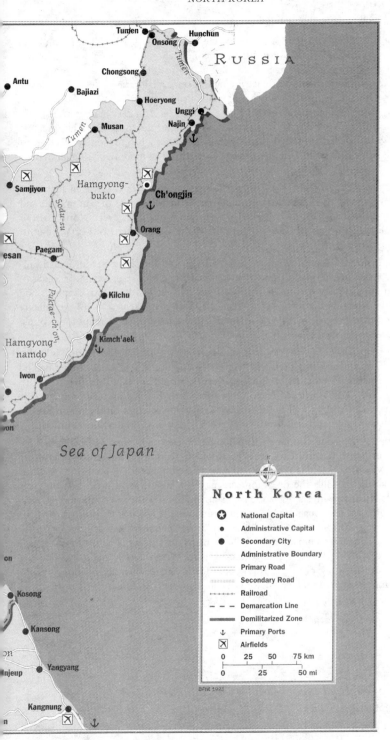

The road to the 38th parallel, no doubt.

The Great Leader departed for the Great Unknown on July 18, 1994, succumbing to illness that he tried vainly to thwart with a combination of meteorology and herbs. Millions of North Koreans have made pilgrimages to the statue and other shrines, openly weeping for a man who they were taught since birth created the dawn of each new day. Literally. It must have come as quite a shock when the sun rose that next morning. Myth and legend shrouded Kim Il Sung. His legendary heroics against the Japanese during World War II, by all historical accounts, never occurred. His greatest victory was a stalemate in the Korean War, at the cost of a half million North Korean lives. He might also claim a victory of sorts in the arrest of more than 20 million people.

North Koreans are taught that Kim was the inventor of everything from centuries-old scientific and physics theories to such modern conveniences as the automobile and the toaster. Some believe he's walked on the moon. By law, every North Korean household must possess at least two portraits of the Great One. Not Gretsky, but of Kim. That's overachievement.

Certainly not overachieving is Kim's son, 53-year-old Kim Jong Il, the Great Leader's heir apparent, who hasn't quite yet assumed the duties of president or leader of the Communist Party due to his extended grieving for his dead dad, despite being tagged the Supreme Leader (or Dear Leader). More than likely, some of the military boys put a rifle to his head and *ordered* him to grieve for a while. Perhaps for a couple of hundred years. Cry, baby, cry.

And they may have a good reason. Reclusive, cognac-guzzling Kim Jong Il is both a reported lush and an alleged terrorist. He's been implicated as the mastermind behind a number of terrorist attacks, including a Korean Air jetliner explosion that took 115 lives in 1987. He is believed responsible for North Korea's nuclear program (the bomb part, anyway), as well as the foiled assassination attempt on the South Korean president in Myanmar that instead blew away 17 high-level South Korean officials.

But the mythmaking continues. Kim Jong Il was actually born in Siberia, but because most North Koreans have never heard of Siberia, Jong Il was reborn near North Korea's Mount Paektu. He is reputed to have written hundreds of books, all epic masterpieces. His face fills the television screens every night, at all times and on every channel. The man who claims "socialism is not administrative and commanding" may have a different relationship with communism and alcohol. He is reported to spend nearly three quarters of a million dollars a year on Hennessy cognac, specifically the Paradis line. That's commanding. Yet, he remains the subject of adulation. Normally bright, responsible scholars and educators from North Korea and abroad reduce themselves to writing driveling, soppy odes to this inglorious, silver-spooned papa's boy. Sample this, written by a doctor at Delhi University in India:

Dear leader Kim Jong Il
Friend of masses, savior of
humanity
Increased efforts of yours inspired
the masses
You have awakened them
To build modern DPRK
Brick by brick

Made them independent and masters
of their own destiny
Dear leader Kim Jong Il
A rising star on the horizon
Shown the path of salvation
Of realism
Removed flunkeyism in the face of
Severe odds
Dear leader Kim Jong Il
A versatile personality
I salute you

Removed flunkeyism? Whoa.

The "My Automatic Rifle" Dance

In North Korea, propaganda has become an art form. Perhaps the most entertaining reading we've come across at DP are the "consumer" magazines (actually, there's only one) that come out of Pyongyang—in particular, *Korea Today*, the *People Magazine* of the DPRK. There are magnificent book reviews, all on Kim Jong Il's hundreds of books. No room for anything else. And no comments such as, "The plot is frayed; the characters develop like a fungus. The author has talent, but should have restricted it to flyer writing for the PTA." Nope, nothing like that. You'd end up in the gulag for a few centuries.

The harshest criticism we spotted was surprisingly scathing, though: "Many of the world's people call Kim Jong Il the giant of our times. This means that he is unique and distinguished in all aspects—wisdom, leadership, ability, personality and achievements." (*Korea Today*, No. 3, 1992.). The writer was anonymous, fearing for his life if his byline were to be published. There's coverage of some great plays and performing arts shows. One particularly caught our attention, a tear-jerking rendition of the "My Automatic Rifle Dance," performed by two voluptuous actresses prancing about the stage with their AKs.

Korea Today publishes cutting-edge, bohemian poetry that mainstream periodicals wouldn't have the balls to print:

My song, echo all the way home from the trenches.
When I smash the American robbers of happiness,
And I return home with glittering medals on my chest,
All my beloved family will be in my arms.

Cool stuff. Want to subscribe? Write: The Foreign Language Magazines, Pyongyang, DPRK.

For more laughs, write The Korean People's Army Publishing House (Pyongyang, DPRK) for a copy of their enormously popular *Panmunjom*, a chronicle of North Korea's innumerable military accomplishments. There are some great combat shots, with captions like, "U.S. imperialist troops of aggression training south Korean puppet soldiers to become cannon fodder in their aggressive war against the northern half of Korea." Another innocuous shot of a group of soldiers is depicted as, "A U.S. military advisor and the south Korean stooges are on the spot to organize the armed invasion of the northern half of Korea." Another photo shows a 1953 armistice meeting between North Korean and UN officials breaking up, and is appropriately captioned:

"The U.S. imperialist troops of aggression hastily leave after their crimes have been exposed at a meeting held at the scene of the crime."

But the DP runner-up in the book goes to a 1976 shot of an American soldier using a chain saw to cut down a tree. The caption: "The U.S. imperialist troops of aggression committed a grave provocation, cutting down a tree."

And the winner? A fuzzy shot of a letter from Secretary of State John Foster Dulles to a South Korean colonel, dated June 20, 1950. The caption reads: "Secret messages exchanged between the south Korean puppets and the U.S. imperialists to invade the north, and Dulles' secret letter instigating the puppets to start a war." It took a magnifying glass, but we read the letter:

The dinner which you gave in our honor last night was something I shall always remember. The setting was really glorious, the company distinguished, the entertainment most interesting to us and last, but not least, the food was delicious. The antique vase (you gave us) will grace Mrs. Dulles' living room in New York and always keep fresh the memory of our visit with you.

The Scoop

No one's quite sure. North Korea is perhaps the most closed society on the globe. It is also perhaps the most lobotomized. Obtaining information from abroad is illegal, as is picking up hitchhikers (who might reveal contaminating Western secrets, such as John Travolta actually is a decent actor). North Koreans can't even visit many areas in North Korea. Talking to a foreigner is grounds for arrest.

For sure, the pawns of Pyonyang have nuke capabilities, scaring the hell out of the U.S. puppet imperialists to the south and, of course, Japan. So much so, that Uncle Sam has gone to the brink of (dread!) normalizing relations with Pyongyang. When a U.S. military chopper strayed over North Korean airspace toward the end of 1994 and was shot down, killing one of the two pilots, Bill and Hillary didn't get back the remains for 10 days, and the live one for another week after that largely, and curiously, without any significant protest from Washington. Clintons are taking them seriously, at least for the moment.

North Korea's a damn difficult place to get around. Number one, there aren't any cars (bicycles were even illegal in many areas until the early 1990s). Western tourists can only visit selected areas of the country and only under the chaperoned and watchful eye of a government guide. At the time of this writing, American's weren't permitted to enter North Korea, but this was expected to change as Washington-Pyongyang relations began thawing at the end of 1994 to the temperature of Hudson Bay in January. But don't expect the red carpet. Instead, consider getting a fake Canadian passport (they can be had in Hong Kong and Bangkok) or a fake Nigerian passport (they can be had anywhere on the streets of Abuja).

The Players

Kim Il Sung

Yeah, he's dead. But long live the Kim. The effects of playing God for 46 years don't go away overnight. The North Koreans still show, and will continue to show for years, blinding adoration of their beloved pinko deity except for, perhaps, the estimated 20,000 political prisoners held in the country. But, remember, in North Korea, you're a political prisoner if you don't turn on your television in the morning.

Kim Jong Il

The Dear Leader isn't seen around a lot. Rumor has it he's in Il health. But more likely he's at a Blockbuster somewhere in L.A. either stocking up on copies of *Rambo*, *Godzilla*, and *Goodfellas* or abducting waitress/actresses. Jong's a movie freak; he owns perhaps 20,000 videotapes. It's also widely believed that Jong once kidnapped a South Korean actress and director and held them captive for nearly a decade while he played Dino de Laurentis. He shot a series of anti-Japanese films that make Crichton's *Rising Sun* look like the Meiji Constitution.

Kim Pyong Il

Half brother of Kim Jong Il. A January 1995 shootout occurred in the streets of Pyongyang between followers of Kim Jong Il and Kim Pyong Il, suggesting a power struggle between the two. Jong's response? He banished his half-brother to one place on earth more miserable to live than North Korea. He made him ambassador to Finland.

Jimmy Carter

Jimmy goes where no Bill dares. Carter was instrumental in brokering the October 1994 nuclear agreement between Pyongyang and Washington. Carter was born to be an ex-president. Enjoying the now popular and strong credentials of having been weak in office, this ex has been globe trotting to the nastiest places on earth, meeting face-to-face with bullies, warlords, pranksters and gangsters and washing his hands later. For the most part, it's worked.

The Military

North Korea has approximately 1.2 million troops, most of them massed along the border with South Korea. Fortunately, for the time being, Jong has their support. The biggest reason is that the Dear Leader apparently has no plans to socialize the military, whose elite members enjoy such Western luxuries as Mercedes, Marlboros and mint-flavored Crest.

Getting In

Passport and visa are required. Visas must be arranged prior to arrival in Pyongyang, usually through a tour packager. The best places to procure North Korean visas are in Bangkok and Macau. You must pay for your entire trip before you depart, as you will be part of a government organized tour. The North Korean Visa Office is a better bet than the North Korean embassy in Beijing. Perhaps even a better bet is through M.K. Ways in Bangkok *(57/11 Wireless Road, Bangkok 10330;* ☎ *66-2-254-4765, 255-3390, 254-7770, 255-2892).* The company specializes in tour packages to Indochina, but has introduced packages to North Korea in an exclusive agreement with the government.

Tours of North Korea vary in length, but most are for 14 days. You'll need three passport photos and approximately US$15 for the visa. If you are asked if you are a journalist, it would help facilitate the process to say no. Inside the country, you may be able to extend your visa, but, again, you'll have to pay in advance for accommodations and guide services. Your guide should be able to make the necessary arrangements.

By air, you can get to Pyongyang via Beijing on Air China or Korean Airways. By train, you can enter North Korea from Beijing via Tianjin, Tangshan, Dandong and Shinuiju. You'll be met at the Pyongyang station by your guide. By boat, you may want to try the ship that runs from Nagasaki, Japan to Wonsan on North Korea's east coast.

It would be foolish to try and enter North Korea illegally. You won't get back out.

Getting Around

You won't have much choice in the matter. Most likely, you'll be with a government guide in a government vehicle and you'll go where the government wants you to go. There exists only the skeleton of a public transit system in North Korea: very few buses, virtually no cars and no domestic flights. Travel by train is your best bet if you're not traveling by car. Again, you'll have no say. But trains are usually used to visit some of the more popular tourist sites (which sites aren't?).

Dangerous Places

The Entire Country if you are an American: The North Koreans think all Westerners who visit the country are spies. North Korea is host to few foreign tourists, and those who do get in will only see areas of the country targeted by the government for them to see. All visitors are accompanied by a government guide. You will be subjected to intense propaganda wherever you go. And you will never be permitted to stray off the beaten path unattended, although you might be occasionally permitted an unattended evening stroll around Pyongyang. Crime is not a problem in North Korea. There is wide speculation that thieves and criminals get the death penalty. In this regard, no area of North Korea can be catgorized as unsafe.

Dangerous Things

Insulting the Great Leader or the Dear Leader

Want to end up in the slammer fast? Here's how. Tell your guide that Kim Jong Il wears his mother's (Kim Jong-suk) army boots. Or, perhaps, mention you believe that the U.S. would kick North Korea's ass in soccer or in a ground war. Or mutter your suspicion that Kim Il Sung was gay. You get the point.

Giving Gifts

Never give North Koreans whom you meet gifts of any nature, especially Western items, foreign currency or any currency. Although the individual might gracefully accept your generosity (most won't), you're setting that person up for trouble. Remember, you're a spy. Anyone you come into contact with will be assumed to be collaborating with your efforts to pass information and gather intelligence. Silly, but true.

Touching a North Korean Woman

Regardless of how she might come on to you (she won't, by the way), never touch a North Korean woman. Do not even shake hands. This will be construed as an immoral act and will undoubtedly get you both in trouble.

Getting Sick

North Korea has a shortage of medical supplies, facilities and doctors. Western medicines and remedies are even more rare. On the plus side, the water is potable, and the hygiene and sanitation very good. Also, you won't find the food stalls that are found throughout the rest of Asia. North Korea is squeaky clean.

Nuts & Bolts

After the Japanese surrender of 1945, Korea was divided into two directorates: the U.S.S.R. occupied the north, while the U.S. controlled the south below the 38th parallel. In 1948, the division between the two zones was made permanent. Trade was cut off between the two zones at the advent of the cold war in the late 1940s.

The Democratic Peoples Republic of Korea (DPRK) is very much a communist nation. Before the demise of the Soviet Union, the DPRK imported nearly three quarters of a million tons of oil from the U.S.S.R. per year. These supplies have been essentially cut off. North Korea is nearly US$6 billion in debt.

The country is covered almost entirely by north-south mountain ranges and is about the size of Pennsylvania.

The language in North Korea is Korean, with indigenous elements in the vocabulary. Religions in North Korea include Buddhism and Confucianism. However, religious activities within the country basically don't exist. There is no public worshipping of deities in the DPRK. The currency is the won. The won=100 jon. Per capita income is US$1000.

The time in North Korea is GMT plus nine hours. Electricity is 220 V/60 Hz. Overseas phone calls can be made from the major hotels and IDD is available in certain establishments. Mail can be received at some hotels and the Korea International Tourist Bureau. But it will be read by the government. Fax services are readily available.

The climate in North Korea is cold and dry in the winter with warm summers. More than 60 percent of the annual rainfall occurs from June through September.

The capital of North Korea is Pyongyang.

Dangerous Days

11/12/94	An American army helicopter was shot down in North Korean airspace. One pilot died in the crash and the other repatriated more than two weeks later.
07/18/94	The death of the Great Leader, Kim Il Sung.
07/27/53	The armistice ending the Korean War was signed.
09/15/50	U.N. Commander General Douglas MacArthur made an amphibious landing at Inchon, behind North Korean lines, and routed the North Korean army.
06/27/50	U.S. President Harry Truman ordered U.S. combat units into action to enforce the U.N. condemnation of North Korea's invasion of South Korea.
06/27/50	The United Nations condemned North Korea's attack of South Korea and decreed a withdrawal of the invading forces.
06/25/50	North Korea mounts a surprise invasion of South Korea.
05/01/48	The establishment of the Democratic Peoples Republic of Korea.

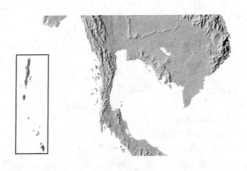

Sentinel Island and the Andamans

Lost People of the Black Waters

In the 13th century, Marco Polo described them as "idol worshippers, a bestial tribe with the head, eyes and teeth of dogs."

"The Sentinel Islanders have a cruel nature," he said, "and kill and eat all those who are not of their own people." In 1890, Sir Arthur Conan Doyle described them as "fierce, morose and intractable."

For centuries, these remote islands have sat in view of crowded shipping lanes. Ancient sailors knew that a shipwreck on the Andaman Islands meant certain death. Tales were told of shipwrecked survivors being cooked and eaten by cannibals. The Andaman islanders in all probability never dined on their victims, but one can understand how the rumors were born. The islanders' favorite piece of jewelry is the jawbone of a favorite relative, which hangs around their necks. However, rather than the natives who were the scourge of the marine merchants, it was Malay pirates doing the dirty deeds to protect their lush hideaway.

There are still island inhabitants on Sentinel Island who have not yet discovered fire, who live much like humans did 15,000 years ago. There have been discoveries of Stone Age tribes in other parts of the world in the recent past: the Tasaday in the Philippines (1960s), the Yanomami in the Amazon (the 1950s) and the Dani of Papua New Guinea (1940s). But these folks used fire, spoke complex languages and established relatively congenial relations fairly quickly with the outside world after they were "discovered." However, in the Andaman Islands, there is still a forbidden place that awaits the adventurer. The Indian government has banned any travel to the island of Sentinel in an effort to protect the inhabitants from disease and social interaction with modern humanity. Only a few anthropologists are allowed on the island to help unlock the mysteries of one of the world's most isolated communities.

The Last Stone Age Tribe in Asia

When the first anthropological expedition reached Sentinel Island in 1967, the Sentinelese hid in the jungle. When teams returned in 1970 and again in 1973, the scientists were attacked with arrows. On March 28, 1974, using police protection, a team of anthropologists entered the natives hastily abandoned huts and exchanged their bows, arrows and other artifacts for gifts of plastic buckets, cloth, sweets, a live pig and utensils. Raghibur Singh, a photographer who accompanied the expedition, created a series of photographic exhibits seen in *GEO* and a documentary film on the tribe entitled *In Search of Man.*

North Sentinel Island: North Sentinel Island, an isolated island 1200 km off the east coast of India near Myanmar is just one of the 200 or so islands that make up the Andaman group. An estimated 100 to 200 aborigines living on the 30 square miles of North Sentinel Island have, until just recently, resisted any overtures by missionaries, scientists and outsiders to meet with them. Any attempt by a foreigner to land on the tiny island would send the inhabitants fleeing or have them launching a volley of spears and poison arrows.

The Sentinelese are more Negroid than Indian; they have black skin, round faces and snow-white teeth. Negritos were the original peoples of Southeast Asia and can be found as distant from Africa as the highlands of Malaysia. Their teeth are strong enough to husk coconuts. The inhabitants use fire and won't abandon sites where fire is burning, terrified the fire will go out. They do not know how to set fire.

They protect themselves with long bows and arrows made from iron salvaged from the many shipwrecks on the island. They live off the sea, living mostly on fish and turtles, and supplement their diet by hunting wild pig or the large monitor lizards. Their culture is the paragon of simplicity; they wear no clothes, have no political structure and can only count to two ("one" and "more than one"). Even their music employs only two notes. The people paint their bodies in wavy patterns of white or ochre.

The first friendly encounter with Sentinelese was made by Indian anthropologist Professor Triloknath Pandit on January 4, 1991, 24 years after he first attempted to make contact with the islanders. Pandit and his colleagues were greeted on the beach by an unarmed party of 28 men, women and children. The anthropologists greeted the tribesmen with the traditional Sentinelese greeting of sitting in a new friend's lap, slapping your right buttock vigorously. This was a far cry from earlier visits, when they were fired upon with arrows. The tribesmen gave the team the Sentinelese version of the finger by first turning their backs then stooping on their haunches as if relieving themselves.

When rare "guests" arrive on the island, they must remove all their clothes, jewelry and even eyeglasses. If they don't, the Sentinelese will do a strip search anyhow, just to see what the newcomers are hiding.

It would be best to leave these Stone Age people alone; other Andaman tribes haven't fared so well. Women have been enslaved into brothels and offered at high prices as exotic encounters. The men have been paid with opium and alcohol by fortune hunters for the edible birds' nests that are then sold to the Chinese as a delicacy.

The Great Andaman Islands (North, Middle & South): The slow assimilation of the aboriginals of the Great Andaman Islands began when British Karen tribesmen of Burma came to the islands as timber workers in 1840. In the 1850s, the British allowed released convicts to settle on the islands. Former soldiers and workers from Bihar were given land, as were refugees from East Bengal (Bangladesh) and Ceylon (Sri Lanka).

The British inherited the islands after their colonial wars with the Danes and Austrians as spheres of influence around the Bay of Bengal. The Brits established a supply base in the islands' main town, Port Blair. Following the Sepoy Mutiny, the British began using the remote Andamans as a penal colony in 1794, completing a massive cellular jail in Port Blair in 1910 to house prisoners that had formerly spent their incarceration in Sumatra. A recent flood of settlers from overcrowded areas on the mainland has caused the population of the Andaman and Nicobar islands to increase 900 percent since 1950, doubling in the past decade alone to 315,000.

In the 1850s, the Andaman Islands tribal population was estimated at about 5000. When the aboriginals fought to repulse the intruders, the British responded by slaughtering them. Today, there are less than 400 aboriginals left (the Sentinelese, Great Andamanese, the Onge and the Jarawa) among the 200,000 others living on the chain of 361 islands.

The prisoners didn't fare so well, either.

In the first year of penal facilities on the islands, 64 of 773 convicts died of disease or heat, 87 were hanged, one committed suicide, and 140 escaped into the jungle. No one ever bothered searching for the escapees. The British in the colony faced repeated attacks from the aborigines involving pitched battles. In fact, five British citizens were awarded the Victoria Cross for killing 70 natives on Little Andaman Island alone, and hundreds of Great Andamanese warriors were slaughtered in the battle of Aberdeen, on the site where Port Blair's bazaar is situated today.

When the British arrived on the Andamans, there were an estimated 5000 to 8000 Great Andamanese. By the beginning of this century, when anthropologist Alfred Radcliffe-Brown surveyed them for his treatise on the islanders, there were 625. Today, only 28 Great Andamanese live on a reserve, the formerly uninhabited Strait Island. However, their numbers are beginning to rise.

The Andamans have always been a rich source of timber. The British established Asia's largest sawmill complex on Chatham Island, just off Port Blair. The current Indian government has declared its intent to stop any further cutting in the jungles. However, an estimated 100,000 hectares (close to 250,000 acres) have already been cleared to feed the sawmills. The cleared timber is dragged out of the woods by work elephants, and today, 1000 workers still work the antique equipment in the 140-year-old sawmill.

Officially, the government claims that 82 percent of the islands are covered by forests, but the reality is closer to 21 percent. The cleared land has been replaced by coconut and coffee plantations.

Little Andaman Island: The Onge of Little Andaman Island number only 98. Formerly hunter-gatherers, they have become addicted to tea and tobacco. Since 1967, the Onge have lived in a government settlement where they were placed to insure that they wouldn't interfere with the island's 3000 (mostly Indian) settlers. In exchange for their land, the natives' needs are generously supplied: their natural forest resources have been reduced from 731 to 110 square kilometers.

There are an estimated 200 Jarawa living on South and Middle Andaman islands. Built in the early 1980s, the 276-kilometer-long Great Andaman Trunk Road runs through the heart of the tribal habitat of the Jarawas. The construction of the route enabled many settlers to penetrate the protected area and occupy parcels of land along the road. Traversing it requires bringing along one of the 360 bush policemen who are posted at 10 stations. Originally built to preserve the tribal habitat on one side of the Trunk, the road now permits access to the area to game hunters from Bihar, who hunt wild boar, deer and swipe the islanders' scarce resources of honey and amber.

Understandably, the Jarawas have started shooting settlers with their arrows. Clashes occur mainly during the dry season, when the Jarawa are out looking for drinking water at the same time settlers are driving their cattle into the jungle. In 1990, a policeman and a settler were killed; seven other settlers were injured. In 1991, eight settlers were injured and one killed. In 1992, one person was injured in clashes with the natives.

Interview Island: Interview Island possesses a herd of formerly domesticated timber elephants which has been running wild, and has now multiplied to about 30 of the beasts. The government is considering resettling the Jarawa here, but would have to remove the rogue elephants first.

Getting In

Tourism is hoped to replace forestry as the islands' principal income source, but it may take awhile. The Andaman Islands are very remote with few facilities. The aborigines are strictly sealed off from tourists and foreigners. Not even foreign anthropologists are granted permission to visit Sentinel Island. However laborers have been found salvaging wrecks in the region, and the intrepid can still charter boats, as there are no police patrols off the island. Remember that the natives are highly susceptible to Western diseases such as polio and smallpox. Even the flu can kill them off.

Getting to Port Blair requires a two-hour flight via India Air from Calcutta and Madras. You can travel by ship if you have two to three days each way (in Calcutta, contact the Shipping Corporation of India on *13 Strand Road*, ☎ *232354*, or in Madras, the same company at *Rajaji Street;* ☎ *514401*). Cost from Calcutta is about 1500 rupees. Steerage will run you only 400 rupees. The fare is cheaper from Madras. If you arrive by air you can get a visa for 30 days but you will not be allowed to visit tribal areas or the restricted islands. Indians can visit the Andamans and Nicobars but must get a permit at Car Nicobar from the Dy Comniisionare in Port Blair.

Getting Around

The Andamans have basic tourist facilities including taxis, ferries and buses. You can even rent bikes in the larger towns. Diving and snorkeling are popular but it is illegal to collect shells or coral.

It is about 80 km by sea from Port Blair to North Sentinal. Little Andaman is over 100 km away, and Great Nicobar is almost 1000 Km south. Depending on your interest and/or purpose, a little conversation and credentials can gain you a ship and access to the forbidden islands. You can cruise certain parts of the Nicobars by contacting Oceanic Company, on MG Road in Middle Point. The well-heeled can inquire about renting the helicopter used for island hopping. Contact the Marine Department to see what type of vessels can be hired.

Getting Out

Once word is out that you have landed, it may be best to charter the boat to take you back to Calcutta—chop, chop.

Coming Attractions

In the last 10 years there have been over 100 wars and 20 million fatalities. It would take a moronically optimistic person to assume that the next millennium will bring love, music and happiness to this planet. For those who travel in harm's way we have shoved all the Little-League wars, nasty places, brewing discontents and things into this overly cute chapter.

As you probably have guessed, this book was out of date the second the ink hit the paper. When I started this book Chechnya and Rwanda were my favorite picks for coming attractions. Since then, half a million Tutsis were turned into worm food and Chechnya went from a cocky little gangster land to little Afghanistan to a wasteland. So with some trepidation and a roll of the dice we lay our selves open to ridicule and present our low-budget trailer of things to come in the next *Dangerous Places*.

Oh, by the way, you will be happy to know that the U.N. has 70,000 soldiers playing referee in 17 different peacekeeping operations.

Chad

Pieces in Our Time

A litany of coups, failures, factionalism and failed peace, Chad is perpetually embroiled in the same tensions its volatile neighbors share. What kind of chance does a country that's bordered by Libya, the Sudan and Nigeria have? Not much of one.

Chad, though, has had the dubious distinction of kicking Qaddaffi's butt on the battlefield. It was back in 1987 and had the tacit support of the French, but it had a lot of mercenaries licking their chops.

Qaddaffi may talk as if he can take on the Great Satan, but he has more than he can chew with the Little Chadian.

How bad is it here? Chad's in pieces. Political tension is high in both N'Djamena and the countryside, especially in the southern and eastern portions of Chad, as well as north of Lake Chad. Armed conflicts between government and opposition groups occur regularly. Ethnic and religious demonstrations in the major cities usually result in violent outbreaks. Chad's northern provinces bordering Libya constitute a military zone and remain heavily mined. Travel to this area is extremely dangerous and may be prohibited. Travel across the southwestern border by Cameroon is hazardous because of continuing bloodshed.

As a result of the anarchy in Chad, extraordinary security precautions are in effect. You'll definitely run into a number of nasty roadblocks—if you get that far—in N'Djamena and elsewhere in the countryside. Overland travel undertaken after dark is a death wish.

And where there isn't war, pickpockets and purse snatchers are endemic, particularly in market and commercial areas. Vehicle thefts and the breaking and entering of homes are commensurate with the rise in temperature.

Helluva place Chad is.

Ecuador

Rumble in the Jungle

What do you get when you have a border that no one can see and that changes like a baking loaf of bread? And with hot heads baking it? Why, Equador and Peru, of course. Ecuador and Peru fought a war over this 1000-mile-long swamp in the Amazon basin back in 1941 and they haven't forgotten about it. In fact, they duked it out again in 1981 and almost came to blows yet another time in 1991. There was even a bullet pinball game in early 1994.

This time it's over a 50-mile stretch in the lush, jungle-covered mountains of Cordillera del Condor that would give Equador access to the Amazon and Maranon rivers—if they had it. Although no one seems to be able to prove it, the area is supposedly rich in gold deposits. Just the rumor alone is apparently enough to raise rifles.

The Protocol of Rio de Janeiro was signed in 1942 to end that first war, but Ecuador later said "screw you" after getting their hands on one of the world's first portable calculators and realizing the ramifications of losing half their territory—nearly 77,220 square miles, to Peru. The problem with the Rio Pact was that it defined part of the border between the two countries as "the river flowing into the Santiago River." Well, there are two rivers flowing into the Santiago River. Sprinkle some gold between the two and you've got a good fight. Even though Pope John Paul II has issued a call to both countries to stop the fighting, no one's listening.

The Philippines

The Crescent and the Cross

There are about six million Muslims in the Philippines, so it isn't surprising that a number of them have gotten bitten by the Ayatollah bug. Nearly 1000 kilometers from Manila, yet only a short boat ride from the principally Muslim Malaysian and Indonesian island of Borneo, secessionists on the two main islands, Basilan and Jolo, have for centuries sought their independence.

Many of the Muslim people who inhabit the Sulu Archipelago have been split by modern national borders, and as a result, they travel frequently and freely between neighboring countries.

Numerous Muslim groups have emerged from the poor fishing villages scattered across the islands but most have evaporated over the years, taking a more conciliatory path or becoming entangled with more radical factions. As the Moros (the Moro National Liberation Front, or MNLF) work out a peace agreement with the Philippine government a new, more radical group has emerged.

The Abu Sayyaf Group (ASG) is an Islamic fundamentalist faction with zero tolerance for a Christian government. The ASG began as Tabligh (Spread the Word), an organization founded in 1972 by Iranian missionaries who came to the Philippines to spread the doctrines of Ayatollah Ruhollah Khomeini. The Abu Sayyaf Group has chosen to wage its secessionist jihad or holy war, in the idyllic Philippines.

Abu Sayyaf has also been allegedly behind a number of bomb blasts, assassinations, grenade attacks and ambushes. The group's first attack came in August 1991 when a grenade was thrown into a crowd of people in Zamboanga, killing two missionaries and wounding 40 others. In February 1993, 22 marines and four rebels were killed in an ambush.

Since then, government officials have attributed more than 15 violent incidents to the group, including another reprisal attack for the Jolo assault in June which killed three people and injured 28 in a shopping centre in General Santos City on the southern island of Mindanao.

The ASG leader is the charismatic Abdurajak Janjalani Abubakar, a Filipino trained in Libya and fluent in Arabic. He was reported killed in combat with government troops on January 13 but DP has heard that he is still very much alive. Janjalani is the son of a poor fisherman. He studied Islam and Arabic in Saudi Arabia in the 1980s and continued his studies in Libya. He returned to the Philippines, where he traveled throughout the Muslim regions giving lectures and preaching Islamic fundamentalism, its ultimate goal being the creation of an independent fundamentalist state in the southern Philippines.

However, the separatist movement in the Philippines began well before Janjalani. It started in 1972 with the MNLF which, with Arab support, was unsuccessful in liberating the large Islamic community in the region. Libya stepped in to broker a cease fire and, today, the Moros are essentially a mainstream political entity. The Abu Sayyaf group first appeared in August 1991.

Tabligh's military arm is called the Mujahedeen Commando Freedom Fighters (MCFF), also referred to as the Abu Sayyaf group and after Janjalini, who goes by the handle of Abu Sayyaf (Father of the Sword). The group is based in Darayan, Patikul and Sulu and can muster only about 120 armed combatants, although they're fierce, namely because they can afford to be. They are supported by Libya and Iran and generate their own funds by kidnapping business people. On January 23, 1995, Muslim rebels kidnapped a businesswoman and her companion in the southern Philippines and demanded one million pesos and 100 cattle for their safe return. The Abu Sayyaf group also held five journalists for four days before releasing them unharmed on January 23, 1995. Scores of people, including foreign missionaries, have been kidnapped in the southern Philippines.

Since August of 1992, the rebels have typically attacked members of the Roman Catholic Church. They kidnap priests, missionaries and nuns, usually releasing them after a lengthy captivity. The MCFF also provides protection for the many smugglers and pirates that navigate the Sulu Sea. There have been reports of Mujahedeen veterans from the Afghan war providing training in guerrilla tactics and explosives.

It is believed that the ASG is at least partially financed by Iran and Pakistan, as evidenced by the recent arrest of four foreigners for visa irregularities. The men were from Jordan, Pakistan and Iran. One of them carried a large amount of cash. One of the Jordanians was Mahmoud Abdel-Jalil, the Jordanian regional director of the International Islamic Relief Organization. Although Abdel-Jalil is a 10-year resident of the Philippines, it is suspected that he has ties to Islamic extremists in Pakistan and Iran.

The current MNLF chairman, Nur Misuari, operating from an unknown base in Saudi Arabia, is opposed to Abu Sayyaf's attacks on clerics and has publicly asked the group to release their hostages. Abu Sayyaf has divorced itself from the Moros who are now working with the army to free hostages and turn in Abu Sayyaf members.

On January 17, 1995, the government sent in 200 additional soldiers to the remote southern island of Basilan to "neutralize" the Abu Sayyaf group, adding to the strength of more than 2000 soldiers already deployed in the area, who face perhaps 200 guerrilla soldiers. Basilan has been the group's base of operations. On January 13, 33 guerrillas and seven soldiers were killed and 15 other rebels and eight troopers were wounded in a major firefight between the two forces.

A large shipment of arms from Afghanistan arrived in Cotabatu in January 1995 for the MCFF. Estimates put the shipment at some 3500 high-powered guns. There were reports the cache included surface-to-air missiles.

A major government offensive against the Abu Sayyaf was launched on Basilan in January 1995, killing Abu Sayyaf's leader Janjalani. Philippines president Ramos de-

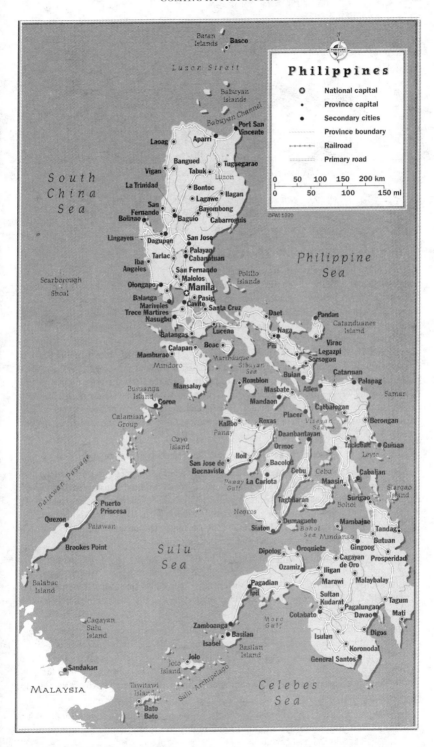

clared Basilan Island under a "state of calamity." He also whined about the $38,000 a day it was costing him to chase down the fanatics. Meanwhile the legislature authorizes the purchase of 2 billion dollars worth of arms over the next five years.

Watch out for these guys.

OUCH...

A former communist rebel in the Zamboanga del Norte region of Datangan who believed his life was being threatened was killed when a grenade he was carrying for protection detonated while he was sleeping. The blast also killed the man's son and a relative, as well as injuring his wife and daughter and four other relatives. The man was sleeping with the grenade in his trousers pocket. Meanwhile, airport security officers in Manila were seizing aerosol sprays, perfumes and lotions from passengers bound for the U.S. No word on whether officials were seeking to prevent these items from blowing up in the pockets of passenger's trousers at 37,000 feet.

Getting Out

If you find yourself in a pinch, or need quick transport out of the Philippines, you can charter a boat from Sitangkai for the 40-km trip to Semporna in the Malaysian state of Sabah. This, of course, is completely illegal. However, there are a slew of boats that make the trip to the busy market in Semporna. Keep in mind that Sabah has its own customs and immigration requirements, so you'll need a separate stamp when you move back and forth from Sabah to peninsular Malaysia. These waters are also home to Sulu pirates, actually a combination of minor smugglers and armed thugs who prey on large commercial vessels. Pirates have also been known to rob banks and terrorize entire towns in coastal Sabah. Just inquire at any fishing village or dockside hangout in Sitangkai. Usually, you'll have to cross at night and don't be surprised to pay two to three times the normal rate of P150. Going the other way is also easy; there are boatmen who can hook you up with the many speedboats that are for rent in Semporna. Be careful dealing with the Ray-Banned entrepreneurs you meet along the docks. They might turn you in for the reward money and simply pocket the sizeable fee you paid them to get you across.

The Pirates of Zamboanga

Zamboanga is a colorful, dangerous place and home to pirates, smugglers, terrorists and the most charming people I have met. The name Zamboanga is derived from the Samal word *samboangan*, meaning "anchorage." The Samals live in stilt houses built over the shallow waters. The children play in the "front yards" just like children play on grass, but in the water. They travel to market to visit neighbors in tiny dugout canoes. They find it quite exciting when foreigners visit; they wave and hold up their children for a picture when strangers are in town.

Zamboanga is a city of half a million people and is the center for the export of copra timber and other natural products. The population is 75 percent Christian and 25 percent Muslim. Originally a Christian outpost surrounded by Muslims, the city was occupied by American troops in 1899. The Army's 1911 Colt 45 caliber pistol was actually developed because the smaller-caliber bullets would not stop the drug-crazed Moros.

Filipino Muslims have been called *moros* since Spanish colonial times (the word moro means "Moor" or "Muslim" in Spanish). They believe that Sabah, the oil- and timber-rich state of Malaysia, should be part of the Philippines. They base their claim on the historic rights, going back to the 16th century, belonging to the Sultanate of Sulu. One of the sultans leased Sabah to a private firm, The British North Borneo Company, in 1878 even though the boundaries were ill-defined and disputed by other rulers in the region.

In 1946, the company handed Sabah over to the British government which, in turn, ceded it to Malaysia in 1963. But Manila claims that the Sultan of Sulu had already transferred his rights to the

Philippines in 1962. The ancient 16th-century document is considered a gimmick by Manila, similar to selling a tourist the Brooklyn Bridge, as both the Sultan of Sulu (or Sooloo) and the Sultan of Brunei grandly claimed all the islands in the region even though they had little idea of just how large Borneo really was.

Even now, the Philippines has never renounced its formal claims to Sabah, principally because the Philippines congress would have to ratify such a step.

The Muslims living in southwestern Mindanao and on the Sulu islands have been trading for centuries with their fellow Muslims in Sabah to the west and Sulawesi (Indonesia) to the south without considering that anyone would create a demarcation line between them. There are between 300,000 and 700,000 illegal immigrants from the southern Philippines living in Sabah, as well as Timorese from the Indonesian island of Timor. They work cheaply, but are a growing concern for the Sabahans because the Sabahans are outnumbered.

Zamboanga is a historic trading center where luxury goods from Indonesia, Malaysia, Singapore and China are as plentiful as the raw materials from the sea and jungles that surround the city. The goods are brought in on *tora-toras*, flat-bottom boats that are usually loaded to the gunnels with cheap TVs, beer, cigarettes and other prized items.

The "pirate" ships are an assortment of rusting freighters, aging ferries, modern speedboats, basligs—the large boats with outriggers to avoid capsizing in the heavy seas—and speedy canoe-like vintas with their colorful sails.

The amount of trade in high-ticket items from duty-free ports such as Labuan in Brunei make legitimate traders easy targets for pirates who employ everything from parangs (machetes) to machine guns to kill their victims.

There is also an intriguing group of people who carry on the centuries-old tradition of living on the sea. The 10,000 to 20,000 Bajau or sea gypsies, are a nomadic people who roam the Sulu seas, only landing to trade and, some say, to die. Their 30-foot-long boats formerly were intricately carved and painted. However, these days, they're getting simpler and less ornate. The inhabitants catch and then sun-dry fish topside; most of the boats carry chickens. The boat people cook on open fires and carry all the staples they need to be self-sufficient. Some dive for giant clams and other shellfish, while others catch barracuda and slice them into artistic shapes to dry.

Kurdistan

Blowing Your Kurds Away

After waging ten years of all-out warfare with the PKK someone in the Turkish government decided to add up the cost: $179 billion dollars and 22,000 people dead. That radically changes the official estimate of only 12,500 dead.

The Kurds are a divisive, independent group of tribes from East Turkey, Iraq, Iran and Syria. Although there has been ongoing war between Turkey and the PKK, the Kurds as a people do not necessarily condone or even care about the terrorist groups actions. The actions of the PKK do little to help the Kurds gain political and financial clout. The possibility of creating a new country carved out of Iran, Iraq, Turkey and Syria is as likely as Saddam taking a military planning job at the Pentagon. In the meantime, warfare and fear grip Eastern Turkey. The army and the PKK have killed over 12,000 people and demolished over 2000 villages during the last seven years in an attempt to erase their presence. After President Bush gallantly came to the aid of Kuwait, a country weakened by too many late nights at the disco, the Kurds thought they were next in line to be liberated from big bad Saddam. Obviously the Iraqi Kurds never studied postwar Eastern European history or oil exploration. The U.S. did send them bread. We save the military stuff for rich backward people; until they get that oil out of the ground they will have to be poor backward people. For now the Kurds have possession of frozen windswept mountains in a country they call Kurdistan. The capital of Kurdistan is Erbil, a hellish limbo with little chance of being granted independence. A third of Turkey's members of parliament and foreign ministers have Kurdish backgrounds.

The Players

Patriotic Union of Kurdistan

Led by Jalal Talbani who lives in Damascus. Supported by the Turkish Army.

Democratic Party of Kurdistan

Led by Massud Barzini and backed by Iran and Iraq because they consider him the lesser of two evils. They consider Talbani to be a pawn of the CIA and Turkey.

Kurdish Hezbollah

A Kurdish fundamentalist group backed by Iran.

The Turkish Military and Police forces

The presence of over 160,000 military and police has turned Eastern Turkey into a war zone and travel is strictly controlled.

The Kurds

Kurdistan became part of the Ottoman Empire about a thousand years ago. It was a feudalistic system holding together a mixture of mountain people. Today, Kurdistan is a poor region, backward, difficult to reach, underdeveloped by Turkey for fear their neighbors, the former Soviet Union, would annex the region.

The Kurds were considered as bandits ("*eksiya*" in Turkish). Stubborn, backward people they refused to fit into the societies that had built countries around them. For years police and military dealt harshly with the Kurds who not only rebelled against outside authority but continually warred amongst themselves.

Ataturk

In 1928, Mustafa Kemal or Ataturk began the process of unifying Turkey. As with many strong nationalistic movements his required the assimilation and subjugation of the many political and ethnic groups into one stronger group. Ataturk (Father of the Turks) chose to align Turkey with the West rather than the East. The changes meant going so far as to change the written language from the Arabic form to the Latin and even banning the fez. Although the seat of the government is in Ankara and the major focus of Turks is Istanbul it did not address the needs of the 20 million or so Kurds who inhabit the poorer east. Kurds also are the major minority in southeastern Turkey. The Kurds are the major minority in the bordering areas of Iraq, Iran and Syria. Turkey's new love affair with the west meant that they found themselves with their Kurdish language banned and their customs under siege because of the need to Westernize all aspects of Turkish life.

The Kurdish Worker's Party (PKK)

Formed November 27, 1978 in Siverek and led by Abdullah Ocalan who runs the operation out of a comfortable house in Damascus, Syria.The PKK was outlawed by the Turkish military government in 1980; full scale warfare erupted in 1985 starting in Siverek. In 1987 Turkey declared war on the PKK . PKK guerrillas are recruited from the villages of Eastern Turkey and the refugee camps in Northern Iraq. They are trained in terrorist training camps in Lebanon and Iraq. One of the main PKK bases is in Zaleh near the Iranian border with Turkey. The PKK has been responsible for the deaths of over 12,000 people.

Politically the Kurds also found themselves a long way down in the pecking order when it came to representation, financial aid and clout, since the Turkish government has been loathe to develop the east because of the threat of invasion from former Soviet Union, Iran and Iraq.

To fight for their rights a Marxist group called the PKK or Kurdish Worker's Party was formed to create an independent Kurdistan. Initially the PKK pursued its demands through political actions. There were various Kurdish political parties but none that demanded absolute autonomy to the party and carried out acts of murder and intimidation like the PKK. The PKK was outlawed in 1980 for its terrorist activities against the government. Although there had been terrorist incidents since the 70s, full scale warfare erupted in 1985 starting in Siverek (see "In a Dangerous Place: Eastern Turkey") and has continued uninterrupted now for ten years.

In 1987 Turkey essentially declared war on the PKK and locked down the entire eastern Provinces. The presence of over 160,000 military and police has turned eastern Turkey into a war zone and travel is strictly controlled. As of this writing there are major military operations against the Kurds near Tuncelli and sporadic firefights and sabotage throughout southeastern Turkey.

PKK guerrillas are recruited from the villages of eastern Turkey and the refugee camps in Northern Iraq. They are trained in terrorist training camps in Lebanon and Iraq.One of the main PKK bases is in Zaleh near the Iranian border with Turkey. Before and after the Gulf War Iraq carried out a campaign of genocide to effectively push the Kurds out of Iraq and into Turkey. In 1989, Turkey accepted 150,000–300,000 Iraqi Kurds who were fleeing extermination by Saddam Hussein. It is estimated that Hussein's brutal campaign pushed 1.5 million Kurdish refugees into Northern Iraq and Southeastern Turkey where many live in makeshift camps.

Iran supports the Kurds since they create conflict in one of the more Westernized and liberal Muslim nations.

The greatest damage the Kurds do to Turkey is to realign this wealthy and sophisticated country with its more backward but equally fractured Eastern neighbors. The chances of Turkey joining the EC are slim and the increasing force that the local and national governments use against the PKK is reinforcing the brutal genocidal image the Armenians have projected.

On the other hand, the PKK has broken the cardinal rule of terrorist groups in alienating the Western press and governments. There is little sentiment for the PKK's extortion tactics against its own people. The PKK is a revolution run by an absentee landlord. They have effectively removed any constructive voice for change by being banned as a political party in Turkey. They are ineffective in providing normal fundraising or publicity by being banned in Europe. They cannot form a workable government to take care of their own people, forcing the U.S. and U.N. to effectively run Kurdistan as an aid station in Northern Iraq. This does not give them a solid footing in the international community. The atrocities committed against unarmed schoolteachers, Kurdish women, children and old men are publicized by the Turkish government and media.

Kurdistan or Northern Iraq

The outlook for the Kurds is dim since their demands for a new homeland would not only remove a major chunk of Turkey but a major portion of Iran, Iraq and Syria as well. They also run up against Turkey's goal of uniting the various peoples within its border and the call for peaceful and political settlements to rights, but they maintain a hard line on secessionist groups. Even if Turkey was to be conciliatory, many people forget that the PKK is waging a battle on four fronts (not including its terrorist activities in Europe) and has little chance of convincing the hardline governments of Iraq, Iran and Syria to give them concessions.

The PKK targets the local population and is on the run from the Turkish Special Ops teams. The PKK control the countryside at night and the government controls the major cities. There is continual warfare on a daily basis as the Turkish government seeks to annihilate the 10,000 or so ground troops the PKK has in the country. The PKK shows no quarter to Kurds they think are sympathizers, yet are surprisingly lenient with foreigners they kidnap. Of the 20 or so foreigners they kidnap in a year, all are released without harm.

Welcome to Turkey, Now Duck

In 1993 the Kurds began a sporadic bombing campaign in Istanbul and Antalya designed to scare off Western tourists. In Europe in 1993, the Kurds created global publicity when they executed a series of terrorist activities against Turkish embassies and businesses (airline offices, banks and travel agents). Germany, with a Turkish community of over 2 million (a quarter of them, Kurds) was understandably nervous about becoming a battleground and quickly banned 36 Kurdish political organizations.

France also banned two Kurdish political groups and Great Britain is trying to figure out how to stop the regular extortion of Turkish emigrants and/or their businesses by the Kurds.

Their efforts have been successful in creating sympathy for a people deposed. In our own humble opinion, one of the most powerful opinion shapers was Coskun's photos of the Kurdish refugees fighting for bread featured in news magazines around the world including *Time* magazine. The problem is that there is little even a sympathetic person can do to help the Kurds.

While the U.S. turns a blind eye to the PKK atrocities in Turkey they are actively using the Kurds to help destabilize Hussein in Iraq. "Kurdistan" was effectively created when the U.S and Turkish military (Operation Provide Comfort) created a safe zone for the 1.5 million Kurds displaced by Hussein's attempt to eliminate the Kurds. During the three year military occupation by the Americans they managed to form two major political parties from the diverse group of Kurds. There were actually democratic elections held among the area's 3.5 million residents in 1992. The area is essentially divided into East and West. The West is controlled by the Kurdish Democratic Party (KDP) and the east by the Patriotic Union of Kurdistan (PUK) led by Jalal Talabani with the center being the regional capital of Arbil, which is still equally contested between the two parties.

In May of 1994 fighting broke out between the two parties after a PUK leader was assassinated. The two parties then decided to settle their differences without the aid of a ballot box. Using anti-aircraft guns and other heavy weaponry, they duked it out in the central mountain town of Shaqlawa.

The Iraqi National Congress with the appropriate acronym INC, an organization set up with covert Western support to unite the Iraqi factions fighting Saddam Hussein, is trying to resolve the conflict between the two sides. The INC's military wing has even acted as a buffer force.

About 200 people have been killed in a war that was conducted while the leader of the PUK was in Damascus.

China

The Next U.S.S.R.?

China possesses no known terrorist groups, but a ride on one of their domestic airliners may make you wish they did—so the plane could be hijacked to a country with decent air traffic control. Unlike in other parts of the world, hijackers in China aren't trying to draw world attention to a cause (they wouldn't get it, anyway). They're not likely to make ransom demands. And it's not done for the love of God. They're simply trying to get the hell out. Taiwan is the favored destination. There were 10 hijackings to Taipei in 1993 and three other foiled attempts. However, the hijacking problem may be more serious than these figures reflect. A May 25, 1994 report carried by the Beijing-controlled Hong Kong China News Agency said that airport police in Shenzhen, the Special Economic Zone near Hong Kong, claimed to have successfully prevented 16 hijacking attempts to that date in 1994.

Safety on China's roads, railways, boats and aircraft is also questionable. In 1993, 73 people were killed in three separate air crashes. Hundreds of other people have been killed in road, rail and boating accidents and China now has a growing reputation with foreign tourists as one of the least safe places to travel in the world, although this isn't entirely justified.

There is no real terrorist threat to Americans traveling to, or doing business in, the People's Republic of China (PRC). An insignificant 39 terrorist incidents and other forms of political violence have been reported since 1988, however; 21 of these occurred in 1993. Americans as a specific group are not targeted by the Chinese but will, as all foreigners to this relatively closed society, continue to receive the usual close scrutiny of the native inhabitants.

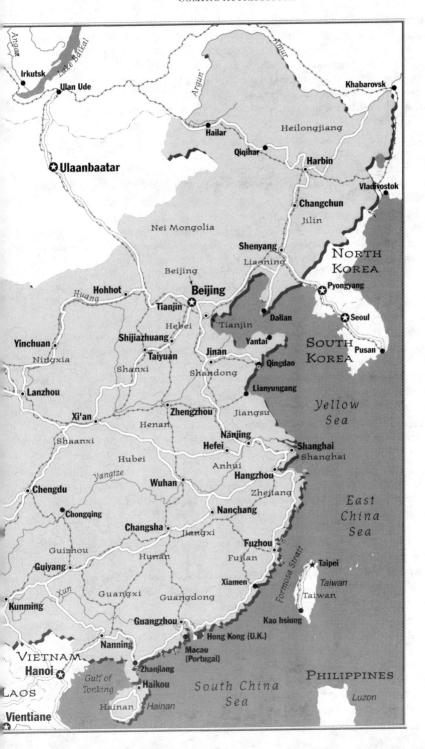

Although the crime rate is rising, it is lower than those rates found in the West. Crimes are generally nonviolent; thefts form the crux of them. However, some analysts forecast that the thrusting of the Chinese economy in recent years is creating an environment that may breed disorder in the future. They cite burgeoning social conflicts, including racial and religious disputes, which may endanger stability. Indicators include a surge in major crimes, gang activities, social evils, fraud, violence and industrial accidents. Major crime incidents have risen by nearly 20 percent annually in the past four years.

White-collar crime seems to have arrived in China. Some of these S&L wanna-bes give bribes to banking officials to launder and move tremendous amounts of foreign exchange out of the country. The number of assaults on public security officers has also risen. The number of injuries rose from about 600 in 1985 to more than 8000 in 1993; 275 officers were killed.

As China becomes more stratified, the lower classes are becoming more prone to commit crimes. China is not a dangerous place if you stay in the tourist ruts. However, you may find yourself in trouble in some of the out-of-way places. The most dangerous places for highway robbery are in the remote mountainous regions. Other dangers include organized raids on passenger trains and simple thefts from hotels. There was a 36-hour orgy of rioting in Guangdong Province when the Ling Xiao Yan resort came under attack by locals. The resort caters to Chinese visitors from Hong Kong and Macau. In March, 1994, 24 Taiwanese tourists were killed on Qiandao Lake.

The Chinese Public Security Ministry has admitted the country does not have the resources to protect tourists from the rising rate of crime across the mainland. The Qiandao Lake incident may be a precursor of what's to come. There have been numerous recent incidents where tourists have been robbed, beaten and even murdered. There was one occasion in Zhejiang involving 70 participants and 80 police where local residents battled with a tour group.

A secret Pentagon report (China in the Near Term) predicted that when the Chinese leader Deng Xiaoping dies—which is expected any day—there's a 50 percent chance that China will break up like the USSR did.

This isn't good news for tourists and even worse news for the government because tourism to China has been surging in recent years. About 1.74 million foreign tourists visited Beijing alone in 1992, compared with less than 300,000 in 1978. In the first six months of 1993, 882,600 foreigners visited the capital city, up 13 percent over the corresponding period the preceding year. Throughout China, tourism brought in a whopping US$1.69 billion in the first five months of 1993, up 22.2 percent over the same period in 1992. That figure is a record.

The U.S. Department of State published the following general crime report on February 3, 1994. It includes coverage for Beijing, Chengdu, Guangzhou, and Shenyang Consular Districts.

"China continues to enjoy economic prosperity though it has been somewhat tempered in recent months by inflationary trends. Its political structure continues to exert strong control over all sectors of Chinese society with only minor disruptions in the countryside over payment of taxes and loss of some government subsidies. Americans are not specifically targeted as a distinct subgroup of foreigners, but do experience the same degree of scrutiny that all other classes of non-ethnic Chinese receive.

"China experiences a low, but gradually rising crime rate. Crime has increased principally in the major cities where economic progress is most evident. Most crime is nonviolent in nature, with pickpockets and purse snatchers accounting for the bulk of petty thefts.

"Police are only moderately effective in providing assistance throughout the country. Most police have only a little formal education and their equipment and training are below those standards set by American enforcement agencies. Response to an emergency may take between 15 and 30 minutes. Police generally speak little English; in Beijing, foreigners may call the police foreign control unit at ☎ 552729 for an English speaker.

"Americans and other foreign visitors to China are occasionally victims of criminals. Most crime remains nonviolent, with the victim's lack of awareness of his/her surroundings being the major contributor to incidents. Crowded public areas such as hotel lobbies, bars and restaurants, or public transportation and tourist sites are major risk areas that account for almost all of the reported crime scenes where thefts have occurred. Travelers should avoid using unmarked taxis. Legal taxis are clearly marked, are metered, and should have the driver's identification clearly displayed.

"Travelers must protect all their valuables assiduously. All identification media and travel documents, such as passports and airline tickets, need to be safeguarded. Hotel safe deposits can be used for this purpose. Travelers should limit the items they carry on the street to a minimum. They should carry identification and utilize a money belt or concealed abdominal pack in which to secure it."

The following constitutes Shanghai's 1993 report on crime and safety information:

"Major civil disturbances, by Western standards, are rare in Shanghai. However, even mundane situations such as traffic accidents or arguments can draw a large crowd almost instantly. Though these situations seldom get out of control, visitors should not attempt to photograph or videotape the incident. Involved parties or police authorities may take exception to having their photo taken without prior approval and the photographer may suddenly find himself at the center of attention. Americans are not specifically targeted as a distinct subgroup of foreigners, but do experience the same degree of scrutiny that all other classes of non-ethnic Chinese receive.

"Shanghai experiences a low, but steadily rising crime rate. Most crime is nonviolent in nature, with pickpockets, purse snatchings, and bicycle thefts accounting for the bulk of criminal incidents. Burglaries of residences and thefts from hotel rooms are on the rise.

"Police are moderately effective in providing assistance, considering the low crime threat environment. Levels of authority and functional responsibilities are more specialized among Shanghai police authorities in comparison to American counterparts. Shanghai police officers often have a specific function, i.e. traffic control, and are generally not trained to deal with situations beyond the scope of their specialty. The training and equipment they do receive is below those standards set by American law enforcement agencies. Response to an emergency may take between 15 and 30 minutes. Police generally do not speak English, but will generally attempt to overcome language barriers to help foreigners requiring assistance. Foreigners may call the police foreign control unit at ☎ 321-1997 for an English speaker.

"Americans and other foreign visitors to Shanghai are occasionally victims of criminals. Most crime remains non-violent, with the victim's lack of awareness of his/her surroundings being the major contributor to incidents. Crowded public areas such as shopping areas, bars, public transportation and tourist sites are major risk areas that account for almost all of the reported thefts. Travelers should avoid using unmarked taxis. Legal taxis are clearly marked and metered and should have the driver's identification clearly displayed.

"Travelers must protect their valuables assiduously. All identification, media and travel documents, such as passports and airline tickets, need to be safeguarded. Hotel safe deposits can be used for this purpose. Travelers should limit the items they carry on the street to the minimum. They should carry identification and utilize a money belt or concealed abdominal pack in which to secure it."

Getting In

Passports and visas are required. Most tourist visas are valid for only one entry. Travelers are required to obtain new visas for additional entries into China. Those who arrive without a visa will be fined a minimum of $400 at the port of entry and might not be allowed to enter China (or get out!). A transit visa is required for any stop (even if one does not exit the plane or train) in China. Specific information is available through the Embassy of the People's Republic of China or from one of the consulates general in Chicago, Houston, Los Angeles, New York or San Francisco.

Chinese Embassy in the U.S.

2300 Connecticut Avenue, NW
Washington, DC 20008
☎ *(202) 328-2500.*

U.S. Embassy in China

Xiu Shui Dong Jie 3
Beijing -100600
☎ *[86] (1) 532-3831*

Macedonia

Witch's Brew

Here, in the most southern of the Yugoslavian republics, a witch's brew of ethnic and religious hatred is stirring. As the various ethnic factions vie for dominance in this landlocked domain which was once part of the former Yugoslavia, the United Nations is busy conducting a census of Macedonia's two million people to create at least a mildly accurate picture of this country's explosive ethnic composition. Serbs, Turks, Vlachs, Greeks, Bulgarians, Gypsies and others want to wield political power. When it's all said and done, there aren't enough flag designs left to accommmodate separate countries for each of these ethnic subdivisions.

Guatemala

Body Parts

Guatemala's 33-year-old insurgency was supposedly put to rest by a covert war organized, financed and efficiently run by Uncle Sam in eastern Guatemala in 1968. It then blossomed to include a western highlands uprising in the 1970s after 500,000 Indians took their cue from the success of the Sandinistas in Nicaragua and revolted against the Guatemalan government.

Of a total Guatemala population of 9.5 million, some 150,000 were killed in the ensuing fighting. More than 440 villages were entirely destroyed and 45,000 people fled to Mexico and the United States. Since then the government since has kept Guatemalans on a short leash by militarizing the country. Today, there are only 45,000 soldiers holding that leash.

The **Guatemalan National Revolutionary Unit** (Unidad Revolucionaria Nacional Guatemalteca or, URNG) is what remains of previous rebel groups. Although the government believes only 800 members of the URNG still exist, the actual figure and its sphere of influence may be much larger. In September1993, an arms cache of more than 750 machine guns, 310 kilos of explosives, as well as rocket and grenade launchers, was discovered in Nicaragua en route to the URNG in Guatemala. Nontheless, the core of the URNG has been forced back into the highlands of the northwest, northern Peten province and along the Pacific coast in the volcanic regions.

Although the URNG has been in peace negotiations with the government, the group has been busy blowing up bridges, tossing bombs and engaging in spirited fire-fights with the Guatemalan army. In the fall of 1993, in San Marcos province, three soldiers were killed and 27 wounded in a 100-hour firefight. There were approximately 300 soldiers killed in 1992, up from 27 killed in 1991. The military claimed it killed 125 guerrillas in that period.

With the URNG receiving support from Fidel Castro, Nicaragua and income derived from drug trafficking and through the government's continued hard-line stance with the guerrillas, there appears little chance of a breakthrough in the peace process.

In 1993, there were three URNG hit-and-run attacks on the military, numerous mines laid and the destruction of power lines and generators in Quiche, Huehuetenango, Alto Verapaz and the outskirts of Guatemala City.

The URNG has also been engaged in eco-terrorism made popular by Saddam Hussein during the Gulf War. Near the end of 1993, rebels began striking oil tanker convoys in the Peten and Alta Verapaz regions, spilling 400,000 gallons of fuel and crude oil into the countryside.

Although 50 percent of Guatemala's population is Indian, its government remains nothing more than a penny arcade parade of military strongmen backed by the U.S. government.

BOXING MAGDELENA

Small babies are a big thing in Guatemala. A lot of Americans like to go down there to pick one up and raise it at home. The problem is, most Guatemalans think that Yankees are buying the babies for body parts. Stranger than fiction, but true. The Guatemalan newspaper Prensa Libre *recently published a story showing the prices for human organs. Shortly afterward, a group of farmers beat an American woman to death.*

Janice Vogel adopted a young Guatemalan girl. Four days later she was trapped by an angry mob who assumed she was going to sell her adopted child for body parts. Babies do get stolen in Guatemala for illegal adoptions—young boys are worth about US$500—but not for body parts. Try telling that to the Guatemalans, who can't tell the difference between a stolen Blazer and a little boy.

Indonesia

Timor Bomb

Indonesia is an archipelago of more than 13,000 islands, the largest of which are Kalimantan (Indonesian Borneo), Sumatra, Irian Jaya (West Irian), Sulawesi and Java. Nearly two-thirds of the population lives on Java, one of the most densely populated areas in the world. Sumatra contains 25 percent of Indonesia's land area and 20 percent of its population.

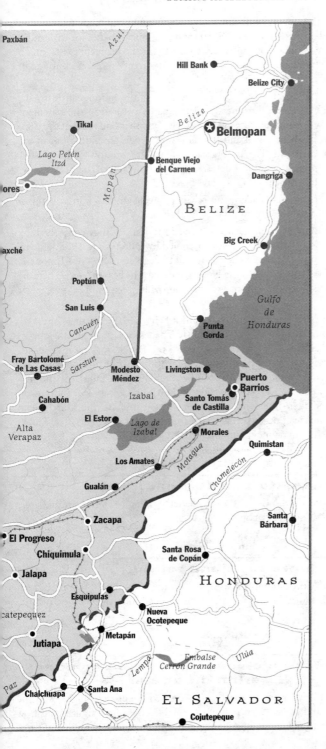

But it's on the far flung island of Timor where a lingering insurgency festers. The Timorese are not fond of their Indonesian rulers and continue to battle for their independence. The Indonesian government is reticent to admit the problem exists, much less the gravity of it. Nonetheless, at least 450 armed Timorese insurgents continue to wreak havoc among the occupying Indonesian forces.

The biggest hotel in Dili was formerly the headquarters of the Indonesian Army Intelligence Group. East Timorese prisoners were regularly tortured in the basement here and then taken away for execution. Some estimates say that one third of the population of East Timor has been killed and the remaining rebels are hiding out in the most remote areas of the island. The Indonesian military's reputation for brutal suppression of this 16-year uprising has not deterred efforts, however, of the Jakarta government to develop tourism facilities in the area.

On the other end of the archipelago, the rebels of Aceh, on the northern tip of Sumatra, have all but ceded their war of independence.

The Portuguese were the first Europeans to arrive in Indonesia; they controlled the eastern half of the island of Timor until it was occupied by Indonesia in 1975. Slowly, the Dutch gained control of most of the islands and occupied them until Indonesia was granted independence in 1949. As the Netherlands East Indies, Indonesia became one of the world's most lucrative colonial outposts providing tea, rubber, rice, sugar and petroleum.

The Indonesian independence movement began early in the 20th century, but it really didn't get a head of steam until World War II. Japanese forces occupying the islands in 1942 induced in the natives hostility toward the Dutch, making it easier for them to control the region. In this case, it made a great ingredient to successful freedom fighting. After the Japanese lost the war and were no longer around, the Indonesians decided they weren't into any outside domination. In 1945, Indonesian nationalists proclaimed their independence and said "get lost" to the Dutch, who failed in their opportunistic efforts to retake what they thought was theirs. The Dutch caved in and granted Indonesia independence in 1949.

Mali

Timbuktu and Tuaregs, too

The Tuaregs, the nomadic dispossessed of the Sahel, continue to fight a mean desert war of revolution in this hot dusty country.

Morocco

More rock and rolling

The Government of Morocco informs us that there are currently 30 foreign backed Islamic fundamentalists working to advance their causes. Hide the Barbies and the John Wayne movies dudes.

Nigeria

Grow hair, pick up chicks and make big money in Nigerian oil deals!

Travelers know that traveling to corrupt, impoverished Nigeria can make even the hardened swear off travel to Africa entirely. But now Nigerians have figured out how to bring corruption and misery straight to you without your leaving the comfort of your office. Nigerian business scams are confidence schemes, designed to exploit the trust you develop in your Nigerian partner and to bilk you of goods, services or money. The scams are flexible and operators adapt them to take the greatest advantage of the target—you.

Every week the U.S. Embassy in Lagos tries to console victems of these scams where businessfolks have lost sums ranging from a few thousand to upwards of one million dollars. Patsies who have traveled all the way to Nigeria to clinch these "lucrative"deals have been threatened, assaulted or even killed. Local police couldn't care less and Nigerian officials find the whole thing funny. The U.S. embassy can't do much more than lend you a toothbrush and a quarter to call your mother for airfare. Some Nigerian immigration officials have begun to warn folks upon arrival at Lagos airport but the lemmings keep arriving to pick up their pot of gold.

Scams range from attempts to engage American businesspeople in fictitious money-transfer schemes to fraudulent solicitations to supply goods in fulfillment of nonexistent Nigerian government contracts. Most scam operators are sophisticated and may take victims to staged meetings, often held in borrowed offices at Nigerian government ministries. They do their research and can often provide plausible, but nonexistent, orders written on seemingly genuine Ministerial stationery replete with official stamps and seals. Nigerian business scams are not always easy to recognize and any unsolicited business proposal should be carefully scrutinized.

It is not possible to describe here how each of several hundred different scams works but they all center on greed (yours), gullibility (yours), and money (yours). Here are brief descriptions of the most common schemes:

The Money Transfer

The operator claims to have a large sum of money, usually millions of dollars worth of ill-gotten gains, which needs to be transferred to a safe bank account abroad. The Central Bank of Nigeria is often, though by no means always, mentioned. You, as the bank account owner, are promised a percentage of the huge sum, just for use of your account. You may be asked to provide blank, signed invoices, letterhead and bank account information, or to send money for transfer taxes. Some businesses have found their accounts looted by the persons to whom they sent account information.

The Fraudulent Order

The operator usually places a small ($1000 or so) order, paying with a genuine cashier's check drawn on a European bank. The operator then places another, somewhat larger order again paying with a genuine instrument. Then, you receive an order by DHL. Your Nigerian partner urgently needs a large quantity of your product air-shipped. Confident in your partner, you ship, but, this time, the cashier's check (which looks the same as before) is fake. Experienced U.S. businesspeople today usually require either full payment in advance of shipment or an irrevocable letter of credit confirmed by a U.S. bank.

The Charitable Donation

The operator offers to make a donation to your organization, asking for bank account information. Then, the operator loots your account or asks for advance payment of a fee to ensure conversion of *naira* into dollars.

The Contract

The operator claims to have a Nigerian government contract and needs your company's expertise to do the job. The operator scams you by collecting thousands of dollars in fees before you can do business. When fees are legitimate, they are published by Ministries and do not exceed $215.

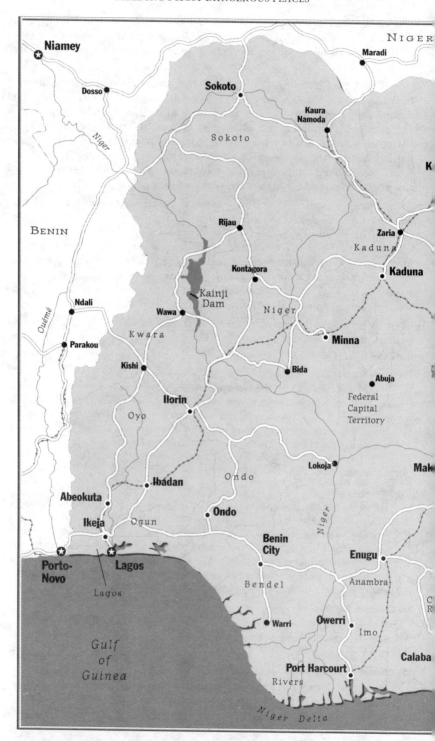

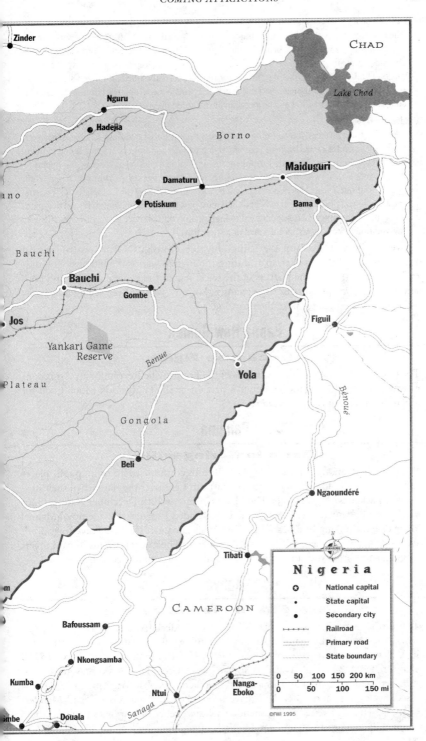

The Crude Oil Deal

The operator claims to have an allocation of crude oil to sell you cheap. Sometimes, the operator claims to be working on behalf of the Nigerian National Petroleum Corporation. Then come demands for various fees to supply you with the crude; of course, you never get your cargo. The Crude Oil Marketing Division of the NNPC is the only authorized seller of the Corporation's crude. Businesses lacking experience with Nigeria's petroleum industry should approach with great caution any proposal involving crude oil sales.

The Business Opportunity

The operator convinces you to explore a business opportunity by visiting Nigeria. Once you arrive, the operator takes charge of your life, trying to keep you from contacting friends, family or the U.S. Embassy. Then by various means, including violence or threats, the operator extracts money from you. This type of scam becomes dangerous for a victim who has entered Nigeria without a valid Nigerian visa, issued by a Nigerian Embassy or Consulate. All travelers must have a visa prior to arrival in Nigeria and must pass through immigration formalities upon entry into the country. Letters addressed to immigration officials have no validity. Anyone telling you otherwise is either misinformed or a scam artist.

So we won't even dwell on the natural division (Muslim North versus Christian South) that ripped the country apart during the Biafran war or the billions of oil dollars that go straight into the pockets of the select few or the general poverty and population growth that plague this large country. For now we just keep seeing how many people will travel there to make their fortune.

Papua New Guinea

Treehouse Fight

The poorly equipped but dogged rebels of the Bouganville Revolutionary Army control tiny pockets of Bouganville, about 5 percent in all. Things don't look good for these rebels wielding rusty shotguns.

Panama

Down in Noriegaville

Panama is a mean, dirty poor little place. Bombs continue to go off in public places and there's still a hold-out group left that just can't get over the days when their nostrils were packed with speedballs. The M-20 Group (or 20th December National Liberation Group, named after the date the U.S. invaded Panama) is made up of Manuel Noriega's old drinking buddies. These former Panamanian Defense Force folks don't have much of an agenda or even a good press agent. Their goal is to oust the occupiers of Panama and bring the current political administration to justice as traitors.

Kenya

A Rift in the Valley

Tourism to Africa's most "civilized" country has declined due to attacks in game parks, lawlessness in the major cities and continuing tribal clashes in areas such as the Rift Valley. Tourism revenue plummeted from US$400 million in 1991 to US$295 million in 1992. The Gulf War and Somalia were a couple of good reasons. Somali bandits crossed the border and attacked U.N. relief workers in Wajir province. At least 35 security officers and 50 civilians have been killed in Wajir, Garissa and Mandera provinces. The Red Cross has suspended selected relief operations in the northern provinces due to bandit attacks and the theft of materials.

In Nairobi, armed robbers ambush expensive vehicles as they drive in exclusive neighborhoods: Mercedes Gelandwagons, Land Rover Defenders, Discoveries, Range Rovers, Toyota Land Cruisers and Isuzu Troopers are their favorite targets. In Nairobi, 1224 cars were stolen in the first six months of 1992. Twenty-five were stolen from the UN High Commission for Refugees alone. The M.O.: Carjackers cut off the intended victim, occasionally utilizing an accomplice to cut off a rear escape. Most carjackings take place after 7:00 p.m., but there have been incidents during daylight hours in populated places.

With more than half of the population of Kenya under the age of 15 and unemployment at over 60 percent, there is ample motivation for criminal behavior. Average per capita income in Kenya is below US$450 a year. Add to the soup bloodthirsty cops and more than 330,000 refugees and thousands of automatic weapons from Somalia and the continent becomes darker indeed. Displaced by the war in Somalia, rugged hardy bands of desperate Somali men go south in search of anything of value. Just hope you don't have what they want.

Kenyan police enjoy bragging that they've killed (not apprehended) 70 percent of the bandits operating in the game park regions. But that's little solace. There's no guarantee you won't run into elements of the other 30 percent.

No unraveling republic would be complete without a little religious clan violence. Although religion-based political parties are banned in Kenya, there are outlaws who love to whoop it up. The Mombasa-based Islamic Party of Kenya gets involved in frequent clashes with the pro-government United Muslims of Africa party. In the Rift Valley, it's everyone for themselves, as Daniel Arap Moi's Kalenjin tribe battles with the dominant Kikuyu tribe in the valley. More than 1000 people have been killed in such violence since 1991.

South Africa

Just Another Day

The free and democratic election of Nelson Mandela didn't make everyone completely happy. In fact, Mandela did what most politicians do when they are on a roll—they give themselves a raise. Mandela's predecessor, F.W. de Clerk, pulled down US$73,817 a year as well as US$6000 for expenses. He also received a US$77,770 car allowance every 4 years. And he didn't drive to the UN once. Mandela, on the other hand, decided he was going to make up for what he had been missing all those years in prison and he bumped his compensation to US$191,660 a year. The average annual wage in South Africa for whites is about US$4000; blacks in the townships make considerably less. Members of parliament aren't complaining though they jacked their salaries from US$34,160 up to US$ 44,720.

Under apartheid in South Africa, thousands of blacks were sent to prison or exiled because of their beliefs. Millions were displaced from their homes at gunpoint. Most estimates put the number of people detained without being charged at above 50,000. Hundreds of others were tortured and even murdered while under custody. Government-sponsored death squads roamed the globe and were responsible for the assassinations in South Africa and abroad of at least 225 anti-apartheid activists.

With Mandela driving now and de Klerk in the back seat, it's time for finger pointing—and, boy, are they. While the new governments in countries such as Argentina, El Salvador, Chile and Ethiopia have established "truth commissions" to investigate crimes against humanity (i.e., war crimes) committed by previous regimes, South Africa has become embattled in whether or not to finger the culprits and, if so, what to do about them. There have been secret attempts to grant limited immunity to nearly 3480 members of the country's security forces, in addition to the police commissioner and right-wing former cabinet members. Mandela accused de Clerk of knowing about the covert immunity grants. De Clerk got pissed-off and brought the already rocky relationship to new depths. However, the new truth commission in South Africa moves unsteadily on, unsure of who to charge and what to charge them with.

Meanwhile, on January 28, 1995, 11 people died in random violence. Just another day in South Africa.

Somalia

Recipe for Strife

Chalk another one up for lawlessness. The UN is sticking its tail between its legs again and heading for the hills. U.S. Marines are again arriving in the area, but this time unillustriously in Mombasa, Kenya. Not to storm the beaches of Mogadishu under the bravado of the world media's camcorder lights, but to "quietly" perform the evacuation of UN troops from Somalia. Although the U.S. received assurances from the principal warlords that the evacuation would be unimpeded, tell it to the rogues in those beat-up, gun-mounted pickups.

The clan-riddled terror zone called Somalia is being left to stone and machine-gun itself back into the Stone Ages. Aidid and his boys just like to kill. Nine days of inter-clan fighting in Mogadishu left at least 37 dead in October 1994. On January 16, 1995, the last civilians in the downtown Mogadishu UN compound (formerly the 80-acre spread of the U.S. embassy) were evacuated. Other abandoned UN administrative buildings have been hotly contested for by thugs of rival warlords—notably the Abdal and Habre Gedir clans. The UN announced it was getting the hell out back on November 4, 1994. Aidid promised to help the limping world body out of hell, but condemned it for not attending and supporting his self-styled "constitutional convention."

Both Aidid and Ali Mahdi said they would establish "broad based" governments. However, as they refuse to let each other participate, "broad" is the range of an M-60.

Other clans like the Marewhan and the Harte clans are busy blowing bullets at each other trying to gain control of Kismayu. The UN has decided to leave nothing behind and are shipping out or destroying everything they brought in.

Party on, dudes!

Sierra Leone

Nun-napping

Seven foreigners were grabbed in two days by RUF rebels. Then the insurgents went out and snatched seven nuns. That was enough; foreigners in Sierra Leone scrambled to get out of the country as the government mobilized all available troops to prevent the insurgents from getting any closer to Freetown. To date, more than 24,000 Sierra Leoneans have fled into Guinea. The eastern areas of Sierra Leone are especially volatile.

The Spratleys

Makin' Mischief

These flyspeck islands are custom-made for a international dispute. This group of islands just north of Borneo are floating on oil close to nowhere. China, Brunei, the Philippines, Vietnam and anybody else in the neighborhood who has a half-assed reason to lay claim to these isles is talking tough and showing off military hardware like gangbangers in a schoolyard. China has occupied the aptly named Mischief reef. The Philippines sent its entire fighter airforce (nine planes) to sit nearby and look tough. The other countries have gone running to the world court to mediate. Meanwhile China has built ramshackle fishing-boat shelters to get squatters rights. Looks like the court may have to separate the kids in this messy divorce.

DANGEROUS THINGS

Dangerous Diseases

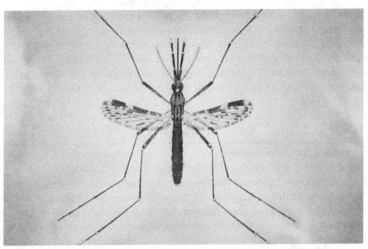

My favorite method of camping in East Africa is flat on my back under the stars. The soft wind carries past scents of the African savanna. I have spent nights listening to the lions bellow and cough their disapproval at the intruder's gall. Later the sound of hyenas screaming and fighting raises the hair on the back of my neck a few more notches. During the night I know the leopards will come unseen and unheard leaving only footprints around our campsite as evidence. The only thing I am afraid of is the sound of mosquitoes sucking my blood and possibly infecting me with deadly or disabling diseases.

Each time I stop in at my doctor's office (a tropical disease specialist with time in Vietnam) he asks me why the hell I do what I do. He couldn't care less about damage I might sustain from a bullet or a land mine since that damage can usually be patched up. He takes great pains to describe the symptoms of the many and sundry tropical diseases that await me in the Third World. His lectures usually center around the life-long pain and debilitation that can be inflicted on travelers who inadvertently ingest an amoeba, get bitten by a mosquito or become the host for a degenerative bug. I take his advice seriously and I am as fastidious as I can be in adverse conditions. I am very careful about what I eat, how I sleep and follow the rules of common sense when it comes to avoiding infection. Despite this, I have spent nights shivering and delirious, lying in puddles of my own sweat on cement floors in the Sahara desert. I pay his bill gladly and trust to the cosmos and good common sense.

With this in mind, do not assume that this chapter is the be-all end-all reference source for tropical diseases. ALWAYS CONFER WITH A SPECIALIST BEFORE TAKING ANY TRIP. This way you understand the odds, the penalties and can make an educated decision on the risks involved. Secondly, ALWAYS HAVE FULL MEDICAL TESTS UPON YOUR RETURN. This means giving a little bit of yourself to the lab to run blood, stool and urine tests. Your doctor may ask you to come back again due to the long incubation time of some of these nasties. This is not hypochondria but common sense. Many people are terrified of taking an HIV test thinking that some '80s dalliance may make them a pariah. The truth is, early detection in all diseases will increase your odds of successful treatment and in the worst case allow for a better understanding of your chances.

The odds of coming down with a bug are pretty good once you leave the antiseptic Western world. I used to think that the locals had built up resistance to the various bugs that strike down Westerners. Once in-country you realize what a toll disease takes on the Third World. Not only are many people riddled with malaria, river blindness, intestinal infections, hepatitis, sexual diseases and more, but they are also faced with malnutrition, poor dental care, toxic chemicals and hard environmental conditions.

Worms

My least favorite are the helminthic infections or diseases caused by intestinal worms. Unlike the more dramatic and deadly diseases, these parasites are easily caught through ingestion of bad water and food and cause long term damage. Just to let you know what's out there, you can choose from angiostrongyliasis, herring worm, roundworm, schistsomiasis, capillariasis, pin worm, oriental liver fluke, fish tapeworm, guinea worm, cat liver fluke, tapeworm, trechinellosis and the ominous sounding giant intestinal fluke (who's eating who here?). All these little buggers create havoc with your internal organs and some will make the rest of your life miserable. Your digestive system will be shot, your organs under constant attack and the treatment or removal of these buggers is downright depressing. These can be prevented by maintaining absolutely rigid standards in what you throw or breathe into your body. Not easy since most male travelers find wearing a biohazard suit a major impediment to picking up chicks or doing the limbo.

Think of yourself as a sponge, your lungs as an air filter, and all the moist cavities of your body as ideal breeding grounds for tropical diseases. It is better to think like Howard Hughes than Pig Pen when it comes to personal hygiene.

The Fevers

The classic tropical diseases that incapacitated Stanley, Livingstone, Burton and Speke are the hemorrhagic fevers. Many of these diseases kill but most make your life a living hell and then disappear. Some come back on a regular basis. It is surprising that most of the African explorers lived to a ripe old age. The hemorrhagic fevers are carried by mosquitoes, ticks, rats feces or even airborne dust that gets into your bloodstream, and let you die a slow, demented death as your blood turns so thin it trickles out your nose, gums, skin and eyes. Coma and death can occur in the second week. There are so many versions they just name them after the places where you will stumble across them. Needless to say these are not featured in any glossy brochures for the various regions. Assorted blood thinning killers are called Chikungunya, Crimean, Congo, Omsk, Kyasanur Forest, Korean, Manchurian, Songo, Ebola, Argentinian, Hantaan, Lassa and yellow fever. The recent outbreak of the Hanta virus in the U.S. shows that North America is not immune from these insect, rodent and airborne afflictions. The outbreak of plague in India also has travelers a little edgy about the whole concept of adventurous travel. There are real dangers in every part of the world and the more knowledgeable you are about them the better your chances for surviving.

Insects

Bugs, not terrorists are the worst enemy of the traveler. Mosquitoes should be the most feared. Over a million people in Africa are killed by malaria every year. It is estimated that there are over 300 million people with malaria worldwide. The female *anopheles* mosquito is small, pervasive and hungry for your blood. As they seek out blood to nurture their own procreation they leave the Plasmodium parasites in your blood system. The symptoms can start with a flu-like attack followed by fever, chills, then lead to failure of multiple organs and then death. In many cases the symptoms of malaria do not start until the traveler has returned home and is in a nonmalarial zone. Remember that current chemoprophylaxis does not prevent malaria. Lariam, Fansidar, and chloroquinine can lower the chances of getting malaria but do not provide any guarantee of being malaria-proof. Two of my fellow travelers (one in Africa and one in Borneo) did not realize they had malaria because they believed that Lariam would prevent or protect them from the disease. Luckily they sought treatment in time.

Malaria is a very real and common danger in most tropical countries. Most malaria in Asian and African areas is quinine-resistant and requires multiple or more creative dosages to avoid the horrors of malaria. Malaria is carried by the anopheles mosquito, a tiny and commonly found mosquito that likes to bite in the cool hours before and after sunset. The most vicious strain of malaria (*Plasmodium falciparum*) attacks your liver and red blood cells creating massive fevers, coma, acute kidney failure, and eventually death. There are four types of malaria in the world: *plasmodium falciparum* is the most dangerous, *plasmodium malariae, plasmodium vivax* and *plasmodium ovale* (found only in West Africa).

The *Anopheles* mosquito is the most dangerous insect in the world and there are few contenders for its crown. Other biting insects that can cause you grief include the *Aedes aegypti* mosquito which carries Yellow fever. His kissing cousins, the *Culex, Haemogogus, Sabethes* and *Mansonia*, can give you filariasis, viral encephalitis, dengue and other great hemorrhagic fevers. Next on the list are tsetse flies, fleas, ticks, sandflies, mites and lice. We won't even bother to discuss wasps, horseflies, African Killer Bees, deerflies, or other clean biters.

These insects are an everyday part of life in tropical, endemic or Third World countries. They infect major percentages of the local population and it is only a matter of time and luck before you become a victim.

Prevention is rather simple but ineffective. Protect yourself from insects by wearing long sleeved shirts and long pants. Use insect repellent, sleep under a mosquito net, avoid swampy areas, use mosquito coils, don't sleep directly on the ground, check yourself for tick and insect bites daily and, last but not least, understand the symptoms and treatment of these diseases so you can seek immediate and effective treatment no matter what part of the world you are in.

Sex

The quest for sexual adventure used to be a major part of the joy of travel. The full range of sexual diseases available to the common traveler would fill an encyclopedia. Despite the continual global publicity on the dangers of AIDS there are few good results. Whorehouses around the world have not gone out of business, junkies still share needles and dentists in many Third World countries still grind and yank away with improperly sterilized instruments. Diseases like HIV, Hepatitis B and other sexually transmitted diseases that Westerners blame on the Third World, and the Third World blames on the West are very preventable and require parking your libido. How do you avoid sexually transmitted diseases, some people ask? Well, keeping your romantic agenda on the platonic side is a good start. The use of condoms is the next best thing. Realistically the chances of catching AIDS through unprotected sex depends on frequency and type of contact. A person waddling painfully out of a gay bathhouse after pulling an all-night train is at a different risk level than someone who has had a romantic fling with a newly divorced 50-year-old. But before you slap on the Old Spice and dust off the Englebert Humperdinck records remember the wild cards: People infected by blood transfusions, prostitutes, frequent drug users, hemophiliacs, homosexuals, and the millions of people who will get HIV this year from heterosexual sex will continue to make HIV a danger, if not an overwhelmingly ominous one.

Old Fashioned Diseases

Many travelers are quite surprised to find themselves coming down with measles or mumps while traveling. Unlike the U.S. which has eradicated much of the childhood and preventable viruses through inoculation, the rest of the world is more concerned about feeding than vaccinating their children. The recent outbreak of plague in India is a good example of what you should watch out for. Whooping cough, mumps, measles, polio and tuberculosis are common in Third World countries. Although some of the symptoms are minor, complications can lead to lifelong afflictions. Make sure you are vaccinated against these easily preventable diseases.

But don't just run off to be the next bubble boy and spend the rest of your life in a hermetically sealed dome. For travelers, these diseases are relatively rare and avoidable. To put the whole thing in perspective, the most common complaint tends to be diarrhea followed by a cold (usually the result of lowered resistance caused by fatigue, dehydration, foreign microbes and stress). The important thing is to know when you are sick versus very sick. Tales of turn-of-the-century explorers struck down by a tiny mosquito bite are now legend. Malaria is still a very real and common threat. Just for fun, bring back a sample of local river water from your next trip and have the medical lab analyze it. You may never drink water of any kind again.

This is not to say that as soon as you get off the plane you will automatically be struck down with Ebola River fever and have blood oozing out from your eyes. You can travel bug-free and suffer no more than a cold caused by the air conditioning in your hotel room. It is important to at least understand the relative risks and gravity of some diseases. You would be very foolish indeed to assume that absorbing local culture also includes catching the local bugs.

Diseases listed below with all caps are important and you should be conversant with both symptoms and cures. Please do not assume that this is medical advice. It is designed to give you an overview of the various nasties that await you.

Tropical countries are the most likely to cause you bacterial grief. Keep in mind that most of these diseases are a direct result of poor hygiene, travel in infected areas and contact with infected people. In other words, stay away from people if you want to stay healthy. Secondly, follow the common sense practice of having all food cooked freshly and properly. Many books tell you to wash fruit and then forget that the water is probably more bug-filled than the fruit. Peel all fruits and vegetables and approach anything you stick in your body with a healthy level of skepticism and distrust. If you are completely anal you can exist on freeze dried-foods, Maggi Mee (noodles) fresh fruit (peeled remember) and tinned food.

It is considered wise to ask local experts about dangers that await. If you do not feel right for any reason, contact a local doctor. It is not advisable to enter a medical treatment program while in a developing country. There are greater chances of you catching worse afflictions once you are in the hospital. Ask for temporary medication and then get your butt back to North America or Europe.

Remember that the symptoms of many tropical diseases may not take effect until you are home and back into your regular schedule. It is highly advisable that you contact a tropical disease specialist and have full testing done (stool, urine, blood, physical) just to be sure. Very few American doctors are conversant with the many tropical diseases by virtue of their rarity.This is not their fault since many tourists do not even realize that they have taken trips or cruises into endemic zones.People can catch malaria on a plane between London and New York from a stowaway mosquito that just came in from Bombay. Many people come in close contact with foreigners in buses, subways and on the street from Los Angeles to New York. Don't assume you have to be up to your neck in Laotian pig wallows to be at risk.

Many labs do not do tests for some of the more exotic bugs. Symptoms can also be misleading. It is possible that you may be misdiagnosed or mistreated if you do not fully discuss the possible reasons for your medical condition. Now that we have scared the hell out of you, your first contact should be with the Centers for Disease Control in Atlanta.

African Sleeping Sickness (African trypanosomiasis)

Found: Tropical Africa.

Cause: A tiny protozoan parasite that emits a harmful toxin.

Carrier: Tsetse fly. Tsetse flies are large biting insects about the size of a horsefly found in East and West Africa.

Symptoms: Eastern trypanosomiasis: 2–31 days after the bite recurrent episodes of fever, headaches and malaise. Can lead to death in 2–6 weeks.Western trypanosomiasis: produces a skin ulcer within 5 to 10 days after being bitten. The symptoms then disappear in 2–3 weeks. Symptoms reappear 6 months to 5 years after the initial infection resulting in fevers, headaches, rapid heart beat, swelling of the lymph glands located in the back of the neck, personality changes, tremors, a lackadaisical attitude and then stupor leading eventually to death.

Treatment: Suramin (Bayer (205), pentamidine (Lomodine, melarasoprol (Mel B)

How to Avoid: Do not travel to infested areas, insect repellent, light colored clothing, covering skin areas.

AIDS (Acquired Immune Deficiency Syndrome)

Found: Worldwide.

Cause: Advanced stage of HIV (Human Immunodeficiency Syndrome) which causes destruction of the natural resistance of humans to infection and other diseases. Death by AIDS is usually a result of unrelated diseases which rapidly attack the victim. These ranges of diseases are called ARC (AIDS-related complex).

Carrier: Sexual intercourse with infected person, transfusion of infected blood or even from infected mother through breast milk. There is no way to determine if someone has HIV except by blood test. Male homosexuals, drug users, prostitutes are high risk groups in major urban centers in the West. AIDS is less selective in developing countries with Central and Eastern Africa being the areas of highest incidence.

Symptoms: Fever, weight loss, fatigue, night sweats, lymph node problems. Infection by other opportunistic elements such as Karposi's sarcoma and pneumonia are highly probable and will lead to death.

Treatment: There is no known cure.

How to Avoid: Use condoms, refrain from sexual contact, do not receive injections or transfusions in questionable areas. Avoid live vaccines such as gamma globulin and Hepatitis B in developing countries.

Amebiasis

Found: Worldwide.

Cause: A protozoan parasite carried in human fecal matter. Usually found in areas with poor sanitation.

Carrier: Entamoeba histolyica is passed by poor hygiene. Ingested orally in water, air or food that has come in contact with the parasite.

Symptoms: The infection will spread from the intestines and causes abscesses in other organs such as liver, lungs and brain.

Treatment: Metronidazole, iodoquinol, diloxanide furoate, paromomycin, tetracycline plus chloroquinine base.

How to Avoid: Avoid uncooked foods. Boil water. Drink bottled liquids. Be sure that food is cooked properly. Peel fruits and vegetables.

Bartonellosis (Oroya fever, Carrion's disease)

Found: In valleys of Peru, Ecuador and Colombia.

Cause: Bartonella bacilliformis, a bacterium.

Carrier: Sandflies that bite at night.

Symptoms: Pain in muscles, joints and bones along with fever occur within three weeks of being bitten. Oroya fever causes a febrile fever leading to possible death. Verruga peruana creates skin eruptions.

Treatment: Antibiotics with transfusion for symptoms of anemia.

How to Avoid: High boots, groundsheets, hammocks and insect repellent

Brucellosis (undulant fever)

Found: Worldwide.

Cause: Ingestion of infected dairy products

Carrier: Untreated dairy products infected with the brucellosis bacteria

Symptoms: Intermittent fever, sweating, jaundice, rash, depression, enlarged spleen and lymph nodes. The symptoms may disappear and go into permanent remission after three to six months.

Treatment: Tetracyclines, sulfonamides and streptomycin.

How to Avoid: Drink pasteurized milk. Avoid infected livestock.

Chagas' Disease (American trypanosomiasis)

Found: Central and South America.

Cause: Protozoan parasite carried in the feces of insects.

Carrier: Kissing or Assassin bugs (Triatoma insects or reduviid bugs). Commonly found in homes with thatched roofs. It can also be transmitted through blood transfusions, breast milk and in utero from infected people.

Symptoms: A papule and swelling at the location of the bite, fever, malaise, anorexia, rash, swelling of the limbs, gastrointestinal problems, heart irregularities and heart failure.

Treatment: Nifurtimox (Bayer 2502).

How to Avoid: Do not stay in native villages; use bednetting and insect repellent.

Cholera

Found: Worldwide; primarily developing countries.

Cause: Intestinal infection caused by the toxin Vibrio Cholerae O group bacteria.

Carrier: Infected food and water contaminated by human and animal waste.

Symptoms: Watery diarrhea, abdominal cramps, nausea, vomiting and severe dehydration as a result of diarrhea. Can lead to death if fluids are not replaced.

Treatment: Tetracycline can hasten recovery. Replace fluids using an electrolyte solution.

How to Avoid: Vaccinations before trip can diminish symptoms up to 50 percent for a period of three to six months. A threat in refugee camps or areas of poor sanitation. Use standard precautions with food and drink for developing countries.

Chikungunya Disease

Found: Sub-Saharan Africa, Southeast Asia, India, Philippines in sporadic outbreaks.

Cause: Alphavirus transmitted by mosquito bites.

Carrier: Mosquitoes who transmit the disease from the host (Monkeys).

Symptoms: Joint pain with potential for hemorrhagic symptoms.

Treatment: None, but symptoms will disappear. If hemorrhagic, avoid aspirin.

How to Avoid: Standard precautions to avoid mosquito bites. Use insect repellent, mosquito nets, cover exposed skin areas.

Ciguatera Poisoning

Found: Tropical areas.

Cause: Ingestion of fish containing the toxin produced by the dinoflagellate Gambierdiscus toxicus.

Carrier: 425 species of tropical reef fish.

Symptoms: Up to six hours after eating victims may experience nausea, watery diarrhea, abdominal cramps, vomiting, abnormal sensation in limbs and teeth, hot-cold flashes, joint pain, weakness, skin rashes and itching. In very severe cases victims may experience blind spells, low blood pressure and heart rate, paralysis and loss of coordination. Symptoms may appear years later.

Treatment: There is no specific medical treatment other than first aid. Induce vomiting.

How to Avoid: Do not eat reef fish (including sea bass, barracuda, red snapper or grouper).

Colorado Tick Fever

Found: North America.

Cause: Arbovirus transmitted by insect or infected blood.

Carrier: The Wood Tick (Dermacentor andersoni); also through transfusion of infected blood.

Symptoms: Aching of muscles in back and legs, chills, recurring fever, headaches, eye pain, fear of brightly lit area.

Treatment: Since symptoms only last about three weeks, medication or treatment is intended to relieve symptoms.

How to Avoid: Ticks are picked up when walking through woods. Wear leggings, tall boots and insect repellent.

Dengue Fever (Breakbone fever)

Found: South America, Africa, South Pacific, Asia, Mexico, Central America, Caribbean.

Cause: An arbovirus transmitted by mosquitoes.

Carrier: Mosquitoes in tropical areas, usually bite during the daytime.

Symptoms: Two distinct periods. First period consists of severe muscle, joint and headaches combined with high fever (the origin of the term "break bone fever"). The second phase is sensitivity to light, diarrhea, vomiting, nausea, mental depression and enlarged lymph nodes.

Treatment: Designed to relieve symptoms. Aspirin should be avoided due to hemorrhagic complications.

How to Avoid: Typical protection against daytime mosquito bites: Insect repellent with high DEET levels, light colored long sleeve pants and shirts.

Diarrhea

Found: Worldwide

Cause: There are many reasons for travelers to have the symptoms of diarrhea. It is important to remember that alien bacteria in the digestive tract is the main culprit. Most travelers to Africa, Mexico, South America and the Middle East will find themselves doubled up in pain, running for the nearest stinking toilet wondering why the hell they ever left their comfortable home.

Carrier: Bacteria from food, the air, water or other people can be the cause. Dehydration from long airplane flights, strange diets, stress and high altitude can also cause diarrhea. It is doubtful you will ever get to know your intestinal bacteria on a first name basis but Aeromonas hydrophila, Campylobacter, jejuni Pleisiomonas, salmonellae, shigellae, shielloides, Vibrio cholerae (non-01), Vibrio parahaemolyticus, Yersinia enterocoliticia and Escherichia coli are the most likely culprits. All these bugs would love to spend a week or two in your gut.

Symptoms: Loose stools, stomach pains, bloating, fever and malaise.

Treatment: First step is to stop eating and ingest plenty of fluids and salty foods; secondly, try Kaopectate or Pepto Bismol. If diarrhea persists after three to four days; seek medical advice.

How to Avoid: Keep your fluid intake high when traveling. Follow commons sense procedures when eating, drinking and ingesting any food or fluids. Remember to wash your hands carefully and frequently since you can transmit a shocking number of germs from your hands to your mouth, eyes and nose.

Diphtheria

Found: Worldwide

Cause: The bacterium Corynebacterium diptheriae, a producer of harmful toxins that is usually a problem in populations that have not been immunized against diphtheria.

Carrier: Infected humans can spread the germs by sneezing, or contact.

Symptoms: Swollen diphtheritic membrane which may lead to serious congestion. Other symptoms are pallor, listlessness, weakness and increased heart rate. May cause death due to weakened heart or shock.

Treatment: Immunization with the DPT vaccine at an early age (three years) is the ideal prevention, treatment with antitoxin, if not.

How to Avoid: Avoid close contact with populations or areas where there is little to no vaccination program for diphtheria.

Ebola River Fever

Found: Found among local populations in Zaire.

Cause: A very rare but much publicized affliction.

Carrier: Unknown, but highly contagious. In 1989 the virus was found in lab monkeys in Reston, Virginia. The monkeys were quickly destroyed. At press time an outbreak in Zaire was rampant.

Symptoms: The virus is described as melting people down, causing blood clotting, loss of consciousness and death.

Treatment: None.

How to Avoid: Unknown.

Encephalitis

Found: Southeast Asia, Korea, Taiwan, Nepal and Eastern CIS countries and eastern European countries.

Cause: A common viral infection carried by insects.

Carrier: The disease can be carried by the tick or mosquito. The risk is high during late summer and fall. The most dangerous strain is tickborne encephalitis transmitted by ticks in the summer in the colder climates of Russia, Scandinavia, Switzerland and France.

Symptoms: Fever, headache, muscle pain, malaise, runny nose and sore throat followed by lethargy, confusion, hallucination and seizures. About one-fifth of encephalitis infections have led to death.

Treatment: A vaccine is available.

How to Avoid: Avoid areas known to be endemic. Avoid tick-infested areas such as forests, rice growing areas in Asia (mosquitoes) or areas that have large number of domestic pigs (tick carriers). Use insect repellent. Do not drink unpasteurized milk.

Filariasis (lymphatic, river blindness)

Found: Africa, Central America, Caribbean, South America, Asia

Cause: A group of diseases caused by long, thin roundworms carried by mosquitoes.

Carrier: Mosquitoes and biting flies in tropical areas.

Symptoms: Lymphatic filariasis, onchocerciasis (river blindness), loiasis, mansonellasis all have similar and very unpleasant symptoms. Fevers, headaches, nausea, vomiting, sensitivity to light, inflammation in the legs including the abdomen and testicles, swelling of the abdomen, joints and scrotum, enlarged lymph nodes, abscesses, eye lesions that lead to blindness, rashes, itches and arthritis.

Treatment: Diethylcarbamazine (DEC, Hetrazan, Notezine) is the usual treatment.

How to Avoid: Avoid bites by insects with usual protective measures and insect repellent.

Flukes

Found: Caribbean, South America, Africa, Asia.

Cause: The liver fluke (Clonorchis sinensis) and the lung fluke (Paragonimus westermani) which lead to paragonimasis.

Carrier: Carried in fish that has not been properly cooked.

Symptoms: Obstruction of the bile system, along with fever, pain, jaundice, gallstones, inflammation of the pancreas. There is further risk of cancer of the bile tract after infection. Paragonimasis affects the lungs and causes chest pains.

Treatment: Treatment for paragonimasis is with Prazanquantel. Obstruction of the bile system can require surgery.

How to Avoid: To avoid liver flukes do not eat uncooked or improperly cooked fish—something most sushi fans will decry. Paragonimasis is found in uncooked shellfish, like freshwater crabs, crayfish and shrimp.

Giardiasis

Found: Worldwide.

Cause: A protozoa Giardi lamblia that causes diarrhea.

Carrier: Ingestion of food or water that is contaminated with fecal matter.

Symptoms: Very sudden diarrhea, severe flatulence, cramps, nausea, anorexia, weight loss and fever.

Treatment: Giardiasis can disappear without treatment but Furazolidone, metronidizole, or quinacrine HCI is the usual method of treatment.

How to Avoid: Cleanliness, drink bottled water and strict personal hygiene in eating and personal contact.

Guinea Worm Infection (dracontiasis, dracunculiasis)

Found: Found in tropical areas like the Caribbean, the Guianas, Africa, Middle East and Asia.

Cause: Ingestion of waterborne nematode Dracunculus medinensis.

Carrier: Water systems that harbor Dracunculus medinensis.

Symptoms: Fever, itching, swelling around the eyes, wheezing, skin blisters and arthritis.

Treatment: Doses of niridazole, metronidazole or thiabendazole are the usual method. Surgery may be required to remove worms.

How to Avoid: Drink only boiled or chemically treated water.

HEMORRHAGIC FEVERS

Some of the more well-known hemorrhagic fevers are yellow fever, dengue, lassa fever and the horror movie caliber Ebola fever. Outbreaks tend to be localized and subject to large populations of insects, or rats. Don't let the exotic sounding names lull you into a false sense of security; there was a major outbreak in the American Southwest caused by rodents spreading the disease.

Found: Worldwide.

Cause: Intestinal worms carried by insects and rodents.

Carrier: Depending on the disease it can be transmitted by mosquitoes, ticks, rodents (in urine and feces).

Symptoms: Headache, backache, muscle pain and conjunctivitis. Later on, the thinning of the blood will cause low blood pressure, bleeding from the gums and nose, vomiting and coughing up blood, blood in your stool, bleeding from the skin and hemorrhaging in the internal organs. Coma and death may occur in the second week.

Treatment: Consult a doctor or medical facility familiar with the local disease.

How to Avoid: Avoid mosquitoes, ticks, and areas with high concentrations of mice and rats.

Hepatitis, A, B, Non-A, Non-B

Found: Worldwide.

Cause: A virus that attacks the liver. Hepatitis A, Non-B and Non-A can be brought on by poor hygiene Hepatitis B is transmitted sexually or through infected blood.

Carrier: Hepatitis A is transmitted by oral-fecal route, person to person contact, or through contaminated food or water. Hepatitis B is transmitted by sexual activity or the transfer of bodily fluids. Hepatitis Non-A and Non-B are spread by contaminated water or from other people.

Symptoms: Muscle and joint pain, nausea, fatigue, sensitivity to light, sore throat, runny nose. Look for dark urine and clay colored stools, jaundice along with liver pain and enlargement.

Treatment: Rest and a high calorie diet. Immune Globulin is advised as a minor protection against Hepatitis A. You can be vaccinated against Hepatitis B.

How to Avoid: Non-A and Non-B require avoiding infected foods. Hepatitis B requires no unprotected sexual contact, avoiding unsterile needles, dental work and infusions. Hepatitis A requires proper hygiene, avoiding infected water and foods.

Hydatid Disease (echinococcosis)

Found: Worldwide.

Cause: A tapeworm found in areas with high populations of pigs, cattle and sheep.

Carrier: Eggs of the echinococcosis.

Symptoms: Cysts form in organs in the liver, lungs, bone or brain.

Treatment: Surgery for removal of the infected cysts. Mebendazole and albendazole are used as well.

How to Avoid: Boil water, cook foods properly, avoid infected areas.

Leishmaniasis

Found: Tropical, subtropical regions.

Cause: Protozoans of the genus Leishmania.

Carrier: Phlebotomine sandflies in tropical and subtropical regions.

Symptoms: Skin lesions, cutaneous ulcers, mucocutaneous ulcers in the mouth, nose and anus. intermittent fever, anemia and enlarged spleen.

Treatment: Sodium stibogluconate, rifampin, and sodium antimony gluconate. Surgery is also used to remove cutaneous and mucocutaneous.

How to Avoid: Use insect repellent, a ground cover when sleeping, bednets and cover arms and legs.

Leprosy (Hansen's disease)

Found: Africa, India and elsewhere

Cause: The bacterium *Mycobacterium leprae* that infects the skin, eyes, nervous system and testicles.

Carrier: It is not known how leprosy is transmitted but direct human contact is suspected.

Symptoms: Skin lesions, and nerve damage that progresses to loss of fingers and toes, blindness, difficulty breathing and nerve damage.

Treatment: Dapsone, rifampin and clofazimine.

How to Avoid: Leprosy is a tropical disease with over half the cases worldwide occurring in India and Africa. There is no known preventive method.

Loaisis

Found: West and Central Africa.

Cause: The loa loa parasite.

Carrier: Chrysops Deer flies or tabanid flies in West and Central Africa.

Symptoms: Subcutaneous swellings that come and go, brain and heart inflammation.

Treatment: Diethylcarbamazine.

How to Avoid: Deerflies are large and their bites can be avoided by wearing full sleeved shirts and thick pants. Hats and bandannas can protect head and neck areas.

Lyme Diseases

Found: Worldwide

Cause: A spirochete carried by ticks.

Carrier: The Ixodes tick, found worldwide and in great numbers during the summer. Ticks are found in rural areas and burrow into skin to suck blood.

Symptoms: A pronounced bite mark, flu-like symptoms, severe headache, stiff neck, fever, chills, joint pain, malaise and fatigue.

Treatment: Tetracyclines, phenoxymethylpenicillin or erythromycin if caught early. Advanced cases may require intravenous penicillin.

How to Avoid: Do not walk through wooded areas in the summer. Check for ticks frequently. Use leggings with insect repellent.

Malaria

Malaria is by far the most dangerous disease and the one most likely for travelers to pick up in Third World countries. Protection against this disease should be your first priority. As a rule, be leery of all riverine, swampy or tropical places. Areas such as logging camps, shantytowns, oases, campsites near slow moving water, resorts near mangrove swamps are all very likely to be major areas of malarial infection. Consult with a local doctor to understand the various resistances and the prescribed treatment. Many foreign doctors are more knowledgeable about the cure and treatment of malaria than domestic doctors.

Found: Africa, Asia, Caribbean, Southeast Asia, Middle East.

Cause: The plasmodium parasite is injected into the victim while the mosquito draws blood.

Carrier: The female anopheles mosquito.

Symptoms: Fever, chills, enlarged spleen in low level versions, plasmodium falciparum or cerebral malaria can also cause convulsions, kidney failure, hypoglycemia.

Treatment: Chloroquinine, quinine, pyrimethamine, sulfadoxine and mefloquine. Note: Some people may have adverse reactions to all and any of these drugs.

How to Avoid: Begin taking a malarial prophylaxis before your trip, during and after (consult your doctor for a prescription). Avoid infected areas, protect yourself from mosquito bites, (netting, insect repellent, mosquito coils, long sleeve shirts and pants) especially during dusk and evening times.

Measles (rubeola)

Found: Worldwide.

Cause: A common virus in unvaccinated areas.

Carrier: Sneezing, saliva and close contact with infected or unvaccinated humans.

Symptoms: Malaise, irritability, fever, conjunctivitis, swollen eyelids and hacking cough appear nine to 11 days after exposure. Fourteen days after exposure the typical facial rash and spots appear.

Treatment: Measles will disappear but complications can occur.

How to Avoid: Vaccination or gamma globulin shots within five days of exposure.

Meliodosis

Found: Worldwide.

Cause: An animal disease (the bacillus *Pseudomonas pseudomallei*) that can be transferred to humans.

Carrier: Found in infected soil, water and transmitted through skin wounds.

Symptoms: Various types including fever, malaise, pneumonia, shortness of breath, headache, diarrhea, skin lesions, muscle pain and abscesses in organs.

Treatment: Antibiotics such as tetracyclines, sulfur drugs.

How to Avoid: Clean and cover all wounds carefully.

Meningitis

Found: Africa, Saudi Arabia.

Cause: Bacteria: Neisseria meningitis, Streptococcus pneumoniae and Haemophilus influenzae. Children are at most risk. There are frequent outbreaks in Africa and Nepal.

Carrier: Inhaling infected droplets of nasal and throat secretions.

Symptoms: Fever, vomiting, headaches, confusion, lethargy, and rash.

Treatment: Penicillin G.

How to Avoid: Meningococcus polysaccharide vaccine. Do not travel to areas where outbreaks occur (the Sahel from Mali to Ethiopia) in the dry season.

Mumps

Found: Worldwide.

Cause: A virus found worldwide. Common in early spring and late winter and in unvaccinated areas.

Carrier: Infected saliva and urine.

Symptoms: Headache, anorexia, malaise. Pain when chewing or swallowing.

Treatment: Mumps is a self-innoculating disease. There can be complications which can lead to more serious lifetime afflictions.

How to Avoid: Vaccination (MMR).

Plague

Found: India, Vietnam, Africa, South America, Middle East, Russia.

Cause: A bacteria (Yersinia pestis) that infects rodents and the fleas they carry.

Carrier: Flea bites that transmit the bacteria to humans. Ticks, lice, corpses and human contact can also spread the disease.

Symptoms: Swollen lymph nodes, fever, abdominal pain, loss of appetite, nausea, vomiting diarrhea, gangrene of the extremities.

Treatment: Antibiotics like streptomycin, tetracyclines and chloramphenicol can reduce the mortality rate.

How to Avoid: Stay out of infected areas, avoid contact.

Poliomyelitis (Polio)

Found: Worldwide.

Cause: A virus that destroys the central nervous system.

Carrier: Occurs through direct contact.

Symptoms: A mild febrile illness that may lead to paralysis. Polio can cause death in five to 10 percent of cases in children and 15–30 percent in adult cases.

Treatment: There is no treatment.

How to Avoid: Vaccination during childhood with a booster before travel is recommended.

Rabies

Found: Worldwide.

Cause: A virus that affects the central nervous system.

Carrier: Rabies is transmitted through the bite of an infected animal. Found in wild animals although usually animals found in urban areas are most suspect: dogs, raccoons, cats, skunks, and bats. Although most people will automatically assume they are at risk for rabies, there are only about 16,000 cases reported worldwide. The risk is the deadly seriousness of rabies and the short time in which death occurs.

Symptoms: Abnormal sensations or muscle movement near the bite followed by fever, headaches, malaise, muscle aches, tiredness, loss of appetite, nausea, vomiting, sore throat and cough. The advanced stages include excessive excitation, seizures and mental disturbances leading to profound nervous system dysfunction and paralysis. Death occurs in most cases four to 20 days after being bitten.

Treatment: Clean wound vigorously, injections of anti rabies antiserum and antirabies vaccine. People who intend to come into regular contact with animals in high risk areas can receive HDCV (human diploid cell rabies vaccine) shots.

How to Avoid: Avoid confrontations with animals.

Relapsing Fever

Found: The louseborne version is found in poor rural areas where infestation by lice is common.

Cause: *Borrelia* spirochetes.

Carrier: Lice and ticks. Ticks are found in wooded areas and bite mainly at night.

Symptoms: The fever gets its name from the six days on and six days off of high fever. Other symptoms include headaches, muscle pains, weakness and loss of appetite.

Treatment: Antibiotics.

How to Avoid: Avoid infected areas, check for ticks.

Rift Valley Fever

Found: Egypt and East Africa.

Cause: A virus that affects humans and livestock.

Carrier: Mosquitoes, inhaling infected dust, contact with broken skin and ingesting infected animal blood or fluids.

Symptoms: Sudden one-time fever, severe headaches, muscle pain, weakness, sensitivity to light, eye pain, nausea, vomiting, diarrhea, eye redness and facial flushing. Blindness, meningitis, meningoencephalitis and retinitis may also occur.

Treatment: Seek medical treatment for supportive care.

How to Avoid: Avoid contact with livestock in infected areas; protect yourself against mosquito bites.

River Blindness (onchocerciais)

Found: Equatorial Africa, Yemen, the Sahara and parts of Central and South America.

Cause: The roundworm Onchocerca volvulus.

Carrier: Transmitted by blackflies found along rapidly flowing rivers.

Symptoms: Itching, skin atrophy, mottling, nodules, enlargement of the lymph nodes, particularily in the groin, and blindness.

Treatment: Invermectin or Diethylcarbamazine(DEC) followed by suramin followed by DEC again.

How to Avoid: Insect repellant, long sleeve shirts and long pants. Avoid blackfly bites.

Rocky Mountain Spotted Fever

Found: Found only in the Western Hemisphere.

Cause: A bacterial disease transmitted by tick bites.

Carrier: Rickettsial bacteria are found in rodents and dogs. The ticks pass the bacteria by then biting humans.

Symptoms: Fever, headaches, chills, rash (after fourth day) on the arms and legs. Final symptoms may include delirum, shock and kidney failure.

Treatment: Tetracyclines or chloramphenicol.

How to Avoid: Ticks are found in wooded areas. Inspect your body after walks. Use insect repellent. Wear leggings or long socks or long pants.

Salmonellosis

Found: Worldwide.

Cause: A common bacterial infection; *Salmonella gastroenteritis* that is commonly described as food poisoning.

Carrier: Found on fecally contaminated food, unpasteurized milk, raw foods, water.

Symptoms: Abdominal pain, diarrhea, vomiting, chills and fever usually within eight to 48 hours of ingesting infected food. *Salmonella* only kills about one percent of its victims, usually small children or the aged.

Treatment: Purge infected food, replace fluids. Complete recovery is within two to five days.

How to Avoid: Consume only properly prepared foods.

Sandfly Fever (three day fever)

Found: Africa, Mediterranean.

Cause: Phleboviruses injected by sandfly bites.

Carrier: Transmitted by sandflies, usually during the dry season.

Symptoms: Fever, headache, eye pain, chest muscle pains, vomiting, sensitivity to light, stiff neck, taste abnormality, rash and joint pain.

Treatment: There is no specific treatment. The symptoms can reoccur in about 15 percent of cases, but typically disappear.

How to Avoid: Do not sleep directly on the ground. Sandflies usually bite at night.

Schistosomiasis (bilharzia)

Bilharzia is one of the meanest bugs to pick up in your foreign travels. The idea of nasty little creatures actually burrowing through your skin and lodging themselves in your gut is menacing. If not treated it can make your life a living hell with afternoon sweats, painful urination, weakness and other good stuff. There is little you can do to prevent infection since the Schistosoma larva and flukes are found where people have fouled freshwater rivers and lakes. Get treatment immediately since the affliction worsens as the eggs multiply and continue to infect more tissues. About 250 million people around the world are believed to be infected.

Found: Worldwide.

Cause: A group of parasitic Schistosoma flatworms (*Schistosoma mansoni*, *Schistosoma japonicum* and *Schistosoma haematobium*) found in slow moving, tropical fresh water.

Carrier: The larvae of Schistosoma are found in slow moving waterways in tropical areas around the world. They actually enter the body through the skin and then enter the lymph vessels and then migrate to the liver.

Symptoms: Look for a rash and itching at the entry site followed by weakness, loss of appetite, night sweats, hive-like rashes, and afternoon fevers in about four to six weeks. Bloody, painful and frequent urination, diarrhea. Later victims become weaker and may be susceptible to further infections and diseases.

Treatment: Elimination of *S. mansoni* requires oxamniquine and praziquantel. *S. japonicum* responds to praziquantel alone and *Schistosoma haematobium is treated with* praziquantel and metrifonate.

How to Avoid: Stay out of slow moving fresh water in all tropical and semitropical areas. This also means wading or standing in water.

Tainiasis (tapeworms)

Found: Worldwide.

Cause: A tapeworm is usually discovered after being passed by the victim.

Carrier: Ingestion of poorly cooked meat infected with tapeworms.

Symptoms: In advanced cases there will be diarrhea and stomach cramps. Sections of tapeworms can be seen in stools.

Treatment: Mebendazole, niclocsamide, paromomysi and praziqunatel are effective in killing the parasite.

How to Avoid: Tapeworms come from eating meats infected with tapeworm or coming into contact with infected fecal matter.

Tetanus (lockjaw)

Found: Worldwide.

Cause: A bacteria caused by the bacteria Clostridiium tetani.

Carrier: Found in soil and enters body through cuts or punctures.

Symptoms: Restlessness, irritability, headaches, jaw pain, back pain and stiffness and difficulty in swallowing. Then within two to 56 days stiffness increases with lockjaw and spasms. Death occurs in about half the cases, usually affecting children.

Treatment: If infected, human tetanus immune globulin is administered with nerve blockers for muscle relaxation.

How to Avoid: Immunization is the best prevention with a booster recommended before travel.

Trachoma

Found: Common in Africa, the Middle East and Asia.

Cause: A chlamydial infection of the eye, that is responsible for about 200 million cases of blindness.

Carrier: Flies, contact, wiping face or eye area with infected towels.

Symptoms: Constant inflammation under the eyelid that causes scarring of the eyelid, in turned eyelashes and eventual scarring of the cornea and then blindness.

Treatment: Tetracyclines, erythromycin, sulfonamide, surgery to correct turned-in lashes.

How to Avoid: It is spread primarily by flies. Proper hygiene and avoidance of fly infested areas are recommended.

Trichinosis

Found: Worldwide.

Cause: Infection of the *Trichinella spiralis* worm.

Carrier: Pig meat (also bear and walrus) that contain cysts. The worm then infects the new hosts tissues and intestines.

Symptoms: Diarrhea, abdominal pain, nausea, prostration and fever. As the worm infects tissues, fever, swelling around the eyes, conjunctivitis, eye hemorrhages, muscle pain, weakness, rash and splinter hemorrhages under the nails. Less than 10 percent of the cases result in death.

Treatment: Thiabendazole is effective in killing the parasite.

How to Avoid: Proper preparation, storage and cooking of meat.

Tuberculosis

Found: Worldwide.

Cause: A disease of the lungs caused by the *Mycobacterium tuberculosis* bacteria or *Mycobacterium bovis*.

Carrier: By close contact with infected persons, (sneezing, coughing) or in the case of *Mycobacterium bovis* contaminated or unpasteurized milk.

Symptoms: Weight loss, night sweats and a chronic cough usually with traces of blood. If left untreated death results in about 60 percent of the cases after a period of two and a half years.

Treatment: Isoniazide, rifampin can control the disease.

How to Avoid: Vaccination and isoniazid prophylaxis.

Tularaemia (Rabbit fever)

Found: Worldwide.

Cause: A fairly rare disease (about 300 cases per year) caused by the bacteria, *Francisella tularnesis* passed from animals to humans via insects.

Carrier: The bite of deerflies, ticks, mosquitoes and even cats can infect humans.

Symptoms: Fever, chills, headaches, muscle pain, malaise, enlarged liver and spleen, rash, skin ulcers and enlargement of the lymph nodes.

Treatment: Vaccination to prevent those at risk from handling animals. Streptomycin primarily. Tetracycline and chloramphenicol are effective.

How to Avoid: Care when handling animal carcasses, removal of ticks and avoidance of insect bites.

Typhoid Fever

Found: Africa, Asia, Central America

Cause: The bacterium Salmonella typhi.

Carrier: Transmitted by contaminated food and water in areas of poor hygiene.

Symptoms: Fever, headaches, abdominal tenderness, malaise, rash, enlarged spleen. Later symptoms include delirium, intestinal hemorrhage and perforation of the intestine.

Treatment: Chloramphenicol.

How to Avoid: Vaccination is the primary protection although the effectiveness is not high.

Typhus Fever

Found: Africa, South America, Southeast Asia, India.

Cause: Rickettsia.

Carrier: Transmitted by fleas, lice, mites and ticks found in mountainous areas around the world.

Symptoms: Fever, headache, rash, and muscle pain. If untreated death may occur in the second week due to kidney failure, coma and blockage of the árteries.

Treatment: Tetracyclines or chloramphenicol.

How to Avoid: Check for ticks, avoid insect bites, hygiene to prevent lice and avoiding mountainous regions.

Yellow Fever

Found: Africa, South America.

Cause: A virus transmitted by mosquito bites.

Carrier: The tiny banded-legged aedes aegpyti is the source for urban yellow fever and the haemogogus and sabethes mosquito carries the jungle version.

Symptoms: In the beginning, fever, headaches, backaches, muscle pain, nausea, conjunctivitis, albumin in the urine and slow heart rate. Followed by black vomit, no urination and delirium. Death affects only five to 10 percent of cases and occurs in the fourth to sixth day.

Treatment: Replace fluids and electrolytes.

How to Avoid: Vaccination is mandatory when entering or leaving infected areas.

Terrorism

I Hear You Knocking, but You Can't Come In

Terrorism can be easily defined as "premeditated, politically motivated violence perpetrated against noncombatant targets by subnational groups or clandestine agents usually intended to influence an audience" as it is by United States Code Section 2656(d). This definition is obviously the work of leaders of established and recognized countries, most with democratic political processes. It should be remembered that the United States of America, Russia, China, France and Israel, along with numerous other now respectable countries, began their road to independence using terrorist methods and actions against their past leaders.

Today few can argue that terrorism is a legitimate and sadly productive method to gain international attention, demand concessions and eventually establish legitimate states and political parties. Despite what the world governments espouse, there are few minority groups who can use the existing political process to gain their independence or freedom without resorting to outrageous tactics.

The less potent the group is as a political force and the thinner the support base, the more likely the group will resort to more dramatic methods to secure world attention.

The leaders of these groups tend to be from the upper classes, well educated, creative, egotistical and flamboyant almost to the point of ridiculousness. Che Guevara, Yasir Arafat, Carlos the Jackal and most recently, Rafael Sebastin Guillen Vicente a.k.a Subcommandante Marcos, the pipe smoking, wisecracking son of a furniture salesman.

There are various proven methods of gaining the world's attention. The first is to execute or kidnap Americans while they are abroad. This will guarantee at least two to five minutes on CNN with 30 minute repeats every half-hour until the situation is resolved.

The next is usually hijacking; the third and most frequent is bombing, the last and possibly least effective are attacks on military or police forces. Sending a well-written political proposal with workable, fair solutions to the ruling party won't even get you a return phone call. You gotta have a gimmick and fear among the populace will definitely get you attention.

There is another level of terrorism activity that doesn't make the headlines but is necessary for the ongoing support of organizations and activities. If terrorist groups are not funded by a government (such as Iran, Iraq, Libya, Pakistan or private sources) they must resort to extortion (demanding money in exchange for lack of violent attacks), robbery (theft of money or possessions by force or threat of force) kidnapping (abducting people who then are released in exchange for negotiated amounts of money), drug or weapons smuggling (payment for safe transport of illegal goods). Other groups are for hire and will conduct assassinations, kidnappings, warfare, bombings or other criminal attacks for a fee. Many times these acts are carried out under the name of a terrorist group but are simply criminal acts. There are various freelance terrorists like Abu Nidal and the now forcibly retired Carlos. They would provide spectacular sound bites and video clips for a fee and/or a piece of the action. All that was missing was a director and a producer.

It is important to note that terrorists would like to attack at the heart of the intended enemies' strongholds but are neither strong, smart or powerful enough. Worse yet, there are no terrorist groups who can handle the ideologically numbing bureaucracy. Just look at the poor Palestinians who are now faced with beating their own people to quell rioting and protect Israelis. So most groups content themselves with chipping away at the public confidence, gaining a hollow importance but taking no real steps toward bettering the plight of the people they represent. Some groups like *Hezbollah* and Hamas are strong political entities with equally strong military arms. Other groups like the Kurdish groups and the PKK are caught in a Catch-22 and have had political structures that were banned as representing terrorist organizations.

The three most dramatic terrorist acts have been the bombing of the Marine Barracks in Beirut, the February 26th bombing of the World Trade Center in New York and the downing of Pan Am 107 over Lockerbie, Scotland. It is important to note that in each one of these cases the perpetrators were either apprehended, identified, or were killed in the act. The former and current supporters of terrorism against the West find themselves banished from the world marketplace and proudly trying to pretend they never needed all that Western money anyway. Libya, Iraq and Iran all make hollow speeches while privately their emissaries desperately try to get invited back into the real world's economic cocktail party. When you make it big in the terrorism network you are guaranteed to have a short career. When Carlos was an embarrassment to the terror network he was shuffled between Libya, Iraq, Jordan, Syria and Yemen and finally ended up in the Sudan before he was then served up to the French.

That means that terrorism will continue to be a threat to all Western travelers. The savvy traveler will need to understand the difference between the Algerian terrorist (who will cut your throat without even rifling through your pockets), a Mexican terrorist (who has no reason to harm an American tourist), a Filipino terrorist (who will trade you like a used car salesman), a Kurdish terrorist (who will use you as a political pawn and usually release you unharmed and well fed) or a plain ol' thug who may have been fighting for some funky acronymic bunch but just likes the Rolex you have and can't be bothered asking you politely for it.

As you head into dangerous places, the lack of other tourists dramatically raises your profile and the chances of your being a target increase. In America the bulk of the terrorist incidents have been in the North Central region (12) and Puerto Rico (11) with seven in the West and only two in the northeast.

Is terrorism a real and present danger? Yes, if you choose to head into areas where foreigners are currently being targeted for kidnapping or execution—Algeria, Turkey, Egypt, Sri Lanka, Cambodia or the Philippines. Is terrorism your biggest fear other than in the above countryies? No. You stand a better chance of being robbed, infected or injured in an accident.

The Forces of Terror—*Jihad* (Holy War) The Crusade Against the Infidels

The beginning of an empire is never heralded until its first major victory. There is a new empire emerging and it has embarked on its great crusade. With the destruction of the Soviet empire there remained a void in the political balance. The U.S. is considered to be a superpower but it is absolutely Judeo-Christian in structure and blindly enthusiastic in its approach to defending its financial and political interests abroad.

Unfortunately, the U.S. has little or no influence in most of Asia, Africa and the Middle East. Its policy of buying peace can only work in poor nations which have economic and philosophical ties to the U.S. The one flashpoint is America's support of Israel (Jews) over the rights of the Arabs (Muslims). The Arabs quite rightly believe that Israel is the invader who has taken advantage of the Arabs' lack of political and military strength in order to establish themselves around one of the Jews' most holy sites (Jerusalem). This scenario is a repeat of the situation that led to the launching of the crusades when the Muslims had taken control of the Christians' most holy site (Jerusalem). Now it is the East's turn to remove the infidels from the Holy Land and restore Islam.

Anyone who reads the Koran will understand the Arabs intolerance for nonbelievers and Jews. Traditional Islam cannot coexist with the current Judeo-Christian ethic. There is no "love thy neighbor" or any other mediating statement to sway a true believer that there is any option other than the complete annihilation (or conversion) of the West and the total elimination of the Jews.

The Role of the United States and the U.N. in Making the World a Dangerous Place

There is little effort by Americans to understand the religion of Islam. Muslims are generally lumped into stereotypical Arab cartoon caricatures or characters from *1001 Arabian Nights*. Recently, America defended Kuwait; a Muslim country run by a wealthy Arab dictator whose government is made up of family members. Iraq believed that Kuwait is part of Iraq (which it is) and was just one of many tribal areas that should be brought under control. Kuwait not only could not defend itself, but the leaders chose to hightail it out of the country and leave the sandblown region to the Iraqi army. After the war, the U.S. decided to break a chunk of northern Iraq off and call it Kurdistan. Kurdistan is not on any map but it's a U.S. occupied territory carved out (like the British carved out Palestine) for the benefit of an oppressed minority. What would happen if the United States occupied Quebec and gave it to the Quebecois?

It is no wonder that the Middle East and Asia view the U.S. as a culturally retarded, schoolyard bully. The U.N and the U.S. have been called upon to settle backyard fights in Bosnia-Herzegovina, Cambodia, Somalia, Cuba, Haiti, Panama and other banana republics. In every case the warring sides do not kiss and makeup but use the time to grab as much land as possible. Nobody wins and there is little, if any, positive political solution once America or the U.N. leave.

The last good fist fight American had was the Gulf War. The American military was designed to kick the Soviet's butt in conventional ground and air combat. The Iraqi army, with its Soviet deep-discount army used tanks, planes and supplies, was the perfect enemy for us. We even got to try out all of our new Pentagon toys and Air Force gizmos to see if they worked.

Not only is America viewed as lumbering, it is also seen as cowardly. In Somalia, instead of annihilating Aidid as any self-respecting war lord would have done, cutting the throat of every man, woman, child and goat, the U.S. once again used conventional tactics in a street brawl. As soon as they took a few casualties they pulled out under public pressure to let the "thugs kill each other off." Few Americans knew that Aidid deliberately and successfully waged a war of terrorism against the U.N. and won.

The lesson in this simplistic political diatribe is that fundamentalist Muslim terrorists view Americans as meddling evil people who overreact when a citizen is murdered or terrorized. You, as a Westerner, are on the front lines whether you want to be or not.

The War At Home

The next big war is being fought right now on the streets of America. WWII started for Americans when the Japanese bombed Pearl Harbor. We think of bombing as something being done by an airplane from a belligerent nation. Few Americans could foresee that the first major bombing attack would be against the World Trade Center, which could be bombed by a rented pickup truck and a homemade bomb. It was a day that will equally live in infamy.

The bomb wasn't delivered by a Soviet bomber, submarine or even a guided missile it was delivered by a beat-up rental van. What if the van had contained an atomic bomb instead of conventional explosives? Would America send its B2s to bomb Tehran, the Bekaa Valley, the homes of American Muslims? Who is the enemy?

Shatun-e-Buzorg (The Great Satan)

The enemy of America is a political and military group called Hezbollah (variously translated as Followers of God, Party of God, Army of God, etc.) Hezbollah is based in Southern Lebanon under the protection of Syria, financed by Iran and is currently expanding and maintaining cells on all continents. The members consider themselves at war with the United States and Israel. Hezbollah is a Shia Muslim group and they are responsible for the destruction of the Marine Barracks in Beirut in October 1983, the bombing of the U.S. Embassy annex in 1984, the 1985 TWA hijacking and the kidnapping of the U.S. and other Western hostages in Lebanon. They most recently blew up the Israeli Embassy in Buenos Aires in 1992. They continually launch attacks into Israel from their base in the Bekaa Valley.

Sudan has joined in its attempt to further Tehran's fundamentalist goals and has created and harbored the Armed Islamic Movement (AIM) popularly known as the International Legion of Islam. AIM is an umbrella organization headquartered in Khartoum, Sudan. The most hard-core and admired members are the Afghans or veterans from Pakistan who trained with the mujahadeen or who have fought in the Afghan war.

AIM and the Shiite Hezbollah have combined to create a strike force that operates on behalf of the interests of fundamentalist governments based in Tehran, Damascus and Khartoum. Various factions in Algeria, Egypt, Israel, Lebanon, Nigeria, Somalia, Jordan, Pakistan, India and others benefit from their association with Hezbollah and the funds from their patrons.

The Hezbollah's operational center is in Lebanon and AIM has its operational centers in Sudan, Pakistan and Afghanistan with its major center of control and direction coming from Iran.

The chaos of southern Lebanon provides a hellish setting for Hezbollah. The French call them the "lunatics of Allah." The poppy fields of the Bekaa Valley were once lucrative sources of funding for their operations. Make no mistake, Hezbollah is not a collection of whacked-out religious fanatics or David Koresh (Branch Davidian)-style rejects. They are a well financed, tightly structured group of highly trained politicians, soldiers and administrators who carry-out the political and religious goals of Iran.

In fact, the consolidation of the political agendas of Sudan, Iran and Syria has created a new Axis similar to the new "Antichrist" mentioned in the Apocalypse. The difference is that this enemy has no shining headquarters, no uniform, no central base and very little for the ponderous Western military machine to attack.

The Holy War

Unlike wars of geographical expansion, the war of Iran is for the mind and soul. Theirs is truly a jihad—a holy war. Although certain elements are motivated by profit and glory, the leadership truly believes in furthering the interests of Islam and the Koran. Their radical Shiite interpretation of the Koran does not allow them the liberalism or Western influence other Islamic nations enjoy.

The Shia Muslims of Iran view the western world as weakened by moral decay, factional squabbling, lassitude and an almost Roman-style decline in morality and diligence. The Iranians are also promoting their hard and ascetic world as being correct, much the same way that Mao and Lenin played up hardship and sacrifice as necessary for success and fulfillment. The leaders of Hezbollah find many a responsive listener when they blame the West for their troubles. Hiding behind the Koran, they preach hatred and intolerance to an eager and angry audience.

While Westerners believe that each person can change his, and his country's, destiny based on individual contribution and democratic principals, the radical Eastern Muslim believes that Allah will determine the outcome of his life and his country's existence. Some may say this naive and fatalistic view of the world cannot bring out the best in a people, but in the eyes of the Islamic fundamentalists, the West's moral decline and incursion into Muslim regions is evidence of the fall of Western values.

The Iranians believe that the imposition of Western values (particularly under the Shah) has created a ruling class of corrupt and greedy cliques. People shut out from the benefits of industrialization and education seek solace in tribal, religious or ethnic self-identities. Impoverished and with little chance for betterment, the youth of Iran find solidarity and hope in the fervent religious message of the mullahs.

The New Antichrist

The CIA was not ashamed to admit that the Shah was an anachronistic and convenient puppet who protected Western interests and provided a safe buffer against the Russians and other Muslim states. His hold on the country was brutal and total with the help of SAVAK, the secret police. His downfall came from trying to force Western morals on a people who saw and derived no benefit from being Westernized.

The Shiite cleric Ayatollah Khomeini was not the Antichrist. He was a quiet but stern cleric who returned from exile in Paris in February of 1979 to turn back the Westernization and destruction of Iran's culture. Iran had enjoyed Western support because of its vast oil reserves. The education of its upper classes and the Westernization of its culture was held up as an example of how the ignorant Muslim could be brought up to quasi-European and Western standards. His major goal was to bring together all Muslims into a single nation (Ummah) and support all and any Islamic movement who fought against Western interests.

Khomeini immediately declared war on a vaguely defined enemy. His armies were equally ill defined. The one constant was Iran's need to provide a strong and aligning philosophy to all Islamic groups that would work to install a love of Islam and acceptance of Spartan third world values. In any case, it is always a good idea to have your young men fighting wars instead of looking for jobs that will never exist.

Many of these young men fought in the eight-year war with Iraq, a set piece war complete with trenches, artillery battles and shocking deaths.

The Ayatollah also opened the door for a new kind of terrorist, unlike the godless terrorists trained by Russia to liberate the oppressed from imperialist and colonialist masters. Employing the techniques they had used to train soldiers to fight the forces of the Shah, Iran began to manufacture terrorists for God who would strike the infidels and spread the word of the Mohammed.

The Education of Terrorists

During the 1970s thousands of terrorists were trained in South Yemen by East German and Bulgarian trainers. Training camps in Baalbek and Rashidyah in Lebanon and the as-Syada Zaynab camp turned out fanatic Muslims who had managed to transfer their hatred of the Soviet Union to hatred of America.

The training of Iranians by Palestinian groups like Yasir Arafat's al-Fatah and Ahmad Jibril's PLFP-GC led to the creation of militias such as Harakat Amal (the first Shiite militia in Lebanon) who were used to overthrow the Shah and track down and kill SAVAK members. There were estimated to be 10,000 anti-Shah guerrillas who were later to become the Pasdaran or Islamic Revolutionary Guards (IRGC).

The intent of Iran to spread revolution could be seen in its willingness to work with Sunni Muslims like Qaddafi, Christian groups like George Ibrahim Abdallah and LARF (a Lebanese based terrorist group that was active in Europe in the early 80s) and Varoudijian Garabedjian and ASALA (the Armenian Secret Army for the Liberation of Armenia).

The International Conference of the World Center for Resistance of Imperialism, Zionism, Racism, Reaction and Fascism was the first embryonic notion of what was to come. The meeting was organized by the Soviets and their allies. The strange meeting took place in mid-June 1982 in Tripoli, Libya. Representatives from 240 anti-western organizations in 80 countries met to create a unified program of revolution. The bankruptcy of the Soviet bloc allowed Iran to replace the Soviets on a bargain-basement-level sponsorship.

The first Iranian terrorist camp was Manzarieh, in northern Tehran, set up in February of 1981. Here, eager young men, many non-Iranian, were trained in both Islamic doctrine and military skills. Only the best became terrorists. Of the first class of 175, only 150 graduated six months later. By 1985 there were 15–18 terrorist training schools in Iran, supported by Soviet bloc instructors who came from North Korea, Russia, Palestine and other countries. Muslim youths from Africa, Asia and Europe were systematically trained in everything including suicide operations. There were even schools for female terrorists, including American and Irish citizens.

It is estimated that there were 3000 graduates between 1981 and 1985. Today the Manzarieh Park camp is the largest and has between 900 and 1000 students at any one time. The camp is run by Muhammad Shamkani and is the home of a suicide unit, which goes through expanded Islamic training including lengthy lectures and even listening to passages of the Koran on cassette. Once they pass the mental indoctrination they are trained in terrorist tactics. Upon graduation they receive signed diplomas.

Graduate work for suicide units is carried out at the Marvdasht camp near Persepolis. Here the students learn how to build and handle bombs, as well as tactics. It is said that suicide training was first conducted with prisoners condemned to death who could be motivated to drive explosive-loaded trucks into each other at the command of an instructor, according to an Iranian defector, Col. Ali Vesseghi who served there until 1983.

Another suicide unit was trained in Bushehr air base in Iran. Here pilots learned to fly suicide missions using 80 *Pilatus Porter PC-7* aircraft loaded with explosives. After three graduates died in low level crashes before ever arriving at their Iraqi targets, the training was shifted to the Won Son air base in North Korea using more experienced pilots. Later these more experienced pilots, in their Swiss built STOL planes, were used to target palaces of the heads of state of the Gulf states and the U.S. 6th fleet in Lebanon. Other planes used for suicide training were 25 *Cessna Citations*, 15 *Falcon Fanjets* and even aging *DC-3s*.

There is also a naval warfare training camp in Bandar Abbas. Here terrorists train to mine ships and conduct UDT warfare. A camp in Isfahan specializes in the handling of high-end explosive devices and booby traps.

Airport attacks and hijackings were taught at Wakilabad near Mashhad. The entire Western-built airport was used for training including using a *Boeing 707* and *727*. A *Boeing 747* would at times be sent down for special classes. A second hijacking school was set up in Shiraz airport with an Iran Air *A300 Airbus* for training.

Where are these graduates now? Well, reunions would be sparsely attended. Many graduates were killed, arrested and detained during the tumultuous late'80s. More frightening, the majority of these graduates were deliberately sent to Western countries to ask for asylum (taught as part of their course) to await activation in later years. Any of these "submarines," when subsequently arrested for terrorist activities, had been resident for up to 10 years.

"We are the Soldiers of God and We Crave Death:"
The Birth of Hezbollah

So said the anonymous caller for Islamic Jihad after the bombing of the U.S. Marine barracks in Beirut on October 23, 1983. Back then few could make sense of just who was behind the kidnapping, bombing and suicide attacks. Today we know that the single most powerful force for radical Islamic revolution is Hezbollah, or the Party of God.

Hezbollah was created in 1973 by Ayatollah Mahmoud Ghaffani. Ghaffani was the man primarily responsible for planning the revolution against the Shah of Iran. However, he did not live to see the successful completion of his plans. He was captured, tortured and killed by SAVAK, the Shah's secret police. He is alleged to have cried out in his final moments that there is but one party and that is the party of God. The organization languished but survived until the Ayatollah Khomeini resurrected it in 1979. In 1982 Khomeini used the slogan "only one party, the party of Allah, only leader, Ruhollah." He also ordered all other Islamic revolutionary groups to merge under the banner of Hezbollah. During Khomeini's time it is estimated that he spent between $15–50 million a year to support the group's activities.

Today, the most dangerous terrorist group in the world is Hezbollah (see the "Lebanon" chapter) under the religious guidance of Sheikh Fadlallah, the most senior cleric in Lebanon. The members of Hezbollah in southern Lebanon are primarily Shiites recruited from the various Palestinian refugee camps. The Israelis conducted numerous retaliatory attacks against these camps in revenge for the shelling of Israel by Palestine troops.

Shortly after the revolution in Iran, Iranians began recruiting the most fanatical Shiites and setup their first major military base outside Iran in Zabadani, Syria. The Iranians sent in about 5000 Pasadaran to Lebanon to help the fight against Israel; 1000 of these troops fought the Israelis in the Shouf mountains. After the fighting ended 500 Iranians stayed behind in the Bekaa (or Biqaa) Valley under the protection of Syrian forces. The Baalbek area became a fertile ground for terrorism with many special interest groups, from Abu Nidal's organization to the Libyans. The Bekaa Valley became the world headquarters for terrorism in 1982. Supplied from Damascus and supported by Iran, the Iranians quickly consolidated their dominance of Hezbollah.

Here the 500 or so followers of Sheikh Fadlallah gathered to become the core group of Hezbollah which would soon be a federation of 13 Islamic terrorist movements (11 Shiite and two Sunni).

Decisions are made by a religious council and though Sheikh Sayyid Muhammad Hussein Fadlallah says he is not the leader, it is known that his authority is absolute even if not secured with a title.

Sheikh Sayyid Muhammad Hussein Fadlallah was born in 1943 or '44 in Najaf, Iraq to a family originally from Lebanon. He rose to prominence after the Iranian revolution due to his abilities and strength of conviction in an Islamic world. He is an author of two books on Islam, including *Islam and the Concept of Power and Dialogue in the Koran*. His religious preachings and his political beliefs are one and the same: Jihad is absolute and all encompassing and the war must be fought by whatever means necessary.

The War Begins in Earnest

The first major blow struck by Sheikh Sayyid Muhammad Hussein Fadlallah was against the U.S. Embassy in Beirut on April 18, 1983. The KGB let Hezbollah know that the Beirut station chief for the CIA, along with high level CIA operatives for the Beirut area, would be in the U.S. Embassy. There was also an operative planted in the PLO, and 17 Lebanese being trained to steal a Syrian missile. Hezbollah assigned a suicide driver but it was considered too important so a Druze driver was asked to park the GMC van outside the embassy. At 1:05p.m. the terrorists detonated the bomb with the unsuspecting driver inside and killed 63 people including most of the high level CIA operatives for the Middle East.

On October 23 in 1983 two terrorists from the Bekaa Valley were in Beirut. They woke up at 5:00 a.m., said their prayers and had tea and cookies (which were laced with a drug). An hour later each drove an explosive-filled truck—one into the American Marine barracks and the other into the French headquarters. Two hundred forty-five Americans were dead and 146 were wounded; 58 French were killed and 15 wounded. Islamic Jihad, a *nom de guerre* of Hezbollah, was used to claim responsibility for all attacks.

On February 26, 1993 the World Trade Center was bombed. The 1000lb bomb was made out of $400 worth of simple chemicals and an alarm clock timer. The war is not over by a long shot.

At the Tehran Terrorist Conference held on October 18–22, 1991 in Iran, over 400 delegates from 45 countries reaffirmed their "all out battle against the global alliance of arrogance" in a torrent of biblical rhetoric and open threats. By the end of the conference it was clear that the main items on the terrorists' agenda include liberating Palestine, eliminating Israel and striking back at the Great Satan: America.

Terrorism in the Americas

No one would or could compare the danger in downtown New York with that of London or Beirut in the '80s. But for such a rigid, controlled land it is just not right that people choose to fight their wars in our land. Of course it doesn't dawn on most harried commuters and white collar workers that we are fighting wars in their lands. Every time a CIA bought rocket smashes into a house in Kabul, or Israeli rockets take out a south Lebanon falafel stand, it is just another reminder that the U.S. has chosen to pick sides in the world's wars.

TERRORIST INCIDENTS IN THE U.S.	1989	1990	1991	1992	1993
Terrorist Incidents	4	7	5	4	12
U.S. Suspected Incidents	16	1	1	0	2
Terrorism Preventions	7	5	4	0	7
TOTAL	27	13	10	4	21

Source: FBI

Luckily, the terrorists' batting average is not as great as the chart shows. What the chart doesn't show is that when our team plays away from home in the coca fields of Colombia or small villages in East Turkey, we don't even stand a chance. Most terrorist organizations focus on attacking U.S. and foreign interests on their home turf.

With the bombing of the World Trade Center it is important to understand that terrorism is not just blowing up public buildings. Iran is very interested in acquiring technology. A Hezbollah operative, Muhammad Harafdini, was arrested with blueprints of components of *F-111* aircraft and missiles. The 1989 pipe bomb attack on Sharon Lee Rogers is another home delivery terror-gram. Rogers was the wife of the captain of the U.S.S. *Vincennes*, the ship that shot down an Iranian airliner by mistake on July 3, 1988. It is speculated that the 30,000 or so Iranian students in the U.S. may contain a hard-core group of 1000 militant "submarines" awaiting the call to action. Most attacks have been sporadic and generally unsuccessful. Iran, for all its boasting, still has financial problems and the more umbilical cords it creates, the weaker mother Iran will become. For now the terrorists get more points for enthusiasm than for skill.

Unlike the expansionist policy of America or Soviet Russia, the battle for Islam does not deliver rich rewards of land, industries and raw goods. It does create more and more fanatics trained in killing and terrorism.

We are at war with religious fundamentalists who lust after a signed fatwah (a formal document that determines their place in eternity) from a religious leader more than a brick layer wants to win the New Jersey lottery.

The conference chairman of the 1991 Tehran Terrorist Conference, Hojjat ol-Islam Abdul-Vahed Mussavi-Lari said the forces of Islam will continue to train Muslim Palestinian fighters, to counter the Jewish migration to the Occupied Territories.

The leader of Hezbollah in Lebanon, Sayyid Abbas al-Mussawi vowed that they will hold out their struggle until the city of Quds (Jerusalem) is liberated.

Organizations supportive of HAMAS in the U.S. are:

The United Association for Studies and Research in Springfield, Virginia

The Islamic Association for Palestine, Dallas, Texas is a reputed major source of funds and publications for HAMAS.

The Monitor and the Al-Zaituni (Olive Tree) in Arabic

The Islamic Committee for Palestine

Muslim Youth League

Mostazafan Foundation in New York

Muslim Students' Association in US and Canada

Al-Da'wa (the Call)

Jundulah (Soldiers of God)

Hezbollah
>   *Mekteb-1 Hezbollah*
>   *South Suburb*
>   *Bir-al Abed*
>   *Beyrouth, Lebanon*

Terrorism in Europe

In the spring of 1992 there were 5 million non-European immigrants living in Germany of which 45,000 were known to be members of extremist groups. Half (23,000) of this latter group were considered to be prepared for violence.

The total numbers are not impressive but the support they provide to terrorism groups is. Western Europe had 180 terrorist attacks in 1993. A rough estimate of expats from countries with potential sympathies to terrorist groups include: 70,000 Tamils and Sikhs, 30,000 Afghans, 300,000 Kurds (3500 are known members of PKK), 650,000 Yugoslavs and 70,000 Palestinians, 85,000 Iranians. The disenchantment of these recent immigrants and the intolerance shown by their host countries (some with insurmountable citizenship laws) has created fertile ground for groups like Hezbollah and the PKK.

The PKK has a network that covers 26 cities in Western Europe; the PFLP is estimated to have 50–60 terrorists in Europe; al-Fatah has 1700 supporters in West Germany; the PFLP-GC has 30 expert terrorists in West Germany. A sleeper network of Abu Nidal was exposed in Portugal and the ranks are growing, not shrinking, despite a get tough attitude by Germany, Spain and France.

P.K.K.

> *Mekte-Bi Amele-1 Kurdestan*
> *Barelias-Chotura*
> *West Bekaa, Lebanon*

Qaddafi was an ardent supporter of the IRA training Irish Republican soldiers and providing explosives and arms. Libya also supports the Basque ETA rebels and the Muslims in Bosnia. These groups are now being supplied by Iran and Syria. The new austerity of the '90s was evidenced by the dropping of the expensive SEMTEX as an explosive device and shifting to more available and cheaper fertilizer chemicals for explosives.

For more information on terrorists, call *1-800-KA-BOOM*. (Just kidding.)

The FAL (Fusil Automatique Leger)

Although the AK47 is the Volkswagen of assault rifles, the Chevy of rifles may be the FAL. The Belgium-designed FAL was finally adopted in 1953 by Canada and soon thereafter by Britain, Australia and then finally by NATO. Most FALs are semiautomatic, not fully automatic. Although only about 3 million FALs have been sold, they are in use in 79 countries. The FAL is very powerful but wildly inaccurate when fired at a rapid rate. It is very accurate when fired single-shot. The FAL also has serious problems in sandy and muddy conditions unless modified with sand cuts along the bolt carrier and receiver. The FAL had a lot of negative points: it was too big at 40 inches long, it was too heavy and the 7.62 ammunition was also heavy and too powerful.

In full automatic, the C21A version can fire off 700 rounds per minute but should be used with a bipod. The FAL fell out of favor in the late 70s when the lighter 5.56 NATO cartridge was favored. The rifle is no longer manufactured.

Bribes

Crime Does Pay

Mordida, dash, spiffs, baksheesh, cadeaus, special fees, fines, gifts or whatever they are called are a regular part of travel in the Third World. In many cases military, police and government officials will expect a gratuity to allow passage, payment of minor infractions or to issue visas. There are a few guidelines to this indelicate art.

Paying Your Dues

Most travelers put in jail are involved in traffic or drug related offenses. Naturally many countries have an unofficial method of dealing with these problems efficiently and profitably. It serves no purpose for small or poor countries to incarcerate you for lengthy periods of time. It also does not serve the purpose of many policemen to spend their time filling out paperwork when they can resolve the problem and teach you a lesson on the spot. From Minnesota to Malaysia to Mexico I have been amazed at the solid financial education police officers have been given. (Which is better? $100 in your pocket or the county's pocket?) There are many officers who do not accept or want bribes. The way to tell is simple. The officer will try to resolve a problem rather than write you up, handcuff you or arrest you. If you feel an opening gambit has been made, then you are expected to explain to the officer your desire for a speedy amicable resolution of your problem. In most cases the officer will feel somewhat uncomfortable about having to take you all the way back to the station (always in the opposite direction you are traveling) to wait for the judge who is typically fishing or out until next week.

If he offers to take the fine back for you or to let you pay it on the spot, then bingo, the chiseling begins. Remember that bribes are a "cash only" business and the amount you can pay will be limited to the amount of cash you have on you at that moment. Now that you have the rules of the game please remember that offering any financial inducement to an officer, however innocently, is illegal and will put you in jail.

Delivering a Bribe

One must never discuss money or the amount or the reason for the gift. Typically you will be presented with a "problem" that can be solved but will take time, money, or approval by a higher authority. You will naturally need to have this problem solved. You may ask if there is a fee that will expedite the solution of this problem or if the local language fails you, you can point out your urgency and present a passport, ticket or papers with a single denomination of currency.

DP'S GUIDE TO BRIBES	
Minor traffic violation (speeding, imaginary stop signs, burned out tail lights that magically work; usually levied on Fridays or Saturday afternoons).	$5–$10
Traffic violations (real stop signs, real speeding tickets).	$10–$50
Serious traffic violations (DUI, very serious speeding or racing).	$50–$500
Very serious traffic problem (accident with no fatalities).	$500–$1000
Accidents that involve fatalities require the application of funds to a judge, your lawyer, prosecutor and probably the police chief. Costs are usually in the $2000–$6000 range and, yes, they will wait while your credit card clears. You will also be waiting in a jail.	$2000–$6000
If you are involved in something shady and need to correct the problem, it is wise to hire a lawyer. To make sure you get a lawyer who is sympathetic to the needs of the police, simply ask the police to recommend a good lawyer. The lawyer will negotiate fees for himself, the judge and the police.	$10,000–$45,000

The Price for Doing Bad Things

Bribes do not work if you are caught by the military, make the local papers or happen to be doing something the government is busy eradicating (usually with U.S. funds) at the time. Smuggling drugs, weapons or people requires the support of a large, covertly sanctioned organization. Freelancers are usually treated roughly with little opportunity to buy their way out. Depending on how big a fish they think you are, you can expect to start at about $12,000 to get out of a South or Central American jail. It is not uncommon to have to pay $30,000–$120,000 to beat a major drug rap.

If you are kidnapped by terrorists you might feel lucky. They will typically hit up your government of origin for your ransom. Americans fetch between $100,000 to $2 million depending on what your carcass is worth. Many times guerrillas will attach other demands. This lowers your chances of freedom dramatically since most governments have stated policies about negotiating with terrorists, though they are fairly helpful with kidnapping cases. The catch is that your government will expect you to pay them back.

Other reasons for bribes are to bring in cars, contraband, machine parts, business samples, cash or even a wife. In many countries the police derive their sustenance from local businesses. A recent article in *Newsweek* estimated that in Hong Kong, brothels provide $120–$600 a month. In Bangkok, the city's 1000 "entertainment houses" pay $600,000 a month to the local police. Strangely these types of businesses can provide favors to travelers if you find yourself in a squeeze or need help approaching the police on a sensitive issue.

The best way to check out bribes is to contact the local embassy, expats who live in the area, local journalists (not foreign journalists) and local lawyers. It should be stated that in many cases a demand for a bribe can be talked down if you are doing nothing wrong. Many junior customs officials will spot first timers and shake them down for everything from their *Playboys* to their underwear. Feel free to protest, but when the man with the big hat and gold stars agrees with the peon, it's time to start rolling off the twenties.

When It Is Better to Give Than to Receive

Many people view bribery as reprehensible and evil. These are usually the ones who have to pay the bribes. Others view the practice as a normal way to supplement meager government wages (you can guess who they are). All countries including America have this affliction. Africa is the worst place for bribery, followed by South America and Central America with Northern Europe being the most incorruptible nation. Nigeria has the worst reputation for "dash" but you can expect any minor official in most poor African nations to ask for a "cadeau" or gift in exchange for providing a higher level of service. Expats detest this practice because they have to go through customs and refuse to pay it. Tourists are more easily intimidated and usually have much more to lose if they miss a flight, connection or cruise because of unnecessary delays.

Remember that bribes are used to facilitate or secure services that can be withheld or denied. Usually tightwads will be processed but at the back of the line. Obnoxious tightwads who like to make loud speeches about corruption may find themselves with insurmountable visa irregularities ("The stamp in your passport must be green ink for a fifteen day visa.")

A carton of cigarettes will ensure that you are speedily processed in most African countries. A bottle of Johnny Walker will not get you far in a Muslim country but will definitely expedite your exit visa in Colombia. Border crossings into most Central American countries can be done for a one hundred dollar bill and you can drive as fast as you want in Mexico if you have a good supply of twenty dollar bills. This will remove the need for a visa and will cause the customs official to forgo even a cursory inspection of your vehicle.

If you need to be smuggled out of a country, it is a little more complicated. First, the boatman will demand about twice the normal fee for your departure. Secondly, the matter of securing an exit visa without the benefit of an entry visa will cost you between $100 and $200 dollars in most Asian and Latin American countries. Eastern European and CIS countries can be crossed for as little as US$5, with no guarantee that you will not be finked on 10 miles down the road.

You don't have to be a criminal to pay bribes. Criminals take great pride in their ability to extract bribes or "protection money" from honest folks. For example, in Russia, 150 criminal gangs control 40,000 businesses. Moscow has 12 major organized crime groups who can extract up to 30 percent of monthly profits from businesses.

In summary, using bribery is like kissing in junior high school. Both parties must be willing but you have to be given an opening before you make your move. If you are brash or unwise you will be severely rebuked.

Land Mines

The world has 105 million land mines in 62 countries, according to the United Nations. Most of them were laid in the last 50 years with most planted in the last 20 years. It is known that every week 150 people, most of them civilians, are killed or injured by land mines. Eighty-five percent of those casualties are in Afghanistan, Angola and Cambodia. Eighteen African countries have 18–30 million mines; Angola has the least, between nine and 20 million uncleared mines, and the countryside of Mozambique is so heavily mined that most roads are unusable and the wildlife has long since disappeared. Somalia has a million mines; Sudan has two million; Zimbabwe and Ethiopia have major uncleared minefields.

Cambodia is the most mined country in the world. All of East Asia has 15–23 million land mines. The Middle East has 17–24 million land mines mainly in Iraq, Iran, Kuwait and the Israeli border. Europe is home to 7 million mines, mostly along the former Soviet border. Russia has both new minefields and WWII fields that were never cleared. Former Yugoslavia has many uncleared fields and new mines are being laid at a rate of 60,000 a week.

Up to a million uncleared mines are left in South America. Some areas of the Falklands are permanently off limits because the British could not spare the men to clear the minefields. There is a lot of splattered mutton every week in the Falklands.

Minefields are laid according to preset patterns with careful maps kept on their layout. Guerillas don't follow patterns. Mines are being used as booby traps and planted specifically to kill civilians in minor wars.

Greenpeace says that about 800 people are killed each month from land mines, some as old as WWI. Other groups say that someone is killed or maimed every 15 minutes. In any case, death by land mine is a nasty and lonely death. Most victims bleed to death in remote places.

The United Nations called for a worldwide ban on land mines. The U.S. asked the 44 countries that manufactured land mines to voluntarily suspend exports for three years. Other estimates say there are 340 different types of mines being manufactured in 48 countries. Together they produce about 10–20 million units a year.

In Cambodia it is estimated it will cost US$12 million annually for 10 years to remove the 10 million land mines left from the war. There is no money designated for that purpose.

In 1993, 80,000 were removed around the world at a cost of $100 million. Unfortunately 2.5 million were put in the ground or dropped during the same period.

The Valmara 69, or "Bouncing Betty," has a kill zone of about 60 feet. It can be recognized by the spikes coming out of the top.

Land mines are laid about six feet apart. One such NATO pattern is an A pattern with one antitank mine surrounded by three antipersonnel mines: one above and one on each side like a triangle with the antitank in the middle.

There were 7 million land mines laid in Iraq and Kuwait before and during the Gulf War.

Land mines are supposed to be laid according to pre-agreed patterns. The area should be marked and maps kept to facilitate cleanup. That is wishful thinking, since the most effective way to sow land mines is to drop millions of small plastic mines by shell or from aircraft. Small bomblets, 247 to a pod, are dropped as part of cluster bombs.

LAND MINES

PMN—Antipersonnel mine

The plastic, four-inch mine contains enough explosive to remove a leg at the hip.

Made by: Chinese, former Soviet state arsenals.

Cost: US$3.00

Found in: Zones throughout Africa, Middle East and Southeast Asia.

Est. in-ground: 20 million.

TYPE 72-A—Antipersonnel mine

Tiny, cheap and difficult to detect because of its plastic case. The perfect recipe for a best selling land mine.

Made by: China North Industries (Beijing).

Cost: US$3.00

Found in: Afghanistan, Angola, Cambodia, Iraq, Mozambique, Somalia, Thailand, Vietnam, Kuwait.

Est. in-ground: 20 million.

POM-Z-2—Antipersonnel fragmentation mine

Small and crude, the POM is mounted on a stick and has the same force as a hand grenade.

Made by: Chinese and former Soviet state arsenals.

Cost: US$3.30.

Found in: Zones worldwide.

Est. in-ground: 16 million.

PRB 409—Antipersonnel mine

Three inches wide, mildly powerful, popular with rebel groups.

Made by: Paoudres Reunie de Belgue, a subsidiary of Giat Industries (Versailles, France).

Cost: US$4.00

LAND MINES

Found in: Afghanistan, Iraq, Iran, Mozambique, Somalia, Lebanon.

Est. in-ground: 11 million.

PT-MI-BA III—Antitank mine

Made of plastic, the 13-inch mine contains 16 pounds of explosive, enough to disable heavily armored vehicles.

Made by: Czechoslovakian state factories.

Cost: US$38.00

Found in: Iran, Iraq, Kuwait, Mozambique, Somalia.

Est. in-ground: 11 million.

VS 2.2—Antitank mine

Plastic, nine-inch diameter mine containing 2.2 kilograms (4.8 pounds) of explosive.

Made by: Valsella Mecannotecnica S.P.A., a subsidiary of Fiat Motors (Brescia, Italy).

Cost: US$26.00

Found in: Afghanistan, Iraq, Iran, Kuwait.

Est. in-ground: 10 million.

L-9—Antitank mine

The "bar" mine is pressure sensitive along its entire 47-inch length. Buried under roads it is designed to destroy small personnel carriers and disable tanks by blowing off their tracks.

Made by: Royal Ordnance, a division of British Aerospace (London).

Cost: US$38.00

Found in: Iraq, Kuwait.

Est. in-ground: Six million.

M18A1 'Claymore'—Antipersonnel mine

A rectangular mine usually mounted as part of defensive construction or used for ambushes. The Claymore has a killing zone 50 yards wide and comes with helpful notice telling you which side to face towards the enemy.

Made by: Thiokol Corporation (Shreveport, LA.); widely imitated.

Cost: US$27.47

Found in: Angola, Mozambique, Central America, Southeast Asia.

Est. in-ground: Six million.

The Land Mine Top Ten

Afghanistan	Angola
Cambodia	Ethiopia
Sudan	Yugoslavia (former)
Mozambique	Somalia
Iraq	Laos

Kidnapping

"I'll see your envoy and raise you two hostages."

You're in Good Hands

Kidnappings by such groups as the PKK in Turkey, Abu Sayeff in the Philippines, the Khmer Rouge in Cambodia and Hezbollah in Lebanon have made travelers realize that they are targets just by being Westerners. Kidnapping is an ancient sport designed to generate cash, embarrass your enemies and, in some countries, find wives. Today, it is a big business. Consider yourself a blue chip, a pork belly, a regular over-the-counter commodity. A mid-level American executive can fetch US$500,000–800,000 for the kidnappers; ransoms of US$2 million for corporate brass aren't unusual. In areas such as Colombia, Venezuela and Russia—where kidnappers have perfected kidnapping to a fine art—people don't hesitate to meet the kidnappers' demands to get their boys home safe. In countries like Pakistan, the U.S. and the Philippines, negotiators can usually work out a discount.

Hijacking is a more lucrative and dangerous version of kidnapping. Chechens have found that they can squeeze bonzo rubles out of cash-poor Moscow by commandeering buses and airplanes.

The trick is not to get greedy. Once kidnappers become too outrageous in their demands, it is much easier to send in groups of specially-trained (or in the case of the Russians, specially-untrained) commandos to rescue the hostages. This usually results in success, but there have been bloodbaths.

Before you head out on your next trip or business posting take this brief test. You may want to apply for the ambassadorship to Disneyland instead.

- Are you traveling to a country that is hostile to American political policy?
- Are you traveling to a country that has regular kidnappings?
- Do you work for an American Company?
- Is it a Fortune 500 company?
- Is your business in oil, mining or food ?
- Are you a non-Muslim?
- Do you have substantial personal assets?

You've got the point. But there is hope.It's called abduction insurance or KR&E (Kidnapping, Rescue and Extortion insurance). It makes it easier for the bad guys, and it makes it easier for the good guys.

These days, Chubb, Fireman's Fund, Kroll & Associates, AIG and Lloyds of London will insure your sorry carcass if you get abducted. The premiums run from US$1000 to $100,000 a year depending on where you plan to go and how long you plan to stay. Lloyds of London has experienced a 50 percent jump in policies written over the last five years, and more insurance companies are looking into offering the coverage.

What do you get for your money? Actually quite a bit. Insurers will pay the ransom payment, medical treatment, interpreters and even your salary while you are gagged and bound. If you hire a free-lance Rambo or security company to help spring you, it's included in the coverage.

Chubb has the best deal in town; annual payments total about US$1000 for every $10 million of ransom payments released. If you are deemed to be "high profile," or the target of previous kidnapping attempts, the premium skyrockets to US$25,000 a year. The insurance is not available in Colombia or Germany, where the governments feel that it can encourage kidnapping.

Who is high profile? Senior American executives who work for high-profile companies overseas. Where are you most likely to get snatched?

The World's Most Dangerous Places for White Collar Expats

Brazil	Colombia
India	Italy
Lebanon	Mexico
Pakistan	Peru
Philippines	Spain
United States	Venezuela

These 12 countries are the sites for 90 percent of all kidnappings.The hot spots are South and Central America and Mexico. Lawlessness in Russia and Eastern Europe will soon put these areas toward the top of the list. The number of kidnappings worldwide grew from 369 in 1984 to 851 in 1990. It is important to remember that a large number of kidnappings are never reported for fear of attracting further attempts.

What is the real danger of being held hostage? The primary motivation of most kidnapers is to generate cash—lots of it. So being worth more alive than dead is comforting. According to Control Risks Group out of London, about 40 percent of all hostages are released safely after the ransom is paid. Having an insurance policy will make your chances of generating the necessary number of bucks a lot easier. But you won't have a choice should someone try to storm the joint in a rescue effort. About 34 percent of hostages are rescued from their captives before the ransom is paid. This is perhaps a hostage's greatest threat. A lot of confusion and panic can occur in these operations, and the moment Rambo springs through the door with an M-60, you ain't worth squat any longer.

Approximately 9 percent of all hostages are killed as a result of being kidnapped. Nearly 11 percent of kidnapping victims are released without payment, either through negotiation or the abductors' realization that no one really gives a damn you took their sorry-ass employee, who was about to get fired anyway.

Escape is a possibility. About 5 percent get out before the ransom is paid. But the stats for American businessmen aren't so great.

- Although only 25 executives of American companies were kidnapped between 1987 and 1991 (12 of them U.S. citizens), nine of them were killed. That's about every third kidnapping victim.

Want to know how to avoid being kidnapped? First make sure you answered "no" to each of the questions in our rigged quiz. Secondly, follow these slightly paranoid tips:

- Try to de-Westernize your mode of dress. Do not wear jewelery or American flag accessories.

- Do not follow a regular routine.

- Do not enter taxis, buildings, cars or areas where you feel you have been seen often. Avoid public transport, expensive cars or limosines.

- Do not book hotels or restaurants in a corporate name or even your name.

- Keep family, colleagues and other trusted people informed of your whereabouts. Do not use a celluar phone to do this.

- Remember that most victims are snatched as they are traveling between places in relatively close proximity to each other.

Security Firms/Hostage Negotiation/ Rescue Firms

Pinkerton Risk Assesment Services

1600 Wilson Boulevard, Suite 901
Arlington, VA 22209
☎ *(703) 525-6111*
FAX (703) 525-2454
Once on the trail of bank robbers in the wild west, Pinkerton has gone global and high-tech. Today you can get risk assessments of over 200 countries on-line or in-person. Pinkerton offers access to a database of more than 55,000 terrorist actions and daily updated reports on security threats. For the non-techie, you can order printed publications that range from daily risk assesment briefings to a monthly newsletter. Their services are not cheap, but how much is your life

worth? Annual subscriptions to the on-line service start at about US$7000, and you can order various risk and advisory reports that run from US$200–700 each. Pinkerton gets down and dirty with its counterterrorism programs, hostage negotiators, crisis management and travel security seminars.

The service is designed for companies who send their employees overseas or need to know what is going on in the terrorist world. Some reports are mildly macabre, with their annual business-like graphs charting maimings, killings, assaults and assassinations. Others are truly enlightening. In any case, Pinkerton does an excellent job of bringing together the world's most unpleasant information and providing it to you in concise, intelligent packages.

Unlimited on-line access to their database on 230 countries will run you US$6000 a year. You will find the information spotty, with a preponderance of information on South and Central America. Many of the write-ups on everything from Kurds to the Islamic Jihad are written by young college students with little in-country experience. On the other hand, there are many holes that are filled by CIA country profiles (available at any library for free).

If you want to save a few bucks, for US$4000 a year (US$5000 overseas), you can get a full subscription of daily, weekly, quarterly and annual risk assessments, as well as analysts' commentaries, a world status map and a fax service that keeps you abreast of fast breaking events.

Cheapskates can opt for the US$2250 standard package, which eliminates the daily reports sent via fax, but provides you most of the other elements. If you want to order á la carte, expect services that range from a US$30 personalized trip package to US$250 printouts of existing risk and travel advisories to accessing the company's Country Data bank for US$1000 per country.

Control Risks Group

8200 Greensboro Drive, Suite 1010
McLean, Virginia 22102
☎ *(703) 893-0083*
FAX (703) 893-8611

Organization Resources Counselors

Michal Fineman
Director of International Client Services
Rockefeller Center, 1211 Avenue of the Americas
New York, New York 10036
☎ *(212) 719-3400*
FAX (212) 398-1358

Employment Conditions Abroad

Anchor House, 15 Britten Street
London SW3 3TY
☎ *071-351-7151*
FAX 071-351-9396

The American Society for Industrial Security (ASIS)

FAX (703)-243-4954
Holds three day meetings where topics ranging from terrorism, espionage and neo-Naziism are discussed.

Getting Arrested

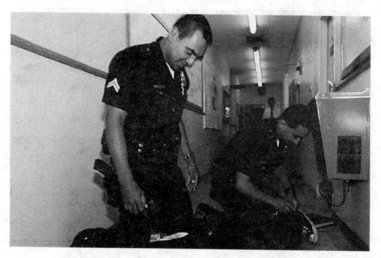

Oh Won't You Stay...Just a Little Bit Longer

You're catching some rays on the beach in Manzanillo. The low tangerine shafts of sunlight trickle across the purple Pacific as you wipe the piña colada foam from your lips. It's your last day. Monday, it's back behind the desk at Shrapnel-Wesson Bros., the brokerage people, in beautiful downtown Gary, Indiana. You lament the week ahead as you notice the young Mexican kid approach your towel. Another souvenir or massage parlor tout. Jeez, they get these kids young, you think. Instead of balsawood dolphins, hammocks or whorehouse flyers, the kid pulls from his pocket a bag of weed. You do a doubletake. *Sensimilla*, the kid says. Twenty bucks. What the hell, you say. It's your last day. You're grabbed from behind. Someone's got your hair. Your face gets stuffed into the sand. Then a boot in the left ear. Christ, that hurt! Thirty minutes later, you're pissing against a stained cement wall. Your left eye has swollen over. You've signed a confession.

What the hell. It's your last day.

Approximately 3000 Americans are arrested abroad every year, about one percent of all U.S. international travelers. At the end of 1993, there were 2559 Americans in foreign jails, according to the U.S. State Department. The majority (about 66 percent) of the cases are drug related. Mexico and Jamaica are responsible for the bulk of the drug related incarcerations, filing 71 percent of all drug charges against Americans traveling abroad (as of 1993).

The top five destinations for Americans seeking free room and board are Mexico, Germany, Canada, Jamaica and Great Britain. At the end of 1993, Mexico had 429 gringos on ice and had arrested 766 that year. Fifty-seven of those weren't happy campers and filed complaints of mistreatment.

Even those folks had it good. In places like Malaysia and Singapore, move dope and die. Zero tolerance. Deal dope and you'll get the rope. Getting beaten up in a Mexican jail may be inconvenient, but at least the *federales* are trying to teach you a lesson, a lesson you might learn from in later life. In Southeast Asia, there is no later life.

Here are a few survival tips (at the risk of sounding like your mother) for those who don't want to die as a skinny, frazzled, psychotic wimp in a Pakistani jail.

Have nothing to do with drugs or the drug culture.

Those pleasant men in pressed uniforms are employed for a single purpose, to find your drugs. Once they've found them, make no mistake, you will be busted. Once you're tried (if you ever are), you will be going away for a long time. And then it will take a lot of money to get you out. A lot of it. And you'll look different, too. Not good.

Do not take anything illegal through customs, or anything that doesn't belong to you.

Do not be an unwitting mule and carry a package for a friend. Do not think you can sneak a few joints through. Customs officers live by two words: How much? How much is it going to cost you to get out of this mess? How much time are you going to do? How much will it cost to repatriate your remains?

Be careful with unmarked drugs.

Combining drugs or putting prescription drugs into reminder boxes may create questions of legality. Your personal appearance, the quantity of the drugs and the general demeanor of your inquisitor will determine if you are let off.

Avoid driving.

Car accidents are a great way to go to jail. In many countries, the Napoleonic code of justice is utilized. In other words, by law, you are guilty until proven innocent. For instance, if someone smacks into your car in Mexico, you'll go to jail. No witnesses and it may be a long time. Hire a driver and you're off the hook.

Be judicious in your enthusiasm to photograph military or government facilities.

Soldiers in Africa love camera equipment. If you want it back, you'll have to pay a fine. Most of the former Soviet republics will arrest you for taking pictures of army bases or airports. We have spent plenty of time fast-talking our way out of jail simply for carrying cameras in countries that demand you have national and regional permits to carry them.

Get the right kind of help.

The U.S. embassy will not lift a finger to get you out of jail. They may assist you, but if you have broken the law in that country, you are expected to do the time. Many countries will assume you are guilty and hold you until trial. It may take an extraordinary amount of time for your case to go to trial, and you may even be required to pay your room and board while in jail. Hire a local lawyer and explore all options for your release, including bribes and being smuggled out. Communicate your case to friends and tell them to contact journalists in the local and national media. If you really did something stupid and you don't have any money, be prepared for the worst. As we said, if you're caught trafficking narcotics in Malaysia, you will be executed.

U.S. Citizens in Custody Abroad

Country	Currently in Custody	Country	Currently in Custody
Antigua & Barbuda	23	Italy	46
Australia	57	Jamaica	111
Austria	14	Japan	54
Bahamas	29	Korea	25
Barbados	20	Mexico	429
Belize	21	Netherlands	36
Bermuda	24	Netherlands Antilles	21
Bolivia	10	Nigeria	10
Brazil	27	Panama	34
Canada	189	Peru	35
Colombia	40	Philippines	46
Costa Rica	22	Russia	7
Cuba	11	Saudi Arabia	11
Denmark	10	South Africa	17
Dominican Republic	79	Spain	58
Ecuador	34	Sweden	12
France	39	Switzerland	40
Germany (Fed Rep)	225	Taiwan	12
Greece	37	Thailand	71
Guatemala	16	Trinidad & Tobago	27
Honduras	8	United Arab Emirates	11
Hong Kong	11	United Kingdom	106
India	16	Venezuela	50
Ireland	10	Yemen Arab Republic	7
Israel	86	Zambia	5

Drugs

War's Bastard Son

When Muslims blow the hell out of Jews and American Marines in suicide bombings, they do so in the belief that theirs is an act of holiness, of divine intervention; that they will be bestowed an afterlife of eternal peace by a God who pays no heed to body counts in the struggle to establish an earthly homeland for His flock. The deed is good.

Drug traffickers subscribe to no such piety. And they couldn't give a damn. They don't justify what they do with a scripture, ancient scrolls and engraved tablets. Producing and running drugs has only one justification: hard cash. Of course, hard cash is needed by holy warriors, as well, to ensure the longevity of their ability to murder and maim. Hey, if a few mountainsides of poppies can finance the battle against Satan, why not? Besides, most of the stuff ends up in America, anyhow. That's who we're fighting, right?

No list of dangerous things would be complete without mentioning drugs. Not the danger of drugs, but the drugs that cause danger, and the lands that are dangerous because of them.

Heroin

Behold the lowly *Papaver somniferum*, or Eurasian poppy. This innocent little flower originally came from the Mediterranean area. It's now grown up and discovered it's the half-brother of war. Lebanon, Turkey, India, Myanmar, China, Pakistan, Laos, Thailand, Mexico and Afghanistan are the troubled homes of this gentle, unassuming weed that blows in the wind. Wars have been fought over opium since the 1839–1842 Opium War between Britain and China. Today, the battles are taking place on the streets of St. Louis, Miami, L.A. and small-town America. Millions of people are currently enslaved by the by-products of the opium poppy. Eighty percent of all illicit drugs in the U.S. are heroin originating in the land of desperadoes—the Golden Triangle of Southeast Asia. The current purity of heroin found on the street in the United States has jumped from an average seven percent in 1984 to 36 percent today, a testament not only to its grip on a nation, but to the seemingly ceaseless world supply of the narcotic. Heroin shipped into the U.S. comes from at least 11 different countries.

Poppies can be grown in the cool plateaus above 1500 meters. The plants grow rapidly and propagate easily. Planted at the end of the wet season (in Asia in September and October), the poppy heads are later scraped after the petals fall off. The scraping creates an oozing sap that is removed from the plant and packed tightly into banana leaves. The crude opium is then packed out of the hills via pony or armed human convoys to the middlemen. For those who grow opium, few are spared. Hilltribe growers swiftly become addicts themselves. Up to 30 percent of Southeast Asia's Hmong tribe is addicted to opium. Most of the income into northern Laos is dope money. In fact small nickel bags, or *parakeets* as they are called locally, can be used as a form of currency.

The poppy is usually cultivated in third world countries with little or no political, military or police interference. Mexico, Lebanon and Turkey have faded from the scene and been replaced by Afghanistan, Pakistan, Laos and Myanmar. The DEA says that 60–70 percent of the heroin coming into America is brought in by four groups: The United Wa State Army and Khun Sa in Southeast Asia, and the Quetta Alliance and the Haji Baig Organization in Pakistan.

Opium has been used to kill pain, cure diarrhea and even as a social drug since 300 BC. Today, the legal use of opium is mainly to create morphine and codeine for medicinal purposes. Worldwide, there were an estimated 4000 metric tons of the stuff in 1993 double the amount produced in 1986.

Heroin (from the Greek root, meaning "Hero") is the most refined by-product of the opium poppy and causes a sense of power, creates a feeling of euphoria, relieves pain and induces sleep. Heroin has only been around since 1874 and was originally used for medicinal purposes without knowledge of its addictive properties. Today, 60 percent of the world's heroin supply comes from Myanmar and Laos, not northern Thailand as assumed by most tourists. The U.S. government has vacillated between encouraging the production of heroin (as it did in its support of Laotian rebels during the Vietnam War) and condemning it (through its covert military ops in Thailand aimed at stemming the heroin tide washing up on the shores of New York streets).

Even in its heavily-cut street form (nickel bags diluted with sugar, starch, powdered milk or quinine to less than 10 percent purity) it is highly addictive, and its victims require larger and larger doses and more direct methods of ingestion to deliver a high. In New York City, nickel bags of heroin go for $10; its dearth of purity means junkies can snort it instead of having to inject it. Some estimates tag the heroin trade as a US$4 to 10 billion a year business. There are about 600,000 users; half of them are concentrated in New York City. Heroin is becoming more popular; there was a 50 percent increase in heroin-induced overdoses as tracked by ER rooms in the first half of 1993 in the U.S.

Morphine is bitter to the taste, darkens with age and is derived from opium (at a strength of between 4–21 percent). Most of its addicts are former soldiers who were treated with morphine as a pain killer after being wounded in combat.

Codeine (0.7 percent to 2.5 percent concentration of opium) is an alkaloid by-product of the poppy and is found in a variety of patent medicines around the world. In the

U.S., codeine is only available in prescribed medications. However, these same medicines (i.e., Tylenol with Codeine) can be had over the counter in many countries, particularly in Central and South America and Southeast Asia.

The Golden Triangle

Just under 70 percent of the world's heroin seized by U.S. law enforcement in 1993 came from the Golden Triangle. The Golden Triangle is not really a geographic triangle but a loosely defined area that covers eastern Myanmar, northern Laos and scattered parts of northern Thailand. The common elements are remoteness and inaccessibility, lack of law enforcement and the right altitude and climate to permit the cultivation of poppies.

Visitors to this area will find the locals decidedly reserved and openly belligerent if pressed for details on their trade. The U.S. State Department estimates that Myanmar exports about 2300 tonnes of raw opium a year, primarily from the Kachin and North Shan states. Laos moves about 300 tonnes and Thailand about 30 tonnes.

The Hill Tribes

The real dirty work is taken care of by the region's poor but industrious hill tribes. Poppies in the Golden Triangle are grown and harvested by the Lahu, Lisu, Nfien and Hmong tribes, and cultivated among less odius but less profitable crops like maize. Since smart farmers maximize the use of their land and labor, it's not surprising that the annual opium production has tripled in Myanmar in the last ten years. Depending on which drug lord's auspices the farmer falls under, the raw product is sent to processing labs either along the Chinese border (Wa) or along the Thai border (Shan).

The Shan United Army

The hill people pack or carry the opium out and into the hands of major processors and exporters like Myanmar's notorious Khun Sa. Khun Sa, 61, lives in the village of Wan Ho Mong, nine miles from the Thai border. Wan Ho Mong is a wealthy, well-administered town with little use for outside visitors or missionaries. Khun Sa has his own army, the Shan United Army, a group of 19,000 men who, in addition being an industrial security force, also carry a big political club when the outside world threatens to crack down. Depending which PR spin you like, he is either an oppressed freedom fighter forced to tax drug growers to support his peoples' fight for freedom, or a greedy drug king who enslaves an ethnic minority to do his dirty work. Nonetheless, Khun Sa has a knack for business. He's just introduced a line of ladies' footwear. The shoes are bought from England and adorned with Burmese rubies and gems before fetching up to US$20,000 a pair back in countries such as England and Australia. Robin Leach may be paying a visit to Wan Ho Mong in the near future.

The United Wa Army

Khun Sa's biggest competitor is the United Wa State Army. Back in 1989, the Wa decided to dump Khun Sa as an ally and get into bed with the generals who run Myanmar. The Wa is run by two men, Chao Nyi-Lai and Wei Hsueh-Kang, who operate out of the town of Pan Hsang in the most easterly corner of Myanmar. They control an army of between 15,000 to 35,000 men and once provided raw opium to Khun Sa. The two leaders have political ambitions and claim that they want to shift the Wa people into legitimate crops once they have representation within the country of Myanmar, a country who's leaders are allegedly benefiting from everything from timber smuggling to drug trafficking.

A third group led by Ai Hsiao-shih and Wei Hsueh-kang specializes in the transportation of raw and processed heroin into China and Thailand.

The Wa and the Shan, or more accurately Khun-Sa and Nyi-Lai/Hsueh-kang, account for 75 percent of the opium leaving the Golden Triangle. Most of Myanmar's opium is transported in pony caravans along simple trails into China's Yunnan province and eventually to the drug syndicates in Hong Kong; or it moves south through Chiang Mai in northern Thailand down to

Bangkok. Once the pony caravans reach minor towns, the heroin is then trucked to major cities from where it is shipped or flown to the United States or Mexico.

A third route is from Moulmein in southern Burma into Bangkok and, surprisingly, into Malaysia and Singapore. Malaysia and Singapore widely publicize their imposition of a mandatory death penalty for drug smuggling while also serving as major centers for the export of drugs.

Afghanistan

A common harvest of lawlessness is drugs. When the Soviets pulled out of Afghanistan they left little government and less of an economy. So the gaps were filled in by industrious Afghans who raised poppies and sold them to the equally industrious Pakistanis. The Pakistanis jumped in when Iran's fundamentalist government got tough on drugs and Afghan routes to the west were interrupted by war. Today, Pakistan exports between 65–80 tons of heroin every year. Not much when you compare it to the 2630 tonnes from the Golden Triangle, but enough to generate U.S.$1.5 billion in revenue.

The Haji Baig Organisation

This is a Lahore, Pakistan-based group loosely modeled after the 1980s American S&L structure; in other words, most of the key players are currently in jail while making millions of dollars. This organization lacks the political halo and the tens of thousands of armed men the Myanmar groups possess, and they are paying the price. Haji Mirza Iqbal Baig, 66, Anwar Khan Khattak, 44, and Tariq Waheed Butt, 44, are all killing time in Pakistan on drug charges awaiting extradition to the States. Meanwhile, their organization relies on Haji Ayub Afridi to carry on business as usual. Afhdi lives a half hour outside Peshawar in a compound protected by anti aircraft guns and armed tribesmen. His responsibility is to keep the flow of heroin and hashish moving to local distribution and sales groups in New York; Newark, NJ; L.A. and San Francisco.

The Quetta Alliance

The DEA-named Quetta Alliance is a coalition of Afghan tribes (the Issa, Notezai and the Rigi) based along the Pakistan-Afghani border. The tribes control the output and shipment of processed opium (mostly morphine) to Turkey for further processing into heroin. The PKK and other terrorist groups in Turkey and Iran take care of security, and the final product is trucked from Istanbul to Europe for the last leg of the journey into America. The leader of the Notezai, Sakhi Dost Jan Notezai, is serving his third term in the provincial assembly, while concurrently serving time in prison on drug charges.

Drugs are also sent from Quetta to the Makran coast, where they are shipped via freighter to Marseilles and New York.

Crack

Crack has replaced heroin as the new "Jones" that is dragging down the inner city. Not as addictive as heroin, it has an intense high that is psychologically addictive. In some American cities, 2 out of 100 first-graders are addicted to crack, thanks to their mothers. In 1992, 16.9 per 1000 live births were crack babies. Crack pushes users to violent criminal acts, sexual trading and other desperate measures to feed their habit. According to the Bureau of Justice Statistics, the typical crack user is low-income, white (49.9%) and desperate; 35.9% are black and 14.2% Latino.

Dangerous Jobs

In 1992, 1216 acts of violence took place at work; 1001 were homicides, 822 by firearms and 82 stabbings.

A 1992 study by the U.S. Department of Labor shows that homicides in the workplace were second to vehicle accidents as a cause of death while on the job. Murders were the cause of 17 percent of work related deaths.

The most dangerous jobs don't include one hairy chested occupation in the lot:

The World's Most Dangerous Jobs or why don't we see more action/adventure shows starring these folks?

1. Taxi Driver

2. Convenience Store Operator

3. Service Station Attendant

4. Bank Teller

Victims of violent crime according to the U.S. Justice Department

Private company	61%
Government	30%
Self-employed	8%
Working without pay	1%

The locations where these crimes took place:

Restaurant, bar or nightclub	13%
Office, factory or warehouse	14%
Other commercial sites	23%
On school property	9%
Parking Lot/Garage	11%
On public property	22%
Other	8%

Being a man is dangerous. Besides having a short life span, 93 percent of people killed on the job are men.

Texas is the most dangerous place to work with workplace homicide accounting for 22 percent of all occupational fatalities. During 1991 and 1992 there were 199 employees slain at work in Texas. Ten of them were police but 57 of them were service station and convenience store clerks.

Who's out there?

The typical whacko who freaks out at work and starts banging away is typically a middle age male over 35, withdrawn, owner of a gun, has served in the military and probably drinks or snorts too much of some substance.

What's danger worth?

The U.S. Department of State thinks employees who work in dangerous places should receive an additional payment of 25 percent of their normal salary. French companies will pay up to double the standard rate to do business in remote or dangerous places. Americans are the preferred targets. In 1989 Americans were targets in 33 percent of the 177 anti-U.S. attacks. Latin America is the most likely place for anti-American attacks with the Middle East just behind. The Middle East was the site of choice for half of all terrorist attacks in 1989.

Don't think that it matters to the paymaster whether you are an American or a former Colombian sent to work in Colombia? You will get preferential treatment: 92 percent of U.S. companies pay the same incremental amount regardless of race or country of origin.

CIA

Everyone knows that the CIA is looking for a few good men. The newest job category that might attract MBA/Adventurers is the opportunity to work in *nonofficial cover*. Opportunity is knocking or NOC'ing for a few lucky business grads. Dissatisfied with the traditional foreign embassy bureaucrat or aid worker as a cover for its operatives, the CIA has decided to get creative. The CIA now recruits young executives through bogus companies usually based in northern Virginia. The ads appear in major periodicals and newspapers and seek recent business school grads who want to work overseas. The job pays wells but requires training. The NOC's are not trained in Camp Peary nor do they ever appear on any CIA database to keep them safe from moles. Sounds like a great movie plot, so far.

The successful graduates are then posted with real companies overseas. Many large American corporations gladly accept these folks since they get a real business grad who works long hours for free. Each NOC has a liaison person or handler who must handle the intel that is provided by his charge. Many of these positions are with banks, import-export firms and companies which have a reason to be in some of our colder countries. North Korea, Iraq, Iran, Colombia and other nasty places are great locations for NOC's. The CIA has to cut corners on its $28 billion dollar annual budget but NOC's cost more to train, more to support but hopefully can provide hard information in countries where the embassy is a little light on cocktail party chatter.

If you are exposed or captured you are officially a spy and not protected by a diplomatic passport.

Navy SEAL

Specialists in Naval Special Warfare, the SEALs (SEa Air, Land) evolved from the frogman of WWII. The SEALs have been glorifed in films and books. Their most recent brush with fame was their less-than-secret invasion of Kuwait City with the world's press watching and filming with high powered camera lights.

In 1989 the SEALs were the first into Panama, using rebreathers and midget subs. In the Gulf war they even used custom-made dune buggies to operate behind enemy lines.

The SEALs go through 25 weeks of training, either in Coronado in San Diego or on the east coast. The training starts with extreme physical and mental abuse. The focus is on teamwork and surviving the constant harassment. The first test is hell week, six days of misery and physical torture with little or no sleep. Then there is extensive classroom and underwater training in SCUBA (Self Contained Underwater Breathing Apparatus) diving. This phase ends with another serious physical challenge. The third and final phase is the UDT and above water training on San Clemente Island.

SEAL teams must practice close quarter battle drills by firing 300 or more rounds of 9 mm ammunition weekly. Each of the six line SEAL teams is given 1.5 million rounds of ammunition annually to train its five 16 man platoons. According to the specs on their Beretta 92F pistols this means they burn out one handgun a year. Their MP5 machine guns last a little longer.

Cab Driver

Taxis were introduced in 1907 in New York City. Today it is a job usually taken by recent immigrants. In New York City there are 11, 787 Yellow Cabs, 30,000 livery cars and between 5000 and 9000 illegal gypsy cabs. Cab drivers are independent contractors who lease their cabs from a cab company. In New York a cabbie pays about $40 a day for the cab and maybe about $20 for gas. He gets to keep everything after that. The term for breaking even is "making the knot." There are no benefits, no workers comp or holidays. The hours are flexible and you meet a lot of interesting people, albeit briefly. The Lexan dividers in some cabs have been credited with saving lives, but driving a cab is still a dangrous business.

In 1993 in New York City there were 42 murders of cabbies; most were drivers of livery or gypsy cabs. In a five year period 187 drivers were killed. There were also 3500 robberies in 1993 and 3675 in 1992. The average amount of the theft was $100 in cash.

Army Rangers

The Ranger course is 68 days and emphasizes patrolling and raiding. The course is being restricted and very few non-infantry soldiers will be able to attend in the future. Troops from other branches can attend if they are being sent to jobs with a specific need for Ranger skills. The Ranger school is considered the toughest course in the army.

Smokejumper

If the thought of being parachuted into a raging inferno and having to fight your way back until you can be airlifted out many sleepless nights later appeals to you, then you should try smokejumping. Smokejumpers are firefighters who must be in the air within 10 minutes and parachute into remote areas to fight fires. Dropped from small planes as low as 1500 feet in altitude, they quickly must hike to the scene of the fire, and instantly begin to chop and backburn areas to head off forest fires before they get too big. The work is all manual, requires strength, endurance and an ability to work around the clock if need be.

Most smokejumpers are attracted by the danger and the camaraderie this jobs affords. They are known as party animals, close friends and hard workers

Although the death of 14 firefighters in Glenwood Springs, Colorado on July 6, 1994 reminded people that smokejumping is dangerous, the fact that there are only 387 in the U.S. makes those deaths even more significant. The last time any smokejumpers were killed was in 1949 during the Mann Gulch blaze in Montana. During this 45-year period of calm one jumper pancaked into the ground due to chute failure and another hanged himself when he tried to get out of a tree that he had landed in.

Like most dangerous jobs, the goal is to stay alive and healthy and you definitely don't do it for the money. Pay for smokejumpers starts at about $9 an hour and there is additional pay during fires and with overtime. Most are part time jumpers who earn the money during the hot summer fire season.

There are nine U.S. Forest Service and Bureau of Land Management regional jumper bases in the West. The supervisors react quickly to fires and send in anywhere from two or more jumpers depending on the size of the fire. If a lightening strike starts a small blaze, firejumpers can deal with it quickly and effectively before calling in the water bombers. Supplies can be parachuted in once the jumpers are on the ground. Once done, the jumpers then get to hike out with their equipment or be picked up by helicopter.

Training requires federal certification to fell large trees and to be able to climb in and more likely out of trees. They maintain their own chainsaws and other equipment. Their protective Kevlar suits hold their equipment and protect then when landing in trees. Forest Service jumpers use round shoots and jump at 1500 feet BLM; jumpers use the more modern rectangular chutes and exit at 3000 feet.

Bicycle Messenger

You would risk your life for this?

Goon

When management gets tough with strikers they call in the professionals, the strike-breakers. These men are there to make sure the scabs can get to work unscathed. Being a strikebreaker doesn't mean you get to crack heads. It means you get to be the target of insults, epithets, rocks, bottles, spittle, feces and even nasty names. It helps to be big and to have thick skin. Employers look for military or law enforcement training. One firm that specializes in providing a few good men is Falcon Global in Philadelphia, Pennsylvania.

Blowout Control

If you like your work hot and dangerous, try containing oil blowouts. The most famous of these workers is, of course, Red Adair's group which inspired a movie starring John Wayne. Despite the dramatic footage of men covered in oil and being roasted, safety comes first. Red is retired but the company lives on.

The general idea is that when oil wells catch on fire or blow out, there is a lot of money being sprayed into the air. So these people have to work fast. Saddam Hussein overtaxed companies from eight countries when he set the Kuwaiti fields alight. There were 732 oil wells in need of capping, but not before US$60 billion worth of oil had disappeared.

Even though the companies can be paid up to a million dollars a job (mostly for equipment and expenses), a more realistic fee is between US$20,000 and US$200,000 to control a blowout. The crew makes about US$300 to US$1000 a day each plus room and board. The work requires a drilling background. It is tough, hard and dirty work. You also can't pick your customers since blowouts happen anywhere, anytime.

Safety Boss
Red Deer, Alberta, Canada
☎ *(403) 342-1310*

Boots & Coots
Houston, TX
☎ *(713) 931-8884*

Red Adair
Dallas, TX
☎ *(713) 462-4282*

Mine Sweeper

Land mines kill or maim someone on this planet every hour. There is a big demand for former explosives and munitions experts to clean up these killers. Mine clearance personnel are paid about US$90,000 a year. There are about 20 companies that specialize in the detection and removal of land mines. Kuwait is spending about US$1 billion to clean up the seven million land mines sewn during the five-month occupation of Kuwait by Iraq; 83 mine clearance experts have been killed just in Kuwait. If you are looking for big money, be aware that local minesweepers in Angola make only US$70 a day.

Explosive Ordnance Disposal World Services

Fort Walton Beach, FL
☎ (904) 864-3454

UXB

Chantilly, VA
☎ (703) 803-8904

CTA Environmental

Norcross , GA
☎ (404) 728-9217

Ronco

Berkeley, CA
☎ (510) 548-3922

Royal Ordnance

a subsidary of British Areospace
London, England
☎ 81-012-52-37-32-32

Cop

Being a cop means meeting the criminal, the drunk, the wasted, on a daily basis. For this you will get paid about US$30,000–US$50,000 a year. You will get to retire in about 40 years with full pension and there are good benefits in some areas. Competition is stiff and you can expect the domestic, drug, health and other problems that come with stress.

Bounty Hunter

For those of you who can't hold a day job, you might consider bounty hunting. Since the romantic notion of men being brought in dead or alive for a price on their head is almost gone, you end up working for bail bondsmen, not the most romantic of employers. They will pay you a finder's fee so they don't have to cough up the entire amount of the court imposed bail when their client doesn't show.

The job does not require much training or even much of anything except a pair of handcuffs and a little skip tracing education. What you get for bringing in bad people is between 10–30 percent of the fugitives' bail from the grateful bondsmen. Your clients will not be happy to see you and in most cases they will try to elude you since you have neither an attractive uniform nor a big gun. If you have a permit to carry a gun you are not always allowed to use it. You are essentially making a citizen's arrest, and if you end up with broken bones or holes in you, it's your problem. Some states don't like bounty hunters so you can't practice your business in Illinois, Kentucky or Oregon.

There are about 50–100 active bounty hunters in the U.S. with about 20,000 fugitives returned each year. Most of these hunters don't make much money. The lower the bail, the less serious the crime, the less money one makes, the easier the errant crooks or fugitives (Don't forget they are innocent until proven guilty.) are to find.

There is a market for high-end bounty hunters. There are many terrorists with very big prices on their head. You will need a working command of Arabic, Persian, French and some tribal dialects. You will need to be fully conversant with Islam and the Koran and be able to pass for a Sunni or a Shiite. If you're caught you will be lucky if you are shot. The government was recently offering US$2 million for the ring leader of the World Trade Center bombing. He was found in Pakistan and whisked back to New York.

If you want to know more about bounty hunting contact

Bob Burton

National Institute of Bail Enforcement
P.O. Box 1170
Tombstone, AZ 85638
☎ *(520) 457-9360*

How many sailors does it take to sail a desk?

There are 33,574 British sailors and only 114 ships. We do not know how many desks there are and whether they float.

How to Track Mortars

When a mortar shell impacts, the casing explodes into dozens of sharp edged pieces of shrapnel. The tip or fuse is a solid piece and is driven into the ground. If you poke a stick into the hole made by the tip you can determine from where the shell came. Originally this simple method was used to direct counter-fire but is now used by the UN to determine blame for civilian casualties in Bosnia.

Adventure Calls

There is no one perfect source for information on travel or adventuring to far-flung places. This is only a sampler of what is out there. We encourage readers to send in any sources they have come across to expand our list and to report on the experience.

A couple of things to keep in mind when dealing with these folks. Tell them why you are calling. Ask them for more information. Ask them to describe the typical member, client etc., and then ask for references. Do not take brochure or PR material at face value.

There is no one way to join or organize an expedition. By definition all you have to do is walk out your door. Most expeditions have goals, structure, deadlines, budgets, etc. and require more planning than execution. Most are scientific in nature. Many are adventurous or exploratory with little of the painstaking information-recording required of expeditions in the old days.

Expeditions

Expeditions are simply formalized trips. Like any great endeveavor they should have an objective, a unique sense of purpose and maybe a dash of insanity. A lot of people dream about doing great things and being lauded for their superhuman status.

An expedition is a way to say "Here is what we said we would do and here is what we did." There is little to no reward for climbing Mt. Everest blindfolded or swimming the Atlantic while towing a barge. There is far more reward in being an actor portraying the adventurer. Sigourney Weaver made more money acting as Dian Fossey and Patrick Bergen put more in the bank than their characters ever made in a lifetime—a sobering thought. Fame does await the bold. And after that fame comes an endless procession of rubber chicken dinners and outdoor store openings. The more literate will write a book that will grace remainder lists for years to come. So consider an expedtion as a good use of your skills and talents with the only reward being the satisfaction of fellowship, a job well done and a better understanding of our world. Along the way you will enter an elite club of men and women who have tested themselves and found themselves to be comfortably mortal.

Now a warning to the adventurous who view expeditions as an interesting way to see the world. All expeditions have some hardship involved. In fact more and more of them seem to feature physical discomfort. Rannulph Fiennes' jaunt to the pole on skis is an example of this craziness. He could have flown but he wanted to do something that had never been done before. Other expeditions like the recent attempt to climb Mt. Kinabalu in Borneo turned into a fiasco because a group of men decided to do whatever they felt like and got lost. They were found later, close to starvation. Expeditions are usually led by tough experienced men who think there is nothing unusual about forcing physical and mental discomfort on others. So it is not surprising than many expeditions tend to be run either by emotionless sado-masochistics, raving egomaniacs, men who were dressed as girls when they were young or questionable characters with overstated credentials who are forced by their lack of job skills to make their living in godforsaken places.

If you can combine all these characteristics into one person, then you stand the chance of mounting a successful expedition. Why would someone want to walk to the North Pole, bake in the Sahara or pick ticks out of their private parts, you may well ask? The answer is always unsatisfactory. Most expedition junkies are always testing themselves, proving other people wrong and seeking to top themselves in their next hair-brained adventure.

Why do I sound so cynical here? Maybe because I have watched various expedition leaders lose it and seen many of my well-trained friends throw their hands up in disgust. The biggest single enemy of the expedition is bad chemistry usually caused by the fearless leader's inability to lead men by example rather than brute force.

My more pleasurable expeditions have always seemed leaderless, where the group reacted in unison allowing creative interpretation of directions, deadlines and goals. Secondly, you must truly know your fellow expedition members. Men and women react very strangely under stress. Some revert to childish whining, others become combative and other simply lose it both mentally and physically.

The best way to see if you have picked the right partners in an expedition is to have a dry run that includes at least 48 hours without sleep, in adverse conditions. Sleep deprivation combined with some mental and physical abuse at the 36 hour stage will show a person's real mettle. Strangely enough, in my experience white collar workers, physical fitness nuts, city dwellers, businessmen, triatheletes and sportsmen do very poorly in the ill-defined non-competitive expedition environment. People with military experience, medical personnel, photographers, blue collar laborers, rural backgrounds do very well.

The attributes to look for are experience in hard conditions, physical fitness, a sense of humor, a level-headed approach to stress, pain and discomfort and a genuine desire for knowledge and fellowship.

Expedition members should be chosen for specific knowledge such as medical, language—or bushlore, always get references. Members should never be chosen for prestige, ability to provide funding, university credentials, and absolutely stay away from taking on journalists, relatives of backers and good looking members of the opposite sex.

How to launch an expedition

1. Pick a region or topic that is newsworthy or beneficial to sponsors.

2. Select a specific task that you will accomplish and how that will make the world a better place or create publicity.

3. State specifically how you will generate publicity (book, speeches, press releases, photographs, magazine articles).

4. Write a one page query letter that states your purpose, method of execution and perceived result. Ask for a written show of support (do not ask for money) and other people who should be made aware of your expedition.

5. Gather letters of support from high profile politicians, community members, scientists and include them in your proposal.

6. Write an expedition (much like a business plan) plan and explain the benefits to the backers and sponsors.

7. Create a sponsorship program. Tell and show the primary sponsor what they will get, secondary sponsor and so on. As a rule of thumb ask for twice as much money as you predict you will need and come up with something to present to a recognized non-profit charity at the end of your expedition.

8. Once you have your expedition goal figured out and raison d'etre, send a one page press release and your outline to all news organizations telling them that you are going to do this and you need sponsors. It is important to set a date to let sponsors know that you are going with or without their funds.

9. Gather lists of potential sponsors and then phone to get the owner, president or founder's name.Send in your pitch along with any early PR you generated. If the president or owner likes it they will delegate it downward. If you send it in blind, most companies will put you in the "talk to our PR company who then promise to talk to the client" loop.

10. Follow up with a request for a meeting (money is never pledged over the phone) and thrill them with your enthusiasm and vision.

11. Send a thank you letter with a specfic follow-up and or commitment date. Promise to follow up with a phone call on a certain date and time.

Do this thousands of times and you will have enough money to do any hairbrained thing you want.

Just as Columbus had to sweet-talk Isabella after the banks turned him down, you have to be creative and ever hopeful. Everyone wishes they could go with you and their investment is just a way of saying I am part of this adventure.

Advice, comfort and a shoulder to cry on

The best sources for tough expeditions are the Royal Geographical Society in London and the National Geographic Society in Washington. Local newspapers will carry features on "brave young men and women" who are setting out to do whatever has not been done. In most cases they will be looking for money (always an automatic entree into an expedition) or someone with multiple skills (doctor, cook, masseuse)to fill out the team. Be careful, since it all comes down to personality fit. Many people have never spent more than a weekend in close proximity to their spouse let alone a total stranger; shake-down cruises are well advised, and go with your first impression. Things usually only get worse.

The up side is that you can be the first person on your block to pogo stick to the North Pole, balloon across the Sahara or kayak Lake Baikal. Fame and fortune may await. You will need lots of money, time and the enthusiasm of a Baptist preacher. Remember that 99 percent of your time will be spent raising funds and planning. The best single source in the world is the Expedition Advisory Centre of the Royal Geographical Society in London.

Usually funded by universities or governments, there are no real grapevines other than reading scientific journals, staying in touch with universities or talking to expeditioners and outfitters. Most participants will be scientists and will often bring interns (for a fee) to help defray costs. The best way to find out what is happening is to contact a university directly to see if any expeditions are being mounted.

RGS Expedition Advisory Centre

1 Kensington Gore
London, England SW7 2AR
☎ *(071) 5812057*
Contact Shane Winser of the Expedition Advisory Center. Don't be shy about calling or ordering any one of their excellent (but very British) books on expedition planning. Besides an incredible selection of how-to books, you can also get listings of past expeditions, contact other people interested in expeditions and get in touch with experts who have been to your area of interest.They do not sponsor expeditions but have a handbook on how to raise money.

All inclusive expeditions

The line between soft adventure and hard adventure is the word expedition. Experienced rafters, climbers, canoeists, hikers and divers usually seek out the small category of hard core trips that may or may not provide any touristic benefit but push them to the limit. The common goal is to do something first, more intensely or just better than anyone has done before.

Mountain Travel/Sobek Inc.

6420 Fairmont Avenue
El Cerrito, California 94530
☎ *(800) 227-2384*
MTS is always trying to open up new areas or try new rivers. Usually trips are offered as part of their catalog or if you call them directly they might have the same idea you have and help you put together a run (at a cost of course). MTS does the old-fashioned type of expediting and running expeditions.

The Sports Advisory Bureau

Sports Council
16 Upper Woburn Place
London, England WC1H 0PQ
☎ *071 388 1277*
They can put you in touch with the major specialist sport and adventure groups in the UK. From there you can ask around as to who's climbing what mountain or running what river.

Expedition Organizers

If you would like to do more than wander around a country, try joining an expedition. Americans haven't quite caught on to this method of travel but the British are crazy about it. Accordingly, they offer a lot more variety than some of their stateside counterparts.

Brathay Exploration Group

Brathay Hall
Ambleside
Cumbria, England LA22 0HP
☎ *(05394) 33942*
The Brathay Group has launched over 550 expeditions since 1947. Every year about 125 young people (15–25 years old) in groups of about 20 set off on a variety of scientific trips. There are sponsorships for the financially disadvantaged and most members contribute toward the cost of each expedition.

Trekforce Expeditions

134 Buckingham Palace Road
London, England SW1W 9SA
☎ *(071) 824 8890, FAX (071) 824 8892*
Trekforce has six week expeditions to Indonesia between June and November. Trips include four days of jungle training and the ability to work side by side with scientists working at a variety of scientific sites. Some of the projects have included Sumatran Rhino surveys, trips to the Baliem valley in Irian Jaya, grasshopper studies and even restoring a British fort in Sumatra. You must be over 18 years old and are expected to raise the $4000 or so it takes for airfare and your expenses.

Environmental Careers Organization

68 Harrison Avenue
Boston Massachusetts 02111
Helps find paid, short-term positions for college students and graduates.

Earthwork

The Student Conservation Association
Post Office Box 550
Charlestown, New Hampshire 03603
Provides lists of internships for students in the natural resources area.

Institute for Central America Developmental Studies

Post Office Box 025216
Miami, Florida 33102
Educational and environmental internships in Central America.

Green Corps

Field School for Environmental Organizing
3507 Lancaster Avenue
Philadelphia, Pennsylvania 19104
☎ *(215) 879-1760*
Selected applicants can join annual training programs in environmental studies and campaign organizing.

International Research Expeditions

140 University Drive
Menlo, California 94025
☎ *(415) 323-4228*

University Research Expeditions Program

University of California
Berkeley, California 94720
☎ *(510) 642-6586*
Local and worldwide field research programs are available throught the California State University Network.

Oceanic Society Expeditions

Fort Mason Center
Building "E"

San Francisco, California 94123
☎ *(415) 441-1106*
Marine research studies in the Caribbean and South America.

EarthWatch

680 Mount Auburn Street
Post Office Box 403
Watertown, Massachussetts 02272
☎ *(617) 926-8200*

Wexas International

45 Brompton Road
London, England SW3 1DE
☎ *(071) 589 3315, FAX (071) 589 8418*
A British travel club with members in 130 countries. Its *Traveller* magazine is a good source for finding expedition members, discounts or travel partners. You can also find deals on airfares, insurance, car rental and hotels.

World Challenge Expeditions

Soane House
305-315 Latimer Road
London, England W10 6RA
☎ *(081) 964 1331, FAX (081) 964 5298*
World Challenge Expeditions puts together young people in groups of 12–16 members, and sends them off to foreign lands to conduct an environmental field project.These are not real scientific projects but tasks designed to build leadership skills and self reliance. Each member of the team has a chance to lead at least once during the month-long expedition.

Applicants must be between 16–20 years old and the cost runs about $3000. Applications should be in before February.

Volunteer Vacations

For those of you who flunked science but still want to do something meaningful with your time, consider volunteering in a foreign region. You can do anything from writing pamphlets to cleaning toilets. In most cases there will be a "goal" and you will help in "achieving that goal." You, of course, will pay for all the expenses involved and will have to make a donation as well. Once on site you will be working with motivated people who are trying to change whatever it is that causes problems in the local region. It can be lonely, frustrating and ultimately depressing. On the other hand, there is no better way to understand the world's problems. There are thousands upon thousands of opportunities for people who want to give of their time and skills. There are even more opportunties for people who don't mind paying to volunteer. In some cases state agencies have replaced paid workers with paying volunteers for maintenance of trails, parks, etc. Archeological digs are popular as are works projects in Third World countries. The list and choice of volunteer vacations is so extensive that there are over 40 books and directories currently in print on the subject. There are enough of these opportunites to ensure that you will end up in the dangerous place of your choice, whether it's digging ditches in Sierra Leone, working on a Kibbutz in areas occupied by Israel or counting trout in the good old USA. You can choose from mild to wild.

An excellent resource is *Volunteer Vacations* by Bill McMillon published by the Chicago Review Press or call any one of the clearing houses for volunteer opportunities listed below.

Archaeological Institute of America

675 Commonwealth Avenue
Boston Massachussets 02215
☎ *(800) 338-5578, (617) 353-9361, FAX (617) 353-6560*
Call to order their annual listings of digs around the world that are looking for volunteers.

Council on International Educational Exchange

205 East 42nd Street
New York, New York 10017
☎ *(212) 661-1414*
Offers field programs and summer academic programs in Latin and South America.

GAP Activity Projects Limited

44 Queen's Road
Reading
Berkshire, England RG1 4BB
☎ *(0734) 594914, FAX (0734) 576634*
The "gap" is a British term to describe the year between grade school and college. The GAP places young people in a variety of work situations in Russia, Hungary, Japan, China and Poland. Positions include business, medical, adventure training, conservation and teaching.

Institute for International Cooperation and Development

Post Office Box 103-F
Williamstown, Massachussetts 01267
☎ *(413) 458-9828*
Semester-long programs worldwide that combine cultural and educational experiences.

Raleigh International

Raleigh House
27 Parsons Green Lane
London, SW6 4HZ England
☎ *(071) 371 8585, FAX (071) 371 5116*
Can you swim 500 meters? Can you speak English? Good, you're on. Raleigh International sends eager young (17–25 years old) volunteers to the far corners of the world. The goal is to work on community, research and conservation projects while having a bit of adventure. The charity likes to challenge young people and develop their leadership skills and self confidence.

UNIPAL (Universities' Education Fund for Palestinian Refugees)

33A Islington Park Street
London, N1 1QB, England
☎ *(071) 2267997, FAX (071) 2260880*
UNIPAL provides teaching and social services to the Palestinians in Israel and Jordan.

Volunteers for Israel

330 West 42nd Street
Suite 1318
New York, New York
☎ *(212) 643-4848*
Those who want to work on kibbutzim, Israel Defense Fund bases or in hosptitals can expect to pay between $500 and $1000 for the privilege. Age is no object, other than you must be over 18; over 15,000 people have signed up with this 13-year-old agency.

Volunteers for Peace

43 Tiffany Road
Belmont, Vermont 05730
☎ *(802) 259-2759*
A work camp-type environment with placement worldwide.

Volunteers in Technical Assistance

1815 North Lynn Street
Suite 200
Arlington, Virginia 22209
☎ *(703) 276-1800*
If you have a specific technical skill that you would like to share or apply with others, contact this group. They prefer to communicate by mail and will ask you some specific questions before referring you to one of the many volunteer groups in their listings.

Volunteer, The National Center

1111 North 19th Street
Suite 500
Arlington, VA 22209
☎ *(703) 276-0542*
If you want to narrow down your choices make this group your first stop. They will simply refer you to a group of organizations they think will match your interests.

Working Overseas

Working overseas is a lot more romantic than it is financially rewarding. My stepfather pulled down a mediocre wage looking for oil in Canada but managed to get a six figure tax-free salary with a simple idea. He figured he would find the thing of most value to the wealthiest people in the world. What's that you ask? Water and the Saudi's, of course. Most jobs overseas require training and lengthy job searches. There are some shortcuts: the military, the diplomatic corp, multinational corporations, airline stewards, aircraft ferry pilots, even foreign correspondents all will guarantee you air time and broken marriages. On the other hand, the world will be your playground and you will develop an understanding and enjoyment of the world few people will ever appreciate.

National Director of Internships

National Society of Internships and Experiential Education
Suite 207, 3509 Haworth Drive
Raleigh, North Carolina 27609

The Job Seeker

Post Office Box 16
Route 2
Warrens, Wisconsin

Vacation Work Publications

9 Park End Street
Oxford, England OX1 1HJ
☎ *0865 241978*
FAX 0865 790885
A British source for publications on summer jobs, volunteer positions and other new ways of travel. If you cover the postage they will send you their latest catalog about books and specific publications on subjects that cover teaching or living and working in various countries around the world. A small sampling of publications can show you how to teach English in Japan, work on a kibbutz in Israel, choose an adventure holiday, get au pair and nanny jobs, find summer employment in France and much more.

EcoNet and PeaceNet

18 De Boom Street
San Francisco, California 94107
☎ *(415) 442-0220*
An on-line group that can link you up with like-minded conservationists and possibly a job.

Environmental Opportunities

Post Office Box 4957
Arcata, California 95521
☎ *(707) 839-4640*

Foundation for Field Research Programs

Post Office Box 2010
Alpine, California 91903
☎ *(619) 445-9264*
A comprehensive directory of Field Research Programs around the world.

Archaeology Abroad

31-34 Gordon Square
London, WC1H 0PY England
AA puts out three bulletins a year advertising overseas excavations that need volunteers and staff. They are primarily looking for people with excavation experience (grave digging and gardening don't necessarily qualify you).

The Astrid Trust

Training Ship Astrid
9 Trinity Street
Weymont, DT4 8TW England

☎ *(0305) 761916*
Every year the square rigger "Astrid" offers two 3-month, transatlantic voyages for 26 young people. The seven-week trip heads to the Caribbean from Weymouth in September and from St. Lucia to Weymouth in mid-May. There are also short summer cruises while in England where the crew can learn to sail, scuba dive and take part in expeditions onshore.

Rules of Politically Correct Travel

• *Try to learn and use the local language.*

• *Dress conservatively.*

• *Try to use nonpolluting conveyances(bike, hike, canoe).*

• *Use public transport (bus, train, plane) to save fuel.*

• *Stay to marked paths, do not litter.*

• *Respect local cultures.*

• *Try to choose locally run establishments (restaurants, hotels, tour guides) rather than chains.*

• *Hire a local guide to add to your knowledge and exchanges with locals.*

Destination: Adventure

For the less organized and mildy impetuous we offer straight shots into the unknown. We all yearn to stuff a few things into a faded knapsack and hit the road. For those who look a little farther down the road it means a dirt cheap ticket from a bucket shop and a bunch of needles and expensive pills. Where do you want to go? We have put together a smattering of rough and tumble places that will get you started. For those who like a babysitter to keep them out of trouble, I have included the addresses of tour packagers and outfitters.

Say, "Cheese!"

A plane ride is a plane ride but when they crack open those aluminum doors and the heat and smell clobbers you like a hammer, you know you have arrived. Outside the heat rises in waves and the reddish brown earth tells you that you have come a long way. On one such trip I had to take a picture of the UTA DC-10 on the broken and potholed tarmac. I had to capture the silver bird crowned by a single monstrous cumulus cloud incongruously surrounded by soldiers with faded green uniforms. No sooner had I raised my camera to my eye than I was arrested by two scowling soldiers. Stupid, I should have known better than to take a picture in a West African airport. Thinking quickly as they grabbed for my Leica, I waved towards the cockpit. The soldiers balked trying to figure out who I was waving to. Why of course I was taking a picture of the pilot. I explained quickly to the French ground crews to tell the pilot that I had taken a picture of him not the airplane. The guards frog-marched me up the ladder and to my relief the pilots played along. The soldiers let me go and explained how lucky I was that I wasn't taking pictures of the airport. There was no law as far as they knew against taking pictures of the pilots.

Arctic/Antarctic

We used to say the Arctic was a great place to live if you were a Fudgsicle. Having been born in Edmonton, Alberta and having participated in snowshoe marathons in my youth, all I can say is the frozen food section in the grocery store is about as close as I want to get to the colder climes these days. But don't let me stop you if your idea of fun is trying to unstick your private parts from your zipper after relieving yourself in a blizzard.

The most popular places are: Antarctica, for cold-weather travel where legions of red survival suited tourists create more photos of penguins and icebergs than ever could be viewed by their warmer relatives; second is Alaska and then the Northwest Territories. Siberia and Kamchatka a distant fourth but ripe for development. People who venture to the poles have to be a little crazy since there is essentially nothing to see. The folks who pay a minimum of ten grand to get to the North Pole are really sitting over a mass of water. Weather permitting, you get a few hours before you are bundled back on the plane for the long return flight. April is really the only hospitable month that the Pole can be visited with some certainty. There is some awe-inspiring and desolate scenery along the way and you will be sick of flying as you must first get to Yellowknife, then Resolute then a weather station on the edge of Ellesmere Island. From there you wait until the weather clears and off you go. Make sure you know there is a geographic North Pole and a magnetic North Pole. The Magnetic North Pole wanders around like a bedouin looking for an oasis. A visit to the geographic North Pole may be all in good fun but a visit to the South Pole is a different story. As bad as the weather is up north, it is much worse in the south. The vibes are very different as well. Scientists want nothing to do with the variety of adventurers, tourists and nuts who want to do everthing from ski to motorcycle to the South Pole. Most of these people require very expensive and difficult extraction once they come face to face with the harsh realities of Antarctica. Cruise ships are considered a major evil with their disturbance of animal populations, litter and general disruption of this pristine area.

Is it dangerous in the colder climes? Well, what to you think? You can start with the cold. Hypothermia, exposure, frostbite and plain old freezing to death are the constants. Falling through thin ice, predatory polar bears, crevasses, fires caused by unattended heaters and the list goes on. Being an old hand in the north I won't bore you with long descriptions of 100-mph winds, helicopter crashes, drilling through blood blisters with pocket knives to relieve the pain, how flesh sticks to metal, why engines have to be run 24 hours a day and what frostbite can do to your toes. If you want all the gory details contact the following.

Adventure Canada

1159 West Broadway
Vancouver, British Columbia, Canada V6H 1G1
☎ *(604) 736-7447*
OK, you've been there, done that, visited all 235-some-odd countries. What is left to impress your friends? How about a round of golf on the North Pole? You can also claim to visit Greenland, Russia, Canada and the USA as you whack your ball around the four international zones that meet at the North Pole. The trip costs $10,200 and golf clubs are provided.

Adventure Network International

200-1676 Dranleau Street
Vancouver, British Columbia, Canada V6H 3S5
☎ *(604) 683-8033, FAX (604) 689-7646*
Nothing to do in late November or early December? Then the Antarctic is the place to be. Pat Morrow and those crazy adventurers at ANI (founded in 1985 by a group of expedition guides) have put together a two week ski and snowmobile trip where an intrepid few can stay at Patriot Hills basecamp (the only private basecamp in the Antarctic) and then visit the surrounding area on skis via or snowmobile. Flights are available to overfly Mt Vinson and the Ellesworth mountains. Campers can participate in the two week ski trip that includes outside camping. If that sounds too tame, how about flying down to the South Pole and driving some *Ski-Doos* back to the basecamp? All you need is $50,000 (that's not a typo) for the three week stint. If this seems cheap, then get in line for a month long trip that crosses the Ross Ice Shelf to Cape Evans where you will be met by an expedition ship. The ticket is $100,000 per person. That's a lifetime of Club Meds for most folks.

Arctic Experience

29 Nork Way
Banstead SM7 1PB, England
☎ *(0737) 362321*
A small outfit specializing in putting together European-based Arctic expeditions for small groups.

Borton Overseas

5516 Lyndale Avenue South
Minneapolis, Minnesota 55419
☎ *(800) 843-0602, FAX (612) 827-1544*
Every spring Borton runs eight day tours of Greenland that include two days of dog sledding. Participants can visit a remote Inuit village as well as tour Ammasalik and Sarfagajik Fjord.

Ecosummer Expeditions

1516 Duranleau Street
Vancouver, British Columbia, Canada V6H 3S4
☎ *(604) 669-7741*
A neighbor of ANI on picturesque Granville Island, this group is the best kayak outfitter in North America. They will send you to both warm and cold climates to get eye level with the world. Their trips to Ellesmere Island are not strenuous and cover only about five–20 miles a day, leaving plenty of time to get to see the wide variety of wildlife that comes visible in the summer.

Special Odysseys

3430 Evergreen Point Road
Post Office Box 37A
Medina, Washington 98039

☎ *(206) 455-1960*
If you really want to get to the North Pole it will cost you about eight days and 10 grand just to land, walk around and then get back in the plane the same day. The trip leaves every April and I am sure can provide you with some type of sporting event other than golf.

Arctic Adventure ApS

Aaboulevarden 37, DK-1960
Frederiksberg
Copenhagen, Denmark
☎ *(45) 1 37 12 33*
The experts on the massive island of Greenland . They can get you there just about any time you want to go.

Quark Expeditions

Stamford Connecticut
☎ *(800) 223-5688*
Eighteen grand will put you in a nuclear powered Russian icebreaker with a bunch of prefab living quarters bolted on. The 500' Sovetskiy Soyuz puts its 75,000 horses into crushing through up to 16 feet of ice. Quark puts an *eco-spin* on this trip so expect to be educated by scientists and come back knowing more about the Arctic that you ever wanted to know. The Soyuz will cut a hole right on up to the geographic North Pole (the magnetic pole is too flakey).

Adventure Trips

For those who have no particular method of transportation in mind, you might want to contact these groups.

Turtle Tours

5924 East Gunsight Road
Cave Creek, Arizona 85331
☎ *(602) 488-3688*
FAX (602) 488-3406
Post Office Box 1147
Carefree, Arizona 85377
For nine years Irma Turtle has specialized in introducing small groups of travelers to the world's dwindling nomadic and tribal peoples. Starting with trips to the Sahara to visit the Turegs, she has expanded her offerings to cover South America, the Middle East and Asia. If you want to experience the Wodaabe gerewol festival in Niger, the Pushkar Camel fair in Rajashtan in India or the Asmats of Irian Jaya, she can provide an existing itinerary or put together a custom trip. Turtle offers a good selection of destinations for groups as small as two. Choose from Trans Sahara, The Empty Quarter, Northern Kenya, Namibia, Ethopia—all designed to add an element of contact with culture and peoples that other operators don't offer. Ground costs, per person for group tours run about $3500 for 14–18 day trips.

Discovery Expeditions

Expedition Base
Motcombe, near Shaftesbury
Dorset, England SP7 9PB
☎ *(0747) 54456*
Colonel John Blashford-Snell runs a variety of very adventurous and very rewarding trips for "active mature adults." There is no age limit or special requirements but they do ask that prospective team members get together at a briefing weekend (in England) to determine their compatibility and are briefed on the realities that await them. Blashford-Snell's reputation as a "famous explorer" truly has the credentials to make any expedition interesting and worthwhile.

Backroads

1516 5th Street
Berkeley, California 94710
☎ *(800) GO ACTIVE, FAX 510-527-1444*

Twickers World

20/22 Church Street

Twickenham, EnglandTW1 3NW
☎ *(081) 892 7851, FAX (081) 892 8061*

A tour company specializing in naturalists and birdwatching.

Explore Worldwide

Aldershot, England GU11 1LQ
☎ *(0252) 344161 (24 hr)*

Karakoram Experience

32 Lake Road
Keswick, Cumbria C12 5DQ
☎ *(07687) 73966, FAX (07687) 74693*

Foundation for Field Research

P.O. Box 2010
Alpine California
☎ *(619) 445-9264*

Brathay Exploration Group

Brathay Hall
Ambleside, Cumbria LA22 OHP
☎ *(05394) 33942*

InnerAsia

☎ *(800) 777-8183*

Butterfield and Robinson

☎ *(800) 678-1147*

Bolder Adventures

P.O. Box 1279
Boulder, Colorado 80306
☎ *(800) 642-ASIA*

Bike Africa

4887-04 Columbia Drive South
Seattle, Washington 98108
No phone numbers listed for the organization.
Provides 2–4 week trips to remote areas by bike.

Adventure Center

1311-E 63rd Street
Everyville, California 94608
☎ *(800) 227-8747*

Earthwatch

Belsyre Court
57 Woodstock Road
Oxford, England OX2 6HU
☎ *(0865) 516366, FAX (0865) 311383*

Ecotour Expeditions

Post Office Box 1066
Cambridge, Massachusetts 02238
☎ *(800) 688-1822, (617) 876-5817*

International Expeditions

1 Environs Park
Helena, Alabama 35080
☎ *(800) 633-4734*

Natural Habitat Wildlife Adventures

1 Sussex Station
Sussex, New Jersey 07461
☎ *(800) 543-8917 (201) 702-1525*

National Audubon Society

700 Broadway
New York, New York 10003
☎ *(212) 979-3066*

The Nature Conservancy

International Trips Program

1815 North Lynn Street
Arlington, Virginia 22209
☎ (703) 841-4880

Sierra Club Outings

730 Polk Street
San Francisco, California 94109
☎ (415) 923-5630

Tread Lightly

1 Titus Road
Washington Depot, Connecticut 06794
☎ (203) 868-1710

University Research Expeditions

University of California
Berkeley, California 94720
☎ (510) 642-6586

Wilderness Southeast

711-J Sandtown Road
Savannah, Georgia 31410
☎ (912) 897-5108

World Wildlife Fund Travel Program

1250 24th Street, NW
Washington D.C. 20037
☎ (202) 293-4800

Overseas Adventure Travel

349 Broadway
Cambridge, Massachusetts 02139
☎ (800) 221-0814

Ballooning/Hang gliding/Soaring

Not really a method of travel unless you are Richard Branson. Balloons are expensive, vicarious and sometimes deadly as a method of long distance travel. As a vehicle for short, breathtaking ascents they are a blast. Zeppelins have fallen out of favor (and out of the sky), so for now any desire to float through the sky is limited to balloon tour operations, hang gliding and soaring (glider flight). The newest adventure twist is bungee jumping from balloons.

Balloons travel with the prevailing wind so you can't really determine your path. A variety of balloon safaris are available in Africa. For example, a balloon ride with champagne breakfast in the Masai Mara in Kenya will set you back about $250 per person for the four hour event. If you are really nutso about starting every day with a balloon ride, then give these folks a call:

Adventure Balloons

3 Queens Terrace
Hanwell
London, England W7 3TS
☎ (44) 81 840-0108
A specialist in balloon holidays in Great Britain, France and Ireland.

Air Escargot

Remigny, France 71150
☎ (33) 8587 1230
Balloon trips in the Burgundy area with evenings at fine restaurants. Expect to pay about $300 a day per person and stay in luxury accommodations complete with daily balloon rides.

Bombard Balloon Adventures

6727 Curran Street
McLean, Virginia 22101
☎ (800) 862-8537, (703) 883-0985
Where would you like to go? Bombard is the world's largest balloon tour operator and can take you just about anywhere you want to go. They claim to have sent more than 14,000 people on trips over the last 18 years.

Bicycle

Healthy unless you are ingesting cubic yards of diesel-filled air. Painful if you fall, and you can get cramps. Consumes massive calories resulting in huge legs and a scrawny upper chest. You are married to your bike. Probably the most dangerous method of travel due to exposure to theft, accident and health problems. Most gung-ho bikers do not stoop to organized tours, but just head out. Others realize the benefits of having a van carry all their junk. When I first biked throughout Europe and the mountains of British Columbia, it was considered "de riguer" to run road bikes without the benefit of touring gears. Mountain bikes have now actually made it fun to ride through mountainous and rough terrain. The major players in packaged bike tours are:

Backroads

1516 5th Street
Berkeley, California 94710
☎ *(800) 245-3874, (510) 527-1555*
Probably the biggest and most successful bike outfitter out there and with probably with the largest group because of it success and size.

Butterfield and Robinson

70 Bond Street
Toronto, Ontario Canada M5B 1X3
☎ *(800) 387-1147, in Canada (800) 268-8415*
Rather cushy tours with great meals, fine hotels and tour guides. If you're going to "wuss out," why not do it in style! You know it's not cheap.

Forum Travel International

91 Gregory Lane
Suite 21
Pleasant Hill, California 94523
☎ *(510) 671-2900*
A clearing house for a lot of smaller groups. Seekers of the exotic will find more to their liking here especially in Latin America and Asia.

REI Adventures

Post Office Box 88126
Seattle, Washington 98138
☎ *(800) 622-2236*
An adventure store with a co-op policy, REI also runs some pretty whacko tours to Russia, China and Nepal. Prices aren't too steep because of their business structure.

Canoes

Much of the world was explored by canoe. North America used a system of river highways to spread religion and gather furs. Every spring after the ice broke, trappers would paddle their furs, trapped over the winter season, to the great meeting places of America. Unlike the big business of rafting, canoeing in the Third World is still pretty much a BYOC proposition, unless you enjoy traveling in pirogues made of three flimsy planks. There are so many choices in Canada and the U.S. that geographic proximity is the best way to start. The top canoe routes are Boundary Waters Canoe Area in Minnesota with over 150,000 visitors each year. I prefer the more remote northern rivers like the MacKenzie, Ottawa River and even the Nahanni. To find out about domestic canoe outfitters contact:

National River Guides Association

Post Office Box 1348
Knoxville, Tennessee 37901
☎ *(615) 524-4814, FAX (615) 525-4765*

National Association of Canoe Liveries and Outfitters

Route 27 and Catro Route 2
Box 2119
Butler, Kentucky 41006
☎ *(606) 654-4111*

Cruise Ships/Expedition Vessels

Cruise ships are essentially floating hotels that don't pay property or bed taxes. It is no surprise that there are about 5 million people who will be taking cruises this year. You have about 150 major and minor ships to choose from. The rates run about $200 to $800+ a day. The cruise industry is busy ruining much of the Caribbean since up to 1000 people are disgorged into T-shirt shops on small islands. Other complaints about the refuse and lack of local economic support are being dealt with but, for now, cruises are the best way to see exotic places and still get a warm bed, western meal and a hot shower every day. Cruises have been blamed for the growing pollution found in Antarctica and the Galapagos. Although it is minor now, many countries are taking steps to reduce the negative effects of what are essentially the world's largest tour buses (like the recent ban on large cruise ships to the Galapagos and restrictions in the Seychelles). Other expedition ships manage to bring small groups of people into remote regions with less destructive results. For now, cruising along with eco-tourism is a rapidly growing travel segment.

The best for info about this can be found in *Fielding's Guide to Worldwide Cruises*, the first and still the best selling guide to cruises.

Abercrombie & Kent	☎ *(800) 323-7308*
Alaska Sightseeing/Cruise West	☎ *(800) 426-7702*
Clipper Cruises	☎ *(800) 325-0010*
Quark Expeditions	☎ *(800) 356-5699*
Special Expedtions	☎ *(800) 762-0003*
Tall Ship Adventures	☎ *(800) 662-0090*

Four-wheel drive

This is the best way and sometimes only way to see most of the rugged areas of the world. Most people will use four-wheel drive vehicles to cover bad roads and primitive conditions. Others will use them like tractors, yet others will only go shopping in them. Travel by four-wheel drive requires considerable planning, paperwork and expense—you then get to see some of the worst roads in the world. Travelers to Central Africa stare in amazement at potholes that can sink an entire Bedford truck. Washboard desert pistes in the Sahara can rattle every bolt, and many people come back from central America and Mexico proudly displaying bullet holes and pry marks on their vehicle. In any case, if you frequent third world countries you will find yourself driving a four-wheel drive vehicle whether you planned it or not. The top areas for off-road driving are areas with large networks of rough trails and spectacular scenery: North Africa, Mexico, British Columbia, South America, Malaysia and Australia.

The ultimate off-road trip is actually open to all comers. Imagine an event that picks the best drivers of 12 nations, drops them into a third world country in brand new Land Rovers and then lets them turn them into junk two weeks later. The competitors train for six months in everything from compass reading to overhauling transmissions in an effort to win a tin trophy. Strange but true. Over 1.6 million people around the world try to get one of the 64 spots in each year's event. The event is rough with little to no sleep, rolled vehicles, plenty of winching, physical exertion and a host of abuses that make basic training seem like Sunday school.

The Camel Trophy

Once a bizarre real life recreation of a cigarette ad, the Camel Trophy has gone from being the toughest off-road endurance test/cigarette commercial to eco-friendly/off-road-but-with-physical-challenges/clothing-and-sport-utility commercial.

When I ran the Camel Trophy we were there to compete and not pay attention to the video film and still photographers that hovered around our every discomfort. The people that make the cut come from over one dozen nations and must compete in physical, mental, driving, survival and team skills. The goal is to make it across a specific distance with competitive sections at the beginning, middle and end. Journalists are flown in from around the world to cover the event. And the winner gets a trophy and thats it.

The actual event can range from comical to magical to pathetic as the organizers try to create as much havoc and "toughness" as possible. I enjoy the camaraderie and exotic locations of the event, but the overall mindset of the organizers should be questioned once in a while. My claim to fame in Africa was having a knife pulled on me by event leader Ian Chapman who was terrified that I would throw him in the swimming pool with his pretty little kilt on.

The Camel Trophy does afford the regular Joe an opportunity to compete for and get a spot in a world class competition that pits him against the best that other countries have to offer. Rather than compete, the participants are united by adversity and winning the team spirit award can provide a lot more weight than the actual trophy. The team spirit award is voted on by the competitors while the overall Trophy is decided by some voodoo method only the organizers understand.

What kind of people make the cut? Triathletes, joggers, weightlifters and racers shouldn't even waste the postage. The key is teamwork, a sense of humor and the stamina to go through a lot of crap and keep smiling. Hard core athletes rarely have the team spirit or stamina required for a two week event. Musclemen and racers couldn't handle the bad days when two to three miles seems like a long way. Finally, who makes it? Stable, good humored people, who can endure being squeezed in a vehicle with three other people for two weeks. Professional racers are disqualified automaticaly and females are welcome, although no American women have made the cut so far.

The initial cut is based on experience—can you drive off-road, pitch a tent, read a map or change a tire? Once accepted you will spend a miserable frozen weekend in Grand Junction, Colorado with team organizer Tom Collins. You will be run through the standard officer canditate tests, silly things like sliding people through rope webs, balancing on a log, even winching vehicles places they should never fit into. Forty-eight hours later-sleepless, bagged and tired, you will find out if you made the first cut. If you make it you get to go to the finals usually held in Europe. Here they mess with your mind and run you through junior commando school, fun things like dragging a Land Rover half a mile with its wheels locked the wrong way (it can be done), building bridges, getting dumped in freezing cold water and playing the Flying Wallendas while crossing high wires—all posed for the cameras and designed to generate a sinking feeling of self-doubt for the real event.

The real event is quite different. A convoy of yellow vehicles will snake its way across some fetid hellhole. There are few roads and fewer reasons why trucks should pass here.The event is usually run in the wet season so that there are plenty of opportunities to use your winch or slide down hills. The competitions are great fun and deadly serious. High speed driving is not a factor in any of this. Rally driving is being phased out in favor of more eco-sensitive events like building research facilities. You are graded on how well you perform in these tasks as well as how you perform as an overall team member.

Few people can claim the honor of having been on the Trophy and most people would never want to. But, hey that's adventure.

Probably the best single proponent of off-road adventuring in North America is Tom Collins. Tom has been the major reason for the growth of the Camel Trophy Stateside. He selected, trained and motivated the U.S. team to its first place win against 12 other countries in Borneo in '94. Soft-spoken, lanky and ever energetic, Tom has set a standard that will be hard to match. He has driven the Camel Trophy in Mexico, Argentina, Brazil, Chile, Guyana, Paraguay, Siberia, Indonesia, Burundi, Tanzania and Madagascar.

Since Tom works out of his house, he has asked me to provide his FAX number and address for Camel Trophy hopefuls. Tom also runs the Land Rover schools for folks that want a first class off-road adventure. Tom is a unique individual, having spent his early years doing four-wheel drive expeditions. The problem is that he did them with two-wheel drive station wagons. He moved to Aspen, Colorado and immediately got into motocross racing and downhill racing in the early 70's. To support his hobby he worked as a waiter and a carpenter and rode bareback bulls and broncs. In 1986 he applied for and was accepted for the Camel Trophy in Madagascar and has been involved ever since. He has run prescouts and events ever since. In the off season he has taught the Land Rover schools, created the Great Divide expedition and even managed to run the Baja 1000 in 1992.

Contact Tom by writing to his address in Snowmass. He promises to get back to each and every person.

The Camel Trophy

Tom Collins
U.S. Camel Trophy Team Coordinator
Snowmass, Colorado
FAX (303) 927-9308

Intrigued by spending two weeks with sweaty, foul smelling men? If you want to be a competitor for the Camel trophy you should have the following skills:

You must know how to make knots, hitches and lashing. You must know how to operate a winch safely and neatly. Off-road driving skills are a must. This means careful, consistent driving. Medical skills are a plus but you must have basic knowledge of CPR and first aid. Orienteering is a major part of the competitive sections; you must know how to operate a compass and GPS (Global Positioning System) as well as read maps. Rally math is used to manually figure out average times. Believe it or not, you will be asked to calculate average speeds using a manual calculator, tulip rally map, odometer and stopwatch while driving at high speeds, at night with no sleep over rough trails. It is truly an experience.

Mechanical skills are expected of all contestants. You must be able to change front and rear axles, shocks, alternator and clutch as well as change tires under extreme conditions. In Africa some teams had to replace engines and transmissions in the bush—an interesting introduction to advanced auto mechanics.

Your engineering skills will be put to the test as you build crude bridges from logs, rope and aluminum ladders. Roads are built and rebuilt countless times every day and vehicles that have been rolled or submerged must be extracted quickly with little time for rumination.

The ability to work together and function as a team is a critical part of any success. After not sleeping for three to four days, tempers get tight and situations are always less than ideal. There is no one leader, so decisions must be made intuitively and quickly.

Finally, physical skills are the most important. Besides the general stamina required to endure tropical conditions, lack of sleep, dampness, lack of food, bruises, cuts and exhaustion, you must have sufficient energy reserves to actually compete in swimming, running, hiking and whatever challenges are part of the formal competitions.

For example, just to qualify you must run a 10-mile course that includes orienteering, obstacle courses, rope climbing, wire bridges and other inhumanities. These courses seem to pop knees like wishbones on Thanksgiving. The other attribute is putting up with the general stupidness the organizers will throw at you.

If you would like to apply to become a U.S. team member for the Camel Trophy you must be a U.S. Citizen, be over 21, have a valid drivers licence and have never held a professional race or rally license. You will be asked about your experience with map and compass, travel, swimming, running, racing and four-wheel drive experience.

Other Off-Road Adventurers

Alies Kar, The Adventure Company, Inc.

8855 Apian Way
Los Angeles, California 90046
☎ *(213) 848-8685*

Everthing's clear to this outfitter that can take you on four-wheel drive tours around Southern California and Baja.

Bush Trek 4WD Services

44 Tulloch Avenue
Maryland, New South Wales 2287
☎ *(049) 515815*
Garry Walthers will yank you out of a tight spot, train you not to get into a tight spot or set up four-wheel drive tours.

Four-Wheel Drive

Cape York Guides
Post Office Box 908
Atherton, Queensland 4883
☎ *(070) 911978*
FAX (070)912545
Four-wheel drive trips through the top end of Australia. You can bring your own or rent one of theirs. Travelers can rely on good cooking and expert guidance.

The Lost Patrol

Suite 172
11919 North Jantzen Avenue
Portland, Oregon 97217
☎ *(503) 731-3030*
Billed as the longest, coldest, toughest winter rally in the world, the Lost Patrol is a quick run up the Alcan highway in the dead of winter. Using standard TSD rally methods, the idea is to have the most accurate and consistent times. Sometimes this means driving as fast as the law of gravity and friction will allow and sometimes crawling to make up time. The Rally leaves Seattle at the beginning of February with about 30 entries and ends up in the Arctic about a week later.

The winner might pick up about a grand (depending on who donates the purse) and side bets are encouraged. Economically, the entry fee of $2500 doesn't make this a paying proposition, but what better things could you be doing in the dead of winter?

Rovers North

Route 128
Westford, Vermont
☎ *(802) 879-0032*
One of the few places where you can squeeze yourself into a funky old Series II or III Landrover and bump around the Northeast. Having some experience with these folks, I guarantee you there is no mechanical obstacle that will keep you from having a good time.

The Trans Pen

The Trans Pen is an annual four-wheel drive expedition to the most remote parts of Malaysia. Not an endurance trial per se, it sometimes becomes one. The 10-day event covers more ground over rougher terrain than the Camel Trophy without all the poseur stuff required by the press. The event is the idea of the local four-wheel drive club. Every year there are a revolving group of characters who enliven the proceedings. The competitors are mostly Chinese and Malaysians who love the outdoors. Because they spend the good part of a year searching out remote regions, you are guaranteed to see places no tourist will ever see.

United Four-Wheel Drive Association

4505 West 700 Street
Shelbyville Indiana 46176
☎ *800-44-UFWDA*
UFWDA can let you know about local events, clubs and schools in the northern and midwest region.

Warn Adventure

G.P.S Expeditions
Antonia Lopez, 115
28026 Madrid Spain
☎ */FAX: 34-1475-6841*

If you have a hankering to explore the uncharted terrain of the North African desert, try this event sponsored by Warn Winches (who sponsered a muddy and cold trip to Transylavnia a while back). The event is called Adventure Morocco and is looking for 20 teams comprised of three trucks and six participants. You need to be 17, healthy, have insurance and a properly outfitted vehicle. The event is a competition that stresses teamwork. There are a series of events that must be performed to gain points. Although like most adventure concepts this one stresses that every challenge can be met by protecting the environment through "ecological sensitivity," there is no supervision of the tasks. All team members simply show a Polaroid of the checkpoint. The entry fee for each vehicle is a paltry $450 with the ferry from Spain to Morrocco about $250 per car. Contestants must supply all food, lodging etc. If you win you will receive an unspecifed prize.This year the five day event kicks off in the Spring and will wind thorugh the Atlas mountains through forests, across river beds and finally into the great sand dunes of the Sahara.

Horseback

Who can resist the sun and wind-burnt look of three weeks in the saddle. Horses, like old Jeeps or Land Rovers, mean adventure. Horses mean wild rugged landscapes with endless horizons and clear blue skies. Dude ranches have surged in popularity as families try to capture this simple and pure way of life.Remember that horses can only travel about 30–50 kms depending on the terrain, while camels, yaks, mules and elephants will do about half of that distance.

Equestrian vacations do not necessarily mean fox hunting in England or overcrowded dude ranches in Arizona. You can go on a horseback safari in Africa, race the desert wind in Morocco or even tour the wilds of Spain.

If you want to spend some time in the saddle, contact:

Equitours
> *Bitterroot Ranch*
> *Post Office 807*
> *Dubois, Wyoming 82513*
> ☎ *(800) 545-0019, (307) 455-2778*
> Your first stop should be with Equitours. They set up tours around the world and make sure the horses are up to their standards.

FITS Equestrian
> *2011 Alamo Pintalo Road*
> *Solvang, California 93463*
> ☎ *(800) 666-FITS, FAX (805) 688-2943*
> FITS will get you to many of the places Equitours can and then some. They have a great selection in France.

Jungle Trekking

Many people would never think of going to a tropical jungle with a tour operator while others wouldn't think of going without one. Keep in mind that most of these folks will hook you up with local ground operators, so expect to find the same trips offered by many agencies. Top jungle destinations are Irian Jaya, Papua New Guinea, Borneo, Sumatra, Vietnam and the Amazon; the most popular are Costa Rica and Belize.

Adventure Center
> *1311 63rd Street*
> *Suite 200*
> *Emeryville, California 95608*
> ☎ *(800) 227-8747*
> ☎ *(510) 654-1879*
> A lower cost alternative.

Ecosummer Expeditions
> *1516 Duranleau Street*
> *Vancouver, British Columbia Canada V6H 3S4*
> ☎ *(604) 669-7741*

I know you are getting sick of "sea"ing this company in here, but it just so happens that they are one of the best packagers to Papua, New Guinea.

Journeys/Wildland Adventures

4011 Jackson Road
Ann Arbor, Michigan 48103
☎ *(800) 255-8735*
An excellent choice for trips to Madagascar, Brazil and Venezuela.

Mountain Travel/Sobek Inc.

6420 Fairmont Avenue
El Cerrito, California 94530
☎ *(800) 227-2384*
Although they are primarily a rafting company, they have developed good contacts and a good nose for exotic tours.

SafariCenter

3201 North Sepulveda Boulevard
Manhattan Beach, California 90266
☎ *(800) 223-6046, In California (800) 624-5342*
An excellent selection of adventure and jungle tours.

Kayaks

The Shotover in New Zealand, The Sun Khosi in Nepal, The Rogue River in Oregon and the Cheat, the Upper Yough, the Gauley and the Tygart (all found in the Allegheny mountains in West Virginia) are some of the top spots. West Virginia probably offers the widest selection of Class IV to V runs on the continent. Rafters can conquer these rivers with impunity, but kayakers need a healthy dose of Class IV skills before venturing out. Kayakers need look no further than Ecosummers located in Vancouver for the widest selection of kayak trips.

Ecosummer Expeditions

1516 Duranleau Street
Vancouver, British Columbia, Canada V6H 3S4
☎ *(604) 669-7741*
Ask for their annual catalog of trips along the west coast of North America as well as some intriguing Arctic and foreign destinations

Motorcycle

Motorcycle touring comes in four flavors: the classic Harley/Gold Wing big butt road riders; the leather clad, bug splatter BMW crowd; the brightly colored and over-revved sport Tourers; and the sunburnt, trans-Sahara off-road crowd. All can be considered adventurous and dangerous but the choice is ultimately yours. There is a law of diminishing returns if you are crossing Mali dehydrated, stricken with dysentery and nursing a broken ankle. You will probably dream of cruising the Grand Tetons adjusting the air suspension and the radio on your Gold Wing. There are happy mediums. Usually BMWs are found in scenic places like New Zealand, California and the Alps. If you want to ship your own bike, expect to pay between $1500–$3000 for the round trip. You might want to look into BMWs European delivery plan where you will pay about what the discounted price is in the States. You then pick up your bike in Munich, drive all over Europe and bring it back to Munich where they will pay for the crating, shipping and taxes. You can also look into buy-back deals where you sell the bike back at the end of the trip. Stateside you can arrange rentals through Von Thielman or Western States Motorcycle Tours. Bikes rent for about $500–$800 per week with insurance extra. If you are interested in touring Vietnam, I should plug Wink Dulles' book *Vietnam on 2 Wheels*, the best (and only) guide to motorcycling through South Vietnam. ☎ *(800) FW-2-GUIDE* to order your copy.

The first step is to contact the companies that strike your fancy and then start packing your leathers:

Alaska Motorcycle Tours

Post Office Box 622
Bothell, Washington 98041

☎ *(800) 642-6877, (206) 487-3219*
Timothy McDonnel runs shiny new Honda Gold Wings through the summer wilds of Alaska. The tour covers about 1600 miles over seven days. Figure on about $250 a day; that includes your gas, high end hotels and the bike rental. You pay for your own food.

Adventure Center

1311 63rd Street
Suite 200
Emeryville, California 95608
☎ *(800) 227-8747, (510) 654-1879*
The Center reps the Australian Motorcycle Touring ☎ *(011 61) 3 233-8891* where owner Geoff Coat runs eight and 10-day trips beginning in Melbourne. You can expect a well serviced BMW R80 and twin share accommodations. Tours run about $120 a day and watch out for those kangaroos.

Baja Off Road Tours

25108 Marguerite Parkway
Suite B-126
Mission Viejo, California
☎ *(714) 830-6569*
A former Team-Honda dirt bike racer will put you on a Honda 250 or 600cc dirt bike and send you off to La Paz (seven days) or San Felipe (four days). You will experience one of the primo desert riding and scenic runs in Mexico. The all-inclusive trips will cost you about $300–$400 a day. You pay the airfare to Southern California.

Beach's Motorcycle Tours

2763 West River Parkway
Grand Island, New York 14072
☎ *(716) 773-4960, FAX (716) 773-5227*
Why not buy your bike overseas? The Beach's will set you up on a rental or your very own BMW as you tour the Alps. They also have trips to New Zealand, Great Britain and Australia. You can also ship your own bike for the ride. Beach's will handle the crating, shipping and customs involved. Expect to pay about $800–$1800 each way to Europe; New Zealand is about 30 percent more. Tours are longer than most (16–22 days) but are great deals and highly recommended. Costs are about $200 a day plus about $50 a day for the rental of the bike.

Desmond Adventures

1280 South Williams Street
Denver, Colorado 80210
☎ *(303) 733-9248, FAX (303) 733-9601*
One of the best ways to see the Alps is on a 16-day Alpentour devised by the Desmonds. You can choose from East or West. Expect to pay about $4000 per rider and about $500 less for the passenger. It includes roundtrip airfare from New York, meals, bike rental and insurance. The trip is van-supported so bring lots of camera gear and luggage. You can also choose your weapon from mighty CBR 1100cc sport bikes to nimble Honda Trans Alps (Beemers, Trans Alps, CBR's Katanas sport bikes or Kawasaki Concours).

Edelweiss Bike Travel

Armonk Travel
146 bedford Road
Armonk, New York 10504
☎ *(800)255-7451, (914) 273-8880*
The U.S. agents for Edelweiss Bike Travel (*Steinreichweg 1, A6414 Meiming, Austria*) can send you just about anywhere including the CIS. Its homegrown 12-day Alpine ride is one of the most popular (and the best deal) for mountain rippers. They like to stick you on BMW 750s, the rideable but standard for many bike rentals, but larger bikes are available for 10–20 percent more. Edelweiss provides support vans.

Explo-Tours

Arnulfstasse 134
8000 Munich 19 Germany
☎ *(49) 89 160 789, FAX (49) 89 161 716*

Africa nuts who like chipped teeth and sandblasted eyeballs will love the offerings of Explo-Tours. They arrange tours across the Sahara, through Central Africa and into South Africa on Spartan but reliable Yamaha XT350s. Naturally only Germans are crazy enough to keep this company in business, but most Germans speak English. This is some serious riding, so participants must be physically fit and ready to ride thousands of miles in sweltering heat. The trips are great bargains at about $150 a day including bike rental. There is a support van if you or your bike conk out, and when you return, you'll know more than a plasterer about mud and sand.

Great Motorcycle Adventures

8241 Heartfield Lane
Beaumont, Texas 77706
☎ *(800) 642-3933, (409) 866-7891*
If you are looking for a little danger how about a mix of Mexican roads and fast bikes? Well, OK, how about off-roading on slow bikes? GMA organizes off-road trips to Copper Canyon, the Yucatan and the Sierra Madre mountains on dual purpose bikes. Tour costs include food, lodging, tours, gas and insurance. Trips are about $160 a day not including bike rental (dual purpose bikes are only $500 a week). If you really want to do it on a fast road bike, then expect to pay another $600 dollars a week.

MHS Motorradtouren GmbH.

Donnersbergerstrasse 32
D-8000, Munich, Germany
☎ *(011 49) 89 168 4888*
FAX (011 49) 89 1665 549
MHS offers a wide array of bike tours (including Southern California). You can choose from their popular week in Southern Italy tour or any one of the other tours including Northern Italy, Kenya, Sicily, Tunisia, Hungary, the U.S.A. and South Africa. European tours run about $150 a day with bike rentals (BMWs or Suzukis) costing about $900 a week. A cool idea for Easy Rider-wannabe's is the one-way Drive USA program where riders can pick up a bike at either coast and drop it off on the other.

Motorrad-Reisen

Jean Fish
Post Office Box 591
Oconomowoc, Wisconsin 53066
☎ *(414) 567-7548*
The U.S agent for Motorrad-Reisen (*Postfach 44 01 48, D-8000 Munich 44, Germany*
☎ *(011 49) 89 34 48 32)* can send you on a motorcycle adventure (we don't use the word holiday) to Kenya, southern France, the Alps, Italy or Russia. As with most German companies, tours are lower in cost but offer less frills. You can also purchase a new BMW, ride it on your trip and ship it back home.

Villa Moto-Tours

9437 E.B. Taulbee
El Paso, Texas
☎ *(800) 233-0564*
☎ *(915)757-3032*
One of the few companies that can stick you on a Harley. As you guessed from the name, Pancho Villa specializes in tours through Mexico down to the Yucatan Peninsula. They also can take you through Costa Rica, Baja, the Sierra Madre Central Coast and the Southwest U.S. Harleys and the Southwest—what a combo. The prices are fair, about $110 a day with bike rental running about $50–100 a day extra.

Rocky Mountain Moto Tours Ltd.

Post Office Box 7152
Station E
Calgary, Alberta T3C 3M1
☎ *(403) 244-6939*
FAX (403) 229-2788

Touring the dramatic countryside of Alberta and British Columbia may be a good second choice to the Alps. Using Honda 600cc dual purpose machines, RMMT takes you on the remote backcountry routes. Their rates of about $120 a day including bike rental are downright cheap. Choose from seven day tours of the Bugaboos and 10-day trips through Big Sky country.

Western States Motorcycle Tours

1823 East Seldon Lane
Phoenix, Arizona 85021
☎ *(602) 943-9030*
Western states will put a fire-breathing Harley between your legs and point you in the right direction. You can arrange a buy-back deal if you plan on being gone a long time or you can rent everything from a Gold Wing to a Harley for about $100 a day.

Von Theilman Tours

Post Office Box 87764
San Diego, California 92138
☎ *(619) 463-7788*
FAX (619) 234-1558
If you are a jaded biker and view the Alps and New Zealand as commonplace, then Von Theilman has the antidote. This company has been around long enough to put together tours that bring the jaded back. How about Southern California, Thailand, China, Argentina or even Jamaica? The company has really got its act together. They can send you out alone, help you buy a new bike, ship yours or give you a wide selection of dual purpose and touring bikes.

Mountaineering

There is little argument that the Hindu Kush in Nepal is the *ne plus ultra* of peaks and trekking. Only about 40 years ago the ascent of a major peak would put you on the rubber chicken circuit until you grew old. Now even Mount Vinson in the Antarctica has had 130 successful summit trips. Up and coming places include the peaks of Alaska, Argentina and Pakistan with the Alps looking like a drive-through window at McDonald's. The holy grail is to conquer the seven summits or climb the highest mountain on each continent. Many guides will require that you have proof of your skills before taking you along.

The international UIAGM or the local AMGA provides certification and standards for guides. See the listings under Schools in the back of the book, or to find out more about schools, guides and programs contact:

American Mountain Guides Association

Post Office Box 2129
Estes Park, Colorado 80517
☎ *(303) 586-0571*

Canadian Mountain Guide Association

Post Office Box 1537
Banff, Alberta, T0L 0C0Canada

Himalayan Kingdoms

20 The Mall
Clifton
Bristol, BS8 4DR England
☎ *(44) 272 237163, FAX (44) 272 744993*
One of the leaders in expedition and advanced quality climbs.

Summits

Post Office Box 214
Mount Ranier, Washington 98304
☎ *(206) 569-2992, FAX (206) 569-2993*

Overlanding

Although not technically four-wheel driving , you will be sitting in a four- or six-wheel drive Bedford as you bump and lurch across Africa. Any old African hand knows that you use a Bedford to pull out a Land Rover and you will need a tank to pull out a Bedford.

Overlanding became all the rage in the early seventies when companies could take you all the way from London to South Africa for only $1200 bucks. Today, prices are up around $5000 and the conditions and roads have since worsened. Most overlanding is done on a communal basis. Cooking and other camp chores are usually shared. Most only invite young people along. You can imagine the social dynamics of young people usually on their first or second major trip away from home. Cliques emerge, rebellions soon form, people leave and seats, toilet paper and girlfriends are fought over. In the end, everyone departs firm friends.

Himalayan Travel, Inc.

Post Office Box 481
Greenwich, Connecticut 06836
☎ *(800) 225-2380, (203) 622-6777*

The agent or Tracks Africa can send you on a 15-week overland trip from Fez in Morocco to Dar es Salaam in Tanzania. The route changes or the trip is cancelled depending on who's killing who along the way. If things are relatively quiet-expect to pay about $4000 per person.

Dragoman c/o Adventure Center

1311 63rd Street
Suite 200
Emeryville, California 95608
☎ *(800) 227-8747, (510) 654-1879*

Contact the Adventure Center if you want more punishment than Tracks Africa delivers. If you want to do 19 weeks, Trans-Africa will weave you through West Africa as well as hit most countries in Central and East Africa. Dragoman is a British company that uses Mercedes trucks. The 20-year-old company can also take you on a 7-week tour down the spine of South America.

Forum Travel International

91 Gregory Lane
Suite 21
Pleasant Hill, California 94523
☎ *(510) 671-2900, FAX (510) 946-1500*

If you want to travel 5000 miles from the headlands of the Amazon to the tip of Patagonia, then mark five months off your calendar and call Forum Travel. Probably a little too much of South America for anyone, so you can bail on any one of the 11 sections, each lasting about 12 days. The cost is $1800 per stage but do you really want to spend $20,000 bouncing around in a modified Mercedes troop truck?

Trans Continental Safaris

James Road
Clare, South Australia 5453
☎ *(61) 88 423 469, FAX (61) 88 422 586*

The continent of Australia may look small but it is very big from the windshield of a Toyota Land Cruiser about to run out of gas. Althought there are many operators who will run you around in a four-wheel drive truck for the day, it is best to stick with a pro who puts together long distance safaris. TCS will provide one-37-day tours of Australia's outback complete with driver/cooks/guides who know how to fix the air conditioning and also tell you enough dirty jokes to make the long distances bearable. They supply all the camping equipment you will need; all *you* need is the stamina.

World Expeditions

Suite 747
920 Yonge Street
Toronto, Ontario Canada M4W 3C7
☎ *(800) 387-1483*

World Expeditions will show you the most remote sections of the Australian outback on a 15 day trip from Marlin Coast to Cape York. Starting and returning in Cairns, they will introduce you to the aborigines, the Australian rain forest and the rugged scenery of Northern Australia.

Scouting

Scouts are the best way to introduce children and young adults to the outdoors. If they get serious there is a global brotherhood of fellow scouts and a wide range of travel opportunities, kind of like adventure with training wheels. If you have a young boy who wants to get into the adventurous lifestyle, the Scouts are your best bet.

As for Girl Scouts, my daughters sum it up by saying "The boys get to do all the cool stuff like camping." The current Girl Scout's philosophy is firmly entrenched in the mid-fifties and has very little to do with what the Boy Scout program can offer.

Boy Scouts of America

1325 Walnut Hill Lane
Post Office Box 152079
Irving, Texas 75015
☎ *(214) 580-2000*

Girl Scouts of the U.S.A.

830 3rd Avenue & 51st Street
New York, New York 10022
☎ *(212) 940-7500*

The Scout Association

International Secretary
Baden-Powell House
Queen's Gate
London, SW7 5JS England
☎ *(071) 584 7030, FAX (071) 581 9953*

I know you are probably a little old for merit badges and singing around campfires but you have to start somewhere. The Scouts movement was started in 1907 by Robert Baden-Powell and now has 16 million members. Many an adventurer has started by being a cub, a brownie or a scout. The goal is to encourage the spiritual, physical and mental development of young people so that they can take a constructive place in society. What it really means is you get to do a lot of cool stuff, go camping, wear dorky uniforms and compare merit badges. You can start off at age eight and you are considered too old at 20. Adults can be scout leaders and volunteer their time. Among the scouting brother/sisterhood lie many opportunities for expeditions, trips, foreign exchange programs or even just having a like-minded pen pal.

Scuba

Self Contained Underwater Breathing Apparatus was invented by Jacque-Yves Cousteau and a partner back in the 1940s. Since then SCUBA tourism has taken Americans to some of the most beautiful places on the planet.

The highest percentage of species is found around the island of Borneo, decreasing as you get farther away. The U.S. has only about 250 species, Hawaii about 450, Indonesia has about 2500. There is much talk about where the best dive sites are. There is always a hard core crowd that will always travel to the next best place. I was on Sipadan in Sabah, Malaysia during the early years and it was spectacular. At that time they were busy creating a new dive site in Indonesian Borneo; Kalimantan. Now that Sipadan is known worldwide, there are many more dive sites waiting to be discovered in Indonesia. The best dive sites in the world for pure color and variety are in Indonesia, followed by Thailand, Malaysia and then the South Pacific and the Red Sea. The adventurous will choose the Sea of Cortez for its amazing proliferation of large fish; others prefer wreck diving in Truk or even the frigid waters of the Inside Passage in British Columbia. Having dived from the Seychelles to Hawaii, my personal preference are the island of Sipadan and live-aboards in the remote Nusa tenggera islands of Indonesia. The more adventurous claim that Papua New Guinea has much to be explored and that the Galapagos is the next big place. The top dive sites are Indonesia, Micronesia, Truk, Bajal, Australia, Hawaiil and Papua New Guinea.

As you probably already know, you need to be certified to dive (although I was on a dive trip where Mexican dive masters certified the rookies with about 90 seconds of boatside instruction).

Most dive tour companies will link you up with the dive site of your choice. Don't hold high hopes for luxury or gourmet food.

Many people can't decide whether to bring all their shiny new gear or to rent. If you just spent $3000 on all the gear, then you are more than likely going for one reason, so bring the whole kit. Many airlines offer extended luggage or weight allowances if one of your bags is dive gear. If you are going to bring your gear, bring a small took kit including spare O-rings, straps and batteries.

My experience is that at a minimum, it is best to bring your mask along with octopus, with regulator and gauges. The next level would be booties and BC. Lose the dive knife, tanks, flippers and wet suit for warm water dives. Photographers will want to bring their certification card, logbook, camera, film, flash, batteries and maintenance pack.

There is a caveat. I ran out of air at 90 feet below in the clear waters of the Cayman Islands. The reason? The vibration from the plane flight had loosened my regulator and, I went through 3000 psi of air in about eight minutes. Speaking of close calls, there is also divers insurance that will make sure you get repatriated or flown to the nearest decompression center. Contact **Divers Alert Network** ☎ *(800) 446-2671* or **Divers Security Insurance** ☎ *(800) 288-4810*. Remember to wait that extra day to fly home after diving. To start planning your next great dive trip contact:

Innerspace Adventures

13393 Sorrento Drive
Key Largo, Florida 34644
☎ *(800) 833-SEAS, FAX (813) 596-3891*
A 20-plus year old dive travel agency that can get you deals as well as great dive sites. Micronesia is a specialty.

Island Dreams Travel

7887 Katy Freeway
Suite 105
Houston, Texas 77024
☎ *(800) 346-6116*
Specialists in the Western Caribbean.

Sea Safaris Travel, Inc.

3770 Highland Avenue
Suite 102
Manhattan Beach, California 90266
☎ *(800) 821-6670, in California (800) 262-6670*
An agency staffed by divers that can set you up in Asia, the Caribbean, the South Pacific and the MiddleEast.

See & Sea Travel Service, Inc.

50 Francisco Street
Suite 205
San Francisco, California 94133
☎ *(800) 348-9778, (415) 434-3400*
A good choice for more exotic and far flung dive trips. Sea & Sea has an excellent selection of live-aboards.

Safaris

Arguably, safaris were the first adventure or eco-tour. Back then you would save wildlife by collecting samples for museums by shooting and mounting them. Now all you hear is the clicking of cameras and whirring of videotapes. Most safaris in Africa today are nothing more than small bus tours complete with zebra striped buses and clusters of floppy bush hats brandishing new auto-everything cameras.

Masai Mara and Kruger Parks are glorified zoos without bars. The sight is still spectacular and the photographs make everyone feel like they were the first one to set eyes on a lion kill or multi-hued African sunset. Despite the rampant commercialism there is still a primitive joy in drinking a bloody Mary while watching the sun go down in Africa. I also enjoy the raw fear of camping without a tent in hunting areas of Tanzania and listening to the lions coughing and roaring at the intruders.

It is quite easy to fly directly to Nairobi or Dar es Salaam and book your own safari. You can also rent your own four-wheel drive vehicle and stay at the various game parks or campsites. In fact, *Fielding's Guide to Kenya* is the most complete guide to homestays, game lodges and campsites and will show you how easy it is.

The best safaris in the world are private tented safaris to the lesser visited areas of Africa's parks. In terms of wildlife, South Africa has an overabundance of wildlife along with clean, effiencient facilities. Kenya has the creaky colonial ambience many people expect and Tanzania is the stronger and more realistic of the two. My personal favorite is the rugged and remote Ruaha in Tanzania.

If you want to get your money's worth, the best way to get around is by air. That way you can hit as many regions as you want and get a good grounding in geography as you bump and shudder through the hot African sky. Masai Mara has the most wildlife per square foot but has an equal number of tourists. Northern Kenya is plagued with bandits but has more dramatic scenery. Tanzania can be tedious (Selous) or dramatic (Ngorongoro Crater) but is what most people expect Kenya to look like. The Okavongo Delta and Namibia are becoming ideal second safari areas and regions in Uganda, once the most beautiful country in Africa, are supposed to be coming back slowly. When it comes to choosing lodges, home stays, parks or accomodations, and Fielding publishes the best single book on Kenya. If you want to set up a safari in Africa we reccomend these groups.

Abercrombie & Kent

1520 Kensington Road,
Oak Brook, Illinois 60521
☎ *(800) 323-7308, (708) 954-2944*
The most famous African Safari and adventure tour operator does tours on the "cushy side" but the Kents run a first class show. They also can put together custom expeditions since they know most of the major ground operators on every continent.

American Museum of Natural History Discovery Tours

Central Park West at 79th Street
New York, New York 10024
☎ *(800) 462-8687, (212) 769-5700*
One of the best sources for high end natural history tours. Although the tours are set up using a variety of ground operators, the museum provides stimulating guides and guest lecturers.

Borton Overseas

5516 Lyndale Avenue South
Minneapolis, Minnesota 55419
☎ *(800) 843-0602, (612) 824-4415*
A ground operator who specializes in Tanzania.

Ker, Downey, Selby

Box 41822
Nairobi, Kenya
☎ *(254) 2 556466*
The classic tented safari is the speciality of this group of independent outfitters and former big game hunters.

Tamu Safaris

Post Office Box 247
West Chesterfield
N.H. 03466
☎ *(800) 766-9199)*

Wildland Adventures

3516 Northeast 155th
Seattle, Washington, 98155
☎ *(800) 345-4453*

Walking/Trekking

This is the most laid back method of travel. You will meet people, get healthy and presumably do most of your travel in the world's most beautiful places. There is some danger of kidnapping and robbery as well as the usual penalties caused by tripping, falling and general wear and tear. Most trekkers hire porters and spend the evenings in small huts or villages. Trekking does not have to be set up from home since most countries that are known for trekking supply the manpower for tour packagers overseas. Make sure however, that you bring all the camping do-dads and clothing you will need.

The most popular trekking sites are Annapurna in Nepal, Zanskar in Ladakh, Bernese Oberland in the Alps, The Milford Track in New Zealand and Chiang Mai in Northern Thailand.

The Ramblers Association

1 -5 Wandsworth Road
London, SW8 2XX, England
A group that can advise you on where to hike in Britain and set you up with the resources you might need for a European walking holiday. As you may have guessed from the name of this group, their members are not triathletes or mountain climbers. For actual tours contact Rambler's Holidays below.

Mountain Travel-Sobek

6420 Fairmount Avenue
El Cerrito, California 94530
☎ *(800) 227-2384*
The IBM and GM of adventure tours can send you anywhere that's worth trekking to. Although their expertise is really rafting and climbing, their trekking expeditions make use of many of the same contacts and guides.

Rambler's Holidays

P.O. Box 43
Welwyn Garden City AL8 6PQ, England
☎ *(0707) 331133*
A British group that can set up walking tours in Europe and Britain.

The Sierra Club

730 Polk Street
San Francisco, CA 94109
☎ *(415) 776-2211*
One of the better sources for trekking, hiking or climbing trips around the United States and the world.

White-Water Rafting

Rafting has captured the imagination of Americans. In fact, when you ask most people what adventure is, they will reply, "a rafting trip on the Colorado." The truth is that rafting is among the safer aquatic sports. Bobbing like a cork on thundering white water, large flexible rafts carry thousands of people a year down the nation's major rafting rivers. As a method of travel rafts, canoes and kayaks are a pain. They must be trucked in to the river, trucked out and you are always wet and soggy and cold. But rafts and canoes provide the the best way to see a lot of the primitive world. I have traveled by canoe in Africa, North America and Asia and found that the purity and simplicity cannot be beaten for communing with nature. I also have despised the primitive method of transportation after carrying a water logged six man canoe across the nine mile Grand Portage.

The top domestic rivers for white-water rafting are the Tatshenshini in Alaska, the Colorado in Arizona, the Chiclo/Chicoltin in British Columbia, Canada and the Upper Youghiogheny in West Virginia. Internationally there are many rivers yet to be run, among them the upper reaches of the Mahakam in Borneo, the Bio Bio in Chile, the Obihingoú in the CIS and the Zambesi in Zimbabwe.

To find out where you can eat H_2O contact U.S.A. Whitewater at ☎ *(800) USA-RAFT* for a selection of outfitters in the U.S.

In this country, these two outfitters stand head and shoulders above the rest:

Mountain Travel/Sobek Inc.

6420 Fairmont Avenue
El Cerrito, California 94530
☎ *(800) 227-2384*

The granddaddy of adventure tour companies, Sobek joined with Mountain Travel to create the Thomas Cook's of eco-tourism. I once stayed with a remote tribe in Borneo who used the word "sobek" to ask for money. They explained that an American rafting expedition had been through and when the natives said the word "sobek" the rafters gave them money. Such is eco-tourism. MTS has specialized in Asia and Africa and are really the only sources for reliable rafting trips in Papua New Guinea, Ethiopia and Borneo.

Steve Curry Expeditions Inc.

Post Office Box 1574
Provo, Utah 84603
☎ *(801) 224-6797*

The master of the Yangtze in China, Currey also provides expertise in Latin America and the Soviet Union.

Expedition Information

The National Geographic Society

The august and venerable National Geographic Society has become the best and most popular means for the world to understand itself. Back in 1888 it was simply a group of philanthropists who wanted to increase and diffuse geographical knowledge. Since then they have funded almost 5000 expeditions, educated and entertained hundreds of millions and are the largest geographic group of any kind on this planet. They manage to maintain a rough edge and an accessible front. Unlike the tiny, musty adventurers clubs, the National Geographic Society has gone global. You can sit in your own musty den and travel to more countries, experience more expeditions and learn more about our world thanks to their efforts.

Many adventurers were weaned on their yellow tomes. A generation further back were titillated by sights of unclothed natives and exotic locales. If any magazine could be called adventurous it would be good old *National Geo.*

National Geographic Society has 9.7 million members in almost 200 countries. Over 44 million people read each issue of their magazine, 40 million watch their documentaries on PBS and 15 million watch "On Assignment" each month. Though not exactly an elite group, being featured in or by a National Geographic publication thrusts you into the mainstream of adventure/entertainment. If you are written up or have an article in the *National Geographic Magazine*, you can work the rubber chicken circuit for the next decade. If you are featured on any of their television specials, like Jacques-Yves Cousteau *(The Voyages of the Calypso)* or Bob Ballard *(The Search for the Titanic)*, you can contemplate licensing and even your own TV series.

Despite being Valhalla for adventureres, the *National Geographic* does their bit to generate content. In 1992 the Society awarded 240 grants for field research and exploration. The Nat Geo is also on a mission to create higher awareness of geography among students because they would have little product to sell if people didn't know the difference between Bahrain and the Bahamas. If you are young and a whiz at geography you can try to join the 6 million people who take part in the National Geographic Bee.

The National Geographic is probably the biggest and best source for just about any information about the world and adventure. They offer a staggering range of books on everything from the Amazon to Zaire. They now offer *World*, a kids magazine with three million readers a month, *Traveler Magazine* with another 3 million and *National Geographic Explorer* (8 million viewers a month), a radio station (a million listeners a day) and home videos with 5.4 million viewers a year. You wouldn't think there was enough adventure, geography and science info out there but *Nat Geo* just keeps on churning it out with CD-ROMs, Geoguides, pop-up action books, news features, on-line services, globes, atlases, a museum and more. How do they do it? For starters they pull in about half a billion dollars in tax free-income. Just call ☎ *(800) 638-4077* for a catalog of what interests you and join today.

National Geographic Research & Exploration Quarterly

1145 17th Street North West
Washington, D.C. 20036
☎ *(800) 638-4077*
A quarterly journal with a definitely scientific bent. Better laid out and illustrated than other dry journals.

National Geographic Magazine

1145 17th Street North West
Washington, D.C. 20036
☎ *(800) 638-4077*
The old standard (requires membership) at $21 a year is still a great bargain. Editorial stance is getting tougher. More articles on pollution, politics, natural threats in addition to the standard "purdy" pictures. The magazine has launched a small but well traveled group of photographers who capture the world for $800 a day (check with Nat Geo).

The Royal Geographical Society

1 Kensington Gore
London, England SW7 2AR
☎ *(071) 589 5466*
The fabled exploration society that still requires nomination by an existing member to join. I highly recommend contacting their Expedition Advisory Center and checking the range of publications they offer. When in London nonmembers can visit the Map Room in their creaky Victorian headquarters on Hyde Park near Albert Hall. They also have an impressive photo archives and reference book selection.

The Royal Geographical Society Magazine

Stephenson House, 1st Floor
Bletchley, Milton Keynes
MK2 2EW
☎ *(0908) 371981*
A monthly magazine that is a lot dryer and a lot less pretty than a *Nat Geo* publication but much tougher and smarter in its editorial focus. Covers expeditions, environment, travel, adventure—all with a scientific bent.

Air Ambulance Services

Air Ambulance Inc.
Hayward, CA, ☎ *800-982-5806/510-786-1592*

Aero Ambulance International
Ft. Lauderdale, FL, ☎ *800-443-8042/305-776-6800*

Air Ambulance Network
Miami, FL, ☎ *300-327-1966/305-387-1708*

Air-Evac International
8665 Gibbs Drive
Suite 202
San Diego, California 92123
☎ *(800) 854-2569*

Air Medic—Air Ambulance of America
Washington, PA, ☎ *800-321-4444/412-228-8000*

Care Flight—Air Critical Care Intl.
Clearwater, FL, ☎ *800-282-6878/813-530-7972*

National Air Ambulance
Ft. Lauderdale, FL, ☎ *800-327-3710/305-525-5538*

International Medivac Transport
Phoenix, AZ, ☎ *800-468-1911/602-678-4444*

International SOS Assistance
Philadelphia, PA, ☎ *800-523-8930/215-244-1500*

Mercy Medical Airlift

Manassas, VA, ☎ *800-296-1217/703-361-1191*
(Service area: Caribbean and Canada only. If necessary, will meet commercial incoming patients at JFK, Miami and other airports.)

Health and Safety

Access America, Inc.

Post Office Box 90310
Richmond, Virginia 23230
☎ *(800) 284-8300*

Adventure Link, Inc.

Post Office Box 510434
Melbourne Beach, Florida 32951
☎ *(407) 724-5368*
Oceanese waterproof reference cards provide medical information on how to treat injuries from marine animals. They also have illustrations of varmints for easy identification and avoidance. The information is sparse but could save your life. There is one card for the Atlantic and another for the Pacific, they run $4.95 each.

Alan Pharmaceuticals, Ltd.

204 Essex Road
London N1 3AP, United Kingdom
☎ *44-71-226-6246*
FAX 44-71-704-9348

American Society of Tropical Medicine and Hygiene

6436 31st St. NW
Washington, D.C. 20015-2342
☎ *(301) 496-6721*
Ask for *Health Hints for the Tropics* ($ 4).

Centers for Disease Control and Prevention

1600 Clifton Rd., N.E.
Atlanta, GA 30333
☎ *(404) 639-3311*
The Centers for Disease Control in Atlanta maintains the international travelers hotline at ☎ *404-332-4559*.

Citizens Emergency Center

☎ *202-647-5225*
U.S. State Department Consular Information Sheets and Travel Warnings may be heard anytime by dialing the Citizens Emergency Center using a touch tone phone, or by contacting any of the 13 regional passport agencies, field offices of the U.S. Department of Commerce and U.S. embassies and consulates abroad, or, by writing and sending a self-addressed, stamped envelope to the Bureau of Consular Affairs,

The Citizens Emergency Center maintains a travel notice on HIV/AIDS entry requirements. Call to obtain these requirements. A number of countries require foreign visitors to be tested for the AIDS virus as a requirement for entry. This applies mostly to those planning to reside overseas. Before traveling, check the latest entry requirements with the foreign embassy of the country to be visited.

Foreign Entry Requirements

A listing of foreign entry requirements is available for 50 cents from the Consumer Information Center, *Pueblo, CO 81009*.

Directory of Medical Specialists

The authoritative reference is published for the American Board of Medical Specialists and its 22 certifying member boards; it contains detailed information on physicians abroad. This publication should be available in your local library. If abroad, a list of hospitals and physicians can be obtained from the nearest American embassy or consulate.

Drugstore Olskouvara Co.

35, Agorakitou Street
10440 Athens Greece
☎ *30-1-822-27-685*
FAX 30-1883-1680

Emergency Medical Payment/Information Services

Available to American Express

1) A directory of *U.S. Certified Doctors Abroad* (Price: $3.00)

2) A health insurance plan is available through the Firemens Fund Life Insurance Company, *1600 Los Gamos Rd., San Raphael, CA 94911.* Attention: American Express Card Service.

Health Information for International Travelers

by the Centers for Disease Control

(Publication No. HHS-CDC 90-8280, $6.00 each) is an annual global rundown of disease and immunization advice and other health guidance, including risks in particular countries; may also be obtained from the Government Printing Office.

Healthcare Abroad

243 Church Street, N.W.
Suite 100-D
Vienna, Virginia 22180
☎ *(800) 237-6615*
☎ *(703) 281-9500*

IAMAT International Association for Medical Assistance to Travelers

736 Center Street
Lewiston, NY 14092
☎ *716-754-4883*
A medical directory, clinical record and a malaria risk chart are sent without charge; however, a contribution is requested for World Climate Charts.

Immunization Alert

P.O. Box 406
Storrs, CT 06268
☎ *203-487-0611*
For $25 a traveler is provided with an up-to-date, detailed and personalized health report on up to six countries to be visited. It will tell you what diseases are prevalent and what precautions are recommended or advisable.

International SOS Assistance

1 Neshaminy Interplex
Suite 310 Trevose, Pennsylvania 19047
☎ *(800) 523-8930/(215) 244-1500*

Life Extension Foundation

800-841-5433
World Research Foundation
☎ *(818) 907-5483*

The following are vendors who can supply non FDA approved drugs. Remember it is best to use Federal Express to ship drugs.

Masters Marketing, Co. Ltd

Masters House
Number 1, Marlborough Hill
Harrow, Middlesex HA1 ITW, United Kingdom
☎ *44-81-427-9978*
FAX 44-81-427-1994

Medical Sea Pak Company

1880 Ridge Road East, Suite 4

Rochester, New York 14622
☎ (800) 832-6054

Most first aid kits are great for homes and construction sites but what about for divers? How about Sea Paks, a selection of four different kits for divers? The largest is the $900, 30-pound Trans Ocean Pak and the smallest is the Day Pak, a seven-pound, 15"x 6"x 3"day pack with instruction booklet.

Near, Inc.

450 Prairie Avenue
Suite 101
Calumet City, Illinois 60409
☎ (800) 654-6700

Travel Assistance International

1133 15th Street, N.W.
Suite 400 Washington, DC 20005
☎ (800) 821-2828/(202) 331-1609

Travmed

Post Office Box 10623
Baltimore, Maryland 21285
☎ (800) 732-5309

World Care Travel Assistance

1150 South Olive Street
Suite T-2233 Los Angeles, California 90015
☎ (800) 253-1877

Military/Adventure

Books International

69B Lynchford Road
Farnborough
Hampshire GU14 6EJ
☎ 01252-376564
FAX 01252-370181

Books International specializes in military reference books for the modeler, collector, researcher or curious. You won't find too many cerebral products here but plenty of hard-to-find illustrated books on past wars, equipment, history and miltary reference works. Where else would you find an illustrated reference guide to Polish miltary helicopters or a real life photo book of the Navy SEALS?

Brassey's Inc.

8000 Westpark Drive
First Floor
McLean, Virginia 22102
☎ (703) 442-4535
FAX (703) 790-9063

Brassey's is the publisher of choice when British military men want to fill their mahogany book-cases. They are known for their annual *Defence* yearbook that keeps the Brits up to date on the rest of the world. Each issue has essays and intros on the leading political and military topics. If you want to be the model of a modern major general you should look into their books on biological, nuclear, naval, historical and military warfare. Their annual update of *The World in Conflict* is a must read for professional adventurers. There are drier books on ammunition, land force logistics, radar and other technical reference manuals. It is no surprise that their U.S. rep is based in McLean, Virginia.

Covert Action

1500 Massachusetts Ave., NW. #732,
Washington D.C. 20005
☎ (202) 331-9763
FAX (202) 331-9751

A magazine written by some ex-company folks who have no qualms about telling it like it is. Plenty of facts, numbers, dates, photos and other material to back their statements up.

For Your Eyes Only

Tiger Publications
Post Office Box 8759
Amarillo, Texas 79114
☎ *(805) 655-2009*

Billed as an open intelligence summary of current military affairs. Editor Stephan Cole puts together the biweekly eight-page newsletter to provide an excellent update on military, political and diplomatic events around the world. Somewhat right wing and hardware oriented, it still provides a balanced global view of breaking events. An annual subscription costs $65 (26 issues). Sample copies are $3 each. Back issues are available for $1.25–$2 depending on how many you order. FYEO is also available on NewsNet ☎ *(800) 952-0122* or *(215) 527-8030.*

Greenhill Books

Park House
1 Russell Gardens
London NW11 9NN
☎ *(081) 458-6314*
FAX (081) 905-5245

A publisher of military books from Alexander the Great to the Gulf War.

Jane's Information Group

1340 Braddock
Suite 300
Alexandra Virginia 22314
☎ *(703) 683-3700*
FAX (703) 836-1593

Jane's is the undisputed leader in military intelligence for the world's armies. About a quarter of a million people subscribe to their annual guide on aircraft but only about 11,000 need to know what's new in nuclear, biological and chemical protection clothing. Just as teenagers await the new car catalogs in the fall, the world's generals eagerly await the new Janes reports on weapon systems, aircraft, ships, avionics, strategic weapons and other hardware. Esoteric fans thumb through their yearbooks on "Electro-optics, Image Intensifier Systems" (not to be confused with their guide to thermal imaging systems) or Air Launched Weapons. Arms dealers never travel without their *World Markets for Armoured and Military Logistics Vehicles.* Prices for the books or CD-ROMS run between $400 and $9000. If you are buying an update of an existing book or CD-ROM the price drops about 25 percent. For your money you get one annual guide, eleven monthly updates and a summary report. Jane's also publishes a monthly intelligence review, *Jane's Intelligence Review,* that provides background on global conflicts, terrorist groups and arsenals.

A new service is "Jane's Sentinel," a series of regional security assessments with monthly updates and a broadcast FAX service. Sentinel breaks down the world into six regions and provides reports on physical features, infrastructure, defence and security as well as general information like maps and graphs.

In case the world is smitten with a bad case of peacefulness, Jane's also dabbles in the mundane. They have guides to airports, the container business and railways.

Jane's Security and Counter-Insurgency Equipment Yearbook

edited by Ian Hogg

If you have ever have been torn between buying a Vigiland Survellance Robot or a Magnavox Thermal Sniper Scope, Jane's makes it as easy as shopping at Victoria's Secret. The book contains an overview and listing of all major equipment used by security, antiterrorist and civil defence organizations.

The New Press

450 West 41st Street
New York, New York 10036
☎ *(212) 629-8802*
FAX (212) 268-6349

This publisher of "serious books" can be counted on for interesting new books. Their titles include *Civil Wars: From L.A. to Bosnia* by Hans Magnus Enzensberger, a book that helps readers understand the new forces that shape conflicts and two books by Gabriel Kolko— *Century of War*, a new view of wars since 1914 with some excellent insights to war after WWII; *Anatomy of a War*, the story of the Vietnam conflict from the Vietnamese, U.S. and Communist Party viewpoint.

Paladin Books

Post Office Box 1307
Boulder, CO 80306
The most infamous source for militaria, gung ho adventure books and such classics as *Advanced Weapons Tactics for Hostage Rescue Teams*. Send for a listing or catalog. Most of the material is borderline plagarism from military manuals or fantasy tough guy stuff. But there are some gems among the stones.

Soldier of Fortune

5735 Arapahoe Aenue
Boulder, Colorado 80303
☎ *(800) 877-5207 (subscriptions)*
☎ *(303) 449-3750 (editorial)*
The political left imagines the SOF reader as a gun polishing, beer drinking, closet Rambo who cleaned latrines in the Nam. Well, they are probably half right. Its other half that is impressive. For every three articles on self defence, gun control or new fighting knives, there is a good firsthand description of one of the world's dirty little wars. SOF does provide some very interesting on-the-ground reporting from countries undergoing third world turmoil. Their editorial position is somewhat to the right of Ronald Reagan and Wyatt Earp but the magazine is still an important source for information on weapons and little-known conflicts. Subscriptions are $28 a year with newstand issues going for $4.75

The Stockholm International Peace Research Institute

FAX (46 8 655 97 33)
This group publishes an 870 page annual on the world's military expenditures, arms production and trade.

Political and World Affairs

CIA World Factbook

An accurate if frumpy look at 250-odd countries of the world. Covers government statistics, economics.

État des Drogues, Drogue des États

Hachette ISBN 2 01 278701 0
A 322-page, annually updated guide to the world of illegal drugs from the Geopolitical Observatory of Drugs in Paris.

This unique guide breaks down the world of illicit drugs into three levels of intensity. It provides a country-by-country analysis of of the global drug trade. With sixty-three sections on individual countries. Identifies "Narco states" such as Myanmar, states under the influence like Colombia, and "Fragile States" like Italy where corrruption as a result of drug trafficking is a problem.

National Institute of Standards and Technology (NIST)

$32, on disc $140
The CIA/KGB factbook is also available on CD-ROM from Compton New Media for $40.

Pinkerton Risk Assessment Services

1600 Wilson Boulevard
Suite 901
Arlington VA 22209
☎ *(703) 525-6111*
FAX (703) 525-2454

Pinkerton provides risk assessements of over 200 countries on-line or in person. Some are in-depth and some are simply rehashes of outdated State Department info. They offer access to a database of over 55,000 terrorists' actions and daily updated reports on security threats. The nontechie can order printed publications that range from daily risk assesment briefings to a monthly newsletter. Their services are not cheap, but then again, how much is your life worth? Annual subscription to the on-line service starts at about $7000 and you can order various risk and advisory reports that run from $200–$700 each. Pinkerton's can still get down and dirty with counterterrorism programs, hostage negotiators, crisis management and Travel Security seminars.

The service is designed for companies who send their employees overseas or need to know what is going on. Some reports are mildly macabre with their annual report-like graphs of maimings, killings, assaults and assassinations. Others are downright enlightening. In any case, Pinkerton does an excellent job of bring together the world's most unpleasant information and providing it to you in concise, intelligent packages.

Reporters Sans Frontières Annual Report

John Libbey & Co. Ltd.
13 Smiths Yard
Summerley Street
London SW18 4HR
☎ *(44) 81-947 2777, FAX (44) 81-947 2664*

This 391-page book covers the state of the freedom of the press in every country in the world and tells you the scoop on what to expect in the way of murders and disappearances, arrest, imprisonment, and torture, threats and harassment, administrative, legal or economic pressure and obstacles to the international free flow of information. It is an exhaustive, informative and obviously self-serving reference book that should be required reading for every traveling jour-nalist.

I.B. Tauris

c/o St Martins Press
257 Park Avenue South
18th Floor
New York, New York 10010
☎ *(212) 982-3900*
FAX (212) 777-6359

I.B. Tauris is an English publisher who specializes in political and nontraditional books on world affairs. Their coverage of the Middle East, Yugoslavia and Islam is excellent. Titles like *A Modern History of the Kurds*, *The Making of the Arab-Israeli Conflict* and *Violence and Diplomacy in Lebanon* are useful reference guides. They also publish books on Yemen, Turkey, Jordan, Algeria, Pakistan, Iran, Syria and Albania. Books on assassins, gypsies, mythology, pol-itics, war and Africa are a great addition to the politically astute reader's library.

Understanding Global Issues

FREEPOST GL496
The Runnings
Cheltenham GL51 9BR
☎ *01242-245252*
FAX 01242-224137

UGI publishes 10 minibriefings (18–22 pages) that range from *The Kurds, Caught Between Two Nations* to *The Rubbish Mountain, Tackling Europe's Waste*. The almost monthly mail-ings are well illustrated, somewhat simplistic (which in this case is good), politically unaligned and an ideal overview of the world's global issues. Although it is published by a German schoolbook company, the teenage-level presentation complete with charts, graphs, maps and photos does provide an easy entry point into complex social issues.

An annual subscription (10 issues) is 22.50 pounds; back issues are 2.50 pounds. You can order your binder for 4.95 pounds.

The World Bank

1818 H Street, N.W.

Washington, D.C. 20433
☎ *(202) 473-2941*
The World Bank can provide you with some interesting information on world population projections, saving the rain forest, health care, literacy and general information on global financial topics. Although this agency has been blamed for many of the world's woes by financing large mining, development and dam projects, it would be best to understand why they are so busy developing the world while some ecologists are busy trying to undevelop it.

The World's Statistics on CD-ROM

DSI Data Service & Information
CD-ROM Department
Post Office Box 1127
D-47476 Rheinberg, Germany
☎ *(49) 2843 3220*
FAX (49) 2843 3230
or American Overseas Book Company
550 Walnut Street
Norwood, New Jersey 07648
☎ *(201) 767-7600*

Number crunchers can pig out with statistics from the United Nations, Europe, even census information from a variety of countries. The information is very expensive but worth it for those who make their living by knowing the right numbers. Relevent titles would be *International Statistical Yearbook* (DM 5000), *World Climate Disc* (DM2300), *United Nations* (on CD-ROM contains over one million entries for all countries and regions of the world) and the CD *Atlas of France* (DM 2600).

State Department Updates/Reports

The State Department issues Consular Information Sheets for every country in the world. They include such information as the location of the U.S. embassy or consulate in the subject country, health conditions, political disturbances, unusual currency and entry regulations, crime and security information, and drug penalties. The State Department also issues Travel Warnings. These are issued when the State Department decides, based on all relevant information, to recommend that Americans avoid travel to a certain country. Countries where avoidance of travel is recommended will have Travel Warnings as well as Consular Information Sheets.

Bureau of Consular Affairs

Room 4811, N.S.
U.S. Department of State
Washington, DC, 20520
☎ *(202) 647-1488*

Consular Affairs Automated FAX System

☎ *(202) 647-3000.*
Information Sheets, Warnings and publications can be FAXed to you by dialing from a FAX machine that is equipped with a phone handset.

Consular Affairs Bulletin Board—(CABB)

Modem Number: (202) 647-9225
If you have a personal computer, modem and communications software, you can access the Consular Affairs Bulletin Board or CABB. This service is free. Modem Speed: The CABB will accomodate modems operating at 300, 1200, 2300, 9600 or 14400 bps. Set your terminal communications program to N-8-1 (No parity, 8 bits, 1 stop bit).

OAG Electronic Edition

☎ *(800) 323-4000*
If you have a personal computer and a modem, you can also access Consular Information Sheets and Travel Warnings through the Official Airlines Guide (OAG). The OAG provides the full text of Consular Information Sheets and Travel Warnings on many on-line computer services. You can obtain information on accessing Consular Information Sheets and Travel Warnings through OAG on any of the following computer services:

CompuServe (CompuServe subscribers may type GO STATE at any "!" prompt.)

Dialcom

Dialog

Dow Jones News/Retrieval

General Videotex-Delphi

NewsNet

GEnie

IP Sharp

iNet-America

iNet-Bell of Canada

Telenet

Western Union-Easylink

Infosys America

☎ *(314) 625-4054*
Infosys America Inc. also provides the full text of Consular Information Sheets and Travel Warnings through Travel On-line BBS on the SmartNet International Computer Network in the U.S., Canada and overseas. The (modem) telephone number for Travel+Plus is ☎ *(617) 876-5551* or ☎ *(800) 544-4005.* Interactive Office Services, Inc. offers on-line travel information in Travel+Plus through the networks listed below. For information on access, call

Travel+Plus.

Delphi, MCI (RCA Hotline)

Unison

Bell South TUG

FTCC Answer Bank

Overseas Security Electronic Bulletin Board

Executive Director
Overseas Security Advisory Council
(DS/OSAC)
U.S. Department of State
Washington, DC 20522-1003
☎ *(202) 647-5225 Travel Advisory*
☎ *(202) 647-9225 Bulletin Board*
The Overseas Security Electronic Bulletin Board provides State Department Consular Information Sheets and Travel Warnings as a free service (purchase of necessary software required) for American firms doing business overseas.

The following computer reservation systems (CRS) maintain State Department Consular Information Sheets and Travel Warnings. This information can be accessed by entering the CRS codes listed below.

APOLLO—For the index, enter: S*BRF/TVLADV. For the full text of Consular Information Sheets and Travel Warnings, enter: TD*DS/ADV

DATAS II—For full text of Consular Information Sheets and Travel

Warnings, enter: G* _ (country)_

PARS—For the index, enter: G/AAI/TVL

Travel Document Systems, Inc.

Travel Document Systems, Inc. provides the full text of Consular Information Sheets and Travel Warnings to the following reservation systems:

SABRE—Enter: N*/ADVISORY INDEX

SYSTEM ONE—Enter: GG SUP TD ADV

In Western Europe, SYSTEM ONE is accessed through the AMADEUS system and APOLLO through the GALILEO system.

Travel/Recreation

Business Traveler International

51 East 42nd Street
New York, NY 10017
☎ *(212) 697-1700*
FAX (212) 697-1005
Geoffrey H. Perry has about 40,000 avid readers who need to know facts, not gushy descriptions of the world's regions. The magazine can be counted on to provide on-the-ground information, comparative charts and travel tips that are always useful. A year's subscription is $29.97. Single copies are $3.

EcoTraveler

9560 S.W. Nimbus Avenue
Beaverton, Oregon 97008
☎ *(800) 285-5951*
Definitely on the fluffy side, an adventure magazine in the genre of : "Oh muffy, won't we look so butch in hiking boots!" This is the latest in the wave of new eco-zines that channels college guilt into politically correct travel experiences. This bimonthly lacks the veracity of *Escape* but does cover faraway regions. I can't help feeling like I'm being scolded as I am being lectured on proper etiquette for scuba divers ("Get involved in local environmental issues"). There are lots of "I was there and this is what I did" articles for the politically correct and ecologically aware. On the positive side there are lots of local getaways, plenty of pictures and of course lots of ads. A subscripton to *EcoTraveler* costs $11.97 for a year (six issues) or you can buy it off the rack for $3.95

The Educated Traveler

P.O. Box 220822
Chantilly Virginia 22022
☎ *(800) 648-5168*
A newsletter that covers museum-sponsored tours, learning vacations, cultural tourism and more for $65 a year. A little stuffy but a good source for unusual travel opportunities.

Escape Magazine

3205 Ocean Park
Santa Monica, California 90405
☎ *(800) 738-5571*
An outdoor /adventure/world music pub that features a good mix of Third World adventure stories with practical info. The editor/founder, Joe Robinson, has a good eye and ear for real adventure and you never know what will crop up in this quarterly, soon to be bimonthly, magazine. *Escape* also covers world music and socio-political issues in between writing about blisters and leeches. Good stuff and available at major bookstores or by subscription.

Great Expeditions

5915 West Boulevar
Vancouver, British Columbia
☎ *(604) 257-2040*
A magazine that gets down and dirty with first hand information on trips by its readers to exotic places. The magazine is tough to find but worth it for the up-close info it provides.

Maplink

25 E. Mason
Santa Barbara, CA 93101
☎ *(805) 965-4402*

South American Explorers Club

Lima Clubhouse
Avenida Portugal146
Brena District
Lima Peru

Mailing address:

Casilla 3714
Lima 100, Peru

US Associate address:

126 Indian Creek Rd.
Ithaca, NY 14650
☎ *(607) 277-0488*

Books, maps, trip reports, rain forest advice.The main clubhouse in Peru has an excellent library of maps and other helpful publications. Membership is open to all and includes their magazine: *The South American Explorer.*

Travel Guides

Travel guides are an odd source of travel information, more for what they don't tell you than what you can find inside. Most travel writers write champagne tour guides on beer budgets. Budget guides tend to stick to inner cities, known hiking trails or tourist ruts (even though they profess not to) simply because they avail themselves of the local tourism industry to get around. The other problem is that the data can be horribly outdated or wrong. Check the copyright in the front of the book, get to know the writer and get a least a couple of opinions before you go.

Fielding Worldwide, Inc.

308 South Catalina Avenue
Redondo Beach, CA 90277
☎ *(800) FW -2 GUIDE*
FAX (310) 376-8064

Hey, its my company, so I get to plug it shamelessly. FWI was started by a New England blue blood that got his start writing disinformation pamphlets for Tito while in the employ of the OSS in World War II. After that auspicious start, he also wrote one of the wittiest, right on travel guides to Europe back in 1947. Since Temple Fielding's passing on in 1983, Fielding guides have focused on the unusual, the unknown and the unique.

FWI does its best to gather firsthand information from people on the ground. Our authors range from college professors who read Mayan hieroglypics to war correspondents to Brazilian music reviewers—not just folks with a notebook and a penchant for freebies. We look beyond the standard tourism ruts to deliver fresh information. Of course, when we cover areas like the Caribbean, Hawaii and Europe we also focus our laser-sharp eye on the standards and experience the tourism industry provides. Our books are controversial, (our travel guide to Vietnam is forbidden in Vietnam), a little wacky (you bought this book, didn't you?) and never boring. Well, OK, maybe our guide to Holland will never make the *New York Times* bestseller list.

The Government Printing Office

Superintendent of Documents
U.S. Government Printing Office,
Washington, DC 20402
☎ *(202) 783-3238*

If you trust and believe our government, then you might want to try their version of travel guides. The information is surprisingly helpful. The following publications are available for $1.25:

Your Trip Abroad—offers tips on obtaining a passport, considerations in preparing for your trip and traveling, and other sources of information.

Also available for $1 each from the U.S. Government Printing Office:

Safe Trip Abroad—contains helpful precautions one can take to minimize the chance of becoming a victim of terrorism or crime, and other safety tips.

Tips for Americans Residing Abroad—offers information for U.S. citizens living abroad on dual citizenship, tax regulations, voting, and other overseas consular services.

Passports—Applying for Them the Easy Way—gives detailed information on how and where to apply for your U.S. passport. It is available for 50 cents from the Consumer Information Center, *Pueblo, CO 81009.*

Background Notes are brief, factual pamphlets describing the countries of the world. They contain the most current information on each country's people, culture, geography, history, government, economy and political conditions. Single copies are available from the U.S. Government Printing Office for about $1 each. Yearly subscription for updated copies is available. Confirm price by calling ☎ *(202) 783-3238.*

Health Information for International Travel contains detailed information on international health requirements and is available from the U.S. Government Printing Office for $6.50.

Lonely Planet Publications

Embarcadero West,
112 Linden St.,
Oakland, CA 94607
☎ *(415) 893-8555*
The '70s and '80s bible of adventure travelers and expats. Plenty of good practical info served up with a sense of juvenile naiveté. Most of the books are updated on a three-year cycle, so check the copyright date.Tony and Maureen Wheeler built Lonely Planet from the kitchen table to a $22 million publishing business. Their recent shot at guides to civilized countries falls well short of the standard they set for Third World countries. Their books on Asia are excellent.

Moon Publications

722 Wall Street
Chico California 95938
☎ *(800) 345-5473, (916) 345-5473*
A company launched by their flagship book on Indonesia by founder Bill Dalton. Moon is quietly building a following and slowly building a library of good, comprehensive, intelligent books on the world. Well-researched, well-written and very practical. They cover domestic locations very well and are updated when needed.

Rough Guides

1 Mercer Street
London WC3H 9QJ
☎ *(071) 379-3329*
 A new entry over here but over in Europe, Rough Guides have out-lonely planeted Lonely Planet by emphasizing detail, attitude and opinons over facts. They tend to dwell on places you have no intention of going to and their information is lacking on anything above backpacker budgets. Better written than most books.

Stanfords

12 -14 Long Acre
London England WC2E 9LP
☎ *(071) 836 1321*
FAX (071) 836 0189

Also at

156 Regent Street
London, England W1R 5TA
Billed as the world's largest map and travel book shop this is a great source for hard to find maps and books.

Trade & Travel Publications

6 Riverside Court
Riverside Road
Lower Bristol Road
Bath BA2 3DZ
☎ *(01225) 469141, FAX (01225) 469461*

Easily the most compact and well researched travel guides to the world's remote regions. These tiny, expensive travel bibles contain phone numbers, maps, sidebars, intros and just about everything needed for reference. They are thin on accommodation reviews. They began at the turn of the century with their South America guide and have expanded into Asia, the Caribbean and Africa.

Miscellaneous

Nemisis Resource Library

Hudson Ohio
☎ *(216) 656-9706*
30,000 articles books and reports for security and law enforcement professionals.

$50 annual membership fee.

Safe 'n Secure

Phoenix, Arizona
☎ *(602) 870-6004*
A local BBS with four fields—security, legal cases, law enforcement (including links to the FBI Enforcement Bulletin), and emergency disaster managment.

Free to professionals.

Publications

New Internationalist/Third World Guide

Post Office Box 1143
Lewiston, New York 14092
☎ *(905) 946-0407*
FAX (905) 946-0410
Found in 1970, the *New Internationalist* "exists to report on the issues of world poverty and inequality: to focus attention on the unjust relationship between the powerful and powerless in both rich and poor nations..." well you get the point. This rather biased magazine does provide a good second look at the world's people and has some interesting things to add to any cocktail political discussion. A good source for folks looking for information to make their case against the world's military/industrial complex. Subscriptions are $35.98 per year with corporations being dinged $60 (as you would expect from these folks).

Third World Guide

New Internationalist
55 Rectory Road
Oxford OX4 IBW
☎ *(0865) 728 181*
FAX (0865) 793 152
If the *New Internationalist* magazine is a little too strident in its bashing of the UN, big business and first world countries, at least you should own its most illuminating product, fascinating annual called *Third World Guide*. This unusual guide covers 173 countries and is put together by researchers, journalists and academics in Third World countries and provides information on arms, housing, aid, refugees, food and country profiles on newly formed nations. The 630 page '93/'94 issue covers 30 emerging nations, has 55 maps, 780 diagrams and 6800 references . The full sized book will set you back a hefty $38.95 plus $3.95 shipping and handling. Now in its eighth. Stick this hefty guide next to your CIA Handbooks and you have a fairly balanced portrait of the world.

World Press Review

200 Madison Avenue
New York, New York 10016
☎ *(212) 889-5155*
The *World Press Review* consists of material excerpted from the press outside the United States. WPR is a nonprofit organization/educational service and seeks to foster the international exchange of information. The magazine does a good job of providing updates on news

from various countries but more importantly showing the variety of responses on global affairs, whether it is the U.S. invasion of Haiti or what the rest of the world thinks of Saddam Hussein. Their choice of news sources is quite good and varied. The leaning of the publication is noted before the clip (pro-government, centrist, liberal, conservative business etc.) The *Review* also makes good use of political cartoons from around the world. Subscriptions are $24.97 for 12 issues.

The Economist

111 West 57th Street
New York, New York 10019
(212) 541-5730,
☎ *(800) 456-6086*
FAX (212) 541-9378

The granddaddy of world mags is devoid of the cheesy stereo ads of the *New York Times* or the "grow new hair" ads found in *Time* and *Newsweek*. Their readers just don't have time to read the ads. In fact the *Economist* probably has the most time-starved readership of all the news magazines—a blue chip collection of world leaders, policy makers, big business etc. If they get something wrong, chances are the person that they are writing about will contact them to correct it. Their lofty and somewhat ludicrous goal is to "take part in a severe contest between intelligence which presses forward, and an unworthy, timid ignorance obstructing our progress." I suppose they mean that their subscription drives are hampered by stupid people who don't see the value of paying $125 a year (for 51 issues) to bone up on global and financial news. The magazine's easy to use format and impressive attention to facts before opinions make this a must-have for globally aware readers. Their special sections are packed full of first generation information and they even throw in charts, graphs and other helpful graphics. If you can't get enough, the *Economist* also puts out quarterly indexes and some very impressive year-end wrap ups in book form.

Geographical

Post Office Box 425
Woking GU21 1GP
☎ *0483 724122*
FAX 0483 776573

A surprisingly intelligent magazine that explores adventure, science, politics and geography. A monthly published for the Royal Geographic Society. Very little posturing, long on facts, maps and research; the magazine provides coverage other magazines can't deliver. Definitely a recommended publication for adventurers. $57 for an annual subscription or $5.50 on the newstands.

S. Carwin & Sons Ltd.

Post Office 2145
Winnetka, CA 91396
☎ *(800) 562-9182*

Books and videos on military, aviation and naval topics.

United Nations Publications

Sales Sections
2 United Nations Plaza
Room DC2-853, Dept 403
New York, New York 10017
FAX (212) 963-3489

The United Nations provides an enormous amount of important information on the world and its people. The first step is to send away for their catalog of publications. Their rather dry but informative publications cover narcotics, disasters, agriculture economics, hunger, poverty, war and just about anything else of interest. They range from thrilling books like *ESCAP Atlas of Stratigraphy IX: Triassic Biostratigraphy* and *Paleography of Asia—Mineral Resources Development Series and Stratigraphic Correlation Between Sedimentary Basins of the ESCAP Region* to *Urban Crime Global Trends and Policies.*

Health and Safety Information

National Safety Council

Accident Facts
Customer Service
National Safety Council
1121 Spring Lake Drive
Itasca, Illinois 60143
☎ *(708) 285-1121*

Every year the National Safety Council adds up all the dead bodies, severed limbs, infections, and puts together a 115-page guide to what's dangerous in America. It is good reading for people who worry about bacon causing cancer or just how dangerous flying is. Other good sources for health and safety information are:

American Automobile Manufacturers Association

7430 2nd Avenue, Suite 300
Detroit Michigan 48202
☎ *(313) 872-4311*

American National Standards Institute

11 W. 42nd Street, 13th Floor
New York, NY 10036
☎ *(212) 642-4900*

Federal Highway Administration

400 7th Street , SW
Washington, DC 20590
☎ *(202) 366-0660*

Federal Railroad Administration

400 7th Street, SW, Room 8301
Washington, DC 20590
☎ *(202) 366-2760*

Hunter Education Association

P.O. Box 525
Draper, UT 84020
☎ *(801) 571-9461*

Insurance Information Institute

110 William Street
New York, NY 10038
☎ *(212) 669-9200*

Insurance Institute for Highway Safety

1005 N. Glebe Road, Suite 800
Arlington, VA 22201
☎ *(703) 247-1500*

International Association of Chiefs of Police

515 N. Washington Street, 4th Floor
Alexandria, VA 22314
☎ *(703) 836-6767*

Mine Saftey & Health Administration

Health & Saftey Analysis Center
Division of Mining Information
P.O. Box 25367
☎ *(303) 231-5445*

Motorcycle Safety Foundation

2 Jenner Street, Suite 150

Irvine, CA 92718-3812
☎ *(714) 727-3227*

National Center for Health Statistics

6525 Belcrest Road
Hyattsville, MD 20782
☎ *(301) 436-8500*

National Center for Statistics and Analysis

400 7th Street, SW
Washington, DC 20590
☎ *(202) 366-1470*

National Clearinghouse for Alcohol and Drug Information

P.O. Box 2345
Rockville, MD 20847-2345
☎ *(800) 729-6686*

National Collegiate Athletic Association

6201 College Boulevard
Overland Park, KS 66211-2422
☎ *(913) 339-1906*

National Fire Protection Association

P.O. Box 9101
Batterymarch Park
Quincy, MA 02269-0910
☎ *(617) 770-3000 or (800) 344-3555*

National Head Injury Foundation

1776 Massachusetts Ave., NW, Suite 100
Washington, DC 20036
☎ *(202) 296-6443*

National Highway Traffic Safety Administration

400 7th Street, SW
Washington, DC 20590
☎ *(202) 366-0123*

National Institute for Occupational Safety and Health

Clearinghouse for Occupational Safety and Health Information
4676 Columbia Parkway
Cincinnati, OH 45226
☎ *(800) 356-4674*

National Society to Prevent Blindness

500 E. Remington Road
Schaumburg, IL 60173
☎ *(708) 439-4000*

National Spinal Cord Injury Association

600 W. Cummings Park, Suite 2000
Woburn, MA 01801
☎ *(617) 935-2722*

National Sporting Goods Association

1699 Wall Street
Mt. Prospect, IL 60056-5780
☎ *(708) 439-4000*

National Transportation Safety Board

490 L'Enfant Plaza East, SW
Washington, DC 20594
☎ *(202) 382-6735*

Social Security Administration

6401 Security Blvd.
Baltimore, MD 21235
☎ *(410) 965-7700*

Transportation Research Board

> 2101 Consititution Ave., NW
> Washington, DC 20418
> ☎ (202) 334-2935

U.S. Coast Guard

> 2100 2nd Street, SW
> Washington, DC 20593-0001
> ☎ (202) 267-2229

U.S. Consumer Product Safety Commission

> National Injury Information Clearinghouse
> 5401 Westbard Ave., Room 625
> Washington, DC 20207
> ☎ (301) 504-0424

U.S. Department of Commerce

> Bureau of the Census, Public Information
> Office
> Washington, DC 20233-8200
> ☎ (301) 763-4040

U.S. Department of Labor

> Bureau of Labor Statistics
> 2 Massachusette Ave., NE
> Washington, DC 20212
> ☎ (202) 606-7828

OSHA Office of Statistics, Room N-3507

> 200 Consititution Ave., NW
> Washington, DC 20210
> ☎ (202) 219-6463

News Sources

A Takim (A-Team)

American Broadcasting Corporation (ABC)

Amnesty International

Agence France Presse (AFP, French Press Agency)

Associated Press (AP)

Bak & Bakker

Cable News Network (CNN)

Canadian Broadcasting Corporation (CBC)

Canadian Commitee to Protect Journalists

Central Intelligence Agency

CBS

Committee to Protect Journalists

Chinese Wire Service (Xinhua)

Frontline

German Press Agency (DPA)

The Economist

Human Rights Watch

IBC Int'l Country Risk Guide, a Division of IBC USA (Publications) Inc.

Index on Censorship

The Indian Ocean Newsletter (Indigo Publications)

Intelligence Newsletter

International Air Transport Association (IATA)

International Defense Review (IDR)

International Federation of Human Rights

International Federation of Journalists

International Federation of Newspaper Publishers

International Institute for Strategic Studies

International PEN

International Press Institute

International Television News (ITN)

Iraqi News Agency

Jane's

Lawyers Committee for Human Rights

L'Etat du Monde, published by Editions La Découverte

Los Angeles Times

Middle East News Agency (MENA)

NBC

New York Times

KCWD, ABC-Clio, Inc.

Radio France International

Reuters

Soldier of Fortune

Syrian News Agency

Time Magazine

UNESCO

United Press International (UPI)

United States State Department

U.S. News and World Report

Walden Country Reports,

World Development Report, World Bank

Running with the Bulls

Have you ever dreamed of being one of the corredores in the annual "encierro" of Pamplona? Probably not, but many of us have dreamed of running with the bulls ever since we read Hemingway's account of it in the Sun Also Rises. *Little did he know that he would elevate the running of the bulls in the medieval city of Pamplona to the level of the Holy Grail for adventurers. Twelve people have been killed in the run. No one bothers to keep track of the trampled, tripped and torn. The consumption of alcohol is considered to be mandatory and the cost and scarcity of hotel rooms means that sleeping is completely on a "when available/as-needed basis."*

The running of the bulls is part of the Festival of San Fermin, July 6-14th, every year in the Spanish province of Navarre. As if it matters anymore, Saint Fermin was martyred in the third century.

The bulls are let loose from a corral about 800 meters away from the bull ring and they run through the barricaded streets on their way to it.

Tips on running

A rocket is fired off to start the run on Calle Santo Domingo at 7 a.m. on the seventh day of the seventh month. Don't eat breakfast first since it is customary to celebrate afterwards with hot chocolate and deep fried churros, essentially a long Spanish donut. Get there early. The students from the local university tend to be the most enthusiastic members of the crowd. Foreigners are usually too damn serious. The course is a lot shorter and tighter than most people expect it to be. Novices (or Los Valientes, the Brave Ones) get about a five minute head start on the bulls but are quickly overtaken. The most dangerous part of the course is the tight turn onto Estafeta street. Here bulls and corredores discover that two objects can't occupy the same place at the same time. The lack of space is aggravated by lines of policemen who prevent the more timid from bolting over the barricades. The bulls are prodded on by the less valiant (those running behind or spectating) by smacking them with rolled up newspapers. Once bulls and runners stream into the bull ring, free-form amateur bull fighting breaks out. Once you get bored, head into the old quarter for breakfast or to the cafes to continue your celebrating. If you end up feeling like a Union 76 ball on a car antenna, the Red Cross is nearby to attend to any minor injuries.

If for some strange reason you do not spend the evening drinking and carousing, the best accommodations are to be found in the nearby town of Olite, about 40 kilometers away.

In a Dangerous Place: Across East Africa by Land Rover

We had come to see Africa as well as to conquer it. The white man's idea of Africa has always been to test his mettle against this daunting land. We would be following the path of fellow RGS explorers: Burton and Speke, roughly following an old Arab slave trading route in four-wheel drive expedition vehicles. Starting in the rough and tumble port of Dar es Salaam, we will travel a thousand kilometers to the source of Nile, a tiny stream in equally minuscule Burundi. There was a rough track in the dry season but we will attempt it in the height of the rainy season. If we succeeded we would gain nothing but a sense of accomplishment. If we failed we would simply join the millions of people who understand that Africa, after all its death, pestilence, disease, hunger and poverty will always be the dark continent.

As we cruised along country roads, singing stupid songs and dodging potholes the size of small lakes, it felt more like a vacation than an expedition. When we were delayed by overturned trucks or washouts we would amuse ourselves by handing out balloons, baseball cards and candy to delighted children.

As the day progressed, the villages gave way to farmland and farmland to grasslands. As evening fell, we waited for the rest of the convoy at the turnoff that would take us onto our first remote trail. A heavy rain began to fall with a foreboding vengeance; the easy part was over. As the scout in the lead car searched for the path in the tall grass, we watched the villagers stare at us from under the shelter of a giant mango tree.

There is some confusion. Where the road once was, there is now a wall of grass 20 feet high. You could feel the packed ground where a trail has once been. To the right are the remains of a drainage ditch and along the road a clear area still exists. Step one foot off on either side of the narrow path and you would sink into the bottomless, black mud.

We can imagine the thoughts of the villagers as they watch the long yellow column of vehicles idling at the entrance to what looks like a sea of tall grass. Who are these strange white men? Why are they going down that road?

He keeps searching the wet, sucking mud for an entrance to, or even a trace of, a road, muttering that just three months ago on the pre-scout mission he drove this road at 60 miles an hour. The scout tries to convince himself that the tall grass is an illusion or just a temporary barrier. He has obviously not consulted with the locals, or has a hard time comprehending the growth rate of grass in Africa. Three months ago, in the dry season, the locals would have told him that, yes, there is a definite reason the grass grows so tall here and, yes, there was a road here once but probably only for a few days. We are standing knee deep at the entrance to a swamp that stretches not for yards, but for miles.

There is a reason grass can grow 20 feet in three months. We are about to enter the great swamps of East Africa.

Into the Tall Grass

We decide to press forward on this path despite being faced with an endless sea of swamp and tall grass. We inch forward testing the route. The rest of the convoy waits patiently behind, wondering what is going on. This is to be a common pattern over the next few days. At first we try using machetes to clear the path. As we push deeper and deeper into the swamp, we realize that at this rate using machetes will get pretty old after a couple of days. We wonder what surprises await us in the long grass. There are to be quite a few.

The scout runs ahead to feel the path while the drivers follow the lead car. We are 20 yards behind the red taillights leaving enough room in case they need to be towed out of a gully or river. Suddenly the scout comes screaming toward us tearing his clothes off while swearing, "Bloody bastards. Get some water, get some water!" His thick Scottish brogue and apoplectic state make it difficult for us to understand exactly what he wants. Since it is pouring rain it seems a strange request. It is only after he is nearly naked that we realize he has been attacked by red ants. So we dump half of our precious water supply on him in order to ease the pain.

After our first run-in with African wildlife we offer to cut trail. We take a more scientific, more team-oriented approach. We assign responsibilities. One person will stand on the roofrack rides on top with the spotlight looking for the thin ridge of high grass that identifies the center of the road. Webb drives blind, feeling the camber of the road through the steering wheel and angle of the hood. I watch out the passenger side for the slight ridge caused by shorter grass that identifies where trucks have slowed grass growth by soil compression. We decide to abandon the machete method and use our Discovery like a bulldozer to smash our way through the green wall of grass.

The Yellow Weed Whacker

The rain increases in intensity. It is night time and we are surrounded by a solid wall of grass 20 feet high. The powerful driving lights bounce back off the wet grass and illuminate the car like a movie set. What I think is sweat running down my neck is really dozens of inquisitive insects. To say that there are a lot of insects would be an understatement. Not the big fluttery, elegant kind found in Asia but the weird, crawly bugs of Africa. As we slam through the thick, wet grass and bugs of every size and description are flicked onto the hood and inside the truck.

Soon, car and passengers are a furry carpet of prickly grass and crawling insects. It is a truly special and indescribable feeling to be soaking wet and covered from head to toe with insects of every variety. Hundreds of cockroaches, beetles, flies, mantises, spiders, ticks, moths, crickets, ants, earwigs, grasshoppers and walking sticks are crawling over and through our hair, up our noses and inside our clothing.

Giant praying mantises and walking sticks calmly crawl up our necks to stand next to our headmounted flashlights and gorge themselves on the gnats, flies and moths that are attracted to the light. Despite our inquisitive friends, we still have to pay attention to the other surprises that await us in the endless ocean of grass.

An incredible amount of stress comes from driving at speed through a 12- to 18-foot wall of grass. It rains every night, swelling rivers, washing out makeshift bridges and deepening ravines. Fallen tree branches suddenly appear like lances straight out of the green wall. Stream beds present themselves quickly and dramatically as we slam on the brakes to avoid going head over heels into the water. We get our reconfirmation that this has been a road or at least a bridge when we almost plunge into a ten-foot gap created by two naked bridge supports. We have to drive fast because driving slow means getting stuck, and each river we cross is running higher and faster, swollen by the heavy rains. As night turns to day and to night again, all we see is grass. Fording ravines and rivers affords our only break from the monotony.

We are in a hurry to reach Mikumi to make up lost time. Instead of building bridges and laying passable tracks for the teams behind, we decide to smash through swamps and washouts leaving a gooey quagmire for those who follow behind. The rear of the column is getting farther and farther behind—a distance originally measured in hours and now in days. The heavy support vehicles require constant winching through the swamp until the convoy is no longer driving but winching every inch of the way.

The last time we see the rear of the convoy is at a point on the map where a shallow river crossing is marked. Tonight, or rather this morning, it is a raging river with a 20-foot-high waterfall where the road used to be. We decide to stop and sleep for three hours; as the sun comes up, I walk back to visit with the other teams just pulling in to the rear of the column. They are beginning to show the effects of constant driving and winching, their faces showing the strain of no sleep and the endless strain of fighting the swamp. In the weak light of morning, large blue crabs scuttle around the two water-filled ruts the vehicles have left behind us as they winched themselves through the endless bog.

The Elephant Walk

The tedium of the seamless days and nights is punctuated by rain-swollen river crossings. During one wet and exhausting river crossing, we find an unusually large hole through the trees to winch the trucks up from the river. Once the vehicles were across we collapse until the dawn comes an hour and a half later. While sleeping on the roof rack in the rain, I hear slow swishing in the grass and wake up to find elephants, obviously quite disturbed to find these metal intruders blocking their path to the river. Eye to eye with these giants, I keep desperately quiet as they slowly thread their way alongside our vehicles and down to the river.

That morning the car windows are steamed up, the sleeping occupants appearing as if they have been shot dead in their seats; mouths gaping, heads sagging. We realize that we weren't dreaming when we see the huge elephant tracks around the trucks heading down to the river bank.

We have lost radio contact with the rest of the convoy. At last check, we were four days ahead of the last vehicle. Our fuel indicators have been on empty for the last day and a half. In the last six days we have slept exactly six and one half hours. Our eyes have given up focusing—they stare straight ahead. We stare out through the rain-soaked windshield, hallucinating from lack of sleep. We are travelling up through a pass at night. Huge 50- to 150-foot trees bearing monstrous scars loom overhead. Elephants have ripped branches and trunks from the trees, leaving white flesh and jagged ripped skeletons. Illuminated by our eight high-powered driving lights they seem to dance and move. This is elephant, big elephant country.

Finally we emerge from the bizarre forest and re-enter the swamps. We run over what we first think is a giant toad, which turns out to be the head of a very long python. We know it is at least 15 feet long since we can see only 15 feet at one time. Unharmed in the marshy ground, it slithers back into the grass. Later we come across the skeleton of a elephant killed by poachers. We take turn taking pictures of each other standing inside the elephant's pelvis. We tie the massive bones to the fronts of our vehicles in a "skull and crossbones" and then decide to leave the murdered pachyderm's bones in peace.

At last, we come to the long-awaited river crossing—the end of wilderness and the beginning of the road that leads to Mikumi. The water rages under the heavy downpour. Too tired to walk the swollen river, we charge our vehicle across and immediately plunge over the edge of a steep rock ledge and submerge our car for the third time that week. We jump out of the truck and struggle through the heavy current to the opposite bank with the winch line. We hook it up and wait for the driver to pull us across. We wait...and wait. The vehicle is leaning at a grotesque angle. The water is rising and pouring through the open windows. We realize the driver is fast asleep at the wheel, quite comfortably submerged up to his chest in the raging water. We bang on the hood and he finally snaps out of it. We winch it out and our fuel finally runs out 20 feet on the other side.

We don't have time to celebrate the fact that we have made it out of the swamps and are only a few miles from civilization. By now we are zombies as we try make it to a mission, 20 miles up the dirt track. Instead of a navigable dirt road, we experience a wet and furious roller coaster ride through enormous, lake-sized potholes and muddy cane fields. We don't even notice. We drive straight through, not even caring how deep the holes are. We dive underwater again. By now we are so wet, tired and cold we don't notice. We try to stay awake by talking to each other, but we miss chunks of sentences as we doze off and awake mid-sentence. Somehow we get to Mikumi in one piece.

We collapse on the cement floor, only to find ourselves wide awake an hour later and unable to sleep.

Boredom and Death in Mikumi

We have pushed hard for 144 hours (138 hours without sleep), all we can do now is sit and wait for the others to make it through the swamps. The unforeseen delay and hardship have also depleted their fuel, water and vital spare parts.

A military cargo helicopter on loan from the Tanzanian government is pressed into service to fly the needed supplies to the depleted convoy.

We load up fuel, water and a replacement gearbox and wait in a schoolyard to load it onto the helicopter. We wait until the sun goes down. Still no helicopter. We found out the details later: ten minutes after takeoff it crashed into a mountainside, killing the copilot and seriously injuring the other two crew members. The battered old Huey was exactly 50 percent of the Tanzanian Air Force. Since some of the stuck convoy was a few kilometers from a rail line, we resorted to commandeering a rail speeder car for a five-hour trip. The heavy gearbox and diesel fuel were carried in safari style on two poles to the stranded convoy. Later, we regroup and resume our journey.

Out of the swamps and into the scrub

We have left the mud and grass of the swamps far behind us and are now travelling through classic East African savannah. The horizon stretches in a virtually unobstructed 360-degree view, hindered only by gentle acacias and tortured, swollen baobab trees.

Puffy, white clouds form an endless pattern accompanied by the lazy sound of tsetse flies as giraffes watch shyly in the distance. Time seems to slow down and your senses are sharpened. You begin to notice the thousands of purple and yellow flowers that carpet the land. Time passes even slower as vultures aimlessly circle the convoy. We discover more bleached, tuskless skeletons of elephants killed by poachers. The heat paints swirls on the landscape, creating an impressionist painting. The cruel African sun sucks the moisture out of our bodies. Tiny sweat bees hungrily suck the beads of sweat on our arms. We figure they are entitled to it.

Our once-soaked clothes and feet are now dry. Our hands are hard, cracked and calloused, the nails and creases packed with black dirt. The hot sun begins to tan our skin and clear up our rashes, grass cuts and insect bites. We are adapting to the hot, dry savannah days and cool-crisp nights. We come to recognize the unique flora and fauna of the savannah-like spear grass. Thousands of these sharp, barbed weapons are snicked off by the brush guard and embedded in skin and clothing. However, spear grass pales in comparison to the various types of acacia thorns that grow up to five inches long. Just like porcupine thorns, these light, hollow daggers are everywhere and can penetrate right through heavy boots. They become projectiles when they smack through an open window at 40 m.p.h., looking for soft flesh to penetrate.

We also become good friends with the scourge of Africa—the tsetse fly. Built like deer flies with mandibles designed to bite through water buffalo skin, these dudes are vicious. Under constant attack, we smack 'em, roll 'em, crush 'em—and they just get up, shake their heads and attack again. Well-fed tsetse flies are easier to kill. We would catch them on the windows as they were hanging heavy with ketchup bottle like waists. One smack and—blammo!—they would explode in a shower of blood.

We are attacked by African Killer bees that swarm out of their nests to attack us again and again. They will attack even if we pass 20 to 30 meters from their nests. They charge at us in a horde climbing up our noses, into our shirts. The next day I feel like I have been beaten with a baseball bat as I gingerly nurse my swollen body.

The other denizens of the game reserves are somewhat more attractive but less sociable. We passed through many primitive and scenic areas populated by elephants, warthogs, baboons, giraffes, zebras, gazelles and other savannah animals. In the Selous, we stopped to admire a family of elephants playing in the shade of a spreading acacia tree. The bull elephant suddenly took exception to our intrusion, turning on us, ears flapping, shaking his head and loudly trumpeting his displeasure. After his false charge, he lowers his head like a locomotive and charges straight for us again. As we sped off, the ranger cocks his weathered rifle and only takes it down when the elephant gives up.

Finally we find a faint trail, which soon becomes a dirt road. We have crossed the savannah and now see the hills and mountains of Central Africa dead ahead of us. Late that night we pull into the ranger station in Rungwa to refuel, replace tires and sleep. The next morning we are awakened by a glorious, 20-minute long sunrise framed by an unusual double rainbow; it's almost as if the heavens are rewarding us for surviving the long journey. In any case, simple adjectives often cannot describe the beauty and drama of East Africa.

Into the Heart of Africa

Even though no signpost marks the spot, there is a distinct transition between Eastern and Central Africa. The soil turns from black loam to dark, red clay; the weather turns softer, more tropical; and for some reason the people become gentler and shyer. It is also darker and more foreboding. The wild, empty panoramas of Tanzania are replaced by the heavily populated, patchwork agricultural quiltwork of Burundi. Slipping and sliding through muddy banana plantations, the convoy labors over a mountain pass in dense fog. As we reach the crest we are dazzled by the brilliant light and spectacular view.

Before us lays a wide expanse of shimmering silver fronting a mountainous wall of rich green. Stretching as far as the eye can see is a massive wall of dark mountains. Soaring above these magnificent mountains are huge, white thunderheads, below is the fabled Sea of Ujijji, now known as Lake Tanganyika, sparkling like a pool of diamonds.

This unforgettable sight has inspired awe in every explorer since Burton and Speke first set eyes on the lake:

"Nothing could be more picturesque than this first view of the lake," wrote Burton, "A narrow strip of emerald green, marvelously fertile, shelves towards a ribbon of yellow sand and bordered by sedgy rushes.

Like Burton, we had endured the swamps; the long, hot savannah; the wild animals; pests; and pestilence. But what had taken him seven and a half months we have compressed into 3 weeks.

That night we celebrate with the locals, among them the President of Burundi and whatever socialites and party animals Bujumbura can muster. Once the politicians and upper crust go home, 20 days of being in the bush with little sleep is erased by adrenaline and alcohol. One by one the team members start throwing each other in the pool. Soon there are more people in the pool than outside. After we run out of khaki-clad people to toss in, everything else is fair game; Sabena stewardesses, lawn furniture, waiters, pots and pans. Laughing riotously, we pour what beer is left on top of each other's head and jump into the seething pile of debris and people in the once sedate hotel pool. After the hotel runs out of beer, we migrate to an all-night disco on the shores of Lake Tanganyika.

Still dripping wet, we spend the rest of the night dancing and drinking with the local girls. Most try to stay out of fights with jealous boyfriends who are determined to see just how tough these guys are. We didn't come to Africa to prove we were tough; we came here to have a good time. And we did with a vengeance!

As the dawn breaks over Lake Tanganyika, the few that can still walk stagger outside to get one last look at this magical lake in the heart of Africa. As the sun rises over the mist-covered mountains across the golden lake, we know we have entered the soul of Africa and none of us would ever be the same.

History of the Camel Trophy

Just in case you find this exhilarating enough to want to inquire about participation in the Camel Trophy series in the future, here is bit of history on the event.

The Camel Trophy is an annual event that is part reality, part illusion. Heroic images of stalwart men in yellow Land Rovers battling through green tropical hell have earned it the slogan: "The Toughest Test of Man and Machine."

The idea of the best of the best—hard men in solid trucks pitted against the planet's most hostile regions—has definitely struck a responsive chord in off-roaders and adventurers alike. Accordingly, the legend and appeal of The Camel Trophy expeditions have grown greater every year. This year, over a million and a half people from 17 different countries vied for the 68 available seats -each one hoping to add to the legend.

Most people have seen the famous Camel Adventure advertising campaign with the "rugged" outdoorsman usually doing something very "rugged" in a very "rugged" place. The Camel smoker seemed to be one heck of a "rugged" guy. If you have ever smoked nonfilter Camel cigarettes you'd know why!

It seems the Teutons were quite smitten with this image, and it didn't take long for life to imitate art (or advertising) when six Germans drove through Brazil in three ill-prepared Jeeps. The "Camel Trophy" concept instantly captured the imagination of the rest of the world. Originally, only German teams were involved (1980 and 1981), then from 1982 to 1985 the event grew to include teams from countries as far away as Brazil, Hong Kong, Malaysia and Argentina.

American participation has been sporadic. A U.S. team has competed in four of the 11 previous Trophies, with Tom Collins of Colorado and Don Floyd of California placing highest (tying for first place in Madagascar in 1987). Although the biggest fans of The Camel Trophy are still the Germans, Italians, French and Dutch, a whole new world has opened up with the collapse of Communism and the spread of advertising in the Eastern Bloc. The imagery and concept of The Camel Trophy has now caught the fancy of the Russians and Eastern Europeans, particularly since the event was held in Siberia in 1991.

So far The Camel Trophy has challenged the most inhospitable regions of the Amazon, Madagascar, Sulawesi, Borneo, Zaire, Sumatra, Papua New Guinea, Australia and Siberia. Each year has its official story—and the real story. Mysterious stories of mutinies, fights, failure and madness are best told around campfires by ex-Trophyists. Only they could understand them. This is the dark side of men in the wilderness. The Camel Trophy has a strange appeal that brings men back again and again for three weeks of pure hell. It is one of the few great adventures left in this clinical, well-ordered world. Despite its detractors The Camel Trophy is still the foremost—and only genuine—opportunity for everyday people to take part in grand adventure based on merit and sheer guts alone.

Who is a Camel Trophyist? Despite the advertising, he is not a rugged, hairy-chested, chain-smoking stud. In the year I participated, competitors came from an amazing assortment of backgrounds and occupations: carpenters, fighter pilots, mechanics, soldiers, engineers, policemen, bankers, mountain guides, bodyguards, game wardens, airline pilots, students, journalists and even a male nurse. Typically Camel Trophy contestants are between the age of 26 and 32, physically fit, with an intense love of adventure and travel. They are not paid or otherwise compensated for participating. They do, however, sign away their lives. One of the biggest problems for R.J Reynolds is finding a participant who in addition to having the right skills also has the right look, since photos of the event are used in advertising and public relations around the world. The oldest candidate on the East African Expedition was a Polish university professor aged 39.

5-Door, Turbo Diesel Discovery

For the East Africa journey, the vehicles used were Land Rover Discoveries. The equipment list (not including rations) was as follows:

2495 cc intercooled, turbocharged, direct injection diesel with four cylinders in line. Full-time, four-wheel drive with high/low and central diff lock. Fuel capacity, 88.6 liters.

Factory Modifications

- Custom roll bar with integrated roof rack and light bar designed by safety specialists

- Dog guard for luggage area

- 2 Hella fog lamps on bull bar

- Blacked-out hood for night glare from roof driving lights

- Skid plate front and rear with Neoprene padding

- 1 Hand spot

- Brush guard with lamp protectors

- Four sand ladders

- 2 Pintle hooks on front, 1 on rear

- Waterproof seat covers

- Inside and outside winch remote plug

- Waterproof box for winch solenoids under hood

- 80-amp alternator

- Heavy-duty shocks

- Wading plugs

- Michelin XCL radial tires

- Air intake snorkel for deep wading

- Terratrip odometer

- Heavy duty 5.5" x 16" steel wheels

- 8000-lb. Superwinch with extra cable and winch kit (gloves, remote, shackles, snatch block and tree protector)

- Rear light protectors

- Ladder-to-roof rack on back door

- 4 Hella driving lights with rear work light

- 8 Black Pelican cases with Camel Trophy logo

- Axe

- Pick & shovel

- 2 Water containers

- 2 Spare tires on rims

- Yellow (Sable) paint

- Hood locks

- Wire brush protectors with hood release

- Underhood, electrical cutoff switch

- Dual batteries (single system)

- Extensive spares kit

- 6 Inner tubes

- 2 Zargas aluminum boxes (for food)

- Rear shelf with retainers

- Air jack

At Sea With the Yupik

Eben's snow machine has surrendered to the cold. We have to borrow one to drag his gear to the boat, which has been hauled up on the rocks of a steep cape about half a mile up shore from the village. In the plywood haul-sled are a CB for Eben to keep in touch with his wife Leah, two five-gallon jerry cans holding $88.42 worth of gas for the Mercury outboard, our lunch of Crisco sandwiches, a homemade harpoon of wood, bone, brass and twine, Eben's bird gun, his 2-22 for seal or walrus, and his young apprentice's 22 which has a plastic stock of simulated walnut. It's a brilliant spring day and cold. Pack ice still covers much of the sea. We all wear triple layers of wool and rubber hip boots for pushing off in icy shallows.

Eben is 28; Leah 22. They have two kids, five and three. Eben doesn't have the Eskimoe's subcutaneous fat. He's wiry. Two nights ago, we'd run his snow machine out on the tundra on a bird shoot, great flocks of Canada Geese overhead, elegantly slipstreamed formations of swan, but no luck, and his family needed meat, so we kept at it until there was no light, slept tentless on the snow and woke to shoot again. One Canada goose. One swan. It was cold. I wondered how cold he got without the fat, but we'd just met and he looked so nasty, with the wind whipping at his raw-boned features.

In the village there are maybe 60 igloos; none of them ice, all of them patched together with tarpaper and 4x8 sheets of CDX plywood. It turns out that in the Yupik tongue, "igloo" simply means house, and for men like Eben, the big question is whether to hang around the house so you'll be in the village when work comes, or go to sea, or out on the tundra, which is where you have to be when the game comes or no meat. It was a hard question. Nobody had an answer. The best they could do was get together and vote to ban alcohol from the village.

Banging down out of the village, Eben veers out onto shore ice, narrowly skirting treacherous leads which are beginning to open. It's not an uncommon accident, Leah says; snowmobile and rider simply sinking into the ocean.

Clear of the lead, Eben jockeys the machine up a narrow path on the rock face of the cape to where he dry-moors his boat. From below, I can see way up on the rock face an open vessel about ten feet long. An old fiberglass treatment is peeling away from a wooden hull. We begin climbing the rock face. It's not easy. I wonder how we'll horse the boat down.

We horse it down with my heart in my mouth. We load up and push off toward the pack ice and Nunivak Island which looms thirty miles out to sea.

The day is so brilliant; it's the sort of day when the sun hits every crack and crevice, glinting off every swell. We hear walrus, but distantly, trumpeting, always somewhere just beyond. We never see them. We see lots of seals. This is not the pelt harvest of cubs on islands where the animals are clubbed. The prey is mature, it is swimming and all that can be seen is its small gray head as it bobs up in the broad, featureless ocean, a hundred yards off, dives with hardly a hint which direction it's moving, and doesn't surface for another five minutes.

Every shot misses its mark, and meantime, as we race and snake between ice flows, the pack ice keeps threatening to close in on us. Shifting channels narrow, squeeze, crack; Eben has to wheal about in a crunch of wook against ice and focus on getting us safely free. Seals come and go.

Showing no anger, he takes nine hours of frustration, until finally we run low on gas. His family needs meat. He runs straight at a small berg, runs the boat right up on it.

"Now we stuck forever," says his little apprentice Sam as he throws back his head, "I jokes. I jokes."

The idea is to save gas by drifting with the berg, but it doesn't do anything for us, and we push off for another bobbing flow, get out and have a Crisco sandwich on the ice, then push off again. Another flow. We run up on it, get out, drift again, and again it's that dread time to push off, frigid water swirling about our hip boots. We slip deeper into the cold black as the tricky flow suddenly kilters and up-ends beneath our feet.

But then we're off and into the boat and Eben spots a seal. We race after it, even shouting "hoot, hoot" to dazzle the animal. Eben stands in the prow, an erect figure against a huge blue sky, leaning into his rifle. Crack, and a frigid-air echo; crack, as Eben squeezes off his round, carefully but without result.

"Left," he shouts, as his apprentice Sam veers to the right.

"Left," he shouts, and as little Sam starts to protest, Eben flares, "You backtalk, I throw you out the boat, boy."

The seal is gone. As the length of the day seems to expand the immensity of the sky and our isolation, the mesmerising silence is broken by a burble, then another. The outboard.

Water in the gas line. We stall. It takes draining and repeated yanks to get it going again. The wind dies to nothing and the ocean's surface turns as oily-smooth as gun-metal, glinting in the late afternoon sun, merging indistinguishably into a gunmetal gray sky. Somewhere in the distnace, amidst the faint bellowing of walrus, a baby seems to be crying. In the far distance, we spot Abner Truman's boat up on a flow and we veer toward him. Abner is behind the boat, laid out on the ice flow, taking tea with his partner over a sterno stove sitting on the ice, floating on the ocean. When I'd met him a couple of days earlier, there was a big Yupik grin on his face. It was still there. Cradled at the bottom of his boat are two prime spotted seals.

"Caught me two," says Abner. Just like brother Eben.

Eben had caught two seals? When was that?

Over Abner's CB, we can hear the lusty cries of his baby daughter back in the village, along with the gently scolding tones of his wife.

"Week ago Tuesday," says Abner. "Two mighty fine."

"Give it to the people," says Abner. "Mighty fine party. Mmmm! You like seal liver? You like seal liver, you eat it raw. Mmmm!"

The sun cants toward the horizon, blazes red, then clouds over. The wind picks up. No sun, and the wind and the cold lets you know it's there. The outboard has stalled again. This time Eben pulls the plugs and blows out the engine with his mouth as little Sam shoots at mallards. At last, as exhausted as he'd been on the bird hunt, Eben gets the boat going again, Sam finally bags a mallard, and in rapid fire succession, eben brings down two more.

All this amounts to a twelve hour working day and $88.42 worth of gas expended for three ducks. "Seal hunt's fer pardners," says Abner Truman, back in the village. What Eben needs is at least one seasoned partner. Not this greenhorn Sam and a *gusik*, which is the Yupik word for white man.

Eben gives all three birds to Sam, who hurries off with them.

The next day, as I prepare to leave for Bethel, he says; "my meat rack is the one on the right, take whatever you want."

"Canada goose," says Leah. "Swan. At least a ptarmigan. Let me get you a ptarmigan."

It's not bird meat, it's seal that young John Kailukiak wants most of all; seal meat, seal liver, precious seal oil. But that means putting to sea and for days, rough water and fog have holed him up with his pregnant wife Mary and three young sons in a 12 by 15 foot fram and tar-paper igloo in the village of Tanunaq; an isolated settlement of some 300 Yupik Eskimoes on the cold grey shores of the Bering Sea.

John's family needs meat, period, whether seal or bird. There are still some strings of dry herring hanging out on the meat rack, but it's been almost a year since the last herring run. Stocks are running low and here I am on his doorstep, in the shadow of that almost meatless rack, delivering a choice item just for birds—a 12-gauge, pump action Remington with a three inch bore and a long barrel.

So the reluctant decison is made to go out for birds instead of seal and we sit down to a meal of seal oil and raw seal liver, which is tender and sweet and more palatable to my white man's tongue than the oil, which Mary prizes highly.

Man-eating Sharks

Probably the most feared animal in the ocean, sharks are one of the few animals that eat people as opposed to stinging, biting or poisoning you. There are 350 species of sharks, but only a tiny percentage are dangerous to humans. In the U.S. there are about 12 shark attacks each year; only one or two are fatal. Of the species that are dangerous, the large sharks are the most treacherous. Sharks usually attack in murky water close to land. The shark will usually swim away after one bite.

Marine biologists think that sharks mistake swimmers for seals or large fish.

Sharks can see up to 50 feet. At distances greater than this or in low visibility sharks find food by tracking the electrical impulses the prey produces. Sharks also go into a feeding frenzy. Sharks can detect one ounce of blood in a million ounces of seawater.

Man-eating Sharks

The most dangerous sharks are the large sharks, six feet or more. Three species, the white shark, Carcharodon carcharias, the tiger shark, Galeocerdo cuvieri, and the bull shark, Carcharhinus leucas, are responsible for most attacks.

Although there is no firm evidence, it is estimated that some sharks may live to be 75 to 100 years old or longer.

The most dangerous shark is the bull shark. The bull shark can live for long periods in freshwater and has been found 2000 miles upstream in the upper Amazon and in landlocked bodies of water, such as Lake Nicaragua. Bulls like shallow water and have been implicated in a number of unprovoked attacks.

Your chances of being attacked by a shark are slim–about 1 in 300 million– compared to a 1 in 5.5 million chance of being stung by a bee. For those who dislike sharks or like the idea of man eating sharks as opposed to man-eating sharks, take comfort in the fact that for every human bitten by a shark more than 1 million sharks are killed. About 10 to 12 million sharks are eaten every year by shark-eating men and women.

What to Pack

Travel light, wash often, dress casually and buy what you need when you get there. I have traveled with nothing (after all my luggage was stolen) and lots (complete with tripod, tape recorders, video cameras and camera) and nothing is the way to go. Most travelers travel with less and less as they gain experience. The only exception would be specialized expeditions where you are expected to come back with footage or samples of your discoveries. Even if you consider porters for your gear maintain your credo of traveling light.

Luggage:

I prefer a frameless backpack and a fanny pack. Avoid outside pockets or fill them with your dirty laundry. Locks and twist ties from garbage bags are good to slow down thieves.Put everything inside large heavy duty Ziploc Freezer bags and then put those inside large garbage bags. Bring some spares of both types of bags. Some people like to use thick rubber "rafting" stuff sacks but in my experience they are useless being neither waterproof nor durable. Inside my pack I like to put a small Pelican case with the delicates and expensives. I also carry a second fanny pack for toiletries and personal stuff. I use clear Tupperware containers to store first aid, medicines, and other assorted small objects. Don't scrimp on your pack but remember it will come back foul smelling, ripped and covered in dirt.

Tent:

North Face's Bullfrog is about as good and as light as it gets. Not cheap, but I have yet to find anything close in space and weight. Two people won't fit. You can substitute a groundsheet with rope for warmer climes or a jungle hammock. After your first night on the ground in the jungle you will realize why the apes sleep in the trees. It is wet, very wet down on the ground. L.L. Bean *(Freeport, ME 04033;* ☎ *(800) 221-4221)* makes a great jungle hammock (make sure where you are going that there are at least two Land Rovers to hang it from).

Sleeping Bag:

Get a light cotton-lined sleeping bag that has anything but down stuffing. Down does not insulate in the wet. Get a sleeping bag small enough so that it can be washed (it will get funky!).

Toiletry Kit:

Combination comb/brush, toothbrush, toothpaste, floss, deodorant, toilet paper, tampons, condoms, small Swiss Army knife with scissors and nail file, shaver, shampoo, liquid soap.

Compass:

Even if you don't know how to use a compass you should have one. You can use compasses to tell time, measure maps, navigate by the stars, signal airplanes, shave with and, God forbid, even plot your course if you get lost. The best compasses are made by Silva *(P.O. Box 966,*

Binghampton, NY 13902; ☎ *(607) 779-2200)* and are available at just about any sporting goods store.

Flashlight:

There are only two kinds you should consider buying—a small Tekna waterproof flashlight (get a yellow one so you can find it when you drop it); better yet get two or three because they make great gifts for your guide. The other kind is a Petzl or REI waterproof head-mounted flashlight. You will use both. Try putting up a tent with a handheld flashlight. Maglites are great but are a bitch to hold on to in the mud. Get lots of AA Duracell batteries.

Mosquito Netting:

REI sells a nifty mosquito tent. Mosquitoes like to start feeding as soon as you drift off to sleep so this light tent-like mesh will keep your head and arms safe. It can also be used to catch fish, strain chunks out of water and strain gasoline. Bring bug repellent with the highest DEET content. Watch it though, because it may cause some nasty rashes if not washed off. In hotel rooms mosquito coils can make life bearable. They do not scare off large rats.

Clothing:

Cotton is about the only fabric worth wearing and don't get carried away with too many changes. After one week everything you own will be stinky, damp and wrinkled so its best to rotate three shirts, three t-shirts, two pants, one shorts, three socks, three underwear, a hat, poncho, one pair of sneakers, hiking boots and flip-flops. And that's it.

Pants: The plain khaki army fatigues made in Korea are your best bet. You will find the ones I am talking about in any surplus or Army Navy store. Cabellas is also an excellent source. Banana Republic used to be the place for adventurers but the only thing they make that is worthwhile is their correspondent's vest which has to be special ordered. Don't forget.

Light cotton T-shirts: Preferably with the name of where you are from (use as gifts later).

One good pair of pants.

Wool socks: take three pairs; one to wear, one to wash and another to wear because you forgot to wash the first pair. Do not get the high synthetic socks, just the funky ragg type.

Underwear: loose cotton boxers; get groovy looking ones so they can double as swim trunks.

Shirt: Long-sleeved wool.

Poncho: cheap plastic to protect pack and camera gear.

Hat: Wide-brimmed canvas hat. Tilleys are the best but who wants to look like a geriatric on safari? Another choice is to pick up a cheap straw hat when you get there. Natty and disposable. Hiking boots: Lightweight mesh and canvas.

Sneakers: I use Chuck Taylor's Converse in beige. Get 'em one size larger cause your feet will swell up.

Cooking:

I bring a standard stainless steel cooking set that doubles as an eating set: a knife, fork and spoon with a hole in the handle so they can be carried on a belt ring. (That way I am always ready to eat.) Other people just bring the old military mess tin and one spoon. I notice that the more I travel and the friendlier I get, the less I use my own mess kit and end up eating at other people's homes.

If you are on an expedition you need a cooking stove that burns not just stove fuel but diesel and every grade of automotive gasoline. You haven't lived until you have tasted a dinner cooked over diesel fuel. Bring a multifuel stove and a small fuel bottle. They work best with white gas since car fuels clog up the stove and require frequent cleaning (so bring the kit and a spare O-ring). When it comes to freeze-dried don't be swayed by those high-end organic meals. You won't hear many complaints when you serve up those cheese and potato meals they sell at regular supermarkets (at about a tenth of the price). Remember to bring fruits and treats.

I can live off peanut butter, beef jerky and warm beer, but I can't stand some of the healthy meals.

First Aid Kit:

A prescription from your doctor or a letter describing the drugs you are carrying can help. Pack wads of antidiarrheals, electrolyte powder, antibiotics, insect-sting kit, antacids, antihistamines (for itching and colds), antibiotic ointment, iodine, water purifier, foot powder, antifungal ointment and a syringe or two.

Camera:

If you are a total idiot, bring an auto-everything camera and find out when you return how it turns on. If you are an idiot-in-training bring a brand new outfit with too many lenses and never use it. Pros bring two bodies; a 300 2.8, a zoom to cover the middle and then a 20mm. The new autofocus lenses suck in moisture and dust. Try to stick to the old manual metal mount lenses. I shoot with a Leica range finder and R system. Nikon, Canon and Zeiss systems are just as good.

Video:

I love the new Sony TR-200, Hi-8 system and consider it a must-have on any trip. It's light, tiny (even with all the accessories) and easy to shoot.

Binoculars:

Don't bring binoculars. You can always bum somebody else's unless you are going to Africa—then they are a must. Leica and Zeiss roof prisms are the only ones to consider.

Survival Kit:

Down in the bottom of your pack you can put together your talisman kit. Like an African fetish, we hope that just having these items around means we will never have to use them: First Aid kit, two space blankets, Bic lighters, Swiss Army knife (get the one with the saw), a whistle, Power Bars (get one of each flavor), plenty of rope, fishing line with hooks (not too helpful in the desert), candlebutts, Stoptrot or any other electrolite replacement product and headache pills. Bring a sewing kit and buy a surgical needle shaped like a fishhook. You will need this to sew up your skin if you suffer a severe gash. I recommend a tiny first aid manual to refer to if things go wrong.

Water Bottle:

Bring a metal waterbottle that can double as a spare fuel bottle (use a large silver one for your water and a small red one for fuel).

Essentials:

Your passport, airline tickets, money, credit cards, "traveler's cheques", drivers license, malaria pills, Bullfrog sunscreen, lip salve, spare contacts, glasses, sunglasses.

Letters of recommendation:

If you get in a jam or need special dispensations, it doesn't hurt to have plenty of glowing letters about you on fancy stationery. Lots of official stamps help too.

Gifts

Most of the Third World views you as a rich capitalist pig. The fact that you are a poor capitalist pig doesn't let you off the hook when it comes to giving gifts. Keep it simple, memorable and have plenty to go around. Mirrors, beads and shiny paper were big in Columbus' time but you are expected to do better than that. Here are a few suggestions to make you the hit of the village.

Pens:

Call an advertising specialist company to get cheap pens printed with your name and message on them. They will still be as cheap as drug store Bics and a lot cooler.

Stickers:

Buy a bag of them from party stores, if you can't resist a little self-promotion have your own stickers printed up on foil and give 'em out to the eager hordes.

Cigarettes:

I know it is not cool to smoke but male bonding through passing around the smokes is still very big in the rest of the world. In the Muslim world where men don't drink they smoke enough to make up for it. Even if you don't smoke, carry a couple of packs of cigarettes as gifts and ice-breakers. I know for a fact that peoples' intentions to shoot me have been altered by the speed with which I have offered up the smokes.

Balloons:

Kids love the farting sound they make and they will play with the balloons until they mysteriously pop. At which point they will head straight back to you asking you to repair it.

Holograms:

I carry stacks of cheap hologram stickers. They amaze, confuse and delight your hosts.

Weird Stuff No Adventurer Should Be Without

Everyone tells you to pack light (including me) so here are all the little items that can make your day or night in the bush.

Travel Clock Calculator:

I can never find the kind I like so I buy them in the duty free shops. The Sharp EL-470 acts as an international timepiece, alarm clock, calculator, currency converter and business card holder. Some of the new personal assistants put this tiny thing to shame but think about packing one along.

Utility Vest:

Not the kind that holds grenades or ammunition clips but the fishing, cruising or photo vests they sell in various adventure stores. They make great organizers hung over the back of your seat or hanging in the tent. Don't wear the damn thing; you might be mistaken for a tourist .

Books:

Buy them by thickness. My faves are: *Information Please Almanac*, the *Book of Lists*, Penguin compendiums of classic stories and fat chunky adventure novels like *Three Musketeers* or *Les Misrables*. The *Bible* or the *Koran* will do in a pinch and I have been known to write a book out of boredom. Trade 'em or give them away as gifts along the way. We hope the first thing you pack is a Fielding guidebook. Also think about phrase books, survival manuals and even poetry if you know all is lost. Address books are useful too.

Maps:

Good maps are very difficult to get in third world countries. Especially in war zones. Spraying them with a spray fixative available at any art store will waterproof them.

Cash:

Its amazing how useless credit cards and "traveler's cheques" are in the desert or jungle. If you are going deep into the dark places bring about $1000 in U.S. twenties, tens and hundreds. Get new ones, wrap them in a freezer bag and hope you won't have to use them. Stash some of it in secret hidey holes in case you lose your stash. Many people sew their mad money into their jackets (chancey) or wear them around their necks (dumb). I stick mine in the lining of my... Hey, I'm not going to tell you. I'll give you a hint. It's a place that is dark, it's a spare and it's never opened except when it's empty.

Business or Calling Cards:

If you are the sociable type have a bunch of cheap cards with plasticized ink made up (make sure moisture doesn't make the ink run). Look in the phone book for a translator if you would like them in two languages. Leave enough room for your new friends to write their name and address on them.

Short Wave Radio:
Now that Sony makes those teensy-weensy shortwave receivers you need never spend a ten-hour bus ride without entertainment.

A Laptop Computer:
We may be pushing it here but I drag my Powerbook to the world's roughest and toughest places. You'll have plenty of time to use it (with a car or solar charger). You can also carry the equivalent of an entire reference library on the hard disk as well. Mine was finally stolen in New York City of all places with three books in process that I had not backed-up.

A Notebook and Pens:
For the nontechnical a notebook is an indispensable part of the travel experience. You will have plenty of time to wax poetic and capture your thoughts.

Caribiners:
Use them to snap your pack to a bus rail, be framed, hold items on your belt, hang things from trees, rescue people and use as a belt when you lose weight.

Yellow and Black Danger Zone Tape:
I use the heavy striped tape to mark my luggage, tape rips, pack boxes and even fix my runners.

Syringes:
Just visit a third world hospital.

Razor Blades:
Boils, slivers, infected cuts—all may require a little field surgery.

Hydrogen Peroxide:
Cleans out cuts, hurts like hell, stops major infections.

Ziploc Freezer Bags:
Organizes, holds anything, waterproofs everything from passports to cameras. Use it for everything but food. The plastic transmits an icky plastic taste to food when kept in hot climates.

Trash Bags:
Heavy-duty garbage bags make great waterproofers. They also double as ponchos, groundcovers, umbrellas, water catchers, spare windows, sails and even garbage bags.

Tupperware:
Organizes, waterproofs, you can eat out of it, give it away as gifts. Get the clear stuff and size it to the pockets or corners in your luggage.

Bubblegum:
Get the kind that Amerol makes in the tape form. It's sold in a plastic snuff tin. Get the dayglo pink stuff; it drives the natives crazy to watch you blow those bubbles.

Drugs:
Many foreign countries will dispense uppers, painkillers, antibiotics and other full—strength medicines that normally require a prescription in the States. Stop at a local doctor and ask him about what works for malaria locally.

Extra Passport Photos:
You need them for visas, for newly found sweethearts, friends and even the police need them sometimes to file reports. Easy to order extras at home, but a bitch to get when you need six of them for visas in Laos.

Empty Film Cannisters:
The clear kind that Fuji film comes in. Take the top off, squeeze them and they act like suction cups. Squeeze them with the tops and they are like tiny popguns. You can amuse the little ones for hours.

Polaroid Camera:

I could create peace in the world and brotherly love if I just had enough Polaroid film to take pictures of every headhunter, mercenary, tribal warrior, soldier and politician. They love it, and smiles break out all around. Think about it: How many times does somebody take your picture where you work and actually give you a copy?

Sex slavery

Cambodia is in danger of attracting sex tourists caused by impoverished families.

Thailand has 800,000 prostitutes under the age of 16.

India has 400,000 child prostitutes.

The Philippines has 200,000 child prostitutes.

Taiwan has 100,000 child prostitutes.

Tourist Offices

If you need information about a country not listed here, call the United Nations at ☎ *(212) 963-1234,* wait through the recorded message for an operator, and ask for the number of the country's U.N. delegation. If they are not a member of the U.N. call the ministry of Tourism or government office in that country directly, using the area code of the capital city.

Antigua and Barbuda

*Antigua and Barbuda Department
of Tourism
610 Fifth Ave., Suite 311
New York, New York 10020*
☎ *(212) 541-4117*

Argentina

*Argentine Government Tourist Office
3550 Wilshire Blvd., Suite 1450
Los Angeles, California 90010*
☎ *(213) 930-0681*

Armenia

*Embassy of Armenia
122 C St. N.W., Suite 360
Washington D.C. 20001*
☎ *(202) 393-5983*

Aruba

*Aruba Tourism Authority
1000 Harbor Blvd.
Weehawken, New Jersey 07087*
☎ *(800) 862-7822 or (201) 330-0800.*

Australia

*Australian Tourist Commission,
2121 Avenue of the Stars, Suite 1200
Los Angeles, California 90067*
☎ *(310) 552-1988*

Austria

*Austrian National Tourist Office
11601 Wilshire Blvd., Suite 2480
Los Angeles, California 90025*
☎ *(310) 477-3332*

Bahamas

*Bahamas Tourist Office
3450 Wilshire Blvd., Suite 208
Los Angeles, California 90010*
☎ *(213) 385-0033.*

Barbados

*Barbados Tourism Authority
3440 Wilshire Blvd., Suite 1215
Los Angeles, California 90010*
☎ *(213) 380-2198*

Belgium

*Belgian Tourist Office
780 Third Ave., Suite 1501
New York, New York 10017*
☎ *(212) 758-8130*

Belize

*Consulate General of Belize
5825 Sunset Blvd., Suite 203
Hollywood, California 90028*
☎ *(213) 469-7343*

Bermuda

*Bermuda Department of Tourism
310 Madison Ave., Suite 201
New York, New York 10017*
☎ *(212) 818-9800*

Bhutan

*Bhutan Travel Service
120 East 56th St., Suite 1130
New York, New York 10022*
☎ *(212) 838-6382*

Bolivia

*Embassy of Bolivia
Tourist Information
3014 Massachusetts Ave.
N.W. Washington D.C. 20008*
☎ *(202) 483-4410*

Bonaire

*Tourism Corporation Bonaire
444 Madison Ave., Suite 2403
New York, New York 10022*
☎ *(800) 826-6247 or (212) 832-0779*

Brazil

Consulate General of Brazil
Brazilian Trade Center
Tourist Information
8484 Wilshire Blvd.
7th Floor
Beverly Hills, California 90211
☎ (213) 651-2664, ext. 200

British Virgin Islands

British Virgin Islands Tourist Board
1686 Union St., Suite 305
San Francisco, California 94123
☎ (800) 835-8530

Bolivia

97-45 Queens Park, Suite 600
Rego Park
New York, New York 11374
☎ (800) BOLIVIA or (718) 897-7956
FAX (718) 275-3943

Bulgaria

Balkan Holidays
Tourist Information
41 East 42nd St., Suite 508
New York, New York 10017
☎ (212) 573-5530

Canada

Canadian Consulate General
Tourist Information
300 S. Grand Ave.
10th Floor
Los Angeles, California 90071
☎ (213) 346-2700

Caribbean

Caribbean Tourism Organization
20 East 46th St., 4th Floor
New York, New York 10017
☎ (212) 682-0435

Cayman Islands

Cayman Islands Department of Tourism
3440 Wilshire Blvd., Suite 1202
Los Angeles, California 90010
☎ (213) 738-1968

Chile

Chilean Consulate General
Tourist Information
1110 Brickell Ave., Suite 616
Miami, Florida 33131
☎ (305) 373-8623

China, People's Republic of

China National Tourist Office
333 W. Broadway, Suite 201
Glendale, California 91204
☎ (818) 545-7505.

Russia/CIS

(and most former Soviet republics)
Intourist U.S.A. Inc.
610 Fifth Ave., Suite 603
New York, New York 10020
☎ (212) 757-3884

Cook Islands

Cook Islands Tourist Authority
6033 W. Century Blvd., Suite 690
Los Angeles, California 90045
☎ (800) 624-6250 or (310) 216-2872

Costa Rica

Consulate General of Costa Rica
3540 Wilshire Blvd., Suite 404
Los Angeles, California 90010
☎ (213) 380-7915

Curaçao

Curaçao Tourist Board
400 Madison Ave., Suite 311
New York, New York 10017,
☎ (800) 270-3350

Cyprus

Cyprus Tourism Organization
13 East 40th St., 1st Floor
New York, New York 10016
☎ (212) 683-5280.

Czech Republic (and Slovakia)

Cedok Central European Tours & Travel
10 East 40th St., Suite 3604
New York, New York 10016
☎ (212) 689-9720

Denmark

Danish Tourist Board
655 Third Ave., 18th Floor
New York, New York 10017
☎ (212) 949-2333
For information on Greenland contact:
Atuakkiorfik
Post Office Box 840 DK-3900
Nuuk Greenland
☎ (299) 22 122
FAX (299) 22 5 00

Dominican Republic

Consulate General of the Dominican
Republic Tourism Department
1 Times Square, 11th Floor
New York, New York 10036
☎ (212) 768-2481

Ecuador

Ecuadorian Consulate
Tourist Information
548 S. Spring St., Suite 602
Los Angeles, California 90013
☎ (213) 628-3014

Egypt

Egyptian Tourist Authority
8383 Wilshire Blvd., Suite 215
Beverly Hills, California 90211
☎ (213) 653-8815

Estonia

Consulate General of Estonia
Tourist Information
630 Fifth Ave., Suite 2415
New York, New York 10111
☎ (212) 247-7634

Fiji

Fiji Visitors Bureau
5777 W. Century Blvd., Suite 220
Los Angeles, California 90045
☎ (310) 568-1616

Finland

Finnish Tourist Board
655 Third Ave., 18th Floor
New York, New York 10017
☎ (212) 949-2333

France

French Government Tourist Office
9454 Wilshire Blvd., Suite 715
Beverly Hills, California 90212
☎ (310) 479-4426
☎ (900) 990-0040
(calls cost 50 cents a minute)

French Guiana

French Government Tourist Office
9454 Wilshire Blvd., Suite 715,
Beverly Hills, California 90212
☎ (310) 479-4426
☎ (900) 990-0040
(calls cost 50 cents a minute)

Germany

German National Tourist Office
11766 Wilshire Blvd., Suite 750
Los Angeles, California 90025
☎ (310) 575-9799

Ghana

Embassy of Ghana
Tourist Information
3512 International Drive N.W.,
Washington D.C. 20008
☎ (202) 686-4520

Great Britain

British Tourist Authority
551 Fifth Ave., Suite 701
New York, New York 10176
☎ (800) GO2 BRITAIN
Free fax on demand service (213) 628-1216;
you must call from a fax machine

Greece

Greek National Tourist Organization
611 W. 6th St., Suite 2198
Los Angeles, California 90017
☎ (213) 626-6696

Grenada

Grenada Tourist Office
820 Second Ave., Suite 900-D
New York, New York 10017
(800) 927-9554

Greenland

See Denmark

Guadeloupe

See French Government Tourist Office

Guam

Guam Visitors Bureau
1150 Marina Village Parkway, Suite 104
Alameda, California 94501
☎ (800) US3-GUAM

Guatemala

Guatemala Consulate General
2500 Wilshire Blvd., Suite 820
Los Angeles, California 90057
☎ (213) 365-9251

Haiti

Haitian Consulate
271 Madison Ave., 17th Floor
New York, New York 10016
☎ (212) 697-9767

Honduras

Honduras Consulate
3450 Wilshire Blvd., Suite 230
Los Angeles, California 90010
☎ (213) 383-9244

Hong Kong

Hong Kong Tourist Association
10940 Wilshire Blvd., Suite 1220
Los Angeles, California 90024
☎ (310) 208-4582.

Hungary

Ibusz Travel
1 Parker Plaza, 4th Floor
Ft. Lee, New Jersey 07024
☎ (201) 592-8585

Iceland

Icelandic Tourist Board
655 Third Ave., 18th Floor
New York, New York 10017,
☎ (212) 949-2333

India

Government of India Tourist Office
3550 Wilshire Blvd., Suite 204
Los Angeles, California 90010
☎ (213) 380-8855

Indonesia

Indonesia Tourist Promotion Office
3457 Wilshire Blvd., Suite 104
Los Angeles, California 90010
☎ (213) 387-2078

Ireland

Irish Tourist Board
345 Park Ave.
New York, New York 10154
☎ (800) 223-6470 or (212) 418-0800

Israel

Israel Government Tourist Office
6380 Wilshire Blvd., Suite 1700
Los Angeles, California 90048
☎ (213) 658-7462

Italy

Italian Government Tourist Board
12400 Wilshire Blvd., Suite 550
Los Angeles, California 90025
☎ (310) 820-0098

Ivory Coast

Tourism Cote d'Ivorie North America
2424 Massachusetts Ave.
N.W. Washington D.C. 20008
☎ (202) 797-0344

Jamaica

Jamaica Tourist Board
3440 Wilshire Blvd., Suite 1207
Los Angeles, California 90010
☎ (213) 384-1123

Japan

Japan National Tourist Organization
624 S. Grand Ave., Suite 1611
Los Angeles, California 90017
☎ (213) 623-1952

Jordan

Jordan Information Bureau
2319 Wyoming Ave. N.W.
Washington D.C. 20008
☎ (202) 265-1606

Kenya

Kenya Consulate
Tourist Office
9150 Wilshire Blvd., Suite 160
Beverly Hills, California 90212
☎ (310) 274-6635

Korea (South)

Korea National Tourism Corp.
3435 Wilshire Blvd., Suite 350
Los Angeles, California 90010
☎ (213) 382-3435

Latvia

Latvian Embassy
4325 17th St. N.W.
Washington D.C. 20011
☎ (202) 726-8213

Liechtenstein

See Swiss National Tourist Office

Lithuania

Embassy of Lithuania
Tourist Information
2622 16th St. N.W.
Washington D.C. 20009
☎ (202) 234-5860

Luxembourg

Luxembourg Tourist Office
17 Beekman Place
N.Y. 10022
☎ (212) 935-8888

Macau

Macau Tourist Information Bureau
3133 Lake Hollywood Drive
Los Angeles, California 90068
☎ (213) 851-3402

Madagascar

Embassy of Madagascar
Tourist Information
2374 Massachusetts Ave. N.W.
Washington D.C. 20008
☎ (202) 265-5525

Malaysia

Malaysia Tourism Promotion Board
818 West 7th St.
Los Angeles, California 90017
☎ (213) 689-9702.

Malta

Malta National Tourist Office
249 East 35th St.
New York, New York 10016
☎ (212) 213-6686

Martinique

See French Government Tourist Office

Mauritius

Mauritius Tourist Information Service
8 Haven Ave.
Port Washington New York 11050
☎ (516) 944-3763

Mexico

Mexican Government Tourism Office
10100 Santa Monica Blvd., Suite 224
Los Angeles, California 90067
☎ (310) 203-8191

Monaco

Monaco Government Tourist & Convention Bureau
845 Third Ave., 19th Floor
New York, New York 10022
☎ (800) 753-9696 or (212) 759-5227

Morocco

Moroccan National Tourist Office
20 East 46th St.
New York, New York 10017
☎ (212) 557-2520

Myanmar (Burma)

Embassy of Myanmar
2300 S St. N.W.
Washington D.C. 20008,
☎ (202) 332-9044

Nepal

Royal Nepalese Consulate
Tourist Information
820 Second Ave., Suite 202
New York, New York 10017
☎ (212) 370-4188

Netherlands

Netherlands Board of Tourism
225 N. Michigan Ave., Suite 326
Chicago, Ilinois 60601
☎ (312) 819-0300.

New Zealand

New Zealand Tourism Board,
501 Santa Monica Blvd., Suite 300
Santa Monica, California 90401
☎ (800) 388-5494 or (310) 395-7480

Nigeria

Embassy of Nigeria
Tourist Information
2201 M St. N.W.
Washington D.C. 20037
☎ (202) 822-1500

Norway

Norwegian Tourist Board
655 Third Ave., 18th Floor
New York, New York 10017,
☎ (212) 949-2333

Papua New Guinea

Air Niugini
5000 Birch St., Suite 3000
Newport Beach, California 92660
☎ (714) 752-5440

Paraguay

Paraguay Embassy
Tourist Information
2400 Massachusetts Ave. N.W.
Washington D.C. 20008
☎ *(202) 483-6962*

Peru

Peruvian Consulate
Tourist Information
3460 Wilshire Blvd., Suite 1005
Los Angeles, California 90010
☎ *(213) 383-9895*

Philippines

Philippine Department of Tourism
3660 Wilshire Blvd., Suite 216
Los Angeles, California 90010
☎ *(213) 487-4525*

Poland

Orbis Polish Travel Bureau
342 Madison Ave., Suite 1512
New York, New York 10173
☎ *(212) 867-5011*

Portugal

Portuguese National Tourist Office
590 Fifth Ave., 4th Floor
New York, New York 10036
☎ *(212) 354-4403*

Puerto Rico

Government of Puerto Rico Tourism Co.
3575 W. Cahuenga Blvd., Suite 560
Los Angeles, California 90068
☎ *(213) 874-5991*

Romania

Romanian National Tourist Office
342 Madison Ave., Suite 210
New York, New York 10173
☎ *(212) 697-6971*

Russia/CIS

(and most former Soviet Republics)
Intourist U.S.A. Inc.
610 Fifth Ave., Suite 603
New York, New York 10020
☎ *(212) 757-3884*

St. Barthelemy

See French Government Tourist Office

St. Kitts and Nevis

St. Kitts and Nevis Tourist Office
414 East 75th St., 5th Floor
New York, New York 10021
☎ *(212) 535-1234*

St. Lucia

St. Lucia Tourist Board
820 Second Ave., 9th Floor, Suite 900E
New York, New York 10017
☎ *(800) 456-3984 or (212) 867-2950*

Sint Maarten

Sint Maarten Tourist Office
275 Seventh Ave., 19th Floor
New York, New York 10001-6788
☎ *(212) 989-0000*

St. Martin

See French Government Tourist Office

St. Vincent

St. Vincent & the Grenadines Tourist Office
801 Second Ave., 21st Floor
New York, New York 10017
☎ *(212) 687-4981*

Samoa

American Samoa Government Office
Tourism Information
401 Waiakamilo Road, Suite 201
Honolulu, Hawaii 96817
☎ *(808) 847-1998*

Senegal

Senegal Tourist Office
888 Seventh Ave., 27th Floor
New York, New York 10106
☎ *(202) 234-0540*

Seychelles

Seychelles Tourist Office
820 Second Ave., Suite 900-F
New York, New York 10017
☎ *(212) 687-9766*

Singapore

Singapore Tourist Promotion Board
8484 Wilshire Blvd., Suite 510
Beverly Hills California 90211
☎ *(213) 852-1901*

Slovakia

Cedok Central European Tours & Travel
10 East 40th St., Suite 3604
New York, New York 10016
☎ *(212) 689-9720*

Slovenia

Slovenian Tourist Office
122 East 42nd St., Suite 3006
New York, New York 10168-0072
☎ *(212) 682-5896*

Solomon Islands

Solomon Islands Tourist Authority
P.O. Box 321
Honiara, Solomon Islands
☎ *(011) 677-22-442*

South Africa

South African Tourist Board
9841 Airport Blvd., Suite 1524
Los Angeles, California 90045
☎ *(800) 782-9772 or (310) 641-8444*

Spain

National Tourist Office of Spain
8383 Wilshire Blvd., Suite 960
Beverly Hills, California 90211
☎ *(213) 658-7188*

Sri Lanka

Embassy of Sri Lanka
Tourist Information
2148 Wyoming Ave. N.W.
Washington D.C. 20008
☎ *(202) 483-4025*

Sweden

> Swedish Travel & Tourism Council
> 655 Third Ave., 18th Floor
> New York, New York 10017
> ☎ (212) 949-2333

Switzerland

> Swiss National Tourist Office
> 222 N. Sepulveda Blvd., Suite 1570
> El Segundo, California 90245
> ☎ (310) 335-5980

Tahiti (French Polynesia)

> Tahiti Tourism Board
> 300 N. Continental Blvd., Suite 180
> El Segundo, California 90245
> ☎ (310) 414-8484

Taiwan (Republic of China)

> Taiwan Visitors Assn.
> 166 Geary St., Suite 1605
> San Francisco, California 94108
> ☎ (415) 989-8677

Tanzania

> Tanzania Mission to the U.N.
> 205 East 42nd St., Suite 1300
> New York, New York 10017
> ☎ (212) 972-9160

Thailand

> Tourism Authority of Thailand
> 3440 Wilshire Blvd., Suite 1100
> Los Angeles, California 90010
> ☎ (213) 382-2353

Tonga

> Tonga Consulate General
> Tourist Information
> 360 Post St., Suite 604,
> San Francisco, California 94108
> ☎ (415) 781-0365.

Trinidad & Tobago

> Trinidad & Tobago Tourism
> Development Authority
> 25 West 43rd St., Suite 1508
> New York, New York 10036
> ☎ (800) 232-0082

Tunisia

> Embassy of Tunisia
> Tourist Information
> 1515 Massachusetts Ave.
> N.W. Washington D.C. 20005
> ☎ (202) 862-1850

Turkey

> Office of Tourism Information Attache
> 821 United Nations Plaza
> New York, New York 10017
> ☎ (212) 687-2194

Ukraine

> Kobasniuk Travel
> 157 Second Ave.
> New York, New York 10003
> ☎ (212) 254-8779

Uruguay

> Consulate of Uruguay
> Tourist Information

> 747 3rd Ave., 21st Floor
> New York, New York 10017
> ☎ (212) 753-8191

Vanuatu

> National Tourism Office of Vanuatu
> 520 Monterey Drive
> Rio del Mar, California 95003
> ☎ (408) 685-8901

U.S. Virgin Islands

> U.S. Virgin Islands Division of Tourism
> 3460 Wilshire Blvd., Suite 412
> Los Angeles, California 90010
> ☎ (213) 739-0138

Venezuela

> Embassy of Venezuela
> Tourist Information
> 1099 30th St. N.W.,
> Washington D.C. 20007
> ☎ (202) 342-6850

Zambia

> Zambia National Tourist Board
> 237 East 52nd St.
> New York, New York 10022,
> ☎ (212) 308-2155.

Getting a Passport

First-time Passport

To get a passport you will need:

1. Evidence of United States citizenship or nationality such as: a certified copy of a birth certificate for all applicants born in the U.S.; a Certificate of Naturalization or Citizenship; an expired U.S. passport; or other evidence acceptable for passport purposes.

2. Evidence of identity which contains applicant's signature and photograph or physical description. Temporary or expired documents are not generally acceptable.

3. Two passport photographs which are identical and a reasonably good likeness (normally taken within the last six months). The photographs must be 2 x 2 inches with an image size between 1 and 1-3/8 inches. Photographs must be a front view, full face, taken in normal street attire without a hat or dark glasses, and printed on thin paper with a plain white or off-white background. They must be capable of withstanding a mounting temperature of 225 degrees Fahrenheit (107 degrees Celsius).

4. Passport fees are $65 if the applicant is 18 years of age or over and $40 if under 18. The actual passport fee is $55 for adults and $30 for minors and an additional fee of $10 for execution of the passport application is applied. Generally fees may be paid by check or money order but you should check with the office which will execute your application for specific instructions. There is a $25 returned check service charge.

5. A completed passport application form (DSP-11) which contains all the requested information, except your signature, must be signed in the presence of an authorized executing official.

Passport Renewal

Passport applicants who have had a previous passport and meet the following criteria may be eligible to apply by mail: If your most recent passport was issued within the past 12 years, you were 18 when the passport was issued, you have the same name or you can substantiate the name change with a court order or marriage certificate and you can send in your previous passport, you can apply by mail.

Send in:

1. Evidence of citizenship in the form of your most recently issued passport.

2. Two passport photographs which are identical and a reasonably good likeness (normally taken within the last six months). The photographs must be 2 x 2 inches with an image size between 1 and 1-3/8 inches. Photographs must be a front view, full face, taken in normal street attire without a hat or dark glasses, and printed on thin paper with a plain white or off-

white background. They must be capable of withstanding a mounting temperature of 225 degrees Fahrenheit (107 degrees Celsius).

3. Passport fees are $55 if you are 18 years of age or over and $30 if you are under 18. Fees must be paid by check or money order made payable to Passport Services. There is a $25 returned check service charge.

4. A completed passport application form (DSP-82) which contains all the requested information and is signed and dated. These applications should be mailed to:

Passport Lockbox
P.O. Box 371971
Pittsburgh, PA 15250-7971

Passport Fees

The fee for an adult's (18 years of age and older) first-time, 10 year passport is $65.00. This includes the $55.00 passport fee and the $10.00 execution fee. The fee for a child's (under 18 years of age) first-time, 5 year passport is $40.00. This includes the $30.00 passport fee and the $10.00 execution fee. The fee for the application to receive a Passport by Mail for a person 18 years of age and older is $55.00. There is no execution fee and the passport is valid for 10 years. The fee for the application for Passport by Mail for a person 16 years of age up to 18 years of age is $30.00. There is no execution fee and the passport is valid for 5 years. MORE ON VALIDITY: Unless specifically authorized by a passport issuing office, no person may have more than one valid, or potentially valid, U.S. passport of the same type at any one time.

Note: All U.S. citizens are required to obtain individual passports in their own names. The inclusion of minors over the age of 13 in U.S. passports was discontinued effective January 1, 1978. The inclusion of a spouse was discontinued January 14, 1980. The inclusion of children under the age of 13 was discontinued January 1, 1981.

Best Time and Place to Get a Passport

Your best bet is to apply through a Clerk of Court or Post Office nearest your locale which accepts passport applications. Passport Agencies have extremely long lines during the spring and the summer which results in longer waiting times for people applying in person at a passport agency. The best time to get your passport is in the fall when workload volume is at its lowest. You should also apply at least four to six weeks prior to any scheduled international travel. This will allow sufficient time to correct application deficiencies, should there be any, and would allow time for visas to be obtained, if needed, without jeopardizing scheduled travel plans. Clerk of Court or Post Offices tend to have much shorter lines. There are over 2500 courts and 900 post offices in the United States that accept passport applications.

Heavy-Duty Passports for Industrial Strength Travel

If you plan to do a lot of traveling or travel to Third World countries where officials in cheap polyester uniforms like to make you sign in at every police post, ask for the 48-page passport which can be issued in lieu of a 24-page passport at no extra charge. You can request this one when you apply for your passport.

If you have no more space in your passport for visa stamps, additional visa pages may be placed in your passport. There is no charge for this service. You must submit your current, valid passport and a completed Form DSP-19 to the nearest passport agency.

If You Lose Your Passport

Don't be without a passport. If your passport is stolen or lost expect it to be used for unsavory purposes. Notify Passport Services or the nearest Passport Agency in writing, or, if abroad, notify the nearest U.S. embassy or consulate. The majority of passports are lost or stolen in the States (60 percent); the balance were lost or stolen while abroad.

If you join the ranks of the over 60,000 people who had their passports stolen between 1980 and 1989, your chances of getting your passport back are slim; only five percent of stolen passports are recovered.

If your passport is stolen, report the theft to police authorities in the locale in which the theft occurred.

If you wish to obtain another passport, you must execute a Form DSP-11 and you must submit a detailed statement explaining the circumstances surrounding the loss or theft of the passport and stating what efforts have been made to recover it. Brief notations such as "lost," "stolen," or "burned" are not sufficient. You must fill out a Form DSP-64, "Statement Regarding Lost or Stolen Passport," or a statement containing the information requested on the DSP-64. You will be required to complete a Form DSP-11 in the prescribed manner, present acceptable identification and submit two new photographs and the required fees. You should submit other acceptable evidence of citizenship in order to avoid delay in issuance of the replacement passport. If the lost passport is recovered subsequent to the issuance of a replacement passport, the recovered passport should be submitted to the nearest passport issuing office.

Replacement Passports

Passports issued to replace lost or stolen valid passports are normally issued for the full period of validity. However, there may occasionally be circumstances in which the replacement passport is limited to a shorter period of time. Upon conclusion of the initial period of validity, the bearer may request that the passport be extended by presenting it to Passport Services, a Passport Agency or a U.S. consular post abroad. There is no fee charged for this extension. The bearer should submit a statement advising whether the previous passport has been recovered. This is usually done with a Form DSP-19, "Passport Amendment/Validation Application." Extension of a passport while abroad may take several weeks for completion. If the lost passport is subsequently recovered, it should be submitted to the nearest passport issuing office along with the limited passport. The recovered passport will normally be cancelled and the limited passport validated for use and returned to the bearer, unless the bearer specifically requests that the recovered passport be validated for use and returned.

Where Your U.S. Passport Will Get You Into Trouble

The Secretary of State has the statutory authority to invalidate U.S. passports for travel to countries with which the United States is at war, where armed hostilities are in progress, or where there is imminent danger to the public health and physical safety of United States travelers.

Currently, a U.S. passport is not valid for travel to Libya, Lebanon and Iraq. The Department of State considers requests for exceptions to these restrictions on a case-by-case basis. The four categories under which a request is considered are as follows:

- Professional reporter

- Representatives of the American Red Cross
- Applicants whose travel is in the national interest
- Applicants who establish that their trip is justified by compelling humanitarian considerations.

To request an exception to these passport restrictions, send a letter including biographical information concerning the individual, the specific reason for traveling to a country where a U.S. passport is invalid, and any supporting documentation to the

Department of State, Office of Citizenship Appeals and Legal Assistance

Room 300, 1425 K Street, N.W.
Washington, D.C. 20522-1705
☎ *(202) 955-0233*

Further, the U.S. Department of the Treasury, (Office of Foreign Assets Control), has imposed economic sanctions upon U.S. citizens traveling to Libya and Iraq. Questions concerning these restrictions, and any exceptions to the restrictions, must be addressed directly to that agency.

Some countries require that your passport be valid at least six months beyond the dates of your trip.

With certain exceptions, it is against U.S. law to enter or leave the country without a valid passport. Generally for tourists, the exceptions refer to direct travel within U.S. territories or between North, South, or Central America (except Cuba).

Note: If you mutilate or alter your U.S. passport, you may render it invalid and expose yourself to possible prosecution under the law (Section 1543 of Title 22 of the U.S. Code).

You will need:

Proof of U.S. Citizenship

A previous U.S. passport, or (if you were born in the U.S.) a certified copy of your birth certificate issued by the state, city, or county of your birth (a certified copy will have a registrars raised, embossed, impressed, or multicolored seal and the date the certificate was filed with the registrar's office).

If you have neither a passport nor a certified birth certificate...

- bring a notice from the registrar of the state where you were born that no birth record exists;
- also, bring as many as possible of the following (To be considered, these documents must show your full name and date and place of birth. Also you should bring a notarized affidavit completed by an older blood relative who has personal knowledge of your birth.):

- a baptismal certificate,
- hospital birth record,
- early census,
- school record, or
- family Bible record.

- If you were born abroad, bring a Certificate of Naturalization, Certificate of Citizenship, Report of Birth Abroad of a U.S. Citizen, or a Certification of Birth (Form FS-545 or DS-1350). If you do not have these documents, check with the acceptance office agent for documents that can be used in their place.

Two Photographs

The photos must have been taken within the past six months, identical, 2 x 2 inches, and either color or black/white. They must show a front view, full face, on a plain, light (white or off-white) background. Always order at least 12 photos. They will be used for your international drivers license, ID badges, visas and just as gifts for people you meet on the road. Remember the photos you get from the arcade machines are not acceptable.

Proof of identity

This can be a previous U.S. passport, a Certificate of Naturalization or Citizenship, a valid driver's license, government or military ID, or corporate ID.

Fees

It costs $65 for a ten-year passport; or $40 for a five-year passport for persons under 18 (these amounts include a $10 execution fee.) Make your check or money order payable to Passport Services. Post offices (and passport agencies) accept cash, but courts are not required to do so.

Social Security Number

A Social Security number is not required for issuance of a passport but Section 603E of the Internal Revenue Code of 1986 requires passport applicants to provide this information. Passport Services will provide this information to the Internal Revenue Service (IRS) routinely. Any applicant who fails to provide the information is subject to a $500 penalty enforced by the IRS. All questions on this matter should be referred to the nearest IRS office.

Passport Agencies That Get You a Passport In a Hurry

Don't assume the passport agency will think you are in a rush. Applications are processed according to the departure date indicated on your application form. If you give no departure date, the passport agency will assume you are not planning any immediate travel. Your passport will be returned to you by mail at the address you provided on your application.

If you need a passport within five working days, apply in person at the nearest passport agency and present your tickets or travel itinerary from an airline, as well as the other required items. Or, apply at a court or post office and have the application sent to the passport agency through an overnight delivery service of your choice (you should include a self-addressed, prepaid envelope for the return of the passport). Be sure to include your dates of departure and travel plans on your application.

Boston Passport Agency
Thomas P. O+Neill Fed. Bldg., Rm. 247
10 Causeway Street
Boston, MA 02222-1094
Information: ☎ *(617) 565-6998**
☎ *(617) 565-6990*

Chicago Passport Agency
Suite 380, Kluczynski Federal Office Bldg.
230 South Dearborn Street
Chicago, IL 60604-1564
Information: ☎ *(312) 353-7155**

Honolulu Passport Agency
Room C-106, New Federal Bldg.
300 Ala Moana Blvd.
Honolulu, HI 96850-0001
Information: ☎ *(808) 541-1919**
☎ *(808) 541-1918*

Houston Passport Agency
Suite 1100, Mickey Leland Fed. Bldg.
1919 Smith Street
Houston, TX 77002-8049
Information: ☎ *(713) 653-3153**

Los Angeles Passport Agency
Room 13100, 11000 Wilshire Blvd.
Los Angeles, CA 90024-3615

Information: ☎ *(213) 575-7070**

Miami Passport Agency
3rd Floor, Claude Pepper Federal Office Bldg.
51 Southwest First Avenue
Miami, FL 33130-1680
Information: ☎ *(305) 536-4681**

New Orleans Passport Agency
Postal Service Building
701 Loyola Ave., Rm T-12005
New Orleans, LA 70113-1931
Information: ☎ *(504) 589-6728**
☎ *(504) 589-6161/62*

New York Passport Agency
Room 270, Rockefeller Center
630 Fifth Avenue
New York, NY 10111-00311
Information: ☎ *(212) 399-5290**

Philadelphia Passport Agency
Room 4426, Federal Bldg.
600 Arch Street
Philadelphia, PA 19106-1684
Information: ☎ *(215) 597-7480**

San Francisco Passport Agency
Suite. 200, Tishman Speyer Bldg.

525 Market Street
San Francisco, CA 94105-2773
Information: ☎ (415) 744-4444 or 4010*

Seattle Passport Agency

Room 992, Federal Office Bldg.
915 Second Avenue
Seattle, WA 98174-1091
Information: ☎ (206) 220-7777*
☎ (206) 220-7788

Stamford Passport Agency

One Landmark Square
Broad and Atlantic Streets
Stamford, CT 06901-2767
Information: ☎ (203) 325-3530*

Washington Passport Agency

1425 K Street, N.W.
Washington, DC 20522-1705
Information: ☎ (202) 647-0518*

If you have any questions about an application that was mailed, write or call:

National Passport Center

31 Rochester Ave.
Portsmouth, NH 003801-2900
☎ (603) 334-0500

*This is a 24-hour information line that includes general passport information, passport agency location and hours of operation and information regarding emergency passport services during non-working hours.

Visas and Entry Requirements

IMPORTANT: THIS LISTING IS PREPARED FROM INFORMATION OB-TAINED FROM THE STATE DEPARTMENT AND FOREIGN EMBASSIES PRIOR TO PUBLICATION. THIS INFORMATION IS SUBJECT TO CHANGE. CHECK ENTRY REQUIREMENTS WITH THE CONSULAR OFFICIALS OF THE COUNTRIES TO BE VISITED WELL IN ADVANCE.

Passports

U.S. citizens who travel to a country where a valid passport is not required will need documentary evidence of their U.S. citizenship and identity. Proof of U.S. citizenship includes an expired passport, a certified (original) birth certificate, Certificate of Naturalization, Certificate of Citizenship, or Report of Birth Abroad of a Citizen of the United States. To prove identity, a valid driver's license or government identification card are acceptable provided they identify you by physical description or photograph. However, for travel overseas and to facilitate reentry into the U.S., a valid U.S. passport is the best documentation available and it unquestionably proves your U.S. citizenship.

Some countries require that your passport be valid at least six months beyond the dates of your trip. If your passport expires before the required validity, you will have to apply for a new one. Please check with the embassy or nearest consulate of the country you plan to visit for their requirements.

Some Arab or African countries will not issue visas or allow entry if your passport indicates travel to Israel or South Africa. Consult the nearest U.S. passport agency for guidance if this applies to you.

A visa is an endorsement or stamp placed by officials of a foreign country on a U.S. passport that allows the bearer to visit that foreign country. VISAS SHOULD BE OB-TAINED BEFORE PROCEEDING ABROAD. Allow sufficient time for processing your visa application, especially if you are applying by mail. Most foreign consular representatives are located in principal cities, and in many instances, a traveler may be required to obtain visas from the consular office in the area of his/her residence. The addresses of foreign consular offices in the United States may be obtained by consulting the Congressional Directory in the library. IT IS THE RESPONSIBILITY OF THE TRAVELER TO OBTAIN VISAS, WHERE REQUIRED, FROM THE AP-

PROPRIATE EMBASSY OR NEAREST CONSULATE OF THE COUNTRY YOU
ARE PLANNING TO VISIT.

Immunizations

Under the International Health Regulations adopted by the World Health Organization, a country may require International Certificates of Vaccination against yellow fever. A cholera immunization may be required if you are traveling from an infected area. Check with health care providers or your records to ensure other immunizations (e.g. tetanus and polio) are up-to-date. Prophylactic medication for malaria and certain other preventive measures are advisable for travel to some countries. No immunizations are required to return to the United States. Detailed health information is included in Health Information for International Travel, available from the U.S. Government Printing Office for $6.50 or may be obtained from your local health department or physician or by calling the Centers for Disease Control on 404/332-4559.

An increasing number of countries have established regulations regarding AIDS testing, particularly for long-term visitors. Although many are listed here, check with the embassy or consulate of the country you plan to visit to verify if this is a requirement for entry.

All international flights are subject to U.S. Immigration and U.S. Customs fees paid in advance as part of your ticket. In addition, many countries have departure fees that are sometimes collected at the time of ticket purchase.

Entry Information for Foreign Countries

COUNTRY	ENTRY
AFGHANISTAN	Passport and visa required. No tourist or business visas are being issued at this time. For further information contact Embassy of the Republic of Afghanistan, *2341 Wyoming Ave., N.W., Washington, D.C. 20008.* ☎ *(202) 234-3770/1 .*
ALBANIA	Passport required. For further information contact the Embassy of the Republic of Albania at *1150 18th Street N.W., Washington, D.C. 20036,* ☎ *(202) 223-4942.*
ALGERIA	Passport and visa required. Obtain visa before arrival. Visa valid up to 90 days, requires 2 application forms, 2 photos, proof of onward/return transportation, sufficient funds and $22 fee (money order or certified check). Company letter (plus 1 copy) required for business visa. Visa not granted to passports showing Israeli visas. Enclose prepaid self-addressed envelope for return of passport by registered, certified or express mail. For currency regulations and other information contact the Consular Section of the Embassy of the Democratic and Popular Republic of Algeria, *2137 Wyoming Ave., N.W., Washington, D.C. 20008,* ☎ *(202) 265-2800.*
ANDORRA	(See France.)
ANGOLA	Passport and visa required. Tourist/business visas require an application form, letter stating purpose of travel, and two color photos. Applications by mail require prepaid return envelope. Yellow fever and cholera immunizations required. For additional information contact Embassy of Angola, *1899 L Street, N.W., 6th Floor, Washington, D.C. 20036* ☎ *(202) 785-1156)* or the Permanent Mission of the Republic of Angola to the U.N., *125 East 73rd Street, New York, NY 10021,* ☎ *(212) 861-5656.*
ANTIGUA AND BARBUDA	Proof of U.S. citizenship required, return/onward ticket and/or proof of funds needed for tourist stay up to 6 months. AIDS test required for immigrant, student and work visas. U.S. test accepted. Check Embassy of Antigua and Barbuda, *Suite 4M, 3400 International Drive, N.W., Washington, D.C. 20008,* ☎ *(202) 362-5122/5166/5211)* for further information.
ARGENTINA	Passport required. Visa not required for tourist stay up to 3 months. Business visa requires company letter detailing purpose of trip and length of stay. For more information contact Argentine Embassy, *1600 New Hampshire Ave., N.W., Washington, D.C. 20009,* ☎ *(202) 939-6400)* or the nearest Consulate: CA ☎ *(213) 739-5959* and ☎ *(415) 982-3050,* FL ☎ *(305) 373-1889,* IL ☎ *(312) 263-7435,* LA ☎ *(504) 523-2823,* NY ☎ *(212) 603-0415,* PR ☎ *(809) 754-6500* or TX ☎ *(713) 871-8935.*
ARMENIA	Passport and visa required. For additional information contact the Consular Section of the Embassy of Armenia, *122 C Street, N.W., Suite 360, Washington, D.C. 20001,* ☎ *(202) 393-5983.*

COUNTRY	ENTRY

ARUBA

Passport or proof of U.S. citizenship required. Visa not required for stay up to 14 days, extendable to 90 days after arrival. Proof of onward/return ticket or sufficient funds for stay may be required. Departure tax $9.50. For further information consult Embassy of the Netherlands ☎ *(202) 244-5300)*, or nearest Consulate General: CA ☎ *(212) 380-3440*, IL ☎ *(314) 856-1429*, NY ☎ *(212) 246-1429* or TX ☎ *(713) 622-8000.*

AUSTRALIA

Passport, visa and onward/return transportation required. Transit visa not necessary for up to 8-hour stay at airport. Visitor visa valid 1 year for multiple entries up to 3 months, no charge, requires 1 application and 1 photo. Applications for a stay of longer than 3 months or with a validity longer than 1 year, require fee of $25 (U.S.). Need company letter for business visa. Departure tax, $20 (Australian), paid at airport. Minors not accompanied by parent require notarized copy of the child's birth certificate and notarized written parental consent from both parents. AIDS test required for permanent resident visa applicants age 15 and over; U.S. test accepted. Send prepaid envelope for return of passport by mail. Allow 3 weeks for processing. For further information contact the Embassy of Australia, *1601 Mass. Ave., N.W., Washington, D.C. 20036,* ☎ *(800) 242-2878,* ☎ *(202) 797-3145* or the nearest Consulate General: CA ☎ *(213) 469-4300* or ☎ *(415) 362-6160,* HI ☎ *(808) 524-5050,* NY ☎ *(212) 245-4000* or TX ☎ *(713) 629-9131.*

AUSTRIA

Passport required. Visa not required for stay up to 3 months. For longer stays check with Embassy of Austria, *3524 International Court, N.W., Washington, D.C. 20008,* ☎ *(202) 895-6767,* or nearest Consulate General: Los Angeles ☎ *(310) 444-9310,* Chicago ☎ *(312) 222-1515* or New York ☎ *(212) 737-6400.*

AZERBAIJAN

Passport and visa required. Visa (no charge) requires 1 application form, 1 photo and a letter of invitation. For additional information contact the Embassy of the Federal Republic of Azerbaijan, *927 15th Street, N.W., Suite 700, Washington, D.C. 20005,* ☎ *(202) 842-0001.*

AZORES

(See Portugal.)

BAHAMAS

Proof of U.S. citizenship, photo ID and onward/return ticket required for stay up to 8 months. Passport and residence/work permit needed for residence and business. Permit required for firearms and to import pets. Departure tax of $15 must be paid at airport. For further information call Embassy of the Commonwealth of the Bahamas, *2220 Massachusetts Ave., N.W., Washington, D.C. 20008,* ☎ *(202) 319-2660* or nearest Consulate: Miami ☎ *(305) 373-6295* or New York ☎ *(212) 421-6420.*

COUNTRY	ENTRY

BAHRAIN

Passport and visa required. No tourist visas issued at this time. Transit visa available upon arrival for stay up to 72 hours, must have return/ onward ticket. Business, work, or resident visas valid for 3 months, single-entry, require 1 application form, 1 photo, letter from company or No Objection Certificate (NOC) from Immigration Dept. in Bahrain and $30 fee ($20 for bearer of NOC). Yellow fever vaccination needed if arriving from infected area. Send SASE for return of passport by mail. For departure tax and other information, contact Embassy of the State of Bahrain, *3502 International Drive, N.W., Washington, D.C. 20008,* ☎ *(202) 342-0741*; or the Permanent Mission to the U.N., *2 United Nations Plaza, East 44th Street, New York, NY 10017* ☎ *(212) 223-6200.*

BANGLADESH

Passport, visa, and onward/return ticket required. Tourist/business visa requires 2 application forms, 2 photos. Business visa also requires company letter. For longer stays and more information consult Embassy of the People's Republic of Bangladesh, *2201 Wisconsin Ave., N.W., Washington, D.C. 20007,* ☎ *(202) 342-8373.*

BARBADOS

U.S. tourists traveling directly from the U.S. to Barbados may enter for up to 3 months stay with proof of U.S. citizenship (original or certified copy of birth certificate), photo ID and onward/return ticket. Passport required for longer visits and other types of travel. Business visas $25, single-entry and $30 multiple-entry (may require work permit). Departure tax of $25 is paid at airport. Check information with Embassy of Barbados, *2144 Wyoming Ave., N.W., Washington, D.C. 20008,* ☎ *(202) 939-9200* or Consulate General in New York ☎ *(212) 867-8435.*

BELARUS

Passport and visa required. Visa requires 1 application form and 1 photo. The visa processing fee is $30 for 7 working days, $60 for next day, and $100 for same day processing. (No charge for official travelers.) Transit visa is required when travelling through Belarus ($20). For additional information contact Embassy of Belarus, *1619 New Hampshire Ave., N.W., Washington, D.C. 20009,* ☎ *(202) 986-1604.*

BELGIUM

Passport required. Visa not required for business/tourist stay up to 90 days. Temporary residence permit required for longer stays. For residence authorization, consult Embassy of Belgium, *3330 Garfield St., N.W., Washington, D.C. 20008,* ☎ *(202) 333-6900,* or nearest Consulate General: Los Angeles ☎ *(213) 857-1244,* Atlanta ☎ *(404) 659-2150,* Chicago ☎ *(312) 263-6624* or New York ☎ *(212) 586-5110.*

BELIZE

Passport, return/onward ticket and sufficient funds required. Visa not required for stay up to 30 days. If visit exceeds 1 month, a stay permit must be obtained from the Immigration Authorities in Belize. AIDS test required for those staying more than 3 months; U.S. test accepted if within 3 months of visit. For longer stays and other information contact Embassy of Belize, *2535 Massachusetts Ave., N.W., Washington, D.C. 20008,* ☎ *(202) 332-9636* or the Belize Mission in New York at ☎ *(212) 599-0233.*

COUNTRY	ENTRY
BENIN	Passport and visa required. Entry/transit visa for stay up to 90 days, requires $20 fee (no personal checks), 2 application forms, 2 photos, vaccination certificates for yellow fever and cholera, proof of return/onward transportation (guarantee from travel agency or photocopy of round trip ticket) and letter of guarantee from employer. Send prepaid envelope for return of passport by certified or express mail. Apply at Embassy of the Republic of Benin, *2737 Cathedral Ave., N.W., Washington, D.C. 20008*, ☎ *(202) 232-6656.*
BERMUDA	Proof of U.S. citizenship, photo ID and onward/return ticket required for tourist stay up to 21 days. Departure tax of $10 is paid at airport. For further information consult British Embassy ☎ *(202) 986-0205.*
BHUTAN	Passport and visa required. Visa requires $20 fee, 1 application and 2 photos. Tourist visas arranged by Tourism Department and issued at entry checkpoints in Bhutan. Apply 2 months in advance. Yellow fever vaccination required if traveling from an infected area. For further information call the Consulate of the Kingdom of Bhutan in New York ☎ *(212) 826-1919.*
BOLIVIA	Passport required. Visa not required for tourist stay up to 30 days. Business visa requires $50 fee and company letter explaining purpose of trip. Send SASE for return of passport by mail. AIDS test required for resident visa. U.S. test sometimes accepted. For more information contact Embassy of Bolivia (Consular Section), *3014 Mass. Ave., N.W., Washington, D.C. 20008*, ☎ *(202) 232-4828 or 483-4410* or nearest Consulate General: San Francisco ☎ *(415) 495-5173*, Miami ☎ *(305) 358-3450*, New York ☎ *(212) 687-0530* or Houston ☎ *(713) 780-8001.* (Check special requirements for pets.)
BOSNIA AND HERZEGOVINA	Passport required. At the time of publication, Bosnia-Herzegovina entry permission is being granted at the border on a case by-case basis.
BOTSWANA	Passport required. Visa not required for stay up to 90 days. For further information contact Embassy of the Republic of Botswana, *Suite 7M, 3400 International Drive, N.W., Washington, D.C. 20008*, ☎ *(202) 244-4990/1* or nearest Honorary Consulate: Los Angeles ☎ *(213) 626-8484*, San Francisco ☎ *(415) 346-4435* or Houston ☎ *(713) 622-1900.*
BRAZIL	Passport and visa required. Visa must be obtained in advance. Multiple-entry visa valid up to 90 days (extendable), requires 1 application form, 1 photo, proof of onward/return transportation, and yellow fever vaccination if arriving from infected area. No charge if you apply in person; $10 service fee if you apply by mail. Provide SASE for return of passport by mail. For travel with children or business visa contact Brazilian Embassy (Consular Section), *3009 Whitehaven St., N.W., Washington, D.C. 20008*, ☎ *(202) 745-2828* or nearest Consulate: CA ☎ *(213) 651-2664*, FL ☎ *(305) 285-6200*, IL ☎ *(312) 464-0244*, LA ☎ *(504) 588-9187* or NY ☎ *(212) 757-3080.*

COUNTRY	ENTRY

BRUNEI — Passport required. Visa not required for tourist/business stay up to 90 days. Yellow fever vaccination needed if arriving from infected area. For more information, contact Embassy of the State of Brunei Darussalam, *Suite 300, 2600 Virginia Ave., N.W., Washington, D.C. 20037* ☎ *(202) 342-0159* or Brunei Permanent Mission to the U.N., *866 United Nations Plaza, Rm. 248, New York, NY 10017* ☎ *(212) 838-1600.*

BULGARIA — Passport required. Tourist visa not required for stay up to 30 days. AIDS test may be required for those staying more than 1 month; U.S. test not accepted. For business visas and other information contact Embassy of the Republic of Bulgaria, *1621 22nd St., N.W., Washington, D.C. 20008,* ☎ *(202) 387-7969.*

BURKINA FASO — Passport and visa required. Single-entry visa valid 3 months for visit up to 1 month, extendable, requires $20 fee, 2 application forms, 2 photos and yellow fever vaccination (cholera immunization recommended). Send passport by registered mail and include postage or prepaid envelope for return by mail. Payment accepted in cash or money order only. For further information call Embassy of Burkina Faso, *2340 Mass. Ave., N.W., Washington, D.C. 20008* ☎ *(202) 332-5577,* or Honorary Consulate in Decatur, GA ☎ *(404) 378-7278,* Los Angeles, CA ☎ *(213) 824-5100* or New Orleans, LA ☎ *(504) 945-3152.*

BURMA — (See Myanmar.)

BURUNDI — Passport and visa required. Obtain visa before arrival to avoid long airport delay. Multi-entry visa valid for 2 months (must be used within 2 months of date of issue) requires $11 fee, 3 application forms, 3 photos, yellow fever and cholera immunizations and return/onward ticket (meningitis immunization recommended). Company letter needed for business travel. Send U.S. postal money order only and SASE for return of passport by mail. For further information consult Embassy of the Republic of Burundi, *Suite 212, 2233 Wisconsin Ave., N.W., Washington, D.C. 20007,* ☎ *(202) 342-2574* or Permanent Mission of Burundi to the U.N. ☎ *(212) 687-1180.*

CAMBODIA (formerly Kampuchea) — Passport and visa required. Airport visa valid for a 1 month stay is available upon arrival in Cambodia from the Ministry of National Security; requires $20 fee. Visas can also be obtained from a Cambodian embassy or consulate in a country which maintains diplomatic relations with Cambodia. There is no Cambodian Embassy in the U.S. at this time.

CAMEROON — Passport and visa required. Obtain visa before arrival to avoid difficulty at airport. Multiple-entry tourist visa for stay up to 90 days, requires $65.22 fee, 2 application forms, 2 photos, yellow fever and cholera immunizations, proof of onward/return transportation and bank statement. If invited by family or friends, visa available for up to 3 months, may be extended 1 month. Invitation must be signed by authorities in Cameroon. Multiple-entry business visa, valid 12 months, requires company letter to guarantee financial and legal responsibility; include exact dates of travel. Enclose prepaid envelope for return of passport by registered, certified or express mail. For additional information contact Embassy of the Republic of Cameroon, *2349 Mass. Ave., N.W., Washington, D.C. 20008,* ☎ *(202) 265-8790 to 8794.*

COUNTRY	ENTRY

CANADA

Proof of U.S. citizenship and photo ID required. Visa not required for U.S. tourists entering from the U.S. for a stay up to 180 days. However, anyone with a criminal record (including a DWI charge) should contact the Canadian Embassy or nearest consulate before travel. U.S. citizens entering Canada from a third country must have a valid passport. For student or business travel, check with the Canadian Embassy, *501 Pennsylvania Ave., N.W., Washington, D.C. 20001,* ☎ *(202) 682-1740* or nearest Consulate General: CA ☎ *(213) 687-7432* and *(415) 495-6021,* GA ☎ *(404) 577-6810,* IL ☎ *(312) 427-1031,* MA ☎ *(617) 262-3760,* MI ☎ *(313) 567-2340,* MN ☎ *(612) 333-4641,* NY ☎ *(212) 768-2400* or *(716) 852-1247,* OH ☎ *(216) 771-0150,* TX ☎ *(214) 922-9806* or WA ☎ *(206) 443-1777.*

CAPE VERDE

Passport and visa required. Single-entry tourist visa (must be used within 120 days of issue), requires $11.31 fee, 1 application form, 1 photo and yellow fever immunization if arriving from infected area. Include SASE for return of passport by mail. For further information contact the Embassy of the Republic of Cape Verde, *3415 Mass. Ave., N.W., Washington, D.C. 20007,* ☎ *(202) 965-6820* or Consulate General, *535 Boylston St., Boston, MA 02116* ☎ *(617) 353-0014.*

CAYMAN ISLANDS

(See West Indies, British.)

CENTRAL AFRICAN REPUBLIC

Passport and visa required. Visa must be obtained before arrival. To obtain a visa you need 2 application forms, 2 recent photos, yellow fever immunization, onward/return ticket , SASE for return of passport by mail, and $30 fee. Company letter needed for business visa. For further information contact Embassy of Central African Republic, *1618 22nd St., N.W., Washington, D.C. 20008,* ☎ *(202) 483-7800* or *7801.*

CHAD

Passport and visa required. Transit visa valid for up to 1 week, requires onward ticket. Single-entry visa valid 2 months for tourist/business stay up to 30 days (extendable), requires $25 fee (no personal checks), yellow fever and cholera vaccinations, 3 application forms and 3 photos. For business visa need company letter stating purpose of trip. Send prepaid envelope for registered/certified return of passport. Apply Embassy of the Republic of Chad, *2002 R St., N.W., Washington, D.C. 20009.* ☎ *(202) 462-4009,* and check specific requirements.

CHILE

Passport required. Visa not required for stay up to 3 months, may be extended. For official/diplomatic travel and other information consult Embassy of Chile, *1732 Mass. Ave., N.W., Washington, D.C. 20036,* ☎ *(202) 785-3159* or nearest Consulate General: CA ☎ *(310) 785-0113* and ☎ *(415) 982-7662,* FL ☎ *(305) 373-8623,* PA ☎ *(215) 829-9520,* NY ☎ *(212) 980-3366,* TX ☎ *(713) 621-5853* or PR ☎ *(809) 725-6365.*

COUNTRY	ENTRY
CHINA, PEOPLE'S REPUBLIC OF	Passport and visa required. Transit visa required for any stop (even if you do not exit the plane or train) in China. Visitors must show hotel reservation and letter of confirmation from the China International Travel Service (CITS) or an invitation from an individual or institution in China. CITS tours may be booked through several travel agencies and airlines in the United States and abroad and are often advertised in newspapers and magazines. Visas for tour group members are usually obtained by the travel agent as part of the tour package. Visa requires $10 fee (no personal checks), 2 application forms and 2 photos. Allow at least 10 days processing time. Medical examination required for those staying 1 year or longer. AIDS test required for those staying more than 6 months. For further information contact Chinese Embassy, *2300 Connecticut Avenue, N.W., Washington, D.C. 20008,* ☎ *(202) 328-2517* or nearest Consulate General: Chicago ☎ *(312) 346-0287,* Houston ☎ *(713) 524-4311,* Los Angeles ☎ *(213) 380-2506,* New York ☎ *(212) 330-7409* or San Francisco ☎ *(415) 563-4857.*
COLOMBIA	Passport, proof of onward/return ticket, and entry permit required for tourist/business stay of up to 6 months. Entry permits are granted by the immigration authorities at the port of entry. Minors (under 18) traveling alone, with one parent or in someone else's custody, must present written authorization signed before a notary and authenticated by the Colombian Embassy or Consulate from the absent parent(s) or guardian. Persons suspected of being HIV-positive may be denied entry. For information about longer stays, business and official travel contact Embassy of Colombia (Consulate), *1825 Conn. Ave., N.W., Washington, D.C. 20009,* ☎ *(202) 332-7476,* or nearest Consulate General: CA ☎ *(213) 362-1137* or ☎ *(415) 362-0080,* FL ☎ *(305) 448-5558,* GA ☎ *(404) 237-1045,* IL ☎ *(312) 341-0658/9,* LA ☎ *(504) 525-5580,* MA ☎ *(617) 536-6222,* MI ☎ *(313) 352-4970,* MN ☎ *(612) 933-2408,* MO ☎ *(314) 991-3636,* OH ☎ *(216) 943-1200,* NY ☎ *(212) 949-9898,* PR ☎ *(809) 754-6885* or TX ☎ *(713) 527-8919.*
COMOROS ISLANDS	Passport and onward/return ticket required. Visa for up to 3 weeks (extendable) issued at airport upon arrival. For further information consult Embassy of the Federal and Islamic Republic of Comoros, *336 East 45th St., 2nd Floor, New York, NY 10017,* ☎ *(212) 972-8010.*
CONGO	Passport and visa required. Single-entry $30 or multiple-entry $50, for tourist/business stay up to 3 months, requires yellow fever and cholera immunizations and onward/return ticket. First-time applicants need 3 application forms and 3 photos, returning visitors need only 2. For business visa must have company letter stating reason for trip. Include SASE for return of passport by mail. Letter of introduction stating reason for trip, 3 applications and 3 photos required. Apply Embassy of the People's Republic of the Congo, *4891 Colorado Ave., N.W., Washington, D.C. 20011,* ☎ *(202) 726-5500* or the Permanent Mission of the Congo to the UN, *14 East 65th St. New York, NY 10021* ☎ *(212) 744-7840.*
COOK ISLANDS	Passport and onward/return ticket required. Visa not needed for visit up to 31 days. For longer stays and further information contact Consulate for the Cook Islands, Kamehameha Schools, #16, *Kapalama Heights, Honolulu, HI 96817,* ☎ *(808) 847-6377.*

COUNTRY	ENTRY

COSTA RICA — Passport required. Travelers are sometimes admitted with (original) certified U.S. birth certificate and photo ID for tourist stay up to 90 days. Tourist card issued upon arrival at airport. U.S. citizens must have onward/return ticket. For stays over 90 days, you must apply for an extension (within the first week of visit) with Costa Rican Immigration and, after 90 days, obtain exit visa and possess a valid U.S. passport. Visitors staying over 90 days must have an AIDS test performed in Costa Rica. For travel with pets and other information contact the Consular Section of the Embassy of Costa Rica, *1825 Conn. Ave., N.W., Suite 211, Washington, D.C. 20009,* ☎ *(202) 328-6628* or nearest Consulate General: CA ☎ *(415) 392-8488,* GA ☎ *(404) 370-0555,* FL ☎ *(305) 377-4242,* IL ☎ *(312) 263-2772,* LA ☎ *(504) 467-1462,* NY ☎ *(212) 425-2620* or TX ☎ *(713) 266-0485.*

COTE D' IVOIRE (formerly Ivory Coast) — Passport required. Visa not required for stay up to 90 days. Visa $33, requires 4 application forms, 4 photos, yellow fever vaccination, onward/return ticket and financial guarantee. Include postage for return of passport by registered mail. For further information contact Embassy of the Republic of Cote D' Ivoire, *2424 Mass. Ave., N.W., Washington, D.C. 20008* ☎ *(202) 797-0300* or Honorary Consulate: CA ☎ *(415) 391-0176.*

CROATIA — Passport and visa required. Visa can be obtained at port of entry. There is no charge for business or tourist visa. Check requirements with Embassy of Croatia, *236 Massachusetts Ave., N.E., Washington, D.C. 20002,* ☎ *(202) 543-5580 or 5586.*

CUBA — Passport and visa required. Tourist visa $26, business visa $36, valid up to 6 months, requires 1 application and photo. Send money order only and SASE for return of passport. Apply Cuban Interests Section, *2639 16th Street, N.W., Washington, D.C. 20009,* ☎ *(202) 797-8609 or 8518.* AIDS test required for those staying longer than 90 days. Attention: U.S. citizens need a Treasury Dept. license in order to engage in any transactions related to travel to and within Cuba. Before planning any travel to Cuba, U.S. citizens should contact the Licensing Division, Office of Foreign Assets Control, Department of the Treasury, *1331 G St., N.W., Washington, D.C. 20220,* ☎ *(202) 622-2480.*

CURACAO — (See Netherlands Antilles.)

CYPRUS — Passport required. Tourist/business visa issued on arrival for stay up to 3 months. Departure tax of $8 paid at airport. AIDS test required for certain entertainers; U.S. test accepted. For other information consult Embassy of the Republic of Cyprus, *2211 R St., N.W., Washington, D.C. 20008* ☎ *(202) 462-5772* or nearest Consulate: CA ☎ *(213) 397-0771,* LA ☎ *(504) 388-8701* or New York ☎ *(212) 686-6016.*

CZECH REPUBLIC — Passport required. Visa not required for stay up to 30 days. All foreigners must register with the proper authorities within 48 hours of arrival. For more information contact Embassy of the Czech Republic, *3900 Spring of Freedom Street., N.W., Washington, D.C. 20008* ☎ *(202) 363-6315.*

COUNTRY	ENTRY

DENMARK (including GREENLAND)

Passport required. Tourist/business visa not required for stay of up to 3 months. (Period begins when entering Scandinavian area: Finland, Iceland, Norway, Sweden.) Special rules apply for entry into the U.S.-operated defense area in Greenland. For further information contact the Royal Danish Embassy, *3200 Whitehaven St., N.W., Washington, D.C. 20008* ☎ *(202) 234-4300* or nearest Consulate General: CA ☎ *(213) 387-4277*, Chicago ☎ *(312) 329-9644* or New York ☎ *(212) 223-4545*.

DJIBOUTI

Passport and visa required. Visas must be obtained before arrival. Single-entry visa valid for 30 days, extendable, requires $15 fee, 2 applications, 2 photos, yellow fever immunization, onward/return ticket and sufficient funds. Company letter needed for business visa. Send prepaid envelope for return of passport by registered, certified, or express mail. Apply Embassy of the Republic of Djibouti, *1156 15th St., N.W., Suite 515, Washington, D.C. 20005* ☎ *(202) 331-0270* or the Djibouti Mission to the U.N., *866 United Nations Plaza, Suite 4011, New York, NY 10017* ☎ *(212) 753-3163*.

DOMINICA

Proof of U.S. citizenship, photo ID and return/onward ticket required for tourist stay up to 6 months. For longer stays and other information consult Consulate of the Commonwealth of Dominica, *820 2nd Ave., Suite 900, New York, NY 10017* ☎ *(212) 599-8478*.

DOMINICAN REPUBLIC

Passport or proof of U.S. citizenship and tourist card or visa required. Tourist card for stay up to 2 months, available from Consulate or from airline serving the Dominican Republic, $10 fee. Visa issued by Consulate, valid up to 5 years, no charge. All persons must pay $10 airport departure fee. AIDS test required for residence permit. U.S. test not accepted. For business travel and other information call the Embassy of the Dominican Republic, *1715 22nd St., N.W., Washington, D.C. 20008* ☎ *(202) 332-6280*, or nearest Consulate General: CA ☎ *(415) 982-5144*, FL ☎ *(305) 358-3221*, IL ☎ *(312) 772-6363*, LA ☎ *(504) 522-1007*, MA ☎ *(617) 482-8121*, NY ☎ *(212) 768-2480*, PA ☎ *(215) 923-3006* or PR ☎ *(809) 725-9550*.

ECUADOR

Passport and return/onward ticket required for stay up to 3 months. For additional information contact the Embassy of Ecuador, *2535 15th St., N.W., Washington, D.C. 20009* ☎ *(202) 234-7166* or nearest Consulate General: CA ☎ *(213) 628-3014* or ☎ *(510) 223-2162*, FL ☎ *(305) 539-8214*, IL ☎ *(312) 329-0266*, LA ☎ *(504) 523-3229*, MA ☎ *(617) 523-2700*, MD ☎ *(301) 889-4435*, MI ☎ *(313) 332-7356*, NV ☎ *(702) 735-8193*, NY ☎ *(212) 683-0170/71*, PR ☎ *(809) 781-4408*, or TX ☎ *(214) 747-6329*.

COUNTRY	ENTRY
EGYPT	Passport and visa required. Transit visa for stay up to 48 hours available. Tourist visa, valid 3 months, requires $15 fee (cash or money order), 1 application form and 1 photo. Visa may be issued at airport upon arrival for fee of $20. For business travel, need company letter stating purpose of trip. Enclose prepaid envelope for return of passport by certified mail. Proof of yellow fever immunization required if arriving from infected area. AIDS test required for workers and students staying over 30 days. Register with local authorities or at hotel within 7 days of arrival. Travelers must declare foreign currency on Form "D" on arrival and show Form "D" and bank receipts upon departure. Maximum Egyptian currency allowed into and out of Egypt is LE20. For additional information consult Embassy of the Arab Republic of Egypt, *2310 Decatur Pl., N.W., Washington, D.C. 20008* ☎ *(202) 234-3903* or nearest Consulate General: CA ☎ *(415) 346-9700*, IL ☎ *(312) 443-1190*, NY ☎ *(212) 759-7120* or Houston ☎ *(713) 961-4915.*
EL SALVADOR	Passport and visa required. (Length of validity of visa will be determined by immigration authorities upon arrival.) Requires 1 application form and 2 photos. Allow 3 working days for processing. Send SASE for return of passport by mail. AIDS test required for premanent residence permit. U.S. test not accepted. Apply Consulate General of El Salvador, *1010 16th St., N.W., 3rd Floor, Washington, D.C. 20036* ☎ *(202) 331-4032* or nearest Consulate: CA ☎ *(213) 383-5776 or (415) 781-7924*, FL ☎ *(305) 371-8850*, LA ☎ *(504) 522-4266*, NY ☎ *(212) 889-3608* or TX ☎ *(713) 270-6239.*
ENGLAND	(See United Kingdom.)
EQUATORIAL GUINEA	Passport and visa required. Obtain visa in advance. For further information contact the residence of the Ambassador of Equatorial Guinea at *57 Magnolia Ave., Mount Vernon, NY* ☎ *(914) 667-9664.*
ERITREA	Passport and visa required. Tourist/business visa valid for a stay of up to 6 months, requires 1 application, 2 photos, $25 fee (no personal checks). Business visa can be extended up to 1 year, requires company letter stating purpose of travel. Include SASE for return of passport by mail. Allow 3 working days for processing. For more information contact the Embassy of Eritrea, *910 17th St., NW, Suite 400, Washington, D.C. 20006* ☎ *(202) 429-1991.*
ESTONIA	Passport required. Visas not required for stay of up to 90 days. AIDS test required for residency and work permits. U.S. test sometimes accepted. For further information check Embassy of the Republic of Estonia, *9 Rockefeller Plaza, Suite J-1421, New York, NY 10020* ☎ *(212) 247-1450.*
ETHIOPIA	Passport and visa required. Tourist/business visa valid for stay up to 2 years, fee $50 or transit visa for 48 hours, $20, requires 1 application, 1 photo and yellow fever immunization. Business visa requires company letter. Send $2 postage for return of passport or $15.30 for Federal Express and $9.95 for Express Mail service. (Money orders only.) Allow 2 weeks for processing. Exit visas are required of all visitors remaining in Ethiopia for more than 30 days. For longer stays and other information contact Embassy of Ethiopia, *2134 Kalorama Rd., N.W., Washington, D.C. 20008* ☎ *(202) 234-2281/2.*

COUNTRY	ENTRY

FIJI
Passport, proof of sufficient funds and onward/return ticket required. Visa issued on arrival for stay up to 30 days and may be extended up to 6 months. For further information contact Embassy of Fiji, *2233 Wisconsin Ave., N.W., #240, Washington, D.C. 20007* ☎ *(202) 337-8320*, or Mission to the U.N., *One United Nations Plaza, 26th Floor, New York, NY 10017* ☎ *(212) 355-7316.*

FINLAND
Passport required. Tourist/business visa not required for stay up to 90 days. (90 day period begins when entering Scandinavian area: Sweden, Norway, Denmark, Iceland.) Check Embassy of Finland, *3216 New Mexico Ave., N.W., Washington, D.C. 20016* ☎ *(202) 363-2430* or nearest Consulate General: Los Angeles ☎ *(310) 203-9903* or New York ☎ *(212) 573-6007.*

FRANCE
Passport required to visit France, Andorra, Monaco, Corsica and French Polynesia. Visa not required for tourist/business stay up to 3 months in France, Andorra, Monaco and Corsica, and 1 month in French Polynesia (officials/diplomats, journalists on assignment, ship or plane crew members, and students are required to obtain a visa in advance). For further information consult Embassy of France, *4101 Reservoir Rd., N.W., Washington, D.C. 20007* ☎ *(202) 944-6200/6215*, or nearest Consulate: CA ☎ *(310) 479-4426 or (415) 397-4330*, FL ☎ *(305) 372-9798*, GA ☎ *(404) 522-4226*, HI ☎ *(808) 599-4458*, IL ☎ *(312) 787-5359*, LA ☎ *(504) 523-5774*, ME ☎ *(617) 482-3650*, MI ☎ *(313) 568-0990*, NY ☎ *(212) 606-3600*, PR ☎ *(809) 753-1700* or TX ☎ *(713) 528-2181.*

FRENCH GUIANA
Proof of U.S. citizenship and photo ID required for visit up to 3 weeks. (For stays longer than 3 weeks, a passport is required.) No visa required for stay up to 3 months. For further information consult Embassy of France, *4101 Reservoir Rd., N.W., Washington, D.C. 20007* ☎ *(202) 944-6200/6215.*

FRENCH POLYNESIA
Includes Society Islands, French Southern and Antarctic Lands, Tuamotu, Gambier, French Austral, Marquesas, Kerguelen, Crozet, New Caledonia, Tahiti, Wallis and Furtuna Islands. Passport required. Visa not required for visit up to 1 month. For longer stays and further information consult Embassy of France ☎ *(202) 944-6200/6215.*

GABON
Passport and visa required. Visas must be obtained before arrival. Single-entry visa valid up to 1 month, multiple-entry visa valid for 2-4 months. Both visas require 2 application forms, 2 photos, small pox and yellow fever vaccinations, and $50 fee (no personal checks accepted). Also need detailed travel arrangements, including flight numbers, arrival and departure dates, accommodations and next destination. Business visa requires company letter stating purpose of trip and contacts in Gabon. Accompanying family must be included in letter. For longer stays and other information call Embassy of the Gabonese Republic, *2034 20th St., N.W., Washington, D.C. 20009*, ☎ *(202) 797-1000*, or the Permanent Mission of the Gabonese Republic to the UN, *18 East 41st St., 6th Floor, New York, NY 10017*, ☎ *(212) 686-9720.*

GALAPAGOS ISLANDS
Passport and onward/return ticket required for visits up to 3 months. For further information consult Embassy of Ecuador ☎ *(202) 234-7166.*

COUNTRY	ENTRY

GAMBIA

Passport and visa required. Tourist/business visa for a stay of up to 3 months, requires 1 application, 1 photo, and yellow fever immunization certificate (no fee. For business visa, you also need company letter stating purpose of visit and itinerary. Allow at least 2 working days for processing. Include prepaid envelope for return of passport by mail. Apply Embassy of the Gambia, *Suite 720, 1030 15th St., N.W., Washington, D.C. 20005* ☎ *(202) 785-1399* or Permanent Mission of The Gambia to the U.N., *820 2nd Ave., 9th floor, New York, NY 10017*, ☎ *(212) 949-6640.*

GEORGIA

Passport, visa and letter of invitation (issued upon arrival) required. For additional information contact the Embassy of the Republic of Georgia, *Suite 424, 1511 K St., N.W., Washington, D.C. 20005*, ☎ *(202) 393-6060.*

GERMANY

Passport required. Tourist/business visa not required for stay up to 3 months. For longer stays, obtain temporary residence permit upon arrival. AIDS test required of applicants for Bavaria residence permits staying over 180 days; U.S. test not accepted. Every foreigner entering Germany is required to provide proof of sufficient health insurance. For further information contact the Embassy of the Federal Republic of Germany, *4645 Reservoir Rd., N.W., Washington, D.C. 20007*, ☎ *(202) 298-4000* or nearest Consulate General: CA ☎ *(415) 775-1061*, FL ☎ *(305) 358-0290*, GA ☎ *(404) 659-4760*, IL ☎ *(312) 263-0850*, MA ☎ *(617) 536-4414*, MI ☎ *(313) 962-6526*, NY ☎ *(212) 308-8700* or TX ☎ *(713) 627-7770.*

GHANA

Passport and visa required. Tourist visa required for stay up to 30 days (extendable). Requires 1 application form, 4 photos, copy of onward/return ticket, bank statement or pay stub and yellow fever immunization. Single-entry visa requires $20 fee, multiple-entry $50. Allow 3 working days for processing. Include prepaid envelope for return of passport by certified mail. For additional information contact Embassy of Ghana, *3512 International Drive, N.W., Washington, D.C. 20008*, ☎ *(202) 686-4520* or Consulate General, *19 East 47th St., New York, NY 10017* ☎ *(212) 832-1300.*

GIBRALTAR

Passport required. Visa not required for tourist stay up to 3 months. For further information consult British Embassy ☎ *(202) 986-0205.*

GILBERT ISLANDS (See Kiribati.)

GREAT BRITAIN AND NORTHERN IRELAND (See United Kingdom.)

GREECE

Passport required. Visa not required for tourist/business stay up to 3 months. If traveling on diplomatic/official passport, visa required and must be obtained in advance. AIDS test required for performing artists and students on Greek scholarships; U.S. test not accepted. For additional information consult Consular Section of the Embassy of Greece, *2221 Mass. Ave., N.W., Washington, D.C. 20008* ☎ *(202) 232-8222* or nearest Consulate: CA ☎ *(213) 385-1447* or ☎ *(415) 775-2102*, GA ☎ *(404) 261-3313*, IL ☎ *(312) 372-5356*, LA ☎ *(504) 523-1167*, MA ☎ *(617) 542-3240*, NY ☎ *(212) 988-5500* or TX ☎ *(713) 840-7522.*

COUNTRY	ENTRY

GREENLAND (See Denmark.)

GRENADA Passport is recommended, but tourists may enter with birth certificate and photo ID. Visa not required for tourist stay up to 3 months, may be extended to maximum of 6 months. For additional information consult Embassy of Grenada, *1701 New Hampshire Ave., N.W., Washington, D.C. 20009* ☎ *(202) 265-2561* or Permanent Mission of Grenada to the U.N. ☎ *(212) 599-0301.*

GUADELOUPE (See West Indies, French.)

GUATEMALA Passport and visa or tourist card required. Visas no charge, valid 1 year, multiple entries of 30 days each, requires passport, 1 application form, 1 photo and $5 fee. Provide SASE for return of passport by mail. For travel by minors and information about tourist cards contact the Embassy of Guatemala, *2220 R St., N.W., Washington, D.C. 20008* ☎ *(202) 745-4952,* or nearest Consulate: CA ☎ *(213) 365-9251/2 or (415) 788-5651,* FL ☎ *(305) 443-4828/29,* IL ☎ *(312) 332-1587,* NY ☎ *(212) 686-3837* or TX ☎ *(713) 953-9531.*

GUIANA, FRENCH (See French Guiana.)

GUINEA Passport and visa required. Tourist/business visa for stay up to 3 months, requires 3 application forms, 3 photos, yellow fever immunization and $25 fee (cash or money order only). Malaria suppressants are highly recommended. For business visa need company letter stating purpose of trip and letter of invitation from company in Guinea. Provide SASE for return of passport by mail. For more information contact the Embassy of the Republic of Guinea, *2112 Leroy Pl., N.W., Washington, D.C. 20008* ☎ *(202) 483-9420.*

GUINEA-BISSAU Passport and visa required. Visa must be obtained in advance. Visa valid up to 90 days, requires 2 application forms, 2 photos, health certificate, financial guarantee to cover stay, letter staying purpose of travel and $12 fee (payment by money order only). Include prepaid envelope for return of passport by express mail. Apply Embassy of Guinea-Bissau, *918 16th St., N.W., Mezzanine Suite, Washington, D.C. 20006* ☎ *(202) 872-4222.*

GUYANA Passport required. For more information consult Embassy of Guyana, *2490 Tracy Pl., N.W., Washington, D.C. 20008* ☎ *(202) 265-6900/03* or Consulate General, *866 U.N. Plaza, 3rd Floor, New York, NY 10017* ☎ *(212) 527-3215.*

HAITI Passport required. For further information consult Embassy of Haiti, *2311 Mass. Ave., N.W., Washington, D.C. 20008* ☎ *(202) 332-4090* or nearest Consulate: FL ☎ *(305) 859-2003,* MA ☎ *(617) 723-5211,* NY ☎ *(212) 697-9767* or PR ☎ *(809) 766-0758.*

HOLY SEE, APOSTOLIC NUN-CIATURE OF THE Passport required (for entry into Italy). For further information consult Apostolic Nunciature of the Holy See, *3339 Mass. Ave., N.W., Washington, D.C. 20008* ☎ *(202) 333-7121* or call Embassy of Italy, ☎ *(202) 328-5500.*

COUNTRY	ENTRY
HONDURAS	Passport and onward/return ticket required. For additional information contact Embassy of Honduras (Consular Section), *Suite 319, 1612 K Street., N.W., Washington, D.C. 20006* ☎ *(202) 223-0185* or nearest Consulate: CA ☎ *(213) 383-9244* and *(415) 392-0076*, FL ☎ *(305) 447-8927*, IL ☎ *(312) 772-7090*, LA ☎ *(504) 522-3118*, NY ☎ *(212) 269-3611* or TX ☎ *(713) 622-4572.*
HONG KONG	Passport and onward/return transportation by sea/air required. Visa not required for tourist stay up to 30 days, may be extended to 3 months. Confirmed hotel and flight reservations recommended during peak travel months. Departure tax 150 Hong Kong dollars (approx. $20 U.S.) paid at airport. Visa required for work or study. For other types of travel consult British Embassy ☎ *(202) 986-0205.*
HUNGARY	Passport required. Visa not required for stay up to 90 days. For business travel and other information check Embassy of the Republic of Hungary, *3910 Shoemaker Street, N.W., Washington, D.C. 20008,* ☎ *(202) 362-6730* or Consulate General, *8 East 75th Street, New York, NY 10021* ☎ *(212) 879-4127.*
ICELAND	Passport required. Visa not required for stay up to 3 months. (Period begins when entering Scandinavian area: Denmark, Finland, Norway, Sweden.) For additional information call Embassy of Iceland, *2022 Conn. Ave., N.W., Washington, D.C. 20008,* ☎ *(202) 265-6653-5* or Consulate General in New York ☎ *(212) 686-4100.*
INDIA	Passport and visa required. Obtain visa in advance. Tourist visa valid for stay up to 1 month, requires $5 fee, up to 6 months $25 fee and up to 12 months $50 fee, 1 application form, 2 photos, onward/return ticket and proof of sufficient funds. Visa must be obtained before arrival. Business visa requires $50 fee, 2 application forms, 2 photos and company letter stating purpose of trip and itinerary. Include prepaid envelope for return of passport by certified mail. Allow 2 weeks for processing. Yellow fever immunization needed if arriving from infected area. AIDS test required for all students and anyone over 18 staying more than 1 year; U.S. test sometimes accepted. Check requirements with Embassy of India, *2536 Mass. Ave., N.W., Washington, D.C. 20008,* ☎ *(202) 939-9839/9850* or nearest Consulate General: Chicago ☎ *(312) 781-6280*, New York ☎ *(212) 879-7800* or San Francisco ☎ *(415) 668-0683.*
INDONESIA	Valid passport and onward/return ticket required. Visa not required for tourist stay up to 2 months (non-extendable). For longer stays and additional information consult Embassy of the Republic of Indonesia, *2020 Mass. Ave., N.W., Washington, D.C. 20036,* ☎ *(202) 775-5200* or nearest Consulate: CA ☎ *(213) 383-5126* or *(415) 474-9571*, IL ☎ *(312) 938-0101*, NY ☎ *(212) 879-0600* or TX ☎ *(713) 626-3291.*
IRAN	Passport and visa required. The United States does not maintain diplomatic or consular relations with Iran. Travel by U.S. citizens is not recommended. For visa information contact Embassy of Pakistan, Iranian Interests Section, *2209 Wisconsin Ave., N.W., Washington, D.C. 20007,* ☎ *(202) 965-4990.*

COUNTRY	ENTRY

IRAQ
Passport and visa required. AIDS test required for stay over 5 days. The United States suspended diplomatic and consular operations in Iraq in 1990. Since February 1991, U.S. passports are not valid for travel in, to, or through Iraq without authorization from the Department of State. Application for exemptions to this restriction should be submitted in writing to Passport Services, U.S. Department of State, *1425 K St., N.W., Washington, D.C. 20524, Attn: CA/PPT/C, Room 300*. Attention: U.S. citizens need a Treasury Dept. license in order to engage in any transactions related to travel to and within Iraq. Before planning any travel to Iraq, U.S. citizens should contact the Licensing Division, Office of Foreign Assets Control, Department of the Treasury, *1331 G St., N.W., Washington, D.C. 20220,* ☎ *(202) 622-2480.* For visa information contact a country that maintains diplomatic relations with Iraq.

IRELAND
Passport required. Tourists are not required to obtain visas for stays under 90 days, but may be asked to show onward/return ticket. For further information consult Embassy of Ireland, *2234 Mass. Ave., N.W., Washington, D.C. 20008,* ☎ *(202) 462-3939* or nearest Consulate General: CA ☎ *(415) 392-4214,* IL ☎ *(312) 337-1868,* MA ☎ *(617) 267-9330* or NY ☎ *(212) 319-2555.*

ISRAEL
Passport, onward/return ticket and proof of sufficient funds required. Tourist visa issued upon arrival valid for 3 months, but can be renewed. Departure tax $15 payable at airport. Consult Embassy of Israel, *3514 International Dr., N.W., Washington, D.C. 20008,* ☎ *(202) 364-5500* or nearest Consulate General: CA ☎ *(213) 651-5700* and ☎ *(415) 398-8885,* FL ☎ *(305) 358-8111,* GA ☎ *(404) 875-7851,* IL ☎ *(312) 565-3300,* MA ☎ *(617) 542-0041,* NY ☎ *(212) 351-5200,* PA ☎ *(215) 546-5556* or TX ☎ *(713) 627-3780.*

ITALY
Passport required. Visa not required for tourist stay up to 3 months. For longer stays, employment or study, obtain visa in advance. For additional information consult Embassy of Italy, *1601 Fuller St., N.W., Washington, D.C. 20009,* ☎ *(202) 328-5500* or nearest Consulate General: CA ☎ *(310) 820-0622* or ☎ *(415) 931-4924,* FL ☎ *(305) 374-6322,* IL ☎ *(312) 467-1550,* LA ☎ *(504) 524-2272,* MA ☎ *(617) 542-0483/4,* MI ☎ *(313) 963-8560,* NJ ☎ *(201) 643-1448,* NY ☎ *(212) 737-9100,* PA ☎ *(215) 592-7329* or TX ☎ *(713) 850-7520.*

IVORY COAST
(See Cote d' Ivoire.)

JAMAICA
Passport (or original birth certificate and photo ID), onward/return ticket and proof of sufficient funds required. (Photo ID is not required for U.S. citizens under 16 using birth certificate.) Tourist card issued on arrival for stay up to 6 months; must be returned to immigration authorities on departure. For business or study, visa must be obtained in advance, no charge. Departure tax $15 paid at airport. Check information with Embassy of Jamaica, *Suite 355, 1850 K St., N.W., Washington, D.C. 20006* ☎ *(202) 452-0660* or nearest Consulate: CA ☎ *(213) 380-9471* or *(415) 886-6061,* FL ☎ *(305) 374-8431,* GA ☎ *(404) 593-1500,* IL ☎ *(312) 663-0023* or NY ☎ *(212) 935-9000.*

COUNTRY	ENTRY

JAPAN

Passport and onward/return ticket required. Visa not required for tourist/business stay up to 90 days. Departure tax $15.50 paid at airport. For specific information consult Embassy of Japan, *2520 Mass. Ave., N.W., Washington, D.C. 20008* ☎ *(202) 939-6800* or nearest Consulate: AK ☎ *(907) 279-8428*, CA ☎ *(213) 624-8305 or (415) 777-3533*, FL ☎ *(305) 530-9090*, GA ☎ *(404) 892-2700*, Guam ☎ *(671) 646-1290*, HI ☎ *(808) 536-2226*, IL ☎ *(312) 280-0400*, LA ☎ *(504) 529-2101*, MA ☎ *(617) 973-9772*, MI ☎ *(313) 567-0120*, MO ☎ *(816) 471-0111*, NY ☎ *(212) 371-8222*, OR ☎ *(503) 221-1811*, TX ☎ *(713) 652-2977* or WA ☎ *(206) 682-9107*.

JORDAN

Passport and visa required. Visa requires 1 application form, 1 photo, letter stating purpose of visit and itinerary. Entry into Jordan is sometimes denied to persons holding passports with Israeli visas stamps. (This is especially true when the holders are U.S./Jordanian dual nationals.) Send SASE for return of passport by mail. For details check Embassy of the Hashemite Kingdom of Jordan, *3504 International Dr., N.W., Washington, D.C. 20008* ☎ *(202) 966-2664*.

KAZAKHSTAN

Passport and visa required. For additional information contact the Embassy of Kazakhstan, *3421 Mass. Ave., N.W., Washington, D.C. 20007* ☎ *(202) 333-4504 or 07*.

KENYA

Passport and visa required. Visa must be obtained in advance. Single-entry visa for tourist/business stay up to 6 months, $10 (money order only); requires 1 application form, 2 photos and onward/return ticket. Yellow fever immunization is recommend. Anti-malaria pills are recommended for those travelling to the western or coastal regions. Multiple-entry business visa valid for up to 1 year, $50. Payment by cashiers check or money order only. Airport departure tax is $20. Consult the Embassy of Kenya, *2249 R St., N.W., Washington, D.C. 20008* ☎ *(202) 387-6101* or Consulate General: Los Angeles ☎ *(310) 274-6635* or New York ☎ *(212) 486-1300*.

KIRIBATI (formerly Gilbert Islands)

Passport and visa required. For additional information consult British Embassy ☎ *(202) 462-1340*.

KOREA, DEMOCRATIC PEOPLE'S REPUBLIC OF (North Korea)

The United States does not maintain diplomatic or consular relations with North Korea and has no third country representing U.S. interests there. Attention: U.S. citizens need a Treasury Dept. license in order to engage in any transactions related to travel to and within North Korea. Before planning any travel to North Korea, U.S. citizens should contact the Licensing Division, Office of Foreign Assets Control, Department of the Treasury, *1331 G St., N.W., Washington, D.C. 20220* ☎ *(202) 622-2480*. Visa information must be obtained from a consulate in a country that maintains diplomatic relations with North Korea.

COUNTRY	ENTRY

KOREA, REPUBLIC OF (South Korea) — Passport required. Visa not required for a tourist stay up to 15 days. For longer stays and other types of travel, visa must be obtained in advance. Tourist visa for longer stay requires 1 application form and 1 photo. Business visa requires 1 application form, 1 photo and company letter. Fine imposed for overstaying visa and for long-term visa holders not registered within 60 days after entry. AIDS test required for anyone staying over 90 days. U.S. test accepted. For further information check Embassy of the Republic of Korea, (Consular Division), *2600 Virginia Ave., N.W., Suite 208, Washington, D.C. 20037* ☎ *(202) 939-5660/63* or nearest Consulate General: AK ☎ *(907) 561-5488*, CA ☎ *(213) 385-9300* and *(415) 921-2251*, FL ☎ *(305) 372-1555*, GA ☎ *(404) 522-1611*, Guam ☎ *(671) 472-6109*, HI ☎ *(808) 595-6109*, IL ☎ *(312) 822-9485*, MA ☎ *(617) 348-3660*, NY ☎ *(212) 752-1700*, TX ☎ *(713) 961-0186* or WA ☎ *(206) 441-1011.*

KUWAIT — Passport and visa required. AIDS test required for work visa; U.S. test accepted. For further information contact the Embassy of the State of Kuwait, *2940 Tilden St., N.W., Washington, D.C. 20008* ☎ *(202) 966-0702* or Consulate, *321 East 44th St., New York, NY 10017* ☎ *(212) 973-4318.*

KYRGYZ REPUBLIC (Kyrgyzstan) — Passport and visa required. Visa requires 1 application form, 2 photos, (a letter of invitation from a Kyrgyz citizen or organization if staying more then 21 days). Multi-entry visa $100 (no personal checks). Include SASE for return of passport by mail (or proper fee for express mail service). For additional information contact the Embassy of the Kyrgyz Republic, *1511 K St., N.W., Suite 707, Washington, D.C. 20005* ☎ *(202) 628-0433.*

LAOS — Passport and visa required. Visa requires $35 fee, 3 application forms, 3 photos, onward/return transportation, sufficient funds, cholera immunization and SASE for return of passport by mail. Transit visas for stay up to 5 days requires onward/return ticket and visa for next destination. Visitor visa are issued for 1 entry and must be used within 3 months of issue date. Period of stay: 1 month, can be extended for another 30 days (visitor visa application must be accompanied by letter from relative or friends in Laos). Tourist visas are issued only to those who apply through a tourist agency. Business visa requires letter from counterpart in Laos and is valid for 1 entry and must be used within 3 months of issue date. Period of stay: 1 month, can be extended for another 30 days. For more information, check with the Embassy of the Lao People's Democratic Republic, *2222 S St., N.W., Washington, D.C. 20008* ☎ *(202) 332-6416/7.*

LATVIA — Passport and visa required. Tourist/business visa issued at Embassy or point of entry. Require 1 application form, 1 photo, and $5 fee. For further information contact Embassy of Latvia, *4325 17th St., N.W., Washington, D.C. 20011* ☎ *(202) 726-8213.*

COUNTRY	ENTRY

LEBANON

Passport and visa required. AIDS test required for those seeking residence permits; U.S. test accepted. Since January 1987, U.S. passports are not valid for travel in, to, or through Lebanon without authorization from the Department of State. Application for exemptions to this restriction should be submitted in writing to Passport Services, U.S. Department of State, *1425 K St., N.W., Washington, D.C. 20524, Attn: CA/PPT/C, Room 300.* For further visa information contact Embassy of Lebanon, *2560 28th St., N.W., Washington, D.C. 20008* ☎ *(202) 939-6300* or nearest Consulate General: Los Angeles ☎ *(213) 467-1253*, Detroit ☎ *(313) 567-0233* or New York ☎ *(212) 744-7905.*

LEEWARD ISLANDS

(See Virgin Islands, British.)

LESOTHO

Passport and visa required. Visa requires 1 form. Single-entry visa requires $5 fee and multiple-entry $10. For more information, check Embassy of the Kingdom of Lesotho, *2511 Mass. Ave., N.W., Washington, D.C. 20008* ☎ *(202) 797-5533.*

LIBERIA

Passport and visa required. Transit visitors with onward ticket can remain at airport up to 48 hours. Other travelers must obtain visas before arrival. Tourist/business entry visa valid 3 months, no fee, requires 2 application forms, 2 photos, cholera and yellow fever vaccinations and medical certificate to confirm that traveler is in good health and free of any communicable disease. Company letter needed for business visa. Include SASE for return of passport by mail. Obtain exit permit from immigration authorities upon arrival, 1 photo required. For business requirements call Embassy of the Republic of Liberia, *5201 16th St., N.W., Washington, D.C. 20011* ☎ *(202) 723-0437* or nearest Consulate: CA ☎ *(213) 277-7692*, GA ☎ *(404) 753-4754*, IL ☎ *(312) 643-8635*, LA ☎ *(504) 523-7784*, MI ☎ *(313) 342-3900* or NY ☎ *(212) 687-1025.*

LIBYA

Passport and visa required. AIDS test required for those seeking residence permits; U.S. test accepted. Since December 1981, U.S. passports are not valid for travel in, to, or through Libya without authorization from the Department of State. Application for exemptions to this restriction should be submitted in writing to Passport Services, U.S. Department of State, *1425 K St., N.W., Washington, D.C. 20524, Attn: CA/PPT/C, Room 300.* Attention: U.S. citizens need a Treasury Dept. license in order to engage in any transactions related to travel to and within Libya. Before planning any travel to Libya, U.S. citizens should contact the Licensing Division, Office of Foreign Assets Control, Department of the Treasury, *1331 G St., N.W., Washington, D.C. 20220* ☎ *(202) 622-2480.* Application and inquiries for visas must be made through a country that maintains diplomatic relations with Libya.

LIECHTENSTEIN

Passport required. Visa not required for tourist/business stay up to 3 months. For further information consult the Swiss Embassy ☎ *(202) 745-7900.*

LITHUANIA

Passport and visa required. Visa requires 1 application form and $25 fee. AIDS test required for pemanent residence permits. U.S. test sometimes accepted. For further information contact Embassy of Lithuania, *2622 16th St., N.W., Washington, D.C. 20009* ☎ *(202) 234-5860.*

COUNTRY	ENTRY

LUXEMBOURG — Passport required. Visa not required for tourist/business stay up to 3 months. For additional information contact Embassy of Luxembourg, *2200 Mass. Ave., N.W., Washington, D.C. 20008* ☎ *(202) 265-4171* or the nearest Consulate: CA ☎ *(415) 788-0816*, FL ☎ *(305) 373-1300*, GA ☎ *(404) 668-9811*, IL ☎ *(312) 726-0355*, MO ☎ *(816) 474-4761*, NY ☎ *(212) 888-6664* or OH ☎ *(312) 726-0355.*

MACAU — Passport required. Visa not required for visits up to 60 days. For further information consult nearest Portuguese Consulate: Washington, D.C. ☎ *(202) 332-3007*, San Francisco ☎ *(415) 346-3400*, New Bedford ☎ *(508) 997-6151*, Newark ☎ *(201) 622-7300*, NY ☎ *(212) 246-4580*, Providence ☎ *(401) 272-2003* or Portuguese Consulate in Hong Kong ☎ *(231-338.*

MACEDONIA, FORMER YUGOSLAV REPUBLIC OF — Entry permission can be obtained at border points. Macedonia does not currently maintain an embassy in the U.S. For more information check with the Former Yugoslav Republic of Macedonia's Office, *1015 15th St., N.W., Suite 402, Washington, D.C. 20005* ☎ *(202) 682-0519.*

MADAGASCAR — Passport and visa required. Visa valid 6 months for single-entry up to 90 days, $22.50; or multiple-entries, $44.15 (no personal checks). Requires 4 application forms, 4 photos, yellow fever and cholera immunizations, proof of onward/return transportation and sufficient funds for stay. Include a prepaid envelope for return of passport by registered mail. Allow 4 months to process visa for longer stay. For additional information contact Embassy of the Democratic Republic of Madagascar, *2374 Mass. Ave., N.W., Washington, D.C. 20008* ☎ *(202) 265-5525/6* or nearest Consulate: NY ☎ *(212) 986-9491*, PA ☎ *(215) 893-3067* or CA ☎ *(800) 856-2721.*

MALAWI — Passport required. Visa not required for stay up to 1 year. Strict dress codes apply for anyone visiting Malawi. Women must wear dresses that cover their shoulders, arms, and knees and may not wear slacks except in specifically designated areas. Men with long hair cannot enter the country. For further information about this and other requirements, contact the Embassy of Malawi, *2408 Mass. Ave., N.W., Washington, D.C. 20008* ☎ *(202) 797-1007* or Malawi Mission to the U.N., *600 3rd Ave., New York, NY 10016* ☎ *(212) 949-0180.*

MALAYSIA (and the Borneo States, Sarawak and Sabah) — Passport required. Visa not required for stay up to 3 months. Yellow fever and cholera immunizations necessary if arriving from infected areas. AIDS test required for work permits. U.S. test somtimes accepted. For entry of pets or other types of visits, consult Embassy of Malaysia, *2401 Mass. Ave., N.W., Washington, D.C. 20008* ☎ *(202) 328-2700* or nearest Consulate: Los Angeles ☎ *(213) 621-2991* or New York ☎ *(212) 490-2722.*

MALDIVES — Passport required. Tourist visa issued upon arrival, no charge. Visitors must have proof of onward/return transportation and sufficient funds (minimum of $10 per person per day). Check with Embassy of Maldives in Sri Lanka, 25 Melbourne Avenue, Colombo 4, Sri Lanka or the Maldives Mission to the U.N. in New York ☎ *(212) 599-6195* for further information.

COUNTRY	ENTRY

MALI
Passport and visa required. Visa must be obtained in advance. Tourist/business visa for stay up to 4 weeks, may be extended after arrival, requires $17 fee (cash or money order), 2 application forms, 2 photos, proof of onward/return transportation and yellow fever vaccination. (Cholera immunization is recommended.) For business travel, must have company letter stating purpose of trip. Send SASE for return of passport if applying by mail. Apply Embassy of the Republic of Mali, *2130 R St., N.W., Washington, D.C. 20008* ☎ *(202) 332-2249.*

MALTA
Passport required. Visa not required for stay up to 3 months (extendable) Extension must be applied for prior to end of 3-month period or expiration of original visa). Visa requires 3 application forms, 2 photos, proof of onward/return transportation and $46 fee (check or money order). Transit visa available for $31. For additional information consult Embassy of Malta, *2017 Conn. Ave., N.W., Washington, D.C. 20008* ☎ *(202) 462-3611/2* or nearest Consulate: CA ☎ *(213) 939-5011* and ☎ *(415) 468-4321,* MA ☎ *(617) 259-1391,* MI ☎ *(313) 525-9777,* MO ☎ *(816) 833-0033,* MN ☎ *(612) 228-0935,* NY ☎ *(212) 725-2345,* PA ☎ *(412) 262-8460* or TX ☎ *(713) 497-2100* or *(713) 999-1812.*

MARSHALL ISLANDS, REPUBLIC OF THE
Proof of U.S. citizenship, sufficient funds for stay and onward/return ticket required for stay up to 30 days (extendable up to 90 days from date of entry). Entry permit not needed to bring in sea-going vessel. Obtain necessary forms from airline or shipping agent serving Marshall Islands. Departure fee $10 (those over age 60 exempt). Health certificate required if arriving from infected areas. AIDS test may be required for visits over 30 days; U.S. test accepted. Check information with Representative Office, *Suite 1004, 1901 Pennsylvania Ave., N.W., Washington, D.C. 20006* ☎ *(202) 234-5414* or the nearest Consulate General: CA ☎ *(714) 474-0331* or HI ☎ *(808) 942-4422.*

MARTINIQUE
(See West Indies, French.)

MAURITANIA
Passport and visa required. Obtain visa before arrival. Visa valid 3 months, requires $10 fee (money order only), 2 application forms, 4 photos, yellow fever and cholera immunizations and proof of onward/return transportation. Business travelers must have proof of sufficient funds (bank statement) or letter from sponsoring company. For further information contact Embassy of the Republic of Mauritania, *2129 Leroy Pl., N.W., Washington, D.C. 20008* ☎ *(202) 232-5700/01* or Permanent Mission to the U.N., *211 East 43rd Street, Suite 2000, New York, NY 10017* ☎ *(212) 986-7963.*

MAURITIUS
Passport, sufficient funds for stay and onward/return ticket required. Visa not required for tourist/business stay up to 3 months. AIDS test required for permanent residence and work permits. U.S. test sometimes accepted. For further information consult Embassy of Mauritius, *Suite 441, 4301 Conn. Ave., N.W., Washington, D.C. 20008* ☎ *(202) 244-1491/2* or Honorary Consulate in Los Angeles ☎ *(818) 788-3720.*

MAYOTTE ISLAND
(See France.)

COUNTRY	ENTRY

MEXICO

Passport and visa not required of U.S. citizens for tourist/transit stay up to 90 days. Tourist card is required. Tourist card valid 3 months for single entry up to 180 days, no charge, requires proof of U.S. citizenship, photo ID and proof of sufficient funds. Tourist cards may be obtained in advance from Consulate, Tourism Office, and most airlines serving Mexico upon arrival. Departure tax $10 is paid at airport. Notarized consent from parent(s) required for children travelling alone, with one parent or in someone else's custody. (This permit is not necessary when a minor is in possession of a valid passport.) For other types of travel and details, check Embassy of Mexico Consular Section, *2827 16th St., N.W., Washington, DC 20009-4260* ☎ *(202) 736-1000* or nearest Consulate General: CA ☎ *(213) 351-6800,* ☎ *(415) 392-5554 and (619) 231-8414,* CO ☎ *(303) 830-6702,* FL ☎ *(305) 441-8780,* IL ☎ *(312) 855-1380,* LA ☎ *(504) 522-3596,* NY ☎ *(212) 689-0456,* PR ☎ *(809) 764-0258* or TX ☎ *(214) 522-9741, (713) 463-9426, (512) 227-9145 and (915) 533-3644.*

MICRONESIA, FEDERATED STATES OF (Kosrae, Yap, Ponape, and Truk)

Proof of citizenship, proof of sufficient funds, and onward/return ticket required for tourist visit up to 6 months, extendable (up to 12 months from date of entry) after arrival in Micronesia. Entry permit may be needed for other types of travel; obtain forms from airline. Departure fee $5 (U.S.). Health certificate may be required if traveling from infected area. Typhoid and tetanus immunizations are recommended. AIDS test required if staying over 1 year. U.S. test is accepted. For further information contact Embassy of the Federated States of Micronesia, *1725 N St., N.W., Washington, D.C. 20036* ☎ *(202) 223-4383* or nearest Consulate: Hawaii ☎ *(808) 836-4775* or Guam ☎ *(671) 646-9154.*

MOLDOVA

Passport and visa required. Visas issued at authorized entry points at the airport or along the Romanian border. Moldova does not currently maintain an Embassy in the United States.

MIQUELON ISLAND

Proof of U.S. citizenship and photo ID required for visit up to 3 months. For further information consult Embassy of France ☎ *(202) 944-6000.*

MONACO

Passport required. Visa not required for visit up to 3 months. For further information consult French Embassy ☎ *(202) 944-6000* or nearest Honorary Consulate of the Principality of Monaco: CA ☎ *(213) 655-8970 or (415) 362-5050,* IL ☎ *(312) 642-1242,* LA ☎ *(504) 522-5700,* NY ☎ *(212) 759-5227* or PR ☎ *(809) 721-4215.*

MONGOLIA

Passport and visa required. Transit visa for stay up to 48 hours requires onward ticket, visa for next destination and $15 fee ($30 for double transit). Tourist visa for up to 90 days requires confirmation from Mongolian Travel Agency (Zhuulchin) and $25 fee. Business visa requires letter from company stating purpose of trip and invitation from Mongolian organization and $25 fee (multiple-entry $50). Submit 1 application form, 2 photos, itinerary and prepaid envelope for return of passport by certified or special delivery mail. AIDS test required for students and anyone staying longer than 3 months; U.S. test accepted. For additional information contact Embassy of Mongolia, *2833 M Street, N.W., Washington, D.C. 20007* ☎ *(202) 333-7117* or the UN Mission of Mongolia, *6 East 77th St., New York, NY 10021* ☎ *(212) 861-9460.*

COUNTRY	ENTRY

MOROCCO Passport required. Visa not required for stay up to 3 months, extendable. For additional information consult Embassy of Morocco, *1601 21st St., N.W., Washington, D.C. 20009* ☎ *(202) 462-7979 to 7982* or Consulate General in New York ☎ *(212) 213-9644.*

MOZAMBIQUE Passport and visa required. Visa must be obtained in advance. Entry visa valid 30 days from date of issuance, requires 2 application forms, 2 photos, immunization for yellow fever and cholera, $20 fee and letter (from company or individual) giving detailed itinerary. Visitors may have to exchange $25 at point of entry and declare all foreign currency. Apply Embassy of the People's Republic of Mozambique, *Suite 570, 1990 M St., N.W., Washington, D.C. 20036* ☎ *(202) 293-7146.*

MYANMAR (formerly Burma) Passport and visa required. Single-entry visas, for stay up to 14 days, requires $16 fee for tourist visa and $30 fee for business visa, 2 application forms, 3 photos and itinerary. Tourists visas are issued for package or group tours as well as Foreign Independent Travelers (FITs). FITs holding tourist visas must change a minimum of $200 (U.S.) upon arrival. Business visa requires company letter and invitation from a Myanmarian company; extendable after arrival. Overland travel into and out of Myanmar is only permitted at certain points (check with Embassy). Enclose prepaid envelope for return of passport by registered/certified mail. Allow 2-3 weeks for processing. Minimum of $100 must be changed for local currency on arrival. For further information contact Embassy of the Union of Myanmar, *2300 S St., N.W., Washington, D.C. 20008* ☎ *(202) 332-9044-5* or the Permanent Mission of Myanmar to the U.N., *10 East 77th St., New York, NY 10021* ☎ *(212) 535-1311.*

NAMIBIA Passport, onward/return ticket and proof of sufficient funds required. Visa not required for tourist or business stay up to 90 days. Consult Embassy of Namibia, *1605 New Hampshire Ave., N.W., Washington, D.C. 20009* ☎ *(202) 986-0540* for further information on entry requirements.

NAURU Passport, visa, onward/return ticket and sponsorship from a resident in Nauru required. For more information contact Consulate of the Republic of Nauru in Guam, *P.O. Box Am, Agana, Guam 96910* ☎ *(671) 649-8300.*

NEPAL Passport and visa required. Tourist visa for stay up to 30 days extendable to 3 months. Single-entry visa $40, double $70 and multiple $100 (postal money order), requires 1 application form and 1 photo. For other types of travel obtain visa in advance. For additional information contact Royal Nepalese Embassy, *2131 Leroy Pl., N.W., Washington, D.C. 20008* ☎ *(202) 667-4550* or Consulate General in New York ☎ *(212) 370-4188.*

NETHERLANDS Passport required. Visa not required for tourist/business visit up to 90 days. Tourists may be asked to show onward/return ticket or proof of sufficient funds for stay. For further information contact Embassy of the Netherlands, *4200 Linnean Ave., N.W., Washington, D.C. 20008* ☎ *(202) 244-5300* or nearest Consulate General: CA ☎ *(213) 380-3440,* IL ☎ *(312) 856-0110,* NY ☎ *(212) 246-1429* or TX ☎ *(713) 622-8000.*

COUNTRY	ENTRY

NETHERLANDS ANTILLES — Islands include Bonaire, Curacao, Saba, Statia, St. Maarten. Passport or proof of U.S. citizenship required. Visa not required for stay up to 14 days, extendable to 90 days after arrival. Tourists may be asked to show onward/return ticket or proof of sufficient funds for stay. Departure tax $10 when leaving Bonaire and Curacao, $4 in Statia, $10 in St. Maarten. For further information consult Embassy of the Netherlands ☎ *(202) 244-5300*, or nearest Consulate General: CA ☎ *(213) 380-3440*, IL ☎ *(312) 856-0110*, NY ☎ *(212) 246-1429* or TX ☎ *(713) 622-8000*.

NEW CALEDONIA — (See French Polynesia.)

NEW ZEALAND — Passport required. Visa not required for tourist/business stay up to 3 months, must have onward/return ticket, visa for next destination and proof of sufficient funds. For additional information contact Embassy of New Zealand, *37 Observatory Circle, N.W., Washington, D.C. 20008* ☎ *(202) 328-4800* or the Consulate General, Los Angeles ☎ *(213) 477-8241*.

NICARAGUA — Passport and onward/return ticket required. Check further information with Embassy of Nicaragua, *1627 New Hampshire Ave., N.W., Washington, D.C. 20009* ☎ *(202) 939-6531 to 34*.

NIGER — Passport and visa required. Visa valid between 7 and 12 months (from date of issuance), depending on type/category of travelers. Requires 3 application forms, 3 photos, yellow fever vaccination (cholera vaccination is recommended, but not required), proof of onward/return transportation, letter of invitation and $56.07 fee. For further information and fees contact Embassy of the Republic of Niger, *2204 R St., N.W., Washington, D.C. 20008* ☎ *(202) 483-4224*.

NIGERIA — Passport and visa required. Visa, no charge, valid for one entry within 12 months, requires 1 photo, yellow fever vaccination, proof of onward/return transportation, and for tourism a letter of invitation is required. Business visa requires letter from counterpart in Nigeria and letter of introduction from U.S. company. For further information contact Embassy of the Republic of Nigeria, *2201 M St., N.W., Washington, D.C. 20037* ☎ *(202) 822-1500 or 1522* or the Consulate General in New York ☎ *(212) 715-7200*.

NIUE — Passport, onward/return ticket and confirmed hotel accommodations required. Visa not required for stay up to 30 days. For additional information consult Embassy of New Zealand ☎ *(202) 328-4800*.

NORFOLK ISLAND — Passport and visa required. Visa issued upon arrival for visit up to 30 days, extendable, requires confirmed accommodations and onward/return ticket. Australian transit visa must also be obtained in advance for travel to Norfolk Island. For both visas consult Australian Embassy ☎ *(202) 797-3000*.

NORWAY — Passport required. Visa not required for stay up to 3 months. (Period begins when entering Scandinavian area: Finland, Sweden, Denmark, Iceland.) For further information contact Royal Norwegian Embassy, *2720 34th St., N.W., Washington, D.C. 20008* ☎ *(202) 333-6000* or nearest Consulate General: CA ☎ *(415) 986-0766 to 7168* and *(213) 933-7717*, MN ☎ *(612) 332-3338*, NY ☎ *(212) 421-7333* or TX ☎ *(713) 521-2900*.

COUNTRY	ENTRY
OMAN	Passport and visa required. Tourist/business visas for single-entry issued for stay up to 3 weeks. Requires $21 fee, 1 application form, 1 photo and cholera immunization if arriving from infected area. AIDS test required for work permits. U.S test not accepted. Allow 1 week to 10 days for processing. For transit and road travel check Embassy of the Sultanate of Oman, *2535 Belmont Rd., N.W., Washington, D.C. 20008* ☎ *(202) 387-1980-2.*
PAKISTAN	Passport and visa required. Visa must be obtained before arrival. Tourist visa requires 1 application form, 1 photo and proof of onward/return transportation. Validity depends on length of visit (minimum 3 months), multiple entries, no charge. Need letter from company for business visa. Include prepaid envelope for return of passport by registered mail. AIDS test required for stays over 1 year. For applications and inquiries in Washington area, contact Consular Section of the Embassy of Pakistan, *2315 Mass. Ave., N.W., Washington, D.C. 20008* ☎ *(202) 939-6295.* All other areas apply to Consulate General, *12 East 65th St., New York, NY 10021* ☎ *(212) 879-5800.*
PALAU, THE REPUBLIC OF	Proof of U.S. citizenship onward/return ticket required for stay up to 30 days (extendable). $50 fee for extension (must apply for extension in Palau). Obtain forms for entry permit from airline or shipping agent serving Palau. For further information consult with Representative Office, *444 N. Capitol St., Suite 619, Washington, D.C. 20001* ☎ *(202) 624-7793.*
PANAMA	Passport, tourist card or visa and onward/return ticket required. Tourist card valid 30 days, available from airline serving Panama for $5 fee. For longer stays and additionall information contact Embassy of Panama, *2862 McGill Terrace, N.W., Washington, D.C. 20008* ☎ *(202) 483-1407.*
PAPUA NEW GUINEA	Passport, onward/return ticket and proof of sufficient funds required. Tourist visa not required for a stay of up to 30 days. Business visa requires 2 application forms, 2 photos, company letter, bio-data and $10.25 fee (single entry) or $154.00 (multiple entry). AIDS test required for work and residency permits; U.S. test accepted. For longer stays and further information contact Embassy of Papua New Guinea, *Suite 300, 1615 New Hampshire Ave., N.W., Washington, D.C. 20009* ☎ *(202) 745-3680.*
PARAGUAY	Passport required. Visa not required for tourist/business stay up to 90 days (extendable). AIDS test required for resident visas. U.S. test sometimes accepted. For additional information consult Embassy of Paraguay, *2400 Mass. Ave., N.W., Washington, D.C. 20008* ☎ *(202) 483-6960.*
PERU	Passport required. Visa not required for tourist stay up to 90 days, extendable after arrival. Tourists may need onward/return ticket. For official/diplomatic passport and other travel, visa required and must be obtained in advance. Business visa requires company letter stating purpose of trip and $27 fee. For further information contact Embassy of Peru, *1700 Mass. Ave., N.W., Washington, D.C. 20036* ☎ *(202) 833-9860-9* or nearest Consulate: CA ☎ *(213) 383-9896* and *(415) 362-5185*, FL ☎ *(305) 374-1407*, IL ☎ *(312) 853-6173*, NY ☎ *(212) 644-2850*, PR ☎ *(809) 763-0679* or TX ☎ *(713) 781-5000.*

COUNTRY	ENTRY

PHILIPPINES

Passport and onward/return ticket required. For entry by Manila International Airport, visa not required for transit/tourist stay up to 21 days. Visa required for longer stay, maximum of 59 days, 1 application form, 1 photo, no charge. Company letter needed for business visa. AIDS test required for permanent residency; U.S. test accepted. For more information contact the Embassy of the Philippines, *1600 Mass. Ave., N.W., Washington, D.C. 20036* ☎ *(202) 467-9300* or nearest Consulate General: CA ☎ *(213) 387-5321* and *(415) 433-6666*, HI ☎ *(808) 595-6316*, IL ☎ *(312) 332-6458*, NY ☎ *(212) 764-1330*, TX ☎ *(713) 621-8609* or WA ☎ *(206) 441-1640.*

POLAND

Passport (must be valid at least 12 months past date of entry) required. Visa not required for stay up to 90 days. Visitors must register at hotel or with local authorities within 48 hours after arrival. Check with the Embassy of the Republic of Poland (Consular Division), *2224 Wyoming Ave., N.W., Washington, D.C. 20008* ☎ *(202) 232-4517* or nearest Consulate General: Chicago, IL, *1530 Lakeshore Dr., 60610* ☎ *(312) 337-8816*, Los Angeles, CA, *3460 Wilshire Blvd., Suite 1200, 90010* ☎ *(213) 365-7900* or New York, NY, *233 Madison Ave., 10016* ☎ *(212) 889-8360.*

PORTUGAL

(Includes travel to the Azores and Madeira Islands.) Passport required. Visa not required for visit up to 60 days (extendable). For travel with pets and other information consult nearest Consulate: Washington., D.C. ☎ *(202) 332-3007*, CA ☎ *(415) 346-3400*, MA ☎ *(617) 536-8740* and *(508) 997-6151*, NJ ☎ *(201) 622-7300*, NY ☎ *(212) 246-4580* or RI ☎ *(401) 272-2003.*

QATAR

Passport and visa required. Single-entry visa $33; multiple-entry visa, valid 3-6 months for $60 fee or 12 months for $115 fee; transit visa $6. Visas require No Objection Certificate from Qatar Ministry of Interior, 2 application forms, 2 photos and SASE for return of passport by mail. Business visa must be obtained through sponsor in Qatar. AIDS test required for work and student visas; U.S. test accepted if within 3 months of visit. For specific information contact Embassy of the State of Qatar, *Suite 1180, 600 New Hampshire Ave., N.W., Washington, D.C. 20037* ☎ *(202) 338-0111.*

REUNION

(See France.)

ROMANIA

Passport and visa required. Transit and tourist visa may be obtained at border in Romania or from the Romanian Embassy or Consulate before departure. Transit visa for stay up to 4 days, single-entry $21 or double-entry $31. Tourist/business visa, single-entry valid 6 months for stay up to 60 days, $31 (multiple-entry $68). No application or photos needed. Provide SASE for return of passport by mail. Allow 1 to 3 days for processing. For additional information consult Embassy of Romania, *1607 23rd St., N.W., Washington, D.C. 20008* ☎ *(202) 232-4747-9* or the Consulate General, New York ☎ *(212) 682-9120, 9121, 9122.*

COUNTRY	ENTRY

RUSSIA
Passport and visa required. Tourist visa, no charge, requires 1 application form, 3 photos, confirmation from tourist agency in the Commonwealth of Independent States (CIS) and processing fee (visa processing fee is $20 for 2 weeks, $30 for one week, and $60 for three days processing time). Business visa requires 1 application, 3 photos, and letter of invitation from a CIS company. Multiple-entry business visa $120 plus processing fee. Fee paid by money order or company check only. AIDS test required for anyone staying over 3 months; U.S. test accepted. For additional information contact the Consular Section of the Embassy of Russia, *1825 Phelps Pl., N.W., Washington, D.C. 20008* ☎ *(202) 939-8907, 8911 or 8913* or the nearest Consulate General: San Francisco ☎ *(415) 202-9800* or Seattle ☎ *(206) 728-1910.*

RWANDA
Passport and visa required. Multiple-entry visa for stay up to 3 months requires, $20 fee, 2 application forms, 2 photos and immunizations for yellow fever. Exact date of entry into Rwanda required with application. Include prepaid envelope or postage for return of passport by certified mail. Apply at one of the following: Embassy of the Republic of Rwanda, *1714 New Hampshire Ave., N.W., Washington, D.C. 20009* ☎ *(202) 232-2882,* Permanent Mission of Rwanda to the U.N., *124 East 39th Street, New York, NY 10016* ☎ *(212) 696-0644/45/46* or the Consulate General in Chicago ☎ *(708) 205-1188* or Denver ☎ *(303) 321-2400.*

SAINT KITTS AND NEVIS
Proof of U.S. citizenship, photo ID and onward/return ticket required for stay up to 6 months. AIDS test required for work permit, residency or student visas; U.S. test is accepted. For further information consult Embassy of St. Kitts and Nevis, *2501 M St., N.W., Washington, D.C. 20037* ☎ *(202) 833-3550* or Permanent Mission to the U.N., *414 East 75th St., Fifth Floor, New York, NY 10021* ☎ *(212) 535-1234.*

SAINT LUCIA
Passport (or proof of U.S. citizenship and photo ID) and return/onward ticket required for stay up to 6 months. For additional information contact Embassy of Saint Lucia, *2100 M St., N.W., Suite 309, Washington, D.C. 20037* ☎ *(202) 463-7378/9* or Permanent Mission to the U.N., *820 Second St., 9th Floor, New York, NY 10017* ☎ *(212) 697-9360.*

ST. MARTIN (Sint Maarten*)
(See West Indies, French or *Netherlands Antilles.)

ST. PIERRE
Proof of U.S. citizenship and photo ID required for visit up to 3 months. For specific information consult Embassy of France ☎ *(202) 944-6000.*

SAINT VINCENT AND THE GRENADINES
Proof of U.S. citizenship, photo ID, and onward/return ticket and/or proof of sufficient funds required for tourist stay up to 6 months. For more information consult the Embassy of Saint Vincent and the Grenadines, *1717 Mass. Ave., N.W., Suite 102, Washington, D.C. 20036* ☎ *(202) 462-7806 or 7846* or Consulate, *801 Second Ave., 21st Floor, New York, NY 10017* ☎ *(212) 687-4490.*

SAN MARINO
Passport required. Visa not required for tourist stay up to 3 months. For additional information contact the nearest Honorary Consulate of the Republic of San Marino: Washington *1899 L St., N.W., Suite 500, Washington, D.C. 20036,* ☎ *(202) 223-3517,* Detroit ☎ *(313) 528-1190* or New York ☎ *(516) 242-2212.*

COUNTRY	ENTRY

SAO TOME AND PRINCIPE

Passport and visa required. Tourist/business visa for visit up to 2 weeks, requires 2 application forms, 2 photos and yellow fever immunization card, letter stating purpose of travel and $15 fee (money orders only). Company letter is required for a business visa. Enclose prepaid envelope or postage for return of passport by certified or special delivery mail. Apply Permanent Mission of Sao Tome and Principe to the U.N., *122 East 42nd Street, Suite 1604, New York, NY 10168* ☎ *(212) 697-4211.*

SAUDI ARABIA

Passport and visa required. (Tourist visas are not available for travel to Saudi Arabia.) Transit visa valid 24 hours for stay in airport, need onward/return ticket. Business visa requires $15 fee (money order only), 1 application form, 1 photo, company letter stating purpose of visit, invitation from Foreign Ministry in Saudi Arabia and SASE for return of passport by mail. Meningitis and cholera vaccinations are highly recommended. Medical report, including AIDS test, required for work permits; U.S. test accepted. For details and requirements for family visits, contact The Royal Embassy of Saudi Arabia, *601 New Hampshire Ave., N.W., Washington, D.C. 20037* ☎ *(202) 342-3800* or nearest Consulate General: Los Angeles ☎ *(213) 208-6566*, New York ☎ *(212) 752-2740* or Houston ☎ *(713) 785-5577.*

SCOTLAND

(See United Kingdom)

SENEGAL

Passport required. Visa not needed for stay up to 90 days. U.S. citizens need onward/return ticket and yellow fever vaccination. For further information contact Embassy of the Republic of Senegal, *2112 Wyoming Ave., N.W., Washington, D.C. 20008* ☎ *(202) 234-0540.*

SERBIA AND MONTENEGRO

Passport required. For further information check with the Embassy of the Former Federal Republic of Yugoslavia (Serbia & Montenegro), *2410 California St., N.W., Washington, D.C. 20008* ☎ *(202) 462-6566.* Attention: U.S. citizens need a Treasury Dept. license in order to engage in any commercial transactions within Serbia & Montenegro. Before planning any travel to Serbia & Montenegro, U.S. citizens should contact the Licensing Division, Office of Foreign Assets Control, Department of the Treasury, *1331 G St., N.W., Washington, D.C. 20220* ☎ *(202) 622-2480.*

SEYCHELLES

Passport, onward/return ticket and proof of sufficient funds required. Visa issued upon arrival for stay up to 1 month, no charge, extendable up to 1 year. Consult Permanent Mission of Seychelles to the U.N., *820 Second Ave., Suite 203, New York, NY 10017* ☎ *(212) 687-9766* for further information.

SIERRA LEONE

Passport and visa required. Single-entry visa valid 3 months, requires 1 application form, 1 photo, return/onward ticket and proof of financial support from bank or employer. Cholera and yellow fever immunizations required and malarial suppressants recommended. Adult travelers (over age 16) must exchange $100 minimum upon arrival and declare other foreign currency on an exchange control form (M), certified and stamped at the port of entry. For further information consult Embassy of Sierra Leone, *1701 19th St., N.W., Washington, D.C. 20009* ☎ *(202) 939-9261.*

COUNTRY	ENTRY

SINGAPORE Passport and onward/return ticket required. Visa not required for tourist/business stay up to 2 weeks, extendable to 3 months maximum. AIDS test required for some work visas. U.S. test is not accepted. For additional information contact Embassy of Singapore, *3501 Int'l Place, N.W., Washington, D.C. 20008* ☎ *(202) 537-3100.*

SLOVAK REPUBLIC Passport required. Visa not required for stay up to 30 days. For longer stays and other types of travel contact Embassy of the Slovak Republic, *2201 Wisconsin Ave., N.W., Suite 380, Washington, D.C. 20007* ☎ *(202) 965-5164.*

SLOVENIA Passport required. Visa not required for stay of up to 90 days. Additional information can be obtained from the Embassy of Slovenia, *1300 19th St., N.W., Washington, D.C. 20036* ☎ *(202) 828-1650.*

SOLOMON ISLANDS Passport, onward/return ticket and proof of sufficient funds required. Visitors permit issued on arrival for stay up to 2 months in 1-year period. For further information consult British Embassy ☎ *(202) 986-0205.*

SOMALIA Passport required. For further information contact Consulate of the Somali Democratic Republic in New York ☎ *(212) 688-9410.*

SOUTH AFRICA Passport required. Visa not required for tourist stay up to 90 days. Malarial suppressants are recommended. For business travel, a visa and company letter are required. For more information contact: Embassy of South Africa, Attn: Consular Office, *3201 New Mexico Ave., N.W., Washington, D.C. 20016* ☎ *(202) 966-1650* or nearest Consulate: CA ☎ *(310) 657-9200,* IL ☎ *(312) 939-7929,* or NY ☎ *(212) 213-4880.*

SPAIN Passport required. Visa not required for tourist stay up to 6 months. For additional information check with Embassy of Spain, *2700 15th St., N.W., Washington, D.C. 20009* ☎ *(202) 265-0190/1* or nearest Consulate General: CA ☎ *(415) 922-2995* and *(213) 658-6050,* FL ☎ *(305) 446-5511,* IL ☎ *(312) 782-4588,* LA ☎ *(504) 525-4951,* MA ☎ *(617) 536-2506,* NY ☎ *(212) 355-4080,* PR ☎ *(809) 758-6090* or TX ☎ *(713) 783-6200.*

SRI LANKA Passport, onward/return ticket and proof of sufficient funds ($15 per day) required. Tourist visa not required for stay up to 90 days. For business or travel on official/diplomatic passport, visa required and must be obtained in advance. Business visa valid 1 month, requires 1 application form, 2 photos, a company letter, a letter from sponsoring agency in Sri Lanka, a copy of an onward/return ticket, and $5 fee. Include $6 postage for return of passport by registered mail. Yellow fever and cholera immunizations needed if arriving from infected area. For further information contact Embassy of the Democratic Socialist Republic of Sri Lanka, *2148 Wyoming Ave., N.W., Washington, D.C. 20008* ☎ *(202) 483-4025* or nearest Consulate: CA ☎ *(805) 323-8975* and *(504) 362-3232,* HI ☎ *(808) 373-2040,* NJ ☎ *(201) 627-7855* or NY ☎ *(212) 986-7040.*

COUNTRY	ENTRY

SUDAN Passport and visa required. Visa must be obtained in advance. Transit visa valid up to 7 days, requires $50 fee (cash or money order), onward/return ticket and visa for next destination, if appropriate. Tourist/business visa for single entry up to 3 months (extendable), requires $50 fee, 1 application form, 1 photo, proof of sufficient funds for stay and SASE for return passport. Business visa requires company letter stating purpose of visit and invitation from Sudanese officials. Malarial suppressants and vaccinations for yellow fever, cholera, and meningitis recommended. Visas not granted to passports showing Israeli or South African visas. Allow 4 weeks for processing. Travelers must declare currency upon arrival and departure. Check additional currency regulations for stays longer than 2 months. Contact Embassy of the Republic of the Sudan, *2210 Mass. Ave., N.W., Washington, D.C. 20008* ☎ *(202) 338-8565 to 8570* or Consulate General, *210 East 49th St., New York, NY 10017* ☎ *(212) 573-6035.*

SURINAME Passport and visa required. Multiple-entry visa requires 2 application forms and 2 photos. Business visa requires letter from sponsoring company. For return of passport by mail, send $5 for registered mail or $9.95 for Express Mail. For additional requirements contact Embassy of the Republic of Suriname, *Suite 108, 4301 Conn. Ave., N.W., Washington, D.C. 20008* ☎ *(202) 244-7488 and 7490* or the Consulate: Miami ☎ *(305) 593-2163.*

SWAZILAND Passport required. Visa not required for stay up to 60 days. Temporary residence permit available in Mbabane for longer stay. Visitors must report to immigration authorities or police station within 48 hours unless lodging in a hotel. Yellow fever and cholera immunizations required if arriving from infected area and anti-malarial treatment recommended. For further information consult Embassy of the Kingdom of Swaziland, *3400 International Dr., N.W., Suite 3M, Washington, D.C.* ☎ *(202) 362-6683.*

SWEDEN Valid passport required. Visa not required for stay up to 3 months. (Period begins when entering Scandinavian area: Finland, Norway, Denmark, Iceland.) For further information check Embassy of Sweden, *Suite 1200, 600 New Hampshire Ave., N.W., Washington, D.C. 20037* ☎ *(202) 944-5600* or nearest Consulate General: Los Angeles ☎ *(310) 575-3383* or New York ☎ *(212) 751-5900.*

SWITZERLAND Passport required. Visa not required for tourist/business stay up to 3 months. For further information contact Embassy of Switzerland, *2900 Cathedral Ave., N.W., Washington, D.C. 20008* ☎ *(202) 745-7900* or nearest Consulate General: CA ☎ *(310) 575-1145* or *(415) 788-2272*, GA ☎ *(404) 870-2000*, IL ☎ *(312) 915-0061*, NY ☎ *(212) 758-2560* or TX ☎ *(713) 650-0000.*

COUNTRY	ENTRY

SYRIA

Passport and visa required. Obtain visa in advance. Single-entry visa valid 6 months or double-entry for 3 months, $15; multiple-entry visa valid 6 months, $30. Submit 2 application forms, 2 photos (signed) and fee (payment must be money order only). Enclose prepaid envelope (with correct postage) for return of passport by mail. AIDS test required for students and others staying over 1 year; U.S. test sometimes accepted. For group visas and other information contact Embassy of the Syrian Arab Republic, *2215 Wyoming Ave., N.W., Washington, D.C. 20008* ☎ *(202) 232-6313.*

TAHITI

(See French Polynesia.)

TAIWAN

Passport required. Visa not required for stay up to 5 days. AIDS test mandatory for anyone staying over 3 months; U.S. test sometimes accepted. For business travel, longer stays or other information contact Coordination Council for North American Affairs (CCNAA), *4201 Wisconsin Avenue, N.W., Washington, D.C. 20016-2137* ☎ *(202) 895-1800.* Additional offices are in Atlanta, Boston, Chicago, Guam, Honolulu, Houston, Kansas City, Los Angeles, Miami, New York, San Francisco, and Seattle.

TAJIKISTAN

Passport and visa required. At the time of publication, visa issuances are being handled by the Russian Consulate. The visa process must be initiated in Tajikistan by the sponsoring agency or by the travel agent involved; no visa request is initiated at the Russian Consulate. Visas are not issued until an approval cable arrives from the Ministry of Foreign Affairs in Tajikistan to the Russian Consulate.

TANZANIA

Passport and visa required. Obtain visa before departure. Visas for mainland Tanzania are valid for Zanzibar. Tourist visa (valid 6 months from date of issuance) for 1 entry up to 30 days, may be extended after arrival. Requires 1 application, 1 form and $10.50 fee (no personal checks). Enclose prepaid envelope for return of passport by certified or registered mail. Yellow fever and cholera immunizations recommended (required if arriving from infected area) and malarial suppressants advised. Allow 1 month for processing. For business visa and other information, consult Embassy of the United Republic of Tanzania, *2139 R St., N.W., Washington, D.C. 20008* ☎ *(202) 939-6125* or Tanzanian Permanent Mission to the U.N. *205 East 42nd St., 13th Floor, New York, NY 10017* ☎ *(212) 972-9160.*

THAILAND

Passport and onward/return ticket required. Visa not needed for stay up to 15 days if arrive and depart from Don Muang Airport in Bangkok. For longer stays obtain visa in advance. Transit visa, for stay up to 30 days, $10 fee; or tourist visa for stay up to 60 days, $15 fee. For business visa valid up to 90 days, need $20 fee and company letter stating purpose of visit. Submit 1 application form, 2 photos and postage for return of passport by mail. Apply Embassy of Thailand, *2300 Kalorama Rd., N.W., Washington, D.C. 20008* ☎ *(202) 234-5052* or nearest Consulate General: CA ☎ *(213) 937-1894,* IL ☎ *(312) 236-2447* or NY ☎ *(212) 754-1770.*

COUNTRY	ENTRY

TOGO
Passport required. Visa not required for stay up to 3 months. Americans travelling in remote areas in Togo occasionally require visas. Yellow fever and cholera vaccinations are required. Check further information with Embassy of the Republic of Togo, *2208 Mass. Ave., N.W., Washington, D.C. 20008* ☎ *(202) 234-4212/3.*

TONGA
Passport and onward/return ticket required. Visa not required for stay up to 30 days. For additional information consult the Consulate General of Tonga, *360 Post St., Suite 604, San Francisco, CA 94108* ☎ *(415) 781-0365.*

TRINIDAD AND TOBAGO
Passport required. Visa not required for tourist/business stay up to 3 months. Business visa requires passport and company letter. For further information consult Embassy of Trinidad and Tobago, *1708 Mass. Ave., N.W., Washington, D.C. 20036* ☎ *(202) 467-6490* or nearest Consulate in New York ☎ *(212) 682-7272.*

TUNISIA
Passport and onward/return ticket required. Visas not required for tourist/business stay up to 4 months. For further information consult Embassy of Tunisia, *1515 Mass. Ave., N.W., Washington, D.C. 20005* ☎ *(202) 862-1850* or nearest Consulate: San Francisco ☎ *(415) 922-9222* or New York ☎ *(212) 272-6962.*

TURKEY
Passport required. Visa not required for tourist/business stay up to 3 months. For other travel, visa required and must be obtained in advance. For further information contact Embassy of the Republic of Turkey, *1714 Mass. Ave., N.W., Washington, D.C. 20036* ☎ *(202) 659-0742* or nearest Consulate: CA ☎ *(213) 937-0118,* IL ☎ *(312) 263-0644,* NY ☎ *(212) 949-0160* or TX ☎ *(713) 622-5849.*

TURKMENISTAN
Passport and visa required. At the time of publication, visa issuances are being handled by the Russian Consulate. The visa process must be initiated in Turkmenistan by the sponsoring agency or by the travel agent involved; no visa request is initiated at the Russian Consulate. Visas are not issued until an approval cable arrives from the Ministry of Foreign Affairs in Turkmenistan to the Russian Consulate.

TURKS AND CAICOS
(See West Indies, British.)

TUVALU
Passport and onward/return ticket and proof of sufficient funds required. Visitors permit issued on arrival. For further information consult British Embassy ☎ *(202) 986-0205.*

UGANDA
Passport required. Immunization certificates for yellow fever and cholera are required (typhoid and malaria suppressants recommended). For business visa and other information contact Embassy of the Republic of Uganda, *5909 16th St., N.W., Washington, D.C. 20011* ☎ *(202) 726-7100-02* or Permanent Mission to the U.N. ☎ *(212) 949-0110.*

COUNTRY	ENTRY

UKRAINE

Passport and visa required. Visas may be obtained at the Ukraine Embassy in the U.S. (visas limited to 3 days may be obtained at airports in Ukraine, or at any border crossing point). Visa requires 1 form, 1 photo and $30-100 fee, depending upon processing time (company check or money order only). AIDS test may be required for anyone staying over 3 months. U.S. test is sometimes accepted. For additional information contact Embassy of Ukraine, *3350 M St., N.W., Washington, D.C. 20007* ☎ *(202) 333-7507* or the nearest Consulate: IL ☎ *(312) 384-6632* or NY ☎ *(212) 505-1409.*

UNITED ARAB EMIRATES

Passport and visa required. Tourist visa must be obtained by relative/sponsor in UAE, and sponsor must meet visitor at airport. Business visas issued only by Embassy, and require company letter and sponsor in UAE to send a fax or telex to Embassy confirming trip. Single-entry visa valid 2 months for stay up to 30 days, $18 fee. Multiple-entry visa (for business only), valid 6 months from date of issue for maximum stay of 30 days per entry, $225 fee, paid by cash, money order or certified check. Submit 2 application forms, 2 photo and prepaid envelope for return of passport by certified/registered mail. AIDS test required for work or residence permits; testing must be performed upon arrival; U.S. test not accepted. For further information contact Embassy of the United Arab Emirates, *Suite 740, 600 New Hampshire Ave., N.W., Washington, D.C. 20037* ☎ *(202) 338-6500.*

UNITED KINGDOM (England, Northern Ireland, Scotland, and Wales)

Passport required. Visa not required for stay up to 6 months. AIDS test required for anyone staying over 6 months and for resident and work visas; U.S. test usually accepted. For additional information consult the Consular Section of the British Embassy, *19 Observatory Circle, N.W., Washington, D.C. 20008* ☎ *(202) 986-0205* or nearest Consulate General: CA ☎ *(310) 477-3322,* GA ☎ *(404) 524-5856,* IL ☎ *(312) 346-1810,* MA ☎ *(617) 437-7160,* NY ☎ *(212) 752-8400,* OH ☎ *(216) 621-7674* or TX ☎ *(713) 659-6210.*

URUGUAY

Passport required. Visa not required for stay up to 3 months. For additional information consult Embassy of Uruguay, *1918 F St., N.W., Washington, D.C. 20008* ☎ *(202) 331-1313-6* or nearest Consulate: CA ☎ *(213) 394-5777,* FL ☎ *(305) 358-9350,* IL ☎ *(312) 236-3366,* LA ☎ *(504) 525-8354* or NY ☎ *(212) 753-8191/2.*

UZBEKISTAN

Passport and visa required. Apply Uzbekistan Consulate, *866 United Nations Plaza, Suite 326, New York, NY 10017* ☎ *(212) 486-7570.*

VANUATU

Passport and onward/return ticket required. Visa not required for stay up to 30 days. For further information consult the British Embassy ☎ *(202) 986-0205.*

VATICAN

(See Holy See.)

COUNTRY	ENTRY

VENEZUELA Passport and tourist card required. Tourist card can be obtained from airlines serving Venezuela, no charge, valid 60 days, cannot be extended. Multiple-entry visa valid up to 1 year, extendable, available from any Venezuelan Consulate, requires $30 fee (money order or company check), 1 application form, 1 photo, onward/return ticket, proof of sufficient funds and certification of employment. For business visa, need letter from company stating purpose of trip, responsibility for traveler, name and address of companies to be visited in Venezuela and $60 fee. All travelers must pay departure tax ($12) at airport. Business travelers must present a Declaration of Income Tax in the Ministerio de Hacienda (Treasury Department). For additional information contact the Consular Section of the Embassy of Venezuela, *1099 30th Street, N.W., Washington, DC 20007* ☎ *(202) 342-2214* or the nearest Consulate: CA ☎ *(415) 512-8340*, FL ☎ *(305) 577-3834*, IL ☎ *(312) 236-9655*, LA ☎ *(504) 522-3284*, MA ☎ *(617) 266-9355*, NY ☎ *(212) 826-1660*, PR ☎ *(809) 766-4250* or TX ☎ *(713) 961-5141.*

VIETNAM Passport and visa required. Tourist visa, valid 30 days, requires application form(s), 2 photos and $90 fee. Allow at least 3 weeks for processing. (Visas are not being issued in the U.S. at this time. You must apply in a country that maintains diplomatic relations with Vietnam.) For other types of travel and more information contact the Vietnamese Permanent Mission to the U.N., *20 Waterside Plaza, New York, NY 10010* ☎ *(212) 679-3779.*

VIRGIN ISLANDS, British Islands include Anegarda, Jost van Dyke, Tortola and Virgin Gorda. Proof of U.S. citizenship, photo ID, onward/return ticket and sufficient funds required for tourist stay up to 3 months. AIDS test required for residency or work; U.S. test accepted. Consult British Embassy for further information ☎ *(202) 986-0205.*

WALES (See United Kingdom.)

WEST INDIES, British Islands include Anguilla, Montserrat, Cayman Islands, Turks and Caicos. Proof of U.S. citizenship, photo ID, onward/return ticket and sufficient funds required for tourist stay up to 3 months. AIDS test required for residency or work; U.S. test accepted. Consult British Embassy for further information ☎ *(202) 986-0205.*

WEST INDIES, French Islands include Guadeloupe, Isles des Saintes, La Desirade, Marie Galante, Saint Barthelemy, St. Martin and Martinique. Proof of U.S. citizenship and photo ID required for visit up to 3 weeks. (For stays longer than 3 weeks a passport is required.) No visa required for stay up to 3 months. For further information consult Embassy of France ☎ *(202) 944-6200/6215.*

WESTERN SAMOA Passport and onward/return ticket required. Visa not required for stay up to 30 days. For longer stays contact the Western Samoa Mission to the U.N., *820 2nd Avenue, Suite 800, New York, NY* ☎ *(212) 599-6196.*

COUNTRY	ENTRY

YEMEN, REPUBLIC OF-

Passport and visa required. Visa valid 30 days from date of issuance for single entry, requires 1 application form and 2 photos. For tourist visa need proof of onward/return transportation and employment and $20 fee. Visitors visa requires letter of invitation and $20 fee. Business visa requires $20, company letter stating purpose of trip. Payment by money order only and include postage for return of passport by registered mail. Entry not granted to passports showing Israeli or South African visas. Yellow fever and cholera vaccinations and malaria suppressants recommended. Check information with Embassy of the Republic Yemen, *Suite 705, 2600 Virginia Ave., N.W., Washington, D.C. 20037* ☎ *(202) 965-4760* or Yemen Mission to the U.N., *866 United Nations Plaza, Rm. 435, New York, NY 10017* ☎ *(212) 355-1730.*

ZAIRE

Passport and visa required. Visa must be obtained before arrival. Transit visa for stay up to 8 days, single-entry $45; double-entry $70. Tourist/business visa, valid 1 month $75-120, 2 months $140-180, 3 months $190-220 and 6 months $264-360, requires 3 photos, 3 applications, yellow fever immunization and onward/return ticket. Business visa also requires company letter accepting financial responsibility for traveler. No personal checks, send money order and enclose SASE for return of passport by mail. Apply Embassy of the Republic of Zaire, *1800 New Hampshire Ave., N.W., Washington, D.C. 20009* ☎ *(202) 234-7690/1* or Permanent Mission to the U.N., *747 Third Ave., New York, NY 10017* ☎ *(212) 754-1966.*

ZAMBIA

Passport and visa required. Obtain visa in advance. Visa valid up to 6 months, requires $10 fee (no personal checks), 2 application forms and 2 photos. Business visa also requires company letter. Yellow fever and cholera immunizations recommended. Apply Embassy of the Republic of Zambia, *2419 Mass. Ave., N.W., Washington, D.C. 20008* ☎ *(202) 265-9717-21.*

ZANZIBAR

(See Tanzania.)

ZIMBABWE

Passport, onward/return ticket and proof of sufficient funds required. Visitors must declare currency upon arrival. For regulations check with Embassy of Zimbabwe, *1608 New Hampshire Ave., N.W., Washington, D.C. 20009* ☎ *(202) 332-7100.*

NOTES:

SASE is self-addressed, stamped envelope.

If applying in person, remember to call about office hours. Many consulates are only open in the morning.

The State Department

Big Brother Abroad

Embassies and Consulates outside the U.S. provide emergency services for American citizens both outside and inside the U.S. The State Department can turn out to be your only friend if things go to hell while traveling and your only lifeline to the U.S. Although they cannot interfere with the local police or judicial process, they can be the only responsible, functional lifeline you have in times of disaster, war, or personal misfortune. When should you contact the local embassy or mission abroad?

If You Are Arrested

Nearly 3000 Americans are arrested abroad each year. Over 30 percent of these arrests are drug related. Over 70 percent of drug related arrests involve marijuana or cocaine.You are on your own when you are arrested out of the United States. Each country is sovereign and its laws apply to everyone who enters regardless of nationality. The U.S. Government cannot release or prevent you from serving time in foreign jails. However, a consul will insist on prompt access to the arrested American, provide a list of reputable attorneys, provide information on the host country's legal system, offer to contact your family or friends, visit on a regular basis, protest mistreatment, monitor jail conditions, provide dietary supplements if needed, and keep the State Department informed. The Citizens Emergency Center is the point of contact in the U.S. for family members and others who are concerned about an American arrested abroad.

The State Department can come to your assistance in emergency situations. Emergency assistance generally pertains to four categories: deaths, arrests, financial/medical problems and welfare/whereabouts queries. The Citizens Emergency Center, working through our embassies and consulates abroad, is a link between the citizen in distress and his or her family in the U.S. The Citizens Emergency Center is also responsible for administering the Department's travel advisory program.

The Citizens Emergency Center deals with emergencies involving Americans abroad—Americans who die, become destitute, get sick, disappear, have accidents, or get arrested. In addition to individual emergencies, the Citizens Emergency Center is the State Department's focal point for major disasters involving Americans abroad: plane crashes, hijackings, natural disasters, terrorist incidents, etc.

The Citizens Emergency Centers
☎ *(202) 647-5225.*
Open 8:15 a.m. to 10:00 p.m. Monday through Friday,
9:00 a.m. to 3:00 p.m. Saturday.

At all other times, including holidays, a duty officer can be reached through the State Department's main number: ☎ *(202) 647-4000.*

If An American Is Killed

Approximately 6000 Americans do die while outside of the U.S. every year. The Citizens Emergency Center assists with the return of remains of approximately 2000. When an American dies abroad, a consular officer notifies the American's family and informs them about options and costs for disposition of remains. Costs for preparing and returning a body to the U.S. are high and are the responsibility of the family. Often local laws and procedures make returning a body to the U.S. for burial a lengthy process.

When an American dies abroad, the Bureau of Consular Affairs must locate and inform the next of kin which can be difficult. If the American's name is known, the Bureau's Office of Passport Services will search for his or her passport application. However, the information there may not be current.

The Bureau of Consular Affairs provides guidance to grieving family members making arrangements for local burial or return of the remains to the U.S. The disposition of remains is affected by local laws, customs, and facilities which are often vastly different from those in the U.S. The Bureau of Consular Affairs relays the family's instructions and necessary private funds to cover the costs involved to the embassy or consulate. The Department of State has no funds to assist in the return of remains or ashes of American citizens who die abroad. Upon completion of all formalities, the consular officer abroad prepares an official Foreign Service Report of Death, based upon the local death certificate, and sends it to the next of kin or legal representative for use in U.S. courts to settle estate matters.

A U.S. consular officer overseas has statutory responsibility for the personal estate of an American who dies abroad if the deceased has no legal representative in the country where the death occurred. The consular officer takes possession of personal effects, such as convertible assets, apparel, jewelry, personal documents and papers. The officer prepares an inventory and then carries out instructions from members of the deceased's family concerning the effects. A final statement of the account is then sent to the next of kin. The Diplomatic Pouch cannot be used to ship personal items, including valuables, but legal documents and correspondence relating to the estate can be transmitted by pouch. In Washington, the Bureau of Consular Affairs gives next of kin guidance on procedures to follow in preparing Letters Testamentary, Letters of Administration, and Affidavits of Next of Kin as acceptable evidence of legal claim of an estate.

If You Have No Money

If you are broke you can turn to a U.S. consular officer abroad for help. The Citizens Emergency Center will help by contacting the destitute person's family, friends, or business associates to raise private funds. It will help transmit these funds to destitute Americans abroad. The Citizens Emergency Center transfers millions of dollars a year in private emergency funds. It can approve small government loans to destitute Americans abroad to tide them over until private funds arrive. Also, the Citizens Emergency Center can approve repatriation loans to pay for destitute Americans' direct return to the U.S.

If You Are Sick Or Injured

The Citizens Emergency Center works with U.S. consuls abroad to assist Americans who become physically or mentally ill while traveling. The Citizens Emergency Center locates family members, guardians, and friends in the U.S., assists in transmitting private funds, and, when necessary, assists in the return of ill or injured Americans to the U.S. by commercial carrier.

If you are injured, the embassy or consulate abroad notifies family members in the U.S. The Bureau of Consular Affairs can assist in sending private funds to the injured American; frequently it collects information on the individual's prior medical history and forwards it to the embassy or consulate. When necessary, the State Department assists in arranging the return of the injured American to the U.S. The full expense must be borne by the injured American or his family.

If Your Friends or Family Can't Find You

The Citizens Emergency Center receives approximately 12,000 inquiries a year concerning the welfare or whereabouts of Americans abroad. Many inquiries are from worried relatives who have not heard from the traveler. Others are attempts to notify the traveler about a family crisis at home. Most welfare/whereabouts inquiries are successfully resolved. However, occasionally, a person is missing. It is the responsibility of local authorities to investigate. The State Department and U.S. consuls abroad do not conduct investigations and may not always tell you if they have found someone. Because of the Privacy Act of 1974 consular officers may not reveal information regarding an individual American's location, welfare, intentions, or problems, to anyone, including family members and Congressional representatives, without the expressed consent of that individual.

When concerned relatives call in, officers of the Bureau of Consular Affairs collect the names of any Americans possibly involved in a disaster and pass them to the embassy and consulates. Officers at post attempt to locate these Americans in order to report on their welfare. The officers work with local authorities and, depending on the circumstances, may personally search hotels, airports, hospitals, or even prisons. As they try to get the information, their first priority is Americans—dead or injured.

If You Need Information During a Foreign Crisis

When a natural or political crisis occurs, the State Department sets up a task force or working group to bring together in one set of rooms all the people necessary to work on that event. Usually this Washington task force will be in touch by telephone 24 hours a day with the Ambassador and Foreign Service Officers at the embassy in the country affected. In most cases phones lines are jammed and people in the States cannot get in touch with people in foreign countries. They then usually call the State Department who then contacts the local embassy.

The immediate job of the State Department's Bureau of Consular Affairs is to provide information to relatives and friends who telephone the State Department to find out if their American relatives are safe.

When commercial transportation entering and leaving a country is disrupted during a political upheaval or natural disaster and if it appears unsafe for Americans to remain, the embassy and consulates will work with the task force in Washington to charter special airflights and ground transportation to help Americans leave. The U.S. Government cannot order Americans to leave a foreign country. It can only advise and try to assist those who wish to leave.

Many times people may want to discover your whereabouts but you may prefer being elusive. Remember that the provisions of the Privacy Act of 1974 prevents consular officers from revealing information regarding your location, welfare, intentions, or problems to anyone, including family members and Congressional representatives, without your express consent. Although sympathetic to the distress this can cause concerned families, consular officers must comply with the provisions of the Privacy Act.

If You are Caught in a Political or Natural Crisis

Earthquakes, hurricanes, political upheavals, acts of terrorism, and hijackings are only some of the events threatening the safety of Americans abroad. Each event is unique and poses its own special difficulties. However, for the State Department there are certain responsibilities and actions that apply in every disaster or crisis.

When a crisis occurs, the State Department sets up a task force or working group to bring together in one set of rooms all the people necessary to work on that event. Usually this Washington task force will be in touch by telephone 24 hours a day with the Ambassador and Foreign Service Officers at the embassy in the country affected.

In a task force, the immediate job of the State Department's Bureau of Consular Affairs is to respond to the thousands of relatives and friends who begin to telephone the State Department concerning their American relatives immediately after the news of a disaster is broadcast.

Relatives want information on the welfare of their U.S. family members and on the disaster. For hard information, the State Department relies on its embassies and consulates abroad. Often these embassies and consulates are also affected by the disaster and lack electricity, phone lines, gasoline, etc. Nevertheless, foreign service officers work hard to get information back to Washington as quickly as possible. This is rarely as quickly as the press is able to relay information. Foreign Service Officers cannot speculate; their information must be accurate. Often this means getting important information from the local government, which may or may not be immediately responsive.

As concerned relatives call in, officers of the Bureau of Consular Affairs collect the names of the Americans possibly involved in the disaster and pass them to the embassy and consulates. Officers at post attempt to locate these Americans in order to report on their welfare. The officers work with local authorities and, depending on the circumstances, may personally search hotels, airports, hospitals, or even prisons. As they try to get the information, their first priority is Americans dead or injured.

Sometimes commercial transportation entering and leaving a country is disrupted during a political upheaval or natural disaster. If this happens, and if it appears unsafe for Americans to remain, the embassy and consulates will work with the task force in Washington to charter special airflights and ground transportation to help Americans to depart. The U.S. Government cannot order Americans to leave a foreign country. It can only advise and try to assist those who wish to leave.

If You Need Information on Other Countries

The Citizens Emergency Center administers the State Department's Consular Information Program. Consular Information Sheets and Travel Warnings are issued to inform traveling Americans of conditions of risk abroad which might affect them adversely.

Travel Warnings

Warnings are issued when the State Department decides, based on all relevant information, to recommend that Americans avoid travel to a certain country. Countries where avoidance of travel is recommended will have Travel Warnings as well as Consular Information Sheets issued.

Consular Information Sheets

Consular Information Sheets are available for every country of the world. They include such information as location of the U.S. Embassy or Consulate in the subject country, unusual immigration practices, health conditions, minor political disturbances, unusual currency and entry regulations, crime and security information, and drug penalties. If an unstable condition exists in a country that is not severe enough to warrant a Warning, a description of the condition(s) may be included under an optional section entitled "Areas of Instability." On limited occasions, we also restate in this section any Embassy advice given to official employees. Consular Information Sheets generally do not include advice, but present information in a factual manner so the traveler can make his or her own decisions concerning travel to a particular country.

To access Consular Information Sheets and Travel Warnings you have a variety of options:

By Mail:
Sending away for them by writing and sending a self-addressed, stamped envelope to the Citizens Emergency Center, Bureau of Consular Affairs, *Room 4811, N.S., U.S. Department of State, Washington, DC 20520.* Consular Affairs Bulletin Board - CABB.

By Audiotext:
Calling the State Department's Citizens Emergency Center at ☎ *(202) 647-5225* (24 hours a day).Using a touchtone phone you can hear a continuously updated recording.

In Person:
Reading the posted reports at each of the 13 regional passport agencies across the U.S.

When Traveling:
Asking for them at the U.S. embassies and consulates abroad.

From your Travel Agent
Travel Agents can provide you with the information using their computerized reservations systems.

Via Fax:
You can fax the reports to yourself using the Consular Affairs automated fax system at ☎ *(202) 647-3000.*

Via Modem:
If you have a personal computer, modem and communications software, you can access the Consular Affairs Bulletin Board or CABB. This service is free of charge.

Modem Number: ☎ *202-647-9225.* Modem Speed: Will accommodate 300, 1200, 2400, 9600 or 14400 bps. Terminal Communications Program: Set to N-8-1 (No parity, 8 bits, 1 stop bit).

Via On-Line Services:
You can also access Consular Information Sheets and Travel Warnings through the Official Airlines Guide (OAG). The OAG provides the full text of Consular Information Sheets and Travel Warnings on many on-line computer services. To obtain information on accessing Consular Information Sheets and Travel Warnings through OAG on any of the following computer services, call the OAG Electronic Edition at ☎ *(800) 323-4000.*

Other carriers of State Department Information are :

CompuServe

Dialcom

Dialog

Dow Jones News/Retrieval

General Videotext

Delphi NewsNet

GEnie

IP Sharp

iNet-America

iNet-Bell of Canada

Telenet

Western Union-Easylink.

CompuServe subscribers may type GO STATE at any "!" prompt.

Infosys America Inc. (Travel Online BBS on the SmartNet International Computer Network in the U.S., Canada and overseas. The (modem) telephone number for Infosys America is ☎ *(314) 625-4054.*

Interactive Office Services, Inc. offers on-line travel information in Travel+Plus through the networks listed below. For information on access, call Travel+Plus at ☎ *(617) 876-5551* or ☎ *(800) 544-4005.*

Delphi, MCI (RCA Hotline)

Unison Bell South

TUG FTCC Answer Bank

The Overseas Security Electronic Bulletin Board provides State Department Consular Information Sheets and Travel Warnings as a free service (purchase of necessary software required) for American firms doing business overseas. Apply to the Executive Director, Overseas Security Advisory Council (DS/OSAC), *Department of State, Washington, DC 20522-1003.*

AIDS

Perhaps the most dangerous and most publicized disease is AIDS. AIDS, unlike other terminal illnesses such as cancer, strikes right at the heart of American phobia. Pain for pleasure. AIDS is the terminal phase of HIV (Human immunodeficiency virus). HIV is not life threatening but is usually the precursor to AIDS and then death by cancer, pneumonia and other afflictions that attack the weakened human immune system. It has roughly a 9-year incubation period. AIDS has been shunted off as the gay plague, the African disease.

The reality is that in the late 70s, Americans took a predominantly Central African disease and turned it into the biggest killer of young American men. In San Francisco, AIDS is the number one killer of gay men. Sobering but nothing compared to Uganda where it causes 80% of all deaths.

Zoonosis

AIDS first began near the Zaire-Burundi border. A 1992 Rolling Stone article by AIDS activist Blaine Elswood places the blame on polio vaccines grown in primate kidney cells and then injected into humans in 1957 and 1958. Other researchers had injected malaria-tainted blood from chimpanzees and mangabeys into human volunteers. The first AIDS case is purported to be a British sailor (who had never been to Africa) who died in 1959. The case wasn't officially recognized by the Centers for Disease Control until 1981.

There are two types of human AIDS virus: HIV-1, the most common type, and HIV-2, originally only found in people from Guinea-Bissau in West Africa. HIV-2 is very close to SIV (Simian immunodeficiency virus) found in sooty mangabeys. Curiously, SIV is not found in the Asian macaques normally used for research. Sooty mangabeys are commonly eaten by villagers in Africa. There is no hard proof that AIDS came from monkeys or even from Africa but the preponderance of evidence shows that AIDS may have originated in central Africa within the past 50 years.

Who has AIDS

Originally, America turned AIDS into a predominantly gay, urban affliction. Of the 356,275 cases of AIDS reported in the U.S., the breakdown went like this: 54% were gay men, 24% were heterosexual IV drug users, 7% were gay IV drug users, 1% were hemophiliacs, 2% were recipients of blood transfusions, 6% were infected through heterosexual contact and for 6% the transmission method was not known.

AIDS

More interesting, of the 6% or 23,039 people who contracted AIDS through heterosexual contact, 12,620 had sex with an IV drug user, 213 had sex with a hemophiliac or blood transfusion recipient, 508 had sex with an HIV infected person, 1375 had sex with a bisexual male and 8323 could not specify the origin of the infection.

AIDS is expected to slow population growth, lower life expectancies and raise child mortality rates in many of the world's poorer countries over the next 25 years, according to a report by the U.S. Census Bureau.

By the year 2010, a Ugandan's life expectancy will decline by 45 per cent to 32 years—down from 59 years projected before AIDS. A Haitian's life expectancy will fall to 44 years, also down from 59 years. Life expectancy in Thailand will drop from a projected 75 years to 45.

The Census Bureau's "World Population Profile" estimates that the world population has reached 5,642,000,000 and is expected to top 7.9 billion within 25 years.

Because of AIDS, by the year 2010, Thailand's child mortality rates are expected to increase from the current 20 deaths per 1000 children born to 110 deaths. In Uganda, the jump will be from 90 deaths to 175 deaths out of every 1000 children born. In Malawi, it will soar from 130 to 210 deaths per 1000. Overall, premature death rates in those countries will double by 2010, compared with 1985 levels.

In 16 countries—the African nations of Burkina Faso, Burundi, Central African Republic, Congo, Cote d'Ivoire, Kenya, Malawi, Rwanda, Tanzania, Uganda, Zaire, Zambia and Zimbabwe, plus Brazil, Haiti and Thailand—AIDS will slow population growth rates so dramatically that by 2010, there will be 121 million fewer people than previously forecast. Thailand's population will actually fall by nearly one percent because of AIDS deaths, according to the bureau.

In the United States, AIDS increased the premature death rate last year by 1.5 percent. And in 1992, AIDS became the leading cause of death nationally for men aged 25-44 years. The U.S. Census Bureau also said that in 1994, half of the world's population resided in just six countries. In order of population they were: China (1.2 billion), India (920 million), United States (261 million), Brazil (159 million) and Russia (150 million).

The overall population growth rate for Earth has slowed from 2 per cent per year in the 1960s to 1.5 per cent in the 1990s. According to the bureau, that slowdown had less to do with family planning and contraception than with the aging of people in the industrialized world.

AIDS cases in Myanmar are estimated to be between 100,000 and 200,000, making it the third worst affected country in Asia, after India and Thailand. Only 189 AIDS cases had been reported at the end of 1993 in Yangon, Mandalay and Kengtung. HIV infection rates among Burmese intravenous drug users is the highest in the world.

In the drug area of Bhamo and Myitkyina near the Chinese border, 90% of the users have been infected. Mandalay reported an 84% infection rate among IV drug users. Yangon reports 74%. There are shooting galleries where addicts regularly get hits from shared needles. There are 13,000 registered heroin addicts. Sex workers returning from Thailand to the border regions are causing infection in the general population.

Save Humanity

I always get a little nervous when I see the amount of money and time that go into animal, ecological, art and entertainment special interest groups. The images of small children dying of starvation and disease seem to have less impact than the image of a baby seal having its brains bashed in. We eat animals and we wear their skins on a daily basis, but if you shot a calf on TV and ate it I am sure it would spawn hundreds of letters about cruelty, etc. There is a hidden Darwinian ethos amongst many Westerners who assume that AIDS in San Francsico, starvation in Africa, the plague in India and earthquakes in Indonesia are just God's way of cleaning up the mess. There are others that realize more correctly that civilization is a machine that we do not have the manual for. Humans are constantly learning cause and effect the hard way. Cut down trees to grow crops and the dirt washes away. Start a war over oil and an entire nation is plunged into the Middle Ages. Pocket aid money to buy seed from Western governements and use it to go shopping in Paris and entire populations starve. We don't see the cause a lot of times, but we do see the effect.

Americans are getting thicker hides than the endangered rhino. Reality shows spawn like flies from maggots and people watch the pain and suffering of total strangers interupted every eight minutes by commercials that sell toothpaste and new cars. The 4 o'clock, 6 o'clock, 7 o'clock, 8 o'clock, 9 o'clock and 10 o'clock news cut together the world's woes and wars into 15 minutes complete with snazzy graphics, logos and maps. Designed to stop channel surfers and fire freaks, television zooms in on bang bang with nice clean images of blood, explosions, screaming and "you are there" action. The trouble is you aren't there, and even if you are, television makes it seem more distant, less painful and with the flick of a remote control, fixed.

People helping people can make a difference. It might be teaching kids a song or working for 10 years for their indigenous rights. Every time you do something for someone instead of just watching, a life is changed. Dangerous places need people who can help push back the danger. You don't need to be a bomb disposal expert or a facial reconstuction expert to make a difference; you can also pick up a shovel or mend a net.

Those looking for a productive outlet for their urges to make the world a better place should look into the variety of groups that strive for global peace. Many of the groups are bad hangovers from the cold war era. Some engage in endless discussion to provide solutions, while other groups get their hands dirty and clean up the mess. We would advise you to investigate the results of a group's efforts rather than its intentions. Don't waste your time polluting the world with more hot air.

The solution to the world's problems is simple. The more people that look for solutions and actively carry out the remedies, the better off the world will be. There are groups that can provide an outlet for your need to make the world a better place. Some require major commitments of time; others can take your money and put it toward projects that do good. There is no way we could list every charitable organization that seeks to elevate the position of people in the world, but here is a start:

Life Enhancers

American Field Service Intercultural Programs

313 East 43rd Street
New York, NY 10017
☎ *(212) 949-4242*

The Carter Center

One Copenhill
Atlanta, Georgia 30307
☎ *(404) 331-3900*
FAX (404) 331-0283

Jimmy Carter has been busy these days. His peace negotiatons in North Korea, Haiti and Bosnia have been effective in achieving short-term results as well as angering many hardliners by his friendly approach to our enemies. Carter shows that a mild-mannered, ever smiling good ol' boy from the South could play the perfect good cop to the U.S. military's bad cop. Jimmy Carter seems to be working overtime for the Nobel Peace prize. Not because he needs more stuff to hang on his wall, but because he really believes that all people have good in them and he has a responsibility to make the world a better place.

Jimmy and Rosalynn's "keep busy and do good" organization is the Carter Center. Eternally miffed by Reagan's skunk job on the Iran hostages, Jimmy is in the good guy business in a big way. He works out of a 100,000 sq. ft. complex complete with chapel, library, conference facilities and museum. Seeded by $28 million in donations, the center works to fight disease, hunger, poverty, conflict and oppression in 30 countries. The center is linked to Emory University and is operated by the Federal government. Jimmy Carter has been busy acting as a force for good and justice everywhere, from doing Bill's dirty work in Haiti and North Korea to monitoring elections in Africa. It could be argued that Carter has done better out of office than in.

Some programs could be considered downright useless (preparing for democratice elections in Liberia and teaching CIS TV journalists how to cover elections) to down home practical (like eradicating the Guinea Worm and immunizing kids). The center is always happy to receive donations and resumes of motivated individuals who want to volunteer their time. With Jimmy's upstaging of fellow southerner Clinton you might just be making to Soviet Union, northern Ireland and elsewhere.

Connect US-USSR
☎ *(612) 333-1962*
A nonprofit Minneapolis organization that arranges sister-city projects between the Twin Cities and Novosibirsk, a Soviet city of 1.5 million people. They also develop projects for other Americans and Soviets seeking exchanges and relationships.

Council for a Livable World
20 Park Plaza
Boston, MA 02116
☎ *(617) 542-2282*

Cultural Survival Inc.
215 First Street
Cambridge, Massechussets 02142
☎ *(617) 495-2562*
FAX (617) 621-3814
There is much talk that there is more work being done to save the rain forest than the people who live in it. Nomadic forest dwellers have no money, own no land and in many cases do not integrate into societies who are pushing them out of their homeland. Having seen the havoc wreaked on our own native Indians and Inuit it is difficult to come up with viable alternatives to their eventual extinction.

This is an organization of anthropologists and researchers whose goal is to help indigenous peoples (like tropical forest dwellers) develop at their own pace and with their own cultures intact. Cultural Survival's weapon is the almighty dollar and they put it in the hands of the groups they help. Working with indigenious peoples and ethnic minorities, they import sustainably harvested, non-timber forest products. What are those, you ask? Well, handicrafts, cashew and brazil nuts, babassu oil, rubber, bananas, even beeswax. The end result is that indigenous peoples gain lands, develop cash crops and don't have to live in shantytowns or timber camps to support themselves.

Founded in 1972, the group has a variety of methods of achieving its goals; education programs, importing and selling products, providing expertise to larger aid groups and providing technical assistance to local groups seeking economic viability.

The group has projects in Brazil, Guinea-Bissau, Guatemala, Ecuador, the Philippines and Zambia. Membership ($45) gets you a subscription to the *CSE Matters* and the quarterly journal *Cultural Survival Manual*. Ask for a free catalog of products. By purchasing the products for sale you directly support the peoples who gather and manufacture them, something very rare in this world of markups and middlemen.

If you would like to work as an intern, they are looking for people to help crank out the newsletter, raise funds, handle the office work and expand the network of indigenous groups and supporters. To receive an application contact Pia Maybury-Lewis, Director of Interns, Cultural Survival *46 Brattle Street, Cambridge, Massechussets 02138,* ☎ *(617) 441-5400* or fax your resume and a letter that explains your personal interests to ☎ *(617) 441-5417*.

EarthStewards Network
P.O. Box 10697
Bainbridge Island, WA 98110
☎ *(206) 842-7986*

The Eisenhower Exchange Fellowships Inc.
256 South 16th Street
Philadephia, Pennsylvania 19102

☎ *(215) 546-1738*
FAX (215) 546-4567

You don't have to be a pimply-faced student to do good in the world. Captains of industry, artists, farmers and educators can do their bit too. Based on the premise that the best leadership is by example, the Eisenhower Exchange Fellowship (EEF) is looking for prime examples of successful people from education, business and government. The organization allows you to submit your own ideas on what needs to be done and how you intend to do it. In other cases host countries ask for specific expertise and they try to fill the need. In either case you will find the opportunity offered by the EEF rewarding and stimulating. You can reach out and touch someone and EEF will pick up the bill.

If you have a few years, a little knowledge and a yen for travel but don't have too much money, you might want to apply for an Eisenhower Exchange Fellowship. They offer two shades of the same color, the USA-EEF program and the USA Emerging Democracies Program. The former is a one month gig in October that that will take you and your spouse to a selected foreign country (this years choices are Argentina, Taiwan and Turkey) where you'll speak on topics like journalism, international relations and human rights. The EEF will take care of all the arrangements (and the basic bills) on this short but intense trip.

The Emerging Democracies will require three months of your life and will usually plunk winning candidates in places like the Czech Republic or Romania talking on topics like information technology, arts management and helping extend the growing season in Romania. Candidates should be "mid career professionals who have demonstrated outstanding achievements in their professions." You will compete with other over-acheivers, but once selected expect the foundation to pick up airfare, domestic travel, housing and meals for you and a spouse (yours, of course). Leave the kids at home. You will conduct workshops, attend numerous meetings, get one on one and hopefully inspire and enlighten your hosts. You must be an American citizen and have some experience in leadership and participation in organizations outside of your regular place of work. The bowling league won't cut it.

The Eisenhower Exchange Fellowship was founded in 1953 to honor and emulate then President Eisenhower. Their goal is to promote the exchange of ideas, information and perspectives throughout the world.

Experiment in International Living

Black Mountain Road
Brattleboro, VT 05301
☎ *(802) 257-7751*

National Charities Information Bureau (NCIB)

☎ *212-929-6300*

NCIB regularly publishes listings and reports on charities, monitoring which groups meet their standards. Ask for a copy of their *Wise Giving Guide*. Individual contributions of $25 or more and corporations and foundations contributing $100 or more will be sent the *Wise Giving Guide* for one year. NCIB also publishes detailed evaluations about organizations. As many as three reports at a time are available without charge.

Overseas Development Network

333 Valencia Street, Suite 330
San Francisco, California 94103
☎ *(415 431-4204*
FAX (415) 431-5953

The ODN is primarily for students who want to work overseas in an intern (read no pay) position. This is also called "alternative tourism" in the San Francisco area. The benefit is that you get to get in there and do something about hunger, poverty and social injustice. The 12-year-old organization has placed over 200 interns overseas and in the Appalachian area of the States (yes, the Third World standards do still exist in America). If you want to do your good deeds even closer to home ODN membership($15 Student, $25 for a regular member) will introduce you to other like-minded students. There are also positions with ODN requiring about 12–20 hours a week. You can gain experience organizing, promoting, writing, marketing and are considered to have a good "foot in the door" position if you want to get serious in global affairs. All positions are unpaid and require a minimum commitment of three months and eight hours a week. You can take part in a local ODN chapter, work to build sustainable locally initiated development programs within your local community or just contribute to the ODN's ongoing programs.

The most tangible fund raising program is the annual Bike-Aid program. The "spin" has been toward AIDS awareness over the last two years. The 3600–1000 mile cross-country event is in its eighth year and has raised over $1 million for international grassroots development programs. The idea is for small (25–30) groups of cyclists to cover any one of five routes (Seattle, Portland, San Francisco, Montreal and Austin) converging on Washington D.C. in late August. There is even an all-women route that starts in Portland. You find people to sponsor you at about a buck a mile. Along the way participants meet local leaders and help in community projects about once a week. All ages are welcome. If you are not a bike rider you can help out by hosting riders in your home, sponsoring riders, even acting as a local publicist.

An information packet on the Bike-Aid program will cost you five bucks. They also offer publications that offer insight into opportunities for alternative travel:

Pros and Cons of the Peace Corps ($7)

A compilation of articles written by former Peace Corps members. It also includes a list of publications that can lead you to employment and intern positions around the world.

The Peace Corps and More ($10, students $7)

120 Ways to Work, Study and Travel in the Third World

Last updated in 1993, this book will give you the names addresses and requirements of over 100 organizations that can get you overseas and working

A Handbook for Creating your Own Internship in International Development ($7.95)

This is a how-to book on financing your internship, finding placement with an international development firm, written by interns who have been there and done that. The new 1994 edition is available.

Peace Corps
1990 St., N.W.
Room 9320
Washington, D.C. 20526
☎ *800-424-8580*

When most people in the '60s and '70s thought about how they could change the world, the Peace Corps came to mind. It may surprise you to know that the Vietnam-era hearts and minds division of the U.S. Government is still hard at work making the world a better place without killing or maiming.

The Peace Corps is pure American do-goodism from its Woodstock-style logo (the Peace Corps was formed in 1961) to its Puritan slogan "The Toughest Job You'll Ever Love" and goes straight to the soul of every midwestern farm boy. The Corps appeals to the American love of doing good things in bad places. In the 30 years of the Peace Corps' existence, 140,000 Americans have heeded the call and the world has truly benefited by an outpouring of American know-how. Last year there were about 6500 volunteers spread out over 90 countries. What do you get? Well, the answer is better stated as what do you give. Successful applicants go through two to three months of language, technical and cultural training for each "tour." You will get a small allowance for housing, food and clothing, airfare to and from your posting and 24 days of vacation a year.

While in-country you will work with a local counterpart and may be completely on your own in a small rural village or major city. The pay-off is that you can actually make things happen, understand a different culture and say that you did something about the world. Does the reality meet the fantasy? Apparently it does. The average length of time spent in the Peace Corps is six years with nine months of training. That works out to three two-year tours with the minimum training. All ex-Peace Corps volunteers we talked to said it was among the most rewarding years of their lives.

Getting in is not that easy, but once in, you join a club that can benefit you greatly in your career. Being an ex-Peace Corps member says that you are about giving, hard work and a little more worldly than most.

You must be a U.S. citizen and at least 18 years old and healthy (the Peace Corps feels you must at least be in your twenties to have the maturity required). Most successful applicants have at least a bachelor's degree. You must also have a minimum 2.5 grade point average for educational assignments or experience in the field you want to enter. Although there is no limit on age, the Peace Corps is typically a young person's game and considered to be an excellent way to get a leg up in government and private sector employment. The government will give you $5400 when you get out, find you a job in the government on a noncompetitive basis and even help you apply for the over 50 special scholarships available for ex-Peace Corps members.

The emphasis is on training and education in the agricultural, construction and educational areas. There are not too many fine arts requirements although they do have a category for art teacher. Couples with dependents are a no no, and couples are strongly discouraged. It helps if you know a foreign language, have overseas experience and have teaching/tutoring experience.

The Peace Corps does not mess around in countries that are overtly hostile or dangerous to Americans like Peru, Colombia, Angola, Algeria and Iran. Also you will not be posted to Monaco or Paris. You can be posted to Fiji, Thailand, Central Africa or most countries in the CIS. If you are curious the Peace Corps recruiters hold two-hour evening seminars at their regional offices. Don't be put off by the slightly 80's banner of "Globalize Your Resume." You can meet with returning volunteers and ask all the questions you want.

Philanthropic Advisory Service (PAS)
of the Council of Better Business Bureau (CBBB)
☎ 703-276-0100

The Council and its Philanthropic Advisory Service (PAS) promote ethical standards of business practices and protect consumers through voluntary self-regulation and monitoring activities. They publish a bimonthly list of philanthropic organizations that meet the Council of Better Business Bureau's (CBBB) Standards for Charitable Solicitations. The standards include: Public Accountability, Use of Funds, Solicitations and Informational Materials, Fund Raising Practices and Governance. Ask for a copy of *Give But Give Wisely* ($1.00). Many of the groups have e-mail addresses, databases and on-line services.

Save the Children
50 Wilton Road
Westport, CT 06880
203-226-7272
☎ *(800) 243-5075*

UNICEF
3 U.N. Plaza
New York, NY 10017
☎ *(212-326-7000*

Youth Exchange Service (YES)
4675 MacArthur Court
Suite 830
Newport Beach, CA 92660
☎ *(800) 848-2121*
☎ *(714) 955-2030*

An international teenage exchange-student program dedicated to world peace. If you are interested in hosting an international teenage "ambassador" contact this group.

Medical Aid Groups

There are angels in Rwanda, Somalia, Angola, Afghanistan and Iraq. They are not there to convert souls or play harps. They are not soldiers or politicians but white coated volunteers who sew back limbs, pull out shrapnel from babies' heads and minister to the sick and dying. They are the men and women who try to ease the suffering caused by violent actions. Natural disasters also tax the resources and stamina of aid workers to the limit. If you don't mind stacking bodies like firewood or can live with the ever present stench of too many sick people in one place, you will do just fine.

The world needs people who clean up the mess caused by governments. If there is a disaster, chances are you will see these folks in there long before the journalists and the politicians try to grab air time. These are nondenominational groups that are found in the world's most dangerous places. If you have medical skills and want to save more lives in a day than a tentful of TV evangelists in a lifetime, this is the place to be. Conditions are beyond primitive, usually makeshift refugee camps on the edges of emerging conflicts. Many groups will walk or helicopter in to war-torn regions to assist in treating victims. Many aid workers have been targeted for death because of their policy of helping both sides. There is constant danger from rocket attacks, land mines, communicable diseases and riots. These people are not ashamed to stagger out of a tent after being up 48 hours straight, have a good cry and then get back to work saving more lives. It hurts but it feels good. Contact the following organizations for more information.

American Red Cross

National Headquarters
17th and D Street, NW
Washington, D.C. 20006
☎ *(202) 737-8300*

AmeriCares

161 Cherry Street
New Canaan, CT 06840
☎ *(203) 966-5195*
☎ *(800) 486-4357*

Amnesty International USA

322 Eighth Avenue
New York, NY 10001
☎ *(212) 807-8400*

Amnesty International likes to shine light in dark places. When the London-based organization organizes the dissemination of thousands of letters, they tend to send jailors and governments scattering like cockroaches scurrying for cover. By showing these governments that they are aware, they hope to embarrass or pressure governments into better treatment of political prisoners. Their method is simple and easy to effect. They coordinate the writing and mailing of letters to the captors of prisoners of conscience. Their methods have been proven successful and the international group was awarded the Nobel Peace prize in 1977 for their efforts to promote observance of the UN Universal Declaration of Human Rights.

The membership is over 500,000 people in over 150 countries. Together they can create an avalanche of mail and global protest over the mistreatment of prisoners. Amnesty International has groups that focus on health needs, legal support, human rights awareness and education and even a writers group which will write three prisoner appeals each month to government authorities. There is an Urgent Action network which will step up the pressure to aid prisoners who are in immediate danger of execution or torture.

Amnesty International began in London in 1961 and so far claims they have come to the rescue of 43,000 prisoners. Today the staff of 200 monitors news and information and communications from around the world to seek out cases of mistreatment. Their goal is to pressure governments to end torture, executions, political killings and disappearances, to ensure speedy trials for all political prisoners and to effect the release of prisoners of conscience provided they have neither used nor advocated violence. Many countries with political prisoners (don't be so smug, the U.S. is on their list) insist that they are just meddlers. They are the only global organization that can really apply enough pressure to save the health and life of many political prisoners.

As a member you can provide letter writing assistance, organizing skills or financial support. Memberships run $25 a year ($15 for students) and you are urged to participate in as many programs and networks as you would like. Freedom writers are sent sample letters which are then written and mailed by the member. Lawyers can contribute research and defense skills. Doctors can work to dissuade medical practitioners from participating in torture and executions. Students can join a 2000-school wide student network that works in groups of five to 100 people to write letters, educate peers and gather signatures for petitions. Regular joes can get writer's cramp sending letters to prisoners identified in the Amesty Action newsletter. Amnesty International has local chapters in 47 states as well as four regional offices and their national office in Washington, ☎ *(202) 544-0200*. If you want to attend the monthly orientation session held in New York leave a message on Randy Paul's machine ☎ *(212) 873-1073*.

A few tips on writing letters to governments:

AI encourages members to write letters, but telegrams are are more effective in gaining the attention of the reader. State the purpose of your letter in the first sentence and make sure you end it with your request. If you are writing about a specific person, clearly state his name. The letters should be short. Be polite and state your concern as simply and honestly as possible. Always assume that the person you are writing to is a reasonable person. Tell the reader what you do for a living and what country you are from. Do not bring up politics, religion or opinions. Use the proper title of the addressee, write in English, write it by hand and sign the letter "Yours respectfully."

CARE

Worldwide Headquarters
660 First Avenue
New York, NY 10016
☎ *(212) 686-3110*

Catholic Relief Services

209 West Fayette Street
Baltimore, MD 21201
☎ *(301) 625-2220*

Human Rights Internet

Harvard Law School
Cambridge, MA 02138
☎ *(617) 495-9924*

Human Rights Watch

1522 K Street, NW
Suite 910
Washington, D.C. 20005
☎ *(202) 371-6592*

This organization promotes and monitors human rights worldwide. Human Rights Watch serves as an umbrella organization to Africa Watch, Asia Watch, Americas Watch, Middle East Watch, Helsinki Watch and the Fund for Free Expression.

International League for Human Rights

432 Park Avenue South
New York, NY 10016
☎ *(212) 684-1221*

Medical Aid for the Third World

Oudestraat 34, 2660 Hoboken
Antwerp, BELGIUM
☎ *(32) 3-828-0243*
☎ *(32) 2-513-6626*
FAX (32) 2-513-98-31

Médecin Sans Frontière

Amsterdam
FAX 20-205 170
Equilibre Association L01 1901
France
☎ *72-73-04-14*

Reporters Sans Frontieres

International Secretariat
17, rue Abbe de L'Epee
Paris, France

RSF was founded in 1985 and has offices in Belgium, Canada, France, Germany, Italy, Spain and Switzerland with members in 71 countries. Their job is to defend imprisoned journalists and press freedom around the world.

They will send protest letters, provide lawyers (if possible) and other forms of assistance to reporters in jail. If you want to convert to Journalism after you are jailed these folks can't help you.

Survival International

310 Edgeware Road
London, England W2 1DY

CTU

Don and Judy Feeney, a couple in their early 40s, run a business that provides security firms to local businesses. They also have an à la carte menu of other services that include corporate security, crisis management training and hostage rescue. The fact is that Don is a Delta Force vet and knows a little something about finding or rescuing people. They have carried out successful retrievals of children in Peru, Jordan, Bangladesh and Tunisia.

They specialize in children who have been spirited away to a foreign country, usually by a parent. What they do is completely illegal in some countries, so Don has done a little jail time as a result of his chosen profession. An attempt to rescue a young girl in Iceland got Feeney and his cohort sentenced to two years in prision. He served one year that included six months in isolation after he attempted to escape and was recaptured.

The international rescue missions are pure cloak and dagger stuff where they adopt personaes, and disguises. Their disguises have included movie location scout, investment banker and wine merchant. Typical missions include a lot of close calls, long distance air travel and a little rough stuff when needed, but operatives do not carry guns on missions.

In 1984 after 16 years of military service, Don Feeney, 41, a former army sniper and member of the 1980 hostage team that tried to rescue the hostages in Iran, resigned to avoid disciplinary action. He and other Delta Force men were working undercover in Beirut and were forced to live on small per diems, so they worked out kickbacks with the local hotel owners. Feeney says he was doing what was necessary to get the job done; the Army says he was bending the rules too far.

In any case there aren't a whole lot of people in the phone book under hostage rescue. As of press time we have been unable to obtain contact information on CTU

Political Action Groups

Center on Budget and Policy Priorities

236 Massachusetts Avenue, NE
Washington, D.C. 20002
☎ *(202) 546-9737*

Citizen Exchange Council

12 West 31st Street
New York, NY 10001-4415

☎ *(212) 643-1985*

Foreign Policy Association

729 Seventh Avenue
New York, NY 10019
☎ *(212) 764-4050*

Institute for Policy Studies

1601 Connecticut Avenue, NW
Washington, D.C. 20009
☎ *(202) 234-9382*

Peace Links

729 8th Street SE
Suite 300
Washington, D.C. 20003
☎ *(202) 544-0805*
FAX (202) 544-0809

Founded in 1982 at a kitchen table by Betty Bumpers and a group of friends, Peace Links is a group of about 30,000 citizens (mostly female) who work to eradicate conflict and the threat of nuclear war. Although Peace Links is a relic of the cold war, they feel that the threat of nuclear war is not past and they have shifted their focus to eliminate armed violence, warfare, conflict and other violent ways of settling differences. Peace Links creates local citizen groups to pressure politicians; they provide educational programs to schools on how to resolve conflicts without violence and they have an unusual Pen Pals for Peace program that sends and recieve letters stressing goodwill and peace.

They are developing exchange programs between the CIS, China and the U.S. and are looking for donations to continue their work. You can also buy a Peace Pal Bunny (a 7.5" high stuffed rabbit with the world in her paws) for $10 or a video of a Peace Links' trip to the former Soviet Union.

Contact them about the US/USSR Letter Links, which organizes people from those countries to write and receive letters.

World Policy Institute

777 UN Plaza, 5th floor
New York, NY 10017
☎ *(212) 490-0010*

Educational Organizations

Foundation for Global Community (Formerly Beyond War)

222 High Street
Palo Alto, CA 94301
☎ *(415) 328-7756*
FAX (415) 3328-7785

Before the red AIDS ribbon was the hip lapel pin there was the ubiquitous earth pin, the San Francisco version of the midwesterner's Rotarian pin. The group originally wanted to show the Soviet Union that it could be good-vibed out of existence (maybe it worked) and had to refocus their efforts once the Evil Empire went bankrupt. Since 1991 they have been working on building a global community.

They are a new-agish group whose goals are mired in PC-speak. Their mission statement "Discover, live and communicate what is needed to build a world that functions for the benefit of all life" has a Berkleyish happy face ring to it. Their list of current projects includes the Heroic Choice(learning how to move beyond self interest to a larger purpose) educational process, a Fifth Discipline Team (how to integrate the process of systems thinking) and The Enneagram learning process (understanding the nine personality types to instill a deeper appreciation of people) are probably too obtuse for New Yorkers or Midwesterners. In plainspeak they hope to offer nonviolent alternatives to resolving conflict. They also offer educational programs that teach that all life is one interconnected whole.

For example, they have brought together Armenians and Azeris at the Sequoia Seminar retreat in Ben Lomond, California to discuss how to end the war in Nagorno-Karabakh. They then sent four participants to Azerbaijan to work toward the peace process. It will be interesting to see if the Northern California free thinkers can roll back five centuries of ethnic hate or the Armenian tanks. Some may find the mental gymnastics and endless intellectual stroking a little like showing drive-in intermission films in Somalia. Positive, entertaining but ultimately inneffective.

The important thing is that they search for answers and they try to effect change in people's thinking. It's up to you what you do with all that positive energy and clear thinking. For now they have members in 32 states and offer a variety of materials (audio and video tapes, posters, stickers, cards, pins and books that offer imagery and information that reinforce the idea of a global community). If you are commited to embracing incongruent life-styles, engaging others while learning and want to show that all of life is one interconnected whole, then donate over $25 or order their catalog of materials. The 5000-plus members receive their bimonthly copy of Timeline, a 24 page newsletter.

Global Education Associates
475 Riverside Drive
Suite 456
New York, NY 10115
☎ *(212) 870-3290*

Institute for Peace and Justice
4144 Lindell, #122
St. Louis, MO 63108
☎ *(314) 533-4445*

Military and Paramilitary Organizations

How to travel free, meet interesting people and then kill them

There is a small group of people who think that planting seedlings and buying running shoes made out of recycled garbage bags is not doing enough. Young men who hunger for danger should be lining up to be cabbies or donning the polyester warrior garb of the late night convenience store clerk. Instead, our young are force fed a diet of well armed soldiers barfing out endless rounds of 9mms and steroid-pumped knuckleheads causing serious dental bills. At least on TV. In the inner city there is less plot but a lot more action. With all this violence becoming the Muzak of the nineties it is no surprise that the more ambitious think the best way to make the world a better place is to start by eliminating some of the bad guys. Jimmy Carter doesn't have a show called "Have Mouth Will Travel" and it is unlikely that Stallone will star as a soft-spoken peace broker anytime soon. For now we just shoot first and negotiate later.

But adventure stirs deep in the loins of youth. What can they do to make this world a better place and tell stories to their grandkids? In the old days you could ride off to the Crusades, discover the New World or just raise hell in some wealthy potentate's army. Since then there have been enough great wars to occupy the heroic and romantic. Between our great and not so great wars (when Uncle Sam made you volunteer) poets, thugs and the bloodthirsty have volunteered for a variety of noble causes from the Russian Revolution to the Spanish Civil War. Today those who seek to make a difference by direct action can choose to join an army or group that is actively fighting for independence, freedom or any other cause. Keep in mind that you can lose your American citizenship if you do, and your chances of being summarily executed at the side of the road if captured are high. The shadowy nature and basic illegality of the mercenary business means we can't provide you with neat little addresses and phone numbers of all the people who recruit or hire mercenaries, but we can give a general overview of what is out there and a few interesting highlights of this ancient and much maligned profession.

Happiness is a warm gun

Today's armed forces look pretty good to the hordes of young men and women who can't find jobs. Despite the dire warnings and foreign rumblings there is little chance for good versus evil action in today's globocop environment. The world's businesses are just too tightly interwoven to allow another Axis versus Allied confrontation. The U.S military has offically seen action in Korea, Vietnam, Lebanon, Iraq, Grenada, Panama, Libya, Somalia and Haiti. Strangely none of these have been official wars but rather police actions or international brigades fighting to support victimized countries. There have been few guts and glory movies about action in Angola, Cuba, Cambodia, Nicarauga, El Salvador and numerous other covert operations. Most of our military expenditure and effort have been concentrated on a cold war with the Soviet Union and China. With the lack of clear objectives, simple villains or even positive role models, it is no surprise that the U.S. military is having trouble attracting the caliber of soldier it had with the draft. Scores are down, average IQ levels are down while the equipment and technology gets more complicated. Although political science and analysis is not required of grunts, it is very difficult for modern day veterans of Somalia, Haiti and Beirut to understand why they fought.

It would be hard to get excited about fighting for America's freedom while sitting in a barracks in Beirut or babysitting missiles pointed at Moscow. What can you expect if you sign up in today's army? The Army's nine-week basic training program at Fort Jackson, S.C. transforms civilians to soldiers 60 raw recruits at a time. At bases like Fort Jackson in South Carolina 70,000 military personnel are trained annually, 3 million since the base's opening in 1917.

Upon arrival you can expect to fill out horrendous amounts of paperwork. You spend the first six days at the Reception Battalion where you will pick up your uniforms and get a shaved head, shots and you're given 16-hour doses of KP or kitchen patrol. The second week is filled with 12-hour days (with reveille at 4 a.m. and ending at 8 p.m.) drill and ceremony movements, classroom work, la and navigation course, bayonet assault and an obstacle course centered around the Victory Tower.

The second month begins with basic rifle marksmanship. You will learn to understand and care for your M-16 like no other physical object you will own. You will learn to fire at targets as far as 300 meters away. Based on your peformance you will be called a marksman, sharpshooter or expert. Toward the end of the second month the weaponry gets serious, with the M-60 machine gun, AT4 anti-tank weapon and hand grenades. Instead of firing your weapon you get a taste of what it will be like on the receiving end as you learn how to move around under fire complete with barbwired obstacles, dynamite going off and M-60 rounds being fired over your head as you crawl 300 meters on your belly.

The last week of training intensifies with PT testing and working with explosives. The climax is a three-day field exercise where trainees get to play war by digging foxholes and taking eight-mile hikes with full packs. The last few days are spent cleaning barracks in preparation for the next cadets. How tough is it? New recruits will say very; the old salts will say not as tough as it used to be. Corporal punishment was banned in the mid-1970's and sexual harrassement has been added to the list of subjects taught.

Minor punishment is confined to "smoke-sessions," for the less than motivated. These semi-punitive periods of intense physical training are designed to remind the errant soldier who is in charge. Soldiers are chewed out using the entire spectrum of profanity.

The front-leaning-rest position (a push-up that is never completed) is also used as punishment. There is no form of entertainment since there technically is no rest time. Television, newspapers and radios are taboo. Mail and occasional phone calls are allowed. Three washing machines and five showerheads are considered enough to keep 60 active men clean.

Once out of basic training you can expect to be posted to an area in line with your specialty. The military is still using technology about 10–20 years behind what you find on the outside. The main focus in the military is changing from 40's style ground wars to 70's style rapid deployment tactics. The Army provides lousy pay, good benefits and a chance to pack in two careers in a lifetime. As for furthering a cause or making the world a better place, one only has to look at Lebanon, Kuwait, Somalia and Vietnam to see the results of gunboat diplomacy.

Since McDonald's is not hiring any Green Berets or Navy SEALS to take down Burger Kings, just who is hiring military experts? Well technically, nobody. Although many countries like Brunei (which uses Ghurkas), the Vatican (which has about 100 Swiss guards), the Spanish Foreign Legion (the poor man's legion) and Oman have armies staffed by paid foreigners (about 360 British officers were "seconded" to the Sultan to fight rebels), you will have to be hired out of an existing army (typically the British Army) to be considered. Many foreign armies are happy to enlist your services and the Canadian, British or Australian armed force will even give you citizenship when you are done. Times are tough so there are plenty of people who like the idea of paid housing and training. You can expect stringent entry requirements and a thorough check of your police record and passport. These groups have had a dismal record of mismanagement and failed causes from Beirut to Mogadishu. The recent action in Haiti looked more like a replay of the L.A. riots, except that Haiti had a happy ending. If you endorse the retro concept of keeping the natives from getting restless or just want to hang out with men who have bad tattoos, you might want to consider enlisting in the Foreign Legion.

For those who want to get dangerous we have some other options:

The French Foreign Legion

The more romantic and politically insensitive might want to consider joining the Legion. The Legion does France's colonial housekeeping work, oppressing minorities, liberating missionaries and generally keeping the natives from getting too restless. The Legion knows it does France's dirty work and recruits accordingly. They will take all comers, preferably foreigners and preferably men who will not draw too big a funeral procession. The Legion is tough and disposable.

The best example of the Legion's mind-set is the single most revered object in their possession—the wooden hand of Capt. Jean Danjou on display in the museum in Aubagne. Danjou lost his hand when his musket misfired and blew up. He then died with the 59 worn out survivors defending a hacienda on April 30, 1864 in a small hamlet called Camerone in Mexico. His men, exhausted after a long forced march to evade the 2000 strong Mexican army, decided to die rather than surrender. His wooden hand was found by the tardy relief column and enshrined to commemorate his courage. Over 10,000 legionnaires died at Dien Bien Phu in 1954 in a similar debacle.

One group, the 1er REP, suffered 90 percent losses at Cao Bang only to have 576 out of 700 killed four years later at Dien Bien Phu.

A normal army would tut tut the lack of reinforcement, bad strategies and resulting waste of manpower. The Legion (like all of French Military history) myopically elevates folly into legend and attracts thousands of eager recruits every year. The basic lesson is that with only 75 percent of the Legion being French, they are considered disposable.

Despite its notoriety, the Legion is still army of choice when young men dream of adventure. The legion is the tough guy's army, tailor-made for Hollywood film scripts, home for intellectuals, criminals and outcasts. It's a close knit band of hardy, brutal men who are either escaping misguided pasts or seeking adventure in exotic places and doing heroic deeds. The lure of the legion is communicated to us via simplistic movies like *Beau Geste* or simplistic books that romanticize its violence and bloodshed. What they don't tell you is that the Legion has always been brutal, ill equipped and worst of all, disposable. But you get to learn to be a professional killer and your chances are high that you will get to use those skills on other people.

The legion was created in 1831 by King Louis Phillipe to assist in the conquest of Algeria. The King correctly assumed that paid mercenaries would not complain about the conditions or political correctness in carrying out his orders. Since then the Legion has been used to fight France's dirty little wars in Algeria, Indochina, Africa and the Middle East. Although there have been many heroic battles fought in some of the world's most remote and hostile regions, you are better served by reading the multitudes of book about the Legion. The reality today is that the Legion has been downsized and specialized.

The Legion is one of the few action outfits (like the former Selous Scouts of Rhodesia or Oman's mostly British army) which offers the professional adventurer a steady diet of hardship broken up by short bursts of excitement and danger. This format has attracted many of the world's best trained soldiers, like the SS after WWII or Special Forces vets from Vietnam. The world of adventure is shrinking, however. Today the French Foreign Legion is made up of 8500 officers and men from more than 100 countries. They no longer have any ongoing wars that require constant replacements. They now focus on picking and choosing from amongst the world's tough guys to enable them to field soldiers who are fluent in many languages and specialities without many of the religious, political or ethnic barriers that hamper other peacekeeping or expedition forces.

How to get in

There are 16 Legion recruiting centers in France, the most popular being Fort de Nogent in Paris. Just ask at the police station for the Legion Etrangere. The more focused head straight for Aubagne just outside of the dirty Mediterranean port of Marseille. You will be competing with over 8000 other eager Legionnaire wanna-be's for the 1500 slots available. Candidates are tested for their intelligence, physical fitness and special skills are a definite plus. If you just murdered your wife's boyfriend the week before, be forewarned that all candidates are run through Interpol's data banks and the Legion cooperates with them to weed out murderers. If you just want to escape the IRS or alimony payments, the Legion could care less. After all, what better inducement to staying after your third year in Djibouti than the thought of spending that same time in jail stateside.

You don't have to bring any ID or proof of anything; when you show up you will be assigned a *nom de guerre* and a nationality when you sign up. Being Canadian is popular and calling yourself Rambo is definitely an old joke.

You must pass the same general standards as the French Army, but then the legion takes over. You will learn to march like a mule in hell—long forced marches with heavy packs; jungle, mountain and desert training. You must speak the thick, crude French of the Legionnaire and you must learn to be completely self-sufficient in the world's worst regions. There is basic training in Castelnaudary (between Carcassone and Toulouse, just off the A61), commando training in St Louis near Andorra and mountain training in Corsica. Four weeks into your training you will be given the Kepi blanc, the white pillbox hat of the Legionnaire. Unlike the Navy SEALS or Western elite forces, the accommodations are simple, the discipline swift and other than special prostitutes who service the legion, there is little to look forward to in your first five years. Once you pass basic training you will be trained in a specialty: mountain warfare, explosives or any number of trades that make you virtually unemployable upon discharge (except in another mercenary army). French citizens cannot serve except as officers. Those French officers who do sign on do so for a taste of adventure. In troubled times the Legionnaires are always the first to be deployed to protect French citizens in uprisings or civil wars. Most Legionnaires are Europeans with men from over 100 countries serving at any one time.

With this international makeup it is not surprising that Legionnaires today find themselves as peacekeepers, stationed in the tattered shreds of the French empire or with the U.N. You may be assigned to protect the European space program in Kourou, in the steamy jungles of French Guiana, patrol the desert from Quartier Gaboce, in the hot baked salt pan of Djibouti or be stationed amidst the cold choas of Bosnia. When it hits the fan as in Kolwezi or Chad, you can expect some excitement, a quick briefing, an air drop into a confused and bloody scene followed by years of tedium, training and patrol. Remember the Legion has always been disposable.

Since the legion attracts loners and misfits and since many of them spend their time in godforsaken outposts, it is not hard to understand that the Legion becomes more than a job. In fact the motto of the Legion is "Legio Patria Nostra" or "The Legion Is Our Homeland" which describes the mindset and purpose of the Legion. Men serve out their 20 years, many unable to find work or equally stimulating occupations on the outside.

When you get out you don't get much, either. You get a small pension, and you can become a Frenchman (Legionnaires are automatically granted French citizenship after five years). After a lifetime of adventure, and divorced from their homeland, the men of the Legion can look forward to retirement at Domaine Danjou, a chateau near Puyloubier (12 miles west of St. Maxim, north of the A7) in southern France where close to 200 Legionnaires spend their last years. This is where the Legion looks after its own, its elderly, wounded and infirm. Here the men have small jobs ranging from bookbinding to working in the vineyards. Later they will join their comrades in the stony ground of the country that never claimed them but for which they gave their lives.

Happiness is a Dead Infidel

If the Legion seems a little too Euro or confining you can try the next level down. If you are Muslim, don't mind being completely disposable and hate infidels more than the IRS, maybe you should become an Afghan. The most volunteering folks on this planet are the Afghans, or veterans of the war in Afghanistan against Russia. You should want a front row seat in the Superbowl of religious wars: Jihad. There is always Jihad or the holy war being exported by Iran against Russia, The Great Satan (us) and all its allies. Think of it as the Crusades of the 21st century.

Jihad started in 1979 when the Soviets decided to install a puppet ruler and then back him up with the Soviet Army. As with all foreign countries who decided to roll armies into Afghanistan, they forgot the tribes of Afghanistan love a good fight. In fact, when there is no occupying power they love to fight against themselves.

The Afghans are the direct effect of too much money, training and weapons being funneled into one of the world's poorest regions—Pakistan and Afghanistan. The U.S decided this would be a great time to give the Russians a bloody nose and sent in massive amounts of money to support every tiny tribal religious or political group that hated the Russians. All the Afghan groups had to do was provide a head count, a list of weapons, an area of operations and they were in business. Naturally the real mujahadeen looked upon the money from the infidels warily and the most wacky kept coming back for more.

The result is that the States and the Gulf States (through the CIA, through Pakistan) created an entire 7-11 chain of warrior clans armed to the teeth with the common goal of causing the Russians grief. Simple gun-happy tribesmen were trained in everything from how to make explosives out of fertilizer to how to use Stinger missiles. The CIA not only provided more than enough money, they created an unholy network where these factions could swap war stories and business cards.

Over 10,000 volunteers traveled to Afghanistan to fight the Russians lured by money, principal and a chance to poke the bear in the nose. Many more people, after hearing of the plight of the Afghan people sent funds and were predisposed to the total annihilation of the Russian soldiers in Afghanistan. Recruits and funding were actively sought in 28 states in America, but the number of U.S. volunteers was minuscule.

The war in Afghanistan was the largest covert operation of the Reagan era.Over the course of the war, western countries pumped in between $25 million or $30 million a year to several billion a year. The CIA, Saudi government and Gulf states signed most of the checks with 70 percent of the U.S aid going to training and arming the Islamic radicals.Pakistan was hired to provide training to the volunteers and nobody ever thought about what these people were going to do after the war. The Russian people simply went bankrupt and flushed the Communist party down the drain; the Russian army went into business for itself renting and selling weapons to any social or political group that wanted them and the well-trained and ideologically infused Afghans became terrorists for hire. Keep in mind that the term Afghan refers to fighters who traveled or were trained in Pakistan to fight Russians. They are typically young Muslim men (now in their thirties) turned on by clerical haranguing and with little financial incentive to remain in their home country. Their home countries are usually Muslim, have high birth rates, high unemployment, and have strong representation by Iranian-backed political and religious groups (usually from Egypt, Sudan, Algeria, Libya or Pakistan.)

It is no coincidence then that all the men arrested in the World Trade Center bombing were trained or were involved in the war in Afghanistan.

Ahmad Ajaj, 28 learned how to make bombs in Afghanistan; Mahmud Abouhalima, 34, a New York taxi driver, fought in Afghanistan; Clement Hampton-El, 55,born in American but a veteran of Afghanistan, provided materials to the bombers. Ramzi

Yousef, 26, captured in Islamabad; and their reputed ring leader Sheik Omar Abdel-Rahman, 55, has direct connections with the Afghan resistance movement and even sent two sons to fight the Russians in the Afghan war.

And it is no coincidence that all these men have links to Afghan prime minister,Gulbuddin Hekmatyar. Hekmatyar was the most entrepreneurial and most dedicated anti-Soviet. He spent over $1 billion of U.S. aid during the war against the Soviets. The fact that Hekmatyar hated the West didn't seem to bother Ronald Reagan. In the mid-80's Hekmatyar set up an Afghan refugee center to coordinate and support the works of fundamentalist activities in America. He is now busy fighting for his life in Kabul with 12 other islamic fundamentalist groups.

Most Afghan volunteers he recruited and trained did not come from America but ended up in America as refugees from Afghanistan. The CIA facilitated the handing out of visas and green cards, and many of these recent transplants can be found driving taxis in New York City. Using the funds supplied by the CIA, he set up a center in Brooklyn to raise funds to supply arms to the mujahadeen in Afghanistan and to send volunteers to fight in Afghanistan. The center also organized paramilitary training in the United States for Muslims. One of the refugee center graduates was El Saaid Nosair, charged then acquitted of killing Rabbi Mayer Kahane in a Manhattan hotel. Police have also implicated Mahmud Abouhalima who was alleged to be Nosair's get-away driver. When police investigated Nosair's apartment, they found a variety of training materials, and information in Arabic that later was the beginnings of the WTC bombing. We still hadn't figured out what was going on.

How to get in

If you are a traditional Westerner, forget it. You are the enemy. If you are from Sudan, Pakistan, India, Egypt, Turkey, Syria, the Middle East or a Shiite, you stand a good chance. If you fought in the war against Russia and have contacts, you are in like Flynn. The problem is now finding an employer or a cause. Peshawar is still the major clearing house for Afghans and the headquarters of Sheik Rahman's international network. Peshawar was also the headquarters of Gulbuddin Hekmatyar's party, which trained four of the New York bombing suspects. Today Afghanistan is the wildest and woolliest land in the world. There is no one in charge, no one to stop you from entering. But enter at your own risk. You will be stopped, robbed, murdered and kidnapped by any one of the armed groups that control the regions. If you get into Kabul you can ask for protection, but no group can guarantee it. Once in Pakistan you may find yourself being sent right back to the United States to recruit funds and volunteers.

Realistically you either is or you ain't an Afghan, but you can always try.

Other volunteer activities:

Harkat-ul Jehad Al Islami, or Holy War for Islam, plans to send at least 3000 activists as mujahids, or holy worriers, to Kashmir and is recruiting Bangladeshi volunteers to join Muslim militants fighting Indian troops for the independence of Kashmir, according to Dhaka's privately-run PROBE news agency.

Their founder, Abdur Rahman Faruqi, was among 25 Bangladeshi mujahids killed in Afghanistan in action against the Soviets in 1989. They provided Bangladeshi volunteers during the Soviet occupation of Afghanistan. The current head of the group chief Mufti Shafiqur Rahman, is currently recruiting volunteers but denies that they are being mobilized. The volunteers are being recruited from the Madrashas or Islamic schools in southern districts of Cox's Bazaar and the northeastern district of Sylhet.

Harkatul Jihad al Islami has an organization in Pakistan and provides training in Bangladesh and Pakistan. Bangladesh is a predominately Muslim nation. The young men are being convinced in handouts written by clerics that it is their Islamic duty to fight against Hindu India. There are between 20 and 24 Islamic fundamentalist groups in Bangladesh; some are currently recruiting volunteers to join the Muslim separatist war. It is estimated that there are 3000 new volunteers who are waiting to join the 200 Bangladeshi Moslems currently fighting in the secessionist war that has killed at least 9150 people in Kashmir since 1990. The group insists that any volunteers that end up in Kashmir do so at their own effort and Harkatul Jihad al Islami does not send them.

Volunteers in Armenia

In order to maintain its newly found sovereignty in the Republic of Mountainous Karabakh, Armenia has resorted to press-ganging "volunteers" for duty in Nagorno-Karabakh despite its assertions that no Armenian troops are involved in the fighting against Azerbaijan. The truth lies in the Yeriblu military cemetery on a hill overlooking Yerevan. Here are the remains of hundreds of soldiers from the Armenian capital who died in Nagorno-Karabakh, with new victims interred every day. Many of the three quarter of a million refugees who have fled Armenia over the past year have left to avoid the draft and worsening living conditions.

Volunteers in Russia

The Russian army may be the most active proponent of capitalism. As Moscow loses its control over its vast region, individual army units learn not only to make decisions on their own, but to come up with creative ways to sustain themselves. A captain and two NCOs from a Moscow air-defence regiment were arrested for stealing 650 circuit boards from missiles in order to extract the gold and platinum. An air force general in Siberia was charged with creating his own little airline using heavy bombers to fly entrepreneurs into China. A naval ship was deliberately sunk in shallow water off Baltiisk, allowing its officers to sell the ship bits for scrap.

In early 1992 in the Caucasus military district, 1118 railway wagons, with 20 tons of artillery ammunition on board each railway car, went missing. It didn't take long to figure out that the ammunition was sold by Russian commanders. The Russian army has no money for maintenance, training or even maneuvers. They are so poor that an infantry colonel in a letter to an Army newspaper tells of how he has to carry a light-bulb with him in order to get his work done.

The Russian army has resorted to recruiting men by hiring volunteers, or "contract soldiers" as the Russians call them. It is estimated that there are already 100,000 soldiers serving on contract as volunteers. The volunteers are sent directly to the south to fight against rebels in the Caucasus region. Although the Russian army tries to draft its youth into its crumbling military, over 95 percent of Russian youths manage to avoid the draft. Only 11 percent of the draft dodgers are prosecuted and only 0.18 percent convicted. The Russian army is definitely top heavy with a staggering 5600 generals (in 1987). Russian sources estimate that there are 630,000 officers to command only 544,000 men.

The Russian army is working overtime in the southern republics where the entire 3800-mile long border region is volatile. Tough Russian volunteers are needed to keep peace along the mountainous border where Ossetians, Chechens, Ingush, Kabardins, Balkars and others have sent volunteers to fight on the side of the Ossetians, Chechens and Abkhazians. The loose alliance of breakaway states is called The Confederation of Northern Caucasian Peoples.

Mercenaries

Er, excuse us, we meant to say "volunteers" are a curious career choice for folks who have gone to Military U and can't seem to find a direct application or reward for their skills in the outside world.

The Hague 1907 Convention bans operation on the territory of neutral states of offices for recruitment of soldiers (volunteers or mercenaries) to fight in a country at war. In 1977 part of a supplementary protocol to the 1949 Geneva Convention on the Protection of Civilian Population in Time of War made free-lancers liable to court trial as criminals if they are taken POW. If found guilty they can be simply shot on the spot as bandits.

The U.N. General Assembly reached a consensus on, and accepted in 1989, a convention on recruiting, training, use and financing of mercenaries. If you are interested in volunteering, make sure you understand the laws and penalties that will suddenly apply to you. If you think fighting for money will make you popular and chicks will dig you, think again. On the other hand, if Uncle Sam has spent five years and about half a million dollars turning you into all that you can be, there are employment choices other than flipping burgers or Jiffy Lube.

Americans have not always been the ideal volunteers. In fact the last two great wars showed that the majority held back until they are pushed into it. But once they were in it they finished the job.

For now many foreign armies don't want American volunteers. They want too much money, they complain too much and they create too many political overtones when captured or killed. Recently American mercenaries have fought in Angola, Rhodesia, Guatemala, El Salvador, Nicaragua, Lebanon, Bosnia and Russia. Many are motivated by religion (black Muslims in the Middle East), background (Croats in Yugoslavia), money (Central America) or a misguided sense of adventure (Angola). The U.S. is not adverse to hiring mercenaries, starting back when Benjamin Franklin hired the Prussian officer, Friedrich von Steuben to instill discipline into the Continental Army, or when Claire Chennault was hired to give China grief with his Flying Tigers. In modern times U.S.-hired mercenaries have been as diverse as the Ray-Banned pilots that flew for Air America, the Nung or Montagnard tribes in Vietnam or the doomed Contras in Nicaragua. Mercenaries continue to do *our* dirty or covert work but our government does not like the idea of *you* running off to fight in other people's wars.

Today those who wish to be wild geese or soldiers of fortune will find few clear career paths. You will need the minimum service and training provided by a Western military power. Special forces members, explosives experts, pilots, officers with training experience and other specialized skills are in demand.

Although the need for foreign volunteers cannot be predicted, there are certain hot spots that are excellent starting points. The main centers for recruitment of mercenaries are Johannesburg, Istanbul, Bangkok, Panama City, Belgium, Marseille and Beirut. Remember, if you find a recruiter who is looking for a few good men, they are filling grunt and junior officer levels only. The players have already cut their deal up at the top. There are also recurring stories about hucksters preying on the gullible. Even if you do find someone who has a gig for you, remember that they get paid by the head count and once in that country you can be turned down, arrested or sent into action on your first day without training, weapons, gear or ammo. The reality is that most experienced mercenaries simply fly to the capital city of an emerging war zone and offer their services directly to the military advisors for whichever side they feel is the most gullible. There services usually include rounding up canon fodder like you. Other mercenary groups are organized and funded by local militia funded and directed by CIA operatives. Some like the Falangists and Chamounists in Beirut in the 80s brought in eager French Falangist Party students and trained them, but most look for trained, hardened professionals with special skills.

Because of the old boy network and need for inside contacts, many soldiers of fortune do not make their money fighting on the ground in wars, but make themselves available for transportation contracts using leased aircraft, organizing jail breaks, negotiating hostage releases and other solitary and more lucrative adventures. "Employment with a difference" was how the classified ad placed by Mike Hoare read when he set out to recruit mercenaries to fight in the Belgian Congo. Having neither the budget nor the time to train men, he put together what he called his "Wild Geese," the name of an Irish band of soldiers for hire.

Today's mercenary is not a cigar chomping, muscle bound adventurer with a bandolier of 50mm bullets and grenades hung like Christmas ornaments. He is more likely to be a recently unemployed soldier who can't find work with his specialized skills. The pay is lousy (mercenaries make between $1200–$3500 a month depending on your skills or rank), the benefits slim to none and the chances of getting killed very high. Americans will lose their passport or citizenship if they fight in the service of a foreign army.

Are there any loopholes? Well, if you are hired to invade another country, destroy property, kill or hurt people or even destabilize a democratic or undemocratic government, you are breaking the law. If you do not live in the attacked country, have a foreign citizenship or have come in to rescue someone or are hanging around a war zone you can be shot as a spy or foreign agent. If you are in a country that has declared a state of war remember it is much easier and cheaper to shoot questionable characters than to fill out the paperwork.

If you want to truly be a volunteer like Steiner (the Sudan) or Che Guevara (Bolivia) remember that Steiner was tried, imprisoned and tortured and Che was ventilated by CIA operatives so just because you were too stupid to ask for a paycheck doesn't mean you won't get extinguished.

There are some grey areas that afford some (but little) protection. Make sure you enlist in a recognized foreign army. Join a foreign legion like the Spanish or French Foreign legion; have a civilian work contract for a recognized government. You could fight with a recognized army in a foreign territory (like our army in the Gulf or Vietnam) that is not technically at war but helping someone else win a war.

The skinniest loophole is offering your services for a higher pay rate in a foreign army where you are seconded to another army. Technically you can join as a regular service member if there are no local troops with comparable experience. Will that stop the opposing side from parading you around like a zoo animal, then doing a flamenco dance on your testicles. No.

Be warned that there are a heap of bad books that try to add the luster of righteousness and adventure to the mercenary life. These books tend to be short on facts and long on gun talk. They provide hard to find tips like "never handle explosives carelessley" (from the *Mercenary's Tactical Handbook* by Sid Campbell) to "take no unecessary risks" (from the *African Merc Combat Manual* from Paladin Press). If that is not enough solid advice, you might want to note Mitch Balor's advice in his *Manual of the Mercenary Soldier* in which he warns the reader not to dress like you just came from a military garage sale, or wear T-shirts that say things like "Death from Above." Probably the most practical tip he gives is "Unfortunately some of your peers are nuts." Nobody wants to admit writing this stuff; Paul Balor is a *nom de guerre* or *plume*. One might hazard a guess that the gentleman who is pictured on the front cover wearing fatigues that clearly say "Werbell" is the wellspring for the information in the 300-page book. One can assume that this is Mitch Werbell, proponent of the MAC machine pistol and purported adventurer/arms salesman.

There are some good books on this nasty business, most long out of print and yellowed: *The Brother's War* by John St. Jorre, *Legionnaire* by Simon Murray, *Mercenary* by Mike Hoare, *The Last Adventurer* by Rolf Steine, *Mercenary Commander* by Jerry Puren, and probably the most accurate, well written and depressing of the bunch, the *Whores of War, Mercenaries Today* by Wilfred Burchett and Derek Roebuck. *Whores*, published in 1977 chronicles the misfortunes of 13 American and British mercs in Angola who were captured, tried and executed or imprisoned. Sobering stuff for wanna-bes.

Stay away from the hairy chested fluff put out by gun love organizations which can be more misleading than informative. *Soldier of Fortune* magazine has abandoned its "merc for hire" stance after a landmark lawsuit that made it liable for the actions of a hitman who was hired from their classified pages.

The bottom line is that any time you leave the apron strings of Uncle Sam's army you are on your own, and even if you are not in violation of any laws you will be accused of being a criminal (actually a criminal has rights, you won't) without any rights and dealt with accordingly.

The true movers and shakers in the mercenary world are the classic megalomaniacs, self promoters and verbose ex-soldiers who see their role beyond that of a short term gun toter—as a potential ruler of faraway kingdoms. So our advice, if you are going to get into this nasty business (the retirement program sucks), is to think big, don't take any checks and make sure you remember your hat size when you order your crown.

WARNING: Joining any military or paramilitary organization and/or fighting with a foreign army may subject you to prosecution, imprisonment or execution by other countries. If you are a U.S. citizen you can lose your citizenship and be liable for international crimes. Association or contact with mercenary recruiters and groups can make you subject to investigation by U.S. and international law enforcement agencies.

The Men Who Would Be King

The late sixties and early seventies were the glory years for mercenaries like "Mad" Mike Hoare, "Black" Jacques Schramme, and Bob Denard. Tin pot rulers unable to field trained armies turned to free-lancers so they could continue to rifle treasuries and shop in London and Paris without being overthrown while on vacation. Stories of evil mercs laying waste to natives in the Congo, Angola, Biafra, Uganda, Gabon, Benin, Rhodesia and Mozambique became part of literature and Hollywood screenplays. In some cases the scene became truly Chaplinesque and Kiplingesque.

The Man Who Would Be King: Part I

A more successful attempt was made by Frenchman Bob Denard who actually managed to run the Comoros Islands between 1978 and 1989. The Comoros are another Indian Ocean island group just northwest of Madagascar. The major export of the long forgotten islands is ylang-ylang, a rare flower used in the production of aromatic oils. On May 12, 1978 Denard landed with 46 men in a converted trawler named the *Massiwa*. He had sailed from Europe with his black uniformed crew.

Denard had been here before to train the soldiers of Marxist ruler Ali Soilih. Soilih was busy kicking out Ahmed Abdallah. Abdallah fled to Paris and later, short on funds but high on ambition, offered to cut Denard in on the deal if he would return him to power. Denard enjoyed his new role as man who would be king. He adopted a Muslim name, took wives and settled in to a long life of happiness in his new island kingdom. Abdallah took all the political heat as his puppet. His presence angered the other African states to such a degree that the French arranged for Denard's ouster in 1989. Denard, disappointed and back in South Africa, probably spends his evenings staring at maps looking for his next island hideaway.

The Man Who Would Be King: Part II

The Dogs of War, by Frederick Forsyth was published in 1974. In the book and later film a group of white mercenaries are hired to take over a West African country on behalf of an industrialist who finds it cheaper to take over the country rather than pay for its mineral resources. The movie ends with the mercenaries suddenly having a change of heart and installing an idealistic and honest leader. Naturally the book and the film are fiction. Well, not completely, said an investigative report by London's *Sunday Times*. They claimed that *The Dogs of War* was based on a real incident instigated by the author. The *Times* claimed, that in 1972 Forsyth allegedly put up just under a quarter of a million dollars ($240,000) to overthrow President Francisco Macias Nguema of Equatorial Guinea. Forsyth was no stranger to the murky world of mercenaries since he had spent considerable time in Nigeria covering the Biafran civil war. While he was there he met a Scottish mercenary named Alexander Ramsay Gay. Gay was only too happy to train and equip a small group of men who would set up a homeland for the defeated Biafrans. It is reputed that Gay was able to purchase automatic weapons, bazookas and mortars from a Hamburg arms dealer, then hire 13 other mercenaries along with 50 black soldiers from Biafra. They then purchased a ship called the *Albatross* out of the Spanish port of Fuengirola. The plot was blown when one of the British mercs shot himself after a gun fight with London police. The mercenaries were denied an export permit for their weapons and ammunition and the ship and crew were arrested in the Canary islands en route to their target.

Forsyth denies the story or any participation in the plot and admits to nothing more than writing a solidly researched book.

The Man Who Would Be King: Part III

Dublin born Mad Mike Hoare was hired by persons unknown to take over the Seychelles, a nation of 92 islands 1000 miles off the East African. Hoare served in the Royal Armored Corps in World War II and left with the rank of Major. He emigrated to South Africa after the war and made ends meet by being a safari guide, car dealer and accountant until he was hired by Moise Tshombe in 1964 to help him defeat rebels. Hoare put together about 200 male white mercenaries and led probably the last efficient use of a mercenary army in Africa—to save lives and put down a revolt.

Hoare's last big gig (Major Hoare does not work too often due to his high price tag) was a Keystone Cops affair that would seem to be the result of a bad script writer rather than real political intrigue. They were supposed to overthrow the socialist government of President Albert Rene of the Seychelles and to take control of the idyllic Indian Ocean archipelago. In December of 1981 their plan of flying in as a visiting rugby team quickly unraveled when customs inspectors found heavy weapons in the bottom of their gym bags. A brief shoot-out between the 52 raiders and police ensued on the tarmac with the mercenaries' transportation being quickly hijacked and flown back to safety in South Africa. It was not known for whom or why this was done, but suspicion falls on the South African government. Some analysts believe that Hoare backers were South African businessmen looking for a tax haven. A Durban newspaper charged that several of the mercenaries were South African policemen.

The leniency with which the mercenaries were treated back in South Africa adds to that suspicion. The 44 mercenaries who made it back were put on trial (wearing beach shirts and khakis) not for hijacking the Air India aircraft, which would have meant a mandatory five to 30 years in jail; they were charged with kidnapping which requires no mandatory penalty.

The South African Cabinet also approved the freeing on bail of 39 of the 44 mercenaries on the condition they keep a low profile and not discuss the coup attempt. Five mercenaries were arrested in the Seychelles and it is assumed that three others are dead or hiding in the hills.

Others blame ousted Seychelles President James Mancham who was exiled after Rene's successful 1977 coup. Although Mancham denied the accusation, one of the captured mercenaries had a tape recording of Mancham's victory speech intended for broadcast after the coup. The soldiers for hire were paid $1000 each and were promised a $10,000 if the coup was successful.

The Man Who Would Be King: Part IV

Rolf Steiner was last seen living in a tent camp outside a major German city. Poor, ailing from his many wounds and years in prison, one would never recognize him for what he once was. Steiner was a member of Hitler's Youth or Werewolves, He joined the French Foreign Legion at the age of 17 in 1950. He fought at Dien Bien Phu, and Algeria and made the mistake of joining the anti-de Gaulle OAS. He found himself a drummed out corporal chef and a civilian.

In the fall of 1967 Biafra was busy spending oil money and French secret service funds on hiring mercenaries from Swedish pilot Count von Rosen (pilots were paid between eight and $10,000 per month in cash to fly in supplies) and paying Swiss PR firms to publicize their plight. Money flowed freely; grisly battle scarred veterans like Roger Faulques were paid 100,000 British pounds to hire 100 men for 6 months but only delivered 49. He was asked to leave and one of the mercenaries he had hired stayed behind.

In July of 1968 Steiner asked for and was given a group of commando-style soldiers and had great successes against the Russian-backed Nigerians. He was given the rank of colonel and given command of thousands of soldiers. This created an instant Napoleonic complex and Steiner experienced a series of military defeats and routs. He was reigned in by removal of his Steiner Commando Division and after an angry confrontation with the Biafran leader, Sandhurst-educated General Emeka Ojukwa, he was shipped out of the country in handcuffs.

Steiner then showed up in the Southern Sudan among the Anya Na fighting the Islamic North. He taught agriculture, defense, education and other essential civic skills to the animist tribes. For a brief shining moment he was their de facto leader until he was captured by the Ugandans and put on trial in the mid-70s. He was released after spending three years in a Sudanese prison where he was tortured and beaten. Some say he was a crazed megalomanic; other say he tried to apply his skills to aid a tiny struggling nation.

16 Tons and What Do You Get?

For now the opportunities for mercenaries are limited, driven by financial gain and highly hazardous. An example of a recent operation shows the typical rationale behind the hiring of mercenaries.

Executive Outcomes has trained 4000 to 5000 troops and about 30 pilots. Eeben Barlow is managing director of Executive Outcomes based in Pretoria, South Africa. The firm trains and supplies pilots and security personnel for corporations in Africa. They recruit primarily from the South African military, typically hiring men who have some combat experience against UNITA. Their most recent contract (beginning in September of 1993) was a $140,000 contract to protect a diamond mine in Canfunfo in Lunda Norte, Angola. Soldiers of UNITA (National Union for the Total Independence of Angola) finally overan the mine leaving 36 people dead, most of them from the security firm. The men were provided as miltary trainers and were allowed to carry out pre-emptive strikes against UNITA if they felt they or the mine were threatened.

The New Crusades

Bosnia is the most recent gathering ground of white mercenaries. Called "volunteers," they joined for ethnic and religious reasons. Many came from Croation communities in Canada, Australia and Germany with little or no military experience. Eastern European teenagers, unemployed and seeking thrills, also heeded the call and signed up to fight with the Croats. Slovaks, Czechs, Hungarians and Bulgarians began to arrive, green but eager to accept the paltry wages offered. At least 150 Poles were provided by a Krakow recruiting firm. Western advisors began arriving from Britain to train troops in guerilla warfare.

The appearance of eager volunteers in former Yugoslavia was a direct result of the appeals in the summer of 1991 by the Croatian Defence Force for men and supplies to fight back the Serbs. The number of mercenaries or volunteers has been estimated at between 5000 and 20,000.

Albanian and Turkish guest workers from Germany, Australia and Switzerland fought alongside mujahadeen in the central Bosnian regions of Zenica and Travnik.

In late 1992, to counter this infusion, the Russians became an increasingly visible part of Serbian units. Many of these volunteers are sponsored by the Russian Party, the National Republican Party and the Russian National Legion. The Russian Party has recruitment rallies and operates three training camps in and around St. Petersburg.

The third factor is the Muslim world's response to the Serbian brutality. Muslim countries have sent volunteers and weapons to fight the Serbs. Most of the Muslim volunteers are Afghans or non-Afghan Muslim veterans of the war against the Russians. There were estimated to be about 4000 Muslim volunteers from Turkey, Algeria, Iran and Pakistan. Sheikh Mahmud Abdul Aziz has put together an International Islamic Brigade of some 400 devoted volunteers.

When the Serbian-Croatian war subsided in January, 1992, many advisors moved to Herzegovina. Two British military advisors were captured and tortured to death in Travnik after being kidnapped from their apartment by Serbian forces. There have been documentations and reports of former British and Canadian soldiers who conducted raids and sorties. Many of these volunteers left Bosnia and Herzegovina once they realised the futility of their efforts and lack of funds.

Russians for hire

If it isn't westerners, Muslims or the local folks, it seems to be Russians that volunteer for service in Bosnia. Orthodox Christian Russian volunteers are recruited by cossack, monarchist and right wing groups from Russia, Romania and Greece to try to stem the Muslim threat. In the early part of the war there were 500 Russian volunteers stationed in Bosnia, mostly in battle zones along the Drina river border with Serbia. Many of these Russians came in on three-month contracts making $ 25 a month.

Moscow television has reported that there were only around 200, including veterans of the Afghan war, however information released at the Conference on Armed Forces in the Post-Totalitarian Society held near Moscow estimates that there were about 2000 fighting in former Yugoslavia. The same conference estimated that over 30,000 volunteers and mercenaries have been part of the local conflicts in the former Soviet Union since 1990. It was also estimated that at least 10 percent of the junior and intermediate-level officers of the former USSR armed forces are prepared to let their skills for hire. The Russian officers that find immediate employment are aircraft pilots, snipers, communications experts and anti-aircraft systems experts.

On March 1, 1993 the Russian parliament approved a draft of a law that banned the recruitment, arming, financing and training of mercenaries. Prison sentences up to 10 years could be imposed on Russians caught fighting under a foreign flag.

Coup School

The School of the Americas (SOA) in Fort Benning, Georgia has turned out 56,000 "elite military personnel" since its founding in Panama in 1946. Nicknamed "Escuela de Golpes" (School of Coups), it has been at Fort Benning since 1984 after intense political pressure in Panama forced its relocation. In order to avoid the school being shut down due to base closures, other sites such as Fort Bragg, North Carolina, headquarters of the Green Berets Special Forces and locations in Bolivia are being considered as potential sites.

The SOA operates on a $5.8 million annual budget and has an interesting list of graduates: the ex-dictator of Panama, Manuel Noriega; Bolivia's Hugo Banzer Suarez; Guatemalan intelligence chief in the 1970s and 1980s, General Manuel Antonio Callejas y Callejas; Honduran chief of staff Humberto Regalado and Salvadoran death squad leader Roberto D'Aubuisson.

The school has been under a cloud ever since it was revealed that 19 out of the 27 Salvadoran officers implicated in the San Salvador massacre of six Jesuit priests and their housekeeper in 1989 were SOA graduates. The 1993 United Nations Truth Commission Report on El Salvador cited 60 Salvadoran officers for ordering, carrying out and concealing major atrocities during 10 years of civil war; 48 of the officers were SOA graduates.

Major volunteer groups that provide projects on a global basis:

ASB

Sültzburgstrasse 140
D-5000 Köln Germany
☎ *(0) 221 14 76 050*

Global Missions

c/o Evangelical Lutheran Church
8765 West Higgins Road
Chicago, IL 60631
☎ *(312) 380-2650*

Oxfam America

115 Broadway
Boston, MA 02116
☎ *(617) 482-1211*

Human Rights

Center for Third World Organizing

3861 Martin Luther King Jr. Way
Oakland, CA 94609
☎ *(415) 654-9601*

Simon Wiesenthal Center

9760 West Pico Boulevard
Los Angeles, CA 90035
☎ *(213) 223-5486*

Amanaka's Amazon Network

Post Office Box 1419
New York, NY
☎ *(212) 219-2704*
FAX (212) 274-1773

Organizations for Citizen Diplomacy/Peace

Earthstewards Network

☎ *(206) 842-7986*
A Washington-based group that sponsors dozens of citizen diplomacy trips to the Soviet Union, Northern Ireland and elsewhere.

Peace Organizations

The Arms Control Association

11 Dupont Circle, NW
Washington, D.C. 20036
☎ *(202) 797-4626*

Center for National Security Studies

122 Maryland Avenue, NE
Washington, D.C. 20002

☎ *(202) 544-5380*

Fellowship of Reconciliation

P.O. Box 271
Nyack, NY 10960
☎ *(914) 358-4601*

Jobs with Peace Campaign

76 Summer Street
Boston, MA 02110
☎ *(617) 338-5783*

World Peacemakers, Inc.

2025 Massachusetts Avenue, NW
Washington, D.C. 20036
☎ *(202) 265-7582*

World Priorities, Inc

P.O. Box 25140
Washington, D.C. 20007
☎ *(202) 965-1661*

World Federalist Association

418 Seventh Street, SE
Washington, D.C. 20003
☎ *(202) 546-3950*

Like the Tears for Fears song "Everbody Wants to Rule the World" there is a group of folks who think that it may be possible. The WFA works to promote change in the structure of the U.N. and create a more effective institution that would provide global governance, or so says Walter Cronkite, a high profile member. Other celebs like Peter Ustinov (current president of the group), Steve Allen, Lloyd Bridges and Jean Stapleton also believe that world federalism is the hot ticket for a bright tommorow. With the U.N. up to its armpits in alligators and not making much headway in many hot spots, the practicality of their noble but ambitious cause may be worth looking into. In any case, World Federalists feel that a single world government is inevitable so you might want to cover all bases by joining up (would you want to run the world?). They would like to send you some free info (it would be nice if you tucked in a check to defray the cost of the materials and shipping) on World Federalism so write or call. After all, how could you resist any group that seeks to Abolish War, Preserve the Enviorment, Protect Human Rights and Promote Economic and Social Progress?

Save the Planet

Save the Rain Forest

The statistics fly around like curses at a barroom brawl. Typically like the curses, the numbers are half right, half wrong but rooted in truth. Rain forests comprise only two percent of the planet's surface, yet they contain half the world's species. Half of the world's rain forests have disappeared since World War II, which is understandable when you consider the value of the timber and the need for emerging countries to develop their wilderness into towns, factories and grazing land.

Many conservation groups paint a Disneyesque picture of sunny glades populated with singing birds, bright flowers, romping animals and happy native peoples. The reality is much darker. Triple canopy tropical forests have one of the lowest biomasses of mammals and birds. They are typically dark, dank, still and oppressively hot—ideal incubators for plant life. The native people live in isolation, sometimes culling each other in violent tribal conflicts, a natural thinning process that is also accelerated by disease and early death. When cleared, the land is barren and provides at most two years of scanty crops. Forest dwellers are forced to use swidden, or slash and burn cultivation, a method whereby trees are cleared, the ground burned, crops are planted for one or two years and then the area is left to regenerate for up to 10 years before any nutrients are put back in soil.

The term rain forest pertains to a variety of environments. There is no single way to saving the montane moss forests and the mangrove swamps, since they are in jeopardy from a variety of sources. The major enemies of the Asian forests are logging companies that pull out first generation hardwood using crude and inefficient methods. Because of the low cost of this wood, tropical hardwoods are turned into everything from concrete construction forms to coffee table veneers. Decline is also accelerated by repopulation programs that clear large areas for cultivation and grazing. The country itself has the most to lose, but there are few options. Many countries, like Malaysia, point to our denuded forests and first world prosperity, then ask us why we think we have the right to tell them not to develop the same resources to achieve the same success.

The West's view of the rain forests seems to be as a potential location for tourism (if they ever get there) and as the lungs of the world. The East's view of the rain forests are that they provide short-term jobs and income. They still view the forests as the wilderness and as a symbol that they are not fully developed like the West. Both sides seem to agree that the rain forests are a resource, but the two hemispheres don't see eye to eye on how they should be used. We say to cut at sustainable yields, and they say they need the money now. The hitch is that the valuable timber in those triple canopy forests is well over a hundred years old; unlike our fast growing softwoods, they will not be back in our lifetime. There are answers and there are groups that are coming up with solutions and programs. The major thrust seems to be toward finding higher returns on the same resources. For example, over 70 percent of plant species that may help in the fight against cancer come from the rain forest, yet only one percent of the species have been tested for this property. Many foods such as rice, potatoes, chocolate, tomatoes, oranges and cinnamon have come from the tropical forests.

Although experts on both sides duke it out over how much rain forest is lost every minute, there is no denying that a lot more forest is being cut down than is being planted. Does it matter? Of course. Can you stop it? Of course not. Can you slow it down? Absolutely.

If you want to save the rain forest, or any forest for that matter, there are groups that make a difference. Joining any one of the following groups supports their activities as well as introduces you to other like-minded people. The variety of programs is bewildering, but then the answers required for solid preservation and management are even more complex.

Start by asking for information and attending some meetings. You can communicate with many of these people via computer. Many groups have needs for active volunteers as well as members. If you are looking for more active pursuits, as in the case of Bruno Manser, a Swiss national who helped the Punan organize against the timber companies in Sarawak, they can introduce you to sponsors, legal funds, mentors, etc.

You may just be happy to receive the ever present newsletter and know that your money is supporting a good cause.

American Forests

Post Office Box 2000
Washington, D.C. 20013
☎ *(800) 873-5323*

OK, so everyone wants to save the rain forests, but when was the last time you visited Washington, Alaska or Hawaii? It seems we like to cut our rain forests as fast as our Third World cousins do. The American Forestry Association is about cutting down trees and about growing trees, but mostly about the need to grow trees. I worked on both sides of the fence, both for the Forest Service (basically counting trees) and as a logger (cutting them down). I, like most people, prefer walking through virgin forests to cutting them down. I just don't know whose forests we are going to cut down if we don't rebuild and manage ours.

Both sides of the fray (loggers and environmentalists) agree that we need to preserve trees. They just don't agree about how. Loggers say grow 'em as fast as you cut 'em down, and conservationists say don't cut 'em. Loggers like to ask who is going to supply the timber to build the house you return to after your hike in the woods? The fact is we still consume them a lot faster that we replace them. Joining American Forests puts your money toward replanting trees. Whether you shell out $30 to plant 10 trees or $1000 to plant an entire acre of trees (500) your money gets right to the heart of the matter. The 120-year-old organization is the creator of the Global ReLeaf program and works to make the country and the city a more livable place by planting more trees. It should be known that this group views trees as a renewable resource and not as sacred plants, so the more strident preservationists may want to spend their money with the Sierra Club or other "preservation only" groups. For now, as long as we continue to use wood as a resource, management is the first step to better logging practices. The group also offers trips to forested places like New Zealand and even has a magazine on urban forests.

American Forestry Association (AFA)
☎ *202-667-3300*
(To donate $5.00 for Global ReLeaf, ☎ 900-420-4545)
To plant trees contact their Global ReLeaf Campaign.

Better World Society
☎ *202-331-3770*
Become a BWS video advocate and obtain *Profits from Poison*, a documentary about the dangerous misuse of pesticides in developing countries.

Conservation International
1015 18th Street N.W.
Suite 1000
Washington, D.C. 20036
☎ *(202) 429-5660*
FAX (202) 887-5188
CI tries to integrate people into its conservation efforts. Their major focus is the rain forest in 24 countries in Latin America, Africa and Asia. They strive to integrate economics, community development and scientific solutions. Being down to earth, they tell you exactly what your donation can provide. Whether it is a $100 donation that buys a grinding wheel for making handicrafts from sustainable rain forest products in Ecuador, or $1000 that provides one thousand tree seedlings and planting equipment in Costa Rica, they do a good job of putting your money to work. Their idea of being able to create economic benefit seems a refreshing alternative to the eco-nazis who demand natural preservation at the cost of local development.

Earth Island Institute
300 Broadway, Suite 28
San Francisco, California 94133
☎ *(415) 788 3666*
FAX (415) 788- 7324
EII is somewhat of an incubator for conservation, preservation and restoration projects. In 1982 David Brower, the founder of Friends of the Earth and first executive director of the Sierra Club, set up an institute to support creative solutions to the world's problems. Projects that have sprung from the institute include films, conferences and a variety of organizations. The Rain Forest Action Network, International Rivers Network and the International Marine Mammal Project all went on to become self-sustaining separate organizations. Earth Island Institute supports numerous projects around the world, from protecting mangrove forests to

educating Australian aborgines about uranium waste disposal. Annual membership is $25 and gets you a subscription to the quarterly *Earth Island Journal*.

Greenpeace

☎ *202-462-1177*

Their Toxics Campaign seeks to solve the toxic pollution problem through waste prevention. Greenpeace takes direct action against the polluters, fighting to cut off toxic substances at their source. Ask for a copy of *Toxics: Stepping Lightly on the Earth, Everyone's Guide to Toxics in the Home* (free).

National Audubon Society

☎ *212-832-3200*

Ask for a copy of "The Audubon Activist Carbon Dioxide Diet," a worksheet that explains how to reduce your household's production of carbon dioxide, CFCs and trash ($2.00).

Rainforest Action Network (RAN)

450 Sansome
Suite 700
San Francisco, California 94111
☎ *(415)398-4404*
FAX (415) 398-2732

RAN is a fiesty little group (13 full-time employees) formed in 1985 that yaps around the heels of big business. Their Darth Vader of the rain forest is Mitsubishi, "the worst corporate destroyer of rain forests in the world." They have also targeted oil companies like Texaco and Unocal and anybody who destroys rain forests or endangers indigenous peoples. They use public pressure, direct action and the coordinated actions of hundreds of like-minded groups around the world to force change and conservation.

They claim to have forced Burger King to stop importing beef from Central America—beef raised on land formerly occupied by rain forests. Their boycott caused a 12 percent drop in income and BK now no longer makes whoppers out of Third World cows.

Their biggest weapon is a group of 150 independent Rain Forest Action Groups (RAG) who raise funds, educate their community and conduct campaigns to save the rain forest. RAN is proud of the fact that at least 82 percent of donations go directly towards rain forest preservation. Their most effective program is the Protect-an-Acre program. RAN uses funds to help forest peoples secure communal land titles and helps them develop livelihoods and long-term protection programs. To date they have secured more than 2.5 million acres of land title.

They offer a variety of publications including the monthly *Action Alert* and the quarterly *World Rainforest Report*, and produce numerous fact sheets and brochures targeting specific rain forest issues. There are directories of over 250 groups who are working to save the rain forest in the Amazon and 250 groups in Southeast Asia.

If you would like to get involved you can start your own RAG, join one, support the group with funds or work as an unpaid intern in their San Francisco headquarters. You must put in twelve hours a week eight hours a day for three months.

Sierra Club

739 Polk Street
San Francisco, CA 94109
☎ *(415) 776-2211*
(202) 547-1141 (D.C.)

The granddaddy of eco-clubs, with 102 years under its belt and 600,000 members. The Sierra Club was founded in 1892 by John Muir with the idea that the natural areas of America needed to be saved from the industrialists who were ravaging the west.

Backed up by a staff of 350 paid volunteers, 20 regional field offices, 32 chapter offices and a rapidly growing membership roster, the Sierra Club is by far the most effective voice for conservation in America. They track the environmental profiles and voting history on environmental issues of members of the U.S. Senate and House of Representatives. They support their activities by publishing an impressive array of books, calendars, licensed products and *Sierra* magazine. They also lead about 300 trips every year, fight a number of legal battles from their six Legal Defense Fund Offices in San Francisco, Denver, Juneau, Honolulu and Washington, D.C.

You don't have to be a reformed lumberjack to help out. You can join as a member, or you can apply for a paid (or unpaid job) in their head office in San Francisco or in one of the regional offices. The Sierra Club is looking for low paid, hard working staff to work on books and their magazine. They need human resources, financial, data entry, management, public affairs, travel, conservation and campaign workers. Their Washington office needs lobbyists, support people, media reps and issues specialists. If you are hoping to be paid to hike around the parks and take those amazing photographs in *Sierra* magazine or their books, sorry, its all on spec or freelance. They welcome submissions though, so keep trying if you get turned down the first time. The Sierra Club can give you a reduced fee on one of their outings in exchange for some trail clearing and maintenance work. Twenty lucky interns can work for nothing throughout the organization with the hopes of getting a full time job later. If you do get a job expect full dental, medical and life insurance programs, a pension plan and generous vacation accrual (that means you will work plenty of OT) and discounts on calendars, outings, etc. If you are interested contact the Human Resources Department at ☎ *(415) 923-5581.*

Worldwatch Institute
☎ *202-452-1999*
Ask for publications such as *Clearing the Air: A Global Agenda, Air Pollution, Acid Rain,* and *The Future of Forests,* and *The Bicycle: Vehicle for a Small Planet.*

Other Rain Forest Action Groups

Headwaters
Post Office Box 1075
Grants Pass, Oregon 97526
☎ *(503) 474-6034*

Japan Tropical Forest Action Network
7-1-801 Uguisudani-cho
Shibuya-ku, Tokyo 150 Japan
☎ *81 3 3770 6308*

Native Forest Council
Post Office Box 2171
Eugene Oregon 97402
☎ *(503) 688-2600*

Oregon Natural Resource Council
1050 Yeon Building
522 SW Fifth Avenue
Portland, Oregon 97204
☎ *(503) 223-9009*

Rainforest Alliance
270 Lafayette Street, Suite 512
New York, New York 10012
☎ *(212) 941-1900*

Rainforest Information Center
Post Office Box 368
Lismore 2480 New South Wales, Australia
☎ *61 66 21 8505*

Sahabat Alam Malaysia
19 Kelawei Road
10250 Penang, Malaysia
☎ *(04) 375 705*

Sierra Club of Western Canada
620 View Street, Room 314
Victoria, British Columbia V8W 1J6
☎ *(604) 386-5255*

SKEPHI
Tromol Pos 1410
Jakarta, 13014 Indonesia
☎ *62 21 471 1388*

Western Canada Wilderness Committee
103-1530 West 6th Avenue
Vancouver, British Columbia V6J 1R2
☎ *(604) 683-8220*

The Wilderness Society
1400 Eye Street NW
Washington, D.C. 20005
☎ *(202) 842-3400*

The Environment

These groups provide information and studies on the impact of humans on the tropical environment.

The Center for Environmental Information
99 Court Street
Rochester, New York 14604
☎ *(716) 546-3796*

Organization for Tropical Studies
Box DM
Duke Station
Durham, South Carolina 27706
☎ *(919) 684-5774*

The Smithsonian Tropical Research Institute
Apartado 2072
Balboa, Panama
☎ *(507) 27-6022*

Save the Animals

Animal rights activists are not always bulimic models and washed up celebrities. There are plenty of square jawed park rangers who hunt down and kill poachers on a nightly basis. I spent three days badgering the Tanzanian game wardens in Selous park to take us man hunting with them at night. I found out why they didn't want me along; it seems they left their remote little hut, drove about half a mile away and slept. Oh, well. In any case, you can make a difference whether you are on the ground or in your living room. Your meager contribution is a spit in the ocean and is guaranteed not to save an animal species from extinction, but a lot of people chipping in a few bucks and a few hours will go a long way to doing something concrete.

If you just can't stand by and watch another elephant get chain-sawed for his tusks, then there are also more active outlets for you. One of the best ways to visit dangerous places is to do good. The image of the great white hunter as adventurer has been re-placed by the great white conservationist as adventurer. If you have dreams of getting sunburnt, dusty and wrinkled while bouncing around Africa in an old Land Rover 88, your best bet is to look into the many conservation groups that need volunteers and support. Those who preferred *Indiana Jones* to *Born Free* can also check into the many archaeological digs that need helping hands. If you just want to read about and keep one more white rhino on the planet, then by all means tuck in your love gift and get warm fuzzies (and usually a colorful newsletter).

African Elephant and Rhino Specialist Group (AERSG)

c/o IUCN
Avenue du Mont-Blanc
CH-1196
Gland, Switzerland

African Elephant Conservation Coordinating Group

c/o Dr. David Weston
Wildlife Conservation Intl.
P.O. Box 62844
Nairobi, Kenya

African Wildlife Foundation

1717 Massachusetts Avenue, NW
Washington, D.C. 20036
☎ *(202) 265-8393*

Founded in 1961 with the belief that only Africans can save African wildlife, the AWF operates two colleges of wildlife management. Their colleges have trained hundreds of game wardens and rangers for parks all over Africa. AWF is unique in that it works with Africans, within Africa to manage African wildlife. They also educate children on conservation, help local communities benefit from wildlife preservation and show them ways to make more efficient use of land.

The AWF developed programs and trained staff in Rwanda's Parc des Volcans to protect the remaining 650 mountain gorillas. They have continued their support of the rangers through-out the recent bloodshed and report that no gorillas were harmed. They also run the longest continuous study of elephants in Africa in Kenya. They have been tracking the 790 elephants in Amboseli National Park to understand elephant behaviour and social patterns. There is a field office in Nairobi and a fund raising center in Washington. Supporters receive a thrice yearly newsletter *Wildlife News* and contributions are tax deductible.

Cetacean Society International

P.O. Box 9145
Wethersfield, CT 06109
☎ *(203) 563-6444*

Convention on International Trade in Endangered Species (CITES)

c/o UNEP

DC2-0803 United Nations
New York, NY 10017
☎ (212) 963-8093

The Cousteau Society

Membership Center
870 Greenbriar Circle
Suite 402
Chesapeake, Virginia
☎ (804) 627-1144
☎ (804) 523-9335

This worldwide organization, started in 1973, serves to protect the oceans, marine animals and ultimately humans from pollution and abuse. Their noble but somewhat ambitious goal is to "provide a centralized facility for continuing studies of man and his world." They also strive to "protect and improve the quality of life for present and future generations," another goal that I am sure would be difficult to oppose. The problem I have with the Cousteau Society is determining just what they do. They freely admit that their job is to "bridge the gap between specialists and the public" meaning doing cool things with a scientist as baby sitter. Their methodology might be overly dramatic and Inspector Clouseau/Captain Cousteau's voiceover horribly mangled and poetic, but many of my generation can't imagine going diving without saying at least once: "Luuk at zee leetle feeshes adrrrift in zeee vaaast ocheoon."

Well anyway, join the club and let me know. In the meantime, if you like diving as I do you have to give Jacques-Yves his due for being the co-inventor of the aqualung and making diving such a popular sport.

If you join up you'll get a free bimonthly mag called *The Calypso Log* and the *Dolphin Log* for kids. The money goes toward supporting the activities of the Cousteau Society and toward publicizing their ongoing activities which consist primarily of creating films on various regions of the world and acting as PR agents for whales and other wet things. Cousteau is currently on his rediscovery of the world which means they have pretty much blown through it once before. His shows are bankrolled by Ted Turner and continue to be the best aquatic filmmaking out there. On the down side, Cousteau seems to keep discovering places that people have lived in for thousands of years. Simplification and a somewhat lopsided view of the world (ocean) make for great entertainment but sometimes provide only sketchy scientific content. Oh hell! I admit I love bumper stickers that say things like "Nuke the gay whales for Jesus" and I do eat fish. Can you actually do anything or come along for the ride? No. But you can watch their television specials, buy the books and join the society. Membership is $20 for an individual and $28 for families.

National Wildlife Federation

1400 16th Street, NW
Washington, D.C. 20036
☎ (202)797-6800

The Nature Conservancy

1815 North Lynn Street
Arlington, Virginia 22209
☎ (800) 628-6860
☎ (703) 841-5300
FAX (703) 841-4880

The Nature Conservancy seeks out, develops and works to create conservation areas around the world. The group's goals are to assist in the development of local conservation institutions, provide on-the-ground protection assistance, create sustainable conservation financing and generate improved conservation information. The group sets up Conservation Data Centers for developers trying to avoid vulnerable species and for conservationists designing preserves. The group is active in the Caribbean and Latin America with programs in Mexico, Panama, Costa Rica, Ecudor and Brazil. They also are working to build and protect parks in the South Pacific.

The Student Conservation Association, Inc.

Post Office Box 550
Charlestown, New Hampshire 03603
☎ *(603) 826-4301*
FAX (603) 826-7755

The SCA offers 12-week positions assisting in the management and protection of U.S. national Parks, forests and other conservation areas. You might be maintaining trails, educating visitors, helping archaeology surveys and telling people to turn their ghetto blasters down in campsites. You will get to work in the great outdoors, have food and housing supplied as well as have your travel expenses covered in the U.S.

The year-round program is open to those over 18 and it helps if you have academic qualifications. The list of positions available is published every July and December and is available by contacting the recruitment director.

Wildlife Conservation International

☎ *212-220-5155*

Their Tropical Forest Campaign supports field researchers and conservation action plans at work in 37 tropical forests around the globe.

World Wildlife Fund

1250 24th Street, NW
Washington, D.C. 20037
☎ *202-293-4800*

Save Yourself

or How to Stay Alive and Well for At Least Four Weeks

I guess just about any type of school can be called a survival school (translating Homeric poems from the original Greek could help you survive British boys school reunions). Knowledge is power and power creates self-confidence. America offers little in the normal school curriculum that would help us survive in either urban or rural enviroments. In fact most high school kids don't even know how to open a bank account let alone trap, skin and cook a rabbit.

There are three types of survival schools. The first is sport or location specific (mountain, diving, jungle, jumping); the next deals with bush lore, and the last type is the southern "be a mercenary" school that does little but promote the sales of black t-shirts with skulls, and cheap beer. Having never received any formal military training, I learned my survival skills from a variety of eclectic sources: guides, boatmen, headhunters, Indians, trappers, botanists and others.

The first tool for survival is knowledge, the second is self-confidence and the third is ingenuity. I would like to say that luck is by far the most important element of survival, but let's put that aside for now.

Armies have long known that training can replace thinking in men. If someone is exposed to rote learning, common experience and instinctive reaction, they will often do the unthinkable. In the trenches of WWI, thousands of men crawled out of relative safety to follow their dead comrades into withering machine gun fire. Intensive training can suppress our natural instinct to run away, cower in fear or scream at the top of our lungs.

What does that have to do with survival training? First of all, most people have never been in a life-threatening situation. Or more correctly, most people don't know how to deal with life-threatening situations. Second, most urban people left in remote places don't have the foggiest idea about how to build a fire, construct shelter and find food.

Most adventurers eagerly look forward to the serendipity of being thrust into unforeseen or harsh circumstances. Many of them have a smattering of training and good sense, but few are honest-to-god bushmen, so if you want the odds stacked in your favor, try spending some time at one of the training spots listed in this section.

The best sources for survival training are the special forces or commando sections of the British, American, Australian and French military. Most require a minimum of four to five years and will consume the flower of your youth. You may find yourself with skills that lead you to a life of hard-core adventure since the first place security and mercenary recruiters go is to the bars that the SAS and French Foreign Legion frequent. If you wish to side-step the endless years of boredom spent on military bases and go straight for the good stuff you can look into these schools, many taught by the cream of the SAS or American special forces vets. Don't be shy about setting up a one-on-one itinerary if you have special educational needs.

If you gravitate toward the more earthbound, then be prepared to learn survival the politically correct way: no killing, no field stripping of weapons and a definite slant towards new age thinking. Will these skills save your life when you have to E&E Khmer Rouge terrorists? Maybe. Will they make you more comfortable and secure in the wild? Yes.

Adventure/Recreation Schools

OK, OK, we should say schools for dangerous people, or schools that will make your adventures less dangerous; Oh hell, it sounds better our way. Herein you can find a list of institutions, events and resources that will help the curious and adventurous add to their survival skills.

Bremex

Expedition Leadership Training Scheme
London Information Center
18 Westbourne Park Villas
London, England W2 5EA
☎ *071- 229 9251*
Bremex operates a school in expedition planning, leadership and survival skills. The briefings and lectures are on Tuesday evenings with weekend training wilderness expeditions in the winter. All courses are London based and vary from "Weekend Taster" courses to nine month qualifying courses for expedition leaders. Training includes first aid, survival skills, mountain rescue, leadership studies, canoeing, snow and ice climbing, navigation and orienteering.

Fees are about $50 a month with transportation provided to weekend moor and mountain locations.

National Outdoor Leadership School

Post Office Box AA
Lander, Wyoming 82520
☎ *(307) 332-6973*
FAX (307) 332-3031
This school gets past the superficial imagery of some survival schools and gets right down to business. People who want to make money in the outdoor adventure business come here to learn not only survival aspects, but the nuts and bolts of adventure travel outfitting. You can also take the 34-day, $2100 NOLS instructor's class once you have passed a basic wilderness class. The emphasis here is on safety since your future charges will be less than amused if they end up living off the land because you forgot to pack their favorite pudding. Choose from, sea kayaking, winter camping, telemark skiing, backpacking or mountaineering. Some courses qualify for college credit.

Entry level classes are in reality great adventure vacations depending on your area of interest. Mountaineering classes are taught in Alaska, British Columbia and even Kenya. Expect to spend two weeks to three months on location learning the specialized skills you will need to lead other groups. If you want to cram in a class on your vacation, then opt for their selection of two-week courses on horsepacking, winter skiing, rock climbing or canoeing. If you flunk, well you had a good time on a well organized adventure tour.

School for Field Studies

16 Broadway
Beverly, Massachussets 01915

☎ *(508) 927-5127*
A non-profit group that runs 40 month-long and semester-length programs that allow students to gain field research experience. Targeted to high school and college students, the college credit courses are run all around the world. There is a wide choice of topics from coral reef studies (the Caribbean), marine mammals (Baja, Mexico), tropical rain forests (Australia) and wildlife management (Kenya). Scholarships and interest-free loans are available.

SOLO (Stonehearth Open Learning Opportunity)
Rural Federal District 1
Box 163
Conway, New Hampshire 03818
☎ *(603) 447-6711*
FAX (603) 447-2310
A professional school for professionals, SOLO is designed to teach wilderness guides what to do in an emergency. They offer a four week, $1200 Emergency Wilderness Training Certification course that will get you on the preferred list of just about any expedition. Shorter two day seminars are taught around the country for $100. The areas of specialization are wilderness emergencies (such as frostbite, hypothermia, bites and altitude sickness), climbing rescue, and emergency medicine (wounds, broken limbs, shock and allergy). Participants are expected to have a basic grounding in climbing and outdoor skills.

Bicycle Schools

The Mountain Bike School
800 Mountain Road
Mount Snow, Vermont 05356
☎ *(800) 451-4211*
☎ *(802) 464-3333*
A school on how to ride a bike? Well, you never know when you might need to balance on one wheel or hop down a cliff without going arse over tea kettle. The weekend school also runs trips in Vermont and New Hampshire.

Driving Schools

Adventurers will usually find themselves behind the wheel of a decrepit vehicle on a crumbling road, being overtaken by drunk Mexican holidaymakers or dodging Pakistani truckdrivers.There are many instances where knowledge of advanced driving skills can come in handy. The problem is that most of us learned how to drive from our dad or a mild-mannered driving instructor. When you really need to drive either at high speeds, in inclement conditions or off-road, one wrong move can kill you. There are plenty of racing schools around the country, most designed to create legions of weekend warriors on paved tracks. If you're curious what the most dangerous car is, most people are not surprised that the Chevrolet Corvette takes the prize with 36 driver deaths for every 100,000 miles. According to The Insurance Institute for Highway Safety, the safest car is the Volvo 240 four-door with 0 deaths. That probably says as much about the kind of people who drive the two cars as it does about their relative safety. In both cases training can make the difference between life and death.

Although these schools are not for the timid, they can teach the overly aggressive the gentler skills of driving a car with control and most of all smoothness. Many schools discourage speed or lap times until the students understand the precision and focus required for short lap times.

Skip Barber Racing School
Sears Point International Raceway,
29355 Arnold Drive,
Sonoma, California 95476
West Coast ☎ *(707) 939-8000*
East Coast ☎ *(203) 824-0771*
Skip Barber teaches people how to drive on the street and on the track. Yuppies will want to check out the one- ($450) and two-day ($880) BMW advanced driving schools that let you learn how to drive M3s and 325i sedans to the limit. I understand that students are not allowed to use their cellular phones while racing. The school moves to approximately 19 race tracks around the country, so call for the best place and time. You can also take three-day and five-

day Competition courses. Once certified you're ready for the eight-day Racing course ($3800) that lets you run BMW 3 series and Formula Ford cars. Courses are SCCA and IMSA approved.

Bob Bondurant School of High Performance Driving

Firebird Raceway
Post Office 60968
Phoenix, Arizona 85082
☎ *(800) 842-7223*
☎ *(602) 961-1111*
If you have a hot car and yearn to push it to its limits, the Bondurant School will slot you into the one-day Advanced Highway Driving Course for $450. If you want to let them deal with the maintenance, it costs $650 to use their car. (Bondurant uses specially prepared Mustangs and Formula Fords.) My favorites are the training wheel-equipped Mustangs used to see just how far you can push it on the skid pad. The school offers everything from courses for ignorant teenagers and courses for those with death wishes ($895) to four-day Grand Prix courses ($2495) and four-day anti-terrorist executive protection programs for chauffeurs. Surprisingly, there are no courses for New York cabbies.

Ford-Michelin Ice Driving School

Post Office Box 774167
Steamboat Springs, Colorado 80477
☎ *(303) 879-6104*
Ice driving isn't everyone's favorite sport but it is a skill that becomes mandatory for most of the country four months out of each year. For $80 you can spend a half-day learning how to control Fords and Lincoln-Mercury cars (outfitted with Michelin tires) on ice. Expect to spend some time in the classroom and then a couple of hours on the ice. If you want more, the school offers a full day for $180 and a day-and-a-half Grand Prix course for $300.

Real adventure..right after this word from our sponsor

To introduce the New Nissan Pathfinder in 1988, L.A. ad agency Chiat/Day came up with a novel idea: Why not grab a couple of yuppies and send them on a 6500-mile test drive. But instead of driving around the block, we'll have them run down to Rio from a nice suburb of Chicago.

So off they went from Chicago through Central America and down; six weeks later they arrived at Rio de Janeiro's Copacabana Beach. The cost was only about twice the normal budget for a glitzy television ad. The lucky participants/actors were the Andersons. Kurt, then 33, is a film producer; his wife Martha, or Marty, 35, is a real estate agent and itinerant actress. They competed with 1000 other adventurers to answer a casting call from Chiat/Day advertising. They received about $16,500 each for the 45 days, plus expenses and residuals. The trip covered 2200 miles of the Trans-Amazon; they were accompanied by a crew of 10,

Off-Road Driving Schools

Driving a vehicle through pristine jungles and deserts has never captured the imagination of American travelers. Viewing the vehicle as polluting, noisy and expensive, they tend to gravitate toward more caloric transportation. For the serious adventurer, there are not many options if you have to travel through Angola, Borneo, Siberia or other vast remote regions.There are large areas of the world where there are no buses, no taxis, no rivers and no pack animals. It is then that the four-wheel drive vehicle comes into its own. Most adventure travelers will have need of one at some time in their travels. Surprisingly few understand the skills required to drive comfortably through wilderness regions. Here are a list of schools and events that can help the four-wheeled adventurer:

Ecological 4-Wheeling

2925 College Avenue, Suite A7
Costa Mesa, California 92626
☎ *(714) 540-7731*
Imagine, college courses and guided off-road trips.

Espirit de Four

Four-Wheel Drive Clinics
1765 Yerba Buena Road
San Jose, California 95121
☎ *(408) 723-8628*
This French-sounding but completely American school conducts off-road clinics and training schools for beginning and advanced off-roaders.

Rod Hall's Off-Road Driving School

1360 Kleppe Lane
Sparks, Nevada 89431
☎ *(702) 331-4800*
There are some who think that running out of pavement doesn't mean you should slow down. Rod trains the borderline insane for Baja runs and other high speed off-road racing events.

Land Rover Driver Training

Royal Geographical Society
1 Kensington Gore
London SW7 2AR
☎ *(011 71) 581 2057*
FAX (011 71) 584-4447
"Drive like you have an egg under the accelerator pedal." With that in mind I blasted through the course like a rhino with hemorrhoids. When they barked "Give it a little Wellie," I already had the pedal to the floor and took great pleasure in creating theatrical sheets of brown mud, soaking spectators and team members alike. Shaking his head, the silver-haired instructor felt a pang of pity for whatever vehicle I would captain. I had an absolute blast learning how to push the Land Rover and the Discovery to their limits at Eastnor Castle. Although I had been part of the American Team for the Camel Trophy, my driving has been to a colder more calculating style. You will still not find a better place to learn off roading and expedition driving.

Land Rover offers courses for regular folks and even potential Land Rover owners. Eastnor Castle is 5000 acres of glorious muck and forests, populated by red deer and caravaners (trailer campers). They do cheat here, since the tracks are designed only for Land Rover products. The well worn ruts, cliffs, hills and specially constructed water holes are designed to test the vehicles to their maximum usefulness. Each trail, proper speed and gear are of course memorized by the senior Land Rover trainers but designed to intimidate the uninitiated.

Americans are known for their prowess with the winch, covering many impassable hills, holes and bogs by the creative application of winch cables and motors. After one particularly entertaining section, I used a pocket knife as a remote and lassoed a tree from the front bumper of a 110 as it began to slither down a steep cliff. As the trainers said, "We teach you Yanks how to drive and you teach us how to winch."

The schools are not that exhilarating, but with a little luck you can induce the instructor and others to push these amazing vehicles to the max. The Expedition Advisory Center of the Royal Geographical Society offeres two one-day courses a year where 10 lucky people will try the patience of the venerable Land Rover instructors. Cost is a measly 35 pounds, but you have to get to Eastnor Castle in Hereford, in itself worth a trip.

The Land Rover Driving Academy

1975 North Park Place
Atlanta, Georgia 30339
☎ *(800) 910-6999*
☎ *(404) 850-6890*
If you have no desire to spend two weeks exchanging body odors, but have a thing for Land Rovers, you might opt for The Land Rover Driving Academy. This highfalutin' name is really

just an upscale outing for owners of Range Rovers, Discoverys and Defender models. The upside is that it is taught by Tom Collins and you get to see some pretty spectacular country-side. The one-week event combines training in off-roading, recovery, winching and mechanical skills plus a little driving thrown in to keep you from getting too bored. The cost is $470 per person, single occupancy. You must be a current owner of a fairly new Land Rover vehicle, be over 21 and have a valid drivers license. You can bring a friend who doesn't have a Land Rover. The tab would be $4750 for each person for the week and includes hotel, vehicle, instruction, food and some free clothing. You have to pay the air fare in addition to the course fee.

Every year they dream up some event to test your skills. In 1994 they reran the Great Divide Expedition that wowed the automotive press a few years ago. The driving academy is con-ducted in August and September.

Jean-Paul Luc Winter Driving School

Post Office 774167
Steamboat Springs, Colorado 80477
☎ *(303) 879-6104*
For ABS lovers only. Learn how to drive fast on ice and snow. Brakes optional for this winter and rally driving school.

Kayaking Schools

Class III rapids and above usually require some knowledge of running rivers. I learned from the boatmen and about 4000 miles of canoeing across the continent. You are better off spending a wild weekend at one of these schools so your soggy corpse won't end up like a pickle in a blender in some white water hell.

Boulder Outdoor Center

2510 North 47th Strret
Boulder, Colorado 80301
Seekers of the extreme flock to BOC to learn how to kayak. Star instructors, intense instruction and wild rivers make this one of the better schools.

Nanthala Outdoor Center

US 19W
Post Office Box 41
Bryson City, North Carolina
☎ *(704) 488-2175*
FAX (704) 488-2498
Stay in the rustic bunkhouse and learn how not to drown.The oldest training center for canoe-ists and kayakers must have a secret that keeps them coming back. Classes offered include Basic Canoeing, Intermediate Kayaking, Fast Track Kayaking, Racers Workshop, Rowing Technique and others up to Raft Guide Training. You can also combine instruction with shooting some of the world's great rivers.

Sundance Expeditions, Inc.

14894 Galice Road
Merlin, Oregon 97532
☎ *(503) 479-8508*
Kayakers who graduate from Sundance attest to its good vibes, excellent selection of rivers and professional training. Nine days at the school will set you back about $1200 bucks which also includes a four-day trip down the Deschutes or the Rogue.

Motorcycle Racing Schools

Satisfy the need for speed

Despite the recent invasion of Harley-riding accountants, motorcycle registration is down dramat-icaly (about 25 percent in the last 10 years). Although there were only 2500 people killed in motor-cycle accidents in 1992 (about seven percent of all fatalities), there were 65,000 people injured, so the need to be on top of your game is obvious. We are not advocating that you need to be a racer to ride a motorcycle properly, but it sure helps to know what your bike can do at its limit. Driving at a sedate pace is dangerous enough, but the fact that motorcycling seems to attract the young, wild and crazy makes it a lethal combination. Riding a motorcycle in America is 16 times more dangerous than driving a car. What causes accidents? Well, 54 percent were because of a collision with another vehicle, 15 percent from collisions with fixed objects and a surprisingly 26 percent were noncollision. That means a lot of people screwed up and dumped their bike.The only saving grace is that wearing a helmet makes the cyclist 20–40 percent more likely to survive an accident and there are safety schools that can help keep you out of the grim stats. So you have figured out that motorcycling is dangerous to start with, but the odds stack up against you if you don't know what to do in an emergency. There are two schools that will teach how to squeeze the most from your machine and to do the right thing in an emergency. The right and moral stuff aside, there is also a pure, singular rush that comes from having your head two feet off the blurred pavement, the howl of a big engine at max rpms, sparks flying from red hot kickstands and the smell of tires being shredded into bubblegum. Whatever your rationale, these schools are the next best thing to being an astronaut.

California Superbike School

Post Office Box 3107
Hollywood, California 90078
☎ *(213) 484-9323*
FAX (213) 484-9323
Keith Code is known for his cerebral style of motorcycle racing. He will show how to focus concentration as you wind and curve around any one of the 10 tracks the school travels to. The course teaches all levels and all riders from novices(with license and riding experience) to racers. The school uses videos, on-board audio headsets and classroom sessions. The basic program will give you a minimum of 40 miles of track time and the advanced day course will give you 100 track miles. The coolest course is the racing school held at Willow Springs, near Palmdale in Southern Califronia. Here students pay about $1100 to watch and critique video tapes filmed from their bikes. You must be 18 and have a valid motorcycle licence to enroll.

CLASS, Inc. Safety Schools

15500 West Telegraph Road
Suite C-24
Santa Paula, California 93060
☎ *(800) 235-7228*
The highlight of Reg Pridmore's one-day safety school is when you get to ride behind Reg or his son Jason as they take you around the course at full speed. Most students are somewhat humbled that these two can outlap most racers even with a passenger. It's called a safety school because being called a racing school would send the wrong message. You alternate between classroom and track time as you learn the various tricks of bike riding. You start off slowly and by the end of the day, You're in esctasy drifting your K-1 around hairpin turns and grinding the sides of your boots. The site of the occasional student sliding down the track grinding his shiny new leathers to a ragged buff didn't slow us down one bit because we knew how to ride.The school quite rightly focuses on understanding the dynamics of racing, body English and smooooothness. Students provide their own bikes and it's predominantly Beemer fans who like it fast. There are a lot of repeat attendees. The one-day course is $275 with a laudable discount for young riders under 21 ($175). Young riders, usually with just a few street miles under their belt, have the lifespan of mayflies. A surprising number of CLASS members are repeat attenders who enjoy discounts as well as the special rate ($195) for early birds who sign up for the March classes at Willow Springs or Laguna Seca.

Mountaineering Schools

Alpine Ascents International

16615 Saybrook Drive
Woodinville, Washington 98072
☎ *(206) 788-1951*
This company offers six-day and 13-day mountaineering courses on Mt. Baker to develop skills to intermediate or advanced levels. They offer alpine tours including a Seven Summits program

that allows climbers to experience peaks in Alaska, Argentina, Tanzania, Russia, Irian Jaya and Antarctica.

Alpine Skills International

Post Office Box 8
Norden, California 95724
☎ *(916) 426-9108*
FAX (916) 426-3063
This is not just a climbers school; you can also learn about high altitude skiing. In fact, you can combine an alpine climb and a nerve grinding alpine ski descent. Open year round. AMGA accredited.

American Alpine Association

1212 24th
Bellingham, Washington 98225
☎ *(206) 671-1505*
Choose from six, 12 or 18 courses and then head out on one of their tours. Rock climbing is also offered. AMGA accredited.

Colorado Mountain School

Post Office Box 2062
Estes Park, Colorado 80517
☎ *(800) 444-0730*
☎ *(303) 567-5758*
The school combines intensive training with the opportunity to apply your skills in a wide range of global expeditions that run the gamut from the mild ascent of Kilamanjaro in Tanzania to the more rigorous Aconcagua (the highest mountain in the Western hemisphere at 23,085ft.) in Argentina. AMGA accredited.

Exum Mountain Guides

Grand Teton National Park
Box 56
Moose, Wyoming 83102
☎ *(307) 733- 2297*
Founded in 1935, Exum has turned out more famous climbers, mountain guides and alpinists than just about any other school in North America. The year-round program features mountain rescues, rock climbing, ice climbing and mountaineering. They can put together a custom program and you can join them on their local climbing and ski touring programs. AMGA accredited.

The International Alpine School

Post Office Box 3037
Eldorado Springs, Colorado 80025
☎ *(303) 494- 4904*
IAS provides an unusual ice climbing class during the winter, as well as ski mountaineering and a rigorous full spectrum climbing school. They also can set you up on their expeditions to most major climbing areas.

International School of Mountaineering

Club Vagabond
CH-1854 Leysin, Switzerland
☎ *(011 41) 25 34 1321*
Why not combine a trip to Europe with a one- to three-week mountaineering course. The courses are available in English and you can also combine alpine skiing into your curriculum.

Jackson Hole Mountain Guides and Climbing School

Post Office Box 7477
165 North Glenwood,
Jackson, Wyoming 83001
☎ *(307) 733-4979*
For those who would like to hone their climbing skills in the Grand Tetons, this year-round school prides itself on its small classes and intensive training.

National Outdoor Leadership School

Post Office Box AA
Lander, Wyoming 82520
☎ *(307) 332-6937*
NOLS conducts longer climbing schools than most with three- to five-week courses. They also provide a wide variety of other outdoor skills training courses.

Rainer Mountaineering Inc.

535 Dock Street
Tacoma, Washington 98402
☎ *(206) 627-6242*
Rather specialized since it focuses strictly on climbing Mount Rainer, which at 14,410 feet is still a major climb. The area is excellent for learning crevasse rescue, snow and ice climbing, rock climbing, mountain rescue and joining their annual trip to the top. AMGA accredited

When they leave, the students are expected to recognize hazardous terrain and know how to survive or help others survive if caught in an avalanche.

It is common knowledge that some people can survive avalanches, but avalanche victims have only a 50 percent chance of survival if found within 30 minutes after being buried by an avalanch reaching speeds of 170 mph with a force of 50 tons per square meter. There is precious little time to find, dig out and recover victims. More important is the avoidance of areas prone to avalanches.

Colorado Avalanche School

Silverton, Colorado
☎ *(970) 387-5712*
In Silverton, Colorado there is an avalanche survival school designed for skiers, ski patrollers, search and rescue teams, law enforcement officers and even snowplow operators to learn avalanche survival training. The courses include snow physics, learning how to survive an avalanche and practicing search and rescue techniques. The Colorado Avalanche School opened in 1962 with 24 students. Today, applicants are turned away to limit enrollment to 120 for the four-day school each January. Tuition is $100.

Soaring Schools

Most major urban areas will have a glider school within a few miles. Here are just some of the interesting ones:

High Country Soaring

Post Office Box 70
Minden, Nevada 89423
☎ *(702)782-4944*
FAX (702)782-4384
Minden is a mecca for glider pilots, so why not learn where the gliding is best? Minden delivers some of the longest flights in the world due to its location at the base of the Sierra Nevada mountains. Gliders can climb at 2500 feet per second and there are many pilots who have acheived the 5000 meter (16,404 ft.) height to be awarded a diamond pin. Many pilots use oxygen to fly at altitudes of 25,000 feet.

Kenya Soaring Club

Post Office Box 926
Nyeri, Kenya
The hot flat plains and constant winds below Mt. Aberdare and Mt. Kenya provide dramatic lift year round.

Rent a MIG

MIGS etc., Inc.
☎ *(813) 923-0607*
You can rent, buy or steal just about anything in Russia these days. Whether its purchasing materials for thermonuclear bombs, borrowing tanks for a little siege work or even renting soldiers for a little ethnic cleansing, the Russian military forces are embracing capitalism with a vengeance.

So it comes as no surprise that renting a supersonic *MIG-21* is a rather commonplace way to generate funds for cold war hardware. The outfit is MIGS etc., Inc. and they can put you in a state-of-the-art-Soviet era machine starting at $5500. You get airfare, bad Russian food, lousy accommodations and the ride of your life. You do not need to be a pilot. They will take you through aerobatic maneuvers (including a tailslide) and give you some cheap Russian flight gear as a souvenir. There are other planes available for rent but everyone wants a trip in the big gun *MIG-25*.

Soar Hawaii

266 Poipu Drive
Honolulu Hawaii 96825
☎ *(808) 637-3147*
Why not learn how to soar in Hawaii? Better scenery, better vibes. One-shots are $50 a person. If you want to go all the way, plan on spending about $2000 to get your license. The school flies *Schweizer 233's* and *Grob 103's*.

Adventure Experience Organizations

British Schools Exploring Society

Royal Geographical Society
1 Kensington Gore
London, England SW7 2AR
☎ *071 584 0710*
FAX 071-581 7995
BSES sets up an expedition for young people (16.5 to 20 years old) every year. The six-week expeditions are usually to the arctic regions of Europe (Canada to Russia) and are during the summer holidays. They have been sneaking in expeditions to tropical climes and offer four- to six-month expeditions to Botswanna, Greenland, Alaska and Svalbard.

Over 3000 people have taken part since 1932 and interviews take place in London in November. Participants pay a fee to cover costs; membership to BSES is by election after the successful completion of a BSES expedition.

Castle Rock Center for Enviromental Adventures

412 County Road 6NS
Cody, Wyoming 82414
☎ *(800) 533-3066*
☎ *(307) 527-6650*
FAX (307)527-7196
Here's a place that is about halfway between the Boy Scouts and Outward Bound. Targeted directly to bored teens, you can start 'em off young. Called "Man and His Land Expeditions." These allow you to choose from fishing, ice climbing, white-water rafting, horsepacking, mountain biking, llama trekking or you can do all of them. The eight-week Full West program will pack more rootin' tootin' Western adventure than a year of *National Geographic* TV specials. How about a seven-day backpack trip in the Rockies; then you're off to the Grand Canyon; then you zip over to the Green River for a little white-water rafting, and zoom, you blast up to Mount Rainier for mountain climbing and rescue training. Still not totally bagged? More thrills and spills await as you tour the rain forests of the Olympic Peninsula and then more river running, then in one last eco-adventure blast in the Absaroka Range in Wyoming you spend the next week mountain biking, llama trekking, horsepacking and camping. If there are any survivors, the final week is spent climbing mountains in the Tetons as part of the Exum school of Mountaineering. And all you thought there was for teenagers to do in the summer was play video games and listen to heavy metal.

Earth Skills

570 Shepard Street
San Pedro, CA 90731
☎ *(310) 833-4249*

There is a school where you can learn tracking, survival, plant uses and general bush lore. The Earth Skills school was founded in 1987 by Jim Lowery to introduce people to the great outdoors in a very practical way. Most of the classes are over a three-day weekend and run between $50 to $160. The wilderness skill course is a three-day class that will teach you how to trap, identify edible plants, weave baskets, build shelters, start a fire with an Indian bow, make primitive weapons, purify water and just generally learn how to survive more than 50 miles from a Seven-11.

The one-day classes, usually held on a weekend, teach tracking skills or plant uses. Once you have graduated from tracking or wilderness you can move up to the advanced levels where you can learn earth philosophy. Using the methodology and philosophy of aboriginal peoples, Lowery will show you how to use your inner vision to communicate with the animals. If this is a little too California for some folks, you can skip Earth Philosophy and go into Advanced Tracking and Awareness. This class is taught in the Los Padres mountains at an elevation of 8000 feet in the summer or in Joshua Tree in the winter. Both are spectacular sites.

Ready for graduate work? Once you have completed the above you are ready for the track-reading workshop, a one-day class that teaches you foot movement and biomechanics so you will essentially be reading the animals mind and actions as you follow the tracks of wild animals. If that is not enough, there is a whole weekend of tracking in Nipomo dunes near Pismo Beach. Here you will track coyote, bobcat, raccoons, opossums and other small animals.

The school has had about 3000 graduates who have spent serious "dirt time" with Jim. He recommends his class for nature center leaders, biologists, scout leaders and anyone who wants to understand our world a little better. He offers a quarterly newsletter called *Dirt Times* for $10 a year.

Four Corners School of Outdoor Education

East Route
Monticello, Utah 845535
☎ *(800) 525-4456*
Four Corners provides outdoor skills, natural sciences and land stewardship in the Colorado Plateau. The activities include rafting, jeeping, hiking and backpacking. Costs are between $375 to $2495 with courses given between February and November.

The Hardt School of Wilderness Living and Survival

Post Office Box 231-A
Salisbury Vermont 05769
Ron Hardt and those rugged Vermonters must specialize in the lighter side of survival. Here you can spend six days doing all the things the Indians did without being banished to the wilderness to prove your self-sufficiency. Better yet, you can look forward to a cozy cabin and three robust meals a day while you learn how to skin rabbits and make tepees. The summertime classes cost $525 with a weekend program for about $200.

International Journeys Inc.

☎ *800-622-6525*
Travel up the Amazon on a research vessel ($1695 from Miami), extensions to Macchu Pichu and Cuzco are available.

Outward Bound

384 Field Point Road
Greenwich, Connecticut 06830
☎ *(800) 243-8520*
☎ *(800) 477-2627 (Colorado School)*
☎ *(800) 547-3312 (Pacific Crest School)*
☎ *(203) 661-0797*
Do you want to develop that calm, steely-eyed approach, that strong warmth that exudes from those, '40s male movie stars with an unshakeable faith in your abilities and courage? All right, how about just being able to sleep without your Mickey Mouse nightlight on? Outward Bound starts with the mind and the body follows. The program has been used with the handicapped,

the criminal and the infirm and it creates magical transformations in all. What is the secret? Well, like the tiny train that said, "I think I can, I think I can," OB teaches you to motivate yourself, trust your companions and step past your self-imposed limits. What emerges is self-confidence and a greater understanding of your fellow man.

The idea for the school was developed in 1941. Today there are 31 Outward Bound schools around the world with seven in North America: Colorado, Maine, New York, North Carolina, Oregon, Minnesota and Toronto. The instructors are not strutting, barking ex-marines but warm caring individuals who hold safety and understanding above pushing limits. So now that you're sold, what actually happens to effect this magical change in people? Well, first you must put aside about two grand for the 2-day long programs; shorter programs cost about half that.

You can choose from hiking, rafting, winter camping, climbing, trekking, canoeing and ski mountaineering. Each program is broken into four phases (I sense a heroic structure through these schools.) First students are instructed in the sport-specific skills they need. Phase two is the journey. Small groups of eight to 12 people tackle a specific journey via their chosen mode of travel. Phase three is the Challenge, where students now must go into the wilderness (their instructors check in on them daily) and be self-sufficient, meditate and reflect on their general state of affairs (40 days and 40 nights is probaby too extreme so the usual length of time is one to three days). Phase four lets the students break into smaller groups without the benefit of instructors and complete their own mini-expedition. At the end of the course the students are reunited and they participate in one last activity. Whew! After all that, most students rave about the change in their self-confidence, their lust for life and their re-centering (a California word that means they are on the right track).

If you find this process stimulating and rewarding, Outward Bound has leadership courses to prepare you for positions as a guide o ʾ̄ust to help you teach other people to expand their self-confidence and awareness.

Outward Bound has expanded to include executive training courses, but the results are not as glorious as anticipated. In one recent session instructors in England divided executives into two groups and told them to rescue two injured people on the side of a mountain. One group then proceeded to steal the other's stretcher, brought their "victim" to safety, then stood and cheered while the other victim lay stranded on the mountain. Oh, well. Maybe learning to survive the urban jungle makes men tougher than we thought.

John Ridgeway Adventure School

Ardmore, Rhiconich
By Lairg, Sutherland, Scotland IV27 4RB
☎ *(011 44) 97 182 229*
The Ridgeway School is an established (since 1969) place for young people to learn outdoor skills. For those young people jaded by the choices offered by the wild west, John Ridgeway can put them on a 57-ft. sailing ketch, teach them how to sail a dinghy and provide a different angle on survival training, backpacking, canoeing, rock-climbing and intra-personal skills. Open to 12–15 year olds and 15–18 years old, these two-week summer courses run about $800. An interesting alternative if you are spending the summer in Europe and are looking for something to occupy the teens.

U.S. Space Camp

Huntsville, Alabama
☎ *800-63-SPACE*
All right, this one is not quite a life and death experience, but for the young it is a great way to understand why astronauts need the right stuff. It might be the beginning of a life of adventure for the next generation.

This commerical enterprise (no pun intended) strives to deliver a youthful replica of the space program and will really turn on science geeks and flight nuts. During the week-long experience students will perform water survival training, and eventually earn Space Academy wings.

If you can cough up an additional $75 or $225, trainees can either fly as an observer, or get behind the controls of a *Tampico Club* training aircraft when instructors from the University of North Dakota's aerospace department fly Space Academy and Aviation Challenge trainees in single-engine planes.

More than 183,000 trainees have graduated from U.S. Space Camp programs in Alabama and Florida in the past 12 years, more than enough to supply the next few generation of astronauts. Campuses also are located in Japan and Belgium with Space Camp Canada scheduled to open soon.

Survival Training

Boulder Outdoor Survival School

Post Office Box 3226
Flagstaff, Arizona 86003
Summer ☎ *(801) 335-7404*
Winter ☎ *(208) 356-7446*

If you want to live like a native (no, they do not offer casino management courses) check out the BOSS progam. The big one is the 27-day course in Utah where you will go through four phases. For openers you will spend five days traveling without food or water. The second phase is 12 days with the group learning and practicing your survival skills.The third phase has you spending three to four days on a solo survival quest with minimal tools (no credit cards or Walkmans) living off the land until you finally, make the grade by spending five days in the wild traveling a substantial distance. Graduation ceremonies are somewhat informal and muddy. For this you pay about $1300. Naturally food, accommodations and transportation are not included. One added benefit is that most participants lose about five to eight percent of their body weight after taking the month-long course.

For those who don't have a month to spend on a forced weight-loss system, or can't miss reruns of "McGyver," there are one- to three- week courses that range from basic earth skills and aboriginal knowledge for $550, to winter survival courses that include making snowshoes, mushing dog sleds and cold weather first aid for $565. The one that appeals to me is the seven-day desert and marine (as in water) survival course held in the Kino bay area of Sonora, Mexico. This course teaches who how to find your food underwater and on land, finding water, what there is to eat in arid lands and general desert survival knowledge. BOSS is consistently held above the others as the toughest and most rewarding survival school .

A Great Place to Visit... if You're a Fudgsicle

A sparse naval-science outpost at the base of a towering iceberg at the mouth of Independence Fjord...This is "Cool School," Arctic survival training for the 109th Air National Guard unit from Scotia, N.Y. It's not just a job; it's an ordeal. For 50 hours, the students endure continuous exposure to minus 35 degrees F off the coast of northeastern Greenland, learning how to use the resources from their aircraft and the environment to sustain themselves in an emergency.

Taught by four active-duty airmen from Eielson Air Force Base in Alaska, Cool School is an adaptation of the Arctic survival training course they teach 20 weeks each year in the woods outside Fairbanks, Alaska. The course includes a full day of classroom briefings on the environment, clothing, shelter, signaling and cold injuries, followed by a minimum of two days in survival conditions.

A Great Place to Visit... if You're a Fudgsicle

The 109th airlift group flies missions for the armed forces and National Science Foundation to both the North and South Poles and is one of only two United States military units capable of landing cargo aircraft on skis. All flight crew members are required to complete the training at some point in their guard service; 23 braved the cold at this year's session last month. The Andersons said people can't survive a crisis unless they are fully in touch with their feelings and living in harmony with the people and world around them.

Green Mountain Wilderness Survival School

Post Office Box 125
Waitsfield, Vermont 05673
☎ *(802) 496-5300*

Green Mountain offers a little softer and lower-cost approach to survival, and in the process I am sure that the owner, Mike Casper, has more takers. He runs 10-day courses in the summer in Vermont State Parks and wilderness areas. Students will learn how to gather food via tracking, trapping, hunting or fishing. Edible plant identification, cooking without the aid of pots or pans and finding and purifying water round out the culinary aspect of this $950 course. You don't need to be Hawkeye to join and you might actually have some fun.

International Adventure

7 Melbourne Street
Royston, Hertfordshire, England SG8 7BP
☎ *(011 44) 763 242 867*

This British school will send you off to train under Preben Mortensen, a survival instructor who also provides military survival training to the armed forces. The course is held in the Varmland area of Southern Sweden during the winter and the summer. There is little Indian lore or men barking at the moon—just how to stay alive in wilderness conditions. Expect to pay about a grand for ten days.

Survival School for Reporters

Most reporters brag about trial by fire or the red badge of courage. The reality is that very, very few war correspondents have any military or survival training. It may be this lack of training that pushes them to do crazy things. Much like the effect of those Drivers' Ed. movies in high school, hours of watching mangled bodies and gimpy people might make them think twice about journalistic heroics.

It is safe to say that the 63 journalists who were killed in 1993 didn't deliberately get up in the morning and decide to lay down their lives in hopes of gaining eternal fame. They just screwed up. The wrong place at the wrong time, an overenthusiastic sniper, a left-over land mine, ricochets, booby traps—you name it. There are plenty more journalists' names written on Serbian snipers' bullets or Cambodian land mines.

There is an interesting course designed to at least lower the odds of violent death for journalists. The French Defense Journalists' Association has convinced the French government to provide rudimentary training for journalists on a twice yearly basis. The fee is peanuts ($60) and is only intended to cover the meager army rations served over the three-day course. The miniwar school may even provide a few jollies to the war crazed among us.

In a 19th-century castle pushed up close against the Spanish border, journalists are taught how to stay alive: avoiding snipers, identifying and understanding mines and booby-traps, the effects and damage of weapons of various calibers as well as first aid and basic training rules.

- Learn to estimate the source and direction of shooting

- Understand the various calibers and weapons used.

- Seek cover, stay low (most people shoot high)
- Stay off roof-tops
- Wear dark colors but do not wear green
- Do not carry military equipment, including military food rations
- Stay alert
- Watch all openings for snipers or combatants.
- When entering buildings push windows or doors slowly in case of booby traps

At the end of the course students are tested on their knowledge, including a life-like recreation of working in a combat zone. The journalists are asked to negotiate a confusing area of buildings and narrow alleyways while being shot at by soldiers (luckily the soldiers are shooting blanks, but they are detonating grenades close enough to make your ears ring for days). Our favorite "class" is probably the most harrowing and dangerous scenario to adventurers: checkpoints manned by drunken, bored soldiers. The journalists are asked to drive through a checkpoint manned by commandos pretending to be drunken rebels and are judged on their reaction. If only the real world had a time out in situations like these!

A watered-down version of hand-to-hand combat is taught along with first-aid techniques. The first-aid classes teach more than just how to administer for shock and bleeding as a result of gunshot wounds, The students are shown and then asked to use hypodermic needles on themselves in case they need to inject morphine. To minimize the need for first aid attendees are educated on the amazing variety and types of land mines and booby traps. To reinforce the point they are shown graphic photographs of maimed victims. Land mines are a major threat to journalists.

At the nearby Mont Louis commando base in the Pyrenees there is another survival school for journalists. Taught in French, it is nonetheless a very educational and beneficial concept, copied from a similar program taught by the Australian Army to Aussie journalists.

During a short side trip to the Mont Louis commando base the journalists learn to identify various weapons as commandos live-fire various weapons and explosives. Not quite Fourth of July stuff but close.

This new survival course is highly reccomended since the military center normally operates the two- to four-week courses for the French Foreign Legion and regular French army officers. The three-day classes cost around $60 US and are held twice a year.

For information on the course contact:

The French International Journalists' Association
50 Rue Ezouard Pailleron
Paris, France
☎ *331-42-06-16-50*

Security/Health

Who do you turn to when things get nasty? Chances are you are not going to get shot, kidnapped, beaten up, robbed, infected, conned, knifed, raped, scammed or just sick, but as they say, waste matter happens. The first stop for most folks is the embassy. When they find out just how little the embassy can do for them they usually are referred to other sources.

Emergency/Rescue

If you become seriously ill or injured abroad, a U. S. consular officer can provide assistance in finding medical services and informing your the next-of-kin, family or friends. A consular officer can also assist in the transfer of funds from the United States, but payment of hospital and other expenses is your responsibility.

It is wise to learn what medical services your health insurance will cover overseas before you leave on your trip. If you do have applicable insurance, don't forget to carry both your insurance policy identity card as proof of such insurance, and a claim form. Many health insurance companies will pay customary and reasonable hospital costs abroad, but most require a rider for a medevac flight back to the States. This is usually done via private plane or by removing airline seats. You will be accompanied by a nurse or medical assistant who will also fly back to the country of origin. Medivacs can burn money as fast the *Lear Jet* you charter, so plan on spending a minimun of five grand up to $30,000. If you are really banged up you may need more medical technicians, special equipment and a higher level of care during your flight. The Social Security Medicare program does not provide for payment of hospital or medical services outside the U.S.A.

If you're getting toward the back end of your adventuring career the American Association of Retired Persons (AARP)offers foreign medical care coverage at no extra charge with its Medicare supplement plans. This coverage is restricted to treatments considered elligible under Medicare. In general, it covers 80 percent of the customary and reasonable charges, subject to a $50 deductible for the covered care during the first 60 days. There is a ceiling of $25,000 per trip. This is a reimbursement plan so you must pay the bills first and obtain receipts for submission to the plan. Keep in mind that many insurance policies may not cover you if you were injured in a war zone.

To facilitate identification in case of an accident, complete the information page on the inside of your passport providing the name, address and telephone number of someone to be contacted in an emergency. The name given should not be the same as your traveling companions in case the entire party is involved in the same accident. Travelers going abroad with any pre-existing medical problems should carry a letter from their attending physician. The letter should describe their condition and include information on any prescription medications, including the generic name of any prescribed drugs that they need to take.

Any medications being carried overseas should be left in their original containers and be clearly labeled. Travelers should check with the foreign embassy of the country they are visiting to make sure any required medications are not considered to be illegal narcotics.

Access America, Inc.
Post Office Box 90310
Richmond, Virginia 23230
☎ *(800) 284-8300*

Air Ambulance Services

Air Ambulance Inc.
Hayward, CA, ☎ *800-982-5806/510-786-1592*

Aero Ambulance International
Ft. Lauderdale, FL, ☎ *800-443-8042/305-776-6800*

Air Ambulance Network

> Miami, FL, ☎ 300-327-1966/305-387-1708

Air-Evac International

> 8665 Gibbs Drive
> Suite 202
> San Diego, CA 92123
> ☎ (800) 854-2569

Air Medic - Air Ambulance of America

> Washington, PA, ☎ 800-321-4444/412-228-8000

Care Flight - Air Critical Care Intl.

> Clearwater, FL, ☎ 800-282-6878/813-530-7972

National Air Ambulance

> Ft. Lauderdale, FL, ☎ 800-327-3710/305-525-5538

International Medivac Transport

> Phoenix, AZ, ☎ 800-468-1911/602-678-4444

International SOS Assistance

> Philadelphia, PA, ☎ 800-523-8930/215-244-1500

Mercy Medical Airlift

> Manassas, VA, ☎ 800-296-1217/703-361-1191
> (Service area: Caribbean and Canada only. If necessary, will meet commercial incoming patients at JFK, Miami and other airports.)

AIRescue

> 7435 Valjean Avenue
> Van Nuys, CA 91406
> ☎ (800) 922-4911
> ☎ (818) 994-0911
> FAX (818) 994-0180
> (This number can be called collect by patients and customers from anywhere in the world.)

AIRescue is a company whose services you hope you never have need of. AIRescue was started in 1991by former UCLA MEDSTAR physician Francine Vogler with the primary goal of providing emergency aeromedically trained physician/nurse teams along with chartered aircraft to get your butt back in the U.S.A. Naturally they assume you're sick and that your insurance company won't faint when they see the bill. The cost for getting you home can run up to $100,000. In some cases a small commercial jet can be chartered or normal airliners can be used. In the case of using regularly scheduled airlines you will be dinged for four to 12 seats to accommodate the stretcher, equipment and staff required. The majority of emergency flights are national, but they can come and get you just about anywhere you can call them. · ·

Keep in mind that many insurance policies do not cover repatriation costs, yet the extra coverage is minimal. (Don't tell them you're off to liberate Angola under "Reason for travel.") You can and should buy this coverage if you know you are heading out of town. The older you get and the farther you travel should make the coverage that much more compelling. Don't think the coverage is only for the wild and dangerous. It shouldn't take a car accident in Senegal; it could be a rancid taco in Mexico or a burst appendix in Aruba to make you call in a dustoff.

American Red Cross

> National Headquarters
> 17th and D Street, NW
> Washington, D.C. 20006
> ☎ (202) 737-8300

Anca De Jica

> Worldwide Operations Manager
> International SOS Assistance
> 15 Rue Lombard,
> 1205 Geneva, Switzerland
> ☎ 22-347-6161
> FAX 22-347-6172

Médecin Sans Frontière

Amsterdam
FAX 20-205 170
Equilibre Association L01 1901
France
☎ *72-73-04-14*

Medico International

Frankfurt, Germany
☎ *49-69-94-43-80*

Organizations

The American Society for Industrial Security (ASIS)

FAX (703)-243-4954
They hold three-day meetings where topics ranging from terrorism, espionage and neo-Nazism are discussed.

Control Risks Group

8200 Greensboro Drive, Suite 1010
McLean, Virginia 22102
☎ *(703) 893-0083*
FAX (703) 893-8611

Employment Conditions Abroad

Anchor House, 15 Britten Street
London SW3 3TY
☎ *071-351-7151*
FAX 071-351-9396

Healthcare Abroad

243 Church Street, N.W.
Suite 100-D
Vienna, Virginia 22180
☎ *(800) 237-6615*
☎ *(703) 281-9500*

Organization Resources Counselors

Rockefeller Center, 1211 Avenue of the Americas
New York, New York 10036
☎ *(212) 719-3400*
FAX (212) 398-1358

Reporters Sans Frontieres

International Secretariat
17, rue Abbe de L'Epee
Paris, France
RSF was founded in 1985 and has offices in Belgium, Canada, France, Germany, Italy, Spain and Switzerland with members in 71 countries. Their job is to defend imprisoned journalists and press freedom around the world.

They will send protest letters, provide lawyers (if possible) and other forms of assistance to reporters in jail. If you want to convert to Journalism after you are jailed these folks can't help you.

Travel Assistance International

1133 15th Street, N.W.
Suite 400 Washington, DC 20005
☎ *(800) 821-2828/(202) 331-1609*

Travmed

Post Office Box 10623
Baltimore, Maryland 21285
☎ *(800) 732-5309*

World Care Travel Assistance

1150 South Olive Street
Suite T-2233 Los Angeles, California 90015
☎ *(800) 253-1877*

Paraphernalia

Counter Spy Shop of Mayfair London

6th Floor
360 Madison Avenue
New York, NY 10022
☎ *(212) 557-3040*
FAX (212) 983-1278

The ideal upscale store for the paranoid. Counter Spy sells a variety of gizmos that will put you back in control of your life. Start by securing your phone lines from tapping, bullet proofing your car and body from terrorist attacks and even use a voice stress analyser to see if your spouse is really working late.

For those who never imagined how easy it is for other people to eavesdrop, attack, bug, tail, photograph, track and rob, they offer two videos. The videos are catalogs that provide background and information on intercepting faxes, sniffing out bombs, boobytrapping your valuables, and even scrambling your phone messages.

The videos also give a little insight on how you can be tracking, bugging, snooping and checking up on all those people you know are out to get you before they get you. Counter Spy also has retail outlets in London, Mexico City, New York, Beverly Hills, Miami and Washington.

Tape One (cellular and fax intercept, night vision systems, video and audio survellience, Bulletproof vests, tracking systems and minature transmitters) is $89.00 and tape two (telephone stress analysers, hidden recorders, data encryption, audio recorders, bulletproof cars, lie detection and digital tracking systems) is $79.00 and both are available in English, Spanish, Russian French and Arabic. You can deduct the cost of the tape from your first purchase. You can also order brochures and information by calling:

Executive Protection Products Inc.

1325 Imola Ave. West
#504S
Napa, CA 94559
☎ *(707) 253-7142*
FAX (707) 253-7149

Need another source for spy and surveilance gizmos at discount prices. How about a pinhole video camera system for only $2,500?

Spy Supply, Inc

1212 Boylston Street
#120 Chestnut Hill, MA 02167
☎ *(305) 340-0579*
☎ *(617) 327-7272*

Specialists in phone systems. They can program two phones to one number.

Tele-Adapt

☎ *(408) 370-5105*
FAX (408) 370-5110
UK +44 (0) 81-421-4444

Adaptors for U.S. phone plugs to foreign plugs.

Thugs for hire

The Sunday Times did an investigative piece on an unusual business in Lancing West Sussex, England. Advertising in the back of magazines, Paul Price and his partner Peter Matthews offer to bully, molest, victimize or intimidate the person of your choice. Rates are fairly reasonable if the burly proprietors aren't. A threatening phone call goes for about $50, a car can be vandalized for about $600 and your worst enemy can get a good thrashing for $1,500. The thugs for hire also conduct business as Komodo Investigations. By the time you read this it is assumed that the local police will have convinced the two zealous entrepreneurs of the illegality of their ways.

Security/Hostage Negotiations

Pinkerton Risk Assessment Services

1600 Wilson Boulevard
Suite 901
Arlington, VA 22209
☎ *(703) 525-6111*
FAX (703) 525-2454

Once on the trail of bank robbers in the wild west, Pinkerton has gone global and high tech. Today you can get risk assessments of over 200 countries on-line or in person. They offer access to a database of over 55,000 terrorists' actions and daily updated reports on security threats. The non-techie can order printed publications that range from daily risk assessment briefings to a monthly newsletter. Their services are not cheap, but then again, how much is your life worth? Annual subscription to the on-line service starts at about $7000 and you can order various risk and advisory reports that run from $200–$700 each. Pinkerton's can still get down and dirty with counterterrorism programs, hostage negotiators, crisis management and travel security seminars.

The service is designed for companies that send their employees overseas or need to know what is going on. Some reports are mildly macabre with their annual report-like graphs of maimings, killings assaults and assassinations. Others are downright enlightening. In any case Pinkerton does an excellent job of bringing together the world's most unpleasant information and providing it to you in concise, intelligent packages.

INDEX

A

Abkhazians, 258
Adventure experience organizations, 964–967
Adventure/recreation schools, 956–957
Afghanistan, 133–142
AFL, 326
Afwerki, Issaias, 455
Aideed, Muhammed Farah, 433
Albania, 599–602
al-Bashir, Lt. General Omar Hassan Ahmad, 466
al-Gama'a al-Islamiya, 242
Algeria, 143–150, 668
Algiers, Algeria, 148
Alianza Popular Revolucionaria Americana, 353
al-Qaddafi, Col. Muammar abu Minyar, 653
al-Turabi, Dr. Hassan Abdullah, 466
Andamans, 695–698
Angola, 151–157
Animals, 952–954
Ankara, Turkey, 491
Antioquia Department and Medellin, Columbia, 233
APRA, 353
Arafat, Yasir, 280
Arakan Rohingya Islamic Front, 681
Armed Islamic Group (GIA), 147
Armenia, 159–164
Aryan Nation, 562
Assam, India, 267
Assiyut Province, Egypt, 244
Ataturk, 706
Atlanta, GA, 565
Azerbaijan, 165–172
Azeris, 168

B

Baghdad, Iraq, 637
Bahrain, 668–669
Bandits, 148
Besharati, Ali Mohammed, 622
Bicycle schools, 957
Bizimungu, Augustin, 409
Bogota, Columbia, 233

Bolivia, 173–180
Bombay, India, 268
Bosnia-Herzegovina, 181–189
Brazil, 503–508
Bribes, 759–762
Burundi, 191–197
Buses, 226, 235, 250, 283, 355
Business travel, 42–44

C

Cairo, Egypt, 244
Calcutta, India, 268
Cambodia, 199–226
Camel Trophy, 837–852
Cartagena, Columbia, 233
Carter, Jimmy, 691
Castro, Fidel, 607
CGSB, 230
Chad, 658–659, 699–700
Chechnya, 509–519, 545
Chiapas, Mexico, 530
China, 709–714
Choco Department, Columbia, 233
Civil disorder, 149, 177
Clinton, President Bill, 563
CNPZ, 176
Cochabamba, Bolivia, 177
Colombia, 227–238
Colombo, Sri Lanka, 422
Crime, 186, 195, 225, 244, 251, 341, 481, 491, 546, 595, 610
Criminals, 7–8, 149
Croat-Muslims, 185
Cuba, 603–611
Cuzco, Peru, 356

D

Delhi, India, 267
de Lozada, Gonzalo Sanchez, 177
Democratic Front for the Liberation of Palestine (DFLP), 281, 297
Dev Sol, 488
DFLP, 281, 297
Diseases, 17, 729–745
Djibouti, 434–435
Driving schools, 957–958

Favorite People, Places & Experiences

ADDRESS:	NOTES:

Name

Address

Telephone

Name

Address

Telephone

Name

Address

Telephone

Name

Address

Telephone

Name

Address

Telephone

Name

Address

Telephone

Name

Address

Telephone

Favorite People, Places & Experiences

ADDRESS:	NOTES:
Name	
Address	
Telephone	
Name	
Address	
Telephone	
Name	
Address	
Telephone	
Name	
Address	
Telephone	
Name	
Address	
Telephone	
Name	
Address	
Telephone	
Name	
Address	
Telephone	

Favorite People, Places & Experiences

ADDRESS:	NOTES:

Name

Address

Telephone

Name

Address

Telephone

Name

Address

Telephone

Name

Address

Telephone

Name

Address

Telephone

Name

Address

Telephone

Name

Address

Telephone

Favorite People, Places & Experiences

ADDRESS:	NOTES:

Name

Address

Telephone

Name

Address

Telephone

Name

Address

Telephone

Name

Address

Telephone

Name

Address

Telephone

Name

Address

Telephone

Name

Address

Telephone

Favorite People, Places & Experiences

ADDRESS:	NOTES:

Name

Address

Telephone

Name

Address

Telephone

Name

Address

Telephone

Name

Address

Telephone

Name

Address

Telephone

Name

Address

Telephone

Name

Address

Telephone

Favorite People, Places & Experiences

ADDRESS:	NOTES:

Name

Address

Telephone

Name

Address

Telephone

Name

Address

Telephone

Name

Address

Telephone

Name

Address

Telephone

Name

Address

Telephone

Name

Address

Telephone

Favorite People, Places & Experiences

ADDRESS:	NOTES:

Name

Address

Telephone

Name

Address

Telephone

Name

Address

Telephone

Name

Address

Telephone

Name

Address

Telephone

Name

Address

Telephone

Name

Address

Telephone

Favorite People, Places & Experiences

ADDRESS:	NOTES:

Name

Address

Telephone

Name

Address

Telephone

Name

Address

Telephone

Name

Address

Telephone

Name

Address

Telephone

Name

Address

Telephone

Name

Address

Telephone

Favorite People, Places & Experiences

ADDRESS:	NOTES:

Name

Address

Telephone

Name

Address

Telephone

Name

Address

Telephone

Name

Address

Telephone

Name

Address

Telephone

Name

Address

Telephone

Name

Address

Telephone

Favorite People, Places & Experiences

ADDRESS:	NOTES:

Name

Address

Telephone

Name

Address

Telephone

Name

Address

Telephone

Name

Address

Telephone

Name

Address

Telephone

Name

Address

Telephone

Name

Address

Telephone

Favorite People, Places & Experiences

ADDRESS:	NOTES:

Name

Address

Telephone

Name

Address

Telephone

Name

Address

Telephone

Name

Address

Telephone

Name

Address

Telephone

Name

Address

Telephone

Name

Address

Telephone

Favorite People, Places & Experiences

ADDRESS:	NOTES:

Name

Address

Telephone

Name

Address

Telephone

Name

Address

Telephone

Name

Address

Telephone

Name

Address

Telephone

Name

Address

Telephone

Name

Address

Telephone

Favorite People, Places & Experiences

ADDRESS:	NOTES:

Name

Address

Telephone

Name

Address

Telephone

Name

Address

Telephone

Name

Address

Telephone

Name

Address

Telephone

Name

Address

Telephone

Name

Address

Telephone

Favorite People, Places & Experiences

ADDRESS:	NOTES:

Name

Address

Telephone

Name

Address

Telephone

Name

Address

Telephone

Name

Address

Telephone

Name

Address

Telephone

Name

Address

Telephone

Name

Address

Telephone

Favorite People, Places & Experiences

ADDRESS:	NOTES:

Name

Address

Telephone

Name

Address

Telephone

Name

Address

Telephone

Name

Address

Telephone

Name

Address

Telephone

Name

Address

Telephone

Name

Address

Telephone

Favorite People, Places & Experiences

ADDRESS:	NOTES:

Name

Address

Telephone

Name

Address

Telephone

Name

Address

Telephone

Name

Address

Telephone

Name

Address

Telephone

Name

Address

Telephone

Name

Address

Telephone

Favorite People, Places & Experiences

ADDRESS:	NOTES:

Name

Address

Telephone

Name

Address

Telephone

Name

Address

Telephone

Name

Address

Telephone

Name

Address

Telephone

Name

Address

Telephone

Name

Address

Telephone

Favorite People, Places & Experiences

ADDRESS:	NOTES:

Name

Address

Telephone

Name

Address

Telephone

Name

Address

Telephone

Name

Address

Telephone

Name

Address

Telephone

Name

Address

Telephone

Name

Address

Telephone

Favorite People, Places & Experiences

ADDRESS:	NOTES:

Name

Address

Telephone

Name

Address

Telephone

Name

Address

Telephone

Name

Address

Telephone

Name

Address

Telephone

Name

Address

Telephone

Name

Address

Telephone

Favorite People, Places & Experiences

ADDRESS:	NOTES:

Name

Address

Telephone

Name

Address

Telephone

Name

Address

Telephone

Name

Address

Telephone

Name

Address

Telephone

Name

Address

Telephone

Name

Address

Telephone